BASIC CONTRACT LAW

Eighth Edition

CONCISE EDITION

By

Lon L. Fuller
Late Carter Professor of General Jurisprudence,
Harvard University

Melvin Aron Eisenberg
Koret Professor of Law,
University of California at Berkeley

AMERICAN CASEBOOK SERIES®

THOMSON
WEST

Mat #40516228

American Casebook Series and West Group are trademarks registered in the U.S. Patent and Trademark Office.

© 2006 Thomson/West
        610 Opperman Drive
        P.O. Box 64526
        St. Paul, MN 55164–0526
        1–800–328–9352

Printed in the United States of America

ISBN–13: 978–0–314–17172–6
ISBN–10: 0–314–17172–X

 TEXT IS PRINTED ON 10% POST CONSUMER RECYCLED PAPER

Acknowledgments

In any book of this kind it is impossible to acknowledge all those whose influence has made itself felt. Lon Fuller's work and thought continues to permeate this book. Special thanks are due to Shawn Bayern and Joel Willard, who performed exceptionally valuable work as research assistants, and to Steve Vercelloni for his skill and diligence in helping to prepare the manuscript for publication. I am also indebted to Bob Berring for important suggestions, and to the authors and publishers who generously gave me permission to reprint excerpts from their works.

*

Summary of Contents

PART III. ASSENT

Table of Contents

PART I. WHAT PROMISES SHOULD THE LAW ENFORCE?— THE DOCTRINE OF CONSIDERATION

Table of Cases

The principal cases are in bold type. Cases cited or discussed in the text are roman type. References are to pages. Cases cited in principal cases and within other quoted materials are not included.

Table of Uniform Commercial Code Citations

Table of Uniform Consumer
Credit Code Citations

---

*

Table of Citations to the Restatement of Contracts

Principal citations only.

BASIC CONTRACT LAW

Eighth Edition

CONCISE EDITION

*

Part I

WHAT PROMISES SHOULD THE LAW ENFORCE?—THE DOCTRINE OF CONSIDERATION

The first great question of contract law is, what promises should and does the law enforce? This question is subsumed under the heading of *consideration,* and it is the question that will be addressed in Part I of this Book.

Part I consists of four Chapters. Chapter 1 primarily concerns the enforceability of donative promises, that is, promises to make a gift. Chapter 2 concerns bargain promises. Chapter 3 concerns promises to pay for a benefit that was previously conferred by the promisee upon the promisor. Chapter 4 concerns the limits of contract as a technique for social ordering.

1

Chapter 1

DONATIVE PROMISES, FORM, AND RELIANCE

SECTION 1. SIMPLE DONATIVE PROMISES

Section 1 begins with *simple donative promises*, that is, promises that are made for affective reasons (such as love, friendship, or the like); that are not cast in a form to which modern contract law gives special significance; and that have not been demonstrably relied upon. Section 2 considers donative promises that are cast in a special form. Section 3 considers the effect of reliance.

DOUGHERTY v. SALT

New York Court of Appeals, 1919.
227 N.Y. 200, 125 N.E. 94.

CARDOZO, J. The plaintiff, a boy of eight years, received from his aunt, the defendant's testatrix, a promissory note for $3,000 payable at her death or before. Use was made of a printed form, which contains the words "value received." How the note came to be given, was explained by the boy's guardian, who was a witness for his ward. The aunt was visiting her nephew. "When she saw Charley coming in, she said 'Isn't he a nice boy?' I answered her, yes, that he is getting along very nice, and getting along nice in school, and I showed where he had progressed in school, having good reports, and so forth, and she told me that she was going to take care of that child, that she loved him very much. I said, 'I know you do, Tillie, but your taking care of the child will be done probably like your brother and sister done, take it out in talk.' She said: 'I don't intend to take it out in talk, I would like to take care of him now.' I said, 'Well, that is up to you.' She said, 'Why can't I make out a note to him?' I said, 'You can, if you wish to.' She said, 'Would that be right?' And I said, 'I do not know, but I guess it would; I do not know why it would not.' And she said, 'Well, will you make out a note for me?' I said, 'Yes, if you wish me to,' and she said, 'Well, I wish you would.' " A blank was then produced, filled out, and signed. The aunt handed the note to her nephew

2

with these words, "You have always done for me, and I have signed this note for you. Now, do not lose it. Some day it will be valuable."

The trial judge submitted to the jury the question whether there was any consideration for the promised payment. Afterwards, he set aside the verdict in favor of the plaintiff, and dismissed the complaint. The Appellate Division, by a divided court, reversed the judgment of dismissal, and reinstated the verdict on the ground that the note was sufficient evidence of consideration.

We reach a different conclusion. The inference of consideration to be drawn from the form of the note has been so overcome and rebutted as to leave no question for a jury. This is not a case where witnesses summoned by the defendant and friendly to the defendant's cause, supply the testimony in disproof of value (Strickland v. Henry, 175 N.Y. 372). This is a case where the testimony in disproof of value comes from the plaintiff's own witness, speaking at the plaintiff's instance. The transaction thus revealed admits of one interpretation, and one only. The note was the voluntary and unenforceable promise of an executory gift (Harris v. Clark, 3 N.Y. 93; Holmes v. Roper, 141 N.Y. 64, 66). This child of eight was not a creditor, nor dealt with as one. The aunt was not paying a debt. She was conferring a bounty (Fink v. Cox, 18 Johns. 145). The promise was neither offered nor accepted with any other purpose. "Nothing is consideration that is not regarded as such by both parties" (Philpot v. Gruninger, 14 Wall. 570, 577; Fire Ins. Ass'n. v. Wickham, 141 U.S. 564, 579; Wisconsin & M. Ry. Co. v. Powers, 191 U.S. 379, 386; De Cicco v. Schweizer, 221 N.Y. 431, 438). A note so given is not made for "value received," however its maker may have labeled it. The formula of the printed blank becomes, in the light of the conceded facts, a mere erroneous conclusion, which cannot overcome the inconsistent conclusion of the law (Blanshan v. Russell, 32 App.Div. 103; affd., on opinion below, 161 N.Y. 629; Kramer v. Kramer, 181 N.Y. 477; Bruyn v. Russell, 52 Hun, 17). The plaintiff, through his own witness, has explained the genesis of the promise, and consideration has been disproved (Neg.Instr.Law, sec. 54; Consol.Laws, chap. 43).

We hold, therefore, that the verdict of the jury was contrary to law, and that the trial judge was right in setting it aside. . . .

HISCOCK, CH. J., CHASE, COLLIN, HOGAN, CRANE and ANDREWS, JJ., concur.

Judgment accordingly.

RESTATEMENT, SECOND, CONTRACTS §§ 1, 17, 71, 79

[See Selected Source Materials Supplement*]

NOTE ON THE RESTATEMENT OF CONTRACTS

The American Law Institute (ALI) is an organization composed of lawyers, judges, and legal academics. The ALI's objective is to promote the

---

* References in this casebook to "Selected Source Materials Supplement" are to S. Burton & M. Eisenberg, Contract Law: Selected Source Materials (West Publishing Co.).

clarification and simplification of the law and its better adaptation to social needs. It has sought to achieve this objective in part by preparing "Restatements" of various branches of the common law, including Contracts.

The theory of the Restatements has changed somewhat over time. The introduction to the Restatement [First] of Contracts stated that "The function of the Institute is to state clearly and precisely in the light of the [courts'] decisions the principles and rules of the common law." The present theory is that the ALI "should feel obliged in [its] deliberations to give weight to all of the considerations that the courts, under a proper view of the judicial function, deem it right to weigh in theirs." Wechsler, The Course of the Restatements, 55 A.B.A.J. 147, 156 (1969).

The first Restatement of Contracts (hereafter cited as Restatement First) was published by the ALI in 1932. The Reporter was Samuel Williston of the Harvard Law School. Williston was one of the leaders of a school of thought that is now called classical contract law. This school treated contract law as a set of axioms that were deemed to be self-evident, together with a set of subsidiary rules that were purportedly deduced from the axioms. Among the axioms of classical contract law were that bargains constituted consideration, that bargains were formed by offer and acceptance, and that the remedy for breach of an enforceable promise was expectation damages.

Many of the original Restatements were eventually superseded by revised versions. Restatement, Second, of Contracts (hereafter cited as Restatement Second) was published in 1981. The Reporter for the first portion of Restatement Second was Robert Braucher, then of Harvard Law School. On Professor Braucher's appointment to the bench, he was succeeded as Reporter by Professor Allan Farnsworth of Columbia.

Arthur Corbin of the Yale Law School was, until his death, Consultant to the Restatement Second. From the 1920s through the 1960s, Williston and Corbin were the two giants of contract law. Each authored famous multi-volume treatises on contracts that are still in use. Williston was a leader of the classical school of contract law. Corbin was instrumental in laying the foundation for modern contract law. To a significant extent, the differences in approach between Williston and Corbin are paralleled by differences in approach between Restatement First and Restatement Second. Restatement First had much that is admirable, and Restatement Second marks a considerable advance over Restatement First. However, both the theory of the Restatements and other factors often work to prevent a Restatement from setting out the best possible rule in any given area. The Restatements of Contracts are not exceptions.

NOTE ON THE CONCEPT OF CONSIDERATION

The term *consideration* may be conceived in two very different ways, one broad and one narrow.

Under the *broad* conception, consideration is simply a collective term for the whole set of elements that make promises legally enforceable. Bargain is one such element. As will be seen in subsequent Chapters, there are others, such as reliance.

Under the *narrow* conception of consideration, consideration is equated with the single element of bargain. This narrow conception, often referred to as the "bargain theory of consideration," was adopted in Restatement First and continued in Restatement Second. In Restatement Second, this conception is embodied in section 71(1): "To constitute consideration, a performance or a return promise must be bargained for."

The bargain theory of consideration can produce two kinds of distortion in contract law. The first kind of distortion concerns terminology. As will be seen in succeeding Chapters, a number of elements other than bargain should and do make a promise legally enforceable. Restatement Second recognizes these elements, but only in sections that are grouped in a Topic called "Contracts [Enforceable] Without Consideration." The result is that under the terminology of Restatement Second, a promise needs consideration to be enforceable unless it does not need consideration to be enforceable.

The second distortion produced by the bargain theory of consideration is substantive. If consideration means the whole set of elements that make promises legally enforceable, the meaning of the term will be continually adjusted as it becomes socially desirable to add new elements or drop old ones. In contrast, the bargain theory of consideration suggests a closed system, in which all nonbargain promises are presumptively unenforceable. If taken seriously, such an approach tends to stifle the growth of the law.

The bargain theory of consideration is certainly not mandated by contract doctrine. On the contrary, the theory cannot account for many elements of enforceability, such as reliance, except by relegating these elements to the purgatory of "Contracts [Enforceable] Without Consideration." Nor is the theory mandated by judicial decisions. A number of courts use the term "consideration" as equivalent to bargain, but many other courts use the term in its broader sense to embrace nonbargain elements, such as reliance, that make a promise enforceable.

NOTE ON CONDITIONAL DONATIVE PROMISES

Bargain promises often are made in a conditional form. For example, A may say to B, "If you mow my lawn, I will pay you $20." Donative promises may also be made in conditional form. For example, C may say to D, "If you select a car costing no more than $15,000, I will buy it for you as a graduation present." What's the difference between a conditional bargain promise and a conditional donative promise? In the case of a bargain, the parties view performance of the condition as the *price* of the promise. In the case of a gift, the parties view performance of the condition as the necessary *means* to make the gift, not as the price of the gift. Thus in the first example, B's act of mowing A's lawn is viewed by A and B as the price that B must pay to get $20 from A. (And, of course $20 is viewed by A and B as the price that A must pay to get B to mow her lawn.) In contrast, in the second example, D's act of selecting a car is not viewed by C and D as a price D pays to get the gift, but as a mechanical requisite for making the gift.

How do we know whether performance of a condition in a conditional promise is a bargained-for price or simply the necessary means make the gift?

We make a judgement based on all the circumstances and on our knowledge of how people normally act. All this was well put by Williston, who used a now-famous example:

> It is of course ... possible to make a gratuitous conditional promise. ... [A]ny event may be named in a promise as fixing the moment, on the happening of which a promisor (not as an exchange for the happening but as a mere coincidence in time) will perform a promise intended and understood to be gratuitous. The same thing, therefore, stated as the condition of a promise may or may not be consideration, according as a reasonable man would or would not understand that the performance of the condition was requested as the price or exchange for the promise. If a benevolent man says to a tramp, "if you go around the corner to the clothing shop there, you may purchase an overcoat on my credit," no reasonable person would understand that the short walk was requested as the consideration for the promise, but that in the event of the tramp going to the shop the promisor would make him a gift. Yet the walk to the shop is in its nature capable of being consideration. It is a legal detriment to the tramp to take the walk, and the only reason why the walk is not consideration is because on a reasonable interpretation, it must be held that the walk was not requested as the price of the promise, but was merely a condition of a gratuitous promise.

Williston on Contracts § 112 (3d ed. 1957).

SECTION 2.   THE ELEMENT OF FORM

SCHNELL v. NELL

Supreme Court of Indiana, 1861.
17 Ind. 29, 79 Am.Dec. 453.

PERKINS, J. Action by J.B. Nell against Zacharias Schnell, upon the following instrument:

"This agreement, entered into this 13th day of February, 1856, between Zach. Schnell, of Indianapolis, Marion county, State of Indiana, as party of the first part, and J.B. Nell, of the same place, Wendelin Lorenz, of Stilesville, Hendricks county, State of Indiana, and Donata Lorenz, of Frickinger, Grand Duchy of Baden, Germany, as parties of the second part witnesseth: The said Zacharias Schnell agrees as follows: Whereas his wife, Theresa Schnell, now deceased, has made a last will and testament in which, among other provisions, it was ordained that every one of the above-named second parties, should receive the sum of $200; and whereas the said provisions of the will must remain a nullity, for the reason that no property, real or personal, was in the possession of the said Theresa Schnell, deceased, in her own name, at the time of her death, and all property held by Zacharias and Theresa Schnell jointly, therefore reverts to her husband; and whereas the said Theresa Schnell has also been a dutiful and loving wife to the said Zach. Schnell, and has materially aided him in the acquisition of all property, real and personal, now possessed by him; for, and in consideration of all this and the love and respect he bears to his wife; and, furthermore, in consideration of one cent, received by him of the second parties, he, the said Zach. Schnell, agrees to pay the above named sums of money to the parties of the second part, to wit: $200 to the said J.B. Nell; $200 to the said Wendelin Lorenz; and $200 to the said Donata Lorenz, in the following installments, viz., $200 in one year from the date of these presents; $200 in two years; and $200 in three years; to be divided between the parties in equal portions of $66⅔ each year, or as they may agree, till each one has received his full sum of $200. And the said parties of the second part, for, and in consideration of this, agree to pay the above-named sum of money (one cent), and to deliver up to said Schnell, and abstain from collecting any real or supposed claims upon him or his estate, arising from the said last will and testament of the said Theresa Schnell, deceased. In witness whereof, the said parties have, on this 13th day of February, 1856, set hereunto their hands and seals. Zacharias Schnell. [Seal.] J.B. Nell. [Seal.] Wen. Lorenz. [Seal.]''

The complaint contained no averment of a consideration for the instrument, outside of those expressed in it; and did not aver that the one cent agreed to be paid, had been paid or tendered.

A demurrer to the complaint was overruled.

The defendant answered, that the instrument sued on was given for no consideration whatever.

He further answered, that it was given for no consideration, because his said wife, Theresa, at the time she made the will mentioned, and at the time of her death, owned neither separately, nor jointly with her husband, or anyone else (except so far as the law gave her an interest in her husband's property), any property, real or personal, etc. . . .

The court sustained a demurrer to these answers, evidently on the ground that they were regarded as contradicting the instrument sued on, which particularly set out the considerations upon which it was executed. But the instrument is latently ambiguous on this point. See Ind.Dig., p. 110.

The case turned below, and must turn here, upon the question whether the instrument sued on does express a consideration sufficient to give it legal obligation, as against Zacharias Schnell. It specifies three distinct considerations for his promise to pay $600:

(1) A promise, on the part of the plaintiffs, to pay him one cent.

(2) The love and affection he bore his deceased wife, and the fact that she had done her part, as his wife, in the acquisition of the property.

(3) The fact that she had expressed her desire, in the form of an inoperative will, that the persons named therein should have the sums of money specified.

The consideration of one cent will not support the promise of Schnell. It is true, that as a general proposition, inadequacy of consideration will not vitiate an agreement. Baker v. Roberts, 14 Ind. 552. But this doctrine does not apply to a mere exchange of sums of money of coin, whose value is exactly fixed, but to the exchange of something of, in itself, indeterminate value, for money, or, perhaps, for some other thing of indeterminate value. In this case had the one cent mentioned been some particular one cent, a family piece, or ancient, remarkable coin, possessing an indeterminate value, extrinsic from its simple value, a different view might be taken. As it is, the mere promise to pay six hundred dollars for one cent, even had the portion of that cent due from the plaintiff been tendered, is an unconscionable contract, void, at first blush, upon its face, if it be regarded as an earnest one. Hardesty v. Smith, 3 Ind. 39. The consideration of one cent is, plainly, in this case, merely nominal, and intended to be so. As the will and testament of Schnell's wife imposed no legal obligation upon him to discharge her bequests out of his property, and as she had none of her own, his promise to discharge them was not legally binding upon him, on that ground. A moral consideration, only, will not support a promise. Ind.Dig., p. 13. And for the same reason, a valid consideration for his promise cannot be found in the fact of a compromise of a disputed claim; for where such claim is legally groundless, a promise upon a compromise of it, or of a suit upon it, is not legally binding. Spahr v. Hollingshead, 8 Blackf. 415. There was no mistake of law or fact in this case, as the agreement admits the will inoperative and void. The promise was simply one to make a gift. The past services of his wife, and the love and affection he had borne her, are objectionable as legal considerations for Schnell's promise, on two grounds: (1) They are past considerations. Ind.Dig., p. 13. (2) The fact that Schnell loved his wife and that she had been industrious, constituted no consideration for his promise to pay J.B. Nell, and the Lorenzes, a sum of money. Whether, if his wife, in her lifetime had made a bargain with Schnell, that, in consideration of his promising to pay, after her death, to the persons named, a sum of money, she would be industrious, and worthy of his affection, such a promise would have been valid and consistent with public policy, we need not decide. Nor is the fact that Schnell now venerates the memory of his deceased wife a legal consideration for a promise to pay any third person money.

The instrument sued on, interpreted in the light of the facts alleged in the second paragraph of the answer, will not support an action. The demurrer to the answer should have been overruled. See Stevenson v. Druley, 4 Ind. 519.

Judgment reversed.

———

STATUTES APPLICABLE IN SCHNELL v. NELL. A statute in Indiana, which was in effect when *Schnell v. Nell* was decided, provided as follows: "A failure or want of consideration, in whole or in part, may be pleaded in any action, set–off or counter–claim upon or arising out of any specialty,* bond or deed, except instruments negotiable by the law merchant and negotiated before falling due." 2 Ind.Rev.Stats. 44–45 (1852). Another statute provided, "There shall be no difference in evidence between sealed and unsealed writings; and every writing not sealed, shall have the same force and effect that it would have if sealed. A writing under seal, except conveyances of real estate, or any interest therein, may therefore be changed, or altogether discharged, by a writing not under seal. An agreement in writing,

* A "specialty" is a contract under seal.
(Footnote by ed.)

without a seal, for the compromise or settlement of a debt, is as obligatory as if a seal were affixed." Id. § 492.

———

NOTE ON NOMINAL CONSIDERATION

The problem in *Schnell v. Nell* concerns what is now known as nominal consideration. Essentially, the term *nominal consideration* plays off the bargain theory of consideration. A bargain is a *substantive* transaction, consisting of an exchange in which each party views what he gives up as the price of what he gets. A transaction is said to involve nominal consideration when it has the *form* of a bargain, but not the substance of a bargain, because it is clear that the promisor did not view what she got as the price of her promise. So, for example, it is clear that in *Schnell v. Nell* the promisor, Schnell, did not view one cent as the price of his promise to pay $600. (It is possible that the promisees in *Schnell v. Nell* agreed to do other things, such as not bringing suit against Mrs. Schnell's estate, and that Schnell viewed these other things as the price of his promise. Even if that were the case, however, it remains true that Schnell did not view the one cent as the price of his promise.)

A basic axiom of the classical school was the bargain theory of consideration—that to constitute consideration a promise or performance must be bargained for. Ironically, however, as the bargain theory of consideration was actually elaborated by the classical school, it could be satisfied even though no bargain had been made. Both Holmes and Restatement First took the view that the *form* of a bargain would suffice to make a promise enforceable.

Holmes expressed his view in two well-known aphorisms:

Consideration is as much a form as a seal.

and

[I]t is the essence of a consideration, that, by the terms of the agreement, it is given and accepted as the motive or inducement of the promise. Conversely, the promise must be made and accepted as the conventional motive or inducement for furnishing the consideration. The root of the whole matter is the relation of reciprocal conventional inducement, each for the other, between consideration and promise.

By the term "reciprocal inducement," Holmes meant bargain. By the term "conventional," Holmes apparently meant a formal expression whose meaning and significance is artificially determined, like a bidding convention in the game of bridge. Thus, in Holmes's view, if the parties deliberately adopted the convention—that is, the form—of a bargain, the law would enforce their promises as though they had made an *actual* bargain.

Illustration 1 to Restatement First § 84 reflected the same idea:

A wishes to make a binding promise to his son B to convey to B Blackacre, which is worth $5000. Being advised that a gratuitous promise is not binding, A writes to B an offer to sell Blackacre for $1. B accepts. B's promise to pay $1 is sufficient consideration.

Restatement Second has retained the bargain definition of consideration. In two Illustrations, however, Restatement Second has reversed the position of Restatement First on nominal consideration, and adopted a test that requires a bargain in fact rather than in form:

> 4. A desires to make a binding promise to give $1000 to his son B. Being advised that a gratuitous promise is not binding, A writes out and signs a false recital that B has sold him a car for $1000 and a promise to pay that amount. There is no consideration for A's promise.

> 5. A desires to make a binding promise to give $1000 to his son B. Being advised that a gratuitous promise is not binding, A offers to buy from B for $1000 a book worth less than $1. B accepts the offer knowing that the purchase of the book is a mere pretense. There is no consideration for A's promise to pay $1000.

Although Restatement Second rejects the concept of nominal consideration as a general principle, it does provide that nominal consideration makes a promise enforceable in two specific areas—options and guaranties. (An option is an offer accompanied by an enforceable promise to hold the offer open.) The cases in this area are not entirely consistent. The majority rule under the cases is that a *recital* of nominal consideration does not make an option binding. On the other hand, many of the cases hold that even the most negligible consideration will make an option enforceable if it is *paid*. See, e.g., Board of Control v. Burgess, 45 Mich.App. 183, 206 N.W.2d 256 (1973) ($1 nominal consideration not paid; option unenforceable; it would have been enforceable if the $1 had been paid). The reason for this distinction is not clear. If the consideration is really nominal, it is no less a form just because it is paid. Perhaps actual payment of nominal consideration is viewed as a better form than the mere recital of a bargain, because a physical transfer of money may have more psychological impact than a mere recital.

NOTE ON CONSIDERATION AND THE SEAL

The opinion in *Schnell v. Nell* tells us that Schnell's contract ended as follows: "In witness whereof, the said parties have ... set hereunto their hands and seals. Zacharias Schnell. [Seal.] J.B. Nell. [Seal.] Wen. Lorenz. [Seal.]" Prior to modern statutory reforms, a promise under seal occupied a special status in contract law, differing from an unsealed promise in a number of respects. The most important difference was that a promise under seal was enforceable even though it was donative.

This rule was sometimes expressed by the statement that a seal "imports" or "raises a presumption of" consideration. Under developed English law, the presumption was not rebuttable. 3 W. Holdsworth, A History of English Law 419B20 (3d Ed. 1923). Probably the same held true in most American states prior to modern statutory developments, although some jurisdictions may have treated the presumption as rebuttable. See Cochran v. Taylor, 273 N.Y. 172, 7 N.E.2d 89 (1937); Note, The Status of the Common-Law Seal in Florida, 1 U.Fla.L.Rev. 385, 391–93 (1948).

Originally, a seal consisted of a bit of wax placed at the end of a document and bearing the impression of an individual's signet ring. In early times, a signet ring was a ring incised with a symbol that was intimately identified with the ring's owner, such as the owner's coat of arms or initials. Normally the wax would be heated, dripped onto the paper, and then impressed with the signet. In its origin, therefore, the seal was a "natural formality"—that is, a promissory form that is popularly understood to carry legal significance— involving a writing, a ritual of hot wax, and a physical object, the signet ring, that personified its owner—elements that ensured both deliberation and proof. However, "in the United States the courts have not required either wax or impression. Impressions directly on the paper [usually made with a metal form] were recognized early and are still common for notarial and corporate seals, and gummed paper wafers have been widely used. In the absence of statute decisions have divided on the effectiveness of the written or printed word 'seal,' the printed initials 'L.S.' (locus sigilli, meaning place of the seal), a scrawl made with a pen (often called a 'scroll') and a recital of sealing. Most states in which the seal is still recognized now have statutes giving effect to one or more such devices." Restatement Second § 96, comment *a*. With this development, the seal not only ceased to be a natural formality but became an empty device whose legal consequences were not widely understood.

About two-thirds of the states have now adopted statutory provisions depriving the seal of its binding effect. These provisions fall into four basic categories:

1. *Statutory provisions that allow a lack of consideration to be pleaded as a defense in suits based on sealed instruments.* The first of the two Indiana statutes quoted in the Note on Statutes Applicable in Schnell v. Nell, supra, is an example of such a statute.

2. *Statutory provisions that abolish the distinction between sealed and unsealed instruments.* The second Indiana statute quoted in that Note is an example of this type of statute. See also, e.g. Cal.Civ.Code § 1629. On their face, provisions of this type could be interpreted to mean either that sealed instruments should be treated as if they were unsealed, or the other way around. The former reading is almost certainly the one intended, given the historical context. This type of provision is often accompanied by a related statute which provides that a written instrument, sealed or unsealed, shall be presumptive of or shall import consideration. See, e.g., Cal.Civ.Code § 1614; Iowa Code Ann. § 537A.2. The presumption raised under this type of statute is almost certainly rebuttable.

3. *Statutory provisions that abolish the use of a seal in contracts.* See, e.g., Iowa Code Ann. § 537A.1. This type of provision is often accompanied by the type of statute described in paragraph 1, supra.

4. *Statutory provisions that limit the seal's effect.* Statutes in this category frequently provide that the seal shall be only presumptive evidence of consideration. See, e.g., N.J.Rev.Stat. § 2A:82B3. As with the common law rule, a question can be raised whether the statutory presumption is rebuttable or conclusive. It hardly seems likely that conclusive effect was intended, because if the presumption were conclusive the statute would make no change in the common law, and would therefore be unnecessary. See Note, Contracts Without Consideration; the Seal and the Uniform Obligations Act, 3 U.Chi.L.Rev. 312, 314 (1936).[1]

---

1. In Aller v. Aller, 40 N.J.L. 446 (1878), the New Jersey court held that a statute which   provided "that in every action upon a sealed instrument . . . the seal thereof shall be only

In about one-third of the states there is no statute or decision depriving the seal of its binding effect. Restatement Second Ch. 4, Topic 3 (Introductory Note). Few if any of these states have statutes that explicitly validate the common-law rule, but most do have statutory provisions that recognize in some way a distinction between sealed and unsealed instruments. For example, Mass.Gen.Laws Ann. ch. 4, § 9A provides that "In any written instrument, a recital that such instrument is sealed by or bears the seal of the person signing the same or is given under the hand and seal of the person signing the same, or that such instrument is intended to take effect as a sealed instrument, shall be sufficient to give such instrument the legal effect of a sealed instrument without the addition of any seal of wax, paper or other substance or any semblance of a seal by scroll, impression or otherwise...." (Caveat: Section 2–203 of the Uniform Commercial Code, which governs contracts for the sale of goods in almost every state, provides that "The affixing of a seal to a writing evidencing a contract for sale or an offer to buy or sell goods does not constitute the writing a sealed instrument and the law with respect to sealed instruments does not apply to such a contract or offer." Under section 2–203, a statutory provision, such as that in Massachusetts, that recognizes or gives effect to the seal will usually be inapplicable to contracts for the sale of goods.) In some states, there is some legislative recognition of a distinction between sealed and unsealed contracts, but it is less direct than in a state like Massachusetts, and instead consists of different periods of limitations for the two types of contract. See, e.g., Me.Rev.Stat.Ann. tit. 14, § 751.

It is conceivable that in the absence of the kind of explicit statutory validation found in Massachusetts, a modern court would not regard itself as bound by the common-law rule governing enforceability. See Hartford–Connecticut Trust Co. v. Divine, 97 Conn. 193, 116 A. 239 (1922); cf. Ortez v. Bargas, 29 Hawaii 548 (1927) (instrument is sealed only if it bears actual wax seal, and even if sealed, it may be attacked for lack of consideration). But see Warfield v. Baltimore Gas & Electric Co., 307 Md. 142, 512 A.2d 1044 (1986) (longer statute of limitations applied to a contract that included the printed term "(SEAL)." Alternatively, a modern court could reinterpret the common law rule to mean only that a seal creates a rebuttable presumption of consideration.

SECTION 3. THE ELEMENT OF RELIANCE

The cases in Sections 1 and 2 illustrate that the *moral* obligation to keep a promise is not a sufficient ground for concluding that there is a *legal*

presumptive evidence of a sufficient consideration, which may be rebutted, as if such instrument was not sealed," did not change the common law rule that a *donative* promise under seal was enforceable. "[The statute] does not reach the case of a voluntary agreement, where there was no consideration, and none intended by the parties." Id. at 452. In 1900, the New Jersey statute was amended in a manner that may seem to negate the holding of Aller v. Aller. Nevertheless, the result reached in *Aller* was reaffirmed in a 1941 decision of the New Jersey Court of Errors and Appeals, Zirk v. Nohr, 127 N.J.L. 217, 21 A.2d 766. See also United & Globe Rubber Mfg. Cos. v. Conard, 80 N.J.L. 286, 78 A. 203 (Ct.Err. & App. 1910). In Joseph Linder v. Commissioner, 68 T.C. 792 (1977), the United States Tax Court took the position that a modern New Jersey court would not follow the interpretation of the New Jersey statute given in Zirk v. Nohr. Cf. Whitehead v. Villapiano, 16 N.J.Super. 415, 84 A.2d 731 (1951).

obligation to keep a promise. The moral obligation to keep a promise is a strong starting-point for concluding that there should be a legal obligation to keep a promise, because the courts should take moral norms into account in making law. It is not, however, conclusive, because in making legal rules a lawmaker must also consider social policy and experiential concerns, such as problems of proof.

More generally, that private conduct violates a moral norm does not alone justify the use of collective (governmental) resources to legally sanction the conduct. In some cases, like cutting in line, the injury caused by violation of a moral norm is not significant enough to justify a legal sanction. In other cases, like the failure to support aged parents who cannot support themselves, legal enforceability of a moral norm would intrude too far, without sufficient justification, into intimate areas better governed by social norms. In still other cases, legal enforceability of a moral norm would raise difficult problems of administrability. Thus as stated by Thomas Scanlon, "The fact that some action is morally required is not, in general, a sufficient justification for legal intervention to force people to do it; and the rationale for the law of contracts does not seem to be ... an instance of the legal enforcement of morality."

The issue then is, what additional moral or policy elements, beyond the moral obligation to keep a promise, should make a given type of promise enforceable. This Section explores one such element: a significant injury to the promise; in particular, a cost that the promisee incurs in reliance on the promise.

———

KIRKSEY v. KIRKSEY

Supreme Court of Alabama, 1845.
8 Ala. 131.

Assumpsit by defendant, against the plaintiff in error.

The plaintiff was the wife of defendant's brother, but had for some time been a widow, and had several children. In 1840, the plaintiff resided on public land, under a contract of lease, she had held over, and was comfortably settled, and would have attempted to secure the land she lived on. The defendant resided in Talladega county, some sixty or seventy miles off. On the 10th October, 1840, he wrote to her the following letter:

"Dear Sister Antillico,—Much to my mortification, I heard that brother Henry was dead, and one of his children. I know that your situation is one of grief and difficulty. You had a bad chance before, but a great deal worse now. I should like to come and see you, but cannot with convenience at present ... I do not know whether you have a preference on the place you live on or not. If you had, I would advise you to obtain your preference, and sell the land and quit the country, as I understand it is very unhealthy, and I know society is very bad. If you will come down and see me, I will let you have a place to raise your family, and I have more open land than I can tend; and on the account of your situation, and that of your family, I feel like I want you and the children to do well."

Within a month or two after the receipt of this letter, the plaintiff abandoned her possession, without disposing of it, and removed with her family, to the residence of the defendant, who put her in comfortable houses, and gave her land to cultivate for two years, at the end of which time he notified her to remove, and put her in a house, not comfortable, in the woods, which he afterwards required her to leave.

A verdict being found for the plaintiff, for $200, the above facts were agreed, and if they will sustain the action, the judgment is to be affirmed, otherwise it is to be reversed.

Ormond, J. The inclination of my mind is that the loss and inconvenience which the plaintiff sustained in breaking up and moving to the defendant's a distance of sixty miles is a sufficient consideration to support the promise to furnish her with a house and land to cultivate until she could raise her family. My brothers, however, think that the promise on the part of the defendant was a mere gratuity, and that an action will not lie for its breach.

The judgment of the court below must therefore be reversed, pursuant to the agreement of the parties.

––––––

RESTATEMENT, SECOND, CONTRACTS § 90

[See Selected Source Materials Supplement]

––––––

FEINBERG v. PFEIFFER CO.

Missouri Court of Appeals, 1959.
322 S.W.2d 163.

Doerner, Commissioner. This is a suit brought in the Circuit Court of the City of St. Louis by plaintiff, a former employee of the defendant corporation, on an alleged contract whereby defendant agreed to pay plaintiff the sum of $200 per month for life upon her retirement. A jury being waived, the case was tried by the court alone. Judgment below was for plaintiff for $5,100, the amount of the pension claimed to be due as of the date of the trial, together with interest thereon, and defendant duly appealed.

The parties are in substantial agreement on the essential facts. Plaintiff began working for the defendant, a manufacturer of pharmaceuticals, in 1910, when she was but 17 years of age. By 1947 she had attained the position of bookkeeper, office manager, and assistant treasurer of the defendant, and owned 70 shares of its stock out of a total of 6,503 shares issued and outstanding. Twenty shares had been given to her by the defendant or its then president, she had purchased 20, and the remaining 30 she had acquired by a stock split or stock dividend. Over the years she received substantial dividends on the stock she owned, as did all of the other stockholders. Also, in addition to her salary, plaintiff from 1937 to 1949, inclusive, received each year a bonus varying in amount from $300 in the beginning to $2,000 in the later years.

On December 27, 1947, the annual meeting of the defendant's Board of Directors was held at the Company's offices in St. Louis, presided over by Max Lippman, its then president and largest individual stockholder. The other directors present were George L. Marcus, Sidney Harris, Sol Flammer, and Walter Weinstock, who, with Max Lippman, owned 5,007 of the 6,503 shares then issued and outstanding. At that meeting the Board of Directors adopted the following resolution, which because it is the crux of the case, we quote in full:

"The Chairman thereupon pointed out that the Assistant Treasurer, Mrs. Anna Sacks Feinberg, has given the corporation many years of long and faithful service. Not only has she served the corporation devotedly, but with exceptional ability and skill. The President pointed out that although all of the officers and directors sincerely hoped and desired that Mrs. Feinberg would continue in her present position for as long as she felt able, nevertheless, in view of the length of service which she has contributed provision should be made to afford her retirement privileges and benefits which should become a firm obligation of the corporation to be available to her whenever she should see fit to retire from active duty, however many years in the future such retirement may become effective. It was, accordingly, proposed that Mrs. Feinberg's salary which is presently $350.00 per month, be increased to $400.00 per month, and that Mrs. Feinberg would be given the privilege of retiring from active duty at any time she may elect to see fit so to do upon a retirement pay of $200.00 per month for life, with the distinct understanding that the retirement plan is merely being adopted at the present time in order to afford Mrs. Feinberg security for the future and in the hope that her active services will continue with the corporation for many years to come. After due discussion and consideration, and upon motion duly made and seconded, it was—

"Resolved, that the salary of Anna Sacks Feinberg be increased from $350.00 to $400.00 per month and that she be afforded the privilege of retiring from active duty in the corporation at any time she may elect to see fit so to do upon retirement pay of $200.00 per month, for the remainder of her life."

At the request of Mr. Lippman his sons-in-law, Messrs. Harris and Flammer, called upon the plaintiff at her apartment on the same day to advise her of the passage of the resolution. Plaintiff testified on cross-examination that she had no prior information that such a pension plan was contemplated, that it came as a surprise to her, and that she would have continued in her employment whether or not such a resolution had been adopted. It is clear from the evidence that there was no contract, oral or written, as to plaintiff's length of employment, and that she was free to quit, and the defendant to discharge her, at any time.

Plaintiff did continue to work for the defendant through June 30, 1949, on which date she retired. In accordance with the foregoing resolution, the defendant began paying her the sum of $200 on the first of each month. Mr. Lippman died on November 18, 1949, and was succeeded as president of the company by his widow. Because of an illness, she retired from that office and was succeeded in October, 1953, by her son-in-law, Sidney M. Harris. Mr. Harris testified that while Mrs. Lippman had been president she signed the monthly pension check paid plaintiff, but fussed about doing so, and considered the payments as gifts. After his election, he stated, a new accounting firm employed by the defendant questioned the validity of the payments to plaintiff on several occasions, and in the Spring of 1956, upon its recommendation, he consulted the Company's then attorney, Mr. Ralph Kalish. Harris testified that both Ernst and Ernst, the accounting firm, and Kalish told him there was no need of giving plaintiff the money. He also stated that he had concurred in the view that the payments to plaintiff were mere gratuities rather than amounts due under a contractual obligation, and that following his discussion with the Company's attorney plaintiff was sent a check for $100 on April 1, 1956. Plaintiff declined to accept the reduced amount, and this action followed. Additional facts will be referred to later in this opinion.

Appellant's first assignment of error relates to the admission in evidence of plaintiff's testimony over its objection, that at the time of trial she was sixty-five and a half years old, and that she was no longer able to engage in gainful employment because of the removal of a cancer and the performance of a colocholecystostomy operation on November 25, 1957. Its complaint is not so much that such evidence was irrelevant and immaterial, as it is that the trial court erroneously made it one basis for its decision in favor of plaintiff. As defendant concedes, the error (if it was error) in the admission of such evidence would not be a ground for reversal, since, this being a jury-waived case, we are constrained by the statutes to review it upon both the law and the evidence, Sec. 510.310 RSMo 1949, V.A.M.S., and to render such judgment as the court below ought to have given. Section 512.160, Minor v. Lillard, Mo., 289 S.W.2d 1; Thumm v. Lohr, Mo.App., 306 S.W.2d 604. We consider only such evidence as is admissible, and need not pass upon questions of error in the admission and exclusion of evidence. Hussey v. Robison, Mo., 285 S.W.2d 603. However, in fairness to the trial court it should be stated that while he briefly referred to the state of plaintiff's health as of the time of the trial in his amended findings of fact, it is obvious from his amended grounds for decision and judgment that it was not, as will be seen, the basis for his decision.

Appellant's next complaint is that there was insufficient evidence to support the court's findings that plaintiff would not have quit defendant's employ had she not known and relied upon the promise of defendant to pay her $200 a month for life, and the finding that, from her voluntary retirement until April 1, 1956, plaintiff relied upon the continued receipt of the pension installments. The trial court so found, and, in our opinion, justifiably so. Plaintiff testified, and was corroborated by Harris, defendant's witness, that knowledge of the passage of the resolution was communicated to her on December 27, 1947, the very day it was adopted. She was told at that time by Harris and Flammer, she stated, that she could take the pension as of that day, if she wished. She testified further that she continued to work for another year and a half, through June 30, 1949; that at that time her health was good and she could have continued to work, but that after working for almost forty years she thought she would take a rest. Her testimony continued:

"Q. Now, what was the reason—I'm sorry. Did you then quit the employment of the company after you—after this year and a half? A. Yes.

"Q. What was the reason that you left? A. Well, I thought almost forty years, it was a long time and I thought I would take a little rest.

"Q. Yes. A. And with the pension and what earnings my husband had, we figured we could get along.

"Q. Did you rely upon this pension? A. We certainly did.

"Q. Being paid? A. Very much so. We relied upon it because I was positive that I was going to get it as long as I lived.

"Q. Would you have left the employment of the company at that time had it not been for this pension? A. No.

"Mr. Allen: Just a minute, I object to that as calling for a conclusion and conjecture on the part of this witness.

"The Court: It will be overruled.

"Q. (Mr. Agatstein continuing): Go ahead, now. The question is whether you would have quit the employment of the company at that time had you not relied upon this pension plan? A. No, I wouldn't.

"Q. You would not have. Did you ever seek employment while this pension was being paid to you—A. (interrupting): No.

"Q. Wait a minute, at any time prior—at any other place? A. No, sir.

"Q. Were you able to hold any other employment during that time? A. Yes, I think so.

"Q. Was your health good? A. My health was good."

It is obvious from the foregoing that there was ample evidence to support the findings of fact made by the court below.

We come, then, to the basic issue in the case. While otherwise defined in defendant's third and fourth assignments of error, it is thus succinctly stated in the argument in its brief: " ... whether plaintiff has proved that she has a right to recover from defendant based upon a legally binding contractual obligation to pay her $200 per month for life."

It is defendant's contention, in essence, that the resolution adopted by its Board of Directors was a mere promise to make a gift, and that no contract resulted either thereby, or when plaintiff retired, because there was no consideration given or paid by the plaintiff. It urges that a promise to make a gift is not binding unless supported by a legal consideration; that the only apparent consideration for the adoption of the foregoing resolution was the "many years of long and faithful service" expressed therein; and that past services are not a valid consideration for a promise. Defendant argues further that there is nothing in the resolution which made its effectiveness conditional upon plaintiff's continued employment, that she was not under contract to work for any length of time but was free to quit whenever she wished, and that she had no contractual right to her position and could have been discharged at any time.

Plaintiff concedes that a promise based upon past services would be without consideration, but contends that there were two other elements which supplied the required element: First, the continuation by plaintiff in the employ of the defendant for the period from December 27, 1947, the date when the resolution was adopted, until the date of her retirement on June 30, 1949. And, second, her change of position, i.e., her retirement, and the abandonment by her of her opportunity to continue in gainful employment, made in reliance on defendant's promise to pay her $200 per month for life.

We must agree with the defendant that the evidence does not support the first of these contentions. There is no language in the resolution predicating plaintiff's right to a pension upon her continued employment. She was not required to work for the defendant for any period of time as a condition to gaining such retirement benefits. She was told that she could quit the day upon which the resolution was adopted, as she herself testified, and it is clear from her own testimony that she made no promise or agreement to continue in the employ of the defendant in return for its promise to pay her a pension. Hence there was lacking that mutuality of obligation which is essential to the validity of a contract. . . .

But as to the second of these contentions we must agree with plaintiff. . . .

Section 90 of the Restatement, Law of Contracts states that: "A promise which the promisor should reasonably expect to induce action or forbearance of a definite and substantial character on the part of the promisee and which does induce such action or forbearance is binding if injustice can be avoided only by enforcement of the promise." This doctrine has been described as that of "promissory estoppel," as distinguished from that of equitable estoppel or estoppel in pais, the reason for the differentiation being stated as follows:

> "It is generally true that one who has led another to act in reasonable reliance on his representations of fact cannot afterwards in litigation between the two deny the truth of the representations, and some courts have sought to apply this principle to the formation of contracts, where, relying on a gratuitous promise, the promisee has suffered detriment. It is to be noticed, however, that such a case does not come within the ordinary definition of estoppel. If there is any representation of an existing fact, it is only that the promisor at the time of making the promise intends to fulfill it. As to such intention there is usually no misrepresentation and if there is, it is not that which has injured the promisee. In other words, he relies on a promise and not on a misstatement of fact; and the term 'promissory' estoppel or something equivalent should be used to make the distinction." Williston on Contracts, Rev.Ed., Sec. 139, Vol. 1.

In speaking of this doctrine, Judge Learned Hand said in Porter v. Commissioner of Internal Revenue, 2 Cir., 60 F.2d 673, 675, that " . . . 'promissory estoppel' is now a recognized species of consideration."

As pointed out by our Supreme Court in In re Jamison's Estate, Mo., 202 S.W.2d 879, 887, it is stated in the Missouri Annotations to the Restatement under Section 90 that:

> " 'There is a variance between the doctrine underlying this section and the theoretical justifications that have been advanced for the Missouri decisions.' "

That variance, as the authors of the Annotations point out, is that:

> "This § 90, when applied with § 85, means that the promise described is a contract without any consideration. In Missouri the same practical result is reached without in theory abandoning the doctrine of consideration. In Missouri three theories have been advanced as ground

for the decisions (1) *Theory of act for promise.* The induced 'action or forbearance' is the consideration for the promise.... (2) *Theory of promissory estoppel.* The induced 'action or forbearance' works an estoppel against the promisor.... (3) *Theory of bilateral contract.* When the induced 'action or forbearance' is begun, a promise to complete is implied, and we have an enforceable bilateral contract, the implied promise to complete being the consideration for the original promise." (Citing cases.)

Was there such an act on the part of plaintiff, in reliance upon the promise contained in the resolution, as will estop the defendant, and therefore create an enforceable contract under the doctrine of promissory estoppel? We think there was. One of the illustrations cited under Section 90 of the Restatement is: "2. A promises B to pay him an annuity during B's life. B thereupon resigns a profitable employment, as A expected that he might. B receives the annuity for some years, in the meantime becoming disqualified from again obtaining good employment. A's promise is binding." This illustration is objected to by defendant as not being applicable to the case at hand. The reason advanced by it is that in the illustration B became "disqualified" from obtaining other employment *before* A discontinued the payments, whereas in this case the plaintiff did not discover that she had cancer and thereby became unemployable until *after* the defendant had discontinued the payments of $200 per month. We think the distinction is immaterial. The only reason for the reference in the illustration to the disqualification of A is in connection with that part of Section 90 regarding the prevention of injustice. The injustice would occur regardless of when the disability occurred. Would defendant contend that the contract would be enforceable if the plaintiff's illness had been discovered on March 31, 1956, the day before it discontinued the payment of the $200 a month, but not if it occurred on April 2nd, the day after? Furthermore, there are more ways to become disqualified for work, or unemployable, than as the result of illness. At the time she retired plaintiff was 57 years of age. At the time the payments were discontinued she was over 63 years of age. It is a matter of common knowledge that it is virtually impossible for a woman of that age to find satisfactory employment, much less a position comparable to that which plaintiff enjoyed at the time of her retirement.

The fact of the matter is that plaintiff's subsequent illness was not the "action or forbearance" which was induced by the promise contained in the resolution. As the trial court correctly decided, such action on plaintiff's part was her retirement from a lucrative position in reliance upon defendant's promise to pay her an annuity or pension. In a very similar case, Ricketts v. Scothorn, 57 Neb. 51, 77 N.W. 365, 367, 42 L.R.A. 794, the Supreme Court of Nebraska said:

> "... Having intentionally influenced the plaintiff to alter her position for the worse on the faith of the note being paid when due, it would be grossly inequitable to permit the maker, or his executor, to resist payment on the ground that the promise was given without consideration."

The Commissioner therefore recommends, for the reasons stated, that the judgment be affirmed.

Per Curiam.

The foregoing opinion by DOERNER, C., is adopted as the opinion of the court. The judgment is, accordingly, affirmed.

WOLFE, P.J., and ANDERSON and RUDDY, JJ., concur.

———

HAYES v. PLANTATIONS STEEL CO., 438 A.2d 1091 (R.I.1982). Plantations Steel Co. was founded by Hugo R. Mainelli, Sr., and Alexander A. Dimartino. Hayes was employed by Plantations from 1947 to 1972. In January 1972, Hayes announced his intention to retire in July, because he had worked continuously for fifty–one years. Hayes was then sixty–five, and was Plantation's general manager, a position of considerable responsibility. About a week before his actual retirement, Hayes spoke with Hugo R. Mainelli, Jr., an officer and a shareholder of Plantations. Mainelli, Jr. said that the company "would take care" of Hayes, although there was no mention of a sum of money or a percentage of salary that Hayes would receive. Mainelli, Jr.'s father, Hugo R. Mainelli, Sr., authorized the first payment "as a token of appreciation for the many years of [Hayes's] service." It was implied that payments would continue on an annual basis, and it was Mainelli, Jr.'s personal intention that the payments would continue for as long as he was around. Four annual payments of $5,000 each were made.

After Hayes's retirement, he visited Plantations each year to say hello and renew old acquaintances. During the course of his visits, Hayes would thank Mainelli, Jr. for the previous check, and ask how long the checks would continue, so that he could plan an orderly retirement. In 1976, the DiMartinos assumed full control of Plantations as a result of a dispute between the two founding families. After 1976, the payments to Hayes were discontinued. A succession of several poor business years and the takeover by the DiMartino family contributed to the decision to stop the payments. Hayes brought suit. Held, for Plantations.

"[T]he important distinction between *Feinberg* and the case before us is that in *Feinberg* the employer's decision definitely shaped the thinking of the plaintiff. In this case the promise did not. It is not reasonable to infer from the facts that Hugo R. Mainelli, Jr., expected retirement to result from his conversation with Hayes. Hayes had given notice of his intention seven months previously. Here there was thus no inducement to retire which would satisfy the demands of § 90 of the Restatement. Nor can it be said that Hayes's refraining from other employment was 'action or forbearance of a definite and substantial character.' The underlying assumption of Hayes's initial decision to retire was that upon leaving the defendant's employ, he would no longer work. It is impossible to say that he changed his position any more so because of what Mainelli had told him in light of his own initial decision. These circumstances do not lead to a conclusion that injustice can be avoided only by enforcement of Plantations's promise. Hayes received $20,000 over the course of four years. He inquired each year about whether he could expect a check for the following year. Obviously, there was no absolute certainty on his part that the pension would continue. Furthermore, in the face of his uncertainty, the mere fact that payment for several years did occur is insufficient by itself to meet the requirements of reliance under the doctrine of promissory estoppel.''

———

NOTE ON CONTRACT REMEDIES AND CONSIDERATION

The essential question considered in Part I of this casebook, under the heading "Consideration," is what promises should and does the law enforce? On both a theoretical and a practical level, this question is inseparable from the issue, *to what extent* shall a particular kind of promise be enforced?

When issues of remedy are examined in detail (as they will be in Part II), they present a great number of complexities and policy choices. At this point it is useful to examine some of these issues in a broad way.

Injury. One way to address the issue of damages for breach of an enforceable promise is to ask what injury the promisee has suffered. In a contract setting, the term "injury" to a promisee can have several different meanings. One meaning is that the promisee is worse off than he would have been if the promise had not been made. Another meaning is that the promisee is worse off than he would have been if the promise had been performed. The interests of a promisee that are invaded by these two different types of injuries are known as the *reliance interest* and the *expectation interest,* respectively.

These two distinct meanings of injury correspond to two distinct purposes of damages for breach of contract. Reliance damages have the purpose of restoring a promisee back to the position that he would have been in if the promise had not been made. If this purpose is perfectly achieved, a potential promisee is equally well off whether there is (i) no promise, or (ii) promise, breach, and payment of damages. Expectation damages have the purpose of placing a promisee forward to the position that he would have been in if the promise had been performed. If this purpose is perfectly achieved, the promisee is equally well off whether there is (i) promise and performance, or (ii) promise, breach, and payment of damages.*

Compensation. In our legal system, compensation is measured in money. In contract law, compensation is the sum of money that is sufficient to make the victim of an injury equally well off with the money and the injury as he would have been without the money and the injury. In this sense, compensatory damages are the money equivalent of the injury. The idea of a money equivalent to injury can be clarified with help from economic theory. Economists measure the well-being of individuals by the amount of satisfaction they enjoy, and measure the well-being of firms by their profits. Compensation for an injury is "perfect" if it enables the victim to enjoy the same level of satisfaction (if an individual) or profits (if a firm) as would have prevailed without the injury. Computing compensatory damages involves comparing the victim's uninjured state with the injured state, in order to determine how much money is needed to make up the difference.

Because there are two different conceptions of the uninjured state in a contract setting, there are also two different conceptions of compensation.

* To keep matters simple, other interests and remedies will not be considered in this Note. For the same reason, this Note will not consider remedies other than damages.

Protection of the reliance interest requires an award such that the injured promisee will achieve the level of satisfaction (if an individual) or profits (if a firm) that would have been achieved if the promise had never been made. Under the reliance conception of compensation, therefore, compensation is the amount required to put the injured promisee in a state just as good as if the promise had not been made.

In contrast, protection of the expectation interest requires an award such that the injured party will achieve the level of satisfaction or profits that would have been achieved if the promise had been performed. Under the expectation conception of compensation, therefore, compensation is the amount required to make the promisee indifferent between performance and damages. (Expectation damages are not compensatory in the normal sense of that term, because they make the promisee better off than he was before he encountered the promisor. However, such damages are commonly described as compensatory, and that usage will be followed here.)

Reliance damages. Let us focus here on the reliance conception. What compensation is necessary to put a relying promisee in a state just as good as he would have been in if the promise had not been made? When a promise is made, the promisee may rely upon it by incurring various financial and nonfinancial costs that cannot be fully recouped if the promise is broken. Broadly speaking, these costs fall into two classes—out-of-pocket costs and opportunity costs.

Out-of-pocket-costs. Out-of-pocket costs are the net costs incurred by a promisee in reliance on the promise prior to breach, less the value produced by those costs that can be realized after breach. To illustrate, assume that Aunt promises Niece that she will reimburse Niece for the cost of a $12,000 car. Niece purchases a car for $12,000 cash on January 5, and immediately tells Aunt about the purchase. Aunt immediately states that she will not keep her promise. Niece's out-of-pocket costs are the difference between her outlay of $12,000 and the resale value of the car on January 5.

Opportunity costs. Engaging in an activity often entails forgoing an opportunity to do something else. *Opportunity costs* are the surplus that the promisee would have enjoyed if he had taken the opportunity that the promise led him to forgo. More specifically, if as a result of a breach the injured party must purchase a substitute performance, the opportunity cost equals the difference between the price of the substitute performance and the best alternative contract price that was available to the party at the time of contracting. To illustrate, assume that at a time when Niece is about to buy a certain inexpensive make of car, Aunt promises Niece that if she purchases a certain more expensive make, Aunt will pay the full price. Niece begins shopping for the more expensive make of car, but before she makes the purchase, Aunt revokes her promise. Meanwhile, the less expensive make has gone up in price from $12,000 to $13,000. If Niece then purchases that make of car, she has suffered an opportunity cost of $1,000, because the promise led her to forgo buying that make when it cost $1,000 less.

With this background, let us return to the best measure of damages for breach of a relied-upon donative promise. *Dougherty v. Salt* teaches that a simple unrelied-upon donative promise is normally unenforceable. Section 90 of the Restatement teaches that reliance may make a donative promise enforceable. But to what *extent* should a relied-upon promise be enforceable?

Or, to put it differently, what injury to a relying donative promisee should the law compensate? Since a relied-upon donative promise is enforced because, and only because, it has been relied upon, in the normal case the promise should be enforced to the extent of the reliance, that is, by a reliance (rather than an expectation) measure of damages. For reasons of policy or administrability, however, in at least some cases it might be desirable to employ an expectation measure as a surrogate for reliance. Indeed, when Restatement First was being debated on the floor of the ALI, Williston, the Reporter, went much further, and took the position that the expectation measure should be used in all Section 90 cases:

> MR. WILLISTON: . . . Johnny says, "I want to buy a Buick car." Uncle says, "Well, I will give you $1000." . . . [Uncle] knows that that $1000 is going to be relied on by the nephew for the purchase of a car. . . .

> [MR.] PRICKETT: May I ask the Reporter if in the example he gave of Johnny and the car, his uncle's promise would be enforceable when Johnny buys the car?

> MR. WILLISTON: I should say so, because the promise was made as a direct reply to Johnny's expression of a desire for a car. . . .

> MR. PRICKETT: Suppose Johnny pays no money down.

> MR. WILLISTON: If he has got the car and is liable for the price he gets the $1000 under this Section. . . .

> MR. PRICKETT: My idea is this: If he gets the car and pays no money down, if the car is taken away from him, has he suffered any substantial injury?

> MR. WILLISTON: Oh, I think he has, as long as he is liable for the price. . . .

> [MR.] TUNSTALL: . . . Suppose the car had been a Ford instead of a Buick, costing $600.

> . . . Johnny says, "I want to buy a Ford" and . . . not being familiar with the market price of a Ford, the uncle says, "I will give you $1000." Now, is the uncle obligated for the $1000 or for the price of the Ford?

> MR. WILLISTON: I think he might be bound for the $1000.

> MR. COUDERT: . . . Please let me see if I understand it rightly. Would you say, Mr. Reporter, in your case of Johnny and the uncle, the uncle promising the $1000 and Johnny buying the car—say, he goes out and buys the car for $500—that uncle would be liable for $1000 or would he be liable for $500?

> MR. WILLISTON: If Johnny had done what he was expected to do, or is acting within the limits of his uncle's expectation, I think the uncle would be liable for $1000; but not otherwise . . .

In Restatement Second, Section 90 was revised to explicitly negate Williston's view. This was accomplished by adding a new sentence to Section 90: "The remedy granted for breach may be limited as justice requires." The express purpose of this sentence is to permit the use of a reliance measure of damages in Section 90 cases.

————

GOLDSTICK v. ICM REALTY, 788 F.2d 456 (7th Cir.1986). "As a matter of strict logic one might suppose that the plaintiffs, even if they succeeded in establishing a promissory estoppel, would not necessarily be able to recover the value of the promise.... It would seem they would have to show their actual damages: what they gave up ... in reliance on [the] promise....

"This approach treats promissory estoppel as a tort doctrine for purposes of damages, though it is conventionally classified as a contract doctrine.... Some cases do award just the tort measure of damages in promissory estoppel cases, rather than giving the plaintiff the value of the promise, which he would be entitled to in a breach of contract action.... In Gerson Electric Construction Co. v. Honeywell, Inc., 117 Ill.App.3d 309, 312–13, 72 Ill.Dec. 851, 853, 453 N.E.2d 726, 728 (1983), however, the Illinois Appellate Court held that a plaintiff in a promissory estoppel case could recover damages for the profits he would have made had the defendant kept his promise—provided such an award was necessary to do justice to the plaintiff.

"There is much to be said for using the value of the promise as the measure of damages, simply on grounds of simplicity.... In addition, an expectation measure of damages will frequently cover opportunity costs (which are real, but not out-of-pocket, costs), that the reliance measure would miss...."

————

WALTERS v. MARATHON OIL CO., 642 F.2d 1098 (7th Cir.1981). Marathon Oil was engaged in the business of distributing petroleum products. Mr. and Mrs. Walters contacted Marathon in late December 1978 about the possibility of locating a combination food store and service station on a vacant service station site in Indianapolis. Based upon promises made by, and continuing negotiations with, Marathon representatives, the Walters purchased the service station in February 1979, and continued to make improvements upon it. The negotiations and paperwork proceeded normally, and the Walters delivered to Marathon an agreement signed by them. After the agreement was received, but before it was accepted, Marathon placed a moratorium on considering new applications for dealerships, and refused to sign the agreement. The Walters brought suit.

The trial court held for the Walters, on the theory of promissory estoppel. It found that the Walters lost anticipated profits of six cents per gallon for the 370,000 gallons they were to receive under their allocation for the first year's gasoline sales, totaling $22,200, and awarded this amount in damages. On appeal, Marathon argued that since the Walters succeeded at trial solely on a promissory estoppel theory, loss of profits was not a proper measure of damages. Instead, damages should have been based on the amount of the Walters' reliance, measured by the difference between their expenditures on the site and its present value. Using this measure of damages, the Walters would receive no recovery, because the present value of the site as improved was slightly more than the amount the Walters had expended. The Court of Appeals rejected this argument.

"[I]n reliance upon appellant's promise to supply gasoline supplies to them, appellees purchased the station, and invested their funds and their time. It is unreasonable to assume that they did not anticipate a return of profits from this investment of time and funds, but, in reliance upon appellant's promise, they had foregone the opportunity to make the investment elsewhere. As indicated, the record reflects that had appellant performed according to its promise, appellees would have received the anticipated net profit of $22,200.00. The findings of the trial court in this regard were fully supported by the evidence....

"Since promissory estoppel is an equitable matter, the trial court has broad power in its choice of a remedy...."

————

NOTE ON RELIANCE IN COMMERCIAL CONTEXTS

As originally conceived in Restatement First, the principle of reliance in general, and Section 90 in particular, seemed to be primarily directed to donative promises. However, as evidenced by D & G Stout, Inc. v. Bacardi Imports, Inc., and Walters v. Marathon Oil Co., since the adoption of Section 90 the courts have steadily increased the ambit of the reliance principle, and applied it in a wide variety of commercial contexts where for one reason or another the bargain principle was not sufficient to make a promise enforceable or to redress a perceived injury. Many other cases invoking the reliance principle in commercial contexts will be examined in succeeding Chapters.

————

Chapter 2

THE BARGAIN PRINCIPLE
AND ITS LIMITS

This Chapter introduces the major type of consideration, that is, the bargain. (Indeed, recall that under the terminology used by the Restatement and many courts, the terms "bargain" and "consideration" are almost equivalent.) The first several cases in Section 1 implicitly or explicitly set out *the bargain principle*, under which bargains are not only enforced, but enforced according to their terms. These cases also suggest, again explicitly or implicitly, some of the reasons that lie behind the bargain principle. Section 2 explores the limits placed on the bargain principle by the principle of unconscionability. Sections 3 and 4 explore two further, more technical limits on the bargain principle: the doctrine of mutuality and the legal-duty rule.

SECTION 1. THE BARGAIN PRINCIPLE

WESTLAKE v. ADAMS, 5 C.B. (N.S.) 248, 265 (1858). Byles, J., said: "It is an elementary principle, that the law will not enter into an inquiry as to the adequacy of the consideration.... The jury have, I think, made an end of the question [of consideration]; for they have found (as well they might) that the defendant received what he bargained for, and all that he bargained for."

HAMER v. SIDWAY
Court of Appeals of New York, 1891.
124 N.Y. 538, 27 N.E. 256.

Appeal from an order of the general term of the supreme court in the fourth judicial department, reversing a judgment entered on the decision of the court at special term in the county clerk's office of Chemung county on the 1st day of October, 1889. The plaintiff presented a claim to the executor of William E. Story, Sr., for $5,000 and interest from the 6th day of February,

1875. She acquired it through several mesne assignments from William E. Story, 2d. The claim being rejected by the executor, this action was brought. It appears that William E. Story, Sr., was the uncle of William E. Story, 2d; that at the celebration of the golden wedding of Samuel Story and wife, father and mother of William E. Story, Sr., on the 20th day of March, 1869, in the presence of the family and invited guests, he promised his nephew that if he would refrain from drinking, using tobacco, swearing, and playing cards or billiards for money until he became 21 years of age, he would pay him the sum of $5,000. The nephew assented thereto, and fully performed the conditions inducing the promise. When the nephew arrived at the age of 21 years, and on the 31st day of January, 1875, he wrote to his uncle, informing him that he had performed his part of the agreement, and had thereby become entitled to the sum of $5,000.

The uncle received the letter, and a few days later, and on the 6th day of February, he wrote and mailed to his nephew the following letter: "Buffalo, Feb. 6, 1875, W.E. Story, Jr.—Dear Nephew: Your letter of the 31st ult. came to hand all right, saying that you had lived up to the promise made to me several years ago. I have no doubt but you have, for which you shall have five thousand dollars, as I promised you. I had the money in the bank the day you was twenty-one years old that I intend for you, and you shall have the money certain. Now Willie, I do not intend to interfere with this money in any way till I think you are capable of taking care of it, and the sooner that time comes the better it will please me. I would hate very much to have you start out in some adventure that you thought all right and lose this money in one year. The first five thousand dollars that I got together cost me a heap of hard work.... This money you have earned much easier than I did, besides, acquiring good habits at the same time, and you are quite welcome to the money. Hope you will make good use of it. I was ten long years getting this together after I was your age.... Truly yours, W.E. Story. P.S. You can consider this money on interest."

The nephew received the letter, and thereafter consented that the money should remain with his uncle in accordance with the terms and conditions of the letter. The uncle died on the 29th day of January, 1887, without having paid over to his nephew any portion of the said $5,000 and interest.

PARKER, J.... The defendant contends that the contract was without consideration to support it, and therefore invalid. He asserts that the promisee, by refraining from the use of liquor and tobacco, was not harmed, but benefited; that that which he did was best for him to do, independently of his uncle's promise,—and insists that it follows that, unless the promisor was benefited, the contract was without consideration,—a contention which, if well founded, would seem to leave open for controversy in many cases whether that which the promisee did or omitted to do was in fact of such benefit to him as to leave no consideration to support the enforcement of the promisor's agreement. Such a rule could not be tolerated, and is without foundation in the law. The Exchequer Chamber in 1875 defined "consideration" as follows: "A valuable consideration, in the sense of the law, may consist either in some right, interest, profit, or benefit accruing to the one party, or some forbearance, detriment, loss, or responsibility given, suffered, or undertaken by the other." Courts "will not ask whether the thing which forms the consideration does in fact benefit the promisee or a third party, or is of any substantial value to any one. It is enough that something is promised, done, forborne, or suffered by the party to whom the promise is made as consideration for the promise made to him." Anson.Cont. 63. "In general a waiver of any legal right at the request of another party is a sufficient consideration for a promise." Pars.Cont. *444. "Any damage, or suspension, or forbearance of a right will be sufficient to sustain a promise." 2 Kent.Comm. (12th Ed.) *465. Pollock in his work on Contracts (page 166), after citing the definition given by the Exchequer Chamber, already quoted, says: "The second branch of this judicial description is really the most important one. 'Consideration' means not so much that one party is profiting as that the other abandons some legal right in the present, or limits his legal freedom of action in the future, as an inducement for the promise of the first."

Now, applying this rule to the facts before us, the promisee used tobacco, occasionally drank liquor, and he had a legal right to do so. That right he abandoned for a period of years upon the strength of the promise of the testator that for such forbearance he would give him $5,000. We need not speculate on the effort which may have been required to give up the use of those stimulants. It is sufficient that he restricted his lawful freedom of action within certain prescribed limits upon the faith of his uncle's agreement, and now, having fully performed the conditions imposed, it is of no moment whether such performance actually proved a benefit to the promisor, and the court will not inquire into it; but, were it a proper subject of inquiry, we see nothing in this record that would permit a determination that the uncle was not benefited in a legal sense. Few cases have been found which may be said to be precisely in point, but such as have been, support the position we have taken. . . .

Order appealed from reversed, and judgment of the special term affirmed.*

NOTE ON THE STATUTE OF FRAUDS

William E. Story's original promise was not in writing. Did that affect the issue whether it was legally enforceable? The question, what promises must be in writing to be enforceable (or at least, to be enforceable in full), is addressed by a group of rules known as the Statute of Frauds. This casebook is designed so that Statute of Frauds problems are to be considered continuously, in the context of cases involving oral promises, rather than in one batch. To that end, an extended Note on the Statute of Frauds is set forth at Appendix A. You should study Appendix A generally at this point. Thereafter, whenever a case involves an oral promise you should turn to the relevant sections of Appendix A to consider the impact of the Statute of Frauds on that case.

---

* For historical background to both the definition of consideration and the approach to the issue of consideration employed in Hamer v. Sidway, see Appendix B. (Footnote by ed.)

RESTATEMENT, SECOND, CONTRACTS §§ 71, 72, 79

[See Selected Source Materials Supplement]

BATSAKIS v. DEMOTSIS

Court of Civil Appeals of Texas, 1949.
226 S.W.2d 673.

McGILL, JUSTICE. This is an appeal from a judgment of the 57th judicial District Court of Bexar County. Appellant was plaintiff and appellee was defendant in the trial court. The parties will be so designated.

Plaintiff sued defendant to recover $2,000 with interest at the rate of 8% per annum from April 2, 1942, alleged to be due on the following instrument, being a translation from the original, which is written in the Greek language:

"Peiraeus

April 2, 1942

"Mr. George Batsakis

Konstantinou Diadohou # 7

Peiraeus

"Mr. Batsakis:

"I state by my present (letter) that I received today from you the amount of two thousand dollars ($2,000.00) of United States of America money, which I borrowed from you for the support of my family during these difficult days and because it is impossible for me to transfer dollars of my own from America.

"The above amount I accept with the expressed promise that I will return to you again in American dollars either at the end of the present war or even before in the event that you might be able to find a way to collect them (dollars) from my representative in America to whom I shall write and give him an order relative to this. You understand until the final execution (payment) to the above amount an eight per cent interest will be added and paid together with the principal.

"I thank you and I remain yours with respects.

"The recipient,

(Signed) Eugenia The. Demotsis."

Trial to the court without the intervention of a jury resulted in a judgment in favor of plaintiff for $750.00 principal, and interest at the rate of 8% per annum from April 2, 1942 to the date of judgment, totaling $1163.83, with interest thereon at the rate of 8% per annum until paid. Plaintiff has perfected his appeal.

The court sustained certain special exceptions of plaintiff to defendant's first amended original answer on which the case was tried, and struck therefrom paragraphs II, III and V. Defendant excepted to such action of the court, but has not cross-assigned error here. The answer, stripped of such paragraphs, consisted of a general denial contained in paragraph I thereof, and of Paragraph IV, which is as follows:

"IV. That under the circumstances alleged in Paragraph II of this answer, the consideration upon which said written instrument sued upon by plaintiff herein is founded, is wanting and has failed to the extent of $1975.00, and defendant pleads specially under the verification hereinafter made the want and failure of consideration stated, and now tenders, as defendant has heretofore tendered to plaintiff, $25.00 as the value of the loan of money received by defendant from plaintiff, together with interest thereon.

"Further, in connection with this plea of want and failure of consideration defendant alleges that she at no time received from plaintiff himself or from anyone for plaintiff any money or thing of value other than, as hereinbefore alleged, the original loan of 500,000 drachmae. That at the time of the loan by plaintiff to defendant of said 500,000 drachmae the value of 500,000 drachmae in the Kingdom of Greece in dollars of money of the United States of America, was $25.00, and also at said time the value of 500,000 drachmae of Greek money in the United States of America in dollars was $25.00 of money of the United States of America. The plea of want and failure of consideration is verified by defendant as follows."

The allegations in paragraph II which were stricken, referred to in paragraph IV, were that the instrument sued on was signed and delivered in the Kingdom of Greece on or about April 2, 1942, at which time both plaintiff and defendant were residents of and residing in the Kingdom of Greece, and

"*Plaintiff* (emphasis ours) avers that on or about April 2, 1942 she owned money and property and had credit in the United States of America, but was then and there in the Kingdom of Greece in straitened financial circumstances due to the conditions produced by World War II and could not make use of her money and property and credit existing in the United States of America. That in the circumstances the plaintiff agreed to and did lend to defendant the sum of 500,000 drachmae, which at that time, on or about April 2, 1942, had the value of $25.00 in money of the United States of America. That the said plaintiff knowing defendant's financial distress and desire to return to the United States of America, exacted of her the written instrument plaintiff sues upon, which was a promise by her to pay to him the sum of $2,000.00 of United States of America money."

Plaintiff specially excepted to paragraph IV because the allegations thereof were insufficient to allege either want of consideration or failure of consideration, in that it affirmatively appears therefrom that defendant received what was agreed to be delivered to her, and that plaintiff breached no agreement. The court overruled this exception, and such action is assigned as error. Error is also assigned because of the court's failure to enter judgment for the whole unpaid balance of the principal of the instrument with interest as therein provided.

Defendant testified that she did receive 500,000 drachmas from plaintiff. It is not clear whether she received all the 500,000 drachmas or only a portion of them before she signed the instrument in question. Her testimony clearly shows that the understanding of the parties was that plaintiff would give her the 500,000 drachmas if she would sign the instrument. She testified:

"Q. . . . who suggested the figure of $2,000.00?

"A. That was how he asked me from the beginning. He said he will give me five hundred thousand drachmas provided I signed that I would pay him $2,000.00 American money."

The transaction amounted to a sale by plaintiff of the 500,000 drachmas in consideration of the execution of the instrument sued on, by defendant. It is not contended that the drachmas had no value. Indeed, the judgment indicates that the trial court placed a value of $750.00 on them or on the other consideration which plaintiff gave defendant for the instrument if he believed plaintiff's testimony. Therefore the plea of want of consideration was unavailing. A plea of want of consideration amounts to a contention that the instrument never became a valid obligation in the first place. . . .

Mere inadequacy of consideration will not void a contract. 10 Tex.Jur., Contracts, Sec. 89, p. 150; Chastain v. Texas Christian Missionary Society, Tex.Civ.App., 78 S.W.2d 728, loc. cit. 731(3), Wr. Ref.

Nor was the plea of failure of consideration availing. Defendant got exactly what she contracted for according to her own testimony. The court should have rendered judgment in favor of plaintiff against defendant for the principal sum of $2,000.00 evidenced by the instrument sued on, with interest as therein provided. We construe the provision relating to interest as providing for interest at the rate of 8% per annum. The judgment is reformed so as to award appellant a recovery against appellee of $2,000.00 with interest thereon at the rate of 8% per annum from April 2, 1942. Such judgment will bear interest at the rate of 8% per annum until paid on $2,000.00 thereof and on the balance interest at the rate of 6% per annum. As so reformed, the judgment is affirmed.

Reformed and affirmed.

FURTHER NOTE ON CONSIDERATION AND REMEDIES

It has already been pointed out that the question, what promises should the law enforce, is inseparable from the issue, *to what extent* should a particular type of promise be enforced? This is not a problem when the three basic damage measures—expectation, reliance, and restitution—produce identical results. For example, suppose that Plumber P, whose normal rate is $60 an hour, agrees to perform a repair for Homeowner H, and spends one hour on the job. H fails to pay. P's expectation damages are $60, the value of H's promised performance. P's reliance damages are also probably $60, because the plumbing business being what it is, in accepting H's job, P probably gave up an opportunity to use his time doing plumbing repairs for someone else. Restitution damages may also be deemed to be $60, because H has received $60 worth of plumbing services.

Often, however, the three damage measures will differ. In *Batsakis v. Demotsis*, the defendant argued in effect that the value of what she had received was much less than the value of what she had promised. She was willing to pay the value of what she had received—that is, restitution damages. What the defendant resisted was payment of the value of what she had promised—that is, expectation damages. Conversely, the plaintiff rejected restitution damages and insisted on expectation damages. In short, both parties admitted that the contract was enforceable to some extent; the question was, to what extent. In a very real way, therefore, when the court said that adequacy of consideration will not be reviewed, it was making a damages rule, namely, that when a bargain has been made the normal remedy for breach is expectation damages, and it is no defense that the value of one promised performance exceeded the value of the other.

———

RESTATEMENT, SECOND, CONTRACTS §§ 175, 176

[See Selected Source Materials Supplement]

———

UNIDROIT PRINCIPLES OF INTERNATIONAL COMMERCIAL CONTRACTS ART. 3.9

[See Selected Source Materials Supplement]

———

NOTE ON UNIDROIT

In 1971, the governing council of the International Institute for the Unification of Private Law determined to include a codification of the law of contracts in its program. A Working Group consisting of academics, judges, and civil servants was created in 1980. The members of the Working Group were of different nationalities, but sat in their personal capacities, not to express the views of their governments. The ultimate result was the Unidroit Principles of International Commercial Contracts, which was finalized in 1994. The goal of the Unidroit Principles is to set forth general rules for international commercial contracts. The Principles are intended to enunciate communal principles and rules of existing legal systems, and to select the solutions that are best adapted to the special requirements of international commercial contracts. In preparing the Principles, particular attention was paid to recent codifications of contract and commercial law, including the UCC, the Restatement Second of Contracts, the Netherlands Civil Code, the 1985 Foreign Economic Contract law of the People's Republic of China, the Draft New Civil Code of Quebec, and the Convention for the International Sale of Goods.

The Unidroit Principles are not intended for adoption by any country, and are not legally binding. Instead, they are a sort of international Restatement of Contract Law.

———

PRINCIPLES OF EUROPEAN CONTRACT LAW § 4.108

NOTE ON THE PRINCIPLES OF EUROPEAN CONTRACT LAW

The Principles of European Contract Law are the product of the Commission on European Contract Law, a body of lawyers, drawn from all the member States of the European Union under the chairmanship of Professor Ole Lando. The Principles are a response to a perceived need for a European Union-wide infrastructure of contract law. They are intended to reflect the common core of solutions to problems of contract law. In preparing the Principles, the Commission drew on a wide range of legal materials from both within and outside Europe, including the Uniform Commercial Code and the Restatements of Contracts and of Restitution. Some of the provisions in the Principles reflect suggestions and ideas that have not yet materialized in the law of the European Union States. See Introduction, Principles of European Contract Law, parts I and II (1999).

POST v. JONES, 60 U.S. (19 How.) 150, 15 L.Ed. 618 (1856). The whaling vessel Richmond, with a nearly full cargo of whale oil, was inextricably run aground in a deserted area 5,000 miles from the nearest port of safety. Several days later, the whaling vessels Elizabeth Frith, Panama, and Junior came into the vicinity. These vessels did not have full cargoes, but the Richmond had more whale oil than the three vessels could all take. At the instance of the Junior's captain, the Richmond's captain agreed to hold an auction for its oil. The Frith's captain bid $1 per barrel for as much as he needed, and the captains of the Panama and the Junior bid 75¢ per barrel. The three vessels took enough of the Richmond's oil to complete their cargoes, and returned to port with the oil and the Richmond's crew. The Richmond's owners then brought this action to recover part of the value of the oil taken by the Frith and the Panama, on the theory that while these vessels were entitled to salvage (a maritime concept under which one who saves property is entitled to a reward) for the oil they took, they were not entitled to keep the oil at the auction price. Held, for the owners of the Richmond.

"The contrivance of an auction sale, under such circumstances, where the master of the Richmond was hopeless, helpless, and passive—where there was no market, no money, no competition—where one party had absolute power, and the other no choice but submission where the vendor must take what is offered or get nothing—is a transaction which has no characteristic of a valid contract. It has been contended by the claimants that it would be a great hardship to treat this sale as a nullity, and thus compel them to assume the character of Salvors, because they were not bound to save this property, especially at so great a distance from any port of safety, and in a place where they could have completed their cargo in a short time from their own catchings, and where salvage would be no compensation for the loss of this opportunity. The force of these arguments is fully appreciated, but we think they are not fully sustained by the facts of the case. Whales may have been plenty around their vessels on the 6th and 7th of August, but, judging of the future from the past, the anticipation of filling up their cargo in the few days of the season in which it would be safe to remain, was very uncertain, and barely probable. The whales were retreating towards the North Pole, where they could not be pursued, and, though seen in numbers on one day, they would disappear on the next; and, even when seen in greatest numbers, their capture was uncertain. By this transaction, the vessels were enabled to proceed at once on their home voyage; and the certainty of a liberal salvage allowance for the property rescued will be ample compensation for the possible chance of greater profits, by refusing their assistance in saving their neighbor's property.

"It has been contended, also, that the sale was justifiable and valid, because it was better for the interests of all concerned to accept what was offered, than suffer a total loss. But this argument proves too much, as it would justify every sale to a salvor. Courts of admiralty will enforce contracts made for salvage service and salvage compensation, where the salvor has not taken advantage of his power to make an unreasonable bargain; but they will not tolerate the doctrine that a salvor can take the advantage of his situation, and avail himself of the calamities of others to drive a bargain; nor will they permit the performance of a public duty to be turned into a traffic of profit."

SECTION 2. UNCONSCIONABILITY

WILLIAMS v. WALKER–THOMAS FURNITURE CO.

United States Court of Appeals, District of Columbia Circuit, 1965.
121 U.S.App.D.C. 315, 350 F.2d 445.

J. SKELLY WRIGHT, CIRCUIT JUDGE. Appellee, Walker–Thomas Furniture Company, operates a retail furniture store in the District of Columbia. During the period from 1957 to 1962 each appellant in these cases purchased a number of household items from Walker–Thomas, for which payment was to be made in installments. The terms of each purchase were contained in a printed form contract which set forth the value of the purchased item and purported to lease the item to appellant for a stipulated monthly rent payment. The contract then provided, in substance, that title would remain in Walker–Thomas until the total of all the monthly payments made equaled the stated value of the item, at which time appellants could take title. In the event of a default in the payment of any monthly installment, Walker–Thomas could repossess the item.

The contract further provided that "the amount of each periodical installment payment to be made by [purchaser] to the Company under this present lease shall be inclusive of and not in addition to the amount of each installment payment to be made by [purchaser] under such prior leases, bills or accounts; *and all payments now and hereafter made by [purchaser] shall be credited pro rata on all outstanding leases, bills and accounts due the Company by [purchaser] at the time each such payment is made.*" (Emphasis added.) The effect of this rather obscure provision was to keep a balance due on every item purchased until the balance due on all items, whenever purchased, was liquidated. As a result, the debt incurred at the time of purchase of each item was secured by the right to repossess all the items previously purchased by the same purchaser, and each new item purchased automatically became subject to a security interest arising out of the previous dealings.

On May 12, 1962, appellant Thorne purchased an item described as a Daveno, three tables, and two lamps, having total stated value of $391.10. Shortly thereafter, he defaulted on his monthly payments and appellee sought to replevy all the items purchased since the first transaction in 1958. Similarly, on April 17, 1962, appellant Williams bought a stereo set of stated value of $514.95.[1] She too defaulted shortly thereafter, and appellee sought to replevy all the items purchased since December, 1957. The Court of General Sessions granted judgment for appellee. The District of Columbia Court of Appeals affirmed, and we granted appellants' motion for leave to appeal to this court.

Appellants' principal contention, rejected by both the trial and the appellate courts below, is that these contracts, or at least some of them, are unconscionable and, hence, not enforceable. In its opinion in Williams v. Walker–Thomas Furniture Company, 198 A.2d 914, 916 (1964), the District of Columbia Court of Appeals explained its rejection of this contention as follows:

> "Appellant's second argument presents a more serious question. The record reveals that prior to the last purchase appellant had reduced the balance in her account to $164. The last purchase, a stereo set, raised the balance due to $678. Significantly, at the time of this and the preceding purchases, appellee was aware of appellant's financial position. The reverse side of the stereo contract listed the name of appellant's social worker and her $218 monthly stipend from the government. Nevertheless, with full knowledge that appellant had to feed, clothe and support both herself and seven children on this amount, appellee sold her a $514 stereo set.

> "We cannot condemn too strongly appellee's conduct. It raises serious questions of sharp practice and irresponsible business dealings. A review of the legislation in the District of Columbia affecting retail sales and the pertinent decisions of the highest court in this jurisdiction disclose, however, no ground upon which this court can declare the contracts in question contrary to public policy. We note that were the Maryland Retail Installment Sales Act, Art. 83 §§ 128–153, or its equivalent, in force in the District of Columbia, we could grant appellant appropriate relief. We think Congress should consider corrective legislation to protect the public from such exploitive contracts as were utilized in the case at bar."

We do not agree that the court lacked the power to refuse enforcement to contracts found to be unconscionable. In other jurisdictions, it has been held as a matter of common law that unconscionable contracts are not enforceable.[2] While no decision of this court so holding has been found, the notion that an unconscionable bargain should not be given full enforcement is by no

---

1. At the time of this purchase her account showed a balance of $164 still owing from her prior purchases. The total of all the purchases made over the years in question came to $1,800. The total payments amounted to $1,400.

2. Campbell Soup Co. v. Wentz, 3 Cir., 172 F.2d 80 (1948); Indianapolis Morris Plan Corporation v. Sparks, 132 Ind.App. 145, 172 N.E.2d 899 (1961); Henningsen v. Bloomfield Motors, Inc., 32 N.J. 358, 161 A.2d 69, 84–96, 75 A.L.R.2d 1 (1960). Cf. 1 Corbin, Contracts § 128 (1963).

means novel. In Scott v. United States, 79 U.S. (12 Wall.) 443, 445, 20 L.Ed. 438 (1870), the Supreme Court stated:

> " . . . If a contract be unreasonable and unconscionable, but not void for fraud, a court of law will give to the party who sues for its breach damages, not according to its letter, but only such as he is equitably entitled to. . . ."[3]

Since we have never adopted or rejected such a rule, the question here presented is actually one of first impression.

Congress has recently enacted the Uniform Commercial Code, which specifically provides that the court may refuse to enforce a contract which it finds to be unconscionable at the time it was made. 28 D.C.Code § 2–302 (Supp. IV 1965). The enactment of this section, which occurred subsequent to the contracts here in suit, does not mean that the common law of the District of Columbia was otherwise at the time of enactment, nor does it preclude the court from adopting a similar rule in the exercise of its powers to develop the common law for the District of Columbia. In fact, in view of the absence of prior authority on the point, we consider the congressional adoption of § 2–302 persuasive authority for following the rationale of the cases from which the section is explicitly derived.[4] Accordingly, we hold that where the element of unconscionability is present at the time a contract is made, the contract should not be enforced.

Unconscionability has generally been recognized to include an absence of meaningful choice on the part of one of the parties together with contract terms which are unreasonably favorable to the other party.[5] Whether a meaningful choice is present in a particular case can only be determined by consideration of all the circumstances surrounding the transaction. In many cases the meaningfulness of the choice is negated by a gross inequality of bargaining power.[6] The manner in which the contract was entered is also relevant to this consideration. Did each party to the contract, considering his obvious education or lack of it, have a reasonable opportunity to understand the terms of the contract, or were the important terms hidden in a maze of

3. See Luing v. Peterson, 143 Minn. 6, 172 N.W. 692 (1919); Greer v. Tweed, N.Y.C.P., 13 Abb.Pr., N.S., 427 (1872); Schnell v. Nell, 17 Ind. 29 (1861); and see generally the discussion of the English authorities in Hume v. United States, 132 U.S. 406, 10 S.Ct. 134, 33 L.Ed. 393 (1889).

4. See Comment, § 2–302, Uniform Commercial Code (1962). Compare Note, 45 Va. L.Rev. 583, 590 (1959), where it is predicted that the rule of § 2–302 will be followed by analogy in cases which involve contracts not specifically covered by the section. Cf. 1 State of New York Law Revision Commission, Report and Record of Hearings on the Uniform Commercial Code 108–110 (1954) (remarks of Professor Llewellyn).

5. See Henningsen v. Bloomfield Motors, Inc., supra Note 2; Campbell Soup Co. v. Wentz, supra Note 2.

6. See Henningsen v. Bloomfield Motors, Inc., supra Note 2, 161 A.2d at 86, and authorities there cited. Inquiry into the relative bargaining power of the two parties is not an inquiry wholly divorced from the general question of unconscionability, since a one-sided bargain is itself evidence of the inequality of the bargaining parties. This fact was vaguely recognized in the common law doctrine of intrinsic fraud, that is, fraud which can be presumed from the grossly unfair nature of the terms of the contract. See the oft-quoted statement of Lord Hardwicke in Earl of Chesterfield v. Janssen, 28 Eng.Rep. 82, 100 (1751):

> " . . . [Fraud] may be apparent from the intrinsic nature and subject of the bargain itself; such as no man in his senses and not under delusion would make. . . ."

And cf. Hume v. United States, supra Note 3, 132 U.S. at 413, 10 S.Ct. at 137, where the Court characterized the English cases as "cases in which one party took advantage of the other's ignorance of arithmetic to impose upon him, and the fraud was apparent from the face of the contracts." See also Greer v. Tweed, supra Note 3.

fine print and minimized by deceptive sales practices? Ordinarily, one who signs an agreement without full knowledge of its terms might be held to assume the risk that he has entered a one-sided bargain.[7] But when a party of little bargaining power, and hence little real choice, signs a commercially unreasonable contract with little or no knowledge of its terms, it is hardly likely that his consent, or even an objective manifestation of his consent, was ever given to all the terms. In such a case the usual rule that the terms of the agreement are not to be questioned[8] should be abandoned and the court should consider whether the terms of the contract are so unfair that enforcement should be withheld.[9]

In determining reasonableness or fairness, the primary concern must be with the terms of the contract considered in light of the circumstances existing when the contract was made. The test is not simple, nor can it be mechanically applied. The terms are to be considered "in the light of the general commercial background and the commercial needs of the particular trade or case."[10] Corbin suggests the test as being whether the terms are "so extreme as to appear unconscionable according to the mores and business practices of the time and place." 1 Corbin, op. cit. supra Note 2.[11] We think this formulation correctly states the test to be applied in those cases where no meaningful choice was exercised upon entering the contract.

Because the trial court and the appellate court did not feel that enforcement could be refused, no findings were made on the possible unconscionability of the contracts in these cases. Since the record is not sufficient for our deciding the issue as a matter of law, the cases must be remanded to the trial court for further proceedings.

So ordered.

DANAHER, CIRCUIT JUDGE (dissenting):

The District of Columbia Court of Appeals obviously was as unhappy about the situation here presented as any of us can possibly be. Its opinion in the *Williams* case, quoted in the majority text, concludes: "We think Congress should consider corrective legislation to protect the public from such exploitive contracts as were utilized in the case at bar."

My view is thus summed up by an able court which made no finding that there had actually been sharp practice. Rather the appellant seems to have known precisely where she stood.

---

7. See Restatement, Contracts § 70 (1932); Note, 63 Harv.L.Rev. 494 (1950). See also Daley v. People's Building, Loan & Savings Ass'n, 178 Mass. 13, 59 N.E. 452, 453 (1901), in which Mr. Justice Holmes, while sitting on the Supreme Judicial Court of Massachusetts, made this observation:

" . . . Courts are less and less disposed to interfere with parties making such contracts as they choose, so long as they interfere with no one's welfare but their own. . . . It will be understood that we are speaking of parties standing in an equal position where neither has any oppressive advantage or power. . . ."

8. This rule has never been without exception. In cases involving merely the transfer of unequal amounts of the same commodity, the courts have held the bargain unenforceable for the reason that "in such a case, it is clear, that the law cannot indulge in the presumption of equivalence between the consideration and the promise." 1 Williston, Contracts § 115 (3d ed. 1957).

9. See the general discussion of "Boiler-Plate Agreements" in Llewellyn, The Common Law Tradition 362–371 (1960).

10. Comment, Uniform Commercial Code [§ 2–302].

11. See Henningsen v. Bloomfield Motors, Inc., supra Note 2; Mandel v. Liebman, 303 N.Y. 88, 100 N.E.2d 149 (1951). The traditional test as stated in Greer v. Tweed, supra Note 3, 13 Abb.Pr., N.S., at 429, is "such as no man in his senses and not under delusion would make on the one hand, and as no honest or fair man would accept, on the other."

There are many aspects of public policy here involved. What is a luxury to some may seem an outright necessity to others. Is public oversight to be required of the expenditures of relief funds? A washing machine, e.g., in the hands of a relief client might become a fruitful source of income. Many relief clients may well need credit, and certain business establishments will take long chances on the sale of items, expecting their pricing policies will afford a degree of protection commensurate with the risk. Perhaps a remedy when necessary will be found within the provisions of the "Loan Shark" law, D.C.Code §§ 26–601 et seq. (1961).

I mention such matters only to emphasize the desirability of a cautious approach to any such problem, particularly since the law for so long has allowed parties such great latitude in making their own contracts. I dare say there must annually be thousands upon thousands of installment credit transactions in this jurisdiction, and one can only speculate as to the effect the decision in these cases will have.

I join the District of Columbia Court of Appeals in its disposition of the issues.

RESTATEMENT CONTRACTS, SECOND § 208

[See Selected Source Materials Supplement]

UCC § 2–302

[See Selected Source Materials Supplement]

UNIFORM CONSUMER CREDIT CODE §§ 1.301, 5.108

[See Selected Source Materials Supplement]

FEDERAL TRADE COMMISSION REGULATIONS— DOOR–TO–DOOR SALES

[See Selected Source Materials Supplement]

NOTE ON THE UNIFORM COMMERCIAL CODE

The National Conference of Commissioners on Uniform State Laws (NCCUSL) consists of commissioners appointed by each state. NCCUSL recommends legislation to the states on subjects in which uniformity of law among the states is thought to be desirable. Among its successful projects was the Uniform Sales Act, drafted by Professor Williston.

In 1940, the idea of a Uniform Commercial Code was proposed to NCCUSL, to take the place of numerous disparate statutes, including the Uniform Sales Act, which had direct bearing on commercial transactions. Thereafter the UCC became a joint project of NCCUSL and the American Law Institute (ALI), with Karl N. Llewellyn of Columbia Law School, and later of the University of Chicago Law School, as the Chief Reporter. The UCC was adopted by NCCUSL and the ALI in 1952, and comprehensively revised in 1956; further amendments were promulgated thereafter. It has now been enacted in forty-nine states and the District of Columbia. (Louisiana, whose law is based on a civil code, has not adopted the UCC as such. However, it has adopted most Articles of the UCC other than Article 2 ("Sales") and it has incorporated many of the concepts of Article 2 into its Civil Code.)

Many provisions of the UCC are of major interest in the study of contract law, and will be referred to in this book. Most of these provisions are in Article 2. The direct applicability of that Article is set out in UCC § 2–102, which provides that "Unless the context otherwise requires, this Article applies to transactions in goods...." UCC § 2–105(1) defines "goods" to mean "all things (including specially manufactured goods) which are movable at the time of identification to the contract for sale other than the money in which the price is to be paid, investment securities ... and things in action." Other UCC provisions of interest in the study of contract law are contained in Article 1 ("General Provisions") and Article 9 ("Secured Transactions"). Articles 1 and 2, and selected portions of Articles 3 and 9, are set forth in the Selected Source Materials Supplement.

Within recent years, NCCUSL and the ALI have approved revised versions of, or significant amendments to, four articles of the UCC that bear on contract law—Articles 1, 2, 3, and 9. However, it is important to distinguish between the approval of revisions or amendments to the UCC by NCCUSL and the ALI, and the enactment of those revisions or amendments by the states. Like the UCC itself, revisions and amendments of the UCC that are approved by NCCUSL and the ALI become law only if and to the extent they are enacted by state legislatures. The revised versions of Article 3 and 9 have been widely enacted. In contrast, as of early 2006, the revised version of Article 1, which was approved by NCCUSL and the ALI in 2001, has been enacted by only sixteen states. Furthermore, none of those states adopted the choice-of-law provisions in section 1–301 of the revised Article, and only about half of those states adopted the definition of good faith in new section 1–201(b)(20). Substantial amendments to Article 2, which were approved by NCCUSL and the ALI in 2003, have so far not been enacted by any state, and because of strong opposition might never be enacted. Accordingly, the UCC Articles that are both relevant to contract law and enacted in all or most states are the pre–2001 version of Article 1 (General Provisions); the unamended version of Article 2 (Sales); revised Article 3 (Commercial Paper); and revised Article 9 (Secured Transactions).

PITTSLEY v. HOUSER, 125 Idaho 820, 875 P.2d 232 (App.1994). This was a contract for the purchase and installation of residential carpeting. On the issue whether the contract was governed by the UCC, the court said, "although there is little dispute that carpets are 'goods,' the transaction in this case also involved installation, a service. Such hybrid transactions, involving both goods and services, raise difficult questions about the applicability of the UCC. Two lines of authority have emerged to deal with such situations.

"The first line of authority, and the majority position, utilizes the 'predominant factor' test. The Ninth Circuit, applying the Idaho Uniform Commercial Code to the subject transaction, restated the predominant factor test as:

> The test for inclusion or exclusion is not whether they are mixed, but, granting that they are mixed, whether their predominant factor, their thrust, their purpose, reasonably stated, is the rendition of service, with goods incidentally involved (e.g., contract with artist for painting) or is a transaction of sale, with labor incidentally involved (e.g., installation of a water heater in a bathroom). . . .

"This test essentially involves consideration of the contract in its entirety, applying the UCC to the entire contract or not at all.

"The second line of authority . . . allows the contract to be severed into different parts, applying the UCC to the goods involved in the contract, but not to the nongoods involved, including . . . services as well as other nongoods assets and property. Thus, an action focusing on defects or problems with the goods themselves would be covered by the UCC, while a suit based on the service provided or some other nongoods aspect would not be covered by the UCC. . . .

"We believe the predominant factor test is the more prudent rule. Severing contracts into various parts, attempting to label each as goods or nongoods and applying different law to each separate part clearly contravenes the UCC's declared purpose 'to simplify, clarify and modernize the law governing commercial transactions.' . . . As the Supreme Court of Tennessee suggested in Hudson v. Town & Country True Value Hardware, Inc., 666 S.W.2d 51 (Tenn.1984), such a rule would, in many contexts, present 'difficult and in some instances insurmountable problems of proof in segregating assets and determining their respective values at the time of the original contract and at the time of resale, in order to apply two different measures of damages.' *Id.* at 54.

"Applying the predominant factor test to the case before us, we conclude that the UCC was applicable to the subject transaction. The record indicates that the contract between the parties called for '165 yds Masterpiece #2122—Installed' for a price of $4319.50. There was an additional charge for removing the existing carpet. The record indicates that Hilton paid the installers $700 for the work done in laying Pittsley's carpet. It appears that Pittsley entered into this contract for the purpose of obtaining carpet of a certain quality and color. It does not appear that the installation, either who would provide it or the nature of the work, was a factor in inducing Pittsley to choose Hilton as the carpet supplier. On these facts, we conclude that the sale of the carpet was the predominant factor in the contract, with the installation being merely incidental to the purchase."

UNIDROIT PRINCIPLES OF INTERNATIONAL COMMERCIAL CONTRACTS ART. 3.10

[See Selected Source Materials Supplement]

———

PRINCIPLES OF EUROPEAN CONTRACT LAW §§ 4.109, 4.110

[See Selected Source Materials Supplement]

———

COMMISSION OF THE EUROPEAN COMMUNITIES, COUNCIL DIRECTIVE 93/13/EEC

[See Selected Source Materials Supplement]

———

MAXWELL v. FIDELITY FINANCIAL SERVICES, INC.

Supreme Court of Arizona, En Banc, 1995.
184 Ariz. 82, 907 P.2d 51.

FELDMAN, Chief Justice.

Elizabeth Maxwell petitions us to review a court of appeals opinion affirming a trial court ruling that the doctrine of novation barred Maxwell's claim that a contract was unconscionable and therefore unenforceable. See Maxwell v. Fidelity Fin. Servs., Inc., 179 Ariz. 544, 880 P.2d 1090 (Ct.App. 1993). We granted review . . .

FACTS AND PROCEDURAL HISTORY

The facts, taken in the light most favorable to Maxwell, against whom summary judgment was granted, are that in December 1984, Elizabeth Maxwell and her then husband, Charles, were approached by Steve Lasica, a door-to-door salesman representing the now defunct National Solar Corporation (National). Lasica sold the Maxwells a solar home water heater for a total purchase price of $6,512. Although National was responsible for installation, the unit was never installed properly, never functioned properly, and was eventually declared a hazard, condemned, and ordered disconnected by the City of Phoenix. Thus, although the unit may have been intrinsically worthless, the question of unconscionability is determined as of the time the contract was made. A.R.S. § 47–2302. [U.C.C. § 2–302].

Financing for the purchase was accomplished through a loan to the Maxwells from Fidelity Financial Services, Inc. (Fidelity). The sale price was financed for a ten-year period at 19.5 percent interest, making the total cost nearly $15,000.

At the time of the transaction, Elizabeth Maxwell earned approximately $400 per month working part-time as a hotel maid and her husband earned approximately $1,800 per month working for the local paper. At Fidelity's request, an appraisal was made of the Maxwells' South Phoenix home, where they had resided for the preceding twelve years. The appraisal showed that the Maxwells lived in a modest neighborhood, that their 1,539 square foot home was in need of a significant amount of general repair and maintenance, and that its market value was approximately $40,000.

In connection with the financing transaction, Elizabeth Maxwell signed numerous documents, including a loan contract, a deed of trust, a truth-in-lending disclosure form, and a promissory note and security agreement. The effect of these documents was not only to secure the deferred purchase price with a lien on the merchandise sold, but also to place a lien on Maxwell's house as additional security for payment on the water heater contract. The forms and their terms were unambiguous and clearly indicated that Maxwell was placing a lien on her house. Included in the consumer credit contract between Maxwell and Fidelity was a clause expressly stating that Fidelity was subject to all claims by and defenses that Maxwell could assert against National.

Despite the fact that the water heater was never installed or working properly, Maxwell made payments on it for approximately three and one-half years, reducing the deferred purchase balance to $5,733. In 1988, Maxwell approached Fidelity to borrow an additional $800 for purposes unrelated to the original loan. In making this second loan, Fidelity required Maxwell to again sign a bundle of documents essentially identical to those she signed in 1984. Instead of simply adding $800 to Maxwell's outstanding balance on the 1984 contract, Fidelity created a new contract that included the unpaid balance of $5,733 on the 1984 loan, a term life insurance charge of $313, as well as the new $800 loan. In all, Maxwell financed the sum of $6,976 with this second loan. The terms of this latest loan also included interest at 19.5 interest and payments for a period of six years, making Maxwell's new payments, including interest, total nearly $12,000. The combined amount Maxwell would pay under the two contracts for a non-functioning water heater and the additional $800 loan thus totals approximately $17,000, or nearly one-half the value of her home.

Maxwell continued to make payments until 1990, when she brought this declaratory judgment action seeking, *inter alia*, a declaration that the 1984 contract was unenforceable on the grounds that it was unconscionable.

Following discovery, Fidelity moved for summary judgment asserting, among other things, that the statute of limitations had run on Maxwell's claim of unconscionability and, if not, that the 1988 contract worked a novation, thereby barring any action by Maxwell on the 1984 contract. Maxwell filed a memorandum in opposition to this motion and pointed to sworn testimony in her deposition, which Fidelity submitted with its motion, as raising genuine issues of material fact.

In a brief order, the trial court granted Fidelity's motion on the theory of novation. . . .

The court of appeals affirmed [partly on procedural grounds]. . . .

On review from summary judgment, the appellate court views the record in a light most favorable to the party opposing summary judgment (Maxwell) and will affirm only if no genuine issue of material fact exists. We therefore review this record to determine whether it could support a finding that Maxwell's claim of unconscionability was barred by the 1988 loan.

PRELIMINARY ISSUES

Before discussing the merits of Maxwell's petition, we must address.... [the issue, must Maxwell show an agency relationship between Fidelity and National to defeat Fidelity's motion for summary judgment]....

The court of appeals found that Maxwell failed to establish an agency relationship between National and Fidelity. The court reasoned that, absent such a relationship, Maxwell could not defeat Fidelity's motion for summary judgment on grounds of novation. We fail to see the relationship between establishing agency and defeating a claim of novation or pursuing a claim of unconscionability in this case. Fidelity stands in the shoes of National by virtue of both federal law and the terms of the contract to which it is a party. The 1984 and 1988 consumer credit contracts between Maxwell and Fidelity clearly state, in bold face, capital letters:

ANY HOLDER OF THIS CONSUMER CREDIT CONTRACT IS SUBJECT TO ALL CLAIMS AND DEFENSES WHICH THE DEBTOR COULD ASSERT AGAINST THE SELLER OF GOODS OR SERVICES OBTAINED WITH THE PROCEEDS HEREOF.

Thus, Maxwell need not establish an agency relationship between National and Fidelity to maintain a claim against Fidelity for unconscionability or to overcome Fidelity's claim of novation....

DISCUSSION

A. Unconscionability ...

2. The Test for Unconscionability

The court of appeals found the 1984 contract valid because Maxwell "failed to raise a material issue of fact that the agreement evidenced by [the contract documents] was beyond her reasonable expectations or was unconscionable." It is not clear why the court of appeals applied the test of "reasonable expectations" as this test is more correctly associated with contracts of adhesion, not claims of unconscionability, and the issue of adhesion contracts was neither before the trial court nor briefed or argued on appeal. This court previously has noted the rule that "reasonable expectations" and unconscionability are two distinct grounds for invalidating or limiting the enforcement of a contract and has stated that "even if [the contract provisions are] consistent with the reasonable expectations of the party" they are unenforceable if they are oppressive or unconscionable. Broemmer v. Abortion Serv. of Phoenix, 173 Ariz. 148, 151, 840 P.2d 1013, 1016 (1992) (quoting Graham v. Scissor–Tail, Inc., 28 Cal.3d 807, 171 Cal. Rptr. 604, 611–12, 623 P.2d 165, 172–73 (1981)).

3. The History of Unconscionability ...

... Although U.C.C. § 2–302 recognized and codified the amorphous equitable doctrine [of unconscionability], it did little to provide a set of rules for analyzing claims of unconscionability. Also lacking in the statutory recognition of unconscionability is a definition of that term. Courts and respected commentators alike have grappled with defining and applying unconscionability under the Code since its adoption. To this day, both groups remain divided on the proper method for doing so, though they share some common ground on defining such a test.

Within this common area, the elements of unconscionability can be ascertained to fulfill the Code's obvious intent of protecting against unconscionable contracts while not unnecessarily denying parties the benefit of their bargain. Although no litmus test exists, the cases do provide a reasonable, workable analysis.

4.   Divisions of Unconscionability under the U.C.C.

This court previously has acknowledged that the unconscionability principle involves an assessment by the court of

> whether, in the light of the general commercial background and the commercial needs of the particular trade or case, the clauses involved are so one-sided as to be unconscionable under the circumstances existing at the time of the making of the contract.... The principle is one of the prevention of oppression and unfair surprise ... not of disturbance of allocation of risks because of superior bargaining power.

Seekings v. Jimmy GMC of Tucson, Inc., 130 Ariz. 596, 602, 638 P.2d 210, 216 (1981) (citations omitted). This somewhat circular articulation of the principle, however, is not readily applicable to the infinite variety of cases that may involve the doctrine of unconscionability.

The framework upon which the vast majority of courts construct their analysis consists of the well recognized division of unconscionability into substantive and procedural parts. See, e.g., James J. White & Robert S. Summers, 1 Uniform Commercial Code 204, N. 8 and cases cited therein; John D. Calamari & Joseph M. Perillo, Contracts 406 (3d ed. 1987). Professor Dobbs provides the following explanation of the difference between these two types:

> Procedural or process unconscionability is concerned with "unfair surprise," fine print clauses, mistakes or ignorance of important facts or other things that mean bargaining did not proceed as it should. Substantive unconscionability is an unjust or "one-sided" contract. Substantive unconscionability is important in two ways. First, substantive unconscionability sometimes seems sufficient in itself to avoid a term in the contract. Second, substantive unconscionability sometimes helps confirm or provide evidence of procedural unconscionability.

Dobbs, supra at 706 (footnote omitted). This dichotomy evolved from a distinction made by the late Professor Leff in his oft-cited article Unconscionability and The Code—The Emperor's New Clause, 115 U.Pa.L.Rev. 485, 487 (1967). In his article, Professor Leff distinguished between "bargaining naughtiness" (procedural unconscionability) and overly harsh terms (substantive unconscionability). Id.

Over the years, courts have refined the two divisions of unconscionability and identified several factors that are indicative of each. Procedural unconscionability was well-explained in Johnson v. Mobil Oil Corp.:

> Under the procedural rubric come those factors bearing upon ... the real and voluntary meeting of the minds of the contracting party: age,

education, intelligence, business acumen and experience, relative bargaining power, who drafted the contract, whether the terms were explained to the weaker party, whether alterations in the printed terms were possible, whether there were alternative sources of supply for the goods in question.

415 F.Supp. 264, 268 (E.D.Mich.1976) (internal quotations omitted). As Professors White and Summers have noted, procedural unconscionability bears a strong resemblance to its "common-law cousins" of fraud and duress. White & Summers, supra at 204.

Substantive unconscionability concerns the actual terms of the contract and examines the relative fairness of the obligations assumed. Resource Management Co. v. Weston Ranch & Livestock Co., 706 P.2d 1028, 1041 (Utah 1985). Indicative of substantive unconscionability are contract terms so one-sided as to oppress or unfairly surprise an innocent party, an overall imbalance in the obligations and rights imposed by the bargain, and significant cost-price disparity. Id. (citations and internal quotations omitted).

We believe these authorities provide useful illustrations of both divisions of unconscionability under the U.C.C., although we do not restrict applicability of the doctrine to the factors outlined.

5. Application

The point of agreement by courts on the substantive-procedural elements also marks a point of departure in analyzing claims of unconscionability. See generally White & Summers, supra at 218–20. Many courts, perhaps a majority, have held that there must be some quantum of *both* procedural and substantive unconscionability to establish a claim, and take a balancing approach in applying them. Id. at 219. See also 2 William D. Hawkland, Uniform Commercial Code Series § 2–302:05 (1984) and cases cited therein. Other courts have held that it is sufficient if *either* is shown. See, e.g., Gillman v. Chase Manhattan Bank, N.A., 73 N.Y.2d 1, 537 N.Y.S.2d 787, 794, 534 N.E.2d 824, 829 (1988) ("While determinations of unconscionability are ordinarily based on the court's conclusion that both the procedural and substantive components are present ... , there have been exceptional cases where a provision of the contract is so outrageous as to warrant holding it unenforceable on the ground of substantive unconscionability alone.") (citing State v. Wolowitz, 96 A.D.2d 47, 468 N.Y.S.2d 131 (1983)). In addition to the numerous courts holding that either procedural or substantive unconscionability is sufficient,[12] the leading commentators in this field have also endorsed

---

12. See, e.g., Resource Management Co. v. Weston Ranch & Livestock Co., 706 P.2d 1028, 1043 (Utah 1985) ("Gross disparity in terms, absent evidence of procedural unconscionability, can support a finding of unconscionability."); American Home Improvement, Inc. v. MacIver, 105 N.H. 435, 201 A.2d 886, 889 (1964) (relying explicitly on U.C.S. § 2–302 and finding unconscionable, based on price-value disparity, a contract requiring payment of $1,609 for goods and services valued at "far less"); World Enter., Inc. v. Midcoast Aviation Serv., Inc., 713 S.W.2d 606, 610 (Mo.App.1986) ("Unconscionability is defined as either procedural or substantive."); Frank's Maintenance & Eng'g, Inc. v. C.A. Roberts Co., 86 Ill.App.3d 980, 42 Ill.Dec. 25, 31–32, 408 N.E.2d 403, 409–10 (1980) ("Unconscionability can be either procedural or substantive or a combination of both.") (emphasis added). Cf. Schroeder v. Fageol Motors, Inc., 86 Wash.2d 256, 544 P.2d 20, 23 (1975) (en banc) (recognizing that cases fall within the two classifications of procedural and substantive unconscionability). Indeed, it has long been recognized that gross disparity in terms may satisfy the standard for unconscionability by itself. See Marks v. Gates, 154 F. 481, 483 (9th Cir.1907) (inadequacy of consideration sufficient ground for withholding specific performance if it is so gross as to render the contract unconscionable).

this position. See White & Summers, supra at 220 (advocating the sufficiency of excessive price alone).

The cases that require a showing of both procedural and substantive unconscionability appear to be rather fact-specific, based more on the historical reluctance of courts to disturb contracts than on valid doctrinal underpinning.

> In some cases substantive unconscionability is found because the contract price is grossly excessive (or sometimes grossly inadequate). Most of these cases present additional elements such as actual misrepresentations, gross mistreatment of people who are already disadvantaged, or a subject matter such as premarital settlements that calls for intense state scrutiny by judges. In some of them, the substantive unconscionability really seems to be evidentiary only, that is, as confirming the conclusion that the process of bargaining was itself defective.

Dobbs, supra at 707 (footnote omitted) (emphasis added); see also Calamari & Perillo, supra at 406 ("[C]ontracts involving grossly unequal exchanges almost always involve some impropriety in the negotiating process or disability of a party."); White & Summers, supra at 218 ("Almost all of [the cases finding substantively unconscionable terms] exhibit creditor behavior that may be regarded as both procedurally and substantively unconscionable.").

Additional evidence that the dual requirement position is more coincidental than doctrinal is found within the very text of the statute on unconscionability, which explicitly refers to "the contract *or any clause* of the contract." A.R.S. § 47–2302 (emphasis added). Conspicuously absent from the statutory language is any reference to procedural aspects. That the U.C.C. contemplated substantive unconscionability alone to be sufficient is the most plausible reading of the language in § 47–2302, given that the Code itself provides for *per se* unconscionability if there exists, without more, a substantive term in the contract limiting consequential damages for injury to the person in cases involving consumer goods. See A.R.S. § 47–2719(c) [U.C.C. § 2–719 (c)]. It is wholly inconsistent to assert that unconscionability under § 47–2302 requires some procedural irregularity when unconscionability under § 47–2719 clearly does not.

Therefore, we conclude that under A.R.S. § 47–2302, a claim of unconscionability can be established with a showing of substantive unconscionability alone, especially in cases involving either price-cost disparity or limitation of remedies. If only procedural irregularities are present, it may be more appropriate to analyze the claims under the doctrines of fraud, misrepresentation, duress, and mistake, although such irregularities can make a case of procedural unconscionability. See Resource Management Co., 706 P.2d at 1043.

However, we leave for another day the questions involving the remedy for procedural unconscionability alone. We conclude further that this case presents a question of at least substantive unconscionability to be decided by the trial court. From the face of it, we certainly cannot conclude that the contract as a whole is not unconscionable, given the $6,500 price of a water heater for a modest residence, payable at 19.5 percent interest, for a total time-payment price of $14,860.43. These facts present at least a question of grossly-excessive price, constituting substantive unconscionability. See Dobbs, supra at 707; White & Summers, supra at § 4–5 and cases cited therein. This contract is made even more harsh by its security terms, which, in the event of non-payment, permit Fidelity not only to repossess the water heater but foreclose on Maxwell's home. The apparent injustice and oppression in these security provisions not only may constitute substantive unconscionability but also may provide evidence of procedural unconscionability. See Dobbs, supra at 706–07 (citing Williams v. Walker–Thomas Furniture Co., 350 F.2d 445 (D.C.Cir. 1965)).

Under the U.C.C. as enacted in A.R.S. § 47–2302, the court may "refuse enforcement of the contract altogether." Dobbs, supra at 705; Restatement § 208. The present factual record, before the statutorily required evidentiary hearing, certainly contains some evidence that the entire 1984 contract, including sale price, security provisions, and remedies, is unenforceable. We therefore turn to the effect of the doctrine of novation in such a situation.

B. Novation

1. Can the Doctrine of Novation Preclude an Action to Void a Pre-existing Contract on Grounds of Unconscionability?

The thrust of Maxwell's argument on this issue is that the trial court erred in finding her claim of unconscionability barred by the doctrine of novation. Maxwell argues that a finding of unconscionability with respect to the 1984 contract would have prevented the formation of a valid agreement through the 1988 contract. We agree. "Novation may be defined as the substitution by mutual agreement of . . . a new debt or obligation for an existing one which is thereby extinguished." Western Coach Corp. v. Roscoe, 133 Ariz. 147, 152, 650 P.2d 449, 454 (1982) (citations and internal quotations omitted). In this case, therefore, a valid novation requires a previously enforceable debt, the agreement of all parties to a new contract, the extinguishment of the old debt, and the validity of the new one. See Dunbar v. Steiert, 31 Ariz. 403, 404, 253 P. 1113, 1113 (1927); United Sec. Corp. v. Anderson Aviation Sales Co., 23 Ariz.App. 273, 275, 532 P.2d 545, 547 (1975). The effect of a novation is to discharge the original debt. See Restatement § 280 cmt. b. . . .

2. How Valid Must the Prior Obligation Be to Support a Novation?

. . . If the debt created by the 1984 contract was unconscionable when entered into, then it was unenforceable; therefore Maxwell had no obligation, and there is nothing to novate or substitute for. Because the doctrine of unconscionability forbids using courts as instruments of oppression, under such circumstances the *original* contract obligation would be a nullity. Fidelity cannot revive a dead branch by grafting it onto a living tree. It is not clear, moreover, how simply reciting the terms of the 1984 contract, in a new and substantially identical instrument and under substantially identical circumstances four years later, provides any help to Fidelity.

If anything, Fidelity's argument for novation raises substantial questions about the unconscionability of the 1988 contract, as that contract is nearly identical to the 1984 contract. By the terms of the 1988 contract, the outstanding $5,700 principle balance due on the water heater after Maxwell had already made forty-two payments on the 1984 contract was "bundled" with the unrelated $800 cash loan and a term life insurance policy. The 1988 loan amount, totaling $6,976.92, was financed again at 19.5 percent interest and stretched for another six years, with another $5,000 of precomputed interest added, for a total deferred price of $11,887.20. This amount, when added to what Maxwell had already paid, made the total deferred purchase price of the inoperable water heater and the $800 cash loan more than $17,000. Our unconscionability analysis of the 1984 contract applies a *fortiori* to the 1988 contract. If the 1984 contract was substantively unconscionable, the resulting unenforceability could not be avoided by redrafting the documents with essentially identical provisions under a new date. By preparing a new set of almost identical papers in 1988, Fidelity could not transmogrify the water heater deal made in 1984. Finally, it is necessary to point out that the 1988 contract was not a compromise and settlement of a claim. Fidelity presented no evidence and made no allegation that Maxwell intended to settle a claim of unconscionability or that she even presented a claim when she executed the 1988 contract. Accordingly, we hold that if found to be unconscionable, Maxwell's contracts with Fidelity are invalid for purposes of novation. . . .

CONCLUSION

. . . [W]e vacate the court of appeals' opinion, reverse the trial court's judgment, and remand to the trial court for proceedings consistent with this opinion and A.R.S. § 47–2302.

MOELLER, V.C.J., and CORCORAN and ZLAKET, JJ., concur.

[The opinion of Judge MARTONE, concurring in the judgment, is omitted.]

———

SECTION 3. THE PROBLEM OF MUTUALITY

———

INTRODUCTORY NOTE

For several centuries no suit for breach of an unsealed executory agreement was possible in England. One had generally a suit (in *debt* or *detinue*) for the price of a performance that had been rendered, or a suit (in *covenant*) for breach of a promise under seal. However, one generally could not sue for breach of an unsealed contract that had not been performed on one side. When, toward the end of the sixteenth century, this state of affairs was finally changed, the reform was accomplished with surprising ease. No cumbersome fiction was used to cover the courts' departure from precedent; there was no forcing of the reform into some inappropriate framework furnished by previous law. In the most cited of the cases signaling this development, the report observes simply that "a promise against a promise will maintain an action upon the case." (Strangborough and Warner's Case, 1589, 4 Leon. 3)

The rationalizations and fictions came about three centuries later. During the last part of the nineteenth century and the first part of the twentieth, legal thinking went through a period characterized by an intense interest in the "logical" or internal symmetry of the law. In the common law, "consideration" had by that time acquired a more or less fixed definition, as a detriment incurred by the promisee or a benefit received by the promisor. The question was therefore raised, how can this definition be applied to an executory (that is, not-yet performed) exchange of a promise for a promise? The attempts to answer this question resulted in a considerable body of literature.

The first attempt to answer the question, that of Langdell, was rather quickly rejected. Langdell suggested that if A promises to pay $10 for B's horse, and B promises to sell the horse for $10, the consideration for B's promise lies in the fact that A incurred a detriment in binding himself to pay B. It was soon pointed out that this argument moves in a circle, since it presupposes the binding effect of A's promise, a question as much in issue as the binding effect of B's. After the failure of Langdell's theory to win approval, the explanations diverged along two lines. It was argued either that the detriment is furnished by the making of the promise, considered as a fact without regard to its legal effect (Ames), or that consideration in bilateral contracts rests on "a distinct principle" (Williston). So inconclusive did this whole discussion seem to Sir Frederick Pollock that he was moved to declare: "What logical justification is there for holding mutual promises good consideration for each other? None, it is submitted." (1912, 28 L.Q.Rev. 101) In another place he treats the fact that an exchange of promises results in an enforceable contract as "one of the secret paradoxes of the Common Law." (1914, 30 L.Q.Rev. 129.)

Certainly the fault must lie with legal theory if it is incapable of "explaining" so commonplace a phenomenon as the binding effect of mutual promises. A proper explanation would run, not in terms of definitions or abstract juristic conceptions, but in terms of the policies that underlie the requirement of consideration: *Bargains* serve social-welfare purposes because they create wealth through trade, and because they facilitate private economic planning by allowing actors to allocate risks, and to coordinate economic activity through the acquisition of control over inputs and outputs. *Enforcing bargain promises* furthers the welfare purposes that such promises serve.

Even after it became accepted that bargain promises were enforceable as such—that is, although not under seal and not performed on one side—classical contract law had trouble with certain classes of bargain promises. One of these problems was reflected in the concept of mutuality. In hundreds of American cases, it has been asserted as a general rule of contract law that both parties must be bound or neither is bound. This notion has usually been called "the principle of mutuality."

This principle obviously needs more qualification than it usually receives in judicial opinions.

First, the principle has no application to a unilateral contract. In a *bilateral* contract, the parties exchange a promise for a promise. (For example, Seller agrees to sell Buyer a used car for $2,000, delivery in three days, and Buyer agrees to pay $2,000 on delivery.) In a *unilateral* contract, the parties exchange a promise for an act. (For example, A promises to pay B $50 for mowing A's lawn, and makes clear that only B's act of mowing the lawn, not B's promise to do so, will suffice.) In a unilateral contract, the party who exchanges an act for promise may never be bound, because he is not bound to do anything before he chooses to do the act, and he may not be bound to do anything after he does the act. Thus suppose, in the last example, that B mows the lawn. B was not bound to mow the lawn before he mowed it, and is not bound to A in any way after he mowed it. Nevertheless, A is bound to B.

Second, the principle of mutuality is not applied to bargains in which both parties have made real promises but one party is not legally bound by his promise. For example, suppose A fraudulently induces B to agree to buy Blackacre. Although B is not legally bound, he can enforce the contract, notwithstanding the doctrine of mutuality. The same result follows in many other kinds of cases, such as those in which one but not both parties has a defense under the Statute of Frauds or a defense of incapacity.

(WARNING: In certain equity cases involving the right to specific performance it has been held that this remedy will not be granted to a plaintiff unless the defendant might also have obtained specific performance. This concept, which is described as a requirement of "mutuality of remedy," in contrast to the less stringent requirement of "mutuality of obligation," has been applied only in equity cases. The rule is of doubtful standing today, and is mentioned here only to avoid conveying a misleading impression.)

Williston took the view that cases holding that the various types of cases in which a plaintiff may enforce a contract, even though he cannot be sued on the contract (because, for example, he did not sign the memorandum required by the Statute of Frauds), constitute "an exception to the general principles of consideration." 4th ed., at § 7:13. He argued that if the right to bring suit in these cases (for example, the right of a defrauded party, a minor, or a non-signing party) was spelled out in words in the contract itself, the promise would be held to be "illusory" and therefore insufficient as consideration for the promise of the other party.

Whether these cases are exceptions to the requirement of consideration depends, of course, upon the view taken of the policies that define the requirement. In any event, the existence of these cases shows that under some circumstances a promise by the plaintiff that is not itself binding on him can nevertheless act as consideration for the promise of the defendant, and demonstrates again that the alleged principle of "mutuality" requires a good deal of qualification.

SCOTT v. MORAGUES LUMBER CO.

Supreme Court of Alabama, 1918.
202 Ala. 312, 80 So. 394.

Suit by the Moragues Lumber Company, a corporation, against J.M. Scott, for damages for breach of an agreement of charter party. Judgment for plaintiff, and defendant appeals. Affirmed.

Count 2 of the complaint as amended is as follows:

"The plaintiff claims of the defendant $13,000 as damages from breach of an agreement entered into between the plaintiff and the defendant on the 27th day of June, 1917, consisting of an offer by the defendant that, subject to his buying a certain American vessel, 15 years old, which he was then figuring on and which was of about 1,050 tons and then due in Chile, he would charter said vessel to the plaintiff for the transportation of a cargo of lumber from any port in the Gulf of Mexico to Montevideo or Buenos Aires, for the freight of $65 per thousand feet of lumber, freight to be prepaid, free of discount and of insurance, and the vessel to be furnished to the plaintiff within a reasonable time after its purchase by the defendant, which said offer was accepted by the plaintiff, and the plaintiff avers that although the defendant purchased said vessel, and although the plaintiff was at all times ready, willing, and able to comply with all the provisions of said contract on its part, the defendant without notifying the plaintiff of said purchase, and before said vessel was delivered to him, chartered said vessel to a third person, and thereby rendered himself unable to comply with the said contract." . . .

SAYRE, J. . . . It is said, in the first place, that the alleged contract between the parties was conditioned upon the will of appellant, defendant, and was therefore void for want of consideration or mutuality of obligation. A valid contract may be conditioned upon the happening of an event, even though the event may depend upon the will of the party, who afterwards seeks to avoid its obligation. This principle is illustrated in McIntyre Lumber Co. v. Jackson Lumber Co., 165 Ala. 268, 51 So. 767, 138 Am.St.Rep. 66. Appellant was not bound to purchase the vessel; but, when he did, the offer—or the contract, if the offer had been accepted—thereafter remained as if this condition had never been stipulated, its mutuality or other necessary incidents of obligation depending upon its other provisions and the action of the parties thereunder. Davis v. Williams, 121 Ala. 542, 25 So. 704; 3 Page on Contracts, § 1358. See, also, Jones v. Lanier, 198 Ala. 363, 73 So. 535. . . .

The effect of appellee's acceptance, if communicated while the offer was yet open, was to convert it into a binding contract. 6 R.C.L. p. 605, § 27. In substance, it is alleged in the complaint that appellant's offer was accepted; that appellant purchased the vessel; that appellee was able, ready, and willing to perform the contract on its part; but that appellant disabled himself, or failed and refused to perform on his part. From the order in which the facts are alleged it is to be inferred that appellee accepted appellant's offer before the latter purchased the vessel, and there is no ground of demurrer questioning the sufficiency of the complaint to that effect. Thereupon the offer was converted into a binding contract to be performed, if not otherwise stipulated, within a reasonable time; the promise on either hand constituting the consideration of the promise on the other. Appellant's purchase of the vessel was a condition precedent to the existence of a binding contract, it is true; but that was alleged, as it was necessary that it should be. 13 C.J. p. 724, § 847, citing McCormick v. Badham, 191 Ala. 339, 67 So. 609; Long v. Addix, 184 Ala. 236, 63 So. 982; Flouss v. Eureka Co., 80 Ala. 30. And so with respect to appellee's acceptance of the offer. It was necessary that appellee communicate its acceptance to appellant. 1 Page, § 43. But this communication was a part of the acceptance and was covered by the general allegation of acceptance. . . .

Affirmed.

———————

WICKHAM & BURTON COAL CO.
v. FARMERS' LUMBER CO.

Supreme Court of Iowa, 1920.
189 Iowa 1183, 179 N.W. 417, 14 A.L.R. 1293.

Appeal from District Court, Webster County; R.M. Wright, Judge. Counterclaim asserting that damages were due from plaintiff because of a contract made between plaintiff and defendant. A demurrer to the counterclaim was overruled; hence this appeal. Reversed.

SALINGER, J. The counterclaim alleges that about August 18, 1916, defendant, through an agent, entered into an oral agreement, "whereby plaintiff agreed to furnish and to deliver to defendant orders given them" for carload shipments of coal from defendant f.o.b. mines, "to be shipped to defendant at such railroad yard stations as defendant might direct, at the price of $1.50 a ton on all orders up to September 1, 1916, and $1.65 a ton on all orders from then to April 1, 1917." It is further alleged that "said coal ordered would be and consist" of what was known as plaintiff's Paradise 6 lump, 6 3 egg, or 3 2 nut coal. It is next alleged that defendant has for several years last past been engaged in owning and operating what is commonly known as a line of lumber yards, located at different railroad station points tributary to Ft. Dodge, where defendant has its principal place of business; that at these several lumber yards, among other merchandise and commodities, the defendant handles coal in carload lots, with purpose of selling the same at retail to its patrons.

Then comes an allegation that the agent made oral agreement "that plaintiff would furnish unto defendant coal in carload lots, that defendant would want to purchase from plaintiff" on stated terms, with character of the coal described, and that the oral contract was confirmed by the letter Exhibit 1. It is of date August 21, 1916, and recites that plaintiff is in receipt of a letter from their agent—

> "asking us to name you a price [repeating the price and coal description found in the counterclaim]. Although this is a very low price, our agent, Mr. Spalding, has recommended that we quote you this price, and we hereby confirm it. Any orders received between now and September 1st are to be shipped at $1.50. We would like to have a letter from you accepting these prices, and if this is satisfactory will consider same as a contract."

On August 26, 1916, the defendant responded:

> "We have your favor of the 21st accepting our order for coal for shipment to March 31, 1917."

The basis of the counterclaim, so far as damages are concerned, is the allegation that a stated amount of coal had to be purchased by defendant in the open market at a greater than the contract price, and that therefore there is due the defendant from the plaintiff the sum of $3,090.

The demurrer asserts that the alleged contract is "void for failure of mutuality and certainty;" is void because there is no consideration between the parties; because it appears affirmatively that the offer was simply an offer on part of plaintiff, which might be accepted by giving an order until such time as it was actually withdrawn or expired by limitation, each order and acceptance of a carload lot constituting a separate and distinct contract; and void because the agreement could not be enforced by the plaintiff on any certain or specified amount of tonnage, or for the payment of any specified tonnage.

The demurrer makes, in effect, three assertions: (a) That the arrangement between the parties is void for uncertainty; (b) that it lacks consideration; (c) that it lacks mutuality of obligation. We have given the argument and the citations on the first two propositions full consideration. But we conclude these first two are of no importance if mutuality is wanting....

... [T]he asserted lack of consideration is bottomed on the claim that mutuality is lacking. Appellant does not deny that a promise may be a consideration for a promise. Its position is that this is so only of an enforceable promise. That is the law. If, from lack of mutuality, the promise is not binding, it cannot form a consideration.... Campbell v. Lambert, 36 La.Ann. 35, 51 Am.Rep. 1. In the last-named case it is said that, while a promise may be a good consideration for another promise, this is not so "unless there is an absolute mutuality of engagement, so that each party has the right at once to hold the other to a positive agreement"—citing 1 Parsons on Contracts, 448....

The question of first importance, then, is whether there is a lack of mutuality. In the last analysis the counterclaim is based on the allegation that plaintiff undertook to furnish defendant such described coal "as defendant would want to purchase from plaintiff." The defendant never "accepted." Indeed, it is its position that it gave orders, and that plaintiff did the accepting. But concede, for argument's sake, that defendant did accept. What was the acceptance? At the utmost, it was a consent that plaintiff might ship it such coal as defendant "would want to purchase from plaintiff." What obligation did this fasten upon defendant? It did not bind itself to buy all it could sell. It did not bind itself to buy of plaintiff only. It merely "agreed" to buy what it pleased. It may have been ascertainable how much it would need to buy of some one. But there was no undertaking to buy that much, or, indeed, any specified amount of coal of plaintiff....

The "contract" on part of appellee is to buy if it pleased, when it pleased, to buy if it thought it advantageous, to buy much, little, or not at all, as it thought best.

A contract of sale is mutual where it contains an agreement to sell on the one side, and an agreement to purchase on the other. But it is not mutual where there is an obligation to sell, but no obligation to purchase, or an obligation to purchase, but no obligation to sell. 13 Corpus Juris, 339....

Where one party agrees to cut for the other hay "not to exceed 200 tons," there is lack of mutuality, because the offerant was not bound to deliver any particular quantity of hay, and could cut as little as he pleased. Houston R. Co. v. Mitchell, 38 Tex. 85. So where a defendant who binds himself to receive and pay for all the ties plaintiff could produce and ship at a stated price between stated dates. As to this it was held mutuality was lacking, because there was no enforceable duty to deliver any ties. Hazelhurst v. Supply Co. (C.C.) 166 F. 191. And so of an offer to receive and transport railroad iron, not to exceed a stated number of tons, during specified periods, and at a specified rate per ton. As to this it was held that, though plaintiff answered, assenting to the proposal, there was still no contract, because there was no agreement on his part that he would deliver any iron for transportation. Railroad v. Dane, 43 N.Y. 240; Hoffmann v. Maffioli, 104 Wis. 630, 80 N.W. 1032, 47 L.R.A. 427. An agreement to purchase all that the manufacturer desires to sell at a specified price is void. 13 C.J. at 340. . . .

A contract to sell personal property is void for want of mutuality if the quantity to be delivered is conditioned entirely on the will, wish, or want of the buyer. 13 Corpus Juris, 339; Cold Blast Co. v. Bolt Co., 114 F. 77, 52 C.C.A. 25, 57 L.R.A. 696. So of an agreement to supply all pig iron wanted by defendants in their business between stated dates, at specified prices, even though the other party promised to purchase such iron. The argument advanced is that the buyer did not engage "to want any quantity whatever," nor even agree to continue in their business. Bailey v. Austrian, 19 Minn. 535 (Gil. 465). It is said in Hickey v. O'Brien, 123 Mich. 611, 82 N.W. 241, 49 L.R.A. 594, 81 Am.St.Rep. 227, that in National Furnace Co. v. Manufacturing Co., 110 Ill. 427, the case of Bailey v. Austrian is distinguished by pointing out that in the *Bailey* Case stress is laid on the word "want"; while in the Illinois case the plaintiff agreed to sell to defendant all the iron "needed" in its business during the three ensuing years at $22.35 a ton, and the defendant agreed to take its year's supply at that price. We are unable to find any substantial difference between an "agreement" to buy what one might "want" and what one might "need". Be that as it may, in the case at bar the language was, "would want to purchase." And the *Austrian* Case is well supported in authority. . . .

Three cars of coal were shipped and received. Upon this appellee urges that thereby the so-called contract was completed and made mutual. Part performance was ineffectual in Hoffmann v. Maffioli, 104 Wis. 630, 80 N.W. 1032, 47 L.R.A. 427, to found a case as for breach of contract on refusal to ship more. . . .

If there never was a contract to ship anything, that is still the situation when a contract to ship what has not yet been shipped is asserted as the basis of an action. As said in Cold Blast Co. v. Bolt Co., 114 F. 80, 52 C.C.A. 25, 57 L.R.A. 696, even though there had been some shipments, there was still no consideration and no mutuality in the contract as to any articles which defendant had not ordered, or which plaintiff had not delivered, and therefore the refusal of plaintiff to honor the orders of defendants was no breach of any valid contract, and formed no legal cause of action whereon to base a counterclaim. It was further said:

"As to all undelivered articles, that defect still inheres in the agreement. The plaintiff is not bound to deliver, nor the defendant to take and pay for, any articles that have not been delivered [that is to say, so much as has not been performed still rests upon an agreement which is not enforceable, and for the refusal to honor which there can be no recovery]. . . . The defendant never agreed to order or to pay for any quantity of these undelivered articles. If it had refused to order and take them, no action could have been maintained for its failure, because no court could have determined what amount it was required to take." . . .

Defendant alleges further that, by reason of the conduct of plaintiff in furnishing defendant two carloads at $1.50 per ton under the contract terms, plaintiff is now estopped from claiming there was no binding contract between the parties for furnishing coal to defendant under the contract contended for by defendant. But the claimed estoppel is no broader than the claimed breach of a contract which is no contract.

Cases relied on by appellee do not, on careful consideration, militate with what we have declared. All that Keller v. Ybarru, 3 Cal. 147, holds is that, when one party offers to sell as much as the other wishes, there is a contract after the other declares what quantity he will take. . . .

The demurrer should have been sustained.

Reversed.

———

CORBIN, THE EFFECT OF OPTIONS ON CONSIDERATION, 34 Yale L.J. 571, 574 (1925). "[T]he chief feature of contract law is that by an expression of his will to–day the promisor limits his freedom of voluntary choice in the future. Society controls his future action by affording the stimulus described as *compulsion*. With this element absent we are no longer dealing with what is called contract or with contract law. To fall within this field therefore, a promise must in its terms express a willingness to effect this limitation on freedom of choice. Thus, if A asks B to promise some future performance and B makes no answer, B has made no promise. This is true, even though when the future time arrives B may then be willing to perform as requested and may actually so perform. If, under these circumstances, A thinks that B has made a promise, he is under an illusion. The same is true if instead of making no answer B had replied, 'I predict that when the time comes I shall be willing to do what you ask.' A prediction of future willingness is not an expression of present willingness and is not a promise. To see a promise in it is to be under an illusion. We reach the same result if B's reply to A is, 'I promise to do as you ask if I please to do so when the time arrives.' In form this is a conditional promise, but the condition is the pleasure or future will of the promisor himself. The words used do not purport to effect any limitation upon the promisor's future freedom of choice. They do not lead the promisee to have an expectation of performance because of a present expression of will. He may hope that a future willingness will exist; but he has no more reasonable basis for such a hope than if B had merely made a prediction or had said nothing at all. As a promise, B's words are mere illusion. Such an illusory promise is neither enforceable against the one making it, nor is it operative as a consideration for a return promise."

———

WILLISTON ON CONTRACTS § 103B (Rev. ed. 1937). In this section the author refers to the cases holding that an illusory promise will not serve as consideration to support a return promise. He asserts, however, that this result cannot be explained on the ground that the illusory promise is not in fact bargained for, or is not the requested exchange for the real promise. "[That illusory promises] are frequently . . . so requested with intent to make a bargain cannot be successfully disputed. A contractor or seller is often so eager to obtain work, or a sale, that he will gladly subject himself to an absolute promise in return for one which leaves performance optional with the other party. This is most commonly illustrated in agreements to buy or sell goods where the quantity is fixed by the wishes of one of the parties."

RESTATEMENT, SECOND, CONTRACTS § 77

[See Selected Source Materials Supplement]

NOTE ON ILLUSORY PROMISES

A promise is a commitment to take some future action. By virtue of a promise, therefore, the promisor shrinks the boundaries of her realm of choice. Whatever that realm was before she made the promise, it is slightly smaller after she made the promise, because some action that she was morally free to choose before the promise is no longer an action that she is morally free to choose. The illusory-promise rule is applicable to commercial transactions in which one party, A, makes a real promise, while the other party, B, uses an expression that seems to be a real promise—a commitment—but is not, because it does not shrink the boundaries of B's realm of choice. Under the illusory-promise rule, A is not bound in such a case, despite the fact that *she* made a real promise, on the theory that there was no consideration for her promise. As stated in Restatement Second Section 77, "A promise or apparent promise is not consideration if by its terms the promisor or purported promisor reserves a choice of alternative performances unless . . . each of the alternative performances would have been consideration if it alone had been bargained for. . . ."

The Illustrations to Section 77 exemplify the illusory-promise rule as follows:

1.   A offers to deliver to B at $2 a bushel as many bushels of wheat, not exceeding 5,000, as B may choose to order within the next 30 days. B accepts, agreeing to buy at that price as much as he shall order from A within that time. B's acceptance involves no promise by him, and is not consideration. . . .

2.   A promises B to act as B's agent for three years from a future date on certain terms; B agrees that A may so act, but reserves the power to terminate the agreement at any time. B's agreement is not consideration, since it involves no promise by him.

Illustrations 1 and 2 are classic examples of recurring types of cases in which the illusory-promise rule is applied. In one recurring case, exemplified in Illustration 1, B does not shrink the boundaries of his realm of choice because he only agrees to do whatever he may choose to do. In a second recurring case, exemplified in Illustration 2, B does not shrink the boundaries of his realm of choice because he reserves the right to chose to terminate his apparent commitment at any time.

However, while it is true that if one party to a bargain makes only an illusory promise, the parties have not made a bilateral contract, it is not true that they have not made a bargain. On the contrary: normally in such cases a bargain *has* been made. It is true that in illusory-promise cases there is no *bilateral* contract, because only one party has shrunk the boundaries of her realm of choice. The fallacy of the illusory-promise rule is that it treats transactions involving illusory promises as if they were failed bilateral contracts, intended to involve a promise for a promise. In fact, however, properly understood these transactions typically do not involve failed bilateral contracts. Instead, they involve successful *unilateral* contracts designed to increase the probability of exchange.

Call the person who makes the real promise in an illusory-promise transaction, A, and call the person who makes the illusory promise, B. In illusory-promise cases, like Illustrations 1 and 2 to Restatement Second Section 77, the promisor, A, does not make a promise to B for nothing, as a gift. She makes it to advance her own interests, by increasing the probability of exchange.

Choosing to exchange with one trading partner rather than another is not cost-free. In Illustration 1 to Restatement Second Section 77, A must believe that B is unlikely to trade with her unless A agrees to allow B the choice of ordering as many bushels as he wants to at the stated price during the stated time. In Illustration 2, A must believe that B would be unlikely to retain her as his agent unless she agreed that B could terminate the arrangement at any time. In each Illustration, A presumably makes her promise because she believes that B's incentives to exchange with A, rather than with others, would be insufficient unless the promise is made. In effect, there is a disparity of information and incentives between A and B. A has confidence in the attractiveness of her performance, which she believes that B does not share. A therefore makes a promise to B that is intended to change B's incentives to exchange with A, so as to increase the probability of exchange. A does this by making a commitment that she believes will induce B to give A a *chance* to show that her performance is attractive, either by sampling A's commodities or perhaps simply by giving more serious consideration to purchasing A's commodities than he otherwise would be likely to do.

The value of a chance to increase the probability of exchange is widely evidenced: book clubs give free books for the opportunity to sell future books; developers give free vacations for the opportunity to present a sales pitch; retailers offer free prizes in promotional contests to induce customers to shop; direct sellers pay substantial amounts for mailing lists. Correspondingly, if, in an illusory-promise transaction, B responds to A's inducement by giving A a chance to increase the probability of exchange, the act of giving A the chance concludes a unilateral contract by giving A something of value in a bargained exchange for A's promise.

This proposition can be illustrated by the following hypothetical:

A, a third-year law student whose grades are only fair but whose confidence is great, interviews the well-known Washington litigation firm, F, G & H. After the interview, which A feels went very well, she writes to F, G & H as follows:

Dear F, G & H:

I very much enjoyed meeting you at my recent interview. I know my grades are below the level F, G & H usually requires. However, I also know they are not a fair indicator of my skills, particularly in litigation. (As you may recall, I did exceptionally well in several moot court settings.) I am sure that if you gave me a chance you would be more than pleased with my work. In order to induce you to give me a chance I make the following offer: I will work for you for one year at $60,000 (one-half of your normal starting salary), beginning September 1. You may discharge me at any time, without notice, no questions asked.

Sincerely yours,

A

F, G & H concurs, and A begins work. After three months, however, A leaves for another job, over the firm's objection. F, G & H brings suit against A for breach of contract.

Under the illusory-promise rule, A would not be bound to her promise. Clearly, however, A has made a bargain. If F, G & H had paid $500 for A's promise, that promise would clearly be enforceable. The act of giving A a chance to prove herself may be worth much more to A (and may cost F, G & H much more) than $500. A has received exactly what she bargained for, and should be bound by her promise.

In short, the illusory-promise rule is not so much wrong as irrelevant. Recall that under this rule, as formulated in Restatement Second, "[a] promise or apparent promise is not consideration if by its terms the promisor or purported promisor reserves a choice of alternative performances unless . . . each of the alternative performances would have been consideration if it alone had been bargained for. . . ." That is true, but beside the point. B's "promise or apparent promise" may not conclude a bargain, but B's act of giving A a bargained-for chance does conclude a bargain.

The illusory-promise rule is a creature of classical contract law. Although the rule is still on the books, it is being effectively whittled away under modern contract law, as illustrated by the remaining cases in this Section.

———

LINDNER v. MID–CONTINENT PETROLEUM CORP., 221 Ark. 241, 252 S.W.2d 631 (1952). Lindner leased a filling station to Mid–Continent for three years, with an option in Mid–Continent to renew for two more years. Mid–Continent had the right to terminate the lease at any time, on ten days' notice. Following an attempt by Lindner to cancel the lease, Mid–Continent brought suit to regain possession. Lindner defended on the ground that the lease lacked mutuality. Held, for Mid–Continent. "[T]he requirement of mutuality does not mean that the promisor's obligation must be exactly coextensive with that of the promisee. It is enough that the duty unconditionally undertaken by each party be regarded by the law as a sufficient consideration for the other's promise. . . . In this view it will be seen that Mid–Continent's option to cancel the lease upon ten days' notice to Mrs. Lindner is not fatal to the validity of the contract. This is not an option by which the lessee may terminate the lease at pleasure and without notice; at the very least the lessee bound itself to pay rent for ten days."

———

MATTEI v. HOPPER, 51 Cal.2d 119, 330 P.2d 625 (1958). Plaintiff was a real-estate developer. He was planning to construct a shopping center on a tract adjacent to defendant's land, and wanted to acquire the defendant's land in connection with the development of the shopping center. For several months, a real-estate agent attempted to negotiate a purchase of defendant's land under terms agreeable to both parties. After several of plaintiff's proposals had been rejected by defendant because of the inadequacy of the price that the plaintiff offered, defendant submitted an offer of $57,000, which the plaintiff accepted.

The parties' written agreement was evidenced on a form of deposit receipt supplied by the real-estate agent. Under its terms, plaintiff was required to deposit $1,000 with the real-estate agent, and was given 120 days to "examine the title and consummate the purchase." At the expiration of that period, the balance of the price was "due and payable upon tender of a good and sufficient deed of the property sold." The concluding paragraph of the deposit receipt provided: "Subject to Coldwell Banker & Company [a real-estate broker] obtaining leases satisfactory to the purchaser." Plaintiff wanted this clause, and the 120–day period, to make sure that he could arrange satisfactory leases of the shopping-center buildings prior to the time at which he was finally committed to pay the balance of the purchase price and take title to defendant's land.

Thereafter, defendant's attorney notified plaintiff that defendant would not sell her land under the terms contained in the deposit receipt. Subsequently, defendant was informed that satisfactory leases had been obtained and that plaintiff offered to pay the balance of the purchase price. Defendant failed to tender the deed as provided in the deposit receipt. Plaintiff sued for damages, and defendant argued that the plaintiff's promise was illusory. Held, for plaintiff.

"While contracts making the duty of performance of one of the parties conditional upon his satisfaction would seem to give him wide latitude in avoiding any obligation and thus present serious consideration problems, such 'satisfaction' clauses have been given effect. They have been divided into two primary categories and have been accorded different treatment on that basis. First, in those contracts where the condition calls for satisfaction as to commercial value or quality, operative fitness, or mechanical utility, dissatisfaction cannot be claimed arbitrarily, unreasonably, or capriciously . . . and the standard of a reasonable person is used in determining whether satisfaction has been received. . . . Of the cited cases, two have expressly rejected the arguments that such clauses either rendered the contracts illusory . . . or deprived the promises of their mutuality of obligation. . . .

"[The] multiplicity of factors which must be considered in evaluating a lease shows that this case more appropriately falls within the second line of authorities dealing with 'satisfaction' clauses, being those involving fancy, taste, or judgment. Where the question is one of judgment, the promisor's determination that he is not satisfied, when made in good faith, has been held to be a defense to an action on the contract. . . . Although these decisions do not expressly discuss the issues of mutuality of obligation or illusory promises, they necessarily imply that the promisor's duty to exercise his judgment in good faith is an adequate consideration to support the contract. . . ."

HELLE v. LANDMARK, INC., 15 Ohio App.3d 1, 472 N.E.2d 765 (1984). " 'The modern decisional tendency is against lending the aid of courts to defeat contracts on technical grounds of want of mutuality.' Texas Gas Utilities Co. v. Barrett (Tex.1970), 460 S.W.2d 409, 412. As a contract defense, the mutuality doctrine has become a faltering rampart to which a litigant retreats at his own peril."

———

WOOD v. LUCY, LADY DUFF–GORDON

Court of Appeals of New York, 1917.
222 N.Y. 88, 118 N.E. 214.

CARDOZO, J. The defendant styles herself "a creator of fashions." Her favor helps a sale. Manufacturers of dresses, millinery, and like articles are glad to pay for a certificate of her approval. The things which she designs, fabrics, parasols, and what not, have a new value in the public mind when issued in her name. She employed the plaintiff to help her to turn this vogue into money. He was to have the exclusive right, subject always to her approval, to place her indorsements on the designs of others. He was also to have the exclusive right to place her own designs on sale, or to license others to market them. In return she was to have one-half of "all profits and revenues" derived from any contracts he might make. The exclusive right was to last at least one year from April 1, 1915, and thereafter from year to year unless terminated by notice of 90 days. The plaintiff says that he kept the contract on his part, and that the defendant broke it. She placed her indorsement on fabrics, dresses, and millinery without his knowledge and withheld profits. He sues her for the damages, and the case comes here on demurrer.

The agreement of employment is signed by both parties. It has a wealth of recitals. The defendant insists, however, that it lacks the elements of a contract. She says that the plaintiff does not bind himself to anything. It is true that he does not promise in so many words that he will use reasonable efforts to place the defendant's indorsements and market her designs. We think, however, that such a promise is fairly to be implied. The law has outgrown its primitive stage of formalism when the precise word was the sovereign talisman, and every slip was fatal. It takes a broader view to-day. A promise may be lacking, and yet the whole writing may be "instinct with an obligation," imperfectly expressed (Scott, J., in McCall Co. v. Wright, 133 App.Div. 62, 117 N.Y.S. 775; Moran v. Standard Oil Co., 211 N.Y. 187, 198, 105 N.E. 217). If that is so, there is a contract.

The implication of a promise here finds support in many circumstances. The defendant gave an exclusive privilege. She was to have no right for at least a year to place her own indorsements or market her own designs except through the agency of the plaintiff. The acceptance of the exclusive agency was an assumption of its duties. Phoenix Hermetic Co. v. Filtrine Mfg. Co., 164 App.Div. 424, 150 N.Y.S. 193; W.G. Taylor Co. v. Bannerman, 120 Wis. 189, 97 N.W. 918; Mueller v. Mineral Spring Co., 88 Mich. 390, 50 N.W. 319. We are not to suppose that one party was to be placed at the mercy of the other. Hearn v. Stevens & Bro., 111 App.Div. 101, 106, 97 N.Y.S. 566; Russell v. Allerton, 108 N.Y. 288, 15 N.E. 391. Many other terms of the agreement point the same way. We are told at the outset by way of recital that:

"The said Otis F. Wood possesses a business organization adapted to the placing of such indorsements as the said Lucy, Lady Duff–Gordon, has approved."

The implication is that the plaintiff's business organization will be used for the purpose for which it is adapted. But the terms of the defendant's compensation are even more significant. Her sole compensation for the grant of an exclusive agency is to be one-half of all the profits resulting from the plaintiff's efforts. Unless he gave his efforts, she could never get anything. Without an implied promise, the transaction cannot have such business "efficacy, as both parties must have intended that at all events it should have." Bowen, L.J., in the Moorcock, 14 P.D. 64, 68. But the contract does not stop there. The plaintiff goes on to promise that he will account monthly for all moneys received by him, and that he will take out all such patents and copyrights and trade-marks as may in his judgment be necessary to protect the rights and articles affected by the agreement. It is true, of course, as the Appellate Division has said, that if he was under no duty to try to market designs or to place certificates of indorsement, his promise to account for profits or take out copyrights would be valueless. But in determining the intention of the parties the promise *has* a value. It helps to enforce the conclusion that the plaintiff *had* some duties. His promise to pay the defendant one-half of the profits and revenues resulting from the exclusive agency and to render accounts monthly was a promise to use reasonable efforts to bring profits and revenues into existence. For this conclusion the authorities are ample.

The judgment of the Appellate Division should be reversed, and the order of the Special Term affirmed, with costs in the Appellate Division and in this court.

CUDDEBACK, MCLAUGHLIN, and ANDREWS, JJ., concur. HISCOCK, C.J., and CHASE and CRANE, JJ., dissent.

Judgment reversed, etc.

UCC § 2–306

[See Selected Source Materials Supplement]

NOTE ON REQUIREMENTS AND OUTPUT CONTRACTS

Many agreements for the sale of commodities take the form of requirements or output contracts. In a *requirements* contract (1) a seller promises to supply all of the buyer's requirements of a defined commodity at a stated price (or at a price determined under a stated formula) over a designated period of time, and (2) the buyer promises to purchase all of his requirements of the commodity during that time from the seller at the stated price. In an *output* contract (1) a buyer promises to buy all of a seller's output of a given commodity at a stated price (or at a price determined under a stated formula) over a given period of time, and (2) the seller promises to sell all of her output of the commodity during that time to the buyer at the stated price.

In the era of classical contract law, the courts often refused to enforce requirements contracts in cases where the buyer could choose to have no requirements—because, for example, the buyer had no established business, or was a middleman, or required the commodity only in a part of his operations that he could easily abandon.

However, even in cases where the buyer may choose to have no requirements, by making the agreement the seller reveals that in her view, the value of the chance that the buyer will have requirements exceeds the cost to the seller of making her commitment. Furthermore, even when the buyer may choose to have no requirements, requirements contracts are classical bargains. The seller clearly shrinks her realm of choice. So does the buyer. Before the buyer enters into such a contract, he is morally free to purchase the commodity from anyone he chooses. After the buyer enters into such a contract, if he requires the commodity during the contract period he is morally obliged to purchase the commodity from the seller at the contract price. Because both parties have made real promises—have shrunk their realms of choice—and each has exchanged its promise as the price of the other's, courts that refused to enforce requirements contracts because the buyer might have no requirements violated the bargain principle.

UCC § 2–306(1) now provides that "A term which measures the quantity by the output of the seller or the requirements of the buyer means such actual output or requirements as may occur in good faith, except that no quantity unreasonably disproportionate to any stated estimate or in the absence of a stated estimate to any normal or otherwise comparable prior output or requirements may be tendered or demanded." The Official Comment adds that "Under this article, a contract for output or requirements ... [does not] lack mutuality of obligation since, under this section, the party who will determine quantity is required to operate his plant or conduct his business in good faith and according to commercial standards of fair dealing in the trade so that his output or requirements will approximate a reasonably foreseeable figure." Although UCC § 2–306(1) applies only to the sale of goods, most requirements and output contracts fall into that category. In any event, a modern court would almost certainly hold that all requirements and output contracts have consideration.

GROUSE v. GROUP HEALTH PLAN, INC.

Supreme Court of Minnesota, 1981.
306 N.W.2d 114.

Considered and decided by the court en banc without oral argument.

OTIS, JUSTICE.

Plaintiff John Grouse appeals from a judgment in favor of Group Health Plan, Inc., in this action for damages resulting from repudiation of an employment offer. The narrow issue raised is whether the trial court erred by concluding that Grouse's complaint fails to state a claim upon which relief can be granted. In our view, the doctrine of promissory estoppel entitles Grouse to recover and we, therefore, reverse and remand for a new trial on the issue of damages.

The facts relevant to this appeal are essentially undisputed. Grouse, a 1974 graduate of the University of Minnesota School of Pharmacy, was employed in 1975 as a retail pharmacist at Richter Drug in Minneapolis. He worked approximately 41 hours per week earning $7 per hour. Grouse desired employment in a hospital or clinical setting, however, because of the work environment and the increased compensation and benefits. In the summer of 1975 he was advised by the Health Sciences Placement office at the University that Group Health was seeking a pharmacist.

Grouse called Group Health and was told to come in and fill out an application. He did so in September and was, at that time, interviewed by Cyrus Elliott, Group Health's Chief Pharmacist. Approximately 2 weeks later Elliott contacted Grouse and asked him to come in for an interview with Donald Shoberg, Group Health's General Manager. Shoberg explained company policies and procedures as well as salary and benefits. Following this meeting Grouse again spoke with Elliott who told him to be patient, that it was necessary to interview recent graduates before making an offer.

On December 4, 1975, Elliott telephoned Grouse at Richter Drug and offered him a position as a pharmacist at Group Health's St. Louis Park Clinic. Grouse accepted but informed Elliott that 2 week's notice to Richter Drug would be necessary. That afternoon Grouse received an offer from a Veteran's Administration Hospital in Virginia which he declined because of Group Health's offer. Elliott called back to confirm that Grouse had resigned.

Sometime in the next few days Elliott mentioned to Shoberg that he had hired, or was thinking of hiring, Grouse. Shoberg told him that company hiring requirements included a favorable written reference, a background check, and approval of the general manager. Elliott contacted two faculty members at the School of Pharmacy who declined to give references. He also contacted an internship employer and several pharmacies where Grouse had done relief work. Their responses were that they had not had enough exposure to Grouse's work to form a judgment as to his capabilities. Elliott did not contact Richter because Grouse's application requested that he not be contacted. Because Elliott was unable to supply a favorable reference for Grouse, Shoberg hired another person to fill the position.

On December 15, 1975 Grouse called Group Health and reported that he was free to begin work. Elliott informed Grouse that someone else had been hired. Grouse complained to the director of Group Health who apologized but took no other action. Grouse experienced difficulty regaining full time employment and suffered wage loss as a result. He commenced this suit to recover damages; the trial judge found that he had not stated an actionable claim.

In our view the principle of contract law applicable here is promissory estoppel. Its effect is to imply a contract in law where none exists in fact. *Del Hayes & Sons, Inc. v. Mitchell,* 304 Minn. 275, 230 N.W.2d 588 (1975). On these facts no contract exists because due to the bilateral power of termination neither party is committed to performance and the promises are, therefore, illusory. The elements of promissory estoppel are stated in *Restatement of Contracts* § 90 (1932):

> A promise which the promisor should reasonably expect to induce action or forbearance * * * on the part of the promisee and which does induce such action or forbearance is binding if injustice can be avoided only by enforcement of the promise.

Group Health knew that to accept its offer Grouse would have to resign his employment at Richter Drug. Grouse promptly gave notice to Richter Drug and informed Group Health that he had done so when specifically asked by Elliott. Under these circumstances it would be unjust not to hold Group Health to its promise.

The parties focus their arguments on whether an employment contract which is terminable at will can give rise to an action for damages if anticipatorily repudiated. Compare *Skagerberg v. Blandin Paper Co.*, 197 Minn. 291, 266 N.W. 872 (1936); *Degen v. Investors Diversified Services, Inc.*, 260 Minn. 424, 110 N.W.2d 863 (1961); and *Bussard v. College of St. Thomas, Inc.*, 294 Minn. 215, 200 N.W.2d 155 (1972) with *Hackett v. Foodmaker, Inc.*, 69 Mich.App. 591, 245 N.W.2d 140 (1976). Group Health contends that recognition of a cause of action on these facts would result in the anomalous rule that an employee who is told not to report to work the day before he is scheduled to begin has a remedy while an employee who is discharged after the first day does not. We cannot agree since under appropriate circumstances we believe section 90 would apply even after employment has begun.

When a promise is enforced pursuant to section 90 "[t]he remedy granted for breach may be limited as justice requires." Relief may be limited to damages measured by the promisee's reliance.

The conclusion we reach does not imply that an employer will be liable whenever he discharges an employee whose term of employment is at will. What we do hold is that under the facts of this case the appellant had a right to assume he would be given a good faith opportunity to perform his duties to the satisfaction of respondent once he was on the job. He was not only denied that opportunity but resigned the position he already held in reliance on the firm offer which respondent tendered him. Since, as respondent points out, the prospective employment might have been terminated at any time, the measure of damages is not so much what he would have earned from respondent as what he lost in quitting the job he held and in declining at least one other offer of employment elsewhere.

Reversed and remanded for a new trial on the issue of damages.

NOTE ON GROUSE

Grouse needs to be read against the background of the at-will rule that governs employment contracts. Under this rule, an employer can discharge an employee at will at any time without cause. (Correspondingly, the employee is free to leave at any time without cause.) Moreover, any employment contract in which a fixed duration is neither explicit nor clearly implied is deemed to be at will. Although the at-will rule is often presented as an interpretative rule, in fact it is essentially based on judicial concepts—correct or incorrect—of sound policy.

The at-will rule has come under increasing pressure in recent years, and is now subject to major exceptions. The at-will rule and its exceptions are discussed in Wagenseller v. Scottsdale Memorial Hospital, Chapter 13, infra, and the Note that follows that case.

WHITE v. ROCHE BIOMEDICAL LABORATORIES, INC., 807 F.Supp. 1212 (D.S.C.1992), affirmed, 998 F.2d 1011 (4th Cir.1993). In a case with facts similar to those of *Grouse,* the court held for the employer:

> Plaintiff relies on the decision of the Minnesota Supreme Court in Grouse v. Group Health Plan, 306 N.W.2d 114 (Minn.1981), a case with facts similar to this case, in arguing that an employee may base a promissory estoppel claim on a promise of at-will employment....
>
> Other courts have also held that promissory estoppel may be applicable under these circumstances. *See, e.g.,* Humphreys v. Bellaire Corp., 966 F.2d 1037, 1042 (6th Cir.1992) ("we conclude that reliance on a promise of permanent employment might be considered reasonable" for purposes of promissory estoppel)....
>
> However, numerous courts have reached a contrary result under these or similar circumstances....

See also Paul v. Lankenau Hospital, 524 Pa. 90, 569 A.2d 346 (1990) ("The doctrine of equitable estoppel is not an exception to the employment at-will doctrine. An employee may be discharged with or without cause, and [Pennsylvania] law does not prohibit firing an employee for relying on an employer's promise.")

SECTION 4. PERFORMANCE OF A LEGAL DUTY AS CONSIDERATION; MODIFICATION AND WAIVER OF CONTRACTUAL DUTIES

Just as classical contract law excluded illusory promises from the operation of the bargain principle, so too it excluded promises to perform an act that the promisor was already obliged to do. Under the legal-duty rule, such a promise is not consideration, so that a bargain in which one party only promises to perform an act that he is already obliged to perform is unenforceable. That rule is the subject of this Section.

This Section begins with a series of cases that together illustrate the various facets of the legal-duty rule. Lingenfelder v. Wainwright Brewery Co. concerns a promise to perform an act that the promisor is already obliged to perform under a contract. Foakes v. Beer concerns a common variation of the legal-duty rule, in which the promisor agrees to pay less than she was legally obliged to pay, in exchange for a release from her full obligation. Austin v. Loral explicitly concerns the problem that is implicit in the earlier cases: whether and when a threat to not perform a contract can constitute duress. The remaining cases in this Section show how the legal-duty rule has been substantially eroded under modern contract law.

POLLOCK, PRINCIPLES OF CONTRACT 196 (9th ed. 1921). " ... [N]either the promise to do a thing nor the actual doing of it will be a good consideration if it is a thing which the party is already bound to do either by the general law or by a subsisting contract with the other party. It seems obvious that an express promise by A. to B. to do something which B. can already call on him to do can in contemplation of law produce no fresh advantage to B. or detriment to A."

———

SHADWELL v. SHADWELL, 30 L.J.C.P. 145 (1860). Byles, J., said in this case: "The reason why the doing what a man is already bound to do is no consideration, is not only because such a consideration is in judgment of law of no value, but because a man can hardly be allowed to say that the prior legal obligation was not his determining motive."

———

RESTATEMENT, SECOND, CONTRACTS § 73

[See Selected Source Materials Supplement]

———

LINGENFELDER v. WAINWRIGHT BREWERY CO.

Supreme Court of Missouri, 1891.
103 Mo. 578, 15 S.W. 844.

GANTT, P.J. This was an action by Phillip J. Lingenfelder and Leo Rassieur, executors of Edmund Jungenfeld against the Wainwright Brewery Company upon a contract for services as an architect. . . .

The controversy in the court below finally turned upon the single question whether or not, upon the facts found by the referee and the evidence returned by him, the deceased was entitled to commissions on the cost of the refrigerator plant. In considering the subject it should be borne in mind that Jungenfeld's contract with the brewery company was made on or about the 16th of June, 1883; that under and by it he undertook to design the buildings, and superintend their erection to completion; that the superintending or placing of machinery in the building was no part of his contract, and that the claim for commissions on the cost of the refrigerator plant is based solely on a subsequent promise, the facts of which are thus found and stated by the referee:

"[The refrigerator plant] was ordered not only without Mr. Jungenfeld's assistance, but against his wishes. He was in no way connected with its erection. Plaintiff's claim as to this item rests on a distinct ground, as to which I make the following finding of facts:

"Mr. Jungenfeld was president of the Empire Refrigerating Company, and was largely interested therein. The De la Vergne Ice–Machine Company was a competitor in business. Against Mr. Jungenfeld's wishes, Mr. Wainwright awarded the contract for the refrigerating plant to the De la Vergne Company. The brewery was at the time in process of erection, and most of the plans were made. When Mr. Jungenfeld heard that the contract was awarded he took away his plans, called off his superintendent on the ground, and notified Mr. Wainwright that he would have nothing more to do with the brewery. The defendant was in great haste to have its new brewery completed for divers reasons. It would be hard to find an architect to fill Mr. Jungenfeld's place, and the making of new plans and arrangements when another architect was found would involve much loss of time. Under these circumstances, Mr. Wainwright promised to give Mr. Jungenfeld five per cent on the cost of the De la Vergne ice machine if he would resume work. Mr. Jungenfeld accepted, and fulfilled the duties of superintending architect till the completion of the brewery.

"It is not clear to me how plaintiffs can bring their claim for this extra compensation on special agreement under their petition, which asks for the *quantum meruit* of Mr. Jungenfeld's labor; but I pass all questions of pleading, and treat the claim as properly before me, since it is desirable that this report should present findings as to the merits of all branches of the case.

"What was the consideration for defendant's promise to pay five per cent on the cost of the refrigerating plant, in addition to the regular charges?

"Plaintiffs submit two theories accounting for the consideration: (1) It is claimed that the transaction was the compromise of a doubtful claim. I do not find that Mr. Jungenfeld claimed that defendant had broken the contract, or intended to do so. I infer that Mr. Jungenfeld had confidently expected to get for his 'Empire Company' the contract for putting the refrigerating plant into the Wainwright brewery. When the De la Vergne machine was selected, he felt disappointed, aggrieved, angry; but I can find in the whole record no evidence that he ever claimed that any of his legal rights had been violated. With this understanding of the evidence, I find no basis for upholding defendant's promise to pay commission on this refrigerating plant as the compromise of any doubtful claim.

"(2) Plaintiffs also contend that the original contract between the parties was abrogated; that a new contract was entered into between the parties, differing from the old only in the fact that defendant was to pay a sum over and above the compensation agreed on in the discarded, original contract. The services to be performed (and thereafter actually performed) by Jungenfeld would, in this view, constitute a sufficient consideration. Such a principle has been recognized in a number of cases: Munroe v. Perkins, 9 Pick. 305; Holmes v. Doane, 9 Cush. 135; Lattimore v. Harsen, 14 Johns. 330; Peck v. Requa, 13 Gray 408. Without discussing the legal doctrine involved, (of the accuracy of which I may say, however, I am not convinced), I do not think the case in hand warrants its application. I find in the evidence no substitution of one contract for another. As I understand the facts, and as I accordingly formally find, defendant promised Mr. Jungenfeld a bonus to resume work, and complete the original contract under the original terms. This case seems to me analogous to that of seamen who, when hired for a voyage, under threats of desertion in a foreign port receive promises of additional compensation. It has been uniformly held they could not recover. I accordingly submit that in my view defendant's promise to pay Mr.

Jungenfeld five per cent on the cost of the refrigerating plant was without consideration, and recommend that the claim be not allowed."

The referee's finding of fact is based on the testimony of Adolphus Busch, Philip Stock, Ellis Wainwright, and is amply borne out by the testimony. Upon this state of facts the referee was of opinion that the promise to pay the 5 per cent commissions on the cost of the refrigerator plant was void, and the claim should be rejected; whereas, the learned circuit judge was of opinion that the promise was good in law, and that the commission should be allowed; and this question of law is the sole matter presented by this record....

Was there any consideration for the promise of Wainwright to pay Jungenfeld the 5 per cent on the refrigerator plant? If there was not, plaintiffs cannot recover the $3,449.75, the amount of that commission. The report of the referee and the evidence upon which it is based alike show that Jungenfeld's claim to this extra compensation is based upon Wainwright's promise to pay him this sum to induce him, Jungenfeld, to complete his original contract under its original terms. It is urged upon us by respondents that this was a new contract. New in what? Jungenfeld was bound by his contract to design and supervise this building. Under the new promise he was not to do any more or anything different. What benefit was to accrue to Wainwright? He was to receive the same service from Jungenfeld under the new, that Jungenfeld was bound to render under the original, contract. What loss, trouble, or inconvenience could result to Jungenfeld that he had not already assumed? No amount of metaphysical reasoning can change the plain fact that Jungenfeld took advantage of Wainwright's necessities, and extorted the promise of 5 per cent on the refrigerator plant as the condition of his complying with his contract already entered into. Nor was there even the flimsy pretext that Wainwright had violated any of the conditions of the contract on his part. Jungenfeld himself put it upon the simple proposition that "if he, an architect, put up the brewery, and another company put up the refrigerating machinery, it would be a detriment to the Empire Refrigerating Company," of which Jungenfeld was president. To permit plaintiff to recover under such circumstances would be to offer a premium upon bad faith, and invite men to violate their most sacred contracts that they may profit by their own wrong. "That a promise to pay a man for doing that which he is already under contract to do is without consideration" is conceded by respondents. The rule has been so long imbedded in the common law and decisions of the highest courts of the various states that nothing but the most cogent reasons ought to shake it. [Citation of cases omitted.] But "it is carrying coals to New Castle" to add authorities on a proposition so universally accepted, and so inherently just and right in itself.

The learned counsel for respondents do not controvert the general proposition. Their contention is, and the circuit court agreed with them, that when Jungenfeld declined to go further on his contract, that defendant then had the right to sue for damages, and, not having elected to sue Jungenfeld, but having acceded to his demand for the additional compensation, defendant cannot now be heard to say his promise is without consideration. While it is true Jungenfeld became liable in damages for the obvious breach of his contract we do not think it follows that defendant is estopped from showing its promise was made without consideration.

It is true that as eminent a jurist as Judge Cooley, in Goebel v. Linn, 47 Mich. 489, 11 N.W. 284, held that an ice company which had agreed to furnish a brewery with all the ice they might need for their business from November 8, 1879, until January 1, 1881, at $1.75 per ton, and afterwards, in May, 1880, declined to deliver any more ice unless the brewery would give it $3 per ton, could recover on a promissory note given for the increased price. Profound as is our respect for the distinguished judge who delivered that opinion, we are still of the opinion that his decision is not in accord with the almost universally accepted doctrine, and is not convincing, and certainly so much of the opinion as held that the payment by a debtor of a part of his debt then due would constitute a defense to a suit for the remainder is not the law of this state, nor, do we think, of any other where the common law prevails.

The case of Bishop v. Busse, 69 Ill. 403, is readily distinguishable from the case at bar. The price of brick increased very considerably, and the owner changed the plan of the building, so as to require nearly double the number. Owing to the increased price and change in the plans the contractor notified the party for whom he was building that he could not complete the house at the original prices, and thereupon a new arrangement was made and it is expressly upheld by the court on the ground that the change in the buildings was such a modification as necessitated a new contract.

Nothing we have said is intended as denying parties the right to modify their contracts, or make new contracts, upon new or different considerations, and binding themselves thereby. What we hold is that, when a party merely does what he has already obligated himself to do, he cannot demand an additional compensation therefor, and although by taking advantage of the necessities of his adversary he obtains a promise for more, the law will regard it as *nudum pactum,* and will not lend its process to aid in the wrong. So holding, we reverse the judgment of the circuit court of St. Louis to the extent that it allows the plaintiffs below (respondents here) the sum of $3,449.75, the amount of commission at 5 per cent on the refrigerator plant, and at the request of both sides we proceed to enter the judgment here which, in our opinion, the circuit court of St. Louis should have entered, and accordingly it is adjudged that the report of the referee be in all things approved, and that defendant have and recover of plaintiffs, as executors of Edmund Jungenfeld, the sum of $1,492.17, so found by the referee, with interest from March 9, 1887. All the judges of this division concur.

FOAKES v. BEER

In the House of Lords, 1884.
[1884] 9 App.Cas. 605.

[Dr. Foakes owed Julia Beer, £2090.19s. on a judgment. The parties entered into an agreement which, as interpreted by the Court of Appeal, provided that if Dr. Foakes would pay Mrs. Beer £500 at once, and the remainder of the principal in certain installments, Mrs. Beer would forgive the interest on the debt. This is a suit for the interest brought by Mrs. Beer against Dr. Foakes, alleging that if any agreement to forgive the interest was in fact entered, it was without consideration, since the consideration consisted only in Dr. Foakes' doing what he was already bound to do in paying the principal of the debt. Decision in the Court of Appeal went for Mrs. Beer.]

W.H. HOLL Q.C. for the appellant:—Apart from the doctrine of Cumber v. Wane [that £5 cannot be satisfaction of £15] there is no reason in sense or law why the agreement should not be valid, and the creditor prevented from enforcing his judgment if the agreement is performed. It may be much more advantageous to the creditor to obtain immediate payment of part of his debt than to wait to enforce payment, or perhaps by pressing his debtor to force him into bankruptcy with the result of only a small dividend. Moreover if a composition is accepted friends, who would not otherwise do so, may be willing to come forward to assist the debtor. And if the creditor thinks that the acceptance of part is for his benefit who is to say it is not? ... It is every day practice for tradesmen to take less in satisfaction of a larger sum, and give discount, where there is neither custom nor right to take credit.... It has often been held that a sheet of paper or a stick of sealing wax is a sufficient consideration.... Here the agreement is not to take less than the debt, but to give time for payment of the whole without interest. Mankind have never acted on the doctrine of Cumber v. Wane, but the contrary; nay few are aware of it. By overruling it the House will only declare the universal practice to be good law as well as good sense.

[EARL OF SELBORNE, L.C. Whatever may be the ultimate decision of this appeal the House is much indebted to Mr. Holl for his exceedingly able argument.]

BOMPAS Q.C. (Gaskell with him) for the respondent: ... There is a strong current of authority that what the law implies as a duty is no consideration. Therefore where a debt is due part payment is no reason for giving up the residue. The doctrine is too well settled to be now overthrown.... It is contrary to public policy to make the performance of a legal duty a good consideration....

EARL OF SELBORNE L.C.: ... [T]he question remains, whether the agreement is capable of being legally enforced. Not being under seal, it cannot be legally enforced against the respondent, unless she received consideration for it from the appellant, or unless, though without consideration, it operates by way of accord and satisfaction, so as to extinguish the claim for interest. What is the consideration? On the face of the agreement none is expressed, except a present payment of £500, on account and in part of the larger debt then due and payable by law under the judgment. The appellant did not contract to pay the future instalments of £150 each, at the time therein mentioned; much less did he give any new security, in the shape of negotiable paper, or in any other form. The promise de futuro was only that of the respondent, that if the half-yearly payments of £150 each were regularly paid, she would "take no proceedings whatever on the judgment." ...

The question, therefore, is nakedly raised by this appeal, whether your Lordships are now prepared, not only to overrule, as contrary to law, the doctrine stated by Sir Edward Coke to have been laid down by all the judges of the Common Pleas in Pinnel's Case [that payment of a lesser sum on the day cannot be a satisfaction of a greater sum] ... but to treat a prospective agreement, not under seal, for satisfaction of a debt, by a series of payments on account to a total amount less than the whole debt, as binding in law, provided those payments are regularly made.... The doctrine itself, as laid down by Sir Edward Coke, may have been criticised, as questionable in principle, by some persons whose opinions are entitled to respect, but it has never been judicially overruled; on the contrary I think it has always, since the sixteenth century, been accepted as law. If so, I cannot think that your Lordships would do right, if you were now to reverse, as erroneous, a judgment of the Court of Appeal, proceeding upon a doctrine which has been accepted as part of the law of England for 280 years. . . .

. . . It might be (and indeed I think it would be) an improvement in our law, if a release or acquittance of the whole debt, on payment of any sum which the creditor might be content to receive by way of accord and satisfaction (though less than the whole), were held to be, generally, binding, though not under seal; nor should I be unwilling to see equal force given to a prospective agreement, like the present, in writing though not under seal; but I think it impossible, without refinements which practically alter the sense of the word, to treat such a release or acquittance as supported by any new consideration. . . .

My conclusion is, that the order appealed from should be affirmed, and the appeal dismissed, with costs, and I so move your Lordships.

Lord Blackburn. . . .

What principally weighs with me in thinking that Lord Coke made a mistake of fact is my conviction that all men of business, whether merchants or tradesmen, do every day recognise and act on the ground that prompt payment of a part of their demand may be more beneficial to them than it would be to insist on their rights and enforce payment of the whole. Even where the debtor is perfectly solvent, and sure to pay at last, this often is so. Where the credit of the debtor is doubtful it must be more so. I had persuaded myself that there was no such long-continued action on this dictum as to render it improper in this House to reconsider the question. I had written my reasons for so thinking; but as they were not satisfactory to the other noble and learned Lords who heard the case, I do not now repeat them nor persist in them.

I assent to the judgment proposed, though it is not that which I had originally thought proper. . . .

Lord Fitzgerald. . . . I concur . . . that it would have been wiser and better if the resolution in Pinnel's Case had never been come to. . . . [but we] find the law to have been accepted as stated for a great length of time, and I apprehend that it is not now within our province to overturn it. . . .

NOTE ON THE LEGAL–DUTY RULE

Under the legal-duty rule, as embodied in Restatement Second § 73, performance of a preexisting legal duty is not consideration. Insofar as the preexisting duty is imposed by contract, rather than by law, the cases to which the rule is applicable tend to fall into two basic patterns.

Pattern I is exemplified by Lingenfelder v. Wainwright. This pattern can be illustrated as follows. Conrad Change is under a contractual duty to render Performance P to Cecily Holdfast in exchange for $10,000. Change and Holdfast then agree that Change will render performance P, but Holdfast will pay Change $12,000. Change renders performance P, but Holdfast pays only

$10,000. Change then sues Holdfast under the second agreement for the additional $2,000 that Holdfast had promised. Holdfast defends on the ground that the second agreement is unenforceable under the legal-duty rule.

Pattern II is exemplified by Foakes v. Beer. This pattern can be illustrated as follows. Change owes Holdfast $10,000 for a past-due debt under a contract. Change and Holdfast then agree that if Change pays $8,000, Holdfast will accept that amount in full satisfaction of the debt. Change pays $8,000. Holdfast then sues under the original contract for $2,000, the remainder of the original debt. Change raises the second agreement as a defense. Holdfast responds that the second agreement is unenforceable under the legal-duty rule, so that Change's defense fails.

As a matter of either doctrine or policy, there is no reason to distinguish between these two patterns. As a practical matter, however, the difference in the way cases arise under the two patterns may lead to special issues. For example, in a variation of Pattern I, Holdfast may actually pay $12,000, and later sue to recover the additional $2,000. If Holdfast was under no improper pressure from Change at the time she made the $12,000 payment, she cannot invoke the legal-duty rule as a defense to Change's suit. The legal-duty rule makes a *promise* unenforceable, but in the variation, Change is not trying to enforce Holdfast's promise. Rather, Holdfast is trying to undo a completed transaction—to get back money she has paid. The legal-duty rule is not applicable. An analogy would be a case in which Holdfast makes a donative promise to give Change $2,000. Change could not sue Holdfast to enforce the promise, but if Holdfast actually *pays* the $2,000, Holdfast cannot sue to get the money back.

Suppose, however, that Holdfast paid the additional $2,000 only because Change had put Holdfast under improper pressure at the time she made the payment? That issue is the subject of Austin v. Loral, infra.

———

AUSTIN INSTRUMENT, INC. v. LORAL CORP.

Court of Appeals of New York, 1971.
29 N.Y.2d 124, 324 N.Y.S.2d 22, 272 N.E.2d 533.

FULD, CHIEF JUDGE.

The defendant, Loral Corporation, seeks to recover payment for goods delivered under a contract which it had with the plaintiff Austin Instrument, Inc., on the ground that the evidence establishes, as a matter of law, that it was forced to agree to an increase in price on the items in question under circumstances amounting to economic duress.

In July of 1965, Loral was awarded a $6,000,000 contract by the Navy for the production of radar sets. The contract contained a schedule of deliveries, a liquidated damages clause applying to late deliveries and a cancellation clause in case of default by Loral. The latter thereupon solicited bids for some 40 precision gear components needed to produce the radar sets, and awarded Austin a subcontract to supply 23 such parts. That party commenced delivery in early 1966.

In May, 1966, Loral was awarded a second Navy contract for the production of more radar sets and again went about soliciting bids. Austin bid on all

40 gear components but, on July 15, a representative from Loral informed Austin's president, Mr. Krauss, that his company would be awarded the subcontract only for those items on which it was low bidder. The Austin officer refused to accept an order for less than all 40 of the gear parts and on the next day he told Loral that Austin would cease deliveries of the parts due under the existing subcontract unless Loral consented to substantial increases in the prices provided for by that agreement—both retroactively for parts already delivered and prospectively on those not yet shipped—and placed with Austin the order for all 40 parts needed under Loral's second Navy contract. Shortly thereafter, Austin did, indeed, stop delivery. After contacting 10 manufacturers of precision gears and finding none who could produce the parts in time to meet its commitments to the Navy,[13] Loral acceded to Austin's demands; in a letter dated July 22, Loral wrote to Austin that "We have feverishly surveyed other sources of supply and find that because of the prevailing military exigencies, were they to start from scratch as would have to be the case, they could not even remotely begin to deliver on time to meet the delivery requirements established by the Government. * * * Accordingly, we are left with no choice or alternative but to meet your conditions."

Loral thereupon consented to the price increases insisted upon by Austin under the first subcontract and the latter was awarded a second subcontract making it the supplier of all 40 gear parts for Loral's second contract with the Navy.[14] Although Austin was granted until September to resume deliveries, Loral, in fact, receive parts in August and was able to produce the radar sets in time to meet its commitments to the Navy on both contracts. After Austin's last delivery under the second subcontract in July, 1967, Loral notified it of its intention to seek recovery of the price increases. . . .

The applicable law is clear and, indeed, is not disputed by the parties. A contract is voidable on the ground of duress when it is established that the party making the claim was forced to agree to it by means of a wrongful threat precluding the exercise of his free will. (See Allstate Med. Labs., Inc. v. Blaivas, 20 N.Y.2d 654, 282 N.Y.S.2d 268, 229 N.E.2d 50; Kazaras v. Manufacturers Trust Co., 4 N.Y.2d 930, 175 N.Y.S.2d 172, 151 N.E.2d 356; Adams v. Irving Nat. Bank, 116 N.Y. 606, 611, 23 N.E. 7, 9; see, also, 13 Williston, Contracts [3d ed., 1970], § 1603, p. 658.) The existence of economic duress or business compulsion is demonstrated by proof that "immediate possession of needful goods is threatened" (Mercury Mach. Importing Corp. v. City of New York, 3 N.Y.2d 418, 425, 165 N.Y.S.2d 517, 520, 144 N.E.2d 400) or, more particularly, in cases such as the one before us, by proof that one party to a contract has threatened to breach the agreement by withholding goods unless the other party agrees to some further demand. (See, e.g., Du Pont de Nemours & Co. v. J.I. Hass Co., 303 N.Y. 785, 103 N.E.2d 896; Gallagher Switchboard Corp. v. Heckler Elec. Co., 36 Misc.2d 225, 232 N.Y.S.2d 590; see, also, 13 Williston, Contracts [3d ed., 1970], § 1617, p. 705.) However, a mere threat by one party to breach the contract by not delivering the required items, though wrongful, does not in itself constitute economic duress. It must also appear that the threatened party could not obtain the goods from another source of supply and that the ordinary remedy of an action for breach of contract would not be adequate.

---

13. The best reply Loral received was from a vendor who stated he could commence deliveries sometime in October.

14. Loral makes no claim in this action on the second subcontract.

We find without any support in the record the conclusion reached by the courts below that Loral failed to establish that it was the victim of economic duress. On the contrary, the evidence makes out a classic case, as a matter of law, of such duress.

It is manifest that Austin's threat—to stop deliveries unless the prices were increased—deprived Loral of its free will. As bearing on this, Loral's relationship with the Government is most significant. As mentioned above, its contract called for staggered monthly deliveries of the radar sets, with clauses calling for liquidated damages and possible cancellation on default. Because of its production schedule, Loral was, in July, 1966, concerned with meeting its delivery requirements in September, October and November, and it was for the sets to be delivered in those months that the withheld gears were needed. Loral had to plan ahead, and the substantial liquidated damages for which it would be liable, plus the threat of default, were genuine possibilities. More-over, Loral did a substantial portion of its business with the Government, and it feared that a failure to deliver as agreed upon would jeopardize its chances for future contracts. These genuine concerns do not merit the label " 'self-imposed, undisclosed and subjective' " which the Appellate Division majority placed upon them. It was perfectly reasonable for Loral, or any other party similarly placed, to consider itself in an emergency, duress situation.

Austin, however, claims that the fact that Loral extended its time to resume deliveries until September negates its alleged dire need for the parts. A Loral official testified on this point that Austin's president told him he could deliver some parts in August and that the extension of deliveries was a formality. In any event, the parts necessary for production of the radar sets to be delivered in September were delivered to Loral on September 1, and the parts needed for the October schedule were delivered in late August and early September. Even so, Loral had to "work * * * around the clock" to meet its commitments. Considering that the best offer Loral received from the other vendors it contacted was commencement of delivery sometime in October, which, as the record shows, would have made it late in its deliveries to the Navy in both September and October, Loral's claim that it had no choice but to accede to Austin's demands is conclusively demonstrated.

We find unconvincing Austin's contention that Loral, in order to meet its burden, should have contacted the Government and asked for an extension of its delivery dates so as to enable it to purchase the parts from another vendor. Aside from the consideration that Loral was anxious to perform well in the Government's eyes, it could not be sure when it would obtain enough parts from a substitute vendor to meet its commitments. The only promise which it received from the companies it contacted was for *commencement* of deliveries, not full supply, and, with vendor delay common in this field, it would have been nearly impossible to know the length of the extension it should request. It must be remembered that Loral was producing a needed item of military hardware. Moreover, there is authority for Loral's position that nonperform-ance by a subcontractor is not an excuse for default in the main contract. (See, e.g., McBride & Wachtel, Government Contracts, § 35.10, [11].) In light of all this, Loral's claim should not be held insufficiently supported because it did not request an extension from the Government.

Loral, as indicated above, also had the burden of demonstrating that it could not obtain the parts elsewhere within a reasonable time, and there can be no doubt that it met this burden. The 10 manufacturers whom Loral contacted comprised its entire list of "approved vendors" for precision gears, and none was able to commence delivery soon enough.[15] As Loral was producing a highly sophisticated item of military machinery requiring parts made to the strictest engineering standards, it would be unreasonable to hold that Loral should have gone to other vendors, with whom it was either unfamiliar or dissatisfied, to procure the needed parts. As Justice Steuer noted in his dissent, Loral "contacted all the manufacturers whom it believed capable of making these parts" (35 A.D.2d at p. 393, 316 N.Y.S.2d at p. 534), and this was all the law requires.

It is hardly necessary to add that Loral's normal legal remedy of accepting Austin's breach of the contract and then suing for damages would have been inadequate under the circumstances, as Loral would still have had to obtain the gears elsewhere with all the concomitant consequences mentioned above. In other words, Loral actually had no choice, when the prices were raised by Austin, except to take the gears at the "coerced" prices and then sue to get the excess back.

Austin's final argument is that Loral, even if it did enter into the contract under duress, lost any rights it had to a refund of money by waiting until July, 1967, long after the termination date of the contract, to disaffirm it. It is true that one who would recover moneys allegedly paid under duress must act promptly to make his claim known. (See Oregon Pacific R.R. Co. v. Forrest, 128 N.Y. 83, 93, 28 N.E. 137, 139; Port Chester Elec. Constr. Corp. v. Hastings Terraces, 284 App.Div. 966, 967, 134 N.Y.S.2d 656, 658.) In this case, Loral delayed making its demand for a refund until three days after Austin's last delivery on the second subcontract. Loral's reason—for waiting until that time—is that it feared another stoppage of deliveries which would again put it in an untenable situation. Considering Austin's conduct in the past, this was perfectly reasonable, as the possibility of an application by Austin of further business compulsion still existed until all of the parts were delivered.

In sum, the record before us demonstrates that Loral agreed to the price increases in consequence of the economic duress employed by Austin. Accordingly, the matter should be remanded to the trial court for a computation of its damages.

The order appealed from should be modified, with costs, by reversing so much thereof as affirms the dismissal of defendant Loral Corporation's claim and, except as so modified, affirmed.

[The dissenting opinion of Bergan, J., is omitted.]

Burke, Scileppi and Gibson, JJ., concur with Fuld, C.J.

Bergan, J., dissents and votes to affirm in a separate opinion in which Breitel and Jasen, JJ., concur.

Ordered accordingly.

---

15. Loral, as do many manufacturers, maintains a list of "approved vendors," that is, vendors whose products, facilities, techniques and performance have been inspected and found satisfactory.

NOTE ON CONTRACT PRACTICE

In 1988, Professor Russell Weintraub sent a questionnaire to the general counsels of 182 corporations of various sizes, asking for their views on certain contracts issues. Weintraub, A Survey of Contract Practice and Policy, [1992] Wisc. L. Rev. 1. The survey, which had a response rate of 46%, produced a great deal of extremely valuable information and analysis.

One of the questions in the survey was as follows: "If, because of a shift in market prices, one of your suppliers or customers requested a modification of the contracted-for price, would your company always insist on compliance with the contract?" Virtually all of the respondents (95%) said that their companies would not always insist on compliance with the contract. A follow-up question asked those respondents to list the factors deemed relevant in deciding whether a request for a modification would be granted. In response, 80% of the respondents listed whether relations with the company making the request has been long and satisfactory, and 76% listed whether the request was reasonable under trade practice.

A parallel question asked, "How frequently has your company asked relief from or modification of its contractual obligations?" Only 17% of the respondents said that their companies never made such requests. In contrast, 22% said that their companies made such requests an average of one to five times a year, and 18% said that their companies made such requests an average of over five times a year. In most cases, the respondents reported, the problem was amicably worked out by either a modification of the contract in question or adjustments in future contracts.

SCHWARTZREICH v. BAUMAN–BASCH, INC., 231 N.Y. 196, 131 N.E. 887 (1921). The plaintiff entered into a written agreement with the defendant for a year's employment as a designer of coats and wraps at $90 a week. About a month before his services were to begin, the plaintiff received an offer of a higher salary from another firm. A conversation then took place between the defendant and the plaintiff, which was rather differently recollected by the two parties afterward. According to the defendant, the plaintiff threatened to quit at a time when the defendant had to get his sample line out on the road and could not secure another designer. According to the plaintiff, he merely discussed the offer with the defendant and sought his advice as a friend. In any event, the result of the conversation was that a new typewritten contract was drafted, word for word the same as the first contract except that the salary was stated to be $100. The parties then tore their signatures off the old contract. The jury rendered a verdict for the plaintiff under an instruction that "the test question is whether by word or by act, either prior to or at the time of signing the $100 contract, these parties mutually agreed that the old contract from that instant should be null and void." It was held that judgment should be rendered for the plaintiff on this verdict.

RESTATEMENT, FIRST, CONTRACTS § 406, ILLUSTRATION 1:
"A contracts to build a house for B for which B contracts to pay $25,000. A

does a portion of the work, but finding that he will lose more money by completing the contract than by giving up at once makes B an offer to rescind. B accepts. Both parties are discharged. B is under no duty to pay A for what he has done." Comment *a*: "Where ... there is a bilateral contract, and each party is still subject to some duty thereunder, the agreement of each party to surrender his rights under the contract affords sufficient consideration to the other for his corresponding agreement.... Adequacy of consideration is immaterial.... Therefore, since each party surrenders something which he might have retained, the agreement to rescind is effectual."

———

RESTATEMENT, SECOND, CONTRACTS § 73, Comment d: *"Contractual duty to third person.* The rule that performance of legal duty is not consideration for a promise has often been applied in cases involving a contractual duty owed to a person other than the promisor. In such cases, however, there is less likelihood of economic coercion or other unfair pressure than there is if the duty is owed to the promisee. In some cases consideration can be found in the fact that the promisee gives up his right to propose to the third person the rescission or modification of the contractual duty. But the tendency of the law has been simply to hold that performance of contractual duty can be consideration if the duty is not owed to the promisor. Relief may still be given to the promisor in appropriate cases under the rules governing duress and other invalidating causes...."

———

UCC §§ 3–103(a)(4), 3–104, 3–311

[See Selected Source Materials Supplement]

———

RESTATEMENT, SECOND, CONTRACTS §§ 279, 281

[See Selected Source Materials Supplement]

———

RESTATEMENT, SECOND, CONTRACTS § 89

[See Selected Source Materials Supplement]

———

ANGEL v. MURRAY

Supreme Court of Rhode Island, 1974.
113 R.I. 482, 322 A.2d 630.

ROBERTS, C.J. This is a civil action brought by Alfred L. Angel and others against John E. Murray, Jr., Director of Finance of the City of Newport, the city of Newport, and James L. Maher, alleging that Maher had illegally been paid the sum of $20,000 by the Director of Finance and praying that the defendant Maher be ordered to repay the city such sum. The case was heard by a justice of the Superior Court, sitting without a jury, who entered a judgment ordering Maher to repay the sum of $20,000 to the city of Newport. Maher is now before this court prosecuting an appeal.

The record discloses that Maher has provided the city of Newport with a refuse-collection service under a series of five-year contracts beginning in 1946. On March 12, 1964, Maher and the city entered into another such contract for a period of five years commencing on July 1, 1964, and terminating on June 30, 1969. The contract provided, among other things, that Maher would receive $137,000 per year in return for collecting and removing all combustible and noncombustible waste materials generated within the city.

In June of 1967 Maher requested an additional $10,000 per year from the city council because there had been a substantial increase in the cost of collection due to an unexpected and unanticipated increase of 400 new dwelling units. Maher's testimony, which is uncontradicted, indicates the 1964 contract had been predicated on the fact that since 1946 there had been an average increase of 20 to 25 new dwelling units per year. After a public meeting of the city council where Maher explained in detail the reasons for his request and was questioned by members of the city council, the city council agreed to pay him an additional $10,000 for the year ending on June 30, 1968. Maher made a similar request again in June of 1968 for the same reasons, and the city council again agreed to pay an additional $10,000 for the year ending on June 30, 1969.

The trial justice found that each such $10,000 payment was made in violation of law.... [H]e found that Maher was not entitled to extra compensation because the original contract already required him to collect all refuse generated within the city and, therefore, included the 400 additional units. The trial justice further found that these 400 additional units were within the contemplation of the parties when they entered into the contract. It appears that he based this portion of the decision upon the rule that Maher had a preexisting duty to collect the refuse generated by the 400 additional units, and thus there was no consideration for the two additional payments....

A.

As previously stated, the city council made two $10,000 payments. The first was made in June of 1967 for the year beginning on July 1, 1967, and ending on June 30, 1968. Thus, by the time this action was commenced in October of 1968, the modification was completely executed. That is, the money had been paid by the city council, and Maher had collected all of the refuse. Since consideration is only a test of the enforceability of executory promises, the presence or absence of consideration for the first payment is unimportant because the city council's agreement to make the first payment was fully executed at the time of the commencement of this action.... However, since both payments were made under similar circumstances, our decision regarding the second payment (Part B, infra) is fully applicable to the first payment.

B.

It is generally held that a modification of a contract is itself a contract, which is unenforceable unless supported by consideration. . . .

The primary purpose of the preexisting duty rule is to prevent what has been referred to as the "hold-up game." See 1A Corbin . . . § 171. A classic example of the "hold-up game" is found in Alaska Packers' Ass'n v. Domenico, 117 F. 99 (9th Cir.1902). There 21 seamen entered into a written contract with Domenico to sail from San Francisco to Pyramid Harbor, Alaska. They were to work as sailors and fishermen out of Pyramid Harbor during the fishing season of 1900. The contract specified that each man would be paid $50 plus two cents for each red salmon he caught. Subsequent to their arrival at Pyramid Harbor, the men stopped work and demanded an additional $50. They threatened to return to San Francisco if Domenico did not agree to their demand. Since it was impossible for Domenico to find other men, he agreed to pay the men an additional $50. After they returned to San Francisco, Domenico refused to pay the men an additional $50. The court found that the subsequent agreement to pay the men an additional $50 was not supported by consideration because the men had a preexisting duty to work on the ship under the original contract, and thus the subsequent agreement was unenforceable.

Another example of the "hold-up game" is found in the area of construction contracts. Frequently, a contractor will refuse to complete work under an unprofitable contract unless he is awarded additional compensation. The courts have generally held that a subsequent agreement to award additional compensation is unenforceable if the contractor is only performing work which would have been required of him under the original contract. See, e.g., Lingenfelder v. Wainwright Brewing Co., 103 Mo. 578, 15 S.W. 844 (1891), which is a leading case in this area. . . .

These examples clearly illustrate that the courts will not enforce an agreement that has been procured by coercion or duress and will hold the parties to their original contract regardless of whether it is profitable or unprofitable. However, the courts have been reluctant to apply the preexisting duty rule when a party to a contract encounters unanticipated difficulties and the other party, not influenced by coercion or duress, voluntarily agrees to pay additional compensation for work already required to be performed under the contract. For example, the courts have found that the original contract was rescinded, Linz v. Schuck, 106 Md. 220, 67 A. 286 (1907); abandoned, Connelly v. Devoe, 37 Conn. 570 (1871), or waived, Michaud v. McGregor, 61 Minn. 198, 63 N.W. 479 (1895).

Although the preexisting duty rule has served a useful purpose insofar as it deters parties from using coercion and duress to obtain additional compensation, it has been widely criticized as a general rule of law. . . .

The modern trend appears to recognize the necessity that courts should enforce agreements modifying contracts when unexpected or unanticipated difficulties arise during the course of the performance of a contract, even though there is no consideration for the modification, as long as the parties agree voluntarily.

Under the Uniform Commercial Code, § 2–209(1), which has been adopted by 49 states, "[a]n agreement modifying a contract [for the sale of goods] needs no consideration to be binding." See G.L.1956 (1969 Reenactment) § 6A–2–209(1). Although at first blush this section appears to validate modifications obtained by coercion and duress, the comments to this section indicate that a modification under this section must meet the test of good faith imposed by the Code, and a modification obtained by extortion without a legitimate commercial reason is unenforceable.

The modern trend away from a rigid application of the preexisting duty rule is reflected by [§ 89(a)] of the American Law Institute's Restatement, Second, Law of Contracts. . . .

We believe that [§ 89(a)] is the proper rule of law and find it applicable to the facts of this case.[16] It not only prohibits modifications obtained by coercion, duress, or extortion but also fulfills society's expectation that agreements entered into voluntarily will be enforced by the courts.[17] See generally Horwitz, The Historical Foundations of Modern Contract Law, 87 Harv.L.Rev. 917 (1974). Section [89(a)], of course, does not compel a modification of an unprofitable or unfair contract; it only enforces a modification if the parties voluntarily agree and if (1) the promise modifying the original contract was made before the contract was fully performed on either side, (2) the underlying circumstances which prompted the modification were unanticipated by the parties, and (3) the modification is fair and equitable.

The evidence, which is uncontradicted, reveals that in June of 1968 Maher requested the city council to pay him an additional $10,000 for the year beginning on July 1, 1968, and ending on June 30, 1969. This request was made at a public meeting of the city council, where Maher explained in detail his reasons for making the request. Thereafter, the city council voted to authorize the Mayor to sign an amendment to the [1964] contract which provided that Maher would receive an additional $10,000 per year for the

16. The fact that these additional payments were made by a municipal corporation rather than a private individual does not, in our opinion, affect the outcome of this case. . . .

17. The drafters of [§ 89(a)] of the Restatement Second of the Law of Contracts use the following illustrations in comment (b) as examples of how this rule is applied to certain transactions:

"1. By a written contract A agrees to excavate a cellar for B for a stated price. Solid rock is unexpectedly encountered and A so notifies B. A and B then orally agree that A will remove the rock at a unit price which is reasonable but nine times that used in computing the original price, and A completes the job. B is bound to pay the increased amount.

"2. A contracts with B to supply for $300 a laundry chute for a building B has contracted to build for the government for $150,000. Later A discovers that he made an error as to the type of material to be used and should have bid $1,200. A offers to supply the chute for $1,000, eliminating overhead and profit. After ascertaining that other suppliers would charge more, B agrees. The new agreement is binding.

"3. A is employed by B as a designer of coats at $90 a week for a year beginning November 1 under a written contract executed September

1. A is offered $115 a week by another employer and so informs B. A and B then agree that A will be paid $100 a week and in October execute a new written contract to that effect, simultaneously tearing up the prior contract. The new contract is binding.

"4. A contracts to manufacture and sell to B 2,000 steel roofs for corn cribs at $60. Before A begins manufacture a threat of a nationwide steel strike raises the cost of steel about $10 per roof, and A and B agree orally to increase the price to $70 per roof. A thereafter manufactures and delivers 1,700 of the roofs, and B pays for 1,500 of them at the increased price without protest, increasing the selling price of the corn cribs by $10. The new agreement is binding.

"5. A contracts to manufacture and sell to B 100,000 castings for lawn mowers at 50 cents each. After partial delivery and after B has contracted to sell a substantial number of lawn mowers at a fixed price, A notifies B that increased metal costs require that the price be increased to 75 cents. Substitute castings are available at 55 cents, but only after several months delay. B protests but is forced to agree to the new price to keep its plant in operation. The modification is not binding."

duration of the contract. Under such circumstances we have no doubt that the city voluntarily agreed to modify the 1964 contract.

Having determined the voluntariness of this agreement, we turn our attention to the three criteria delineated above. First, the modification was made in June of 1968 at a time when the five-year contract which was made in 1964 had not been fully performed by either party. Second, although the 1964 contract provided that Maher collect all refuse generated within the city, it appears this contract was premised on Maher's past experience that the number of refuse-generating units would increase at a rate of 20 to 25 per year. Furthermore, the evidence is uncontradicted that the 1967–1968 increase of 400 units "went beyond any previous expectation." Clearly, the circumstances which prompted the city council to modify the 1964 contract were unanticipated. Third, although the evidence does not indicate what proportion of the total this increase comprised, the evidence does indicate that it was a "substantial" increase. In light of this, we cannot say that the council's agreement to pay Maher the $10,000 increase was not fair and equitable in the circumstances.

The judgment appealed from is reversed, and the cause is remanded to the Superior Court for entry of judgment for the defendants.

––––––

WATKINS & SON v. CARRIG, 91 N.H. 459, 21 A.2d 591 (1941). "In common understanding there is, importantly, a wide divergence between a bare promise and a promise in adjustment of a contractual promise already outstanding. A promise with no supporting consideration would upset well and long–established human interrelations if the law did not treat it as a vain thing. But parties to a valid contract generally understand that it is subject to any mutual action they may take in its performance. Changes to meet changes in circumstances and conditions should be valid if the law is to carry out its function and service by rules conformable with reasonable practices and understandings in matters of business and commerce."

––––––

UCC § 2–209

[See Selected Source Materials Supplement]

––––––

CISG ART. 29

[See Selected Source Materials Supplement]

––––––

NOTE ON THE CISG

In 1969, the United Nations Commission on International Trade Law (UNCITRAL) appointed a working group to prepare a new draft of an international convention (treaty) on the sale of goods. The United States was an active participant in the working group. The ultimate result was the Convention for the International Sale of Goods (the CISG), which was adopted in 1980, and came into force in 1988 when it had been ratified by the requisite ten countries. The CISG is binding only in those countries that have ratified it. As of 2000, the CISG had been ratified by fifty-three countries, including the United States, Canada, China, France, Germany, and Mexico.

Although in form the CISG is an international treaty, in substance it is a code, much like Article 2 of the UCC. Article 2 governs contracts for the sale of goods between a seller and a buyer in the United States. The CISG governs contracts for the sale of goods (with certain exclusions, such as consumer goods) between a seller and a buyer who have their places of business in different countries, both of which have ratified the CISG. Accordingly, if, for example, a seller with its place of business in the United States enters into a contract for the sale of goods to a buyer with its place of business in France, then unless the parties otherwise provide, the contract is governed by the provisions of the CISG.

Like the UCC, the CISG does not govern the issue whether a contract is substantively valid; that is, it does not govern matters such as fraud, capacity, duress, mistake, legality, or the like. However, the CISG does govern whether a contract satisfies requisite formal requirements, such as whether a contract is required to be in writing, and also governs such matters as whether a contract was formed and whether a contract is sufficiently definite to be enforceable.

RESTATEMENT, SECOND, CONTRACTS § 84

[See Selected Source Materials Supplement]

RESTATEMENT, SECOND, CONTRACTS § 84, ILLUSTRATIONS 3, 4, 6

3. A employs B to build a house, promising to pay therefor $10,000 on the production of a certificate from A's architect, C, stating that the work has been satisfactorily completed. B builds the house but the work is defective in certain trivial particulars. C refuses to give B a certificate. A says to B, "My architect rightfully refuses to give you a certificate but the defects are not serious; I will pay you the full price which I promised." A is bound to do so, and has no power to restore the requirement of the condition.

4. A, an insurance company, insures B's house for $5000 against loss by fire. The insurance policy provides that it shall be payable only if B gives written notification of any loss within thirty days after its occurrence. An insured loss occurs and B gives only oral notification thereof within thirty days. A tells him, either before or after the lapse of thirty days from the loss, that this notification is sufficient. A cannot thereafter rely upon B's failure to give written notification as an excuse for failure to pay for the loss. . . .

6. In Illustration 4, A can restore the requirement of the condition by notifying B of his intention to do so if there still remains a reasonable time for the occurrence of the condition before the expiration of the thirty-day period, unless such action would be unjust in view of a material change of position by B in reliance on A's waiver. If a reasonable time does not remain, A cannot restore the requirement of the condition by extending the time.

NASSAU TRUST CO. v. MONTROSE CONCRETE PRODUCTS CORP., 56 N.Y.2d 175, 451 N.Y.S.2d 663, 436 N.E.2d 1265 (1982), reargument denied 57 N.Y.2d 674, 454 N.Y.S.2d 1032, 439 N.E.2d 1247 (1982). "Modification ... requires consideration.... [In contrast, waiver does not rest] upon consideration or agreement. A modification, because it is an agreement based upon consideration, is binding according to its terms and may only be withdrawn by agreement.... A waiver, to the extent that it has been executed, cannot be expunged or recalled ... but, not being a binding agreement, can, to the extent that it is executory, be withdrawn, provided the party whose performance has been waived is given notice of withdrawal and a reasonable time after notice within which to perform...."

UCC §§ 1–107,* 2–209

[See Selected Source Materials Supplement]

BMC INDUSTRIES, INC. v. BARTH INDUSTRIES, INC., 160 F.3d 1322 (11th Cir.1998), certiorari denied, 526 U.S. 1132, 119 S.Ct. 1807, 143 L.Ed.2d 1010, (1999). "As an initial matter, we must determine whether, under the UCC, waiver must be accompanied by detrimental reliance.... [C]ourts disagree on whether the UCC retains this requirement. We conclude, however, that the UCC does not require consideration or detrimental reliance for waiver of a contract term.

"Our conclusion follows from the plain language of subsections [2–209(4)] and (5). While subsection (4) states that an attempted modification that fails may still constitute a waiver, subsection (5) provides that the waiver may be retracted unless the non-waiving party relies on the waiver. Consequently, the statute recognizes that waivers may exist in the absence of detrimental reliance—these are the retractable waivers referred to in subsection (5). Only this interpretation renders meaning to subsection (5), because reading subsec-

---

* In 2003, the National Commissioners on Uniform State Laws and the American Law Institute promulgated a revised version of Article 1. The revised version has not been widely adopted by state legislatures. Therefore, the cross-reference in the text is to the pre–2003 version of Article 1. In the revised version, the counterpart to pre–2003 section 1–107 is section 1–306:

Waiver or Renunciation of Claim or Right After Breach

A claim or right arising out of an alleged breach may be discharged in whole or in part without consideration by agreement of the aggrieved party in an authenticated record.

(Footnote by ed.)

tion (4) to require detrimental reliance for all waivers means that waivers would never be retractable. See Wisconsin Knife Works v. National Metal Crafters, 781 F.2d 1280, 1291 (7th Cir.1986) (Easterbrook, J., dissenting) (noting that reading a detrimental reliance requirement into the UCC would eliminate the distinction between subsections (4) and (5)). Subsection (5) would therefore be meaningless.

"Although [some] courts have held that waiver requires reliance under the UCC, those courts have ignored the UCC's plain language. The leading case espousing this view of waiver is Wisconsin Knife Works v. National Metal Crafters, 781 F.2d 1280 (7th Cir.1986) ... in which a panel of the Seventh Circuit addressed a contract that included a term prohibiting oral modifications, and considered whether an attempted oral modification could instead constitute a waiver. Writing for the majority, Judge Posner concluded that the UCC's subsection (2), which gives effect to 'no oral modification' provisions, would become superfluous if contract terms could be waived without detrimental reliance. Judge Posner reasoned that if attempted oral modifications that were unenforceable because of subsection (2) were nevertheless enforced as waivers under subsection (4), then subsection (2) is 'very nearly a dead letter.' Id. at 1286. According to Judge Posner, there must be some difference between modification and waiver in order for both subsections (2) and (4) to have meaning. This difference is waiver's detrimental reliance requirement.

"Judge Posner, however, ignores a fundamental difference between modifications and waivers: while a party that has agreed to a contract modification cannot cancel the modification without giving consideration for the cancellation, a party may unilaterally retract its waiver of a contract term provided it gives reasonable notice. The fact that waivers may unilaterally be retracted provides the difference between subsections (2) and (4) that allows both to have meaning. We therefore conclude that waiver under the UCC does not require detrimental reliance."

Chapter 3

PAST CONSIDERATION

Chapter 3 considers the enforceability of promises that are, for the most part, motivated by a moral obligation that preexists the promise. Such a promise is a special case of donative promise, in the sense that it is not bargained for. It differs from a simple donative promise, because a simple donative promise the promise may *give rise* to a moral obligation, but it is not *based* on a preexisting moral obligation.

RESTATEMENT, SECOND, CONTRACTS §§ 82, 83

[See Selected Source Materials Supplement]

BANKRUPTCY CODE, 11 U.S.C. § 524

[See Selected Source Materials Supplement]

THREE SITUATIONS IN WHICH A PROMISE TO DISCHARGE AN UNENFORCEABLE OBLIGATION IS BINDING

Forming the core of any discussion of the doctrine of "past consideration" are three cases in which a promise to pay based on a past event, rather than a present bargain, was traditionally enforceable. These cases are: (1) A promise to pay a debt barred by the statute of limitations. (2) A promise by an adult to pay a debt incurred when the adult was under legal age (so that the contract was not enforceable against her). (3) A promise to pay a debt that has been discharged in bankruptcy. (The practical significance of the bankruptcy case has been limited by § 524 of the Bankruptcy Code, which creates a number of hurdles that must be jumped to make such a promise enforceable, but the doctrinal significance of this case is likely to persist.)

In all three of these cases, the discussion in the traditional commentaries was not concerned with anticipating the result, which is fairly clear, but in reconciling the result with the requirement of the bargain theory of consideration. There were two competing lines of explanation.

The first explanation was that in all of these cases there exists from the beginning a moral obligation to make compensation for a benefit conferred, which supports and serves as consideration for the later promise. Though the law will not enforce the promise of an infant, or the obligation of a debtor whose debt has been barred by the statute or discharged in bankruptcy, the infant or debtor in these cases ought in morality to pay his obligation unless there exists some meritorious defense against it, such as fraud or the like. When the debtor recognizes this moral obligation by making a new promise to pay, he becomes liable.

The competing—and less satisfactory—explanation for these cases ran along the following lines: In all these situations the creditor really has, prior to the new promise by the debtor, not merely a *moral* claim, but a *legal* claim. This legal claim is, for the time being, unenforceable, since the debtor may assert the defense of infancy, the statute of limitations, or the discharge in bankruptcy. When the new promise is made, the effect is not to create a legal right in the creditor where none existed before (for that would require consideration), but rather to remove from the hands of the debtor a defense against the assertion of a legal right that already exists. This explanation was expressed in a variety of ways. For example, it was said that in the case of the infant's contract, the original contract is not "void," but "voidable," and that when the infant, after coming of age, promises to perform it, he "affirms" the contract, and gives up his power to avoid it. Then in the case of the debt barred by the statute of limitations and the discharged bankrupt, it was said that the new promise of the debtor "waives" the defense of the statute or the discharge, and that a "waiver" does not require consideration.

This general mode of analysis raises at least two questions: (1) If a "legal" obligation can "exist" even though the debtor has a completely effective defense to it, what is the difference between such an obligation and an obligation that is merely "moral"? (2) The analysis assumes that consideration is required to create a legal obligation, but is not required to make effective the debtor's surrender of a defense to an existing obligation. What justification is there for this distinction?

The significant question, addressed by the materials in the remainder of this Chapter, is whether these core cases stand by themselves or are instances of a more general principle.

MILLS v. WYMAN

Supreme Judicial Court of Massachusetts, 1825.
3 Pick. [20 Mass.] 207.

This was an action of assumpsit brought to recover a compensation for the board, nursing, & c., of Levi Wyman, son of the defendant, from the 5th to the 20th of February, 1821. The plaintiff then lived at Hartford, in Connecticut; the defendant, at Shrewsbury, in this county. Levi Wyman, at the time when the services were rendered, was about 25 years of age, and had long ceased to be a member of his father's family. He was on his return from a voyage at sea, and being suddenly taken sick at Hartford, and being poor and in distress, was relieved by the plaintiff in the manner and to the extent above stated. On the 24th of February, after all the expenses had been incurred, the defendant wrote a letter to the plaintiff, promising to pay him such expenses. There was no consideration for this promise, except what grew out of the relation which subsisted between Levi Wyman and the defendant, and Howe, J., before whom the cause was tried in the court of common pleas, thinking this not sufficient to support the action, directed a nonsuit. To this direction the plaintiff filed exceptions.

PARKER, C.J. General rules of law established for the protection and security of honest and fair-minded men, who may inconsiderately make promises without any equivalent, will sometimes screen men of a different character from engagements which they are bound in *foro conscientiae* to perform. This is a defect inherent in all human systems of legislation. The rule that a mere verbal promise, without any consideration, cannot be enforced by action, is universal in its application, and cannot be departed from to suit particular cases in which a refusal to perform such a promise may be disgraceful.

The promise declared on in this case appears to have been made without any legal consideration. The kindness and services towards the sick son of the defendant were not bestowed at his request. The son was in no respect under the care of the defendant. He was twenty-five years old, and had long left his father's family. On his return from a foreign country, he fell sick among strangers, and the plaintiff acted the part of the good Samaritan, giving him shelter and comfort until he died. The defendant, his father, on being informed of this event, influenced by a transient feeling of gratitude, promises in writing to pay the plaintiff for the expenses he had incurred. But he has determined to break this promise, and is willing to have his case appear on record as a strong example of particular injustice sometimes necessarily resulting from the operation of general rules.

It is said a moral obligation is a sufficient consideration to support an express promise; and some authorities lay down the rule thus broadly; but upon examination of the cases we are satisfied that the universality of the rule cannot be supported, and that there must have been some preexisting obligation, which has become inoperative by positive law, to form a basis for an effective promise. The cases of debts barred by the statute of limitations, of debts incurred by infants, of debts of bankrupts, are generally put for illustration of the rule. Express promises founded on such preexisting equitable obligations may be enforced; there is a good consideration for them; they merely remove an impediment created by law to the recovery of debts honestly due, but which public policy protects the debtors from being compelled to pay. In all these cases there was originally a quid pro quo; and according to the principles of natural justice the party receiving ought to pay; but the legislature has said he shall not be coerced; then comes the promise to pay the debt that is barred, the promise of the man to pay the debt of the infant, of the discharged bankrupt to restore to his creditor what by the law he had lost. In all these cases there is a moral obligation founded upon an antecedent valuable consideration. These promises therefore have a sound legal basis. They are not promises to pay something for nothing; not naked pacts; but the voluntary revival or creation of obligation which before existed in natural law, but which had been dispensed with, not for the benefit of the party obliged solely, but principally for the public convenience. If moral obligation, in its fullest sense, is a good substratum for an express promise, it is not easy to perceive why it is not equally good to support an implied promise. What a man ought to do, generally he ought to be made to do, whether he promise or refuse. But the law of society has left most of such obligations to the interior forum, as the tribunal of conscience has been aptly called. Is there not a moral obligation upon every son who has become affluent by means of the education and advantages bestowed upon him by his father, to relieve that father from pecuniary embarrassment, to promote his comfort and happiness, and even to share with him his riches, if thereby he will be made happy? And yet such a son may, with impunity, leave such a father in any degree of penury above that which will expose the community in which he dwells, to the danger of being obliged to preserve him from absolute want. Is not a wealthy father under strong moral obligation to advance the interest of an obedient, well disposed son, to furnish him with the means of acquiring and maintaining a becoming rank in life, to rescue him from the horrors of debt incurred by misfortune? Yet the law will uphold him in any degree of parsimony, short of that which would reduce his son to the necessity of seeking public charity.

Without doubt there are great interests of society which justify withholding the coercive arm of the law from these duties of imperfect obligation, as they are called; imperfect, not because they are less binding upon the conscience than those which are called perfect, but because the wisdom of the social law does not impose sanctions upon them.

A deliberate promise, in writing, made freely and without any mistake, one which may lead the party to whom it is made into contracts and expenses, cannot be broken without a violation of moral duty. But if there was nothing paid or promised for it, the law, perhaps wisely, leaves the execution of it to the conscience of him who makes it. It is only when the party making the promise gains something, or he to whom it is made loses something, that the law gives the promise validity. And in the case of the promise of the adult to pay the debt of the infant, of the debtor discharged by the statute of limitations or bankruptcy, the principle is preserved by looking back to the origin of the transaction, where an equivalent is to be found. An exact equivalent is not required by the law; for there being a consideration, the parties are left to estimate its value: though here the courts of equity will step in to relieve from gross inadequacy between the consideration and the promise.

These principles are deduced from the general current of decided cases upon the subject as well as from the known maxims of the common law. The general position, that moral obligation is a sufficient consideration for an express promise, is to be limited in its application, to cases where at some time or other a good or valuable consideration has existed.

A legal obligation is always a sufficient consideration to support either an express or an implied promise; such as an infant's debt for necessaries, or a father's promise to pay for the support and education of his minor children. But when the child shall have attained to manhood, and shall have become his own agent in the world's business, the debts he incurs, whatever may be their nature, create no obligation upon the father; and it seems to follow, that his promise founded upon such a debt has no legally binding force.

The cases of instruments under seal and certain mercantile contracts, in which considerations need not be proved, do not contradict the principles above suggested. The first import a consideration in themselves, and the second belong to a branch of the mercantile law, which has found it necessary to disregard the point of consideration in respect to instruments negotiable in their nature and essential to the interests of commerce.

Instead of citing a multiplicity of cases to support the positions I have taken, I will only refer to a very able review of all the cases in the note in 3 Bos. & P. 249. The opinions of the judges had been variant for a long course of years upon this subject, but there seems to be no case in which it was nakedly decided, that a promise to pay the debt of a son of full age, not living with his father, though the debt were incurred by sickness which ended in the death of the son, without a previous request by the father proved or presumed, could be enforced by action.

It has been attempted to show a legal obligation on the part of the defendant by virtue of our statute, which compels lineal kindred in the ascending or descending line to support such of their poor relations as are likely to become chargeable to the town where they have their settlement. But it is a sufficient answer to this position, that such legal obligation does not exist except in the very cases provided for in the statute, and never until the party charged has been adjudged to be of sufficient ability thereto. We do not know from the report any of the facts which are necessary to create such an obligation. Whether the deceased had a legal settlement in this common-wealth at the time of his death, whether he was likely to become chargeable had he lived, whether the defendant was of sufficient ability, are essential facts to be adjudicated by the court to which is given jurisdiction on this subject. The legal liability does not arise until these facts have all been ascertained by judgment, after hearing the party intended to be charged.

For the foregoing reasons we are all of opinion that the nonsuit directed by the court of common pleas was right, and that judgment be entered thereon for costs for the defendant.

BACKGROUND NOTE ON MILLS v. WYMAN

Based on an analysis of original judicial and historical records, Professor Geoffrey Watson reports that Levi Wyman's "illness was a protracted one: by all accounts it lasted at least two weeks. Daniel Mills, the Good Samaritan who housed and cared for Levi Wyman, arranged for two men to guard Levi for four days and nights while Levi 'was in his derang'd state.' Levi was so sick that 'he leaped out of a chamber window to the imminent hazard of his life, and to the very great alarm of the family and the boarders.' . . . Mills also hired John Lee Comstock, a prominent Hartfort physician, to care for Wyman. Comstock found Levi 'in a state of indisposition' and, for some time 'in a state of delirium' that required two or three persons 'to prevent him from injuring himself.' [Mills's] expenses amounted to about twenty-two dollars—a consid-erable sum in those days—and included six dollars for fourteen days' board and lodging, three dollars for "Room pine and Candles," one dollar for a gallon of "Spirits," six dollars in expenses for the two men hired to restrain

Levi, and six dollars for Dr. Comstock's fee." Wilson, In the Tribunal of Conscience: Mills v. Wyman Reconsidered, 71 Tul. L. Rev. 1749 (1997). (This article contains a wealth of other information about the facts and background of the case, including facts that suggest that Levi might actually have survived his illness and died much later.)

WEBB v. McGOWIN

Court of Appeals of Alabama, 1935.
27 Ala.App. 82, 168 So. 196.

Action by Joe Webb against N. Floyd McGowin and Joseph F. McGowin, as executors of the estate of J. Greeley McGowin, deceased. From a judgment of nonsuit, plaintiff appeals.

Reversed and remanded. . . .

BRICKEN, PRESIDING JUDGE. This action is in assumpsit. The complaint as originally filed was amended. The demurrers to the complaint as amended were sustained, and because of this adverse ruling by the court the plaintiff took a nonsuit, and the assignment of errors on this appeal are predicated upon said action or ruling of the court.

A fair statement of the case presenting the questions for decision is set out in appellant's brief, which we adopt.

"On the 3d day of August, 1925, appellant while in the employ of the W.T. Smith Lumber Company, a corporation, and acting within the scope of his employment, was engaged in clearing the upper floor of mill No. 2 of the company. While so engaged he was in the act of dropping a pine block from the upper floor of the mill to the ground below; this being the usual and ordinary way of clearing the floor, and it being the duty of the plaintiff in the course of his employment to so drop it. The block weighed about 75 pounds.

"As appellant was in the act of dropping the block to the ground below, he was on the edge of the upper floor of the mill. As he started to turn the block loose so that it would drop to the ground, he saw J. Greeley McGowin, testator of the defendants, on the ground below and directly under where the block would have fallen had appellant turned it loose. Had he turned it loose it would have struck McGowin with such force as to have caused him serious bodily harm or death. Appellant could have remained safely on the upper floor of the mill by turning the block loose and allowing it to drop, but had he done this the block would have fallen on McGowin and caused him serious injuries or death. The only safe and reasonable way to prevent this was for appellant to hold to the block and divert its direction in falling from the place where McGowin was standing and the only safe way to divert it so as to prevent its coming into contact with McGowin was for appellant to fall with it to the ground below. Appellant did this, and by holding to the block and falling with it to the ground below, he diverted the course of its fall in such way that McGowin was not injured. In thus preventing the injuries to McGowin appellant himself received serious bodily injuries, resulting in his right leg being broken, the heel of his right foot torn off and his right arm broken. He was badly crippled for life and rendered unable to do physical or mental labor.

"On September 1, 1925, in consideration of appellant having prevented him from sustaining death or serious bodily harm and in consideration of the injuries appellant had received, McGowin agreed with him to care for and maintain him for the remainder of appellant's life at the rate of $15 every two weeks from the time he sustained his injuries to and during the remainder of appellant's life; it being agreed that McGowin would pay this sum to appellant for his maintenance. Under the agreement McGowin paid or caused to be paid to appellant the sum so agreed on up until McGowin's death on January 1, 1934. After his death the payments were continued to and including January 27, 1934, at which time they were discontinued. Thereupon plaintiff brought suit to recover the unpaid installments accruing up to the time of the bringing of the suit. . . ."

The action was for the unpaid installments accruing after January 27, 1934, to the time of the suit.

The principal grounds of demurrer to the original and amended complaint are: (1) It states no cause of action; (2) its averments show the contract was without consideration; (3) it fails to allege that McGowin had, at or before the services were rendered, agreed to pay appellant for them; (4) the contract declared on is void under the statute of frauds.

The averments of the complaint show that appellant saved McGowin from death or grievous bodily harm. This was a material benefit to him of infinitely more value than any financial aid he could have received. Receiving this benefit, McGowin became morally bound to compensate appellant for the services rendered. Recognizing his moral obligation, he expressly agreed to pay appellant as alleged in the complaint and complied with this agreement up to the time of his death; a period of more than 8 years.

Had McGowin been accidentally poisoned and a physician, without his knowledge or request, had administered an antidote, thus saving his life, a subsequent promise by McGowin to pay the physician would have been valid. Likewise, McGowin's agreement as disclosed by the complaint to compensate appellant for saving him from death or grievous bodily injury is valid and enforceable.

Where the promisee cares for, improves, and preserves the property of the promisor, though done without his request, it is sufficient consideration for the promisor's subsequent agreement to pay for the service, because of the material benefit received. . . . Edson v. Poppe, 24 S.D. 466, 124 N.W. 441, 26 L.R.A. (N.S.) 534.

In Boothe v. Fitzpatrick, 36 Vt. 681, the court held that a promise by defendant to pay for the past keeping of a bull which had escaped from defendant's premises and been cared for by plaintiff was valid, although there was no previous request, because the subsequent promise obviated that objection; it being equivalent to a previous request. On the same principle, had the promisee saved the promisor's life or his body from grievous harm, his subsequent promise to pay for the services rendered would have been valid. Such service would have been far more material than caring for his bull. Any holding that saving a man from death or grievous bodily harm is not a material benefit sufficient to uphold a subsequent promise to pay for the service, necessarily rests on the assumption that saving life and preservation of the body from harm have only a sentimental value. The converse of this is true. Life and preservation of the body have material, pecuniary values, measurable in dollars and cents. Because of this, physicians practice their profession charging for services rendered in saving life and curing the body of its ills, and surgeons perform operations. The same is true as to the law of negligence authorizing the assessment of damages in personal injury cases based upon the extent of the injuries, earnings, and life expectancies of those injured.

In the business of life insurance, the value of a man's life is measured in dollars and cents according to his expectancy, the soundness of his body, and his ability to pay premiums. The same is true as to health and accident insurance.

It follows that if, as alleged in the complaint, appellant saved J. Greeley McGowin from death or grievous bodily harm, and McGowin subsequently agreed to pay him for the service rendered, it became a valid and enforceable contract.

It is well settled that a moral obligation is a sufficient consideration to support a subsequent promise to pay where the promisor has received a material benefit, although there was no original duty or liability resting on the promisor. [Extensive citation of cases omitted.]

The case at bar is clearly distinguishable from that class of cases where the consideration is a mere moral obligation or conscientious duty unconnected with receipt by promisor of benefits of a material or pecuniary nature.... Here the promisor received a material benefit constituting a valid consideration for his promise.

Some authorities hold that, for a moral obligation to support a subsequent promise to pay, there must have existed a prior legal or equitable obligation, which for some reason had become unenforceable, but for which the promisor was still morally bound. This rule, however, is subject to qualification in those cases where the promisor, having received a material benefit from the promisee, is morally bound to compensate him for the services rendered and in consideration of this obligation promises to pay. In such cases the subsequent promise to pay is an affirmance or ratification of the services rendered carrying with it the presumption that a previous request for the service was made....

Under the decisions above cited, McGowin's express promise to pay appellant for the services rendered was an affirmance or ratification of what appellant had done raising the presumption that the services had been rendered at McGowin's request.

The averments of the complaint show that in saving McGowin from death or grievous bodily harm, appellant was crippled for life. This was part of the consideration of the contract declared on. McGowin was benefited. Appellant was injured. Benefit to the promisor or injury to the promisee is a sufficient legal consideration for the promisor's agreement to pay....

Under the averments of the complaint the services rendered by appellant were not gratuitous. The agreement of McGowin to pay and the acceptance of payment by appellant conclusively shows the contrary.

The contract declared on was not void under the statute of frauds (Code 1923, § 8034).

From what has been said, we are of the opinion that the court below erred in the ruling complained of; that is to say, in sustaining the demurrer, and for this error the case is reversed and remanded.

Reversed and remanded.

SAMFORD, JUDGE (concurring). The questions involved in this case are not free from doubt, and perhaps the strict letter of the rule, as stated by judges, though not always in accord, would bar a recovery by plaintiff, but following the principle announced by Chief Justice Marshall in Hoffman v. Porter, Fed.Cas. No. 6,577, 2 Brock. 156, 159, where he says, "I do not think that law ought to be separated from justice, where it is at most doubtful," I concur in the conclusions reached by the court.

WEBB v. McGOWIN

Supreme Court of Alabama, 1936.
232 Ala. 374, 168 So. 199.

Certiorari to Court of Appeals.

Petition of N. Floyd McGowin and Joseph F. McGowin, as executors of the estate of J. Greeley McGowin, deceased, for certiorari to the Court of Appeals to review and revise the judgment and decision of that court in Joe Webb v. McGowin, et al. Ex'rs, 168 So. 196 . . . .

FOSTER, JUSTICE. . . .

The opinion of the Court of Appeals here under consideration recognizes and applies the distinction between a supposed moral obligation of the promisor, based upon some refined sense of ethical duty, without material benefit to him, and one in which such a benefit did in fact occur. We agree with that court that if the benefit be material and substantial, and was to the person of the promisor rather than to his estate, it is within the class of material benefits which he has the privilege of recognizing and compensating either by an executed payment or an executory promise to pay. The cases are cited in that opinion. The reason is emphasized when the compensation is not only for the benefits which the promisor received, but also for the injuries either to the property or person of the promisee by reason of the service rendered.

Writ denied.

ANDERSON, C.J., and GARDNER and BOULDIN, JJ., concur.[*]

HARRINGTON v. TAYLOR, 225 N.C. 690, 36 S.E.2d 227 (1945). According to the complaint, defendant assaulted his wife and she took refuge in plaintiff's house. The next day defendant went there and assaulted his wife

---

[*] In the Capability Problem in Contract Law (2d ed.2004), RichardDanzig and Georfrey R. Watson report that after the decisions by Alabama's Court of Appeals and Supreme Court, upholding Webb's complaint against ademurrer, the case was settled for $900. There was some indication that the McGowin family also gave Webb the use of a home and several acres of land. Danzig and Watson further report that J. Greeley McGowin was the President of W.T. Smith Lumber Co. Id. at 159., 178–79.

again. She knocked him down with an axe and was about to decapitate him. Plaintiff caught the axe, "and the blow intended for defendant fell upon her hand, mutilating it badly, but saving defendant's life. Subsequently defendant orally promised to pay the plaintiff her damages; but after paying a small sum, failed to pay anything more."

A judgment below, sustaining the defendant's demurrer, was affirmed. "The Court is of the opinion that however much the defendant should be impelled by common gratitude to alleviate the plaintiff's misfortune, a humanitarian act of this kind, voluntarily performed, is not such consideration as would entitle her to recover at law."

––––––

RESTATEMENT, SECOND, CONTRACTS § 86

[See Selected Source Materials Supplement]

––––––

RESTATEMENT, SECOND, CONTRACTS § 86, ILLUSTRATIONS 1, 2, 6, 10, 12, 13

1. A gives emergency care to B's adult son while the son is sick and without funds far from home. B subsequently promises to reimburse A for his expenses. The promise is not binding under this Section.

2. A lends money to B, who later dies. B's widow promises to pay the debt. The promise is not binding under this Section. . . .

6. A finds B's escaped bull and feeds and cares for it. B's subsequent promise to pay reasonable compensation to A is binding. . . .

10. A digs a well on B's land in performance of a bargain with B's tenant C. C is unable to pay as agreed, and B promises to pay A the reasonable value of the well. The promise is binding. . . .

12. A, a married woman of sixty, has rendered household services without compensation over a period of years for B, a man of eighty living alone and having no close relatives. B has a net worth of three million dollars and has often assured A that she will be well paid for her services, whose reasonable value is not in excess of $6,000. B executes and delivers to A a written promise to pay A $25,000 "to be taken from my estate." The promise is binding.

13. The facts being otherwise as stated in Illustration 12, B's promise is made orally and is to leave A his entire estate. A cannot recover more than the reasonable value of her services.

––––––

AMERICAN LAW INSTITUTE, 42D ANNUAL PROCEEDINGS
273–74 (1965) (comments of Professor Robert Braucher, the Reporter for the Restatement, Second, of Contracts).

"Section [86] is a new provision. . . .

". . . [W]ith the help of the Advisers we went into the cases where past consideration has been upheld, and it has been a traditional thing to say: Well, there is an orthodox view that past consideration does not make a promise binding; and then there is a scattering of cases which represents a minority view which holds that some kinds of past considerations—or sometimes it is called moral considerations—do make a promise binding.

"Actually, when you go through the cases in which this problem has been raised, it seemed to us that you discover that there is a principle, and so we have tried to capture the principle, although I think it is more of a principle than it is a rule.

"If you look at section [86], it bristles with non-specific concepts; in particular, the qualification that the promise is binding to the extent necessary to prevent injustice would be entirely at large if we did not add subsection (2) which refers to the concept of unjust enrichment.

"I think in the light of the comment the principle takes on meaning, and I think there is not a division here between a majority view and a minority view. One of the famous cases on this subject is the great case of Webb v. McGowin, which is summarily stated . . . as illustration 7.

"Now, that's in Alabama. The cases in Alabama were, I suppose, as firm as the cases anywhere in rejecting the notion of past consideration or moral obligation as consideration; and yet when this case came along the case was decided for the plaintiff, as described in this illustration, and I would suppose that, given those facts and that situation, this would be likely to happen in most courts. What you have, really, is a line of distinction between essentially gratuitous transactions and cases which are on the borderline of quasi-contracts, where promise removes the difficulty which otherwise would bar quasi-contractual relief.

"We strained quite a lot to phrase this as precisely as we could. I think you cannot make it more precise—certainly not very much more precise—than we have it in the black letter here, without getting into something that you are not all able to sustain. If you look through the cases, the cases are a wide variety of miscellany, but we think there is a principle. . . ."

———

NOTE ON PAST CONSIDERATION

Suppose that *A* confers a benefit on *B* without *B's* prior request. The resulting relationship will then fall into one of three categories:

I. *B* is legally obliged to compensate *A* under the law of unjust enrichment, as where *A* has paid *B* money by mistake.

II. *B* is morally but not legally obliged to compensate *A*, as where *A* has suffered a loss in rescuing *B*.

III. *B* is neither legally nor morally obliged to compensate *A*, as where *A* has given *B* a wedding gift.

If a case falls into Category I, a later promise by *B* to compensate *A* does not create a new liability (although if the value of the benefit is unclear, the promise may bear on the extent of *A's* recovery). If a case falls into Category

III, a later promise to compensate A is essentially a donative promise, and also should be unenforceable.

Difficult problems arise, however, where B makes a later promise to compensate A in a case that falls into Category II. Traditionally this kind of promise was characterized as based on "past" or "moral" consideration. The general position of classical contract law, grounded on the bargain theory of consideration, was that promises based on past benefits were unenforceable, with limited exceptions.

This position had little to recommend it. By hypothesis, A has conferred a benefit on B, and B is morally obliged to make compensation. Presumably, therefore, the case is in Category II, rather than Category I, only because it is deemed desirable to protect persons against liability for benefits that they might have declined to accept and pay for if given the choice, and because of the severe difficulty in many such cases of measuring the value of the benefit to B. A later promise to make compensation invariably removes the first obstacle and normally removes the second. Such a promise should therefore be enforceable—or, perhaps more precisely, should render the promisor liable to make compensation.

Fortunately, Restatement Second has dramatically broken away from classical contract law in this area and has adopted a sweeping new principle in section 86. In its emphasis on benefit conferred, this section represents a significant reform; but in its limitation on enforceability, the section has moved too far from its roots in moral principles. To distinguish between those benefits that will and those that will not support a subsequent promise, section 86(2)(a) adopts the test whether "the promisor has ... been unjustly enriched." But if the promisor has been unjustly enriched in a legal sense, the law of unjust enrichment normally permits recovery even without the subsequent promise; and whether the promisor is unjustly enriched in any other sense must turn on concepts of morality. Indeed, even a requirement of unjust enrichment in a moral sense seems too narrow. For example, if A's life or property is rescued by B, who later makes a promise of compensation, it cannot be said that A is unjustly enriched. What is unjust about needing and receiving rescue? The question should simply be whether, at the time he made his promise, A may be morally obliged, by reason of a past benefit conferred, to make some compensation to B. The courts should decide this question, like the question of unconscionability, directly rather than covertly.

Chapter 4

THE LIMITS OF CONTRACT

The term "contract" is ambiguous. The Restatement defines a contract as any legally enforceable promise. Under this definition, a relied-upon donative promise is a contract. For some purposes that is a useful definition, but in everyday life the term "contract" usually means an agreement—especially a legally enforceable agreement. The Chapters succeeding this one will deal for the most part with contracts consisting of commercial bargains, in which legal enforceability is pretty clearly appropriate. In contrast, the cases and materials in this Chapter concern situations in which contract—used in the sense of a legally enforceable bargain—may or may not be an appropriate means of social ordering.

BALFOUR v. BALFOUR, 2 K.B. 571, 578 (1919) (opinion of Atkin, L.J.). "[I]t is necessary to remember that there are agreements between parties which do not result in contracts within the meaning of that term in our law. The ordinary example is where two parties agree to take a walk together, or where there is an offer and an acceptance of hospitality. Nobody would suggest in ordinary circumstances that those agreements result in what we know as a contract, and one of the most usual forms of agreement which does not constitute a contract appears to me to be the arrangements which are made between husband and wife. It is quite common, and it is the natural and inevitable result of the relationship of husband and wife, that the two spouses should make arrangements between themselves.... To my mind those agreements, or many of them, do not result in contracts at all, and they do not result in contracts even though there may be what as between other parties would constitute consideration for the agreement. The consideration, as we know, may consist either in some right, interest, profit or benefit accruing to one party, or some forbearance, detriment, loss or responsibility given, suffered or undertaken by the other. That is a well-known definition, and it constantly happens, I think, that such arrangements made between husband and wife are arrangements in which there are mutual promises, or in which there is consideration in form within the definition that I have mentioned. Nevertheless they are not contracts, and they are not contracts because the parties did not intend that they should be attended by legal consequences.... in respect of these promises each house is a domain into which the king's writ does not seek to run, and to which his officers do not seek to be admitted."

IN RE THE MARRIAGE OF WITTEN

Supreme Court of Iowa, 2003.
672 N.W.2d 768.

TERNUS, Justice.

The primary issue raised on appeal of the district court's decree in this dissolution action is whether the court properly determined the rights of Arthur (known as Trip) and Tamera Witten with respect to the parties' frozen human embryos stored at a medical facility. While we agree with Tamera that the informed consent signed by the parties at the request of the medical facility does not control the current dispute between the donors over the use or disposition of the embryos, we reject Tamera's request that she be allowed to use the embryos over Trip's objection. Therefore, we affirm the trial court's order that neither party may use or dispose of the embryos without the consent of the other party. . . .

I.   BACKGROUND FACTS AND PROCEEDINGS.

The appellee, Arthur (Trip) Witten, and the appellant, Tamera Witten, had been married for approximately seven and one-half years when Trip sought to have their marriage dissolved in April 2002. One of the contested issues at trial was control of the parties' frozen embryos. During the parties' marriage they had tried to become parents through the process of in vitro fertilization. Because Tamera was unable to conceive children naturally, they had eggs taken from Tamera artificially fertilized with Trip's sperm. Tamera then underwent several unsuccessful embryo transfers in an attempt to become pregnant. At the time of trial seventeen fertilized eggs remained in storage at the University of Nebraska Medical Center (UNMC).[1]

Prior to commencing the process for in vitro fertilization, the parties signed informed consent documents prepared by the medical center. These documents included an "Embryo Storage Agreement," which was signed by Tamera and Trip as well as by a representative of UNMC. It provided in part:

> Release of Embryos. The Client Depositors [Trip and Tamera] understand and agree that containers of embryos stored pursuant to this agreement will be used for transfer, release or disposition only with the signed approval of both Client Depositors. UNMC will release the containers of embryos only to a licensed physician recipient of written authorization of the Client Depositors.

The agreement had one exception to the joint-approval requirement that governed the disposition of the embryos upon the death of one or both of the

---

1. No medical testimony was introduced at trial with respect to the cell stage of the parties' fertilized eggs. Therefore, while some cases refer to fertilized eggs in the early stages of division as "pre-zygotes" or "preembryos," we use the term "embryo" in discussing the present appeal, since that is the terminology used in the Wittens' contract with UNMC. This term is used interchangeably with the term "fertilized egg." [Ed.: Compare A.Z. v. B.Z., 431 Mass. 150, 752 N.E.2d 1051 (2000), where the court said "We use the term 'preembryo' to refer to the four-to-eight cell stage of a developing fertilized egg." Id. at footnote 1.]

client depositors. Another provision of the contract provided for termination of UNMC's responsibility to store the embryos upon several contingencies: (1) the client depositors' written authorization to release the embryos or to destroy them; (2) the death of the client depositors; (3) the failure of the client depositors to pay the annual storage fee; or (4) the expiration of ten years from the date of the agreement.

At trial, Tamera asked that she be awarded "custody" of the embryos. She wanted to have the embryos implanted in her or a surrogate mother in an effort to bear a genetically linked child. She testified that upon a successful pregnancy she would afford Trip the opportunity to exercise parental rights or to have his rights terminated. She adamantly opposed any destruction of the embryos, and was also unwilling to donate the eggs to another couple.

Trip testified at the trial that while he did not want the embryos destroyed, he did not want Tamera to use them. He would not oppose donating the embryos for use by another couple. Trip asked the court to enter a permanent injunction prohibiting either party from transferring, releasing, or utilizing the embryos without the written consent of both parties.

The district court decided the dispute should be governed by the "embryo storage agreement" between the parties and UNMC, which required both parties' consent to any use or disposition of the embryos. Enforcing this agreement, the trial court enjoined both parties "from transferring, releasing or in any other way using or disposing of the embryos ... without the written and signed approval and authorization" of the other party.

Tamera has appealed the trial court's order, challenging only the court's resolution of the parties' dispute over the fertilized eggs. She claims the storage agreement is silent with respect to disposition or use of the embryos upon the parties' dissolution because there is no provision specifically addressing that contingency. Therefore, she argues, the court should have applied the "best interests [of the child]" test of Iowa Code chapter 598 (2001) and, pursuant to that analysis, awarded custody of the embryos to her. She makes the alternative argument that she is entitled to the fertilized eggs due to her fundamental right to bear children. Finally, Tamera claims it would violate the public policy of this state if Trip were allowed to back out of his agreement to have children. She claims such an agreement is evidenced by his participation in the in vitro fertilization procedure. . . .

III. DISPOSITION OF EMBRYOS.

A. *Scope of storage agreement.* We first consider Tamera's contention that the storage agreement does not address the situation at hand. As noted earlier, the agreement had a specific provision governing control of the embryos if one or both parties died, but did not explicitly deal with the possibility of divorce. Nonetheless, we think the present predicament falls within the general provision governing "release of embryos," in which the parties agreed that the embryos would not be transferred, released, or discarded without "the signed approval" of both Tamera and Trip. This provision is certainly broad enough to encompass the decision-making protocol when the parties are unmarried as well as when they are married.

The only question, then, is whether such agreements are enforceable when one of the parties later changes his or her mind with respect to the proper disposition of the embryos. In reviewing the scarce case law from other jurisdictions on this point, we have found differing views of how the parties' rights should be determined. There is, however, abundant literature that has scrutinized the approaches taken to date. Some writers have suggested refinements of the analytical framework employed by the courts thus far; some have proposed an entirely new model of analysis. From these various sources, we have identified three primary approaches to resolving disputes over the disposition of frozen embryos, which we have identified as (1) the contractual approach, (2) the contemporaneous mutual consent model, and (3) the balancing test.

Tamera's argument that her right to bear children should override the parties' prior agreement as well as Trip's current opposition to her use of the embryos resembles the balancing test. As for Tamera's alternative argument, we have found no authority supporting a "best interests" analysis in determining the disposition of frozen embryos. Nonetheless, we will first consider whether chapter 598 requires application of that analysis under the circumstances presented by this case. Then, we will discuss and consider the three approaches suggested by decisions from other jurisdictions and the literature on this subject.

B. *"Best interests" test.* [The court began by considering the effect of an Iowa statute, § 598.41. This statute set forth various standards governing the award of child custody in a marital-dissolution case, including a requirement that any custody award reflect "the best interest of the child." The court held that the best-interest standard was not applicable to the issue at hand. "First, we note the purposes of the 'best interest' standard set forth in that statute are to 'assure the child the opportunity for the maximum continuing physical and emotional contact with both parents' and to 'encourage parents to share the rights and responsibilities of raising the child.' Iowa Code § 598.41(1)(*a*). The principles developed under this statute are simply not suited to the resolution of disputes over the control of frozen embryos. Such disputes do not involve maximizing physical and emotional contact between both parents and the child; they involve the more fundamental decision of whether the parties will be parents at all. Moreover, it would be premature to consider which parent can most effectively raise the child when the "child" is still frozen in a storage facility. The principles of section 598.41 do not fit because what is really at issue here is not the custody of children as that concept is generally viewed and analyzed in dissolution cases. Rather, the issue here is who will have decision-making authority with respect to the fertilized eggs."
. . .

C. *Enforcement of storage agreement.* We now consider the appropriateness of the trial court's decision to allow Tamera and Trip's agreement with the medical center to control the current dispute between them. As we noted above, there are three methods of analysis that have been suggested to resolve disputes over frozen embryos. We will discuss them separately.

1. *Contractual approach.* The currently prevailing view—expressed in three states—is that contracts entered into at the time of in vitro fertilization are enforceable so long as they do not violate public policy. *See* [*Kass v. Kass*, 91 N.Y.2d 554, 673 N.Y.S.2d 350, 696 N.E.2d 174, 179 (1998)] (stating agreements between donors "regarding disposition of pre-zygotes should generally be presumed valid and binding"); [*Davis v. Davis*, 842 S.W.2d 588 (Tenn. 1992)], 842 S.W.2d at 597 (holding agreement regarding disposition of

embryos "should be considered binding"); *In re Litowitz,* 146 Wash.2d 514, 48 P.3d 261, 271 (2002) (enforcing parties' contract providing for disposition of preembryos after five years of storage).[2] The New York Court of Appeals expressed the following rationale for this contractual approach:

> [It is] particularly important that courts seek to honor the parties' expressions of choice, made before disputes erupt, with the parties' overall direction always uppermost in the analysis. Knowing that advance agreements will be enforced underscores the seriousness and integrity of the consent process. Advance agreements as to disposition would have little purpose if they were enforceable only in the event the parties continued to agree. To the extent possible, it should be the progenitors—not the State and not the courts—who by their prior directive make this deeply personal life choice.

Kass, 673 N.Y.S.2d 350, 696 N.E.2d at 180.

This approach has been criticized, however, because it "insufficiently protects the individual and societal interests at stake":

> First, decisions about the disposition of frozen embryos implicate rights central to individual identity. On matters of such fundamental personal importance, individuals are entitled to make decisions consistent with their contemporaneous wishes, values, and beliefs. Second, requiring couples to make binding decisions about the future use of their frozen embryos ignores the difficulty of predicting one's future response to life-altering events such as parenthood. Third, conditioning the provision of infertility treatment on the execution of binding disposition agreements is coercive and calls into question the authenticity of the couple's original choice. Finally, treating couples' decisions about the future use of their frozen embryos as binding contracts undermines important values about families, reproduction, and the strength of genetic ties.

[Carl H. Coleman, *Procreative Liberty and Contemporaneous Choice: An Inalienable Rights Approach to Frozen Embryo Disputes,*] 84 Minn. L.Rev. at 88–89. Another legal writer has echoed these concerns:

> Binding a couple to a prior disposition agreement has its roots in contract law. The primary advantage of treating the disposition of preembryos as a contract dispute is that it binds individuals to previous obligations, even if their priorities or values change. This advantage, while maximizing the efficiency of commercial transactions, is ill-suited to govern the disposition of human tissue with the potential to develop into

---

2. Application of the contractual approach in *Kass* resulted in enforcement of the parties' agreement that the fertilized eggs would be donated for research should the parties be "unable to make a decision regarding the disposition of [the] stored, frozen pre-zygotes." 696 N.E.2d at 176–77, 181. In *Litowitz,* the court permitted execution of the parties' previous agreement that the preembryos would be "disposed of" after five years. 48 P.3d at 271. The resolution of the divorcing couple's dispute was more complex in *Davis* because the parties did not have a contract addressing the disposition of any unused preembryos. 842 S.W.2d at 590. Noting that a "prior agreement concerning disposition should be carried out," the court concluded in the absence of such an agreement, "the relative interests of the parties in using or not using the preembryos must be weighed." *Id.* at 604. The court awarded the preembryos to the husband, concluding his interest in not becoming a parent outweighed his former wife's interest in donating the preembryos to another couple for implantation. *Id.* The court noted the issue might be closer if the wife had wanted to use the preembryos herself; but in view of the fact she had "a reasonable possibility of achieving parenthood by means other than use of the preembryos in question," she would not have prevailed even under those circumstances. *Id.*

a child. The potential of the embryo requires that couples be allowed to make contemporaneous decisions about the fate of the embryo that reflect their current values.

Christina C. Lawrence, Note, *Procreative Liberty and the Preembryo Problem: Developing a Medical and Legal Framework to Settle the Disposition of Frozen Embryos,* 52 Case W. Res. L.Rev. 721, 729 (2002) [hereinafter "Lawrence Note"]; *accord J.B. v. M.B.,* 170 N.J. 9, 783 A.2d 707, 718–19 (2001). In response to such concerns, one commentator has suggested an alternative model requiring contemporaneous mutual consent. We now examine that approach.

2. *Contemporaneous mutual consent.* The contractual approach and the contemporaneous mutual consent model share an underlying premise: "decisions about the disposition of frozen embryos belong to the couple that created the embryo, with each partner entitled to an equal say in how the embryos should be disposed." Coleman, 84 Minn. L.Rev. at 81. Departing from this common starting point, the alternative framework asserts the important question is "at what time does the partners' consent matter?" *Id.* at 91. Proponents of the mutual-consent approach suggest that, with respect to "decisions about intensely emotional matters, where people act more on the basis of feeling and instinct than rational deliberation," it may "be impossible to make a knowing and intelligent decision to relinquish a right in advance of the time the right is to be exercised." *Id.* at 98; *see also* Sara D. Petersen, Comment, *Dealing With Cryopreserved Embryos Upon Divorce: A Contractual Approach Aimed at Preserving Party Expectations,* 50 UCLA L.Rev. 1065, 1090 & n. 156 (2003) (stating "surveys of couples that have stored frozen embryos suggest that they may be prone to changing their minds while their embryos remain frozen" and citing a study that found " '[o]f the 41 couples that had recorded both a pre-treatment and post-treatment decision about embryo disposition, only 12(29%) kept the same disposition choice' "(citation omitted)). One's erroneous prediction of how she or he will feel about the matter at some point in the future can have grave repercussions. "Like decisions about marriage or relinquishing a child for adoption, decisions about the use of one's reproductive capacity have lifelong consequences for a person's identity and sense of self":

> When chosen voluntarily, becoming a parent can be an important act of self-definition. Compelled parenthood, by contrast, imposes an unwanted identity on the individual, forcing her to redefine herself, her place in the world, and the legacy she will leave after she dies. For some people, the mandatory destruction of an embryo can have equally profound consequences, particularly for those who believe that embryos are persons. If forced destruction is experienced as the loss of a child, it can lead to life-altering feelings of mourning, guilt, and regret.

Coleman, 84 Minn. L.Rev. at 96–97. To accommodate these concerns, advocates of the mutual-consent model propose "no embryo should be used by either partner, donated to another patient, used in research, or destroyed without the [contemporaneous] mutual consent of the couple that created the embryo." *Id.* at 110. Under this alternate framework,

> advance instructions would not be treated as binding contracts. If either partner has a change of mind about disposition decisions made in advance, that person's current objection would take precedence over the

prior consent. If one of the partners rescinds an advance disposition decision and the other does not, the mutual consent principle would not be satisfied and the previously agreed-upon disposition decision could not be carried out. . . .

When the couple is unable to agree to any disposition decision, the most appropriate solution is to keep the embryos where they are—in frozen storage. Unlike the other possible disposition decisions—use by one partner, donation to another patient, donation to research, or destruction—keeping the embryos frozen is not final and irrevocable. By preserving the status quo, it makes it possible for the partners to reach an agreement at a later time.

Id. at 110–12; *see also id.* at 89 (suggesting "the embryo would remain in frozen storage until the parties reach a new agreement, the embryo is no longer viable, or storage facilities are no longer available"); *accord* Lawrence Note, 52 Case W. Res. L.Rev. at 742. Although this model precludes one party's use of the embryos to have children over the objection of the other party, the outcome under the contractual approach and the balancing test would generally be the same. *See A.Z. v. B.Z.*, 431 Mass. 150, 725 N.E.2d 1051, 1057–58 (2000) ("As a matter of public policy, . . . forced procreation is not an area amenable to judicial enforcement."); *J.B.*, 783 A.2d at 717 (evaluating relative interests of parties in disposition of embryos, concluding husband should not be able to use embryos over wife's objection); *Davis*, 842 S.W.2d at 604 ("Ordinarily, the party wishing to avoid procreation should prevail."); Susan B. Apel, *Disposition of Frozen Embryos: Are Contracts the Solution?,* Vermont Bar Journal, March 2001, at 31 ("Some argue that the party seeking to avoid procreation should prevail, and indeed, this appears to be the one harmonizing rationale of the four reported cases.") [hereinafter "Apel"].

3. *Balancing test.* The New Jersey Supreme Court appears to have adopted an analysis regarding the disposition of frozen human embryos that incorporates the idea of contemporaneous decision-making, but not that of mutual consent. In *J.B.*, the New Jersey court rejected the *Kass* and *Davis* contractual approach, noting public policy concerns in "[e]nforcement of a contract that would allow the implantation of preembryos at some future date in a case where one party has reconsidered his or her earlier acquiescence." 783 A.2d at 718. The court stated:

> We believe that the better rule, and the one we adopt, is to enforce agreements entered into at the time in vitro fertilization is begun, *subject to the right of either party to change his or her mind about disposition up to the point of use or destruction of any stored preembryos.*

Id. at 719 (emphasis added). The court based its decision on "[t]he public policy concerns that underlie limitations on contracts involving family relationships." *Id.; see also A.Z.*, 725 N.E.2d at 1057–58 (refusing, in light of the same public policy concerns, to enforce an agreement that allowed the wife, upon the parties' separation, to use the couple's preembryos for implantation).

The New Jersey court did not, however, adopt the requirement for mutual consent as a prerequisite for any use or disposition of the preembryos. Rather, that court stated that "if there is a disagreement between the parties as to disposition . . . , the interests of both parties must be evaluated" by the court. *J.B.*, 783 A.2d at 719. This balancing test was also the default analysis employed by the Tennessee Supreme Court in *Davis* where the parties had not executed a written agreement. *See Davis,* 842 S.W.2d at 604 (holding in the absence of a prior agreement concerning disposition, "the relative interests of the parties in using or not using the preembryos must be weighed" by the court).

The obvious problem with the balancing test model is its internal inconsistency. *See generally* Lawrence Note, 52 Case W. Res. L.Rev. at 738 (suggesting "[t]he premise of the balancing test . . . is flawed"). Public policy concerns similar to those that prompt courts to refrain from enforcement of contracts addressing reproductive choice demand even more strongly that we not substitute the courts as decision makers in this highly emotional and personal area. Nonetheless, that is exactly what happens under the decisional framework based on the balancing test because the court must weigh the relative interests of the parties in deciding the disposition of embryos when the parties cannot agree. *See J.B.,* 783 A.2d at 719.

D.   *Discussion.* With these alternative approaches in mind, we turn to the present case. . . .

[A]re prior agreements regarding the future disposition of embryos enforceable when one of the donors is no longer comfortable with his or her prior decision? We first note our agreement with other courts considering such matters that the partners who created the embryos have the primary, and equal, decision-making authority with respect to the use or disposition of their embryos. We think, however, that it would be against the public policy of this state to enforce a prior agreement between the parties in this highly personal area of reproductive choice when one of the parties has changed his or her mind concerning the disposition or use of the embryos.

Our statutes and case law evidence an understanding that decisions involving marital and family relationships are emotional and subject to change. For example, Iowa law imposes a seventy-two hour waiting period after the birth of a child before the biological parents can release parental rights. *See* Iowa Code § 600A.4(2)(*g*). In addition, although this court has not abolished claims for breach of promise to marry,[3] only recovery of monetary damages is permitted; the court will not force a party to actually consummate the marriage. *See* Herbert F. Goodrich, *Iowa Decisions on Breach of Marriage Promise,* 4 Iowa L. Bull. 166, 177 (1918). It has also long been recognized in this state that agreements for the purpose of bringing about a dissolution of marriage are contrary to public policy and therefore void. *Barngrover v. Pettigrew,* 128 Iowa 533, 535, 104 N.W. 904, 904 (1905) . . . .

This court has also expressed a general reluctance to become involved in intimate questions inherent in personal relationships. *See Miller v. Miller,* 78 Iowa 177, 179–80, 42 N.W. 641, 641 (1889). In *Miller,* we refused to enforce a contract between husband and wife that required, in part, each "to behave respectfully, and fairly treat the other." *Id.* at 180, 42 N.W. at 641. We explained our refusal on the following grounds:

---

3. This court has not had a breach-of-contract-to-marry case before it in over fifty years. *See Bearbower v. Merry,* 266 N.W.2d 128, 132 (Iowa 1978) (citing *Benson v. Williams,* 239 Iowa 742, 32 N.W.2d 813 (1948)).

[J]udicial inquiry into matters of that character, between husband and wife, would be fraught with irreparable mischief, and forbidden by sound considerations of public policy.

It is the genius of our laws, as well as of our civilization, that matters pertaining so directly and exclusively to the home, and its value as such, and which are so generally susceptible of regulation and control by those influences which surround it, are not to become matters of public concern or inquiry.

Id. at 182, 42 N.W. at 642; *accord Heacock v. Heacock,* 108 Iowa 540, 542, 79 N.W. 353, 354 (1899) ("Husband and wife cannot contract with each other to secure the performance of their marital rights and duties."). Certainly reproductive decisions are likewise not proper matters of judicial inquiry and enforcement.

We have considered and rejected the arguments of some commentators that embryo disposition agreements are analogous to antenuptial agreements and divorce stipulations, which courts generally enforce. *See* Apel, Vermont Bar Journal at 31. Whether embryos are viewed as having life or simply as having the potential for life, this characteristic or potential renders embryos fundamentally distinct from the chattels, real estate, and money that are the subjects of antenuptial agreements. Divorce stipulations are also distinguishable. While such agreements may address custody issues, they are contemporaneous with the implementation of the stipulation, an attribute noticeably lacking in disposition agreements.

In addition to decisional and statutory authority supporting a public policy against judicial enforcement of personal decisions concerning marriage, family, and reproduction, our statutes also anticipate the effect of a couple's dissolution on their prior decisions. For example, Iowa Code section 633.271 provides that if a testator is divorced after making a will, "all provisions in the will in favor of the testator's spouse" are automatically revoked. Similarly, Iowa Code section 633.3107 revokes all provisions in a revocable trust in favor of the settlor's spouse upon divorce or dissolution of the marriage. Similar considerations make enforcement of contracts between partners involving such personal decisions as the use and disposition of their combined genetic material equally problematic. As noted by one commentator, embryos are originally created as "a mutual undertaking by [a] couple to have children together." Coleman, 84 Minn. L.Rev. at 83. Agreements made in that context are not always consistent with the parties' wishes once the mutual undertaking has ended.

We think judicial decisions and statutes in Iowa reflect respect for the right of individuals to make family and reproductive decisions based on their current views and values. They also reveal awareness that such decisions are highly emotional in nature and subject to a later change of heart. For this reason, we think judicial enforcement of an agreement *between a couple* regarding their future family and reproductive choices would be against the public policy of this state.

Our decision should not be construed, however, to mean that disposition agreements *between donors and fertility clinics* have no validity at all. We recognize a disposition or storage agreement serves an important purpose in defining and governing the relationship between the couple and the medical facility, ensuring that all parties understand their respective rights and obligations. *See A.Z.,* 725 N.E.2d at 1057 n. 22 ("We also recognize that agreements among donors and IVF clinics are essential to clinic operations."). In fact, it is this relationship, between the couple on the one side and the medical facility on the other, that dispositional contracts are intended to address. *See generally* Ellen A. Waldman, *Disputing Over Embryos: Of Contracts and Consents,* 32 Ariz. St. L.J. 897, 918 (2000) (noting "courts and most scholarly authorities would transform documents designed to record the transmission of medical information from clinic to couple, and the couple's acceptance of medical treatment, into a binding agreement between the couple itself"). Within this context, the medical facility and the donors should be able to rely on the terms of the parties' contract. *See A.Z.,* 725 N.E.2d at 1057 n. 22 (noting court's decision not to enforce agreement between partners is not an "impediment to the enforcement of such contracts by the clinics or by the donors against the clinics"); *J.B.,* 783 A.2d at 719.

In view of these competing needs, we reject the contractual approach and hold that agreements entered into at the time in vitro fertilization is commenced are enforceable and binding on the parties, "subject to the right of either party to change his or her mind about disposition up to the point of use or destruction of any stored embryo." *J.B.,* 783 A.2d at 719. This decisional model encourages prior agreements that can guide the actions of all parties, unless a later objection to any dispositional provision is asserted. It also recognizes that, *absent a change of heart by one of the partners,* an agreement governing disposition of embryos does not violate public policy. Only when one person makes known the agreement no longer reflects his or her current values or wishes is public policy implicated. Upon this occurrence, allowing either party to withdraw his or her agreement to a disposition that person no longer accepts acknowledges the public policy concerns inherent in enforcing prior decisions of a fundamentally personal nature. In fairness to the medical facility that is a party to the agreement, however, any change of intention must be communicated in writing to all parties in order to reopen the disposition issues covered by the agreement. *Id.*

That brings us, then, to the dilemma presented when one or both partners change their minds and the parties cannot reach a mutual decision on disposition. We have already explained the grave public policy concerns we have with the balancing test, which simply substitutes the court as decision maker. A better principle to apply, we think, is the requirement of contemporaneous mutual consent. Under that model, no transfer, release, disposition, or use of the embryos can occur without the signed authorization of both donors. If a stalemate results, the status quo would be maintained. The practical effect will be that the embryos are stored indefinitely unless both parties can agree to destroy the fertilized eggs. Thus, any expense associated with maintaining the status quo should logically be borne by the person opposing destruction. *See* Coleman, 84 Minn. L.Rev. at 112 ("The right to insist on the continued storage of the embryos should be dependent on a willingness to pay the associated costs.").

Turning to the present case, we find a situation in which one party no longer concurs in the parties' prior agreement with respect to the disposition of their frozen embryos, but the parties have been unable to reach a new agreement that is mutually satisfactory. Based on this fact, under the principles we have set forth today, we hold there can be no use or disposition of the

Wittens' embryos unless Trip and Tamera reach an agreement.[4] Until then, the party or parties who oppose destruction shall be responsible for any storage fees. Therefore, we affirm the trial court's ruling enjoining both parties from transferring, releasing, or utilizing the embryos without the other's written consent. . . .

. . . Disposition.

We affirm the trial court's decree [concerning the disposition of the embryos]. . . .

———

R.R. v. M.H., 426 Mass. 501, 689 N.E.2d 790 (1998). "On a report by a judge in the Probate and Family Court, we are concerned with the validity of a surrogacy parenting agreement between the plaintiff (father) and the defendant (mother). Both the mother and the father are married but not to each other. A child was conceived through artificial insemination of the mother with the father's sperm, after the mother and father had executed the surrogate parenting agreement [under which the father agreed to pay the surrogate mother $10,000, and the surrogate mother agreed] that the father would have custody of the child. [The mother actively sought to become a surrogate and entered into the surrogacy agreement voluntarily, advised by counsel, not under duress, and fully informed.] During the sixth month of her pregnancy and after she had received funds from the father pursuant to the surrogacy agreement, the mother changed her mind and decided that she wanted to keep the child.

"The father thereupon brought this action and obtained a preliminary order awarding him temporary custody of the child. . . .

". . . Policies underlying our adoption legislation suggest that a surrogate parenting agreement should be given no effect if the mother's agreement was obtained prior to a reasonable time after the child's birth or if her agreement was induced by the payment of money. Adoption legislation is, of course, not applicable to child custody, but it does provide us with some guidance. Although the agreement makes no reference to adoption and does not concern the termination of parental rights or the adoption of the child by the father's wife, the normal expectation in the case of a surrogacy agreement seems to be that the father's wife will adopt the child with the consent of the mother (and the father). Under G.L. c. 210, § 2, adoption requires the written consent of the father and the mother but, in these circumstances, not the mother's husband. Any such consent, written, witnessed, and notarized, is not to be executed "sooner than the fourth calendar day after the date of birth of the child to be adopted." *Id.* That statutory standard should be interpreted as providing that no mother may effectively agree to surrender her child for adoption earlier than the fourth day after its birth, by which time she better knows the strength of her bond with her child. Although a consent to surrender custody has less permanency than a consent to adoption, the legislative judgment that a mother should have time after a child's birth to reflect on her wishes concerning the child weighs heavily in our consideration

---

4. We do not mean to imply that UNMC's obligation to store the embryos extends beyond the ten-year period provided in the parties' contract.

whether to give effect to a prenatal custody agreement. No private agreement concerning adoption or custody can be conclusive in any event because a judge, passing on custody of a child, must decide what is in the best interests of the child. . . .

". . . . [We conclude that the] mother's purported consent to custody in the agreement is ineffective because no such consent should be recognized unless given on or after the fourth day following the child's birth. In reaching this conclusion, we apply to consent to custody the same principle which underlies the statutory restriction on when a mother's consent to adoption may be effectively given. Moreover, the payment of money to influence the mother's custody decision makes the agreement as to custody void. Eliminating any financial reward to a surrogate mother is the only way to assure that no economic pressure will cause a woman, who may well be a member of an economically vulnerable class, to act as a surrogate. It is true that a surrogate enters into the agreement before she becomes pregnant and thus is not presented with the desperation that a poor unwed pregnant woman may confront. However, compensated surrogacy arrangements raise the concern that, under financial pressure, a woman will permit her body to be used and her child to be given away. . . .

"We recognize that there is nothing inherently unlawful in an arrangement by which an informed woman agrees to attempt to conceive artificially and give birth to a child whose father would be the husband of an infertile wife. We suspect that many such arrangements are made and carried out without disagreement.

"If no compensation is paid beyond pregnancy-related expenses and if the mother is not bound by her consent to the father's custody of the child unless she consents after a suitable period has passed following the child's birth, the objections we have identified in this opinion to the enforceability of a surrogate's consent to custody would be overcome. Other conditions might be important in deciding the enforceability of a surrogacy agreement, such as a requirement that (a) the mother's husband give his informed consent to the agreement in advance; (b) the mother be an adult and have had at least one successful pregnancy; (c) the mother, her husband, and the intended parents have been evaluated for the soundness of their judgment and for their capacity to carry out the agreement; (d) the father's wife be incapable of bearing a child without endangering her health; (e) the intended parents be suitable persons to assume custody of the child; and (f) all parties have the advice of counsel. The mother and father may not, however, make a binding best-interests-of-the-child determination by private agreement. Any custody agreement is subject to a judicial determination of custody based on the best interests of the child.

"The conditions that we describe are not likely to be satisfactory to an intended father because, following the birth of the child, the mother can refuse to consent to the father's custody even though the father has incurred substantial pregnancy-related expenses. A surrogacy agreement judicially approved before conception may be a better procedure, as is permitted by statutes in Virginia and New Hampshire."

———

NOTE ON SURROGATE–PARENTING LEGISLATION

As of the time this casebook is written, seventeen states have adopted statutes concerning surrogacy. These statutes vary widely. For example, the District of Columbia, Indiana, Michigan, New York, and North Dakota either forbid surrogacy contracts or make such contracts void and unenforceable. See D.C. Code § 16–402; Indiana Code § 31–20–1–1; Mich. Comp.Laws § 722.855; N.Y. Dom.Rel.Law § 122; N.D.Cent.Code § 14–18–05. Arkansas allows surrogacy contracts. See Ark. Code § 9–10–201. Washington allows uncompensated surrogacy contracts. See Wash.Rev.Code §§ 26.26.210–260. New Mexico allows uncompensated surrogacy contracts and payment of the surrogate's medical and similar expenses. See N.M. Stat. §§ 32A–5–34(B), (F). Nebraska renders paid surrogacy contracts unenforceable, but says nothing about unpaid surrogacy. Neb. Rev.Stat. § 25–21,200. Nevada and Virginia allow unpaid surrogacy contracts but only where the prospective parents are married couples. See Nev. Rev. Stat. § 126.045; Va. Code § 20–158.

----

42 U.S. CODE § 274e. PROHIBITION OF ORGAN PURCHASES

(a) *Prohibition.* It shall be unlawful for any person to knowingly acquire, receive, or otherwise transfer any human organ for valuable consideration for use in human transplantation if the transfer affects interstate commerce.

(b) *Penalties.* Any person who violates subsection (a) of this section shall be fined not more than $50,000 or imprisoned not more than five years, or both.

(c) *Definitions.* For purposes of subsection (a) of this section:

(1) The term "human organ" means the human (including fetal) kidney, liver, heart, lung, pancreas, bone marrow, cornea, eye, bone, and skin or any subpart thereof and any other human organ (or any subpart thereof, including that derived from a fetus) specified by the Secretary of Health and Human Services by regulation.

(2) The term "valuable consideration" does not include the reasonable payments associated with the removal, transportation, implantation, processing, preservation, quality control, and storage of a human organ or the expenses of travel, housing, and lost wages incurred by the donor of a human organ in connection with the donation of the organ....

RADIN, MARKET–INALIENABILITY

100 Harvard L.Rev. 1849 (1987).*

Since the declaration of "unalienable rights" of persons at the founding of our republic, inalienability has had a central place in our legal and moral culture. Yet there is no one sharp meaning for the term "inalienable."

----

* This article now forms the basis of a book,
Margaret Jane Radin, Contested Commodities
(1996). (Footnote by ed.)

Sometimes inalienable means nontransferable; sometimes only nonsalable. . . . In this Article I explore nonsalability, a species of inalienability I call market-inalienability. Something that is market-inalienable is not to be sold, which in our economic system means it is not to be traded in the market.

Controversy over what may be bought and sold—blood or babies—pervades our news. . . . About fifteen years ago, for example, Richard Titmuss advocated in his book, *The Gift Relationship,* that human blood should not be allocated through the market; others disagreed. More recently, Elisabeth Landes and Richard Posner suggested the possibility of a thriving market in infants, yet most people continue to believe that infants should not be allocated through the market. . . .

In [one] important set of meanings, inalienability is ascribed to an entitlement, right, or attribute that cannot be voluntarily transferred from one holder to another. Inalienability in these uses may mean nongiveable, nonsalable, or completely nontransferable. If something is nontransferable, the holder cannot designate a successor holder. Nongiveability and nonsalability are subsets of nontransferability. If something is inalienable by gift, it might be transferred by sale; if it is inalienable by sale, it might be transferred by gift. This nonsalability is what I refer to as market-inalienability. In precluding sales but not gifts, market-inalienability places some things outside the marketplace but not outside the realm of social intercourse.

Market-inalienability negates a central element of traditional property rights, which are conceived of as fully alienable. But market-inalienability differs from the nontransferability that characterizes many nontraditional property rights—entitlements of the regulatory and welfare state—that are both nongiveable and nonsalable. [Examples are entitlements to social security and welfare benefits.] Market-inalienability also differs from the inalienability of other things, like voting rights, that seem to be moral or political duties related to a community's normative life; they are subject to broader inalienabilities that preclude loss as well as transfer. Unlike the inalienabilities attaching to welfare entitlements or political duties, market-inalienability does not render something inseparable from the person, but rather specifies that market trading may not be used as a social mechanism of separation. Finally, market-inalienability differs from the inalienability of things, like heroin, that are made nontransferable in order to implement a prohibition, because it does not signify that something is social anathema. Indeed, preclusion of sales often coexists with encouragement of gifts. For example, the market-inalienability of human organs does not preclude—and, indeed, may seek to foster—transfer from one individual to another by gift. . . .

Market-inalienability often expresses an aspiration for noncommodification. By making something nonsalable we proclaim that it should not be conceived of or treated as a commodity. When something is noncommodifiable, market trading is a disallowed form of social organization and allocation. We place that thing beyond supply and demand pricing, brokerage and arbitrage, advertising and marketing, stockpiling, speculation, and valuation in terms of the opportunity cost of production.

Market-inalienability poses for us more than the binary choice of whether something should be wholly inside or outside the market, completely commodified or completely noncommodified. Some things are completely commodified—deemed suitable for trade in a laissez-faire market. Others are completely noncommodified—removed from the market altogether. But many things can be described as incompletely commodified—neither fully commodified nor fully removed from the market. Thus, we may decide that some things should be market-inalienable only to a degree, or only in some aspects.

To appreciate the need to develop a satisfactory analysis of market-inalienability, consider the deeply contested issues of commodification that confront us. Infants and children, fetal gestational services, blood, human organs, sexual services, and services of college athletes are some salient things whose commodification is contested. Our division over whether to place a monetary equivalent on a spouse's professional degree or homemaker services in a divorce; or on various kinds of injuries in tort actions, such as loss of consortium, is another form of contest over commodification. Monetization—commodification—of clean air and water is likewise deeply contested. Moreover, debates about some kinds of regulation can be seen as contested incomplete commodification, with the contest being over whether to allow full commodification (a laissez-faire market regime) or something less. If we see the debates this way, residential rent control, minimum wage requirements, and other forms of price regulation, as well as residential habitability requirements, safety regulation, and other forms of product-quality regulation all become contests over the issue of commodification.

How are we to determine the extent to which something ought to be noncommodified, so that we can determine to what extent market-inalienability is justified? Because the question asks about the appropriate relationship of particular things to the market, normative theories about the appropriate social role of the market should be helpful in trying to answer it. We can think of such theories as ordered on a continuum stretching from universal noncommodification (nothing in markets) to universal commodification (everything in markets). On this continuum, Karl Marx's theory can symbolize the theoretical pole of universal noncommodification, and Richard Posner's can be seen as close to the opposite theoretical pole....

Universal commodification undermines personal identity by conceiving of personal attributes, relationships, and philosophical and moral commitments as monetizable and alienable from the self. A better view of personhood should understand many kinds of particulars—one's politics, work, religion, family, love, sexuality, friendships, altruism, experiences, wisdom, moral commitments, character, and personal attributes—as integral to the self. To understand any of these as monetizable or completely detachable from the person—to think, for example, that the value of one person's moral commitments is commensurate or fungible with those of another, or that the "same" person remains when her moral commitments are subtracted—is to do violence to our deepest understanding of what it is to be human....

---

*

Part II

REMEDIES FOR BREACH
OF CONTRACT

Part II concerns remedies for breach of contract, chiefly in the bargain context.

An introductory Chapter, Chapter 5, explores three themes: (1) The nature and theory of the most characteristic remedy for breach of contract, expectation damages. (2) The question whether contract remedies should be based on the innocent party's loss, or may also take into account the wrongdoer's gain through breach. (3) In that connection, the theory of efficient breach.

Chapter 6 considers the remedy of expectation damages in more detail.

Chapter 7 concerns the remedy of specific performance, under which a breaching party is ordered to perform the contract, rather than only to pay damages for breach.

Finally, Chapter 8 explores the use of the reliance and restitution measures in a bargain context (as opposed to the use of the reliance measure in a donative context, which was explored in Chapter 1).

Chapter 5

AN INTRODUCTION TO CONTRACT DAMAGES

RESTATEMENT, SECOND, CONTRACTS § 344

[See Selected Source Materials Supplement]

HAWKINS v. McGEE

Supreme Court of New Hampshire, 1929.
84 N.H. 114, 146 A. 641.

Assumpsit, against a surgeon for breach of an alleged warranty of the success of an operation. Trial by jury and verdict for the plaintiff. The writ also contained a count in negligence upon which a nonsuit was ordered, without exception.

[The defendant moved to have the verdict set aside on several grounds, one of them being that the damages awarded were excessive. The trial court ordered that the verdict be set aside unless the plaintiff would remit all damages in excess of $500. On the plaintiff's refusal to consent to a reduction, the trial court set the verdict aside as being "excessive and against the weight of the evidence." The plaintiff excepted to this ruling of the trial court; his exception and numerous exceptions taken by the defendant were transferred to the Supreme Court.]

BRANCH, J. 1. The operation in question consisted in the removal of a considerable quantity of scar tissue from the palm of the plaintiff's right hand and the grafting of skin taken from the plaintiff's chest in place thereof. The scar tissue was the result of a severe burn caused by contact with an electric wire, which the plaintiff received about nine years before the time of the transactions here involved. There was evidence to the effect that before the operation was performed the plaintiff and his father went to the defendant's office, and that the defendant in answer to the question, "How long will the boy be in the hospital?" replied, "Three or four days, . . . not over four; then the boy can go home and it will be just a few days when he will go back to work with a perfect hand." Clearly this and other testimony to the same effect would not justify a finding that the doctor contracted to complete the hospital treatment in three or four days or that the plaintiff would be able to go back to work within a few days thereafter. The above statements could only be construed as expressions of opinion or predictions as to the probable duration of the treatment and plaintiff's resulting disability, and the fact that these estimates were exceeded would impose no contractual liability upon the defendant. The only substantial basis for the plaintiff's claim is the testimony that the defendant also said before the operation was decided upon, "I will guarantee to make the hand a hundred per cent perfect hand" or "a hundred per cent good hand." The plaintiff was present when these words were alleged to have been spoken, and, if they are to be taken at their face value, it seems obvious that proof of their utterance would establish the giving of a warranty in accordance with his contention.

The defendant argues, however, that, even if these words were uttered by him, no reasonable man would understand that they were used with the intention of entering into any "contractual relation whatever," and that they could reasonably be understood only "as his expression in strong language that he believed and expected that as a result of the operation he would give the plaintiff a very good hand." It may be conceded, as the defendant contends, that, before the question of the making of a contract should be submitted to a jury, there is a preliminary question of law for the trial court to pass upon, i.e. "whether the words could possibly have the meaning imputed to them by the party who founds his case upon a certain interpretation," but it cannot be held that the trial court decided this question erroneously in the present case. It is unnecessary to determine at this time whether the argument of the defendant, based upon "common knowledge of the uncertainty which attends all surgical operations," and the improbability that a surgeon would ever contract to make a damaged part of the human body "one hundred per cent perfect," would, in the absence of countervailing considerations, be regarded as conclusive, for there were other factors in the present case which tended to support the contention of the plaintiff. There was evidence that the defendant repeatedly solicited from the plaintiff's father the opportunity to perform this operation, and the theory was advanced by plaintiff's counsel in cross-examination of defendant that he sought an opportunity to "experiment on skin grafting," in which he had had little previous experience. If the jury accepted this part of plaintiff's contention, there would be a reasonable basis for the further conclusion that, if defendant spoke the words attributed to him, he did so with the intention that they should be accepted at their face value, as an inducement for the granting of consent to the operation by the plaintiff and his father, and there was ample evidence that they were so accepted by them. The question of the making of the alleged contract was properly submitted to the jury.

2. The substance of the charge to the jury on the question of damages appears in the following quotation: "If you find the plaintiff entitled to anything, he is entitled to recover for what pain and suffering he has been made to endure and for what injury he has sustained over and above what injury he had before." To this instruction the defendant seasonably excepted. By it, the jury was permitted to consider two elements of damage, (1) pain and suffering due to the operation, and (2) positive ill effects of the operation upon the plaintiff's hand. Authority for any specific rule of damages in cases of this kind seems to be lacking, but, when tested by general principle and by analogy, it appears that the foregoing instruction was erroneous.

"By 'damages,' as that term is used in the law of contracts, is intended compensation for a breach, measured in the terms of the contract." Davis v. New England Cotton Yarn Co., 77 N.H. 403, 404, 92 A. 732, 733. The purpose of the law is "to put the plaintiff in as good a position as he would have been in had the defendant kept his contract." 3 Williston Cont. § 1338; Hardie–Tynes Mfg. Co. v. Easton Cotton Oil Co., 150 N.C. 150, 63 S.E. 676, 134 Am.St.Rep. 899. The measure of recovery "is based upon what the defendant should have given the plaintiff, not what the plaintiff has given the defendant or otherwise expended." 3 Williston Cont. § 1341. "The only losses that can be said fairly to come within the terms of a contract are such as the parties must have had in mind when the contract was made, or such as they either knew or ought to have known would probably result from a failure to comply with its terms." Davis v. New England Cotton Yarn Co., 77 N.H. 403, 404, 92 A. 732, 733, Hurd v. Dunsmore, 63 N.H. 171.

The present case is closely analogous to one in which a machine is built for a certain purpose and warranted to do certain work. In such cases, the usual rule of damages for breach of warranty in the sale of chattels is applied and it is held that the measure of damages is the difference between the value of the machine if it had corresponded with the warranty and its actual value, together with such incidental losses as the parties knew or ought to have known would probably result from a failure to comply with its terms. . . .

We therefore conclude that the true measure of the plaintiff's damage in the present case is the difference between the value to him of a perfect hand or a good hand, such as the jury found the defendant promised him, and the value of his hand in its present condition, including any incidental consequences fairly within the contemplation of the parties when they made their contract. 1 Sutherland, Damages (4th Ed.) § 92. Damages not thus limited, although naturally resulting, are not to be given.

The extent of the plaintiff's suffering does not measure this difference in value. The pain necessarily incident to a serious surgical operation was a part of the contribution which the plaintiff was willing to make to his joint undertaking with the defendant to produce a good hand. It was a legal detriment suffered by him which constituted a part of the consideration given by him for the contract. It represented a part of the price which he was willing to pay for a good hand, but it furnished no test of the value of a good hand or the difference between the value of the hand which the defendant promised and the one which resulted from the operation.

It was also erroneous and misleading to submit to the jury as a separate element of damage any change for the worse in the condition of the plaintiff's hand resulting from the operation, although this error was probably more prejudicial to the plaintiff than to the defendant. Any such ill effect of the operation would be included under the true rule of damages set forth above, but damages might properly be assessed for the defendant's failure to improve the condition of the hand, even if there were no evidence that its condition was made worse as a result of the operation.

It must be assumed that the trial court, in setting aside the verdict, undertook to apply the same rule of damages which he had previously given to the jury, and, since this rule was erroneous, it is unnecessary for us to consider whether there was any evidence to justify his finding that all damages awarded by the jury above $500 were excessive.

3. Defendant's requests for instructions were loosely drawn, and were properly denied. A considerable number of issues of fact were raised by the evidence, and it would have been extremely misleading to instruct the jury in accordance with defendant's request No. 2, that "The only issue on which you have to pass is whether or not there was a special contract between the plaintiff and the defendant to produce a perfect hand." Equally inaccurate was defendant's request No. 5, which reads as follows: "You would have to find, in order to hold the defendant liable in this case, that Dr. McGee and the plaintiff both understood that the doctor was guaranteeing a perfect result from this operation." If the defendant said that he would guarantee a perfect result, and the plaintiff relied upon that promise, any mental reservations which he may have had are immaterial. The standard by which his conduct is to be judged is not internal, but external.... Defendant's request number 7 was as follows: "If you should get so far as to find that there was a special contract guaranteeing a perfect result, you would still have to find for the defendant unless you further found that a further operation would not correct the disability claimed by the plaintiff." In view of the testimony that the defendant had refused to perform a further operation, it would clearly have been erroneous to give this instruction. The evidence would have justified a verdict for an amount sufficient to cover the cost of such an operation, even if the theory underlying this request were correct....

New trial.

MARBLE, J., did not sit: the others concurred.

SULLIVAN v. O'CONNOR, 363 Mass. 579, 296 N.E.2d 183 (1973). "It has been suggested on occasion that agreements between patients and physicians by which the physician undertakes to effect a cure or to bring about a given result should be declared unenforceable on grounds of public policy. See Guilmet v. Campbell, 385 Mich. 57, 76 (dissenting opinion). But there are many decisions recognizing and enforcing such contracts, see Annotation, 43 A.L.R.3d 1221, 1225, 1229–1233, and the law of Massachusetts has treated them as valid, although we have had no decision meeting head on the contention that they should be denied legal sanction....

"It is not hard to see why the courts should be unenthusiastic or skeptical about the contract theory. Considering the uncertainties of medical science and the variations in the physical and psychological conditions of individual patients, doctors can seldom in good faith promise specific results. Therefore it is unlikely that physicians of even average integrity will in fact make such promises. Statements of opinion by the physician with some optimistic coloring are a different thing, and may indeed have therapeutic value. But patients may transform such statements into firm promises in their own minds, especially when they have been disappointed in the event, and testify in that sense to sympathetic juries.[1] If actions for breach of promise can be readily maintained, doctors, so it is said, will be frightened into practicing 'defensive

---

1. Judicial skepticism about whether a promise was in fact made derives also from the possibility that the truth has been tortured to give the plaintiff the advantage of the longer period of limitations sometimes available for actions on contract as distinguished from those in tort or for malpractice. See Lillich, The Malpractice Statute of Limitations in New York and Other Jurisdictions, 47 Cornell L.Q. 339; annotation, 80 A.L.R.2d 368.

medicine.' On the other hand, if these actions were outlawed, leaving only the possibility of suits for malpractice, there is fear that the public might be exposed to the enticements of charlatans, and confidence in the profession might ultimately be shaken. See Miller, The Contractual Liability of Physicians and Surgeons, 1953 Wash.L.Q. 413, 416–423. The law has taken the middle of the road position of allowing actions based on alleged contract, but insisting on clear proof. Instructions to the jury may well stress this requirement and point to tests of truth, such as the complexity or difficulty of an operation as bearing on the probability that a given result was promised. See annotation, 43 A.L.R.3d 1225, 1225–1227.

"If an action on the basis of contract is allowed, we have next the question of the measure of damages to be applied where liability is found. Some cases [such as Hawkins v. McGee] have taken the simple view that the promise by the physician is to be treated like an ordinary commercial promise, and accordingly that the successful plaintiff is entitled to a standard measure of recovery for breach of contract—'compensatory' ('expectancy') damages, an amount intended to put the plaintiff in the position he would be in if the contract had been performed, or, presumably, at the plaintiff's election, 'restitution' damages, an amount corresponding to any benefit conferred by the plaintiff upon the defendant in the performance of the contract disrupted by the defendant's breach. . . .

"Other cases, including a number in New York, without distinctly repudiating the *Hawkins* type of analysis, have indicated that a different and generally more lenient measure of damages is to be applied in patient-physician actions based on breach of alleged special agreements to effect a cure, attain a stated result, or employ a given medical method. This measure is expressed in somewhat variant ways, but the substance is that the plaintiff is to recover any expenditures made by him and for other detriment (usually not specifically described in the opinions) following proximately and foreseeably upon the defendant's failure to carry out his promise. . . . This, be it noted, is not a 'restitution' measure, for it is not limited to restoration of the benefit conferred on the defendant (the fee paid) but includes other expenditures, for example, amounts paid for medicine and nurses; so also it would seem according to its logic to take in damages for any worsening of the plaintiff's condition due to the breach. Nor is it an 'expectancy' measure, for it does not appear to contemplate recovery of the whole difference in value between the condition as promised and the condition actually resulting from the treatment. Rather the tendency of the formulation is to put the plaintiff back in the position he occupied just before the parties entered upon the agreement, to compensate him for the detriments he suffered in reliance upon the agreement. This kind of intermediate pattern of recovery for breach of contract is discussed in the suggestive article by Fuller and Perdue, The Reliance Interest in Contract Damages, 46 Yale L.J. 52, 373, where the authors show that, although not attaining the currency of the standard measures, a 'reliance' measure has for special reasons been applied by the courts in a variety of settings, including noncommercial settings. See 46 Yale L.J. at 396–401.[2]

2. Some of the exceptional situations mentioned where reliance may be preferred to expectancy are those in which the latter measure would be hard to apply or would impose too great a burden; performance was interfered with by external circumstances; the contract was indefinite. See 46 Yale L.J. at 373–386; 394–396.

"For breach of the patient-physician agreements under consideration, a recovery limited to restitution seems plainly too meager, if the agreements are to be enforced at all. On the other hand, an expectancy recovery may well be excessive. . . .

"There is much to be said, then, for applying a reliance measure to the present facts, and we have only to add that our cases are not unreceptive to the use of that formula in special situations. . . .

"The question of recovery on a reliance basis for pain and suffering or mental distress requires further attention. . . . Suffering or distress resulting from the breach going beyond that which was envisaged by the treatment as agreed, should be compensable on the same ground as the worsening of the patient's conditions because of the breach. Indeed it can be argued that the very suffering or distress 'contracted for'—that which would have been incurred if the treatment achieved the promised result—should also be compensable on the theory underlying the New York cases. For that suffering is 'wasted' if the treatment fails. Otherwise stated, compensation for this waste is arguably required in order to complete the restoration of the status quo ante."

UNIDROIT PRINCIPLES OF INTERNATIONAL COMMERCIAL CONTRACTS ART. 7.4.2

[See Selected Source Materials Supplement]

COOTER & EISENBERG, DAMAGES FOR BREACH OF CONTRACT

73 Calif.L.Rev. 1434 (1985).*

The damage rules that the courts apply should be both fair and efficient. Contracts negotiated under ideal conditions will be efficient, and enforcing the terms of such contracts will usually be regarded as fair. Thus we take as a theorem that a damage rule is both fair and efficient if it corresponds to the terms that rational parties situated like the contracting parties would have reached when bargaining under ideal conditions.

The question then is, why might rational parties, who address the issue, choose an expectation measure over a reliance measure? One reason is administrative: it is usually easier to establish in court the value of performance than the extent of reliance. The very fact of reliance is often difficult to prove, as in cases where the reliance consists of passive inaction (such as failure to pursue alternatives) rather than a positive change of position. Even if the fact of reliance can be proved, reliance damages may be difficult to measure. In a noncompetitive market, for example, reliance damages would normally be calculated by the [victim's opportunity cost], which requires determining the forgone price. Often, however, the forgone price is very hard to determine, as where the buyer breaches and the commodity is so unusual

---

* The text is somewhat revised and reorganized from the original. (Footnote by ed.)

that there is no way to establish exactly what the next-best alternative buyer would have paid. In contrast, expectation damages are based on the contract price, which is known, rather than the forgone price, which is speculative. This administrative consideration has implications for both fairness and efficiency. In terms of fairness, the difficulty of proving reliance damages might, paradoxically, result in a failure to protect the reliance interest unless an expectation measure is chosen. In terms of efficiency, a damage measure that was difficult to prove, and therefore unreliable, would undercut the goal of facilitating private planning.

An intimately related set of considerations has to do with the incentive effects of the expectation and reliance measures. Most contracts are made with the expectation of mutual gain. . . . The total gain to both parties—the surplus from exchange—is the value created by the contract. The terms of a contract have incentive effects upon behavior that influence how much value the contract will create. Accordingly, one index to whether a damage rule would have been agreed to by rational parties situated like the contracting parties, and bargaining under ideal conditions, is whether the rule provides incentives for efficient behavior. . . .

We begin with the incentive effects of damage measures on the decision whether to perform, that is, on the rate of breach. A contract involves a promise by at least one party, and it is always possible that events will induce a promisor to refuse to perform, either because performance has become unprofitable or because an alternative performance has become more profitable. If a promisor were liable only for the promisee's reliance damages, the value of the promisor's performance to the promisee would not enter into a purely self-interested calculation by the promisor whether to perform. In contrast, expectation damages place on the promisor the promisee's loss of his share of the contract's value in the event of breach, and thereby sweep that loss into the promisor's calculus of self-interest.

The effect of expectation damages on the promisor's calculations can be stated in terms of externalities. Economists say that an externality exists when one person imposes a cost upon another without paying for it. Incentives for performance are efficient if they compel a promisor to balance the cost to him of performing against the losses to himself and to others that will result if he does not perform. If the promisor does not perform, the promisee loses his share of the value of the contract. If the promisor is liable for that loss, he internalizes not only his own loss but the losses to the promisee that result from his failure to perform. In contrast, if the promisor is liable only for reliance damages, he will not internalize the full value of performance to the promisee. Thus expectation damages create efficient incentives for the promisor's performance, while reliance damages do not, unless they are identical to expectation damages.

By directly affecting the probability that the promisor will perform, the expectation measure has an indirect effect upon the promisee's behavior, which can be stated in terms of planning. Knowing that expectation damages give the promisor strong incentives to perform, the promisee will be more confident that his reliance on the promisor will not expose him to undue risk. The promisee can therefore plan more effectively, because once a contract is made he can order his affairs with the confidence that he will realize its value, whether by performance or damages. In contrast, under a regime of reliance damages, a promisee could plan only on the basis that if breach occurs the law will put him back to where he was when he started. Since planning is by nature forward-looking, this backward-looking nature of reliance damages would be a shaky foundation for ordering complex affairs. Furthermore, it is in the promisor's interest that the promisee be able to plan reliably, because the ability to do so will make the promisee willing to pay a higher price for the promise.

These ideas can also be expressed in institutional terms. The purpose of the social institution of bargain is to create joint value through exchange. In recognition of the desirability of creating value in this manner, the legal institution of contract supports the social institution of the bargain with official sanctions. It is rational to design the legal sanctions so that the joint value from exchange is maximized. This goal is achieved by protecting the expectation interest.

UNITED STATES NAVAL INSTITUTE v. CHARTER COMMUNICATIONS, INC.

United States Court of Appeals, Second Circuit, 1991.
936 F.2d 692.

Before KEARSE, WINTER and ALTIMARI, CIRCUIT JUDGES.

KEARSE, CIRCUIT JUDGE:

This case returns to us following our remand in *United States Naval Institute v. Charter Communications, Inc.,* 875 F.2d 1044 (2d Cir.1989) ("*Naval I*"), to the United States District Court for the Southern District of New York, Pierre N. Leval, *Judge,* for the fashioning of relief in favor of plaintiff United States Naval Institute ("Naval") against defendant Charter Communications, Inc., and Berkley Publishing Group (collectively "Berkley"), for breach of an agreement with respect to the publication of the paperback edition of *The Hunt For Red October* ("*Red October*" or the "Book"). On remand, the district court awarded Naval $35,380.50 in damages, $7,760.12 as profits wrongfully received by Berkley, and $15,319.27 as prejudgment interest on the damages awarded, plus costs. Naval appeals from so much of the judgment as failed to award a greater amount as profits, denied prejudgment interest on the profits awarded, and refused to award attorney's fees under the Copyright Act of 1976, 17 U.S.C. § 101 *et seq.* (1988) (the "Copyright Act" or the "Act"). Berkley cross-appeals from the judgment as a whole and from such parts of it as awarded moneys to Naval. For the reasons below, we reverse the award of profits; we affirm the award of damages, the award of prejudgment interest, and the denial of attorney's fees.

I. BACKGROUND

The events leading to this action are fully set forth in *Naval I,* 875 F.2d at 1045–47, and will be summarized here only briefly. Naval, as the assignee of the author's copyright in *Red October,* entered into a licensing agreement with Berkley in September 1984 (the "Agreement"), granting Berkley the exclusive license to publish a paperback edition of the Book "not sooner than October 1985." Berkley shipped its paperback edition to retail outlets early, placing those outlets in position to sell the paperback prior to October 1985. As a result, retail sales of the paperback began on September 15, 1985, and early sales were sufficiently substantial that the Book was near the top of paperback bestseller lists before the end of September 1985.

Naval commenced the present action when it learned of Berkley's plans for early shipment, and it unsuccessfully sought a preliminary injunction. After trial, the district judge dismissed the complaint. He ruled that Berkley had not breached the Agreement because it was entitled, in accordance with industry custom, to ship prior to the agreed publication date. On appeal, we reversed. Though we upheld the district court's finding that the Agreement did not prohibit the early shipments themselves, we concluded that if the "not sooner than October 1985" term of the Agreement had any meaning whatever, it meant at least that Berkley was not allowed to cause such voluminous paperback retail sales prior to that date, and that Berkley had therefore breached the Agreement. *Naval I*, 875 F.2d at 1049–51. Accordingly, we remanded for entry of a judgment awarding Naval appropriate relief.

On the remand, Naval asserted that it was entitled to recovery for copyright infringement, and it sought judgment awarding it all of Berkley's profits from pre-October 1985 sales of the Book; it estimated those profits at $724,300. It also requested prejudgment interest, costs, and attorney's fees. Berkley, on the other hand, challenged Naval's right to any recovery at all, contending, *inter alia,* that Berkley could not be held liable for copyright infringement since the Agreement had made it the exclusive licensee of the paperback edition copyright as of September 14, 1984; it argued that Naval therefore had at most a claim for breach-of-contract but that Berkley could not be held liable on that basis because Naval had disavowed its pursuit of a contract claim. Berkley also argued that the profits attributed to it by Naval were inflated, and it opposed any award of prejudgment interest or attorney's fees.

In a Memorandum and Order dated July 17, 1990, 1990 WL 104027 ("July 17 Order"), the district judge rejected Berkley's claim that "its premature publication of the paperback edition constituted only a contract violation and not an infringement of Naval's copyright." *Id.* at 8. He found that Naval's copyright was infringed by the early publication because, though "the *extent* of the breach was a relatively trivial matter of two weeks of sales, the *term* breached was crucial to the scope of the license, as it governed when the license would take effect." *Id.* (emphasis in original). He concluded that Naval was entitled to recover damages for copyright infringement, comprising actual damages suffered by Naval plus Berkley's profits "attributable to the infringement," 17 U.S.C. § 504(b).

The court calculated Naval's "actual damages from Berkley's wrongful pre-October 'publication'" as the profits Naval would have earned from hardcover sales in September 1985 if the competing paperback edition had not then been offered for sale. July 17 Order at 8. Noting the downward trend of hardcover sales of the Book from March through August 1985, the court found that there was no reason to infer that Naval's September 1985 sales would have exceeded its August 1985 sales. The court calculated Naval's lost sales as the difference between the actual hardcover sales for those two months, and awarded Naval $35,380.50 as actual damages.

The district judge held that Berkley's profits "attributable to the infringement" were only those profits that resulted from "sales to customers who would not have bought the paperback but for the fact it became available in September." July 17 Order at 10. He found that most of the September paperback sales were made to buyers who would not have bought a hardcover edition in September, and therefore only those September sales that displaced hardcover sales were attributable to the infringement. Berkley's profit on the displacing copies totaled $7,760.12, and the court awarded that amount to Naval.

The court awarded Naval prejudgment interest (totaling $15,319.27) on the $35,380.50 awarded as actual damages but denied such interest on the award of Berkley's profits. It also denied Naval's request for attorney's fees.

Judgment was entered accordingly, and these appeals followed.

II. Discussion . . .

A. Naval's Claim of Copyright Infringement . . .

The Agreement between Naval and Berkley, headed "Agreement made this 14th day of September 1984," granted Berkley, in & 1, "the exclusive right to publish and reproduce, distribute and sell English-language paperback editions" of the Book in the United States and certain other areas. Paragraph 2 of the Agreement stated that "[t]he term of this license will begin on the date written above"; it stated that the term of the license would continue until at least five years after the date of Berkley's "first publication" of the Book. Paragraph 4 provided that Berkley was to publish the paperback edition "not sooner than October 1985."

These provisions contradict the district court's finding that Berkley's publication date "governed when the license would take effect." Paragraph 2 provided that the license took effect on "the date written above"; since September 14, 1984, was the only date mentioned in the Agreement prior to & 3, the license term began on that date. Further, & 2's distinct references to (a) "the date written above" to define the start of the license term, and (b) Berkley's "first publication" date to anchor the continuation of the license term reveal that the parties deliberately did not define the start of the term by Berkley's first publication date. Thus, according to the express provisions of the Agreement, Berkley became the owner of the right to publish the paperback edition of the book in September 1984 and remained the owner of that right for at least five years after its first publication of that edition in 1985. Its publication of that edition in 1985 therefore could not constitute copyright infringement. . . .

B. Contract Damages

Our ruling that Naval is not entitled to recover under the Copyright Act does not, as Berkley would have it, require the entry of judgment in favor of Berkley. Though Berkley argues that Naval had abandoned its contract claim for money damages prior to trial, we thereafter ruled in *Naval I* that Naval was entitled to recover for breach of contract. . . . Our ruling in *Naval I* that Naval was entitled to recover for breach of the Agreement is the law of the case. . . .

As Naval has renounced any effort at rescission and has accepted Berkley's payments of substantial copyright royalties for paperback sales under the

Agreement, plainly the relief to which Naval is entitled on its meritorious breach-of-contract claim is money damages.

The damages awarded by the district court on remand had two components: (1) Naval's lost profits resulting from Berkley's early publication of the paperback edition of the Book, and (2) Berkley's profits attributable to its assumed infringement. For the reasons discussed above, the latter component of the award cannot stand. The former component, however, may properly measure damages under a breach-of-contract theory.

Since the purpose of damages for breach of contract is to compensate the injured party for the loss caused by the breach, 5 *Corbin On Contracts* '1002, at 31 (1964), those damages are generally measured by the plaintiff's actual loss, *see, e.g., Restatement (Second) of Contracts* § 347 (1981). While on occasion the defendant's profits are used as the measure of damages, *see, e.g., Cincinnati Siemens–Lungren Gas Illuminating Co. v. Western Siemens–Lungren Co.,* 152 U.S. 200, 204–07, 14 S.Ct. 523, 525–26, 38 L.Ed. 411 (1894); *Murphy v. Lischitz,* 183 Misc. 575, 577, 49 N.Y.S.2d 439, 441 (Sup.Ct.N.Y. County 1944), *aff'd mem.,* 268 A.D. 1027, 52 N.Y.S.2d 943 (1st Dep't), *aff'd mem.,* 294 N.Y. 892, 63 N.E.2d 26 (1945), this generally occurs when those profits tend to define the plaintiff's loss, for an award of the defendant's profits where they greatly exceed the plaintiff's loss and there has been no tortious conduct on the part of the defendant would tend to be punitive, and punitive awards are not part of the law of contract damages. *See generally Restatement (Second) of Contracts* § 356 comment *a* ("The central objective behind the system of contract remedies is compensatory, not punitive."); *id.* comment *b* (agreement attempting to fix damages in amount vastly greater than what approximates actual loss would be unenforceable as imposing a penalty); *id.* § 355 (punitive damages not recoverable for breach of contract unless conduct constituting the breach is also a tort for which such damages are recoverable).

Here, the district court found that Berkley's alleged $724,300 profits did not define Naval's loss because many persons who bought the paperback in September 1985 would not have bought the book in hardcover but would merely have waited until the paperback edition became available. This finding is not clearly erroneous....

[The court then held that Naval had proved with sufficient certainty the damages of $33,380.50 awarded by the trial court as the profits Naval would have earned on hardcover sales in September 1985 if the paperback edition had not then been offered for sale.]

CONCLUSION

... For the foregoing reasons, we reverse so much of the judgment as granted Naval $7,760.12 as an award of Berkley's profits. In all other respects, the judgment is affirmed.

No costs.

———

COPPOLA ENTERPRISES, INC. v. ALFONE

Supreme Court of Florida, 1988.
531 So.2d 334.

KOGAN, Justice. . . .

On April 18, 1978, Helen Alfone contracted with Coppola Enterprises, Inc. (Coppola) to purchase a residential lot and single family home to be constructed by Coppola (Unit 53). The purchase price of Unit 53 was $105,690.00. Alfone placed a $10,568.00 deposit on the property.

Closing was projected for "Winter 1978–79" but did not take place until late summer 1980 due to construction delays. The contract provided that the closing was to occur after ten days written notice from the seller to the purchaser.

Upon receipt of the letter informing her of the tentative date set for closing, Alfone immediately sought financing to purchase the property. However, when she was unable to acquire the necessary financing within the time required, Alfone's attorney requested additional time within which to pay the balance due on the property. Taking the position that time was of the essence, Coppola refused Alfone's request and subsequently resold the property for $170,000.00.

The trial court found that Coppola failed to exercise good faith by refusing Alfone a reasonable time to close and by terminating the contract. Final judgment was entered for Alfone, and she was awarded "benefit of bargain" damages of $64,310.00 together with prejudgment interest of $43,295.38. The Fourth District Court of Appeal affirmed the judgment and damages award, holding the "award of damages to a contractual vendee [includes] the profit made by the vendor on the sale of the property to a subsequent purchaser even though there is no proof of fraud or bad faith." 506 So.2d at 1181.

The district court was correct to award damages to Alfone equal to the profit made by Coppola on the subsequent sale.[2] Under this Court's opinion in *Gassner v. Lockett*, 101 So.2d 33, 34 (Fla.1958), "where a vendor is unable to perform a prior contract for the sale of the lands because of a subsequent sale of the same land, he should be held, to the extent of any profit in the subsequent sale, to be a trustee for the prior vendee and accountable to such vendee for any profit." In *Gassner* the seller, who was old and extremely forgetful, conveyed certain property to the buyer. Some months later he conveyed the same property to a subsequent purchaser. This Court concluded the record showed the transaction was not made in bad faith, but nevertheless the seller should not be permitted to profit from his mistake, even though it was made in good faith. The Court awarded, among other things, damages to the buyer that included any profit the seller may have made as a result of the second sale.

The *Gassner* rationale also applies here. Coppola was obligated to sell Unit 53 to Alfone under their contract. The provisions of the contract making time of the essence were waived because construction delays postponed the

---

2. The award should also include a return to Alfone of her initial deposit on Unit 53. (Footnote relocated by ed.)

closing for more than a year and a half past the "Winter 1978–1979" date originally set for closing. Under these circumstances Alfone was entitled to a reasonable time in which to acquire the funds to pay the balance due on the property. Once Coppola breached its contract with Alfone and was unable to perform due to the sale of Unit 53 to a subsequent purchaser, Alfone was entitled to damages equal to Coppola's profits from the sale.

We need not address whether Coppola's decision to sell Unit 53 to a subsequent purchaser involved bad faith. Resolution of that issue is not dispositive here. As in *Gassner* the buyer is entitled to these damages whether the sale to the subsequent purchaser involved bad faith or was merely the result of a good-faith mistake. A seller will not be permitted to profit from his breach of a contract with a buyer, even absent proof of fraud or bad faith, when the breach is followed by a sale of the land to a subsequent purchaser. . . .

It is so ordered.

EHRLICH, C.J., and OVERTON, McDONALD, SHAW and GRIMES, JJ., concur.

BARKETT, J., did not participate in this case.

———

LAURIN v. DeCAROLIS CONSTRUCTION CO., 372 Mass. 688, 363 N.E.2d 675 (1977). In March 1971, the Laurins agreed to purchase a home that DeCarolis was then constructing. The home was situated on a well-wooded lot. Prior to the closing, the Laurins found that after the contract had been signed, DeCarolis had bulldozed many of the trees on the property. The Laurins ordered DeCarolis to desist, but DeCarolis continued to bulldoze trees and also removed gravel and loam worth $6,480. The Laurins paid the purchase price of $26,900 at the closing, and then sued DeCarolis for the value of the trees, gravel, and loam that DeCarolis had removed.

The case was tried by a master, who concluded that the Laurins were the "equitable owners" of the property from and after the signing of the agreement, so that DeCarolis had unlawfully converted the trees, gravel, and loam. In other words, the master reasoned that the Laurins were entitled to disgorgement under a property theory. The Massachusetts Supreme Judicial Court rejected this reasoning, on the ground that under Massachusetts law, "the rights of the purchaser of real property prior to closing are contract rights rather than property rights." Accordingly, the Court concluded, "[this] case must be decided, not as [an] action for injury to or conversion of property, but as a claim for a deliberate and willful breach of contract. . . ."

This left the contract theory. The problem was that taking the trees, gravel, and loam had not diminished the value of the property. Therefore, although DeCarolis had made a gain from breach, the Laurins had not suffered a loss. Nevertheless, the Court held that the Laurins were entitled to disgorgement, because DeCarolis should not be allowed to retain its gains from a willful breach of contract:

> . . . Particularly where the defendant's breach is deliberate and willful, we think damages limited to diminution in value of the premises may sometimes be seriously inadequate. "Cutting a few trees on a timber

tract, or taking a few hundred tons of coal from a mine, might not diminish the market value of the tract, or of the mine, and yet the value of the wood or coal, severed from the soil, might be considerable. The wrongdoer would, in the cases instanced, be held to pay the value of the wood and coal, and he could not shield himself by showing that the property from which it was taken was, as a whole, worth as much as it was before." *Worrall v. Munn, 53 N.Y. 185, 190 (1873)*. This reasoning does not depend for its soundness on the holding of a property interest, as distinguished from a contractual interest, by the plaintiffs. Nor is it punitive; it merely deprives the defendant of a profit wrongfully made, a profit which the plaintiff was entitled to make. . . .

NOTE ON THE THEORY OF EFFICIENT BREACH

A well-known theory in the law-and-economics of contract is the theory of efficient breach. This theory holds that breach of contract is efficient, and therefore desirable, if the promisor's gain from breach, after payment of expectation damages, will exceed the promisee's loss from breach. Probably the best-known exposition of the theory of efficient breach is that given by Richard Posner in his book, *Economic Analysis of Law*. This exposition has changed somewhat over the six editions of that book. Here is the core of the exposition in the first edition:

> . . . [I]n some cases a party [to a contract] would be tempted to breach the contract simply because his profit from breach would exceed his expected profit from completion of the contract. If his profit from breach would also exceed the expected profit to the other party from completion of the contract, and if damages are limited to loss of expected profit, there will be an incentive to commit a breach. There should be.

Although the theory of efficient breach is typically presented in very generalized terms, in fact the theory can only be properly understood and evaluated in the context of paradigm cases to which it might meaningfully be applied. The most salient paradigm for present purposes is one that might be called the Overbidder Paradigm. In this Paradigm, a seller who has contracted to sell a commodity to a buyer breaches the contract in order to sell the commodity to a third party who comes along later and offers a higher price.

The Resale Paradigm is the poster child of the theory of efficient breach. Proponents of the theory, including Posner, typically include an illustration that exemplifies this Paradigm as part of their argument for the theory. Here is the centerpiece illustration of the theory of efficient breach in the first edition of Posner's *Economic Analysis of Law*:

> . . . I sign a contract to deliver 100,000 custom-ground widgets at $.10 apiece to A, for use in his boiler factory. After I have delivered 10,000, B comes to me, explains that he desperately needs 25,000 custom-ground widgets at once since otherwise he will be forced to close his pianola factory at great cost, and offers me $.15 apiece for 25,000 widgets. I sell him the widgets and as a result do not complete timely delivery to A, who sustains $1000 in damages from my breach. Having obtained an additional profit of $1250 on the sale to B, I am better off even after

reimbursing A for his loss. Society is also better off. Since B was willing to pay me $.15 per widget, it must mean that each widget was worth at least $.15 to him. But it was worth only $.14 to A—$.10, what he paid, plus $.04 ($1000 divided by 25,000), his expected profit. Thus the breach resulted in a transfer of the 26,000 widgets from a lower valued to a higher valued use.

There are two major criteria under which the theory of efficient breach needs to be evaluated. One is whether the predicates of the theory are correct; the other is whether if the predicates of the theory are correct the theory is justified on the ground that it promotes efficiency. The theory could be valid only if it satisfies both criteria.

Predicates. The theory of efficient breach rests on two basic predicates, both of which feature in Posner's illustration. The first predicate is that the expectation measure makes the promisee indifferent between performance and damages. This predicate is incorrect because expectation damages do not have that effect. For example, expectation damages are based on objective rather than subjective value; the recovery of a buyer's lost profits under the expectation measure is often cut off by the principle of Hadley v. Baxendale, the certainty rule, or both (see Chapter 6, infra); expectation damages do not include legal fees and other costs of litigation; and prejudgment interest for breach of contract is often not awarded, and when awarded is almost invariably less than the time value of the gains that the promisee would have made from performance.

The second predicate of the theory of efficient breach is that at the time of the perform-or-breach decision, the promisor knows the value that the promisee places on the commodity. In the context of the Overbidder Paradigm, this predicate is incorrect because the seller will seldom know what value the buyer puts on a contracted-for commodity. At least in the case of differentiated commodities (which is the only case in which the theory of efficient breach is relevant), at the time of contract formation a buyer will rarely if ever tell a seller what profits he expects to make from a contract, because a seller could use that information to lever up the price. Even if the buyer did disclose that information, the seller would normally have no way of knowing what profits the buyer expected to make at the time of the perform-or-breach decision, because between the time of contract-formation and the time of that decision, markets may have shifted, or the buyer may have increased his potential profits through investment in beneficial reliance such as advertising or the purchase of complimentary commodities.

Efficiency. Even assuming, counterfactually, that the predicates of the theory of efficient breach were correct, the encouragement of breach in the Overbidder Paradigm would decrease rather than promote efficiency. The efficiency justification of the theory is that if a seller's gain on sale to an overbidder exceeds the buyer's loss, breach is an instrument for transferring a commodity to a higher-valued use. However, in a world without transaction costs, commodities will always flow to higher-valued uses, so that if the overbidder values the commodity more than the buyer, he will end up with the commodity even under a performance regime. Commodities will also normally flow to higher-valued uses in a world *with* transaction costs. If a third party values the commodity more than the buyer, and knows the buyer's identity, he will purchase from the buyer either an assignment of the contract or the commodity itself. If the third party does not know the buyer's identity, a rational seller will either negotiate with the buyer to be released from the contract, so that she can sell to the overbidder, or will sell the overbidder's identity to the buyer, or the buyer's identity to the overbidder. Posner more or less admitted that if an overbidder values the contracted-for commodity more than the buyer, the overbidder will end up with the commodity even if the seller is not allowed to breach, and fell back on an argument that the transaction costs of moving a commodity to an overbidder will be less in an efficient-breach regime than in a performance regime. However, it is impossible to establish that the transaction costs of moving commodities to higher-valued uses would be less under an efficient-breach regime than under a performance regime. Indeed, given the cost of litigation, the transaction costs of such movements would almost certainly be greater in an efficient-breach regime.

In short, in the context of the Overbidder Paradigm there is no convincing efficiency justification for the theory of efficient breach. Moreover, if the theory was widely followed, it would lead to inefficiency, by remaking the parties' contract, reducing the rewards for planning and investing, and weakening the contracting system.

Remaking Contracts. The efficiency of a contract rule can normally be measured by asking whether it is the rule that well-informed contracting parties would normally agree upon if bargaining were cost-free. There is an easy way to determine whether the theory of efficient breach corresponds to what contracting parties in the Overbidder Paradigm would normally agree upon. Suppose a seller and a buyer have negotiated a contract under which the seller agrees to sell a differentiated commodity to buyer—say, a home to live in, or a used machine that the buyer will employ as a factor of production. As the parties are about to sign a written contract, the seller says, "In all honesty, I should tell you that although I have no present intention to breach this contract, neither do I have a present intention to perform. If a better offer comes along, I will take it and pay you expectation damages. In fact, I will begin actively looking for a better offer right after we sign this contract. Let's insert a provision that recognizes that I will do just that."

What would be the buyer's likely response? Under the theory of efficient breach, the buyer would say, "Of course, I expect no more." Experience strongly suggests, however, that in real life most buyers would be surprised if not shocked by such a statement, and would either walk away; insist on an explicit contractual provision stating that the seller has a present intent to perform and that any profit on breach and resale will go to buyer; or demand a payment, in the form of a reduced price, for the seller's right to resell. Buyers will react this way because normally one of the very points of a bargain promise is to convince the promisee that the promisor has an intent to perform.

Moreover, at the time a contract for the sale of a differentiated commodity is made, the buyer and the seller know that an overbid might later be forthcoming. Because the buyer and the seller know this, the buyer will need to pay the seller an implicit premium for taking the risk of forgoing an overbid. The amount of this premium will be the expected value of an overbid, based on a rough probability-weighted average of potential overbid prices. To put this differently, if the seller is economically rational, her price will include a premium paid by the buyer to ensure that the seller will take the contract-ed-for commodity off the market–a premium equal to the reduction in price that the buyer would demand for giving the seller a right to resell to an overbidder. Allowing the seller to obtain and retain the amount of this premium takes from the buyer an amount that he has bought and paid for, and inefficiently remakes the parties contract.

Reducing the rewards for planning and investing. The theory of efficient breach also inefficiently reduces the rewards for planning and investing. Where the buyer's damages are based on the difference between contract price and market price, under the theory of efficient breach the seller will gain from breach only if the price paid by the overbidder exceeds the market price. There are two basic reasons why an overbidder may pay more than market price.

First, market price is an inexact, midpoint construct based on extrapolations from comparable transactions, and the overbidder may be willing to pay a price above the artificial midpoint. In that case the theory has no positive efficiency implication: there is no reason to believe that the overbidder values the commodity more highly than the buyer, because the buyer may also have been willing to pay a price above the constructed market price.

Second, the overbidder may have a special strategic need for the commodity that leads him to place a higher value on the commodity than anyone else, and the constructed market price is almost certain to be less than that value. However, if the third party had a special strategic need for the commodity when he made his overbid, he probably had a prospect of the strategic need when the original contract was made. The question then arises, why didn't the overbidder make a contract with the seller at that time? The answer to this question is likely to involve issues of foresight and investment. For example, it may often be that the commodity takes time to produce, and the buyer foresaw a future need for the commodity and was willing to invest in a contract for production of the commodity, at a time when the overbidder lacked the foresight, was unwilling to make the investment, or both. Or, it may be that the commodity essentially consists of productive capacity, and the buyer foresaw a future need for that capacity, and was willing to invest in a contract to lock up that capacity, at a time when the overbidder lacked the foresight, was unwilling to make the investment, or both.

In either type of case, the overbidder may be willing to pay more than the constructed market price because the supply or productive capacity that he needs has now become highly constrained. However, providing the seller with an incentive to sell the commodity to the overbidder in either type of case would deny the buyer the benefit of his foresight and investment. Efficient incentives should be just the other way around. The law should reward the ant, not the grasshopper. It is the buyer who has earned the opportunity to acquire the commodity, by having foresight and investing when the third party was either not smart enough or willing enough to do so. Accordingly, in such cases too, the theory of efficient breach would have efficiency costs, because it would reduce the rewards for planning and investing.

Weakening the contracting system. There is a third way the theory of efficient breach, if widely followed, would reduce efficiency. The theory of efficient breach is based on a static and short-run approach to the issue of breach, because it addresses only the efficiency of performing or breaching an individual contract. In contrast, a dynamic, long-run approach to the issue of breach addresses the efficiency of the contracting system as a whole. From that perspective, the theory of efficient breach is inefficient because if widely followed, it would diminish the efficiency of that system.

The efficiency of the contracting system does not rest, as the theory of efficient breach implies, solely on legal remedies. Rather, the efficiency of the contracting system rests on a tripod whose legs are legal remedies, reputational constraints, and the internalization of social norms, in particular, the moral norm of promise-keeping. These three legs are mutually supportive. Legal rules rest in significant part on social norms, reputational effects rest principally on social norms, and moral norms are reinforced by legal rules and supported by reputational effects.

All three of these legs are necessary to ensure the reliability of the contracting system. Legal rules are not alone sufficient, because dispute-settlement under law is expensive and chancy. The moral norm of promise-keeping is not alone sufficient, because not all actors fully internalize moral norms and there are limits on the power of norms. Reputational effects are not alone sufficient, because reputations are fully effective only if third parties have reliable knowledge concerning a promisor's history of breach, and this kind of information is hard to come by, both because many breaches do not become widely known and because many promisors will often claim that they had a valid excuse for not performing.

Because all three legs are necessary to support the efficiency of the contracting system, anything that weakens one leg seriously threatens the efficiency of the system. The theory of efficient breach, if widely adopted, would do precisely that, because the effect of the theory is to remove the moral force of promising in a bargain context. The moral meaning of making a promise is to commit yourself to take a given action in the future even if, when the action is due to be taken, all things considered you do not wish to take it. The theory of efficient breach turns this upside down. Under that theory, if you don't wish to take a promised action when it is due, because all things considered you believe that the cost to you of taking the action would exceed the gain to the promise, you not only needn't, but shouldn't keep the promise. As Posner states, if the seller's gain from breach will exceed the buyer's loss, then "if damages are limited to loss of expected profit, there will be an incentive to commit breach. *There should be.*"

Given the dilution or elimination of the moral force of promises under the theory of efficient breach, that theory, if widely adopted, would decrease the efficiency of the contracting system in three ways. (1) It would increase the need to resort to litigation, which is very expensive, as opposed to achieving performance of contracts through the internalization of the moral norm of promise-keeping, which is very inexpensive. (2) It would lead contracting parties to make greater use of costly noncontractual measures to ensure performance, such as self-enforcing deposits. (3) It would diminish the force of reputational constraints, because reputational constraints rest in part on a moral basis.

To summarize, in the context of the Overbidder Paradigm the theory of efficient breach is inefficient in three major respects. First, the theory would inefficiently remake the parties' contract by converting a contract under which the seller agrees to provide a commodity, and to not search for or sell to an overbidder, into a contract that allows and indeed encourages sellers to both search for and sell to overbidders. Second, the theory would reduce the rewards for planning and investing, by encouraging sellers to transfer commodities away from buyers who have planned and invested, to overbidders who have done neither. Third, the theory would reduce the efficiency of the contracting system by seriously weakening one of the three legs upon which that efficiency rests.

GREER PROPERTIES, INC. v. LaSALLE NATIONAL BANK, 874 F.2d 457 (7th Cir. 1989). In February 1987, the Sellers contracted to sell a parcel of real estate to Searle Chemicals for approximately $1,100,000. Searle had the right to terminate the contract if the soil was contaminated by environmental waste. The deal fell through because an environmental consulting firm that Searle hired reported that the site was contaminated, and that a clean-up would cost more than $500,000.

The Sellers then contracted to sell the property to Greer for $1,250,000. Under this contract the Sellers were required to remove the environmental contamination at their own expense, but were allowed to terminate the contract if the cost of the clean-up became economically impracticable. The Sellers then retained a soil consultant, who estimated the cost of the clean-up at $100,000—$200,000. At that point, the Sellers went back to Searle and entered into a new round of negotiations. A purchase price of $1,455,000 was proposed in these negotiations and embodied in a draft contract prepared by Searle. The Sellers then terminated the contract with Greer, purportedly under the clean-up provision.

Greer brought an action for specific performance and damages. The district court held for Sellers, on the ground that upon receipt of the soil consultant's study, Sellers had broad discretion to terminate the contract under the clean-up provision. The Seventh Circuit reversed, on the ground that by making the contract with Searle, Sellers had given up their right to look for a better price:

> Under Illinois law, "every contract implies good faith and fair dealing between the parties to it." ... This implied obligation of good faith and fair dealing in the performance of contracts acts as a limit on the discretion possessed by the parties.... With this limitation on the discretion of the Sellers in mind, their decision to terminate the contract must be analyzed to determine if they acted in good faith. If the Sellers terminated the contract to obtain a better price from Searle, their action would have been in bad faith. *When the Sellers entered the contract with Greer and Greer agreed to pay them a specific price for the property, the Sellers gave up their opportunity to shop around for a better price.* By using the termination clause to recapture that opportunity, the Sellers would have acted in bad faith. (Emphasis added.)

NOTE ON PUNITIVE DAMAGES

It is often said that punitive damages are normally unavailable for breach of contract. Thus Restatement Second § 355 states that "Punitive damages are not recoverable for a breach of contract unless the conduct constituting the breach is also a tort for which punitive damages are recoverable."

Under § 355, punitive damages are available if the conduct constituting the breach is independently a tort. Some of the "torts" in question look suspiciously like breaches of contract. For example, under Illustration 3 to Section 355:

> A, a telephone company, contracts with B to render uninterrupted service. A, tortiously as well as in breach of contract, fails to maintain service at night and B is unable to telephone a doctor for his sick child. B's right to recover punitive damages is governed by Restatement, Second, Torts § 908.

Punitive damages may be available for a breach of the duty of good faith, on the theory that a breach of good faith is tortious. It is now well accepted that there is a duty to perform contractual duties in good faith. Accordingly, this exception, if rigorously followed, could have a very wide ambit. In practice, however, the exception has been relatively limited. Its most significant application has been in suits by insureds against their insurance companies for failure to settle or defend in good faith. See Comunale v. Traders & General Insurance Co., 50 Cal.2d 654, 328 P.2d 198 (1958). Some cases have also applied the exception in cases involving a breach of an employment contract by an employer, and in certain other limited contexts, see, e.g., Nicholson v. United Pacific Insurance Co., 219 Mont. 32, 710 P.2d 1342 (1985). However, in Foley v. Interactive Data Corp., 47 Cal.3d 654, 254 Cal.Rptr. 211, 765 P.2d 373 (1988), the California Supreme Court held that punitive damages were not available for breach of the duty of good faith by an employer.

Many jurisdictions have adopted tests that are more expansive than that of Section 355. For example, in Suffolk Sports Center, Inc. v. Belli Construction Corp., 212 A.D.2d 241, 628 N.Y.S.2d 952 (1995), a landlord had barricaded the entrances to the tenant's leased sports facilities during a dispute concerning the lease. In approving punitive damages against the landlord, the court said that punitive damages were available where the breach evinces a " 'high degree of moral turpitude' or is 'actuated by evil and reprehensible motives,' and demonstrates 'such wanton dishonesty as to imply a criminal indifference to civil obligations.' " In Miller v. Byrne, 916 P.2d 566 (Colo.App. 1995), the court said that "Punitive damages are available ... when a plaintiff is able to prove beyond a reasonable doubt that the defendant engage in 'willful and wanton' misconduct. Willful and wanton conduct means conduct purposefully committed which the actor must have realized is dangerous, done heedlessly and recklessly, without regard to consequences, or of the rights and safety of others, particularly of the plaintiff."

In practice, punitive damages for breach of contract are not that uncommon. Marc Galanter analyzes data concerning contract litigation in his article, Contract in Court; Or Almost Everything You May or May Not Want to Know about Contract Litigation, 2001 Wis. L. Rev. 577. Among Galanter's sources is a Bureau of Justice Statistics study of contract litigation in 1992 in the seventy-five largest counties in the United States, which account for about one-third of the population. That study, Galanter reports, found that 12% of all winning plaintiffs in jury-tried contracts cases were awarded punitive damages (as compared to only 4% of winning plaintiffs in jury-tried tort cases). Even in judge-tried contracts cases, which outnumbered jury-tried cases by two to one, winning plaintiffs in contracts cases were awarded punitive damages 3.6% of the time.

———

Chapter 6

THE EXPECTATION MEASURE

Chapter 6 considers the basic principle of expectation damages, that is, the principle that upon breach of a bargain contract the injured party should be put in the position she would have been in if the contract had been performed. When that very general principle is applied to concrete, recurring kinds of cases, like breach of contracts for the sale of goods, much more specific rules are applied. The first few Sections of Chapter 6 examine some of these rules—specifically, the rules that apply to breach of a contract for services by the person who contracted to perform the services (Section 1(a)); breach of a contract for services by the person who contracted to have the services performed (Section 1(b)); breach of a contract for the sale of goods by the seller (Section 2(a)); breach of a contract for the sale of goods by the buyer (Section 2(b)); and breach of an employment contract by the employer (Section 3). The remaining the materials in Chapter 6 concern limits that the law sets on the principle of expectation damages. These include the innocent party's duty to mitigate (minimize) damages, the requirement that the damages that were incurred were reasonably foreseeable at the time of breach, and the certainty with which damages must be established. The last Section of Chapter 6 concerns the test for the enforceability of "liquidated damages" provisions, that is, contractual provisions in which the parties themselves set the damages for breach.

SECTION 1. DAMAGES FOR BREACH OF A CONTRACT TO PERFORM SERVICES

(a) Breach by the Person Who Has Contracted to Perform Services

LOUISE CAROLINE NURSING HOME, INC. v. DIX CONSTRUCTION CO.

Supreme Judicial Court of Massachusetts, 1972.
362 Mass. 306, 285 N.E.2d 904.

Before Tauro, C.J., and Reardon, Quirico, Braucher and Hennessey, JJ.

Quirico, Justice.

This is an action of contract in which Louise Caroline Nursing Home, Inc. (Nursing Home) seeks damages from Dix Construction Corp. (Dix) for breach of a contract to build a nursing home. . . .

The case was referred to an auditor for hearing pursuant to a stipulation of the parties that his findings of fact would be final. After hearing the parties, the auditor filed a report in which he found generally: (1) that the Nursing Home had fulfilled all of its contractual obligations to Dix; (2) that Dix had committed a breach of its contractual obligations to the Nursing Home by failing, without justification, to complete the contract within the time agreed. . . . However, he further found that the Nursing Home "suffered no compensable damages as a result of the breach by Dix . . . in that the cost to complete the nursing home . . . was within the contract price . . . less what had been paid to Dix. . . ." . . .

. . . Two of the Nursing Home's objections relate to the measure of the damages applied by the auditor in reaching his conclusion that it suffered no "compensable damages." The rule of damages applied by the auditor was that if the cost of completing the contract by the use of a substitute contractor is within the contract price, less what had already been paid on the contract, no "compensable damages" have occurred. The Nursing Home argues that the proper rule of damages would entitle it to the difference between the value of the building as left by Dix and the value it would have had if the contract had been fully performed. Under this rule the Nursing Home contends that it was entitled to the "benefits of its bargain," meaning that if the fair market value of the completed building would have exceeded the contractual cost of construction, recovery should be allowed for this lost extra value. It bases this argument primarily upon our statement in Province Sec. Corp. v. Maryland Cas. Co., 269 Mass. 75, 94, 168 N.E. 252, 257, that "[i]t is a settled rule that the measure of damages where a contractor has failed to perform a contract for the construction of a building for business uses is the difference between the value of the building as left by the contractor and its value had it been finished according to contract. In other words the question is how much less was the building worth than it would have been worth if the contract had been fully performed. Powell v. Howard, 109 Mass. 192. White v. McLaren, 151 Mass. 553, 24 N.E. 911. Norcross Brothers Co. v. Vose, 199 Mass. 81, 95, 96, 85 N.E. 468. Pelatowski v. Black, 213 Mass. 428, 100 N.E. 831." This statement was probably not necessary to the court's decision in the *Province Sec. Corp.* case and, in any event, must be read in light of the cases cited by the court in support of it. All of these cases involved failure of performance in the sense of defective performance, as contrasted with abandonment of performance. In one of the cases, Pelatowski v. Black, 213 Mass. 428, 431, 100 N.E. 831, 832, the court expressly distinguished "cases where a contractor has abandoned his work while yet unfinished."

The fundamental rule of damages applied in all contract cases was stated by this court in Ficara v. Belleau, 331 Mass. 80, 82, 117 N.E.2d 287, 289, in the following language: "It is not the policy of our law to award damages which would put a plaintiff in a better position than if the defendant had carried out his contract.... 'The fundamental principle upon which the rule of damages is based is compensation.... Compensation is the value of the performance of the contract, that is, what the plaintiff would have made had the contract been performed.' F.A. Bartlett Tree Expert Co. v. Hartney, 308 Mass. 407, 412, 32 N.E.2d 237, 240.... The plaintiff is entitled to be made whole and no more."

Consonant with this principle we have held that in assessing damages for failure to complete a construction contract, "[t]he measure of the plaintiffs' damages (at least in the absence of other elements of damage, as, for example, for delay in construction, which the master has not found here) can be only in the amount of the reasonable cost of completing the contract and repairing the defendant's defective performance less such part of the contract price as has not been paid." Di Mare v. Capaldi, 336 Mass. 497, 502, 146 N.E.2d 517, 521. This principle was recently reiterated in Providence Washington Ins. Co. v. Beck, 356 Mass. 739, 255 N.E.2d 600. In the face of this principle the Nursing Home's arguments attempting to demonstrate the amount of alleged "benefits of its bargain" lost are to no avail. In any event, it should be noted that any such "benefits of its bargain" as would derive from obtaining a building worth much more than the actual costs of construction are preserved if the building can be completed at a total cost which is still within the contract price, less any amount which has already been paid on the contract. The auditor was correct in applying the "cost of completion" measure of damages which excluded any separate recovery for lost "benefits of its bargain."

The Nursing Home additionally contends that even under the rule of damages applied by the auditor they were entitled, in the words of the *DiMare* case, *supra,* to recover "other elements of damage, as, for example, for delay in construction." 336 Mass. at 502, 146 N.E.2d at 521. The short answer to this contention is the auditor's express statement, in his summary of the evidence, that "[t]here was no specific evidence as to the costs of delay, if any." ...

... For the foregoing reasons the Nursing Home's exceptions to the denial of its motion to recommit the auditor's report and to the granting of Reliance's motion for entry of judgment in accordance with the auditor's report must be overruled.

Exceptions overruled.

HAWKINS v. McGEE

Chapter 5, supra

PEEVYHOUSE v. GARLAND COAL & MINING CO.

Supreme Court of Oklahoma, 1962.
382 P.2d 109, cert. denied, 375 U.S. 906, 84 S.Ct. 196, 11 L.Ed.2d 145 (1963).

Jackson, J. In the trial court, plaintiffs Willie and Lucille Peevyhouse sued the defendant, Garland Coal and Mining Company, for damages for breach of contract. Judgment was for plaintiffs in an amount considerably less than was sued for. Plaintiffs appeal and defendant cross-appeals.

In the briefs on appeal, the parties present their argument and contentions under several propositions; however, they all stem from the basic question of whether the trial court properly instructed the jury on the measure of damages.

Briefly stated, the facts are as follows: plaintiffs owned a farm containing coal deposits, and in November, 1954, leased the premises to defendant for a period of five years for coal mining purposes. A "strip-mining" operation was contemplated in which the coal would be taken from pits on the surface of the ground, instead of from underground mine shafts. In addition to the usual covenants found in a coal mining lease, defendant specifically agreed to perform certain restorative and remedial work at the end of the lease period. It is unnecessary to set out the details of the work to be done, other than to say that it would involve the moving of many thousands of cubic yards of dirt, at a cost estimated by expert witnesses at about $29,000.00. However, plaintiffs sued for only $25,000.00.

During the trial, it was stipulated that all covenants and agreements in the lease contract had been fully carried out by both parties, except the remedial work mentioned above; defendant conceded that this work had not been done.

Plaintiffs introduced expert testimony as to the amount and nature of the work to be done, and its estimated cost. Over plaintiffs' objections, defendant thereafter introduced expert testimony as to the "diminution in value" of plaintiffs' farm resulting from the failure of defendant to render performance as agreed in the contract—that is, the difference between the present value of the farm, and what its value would have been if defendant had done what it agreed to do.

At the conclusion of the trial, the court instructed the jury that it must return a verdict for plaintiffs, and left the amount of damages for jury determination. On the measure of damages, the court instructed the jury that it might consider the cost of performance of the work defendant agreed to do, "together with all of the evidence offered on behalf of either party".

It thus appears that the jury was at liberty to consider the "diminution in value" of plaintiffs' farm as well as the cost of "repair work" in determining the amount of damages.

It returned a verdict for plaintiffs for $5000.00—only a fraction of the "cost of performance", *but more than the total value of the farm even after the remedial work is done.*

On appeal, the issue is sharply drawn. Plaintiffs contend that the true measure of damages in this case is what it will cost plaintiffs to obtain performance of the work that was not done because of defendant's default.

Defendant argues that the measure of damages is the cost of performance "limited, however, to the total difference in the market value before and after the work was performed".

It appears that this precise question has not heretofore been presented to this court. In Ardizonne v. Archer, 72 Okl. 70, 178 P. 263, this court held that the measure of damages for breach of a contract to drill an oil well was the reasonable cost of drilling the well, but here a slightly different factual situation exists. The drilling of an oil well will yield valuable geological information, even if no oil or gas is found, and of course if the well is a producer, the value of the premises increases. In the case before us, it is argued by defendant with some force that the performance of the remedial work defendant agreed to do will add at the most only a few hundred dollars to the value of plaintiffs' farm, and that the damages should be limited to that amount because that is all plaintiffs have lost.

Plaintiffs rely on Groves v. John Wunder Co., 205 Minn. 163, 286 N.W. 235, 123 A.L.R. 502. In that case, the Minnesota court, in a substantially similar situation, adopted the "cost of performance" rule as opposed to the "value" rule. The result was to authorize a jury to give plaintiff damages in the amount of $60,000, where the real estate concerned would have been worth only $12,160, even if the work contracted for had been done.

It may be observed that Groves v. John Wunder Co., supra, is the only case which has come to our attention in which the cost of performance rule has been followed under circumstances where the cost of performance greatly exceeded the diminution in value resulting from the breach of contract. Incidentally, it appears that this case was decided by a plurality rather than a majority of the members of the court.

Defendant relies principally upon Sandy Valley & E.R. Co. v. Hughes, 175 Ky. 320, 194 S.W. 344; Bigham v. Wabash–Pittsburg Terminal Ry. Co., 223 Pa. 106, 72 A. 318; and Sweeney v. Lewis Const. Co., 66 Wash. 490, 119 P. 1108. These were all cases in which, under similar circumstances, the appellate courts followed the "value" rule instead of the "cost of performance" rule. Plaintiff points out that in the earliest of these cases (Bigham) the court cites as authority on the measure of damages an earlier Pennsylvania *tort* case, and that the other two cases follow the first, with no explanation as to why a measure of damages ordinarily followed in cases sounding in tort should be used in contract cases. Nevertheless, it is of some significance that three out of four appellate courts have followed the diminution in value rule under circumstances where, as here, the cost of performance greatly exceeds the diminution in value.

The explanation may be found in the fact that the situations presented are artificial ones. It is highly unlikely that the ordinary property owner would agree to pay $29,000 (or its equivalent) for the construction of "improvements" upon his property that would increase its value only about ($300) three hundred dollars. The result is that we are called upon to apply principles of law theoretically based upon reason and reality to a situation which is basically unreasonable and unrealistic.

In Groves v. John Wunder Co., supra, in arriving at its conclusions, the Minnesota court apparently considered the contract involved to be analogous to a building and construction contract, and cited authority for the proposition that the cost of performance or completion of the building as contracted is ordinarily the measure of damages in actions for damages for the breach of such a contract.

In an annotation following the Minnesota case beginning at 123 A.L.R. 515, the annotator places the three cases relied on by defendant (Sandy Valley, Bigham and Sweeney) under the classification of cases involving "grading and excavation contracts".

We do not think either analogy is strictly applicable to the case now before us. The primary purpose of the lease contract between plaintiffs and defendant was neither "building and construction" nor "grading and excavation". It was merely to accomplish the economical recovery and marketing of coal from the premises, to the profit of all parties. The special provisions of the lease contract pertaining to remedial work were incidental to the main object involved.

Even in the case of contracts that are unquestionably building and construction contracts, the authorities are not in agreement as to the factors to be considered in determining whether the cost of performance rule or the value rule should be applied. The American Law Institute's Restatement of the Law, Contracts, Volume 1, Sections 346(1)(a)(i) and (ii) submits the proposition that the cost of performance is the proper measure of damages "if this is possible and does not involve *unreasonable economic waste*"; and that the diminution in value caused by the breach is the proper measure "if construction and completion in accordance with the contract would involve *unreasonable economic waste*". (Emphasis supplied.) In an explanatory comment immediately following the text, the Restatement makes it clear that the "economic waste" referred to consists of the destruction of a substantially completed building or other structure. Of course no such destruction is involved in the case now before us.

On the other hand, in McCormick, Damages, Section 168, it is said with regard to building and construction contracts that ". . . in cases where the defect is one that can be repaired or cured without *undue expense* "the cost of performance is the proper measure of damages, but where" . . . the defect in material or construction is one that cannot be remedied without *an expenditure for reconstruction disproportionate to the end to be attained* "(emphasis supplied) the value rule should be followed. The same idea was expressed in Jacob & Youngs, Inc. v. Kent, 230 N.Y. 239, 129 N.E. 889, 23 A.L.R. 1429, as follows:

"The owner is entitled to the money which will permit him to complete, unless the cost of completion is grossly and unfairly out of proportion to the good to be attained. When that is true, the measure is the difference in value."

It thus appears that the prime consideration in the Restatement was "economic waste"; and that the prime consideration in McCormick, Damages, and in Jacob & Youngs, Inc. v. Kent, supra, was the relationship between the expense involved and the "end to be attained"—in other words, the "relative economic benefit".

In view of the unrealistic fact situation in the instant case, and certain Oklahoma statutes to be hereinafter noted, we are of the opinion that the "relative economic benefit" is a proper consideration here. This is in accord with the recent case of Mann v. Clowser, 190 Va. 887, 59 S.E.2d 78, where, in applying the cost rule, the Virginia court specifically noted that " ... the defects are remediable from a practical standpoint and the costs *are not grossly disproportionate to the results to be obtained*" (Emphasis supplied).

23 O.S.1961 §§ 96 and 97 provide as follows:

> "§ 96. . . . Notwithstanding the provisions of this chapter, no person can recover a greater amount in damages for the breach of an obligation, than he would have gained by the full performance thereof on both sides. . . .

> "§ 97. . . . Damages must, in all cases, be reasonable, and where an obligation of any kind appears to create a right to unconscionable and grossly oppressive damages, contrary to substantial justice no more than reasonable damages can be recovered."

Although it is true that the above sections of the statute are applied most often in tort cases, they are by their own terms, and the decisions of this court, also applicable in actions for damages for breach of contract. It would seem that they are peculiarly applicable here where, under the "cost of performance" rule, plaintiffs might recover an amount about nine times the total value of their farm. Such would seem to be "unconscionable and grossly oppressive damages, contrary to substantial justice" within the meaning of the statute. Also, it can hardly be denied that if plaintiffs here are permitted to recover under the "cost of performance" rule, they will receive a greater benefit from the breach than could be gained from full performance, contrary to the provisions of Sec. 96.

An analogy may be drawn between the cited sections, and the provisions of 15 O.S.1961 §§ 214 and 215. These sections tend to render void any provisions of a contract which attempt to fix the amount of stipulated damages to be paid in case of a breach, except where it is impracticable or extremely difficult to determine the actual damages. This results in spite of the agreement of the parties, and the obvious and well known rationale is that insofar as they exceed the actual damages suffered, the stipulated damages amount to a penalty or forfeiture which the law does not favor.

23 O.S.1961 §§ 96 and 97 have the same effect in the case now before us. *In spite of the agreement of the parties,* these sections limit the damages recoverable to a reasonable amount not "contrary to substantial justice"; they prevent plaintiffs from recovering a "greater amount in damages for the breach of an obligation" than they would have "gained by the full performance thereof".

We therefore hold that where, in a coal mining lease, lessee agrees to perform certain remedial work on the premises concerned at the end of the lease period, and thereafter the contract is fully performed by both parties except that the remedial work is not done, the measure of damages in an action by lessor against lessee for damages for breach of contract is ordinarily the reasonable cost of performance of the work; however, where the contract provision breached was merely incidental to the main purpose in view, and where the economic benefit which would result to lessor by full performance of the work is grossly disproportionate to the cost of performance, the damages which lessor may recover are limited to the diminution in value resulting to the premises because of the non-performance.

We believe the above holding is in conformity with the intention of the Legislature as expressed in the statutes mentioned, and in harmony with the better-reasoned cases from the other jurisdictions where analogous fact situations have been considered. It should be noted that the rule as stated does not interfere with the property owner's right to "do what he will with his own" (Chamberlain v. Parker, 45 N.Y. 569), or his right, if he chooses, to contract for "improvements" which will actually have the effect of reducing his property's value. Where such result is in fact contemplated by the parties, and is a main or principal purpose of those contracting, it would seem that the measure of damages for breach would ordinarily be the cost of performance.

The above holding disposes of all of the arguments raised by the parties on appeal.

Under the most liberal view of the evidence herein, the diminution in value resulting to the premises because of nonperformance of the remedial work was $300.00. After a careful search of the record, we have found no evidence of a higher figure, and plaintiffs do not argue in their briefs that a greater diminution in value was sustained. It thus appears that the judgment was clearly excessive, and that the amount for which judgment should have been rendered is definitely and satisfactorily shown by the record.

We are asked by each party to modify the judgment in accordance with the respective theories advanced, and it is conceded that we have authority to do so. 12 O.S.1961 § 952; Busboom v. Smith, 199 Okl. 688, 191 P.2d 198; Stumpf v. Stumpf, 173 Okl. 1, 46 P.2d 315.

We are of the opinion that the judgment of the trial court for plaintiffs should be, and it is hereby, modified and reduced to the sum of $300.00, and as so modified it is affirmed.

WELCH, DAVISON, HALLEY, and JOHNSON, JJ., concur.

WILLIAMS, C.J., BLACKBIRD, V.C.J., and IRWIN and BERRY, JJ., dissent.

IRWIN, JUSTICE (dissenting).

By the specific provisions in the coal mining lease under consideration, the defendant agreed as follows:

"... 7b Lessee agrees to make fills in the pits dug on said premises on the property line in such manner that fences can be placed thereon and access had to opposite sides of the pits.

"[7]c Lessee agrees to smooth off the top of the spoil banks on the above premises.

"7d Lessee agrees to leave the creek crossing the above premises in such a condition that it will not interfere with the crossings to be made in pits as set out in 7b.

. . .

"7f Lessee further agrees to leave no shale or dirt on the high wall of said pits. . . ."

Following the expiration of the lease, plaintiffs made demand upon defendant that it carry out the provisions of the contract and to perform those covenants contained therein.

Defendant admits that it failed to perform its obligations that it agreed and contracted to perform under the lease contract and there is nothing in the record which indicates that defendant could not perform its obligations. Therefore, in my opinion defendant's breach of the contract was wilful and not in good faith.

Although the contract speaks for itself, there were several negotiations between the plaintiffs and defendant before the contract was executed. Defendant admitted in the trial of the action, that plaintiffs insisted that the above provisions be included in the contract and that they would not agree to the coal mining lease unless the above provisions were included.

In consideration for the lease contract, plaintiffs were to receive a certain amount as royalty for the coal produced and marketed and in addition thereto their land was to be restored as provided in the contract.

Defendant received as consideration for the contract, its proportionate share of the coal produced and marketed and in addition thereto, the *right to use* plaintiffs' land in the furtherance of its mining operations.

The cost for performing the contract in question could have been reasonably approximated when the contract was negotiated and executed and there are no conditions now existing which could not have been reasonably anticipated by the parties. Therefore, defendant had knowledge, when it prevailed upon the plaintiffs to execute the lease, that the cost of performance might be disproportionate to the value or benefits received by plaintiff for the performance.

Defendant has received its benefits under the contract and now urges, in substance, that plaintiffs' measure of damages for its failure to perform should be the economic value of performance to the plaintiffs and not the cost of performance.

If a peculiar set of facts should exist where the above rule should be applied as the proper measure of damages, (and in my judgment those facts do not exist in the instant case) before such rule should be applied, consideration should be given to the benefits received or contracted for by the party who asserts the application of the rule.

Defendant did not have the right to mine plaintiffs' coal or to use plaintiffs' property for its mining operations without the consent of plaintiffs. Defendant had knowledge of the benefits that it would receive under the contract and the approximate cost of performing the contract. With this knowledge, it must be presumed that defendant thought that it would be to its economic advantage to enter into the contract with plaintiffs and that it would reap benefits from the contract, or it would have not entered into the contract.

Therefore, if the value of the performance of a contract should be considered in determining the measure of damages for breach of a contract, the value of the benefits received under the contract by a party who breaches a contract should also be considered. However, in my judgment, to give consideration to either in the instant action, completely rescinds and holds for naught the solemnity of the contract before us and makes an entirely new contract for the parties. . . .

In Great Western Oil & Gas Company v. Mitchell, Okl., 326 P.2d 794, we held:

"The law will not make a better contract for parties than they themselves have seen fit to enter into, or alter it for the benefit of one party and to the detriment of the others; the judicial function of a court of law is to enforce a contract as it is written."

I am mindful of Title 23 O.S.1961 § 96, which provides that no person can recover a greater amount in damages for the breach of an obligation than he could have gained by the full performance thereof on both sides, except in cases not applicable herein. However, in my judgment, the above statutory provision is not applicable here.

In my judgment, we should follow the case of Groves v. John Wunder Company, 205 Minn. 163, 286 N.W. 235, 123 A.L.R. 502, which defendant agrees "that the fact situation is apparently similar to the one in the case at bar", and where the Supreme Court of Minnesota held:

"The owner's or employer's damages for such a breach (i.e. breach hypothesized in 2d syllabus) are to be measured, not in respect to the value of the land to be improved, but by the reasonable cost of doing that which the contractor promised to do and which he left undone."

The hypothesized breach referred to states that where the contractor's breach of a contract is wilful, that is in bad faith, he is not entitled to any benefit of the equitable doctrine of substantial performance.

In the instant action defendant has made no attempt to even substantially perform. The contract in question is not immoral, is not tainted with fraud, and was not entered into through mistake or accident and is not contrary to public policy. It is clear and unambiguous and the parties understood the terms thereof, and the approximate cost of fulfilling the obligations could have been approximately ascertained. There are no conditions existing now which could not have been reasonably anticipated when the contract was negotiated and executed. The defendant could have performed the contract if it desired. It has accepted and reaped the benefits of its contract and now urges that plaintiffs' benefits under the contract be denied. If plaintiffs' benefits are denied, such benefits would inure to the direct benefit of the defendant.

Therefore, in my opinion, the plaintiffs were entitled to specific performance of the contract and since defendant has failed to perform, the proper measure of damages should be the cost of performance. Any other measure of damage would be holding for naught the express provisions of the contract; would be taking from the plaintiffs the benefits of the contract and placing those benefits in defendant which has failed to perform its obligations; would be granting benefits to defendant without a resulting obligation; and would be completely rescinding the solemn obligation of the contract for the benefit of the defendant to the detriment of the plaintiffs by making an entirely new contract for the parties.

I therefore respectfully dissent to the opinion promulgated by a majority of my associates.

———

NOTE

In a petition for rehearing, plaintiffs argued that the trial court had wrongfully excluded evidence they presented to show that the diminution in the value of their farm was greater than $300 because the farm consisted not merely of the 60 acres covered by the coal-mining lease, but other lands as well. The court held, 5–4, that the evidence was properly excluded because the complaint related only to the 60 acres covered by the lease and the case had been tried and argued by plaintiffs on a cost-of-performance rather than a diminished-value theory.

RESTATEMENT, SECOND, OF CONTRACTS § 348(2)

[See Selected Source Materials Supplement]

NOTE ON ADDITIONAL FACTS IN PEEVYHOUSE

1. The following excerpt from defendant's brief in *Peevyhouse* (as brought out by Professor Richard Danzig in unpublished materials) proposes an explanation why Garland, the defendant-appellee, did not perform the remedial work:

A review of the testimony of the witness, G.B. Cumpton, will indicate that the defendant, at time of execution of the contract, had [a] good faith intention of complying with all of the terms; but, after partial performance, it became apparent that the amount of coal under the leased property was limited; and the operations were not extended far enough toward the southeastward to permit economic compliance with the terms of the lease requiring remedial work.

Attention of the court is specifically invited to the following excerpt from the testimony of Mr. Cumpton: . . .

"Q. Now then, you were asked also by Mr. McConnell if when you executed this lease you intended to comply with the provisions for installing a fence. And I will ask you if you had been able economically to mine further coal toward the southeast, would you have been able to establish that fence on the spoil bank?

"A. Yes, we could have.

"Q. Having stopped when you ran out of coal down in here, can you now establish that fence line without putting in a very useless and expensive fill?

"A. No. . . ."

From all the testimony of Mr. Cumpton and the engineer, Curry, it is obvious that the Appellee, at the inception of the contract, intended to comply with the terms; but, after it became economically impossible to complete performance of mining operations across the entire tract of land, construction of dikes for erection of fences became impracticable. Appellee went as far with performance of the remedial work as could reasonably be expected under the circumstances, without futile expenditure of money which would accomplish no constructive purpose.

It is respectfully submitted that Appellee did not willfully, or in bad faith, enter into a contract which it did not intend to perform.

2. In Peevyhouse v. Garland Coal & Mining Co. Revisited: The Ballad of Willie and Lucille, 89 Nw.U.L.Rev. 1341 (1995), Professor Judith Maute reports that the Peevyhouses were reluctant to allow mining on their land, while Garland needed immediate access to the land to divert a creek from a neighboring piece of land that it was already mining. Thus the Peevyhouses seem to have had a relatively strong bargaining position. What they negotiated for was Garland's promise to do the restorative work on their land. The standard strip-mining lease used in the area did not contain provisions for restorative work. Instead, lessors typically received an up-front per-acre payment to compensate them for the damage that would be done to their land in the course of the mining. This amount would usually equal the total value of the land before mining began. The Peevyhouses were aware of this standard provision, and they had seen the damage done to their neighbors' land over the years. The Peevyhouses gave up the standard advance payment for surface damage, which in their case would have been $3,000, in return for Garland's promise to do certain restorative work on their land.

Maute questions Garland's claim that because the coal on the Peevyhouse's land was less accessible than Garland expected, the promised restoration was much more costly to implement than Garland had anticipated.

EASTERN STEAMSHIP LINES, INC. v. UNITED STATES, 125 Ct.Cl. 422, 112 F.Supp. 167 (1953). The United States Government chartered the steamship *Acadia* as a troop transport during World War II. The charter provided:

> Clause 7.... Before redelivery, the Charterer [that is, the Government], at its own expense, and on its time, shall restore the Vessel to at least as good condition and class as upon delivery, ordinary wear and tear excepted, and do all work and make all repairs necessary to satisfy any outstanding classification or steamboat inspection requirements necessary to place her in such condition and class.... [provided] that at the Charterer's option, redelivery of the Vessel to the Owner may be made prior to satisfying such requirements or prior to completion of such repairs or work, in which event the Charterer shall pay to the Owner the amount reasonably expended to place the Vessel in such class and condition....

After the war, the owner sued the government for $4,000,000, which the owner claimed to be due under Clause 7 of the charter as the estimated cost of restoring the *Acadia* to its pre-war condition. The Government claimed that it was not bound to pay more than $2,000,000, the estimated value of the ship after restoration, and that it was not bound to pay anything until the ship was restored. The court rejected the owner's claim:

[We will assume, based on the evidence] that after some $4,000,000 had been spent in restoring the ship, it would be worth $2,000,000. . . .

. . . According to the plaintiff's interpretation [of the charter] the Government has now become obligated to pay it $4,000,000. Candor compels the plaintiff to say that it will not feel obliged to spend the $4,000,000 when it gets it, to restore the *Acadia*. Common sense and reality tell us that it will not so spend the money, since after the expenditures it would have only a $2,000,000 ship. The result would be that the Government would pay out $2,000,000 more than the plaintiff had lost by the Government's chartering and use of its ship. The extra $2,000,000 would not be a subsidy to get ships built or sailing. The *Acadia* would still rust at anchor. We decline to . . . produce such a result.

. . . We think that neither party anticipated what actually happened, *viz.* that the market for old ships on the one hand, and the market for labor and materials, on the other, would be such as to make the restoration of old ships a useless and wasteful expenditure of public funds. . . .

The plaintiff has urged that, regardless of the waste of public money that would be entailed by compelling the Government to pay $4,000,000 when the plaintiff's loss is $2,000,000 the weight of authority is that what is "nominated in the bond" will be compelled, regardless of economic waste. We think that is not the law. . . .

. . . The case will be assigned to a commissioner of this court for trial upon the question of the value of the *Acadia*.

CITY SCHOOL DISTRICT OF THE CITY OF ELMIRA v. McLANE CONSTRUCTION CO., 85 A.D.2d 749, 445 N.Y.S.2d 258 (1981). In 1976, the Elmira school district contracted with McLane Construction Company for the construction of a swimming-pool building, which was to feature a roof consisting of natural-wood decking supported by laminated-wood beams. The appearance of the beams was central to the aesthetics of the architectural scheme, which contrasted the natural beauty of the beams with the relatively stark unfinished concrete that comprised the balance of the structure. Even the effectiveness of the indirect lighting system employed in the building depended on the beams. As the building was to be a showplace, and the site of large regional swimming competitions, the design was intentionally dramatic. It was contemplated that the beams, properly treated, would be essentially maintenance-free. However, Weyerhauser Company, which supplied the beams, and was aware of the plans and specifications, used a method of treating the beams that it knew would result in staining and discoloration, and the beams became permanently discolored.

The school district recovered a verdict of $357,000 against Weyerhauser, based on the cost of replacing the beams. On appeal, Weyerhauser argued that damages should have been limited to $3,000, the difference between the value of the structure as built and its value if the beams had been as agreed-upon. Held, for the school district.

"[W]here the contractor's performance has been incomplete or defective, the usual measure of damages is the reasonable cost of replacement or completion (*American Std. v. Schectman*, 80 A.D.2d 318, 321, 439 N.Y.S.2d 529). That rule does not apply if the contractor performs in good faith but defects nevertheless exist and remedying them could entail economic waste. Then, diminution in value becomes the proper measure of damages. A classic illustration of when the general rule is abandoned in favor of this exception is *Jacob & Youngs v. Kent*, 230 N.Y. 239, 129 N.E. 889, where the contractor did not use the brand of pipe specified in the contract, but other brands of like quality. Inasmuch as the cost of replacing the pipe was grievously out of proportion to any damages actually suffered by the house owner, the proper award was the nominal difference in value of the house with and without the specified brand of pipe.

"But Weyerhaeuser does not come within this exception, for here the defect, in relation to the entire project, was not of inappreciable importance. One of the school district's principal objectives was to have an aesthetically prepossessing structure, and that goal has by all accounts been frustrated. Moreover, as the facts already recited indicate, Weyerhaeuser's conduct cannot be said to be innocent oversight or inattention...."

————

ADVANCED, INC. v. WILKS, 711 P.2d 524 (Alaska 1985). "An owner's recovery is not necessarily limited to diminution in value whenever that figure is less than the cost of repair. It is true that in a case where the cost of repair exceeds the damages under the value formula, an award under the cost of repair measure may place the owner in a better economic position than if the contract had been fully performed, since he could pocket the award and then sell the defective structure. On the other hand, it is possible that the owner will use the damage award for its intended purpose and turn the structure into the one originally envisioned. He may do this for a number of reasons, including personal esthetics or a hope for increased value in the future. If he does this his economic position will equal the one he would have been in had the contractor fully performed. The fact finder is the one in the best position to determine whether the owner will actually complete performance, or whether he is only interested in obtaining the best immediate economic position he can. In some cases, such as where the property is held solely for investment, the court may conclude as a matter of law that the damage award can not exceed the diminution in value. Where, however, the property has special significance to the owner and repair seems likely, the cost of repair may be appropriate even if it exceeds the diminution in value."

————

(b) Breach by a Person Who Has Contracted to Have Services Performed

AIELLO CONSTRUCTION, INC. v. NATIONWIDE TRACTOR TRAILER TRAINING AND PLACEMENT CORP.

Supreme Court of Rhode Island, 1980.
122 R.I. 861, 413 A.2d 85.

Opinion

WEISBERGER, JUSTICE.

This case comes before us on appeal from a judgment of the Superior Court which awarded damages to the plaintiffs for a breach of contract allegedly committed by the defendant when it failed to make certain installment payments required by the contract. The case was tried by a justice sitting without the intervention of a jury. The facts as found in his decision are as follows.

The plaintiffs, Aiello Construction, Inc., and Smithfield Peat Co., Inc., as joint venturers, entered into a written contract with defendant in March of 1973. The contract required plaintiffs to haul fill and perform grading work in order to bring a large area owned by defendant to an approximately level condition. The contract further provided that plaintiffs would remove ledge on a portion of the premises, grade eight inches of bank run gravel over the entire yard, grade two inches of crushed run gravel over the entire yard, and finally apply penetration and seal coats of oil topped by application of peastone. The surface was then to be rolled. The defendant was in the trucking business and also engaged in the training and instruction of tractor-trailer operators. The yard area was to be used in the operation of this training enterprise.

In payment for the work to be performed and the material to be furnished, defendant agreed to pay $33,000 in five monthly installments of $6,600 each. The installments were to become due on April 15, May 15, June 15, July 15, and August 15, all during the year 1973. The contract provided that any amount not paid would bear a service charge of 1½ percent per month.

The plaintiffs began work in late March 1973 and continued the work until on or about May 10, 1973, at which time all of the preliminary work had been done save applying and grading the two inches of crushed run gravel, which was a prerequisite to the performance of the oiling. The plaintiffs then stopped work to allow the ground to settle. Meanwhile, defendant paid the monthly installment that was due on April 15. Thereafter, defendant did not pay the May installment, although over a period from June to August of 1973 it did make partial payments which, when added to the April installment, aggregated $10,500. No further payments were made, and the president of the defendant company indicated that funds were not available to make the payments that were due. As a result of the failure to make payments, plaintiffs did not resume work. The plaintiffs brought the instant action for breach of contract....

The trial justice found as a fact that defendant was in breach of the contract and that this breach relieved plaintiffs of the obligation to perform any further work under the contract.... The trial justice awarded damages for the breach of contract by calculating the costs which plaintiffs had incurred in the performance of the work up to the time they withdrew from the project as a result of the breach. He found that the costs amounted to $21,500. To this sum he added $3,000 which he determined from the testimony to be the profit which plaintiffs would have made had the contract been completely performed by both parties. From the sum of $24,500 the trial justice deducted the payments made by defendant in the amount of $10,500. He ordered judgment to enter for plaintiffs in the amount of $14,000 together with interest at the rate of 8 percent per annum from the time of filing of the complaint to the date of judgment.... Thus judgment was entered for the plaintiffs for $16,800. This appeal ensued....

The defendant argues that the trial justice did not correctly assess damages. He cites in support of his argument *George v. George F. Berkander, Inc.*, 92 R.I. 426, 169 A.2d 370 (1961). In that case the rule of damages for breach of contract was stated to be such "as will serve to put the injured party as close as is reasonably possible to the position he would have been in had the contract been fully performed." *Id.* at 430, 169 A.2d at 372. It is precisely this rule that the trial justice attempted to apply. Although the measure of damages may be variously stated under the principle of our holding in *Berkander,* certain alternatives are well set forth in Restatement *Contracts* § 346(2) as follows:

> "For a breach by one who has promised to pay for construction, if it is a partial breach the builder can get judgment for the instalment due, with interest; and if it is a total breach he can get judgment, with interest so far as permitted by the rules stated in § 337, for either
>
> "(a) the entire contract price ... less installments already paid and the cost of completion that the builder can reasonably save by not completing the work; or
>
> "(b) the amount of his expenditure in part [pe]rformance of the contract, subject to the limitations stated in § 333."[1]

The general rules set forth in the Restatement are further elucidated by the commentary. A portion of the comment on subsection (2) of Restatement § 346 reads as follows:

> "*h.* Another common form of stating the measure of recovery is as follows: Damages, measured by the builder's actual expenditure to date of breach less the value of materials on hand, plus the profit that he can prove with reasonable certainty would have been realized from full performance. * * * The builder has a right to his expenditures as well as his profits, because payment of the full price would have reimbursed those expenditures in full and given him his profit in addition * * *."

An examination of the record in this case discloses that the trial justice scrupulously followed this method of assessment of damages, that his findings

---

1. Restatement *Contracts* § 333 (1932) reads in part as follows:

"(a) Such expenditures are not recoverable in excess of the full contract price promised by the defendant.

"(b) Expenditures in preparation are not recoverable unless they can fairly be regarded as part of the cost of performance in estimating profit and loss.

"(c) Instalments of the contract price already received and the value of materials on hand that would have been consumed in completion must be deducted.

"(d) If full performance would have resulted in a net loss to the plaintiff, the amount of this loss must be deducted, the burden of proof being on the defendant."

of fact were amply supported by the evidence, and that he did not overlook or misconceive the evidence in arriving at his conclusion.... [A] court must select the most appropriate remedy depending upon the factual posture of the case and the election of remedy by the plaintiff. The remedy selected by the trial justice in this case was appropriately relevant to the factual posture and the remedy sought by plaintiffs. Therefore, the trial justice cannot be faulted for his assessment of damages either in regard to the law or to the facts....

For the reasons stated, the defendant's appeal is denied and dismissed, the judgment of the Superior Court is affirmed, and the case is remitted to the Superior Court.

DORIS, J., did not participate.

NOTE ON FORMULAS FOR MEASURING DAMAGES FOR BREACH BY A PERSON WHO HAS CONTRACTED TO HAVE SERVICES PERFORMED

Call a person who agrees to perform services a Contractor, and call the person for whom the services are to be performed the Owner. The trial court in *Aiello* measured the Contractor's damages for breach by the Owner under the following formula: (i) expenditures incurred prior to breach, plus (ii) lost profits, offset by (iii) the amount paid by the Owner prior to the breach. As the Rhode Island Supreme Court pointed out, this formula is reflected in Comment h to Restatement First § 346.

The Supreme Court also pointed out that a different (and algebraically equivalent) formula is reflected in the black letter of § 346: (i) contract price, less (ii) the cost of completion that the builder saved by not completing the work, offset by (iii) the amount paid by the Owner prior to the breach.

Although the two formulas are algebraically equivalent, the second formula is the one that is usually employed. Under the first formula, the court must determine lost profits. Since profits equal contract price minus costs (by definition), to apply the first formula the court must calculate (i) all the costs the Contractor incurred prior to breach and (ii) all the costs remaining to be incurred at that point. In contrast, to apply the second formula the court need only calculate the costs remaining to be incurred at the time of breach.

For a demonstration that the two measures are equivalent, see Petropoulos v. Lubienski, 220 Md. 293, 152 A.2d 801, 804–05 (1959).

Although § 346 and Comment h are in terms limited to construction contracts, the formulas they embody are generally applicable to the breach of any contract for the performance of services.

RESTATEMENT, SECOND, CONTRACTS § 347, Illustrations 6, 7: "6. A contracts to build a house for B for $100,000. When it is partly built, B repudiates the contract and A stops work. A would have to spend $60,000 more to finish the house. The $60,000 cost avoided by A as a result of not having to finish the house is subtracted from the $100,000 price lost in determining A's damages. A has a right to $40,000 in damages from B, less any progress payments that he has already received.

"7. The facts being otherwise as stated in Illustration 6, A has bought materials that are left over and that he can use for other purposes, saving him $5,000. The $5,000 cost avoided is subtracted in determining A's damages, resulting in damages of only $35,000 rather than $40,000."

SECTION 2.   DAMAGES FOR BREACH OF A CONTRACT FOR THE SALE OF GOODS

(a) Breach by the Seller

NOTE ON DAMAGES FOR THE SELLER'S BREACH OF A CONTRACT FOR THE SALE OF GOODS

The remedies for breach of a contract for the sale of goods are governed by the Uniform Commercial Code. A buyer's remedies for breach by the seller fall into two broad categories—specific relief (in which the buyer is awarded the actual goods) and damages. Specific relief will be covered in Chapter 7, infra.

The buyer's damage remedies, in turn, fall into several subcategories. One subcategory consists of the buyer's remedies when the seller fails to deliver or the buyer properly rejects the goods or rightfully revokes his acceptance (UCC §§ 2–712, 2–713). A second subcategory consists of the buyer's remedies when the buyer has accepted the goods, and cannot or does not want to rightfully revoke his acceptance, but the goods are defective (UCC § 2–714). Typically, such an action is for breach of warranty.

UCC §§ 2–711(1), 2–712, 2–713, 2–714, 2–715(1), 2–723, 2–724

[See Selected Source Materials Supplement]

CISG ARTS. 45, 49, 50, 74, 75, 76

[See Selected Source Materials Supplement]

CONTINENTAL SAND & GRAVEL, INC. v. K & K SAND & GRAVEL, INC., 755 F.2d 87 (7th Cir.1985). Defendant sold buyer certain mobile equipment (front-loaders, cranes, and so forth) for $50,000, and made various express warranties concerning the equipment. The warranties were breached, and plaintiff sued for damages. The trial court awarded $104,206.75, the cost of repairs to bring the equipment up to the warranted condition. Affirmed.

"Defendants argue that, since the clear bargain of the parties was to sell and purchase the mobile equipment for $50,000, the plaintiff is only entitled to receive an amount of damages that represents the diminution in value from the purchase price as the result of the breach of warranty. In other words, defendants contend that the maximum amount of recoverable damages is the difference between the fair market value of the equipment as accepted, which they define as $50,000, and the fair market value of the equipment in the defective condition. Under this method of computing damages, Continental would be entitled to recover no more than the $50,000 purchase price, and as little as nothing, depending on the court's assessment of the value of the equipment in the defective condition. . . .

"The court below rejected this argument, and instead applied section 2–714(2) of the Illinois Uniform Commercial Code, . . . which provides that damages generally should represent the difference between the value of the goods at the time of acceptance and the value they would have had if they had been as warranted. The court stated that under this section the cost of repair is the proper standard. This was the correct approach under Illinois law, as well as under the general commercial law. . . . As the district court noted, it is not unusual for damages in a breach of warranty case to exceed the purchase price of the goods. . . . This result is logical, since to limit recoverable damages by the purchase price, as defendants suggest, would clearly deprive the purchaser of the benefit of its bargain in cases in which the value of the goods as warranted exceeds that price. Thus we find that the district court properly computed the damages recoverable for the defendants' breach of the warranties."

MANOUCHEHRI v. HEIM, 123 N.M. 439, 941 P.2d 978 (N.M. Ct. App. 1997). "Although [U.C.C. §] 2–714(2) sets the measure of direct damages for breach of warranty as the difference between the value of the goods as warranted and the value of the goods as accepted, often that difference can be approximated by the cost to repair the goods so that they conform to the warranty. For example, if it costs $200 to fix [a] machine so that it performed as [warranted,] then one could assume that the unrepaired machine (the 'goods accepted') was worth $200 less than the repaired machine (the goods 'as warranted'). Thus, the cost of repair is commonly awarded as the direct damages."

EGERER v. CSR WEST, LLC

Court of Appeals of Washington, 2003.
116 Wash.App. 645, 67 P.3d 1128.

BECKER, C.J.

Appellant CSR West breached a contract to supply fill for land development. Issues on appeal include the calculation of damages based on "hypothetical cover". . . . We affirm in all respects.

According to unchallenged findings of fact entered after a bench trial, Robert Egerer owned a 10 acre parcel of land in Skagit County that he planned to develop into commercial property. The property required a considerable amount of fill to make it suitable for development.

Egerer first purchased fill material in 1995, when he contracted at the rate of $1.10 per cubic yard to have Wilder Construction haul to his property some material being excavated from the shoulders of Interstate 5 as a part of a highway improvement project. In its suitability to serve as structural fill, the shoulder material resembled a gravel known as "pit run", but it was cheaper than pit run because it contained asphalt grindings.

Beyond what Wilder Construction could supply, Egerer needed roughly 17,000 cubic yards of fill material. In May 1997, Egerer learned that CSR West had contracted with the Washington State Department of Transportation to excavate material from the shoulder areas of Interstate 5 near Lake Samish. He met with John Grisham, CSR's sales manager, and they reached an agreement to have CSR transport "all" the shoulder excavations from the project to Egerer's site at the rate of $.50 per cubic yard.

CSR brought fill material to Egerer's property on only two nights: July 9 and 10, 1997. Shortly thereafter, the Department of Transportation issued a change order that allowed CSR to use the excavated shoulder material in the reconstruction of the shoulder area. It was more profitable for CSR to supply the material for the State's use than to fulfill its contract with Egerer. CSR excavated a total of 16,750 cubic yards of material during its work on the shoulder project in 1997, and supplied virtually all of it to the Department of Transportation.

Egerer did not purchase replacement fill at the time of the breach in July 1997. Asked about this at trial, he explained that it would have been too expensive, and he also did not think there was time to find replacement fill and get it onto his property before the end of the summer. Egerer said that his window of opportunity to place fill on the property was June through September, before the weather became too wet. In January and February 1998, he obtained price quotes for pit run ranging from $8.25 per cubic yard to $9.00 per cubic yard. These prices exceeded Egerer's budget, and he did not contract for replacement fill at that time either.

In the summer of 1999, Egerer learned of an unexpected landslide at a gravel pit not far from his property. The company agreed to sell Egerer the unwanted slide material at a cost of $6.39 per cubic yard, including the cost of hauling and spreading.

Egerer filed suit in November 2000, alleging that CSR breached its contract by failing to deliver all the excavated shoulder material in the summer of 1997. After a bench trial, the court found breach. The court then turned to the Uniform Commercial Code to determine the measure of damages. CSR raises several legal issues with respect to the award of damages. . . .

Where a seller fails to make delivery of goods sold to a buyer, the buyer has two alternative remedies under the Uniform Commercial Code. One is the remedy of "cover": the buyer may purchase substitute goods and recover as damages the difference between the cost of this cover and the contract price, provided the buyer covers in good faith and without unreasonable delay. U.C.C. § 2–712.* The other, a complete alternative, is damages for non-delivery, also known as "hypothetical cover"[1]: the buyer may recover as damages from the seller "the difference between the market price at the time when the buyer learned of the breach and the contract price".** U.C.C. § 2–713. This measure applies only when and to the extent that the buyer does not cover. Uniform Commercial Code Comment 5, § 2–713. "The general baseline adopted in this section uses as a yardstick the market in which the buyer would have obtained cover had he sought that relief." U.C.C. Comment 1, § 2–713. "The market or current price to be used in comparison with the contract price under this section is the price for goods of the same kind and in the same branch of trade." U.C.C. Comment 2, § 2–713.

The court determined that Egerer was limited to damages for non-delivery under section 2–713: "Mr. Egerer is limited to damages reflecting the difference between CSR contract price and the price he could have obtained replacement material for at the time of the breach in 1997. *See* U.C.C. § 2–713(1) and Comment 3." The court found that Egerer could have obtained replacement material at the time of the breach for a cost of $8.25 per cubic yard—a price quoted to Egerer in early 1998. The court calculated his damages for the non-delivery of fill to be $129,812.50, which was the difference between the market price of $8.25 per cubic yard and the contract price of $.50 per cubic yard.

CSR accepts the trial court's decision to apply the remedy furnished by section 2–713, but contends the court erred by calculating damages based on a market price of $8.25 per cubic yard for pit run. CSR argues that $8.25 was not "the price for goods of the same kind" (as U.C.C. Comment 2 calls for) because pit run is a product superior to shoulder excavations containing asphalt grindings. CSR further argues that $8.25 was not "the market price at the time when the buyer learned of the breach" (as section 2–713 calls for) because the breach was in July 1997 and the $8.25 price was as of six months later—in January, 1998. CSR takes the position that the trial court should instead have used the $1.10 per cubic yard price reflected in Egerer's 1995 contract with Wilder Construction, because that was the only evidence in the record of a price for shoulder excavations. Use of the much higher price for pit run resulted in a windfall for Egerer, according to CSR.

The trial court expressly relied on Comment 3 to U.C.C. 2–713 in determining that $8.25 per cubic yard was the price for which Egerer could have obtained replacement material at the time of the breach. That comment states in part, "When the current market price under this section is difficult to prove the section on determination and proof of market price is available to permit a showing of a comparable market price or, where no market price is

---

* For simplicity, citations to the UCC have been inserted in place of citations to the counterpart sections of the Washington UCC. (Footnote by ed.)

1. *Allied Canners & Packers, Inc. v. Victor Packing Co.*, 162 Cal.App.3d 905, 911–12, 209 Cal.Rptr. 60, 61 (1984).

** The more conventional name for the damages that the court refers to as "hypothetical cover" is "market-price damages." (Footnote by ed.)

available, evidence of spot sale prices is proper." U.C.C. Comment 3, § 2–713. The section on determination and proof of market price provides,

> If evidence of a price prevailing at the times or places described in this Article is not readily available the price prevailing within any reasonable time before or after the time described or at any other place which in commercial judgment or under usage of trade would serve as a reasonable substitute for the one described may be used, making any proper allowance for the cost of transporting the goods to or from such other place.

U.C.C. § 2–723(2).

A court is granted a "reasonable leeway" in measuring market price under section 2–723. *Sprague v. Sumitomo Forestry Co., Ltd.,* 104 Wash.2d 751, 760, 709 P.2d 1200 (1985). Contrary to CSR's argument, a trial court may use a market price for goods different in quality from those for which the buyer contracted. That possibility is encompassed in the reference to "price . . . which in commercial judgment or under usage of trade would serve as a reasonable substitute for the one described". And section 2–723 expressly permits looking to a price "prevailing within any reasonable time before or after the time described."

We conclude the trial court did not misapply the law in concluding that the January 1998 price for pit run was the relevant market price. The court found the 1998 quotes for replacement material and hauling "were reasonable and customary", and noted that CSR "did not offer evidence that suitable replacement material was available at a lower price at the time of breach." There was testimony that shoulder excavation material, though cheap when available, is rarely available. John Grisham, CSR's sales manager, acknowledged that it would have been difficult for Egerer to locate an alternative supplier of shoulder excavations in 1997 because "quantities like that are few and far between". Grisham said he was unaware of any other pit in the area that would have had similar material available at a price anywhere near $.50 per cubic yard in the summer of 1997. Egerer's eventual purchase in 1999 was possible only because of the landslide that unexpectedly deposited unwanted fill material in a local gravel pit. If Egerer had covered at the time of the breach, higher-priced pit run would have been a reasonable substitute for the shoulder excavations. . . .

Affirmed.

WE CONCUR: SCHINDLER, COX, JJ.

———

PANHANDLE AGRI–SERVICE, INC. v. BECKER, 231 Kan. 291, 644 P.2d 413 (1982). "Failure of the buyer to utilize the remedy of cover when such is reasonably available will preclude recovery of consequential damages, such as loss of profits. . . . However, [UCC §] 2–712, which provides for cover, i.e., the buyer's procurement of substitute goods, states:

> '(3) Failure of the buyer to effect cover within this section does not bar him from any other remedy.'

"Therefore, cover is not a mandatory remedy for the buyer. The buyer is free to choose between cover and damages for nondelivery."

DELCHI CARRIER SpA v. ROTOREX CORP.

United States Court of Appeals, Second Circuit, 1995.
71 F.3d 1024.

WINTER, Circuit Judge:

Rotorex Corporation, a New York corporation, appeals from a judgment of $1,785,772.44 in damages for lost profits and other consequential damages awarded to Delchi Carrier SpA following a bench trial before Judge Munson. The basis for the award was Rotorex's delivery of nonconforming compressors to Delchi, an Italian manufacturer of air conditioners. Delchi cross-appeals from the denial of certain incidental and consequential damages. We affirm the award of damages; we reverse in part on Delchi's cross-appeal and remand for further proceedings.

BACKGROUND

In January 1988, Rotorex agreed to sell 10,800 compressors to Delchi for use in Delchi's "Ariele" line of portable room air conditioners. The air conditioners were scheduled to go on sale in the spring and summer of 1988. Prior to executing the contract, Rotorex sent Delchi a sample compressor and accompanying written performance specifications. The compressors were scheduled to be delivered in three shipments before May 15, 1988. Rotorex sent the first shipment by sea on March 26. Delchi paid for this shipment, which arrived at its Italian factory on April 20, by letter of credit. Rotorex sent a second shipment of compressors on or about May 9. Delchi also remitted payment for this shipment by letter of credit. While the second shipment was en route, Delchi discovered that the first lot of compressors did not conform to the sample model and accompanying specifications. On May 13, after a Rotorex representative visited the Delchi factory in Italy, Delchi informed Rotorex that 93 percent of the compressors were rejected in quality control checks because they had lower cooling capacity and consumed more power than the sample model and specifications. After several unsuccessful attempts to cure the defects in the compressors, Delchi asked Rotorex to supply new compressors conforming to the original sample and specifications. Rotorex refused, claiming that the performance specifications were "inadvertently communicated" to Delchi.

In a faxed letter dated May 23, 1988, Delchi cancelled the contract. Although it was able to expedite a previously planned order of suitable compressors from Sanyo, another supplier, Delchi was unable to obtain in a timely fashion substitute compressors from other sources and thus suffered a loss in its sales volume of Arieles during the 1988 selling season. Delchi filed the instant action under the United Nations Convention on Contracts for the International Sale of Goods ("CISG" or "the Convention") for breach of contract and failure to deliver conforming goods. On January 10, 1991, Judge Cholakis granted Delchi's motion for partial summary judgment, holding Rotorex liable for breach of contract.

After three years of discovery and a bench trial on the issue of damages, Judge Munson, to whom the case had been transferred, held Rotorex liable to Delchi for $1,248,331.87. This amount included consequential damages for: (i) lost profits resulting from a diminished sales level of Ariele units, (ii) expenses that Delchi incurred in attempting to remedy the nonconformity of the compressors, (iii) the cost of expediting shipment of previously ordered Sanyo compressors after Delchi rejected the Rotorex compressors, and (iv) costs of handling and storing the rejected compressors. The district court also awarded prejudgment interest under CISG art. 78.

The court denied Delchi's claim for damages based on other expenses, including: (i) shipping, customs, and incidentals relating to the two shipments of Rotorex compressors; (ii) the cost of obsolete insulation and tubing that Delchi purchased only for use with Rotorex compressors; (iii) the cost of obsolete tooling purchased only for production of units with Rotorex compressors; and (iv) labor costs for four days when Delchi's production line was idle because it had no compressors to install in the air conditioning units. The court denied an award for these items on the ground that it would lead to a double recovery because "those costs are accounted for in Delchi's recovery on its lost profits claim." It also denied an award for the cost of modification of electrical panels for use with substitute Sanyo compressors on the ground that the cost was not attributable to the breach. Finally, the court denied recovery on Delchi's claim of 4000 additional lost sales in Italy.

On appeal, Rotorex argues that it did not breach the agreement, that Delchi is not entitled to lost profits because it maintained inventory levels in excess of the maximum number of possible lost sales, that the calculation of the number of lost sales was improper, and that the district court improperly excluded fixed costs and depreciation from the manufacturing cost in calculating lost profits. Delchi cross-appeals, claiming that it is entitled to the additional out-of-pocket expenses and the lost profits on additional sales denied by Judge Munson.

DISCUSSION

The district court held, and the parties agree, that the instant matter is governed by the CISG, reprinted at 15 U.S.C.A. Appendix (West Supp.1995), a self-executing agreement between the United States and other signatories, including Italy.[2] Because there is virtually no caselaw under the Convention, we look to its language and to "the general principles" upon which it is based. See CISG art. 7(2). The Convention directs that its interpretation be informed by its "international character and ... the need to promote uniformity in its application and the observance of good faith in international trade." See CISG art. 7(1); see generally John Honnold, Uniform Law for International Sales Under the 1980 United Nations Convention 60–62 (2d ed. 1991) (addressing principles for interpretation of CISG). Caselaw interpreting analogous provisions of Article 2 of the Uniform Commercial Code ("UCC"), may also inform a court where the language of the relevant CISG provisions tracks that of the

---

2. Generally, the CISG governs sales contracts between parties from different signatory countries. However, the Convention makes clear that the parties may by contract choose to be bound by a source of law other than the CISG, such as the Uniform Commercial Code. See CISG art. 6 ("The parties may exclude the application of this Convention or ... derogate from or vary the effect of any of its provisions.") If, as here, the agreement is silent as to choice of law, the Convention applies if both parties are located in signatory nations. See CISG art. 1.

UCC. However, UCC caselaw "is not per se applicable." Orbisphere Corp. v. United States, 726 F.Supp. 1344, 1355 (Ct.Int'l Trade 1989).

We first address the liability issue. We review a grant of summary judgment de novo. Burgos v. Hopkins, 14 F.3d 787, 789 (2d Cir.1994). Summary judgment is appropriate if "there is no genuine issue as to any material fact" regarding Rotorex's liability for breach of contract. See Fed. R.Civ.P. 56(c).

Under the CISG, "[t]he seller must deliver goods which are of the quantity, quality and description required by the contract," and "the goods do not conform with the contract unless they . . . [p]ossess the qualities of goods which the seller has held out to the buyer as a sample or model." CISG art. 35. The CISG further states that "[t]he seller is liable in accordance with the contract and this Convention for any lack of conformity." CISG art. 36.

Judge Cholakis held that "there is no question that [Rotorex's] compressors did not conform to the terms of the contract between the parties" and noted that "[t]here are ample admissions [by Rotorex] to that effect." We agree. The agreement between Delchi and Rotorex was based upon a sample compressor supplied by Rotorex and upon written specifications regarding cooling capacity and power consumption. After the problems were discovered, Rotorex's engineering representative, Ernest Gamache, admitted in a May 13, 1988 letter that the specification sheet was "in error" and that the compressors would actually generate less cooling power and consume more energy than the specifications indicated. Gamache also testified in a deposition that at least some of the compressors were nonconforming. The president of Rotorex, John McFee, conceded in a May 17, 1988 letter to Delchi that the compressors supplied were less efficient than the sample and did not meet the specifications provided by Rotorex. Finally, in its answer to Delchi's complaint, Rotorex admitted "that some of the compressors . . . did not conform to the nominal performance information." There was thus no genuine issue of material fact regarding liability, and summary judgment was proper. See Perma Research & Dev. Co. v. Singer Co., 410 F.2d 572, 577–78 (2d Cir.1969) (affirming grant of summary judgment based upon admissions and deposition testimony by nonmoving party).

Under the CISG, if the breach is "fundamental" the buyer may either require delivery of substitute goods, CISG art. 46, or declare the contract void, CISG art. 49, and seek damages. With regard to what kind of breach is fundamental, Article 25 provides:

> A breach of contract committed by one of the parties is fundamental if it results in such detriment to the other party as substantially to deprive him of what he is entitled to expect under the contract, unless the party in breach did not foresee and a reasonable person of the same kind in the same circumstances would not have foreseen such a result.

CISG art. 25. In granting summary judgment, the district court held that "[t]here appears to be no question that [Delchi] did not substantially receive that which [it] was entitled to expect" and that "any reasonable person could foresee that shipping non-conforming goods to a buyer would result in the buyer not receiving that which he expected and was entitled to receive." Because the cooling power and energy consumption of an air conditioner compressor are important determinants of the product's value, the district court's conclusion that Rotorex was liable for a fundamental breach of contract under the Convention was proper.

We turn now to the district court's award of damages following the bench trial. A reviewing court must defer to the trial judge's findings of fact unless they are clearly erroneous. Anderson v. City of Bessemer, 470 U.S. 564, 575, 105 S.Ct. 1504, 1512, 84 L.Ed.2d 518 (1985); Allied Chem. Int'l Corp. v. Companhia de Navegacao Lloyd Brasileiro, 775 F.2d 476, 481 (2d Cir.1985), cert. denied, 475 U.S. 1099, 106 S.Ct. 1502, 89 L.Ed.2d 903 (1986). However, we review questions of law, including "the measure of damages upon which the factual computation is based," de novo. Wolff & Munier, Inc. v. Whiting–Turner Contracting Co., 946 F.2d 1003, 1009 (2d Cir.1991) (internal quotation marks and citation omitted); see also Travellers Int'l, A.G. v. Trans World Airlines, 41 F.3d 1570, 1574–75 (2d Cir.1994).

The CISG provides:

> Damages for breach of contract by one party consist of a sum equal to the loss, including loss of profit, suffered by the other party as a consequence of the breach. Such damages may not exceed the loss which the party in breach foresaw or ought to have foreseen at the time of the conclusion of the contract, in the light of the facts and matters of which he then knew or ought to have known, as a possible consequence of the breach of contract.

CISG art. 74. This provision is "designed to place the aggrieved party in as good a position as if the other party had properly performed the contract." Honnold, supra, at 503.

Rotorex contends, in the alternative, that the district court improperly awarded lost profits for unfilled orders from Delchi affiliates in Europe and from sales agents within Italy. We disagree. The CISG requires that damages be limited by the familiar principle of foreseeability established in Hadley v. Baxendale, 156 Eng.Rep. 145 (1854). CISG art. 74. However, it was objectively foreseeable that Delchi would take orders for Ariele sales based on the number of compressors it had ordered and expected to have ready for the season. The district court was entitled to rely upon the documents and testimony regarding these lost sales and was well within its authority in deciding which orders were proven with sufficient certainty.

Rotorex also challenges the district court's exclusion of fixed costs and depreciation from the manufacturing cost used to calculate lost profits. The trial judge calculated lost profits by subtracting the 478,783 lire "manufacturing cost"—the total variable cost—of an Ariele unit from the 654,644 lire average sale price. The CISG does not explicitly state whether only variable expenses, or both fixed and variable expenses, should be subtracted from sales revenue in calculating lost profits. However, courts generally do not include fixed costs in the calculation of lost profits. See Indu Craft, Inc. v. Bank of Baroda, 47 F.3d 490, 495 (2d Cir.1995) (only when the breach ends an ongoing business should fixed costs be subtracted along with variable costs); Adams v. Lindblad Travel, Inc., 730 F.2d 89, 92–93 (2d Cir.1984) (fixed costs should not be included in lost profits equation when the plaintiff is an ongoing business whose fixed costs are not affected by the breach). This is, of course, because the fixed costs would have been encountered whether or not the breach occurred. In the absence of a specific provision in the CISG for calculating lost profits, the district court was correct to use the standard formula employed by most American courts and to deduct only variable costs from sales revenue to arrive at a figure for lost profits.

In its cross-appeal, Delchi challenges the district court's denial of various consequential and incidental damages, including reimbursement for: (i) shipping, customs, and incidentals relating to the first and second shipments—rejected and returned—of Rotorex compressors; (ii) obsolete insulation materials and tubing purchased for use only with Rotorex compressors; (iii) obsolete tooling purchased exclusively for production of units with Rotorex compressors; and (iv) labor costs for the period of May 16–19, 1988, when the Delchi production line was idle due to a lack of compressors to install in Ariele air conditioning units. The district court denied damages for these items on the ground that they "are accounted for in Delchi's recovery on its lost profits claim," and, therefore, an award would constitute a double recovery for Delchi. We disagree.

The Convention provides that a contract plaintiff may collect damages to compensate for the full loss. This includes, but is not limited to, lost profits, subject only to the familiar limitation that the breaching party must have foreseen, or should have foreseen, the loss as a probable consequence. CISG art. 74; see Hadley v. Baxendale, supra.

An award for lost profits will not compensate Delchi for the expenses in question. Delchi's lost profits are determined by calculating the hypothetical revenues to be derived from unmade sales less the hypothetical variable costs that would have been, but were not, incurred. This figure, however, does not compensate for costs actually incurred that led to no sales. Thus, to award damages for costs actually incurred in no way creates a double recovery and instead furthers the purpose of giving the injured party damages "equal to the loss." CISG art. 74.

The only remaining inquiries, therefore, are whether the expenses were reasonably foreseeable and legitimate incidental or consequential damages. The expenses incurred by Delchi for shipping, customs, and related matters for the two returned shipments of Rotorex compressors, including storage expenses for the second shipment at Genoa, were clearly foreseeable and recoverable incidental expenses. These are up-front expenses that had to be paid to get the goods to the manufacturing plant for inspection and were thus incurred largely before the nonconformities were detected. To deny reimbursement to Delchi for these incidental damages would effectively cut into the lost profits award. The same is true of unreimbursed tooling expenses and the cost of the useless insulation and tubing materials. These are legitimate consequential damages that in no way duplicate lost profits damages.

The labor expense incurred as a result of the production line shutdown of May 16–19, 1988 is also a reasonably foreseeable result of delivering nonconforming compressors for installation in air conditioners. However, Rotorex argues that the labor costs in question were fixed costs that would have been incurred whether or not there was a breach. The district court labeled the labor costs "fixed costs, but did not explore whether Delchi would have paid these wages regardless of how much it produced. Variable costs are generally those costs that "fluctuate with a firms' output," and typically include labor (but not management) costs. Northeastern Tel. Co. v. AT & T, 651 F.2d 76, 86 (2d Cir.1981). Whether Delchi's labor costs during this four-day period are variable or fixed costs is in large measure a fact question that we cannot answer because we lack factual findings by the district court. We therefore remand to the district court on this issue.

The district court also denied an award for the modification of electrical panels for use with substitute Sanyo compressors. It denied damages on the ground that Delchi failed to show that the modifications were not part of the regular cost of production of units with Sanyo compressors and were therefore attributable to Rotorex's breach. This appears to have been a credibility determination that was within the court's authority to make. We therefore affirm on the ground that this finding is not clearly erroneous.

Finally, Delchi cross-appeals from the denial of its claimed 4000 additional lost sales in Italy. The district court held that Delchi did not prove these orders with sufficient certainty. The trial court was in the best position to evaluate the testimony of the Italian sales agents who stated that they would have ordered more Arieles if they had been available. It found the agents' claims to be too speculative, and this conclusion is not clearly erroneous.

CONCLUSION

We affirm the award of damages. We reverse in part the denial of incidental and consequential damages. We remand for further proceedings in accord with this opinion.

_____

(b) Breach by the Buyer

_____

UCC §§ 2–501(1), 2–703, 2–704(1), 2–706, 2–708, 2–709, 2–710, 2–723, 2–724

[See Selected Source Materials Supplement]

_____

CISG ARTS. 61, 62, 64, 74, 75, 76

[See Selected Source Materials Supplement]

_____

NERI v. RETAIL MARINE CORP.

Court of Appeals of New York, 1972.
30 N.Y.2d 393, 334 N.Y.S.2d 165, 285 N.E.2d 311.

GIBSON, JUDGE. The appeal concerns the right of a retail dealer to recover loss of profits and incidental damages upon the buyer's repudiation of a contract governed by the Uniform Commercial Code. This is, indeed, the correct measure of damage in an appropriate case and to this extent the code (§ 2–708, subsection [2]) effected a substantial change from prior law, whereby damages were ordinarily limited to "the difference between the contract price and the market or current price".[8] Upon the record before us, the courts below erred in declining to give effect to the new statute and so the order appealed from must be reversed.

The plaintiffs contracted to purchase from defendant a new boat of a specified model for the price of $12,587.40, against which they made a deposit of $40. They shortly increased the deposit to $4,250 in consideration of the defendant dealer's agreement to arrange with the manufacturer for immediate delivery on the basis of "a firm sale", instead of the delivery within approximately four to six weeks originally specified. Some six days after the date of the contract plaintiffs' lawyer sent to defendant a letter rescinding the sales contract for the reason that plaintiff Neri was about to undergo hospitalization and surgery, in consequence of which, according to the letter, it would be "impossible for Mr. Neri to make any payments". The boat had already been ordered from the manufacturer and was delivered to defendant at or before the time the attorney's letter was received. Defendant declined to refund plaintiffs' deposit and this action to recover it was commenced. Defendant counterclaimed, alleging plaintiffs' breach of the contract and defendant's resultant damage in the amount of $4,250, for which sum defendant demanded judgment. Upon motion, defendant had summary judgment on the issue of liability tendered by its counterclaim; and Special Term directed an assessment of damages, upon which it would be determined whether plaintiffs were entitled to the return of any portion of their down payment.

Upon the trial so directed, it was shown that the boat ordered and received by defendant in accordance with plaintiffs' contract of purchase was sold some four months later to another buyer for the same price as that negotiated with plaintiffs. From this proof the plaintiffs argue that defendant's loss on its contract was recouped, while defendant argues that but for plaintiffs' default, it would have sold two boats and have earned two profits instead of one. Defendant proved, without contradiction, that its profit on the sale under the contract in suit would have been $2,579 and that during the period the boat remained unsold incidental expenses aggregating $674 for storage, upkeep, finance charges and insurance were incurred. Additionally, defendant proved and sought to recover attorneys' fees of $1,250.

The trial court found "untenable" defendant's claim for loss of profit, inasmuch as the boat was later sold for the same price that plaintiffs had contracted to pay; found, too, that defendant had failed to prove any incidental damages; further found "that the terms of section 2–718, subsection 2(b), of the Uniform Commercial Code are applicable and same make adequate and fair provision to place the sellers in as good a position as performance would have done" and, in accordance with paragraph (b) of subsection (2) thus relied upon, awarded defendant $500 upon its counterclaim and directed that plaintiffs recover the balance of their deposit, amounting to $3,750. The ensuing judgment was affirmed, without opinion, at the Appellate Division, 37

---

8. Personal Property Law, Consol.Laws, c. 41, §145, repealed by Uniform Commercial Code, § 10–102 (L.1962, ch. 553, eff. Sept. 27, 1964); Lenobel, Inc. v. Senif, 252 App.Div. 533, 300 N.Y.S. 226.

A.D.2d 917, 326 N.Y.S.2d 984, and defendant's appeal to this court was taken by our leave.

The issue is governed in the first instance by section 2–718 of the Uniform Commercial Code which provides, among other things, that the buyer, despite his breach, may have restitution of the amount by which his payment exceeds: (a) reasonable liquidated damages stipulated by the contract or (b) absent such stipulation, 20% of the value of the buyer's total performance or $500, whichever is smaller (§ 2–718, subsection [2], pars. [a], [b]). As above noted, the trial court awarded defendant an offset in the amount of $500 under paragraph (b) and directed restitution to plaintiffs of the balance. Section 2–718, however, establishes, in paragraph (a) of subsection (3), an alternative right of offset in favor of the seller, as follows: "(3) The buyer's right to restitution under subsection (2) is subject to offset to the extent that the seller establishes (a) a right to recover damages under the provisions of this Article other than subsection (1)".

Among "the provisions of this Article other than subsection (1)" are those to be found in section 2–708, which the courts below did not apply. Subsection (1) of that section provides that "the measure of damages for non-acceptance or repudiation by the buyer is the difference between the market price at the time and place for tender and the unpaid contract price together with any incidental damages provided in this Article (Section 2–710), but less expenses saved in consequence of the buyer's breach." However, this provision is made expressly subject to subsection (2), providing: "(2) If the measure of damages provided in subsection (1) is inadequate to put the seller in as good a position as performance would have done then the measure of damages is the profit (including reasonable overhead) which the seller would have made from full performance by the buyer, together with any incidental damages provided in this Article (Section 2–710), due allowance for costs reasonably incurred and due credit for payments or proceeds of resale."

The provision of the code upon which the decision at Trial Term rested (§ 2–718, subsection [2], par. [b]) does not differ greatly from the corresponding provisions of the prior statute (Personal Property Law, § 145–a, subd. 1, par. [b]), except as the new act includes the alternative remedy of a lump sum award of $500. Neither does the present reference (in § 2–718, subsection [3], par. [a]) to the recovery of damages pursuant to other provisions of the article differ from a like reference in the prior statute (Personal Property Law, § 145–a, subd. 2, par. [a]) to an alternative measure of damages under section 145 of that act; but section 145 made no provision for recovery of lost profits as does section 2–708 (subsection [2]) of the code. The new statute is thus innovative and significant and its analysis is necessary to the determination of the issues here presented.

Prior to the code, the New York cases "applied the 'profit' test, contract price less cost of manufacture, only in cases where the seller [was] a manufacturer or an agent for a manufacturer" (1955 Report of N.Y.Law Rev.Comm., vol. 1, p. 693). Its extension to retail sales was "designed to eliminate the unfair and economically wasteful results arising under the older law when fixed price articles were involved. This section permits the recovery of lost profits in all appropriate cases, which would include all standard priced goods." (Official Comment 2, McKinney's Cons.Laws of N.Y., Book 62½, Part 1, p. 605, under Uniform Commercial Code, § 2–708.) Additionally, and "[i]n all cases the seller may recover incidental damages" (id., Comment 3). The buyer's right to restitution was established at Special Term upon the motion for summary judgment, as was the seller's right to proper offsets, in each case pursuant to section 2–718; and, as the parties concede, the only question before us, following the assessment of damages at Special Term, is that as to the proper measure of damage to be applied. The conclusion is clear from the record—indeed with mathematical certainty—that "the measure of damages provided in subsection (1) is inadequate to put the seller in as good a position as performance would have done" (Uniform Commercial Code, § 2–708, subsection [2]) and hence—again under subsection (2)—that the seller is entitled to its "profit (including reasonable overhead) . . . together with any incidental damages . . ., due allowance for costs reasonably incurred and due credit for payments or proceeds of resale."

It is evident, first, that this retail seller is entitled to its profit and, second, that the last sentence of subsection (2), as hereinbefore quoted, referring to "due credit for payments or proceeds of resale" is inapplicable to this retail sales contract.[9] Closely parallel to the factual situation now before us is that hypothesized by Dean Hawkland as illustrative of the operation of the rules: "Thus, if a private party agrees to sell his automobile to a buyer for $2,000, a breach by the buyer would cause the seller no loss (except incidental damages, i.e., expense of a new sale) if the seller was able to sell the automobile to another buyer for $2000. But the situation is different with dealers having an unlimited supply of standard-priced goods. Thus, if an automobile dealer agrees to sell a car to a buyer at the standard price of $2000, a breach by the buyer injures the dealer, even though he is able to sell the automobile to another for $2000. If the dealer has an inexhaustible supply of cars, the resale to replace the breaching buyer costs the dealer a sale, because, had the breaching buyer performed, the dealer would have made two sales instead of one. The buyer's breach, in such a case, depletes the dealer's sales to the extent of one, and the measure of damages should be the dealer's profit on one sale. Section 2–708 recognizes this, and it rejects the rule developed under the Uniform Sales Act by many courts that the profit cannot be recovered in this case." (Hawkland, Sales and Bulk Sales [1958 ed.], pp. 153–154; and see Comment, 31 Fordham L.Rev. 749, 755–756.)

The record which in this case establishes defendant's entitlement to damages in the amount of its prospective profit, at the same time confirms defendant's cognate right to "any incidental damages provided in this Article (Section 2–710)"[10] (Uniform Commercial Code, § 2–708, subsection [2]). From

---

9. The concluding clause, "due credit for payments or proceeds of resale", is intended to refer to "the privilege of the seller to realize junk value when it is manifestly useless to complete the operation of manufacture" (Supp. No. 1 to the 1952 Official Draft of Text and Comments of the Uniform Commercial Code, as Amended by the Act of the American Law Institute of the National Conference of Commissioners on Uniform Laws [1954], p. 14). The commentators who have considered the language have uniformly concluded that "the reference is to a resale as scrap under . . . Section 2–704" (1956 Report of N.Y.Law Rev. Comm., p. 397; 1955 Report of N.Y.Law Rev. Comm., vol. 1, p. 761; New York Annotations, McKinney's Cons.Laws of N.Y., Book 62½, Part 1, p. 606, under Uniform Commercial Code, § 2–708; 1 Willier and Hart, Bender's Uniform Commercial Code Service, § 2–708, pp. 1–180—1–181). Another writer, reaching the same conclusion, after detailing the history of the clause, says that " 'proceeds of resale' previously meant the resale value of the goods in finished form; now it means the resale value of the components on hand at the time plaintiff learns of breach" (Harris, Seller's Damages, 18 Stanf.L.Rev. 66,104).

10. Incidental damages to an aggrieved seller include any commercially reasonable charges, expenses or commissions incurred in stopping delivery, in the transportation, care

the language employed it is too clear to require discussion that the seller's right to recover loss of profits is not exclusive and that he may recoup his "incidental" expenses as well (Proctor & Gamble Distr. Co. v. Lawrence Amer. Field Warehousing Corp., 16 N.Y.2d 344, 354, 266 N.Y.S.2d 785, 792, 213 N.E.2d 873, 878). Although the trial court's denial of incidental damages in the uncontroverted amount of $674 was made in the context of its erroneous conclusion that paragraph (b) of subsection (2) of section 2–718 was applicable and was "adequate . . . to place the sellers in as good a position as performance would have done", the denial seems not to have rested entirely on the court's mistaken application of the law, as there was an explicit finding "that defendant completely failed to show that it suffered any incidental damages." We find no basis for the court's conclusion with respect to a deficiency of proof inasmuch as the proper items of the $674 expenses (being for storage, upkeep, finance charges and insurance for the period between the date performance was due and the time of the resale) were proven without objection and were in no way controverted, impeached or otherwise challenged, at the trial or on appeal. Thus the court's finding of a failure of proof cannot be supported upon the record and, therefore, and contrary to plaintiffs' contention, the affirmance at the Appellate Division was ineffective to save it.

The trial court correctly denied defendant's claim for recovery of attorney's fees incurred by it in this action. Attorney's fees incurred in an action such as this are not in the nature of the protective expenses contemplated by the statute (Uniform Commercial Code, § 1–106, subd. [1]; § 2–710; § 2–708, subsection [2]) and by our reference to "legal expense" in Procter & Gamble Distr. Co. v. Lawrence Amer. Field Warehousing Corp. (16 N.Y.2d 344, 354–355, 266 N.Y.S.2d 785, 792–793, 213 N.E.2d 873, 878–879, supra), upon which defendant's reliance is in this respect misplaced.

It follows that plaintiffs are entitled to restitution of the sum of $4,250 paid by them on account of the contract price less an offset to defendant in the amount of $3,253 on account of its lost profit of $2,579 and its incidental damages of $674.

The order of the Appellate Division should be modified, with costs in all courts, in accordance with this opinion, and, as so modified, affirmed.

FULD, C.J., and BURKE, SCILEPPI, BERGAN, BREITEL, and JASEN, JJ., concur.

Ordered accordingly.

———

LAZENBY GARAGES LTD. v. WRIGHT, [1976] 2 All E.R. 770, [1976] 1 W.L.R. 459 (Ct.App. Eng. 1976) (Lord Denning M.R.) "Mr. Wright works on the land. On February 19, 1974 he went to the showrooms of motor dealers called Lazenby Garages Ltd. He saw some secondhand cars there. He agreed to buy a BMW 2002. He signed a contract to pay £1,670 for it. It was to be delivered to him on March 1, 1974. He went back home to his wife and told her about it. She persuaded him not to buy it. So next day he went back to the garage and said he would not have it after all. They kept it there offering it

and custody of goods after the buyer's breach, in connection with return or resale of the   goods or otherwise resulting from the breach (Uniform Commercial Code, § 2–710).

for re-sale. Two months later on April 23, 1974 they re-sold it for £1,770, that is, for £100 more than Mr. Wright was going to pay.

"Notwithstanding this advantageous re-sale, the garage sued Mr. Wright for damages. They produced evidence that they had themselves bought the car secondhand on 14th February 1974, that is five days before Mr. Wright had come in and agreed to buy it. They said that they had bought it for £1,325. He had agreed to buy it from them for £1,670. So they had lost £345 and they claimed that sum as damages.

"In answer Mr. Wright said: 'You haven't lost anything; you've sold it for a higher price.' The garage people said that they were dealers in secondhand cars; that they had had a number of cars of this sort of age and type, BMW 2002s; and that they had lost the sale of another car. They said that, if Mr. Wright had taken this car, they would have been able to sell one of those other cars to the purchaser. So they had sold one car less and were entitled to profit accordingly. . . .

". . . Now there is an appeal to this court. The cases show that if there are a number of new cars, all exactly of the same kind, available for sale, and the dealers can prove that they sold one car less than they otherwise would have done, they would be entitled to damages amounting to their loss of profit on the one car. . . .

"But it is entirely different in the case of a secondhand car. Each secondhand car is different from the next, even though it is the same make. The sales manager of the garage admitted in evidence that some secondhand cars, of the same make, even of the same year, may sell better than others of the same year. Some may sell quickly, others sluggishly. You simply cannot tell why. But they are all different.

"In the circumstances the cases about new cars do not apply. . . ."

SECTION 3. MITIGATION; CONTRACTS FOR EMPLOYMENT

ROCKINGHAM COUNTY v. LUTEN BRIDGE CO.

Circuit Court of Appeals, Fourth Circuit, 1929.
35 F.2d 301.

PARKER, CIRCUIT JUDGE. This was an action at law instituted in the court below by the Luten Bridge Company, as plaintiff, to recover of Rockingham county, North Carolina, an amount alleged to be due under a contract for the construction of a bridge. The county admits the execution and breach of the contract, but contends that notice of cancellation was given the bridge company before the erection of the bridge was commenced, and that it is liable only for the damages which the company would have sustained, if it had abandoned construction at that time. The judge below . . . excluded evidence offered by the county in support of its contentions as to notice of cancellation and damages, and instructed a verdict for plaintiff for the full amount of its claim. From judgment on this verdict the county has appealed.

The facts out of which the case arises, as shown by the affidavits and offers of proof appearing in the record, are as follows: On January 7, 1924, the board of commissioners of Rockingham county voted to award to plaintiff a contract for the construction of the bridge in controversy. Three of the five commissioners favored the awarding of the contract and two opposed it. Much feeling was engendered over the matter, with the result that on February 11, 1924, W.K. Pruitt, one of the commissioners who had voted in the affirmative, sent his resignation to the clerk of the superior court of the county. The clerk received this resignation on the same day, and immediately accepted same and noted his acceptance thereon. Later in the day, Pruitt called him over the telephone and stated that he wished to withdraw the resignation, and later sent him written notice to the same effect. The clerk, however, paid no attention to the attempted withdrawal, and proceeded on the next day to appoint one W.W. Hampton as a member of the board to succeed him.

After his resignation, Pruitt attended no further meetings of the board, and did nothing further as a commissioner of the county. Likewise Pratt and McCollum, the other two members of the board who had voted with him in favor of the contract, attended no further meetings. Hampton, on the other hand, took the oath of office immediately upon his appointment and entered upon the discharge of the duties of a commissioner. He met regularly with the two remaining members of the board, Martin and Barber. . . .

At one of these meetings, a regularly advertised called meeting held on February 21st, a resolution was unanimously adopted declaring that the contract for the building of the bridge was not legal and valid, and directing the clerk of the board to notify plaintiff that it refused to recognize same as a valid contract, and that plaintiff should proceed no further thereunder. This resolution also rescinded action of the board theretofore taken looking to the construction of a hard-surfaced road, in which the bridge was to be a mere connecting link. The clerk duly sent a certified copy of this resolution to plaintiff.

At the regular monthly meeting of the board on March 3d, a resolution was passed directing that plaintiff be notified that any work done on the bridge would be done by it at its own risk and hazard, that the board was of the opinion that the contract for the construction of the bridge was not valid and legal, and that, even if the board were mistaken as to this, it did not desire to construct the bridge, and would contest payment for same if constructed. A copy of this resolution was also sent to plaintiff. . . .

At the time of the passage of the first resolution, very little work toward the construction of the bridge had been done, it being estimated that the total cost of labor done and material on the ground was around $1,900; but, notwithstanding the repudiation of the contract by the county, the bridge company continued with the work of construction.

On November 24, 1924, plaintiff instituted this action against Rockingham county. . . .

As the county now admits the execution and validity of the contract, and the breach on its part, the ultimate question in the case is one as to the measure of plaintiff's recovery, and the exceptions must be considered with this in mind. Upon these exceptions, [the question arises]. . . . whether plaintiff, if the notices are to be deemed action by the county, can recover under the contract for work done after they were received, or is limited to the recovery of damages for breach of contract as of that date. . . .

Coming, then, to . . . the measure of plaintiff's recovery—we do not think that, after the county had given notice, while the contract was still executory, that it did not desire the bridge built and would not pay for it, plaintiff could proceed to build it and recover the contract price. It is true that the county had no right to rescind the contract, and the notice given plaintiff amounted to a breach on its part; but, after plaintiff had received notice of the breach, it was its duty to do nothing to increase the damages flowing therefrom. If A enters into a binding contract to build a house for B, B, of course, has no right to rescind the contract without A's consent. But if, before the house is built, he decides that he does not want it, and notifies A to that effect, A has no right to proceed with the building and thus pile up damages. His remedy is to treat the contract as broken when he receives the notice, and sue for the recovery of such damages as he may have sustained from the breach, including any profit which he would have realized upon performance, as well as any other losses which may have resulted to him. In the case at bar, the county decided not to build the road of which the bridge was to be a part, and did not build it. The bridge, built in the midst of the forest, is of no value to the county because of this change of circumstances. When, therefore, the county gave notice to the plaintiff that it would not proceed with the project, plaintiff should have desisted from further work. It had no right thus to pile up damages by proceeding with the erection of a useless bridge.

The contrary view was expressed by Lord Cockburn in Frost v. Knight, L.R. 7 Ex. 111, but, as pointed out by Prof. Williston (Williston on Contracts, vol. 3, p. 2347), it is not in harmony with the decisions in this country. The American rule and the reasons supporting it are well stated by Prof. Williston as follows:

> "There is a line of cases running back to 1845 which holds that, after an absolute repudiation or refusal to perform by one party to a contract, the other party cannot continue to perform and recover damages based on full performance. This rule is only a particular application of the general rule of damages that a plaintiff cannot hold a defendant liable for damages which need not have been incurred; or, as it is often stated, the plaintiff must, so far as he can without loss to himself, mitigate the damages caused by the defendant's wrongful act. The application of this rule to the matter in question is obvious. If a man engages to have work done, and afterwards repudiates his contract before the work has been begun or when it has been only partially done, it is inflicting damage on the defendant without benefit to the plaintiff to allow the latter to insist on proceeding with the contract. The work may be useless to the defendant, and yet he would be forced to pay the full contract price. On the other hand, the plaintiff is interested only in the profit he will make out of the contract. If he receives this it is equally advantageous for him to use his time otherwise."

The leading case on the subject in this country is the New York case of Clark v. Marsiglia, 1 Denio (N.Y.) 317, 43 Am.Dec. 670. In that case defendant had employed plaintiff to paint certain pictures for him, but countermanded the order before the work was finished. Plaintiff, however, went on and completed the work and sued for the contract price. In reversing a judgment for plaintiff, the court said:

> "The plaintiff was allowed to recover as though there had been no countermand of the order; and in this the court erred. The defendant, by requiring the plaintiff to stop work upon the paintings, violated his contract, and thereby incurred a liability to pay such damages as the plaintiff should sustain. Such damages would include a recompense for the labor done and materials used, and such further sum in damages as might, upon legal principles, be assessed for the breach of the contract; but the plaintiff had no right, by obstinately persisting in the work, to make the penalty upon the defendant greater than it would otherwise have been." . . .

. . . It follows that there was error in directing a verdict for plaintiff for the full amount of its claim. The measure of plaintiff's damage, upon its appearing that notice was duly given not to build the bridge, is an amount sufficient to compensate plaintiff for labor and materials expended and expense incurred in the part performance of the contract, prior to its repudiation, plus the profit which would have been realized if it had been carried out in accordance with its terms. . . .

. . . The judgment below will accordingly be reversed, and the case remanded for a new trial.

Reversed.

————

RESTATEMENT, SECOND, CONTRACTS § 350

[See Selected Source Materials Supplement]

————

UCC §§ 2–704(2), 2–715(2)

[See Selected Source Materials Supplement]

————

CISG ART. 77

[See Selected Source Materials Supplement]

————

UNIDROIT PRINCIPLES OF INTERNATIONAL COMMERCIAL CONTRACTS ARTS. 7.4.7, 7.4.8

[See Selected Source Materials Supplement]

————

PRINCIPLES OF EUROPEAN CONTRACT
LAW ARTS. 9.504, 9.505

[See Selected Source Materials Supplement]

SHIRLEY MacLAINE PARKER v. TWENTIETH
CENTURY–FOX FILM CORP.

California Supreme Court, 1970.
3 Cal.3d 176, 89 Cal.Rptr. 737, 474 P.2d 689.

BURKE, J. Defendant Twentieth Century–Fox Film Corporation appeals from a summary judgment granting to plaintiff the recovery of agreed compensation under a written contract for her services as an actress in a motion picture. As will appear, we have concluded that the trial court correctly ruled in plaintiff's favor and that the judgment should be affirmed.

Plaintiff is well known as an actress, and in the contract between plaintiff and defendant is sometimes referred to as the "Artist." Under the contract, dated August 6, 1965, plaintiff was to play the female lead in defendant's contemplated production of a motion picture entitled "Bloomer Girl."* The contract provided that defendant would pay plaintiff a minimum "guaranteed compensation" of $53,571.42 per week for 14 weeks commencing May 23, 1966, for a total of $750,000. Prior to May 1966 defendant decided not to produce the picture and by a letter dated April 4, 1966, it notified plaintiff of that decision and that it would not "comply with our obligations to you under" the written contract.

By the same letter and with the professed purpose "to avoid any damage to you," defendant instead offered to employ plaintiff as the leading actress in another film tentatively entitled "Big Country, Big Man" (hereinafter, "Big Country"). The compensation offered was identical, as were 31 of the 34 numbered provisions or articles of the original contract.[11] Unlike "Bloomer Girl," however, which was to have been a musical production, "Big Country"

---

* Victor Goldberg reports that *Bloomer Girl* was an adaptation of a stage musical written by Harold Arlen and Yip Harburg, which ran for 654 performances on Broadway in the mid–1940's. Harburg's son summarized the play's plot and political themes as follows:

Bloomer Girl concerns the political activities of Amelia (renamed Dolly) Bloomer and the effect they have on a pre-Civil War family of her brother-in-law, hoopskirt king Horace Applegate, and his feminist daughter, Evalina. Evalina is the youngest and only remaining unmarried Applegate daughter; her older sisters are all married to company salesmen, and as *Bloomer Girl* begins, Horace is trying to unify business and family by encouraging his chief Southern salesman, Jefferson Calhoun, to court Evalina. On the eve of the Civil War, *Bloomer Girl* centers around Evalina's tutelage of Jeff in matters of gender and racial equality. Evalina, Dolly, and the other feminists of Cicero Falls not only campaign against Applegate's hoopskirts and sexism but also stage their own version of Uncle Tom's Cabin and conceal a runaway slave—Jeff's own manservant, Pompey. It was, said Yip, a show about "the indivisibility of human freedom."

Bloomer Girl interweaves the issues of black and female equality and war and peace with the vicissitudes of courtship and pre-Civil War politics.... [I]t was at no point an escapist entertainment....

Goldberg, "Bloomer Girl Revisited or how to Frame an Unmade Picture," 1998 *Wisconsin Law Review* 1051 (1998) (quoting Harold Meyerson and Ernie Harburg, *Who Put the Rainbow in* The Wizard of Oz? *Yip Harburg, Lyricist* (1993)). (Footnote by ed.)

11. Among the identical provisions was the following found in the last paragraph of Article 2 of the original contract: "We [defendant] shall not be obligated to utilize your [plain-

was a dramatic "western type" movie. "Bloomer Girl" was to have been filmed in California; "Big Country" was to be produced in Australia. Also, certain terms in the proffered contract varied from those of the original.[12] Plaintiff was given one week within which to accept; she did not and the offer lapsed. Plaintiff then commenced this action seeking recovery of the agreed guaranteed compensation.

The complaint sets forth two causes of action. The first is for money due under the contract; the second, based upon the same allegations as the first, is for damages resulting from defendant's breach of contract. Defendant in its answer admits the existence and validity of the contract, that plaintiff complied with all the conditions, covenants and promises and stood ready to complete the performance, and that defendant breached and "anticipatorily repudiated" the contract. It denies, however, that any money is due to plaintiff either under the contract or as a result of its breach, and pleads as an affirmative defense to both causes of action plaintiff's allegedly deliberate failure to mitigate damages, asserting that she unreasonably refused to accept its offer of the leading role in "Big Country."

Plaintiff moved for summary judgment under Code of Civil Procedure section 437c, the motion was granted, and summary judgment for $750,000 plus interest was entered in plaintiff's favor. This appeal by defendant followed.

The familiar rules are that the matter to be determined by the trial court on a motion for summary judgment is whether facts have been presented which give rise to a triable factual issue. The court may not pass upon the issue itself. Summary judgment is proper only if the affidavits or declarations in support of the moving party would be sufficient to sustain a judgment in his favor and his opponent does not by affidavit show facts sufficient to present a triable issue of fact. . . .

The general rule is that the measure of recovery by a wrongfully discharged employee is the amount of salary agreed upon for the period of

tiff's] services in or in connection with the Photoplay hereunder, our sole obligation, subject to the terms and conditions of this Agreement, being to pay you the guaranteed compensation herein provided for."

12. Article 29 of the original contract specified that plaintiff approved the director already chosen for "Bloomer Girl" and that in case he failed to act as director plaintiff was to have approval rights of any substitute director. Article 31 provided that plaintiff was to have the right of approval of the "Bloomer Girl" dance director, and Article 32 gave her the right of approval of the screenplay.

Defendant's letter of April 4 to plaintiff, which contained both defendant's notice of breach of the "Bloomer Girl" contract and offer of the lead in "Big Country," eliminated or impaired each of those rights. It read in part as follows: "The terms and conditions of our offer of employment are identical to those set forth in the 'Bloomer Girl' Agreement, Articles 1 through 34 and Exhibit A to the Agreement, except as follows:

"1. Article 31 of said Agreement will not be included in any contract of employment re-

garding 'Big Country, Big Man' as it is not a musical and it thus will not need a dance director.

"2. In the 'Bloomer Girl' agreement, in Articles 29 and 32, you were given certain director and screenplay approvals and you had preapproved certain matters. Since there simply is insufficient time to negotiate with you regarding your choice of director and regarding the screenplay and since you already expressed an interest in performing the role in 'Big Country, Big Man,' we must exclude from our offer of employment in 'Big Country, Big Man' any approval rights as are contained in said Articles 29 and 32; however, we shall consult with you respecting the director to be selected to direct the photoplay and will further consult with you with respect to the screenplay and any revisions or changes therein, provided, however, that if we fail to agree . . . the decision of . . . [defendant] with respect to the selection of a director and to revisions and changes in the said screenplay shall be binding upon the parties to said agreement."

service, less the amount which the employer affirmatively proves the employee has earned or with reasonable effort might have earned from other employment.... However, before projected earnings from other employment opportunities not sought or accepted by the discharged employee can be applied in mitigation, the employer must show that the other employment was comparable, or substantially similar, to that of which the employee has been deprived; the employee's rejection of or failure to seek other available employment of a different or inferior kind may not be resorted to in order to mitigate damages. (Gonzales v. Internat. Assn. of Machinists (1963) 213 Cal.App.2d 817, 822–824 [29 Cal.Rptr. 190]; Harris v. Nat. Union etc. Cooks, Stewards (1953) 116 Cal.App.2d 759, 761 [254 P.2d 673].... de la Falaise v. Gaumont–British Picture Corp., 39 Cal.App.2d 46 [103 P.2d 447 (1940)]....

In the present case defendant has raised no issue of *reasonableness of efforts* by plaintiffs to obtain other employment; the sole issue is whether plaintiff's refusal of defendant's substitute offer of "Big Country" may be used in mitigation. Nor, if the "Big Country" offer was of employment different or inferior when compared with the original "Bloomer Girl" employment, is there an issue as to whether or not plaintiff acted reasonably in refusing the substitute offer. Despite defendant's arguments to the contrary, no case cited or which our research has discovered holds or suggests that reasonableness is an element of a wrongfully discharged employee's option to reject, or fail to seek, different or inferior employment lest the possible earnings therefrom be charged against him in mitigation of damages.[13]

Applying the foregoing rules to the record in the present case, with all intendments in favor of the party opposing the summary judgment motion— here, defendant—it is clear that the trial court correctly ruled that plaintiff's failure to accept defendant's tendered substitute employment could not be applied in mitigation of damages because the offer of the "Big Country" lead was of employment both different and inferior, and that no factual dispute was presented on that issue. The mere circumstance that "Bloomer Girl" was to be a musical review calling upon plaintiff's talents as a dancer as well as an actress, and was to be produced in the City of Los Angeles, whereas "Big Country" was a straight dramatic role in a "Western Type" story taking place in an opal mine in Australia, demonstrates the difference in kind between the

---

13. Instead, in each case the reasonableness referred to was that of the *efforts* of the employee to obtain other employment that was not different or inferior; his right to reject the latter was declared as an unqualified rule of law. Thus Gonzales v. Internat. Assn. of Machinists, supra, 213 Cal.App.2d 817, 823–824, holds that the trial court correctly instructed the jury that plaintiff union member, a machinist, was required to make "such *efforts* as the average [member of his union] desiring employment would make at that particular time and place" (italics added); but, further, that the court *properly rejected* defendant's offer of proof of the availability of other kinds of employment at the same or higher pay than plaintiff usually received and all outside the jurisdiction of his union, as plaintiff could not be required to accept different employment or a non-union job.

In Harris v. Nat. Union etc. Cooks, Stewards, supra, 116 Cal.App.2d 759, 761, the issues were stated to be, inter alia, whether comparable employment was open to each plaintiff employee, and if so whether each plaintiff made a *reasonable effort* to secure such employment. It was held that the trial court *properly sustained an objection to an offer to prove a custom of accepting a job in a lower rank* when work in the higher rank was not available, as "The duty of mitigation of damages ... does not require the plaintiff 'to seek or to accept other employment of a different or inferior kind.'" (P. 764[5].)

See also: Lewis v. Protective Security Life Ins. Co. (1962) 208 Cal.App.2d 582, 584 [25 Cal.Rptr. 213]: "*honest effort* to find similar employment...." (Italics added.) ...

De La Falaise v. Gaumont–British Picture Corp., supra, 39 Cal.App.2d 461, 469: "reasonable effort."

two employments; the female lead as a dramatic actress in a western style motion picture can by no stretch of imagination be considered the equivalent of or substantially similar to the lead in a song-and-dance production.

Additionally, the substitute "Big Country" offer proposed to eliminate or impair the director and screenplay approvals accorded to plaintiff under the original "Bloomer Girl" contract (see fn. 2, ante), and thus constituted an offer of inferior employment. No expertise or judicial notice is required in order to hold that the deprivation or infringement of an employee's rights held under an original employment contract converts the available "other employment" relied upon by the employer to mitigate damages, into inferior employment which the employee need not seek or accept. (See Gonzales v. Internat. Assn. of Machinists, supra, 213 Cal.App.2d 817, 823–824; and fn. 5. . . .)

Statements found in affidavits submitted by defendant in opposition to plaintiff's summary judgment motion, to the effect that the "Big Country" offer was not of employment different from or inferior to that under the "Bloomer Girl" contract, merely repeat the allegations of defendant's answer to the complaint in this action, constitute only conclusionary assertions with respect to undisputed facts, and do not give rise to a triable factual issue so as to defeat the motion for summary judgment. . . .

In view of the determination that defendant failed to present any facts showing the existence of a factual issue with respect to its sole defense— plaintiff's rejection of its substitute employment offer in mitigation of damages—we need not consider plaintiff's further contention that for various reasons, including the provisions of the original contract set forth in footnote 1, ante, plaintiff was excused from attempting to mitigate damages.

The judgment is affirmed.

McComb, J., Peters, J., Tobriner, J., Kaus, J.,* and Roth, J.,** concurred.

[The dissenting opinion of Sullivan, Acting C.J., is omitted.]

Mosk, J., did not participate.

———

MR. EDDIE, INC. v. GINSBERG, 430 S.W.2d 5 (Tex.Civ.App.1968). Ginsberg was wrongfully dismissed by defendant early in the term of a three-year employment contract. Immediately after the dismissal Ginsberg took another job, which he held for thirty-four weeks, earning $13,760. After Ginsberg left that job, he spent $1,340 unsuccessfully seeking further employment. Held, Ginsberg was entitled to recover his remaining salary under his contract with defendant, minus the $13,760 earned on the other job, but plus the $1,340 he unsuccessfully expended in looking for further employment. As to the $1,340 expense, the court said, "the rule in such cases is . . . as follows: 'The expenses for which a recovery may be had include necessary and reasonable disbursements made in an effort to avoid or mitigate the injurious consequences of the defendant's wrong. . . . if such expenses are the result of a

---

* Assigned by the Acting Chairman of the Judicial Council.

** Assigned by the Acting Chairman of the Judicial Council.

prudent attempt to minimize damages they are recoverable even though the result is an aggravation of the damages rather than a mitigation.' "

SOUTHERN KESWICK, INC. v. WHETHERHOLT, 293 So.2d 109 (Fla.App.1974). This was an action for breach of an employment contract. The jury was instructed, "[It is] the general rule that employment of different or inferior nature cannot be used in reduction of damages." Reversed. "While we would agree that a wrongfully discharged employee is not obliged to *seek* employment of a different or inferior nature, if he in fact *obtains* such employment within the contract period his earnings should be used in mitigation of damages. The foregoing charge was therefore clearly wrong. . . ." (Emphasis added.)

SECTION 4. FORESEEABILITY

HADLEY v. BAXENDALE

In the Court of Exchequer, 1854.
9 Exch. 341.

... At the trial before Crompton, J., at the last Gloucester Assizes, it appeared that the plaintiffs carried on an extensive business as millers at Gloucester; and that, on the 11th of May, their mill was stopped by a breakage of the crank shaft by which the mill was worked. The steam-engine was manufactured by Messrs. Joyce & Co., the engineers, at Greenwich, and it became necessary to send the shaft as a pattern for a new one to Greenwich. The fracture was discovered on the 12th, and on the 13th the plaintiffs sent one of their servants to the office of the defendants, who are the well-known carriers trading under the name of Pickford & Co., for the purpose of having the shaft carried to Greenwich. The plaintiffs' servant told the clerk that the mill was stopped, and that the shaft must be sent immediately; and in answer to the inquiry when the shaft would be taken, the answer was, that if it was sent up by twelve o'clock any day, it would be delivered at Greenwich on the following day. On the following day the shaft was taken by the defendants before noon, for the purpose of being conveyed to Greenwich, and the sum of £2, 4s. was paid for its carriage for the whole distance; at the same time the defendants' clerk was told that a special entry, if required, should be made to hasten its delivery. The delivery of the shaft at Greenwich was delayed by some neglect; and the consequence was, that the plaintiffs did not receive the new shaft for several days after they would otherwise have done and the working of their mill was thereby delayed, and they thereby lost the profits they would otherwise have received.*

* In The Capacity Problem in Contract Law (2d ed.2004), RichardDanzig and Georffrey R. Watson set out the following statement from the Assize Report in August 8, 1853, edition of the Times of London:"[Instead of being forwarded by wagon immediately, [the crankshaft] waskept for several day in London, and was at length forwarded by water on the 20th,

On the part of the defendants, it was objected that these damages were too remote, and that the defendants were not liable with respect to them. The learned Judge left the case generally to the jury, who found a verdict with £25 damages beyond the amount paid into Court.**

WHATELEY, in last Michaelmas Term, obtained a rule nisi for a new trial, on the ground of misdirection.

KEATING and DOWDESWELL (Feb. 1) showed cause. The plaintiffs are entitled to the amount awarded by the jury as damages. These damages are not too remote, for they are not only the natural and necessary consequence of the defendants' default, but they are the only loss which the plaintiffs have actually sustained. The principle upon which damages are assessed is founded upon that of rendering compensation to the injured party....

[PARKE, B. The sensible rule appears to be that which has been laid down in France, and which is declared in their code—Code Civil, liv, iii, tit. iii. ss. 1149, 1150, 1151, and which is thus translated in Sedgwick [on Damages, p. 67]: "The damages due to the creditor consist in general of the loss that he has sustained, and the profit which he has been prevented from acquiring, subject to the modifications hereinafter contained. The debtor is only liable for the damages foreseen, or which might have been foreseen, at the time of the execution of the contract, when it is not owing to his fraud that the agreement has been violated. Even in the case of non-performance of the contract, resulting from the fraud of the debtor, the damages only comprise so much of the loss sustained by the creditor, and so much of the profit which he has been prevented from acquiring, as directly and immediately results from the non-performance of the contract."] If that rule is to be adopted, there was ample evidence in the present case of the defendants' knowledge of such a state of things as would necessarily result in the damage the plaintiffs suffered through the defendants' default....

[... MARTIN, B. Take the case of the non-delivery by a carrier of a delicate piece of machinery, whereby the whole of an extensive mill is thrown out of work for a considerable time; if the carrier is to be liable for the loss in that case, he might incur damages to the extent of 10,000*l*....] These extreme cases, and the difficulty which consequently exists in the estimation of the true amount of damages, supports the view for which the plaintiffs contend, that the question is properly for the decision of a jury, and therefore that this matter could not properly have been withdrawn from their consideration....

WHATELEY, WILLES, and PHIPSON, in support of the rule (Feb. 2). It has been contended, on the part of the plaintiffs, that the damages found by the jury are a matter fit for their consideration; but still the question remains, in what way ought the jury to have been directed? It has been also urged, that, in awarding damages, the law gives compensation to the injured individual. But it is clear that complete compensation is not to be awarded; for instance, the non-payment of a bill of exchange might lead to the utter ruin of the holder, and yet such damage could not be considered as necessarily resulting from the breach of contract, so as to entitle the party aggrieved to recover in respect of it. Take the case of the breach of a contract to supply a rick-cloth, whereby

along with many tons of iron goods which had been consigned to the same parties." Id. at 59 n. 5.

** According to the report of the case, the amount which the defendant had paid into

court was £25. See 9 Exch.Rep. at 343. (Footnote by ed.)

and in consequence of bad weather the hay, being unprotected, is spoiled, that damage would not be recoverable. Many similar cases might be added.... Sedgwick says [p. 28], "In regard to the quantum of damages, instead of adhering to the term compensation, it would be far more accurate to say, in the language of Domat, which we have cited above, 'that the object is to discriminate between that portion of the loss which must be borne by the offending party and that which must be borne by the sufferer.' The law in fact aims not at the satisfaction but at a division of the loss." ... This therefore is a question of law, and the jury ought to have been told that these damages were too remote; and that, in the absence of the proof of any other damage, the plaintiffs were entitled to nominal damages only....

The judgment of the Court was now delivered by Alderson, B.

We think that there ought to be a new trial in this case; but, in so doing, we deem it to be expedient and necessary to state explicitly the rule which the Judge, at the next trial, ought, in our opinion, to direct the jury to be governed by when they estimate the damages.

It is, indeed, of the last importance that we should do this; for, if the jury are left without any definite rule to guide them, it will, in such cases as these, manifestly lead to the greatest injustice. The Courts have done this on several occasions; and, in Blake v. Midland Railway Company, 18 Q.B. 93, the Court granted a new trial on this very ground, that the rule had not been definitely laid down to the jury by the learned Judge at Nisi Prius.

"There are certain established rules," this Court says, in Alder v. Keighley, 15 M. & W. 117, "according to which the jury ought to find." And the Court, in that case, adds: "and here there is a clear rule, that the amount which would have been received if the contract had been kept, is the measure of damages if the contract is broken."

Now we think the proper rule in such a case as the present is this:— Where two parties have made a contract which one of them has broken, the damages which the other party ought to receive in respect of such breach of contract should be such as may fairly and reasonably be considered either arising naturally, i.e., according to the usual course of things, from such breach of contract itself, or such as may reasonably be supposed to have been in the contemplation of both parties, at the time they made the contract, as the probable result of the breach of it. Now, if the special circumstances under which the contract was actually made were communicated by the plaintiffs to the defendants, and thus known to both parties, the damages resulting from the breach of such a contract, which they would reasonably contemplate, would be the amount of injury which would ordinarily follow from a breach of contract under these special circumstances so known and communicated. But, on the other hand, if these special circumstances were wholly unknown to the party breaking the contract, he, at the most, could only be supposed to have had in his contemplation the amount of injury which would arise generally, and in the great multitude of cases not affected by any special circumstances, from such a breach of contract. For, had the special circumstances been known, the parties might have specially provided for the breach of contract by special terms as to the damages in that case; and of this advantage it would be very unjust to deprive them. Now the above principles are those by which we think the jury ought to be guided in estimating the damages arising out of any breach of contract. It is said, that other cases such as breaches of contract in the non-payment of money, or in the not making a good title to land, are to be treated as exceptions from this, and as governed by a conventional rule. But as, in such cases, both parties must be supposed to be cognizant of that well-known rule, these cases may, we think, be more properly classed under the rule above enunciated as to cases under known special circumstances, because there both parties may reasonably be presumed to contemplate the estimation of the amount of damages according to the conventional rule. Now, in the present case, if we are to apply the principles above laid down, we find that the only circumstances here communicated by the plaintiffs to the defendants at the time the contract was made, were, that the article to be carried was the broken shaft of a mill, and that the plaintiffs were the millers of that mill. But how do these circumstances [show] reasonably that the profits of the mill must be stopped by an unreasonable delay in the delivery of the broken shaft by the carrier to the third person? Suppose the plaintiffs had another shaft in their possession put up or putting up at the time, and that they only wished to send back the broken shaft to the engineer who made it; it is clear that this would be quite consistent with the above circumstances, and yet the unreasonable delay in the delivery would have no effect upon the intermediate profits of the mill. Or, again, suppose that, at the time of the delivery to the carrier, the machinery of the mill had been in other respects defective, then, also, the same results would follow. Here it is true that the shaft was actually sent back to serve as a model for a new one, and that the want of a new one was the only cause of the stoppage of the mill, and that the loss of profits really arose from not sending down the new shaft in proper time, and that this arose from the delay in delivering the broken one to serve as a model. But it is obvious that, in the great multitude of cases of millers sending off broken shafts to third persons by a carrier under ordinary circumstances, such consequences would not, in all probability, have occurred; and these special circumstances were here never communicated by the plaintiffs to the defendants. It follows, therefore, that the loss of profits here cannot reasonably be considered such a consequence of the breach of contract as could have been fairly and reasonably contemplated by both the parties when they made this contract. For such loss would neither have flowed naturally from the breach of this contract in the great multitude of such cases occurring under ordinary circumstances, nor were the special circumstances, which, perhaps, would have made it a reasonable and natural consequence of such breach of contract, communicated to or known by the defendants. The Judge ought, therefore, to have told the jury, that, upon the facts then before them, they ought not to take the loss of profits into consideration at all in estimating the damages. There must therefore be a new trial in this case.

Rule absolute.

————

KOUFOS v. C. CZARNIKOW, LTD. [THE HERON II], [1969] A.C. 350 (H.L.1967). The facts in this case were stated by Lord Reid as follows:

By charter party of Oct. 15, 1960, the respondents chartered the appellant's vessel, Heron II, to proceed to Constanza, there to load a cargo of three thousand tons of sugar; and to carry it to Basrah, or, in the charterers' option, to Jeddah. The vessel left Constanza on Nov. 1. The option was not exercised and the vessel arrived at Basrah on Dec. 2. The umpire has found that "a reasonably accurate prediction of the length of the voyage was twenty days". But the vessel had in breach of contract made deviations which caused a delay of nine days.

It was the intention of the respondent charterers to sell the sugar "promptly after arrival at Basrah and after inspection by merchants". The appellant shipowner did not know this, but he was aware of the fact that there was a market for sugar at Basrah. The sugar was in fact sold at Basrah in lots between Dec. 12 and 22 but shortly before that time the market price had fallen partly by reason of the arrival of another cargo of sugar. It was found by the umpire that if there had not been this delay of nine days the sugar would have fetched £32 10s. per ton. The actual price realized was only £31 2s.9d. per ton. The charterers claim that they are entitled to recover the difference as damage for breach of contract. The shipowner admits that he is liable to pay interest for nine days on the value of the sugar and [plaintiff's cable] expenses but denies that fall in market value can be taken into account in assessing damages in this case.

All of the judges agreed that on these facts the shipowner was liable for damages measured by the fall in the sugar price. Again, Lord Reid:

> ... There is no finding that [the charterers] had in mind any particular date as the likely date of arrival at Basrah or that they had any knowledge or expectation that in late November or December there would be a rising or a falling market. The shipowner was given no information about these matters by the charterers. He did not know what the charterers intended to do with the sugar. But he knew there was a market in sugar at Basrah, and it appears to me that, if he had thought about the matter, he must have realized that at least it was not unlikely that the sugar would be sold in the market at market price on arrival. And he must be held to have known that in any ordinary market prices are apt to fluctuate from day to day: but he had no reason to suppose it more probable that during the relevant period such fluctuation would be downwards rather than upwards—it was an even chance that the fluctuation would be downwards....

While all the judges concurred in the result, they differed on how the principle of Hadley v. Baxendale should be expressed. The phrases "liable to result," "real danger," and "serious possibility," met general approval. Lord Reid somewhat querulously disagreed even with these phrases, but made some interesting comments:

> The modern rule of tort is quite different [from that in contract] and it imposes a much wider liability. The defendant will be liable for any type of damage which is reasonably foreseeable as liable to happen even in the most unusual case, unless the risk is so small that a reasonable man would in the whole circumstances feel justified in neglecting it. And there is good reason for the difference. In contract, if one party wishes to protect himself against a risk which to the other party would appear unusual, he can direct the other party's attention to it before the contract is made, and I need not stop to consider in what circumstances the other party will then be held to have accepted responsibility in that event.... [I]n tort, there is no opportunity for the injured party to protect himself in that way, and the tortfeasor cannot reasonably complain if he has to pay for some very unusual but nevertheless foreseeable damage which

results from his wrongdoing. I have no doubt that today a tortfeasor would be held liable for a type of damage as unlikely as was the stoppage of Hadley's Mill for lack of a crank shaft: to anyone with the knowledge the carrier had that may have seemed unlikely but the chance of it happening would have been seen to be far from negligible.

A passage in Lord Reid's opinion also suggests, by inference, some outer limits for determining whether an event should be reasonably foreseeable under the principle of Hadley v. Baxendale. "Suppose one takes a well-shuffled pack of cards, it is quite likely or not unlikely that the top card will prove to be a diamond: the odds are only three to one against. But most people would not say that it is quite likely to be the nine of diamonds for the odds are then fifty-one to one against." If this metaphor is to be taken seriously, it suggests that if, at the time of contract formation, there is a 25 percent chance that a given type of damage will occur in the event of breach, the damage will be compensable under Hadley v. Baxendale, but if there is only a 2 percent chance that a given type of damage will occur, the damage will not be compensable.

————

RESTATEMENT, SECOND, CONTRACTS § 351

[See Selected Source Materials Supplement]

————

UCC §§ 2–713, 2–715(2)

[See Selected Source Materials Supplement]

————

PANHANDLE AGRI–SERVICE, INC. v. BECKER, 231 Kan. 291, 644 P.2d 413 (1982). "Consequential damages are limited under [UCC §] 2–715(2)(a) to those instances where it is established that the loss could not reasonably be prevented by cover or otherwise. A buyer does not have to cover under [UCC §] 2–712(3); however, on failure to attempt cover, consequential damages, including loss of profits, cannot be recovered. [UCC §] 2–715(2)(a)."

————

CISG ART. 74

[See Selected Source Materials Supplement]

————

UNIDROIT PRINCIPLES OF INTERNATIONAL COMMERCIAL CONTRACTS ART. 7.4.4

[See Selected Source Materials Supplement]

PRINCIPLES OF EUROPEAN CONTRACT LAW ART. 9.503

[See Selected Source Materials Supplement]

SECTION 5. CERTAINTY

KENFORD CO. v. ERIE COUNTY

New York Court of Appeals, 1986.
67 N.Y.2d 257, 502 N.Y.S.2d 131, 493 N.E.2d 234.

PER CURIAM.

The issue in this appeal is whether a plaintiff, in an action for breach of contract, may recover loss of prospective profits for its contemplated 20–year operation of a domed stadium which was to be constructed by defendant County of Erie (County).

On August 8, 1969, pursuant to a duly adopted resolution of its legislature, the County of Erie entered into a contract with Kenford Company, Inc. (Kenford) and Dome Stadium, Inc. (DSI) for the construction and operation of a domed stadium facility near the City of Buffalo. The contract provided that construction of the facility by the County would commence within 12 months of the contract date and that a mutually acceptable 40–year lease between the County and DSI for the operation of said facility would be negotiated by the parties and agreed upon within three months of the receipt by the County of preliminary plans, drawings and cost estimates. It was further provided that in the event a mutually acceptable lease could not be agreed upon within the three-month period, a separate management contract between the County and DSI, as appended to the basic agreement, would be executed by the parties, providing for the operation of the stadium facility by DSI for a period of 20 years from the completion of the stadium and its availability for use.

Although strenuous and extensive negotiations followed, the parties never agreed upon the terms of a lease, nor did construction of a domed facility begin within the one-year period or at any time thereafter. A breach of the contract thus occurred and this action was commenced in June 1971 by Kenford and DSI.

Prolonged and extensive pretrial and preliminary proceedings transpired throughout the next 10 years, culminating with the entry of an order which affirmed the grant of summary judgment against the County on the issue of liability and directed a trial limited to the issue of damages (*Kenford Co. v.*

County of Erie, 88 A.D.2d 758, *lv dismissed* 58 N.Y.2d 689). The ensuing trial ended some nine months later with a multimillion dollar jury verdict in plaintiffs' favor. An appeal to the Appellate Division resulted in a modification of the judgment. That court reversed portions of the judgment awarding damages for loss of profits and for certain out-of-pocket expenses incurred, and directed a new trial upon other issues (*Kenford Co. v. County of Erie,* 108 A.D.2d 132). On appeal to this court, we are concerned only with that portion of the verdict which awarded DSI money damages for loss of prospective profits during the 20–year period of the proposed management contract, as appended to the basic contract. That portion of the verdict was set aside by the Appellate Division and the cause of action dismissed. The court concluded that the use of expert opinion to present statistical projections of future business operations involved the use of too many variables to provide a rational basis upon which lost profits could be calculated and, therefore, such projections were insufficient as a matter of law to support an award of lost profits. We agree with this ultimate conclusion, but upon different grounds.

Loss of future profits as damages for breach of contract have been permitted in New York under long-established and precise rules of law. First, it must be demonstrated with certainty that such damages have been caused by the breach and, second, the alleged loss must be capable of proof with reasonable certainty. In other words, the damages may not be merely speculative, possible or imaginary, but must be reasonably certain and directly traceable to the breach, not remote or the result of other intervening causes (*Wakeman v. Wheeler & Wilson Mfg. Co.,* 101 N.Y. 205). In addition, there must be a showing that the particular damages were fairly within the contemplation of the parties to the contract at the time it was made (*Witherbee v. Meyer,* 155 N.Y. 446). If it is a new business seeking to recover for loss of future profits, a stricter standard is imposed for the obvious reason that there does not exist a reasonable basis of experience upon which to estimate lost profits with the requisite degree of reasonable certainty (*Cramer v. Grand Rapids Show Case Co.,* 223 N.Y. 63; 25 CJS, Damages, § 42[b]).

These rules must be applied to the proof presented by DSI in this case. We note the procedure for computing damages selected by DSI was in accord with contemporary economic theory and was presented through the testimony of recognized experts. Such a procedure has been accepted in this State and many other jurisdictions (*see, De Long v. County of Erie,* 60 N.Y.2d 296). DSI's economic analysis employed historical data, obtained from the operation of other domed stadiums and related facilities throughout the country, which was then applied to the results of a comprehensive study of the marketing prospects for the proposed facility in the Buffalo area. The quantity of proof is massive and, unquestionably, represents business and industry's most advanced and sophisticated method for predicting the probable results of contemplated projects. Indeed, it is difficult to conclude what additional relevant proof could have been submitted by DSI in support of its attempt to establish, with reasonable certainty, loss of prospective profits. Nevertheless, DSI's proof is insufficient to meet the required standard.

The reason for this conclusion is twofold. Initially, the proof does not satisfy the requirement that liability for loss of profits over a 20–year period was in the contemplation of the parties at the time of the execution of the basic contract or at the time of its breach (*see, Chapman v. Fargo,* 223 N.Y. 32; 36 N.Y.Jur.2d, Damages, §§ 39, 40, at 66–70). Indeed, the provisions in the contract providing remedy for a default do not suggest or provide for such a heavy responsibility on the part of the County. In the absence of any provision for such an eventuality, the commonsense rule to apply is to consider what the parties would have concluded had they considered the subject. The evidence here fails to demonstrate that liability for loss of profits over the length of the contract would have been in the contemplation of the parties at the relevant times.

Next, we note that despite the massive quantity of expert proof submitted by DSI, the ultimate conclusions are still projections, and as employed in the present day commercial world, subject to adjustment and modification. We of course recognize that any projection cannot be absolute, nor is there any such requirement, but it is axiomatic that the degree of certainty is dependent upon known or unknown factors which form the basis of the ultimate conclusion. Here, the foundations upon which the economic model was created undermine the certainty of the projections. DSI assumed that the facility was completed, available for use and successfully operated by it for 20 years, providing professional sporting events and other forms of entertainment, as well as hosting meetings, conventions and related commercial gatherings. At the time of the breach, there was only one other facility in this country to use as a basis of comparison, the Astrodome in Houston. Quite simply, the multitude of assumptions required to establish projections of profitability over the life of this contract require speculation and conjecture, making it beyond the capability of even the most sophisticated procedures to satisfy the legal requirements of proof with reasonable certainty.

The economic facts of life, the whim of the general public and the fickle nature of popular support for professional athletic endeavors must be given great weight in attempting to ascertain damages 20 years in the future. New York has long recognized the inherent uncertainties of predicting profits in the entertainment field in general (*see, Broadway Photoplay Co. v. World Film Corp.*, 225 N.Y. 104) and, in this case, we are dealing, in large part, with a new facility furnishing entertainment for the public. It is our view that the record in this case demonstrates the efficacy of the principles set forth by this court in *Cramer v. Grand Rapids Show Case Co.* (223 N.Y. 63, *supra*), principles to which we continue to adhere. In so doing, we specifically reject the "rational basis" test enunciated in *Perma Research & Dev. Co. v. Singer Co.* (542 F.2d 111, *cert. denied* 429 U.S. 987) and adopted by the Appellate Division.

Accordingly, that portion of the order of the Appellate Division being appealed from should be affirmed.

Chief Judge WACHTLER and Judges MEYER, ALEXANDER, TITONE and KANE* concur in Per Curiam opinion; Judges Simons, Kaye AND Hancock, Jr., TAKING NO PART.

Order insofar as appealed from affirmed, with costs.

NOTE ON THE NEW–BUSINESS RULE

In the past, a major application of the uncertainty principle was the "new-business rule." This rule prohibits recovery of lost profits that a

---

* Designated pursuant to N.Y. Constitution, article VI, § 2.

plaintiff claims would have been generated by a proposed new business, on the ground that in such cases profits are too speculative. (In one typical fact-pattern, the plaintiff had leased premises for its new business from the defendant, who then broke the lease before the plaintiff even moved in.) The new-business rule still surfaces in some cases, but there is a definite trend toward abrogating the rule, and reconstruing the older cases as resting only on the particular facts involved, rather than on a special rule. For example, in Fera v. Village Plaza, Inc., 396 Mich. 639, 242 N.W.2d 372 (1976), plaintiffs executed a ten-year lease for a "book and bottle" shop in defendants' proposed shopping center. Later, plaintiffs were refused their space, because defendants had misplaced the lease and rented the space to other tenants. Plaintiffs brought suit, claiming lost profits. The jury returned a verdict against the defendants for $200,000. The Court of Appeals (an intermediate appellate court) reversed, partly on the basis of the new-business rule. The Michigan Supreme Court reinstated the jury verdict:

> [Earlier Michigan cases] should not be read as stating a rule of law which prevents *every* new business from recovering anticipated lost profits for breach of contract. The rule is merely an application of the doctrine that "[i]n order to be entitled to a verdict, or a judgment, for damages for breach of contract, the plaintiff must lay a basis for a reasonable estimate of the extent of his harm, measured in money." 5 Corbin on Contracts, § 1020, p. 124. The issue becomes one of sufficiency of proof. . . .

> The Court of Appeals based its opinion reversing the jury's award on two grounds: First, that a new business cannot recover damages for lost profits for breach of a lease. We have expressed our disapproval of that rule. Secondly, the Court of Appeals held plaintiffs barred from recovery because the proof of lost profits was entirely speculative. We disagree. . . .

> While we might have found plaintiffs' proofs lacking had we been members of the jury, that is not the standard of review we employ. As a reviewing court we will not invade the fact finding of the jury or remand for entry of judgment unless the factual record is so clear that reasonable minds may not disagree. This is not the situation here. . . .

————

ROMBOLA v. COSINDAS, 351 Mass. 382, 220 N.E.2d 919 (1966). Rombola agreed to train, maintain, and race Cosindas's horse, Margy Sampson, for the period November 8, 1962, to December 1, 1963. Rombola was to pay all expenses and receive 75% of all gross purses, and Cosindas was to receive the remaining 25%. In the winter of 1962–63, Rombola maintained and trained the horse at his stable, and in the following spring and summer he raced her twenty-five times. In fall 1963, Rombola entered Margy Sampson in six stake races—races in which horses run against others in their own class, according to the amount of money they have won—to be held at a Suffolk Downs meet ending December 1. Before the meet began, Cosindas took possession of Margy Sampson, and thereby deprived Rombola of his right to race her. The horse was not raced again until after December 1. Rombola sued Cosindas for breach of contract, and the trial judge directed a verdict for Cosindas on the ground that Rombola's damages were too uncertain. Reversed.

... In the year of the contract, of the twenty-five races in which the horse was entered by Rombola, she had won ten and shared in the purse money in a total of twenty races, earning, in all, purses approximating $12,000. In the year following the expiration of Rombola's contract with Cosindas, the horse raced twenty-nine times and won money in an amount almost completely consistent percentagewise with the money won during the period of the contract. . . .

We think ... that Rombola would be entitled to show substantial damages on the theory of loss of prospective profits. . . . [Margy Sampson] had already proved her ability both prior to and while under Rombola's management and training, over an extended period of time, against many competitors and under varying track conditions. Her consistent performance in the year subsequent to the breach negates any basis for an inference of a diminution in ability or in earning capacity at the time of the Suffolk Downs meet. While it is possible that no profits would have been realized if Margy Sampson had participated in the scheduled stake races, that possibility is inherent in any business venture. . . .

CONTEMPORARY MISSION, INC. v. FAMOUS MUSIC CORP., 557 F.2d 918 (2d Cir.1977). Famous Music failed to perform a contract with Contemporary Mission, under which Famous Music had agreed to pay a royalty to Contemporary Mission, in return for the master tape-recording of *Virgin* (a rock opera) and the exclusive right to manufacture and sell records made from the master. Under the agreement, Famous Music was obliged to release at least four separate single records from *Virgin*.

Under the doctrine of Wood v. Lucy (Chapter 2, Section 3, supra), Famous Music had an obligation to use reasonable efforts to promote *Virgin* on a nationwide basis. Prior to the breach, one of the singles from *Virgin* had reached number 80 on the hot soul record charts, and later it reached number 61. At the trial, Contemporary Mission offered a statistical analysis of every song that had reached number 61 during 1974. This analysis showed that 76 percent of the 324 songs that had reached number 61 ultimately reached the top 40; 65 percent reached the top 30; 51 percent reached the top 20; 34 percent reached the top 10; 21 percent reached the top 5; and 10 percent reached number 1. Contemporary Mission also was prepared to offer the testimony of an expert witness who could have converted these measures of success into projected sales figures and lost royalties. The trial judge excluded all this evidence on the ground that it was speculative. Held, the evidence should have been admitted.

"... This is not a case in which the plaintiff sought to prove hypothetical profits from the sale of a hypothetical record at a hypothetical price in a hypothetical market. . . . [T]he record was real, the price was fixed, the market was buying and the record's success, while modest, was increasing. Even after the promotional efforts ended, [and] the record was withdrawn from the marketplace, it was carried, as a result of its own momentum, to an additional 10,000 sales and to a rise from approximately number 80 on the 'Hot Soul Singles' chart of Billboard magazine to number 61. It cannot be gainsaid that if someone had continued to promote it, and if it had not been withdrawn from the market, it would have sold more records than it actually did. Thus, it is certain that Contemporary suffered some damage in the form of lost royalties. . . . ''

UCC § 1–106(1)

[See Selected Source Materials Supplement]

RESTATEMENT, SECOND, CONTRACTS § 352

[See Selected Source Materials Supplement]

UNIDROIT PRINCIPLES OF INTERNATIONAL COMMERCIAL CONTRACTS ART. 7.4.3

[See Selected Source Materials Supplement]

CHAPLIN v. HICKS, [1911] 2 K.B. 786. Hicks, a well-known actor and theater manager, ran a contest for actresses. The prizes were theatrical engagements. The not-very-appealing rules of the contest were as follows: Contestants would send photographs of themselves to Hicks, who would divide England into ten districts and would publish, in a newspaper in each district, photographs of the candidates he had selected. Newspaper readers would then vote for the contestants they considered to be the most beautiful. Hicks would thereafter interview fifty finalists, consisting of the five candidates in each district who had the highest votes. From these fifty finalists, Hicks would select twelve winning contestants, who would receive the theatrical engagements.

Chaplin became one of the fifty finalists, but Hicks did not give her an interview. Chaplin then brought an action against Hicks for the loss of her chance of being selected as one of the twelve winners. At trial, she was awarded damages of £ 100. The Court of Appeal affirmed. Lord Justice Moulton stated:

> Is expulsion from a limited class of competitors an injury? To my mind there can be only one answer to that question; it is an injury and may be a very substantial one. Therefore the plaintiff starts with an

unchallengeable case of injury, and the damages given in respect of it should be equivalent to the loss. . . .

. . . Is there any such rule as that, where the result of a contract depends on the volition of an independent party, the law shuts its eyes to the wrong and says that there are no damages? Such a rule, if it existed, would work great wrong. Let us take the case of a man under a contract of service to serve as a second-class clerk for five years at a salary of £200 a year, which expressly provides that, at the end of that period, out of every five second-class clerks two first-class clerks will be chosen at a salary of £500 a year. If such a clause is embodied in the contract, it is clear that a person thinking of applying for the position would reckon that he would have the advantage of being one of five persons from whom the two first-class clerks must be chosen, and that might be a very substantial portion of the consideration for his appointment. If, after he has taken the post and worked under the contract of service, the employers repudiate the obligation, is he to have no remedy? He has sustained a very real loss, and there can be no possible reason why the law should not leave it to the jury to estimate the value of that of which he has been deprived. Where by contract a man has a right to belong to a limited class of competitors, he is possessed of something of value, and it is the duty of the jury to estimate the pecuniary value of that advantage if it is taken from him.

MEARS v. NATIONWIDE MUTUAL INS. CO., 91 F.3d 1118 (8th Cir. 1996). Mears won a contest in which the prize was two Mercedes–Benz automobiles. The promoter of the contest contended that the contract was too indefinite to enforce because there was a very wide range of Mercedes–Benz used and new models and no model had been specified. Held for Mears.

First, contract terms are interpreted with strong consideration for what is reasonable. . . . Under a reasonable interpretation of the contest contract, the jury could expect the automobiles to be new.

Second, when a minor ambiguity exists in a contract, Arkansas law allows the complaining party to insist on the reasonable interpretation that is least favorable to him. . . . These two factors, taken together, are sufficient to support the jury's conclusion that Nationwide owed Mears two of Mercedes–Benz's least expensive new automobiles as his contest prize."

RESTATEMENT, SECOND, CONTRACTS § 355

[See Selected Source Materials Supplement]

SECTION 6.   LIQUIDATED DAMAGES

WASSERMAN'S INC. v. MIDDLETOWN

Supreme Court of New Jersey, 1994.
137 N.J. 238, 645 A.2d 100.

POLLOCK, J.

Pursuant to a public advertisement for bids, plaintiff Wasserman's Inc. (Wasserman's) and defendant, Township of Middletown (the Township or Middletown), entered into a commercial lease for a tract of municipally-owned property. The agreement contained a clause providing that if the Township cancelled the lease, it would pay the lessee, Wasserman's, a pro-rata reimbursement for any improvement costs and damages of twenty-five percent of the lessee's average gross receipts for one year. In 1989, the Township cancelled the lease and sold the property, but refused to pay the agreed damages. On cross-motions for summary judgment, the Law Division held that the ... cancellation clause [was] enforceable. It subsequently required the Township to pay damages in the amount of $346,058.44 plus interest. In an unreported opinion, the Appellate Division affirmed. We granted certification, 134 *N.J.* 478, 634 A.2d 525 (1993), and now on ... reverse and remand for a plenary trial on damages.... We affirm the award of renovation costs and remand to the Law Division the issue of the enforceability of the stipulated damages clause.

–I–

The Township owned a parcel of approximately 20,500 square feet in a commercial area at 89 Leonardville Road, in the Belford section of the Township. From 1948 to 1968, Wasserman's leased the property from the Township for a 3,200–square-foot general store. In 1969, the Township advertised for bids to lease the property, which the Township evaluated at $47,500. Wasserman's submitted the sole bid. After rejecting Wasserman's bid, the Township again advertised in May 1970. Once again, Wasserman's submitted the only bid. Subsequent negotiations resulted in the Township adopting a resolution approving the lease on September 22, 1970. The parties signed the lease on May 21, 1971.

At the center of the dispute is the cancellation clause in the lease. The bid specifications provided that if the Township cancelled the lease, it would pay the tenant a pro-rata reimbursement of improvement costs. Consistent with the specifications, the clause provides in part for reimbursement: "payment to be made shall be (1.) total value of all improvements made by lessee at time of construction (multiplied by) years remaining in Lease term (divided by) total number of years in Lease term." More controversial is the second half of the clause, the terms of which were not included in the original specifications. That provision requires the Township to pay "(2.) twenty-five percent of the lessee[']s average gross receipts for one year (to be computed by + (adding) the lessee[']s total gross receipts for the lessee[']s three full fiscal years immediately preceding the time of cancellation of the lease and (dividing by)

12 (twelve)[)]." The lease also provided for a fixed monthly rental of $458.33, with no escalation for the entire thirty-year term.

Wasserman's made the agreed improvements, spending $142,336.01 in 1971 on the expansion and renovation of the store, which now is approximately 5,600 square feet. In August 1973, Wasserman's sold "the business," presumably the corporate assets, and sublet the premises to Rocco Laurino doing business as Jo–Ro, Inc. (Jo–Ro). The sublease provided that Jo–Ro was to pay Wasserman's a monthly rent of $1,850. Wasserman's and Jo–Ro, jointly described as "plaintiffs," provided for an allocation of any payments made by the Township if it cancelled the lease.

In 1977, Samuel Krawet and Arnold Kornblum purchased from Laurino all of the Jo–Ro stock for $95,000. In connection with the sale, Laurino executed an affidavit, representing that the lease between Middletown and Wasserman's was in full force and effect. Additionally, the Township sent a letter to Wasserman's stating that the Township would permit subletting the property to Jo–Ro.

By letter dated December 7, 1987, the Township cancelled the lease effective December 31, 1988. Krawet and Kornblum vacated the premises, leaving them without a place for their business. In June 1989, the Township, after advertising the property at public auction, sold it for $610,000, nearly thirteen times the value of the property at the time the Township had leased it to Wasserman's in 1971 . . . .

–II–

Plaintiffs sued for breach of contract, seeking in part damages under the terms of the lease. The Township filed an answer and counterclaim seeking a declaration of invalidity of that part of the cancellation clause that required the Township to pay as damages twenty-five percent of the lessee's gross receipts. Originally the Township also disputed its obligation to reimburse Wasserman's for a pro-rata portion of the cost of renovations, but it now concedes the validity of that provision. The parties filed cross-motions for summary judgment.

The Law Division initially granted plaintiffs a partial summary judgment according "full force and effect" to the lease and the cancellation clause. On a subsequent motion, the court awarded plaintiffs damages of $346,058.44 plus ten-percent prejudgment interest. The trial court calculated damages as follows:

> $142,336.01 (construction costs) multiplied by 11.75 (remaining years) divided by 30 years (term of lease) for a total of $55,748.27.

> $3,483,722.25 (Jo–Ro's gross receipts for the years 1985, 1986, 1987) divided by 12 equalling $290,310.18.

Construction compensation	$ 55,748.27
Gross receipts compensation	+ 290,310.18
Total amount due	$346,058.45 . . .

–IV–

The provision in the termination clause providing for damages based on the lessee's gross receipts presents a more difficult issue [than damages based on renovation costs]. The issue is whether that provision is an enforceable liquidated damages provision or is an unenforceable penalty clause.

Disapproval of penalty clauses originated at early common law when debtors bound themselves through sealed penalty bonds for twice the amount of their actual debts. Charles J. Goetz & Robert E. Scott, *Liquidated Damages, Penalties and the Just Compensation Principle: Some Notes on an Enforcement Model and a Theory of Efficient Breach*, 77 *Colum.L.Rev.*, 554, 554 (1977) (hereinafter Goetz & Scott). Because clauses in penalty bonds "carried an unusual danger of oppression and extortion," equity courts refused to enforce them. *Id.* at 555. "This equitable rule, designed to prevent overreaching and to give relief from unconscionable bargains, was later adopted by courts of law." John D. Calamari & Joseph M. Perillo, *The Law of Contracts*, § 14–31 at 639 (3d ed. 1987) (hereinafter Calamari & Perillo). In a sense, judicial reluctance to enforce penalty clauses is a product of history.

For more than five centuries, courts have scrutinized contractual provisions that specify damages payable in the event of breach. *Wassenaar v. Panos*, 111 *Wis.2d* 518, 331 *N.W.2d* 357, 362 (1983); Goetz & Scott, *supra*, 77 *Colum.L.Rev.* at 554. The validity of these "stipulated damage clauses" has depended on a judicial assessment of the clauses as an unenforceable penalty or as an enforceable provision for "liquidated damage." Thus, " '[l]iquidated damages' and 'penalties' are terms used to reflect legal conclusions as to the enforceability or nonenforceability, respectively, of stipulated damage clauses." Kenneth W. Clarkson et al., *Liquidated Damages v. Penalties: Sense or Nonsense?*, 1978 *Wis.L.Rev.* 351, 351 n. 1 (hereinafter Clarkson).

Thirty years ago, the Appellate Division distinguished liquidated damages and penalty clauses:

> *Liquidated damages* is the sum a party to a contract agrees to pay if he breaks some promise, and which, having been arrived at by a good faith effort to estimate in advance the actual damages that will probably ensue from the breach, is legally recoverable as agreed damages if the breach occurs. A *penalty* is the sum a party agrees to pay in the event of a breach, but which is fixed, not as a pre-estimate of probable actual damages, but as a punishment, the threat of which is designed to prevent the breach.

Parties to a contract may not fix a penalty for its breach. The settled rule in this State is that such a contract is unlawful.

[*Westmount Country Club v. Kameny*, 82 *N.J.Super.* 200, 205, 197 *A.2d* 379 (1964) (citations omitted).]

Stating the distinction, however, has been easier than describing its underlying rationale. " '[T]he ablest judges have declared that they felt themselves embarrassed in ascertaining the principle on which the decisions [distinguishing penalties from liquidated damages] were founded.' " E. Allan Farnsworth, *Contracts* § 12.18 at 937 (2d ed. 1990) (alterations in original) (quoting *Cotheal v. Talmage*, 9 *N.Y.* 551, 553 (1854)); *see also Giesecke v.*

Cullerton, 280 *Ill.* 510, 117 *N.E.* 777, 778 (1917) (observing that "no branch of the law is involved in more obscurity by contradictory decisions").

As the law has evolved, a stipulated damage clause "must constitute a reasonable forecast of the provable injury resulting from breach; otherwise, the clause will be unenforceable as a penalty and the non-breaching party will be limited to conventional damage measures." Goetz & Scott, *supra,* 77 *Colum.L.Rev.* at 554. So viewed, "reasonableness" emerges as the standard for deciding the validity of stipulated damages clauses. *See Wassenaar, supra,* 331 N.W.2d at 361 (noting that "[t]he overall single test of validity is whether the clause is reasonable under the totality of circumstances").

The reasonableness test has developed as a compromise between two competing viewpoints concerning stipulated damages clauses. The Wisconsin Supreme Court has described the policy considerations underlying these viewpoints:

> Enforcement of stipulated damages clauses is urged because the clauses serve several purposes. The clauses allow the parties to control their exposure to risk by setting the payment for breach in advance. They avoid the uncertainty, delay, and expense of using the judicial process to determine actual damages. They allow the parties to fashion a remedy consistent with economic efficiency in a competitive market, and they enable the parties to correct what the parties perceive to be inadequate judicial remedies by agreeing upon a formula which may include damage elements too uncertain or remote to be recovered under rules of damages applied by the courts. In addition to these policies specifically relating to stipulated damages clauses, considerations of judicial economy and freedom of contract favor enforcement of stipulated damages clauses.

> A competing set of policies disfavors stipulated damages clauses, and thus courts have not been willing to enforce stipulated damages clauses blindly without carefully scrutinizing them. Public law, not private law, ordinarily defines the remedies of the parties. Stipulated damages are an exception to this rule. Stipulated damages allow private parties to perform the judicial function of providing the remedy in breach of contract cases, namely, compensation of the nonbreaching party, and courts must ensure that the private remedy does not stray too far from the legal principle of allowing compensatory damages. Stipulated damages substantially in excess of injury may justify an inference of unfairness in bargaining or an objectionable *in terrorem* agreement to deter a party from breaching the contract, to secure performance, and to punish the breaching party if the deterrent is ineffective. [*Wassenaar, supra,* 331 N.W.2d at 362.]

Consistent with the principle of reasonableness, New Jersey courts have viewed enforceability of stipulated damages clauses as depending on whether the set amount "is a reasonable forecast of just compensation for the harm that is caused by the breach" and whether that harm "is incapable or very difficult of accurate estimate." *Westmount Country Club, supra,* 82 *N.J.Super.* at 206, 197 A.2d 379; *accord Monmouth Park Ass'n v. Wallis Iron Works,* 55 N.J.L. 132, 140–41, 26 A. 140 (E. & A. 1892); *Wood v. City of Ocean City,* 85 *N.J.Eq.* 328, 330, 96 A. 489 (Ch.1915); *see 218–220 Market St. Corp. v. Krich– Radisco, Inc.,* 124 *N.J.L.* 302, 305, 11 A.2d 109 (E. & A.1939).

Uncertainty or difficulty in assessing damages is best viewed not as an independent test, Calamari and Perillo, *supra*, § 14–31 at 641; Goetz & Scott, *supra*, 77 *Colum.L.Rev.* at 559 (stating, "liquidated damages provisions have seldom been voided solely because the damages were easy to estimate"), but rather as an element of assessing the reasonableness of a liquidated damages clause, *Wassenaar*, *supra*, 331 *N.W.*2d at 363. Thus, "[t]he greater the difficulty of estimating or proving damages, the more likely the stipulated damages will appear reasonable." *Ibid.*

Some courts in other jurisdictions have also considered whether the parties intended the clause to be one for liquidated damages. Clarkson, *supra*, 1978 *Wis.L.Rev.* at 353. Even those courts recognize that "subjective intent has little bearing on whether the clause is objectively reasonable." *Wassenaar*, *supra*, 331 *N.W.*2d at 363. For the past eighty years, New Jersey courts have relied on the "circumstances of the case and not on the words used by the parties" in determining the enforceability of stipulated damages clauses. *Gibbs v. Cooper*, 86 *N.J.L.* 226, 227–28, 90 *A.* 1115 (E. & A.1914); *see also* Farnsworth, *supra*, § 12.18 at 939 ("the parties' own characterization of the sum as 'liquidated damages' or as a 'penalty' is not controlling"); Clarkson, *supra*, 1978 *Wis.L.Rev.* at 353 (same); *cf. Monmouth Park Ass'n*, *supra*, 55 *N.J.L.* at 141, 26 *A.* 140 (stating, "if it be doubtful on the whole agreement whether the sum is intended as a penalty or as liquidated damages, it will be construed as a penalty, because the law favors mere indemnity"). We conclude that the parties' characterization of stipulated damages as "liquidated damages" or as a "penalty" should not be dispositive.

Although the Appellate Division has indicated that courts should determine the enforceability of a stipulated damages clause as of the time of the making of the contract, *Westmount Country Club*, *supra*, 82 *N.J.Super.* at 206, 197 *A.*2d 379, the modern trend is towards assessing reasonableness either at the time of contract formation or at the time of the breach. Calamari & Perillo, *supra*, § 14–31 at 642 (stating, "there are two moments at which the liquidated damages clause may be judged rather than just one").

Actual damages, moreover, reflect on the reasonableness of the parties' prediction of damages. "If the damages provided for in the contract are grossly disproportionate to the actual harm sustained, the courts usually conclude that the parties' original expectations were unreasonable." *Wassenaar*, *supra*, 331 *N.W.*2d at 364; *see* 5A. *Corbin on Contracts* § 1063 (1951) (Corbin) ("It is to be observed that hindsight is frequently better than foresight, and that, in passing judgment upon the honesty and genuineness of the preestimate made by the parties, the court cannot help but be influenced by its knowledge of subsequent events."). Determining enforceability at the time either when the contract is made or when it is breached encourages more frequent enforcement of stipulated damages clauses. Calamari & Perillo, *supra*, § 14–31 at 642.

Two of the most authoritative statements concerning liquidated damages are contained in the Uniform Commercial Code and the *Restatement (Second) of Contracts*, both of which emphasize reasonableness as the touchstone. Farnsworth, *supra*, § 12.18 at 938. Thus, section 2–718 of the Uniform Commercial Code, adopted in New Jersey as *N.J.S.A.* 12A:2–718, provides:

> (1) Damages for breach by either party may be liquidated in the agreement but only at an amount which is reasonable in the light of the

anticipated or actual harm caused by the breach, the difficulties of proof of loss, and the inconvenience or nonfeasibility of otherwise obtaining an adequate remedy.

Similarly, the Second Restatement of Contracts provides:

> Damages for breach by either party may be liquidated in the agreement but only at an amount that is reasonable in the light of the anticipated or actual loss caused by the breach and the difficulties of proof of loss. A term fixing unreasonably large liquidated damages is unenforceable on grounds of public policy as a penalty. [*Restatement (Second) of Contracts* § 356(1) (1981).]

Consistent with the trend toward enforcing stipulated damages clauses, the Appellate Division has recognized that such clauses should be deemed presumptively reasonable and that the party challenging such a clause should bear the burden of proving its unreasonableness.... Similarly, most courts today place the burden on the party challenging a stipulated damages clause....

In commercial transactions between parties with comparable bargaining power, stipulated damage provisions can provide a useful and efficient remedy.... Sophisticated parties acting under the advice of counsel often negotiate stipulated damages clauses to avoid the cost and uncertainty of litigation. Such parties can be better situated than courts to provide a fair and efficient remedy. Absent concerns about unconscionability, courts frequently need ask no more than whether the clause is reasonable. We do not reach the issue of the enforceability of liquidated damage clauses in consumer contracts. Notwithstanding the presumptive reasonableness of stipulated damage clauses, we are sensitive to the possibility that, as their history discloses, such clauses may be unconscionable and unjust. *Foont–Freedenfeld Corp. v. Electro–Protective Corp.*, 126 *N.J.Super.* 254, 258, 314 A.2d 69 (App.Div.1973), *aff'd o.b.*, 64 *N.J.* 197, 314 A.2d 68 (1974); *Westmount Country Club, supra*, 82 *N.J.Super.* at 206, 197 A.2d 379; Goetz & Scott, *supra*, 77 *Colum.L.Rev.* at 588 (stating that "in the absence of bargaining unfairness, a stipulated damage clause reflects equivalent value").

–V–

The purpose of a stipulated damages clause is not to compel the promisor to perform, but to compensate the promisee for non-performance. Farnsworth, *supra*, § 12.18 at 936. Accordingly, provisions for liquidated damages are enforceable only if "the amount so fixed is a reasonable forecast of just compensation for the harm that is caused by the breach." *Westmount Country Club, supra*, 82 *N.J.Super.* at 206, 197 A.2d 379; *see also Restatement (Second) of Contracts, supra*, § 356 comment a (stating, "The parties to a contract may effectively provide in advance the damages that are to be payable in the event of breach as long as the provision does not disregard the principle of just compensation."). One injured by a breach of contract is entitled only to just and adequate compensation. *McDaniel Bros. Constr. Co. v. Jordy*, 195 So.2d 922, 925 (Miss.1967). Thus, the subject cancellation clause is unreasonable if it does more than compensate plaintiffs for their approximate actual damages caused by the breach.

Whether measured from the time of execution of the contract or from the termination of the lease, *see Westmount Country Club, supra*, 82 *N.J.Super.* at

206, 197 A.2d 379, damages based on gross receipts run the risk of being found unreasonable. Generally speaking, gross receipts do not reflect actual losses incurred because of the cancellation. Gross receipts, unlike net profits, do not account for ordinary expenses; nor do they account for the expenses specifically attributable to the breach. Here, we cannot determine whether the stipulated amount was based on damages that would likely flow from a breach or whether it is an arbitrary figure unrelated to any such damages. . . .

Furthermore, basing damages on gross profits could award the plaintiff a windfall. . . .

We cannot determine from plaintiffs' gross receipts the losses they sustained because of the Township's cancellation of the lease. The subject clause requires the Township to pay damages of twenty-five percent of the lessee's average gross receipts for one year. Under the lease, average gross receipts are calculated by taking an average of the lessee's total gross receipts for three fiscal years immediately preceding the cancellation. So calculated, Jo–Ro's average yearly gross was $1,161,240.75. Twenty-five percent of this figure amounts to $290,310.18.

This amount, however, does not necessarily reflect plaintiffs' actual losses on considering operating expenses or relocation costs and other expenses attributable to defendant's breach. As reflected in Jo–Ro's income-tax returns, Jo–Ro earned a net profit of $3,649 in 1985, $414 in 1986, and sustained a loss of $323 in 1987. We recognize the difference between tax losses and actual losses. Yet, to the extent that tax returns reflect actual profit or loss, they demonstrate the unreasonableness of damages exceeding $290,000, which were calculated on the basis of gross receipts.

The decision whether a stipulated damages clause is enforceable is a question of law for the court. *218–220 Market St. Corp., supra,* 124 *N.J.L.* at 304, 11 A.2d 109; *Robinson v. Centenary Fund,* 68 *N.J.L.* 723, 725–26, 54 *A.* 416 (E. & A. 1902). Although the question is one of law, it may require resolution of underlying factual issues. *Highgate Assocs., Ltd. v. Merryfield,* 157 *Vt.* 313, 597 A.2d 1280, 1282 (1991).

On balance, we believe we should remand this matter to the trial court to consider the reasonableness of the clause in light of this opinion. In resolving that issue, the court should consider, among other relevant considerations, the reasonableness of the use of gross receipts as the measure of damages no matter when the cancellation occurs; the significance of the award of damages based on twenty-five percent of one year's average gross receipts, rather than on some other basis such as total gross receipts computed for each year remaining under the lease; the reasoning of the parties that supported the calculation of the stipulated damages; the lessee's duty to mitigate damages; and the fair market rent and availability of replacement space. We leave to the sound discretion of the trial court the extent to which additional proof is necessary on the reasonableness of the clause. Because stipulated damages clauses are presumptively reasonable, *supra* at 252–253, 645 A.2d at 108, the burden of production and of persuasion rests on the Township.

To summarize, we affirm the judgment of the Appellate Division that the Township is liable to plaintiffs for terminating the lease. We also affirm the judgment of the Appellate Division awarding plaintiffs damages of $55,748.27 for renovation costs. We remand to the Law Division the issue whether the clause requiring payment of stipulated damages based on the lessee's gross receipts is a valid liquidated damages clause.

The judgment of the Appellate Division is affirmed in part, reversed in part, and the matter is remanded to the Law Division.

For affirmance in part, reversal in part and remandment—Chief Justice WILENTZ, and Justices CLIFFORD, HANDLER, POLLOCK, O'HERN, GARIBALDI and STEIN—7.*

————

LEE OLDSMOBILE, INC. v. KAIDEN, 32 Md.App. 556, 363 A.2d 270 (1976). Lee Oldsmobile dealt in Rolls–Royces as part of its business operations. Kaiden learned that Lee had on order, as a part of its allotted 1973 quota of ten or eleven Rolls–Royces, a car of the style and color she wanted, and in August 1973 she sent Lee a $5,000 deposit on the purchase of this car for $29,500. Lee then sent Kaiden an order form, which she signed and returned. The order form contained a clause providing that Lee had the right, upon failure or refusal of the purchaser to accept delivery of the motor vehicle, to retain as liquidated damages any cash deposit made by the purchaser. Apparently there was a dispute concerning the date of delivery, and on November 21, Kaiden notified Lee that she had purchased another Rolls elsewhere, and instructed that her order be canceled. On November 29, Lee notified Kaiden that the car was ready for delivery. She declined to accept and demanded the return of her deposit. Lee refused, and later sold the Rolls to another purchaser. Held, Kaiden was entitled to recover the amount of her deposit, minus actual damages.

"We reject the application of the liquidated damage clause in the present case ... because it is clear that the actual damages are capable of accurate estimation. We do not say this from hindsight made possible because the actual figures claimed were in evidence. We say it because at the time the contract was made, it was clear that the nature of any damages which would result from a possible future breach was such that they would be easily ascertainable...."

————

HUTCHISON v. TOMPKINS, 259 So.2d 129 (Fla.1972). Plaintiffs agreed to sell certain land to the Tompkins for $125,000. Of this amount, $10,000 in cash was deposited with an escrow agent. The contract contained a liquidated damages clause, which provided that if the buyer failed to perform sellers could at their option elect to retain the $10,000 deposit. According to the complaint, the Tompkins breached the contract by refusing to complete the purchase, but the escrow agent improperly returned their $10,000 deposit to them. Plaintiffs brought suit against the Tompkins and the escrow agent to recover the $10,000. The trial court dismissed the complaint on the ground that the liquidated damages clause was invalid as a penalty, relying on a Florida Supreme Court case, Pembroke v. Caudill, 160 Fla. 948, 37 So.2d 538

————

* Victor Goldberg reports that following the decision by the New Jersey Supreme Court, the parties settled for $360,000, "which, after taking into account the time value of money, comes to about sixty cents on the dollar." Goldberg, Framing Contract Law: An Economic Perspective 258. (Footnote by ed.)

(1948). On appeal, the Florida Supreme Court began by discussing *Pembroke* and a later case, Hyman v. Cohen, 73 So.2d 393 (Fla.1954):

> ... [T]he rationale of *Pembroke* may be stated as follows: if damages are readily ascertainable at the time of breach, then a liquidated damage clause will be construed as a penalty, even though the damages were not susceptible of ascertainment at the time the contract was entered into. Conversely, in *Hyman* the Court concluded that it was necessary for the damages to be readily ascertainable *at the time of the drawing of the contract* in order for a liquidated damage clause to constitute a penalty:

> We are convinced that the *Hyman* rationale provides the sounder approach to the problem of ascertainability of damages. Damages, especially in real estate transactions, are nearly always ascertainable at the time a contract is breached, because, as the *Pembroke* opinion points out, the measure of damages involves determining the difference between the agreed purchase price and the market value of the land as of the date of breach. Accordingly, the rule in *Pembroke* must have, when followed in letter and spirit ... a chilling effect on contract negotiations where the parties wish to include a provision for liquidated damages.

> For centuries the concept of liquidated damages has been a part of our law. We have no wish to emasculate it now by following a rule which renders nearly all deposit receipt contracts invalid. The better result, in our judgment, as *Hyman* contemplates, is to allow the liquidated damage clause to stand if the damages are not readily ascertainable at the time the contract is drawn, but to permit equity to relieve against the forfeiture if it appears unconscionable in light of the circumstances existing at the time of breach. For instance, assume a situation in which damages were not readily ascertainable at the time the contract was drawn, and the parties agreed to a liquidated damage provision of $100,000. Purchaser later repudiated the contract; vendor resold the land to another party, which because of fluctuations in the real estate market, resulted in a loss to himself of only $2,000. In such a case a court following the *Hyman* theory would allow the liquidated damage clause to stand, because damages were not readily ascertainable at the time of drawing the contract, but would as a court of equity, relieve against the forfeiture as unconscionable. Under the *Pembroke* theory the liquidated damage clause would be struck down on its face without any consideration of vendor's actual damages.

> The instant case falls squarely within *Hyman*. A contract for the sale of land generally suffers from the same uncertainty as to possible future damages as a lease agreement. The land sale market in Florida fluctuates from year to year and season to season, and it is generally impossible to say at the time a contract for sale is drawn what vendor's loss (if any) will be should the contract be breached by purchaser's failure to close. Accordingly, in the instant case we conclude that the damages which the parties could expect as a result of a breach were not readily ascertainable as of the time the contract was drawn up; therefore, under *Hyman*, ... the liquidated damage provision [was not] a penalty.... Moreover, because the definition of "readily ascertainable" in Pembroke v. Caudill,

supra, is incompatible with the rationale of *Hyman,* we hereby recede from *Pembroke* to the extent of such conflict.

———

UCC § 2–718(1)*

[See Selected Source Materials Supplement]

———

RESTATEMENT, SECOND, CONTRACTS § 356

[See Selected Source Materials Supplement]

———

UNIDROIT PRINCIPLES OF INTERNATIONAL COMMERCIAL CONTRACTS ART. 7.4.13

[See Selected Source Materials Supplement]

———

PRINCIPLES OF EUROPEAN CONTRACT LAW ART. 9.509

[See Selected Source Materials Supplement]

———

NOTE ON LIQUIDATED DAMAGES

All courts agree on the principle that liquidated-damages provisions should be given special judicial scrutiny, although the formulation of the principle varies. In contrast, many commentators have criticized this principle. Most of the critiques have an implicit or explicit three-part structure: (1) They begin by assuming that the major justification for the principle that liquidated-damages provisions should be given special scrutiny is that such provisions lend themselves to blameworthy exploitation of one party by the other, and consequent one-sidedness, in a way that other types of contract

---

* In 2003 the National Conference of Commissioners on State Laws and the American Law Institute promulgated an amended version of Article 2. Amended section 2–718(1) provides as follows:

§ 2–718. Liquidation or Limitation of Damages; Deposits.

(1) Damages for breach by either party may be liquidated in the agreement but only at an amount that is reasonable in the light of the anticipated or actual harm caused by the breach and, in a consumer contract, the difficulties of proof of loss, and the inconvenience or nonfeasibility of otherwise obtaining an adequate remedy. Section 2–719 [Contractual Modification or Liquidation of Remedy] determines the enforceability of a term that limits but does not liquidate damages.

For various reasons, as of early 2006 no state legislature has adopted the amended version of Article 2. At least for the present, therefore, liquidated–damages provisions in contracts for the sale of goods continue to be governed by the pre–2003 version of section 2–718.

provisions do not. (2) They then argue that this justification will not hold. (3) They conclude that the principle is therefore unjustified. So, for example, Goetz and Scott argue that the principle of special scrutiny of liquidated-damages provisions arose in a historical context in which protections against fraud and duress were not available. Given the modern development of unconscionability as a unifying unfairness principle, they suggest, the law should simply collapse the treatment of liquidated damages into that principle. Charles J. Goetz & Robert E. Scott, Liquidated Damages, Penalties and the Just Compensation Principle: Some Notes on an Enforcement Model and a Theory of Efficient Breach, 77 Colum. L. Rev. 554, 592 (1977).

The assumption that special scrutiny of liquidated-damages provisions is justified primarily by a special potential for blameworthy exploitation and one-sidedness does reflect the courts' rhetoric, which is cast in terms of whether or not such provisions are "penalties," and therefore suggests a concern with advantage-taking and oppression. In fact, however, the justification for the special scrutiny of liquidated-damages provisions is not that such provisions are specially amenable to blameworthy exploitation and one-sidedness, but that such provisions are systematically likely to reflect the limits of human cognition.

Classical contract law was based on a rational-actor model of psychology. Under this model, actors who make decisions in the face of uncertainty rationally maximize their subjective expected utility, with all future benefits and costs properly discounted to present value. A great body of theoretical and empirical work in cognitive psychology within the last thirty or forty years has shown that rational-actor psychology often lacks explanatory power. Although rational-actor psychology is the foundation of the standard *economic* model of choice, the empirical evidence shows that this model often diverges from the actual *psychology* of choice, due to limits of cognition. As Amos Tversky and Daniel Kahneman point out, expected-utility (rational-actor) theory "emerged from a logical analysis of games of chance rather than from a psychological analysis of risk and value. The theory was conceived as a normative model of an idealized decision maker, not as a description of the behavior of real people." Amos Tversky & Daniel Kahneman, Rational Choice and the Framing of Decisions, 59 J. Bus. S251 (1986).

In contrast to rational-actor psychology, modern cognitive psychology recognizes various limits of cognition. For purposes of contract law, three kinds of limits of cognition are especially salient: bounded rationality, irrational disposition, and defective capability.

1.   Bounded Rationality

To begin with, an actor may not even consider the alternative that would maximize his utility, because actors limit their search for and their deliberation on alternatives. If the costs of searching for and processing (evaluating and deliberating on) information were zero, and human information-processing capabilities were perfect, then an actor contemplating a decision would make a comprehensive search for relevant information, would process perfectly all the information he acquired, and would then make the best possible substantive decision—the decision that, as of the time made, was better than all the alternative decisions the actor might have made if he had complete knowledge and perfect processing abilities, and which would therefore maximize the actor's subjective expected utility.

In reality, of course, searching for and processing information does involve costs, in the form of time, energy, and perhaps money. Most actors either do not want to expend the resources required for comprehensive search and processing or recognize that comprehensive search and processing would not be achievable at any realistic cost. Actors therefore put boundaries on the amount of search and processing they engage in before making decisions. To put it differently, actors often consciously choose to be in a state of *rational ignorance*—"rational," because the incremental cost of achieving complete knowledge about a decision would be more than the expected gain from making the decision with complete rather than partial knowledge. So, for example, a patient may seek a second or perhaps a third doctor's opinion about treatment, but no more, because he believes it unlikely that consulting an extra five, ten, or fifteen doctors will improve his treatment decision enough to justify spending the extra time and money.

Furthermore, our abilities to process information and solve problems are constrained by limitations of computational ability, ability to calculate consequences, ability to organize and utilize memory, and the like. Hence, actors will often process imperfectly even the information they do acquire. Such imperfections in human processing ability increase as decisions become more complex and involve more permutations.

Accordingly, human rationality is normally bounded both by limited information and limited information-processing ability.

2. *Irrational disposition*

Next, actors are unrealistically optimistic as a systematic matter. (Lawyers do not realize this, because they are trained to be systematically pessimistic.) The dispositional characteristic of undue optimism is strikingly illustrated in a study by Lynn Baker and Robert Emery, appropriately titled, When Every Relationship Is Above Average, 17 Law and Hum. Behav. 439 (1993). Baker and Emery asked subjects who were about to get married to report on their own divorce-related prospects as compared to the divorce-related prospects of the general population. The disparities between perceptions as to the prospects of the general population and the prospects of the subjects were enormous, and were almost invariably in the direction of optimism. For example, the subjects correctly estimated that fifty percent of American couples will eventually divorce. In contrast, the subjects estimated that their own chance of divorce was zero. Similarly, the subjects' median estimate of how often spouses pay all court-ordered alimony was that forty percent paid. In contrast, 100 percent of the subjects predicted that their own spouse would pay all court-ordered alimony.

3. *Defective Capability*

Finally, cognitive psychology has established that actors use certain decision-making rules (heuristics) that yield systematic errors: "[T]he deviations of actual behavior from the normative model are too widespread to be ignored, too systematic to be dismissed as random error, and too fundamental to be accommodated by relaxing the normative system." Tversky & Kahneman, supra, at S252. For example, actors make decisions on the basis of data that is readily available to their memory, rather than on the basis of all the relevant data. (This is known as the "availability heuristic.") In particular, actors systematically give undue weight to instantiated evidence as compared to general statements, to vivid evidence as compared to pallid evidence, and to concrete evidence as compared to abstract evidence. Similarly, actors are systematically insensitive to sample size, and erroneously take small samples as representative samples.

Another defect in capability concerns the ability of actors to make rational comparisons between present and future states. For example, the sample consisting of present events is often wrongly taken to be representative, and therefore unduly predictive, of future events. Actors also systematically give too little weight to future benefits and costs as compared to present benefits and costs. Thus Martin Feldstein concludes that "some or all individuals have, in Pigou's ... words, a 'faulty telescopic faculty' that causes them to give too little weight to the utility of future consumption." Feldstein, The Optimal Level of Social Security Benefits, 100 Q. J. Econ. 303, 307 (1985).

A defect of capability related to faulty telescopic faculties is the systematic underestimation of risks. Based on the work of cognitive psychologists, Kenneth Arrow observes that "[i]t is a plausible hypothesis that individuals are unable to recognize that there will be many surprises in the future; in short, as much other evidence tends to confirm, there is a tendency to underestimate uncertainties." Arrow, Risk Perception in Psychology and Economics, 20 Econ. Inquiry 1, 5 (1982). In fact, empirical evidence shows that actors often not only underestimate but ignore low-probability risks.

4. Liquidated-damages provisions.

The limits of cognition have a special bearing on liquidated-damages provisions. To begin with, bounded rationality and rational ignorance play an important role here. Contracting parties normally will find it relatively easy to evaluate proposed performance terms, such as subject matter, quantity, and price. In contrast, at the time a contract is made it is often impracticable, if not impossible, to imagine all the scenarios of breach. Similarly, the inherent complexity of determining the application of a liquidated-damages provision to every possible breach scenario will often exceed actors' information-processing abilities.

Even on the doubtful assumption that a contracting party could imagine all breach scenarios, and determine the application of a liquidated-damages provision to every possible scenario, the benefits of extensive search and information-processing on these issues will often seem to be very low as compared to the costs. A party who contracts to buy or sell a commodity normally expects to perform. Accordingly, the benefits to the party of deliberating very carefully on performance terms—terms that specify what performance the party is required to render—are compelling, and the costs of such deliberation usually do not outweigh the benefits. In contrast, a party often will not expect that a liquidated-damages provision will ever come into play against him, partly because he intends to perform, and partly because experience will tell him that in general there is a high rate of performance of contracts. For example, if contracts are performed at least ninety-five percent of the time (which observation suggests is likely), all the costs of processing the more remote applications of a liquidated-damages provision would have to be taken into account, but the benefits of such processing would have to be discounted by ninety-five percent. The resulting cost-benefit ratio will often provide a substantial disincentive for processing every possible application of a liquidated-damages provision, even if it were in fact possible to imagine every such application. As a result, contracting parties are often likely to not completely think through liquidated-damages provisions, and are therefore often unlikely to fully understand the implications of such provisions.

The problem of irrational disposition also bears significantly on liquidated-damages provisions. Because actors tend to be unrealistically optimistic, a contracting party probably will believe that his performance is more likely, and his breach less likely, than is actually the case. Accordingly, unrealistic optimism will reduce even further the deliberation that actors give to liquidated-damages provisions.

Finally, defective capabilities have particular relevance to liquidated-damages provisions. The availability heuristic may lead a contracting party to give undue weight to his present intention to perform, which is vivid and concrete, as compared with the abstract possibility that future circumstances may compel him to breach. Because actors tend to take the sample of present evidence as unduly representative of the future, a contracting party is apt to overestimate the extent to which his present intention to perform is a reliable predictor of his future intentions. Because actors have faulty telescopic faculties, a contracting party is likely to overvalue the benefit of the prospect of performance, which will normally begin to occur in the short term, as against the cost of breach, which will typically occur, if at all, only down the road. Because actors tend to underestimate risks, a contracting party is likely to underestimate the risk that a liquidated-damages provision will take effect.

The rationale for giving special scrutiny to liquidated damages provisions affects the point of time on which the scrutiny is focused. If the justification for giving special scrutiny to liquidated damages provisions is that such provisions are especially subject to blameworthy exploitation and one-sidedness, the scrutiny should be focused on the time the contract is made—a "forward looking" test. In contrast, if the justification for special scrutiny is that parties often make cognitive errors in adopting such provisions, the scrutiny should be focused on the time of breach—a "second look" approach, which compares the liquidated damages with actual loss—because a gross discrepancy between forecast and result suggests that the liquidated-damages provision was a product of limited or defective cognition.

About half the states hold that the enforceability of liquidated-damages provisions is to be determined at the time the contract is made, and about half the states hold that enforceability of such provisions is to be determined at the time of the breach. See Kelly v. Marx, 44 Mass.App.Ct. 825, 694 N.E.2d 869 (1998), reversed, Kelly v. Marx, 428 Mass. 877, 705 N.E.2d 1114 (1999). However, even courts that purport to employ a forward-looking test may apply a second-look test in the guise relief against forfeiture, unconscionability in application, or the like. See, e.g., Hutchison v. Tompkins, supra.

––––––––

NOTE ON PROVISIONS THAT LIMIT DAMAGES

In a typical liquidated-damages case, the parties try to either (1) estimate the actual damages that will be suffered if a breach occurs, or (2) craft a penalty, in an amount that is greater than estimated actual damages, to deter breach. In contrast, in many cases the parties adopt a technique to limit damages to an amount that is *less* than estimated actual damages. Such provisions are known as *underliquidated-damages* provisions, and are normally enforced. See, e.g., Global Octanes Texas, L.P. v. BP Exploration & Oil Inc., 154 F.3d 518 (5th Cir.1998); Rassa v. Rollins Protective Services Co., 30 F.Supp.2d 538 (D.Md.1998).

A second technique is to limit or exclude liability for consequential damages.

A third technique is to provide that if the goods are defective, the seller's responsibility is limited to repair or replacement of the goods.

The second and third techniques are explicitly validated, subject to certain limitations, by U.C.C. § 2–719, which provides:

(1) Subject to the provisions of subsections (2) and (3) of this section and of the preceding section on liquidation and limitation of damages,

(a) the agreement may provide for remedies in addition to or in substitution for those provided in this Article and may limit or alter the measure of damages recoverable under this Article, as by limiting the buyer's remedies to return of the goods and repayment of the price or to repair and replacement of nonconforming goods or parts; and

(b) resort to a remedy as provided is optional unless the remedy is expressly agreed to be exclusive, in which case it is the sole remedy.

(2) Where circumstances cause an exclusive or limited remedy to fail of its essential purpose, remedy may be had as provided in this Act.

(3) Consequential damages may be limited or excluded unless the limitation or exclusion is unconscionable. Limitation of consequential damages for injury to the person, in the case of consumer goods is prima facie unconscionable but limitation of damages where the loss is commercial is not.

Note that although repair-or-replace provisions are explicitly validated by Subsection 1(a), Subsection (2) provides that a provision that limits remedies is unenforceable where circumstances cause the limited remedy to "fail of its essential purpose." In a repair-or-replace case, this limitation comes into play where the seller either fails to repair or replace, or does so only in a very dilatory manner.

Frequently, a repair-or-replace provision is coupled with a provision that eliminates liability for consequential damages. The question often arises, if the repair-or-replace provision is held to be unenforceable because it fails of its essential purpose (for example, because of the seller's delay in making the repairs), does a companion provision that eliminates consequential damages remain enforceable, or should it be deemed so closely bound to the repair-or-replace provision that when the latter provision falls, so does the former? "[C]ourts are deeply divided on this issue, and ... about the same number of cases can be marshalled on either side of the question." International Financial Services, Inc. v. Franz, 534 N.W.2d 261 (Minn.1995).

———

Chapter 7

SPECIFIC PERFORMANCE

INTRODUCTORY NOTE

Chapter 7 concerns the remedy of specific performance. Under this remedy, the court, instead of ordering the breaching party to pay damages, orders the breaching party to perform the contract.

The historical background. For centuries the English administration of justice was characterized by the peculiarity that there were two systems of courts administering two different bodies of law. What may be called the "regular" court system consisted of the courts of common law, which had jurisdiction over "actions at law," and administered "regular" law. The other system consisted of courts of "equity" or "chancery," which had jurisdiction over "suits in equity," and applied a body of principles that came to be called "equity." (Note the double linguistic usages involved here. "Law" used: (1) in a broad sense to mean the principles for administering justice, which includes both common law and equity, or (2) in a narrower sense, to mean the principles applied by the common law courts. "Equity" used: (1) in a broad sense, to mean fairness, or (2) in a narrower sense, to mean the established principles administered by a specific system of courts.)

In general, the English equity or chancery courts acted to remedy defects in the rules administered by the common law courts. The equity courts did not have a general jurisdiction over all kinds of disputes; their function was to act in those cases where "the legal remedy was inadequate," that is, where according to the notions of the time, the regular or common law courts did not give the kind of relief that the plaintiff ought to have.

One of the great defects of common law courts was that except in certain extraordinary cases, the procedure in those courts did not contemplate *ordering* the defendant to do anything. If a creditor sued his debtor for £10 and was awarded a judgment at law, the judgment did not take the form of an order commanding the debtor to pay his debt. Instead, in its traditional form the judgement recited that it was "considered that the plaintiff do recover against the defendant his debt." Enforcement of the judgment was accomplished not by commanding the defendant to pay, but by directing the sheriff to levy execution on the defendant's property if the defendant did not pay, so that the plaintiff's claim could be satisfied out of this property.

Where the plaintiff was complaining of a breach of contract by the defendant, this defect prevented the courts from ordering the defendant to perform his promise. Thus, if Seller contracted to convey Blackacre to Buyer, and then broke his promise, there was no way in which Buyer, by appealing to the common law courts, could get a deed to Blackacre, even though Seller had a perfectly good title to the land and was wholly capable of carrying out her contract. Accordingly, the only relief Buyer could obtain from a common law court was an award of money damages.

However, in such a case Buyer could successfully appeal to a court of equity, alleging that his legal remedy (money damages) was inadequate. The equity court would issue a decree ordering Seller to execute a deed in Buyer's favor. If Seller refused to obey this order, she would put herself in contempt of court and be subject to fine or imprisonment.

There are other situations, though, where an appeal to equity to enforce a contract would fail. To put the plainest kind of case, suppose that Seller had sold and delivered a horse to Buyer for $500, and that Buyer, although having ample funds to do so, refused to pay the promised price of the horse. Here conceivably Seller might get a certain spiritual satisfaction out of an order commanding Buyer to pay his debt—an order that the common law courts would not issue. On the other hand, the common law courts would ensure the promised price for Seller through a levy of execution on Buyer's goods. Accordingly in this case the legal remedy was deemed to be adequate, and a suit by Seller in an equity court would be denied.

In other cases, equity refused to enforce contracts not because the legal remedy was adequate, but because it was considered unwise for one or another reasons to attempt specific enforcement. For example, a famous opera singer agrees to sing in the plaintiff's opera–house for three months and then breaks her contract. Here the opera-house proprietor may with much justice assert that his legal remedy of damages is inadequate; an award of money can scarcely be treated as an adequate substitute for actual performance. At the same time, there are obvious objections to attempting to compel a star to sing against her will. Accordingly, this is a case where a court of equity would deny specific performance despite a recognition that the monetary relief granted by the common law courts is an inadequate form of relief.

The relation of law and equity in the United States today. The illustrations provided above give a general view of the way in which the English courts dealt with specific enforcement of contracts at the time the United States began its independent legal existence. Today, most American states no longer have separate courts of law and equity. Instead, in most states the same judges administer both bodies of principles. This does not mean, however, that the two bodies of principles are not to a considerable extent still kept distinct in the thinking of lawyers and judges. If a plaintiff asks the court to issue an order directing the defendant to perform her promise—say, to convey Blackacre—such a suit will be tested by principles called "equity" and derived historically from the English chancery courts. In some jurisdictions, the suit will in fact be labeled as a "suit in equity" even though the judge who tries the suit has the power to try "actions at law" as well. Even in those jurisdictions where no label is attached to the suit to indicate whether it is "at law" or "in equity," the rules applied to the suit will be "equity" rules if the case involves a demand for an order directing the defendant to specifically perform.

LONDON BUCKET CO. v. STEWART

Court of Appeals of Kentucky, 1951.
314 Ky. 832, 237 S.W.2d 509.

STANLEY, COMMISSIONER. This is an appeal from a judgment decreeing specific performance of a contract to properly furnish and install a heating system for a large motel. The basic contention of the appellant, London Bucket Company, is that the remedy of specific performance will not lie for breach of this type of contract.

The chancellor overruled a demurrer to the petition and this is the first assignment of error. Stewart's petition set out the contract, the pertinent parts of which are as follows: "The parties of the first part agree and bind themselves to furnish and install (subletting installation) in said building the following equipment. . . ." The only standard as to the quality of work to be performed was that the defendant was to "guarantee to heat this said court to 75 degrees in winter, and to supervise all work," etc. The plaintiff alleged that the defendant "soon thereafter and within one year installed a plant in an incompleted, unskilled unworkmanlike manner, never finishing same, and of such size, type and inferior quality of materials that same does not to a reasonable degree perform the purpose contemplated." The petition further states: "Plaintiff here now demands of the court of equity that defendant be compelled to specifically perform the terms of said contract and complete said installation and furnish the type of furnace provided in said contract and all the things necessary to properly heat said building and rooms and same to be done forthwith, before the fall of cold weather."

The plaintiff prayed that "immediate specific performance be adjudged" and also asked $8,250 damages for faulty and negligent construction and resulting expense, loss of business, etc. On being required to elect his remedy, he chose specific performance and dismissed without prejudice his action for damages.

The defendant, among other defenses, pleaded there had been a mutual cancellation of the contract insofar as it covered the completion of the job. Upon sharply conflicting evidence, but with some documents strongly supporting the plaintiff's contention, the court found as a fact that there had been no such cancellation. This was an issue necessary to be decided before deciding there could be a decree of specific performance.

The court decreed: "The defendant is hereby mandatorily ordered and directed to comply with the terms of said contract, in its entirety. He shall proceed diligently so to do and continue its obligation, assumed by it under the said contract, therein specifically set out."

No matter what the evidence may have been, the plaintiff's legal right could be no greater than that which the basic facts pleaded authorized. So if the demurrer should have been sustained to his pleading which undertook to state his whole case, that is all the court need consider. In other words, if the plaintiff did not state a cause of action for specific performance, the demurrer should have been sustained instead of overruled. That is the way the trial court treated the case except to find that the work done was defective, the heating system was not properly functioning, and the job was incomplete. In his opinion, the court recognized the difficulty of the question whether the contract and the conditions were such as required specific performance. He considered the familiar principle that such an equitable decree will not be adjudged unless the ordinary common law remedy of damages for a breach of contract is an inadequate and incomplete remedy for injuries arising from the failure to carry out its terms. Edelen v. Samuels & Co., 126 Ky. 295, 103 S.W. 360. The court concluded, nevertheless, that this case was within Schmidt v. Louisville & N.R. Co., 101 Ky. 441, 41 S.W. 1015, 19 Ky.Law Rep. 666, 38 L.R.A. 809, and Pennsylvania Railroad Co. v. City of Louisville, 277 Ky. 402, 126 S.W.2d 840.

It seems to us the two cases are not altogether apt. In the *Schmidt* case it was held a decree of specific performance to operate the railroad under the terms of the lease for the benefit of both holders was proper since there was no adequate remedy at law. The *Pennsylvania Railroad* Case was a suit to declare the rights of the parties and to require several railroad companies to proceed with the elimination of grade crossings as they had contracted to do. Both cases involve matters of great magnitude and were of public interest and welfare. In each case the court in effect said, "Proceed to do what you contracted to do." There was no question of partial or incomplete or faulty performance of a building contract. The *Schmidt* case is distinguished in the leading case of Edelen v. Samuels & Co., supra. In the present case the decree was in effect to direct a building contractor to go back, correct defective work and complete its job. It is the general rule that contracts for building construction will not be specifically enforced because ordinarily damages are an adequate remedy and, in part, because of the incapacity of the court to superintend the performance. 9 Am.Jur., Building and Construction Contracts, § 124; 58 C.J. 1046. The case at bar is not within the exceptions to the rule or of the class where specific performance should be decreed. 49 Am.Jur., Specific Performance, § 12. That there may be difficulty in proving the damages as appellee suggests, is not enough to put the case within the exceptions.

Under our conclusion that specific performance should not have been decreed, the decision on the issue of cancellation of the contract must follow it. This will leave the question open in the common-law action for damages should it be filed.

Wherefore, the judgment is reversed.

———

RESTATEMENT, SECOND, CONTRACTS §§ 359, 360

[See Selected Source Materials Supplement]

———

UNIDROIT PRINCIPLES OF INTERNATIONAL COMMERCIAL CONTRACTS ARTS. 7.2.1, 7.2.2, 7.2.3

[See Selected Source Materials Supplement]

———

PRINCIPLES OF EUROPEAN CONTRACT
LAW ARTS. 9.101, 9.102, 9.103

[See Selected Source Materials Supplement]

––––––––

STOKES v. MOORE, 262 Ala. 59, 77 So.2d 331 (1955). Complainants entered into a contract with Stokes, which provided for his employment by them as manager of their business. The contract also provided that if Stokes's employment was terminated for any reason he would not engage in a similar line of business in Mobile for one year immediately following, and that if this covenant was breached "a restraining order or injunction may be issued and entered against me (employee) in any court of equity jurisdiction." The court stated, "We do not wish to express the view that an agreement for the issuance of an injunction, if and when a stipulated state of facts arises in the future, is binding on the court to that extent. Such an agreement would serve to oust the inherent jurisdiction of the court to determine whether an injunction is appropriate when applied for and to require its issuance even though to do so would be contrary to the opinion of the court. . . . But . . . the provision for an injunction is important in its influence upon an exercise of the discretionary power of the court to grant a temporary injunction."

––––––––

UCC §§ 2–709, 2–716

[See Selected Source Materials Supplement]

––––––––

CISG ARTS. 46, 62

[See Selected Source Materials Supplement]

––––––––

NOTE ON THE TRADITIONAL RULE CONCERNING
SPECIFIC PERFORMANCE OF CONTRACTS
FOR THE SALE OF GOODS

Specific performance for contracts for the sale of goods is now largely governed by UCC § 2–716. Official Comment 1 to that Section refers to the "prior policy as to specific performance." The traditional, pre-UCC rule, inherited from the English legal system, was that in a contract for the sale of goods neither the buyer nor the seller could ordinarily get specific performance unless the goods were "unique." The explanation for this result was that monetary relief is normally adequate in a contract for the sale of goods. To take a simple case, if the seller has broken a contract to deliver 100 bushels of wheat to the buyer, the buyer can cover his needs by buying wheat on the market, and in an action at law the cost of cover is the measure of his right to money damages against the seller. On the other hand, where a contract is for the sale of a unique item, such as a painting or an heirloom, cover on the market was by hypothesis not possible, and specific performance would be granted by a court of equity. The next principal case considers the extent to which the traditional rule is modified by the UCC.

LACLEDE GAS CO. v. AMOCO OIL CO.

United States Court of Appeals, Eighth Circuit, 1975.
522 F.2d 33.

Ross, Circuit Judge. [In 1970, Amoco Oil and Laclede Gas (more accurately, the parties' predecessors in interests) entered into a master contract designed to allow Laclede to provide local propane-gas distribution systems to residential developments in Missouri until natural-gas mains were extended to a development. The master contract contemplated that residential developers would apply to Laclede for a local propane system. Laclede could then ask Amoco to supply propane to the development. Laclede would make these requests in supplemental letters whose form was prescribed by the master agreement. If Amoco decided to supply the propane, it would bind itself to do so by signing the letter. Laclede, for its part, agreed to pay Amoco's posted price for propane plus four cents per gallon. Once a letter agreement covering a given residential development was signed, Amoco was bound to deliver propane to Laclede for that development. In 1973, Amoco breached its letter agreements, by refusing to supply further propane. Laclede brought an action for specific performance.]

Generally the determination of whether or not to order specific performance of a contract lies within the sound discretion of the trial court. Landau v. St. Louis Public Service Co., 364 Mo. 1134, 273 S.W.2d 255, 259 (1954). However, this discretion is, in fact, quite limited; and it is said that when certain equitable rules have been met and the contract is fair and plain "specific performance goes as a matter of right." Miller v. Coffeen, 365 Mo. 204, 280 S.W.2d 100, 102 (1955), quoting, Berberet v. Myers, 240 Mo. 58, 77, 144 S.W. 824, 830 (1912). (Emphasis omitted.)

. . . [W]e have carefully reviewed the very complete record on appeal and conclude that the trial court should grant the injunctive relief prayed. We are satisfied that this case falls within that category in which specific performance should be ordered as a matter of right. See Miller v. Coffeen, supra, 280 S.W.2d at 102.

Amoco contends that four of the requirements for specific performance have not been met. Its claims are: (1) there is no mutuality of remedy in the contract; (2) the remedy of specific performance would be difficult for the court to administer without constant and long-continued supervision; (3) the contract is indefinite and uncertain; and (4) the remedy at law available to Laclede is adequate. The first three contentions have little or no merit and do not detain us for long.

There is simply no requirement in the law that both parties be mutually entitled to the remedy of specific performance in order that one of them be given that remedy by the court. . . .

While a court may refuse to grant specific performance where such a decree would require constant and long-continued court supervision, this is merely a discretionary rule of decision which is frequently ignored when the public interest is involved. See, e.g., Joy v. St. Louis, 138 U.S. 1, 47, 11 S.Ct. 243, 34 L.Ed. 843 (1891); Western Union Telegraph Co. v. Pennsylvania Co., 129 F. 849, 869 (3d Cir.1904). . . .

Here the public interest in providing propane to the retail customers is manifest, while any supervision required will be far from onerous.

Section 370 of the Restatement, Contracts (1932) provides:

> Specific enforcement will not be decreed unless the terms of the contract are so expressed that the court can determine with reasonable certainty what is the duty of each party and the conditions under which performance is due.

We believe these criteria have been satisfied here. As discussed in part I of this opinion, as to all developments for which a supplemental agreement has been signed, Amoco is to supply all the propane which is reasonably foreseeably required, while Laclede is to purchase the required propane from Amoco and pay the contract price therefor. The parties have disagreed over what is meant by "Wood River Area Posted Price" in the agreement, but the district court can and should determine with reasonable certainty what the parties intended by this term and should mold its decree, if necessary accordingly.[3] Likewise, the fact that the agreement does not have a definite time of duration is not fatal since the evidence established that the last subdivision should be converted to natural gas in 10 to 15 years. This sets a reasonable time limit on performance and the district court can and should mold the final decree to reflect this testimony.

It is axiomatic that specific performance will not be ordered when the party claiming breach of contract has an adequate remedy at law. Jamison Coal & Coke Co. v. Goltra, 143 F.2d 889, 894 (8th Cir.), cert. denied, 323 U.S. 769, 65 S.Ct. 122, 89 L.Ed. 615 (1944). This is especially true when the contract involves personal property as distinguished from real estate.

However, in Missouri, as elsewhere, specific performance may be ordered even though personalty is involved in the "proper circumstances." Mo.Rev. Stat. § 400.2–716(1); Restatement, Contracts, supra, § 361. And a remedy at law adequate to defeat the grant of specific performance "must be as certain, prompt, complete, and efficient to attain the ends of justice as a decree of specific performance." National Marking Mach. Co. v. Triumph Mfg. Co., 13 F.2d 6, 9 (8th Cir.1926). Accord, Snip v. City of Lamar, 239 Mo.App. 824, 201 S.W.2d 790, 798 (1947).

One of the leading Missouri cases allowing specific performance of a contract relating to personalty because the remedy at law was inadequate is Boeving v. Vandover, 240 Mo.App. 117, 218 S.W.2d 175, 178 (1949). In that case the plaintiff sought specific performance of a contract in which the defendant had promised to sell him an automobile. At that time (near the end of and shortly after World War II) new cars were hard to come by, and the court held that specific performance was a proper remedy since a new car

---

3. The record indicates that Laclede has now accepted Amoco's interpretation and has agreed that "Wood River Area Posted Price" means Amoco's posted price for propane at its Wood River refinery.

"could not be obtained elsewhere except at considerable expense, trouble or loss, which cannot be estimated in advance."

We are satisfied that Laclede has brought itself within this practical approach taken by the Missouri courts. As Amoco points out, Laclede has propane immediately available to it under other contracts with other suppliers. And the evidence indicates that at the present time propane is readily available on the open market. However, this analysis ignores the fact that the contract involved in this lawsuit is for a long-term supply of propane to these subdivisions. The other two contracts under which Laclede obtains the gas will remain in force only until March 31, 1977, and April 1, 1981, respectively; and there is no assurance that Laclede will be able to receive any propane under them after that time. Also it is unclear as to whether or not Laclede can use the propane obtained under these contracts to supply the Jefferson County subdivisions, since they were originally entered into to provide Laclede with propane with which to "shave" its natural gas supply during peak demand periods.[4] Additionally, there was uncontradicted expert testimony that Laclede probably could not find another supplier of propane willing to enter into a long-term contract such as the Amoco agreement, given the uncertain future of worldwide energy supplies. And, even if Laclede could obtain supplies of propane for the affected developments through its present contracts or newly negotiated ones, it would still face considerable expense and trouble which cannot be estimated in advance in making arrangements for its distribution to the subdivisions.

Specific performance is the proper remedy in this situation, and it should be granted by the district court.

Conclusion

For the foregoing reasons the judgment of the district court is reversed and the cause is remanded for the fashioning of appropriate injunctive relief in the form of a decree of specific performance as to those developments for which a supplemental agreement form has been signed by the parties.

———

WEATHERSBY v. GORE, 556 F.2d 1247 (5th Cir.1977). On March 6, 1973, Weathersby made a contract with Gore, a farmer, under which Gore agreed to sell Weathersby the cotton that Gore produced on 500 acres of land during the 1973 crop year, at 30 cents per pound. On May 3, Gore gave notice that he was cancelling the contract on the ground that Weathersby had failed to provide a required payment bond. Weathersby could have covered, then or later, but did not.

Soon after the May 3 cancellation, cotton was selling for around 35 cents. On September 28, Weathersby sued for specific performance. By this time cotton had soared to 80 cents. The trial court found that Gore had breached the contract, and ordered specific performance. The Court of Appeals remanded for consideration of the issue whether Weathersby had furnished the bond

---

4. During periods of cold weather, when demand is high, Laclede does not receive enough natural gas to meet all this demand. It, therefore, adds propane to the natural gas it places in its distribution system. This practice is called "peak shaving."

within a reasonable time, but held that even if Gore had breached the contract, Weathersby was not entitled to specific performance.

"... The parties are in considerable disagreement over the meaning of [UCC § 2–716(1)]: 'Specific performance may be decreed where the goods are unique or in other proper circumstances.' Various authorities have been cited to the court indicating that crop contracts historically have been treated as susceptible to specific performance treatment more readily than other types of contracts.... However, cotton contracts have not been given such treatment in Mississippi when other cotton was readily available on the open market....

"... Other than to indicate that the Code is intended to 'further a more liberal attitude than some courts have shown in connection with the specific performance of contracts of sale,' the comments accompanying UCC § 2–716 are of little guidance. The comments also state that '[o]utput and requirements contracts involving a particularly or peculiarly available source of market present today the typical commercial specific performance situation,' but the interpretation of this language appears to range from suggesting all output contracts should be specifically enforceable to a mere observation that output contracts form a suitable factual background in most cases in which specific performance may be sought.

"The general rule applicable when specific performance is requested has been stated in Roberts v. Spence, 209 So.2d 623, 626 (Miss.1968): 'Specific performance of a contract will not be awarded where damages may be recovered and the remedy in a court of law is adequate to compensate the injured party.' ... Weathersby was adequately protected from any damages occasioned by Gore's breach of the contract, if any occurred. He could have acquired additional cotton on the open market when Gore informed him he would no longer perform under the contract. He did not do so and thus, if entitled to damages at all, must settle for the difference between the contract and the market price at the time Gore cancelled."

NOTE ON SPECIFIC PERFORMANCE OF CONTRACTS FOR THE SALE OF LAND AND EMPLOYMENT CONTRACTS

1. Contracts for the sale of land. It is well settled that in a contract for sale of land, the buyer can get a decree specifically ordering the seller to execute a deed in his favor. In most states, the seller can also get a decree ordering the buyer to take title to the land and pay the agreed price. Restatement Second § 360, Comment e.

The traditional rationale of the rule that a *buyer* of land can get specific performance has been that damages are inadequate in such cases because: (1) The value of land is always to some extent conjectural, since land usually does not have a clearly defined market price; and (2) Every piece of land is to some extent unique, and therefore the buyer cannot with an award of money damages go out on the market and buy a piece of land exactly like that promised him by the defaulting seller. Statutes now provide for self-executing decrees in such cases; such a decree has the effect of a deed, and can be recorded in the Registry of Deeds.

The *seller's* right to specific performance was often rested on the "affirmative doctrine of mutuality of remedy"—that since the buyer can sue for specific performance, the seller should have a corresponding remedy. That doctrine is now generally discredited; better reasons are the uncertainty of damages measured by the difference between the contract price and the value of the land, and the need for a formal termination of the buyer's interest in the land to facilitate its resale. Partly because constitutional provisions forbid imprisonment for debt, a decree in favor of the seller ordering the buyer to pay money is not ordinarily enforced by contempt. Instead, the decree provides that if the money is not paid by a certain time, the right of the buyer to "redeem" the land by paying the debt is to be cut off, or "foreclosed."

2. *Employment contracts.* Employment contracts are not specifically enforced at the suit of either the employee or the employer. Restatement Second § 367(1). The objections to specific performance here do not lie in a notion that monetary relief is an adequate substitute for the promised performance. Rather, they stem from a belief that it is unwise to attempt to extract, from an unwilling party, a performance involving personal relations. In some cases, the courts, although they will not order the employee to work for the employer, will enjoin the employee from working for a competitor Often, such an injunction could be tantamount to ordering specific performance, because if the employee cannot work for a competitor, she will not be able to earn a living, and therefore will be indirectly forced to work for her original employer. Accordingly, Restatement Second § 367(2) adopts the rule that "[a] promise to render personal service exclusively for one employer will not be enforced by an injunction against serving another if its probable result will be to compel a performance involving personal relations the enforced continuance of which is undesirable or will be to leave the employee without other reasonable means of making a living."

Chapter 8

THE RELIANCE AND RESTITUTION MEASURES

This Chapter considers two damage measures that may be used in a bargain context as an alternative to the expectation measure.

Section 1 concerns the reliance measure as a remedy for breach in a bargain context. (Recall from Chapter 1 that the reliance measure may also be used in a donative context.) As pointed out earlier, the name of this measure is something of a misnomer. Calling it the *cost* measure would be more accurate, and would make it easier to understand the measure's dynamics.

Section 2(a) concerns the restitution measure as a remedy for breach of a bargain contract.

Section 2(b) concerns restitution in favor of a person who is herself in breach.

SECTION 1. RELIANCE DAMAGES IN A BARGAIN CONTEXT

SECURITY STOVE & MFG. CO. v. AMERICAN RYS. EXPRESS CO.

Kansas City Court of Appeals, Missouri, 1932.
227 Mo.App. 175, 51 S.W.2d 572.

BLAND, J. This is an action for damages for the failure of defendant to transport, from Kansas City to Atlantic City, New Jersey, within a reasonable time, a furnace equipped with a combination oil and gas burner. The cause was tried before the court without the aid of a jury, resulting in a judgment in favor of plaintiff in the sum of $801.50 and interest, or in a total sum of $1,000.00. Defendant has appealed.

The facts show that plaintiff manufactured a furnace equipped with a special combination oil and gas burner it desired to exhibit at the American

Gas Association Convention held in Atlantic City in October, 1926. The president of plaintiff testified that plaintiff engaged space for the exhibit for the reason "that the Henry L. Dougherty Company was very much interested in putting out a combination oil and gas burner; we had just developed one, after we got through, better than anything on the market and we thought this show would be the psychological time to get in contact with the Dougherty Company"; that "the thing wasn't sent there for sale but primarily to show"; that at the time the space was engaged it was too late to ship the furnace by freight so plaintiff decided to ship it by express, and, on September 18th, 1926, wrote the office of the defendant in Kansas City, stating that it had engaged a booth for exhibition purposes at Atlantic City, New Jersey, from the American Gas Association, for the week beginning October 11th; that its exhibit consisted of an oil burning furnace, together with two oil burners which weighed at least 1,500 pounds; that, "In order to get this exhibit in place on time it should be in Atlantic City not later than October the 8th. What we want you to do is to tell us how much time you will require to assure the delivery of the exhibit on time."

Mr. Bangs, chief clerk in charge of the local office of the defendant, upon receipt of the letter, sent Mr. Johnson, a commercial representative of the defendant, to see plaintiff. Johnson called upon plaintiff taking its letter with him. Johnson made a notation on the bottom of the letter giving October 4th, as the day that defendant was required to have the exhibit in order for it to reach Atlantic City on October 8th.

On October 1st, plaintiff wrote the defendant at Kansas City, referring to its letter of September 18th, concerning the fact that the furnace must be in Atlantic City not later than October 8th, and stating what Johnson had told it, saying: "Now Mr. Bangs, we want to make doubly sure that this shipment is in Atlantic City not later than October 8th and the purpose of this letter is to tell you that you can *have your truck call for the shipment between 12 and 1 o'clock on Saturday, October 2nd for this.*" (Italics plaintiff's.) On October 2nd, plaintiff called the office of the express company in Kansas City and told it that the shipment was ready. Defendant came for the shipment on the last mentioned day, received it and delivered the express receipt to plaintiff. The shipment contained 21 packages. Each package was marked with stickers backed with glue and covered with silica of soda, to prevent the stickers being torn off in shipping. Each package was given a number. They ran from 1 to 21.

Plaintiff's president made arrangements to go to Atlantic City to attend the convention and install the exhibit, arriving there about October 11th. When he reached Atlantic City he found the shipment had been placed in the booth that had been assigned to plaintiff. The exhibit was set up, but it was found that one of the packages shipped was not there. This missing package contained the gas manifold, or that part of the oil and gas burner that controlled the flow of gas in the burner. This was the most important part of the exhibit and a like burner could not be obtained in Atlantic City.

Wires were sent and it was found that the stray package was at the "over and short bureau" of defendant in St. Louis. Defendant reported that the package would be forwarded to Atlantic City and would be there by Wednesday, the 13th. Plaintiff's president waited until Thursday, the day the convention closed, but the package had not arrived at the time, so he closed up the exhibit and left. About a week after he arrived in Kansas City, the package was returned by the defendant. . . .

The petition upon which the case was tried alleges that ". . . relying upon defendant's promise and the promises of its agents and servants, that said parcels would be delivered at Atlantic City by October 8th, 1926, if delivered to defendant by October 4th, 1926, plaintiff herein hired space for an exhibit at the American Gas Association Convention at Atlantic City, and planned for an exhibit at said Convention and sent men in the employ of this plaintiff to Atlantic City to install, show and operate said exhibit, and that these men were in Atlantic City ready to set up this plaintiff's exhibit at the American Gas Association Convention on October 8th, 1926." . . .

Plaintiff asked damages, which the court in its judgment allowed as follows: $147.00 express charges (on the exhibit); $45.12 freight on the exhibit from Atlantic City to Kansas City; $101.39 railroad and pullman fares to and from Atlantic City, expended by plaintiff's president and a workman taken by him to Atlantic City; $48.00 hotel room for the two; $150.00 for the time of the president; $40.00 for wages of plaintiff's other employee and $270.00 for rental of the booth, making a total of $801.51. . . .

We think, under the circumstances in this case, that it was proper to allow plaintiff's expenses as its damages. Ordinarily the measure of damages where the carrier fails to deliver a shipment at destination within a reasonable time is the difference between the market value of the goods at the time of the delivery and the time when they should have been delivered. But where the carrier has notice of peculiar circumstances under which the shipment is made, which will result in an unusual loss by the shipper in case of delay in delivery, the carrier is responsible for the real damage sustained from such delay if the notice given is of such character, and goes to such extent, in informing the carrier of the shipper's situation, that the carrier will be presumed to have contracted with reference thereto. Central Trust Co. of New York v. Savannah & W.R. Co. (C.C.) 69 F. 683, 685. . . .

Defendant contends that plaintiff "is endeavoring to achieve a return of the status quo in a suit based on a breach of contract. Instead of seeking to recover what he would have had, had the contract not been broken, plaintiff is trying to recover what he would have had, had there never been any contract of shipment"; that the expenses sued for would have been incurred in any event. It is no doubt, the general rule that where there is a breach of contract the party suffering the loss can recover only that which he would have had, had the contract not been broken, and this is all the cases decided upon which defendant relies, including C., M. & St. P. Ry. v. McCaull–Dinsmore Co., 253 U.S. 97, 100, 40 S.Ct. 504, 64 L.Ed. 801. But this is merely a general statement of the rule and is not inconsistent with the holdings that, in some instances, the injured party may recover expenses incurred in relying upon the contract, although such expenses would have been incurred had the contract not been breached. See Morrow v. Railroad, 140 Mo.App. 200, 212, 213, 123 S.W. 1034; Bryant v. Barton, 32 Neb. 613, 616, 49 N.W. 331; Woodbury v. Jones, 44 N.H. 206; Driggs v. Dwight, 17 Wend. (N.Y.) 71, 31 Am.Dec. 283.

In Sperry et al. v. O'Neill–Adams Co. (C.C.A.) 185 F. 231, the court held that the advantages resulting from the use of trading stamps as a means of increasing trade are so contingent that they cannot form a basis on which to rest a recovery for a breach of contract to supply them. In lieu of compensation based thereon the court directed a recovery in the sum expended in preparation for carrying on business in connection with the use of the stamps. The court said, loc. cit. 239:

> "Plaintiff in its complaint had made a claim for lost profits, but, finding it impossible to marshal any evidence which would support a finding of exact figures, abandoned that claim. Any attempt to reach a precise sum would be mere blind guesswork. Nevertheless a contract, which both sides conceded would prove a valuable one, had been broken and the party who broke it was responsible for resultant damage. In order to carry out this contract, the plaintiff made expenditures which otherwise it would not have made. . . . The trial judge held, as we think rightly, that plaintiff was entitled at least to recover these expenses to which it had been put in order to secure the benefits of a contract of which defendant's conduct deprived it." . . .

The case at bar was [not] to recover damages for loss of profits by reason of the failure of the defendant to transport the shipment within a reasonable time, so that it would arrive in Atlantic City for the exhibit. There were no profits contemplated. The furnace was to be shown and shipped back to Kansas City. There was no money loss, except the expenses, that was of such a nature as any court would allow as being sufficiently definite or lacking in pure speculation. Therefore, unless plaintiff is permitted to recover the expenses that it went to, which were a total loss to it by reason of its inability to exhibit the furnace and equipment, it will be deprived of any substantial compensation for its loss. The law does not contemplate any such injustice. It ought to allow plaintiff, as damages, the loss in the way of expenses that it sustained, and which it would not have been put to if it had not been for its reliance upon the defendant to perform its contract. There is no contention that the exhibit would have been entirely valueless and whatever it might have accomplished defendant knew of the circumstances and ought to respond for whatever damages plaintiff suffered. In cases of this kind the method of estimating the damages should be adopted which is the most definite and certain and which best achieves the fundamental purpose of compensation. 17 C.J. p. 846; Miller v. Robertson, 266 U.S. 243, 257, 45 S.Ct. 73, 78, 69 L.Ed. 265. Had the exhibit been shipped in order to realize a profit on sales and such profits could have been realized, or to be entered in competition for a prize, and plaintiff failed to show loss of profits with sufficient definiteness, or that he would have won the prize, defendant's cases might be in point. But as before stated, no such situation exists here.

While it is true that plaintiff already had incurred some of these expenses, in that it had rented space at the exhibit before entering into the contract with defendant for the shipment of the exhibit and this part of plaintiff's damages, in a sense, arose out of a circumstance which transpired before the contract was even entered into, yet, plaintiff arranged for the exhibit knowing that it could call upon defendant to perform its common law duty to accept and transport the shipment with reasonable dispatch. The whole damage, therefore, was suffered in contemplation of defendant performing its contract, which it failed to do, and would not have been sustained except for the reliance by plaintiff upon defendant to perform it. It can, therefore, be fairly said that the damages or loss suffered by plaintiff grew out of the breach of the contract, for had the shipment arrived on time, plaintiff would have had the benefit of the contract, which was contemplated by all parties, defendant being advised of the purpose of the shipment.

The judgment is affirmed.

All concur.

———

BEEFY TRAIL, INC. v. BEEFY KING INT'L, INC., 267 So.2d 853 (Fla.Dist.App.1972) (Owen, J., concurring in part and dissenting in part). "Essentially, the rationale [for granting reliance damages in a bargain context] is this: Normally, had the contract's performance not been prevented by the defendant, and the contract had been a profitable one for the plaintiff, the plaintiff would have recovered over the life of the contract a gain, sufficient not only to fully reimburse him for his expenditures, but also to yield an excess which would be the profit. Since the amount of the gross receipts (i.e., the gain) cannot be determined with the requisite degree of certainty, the amount of the profit cannot be determined and therefore cannot be allowed in the recovery. *But the amount of the gain which would have reimbursed plaintiff for the expenditures incurred in preparation and part performance can be determined by and to the extent of these expenditures,* and therefore *this amount can be allowed in the recovery.*" (Emphasis in original.)

———

L. ALBERT & SON v. ARMSTRONG RUBBER CO., 178 F.2d 182 (2d Cir.1949) (L. Hand, J.). Seller agreed to sell to Buyer four machines designed to recondition old rubber. Seller breached the contract, and Buyer claimed as damages the expenses that it had incurred in reliance upon Seller's promise, including the $3000 cost of a foundation that it had laid for the machines. In the course of his opinion, Hand discussed as follows the issues involved by the possibility that if the contract had been completed it would have resulted in a loss to the plaintiff:

> ... The Buyer ... asserts that it is ... entitled to recover the cost of the foundation upon the theory that what it expended in reliance upon the Seller's performance was a recoverable loss. In cases where the venture would have proved profitable to the promisee, there is no reason why he should not recover his expenses. On the other hand, on those occasions in which the performance would not have covered the promisee's outlay, such a result imposes the risk of the promisee's contract upon the promisor.... It is often very hard to learn what the value of the performance would have been; and it is a common expedient, and a just one, in such situations to put the peril of the answer upon that party who by his wrong has made the issue relevant to the rights of the other. On principle therefore the proper solution would seem to be that the promisee may recover his outlay in preparation for the performance, subject to the privilege of the promisor to reduce it by as much as he can show that the promisee would have lost, if the contract had been performed....

———

SULLIVAN v. O'CONNOR

Chapter 5, supra

WALTERS v. MARATHON OIL CO.

Chapter 1, supra

SECTION 2.   THE RESTITUTION MEASURE

The term "restitution" has both a substantive and a remedial sense. Substantively, restitution refers to the recapture of a benefit conferred on the defendant by the plaintiff, the retention of which would leave the defendant unjustly enriched. Remedially, restitution refers to remedies, including money remedies, that are based on the amount of a defendant's unjust enrichment.

(a) Restitutionary Damages for Breach of Contract

OSTEEN v. JOHNSON

Colorado Court of Appeals, 1970.
473 P.2d 184.

DUFFORD, JUDGE ... This was an action for breach of an oral contract. Trial was to the court, which found that the plaintiffs had paid the sum of $2,500. In exchange, the defendant had agreed to "promote" the plaintiffs' daughter, Linda Osteen, as a singer and composer of country-western music. More specifically, it was found that the defendant had agreed to advertise Linda through various mailings for a period of one year; to arrange and furnish the facilities necessary for Linda to record several songs; to prepare two records from the songs recorded; to press and mail copies of one of the records to disc jockeys throughout the country; and, if the first record met with any success, to press and mail out copies of the second record.

The trial court further found that the defendant did arrange for several recording sessions, at which Linda recorded four songs. A record was prepared of two of the songs, and 1,000 copies of the record were then pressed. Of the pressed records, 340 copies were mailed to disc jockeys, 200 were sent to the plaintiffs, and the remainder were retained by the defendant. Various mailings were made to advertise Linda; flyers were sent to disc jockeys throughout the country; and Linda's professional name was advertised in trade magazines. The record sent out received a favorable review and a high rating in a trade magazine.

Upon such findings the trial court concluded that the defendant had substantially performed the agreement. However, a judgment was entered in favor of the plaintiffs in the sum of $1.00 and costs on the basis that the defendant had wrongfully caused the name of another party to appear on the label of the record as co-author of a song which had been written solely by Linda. The trial court also ordered the defendant to deliver to the plaintiffs certain master tapes and records in the defendant's possession.

1. RIGHT OF RESTITUTION

Although plaintiffs' reasons are not clearly defined, they argue here that the award of damages is inadequate, and that the trial court erred in concluding that the defendant had substantially performed the agreement. However, no evidence was presented during the trial of the matter upon which an award of other than nominal damages could be based. In our opinion, the remedy which plaintiffs proved and upon which they can rely is that of restitution. See 5 A. Corbin, Contracts § 996. This remedy is available where there has been a contract breach of vital importance, variously defined as a substantial breach or a breach which goes to the essence of the contract. See 5 A. Corbin, Contracts § 1104, where the author writes:

> "In the case of a breach by non-performance, ... the injured party's alternative remedy by way of restitution depends upon the extent of the non-performance by the defendant. The defendant's breach may be nothing but a failure to perform some minor part of his contractual duty. Such a minor non-performance is a breach of contract and an action for damages can be maintained. The injured party, however, can not maintain an action for restitution of what he has given the defendant unless the defendant's non-performance is so material that it is held to go to the 'essence'.... A minor breach by one party does not discharge the contractual duty of the other party; and the latter being still bound to perform as agreed can not be entitled to the restitution of payments already made by him or to the value of other part performances rendered." ...

2. BREACH OF CONTRACT

The essential question here then becomes whether any breach on the part of the defendant is substantial enough to justify the remedy of restitution. Plaintiffs argue that the defendant breached the contract in the following ways: First, the defendant did not promote Linda for a period of one year as agreed; secondly, the defendant wrongfully caused the name of another party to appear on the label as co-author of the song which had been composed solely by Linda; and thirdly, the defendant failed to press and mail out copies of the second record as agreed.

The first argument is not supported by the record. Plaintiffs brought the action within the one-year period for which the contract was to run. There was no evidence that during this period the defendant had not continued to promote Linda through the use of mailings and advertisements. Quite obviously the mere fact that the one-year period had not ended prior to the commencement of the action does not justify the conclusion that the defendant had breached the agreement. Plaintiffs' second argument overlooks the testimony offered on behalf of the defendant that listing the other party as co-author of the song would make it more likely that the record would be played by disc jockeys.

The plaintiffs' third argument does, however, have merit. It is clear from the record and the findings of the trial court that the first record had met with some success. It is also clear that copies of the second record were neither pressed nor mailed out. In our opinion the failure of the defendant to press and mail out copies of the second record after the first had achieved some success constituted a substantial breach of the contract and, therefore, justifies the remedy of restitution. Seale v. Bates, 145 Colo. 430, 359 P.2d 356; Colorado Management Corp. v. American Founders Life Insurance Co., 145 Colo. 413, 359 P.2d 665; Bridges v. Ingram, 122 Colo. 501, 223 P.2d 1051. Both parties agree that the essence of their contract was to publicize Linda as a singer of western songs and to make her name and talent known to the public. Defendant admitted and asserted that the primary method of achieving this end was to have records pressed and mailed to disc jockeys. . . .

3. Determining Damages

It is clear that the defendant did partially perform the contract and, under applicable law, should be allowed compensation for the reasonable value of his services. See 5 A. Corbin, Contracts § 1114, where the author writes:

> "[A]ll courts are in agreement that restitution by the defendant will not be enforced unless the plaintiff returns in some way what he has received as a part performance by the defendant."

It shall, therefore, be the ultimate order of this court that prior to restoring to the plaintiffs the $2,500 paid by them to the defendant further proceedings be held during which the trial court shall determine the reasonable value of the services which the defendant rendered on plaintiffs' behalf.

The judgment is reversed, and this case is remanded with directions that a new trial be held to determine the one issue of the amount to which the plaintiffs are entitled by way of restitution. Such amount shall be the $2,500 paid by plaintiffs to defendant less the reasonable value of the services which the defendant performed on behalf of plaintiffs.

Coyte and Pierce, JJ., concur.

RESTATEMENT, SECOND, CONTRACTS §§ 344, 345, 370, 371

[See Selected Source Materials Supplement]

RESTATEMENT, SECOND, CONTRACTS
§ 370, ILLUSTRATIONS 2, 5

2. A contracts to sell B a machine for $100,000. After A has spent $40,000 on the manufacture of the machine but before its completion, B repudiates the contract. A cannot get restitution of the $40,000 because no benefit was conferred on B. . . .

5. A, a social worker, promises B to render personal services to C in return for B's promise to educate A's children. B repudiates the contract after A has rendered part of the services. A can get restitution from B for the services, even though they were not rendered to B, because they conferred a benefit on B. . . .

———

UNITED STATES v. ALGERNON BLAIR, INC.

United States Court of Appeals, Fourth Circuit, 1973.
479 F.2d 638.

CRAVEN, CIRCUIT JUDGE. May a subcontractor, who justifiably ceases work under a contract because of the prime contractor's breach, recover in quantum meruit the value of labor and equipment already furnished pursuant to the contract irrespective of whether he would have been entitled to recover in a suit on the contract? We think so, and, for reasons to be stated, the decision of the district court will be reversed.

The subcontractor, Coastal Steel Erectors, Inc., brought this action under the provisions of the Miller Act, 40 U.S.C.A. § 270a et seq., in the name of the United States against Algernon Blair, Inc., and its surety, United States Fidelity and Guaranty Company. Blair had entered a contract with the United States for the construction of a naval hospital in Charleston County, South Carolina. Blair had then contracted with Coastal to perform certain steel erection and supply certain equipment in conjunction with Blair's contract with the United States. Coastal commenced performance of its obligations, supplying its own cranes for handling and placing steel. Blair refused to pay for crane rental, maintaining that it was not obligated to do so under the subcontract. Because of Blair's failure to make payments for crane rental, and after completion of approximately 28 percent of the subcontract, Coastal terminated its performance. Blair then proceeded to complete the job with a new subcontractor. Coastal brought this action to recover for labor and equipment furnished.

The district court found that the subcontract required Blair to pay for crane use and that Blair's refusal to do so was such a material breach as to justify Coastal's terminating performance. This finding is not questioned on appeal. The court then found that under the contract the amount due Coastal, less what had already been paid, totaled approximately $37,000. Additionally, the court found Coastal would have lost more than $37,000 if it had completed performance. Holding that any amount due Coastal must be reduced by any loss it would have incurred by complete performance of the contract, the court denied recovery to Coastal. While the district court correctly stated the

" 'normal' rule of contract damages,"[1] we think Coastal is entitled to recover in quantum meruit.

In United States for Use of Susi Contracting Co. v. Zara Contracting Co., 146 F.2d 606 (2d Cir.1944), a Miller Act action, the court was faced with a situation similar to that involved here—the prime contractor had unjustifiably breached a subcontract after partial performance by the subcontractor. The court stated:

> For it is an accepted principle of contract law, often applied in the case of construction contracts, that the promisee upon breach has the option to forego any suit on the contract and claim only the reasonable value of his performance.

146 F.2d at 610. The Tenth Circuit has also stated that the right to seek recovery under quantum meruit in a Miller Act case is clear.[3] Quantum meruit recovery is not limited to an action against the prime contractor but may also be brought against the Miller Act surety, as in this case. Further, that the complaint is not clear in regard to the theory of a plaintiff's recovery does not preclude recovery under quantum meruit. Narragansett Improvement Co. v. United States, 290 F.2d 577 (1st Cir.1961). A plaintiff may join a claim for quantum meruit with a claim for damages from breach of contract.

In the present case, Coastal has, at its own expense, provided Blair with labor and the use of equipment. Blair, who breached the subcontract, has retained these benefits without having fully paid for them. On these facts, Coastal is entitled to restitution in quantum meruit:

> The "restitution interest," involving a combination of unjust impoverishment with unjust gain, presents the strongest case for relief. If, following Aristotle, we regard the purpose of justice as the maintenance of an equilibrium of goods among members of society, the restitution interest presents twice as strong a claim to judicial intervention as the reliance interest, since if A not only causes B to lose one unit but appropriates that unit to himself, the resulting discrepancy between A and B is not one unit but two.

Fuller & Perdue, The Reliance Interest in Contract Damages, 46 Yale L.J. 52, 56 (1936).[6]

The impact of quantum meruit is to allow a promisee to recover the value of services he gave to the defendant irrespective of whether he would have lost money on the contract and been unable to recover in a suit on the contract. Scaduto v. Orlando, 381 F.2d 587, 595 (2d Cir.1967). The measure of recovery for quantum meruit is the reasonable value of the performance, Restatement of Contracts § 347 (1932); and recovery is undiminished by any loss which would have been incurred by complete performance. 12 Williston on Contracts § 1485, at 312 (3d ed. 1970). While the contract price may be evidence of reasonable value of the services, it does not measure the value of the

---

1. Fuller & Perdue, The Reliance Interest in Contract Damages, 46 Yale L.J. 52 (1936); Restatement of Contracts § 333 (1932).

3. Southern Painting Co. v. United States, 222 F.2d 431, 433 (10th Cir.1955). See also Great Lakes Constr. Co. v. Republic Creosoting Co., 139 F.2d 456 (8th Cir.1943) (dealing with a prior statute).

6. This case also comes within the requirements of the Restatements for recovery in quantum meruit. Restatement, Restitution § 107 (1937); Restatement, Contracts §§ 347–357 (1932).

performance or limit recovery. Rather, the standard for measuring the reasonable value of the services rendered is the amount for which such services could have been purchased from one in the plaintiff's position at the time and place the services were rendered.

Since the district court has not yet accurately determined the reasonable value of the labor and equipment use furnished by Coastal to Blair, the case must be remanded for those findings. When the amount has been determined, judgment will be entered in favor of Coastal, less payments already made under the contract. Accordingly, for the reasons stated above, the decision of the district court is

Reversed and remanded with instructions.

———

OLIVER v. CAMPBELL, 43 Cal.2d 298, 273 P.2d 15 (1954). Oliver, a lawyer, had agreed to represent Dr. Campbell in a separate-maintenance and divorce action until final judgment, for a fee of $850, including $100 for costs and incidentals. The trial lasted twenty-nine days. After the trial's conclusion, the court indicated its intention to give Mrs. Campbell a divorce. While Mrs. Campbell's proposed findings were under consideration, Dr. Campbell discharged Oliver. At that point, Oliver had been paid $550. Dr. Campbell refused to pay more, and Oliver brought this action to recover the reasonable value of his services, which the court below found to be $5,000. Held, that the trial court should enter a verdict of $300 in Oliver's favor. " 'It is well settled that one who is wrongfully discharged and prevented from further performance of his contract may elect as a general rule to treat the contract as rescinded, may sue upon a *quantum meruit* as if the special contract of employment had never been made and may recover the reasonable value of the services performed even though such reasonable value exceeds the contract price.' ... The question remains, however, of the application of the foregoing rules to the instant case. Plaintiff had performed practically all of the services he was employed to perform when he was discharged. The trial was at an end. The court had indicated its intention to give judgment against Dr. Campbell and all that remained was a signing of findings and judgment. The full sum called for in the contract was payable because the trial had ended. Under these circumstances it would appear that in effect, plaintiff had completed the performance of his service and the rule would apply that: 'the remedy of restitution in money is not available to one who has fully performed his part of a contract, if the only part of the agreed exchange for such performance that has not been rendered by the defendant is a sum of money constituting a liquidated debt.... Rest. Contracts, § 350....' "

Schauer, J., dissenting, was of the opinion that the trial court should be directed to enter a verdict of $5,000 in Oliver's favor on the ground that Oliver had not fully performed at the time of breach. *"The contract plaintiff made with Dr. Campbell did not limit his services to the trial of the case....* Under the contract he agreed to represent the doctor until final judgment, and he told the doctor he *'thought the case would be reversed on appeal.'* " (Emphasis in original.)

———

1 G. PALMER, THE LAW OF RESTITUTION 378–79 (1978). "When the plaintiff has fully performed his obligations under the contract and the defendant's obligation is to pay money, restitution of the value of the plaintiff's performance is regularly denied. The plaintiff's sole remedy is to recover the agreed price.... The principal basis for criticism of the decisions lies in the fact that, for part performance, restitution free of the contract price is recognized by the great weight of authority, and it seems somewhat incongruous that the price should be controlling after full performance. The incongruity is most evident when a plaintiff who has only partly performed is granted restitution of an amount in excess of the contract price for full performance, as has been allowed in numerous decisions."

NOTE ON RESTITUTIONARY AND RELIANCE DAMAGES

In theory, restitutionary and reliance damages are easily distinguishable: restitutionary damages are based on *benefit conferred;* reliance damages are based on *costs incurred.* In practice, however, the distinction is often not easy to maintain, because in an action for restitution the benefit conferred is often effectively measured by the plaintiff's costs. This is particularly true where the action is brought in "quantum meruit," the name of the traditional action that seeks recovery for the reasonable value of work, labor, and services performed at the defendant's request. For example, in Randolph v. Castle, 190 Ky. 776, 228 S.W. 418 (1921), defendant, the owner of a small coal mine, entered into an oral contract with plaintiffs, whereby plaintiffs agreed to work defendant's mine for three years, and defendant agreed to pay plaintiffs $2.10 per ton for coal removed. Defendant later repudiated the contract, and plaintiffs sued for damages. The court said, "... [T]he contract ... was within the statute of frauds.... [and] plaintiffs were entitled to recover, if at all, on the *quantum meruit.* This necessitated plaintiffs showing the value of the services performed.... If the plaintiffs at the instance of defendant's mine foreman remained at the mine, ready, willing and able to work, but were assigned no duties, and thereby lost time, the defendant is liable to them for the reasonable value thereof...."

(b) Restitution in Favor of a Plaintiff in Default*

KUTZIN v. PIRNIE

Supreme Court of New Jersey, 1991.
124 N.J. 500, 591 A.2d 932.

CLIFFORD, J. This is an action on a contract for the sale of residential property. The sellers' real-estate agent prepared the contract, after which defendants, the prospective buyers, signed it, paid a deposit of nearly ten

---

* Logically, the subject-matter of Section 2(b) does not fit under the heading of Part II, because it does not concern a remedy for breach. The subject is nevertheless taken up at this point, partly because it is remedial in nature, and partly because of its close connection with Section 2(a).

percent of the purchase price, and then decided not to go through with the purchase. In the trial court the buyers argued that the contract had been rescinded because attorneys for both parties had sought to amend it during the three-day period provided by the contract's attorney-review clause. The court found the contract to be valid and awarded the sellers compensatory damages, albeit in an amount less than the deposit. The Appellate Division agreed that the contract is binding but held that the sellers are entitled to keep the entire deposit as damages. We granted certification ... to determine whether the contract is enforceable and, if so, whether the sellers should be allowed to keep the deposit. We affirm the Appellate Division holding that the contract is valid but modify that court's judgment on the issue of damages and reinstate the damage award of the trial court.

I

On September 1, 1987, defendants, Duncan and Gertrude Pirnie, and plaintiffs, Milton and Ruth Kutzin, signed a contract for the sale of the Kutzins' house in Haworth for $365,000. The contract, which is the standard-form real-estate sales contract adopted by the New Jersey Association of Realtors, had been prepared by Weichert Realtors (Weichert), the sellers' real-estate agent. Under its terms, the Pirnies agreed to pay a partial deposit of $1,000 on signing the contract and the remainder of the deposit, $35,000, within seven days. In compliance therewith, the Pirnies made out a check for $1,000 to the trust account of Russo Real Estate (Russo), their real-estate agent. The contract does not contain a "forfeiture" or "liquidated damages" clause; with reference to the disposition of the deposit should the sale not take place, the contract merely states, "If this contract is voided by either party, the escrow monies shall be disbursed pursuant to the written direction of both parties."

The contract also contains the following attorney-review provision:

1. *Study by Attorney*

The Buyer or the Seller may choose to have an attorney study this contract. If an attorney is consulted, the attorney must complete his or her review of the contract within a three-day period. This contract will be legally binding at the end of this three-day period unless an attorney for the Buyer or the Seller reviews and disapproves of the contract.

2. *Counting the Time*

You count the three days from the date of delivery of the signed contract to the Buyer and the Seller. You do not count Saturdays, Sundays or legal holidays. The Buyer and the Seller may agree in writing to extend the three-day period for attorney review.

3. *Notice of Disapproval*

If an attorney for the Buyer or the Seller reviews and disapproves of this contract, the attorney must notify the REALTOR(S) and the other party named in this contract within the three-day period. Otherwise this contract will be legally binding as written. The attorney must send the notice of disapproval to the REALTOR(S) by certified mail, by telegram, or by delivering it personally. The telegram or certified letter will be effective upon sending. The personal delivery will be effective upon delivery to the REALTOR(S) office. The attorney may also, but need not, inform the REALTOR(S) of any suggested revision(s) in the contract that would make it satisfactory.

The Kutzins' attorney, Marshall Kozinn, telephoned Russo on September 2nd to communicate his approval of the contract with one exception: he wanted to hold the deposit in his trust account pending closing. Kozinn followed up that conversation by mailing a letter to Russo dated September 3, 1987, with a copy to Joseph Maccarone, the Pirnies' attorney, which read:

> As per our telephone conversation, the above contract is satisfactory to me as Attorney for the Seller with the exception that my clients have requested that I hold the deposit pending closing.

> Would you please forward the One Thousand ($1,000.) Dollars to me, and arrange to have the $35,000 remaining deposit balance made payable to my attorney trust account.

Russo had already complied with Kozinn's request (without discussing the matter with Maccarone) by endorsing the Pirnies' check to Kozinn's trust account and sending it to him on September 2nd.

In a telephone conversation with Kozinn on September 4th, Maccarone agreed to allow Kozinn to hold the deposit but expressed his opinion that the contract prepared by Weichert did not provide adequate protection for the buyers. That same day Maccarone mailed to Kozinn the following letter:

> This office shall be representing the Buyers, Duncan and Gertrude Pirnie with reference to [this] transaction.

> I have reviewed the contracts prepared by the Realtor and I would like to propose the attached amendments which I have taken the liberty to prepare. If these forms meet with your approval, I would appreciate your having them executed by the Sellers and return them to me for execution by the Buyers.

> I shall forward you the balance of the deposit shortly.

Maccarone enclosed with the letter his standard rider for protection of buyers of real estate. Significantly, the rider was silent on the issue of what would happen to the deposit if the sale were not completed.

On September 10th, Maccarone telephoned Kozinn to inquire if the terms of the rider were acceptable. When Kozinn indicated that they were not, the attorneys discussed their differences and eventually agreed on certain changes. During that conversation, Kozinn mentioned that he had not yet received the additional deposit of $35,000 and questioned whether the Pirnies intended to proceed with the purchase. Maccarone assured Kozinn of the Pirnies' intention to buy the house, stating that "if the deposit was to be any demonstration of good faith or what have you [Kozinn] would have the deposit." Kozinn received the Pirnies' check for the balance of the deposit the next day. Thus assured that the sale would occur, the Kutzins left for their Florida home on the 13th of September.

Maccarone revised the rider and on September 21st sent to Kozinn two copies, already signed by the Pirnies, for execution by the Kutzins. Kozinn received the copies of the modified rider on September 22nd and forwarded them to the Kutzins that same day. A letter accompanied the riders requesting, among other things, that the Kutzins sign and return the riders to

Kozinn as soon as the couple returned from Florida. The Kutzins apparently received the letter when they returned to New Jersey on September 24th.

Shortly thereafter the Pirnies instructed their new attorney, Harold Goldman, to write Kozinn the following letter, which was mailed on September 28th:

> Be advised the Purnies [sic: "Pirnies" or "Pirnie" throughout] have retained my office to represent them in their effort to negotiate the purchase of a home in Haworth owned by your client, Milton Kutzin.
>
> Mrs. Purnie has indicated to me that the Purnies are no longer interested in purchasing the subject property. Therefore, please treat this letter as formal notice to withdraw the offer to purchase by the Purnies. I must add that the desire to withdraw the offer to purchase was communicated to Joan Harrison, the listing broker, yesterday by both Mrs. Purnie and [myself].
>
> It is my understanding that you are presently holding in trust deposit monies remitted by the Purnies in regard to the proposed purchase. Please call [me] to arrange for the return of said monies.

The Kutzins refused to return the deposit and promptly sued for specific performance of the contract. The Pirnies counterclaimed for return of their $36,000 deposit, contending that the contract had been validly rescinded either pursuant to the attorney-review provision or by agreement of the parties. Because the Kutzins sold the house to another buyer for $352,500 while the case was pending, they amended their complaint to seek only damages.

The trial court ruled that the parties had entered into a binding contract that had not been rescinded either by agreement or pursuant to the attorney-review clause. Consequently, the court held that the sellers were entitled to $17,325 in damages. That amount consisted of the $12,500 difference between the $365,000 the Pirnies had contracted to pay and the $352,500 for which the house eventually sold; $3,825 in utilities, real-estate taxes, and insurance expenses the Kutzins had incurred during the six-month period between the originally-anticipated closing date and the date of actual sale; and $1,000 the Kutzins had paid for a new basement carpet, which their realtor had recommended they buy to enhance the attractiveness of their house to prospective buyers. The court denied recovery of interest the Kutzins contended they would have earned on the purchase price had the sale to the Pirnies gone through. It also refused to award damages for the increased capital-gains tax the Kutzins had paid as a result of the breach. The court ordered the Kutzins to return the $18,675 balance of the deposit to the Pirnies.

On appeal, the Kutzins argued that they should recover the lost interest and the increased capital-gains tax they had incurred, or, alternatively, that they should be allowed to retain the deposit. On cross-appeal the Pirnies claimed entitlement to the entire deposit, again asserting that the contract had been validly rescinded. In an unreported opinion, the Appellate Division found that the contract between the parties "was enforceable according to its terms" but that "the Kutzins' claims to compensation for their allegedly increased tax liability and lost interest were too speculative to be compensable." The court then noted that "the Kutzins' loss as determined by the trial court was less than the Pirnies' $36,000 deposit," and concluded that "the

Kutzins are entitled to retain the [entire] deposit, but they may not recover any additional amount as damages." ...

III

We [now] determine whether the Kutzins are entitled to retain the entire $36,000 deposit as damages. The issue of whether a seller should be entitled to retain a deposit when a buyer breaches a contract that does not contain a liquidated-damages or forfeiture clause has long troubled courts. As Professor Williston has observed, "Few questions in the law have given rise to more discussion and difference of opinion than that concerning the right of one who has materially broken his contract without legal excuse to recover for such benefit [here, the deposit] as he may have conferred on the other party...." 12 S. Williston, *A Treatise on the Law of Contracts* § 1473 at 220 (3d ed. 1961) (Williston).

-A-

"[T]he common-law rule, which has been very generally followed ..., [was] that where the vendee of real property makes a part payment on the purchase price, but fails to fulfill the contract without lawful excuse, he cannot recover the payment ... even though the vendor may have made a profit by reason of the default." *Quillen v. Kelley*, 216 *Md.* 396, 401–02, 140 A.2d 517, 520 (1958); *see, e.g.,* Annotation, *Modern Status of Defaulting Vendee's Right to Recover Contractual Payments Withheld by Vendor as Forfeited*, 4 A.L.R.4th 993, 997 (1981) (The general rule is that "a vendee in default cannot recover back the money he has paid on an executory contract to his vendor who is not himself in default."). The thought behind that rule is that "restitution should always be refused, for the good and sufficient reason that the [buyer] is guilty of a breach of contract and should never be allowed to have advantage from his own wrong." 5A A. Corbin, *Corbin on Contracts* § 1129 at 37 (1964) (Corbin); *see, e.g., Haslack v. Mayers*, 26 *N.J.L.* 284, 290–91 (Sup.Ct.1857) ("The plaintiff here has deliberately broken his covenant with the defendant.... For the court to aid him[ ] would be to lend its aid to an act of bad faith.... Let him perform his contract ... or ... the loss is the consequence of his own act.").

New Jersey traditionally has adhered to the common-law rule. As the Appellate Division stated in *Oliver v. Lawson*, 92 *N.J.Super.* 331, 333, 223 A.2d 355 (1966), *certif. denied*, 48 *N.J.* 574, 227 A.2d 133 (1967), "It has heretofore generally been held in New Jersey that ... the defaulting buyer may not recover his deposit, irrespective of the actual damages suffered by the seller and regardless of whether the contract contains a forfeiture provision or not." ...

Following [a] long line of cases, the Appellate Division held that the Kutzins are entitled to retain the deposit even though the court was "sympathetic to the trial judge's ruling that the Pirnies were entitled to the return of the balance of their $36,000 contract deposit in excess of the Kutzins' actual damages."

-B-

Despite the ample authority supporting the Appellate Division's disposition of the damages question, "there has been a growing recognition of the injustice that often results from the application of the rule permitting total forfeiture of part payments under a contract of sale." *Great United Realty Co. v. Lewis*, 203 *Md.* 442, 448, 101 A.2d 881, 883 (1954); *see also Quillen v. Kelley, supra,* 216 *Md.* at 402, 140 A.2d at 520 ("In applying [the common-law] rule, there have been instances of harshness and injustice, which have caused a reconsideration of the same, in recent years, by the courts and by learned and renowned scholars and text-writers on the subject of contracts.").

Professor Corbin led the movement favoring departure from the strict common-law rule. In *The Right of a Defaulting Vendee to the Restitution of Installments Paid,* 40 *Yale L.J.* 1013, 1013 (1931) (*Defaulting Vendee*), he stated:

> If a contractor has committed a total breach of his contract, having rendered no performance whatever thereunder, no penalty or forfeiture will be enforced against him; he will be required to do no more than to make the injured party whole by paying full compensatory damages. In like manner, a contractor who commits a breach after he has rendered part performance must also make the injured party whole by payment of full compensatory damages. The part performance rendered, however, may be much more valuable to the defendant than the amount of the injury caused by the breach; and in such case, to allow the injured party to retain the benefit of the part performance so rendered, without making restitution of any part of such value, is the enforcement of a penalty or forfeiture against the contract-breaker.

Corbin went on to declare that if a plaintiff "can and does show by proper evidence that the defendant is holding an amount of money as a penalty rather than as compensation for injury, he should be given judgment for restitution of that amount." *Id.* at 1025–26 (footnote omitted). . . .

Professor Corbin's article . . . was used in the formulation of section 357 of the *Restatement of Contracts* (1932). Section 357 . . . states:

> (1) Where the defendant fails or refuses to perform his contract and is justified therein by the plaintiff's own breach of duty or non-performance of a condition, but the plaintiff has rendered a part performance under the contract that is a net benefit to the defendant, the plaintiff can get judgment, except as stated in Subsection (2), for the amount of such benefit in excess of the harm that he has caused to the defendant by his own breach, in no case exceeding a ratable proportion of the agreed compensation, if
>
> > (a) the plaintiff's breach or non-performance is not wilful and deliberate; or
> >
> > (b) the defendant, with knowledge that the plaintiff's breach of duty or non-performance of condition has occurred or will thereafter occur, assents to the rendition of the part performance, or accepts the benefit of it, or retains property received although its return in specie is still not unreasonably difficult or injurious.
>
> (2) The plaintiff has no right to compensation for his part performance if it is merely a payment of earnest money, or if the contract provides that it may be retained and it is not so greatly in excess of the defendant's harm that the provision is rejected as imposing a penalty. . . .

Section 374(1) of the *Restatement (Second) of Contracts* is based on section 357 but "is more liberal in allowing recovery in accord with the policy behind Uniform Commercial Code § 2–718(2)." *Restatement (Second) of Contracts* § 374 reporter's note (1981). That section sets forth the rule as follows:

> [I]f a party justifiably refuses to perform on the ground that his remaining duties of performance have been discharged by the other party's breach, the party in breach is entitled to restitution for any benefit that he has conferred by way of part performance or reliance in excess of the loss that he has caused by his own breach. [*Id.* § 374(1).]

Particularly relevant to this case is the following illustration:

> A contracts to sell land to B for $100,000, which B promises to pay in $10,000 installments before transfer of title. After B has paid $30,000 he fails to pay the remaining installments and A sells the land to another buyer for $95,000. B can recover $30,000 from A in restitution less $5,000 damages for B's breach of contract, or $25,000. If A does not sell the land to another buyer and obtains a decree of specific performance against B, B has no right to restitution. [*Id.* § 374 illustration 1.]

Since publication of the first *Restatement of Contracts* in 1932, few courts have followed the common-law rule refusing restitution. See 5A Corbin, *supra,* § 1129 at 37–38. The *Restatement* approach of allowing recovery "has steadily increased in favor and probably represents the weight of authority." 12 Williston, *supra,* § 1473 at 222 (footnote omitted). . . .

With the issue squarely presented in this case, we overrule those New Jersey cases adhering to the common-law rule and adopt the modern approach set forth in section 374(1) of the *Restatement (Second) of Contracts.* In Professor Williston's words, "to deny recovery [in this situation] often gives the [seller] more than fair compensation for the injury he has sustained and imposes a forfeiture (which the law abhors) on the [breaching buyer]." 12 Williston, *supra,* § 1473 at 222. The approach that we adopt is suggested to have the added benefit of promoting economic efficiency: penalties deter "efficient" breaches of contract "by making the cost of the breach to the contract breaker greater than the cost of the breach to the victim." R. Posner, *Economic Analysis of Law* § 4.10 at 116 (3d ed. 1986).

-C-

We conclude that the Pirnies are entitled, under the *Restatement* formulation of damages, to restitution for any benefit that they conferred by way of part performance or reliance in excess of the loss that they caused by their own breach. See *Restatement (Second) of Contracts, supra,* § 374(1). We stress, however, that "[o]ne who charges an unjust enrichment has the burden of proving it." *Oliver v. Lawson, supra,* 92 *N.J.Super.* at 336, 223 *A.*2d 355. . . .

The trial court found that the Kutzins had suffered $17,325 in damages, a figure that we accept because it is not challenged in this Court. The Pirnies' deposit of $36,000 exceeded the injury caused by their breach by $18,675, and they are thus entitled to recovery of that amount.

Our holding is not affected by the fact that the $36,000 deposit was less than ten percent of the $365,000 purchase price. *Cf. Krupnick v. Guerriero* . . ., 247 *N.J.Super.* [373,] at 380, 589 *A.*2d [620,] at 624 ("As a general rule a defaulting buyer may not recover a deposit which does not materially exceed 10%. . . ."). Whenever the breaching buyer proves that the deposit exceeds the seller's actual damages suffered as a result of the breach, the buyer may recover the difference.

III

To ensure that our opinion not be misread, we emphasize that the contract at issue does not contain a forfeiture or liquidated-damages clause; it merely states, "If this contract is voided by either party, the escrow monies shall be disbursed pursuant to the written direction of both parties." The contract is otherwise silent on the subject of what would happen to the deposit were the sale not to occur. Had the contract contained a liquidated-damages clause, this case would have been governed by section 374(2) of the *Restatement (Second) of Contracts,* which states:

> To the extent that, under the manifested assent of the parties, a party's performance is to be retained in the case of breach, that party is not entitled to restitution if the value of the performance as liquidated damages is reasonable in the light of the anticipated loss caused by the breach and the difficulties of proof of loss. . . .

IV

We hold that. . . . the Pirnies' refusal to proceed constituted a breach of contract entitling the Kutzins to recover compensatory damages for the loss they suffered as a result of the breach. We also hold that the Kutzins cannot retain the entire deposit as damages. The Pirnies are entitled to restitution of their deposit less the amount of the injury to the Kutzins caused by the Pirnies' breach. To allow retention of the entire deposit would unjustly enrich the Kutzins and would penalize the Pirnies contrary to the policy behind our law of contracts.

The judgment of the Appellate Division is modified to reinstate the trial court's damage award. As modified the judgment is:

Affirmed.

For affirmance—Chief Justice WILENTZ and Justices CLIFFORD, HANDLER, POLLOCK, O'HERN, GARIBALDI and STEIN—7.

Opposed—None.

———

UCC § 2–718(2), (3)

[See Selected Source Materials Supplement]

———

*

Part III

ASSENT

The most common forms of contracts are bargains. A bargain entails assent. What constitutes assent for purposes of the law of contracts is a very difficult issue. That issue is considered in Part III.

Part III begins with Chapter 9, which concerns the basic principles of interpretation in contract law. Although problems of interpretation run through all areas of contract law, they are most salient in the area of assent.

Although bargains can be formed in more than one way, they are most commonly formed by an offer followed by an acceptance. Chapters 10_12 concern problems of offer and acceptance—problems such as what constitutes an offer, whether and when offers are revocable, and what kind of acceptance an offer requires.

Chapter 13 concerns contracts that are formed by implied promises or by conduct, rather than by explicit promises.

Chapter 14 concerns the problems that arise where the terms of an agreement are indefinite or not final.

Finally, Chapter 15 concerns special rules of evidence and interpretation that apply when a contract is in writing.

Chapter 9

AN INTRODUCTION TO INTERPRETATION

This Chapter concerns the interpretation of contractual language. The Chapter consists of three Sections.

Section 1 introduces the role of subjective and objective elements in the principles of interpretation in contract law.

Section 2 concerns the problems of interpreting purposive language.

Section 3 introduces the role of usage, course of dealing, and course of performance in interpretation.

Special rules of interpretation are sometimes applied when a contract is in writing. These rules will be considered later, in Chapter 15, because they reflect policies other than the determination of the parties' intentions.

SECTION 1. SUBJECTIVE AND OBJECTIVE ELEMENTS IN THE PRINCIPLES OF INTERPRETATION IN CONTRACT LAW

INTRODUCTORY NOTE

It is very commonly asserted that a contract requires "a meeting of the minds." In many contexts this statement is scarcely objectionable. For example, if A offers to sell his bicycle to B for $40, and B says that he accepts, provided A will reduce the price to $36, it is obvious that no contract has as yet been entered. One may quite properly justify this conclusion by saying that there has been no "meeting of the minds." On the other hand, difficulties will arise if the requirement of a "meeting of the minds" is taken literally and applied indiscriminately. In Europe there has been much discussion of the problem of the "mental reservation." Could a defendant who had signed a contract with the apparent intention of binding himself escape liability by showing that at the time of the signing he had made a "mental reservation"

234

that he should not be bound? It is obvious that this defense should not be allowed; so obvious is this conclusion that the question has not even been discussed in the case-oriented literature of the common law.

But there are questions of practical import that do present real difficulty, including cases where effective communication fails because one party misinterprets the intention of the others. In these cases, the question may arise whether an expression of intention may be affected by a state of mind that accompanied it. A major theme running through Part III is the tension, in such cases, between subjective intent (state of mind, or what a party "really" meant) and objective intent (what the party expressed, or "seemed" to have meant).

It is sometimes concluded that what a party objectively means is not a question of "intent" at all. That this conclusion rests on a confusion of thought concerning the meaning of intent may be shown by the analogy of legislation. Under our constitutional system, the courts are generally subservient to the legislature. If Congress has properly enacted a law falling within the field of its competence, the courts are bound to follow and apply this law. With respect to the statute, the court's function is conceived as being subordinate. This constitutional relation between courts and statutes is commonly expressed by saying that the "intent" of the legislature governs questions of interpretation of a statute. Yet it is generally recognized that the "intent" that the court must respect is a formalized thing, and not the "actual, inner" intent of particular legislators. A statute becomes law only after it has been enacted in accordance with certain rules; when these rules have been followed the statute stands as law even though Senator Sorghum confides to his dinner partner that he was asleep when the bill was read and did not know what he was voting for.

Similarly, it is sometimes concluded that by emphasizing objective intent, contract law makes no place for subjective intent. This conclusion is equally flawed. The attitude that our courts take toward private agreements rests upon a kind of tacitly accepted constitution. This constitution, like that which regulates the relation of the courts to statutes, is a multi-faceted concept. When this is recognized, there is no longer any need to be disturbed by the fact that judges sometimes hold a person to an agreement he did not subjectively intend and at the same time insist that their purpose in enforcing contracts is to carry out the intention of the parties. Similar paradoxes, proceeding from similar causes, are to be found in most human institutions. The rules of an athletic association, for example, may be intended to ensure that the official record shall go to the fastest runner. At the same time these rules may operate to exclude the fastest runner from the record because his achievement occurred under conditions not satisfying the association's standards of proof. No one argues from this that the association has placed itself in a self-contradictory position, and must either abandon its rules for establishing records or cease pretending that it is interested in the speed of runners. There is as little reason to force upon the law of contracts a similar "either-or" alternative with regard to the treatment of intent.

LUCY v. ZEHMER

Supreme Court of Appeals of Virginia, 1954.
196 Va. 493, 84 S.E.2d 516.

BUCHANAN, JUSTICE. This suit was instituted by W.O. Lucy and J.C. Lucy, complainants, against A.H. Zehmer and Ida S. Zehmer, his wife, defendants, to have specific performance of a contract by which it was alleged the Zehmers had sold to W.O. Lucy a tract of land owned by A.H. Zehmer in Dinwiddie County containing 471.6 acres, more or less, known as the Ferguson farm, for $50,000. J.C. Lucy, the other complainant, is a brother of W.O. Lucy, to whom W.O. Lucy transferred a half interest in his alleged purchase.

The instrument sought to be enforced was written by A.H. Zehmer on December 20, 1952, in these words: "We hereby agree to sell to W.O. Lucy the Ferguson Farm complete for $50,000.00, title satisfactory to buyer," and signed by the defendants, A.H. Zehmer and Ida S. Zehmer.

The answer of A.H. Zehmer admitted that at the time mentioned W.O. Lucy offered him $50,000 cash for the farm, but that he, Zehmer considered that the offer was made in jest; that so thinking, and both he and Lucy having had several drinks, he wrote out "the memorandum" quoted above and induced his wife to sign it; that he did not deliver the memorandum to Lucy, but that Lucy picked it up, read it, put it in his pocket, attempted to offer Zehmer $5 to bind the bargain, which Zehmer refused to accept, and realizing for the first time that Lucy was serious, Zehmer assured him that he had no intention of selling the farm and that the whole matter was a joke. Lucy left the premises insisting that he had purchased the farm.

Depositions were taken and the decree appealed from was entered holding that the complainants had failed to establish their right to specific performance, and dismissing their bill. The assignment of error is to this action of the court.

W.O. Lucy, a lumberman and farmer, thus testified in substance: He had known Zehmer for fifteen or twenty years and had been familiar with the Ferguson farm for ten years. Seven or eight years ago he had offered Zehmer $20,000 for the farm which Zehmer had accepted, but the agreement was verbal and Zehmer backed out. On the night of December 20, 1952, around eight o'clock, he took an employee to McKenney, where Zehmer lived and operated a restaurant, filling station and motor court. While there he decided to see Zehmer and again try to buy the Ferguson farm. He entered the restaurant and talked to Mrs. Zehmer until Zehmer came in. He asked Zehmer if he had sold the Ferguson farm. Zehmer replied that he had not. Lucy said, "I bet you wouldn't take $50,000.00 for that place." Zehmer replied, "Yes, I would too; you wouldn't give fifty." Lucy said he would and told Zehmer to write up an agreement to that effect. Zehmer took a restaurant check and wrote on the back of it, "I do hereby agree to sell to W.O. Lucy the Ferguson Farm for $50,000 complete." Lucy told him he had better change it to "We" because Mrs. Zehmer would have to sign it too. Zehmer then tore up what he had written, wrote the agreement quoted above and asked Mrs. Zehmer, who was at the other end of the counter ten or twelve feet away, to sign it. Mrs. Zehmer said she would for $50,000 and signed it. Zehmer brought it back and gave it to Lucy, who offered him $5 which

Zehmer refused, saying, "You don't need to give me any money, you got the agreement there signed by both of us."

The discussion leading to the signing of the agreement, said Lucy, lasted thirty or forty minutes, during which Zehmer seemed to doubt that Lucy could raise $50,000. Lucy suggested the provision for having the title examined and Zehmer made the suggestion that he would sell it "complete, everything there," and stated that all he had on the farm was three heifers.

December 20 was on Saturday. Next day Lucy telephoned to J.C. Lucy and arranged with the latter to take a half interest in the purchase and pay half of the consideration. On Monday he engaged an attorney to examine the title. The attorney reported favorably on December 31 and on January 2 Lucy wrote Zehmer stating that the title was satisfactory, that he was ready to pay the purchase price in cash and asking when Zehmer would be ready to close the deal. Zehmer replied by letter, mailed on January 13, asserting that he had never agreed or intended to sell.

Mr. and Mrs. Zehmer were called by the complainants as adverse witnesses. Zehmer testified in substance as follows.

He bought this farm more than ten years ago for $11,000. He had had twenty-five offers, more or less, to buy it, including several from Lucy, who had never offered any specific sum of money. He had given them all the same answer, that he was not interested in selling it. On this Saturday night before Christmas it looked like everybody and his brother came by there to have a drink. He took a good many drinks during the afternoon and had a pint of his own. When he entered the restaurant around eight-thirty Lucy was there and he could see that he was "pretty high." He said to Lucy, "Boy, you got some good liquor, drinking, ain't you?" Lucy then offered him a drink. "I was already high as a Georgia pine, and didn't have any more better sense than to pour another great big slug out and gulp it down, and he took one too."

After they had talked a while Lucy asked whether he still had the Ferguson farm. He replied that he had not sold it and Lucy said, "I bet you wouldn't take $50,000.00 for it." Zehmer asked him if he would give $50,000 and Lucy said yes. Zehmer replied, "You haven't got $50,000.00 in cash." Lucy said he did and Zehmer replied that he did not believe it. They argued "pro and con for a long time," mainly about "whether he had $50,000 in cash that he could put up right then and buy that farm."

Finally, said Zehmer, Lucy told him if he didn't believe he had $50,000, "you sign that piece of paper here and say you will take $50,000.00 for the farm." He, Zehmer, "just grabbed the back off of a guest check there" and wrote on the back of it. At that point in his testimony Zehmer asked to see what he had written to "see if I recognize my own handwriting." He examined the paper and exclaimed, "Great balls of fire, I got 'Firgerson' for Ferguson. I have got satisfactory spelled wrong. I don't recognize that writing if I would see it, wouldn't know it was mine."

After Zehmer had, as he described it, "scribbled this thing off," Lucy said, "Get your wife to sign it." Zehmer walked over to where she was and she at first refused to sign but did so after he told her that he "was just needling him [Lucy], and didn't mean a thing in the world, that I was not selling the farm." Zehmer then "took it back over there ... and I was still looking at the dern thing. I had the drink right there by my hand, and I reached over to get a drink, and he said, 'Let me see it.' He reached and picked it up, and when I looked back again he had it in his pocket and he dropped a five dollar bill over there, and he said, 'Here is five dollars payment on it.' . . . I said, 'Hell no, that is beer and liquor talking. I am not going to sell you the farm. I have told you that too many times before.' "[Mrs. Zehmer's testimony was comparable to that of Mr. Zehmer. She added that after Lucy said, "All right, get your wife to sign it." Zehmer came back to where she was standing and said, "You want to put your name to this?" She said "No," but he said in an undertone, "It is nothing but a joke," and she signed it.] . . .

The defendants insist that the evidence was ample to support their contention that the writing sought to be enforced was prepared as a bluff or dare to force Lucy to admit that he did not have $50,000; that the whole matter was a joke; that the writing was not delivered to Lucy and no binding contract was ever made between the parties. . . .

In his testimony Zehmer claimed that he "was high as a Georgia pine," and that the transaction "was just a bunch of two doggoned drunks bluffing to see who could talk the biggest and say the most." That claim is inconsistent with his attempt to testify in great detail as to what was said and what was done. It is contradicted by other evidence as to the condition of both parties. . . . It was in fact conceded by defendants' counsel in oral argument that under the evidence Zehmer was not too drunk to make a valid contract. . . .

The appearance of the contract, the fact that it was under discussion for forty minutes or more before it was signed; Lucy's objection to the first draft because it was written in the singular, and he wanted Mrs. Zehmer to sign it also; the rewriting to meet that objection and the signing by Mrs. Zehmer; the discussion of what was to be included in the sale, the provision for the examination of the title, the completeness of the instrument that was executed, the taking possession of it by Lucy with no request or suggestion by either of the defendants that he give it back, are facts which furnish persuasive evidence that the execution of the contract was a serious business transaction rather than a casual, jesting matter as defendants now contend. . . .

If it be assumed, contrary to what we think the evidence shows, that Zehmer was jesting about selling his farm to Lucy and that the transaction was intended by him to be a joke, nevertheless the evidence shows that Lucy did not so understand it but considered it to be a serious business transaction and the contract to be binding on the Zehmers as well as on himself. . . .

Not only did Lucy actually believe, but the evidence shows he was warranted in believing, that the contract represented a serious business transaction and a good faith sale and purchase of the farm.

In the field of contracts, as generally elsewhere, "We must look to the outward expression of a person as manifesting his intention rather than to his secret and unexpressed intention. 'The law imputes to a person an intention corresponding to the reasonable meaning of his words and acts.' " First Nat. Exchange Bank of Roanoke v. Roanoke Oil Co., 169 Va. 99, 114, 192 S.E. 764, 770.

At no time prior to the execution of the contract had Zehmer indicated to Lucy by word or act that he was not in earnest about selling the farm. They had argued about it and discussed its terms, as Zehmer admitted, for a long time. Lucy testified that if there was any jesting it was about paying $50,000 that night. The contract and the evidence show that he was not expected to pay the money that night. Zehmer said that after the writing was signed he laid it down on the counter in front of Lucy. Lucy said Zehmer handed it to him. In any event there had been what appeared to be a good faith offer and a good faith acceptance, followed by the execution and apparent delivery of a written contract. Both said that Lucy put the writing in his pocket and then offered Zehmer $5 to seal the bargain. Not until then, even under the defendants' evidence, was anything said or done to indicate that the matter was a joke. Both of the Zehmers testified that when Zehmer asked his wife to sign he whispered that it was a joke so Lucy wouldn't hear and that it was not intended that he should hear.

The mental assent of the parties is not requisite for the formation of a contract. If the words or other acts of one of the parties have but one reasonable meaning, his undisclosed intention is immaterial except when an unreasonable meaning which he attaches to his manifestations is known to the other party. Restatement of the Law of Contracts, Vol. I, § 71, p. 74. . . .

So a person cannot set up that he was merely jesting when his conduct and words would warrant a reasonable person in believing that he intended a real agreement. 17 C.J.S., Contracts, § 47, p. 390; Clark on Contracts, 4 ed., § 27, at p. 54.

Whether the writing signed by the defendants and now sought to be enforced by the complainants was the result of a serious offer by Lucy and a serious acceptance by the defendants, or was a serious offer by Lucy and an acceptance in secret jest by the defendants, in either event it constituted a binding contract of sale between the parties.

Defendants contend further, however, that even though a contract was made, equity should decline to enforce it under the circumstances. These circumstances have been set forth in detail above. They disclose some drinking by the two parties but not to an extent that they were unable to understand fully what they were doing. There was no fraud, no misrepresentation, no sharp practice and no dealing between unequal parties. The farm had been bought for $11,000 and was assessed for taxation at $6,300. The purchase price was $50,000. Zehmer admitted that it was a good price. There is in fact present in this case none of the grounds usually urged against specific performance. . . .

The complainants are entitled to have specific performance of the contract sued on. The decree appealed from is therefore reversed and the cause is remanded for the entry of a proper decree requiring the defendants to perform the contract in accordance with the prayer of the bill.

Reversed and remanded.

KELLER v. HOLDERMAN, 11 Mich. 248, 83 Am.Dec. 737 (1863). Suit against the maker of a check for $300, which had been given in return for an old silver watch, worth about $15. The court said, "when the court below found as a fact that 'the whole transaction between the parties was a frolic and a banter, the plaintiff not expecting to sell, nor the defendant to buy the watch at the sum for which the check was drawn,' the conclusion should have been that no contract was ever made by the parties, and the finding should have been that no cause of action existed upon the check to the plaintiff."

RAFFLES v. WICHELHAUS

In the Court of Exchequer, 1864.
2 Hurl. & C. 906.

Declaration. For that it was agreed between the plaintiff and the defendants, to wit, at Liverpool, that the plaintiff should sell to the defendants, and the defendants buy of the plaintiff, certain goods, to wit, 125 bales of Surat cotton, guaranteed middling fair merchant's dhollorah, to arrive ex Peerless from Bombay; and that the cotton should be taken from the quay, and that the defendants would pay the plaintiff for the same at a certain rate, to wit, at the rate of 17¼ d. per pound, within a certain time then agreed upon after the arrival of the said goods in England. Averments: that the said goods did arrive by the said ship from Bombay in England, to wit, at Liverpool, and the plaintiff was then and there ready and willing and offered to deliver the said goods to the defendants, etc. Breach: that the defendants refused to accept the said goods or pay the plaintiff for them.

Plea. That the said ship mentioned in the said agreement was meant and intended by the defendant to be the ship called the Peerless, which sailed from Bombay, to wit, in October; and that the plaintiff was not ready and willing, and did not offer to deliver to the defendants any bales of cotton which arrived by the last-mentioned ship, but instead thereof was only ready and willing, and offered to deliver to the defendants 125 bales of Surat cotton which arrived by another and different ship, which was also called the Peerless, and which sailed from Bombay, to wit, in December.

Demurrer, and joinder therein.

Milward, in support of the demurrer. The contract was for the sale of a number of bales of cotton of a particular description, which the plaintiff was ready to deliver. It is immaterial by what ship the cotton was to arrive, so that it was a ship called the Peerless. The words "to arrive ex Peerless," only mean that if the vessel is lost on the voyage, the contract is to be at an end. [Pollock, C.B. It would be a question for the jury whether both parties meant the same ship called the Peerless.] That would be so if the contract was for the sale of a ship called the Peerless; but it is for the sale of cotton on board a ship of that name. [Pollock, C.B. The defendant only bought that cotton which was to arrive by a particular ship. It may as well be said, that if there is a contract for the purchase of certain goods in warehouse A., that is satisfied by the delivery of goods of the same description in warehouse B.] In that case there would be goods in both warehouses; here it does not appear that the plaintiff had any goods on board the other Peerless. [Martin, B. It is imposing on the defendant a contract different from that which he entered into. Pollock, C.B. It is like a contract for the purchase of wine coming from a particular estate in France or Spain, where there are two estates of that name.] The defendant has no right to contradict by parol evidence, a written contract good upon the face of it. He does not impute misrepresentation or fraud, but only says that he fancied the ship was a different one. Intention is of no avail, unless stated at the time of the contract. [Pollock, C.B. One vessel sailed in October and the other in December.] The time of sailing is no part of the contract.

Mellish (Cohen with him), in support of the plea. There is nothing on the face of the contract to show that any particular ship called the Peerless was meant; but the moment it appears that two ships called the Peerless were about to sail from Bombay there is a latent ambiguity, and parol evidence may be given for the purpose of showing that the defendant meant one Peerless and the plaintiff another. That being so, there was no consensus ad idem, and therefore no binding contract. He was then stopped by the Court.

Per Curiam. There must be judgment for the defendants.

Judgment for the defendants.

————

SIMPSON, CONTRACTS FOR COTTON TO ARRIVE: THE CASE OF THE TWO SHIPS *PEERLESS* 11 Cardozo L. Rev. 287, 295 (1989). "There were reports of at least eleven ships called *Peerless* sailing the seven seas at the time [of the *Peerless* case], for the name was a popular one. The *Mercantile Navy List* for 1863 lists nine British registered sailing vessels of that name, their ports of registration being London, Aberystwyth, Dartmouth, Greennock, Halifax, Windsor (Nova Scotia), Hull, and Liverpool, which boasted two such ships. There were also two American ships named *Peerless* from Boston and Baltimore. The existence of so many vessels of the same or a similar name could obviously cause confusion in shipping movement reports. There was nothing unusual however in this state of affairs. Ships commonly shared the same name, particularly popular names such as *Annie*. But the two vessels with which we are concerned can readily be identified as the two which were registered at Liverpool. At the time it was the practice in the shipping press to differentiate vessels bearing the same name by the names of their captains, not, as one might expect, by using their unique registered number."

————

OSWALD v. ALLEN, 417 F.2d 43 (2d Cir.1969). Dr. Oswald, a coin collector from Switzerland, was interested in Mrs. Allen's collection of Swiss coins. In April 1964 Dr. Oswald was in the United States, and the parties drove to the Newburgh Savings Bank, where two of Mrs. Allen's coin collections were located. Dr. Oswald first examined the coins in Mrs. Allen's Swiss Coin Collection, and was then shown several valuable Swiss coins from Mrs. Allen's Rarity Coin Collection. He took notes on each collection. On the parties' return from the bank, a price of $50,000 was agreed upon for Mrs. Allen's collection of Swiss coins. However, Dr. Oswald thought he was buying all of Mrs. Allen's Swiss coins, while Mrs. Allen thought she was selling only the Swiss Coin Collection, and not the Swiss coins in the Rarity Coin Collection. The evidence showed that each collection had its own key number, and was housed in a labeled cigar box. Dr. Oswald, however, testified that he did not know that some of the Swiss coins he examined were in a separate Collection. Held, no contract was formed. "Even though the mental assent of the parties is not requisite for the formation of a contract . . . the facts . . . clearly place this case within the small group of exceptional cases in which there is 'no sensible basis for choosing between conflicting understandings.' . . . The rule of Raffles v. Wichelhaus is applicable here."

COLFAX ENVELOPE CORP. v. LOCAL NO. 458–3M, 20 F.3d 750 (7th Cir.1994). "*Raffles* and *Oswald* were cases in which neither party was blameable for the mistake. . . . If neither party can be assigned the greater blame for the misunderstanding, there is no nonarbitrary basis for deciding which party's understanding to enforce, so the parties are allowed to abandon the contract without liability. . . . These are not cases in which one party's understanding is more reasonable than the other's. Compare Restatement . . . § 20(2)(b). If rescission were permitted in that kind of case, the enforcement of every contract would be at the mercy of a jury, which might be persuaded that one of the parties had genuinely held an idiosyncratic idea of its meaning, so that there had been, in fact, no meeting of the minds."

EMBRY v. HARGADINE, McKITTRICK DRY GOODS CO.

St. Louis Court of Appeals, Missouri, 1907.
127 Mo.App. 383, 105 S.W. 777.

Action by Charles R. Embry against the Hargadine–McKittrick Dry Goods Company. From a judgment for defendant, plaintiff appeals. Reversed and remanded.

GOODE, J. We dealt with this case on a former appeal (115 Mo.App. 130, 91 S.W. 170). It has been retried, and is again before us for the determination of questions not then reviewed. The appellant was an employee of the respondent company under a written contract to expire December 15, 1903, at a salary of $2,000 per annum. His duties were to attend to the sample department of respondent, of which he was given complete charge. It was his business to select samples for the traveling salesmen of the company, which is a wholesale dry goods concern, to use in selling goods to retail merchants.

Appellant contends that on December 23, 1903, he was re-engaged by respondent, through its president, Thos. H. McKittrick, for another year at the same compensation and for the same duties stipulated in his previous written contract. On March 1, 1904, he was discharged, having been notified in February that, on account of the necessity of retrenching expenses, his services and that of some other employees would no longer be required.

The respondent company contends that its president never re-employed appellant after the termination of his written contract, and hence that it had a right to discharge him when it chose. The point with which we are concerned requires an epitome of the testimony of appellant and the counter testimony of McKittrick, the president of the company, in reference to the alleged re-employment.

Appellant testified: That several times prior to the termination of his written contract on December 15, 1903, he had endeavored to get an understanding with McKittrick for another year, but had been put off from time to time. That on December 23d, eight days after the expiration of said contract, he called on McKittrick, in the latter's office, and said to him that as appellant's written employment had lapsed eight days before, and as there were only a few days between then and the 1st of January in which to seek employment with other firms, if respondent wished to retain his services longer he must have a contract for another year, or he would quit respondent's service then and there. That he had been put off twice before and wanted an understanding or contract at once so that he could go ahead without worry. That McKittrick asked him how he was getting along in his department, and appellant said he was very busy, as they were in the height of the season getting men out—had about 110 salesmen on the line and others in preparation. That McKittrick then said: "Go ahead, you're all right. Get your men out, and don't let that worry you." That appellant took McKittrick at his word and worked until February 15th without any question in his mind. It was on February 15th that he was notified his services would be discontinued on March 1st.

McKittrick denied this conversation as related by appellant, and said that, when accosted by the latter on December 23d he (McKittrick) was working on his books in order to get out a report for a stockholders' meeting, and, when appellant said if he did not get a contract he would leave, that he (McKittrick) said: "Mr. Embry, I am just getting ready for the stockholders' meeting to-morrow. I have no time to take it up now. I have told you before I would not take it up until I had these matters out of the way. You will have to see me at a later time. I said: 'Go back upstairs and get your men out on the road.' I may have asked him one or two other questions relative to the department, I don't remember. The whole conversation did not take more than a minute."

Embry also swore that, when he was notified he would be discharged, he complained to McKittrick about it, as being a violation of their contract, and McKittrick said it was due to the action of the board of directors, and not to any personal action of his, and that others would suffer by what the board had done as well as Embry. Appellant requested an instruction to the jury setting out, in substance, the conversation between him and McKittrick according to his version, and declaring that those facts, if found to be true, constituted a contract between the parties that defendant would pay plaintiff the sum of $2,000 for another year, provided the jury believed from the evidence that plaintiff commenced said work believing he was to have $2,000 for the year's work. This instruction was refused, but the court gave another embodying in substance appellant's version of the conversation, and declaring it made a contract "if you (the jury) find both parties thereby intended and did contract with each other for plaintiff's employment for one year from and including December 23, 1903, at a salary of $2,000 per annum." Embry swore that, on several occasions when he spoke to McKittrick about employment for the ensuing year, he asked for a renewal of his former contract, and that on

December 23d, the date of the alleged renewal, he went into Mr. McKittrick's office and told him his contract had expired, and he wanted to renew it for a year, having always worked under year contracts. Neither the refused instruction nor the one given by the court embodied facts quite as strong as appellant's testimony, because neither referred to appellant's alleged statement to McKittrick that unless he was re-employed he would stop work for respondent then and there.

It is assigned for error that the court required the jury, in order to return a verdict for appellant, not only to find the conversation occurred as appellant swore, but that both parties intended by such conversation to contract with each other for plaintiff's employment for the year from December 1903, at a salary of $2,000. If it appeared from the record that there was a dispute between the parties as to the terms on which appellant wanted re-employment, there might have been sound reason for inserting this clause in the instruction; but no issue was made that they split on terms; the testimony of McKittrick tending to prove only that he refused to enter into a contract with appellant regarding another year's employment until the annual meeting of stockholders was out of the way. Indeed as to the proposed terms McKittrick agrees with Embry, for the former swore as follows: "Mr. Embry said he wanted to know about the renewal of his contract. Said if he did not have the contract made he would leave." As the two witnesses coincided as to the terms of the proposed re-employment, there was no reason for inserting the above mentioned clause in the instruction in order that it might be settled by the jury whether or not plaintiff, if employed for one year from December 23, 1903, was to be paid $2,000 a year. Therefore it remains to determine whether or not this part of the instruction was a correct statement of the law in regard to what was necessary to constitute a contract between the parties; that is to say, whether the formation of a contract by what, according to Embry, was said, depended on the intention of both Embry and McKittrick. Or, to put the question more precisely: Did what was said constitute a contract of re-employment on the previous terms irrespective of the intention or purpose of McKittrick?

Judicial opinion and elementary treatises abound in statements of the rule that to constitute a contract there must be a meeting of the minds of the parties, and both must agree to the same thing in the same sense. Generally speaking, this may be true; but it is not literally or universally true. That is to say, the inner intention of parties to a conversation subsequently alleged to create a contract cannot either make a contract of what transpired, or prevent one from arising, if the words used were sufficient to constitute a contract. In so far as their intention is an influential element, it is only such intention as the words or acts of the parties indicate; not one secretly cherished which is inconsistent with those words or acts. . . .

In Smith v. Hughes, L.R. 6 Q.B. 597, 607, it was said: "If, whatever a man's real intention may be, he so conducts himself that a reasonable man would believe that he was assenting to the terms proposed by the other party, and that other party upon that belief enters into the contract with him, the man thus conducting himself would be equally bound as if he had intended to agree to the other party's terms." . . .

In view of those authorities, we hold that, though McKittrick may not have intended to employ Embry by what transpired between them according to the latter's testimony, yet if what McKittrick said would have been taken by a reasonable man to be an employment, and Embry so understood it, it constituted a valid contract of employment for the ensuing year.

The next question is whether or not the language used was of that character, namely, was such that Embry, as a reasonable man, might consider that he was re-employed for the ensuing year on the previous terms, and act accordingly. We do not say that in every instance it would be for the court to pronounce on this question, because, peradventure, instances might arise in which there would be such an ambiguity in the language relied on to show an assent by the obligor to the proposal of the obligee that it would be for the jury to say whether a reasonable mind would take it to signify acceptance of the proposal.... Embry was demanding a renewal of his contract, saying he had been put off from time to time and that he had only a few days before the end of the year in which to seek employment from other houses, and that he would quit then and there unless he was re-employed. McKittrick inquired how he was getting along with the department, and Embry said they, i.e., the employees of the department, were very busy getting out salesmen. Whereupon McKittrick said: "Go ahead, you are all right. Get your men out, and do not let that worry you." We think no reasonable man would construe that answer to Embry's demand that he be employed for another year, otherwise than as an assent to the demand, and that Embry had the right to rely on it as an assent.... The answer was unambiguous, and we rule that if the conversation was according to appellant's version, and he understood he was employed, it constituted in law a valid contract of re-employment, and the court erred in making the formation of a contract depend on a finding that both parties intended to make one....

The judgment is reversed, and the cause remanded. All concur.

RESTATEMENT, SECOND, CONTRACTS §§ 20, 201

[See Selected Source Materials Supplement]

CISG ART. 8

[See Selected Source Materials Supplement]

UNIDROIT PRINCIPLES OF INTERNATIONAL COMMERCIAL CONTRACTS ARTS. 4.1, 4.2, 4.3

[See Selected Source Materials Supplement]

PRINCIPLES OF EUROPEAN CONTRACT
LAW ARTS. 5.101, 5.102

[See Selected Source Materials Supplement]

MCC–MARBLE CERAMIC CENTER, INC.
v. CERAMICA NUOVA D'AGOSTINO

United States Court of Appeals, Eleventh Circuit, 1998.
144 F.3d 1384.

BIRCH, Circuit Judge:

This case ... [concerns a] dispute governed by the United Nations Convention on Contracts for the International Sale of Goods ("CISG"). The district court granted summary judgment on behalf of the defendant-appellee, relying on certain terms and provisions that appeared on the reverse of a pre-printed form contract for the sale of ceramic tiles. The plaintiff-appellant sought to rely on a number of affidavits that tended to show both that the parties had arrived at an oral contract before memorializing their agreement in writing and that they subjectively intended not to apply the terms on the reverse of the contract to their agreements. The magistrate judge held that the affidavits did not raise an issue of material fact and recommended that the district court grant summary judgment based on the terms of the contract. The district court agreed with the magistrate judge's reasoning and entered summary judgment in the defendant-appellee's favor. We REVERSE.

BACKGROUND

The plaintiff-appellant, MCC–Marble Ceramic, Inc. ("MCC"), is a Florida corporation engaged in the retail sale of tiles, and the defendant-appellee, Ceramica Nuova d'Agostino S.p.A. ("D'Agostino") is an Italian corporation engaged in the manufacture of ceramic tiles. In October 1990, MCC's president, Juan Carlos Monzon, met representatives of D'Agostino at a trade fair in Bologna, Italy and negotiated an agreement to purchase ceramic tiles from D'Agostino based on samples he examined at the trade fair. Monzon, who spoke no Italian, communicated with Gianni Silingardi, then D'Agostino's commercial director, through a translator, Gianfranco Copelli, who was himself an agent of D'Agostino.[1] The parties apparently arrived at an oral agreement on the crucial terms of price, quality, quantity, delivery and payment. The parties then recorded these terms on one of D'Agostino's standard, pre-printed order forms and Monzon signed the contract on MCC's behalf. According to MCC, the parties also entered into a requirements contract in February 1991, subject to which D'Agostino agreed to supply MCC with high grade ceramic tile at specific discounts as long as MCC purchased sufficient quantities of tile. MCC completed a number of additional order forms requesting tile deliveries pursuant to that agreement.

MCC brought suit against D'Agostino claiming a breach of the February 1991 requirements contract when D'Agostino failed to satisfy orders in April,

---

1. Since this case is before us on summary judgment, we consider the facts in the light most favorable to MCC, the non-moving party, and grant MCC the benefit of every factual inference. See Welch v. Celotex Corp., 951 F.2d 1235, 1237 (11th Cir.1992).

May, and August of 1991. In addition to other defenses, D'Agostino responded that it was under no obligation to fill MCC's orders because MCC had defaulted on payment for previous shipments. In support of its position, D'Agostino relied on the pre-printed terms of the contracts that MCC had executed. The executed forms were printed in Italian and contained terms and conditions on both the front and reverse. According to an English translation of the October 1990 contract, the front of the order form contained the following language directly beneath Monzon's signature:

> [T]he buyer hereby states that he is aware of the sales conditions stated on the reverse and that he expressly approves of them with special reference to those numbered 1–2–3–4–5–6–7–8.

R2–126, Exh. 3 ¶ 5 ("Maselli Aff."). Clause 6(b), printed on the back of the form states:

> [D]efault or delay in payment within the time agreed upon gives D'Agostino the right to ... suspend or cancel the contract itself and to cancel possible other pending contracts and the buyer does not have the right to indemnification or damages.

Id. ¶ 6. D'Agostino also brought a number of counterclaims against MCC, seeking damages for MCC's alleged nonpayment for deliveries of tile that D'Agostino had made between February 28, 1991 and July 4, 1991. MCC responded that the tile it had received was of a lower quality than contracted for, and that, pursuant to the CISG, MCC was entitled to reduce payment in proportion to the defects.[2] D'Agostino, however, noted that clause 4 on the reverse of the contract states, in pertinent part:

> Possible complaints for defects of the merchandise must be made in writing by means of a certified letter within and not later than 10 days after receipt of the merchandise....

Maselli Aff. ¶ 6. Although there is evidence to support MCC's claims that it complained about the quality of the deliveries it received, MCC never submitted any written complaints.

MCC did not dispute these underlying facts before the district court, but argued that the parties never intended the terms and conditions printed on the reverse of the order form to apply to their agreements. As evidence for this assertion, MCC submitted Monzon's affidavit, which claims that MCC had no subjective intent to be bound by those terms and that D'Agostino was aware of this intent. MCC also filed affidavits from Silingardi and Copelli, D'Agostino's representatives at the trade fair, which support Monzon's claim that the parties subjectively intended not to be bound by the terms on the reverse of the order form. The magistrate judge held that the affidavits, even if true, did not raise an issue of material fact regarding the interpretation or applicability of the terms of the written contracts and the district court accepted his recommendation to award summary judgment in D'Agostino's favor. MCC then filed this timely appeal.

DISCUSSION

We review a district court's grant of summary judgment de novo and apply the same standards as the district court. See Harris v. H & W

---

2. Article 50 of the CISG permits a buyer to reduce payment for nonconforming goods in proportion to the nonconformity under certain conditions. See CISG, art. 50.

Contracting Co., 102 F.3d 516, 518 (11th Cir.1996). Summary judgment is appropriate when the pleadings, depositions, and affidavits reveal that no genuine issue of material fact exists and the moving party is entitled to judgment as a matter of law. See Fed.R.Civ.P. 56(c).

The parties to this case agree that the CISG governs their dispute because the United States, where MCC has its place of business, and Italy, where D'Agostino has its place of business, are both States Party to the Convention. See CISG, art. 1. Article 8 of the CISG governs the interpretation of international contracts for the sale of goods and forms the basis of MCC's appeal from the district court's grant of summary judgment in D'Agostino's favor.[3] MCC argues that the magistrate judge and the district court improperly ignored evidence that MCC submitted regarding the parties' subjective intent when they memorialized the terms of their agreement on D'Agostino's pre-printed form contract, and that the magistrate judge erred by applying the parol evidence rule in derogation of the CISG.

Subjective Intent Under the CISG

Contrary to what is familiar practice in United States courts, the CISG appears to permit a substantial inquiry into the parties' subjective intent, even if the parties did not engage in any objectively ascertainable means of registering this intent. Article 8(1) of the CISG instructs courts to interpret the "statements ... and other conduct of a party ... according to his intent" as long as the other party "knew or could not have been unaware" of that intent. The plain language of the Convention, therefore, requires an inquiry into a party's subjective intent as long as the other party to the contract was aware of that intent.

In this case, MCC has submitted three affidavits that discuss the purported subjective intent of the parties to the initial agreement concluded between MCC and D'Agostino in October 1990. All three affidavits discuss the preliminary negotiations and report that the parties arrived at an oral agreement for D'Agostino to supply quantities of a specific grade of ceramic tile to MCC at an agreed upon price. The affidavits state that the "oral agreement established the essential terms of quality, quantity, description of goods, delivery, price and payment." See R3–133 ¶ 9 ("Silingardi Aff."); R1–51 ¶ 7 ("Copelli Aff."); R1–47 ¶ 7 ("Monzon Aff."). The affidavits also note that the parties memorialized the terms of their oral agreement on a standard D'Agostino order form, but all three affiants contend that the parties *subjectively* intended not to be bound by the terms on the reverse of that form despite a provision directly below the signature line that expressly and specifically incorporated those terms.

3.   Article 8 provides:

(1) For the purposes of this Convention statements made by and other conduct of a party are to be interpreted according to his intent where the other party knew or could not have been unaware what that intent was.

(2) If the preceding paragraph is not applicable, statements made by and conduct of a party are to be interpreted according to the understanding a reasonable person of the same kind as the other party would have had in the same circumstances.

(3) In determining the intent of a party or the understanding a reasonable person would have had, due consideration is to be given to all relevant circumstances of the case including the negotiations, any practices which the parties have established between themselves, usages and any subsequent conduct of the parties.

CISG, art. 8.

The terms on the reverse of the contract give D'Agostino the right to suspend or cancel all contracts in the event of a buyer's non-payment and require a buyer to make a written report of all defects within ten days. As the magistrate judge's report and recommendation makes clear, if these terms applied to the agreements between MCC and D'Agostino, summary judgment would be appropriate because MCC failed to make any written complaints about the quality of tile it received and D'Agostino has established MCC's non-payment of a number of invoices amounting to $108,389.40 and 102,053,-846.00 Italian lira.

Article 8(1) of the CISG requires a court to consider this evidence of the parties' subjective intent. Contrary to the magistrate judge's report, which the district court endorsed and adopted, article 8(1) does not focus on interpreting the parties' statements alone. Although we agree with the magistrate judge's conclusion that no "interpretation" of the contract's *terms* could support MCC's position, article 8(1) also requires a court to consider subjective intent while interpreting the *conduct* of the parties. The CISG's language, therefore, requires courts to consider evidence of a party's subjective intent when signing a contract if the other party to the contract was aware of that intent at the time. This is precisely the type of evidence that MCC has provided through the Silingardi, Copelli, and Monzon affidavits, which discuss not only Monzon's intent as MCC's representative but also discuss the intent of D'Agostino's representatives and their knowledge that Monzon did not intend to agree to the terms on the reverse of the form contract. This acknowledgment that D'Agostino's representatives were aware of Monzon's subjective intent puts this case squarely within article 8(1) of the CISG, and therefore requires the court to consider MCC's evidence as it interprets the parties' conduct.[4]

II.   ...

... [All this] is not to say that parties to an international contract for the sale of goods cannot depend on written contracts or that ... evidence regarding subjective contractual intent need always prevent a party relying on a written agreement from securing summary judgment. To the contrary, most cases will not present a situation (as exists in this case) in which both parties to the contract acknowledge a subjective intent not to be bound by the terms of a pre-printed writing. In most cases, therefore, article 8(2) of the CISG will apply, and objective evidence will provide the basis for the court's decision. See Honnold, Uniform Law § 107 at 164–65. Consequently, a party to a contract governed by the CISG will not be able to avoid the terms of a contract and force a jury trial simply by submitting an affidavit which states that he or she did not have the subjective intent to be bound by the contract's terms.... Moreover, to the extent parties wish to avoid parol evidence problems they can do so by including a merger clause in their agreement that extinguishes any and all prior agreements and understandings not expressed in the writing.

---

4. Without this crucial acknowledgment, we would interpret the contract and the parties' actions according to article 8(2), which directs courts to rely on objective evidence of the parties' intent. On the facts of this case it seems readily apparent that MCC's affidavits provide *no evidence* that Monzon's actions would have made his alleged subjective intent not to be bound by the terms of the contract known to "the understanding that a reasonable person ... would have had in the same circumstances." CISG, art 8(2).

Considering MCC's affidavits in this case, however, we conclude that the magistrate judge and the district court improperly granted summary judgment in favor of D'Agostino. Although the affidavits are, as D'Agostino observes, relatively conclusory and unsupported by facts that would objectively establish MCC's intent not to be bound by the conditions on the reverse of the form, article 8(1) requires a court to consider evidence of a party's subjective intent when the other party was aware of it, and the Silingardi and Copelli affidavits provide that evidence. This is not to say that the affidavits are conclusive proof of what the parties intended. A reasonable finder of fact, for example, could disregard testimony that purportedly sophisticated international merchants signed a contract without intending to be bound as simply too incredible to believe and hold MCC to the conditions printed on the reverse of the contract.[5] Nevertheless, the affidavits raise an issue of material fact regarding the parties' intent to incorporate the provisions on the reverse of the form contract. If the finder of fact determines that the parties did not intend to rely on those provisions, then the more general provisions of the CISG will govern the outcome of the dispute.[6] . . .

CONCLUSION

MCC asks us to reverse the district court's grant of summary judgment in favor of D'Agostino. The district court's decision rests on pre-printed contractual terms and conditions incorporated on the reverse of a standard order form that MCC's president signed on the company's behalf. Nevertheless, we conclude that the CISG, which governs international contracts for the sale of goods, precludes summary judgment in this case because MCC has raised an issue of material fact concerning the parties' subjective intent to be bound by the terms on the reverse of the pre-printed contract. . . . Accordingly, we REVERSE the district court's grant of summary judgment and REMAND this case for further proceedings consistent with this opinion.

NOTE ON OBJECTIVE AND SUBJECTIVE ELEMENTS IN INTERPRETATION

Recall that one difference between classical contract law and modern contract law is that classical contract law tended to be objective and standardized, while modern contract law tends to include subjective and individualized

---

5. D'Agostino attempts to explain and undermine the affidavit of its representatives during the transaction, by calling Silingardi a "disgruntled" former employee. Appellee's Br. at 11, 39. Silingardi's alleged feelings towards his former employer may indeed be relevant to undermine the credibility of his assertions, but that is a matter for the finder of fact, not for this court on summary judgment.

6. Article 50, which permits a buyer to reduce payment to a seller who delivers nonconforming goods, and article 39, which deprives the buyer of that right if the buyer fails to give the seller notice specifying the defect in the goods delivered within a reasonable time, will be of primary importance. Although we may affirm a district court's grant of summary

judgment if it is correct for any reason, even if not relied upon below, see United States v. $121,100.00 in United States Currency, 999 F.2d 1503, 1507 (11th Cir.1993), and the parties have touched upon these articles in their briefs, they have not provided us with sufficient information to resolve their dispute under the CISG. MCC's affidavits indicate that MCC may have complained about the quality of the tile D'Agostino delivered, but they have provided no authority regarding what constitutes a reasonable time for such a complaint in this context. Accordingly, we decline to affirm the district court's grant of summary judgment on this basis.

elements as well. This difference is particularly striking in the area of interpretation. Classical contract law adopted a theory of interpretation that was purely, or almost purely, objective. As stated in Woburn National Bank v. Woods, 77 N.H. 172, 89 A. 491 (1914):

> A contract involves what is called a meeting of the minds of the parties. But this does not mean that they must have arrived at a common mental state touching the matter in hand. The standard by which their conduct is judged and their rights are limited is not internal but external. In the absence of fraud or incapacity, the question is: What did the party say and do? "The making of a contract does not depend upon the state of the parties' minds; it depends upon their overt acts."

The strict objectivism of classical contract law is also reflected in well-known passages by Williston and Learned Hand. According to Williston:

> It is even conceivable that a contract shall be formed which is in accordance with the intention of neither party. If a written contract is entered into, the meaning and effect of the contract depends on the construction given the written language by the court, and the court will give that language its natural and appropriate meaning; and, if it is unambiguous, will not even admit evidence of what the parties may have thought the meaning to be.

1 Samuel Williston, The Law of Contracts § 95, at 181–82 (1st ed. 1920.)

And according to Learned Hand:

> A contract has, strictly speaking, nothing to do with the personal, or individual, intent of the parties. A contract is an obligation attached by the mere force of law to certain acts of the parties, usually words, which ordinarily accompany and represent a known intent. If, however, it were proved by twenty bishops that either party, when he used the words, intended something else than the usual meaning which the law imposes upon them, he would still be held, unless there were some mutual mistake, or something else of the sort. Of course, if it appear by other words, or acts, of the parties, that they attribute a peculiar meaning to such words as they use in the contract, that meaning will prevail, but only by virtue of the other words, and not because of their unexpressed intent.

> . . . [W]hatever was the understanding in fact of the banks [in this case] . . . of the legal effect of this practice between them, it is of not the slightest consequence, unless it took form in some acts or words, which, being reasonably interpreted, would have such meaning to ordinary men. . . . Yet the question always remains for the court to interpret the reasonable meaning to the acts of the parties, by word or deed, and no characterization of its effect by either party thereafter, however truthful, is material. . . .

Hotchkiss v. National City Bank, 200 F. 287, 293–94 (S.D.N.Y.1911), aff'd 201 F. 664 (2d Cir.1912), aff'd 231 U.S. 50, 34 S.Ct. 20, 58 L.Ed. 115 (1913).

However, contract law is a functional instrument, whose purpose is to effectuate the objectives of parties to a promissory transaction, provided appropriate conditions (such as consideration) are satisfied, and subject to appropriate constraints (such as unconscionability). Accordingly, the principles of interpretation should be responsive not only to objective elements but, where appropriate, to the parties' subjective intentions. Under modern contract law, that is just the case, as illustrated by four central modern principles of interpretation:

Principle I: If the parties subjectively attach different meanings to an expression, neither party knows that the other attaches a different meaning, and the two meanings are not equally reasonable, the more reasonable meaning prevails.

Principle I is adopted in Restatement Second § 201(2)(b):

> Where the parties have attached different meanings to a promise or agreement or a term thereof, it is interpreted in accordance with the meaning attached by one of them if at the time the agreement was made. . . .

> (b) that party had no reason to know of any different meaning attached by the other, and the other had reason to know the meaning attached by the first party.

Principle I is based in significant part on the concept of liability for fault. A is at fault—is negligent—if he uses an expression that he should realize would lead a reasonable person in B's position to understand that A attaches a given meaning, Beta, to the expression, when in fact A attaches meaning Alpha to the expression. If B attaches meaning Beta to the expression, and thereby suffers wasted reliance or the defeat of a legitimate expectation when A insists on meaning Alpha, A should compensate B.

Although *Principle I* is primarily objective, it has a subjective element as well. The more reasonable meaning will prevail only if one of the parties has actually (subjectively) attached that meaning to the expression.

Principle II: If the parties subjectively attach different meanings to an expression, neither party knows that the other attaches a different meaning, and the two meanings are equally reasonable, neither meaning prevails.

Principle II is adopted in the Restatement Second § 20(1):

> There is no manifestation of mutual assent to an exchange if the parties attach materially different meanings to their manifestations and

> (a) neither party knows or has reason to know the meaning attached by the other; or

> (b) each party knows or each party has reason to know the meaning attached by the other.

Principle II is consistent with *Principle I*. If parties to a promissory transaction subjectively attach different meanings to their expressions, and in attaching these different meanings both parties are either equally fault-free or equally at fault, there is no reason why one meaning rather than the other should prevail. *Principle II* is associated with Raffles v. Wichelhaus, the *Peerless* case. To preserve the classical–school program, Holmes argued that the result in *Peerless* could be explained by objective theory. "The true ground of the decision was not that each party meant a different thing from the other . . . but that each said a different thing. The plaintiff offered one thing, the defendant expressed his assent to another." Holmes, The Common Law 309 (1881). But if both parties subjectively meant the December Peerless, Buyer should have been deemed in breach; and if both parties subjectively meant the October Peerless, Seller should have been deemed in breach. Holmes had it backwards: the result in *Peerless* is correct because the parties meant different things, not because the parties said different things.

Principle III: If the parties subjectively attach the same meaning to an expression, that meaning prevails even though it is unreasonable. Principle III squarely reverses the strict objectivism of classical contract law, under which the subjective intention of the parties was irrelevant, even if mutually held. Again, the objectivists had it wrong. Where both parties attach the same, unreasonable, meaning to an expression, both parties may have been at fault in their use of language, but the fault caused no injury. Indeed, a party who in litigation presses a meaning that he did not attach to his expression at the time of contract–formation is himself at fault.

Principle III is adopted in Restatement Second § 201(1). That section provides that "[w]here the parties have attached the same meaning to a promise or agreement or a term thereof, it is interpreted in accordance with that meaning." Under section 201(1), reasonableness becomes relevant only where there is not a mutually held subjective meaning. Thus, Restatement Second stands the classical school's position on its head, by giving primacy to mutually held subjective interpretation, and resorting to an objective or reasonable meaning only in the absence of a mutually held subjective meaning.

Principle IV: If the parties, A and B, attach different meanings, Alpha and Beta, to an expression, and A knows that B attaches meaning Beta, but B does not know that A attaches meaning Alpha, the meaning Beta prevails even if it is less reasonable than the meaning Alpha.

Principle IV is adopted in Restatement Second § 201(2):

> Where the parties have attached different meanings to a promise or agreement or a term thereof, it is interpreted in accordance with the meaning attached by one of them if at the time the agreement was made
>
> (a) that party did not know of any different meaning attached by the other, and the other knew the meaning attached by the first party....

Principle IV is largely subjective. It is supported by a fault analysis. B may have been at fault in attaching meaning Beta to the expression, but A was more at fault in allowing B to proceed on the basis of an interpretation that A knew B held, at least when B did not know that A held a different interpretation.

———

BERKE MOORE CO. v. PHOENIX BRIDGE CO., 98 N.H. 261, 98 A.2d 150 (1953). "The rule which precludes the use of the understanding of one party alone is designed to prevent imposition of his private understanding upon the other party to a bilateral transaction. IX Wig.Ev., 3d Ed., § 2460; Smart v. Huckins, 82 N.H. 342, 348, 134 A. 520. But when it appears that the understanding of one is the understanding of both, no violation of the rule results from determination of the mutual understanding according to that of one alone.

"Where the understanding is mutual, it ceases to be the 'private' understanding of one party. Having thus determined the mutual understanding of the parties, the Court properly interpreted the contract accordingly."

———

SECTION 2.   PROBLEMS OF INTERPRETING PURPOSIVE LANGUAGE

———

FISH, NORMAL CIRCUMSTANCES, LITERAL LANGUAGE, DIRECT SPEECH ACTS, THE ORDINARY, THE EVERYDAY, THE OBVIOUS, WHAT GOES WITHOUT SAYING, AND OTHER SPECIAL CASES

4 Critical Inquiry 625 (Summer 1978).

. . . [A]s Kenneth Abraham observes,

A statute without a purpose would be meaningless . . . to speak of the literal meaning of a statute . . . is already to have read it in the light of some purpose, to have engaged in an interpretation.

In other words, any reading that is plain and obvious in the light of some assumed purpose (and it is impossible not to assume one) is a literal reading, but no reading is *the* literal reading in the sense that it is available apart from any purpose whatsoever.

A sentence is never not in a context. We are never not in a situation. . . . A set of interpretive assumptions is always in force. A sentence that seems to need no interpretation is already the product of one. . . .

[Suppose student X says to student Y, "Let's go to the movies tonight," and student Y replies, "I have to study for an exam." The statement by student X seems to be a proposal, and the statement by student Y seems to be rejection of the proposal. Now suppose student Y replies instead, "I have to eat popcorn tonight" or "I have to tie my shoes." In most circumstances, those statements would not be regarded as a rejection of the proposal. But] is it possible to imagine a set of circumstances in which "I have to eat popcorn tonight" would immediately and without any chain of inference be heard as a rejection of X's proposal? It is not only possible; it is easy. Let us suppose that student Y is passionately fond of popcorn and that it is not available in any of the local movie theaters. If student X knows these facts (if he and student Y mutually share background information), then he will hear "I have to eat popcorn tonight" as a rejection of his proposal. Or, let us suppose that student Y is by profession a popcorn taster; that is, he works in a popcorn manufacturing plant and is responsible for quality control. Again if student X knows this, he will hear "I have to eat popcorn tonight" as a rejection of his proposal because it will mean "Sorry, I have to work." Or, let us suppose that student Y owns seventy-five pairs of shoes and that he has been ordered by a dormitory housemother to retrieve them from various corners, arrange them neatly in one place, and tie them together in pairs so that they will not again be separated and scattered. In such a situation "I have to tie my shoes" will constitute a rejection of student X's proposal and will be so heard. Moreover it is not just "I have to eat popcorn" and "I have to tie my shoes" that could be heard as a rejection of the proposal; given the appropriate circumstances *any* sentence ("The Russians are coming," "My pen is blue," "Why do you behave like that?") could be so heard....

The argument will also hold for "Let's go to the movies tonight." ... Thus if speakers X and Y are trapped in some wilderness, and one says to the other, "Let's go to the movies tonight," it will be heard not as a proposal, but as a joke; or if student X is confined to his bed or otherwise immobilized, and student Y says, "Let's go to the movies tonight," it will be heard not as a proposal, but as a dare....

It is important to realize what my argument does *not* mean. It does not mean that [a] sentence can mean anything at all.... A sentence ... is never in the abstract; it is always in a situation, and the situation will already have determined the purpose for which it can be used. So it is not that any sentence can be used as a request to open the window, but that given any sentence, there are circumstances under which it would be heard as a request to open the window. A sentence neither means anything at all, nor does it always mean the same thing; it always has the meaning that has been conferred on it by the situation in which it is uttered.

HAINES v. NEW YORK

Court of Appeals of New York, 1977.
41 N.Y.2d 769, 396 N.Y.S.2d 155, 364 N.E.2d 820.

GABRIELLI, JUDGE.

In the early 1920's, respondent City of New York and intervenors Town of Hunter and Village of Tannersville embarked upon negotiations for the construction of a sewage system to serve the village and a portion of the town. These negotiations were prompted by the city's need and desire to prevent the discharge of untreated sewage by residents of the area into Gooseberry Creek, a stream which fed a reservoir of the city's water supply system in the Schoharie watershed.

In 1923, the Legislature enacted enabling legislation authorizing the city to enter into contracts with municipalities in the watershed area "for the purpose of providing, maintaining [and] operating systems and plants for the collection and disposal of sewage" (L.1923, ch. 630, § 1). The statute further provided that any such contracts would be subject to the approval of the New York City Board of Estimate and Apportionment.

The negotiations culminated in an agreement in 1924 between the city and intervenors. By this agreement, the city assumed the obligation of constructing a sewage system consisting of a sewage disposal plant and sewer mains and laterals, and agreed that "all costs of construction and subsequent operation, maintenance and repair of said sewage system with the house connections thereof and said disposal works shall be at the expense" of the city. The agreement also required the city to extend the sewer lines when "necessitated by future growth and building constructions of the respective communities". The village and town were obligated to and did obtain the necessary easements for the construction of the system and sewage lines.

The Board of Estimate, on December 9, 1926, approved the agreement and authorized the issuance of $500,000 of "corporate stock" of the City of New York for construction of the system by appropriate resolution. It is interesting to here note that a modification of the original agreement occurred in 1925 wherein the village agreed to reimburse the city for a specified amount representing the expense of changing the location of certain sewer lines. The plant was completed and commenced operation in 1928. The city has continued to maintain the plant through the ensuing years and in 1958 expended $193,000 to rehabilitate and expand the treatment plant and facilities.

Presently, the average flow of the plant has increased from an initial figure of 118,000 gallons per day to over 600,000 gallons daily and the trial court found that the plant "was operating substantially in excess of design capacity". The city asserts, and it is not disputed by any of the parties in this action, that the system cannot bear any significant additional "loadings" because this would result in inadequate treatment of all the sewage and consequently harm the city's water supply. The instant controversy arose when plaintiff, who is the owner of a tract of unimproved land which he seeks to develop into 50 residential lots, applied to the city for permission to connect houses, which he intends to construct on the lots, to existing sewer lines. The city refused permission on the ground that it had no obligation to further expand the plant, which is presently operating at full capacity, to accommodate this new construction.

Plaintiff then commenced this action for declaratory and injunctive relief, in which intervenors town and village joined as plaintiffs, maintaining that the 1924 agreement is perpetual in duration and obligates the city to expend additional capital funds to enlarge the existing plant or build a new one to accommodate the present and future needs of the municipalities. Both the trial court and the Appellate Division, by a divided court, held in favor of plaintiff and intervenors concluding, that, while the contract did not call for perpetual performance, the city was bound to construct additional facilities to meet increased demand until such time as the village or town is legally obligated to maintain a sewage disposal system. Two members of the court dissented in part stating that the agreement should not be construed as requiring the city to construct new or additional facilities.

We conclude that the city is presently obligated to maintain the existing plant but is not required to expand that plant or construct any new facilities to accommodate plaintiff's substantial, or any other, increased demands on the sewage system. The initial problem encountered in ascertaining the nature and extent of the city's obligation pursuant to the 1924 agreement, is its duration. We reject, as did the courts below, the plaintiff's contention that the city is perpetually bound under the agreement. The contract did not expressly provide for perpetual performance and both the trial court and the Appellate Division found that the parties did not so intend. Under these circumstances, the law will not imply that a contract calling for continuing performance is perpetual in duration (*Mitler v. Friedeberg,* 32 Misc.2d 78, 85, 222 N.Y.S.2d 480, 488; *Warner–Lambert Pharm. Co. v. John J. Reynolds, Inc.,* 178 F.Supp. 655, affd. 2 Cir., 280 F.2d 197; *Holt v. St. Louis Union Trust Co.,* 4 Cir., 52 F.2d 1068, 1069; *Town of Readsboro v. Hoosac Tunnel & Wilmington R.R. Co.,* 2 Cir., 6 F.2d 733 [L. Hand, J.]; *Borough of West Caldwell v.*

Borough of Caldwell, 26 N.J. 9, 28–29, 138 A.2d 402, 1 Williston, Contracts [3d ed.], § 38, p. 113).

On the other hand, the city's contention that the contract is terminable at will because it provides for no express duration should also be rejected. In the absence of an express term fixing the duration of a contract, the courts may inquire into the intent of the parties and supply the missing term if a duration may be fairly and reasonably fixed by the surrounding circumstances and the parties' intent (*Warner–Lambert Pharm. Co. v. John J. Reynolds, Inc., supra,* p. 661; *Benham v. World Airways,* 9 Cir., 432 F.2d 359, 361; *Town of Readsboro v. Hoosac Tunnel & Wilmington R.R. Co., supra,* p. 735). It is generally agreed that where a duration may be fairly and reasonably supplied by implication, a contract is not terminable at will (1 Williston, *op. cit.,* p. 112; 10 N.Y.Jur., Contracts, § 412, p. 426; 17 Am.Jur.2d, Contracts, § 487, p. 957; 17A C.J.S. Contracts § 398, p. 480; see, also, Restatement, Contracts 2d [Tent. Draft No. 7], § 230).

While we have not previously had occasion to apply it, the weight of authority supports the related rule that where the parties have not clearly expressed the duration of a contract, the courts will imply that they intended performance to continue for a reasonable time (*Colony Liq. Distrs. v. Daniel Distillery–Lem Motlow Prop.,* 22 A.D.2d 247, 249–250, 254 N.Y.S.2d 547, 549, 550 [Aulisi, J.]; *Metal Assoc. v. East Side Metal Spinning & Stamping Corp.,* 2 Cir., 165 F.2d 163, 165; *Borough of West Caldwell v. Borough of Caldwell, supra,* 138 A.2d p. 412; Simpson, Contracts, § 48, p. 74; 1 Williston, *op. cit.,* pp. 116–117; 10 N.Y.Jur., Contracts, § 413, p. 427). For compelling policy reasons, this rule has not been, and should not be, applied to contracts of employment or exclusive agency, distributorship, or requirements contracts which have been analogized to employment contracts. . . . The considerations relevant to such contracts do not obtain here. Thus, we hold that it is reasonable to infer from the circumstances of the 1924 agreement that the parties intended the city to maintain the sewage disposal facility until such time as the city no longer needed or desired the water, the purity of which the plant was designed to insure. The city argues that it is no longer obligated to maintain the plant because State law now prohibits persons from discharging raw sewage into streams such as Gooseberry Creek. However, the parties did not contemplate the passage of environmental control laws which would prohibit individuals or municipalities from discharging raw, untreated sewage into certain streams. Thus, the city agreed to assume the obligation of assuring that its water supply remained unpolluted and it may not now avoid that obligation for reasons not contemplated by the parties when the agreement was executed, and not within the purview of their intent, expressed or implied.

Having determined the duration of the city's obligation, the scope of its duty remains to be defined. By the agreement, the city obligated itself to build a specifically described disposal facility and to extend the lines of that facility to meet future increased demand. At the present time, the extension of those lines would result in the overloading of the system. Plaintiff claims that the city is required to build a new plant or expand the existing facility to overcome the problem. We disagree. The city should not be required to extend the lines to plaintiffs' property if to do so would overload the system and result in its inability to properly treat sewage. In providing for the extension of sewer lines, the contract does not obligate the city to provide sewage disposal services for properties in areas of the municipalities not presently served or even to new properties in areas which are presently served where to do so could reasonably be expected to significantly increase the demand on present plant facilities.

Thus, those paragraphs of the judgment which provide that the city is obligated to construct any additional facilities required to meet increased demand and that plaintiff is entitled to full use of the sewer lines should be stricken.

Accordingly, the order of the Appellate Division should be modified and the case remitted to Supreme Court, Greene County, for the entry of judgment in accordance with the opinion herein and, as so modified, affirmed, with costs to appellants against plaintiffs-respondents only.

BREITEL, C.J., and JASEN, JONES, WACHTLER, FUCHSBERG and COOKE, JJ., concur.

Order modified, etc.

RESTATEMENT, SECOND, CONTRACTS § 204

[See Selected Source Materials Supplement]

UNIDROIT PRINCIPLES OF INTERNATIONAL COMMERCIAL CONTRACTS ART. 4.8

[See Selected Source Materials Supplement]

SPAULDING v. MORSE

Supreme Judicial Court of Massachusetts, 1947.
322 Mass. 149, 76 N.E.2d 137.

DOLAN, JUSTICE. [George and Ruth Morse were married in 1921. In 1932, Ruth obtained a decree of divorce which made provision for the custody and support of the Morse's two children, Richard and Merilyn. Subsequently, disputes arose between the Morses. As a result, in 1937 they entered into an agreement "intended to supersede in so far as the provisions herein contained are concerned" the provisions made in the decree for the benefit of Ruth, Richard, and Merilyn. The agreement provided that George would make a lump sum payment to Ruth, in installments, as alimony, that Ruth would have custody of Richard, and that George would have custody of Merilyn. In addition, a trustee was appointed for Richard, and it was agreed that George "shall and will pay to the said trustee in trust for his said minor son Richard the sum of twelve hundred dollars ($1,200) per year . . . until the entrance of Richard D. Morse into some college, university or higher institution of learning beyond the completion of the high school grades, and thereupon, instead of said payments, amounting to twelve hundred dollars ($1,200) yearly, he shall and will then pay to the trustee payments in the sum of twenty-two hundred dollars ($2,200) per year for a period of said higher education but not more than four years...."

[Richard completed high school in February 1946, and was immediately inducted into the Army. The trustee brought this action to require George to continue paying $100 a month for Richard while he was in the Army. The trial court held for the trustee, and ordered George to pay $1,500 (the amount which had accrued since Richard's induction) and to continue paying $100 per month to the trustee "until such time, if any, as [Richard] enters college, and, thereupon, and for a period not to exceed four (4) years thereafter, to pay the sum of twenty-two hundred dollars ($2,200) per year to the ... [plaintiff] payable in monthly payments." George appealed.]

"Every instrument in writing is to be interpreted, with a view to the material circumstances of the parties at the time of the execution, in the light of the pertinent facts within their knowledge and in such manner as to give effect to the main end designed to be accomplished.... [The] instrument is to be so construed as to give effect to the intent of the ... [parties] as manifested by the words used illumined by all the attendant factors, unless inconsistent with some positive rule of law or repugnant to other terms of the instrument. An omission to express an intention cannot be supplied by conjecture. But, if the instrument as a whole produces a conviction that a particular result was fixedly desired although not expressed by formal words, that defect may be supplied by implication and the underlying intention ... may be effectuated, provided it is sufficiently declared by the entire instrument." Dittemore v. Dickey, 249 Mass. 95, 104, 105, 144 N.E. 57, 60....

Examining the instrument before us, guided by the settled rule of interpretation set forth above, it is manifest that the main purpose of the parents of Richard was to arrive at an agreement for his maintenance and education and to provide security therefor. At the time of the execution of the agreement he was almost ten years of age. His custody had already been awarded to his mother by the decree of divorce of the Nevada court, concerning the validity of which no question is raised. This being so, it is a fair inference that in so far as Richard was concerned his maintenance and education were the main purposes sought to be accomplished by the trust agreement, the parties to the agreement having in mind his age and recognizing the necessity of his being supported during the years to come, and of his being properly educated in a manner appropriate to the defendant's financial ability and station in life. The instrument specifically provided that the payments to be made by the defendant to the trustee for Richard's benefit should "be applied by ... [his mother] or the trustee upon or toward the maintenance and education and benefit of said Richard, so long as she shall maintain and educate said Richard to the satisfaction of the said trustee." But, as appears by the agreed facts and the record, the education of Richard was interrupted by the second World War and his induction into the armed forces of the United States on February 6, 1946, the day following the completion of his high school grades on February 5, 1946. Since then he had been continuously, and at the time of the hearing and order for decree in the court below was, in the service of the armed forces of the nation. Thus he was actually under the command of his superior officers in that service, his maintenance was provided for during the period here involved by the government, and he was not in the actual custody of his mother and was not a student in any higher institution of learning. Thus neither of the main objects for which the defendant had bound himself to provide existed within the meaning of the trust instrument during the period for which the plaintiff claims payment. In these circumstances we are of opinion that the proper construction of the trust instrument is that the defendant is not required under its terms to perform provisions for the maintenance and education of Richard while he was or is in the armed service of the United States. . . .

It follows from what we have said that the decree entered by the judge must be reversed and that instead a final decree must be entered after rescript dismissing the bill with costs of the appeal.

So ordered.

———

LAWSON v. MARTIN TIMBER CO., 238 La. 467, 115 So.2d 821 (1959). Lawson and Timber Company entered into an agreement on October 14, 1948, which provided that Timber Company had two years to cut and remove timber from Lawson's land, and that "in event of high water after this time [i.e., during the two–year period], . . . Timber Co. is to get additional one year's time." Timber Company cut and removed certain timber from Lawson's land in July 1951, after the original two–year period had expired. Lawson brought an action to recover the value of that timber. The evidence indicated that there was high water during approximately half of the two–year period, but that all the lumber on Lawson's land could have easily been cut and removed during the other half.

The issue was whether the one–year extension was applicable under these circumstances. On the original hearing, a majority of the court held that it was. "[W]hether or not the defendant was prevented from removing the timber within two years from the date of the contract on account of high water . . . is immaterial under the very wording contained in the contract granting defendant an additional year within which to remove the timber 'in event of high water after this time.' The language used in this provision of the contract is clear and unambiguous and we cannot go beyond it with the view of seeking the intention of the parties."

Justice Simon dissented. "The words in the clause standing alone are meaningless. But when taken in context with the preceding language of the contract wherein it is stated that the defendant is given two years in which to cut and remove all of said timber, this clause can have but one objective meaning. . . . It is manifest that, taking the clause as written in the language preceding, it can only mean that if there existed any overflow or high water during the period of two years which would have *prevented* the cutting and removal of this timber within the stated primary term, then the defendant enjoyed the right of so doing during the period of one additional year. . . ."

On rehearing, the court adopted Justice Simon's position.

———

LIEBER, LEGAL AND POLITICAL HERMENEUTICS 17–19 (3d ed. 1880). "Let us take an instance of the simplest kind, to show in what degree we are continually obliged to resort to interpretation. By and by we shall find that the same rules which common sense teaches every one to use, in order to understand his neighbor in the most trivial intercourse, are necessary likewise, although not sufficient, for the interpretation of documents or texts of the highest importance, constitutions as well as treaties between the greatest nations.

"Suppose a housekeeper says to a domestic: 'fetch some soupmeat,' accompanying the act with giving some money to the latter; he will be unable to execute the order without interpretation, however easy and, consequently, rapid the performance of the process may be. Common sense and good faith tell the domestic, that the housekeeper's meaning was this: 1. He should go immediately, or as soon as his other occupations are finished; or, if he be directed to do so in the evening, that he should go the next day at the *usual* hour; 2. that the money handed him by the housekeeper is intended to pay for the meat thus ordered, and not as a present to him; 3. that he should buy such meat and of such parts of the animal, as, to his knowledge, has commonly been used in the house he stays at, for making soups; 4. that he buy the best meat he can obtain, for a fair price; 5. that he go to that butcher who usually provides the family, with whom the domestic resides, with meat, or to some convenient stall, and not to any unnecessarily distant place; 6. that he return the rest of the money; 7. that he bring home the meat in good faith, neither adding any thing disagreeable nor injurious; 8. that he fetch the meat for the use of the family and not for himself. Suppose, on the other hand, the housekeeper, afraid of being misunderstood, had mentioned these eight specifications, she would not have obtained her object, if it were to exclude all *possibility* of misunderstanding. For, the various specifications would have required new ones. Where would be the end? We are constrained then, always, to leave a considerable part of our meaning to be found out by interpretation, which, in many cases must necessarily cause greater or less obscurity with regard to the exact meaning, which our words were intended to convey."

SECTION 3. THE ROLE OF USAGE, COURSE OF DEALING, AND COURSE OF PERFORMANCE IN INTERPRETATION

FOXCO INDUSTRIES, LTD. v. FABRIC WORLD, INC.

United States Court of Appeals, Fifth Circuit, 1979.
595 F.2d 976.

TJOFLAT, Circuit Judge:

In this diversity action Foxco Industries, Ltd. (Foxco), a Delaware corporation, following a jury trial recovered a $26,000 judgment against Fabric World, Inc. (Fabric World), an Alabama corporation, for breaching a contract to purchase certain knitted fabric goods and refusing to pay for merchandise previously purchased. [On appeal, Fabric World argues that] the district court erred in admitting into evidence published standards of the Knitted Textile Association to establish the meaning of a disputed contract term. For the reasons set forth below, we reject the [argument] of Fabric World and affirm.

I

Foxco is in the business of manufacturing knitted fabrics for sale to retail fabric stores and the garment industry. Foxco's principal place of business is in New York City; it has never formally qualified to do business in Alabama. Fabric World is engaged in the retail fabric business and operates a chain of stores in a number of states; its headquarters is in Huntsville, Alabama.

There are two seasons in the fabric industry, a spring season and a fall season. Before the beginning of each season Foxco displays for customers samples of the line of fabrics it will manufacture that season. Customer orders are accepted only from the fabric shown on display. Foxco's manufacturing operation is limited to filling these orders; no fabrics are manufactured merely to be held as inventory. There was some conflict in the testimony as to whether fabric specially knit for one customer, such as Fabric World, could be resold to another customer.

Foxco sells some of its goods to retail fabric stores through manufacturers' representatives, operating on a commission basis, who sell the lines of numerous manufacturers. Foxco furnishes each representative with samples and a price list. Larger retail store customers, such as Fabric World, are handled personally by Foxco's sales manager, Allen Feller, a salaried employee, who supervises all retail fabric store sales. He has responsibility over the approximately twenty-six manufacturers' representatives carrying the Foxco line.

Foxco has never maintained an office in Alabama. At the time of the transactions giving rise to this action, its manufacturers' representative in Alabama was a resident of the state. Foxco's sales manager, Feller, made periodic trips to Alabama to meet with this representative and to obtain orders from Fabric World and Kennemer Company, another large fabric retailer. At the beginning of each season Feller would meet with the manufacturers' representative for two or three days so that the new line of fabrics could be previewed and discussed. In 1974, Foxco's gross sales approximated $14,000,000; Alabama accounted for in excess of $100,000 of that amount. A substantial portion of the Alabama business was with Fabric World, from which three separate orders were obtained.

On April 22, 1974, Feller traveled to Huntsville to show Fabric World the new fall line. His meeting with Glenn Jameson, Fabric World's president, culminated in a written order for "first quality" goods. A dispute subsequently arose regarding the quality of the goods sent to fill the order, and Fabric World refused to pay for the portion of the goods it considered defective.

On October 21, 1974, Feller returned to Huntsville to show Jameson the line for the following spring season. Jameson voiced no complaint about the quality of the goods received pursuant to the previous April 22 order. In fact, he gave Feller a new order, in writing, for 12,000 yards of first quality fabric, at a price of $36,705, to be delivered by January 15, 1975.

A few weeks after the October 21 order was placed, the textile industry began to experience a precipitous decline in the price of yarn. Because of a drop in the price of finished goods, Fabric World wrote Foxco on November 15, 1974, and cancelled its October 21 order. Foxco immediately replied, stating that the manufacture of the order was substantially completed and that it could not accept the cancellation. On November 27, 1974, Foxco's attorney wrote Fabric World that if the goods were not accepted they would be finished and sold and Fabric World sued for the difference between the contract price and the sales price received by Foxco. On December 3, 1974, Fabric World agreed to accept the order, but threatened to return the entire shipment if it contained one flaw. Foxco, believing that it was impossible to produce an order of this magnitude without a single flaw, decided it would not ship the order (which was completed a short time later).

Fabric World established that in December 1974 the fair market value of the October order was approximately 20% less than the contract price. However, Foxco made no attempt to sell the goods from the time Fabric World cancelled the order until September 1975, when the goods had dropped 50% In value. In that month Foxco sold at a private sale without notice to Fabric World approximately 7,000 yards from the order for an average price of between $1.50 and $1.75 per yard, a total consideration of $10,119.50. By the time of trial in April 1976, Foxco had on hand about 5,000 yards of the order worth between $1.25 and $1 per yard, or about $6,250.

During the course of the trial there was much testimony regarding the meaning of the term first quality goods used in the contracts between Foxco and Fabric World. The testimony on behalf of Fabric World was that it meant fabric containing no flaws. Foxco introduced evidence, over the objection of Fabric World, in the form of an exhibit containing standards for finished knitted goods promulgated by the Knitted Textile Association, a large textile industry group to which Foxco belongs. These standards indicated that certain types and amounts of flaws were permissible in first quality fabric. Fabric World is not a member of that association and claimed it had no knowledge of the standards adopted by the association's members. One ground for Fabric World's present appeal is its contention that the standards of a trade association of which it had no knowledge are not admissible to show the meaning of the undefined and disputed contract term "first quality" goods....

Fabric World's [claims] that the district court erred in admitting into evidence the definition of first quality goods contained in the Standards for Finished Knitted Fabrics of the Knitted Textile Association. It contends that it is not a member of the Knitted Textile Association, was unaware of its existence until the time of trial, and that that group's standards were inadmissible because they were a custom or usage of the trade of which Fabric World had no knowledge. We find no error in the trial court's ruling.

A major issue in this case is what was meant by the term "first quality." Under the traditional application of the parol evidence rule, Fabric World's contention may have merit: the private, subjective intent of one party to a contract may well be irrelevant in determining the meaning of a contract term unless it is shown that that intent was communicated to the other party. See Levie, Trade Usage and Custom under the Common Law and the Uniform Commercial Code, 40 N.Y.U.L.Rev. 1101 (1965). In this case there is no direct evidence, as Fabric World argues, that it was put on notice that usage and custom, as embodied in the industry standards, would be used to define the meaning of first quality. Under Alabama sales law, however, that Fabric World did not know of the industry's usage and custom or of the standards in question is of no moment; the parties to a contract such as the one in issue are presumed to have intended the incorporation of trade usage in striking their bargain. U.C.C. section 2–202, Ala.Code tit. 7, § 7–2–202 (1977), explicitly provides that trade usages may help explain or supplement contract terms.[8] As stated in the comment to that provision,

> [Section 2–202(a)] makes admissible evidence of course of dealing, usage of trade and course of performance to explain or supplement the terms of any writing stating the agreement of the parties in order that the true understanding of the parties as to the agreement may be reached. *Such writings are to be read on the assumption that* the course of prior dealings between the parties *and the usages of trade were taken for granted when the document was phrased. Unless carefully negated they have become an element of the meaning of the words used.*

Id., Official Comment (emphasis added). Section 1–205(2) ... defines trade usages. It provides in part that

> A usage of trade is any practice or method of dealing having such regularity of observance in a place, vocation or trade as to justify an expectation that it will be observed with respect to the transaction in question. The existence and scope of such a usage are to be proved as facts.

It further states: "A course of dealing between parties and any usage of trade in the vocation or trade in which they are engaged or of which they are or should be aware give particular meaning to and supplement or qualify terms of an agreement." ... There was uncontroverted testimony that the Knitted Textile Association is an industry group with over 1500 members. Its standards could certainly qualify as trade usages, and thus were admissible notwithstanding Fabric World's unawareness of them. Loeb & Co. v. Martin, 295 Ala. 262, 327 So.2d 711, 715 (1976). See Columbia Nitrogen Corp. v. Royster Co., 451 F.2d 3 (4th Cir. 1971); Chase Manhattan Bank v. First Marion Bank, 437 F.2d 1040 (5th Cir. 1971); Southern Concrete Services, Inc. v. Mableton Contractors, Inc., 407 F.Supp. 581 (N.D.Ga.1975), aff'd 569 F.2d 1154 (5th Cir. 1978).

... Accordingly, the judgment of the district court is AFFIRMED.

RESTATEMENT, SECOND, CONTRACTS
§ 221, ILLUSTRATION 2

2. A, an ordained rabbi, is employed by B, an orthodox Jewish congregation, to officiate as cantor at specified religious services. At the time the contract is made, it is the practice of such congregations to seat men and women separately at services, and a contrary practice would violate A's

---

8. Section 2–202 states:

Final written expression: Parol or extrinsic evidence.

Terms with respect to which the confirmatory memoranda of the parties agree or which are otherwise set forth in a writing intended by the parties as a final expression of their agreement with respect to such terms as are included therein may not be contradicted by evidence of any prior agreement or of a contemporane-ous oral agreement but may be explained or supplemented:

(a) By course of dealing or usage of trade (section 7–1–205) or by course of performance (section 7–2–208); and

(b) By evidence of consistent additional terms unless the court finds the writing to have been intended also as a complete and exclusive statement of the terms of the agreement.

religious beliefs. At a time when it is too late for A to obtain substitute employment, B adopts a contrary practice. A refuses to officiate. The practice is part of the contract, and A is entitled to the agreed compensation.

RESTATEMENT, SECOND, CONTRACTS § 222

[See Selected Source Materials Supplement]

RESTATEMENT, SECOND, CONTRACTS § 222, ILLUSTRATIONS 1–3

1. A contracts to sell B 10,000 shingles. By usage of the lumber trade, in which both are engaged, two packs of a certain size constitute 1,000, though not containing that exact number. Unless otherwise agreed, 1,000 in the contract means two packs.

2. A contracts to sell B 1,000 feet of San Domingo mahogany. By usage of dealers in mahogany, known to A and B, good figured mahogany of a certain density is known as San Domingo mahogany, though it does not come from San Domingo. Unless otherwise agreed, the usage is part of the contract. . . .

3. A and B enter into a contract for the purchase and sale of "No. 1 heavy book paper guaranteed free from ground wood." Usage in the paper trade may show that this means paper not containing over 3% ground wood.

HURST v. W.J. LAKE & CO., 141 Or. 306, 16 P.2d 627 (1932). Buyer and Seller made a contract for the sale of 350 tons of horse meat scraps, "minimum 50% protein," for $50 per ton. Under the contract, if any of the scraps tested at "less than 50% of protein" Buyer was to receive a discount of $5.00 per ton. About 170 tons contained less than 50% protein; of these, 140 tons contained 49.53 to 49.96% protein. Buyer took a $5.00 discount on the entire 170 tons. Seller claimed that Buyer was entitled to a discount on only 30 tons, because under a usage of trade the terms "minimum 50% protein" and "less than 50% protein," when used in a contract for the sale of horse meat scraps, meant that a protein content of not less than 49.5% was equal to a content of 50% protein. The trial court granted Buyer's motion for judgment on the pleadings. Reversed.

"The flexibility of or multiplicity in the meaning of words is the principal source of difficulty in the interpretation of language. Words are the conduits by which thoughts are communicated, yet scarcely any of them have such a fixed and single meaning that they are incapable of denoting more than one thought. In addition to the multiplicity in meaning of words set forth in the dictionaries there are the meanings imparted to them by trade customs, local uses, dialects, telegraphic codes, etc. One meaning crowds a word full of significance, while another almost empties the utterance of any import. The various groups above indicated are constantly amplifying our language; in fact, they are developing what may be called languages of their own. Thus one is justified in saying that the language of the dictionaries is not the only language spoken in America. For instance, the word, 'thousand' as commonly used has a very specific meaning; it denotes ten hundreds or fifty scores, but the language of the various trades and localities has assigned to it meanings quite different from that just mentioned. Thus in the bricklaying trade a contract which fixes the bricklayer's compensation at "$5.25 a thousand" does not contemplate that he need lay actually one thousand bricks in order to earn $5.25 but that he should build a wall of a certain size: Brunold v. Glasser, 25 Misc. 285 (53 N.Y.S. 1021); Walker v. Syms, 118 Mich. 183 (76 N.W. 320). In the lumber industry a contract requiring the delivery of 4,000 shingles will be fulfilled by the delivery of only 2,500 when it appears that by trade custom two packs of a certain size are regarded as 1,000 shingles and that, hence, the delivery of eight packs fulfills the contract, even though they contain only 2,500 shingles by actual count: Soutier v. Kellerman, 18 Mo. 509. And where the custom of locality considers 100 dozen as constituting a thousand, one who has 19,200 rabbits upon a warren under an agreement for their sale at the price of 60 pounds for each thousand rabbits will be paid for only 16,000 rabbits: Smith v. Wilson, 3 Barn. & Adol. 728. . . .

". . . We believe that it is safe to assume, in the absence of evidence to the contrary, that when tradesmen employ trade terms they attach to them their trade significance. If, when they write their trade terms into their contracts, they mean to strip the terms of their special significance and demote them to their common import, it would seem reasonable to believe that they would so state in their agreement. Otherwise, they would refrain from using the trade term and express themselves in other language."

———

RESTATEMENT, SECOND, CONTRACTS § 220, Illustration 9: ". . . A promises to sell and B to buy a certain quantity of 'white arsenic' for a stated price. The parties contract with reference to a usage of trade that 'white arsenic' includes arsenic colored with lamp black. The usage is part of the contract."

———

UCC §§ 1–201(3), (11), 1–205, 2–208

[See Selected Source Materials Supplement]

———

RESTATEMENT, SECOND, CONTRACTS §§ 219–223

[See Selected Source Materials Supplement]

———

CISG ART. 9

[See Selected Source Materials Supplement]

––––––––

UNIDROIT PRINCIPLES OF INTERNATIONAL COMMERCIAL CONTRACTS ART. 1.9

[See Selected Source Materials Supplement]

––––––––

PRINCIPLES OF EUROPEAN CONTRACT LAW ART. 1.105

[See Selected Source Materials Supplement]

––––––––

J. WHITE & R. SUMMERS, UNIFORM COMMERCIAL CODE § 1–2 (5th ed. 2000). "Some of the Article 2 provisions on the formation of contracts for the sale of goods have not only radically altered sales law but have influenced the new Restatement (Second) of Contracts as well. In most fundamental terms, Article Two expands our conception of contract. . . .

"Article Two contracts are . . . more expansive in content than before. Thus 1–201(11) defines 'contract' as the 'total legal obligation which results from the parties' agreement,' and 1–201(3) defines 'agreement' to mean 'the bargain of the parties in fact as found in their language or by implication from other circumstances including course of dealing or usage of trade or course of performance as provided in this Act.' . . . The Code therefore adds to sales agreements much that is not made express by the parties."

––––––––

Chapter 10

THE MECHANICS OF A BARGAIN (I)—OFFER AND REVOCATION

Most bargains are formed by the process of offer and acceptance. Because a bargain is enforceable by expectation damages at the moment it is formed, without regard to whether it has been relied upon, the rules that govern the offer-and-acceptance process often play a central role in contract disputes. These issues are the subject of Chapters 10–12.

Chapter 10 focuses on offers. It consists of three Sections:

Section 1 concerns the issue, what constitutes an offer. If it is determined that a party has made an offer, the legal consequence is to create in the offeree a power of acceptance—that is, a power to conclude a bargain (and therefore a legally enforceable contract) by accepting the offer. Section 2 concerns three kinds of events that can terminate a power of acceptance: lapse of the offer; rejection of the offer; and the making of a counter-offer (or some legal equivalent) by the offeree. Finally, Section 3 concerns the power of an offeror to terminate the offeree's power of acceptance by revoking the offer.

SECTION 1. WHAT CONSTITUTES AN OFFER

RESTATEMENT, SECOND, CONTRACTS § 24

[See Selected Source Materials Supplement]

CISG ART. 14(1)

[See Selected Source Materials Supplement]

UNIDROIT PRINCIPLES OF INTERNATIONAL COMMERCIAL CONTRACTS ART. 2.1.2

[See Selected Source Materials Supplement]

PRINCIPLES OF EUROPEAN CONTRACT LAW § 2.201(1)

[See Selected Source Materials Supplement]

LONERGAN v. SCOLNICK

California Court of Appeal, Fourth District, 1954.
129 Cal.App.2d 179, 276 P.2d 8.

BARNARD, PRESIDING JUSTICE. This is an action for specific performance or for damages in the event specific performance was impossible.

The complaint alleged that on April 15, 1952, the parties entered into a contract whereby the defendant agreed to sell, and plaintiff agreed to buy a 40–acre tract of land for $2,500; that this was a fair, just and reasonable value of the property; that on April 28, 1952, the defendant repudiated the contract and refused to deliver a deed; that on April 28, 1952, the property was worth $6,081; and that plaintiff has been damaged in the amount of $3,581. The answer denied that any contract had been entered into, or that anything was due to the plaintiff.

By stipulation the issue of whether or not a contract was entered into between the parties was first tried, reserving the other issues for a further trial if that became necessary. The issue as to the existence of a contract was submitted upon an agreed statement, including certain letters between the parties, without the introduction of other evidence.

The stipulated facts are as follows: During March, 1952, the defendant placed an ad in a Los Angeles paper reading, so far as material here, "Joshua Tree vic. 40 acres, . . . need cash, will sacrifice." In response to an inquiry resulting from this ad the defendant, who lived in New York, wrote a letter to the plaintiff dated March 26, briefly describing the property, giving directions as to how to get there, stating that his rock-bottom price was $2,500 cash, and further stating that "This is a form letter." On April 7, the plaintiff wrote a letter to the defendant saying that he was not sure he had found the property, asking for its legal description, asking whether the land was all level or whether it included certain jutting rock hills, and suggesting a certain bank as escrow agent "should I desire to purchase the land." On April 8, the defendant wrote to the plaintiff saying "From your description you have found the property"; that this bank "is O.K. for escrow agent"; that the land was fairly level; giving the legal description; and then saying, "If you are really interested, you will have to decide fast, as I expect to have a buyer in the next week or so." On April 12, the defendant sold the property to a third party for $2,500. The plaintiff received defendant's letter of April 8 on April

14. On April 15 he wrote to the defendant thanking him for his letter "confirming that I was on the right land", stating that he would immediately proceed to have the escrow opened and would deposit $2,500 therein "in conformity with your offer", and asking the defendant to forward a deed with his instructions to the escrow agent. On April 17, 1952, the plaintiff started an escrow and placed in the hands of the escrow agent $100, agreeing to furnish an additional $2,400 at an unspecified time, with the provision that if the escrow was not closed by May 15, 1952, it should be completed as soon thereafter as possible unless a written demand for a return of the money or instruments was made by either party after that date. It was further stipulated that the plaintiff was ready and willing at all times to deposit the $2,400.

The matter was submitted on June 11, 1953. On July 10, 1953, the judge filed a memorandum opinion stating that it was his opinion that the letter of April 8, 1952, when considered with the previous correspondence, constituted an offer of sale which offer was, however, qualified and conditioned upon prompt acceptance by the plaintiff; that in spite of the condition thus imposed, the plaintiff delayed more than a week before notifying the defendant of his acceptance; and that since the plaintiff was aware of the necessity of promptly communicating his acceptance to the defendant his delay was not the prompt action required by the terms of the offer. Findings of fact were filed on October 2, 1953, finding that each and all of the statements in the agreed statement are true, and that all allegations to the contrary in the complaint are untrue. As conclusions of law, it was found that the plaintiff and defendant did not enter into a contract as alleged in the complaint or otherwise, and that the defendant is entitled to judgment against the plaintiff. Judgment was entered accordingly, from which the plaintiff has appealed.

The appellant contends that the judgment is contrary to the evidence and to the law since the facts, as found, do not support the conclusions of law upon which the judgment is based. It is argued that there is no conflict in the evidence, and this court is not bound by the trial court's construction of the written instruments involved; that the evidence conclusively shows that an offer was made to the plaintiff by the defendant, which offer was accepted by the mailing of plaintiff's letter of April 15; that upon receipt of defendant's letter of April 8 the plaintiff had a reasonable time within which to accept the offer that had been made; that by his letter of April 15 and his starting of an escrow the plaintiff accepted said offer; and that the agreed statement of facts establishes that a valid contract was entered into between the parties. In his briefs the appellant assumes that an offer was made by the defendant, and confined his argument to contending that the evidence shows that he accepted that offer within a reasonable time.

There can be no contract unless the minds of the parties have met and mutually agreed upon some specific thing. This is usually evidenced by one party making an offer which is accepted by the other party. Section 25 of the Restatement, Law on Contracts reads:

> "If from a promise, or manifestation of intention, or from the circumstances existing at the time, the person to whom the promise or manifestation is addressed knows or has reason to know that the person making it does not intend it as an expression of his fixed purpose until he has given a further expression of assent, he has not made an offer."

The language used in Niles v. Hancock, 140 Cal. 157, 73 P. 840, 842, "It is also clear from the correspondence that it was the intention of the defendant that the negotiations between him and the plaintiff were to be purely preliminary," is applicable here. The correspondence here indicates an intention on the part of the defendant to find out whether the plaintiff was interested, rather than an intention to make a definite offer to the plaintiff. The language used by the defendant in his letters of March 26 and April 8 rather clearly discloses that they were not intended as an expression of fixed purpose to make a definite offer, and was sufficient to advise the plaintiff that some further expression of assent on the part of the defendant was necessary.

The advertisement in the paper was a mere request for an offer. The letter of March 26 contains no definite offer, and clearly states that it is a form letter. It merely gives further particulars, in clarification of the advertisement, and tells the plaintiff how to locate the property if he was interested in looking into the matter. The letter of April 8 added nothing in the way of a definite offer. It merely answered some questions asked by the plaintiff, and stated that if the plaintiff was really interested he would have to act fast. The statement that he expected to have a buyer in the next week or so indicated that the defendant intended to sell to the first-comer, and was reserving the right to do so. From this statement, alone, the plaintiff knew or should have known that he was not being given time in which to accept an offer that was being made but that some further assent on the part of the defendant was required. Under the language used the plaintiff was not being given a right to act within a reasonable time after receiving the letter; he was plainly told that the defendant intended to sell to another, if possible, and warned that he would have to act fast if he was interested in buying the land.

Regardless of any opinion previously expressed, the court found that no contract had been entered into between these parties, and we are in accord with the court's conclusion on that controlling issue. The court's construction of the letters involved was a reasonable one, and we think the most reasonable one, even if it be assumed that another construction was possible.

The judgment is affirmed.

GRIFFIN and MUSSELL, JJ., concur.

———

REGENT LIGHTING CORP. v. CMT CORP., 1997 WL 441297 (M.D.N.C. 1997). On September 1, 1994, Defendant sent a letter to Plaintiff requesting a "firm quotation for winding equipment." The first sentence in this letter stated, "[w]e enclose the following proposal...." The proposal that followed contained a description of the machine, and the price. Included with the proposal was Defendant's "standard terms and conditions." These standard terms stated that "no order shall be binding on SELLER until and unless accepted by SELLER in writing. SELLER may refuse to accept any order for any cause which SELLER deems sufficient and shall not be liable for any claims of any nature because of failure to accept." Held, this term prevented the proposal from being an offer. "An offer 'must be made under circumstances evidencing an express or implied intention that its acceptance shall constitute a binding contract.' Because Defendant reserved the right to not accept an order, its proposal was merely an invitation to submit an offer. Therefore, the proposal sent on September 1, 1994 was not an offer.''

————

LEFKOWITZ v. GREAT MINNEAPOLIS SURPLUS STORE

Supreme Court of Minnesota, 1957.
251 Minn. 188, 86 N.W.2d 689.

MURPHY, JUSTICE. This is an appeal from an order of the Municipal Court of Minneapolis denying the motion of the defendant for amended findings of fact, or, in the alternative, for a new trial. The order for judgment awarded the plaintiff the sum of $138.50 as damages for breach of contract.

This case grows out of the alleged refusal of the defendant to sell to the plaintiff a certain fur piece which it had offered for sale in a newspaper advertisement. It appears from the record that on April 6, 1956, the defendant published the following advertisement in a Minneapolis newspaper:

"Saturday 9 A.M. Sharp

3 Brand New

Fur Coats

Worth to $100

First Come

First Served

$1 Each"

On April 13, the defendant again published an advertisement in the same newspaper as follows:

"Saturday 9 A.M.

2 Brand New Pastel

Mink 3–Skin Scarfs

Selling for $89.50

Out they go

Saturday.

Each.... $1.00

1 Black Lapin Stole

Beautiful,

worth $139.50.... $1.00

First Come

First Served"

The record supports the findings of the court that on each of the Saturdays following the publication of the above-described ads the plaintiff was the first to present himself at the appropriate counter in the defendant's store and on each occasion demanded the coat and the stole so advertised and indicated his readiness to pay the sale price of $1. On both occasions, the defendant refused to sell the merchandise to the plaintiff, stating on the first occasion that by a "house rule" the offer was intended for women only and sales would not be made to men, and on the second visit that plaintiff knew defendant's house rules.

The trial court properly disallowed plaintiff's claim for the value of the fur coats since the value of these articles was speculative and uncertain. The only evidence of value was the advertisement itself to the effect that the coats were "Worth to $100.00," how much less being speculative especially in view of the price for which they were offered for sale. With reference to the offer of the defendant on April 13, 1956, to sell the "1 Black Lapin Stole ... worth $139.50 ..." the trial court held that the value of this article was established and granted judgment in favor of the plaintiff for that amount less the $1 quoted purchase price.

1. The defendant contends that a newspaper advertisement offering items of merchandise for sale at a named price is a "unilateral offer" which may be withdrawn without notice. He relies upon authorities which hold that, where an advertiser publishes in a newspaper that he has a certain quantity or quality of goods which he wants to dispose of at certain prices and on certain terms, such advertisements are not offers which become contracts as soon as any person to whose notice they may come signifies his acceptance by notifying the other that he will take a certain quantity of them. Such advertisements have been construed as an invitation for an offer of sale on the terms stated, which offer, when received, may be accepted or rejected and which therefore does not become a contract of sale until accepted by the seller; and until a contract has been so made, the seller may modify or revoke such prices or terms. . . .

The defendant relies principally on Craft v. Elder & Johnston Co. supra. In that case, the court discussed the legal effect of an advertisement offering for sale, as a one-day special, an electric sewing machine at a named price. The view was expressed that the advertisement was (38 N.E.2d 417, 34 Ohio L.A. 605) "not an offer made to any specific person but was made to the public generally. Thereby it would be properly designated as a unilateral offer and not being supported by any consideration could be withdrawn at will and without notice." It is true that such an offer may be withdrawn before acceptance. Since all offers are by their nature unilateral because they are necessarily made by one party or on one side in the negotiation of a contract, the distinction made in that decision between a unilateral offer and a unilateral contract is not clear. On the facts before us we are concerned with whether the advertisement constituted an offer, and, if so, whether the plaintiff's conduct constituted an acceptance.

There are numerous authorities which hold that a particular advertisement in a newspaper or circular letter relating to a sale of articles may be construed by the court as constituting an offer, acceptance of which would complete a contract. . . .

The test of whether a binding obligation may originate in advertisements addressed to the general public is "whether the facts show that some performance was promised in positive terms in return for something requested." 1 Williston, Contracts (Rev. ed.) § 27.

The authorities above cited emphasize that, where the offer is clear, definite, and explicit, and leaves nothing open for negotiation, it constitutes an offer, acceptance of which will complete the contract. The most recent case on the subject is Johnson v. Capital City Ford Co., La.App., 85 So.2d 75, in which the court pointed out that a newspaper advertisement relating to the purchase and sale of automobiles may constitute an offer, acceptance of which will consummate a contract and create an obligation in the offeror to perform according to the terms of the published offer.

Whether in any individual instance a newspaper advertisement is an offer rather than an invitation to make an offer depends on the legal intention of the parties and the surrounding circumstances. Annotation, 157 A.L.R. 744, 751; 77 C.J.S. Sales § 25b; 17 C.J.S. Contracts § 389. We are of the view on the facts before us that the offer by the defendant of the sale of the Lapin fur was clear, definite, and explicit, and left nothing open for negotiation. The plaintiff having successfully managed to be the first one to appear at the seller's place of business to be served, as requested by the advertisement, and having offered the stated purchase price of the article, he was entitled to performance on the part of the defendant. We think the trial court was correct in holding that there was in the conduct of the parties a sufficient mutuality of obligation to constitute a contract of sale.

2.   The defendant contends that the offer was modified by a "house rule" to the effect that only women were qualified to receive the bargains advertised. The advertisement contained no such restriction. This objection may be disposed of briefly by stating that, while an advertiser has the right at any time before acceptance to modify his offer, he does not have the right, after acceptance, to impose new or arbitrary conditions not contained in the published offer. . . .

Affirmed.

————

FORD MOTOR CREDIT CO. v. RUSSELL, 519 N.W.2d 460 (Minn. Ct. App. 1994). In March 1988, Monticello Ford, an independent dealer, advertised a 1988 Ford Escort Pony in a local newspaper for $7,826, with monthly payments of $159.29, based on 11% financing. On March 15, Dawn Russell sought to purchase a 1988 Escort Pony at the advertised sales price. Monticello Ford contacted three finance companies in an attempt to obtain 11% financing for Russell. Two companies refused to extend credit because of Russell's limited credit history. Ford Motor Credit Company, a subsidiary of Ford Motor Manufacturing Company, offered to finance the purchase at a 13.75% interest rate under a special retail plan for persons with limited or poor credit. Monticello Ford drew up a contract, which Russell signed, providing for the sale of the automobile at a cash price of $7,826 together with the financing arrangements. Monticello Ford subsequently assigned its rights under the contract to Ford Credit. The contract provided that upon default, Ford Credit could accelerate the balance due and repossess the vehicle. In 1990, Russell defaulted on numerous payments. Eventually, Ford Credit repossessed the car, sold it for less than the amount Russell still owed, and sued her for the difference. Russell counterclaimed that the advertisement constituted an offer, which Russell accepted, and therefore Ford Credit breached its contract to sell her a 1988 Ford Escort at 11% financing. Held, for Ford Credit:

> Generally, if goods are advertised for sale at a certain price, it is not an offer and no contract is formed; such an advertisement is merely an invitation to bargain rather than an offer. The test of whether a binding obligation may originate in advertisements addressed to the general public is "whether the facts show that some performance was promised in positive terms in return for something requested." Lefkowitz v. Great Minneapolis Surplus Store, Inc., 251 Minn. 188, 191, 86 N.W.2d 689, 691 (1957)....

> We conclude that the advertisement here did not constitute an offer of sale to the general public. Because not everyone qualifies for financing and Monticello Ford does not have an unlimited number of Ford Escorts to sell, it was unreasonable for appellants to believe that the advertisement was an offer binding the advertiser.

FISHER v. BELL, [1961] 1 Q.B. 394 (1960). The Restriction of Offensive Weapons Act made it unlawful to "offer for sale" a switchblade knife. Defendant, who owned a store known as Bell's Music Shop, was prosecuted under the Act for having displayed such a knife in his shop window accompanied by a ticket upon which the words "Ejector knife–4s. [shillings]" were printed. Held, for defendant. "The sole question is whether the exhibition of that knife in the window with the ticket constituted an offer for sale within the statute. I confess that I think most lay people and, indeed, I myself when I first read the papers, would be inclined to the view that to say that if a knife was displayed in a window like that with a price attached to it was not offering it for sale was just nonsense. In ordinary language it is there inviting people to buy it, and it is for sale; but any statute must of course be looked at in the light of the general law of the country. Parliament in its wisdom in passing an Act must be taken to know the general law. It is perfectly clear that according to the ordinary law of contract the display of an article with a price on it in a shop window is merely an invitation to treat."

RESTATEMENT, SECOND, CONTRACTS § 26

[See Selected Source Materials Supplement]

CISG ARTICLE 14(2)

[See Selected Source Materials Supplement]

PRINCIPLES OF EUROPEAN CONTRACT
LAW ART. 2.201(2), (3)

[See Selected Source Materials Supplement]

———

UNIFORM DECEPTIVE TRADE PRACTICES ACT

[See Selected Source Materials Supplement]

———

FEDERAL TRADE COMMISSION REGULATIONS—
RETAIL FOOD STORE ADVERTISING AND
MARKETING PRACTICES

[See Selected Source Materials Supplement]

———

UCC § 2–328

[See Selected Source Materials Supplement]

———

HOFFMAN v. HORTON, 212 Va. 565, 186 S.E.2d 79 (1972). In this case, the Virginia Supreme Court held that the rule embodied in the second sentence of UCC § 2–328(2) would also be applied to auctions for the sale of land. "[W]hile the Uniform Commercial Code is not controlling here, we think it appropriate to borrow from it to establish the rule applicable to the transaction at hand. To vest the auctioneer crying a sale of land with the same discretion to reopen bidding that he has in the sale of goods is to achieve uniformity and, of more importance, to recognize a rule which is both necessary and fair."

———

SECTION 2. TERMINATION OF THE OFFEREE'S POWER OF ACCEPTANCE: LAPSE, REJECTION, AND COUNTER–OFFER

AKERS v. J.B. SEDBERRY, INC.

Court of Appeals of Tennessee, 1955.
39 Tenn.App. 633, 286 S.W.2d 617, cert. denied by Tenn.S.Ct.

FELTS, JUDGE. These two consolidated causes are before us upon a writ of error sued out by J.B. Sedberry, Inc., and Mrs. M.B. Sedberry, defendants below, to review a decree of the Chancery Court, awarding a recovery against them in favor of each of the complainants, Charles William Akers and William Gambill Whitsitt, for damages for breach of a contract of employment....

J.B. Sedberry, Inc., was a Tennessee corporation with its principal place of business at Franklin, Tennessee. Mrs. M.B. Sedberry owned practically all of its stock and was its president and in active charge of its affairs. It was engaged in the business of distributing "Jay Bee" hammer mills, which were manufactured for it under contract by Jay Bee Manufacturing Company, a Texas corporation, whose plant was in Tyler, Texas, and whose capital stock was owned principally by L.M. Glasgow and B.G. Byars.

On July 1, 1947, J.B. Sedberry, Inc., by written contract, employed complainant Akers as Chief Engineer for a term of five years at a salary of $12,000 per year, payable $1,000 per month, plus 1% of its net profits for the first year, 2% the second, 3% the third, 4% the fourth, and 5% the fifth year. His duties were to carry on research for his employer, and to see that the Jay Bee Manufacturing Company, Tyler, Texas, manufactured the mills and parts according to proper specifications. Mrs. M.B. Sedberry guaranteed the employer's performance of this contract.

On August 1, 1947, J.B. Sedberry, Inc., by written contract, employed complainant Whitsitt as Assistant Chief Engineer for a term of five years at a salary of $7,200 per year, payable $600 per month, plus 1% of the corporation's net profits for the first year, 2% for the second, 3% for the third, 4% for the fourth, and 5% for the fifth year. His duties were to assist in the work done by the Chief Engineer. Mrs. M.B. Sedberry guaranteed the employer's performance of this contract.

Under Mrs. Sedberry's instructions, Akers and Whitsitt moved to Tyler, Texas, began performing their contract duties in the plant of the Jay Bee Manufacturing Company, continued working there, and were paid under the contracts until October 1, 1950, when they ceased work, under circumstances hereafter stated....

[After the employment contracts were made, Mrs. Sedberry acquired the stock of Jay Bee from Glasgow and Byars, and installed a new manager, A.M. Sorenson.] There soon developed considerable friction between Sorenson and complainants Akers and Whitsitt. The Jay Bee Manufacturing Company owed large sums to the Tyler State Bank & Trust Co.; and the bank's officers, fearing the company might fail under Sorenson's management, began talking to Akers and Whitsitt about the company's financial difficulties....

While these matters were pending, Akers and Whitsitt flew to Nashville and went to Franklin to talk with Mrs. Sedberry about them. They had a conference with her at her office on Friday, September 29, 1950, lasting from

9:30 a.m. until 4:30 p.m. As they had come unannounced, and unknown to Sorenson, they felt Mrs. Sedberry might mistrust them; and at the outset to show their good faith, they offered to resign, but she did not accept their offer. Instead, she proceeded with them in discussing the operation and refinancing of the business.

Testifying about this conference, Akers said that, at the very beginning, to show their good faith, he told Mrs. Sedberry that they would offer their resignations on a ninety-day notice, provided they were paid according to the contract for that period; that she pushed the offers aside—"would not accept them", but went into a full discussion of the business; that nothing was thereafter said about the offers to resign; and that they spent the whole day discussing the business, Akers making notes of things she instructed him to do when he got back to Texas.

Whitsitt testified that ... [Mrs. Sedberry].... did not accept the offer, but proceeded with the business, and nothing further was said about resigning.

Mrs. Sedberry testified that Akers and Whitsitt came in and "offered their resignations"; that they said they could not work with Sorenson and did not believe the bank would go along with him; and that "they said if it would be of any help to the organization they would be glad to tender their resignation and pay them what was due them." She further said that she "did not accept the resignation", that she "felt it necessary to contact Mr. Sorenson and give consideration to the resignation offer." But she said nothing to complainants about taking the offer under consideration.

On cross-examination she said that in the offer to resign "no mention was made of any ninety-day notice". Asked what response she made to the offer she said, "I treated it rather casually because I had to give it some thought and had to contact Mr. Sorenson." She further said she excused herself from the conference with complainants, went to another room, tried to telephone Sorenson in Tyler, Texas, but was unable to locate him.

She then resumed the conference, nothing further was said about the offers to resign, nothing was said by her to indicate that she thought the offers were left open or held under consideration by her. But the discussion proceeded as if the offers had not been made. She discussed with complainants future plans for refinancing and operating the business, giving them instructions, and Akers making notes of them.

Following the conference, complainants, upon Mrs. Sedberry's request, flew back to Texas to proceed to carry out her instructions....

On Monday, October 2, 1950, Mrs. Sedberry sent to complainants similar telegrams, signed by "J.B. Sedberry, Inc., by M.B. Sedberry, President", stating that their resignations were accepted, effective immediately. We quote the telegram to Akers, omitting the formal parts:

> "Account present unsettled conditions which you so fully are aware we accept your kind offer of resignation effective immediately. Please discontinue as of today with everyone employed in Sedberry, Inc., Engineering Department, discontinuing all expenses in this department writing." ...

While this said she was "writing", she did not write....

[Akers then wrote] that he was amazed to get her telegram, and called her attention to the fact that no offer to resign by him was open or outstanding when she sent the telegram; that while he had made a conditional offer to resign at their conference on September 29, she had immediately rejected the offer, and had discussed plans for the business and had instructed him and Whitsitt as to things she wanted them to do in the business on their return to Tyler.

This letter further stated that Akers was expecting to be paid according to the terms of his contract until he could find other employment that would pay him as much income as that provided in his contract, and that if he had to accept a position with less income, he would expect to be paid the difference, or whatever losses he suffered by her breach of the contract. [Whitsitt wrote a similar letter.] . . .

As it takes two to make a contract, it takes two to unmake it. It cannot be changed or ended by one alone, but only by mutual assent of both parties. A contract of employment for a fixed period may be terminated by the employee's offer to resign, provided such offer is duly accepted by the employer. . . .

An employee's tender of his resignation, being a mere offer is, of course, not binding until it has been accepted by the employer. Such offer must be accepted according to its terms and within the time fixed. The matter is governed by the same rules as govern the formation of contracts. . . .

An offer may be terminated in a number of ways, as, for example, where it is rejected by the offeree, or where it is not accepted by him within the time fixed, or, if no time is fixed, within a reasonable time. An offer terminated in either of these ways ceases to exist and cannot thereafter be accepted. 1 Williston on Contracts (1936), secs. 50A, 51, 53, 54; 1 Corbin on Contracts (1950), secs. 35, 36; 1 Restatement, Contracts, §§ 35, 40.

The question what is a reasonable time, where no time is fixed, is a question of fact, depending on the nature of the contract proposed, the usages of business and other circumstances of the case. Ordinarily, an offer made by one to another in a face to face conversation is deemed to continue only to the close of their conversation, and cannot be accepted thereafter.

The rule is illustrated by Restatement Contracts § 40, Illustration 2, as follows:

"2. While A and B are engaged in conversation, A makes B an offer to which B then makes no reply, but a few hours later meeting A again, B states that he accepts the offer. There is no contract unless the offer or the surrounding circumstances indicate that the offer is intended to continue beyond the immediate conversation." . . .

Professor Corbin says:

"When two negotiating parties are in each other's presence, and one makes an offer to the other without indicating any time for acceptance, the inference that will ordinarily be drawn by the other party is that an answer is expected at once. . . . If, when the first reply is not an acceptance, the offeror turns away in silence, the proper inference is that the offer is no longer open to acceptance." 1 Corbin on Contracts (1950), section 36, p. 111.

The only offer by Akers and Whitsitt to resign was the offer made by them in their conversation with Mrs. Sedberry. They made that offer at the outset, and on the evidence it seems clear that they expected an answer at once. Certainly, there is nothing in the evidence to show that they intended the offer to continue beyond that conversation; and on the above authorities, we think the offer did not continue beyond that meeting.

Indeed, it did not last that long, in our opinion, but was terminated by Mrs. Sedberry's rejection of it very early in that meeting. While she did not expressly reject it, and while she may have intended, as she says, to take the offer under consideration, she did not disclose such an intent to complainants; but, by her conduct, led them to believe she rejected the offer, brushed it aside, and proceeded with the discussion as if it had not been made.

> "An offer is rejected when the offeror is justified in inferring from the words or conduct of the offeree that the offeree intends not to accept the offer or to take it under further advisement (Rest. Contracts sec. 36)." 1 Williston on Contracts, section 51.

So, we agree with the Trial Judge that when defendants sent the telegrams, undertaking to accept offers of complainants to resign, there was no such offer in existence; and that this attempt of defendants to terminate their contract was unlawful and constituted a breach for which they are liable to complainants....

Finally, defendants contend that if complainants are entitled to any recovery at all, such recovery should have been limited to the ninety-day period from and after October 2, 1950, because complainants themselves admitted that they had offered to resign upon ninety days notice with pay for that period.

The answer to this contention is that their offer to resign on ninety days notice was not accepted, but had terminated, and there was no offer in existence when Mrs. Sedberry undertook to accept their offers of resignation. Such attempt by defendants to terminate their contract was unlawful and was a breach for which they become liable for the measure of recovery as above stated....

All of the assignments of error are overruled and the decree of the Chancellor is affirmed....

The causes are remanded to the Chancery Court for further proceedings not inconsistent with this opinion.

HICKERSON and SHRIVER, JJ., concur.

RESTATEMENT, SECOND, CONTRACTS §§ 38, 41

[See Selected Source Materials Supplement]

CISG ART. 17

[See Selected Source Materials Supplement]

UNIDROIT PRINCIPLES OF INTERNATIONAL COMMERCIAL CONTRACTS ARTS. 2.1.5, 2.1.7

[See Selected Source Materials Supplement]

———

PRINCIPLES OF EUROPEAN CONTRACT LAW ARTS. 2.203, 2.206

[See Selected Source Materials Supplement]

———

NOTE ON THE EFFECT OF THE REJECTION OF AN OFFER

A recurring problem in the area of offer and acceptance concerns the issue whether an expression by the offeree, in response to an offer, terminates the offeree' s power of acceptance. The underlying question in determining whether an offeree's expression terminates his power of acceptance is whether the offeror would reasonably understand that the expression serves to take the offer off the table. If an offer is off the table, the offeree has nothing to accept, any more than if the offer had never been made or if it had lapsed. Furthermore, an offeror is likely to rely on his understanding that the offer is off the table. For example, suppose an offer states that it will be open for ten days. During those ten days, the offeror may take steps to prepare for performance based on his assessment of the probability of acceptance. Suppose now that as a result of an expression used by the offeree on the second day, the offeror reasonably believes the offer is off the table. In that case, the offeror will take no further steps to prepare for performance, and may arrange his affairs on the basis that he will not be entering into a contract. Alternatively, the offeror may make a new offer to a third party that he would not have made in the absence of the offeree's expression. If the offeree then tries to accept on the tenth day, the offeror would be caught short. Moreover, it would be difficult if not impossible for the offeror to prove that he would have acted differently in the absence of the offeree's expression, because the offeror's response to the expression may consist of nonaction or of action that is not related to the expression in an obvious way.

The issue then is, what kinds of expressions by an offeree will lead an offeror to reasonably believe that the offer is off the table. To a very large extent, the law of offer and acceptance deals with this issue through a series of categorical rules, rather than by application of the general principles of interpretation on a case-by-case basis. Under one of these rules, a rejection terminates the offeree's power of acceptance, even if the rejection is communicated before the offer would otherwise have lapsed. It is easy to justify this rule, because it seems virtually certain that under the general principles of interpretation a rejection would be understood by the offeror to take the offer off the table. Although it is conceivable that in a few cases the general principles of interpretation would lead to a different result—because, for example, neither party subjectively viewed the rejection as taking the offer off the table—such a scenario is so unlikely that a categorical rule is supported by administrative justifications. It should be stressed, however, that even in this relatively easy case the categorical rule represents a choice. If the rule is that a rejection terminates the power of acceptance, this is not because a rejection must logically terminate the power of acceptance, but because the rule is perceived to be justified by prudential considerations.

ARDENTE v. HORAN

Supreme Court of Rhode Island, 1976.
117 R.I. 254, 366 A.2d 162.

DORIS, JUSTICE. Ernst P. Ardente, the plaintiff, brought this civil action in Superior Court to specifically enforce an agreement between himself and William A. and Katherine L. Horan, the defendants, to sell certain real property. The defendants filed an answer together with a motion for summary judgment pursuant to Super.R.Civ.P. 56. Following the submission of affidavits by both the plaintiff and the defendants and a hearing on the motion, judgment was entered by a Superior Court justice for the defendants. The plaintiff now appeals.

In August 1975, certain residential property in the city of Newport was offered for sale by defendants. The plaintiff made a bid of $250,000 for the property which was communicated to defendants by their attorney. After defendants' attorney advised plaintiff that the bid was acceptable to defendants, he prepared a purchase and sale agreement at the direction of defendants and forwarded it to plaintiff's attorney for plaintiff's signature. After investigating certain title conditions, plaintiff executed the agreement. Thereafter plaintiff's attorney returned the document to defendants along with a check in the amount of $20,000 and a letter dated September 8, 1975, which read in relevant part as follows:

> "My clients are concerned that the following items remain with the real estate: a) dining room set and tapestry wall covering in dining room; b) fireplace fixtures throughout; c) the sun parlor furniture. I would appreciate your confirming that these items are a part of the transaction, as they would be difficult to replace."

The defendants refused to agree to sell the enumerated items and did not sign the purchase and sale agreement. They directed their attorney to return the agreement and the deposit check to plaintiff and subsequently refused to sell the property to plaintiff. This action for specific performance followed.

In Superior Court, defendants moved for summary judgment on the ground that the facts were not in dispute and no contract had been formed as a matter of law.[1] The trial justice ruled that the letter quoted above constituted a conditional acceptance of defendants' offer to sell the property and consequently must be construed as a counteroffer. Since defendants never

---

1. Although the contract would appear to be within the statute of frauds, defendants did not raise this defense in the trial court, nor do they raise it here. Where a party makes no claim to the benefit of the statute, the court sua sponte will not interpose it for him. Conti v. Fisher, 48 R.I. 33, 36, 134 A. 849, 850 (1926).

accepted the counteroffer, it followed that no contract was formed, and summary judgment was granted. . . .

The plaintiff assigns several grounds for appeal in his brief. He urges first that summary judgment was improper because there existed a genuine issue of fact. The factual question, according to plaintiff, was whether the oral agreement which preceded the drafting of the purchase and sale agreement was intended by the parties to take effect immediately to create a binding oral contract for the sale of the property.

We cannot agree with plaintiff's position. A review of the record shows that the issue was never raised before the trial justice. The plaintiff did not, in his affidavit in opposition to summary judgment or by any other means, bring to the attention of the trial court any facts which established the existence of a relevant factual dispute. Indeed, at the hearing on the motion plaintiff did not even mention the alleged factual dispute which he now claims the trial justice erred in overlooking. The only issue plaintiff addressed was the proper interpretation of the language used in plaintiff's letter of acceptance. This was solely a question of law. . . .

The plaintiff's second contention is that the trial justice incorrectly applied the principles of contract law in deciding that the facts did not disclose a valid acceptance of defendants' offer. Again we cannot agree.

The trial justice proceeded on the theory that the delivery of the purchase and sale agreement to plaintiff constituted an offer by defendants to sell the property. Because we must view the evidence in the light most favorable to the party against whom summary judgment was entered, in this case plaintiff, we assume as the trial justice did that the delivery of the agreement was in fact an offer.[2]

The question we must answer next is whether there was an acceptance of that offer. The general rule is that where, as here, there is an offer to form a bilateral contract, the offeree must communicate his acceptance to the offeror before any contractual obligation can come into being. A mere mental intent to accept the offer, no matter how carefully formed, is not sufficient. The acceptance must be transmitted to the offeror in some overt manner. Bullock v. Harwick, 158 Fla. 834, 30 So.2d 539 (1947); Armstrong v. Guy H. James Constr. Co., 402 P.2d 275 (Okl.1965); 1 Restatement, Contracts § 20 (1932). See generally 1 Corbin, Contracts § 67 (1963). A review of the record shows that the only expression of acceptance which was communicated to defendants was the delivery of the executed purchase and sale agreement accompanied by the letter of September 8. Therefore it is solely on the basis of the language used in these two documents that we must determine whether there was a valid acceptance. Whatever plaintiff's unexpressed intention may have been in sending the documents is irrelevant. We must be concerned only with the language actually used, not the language plaintiff thought he was using or intended to use.

---

2. The conclusion that the delivery of the agreement was an offer is not unassailable in view of the fact that defendants did not sign the agreement before sending it to plaintiff, and the fact that plaintiff told defendants' attorney after the agreement was received that he would have to investigate certain conditions of title before signing the agreement. If it was not an offer, plaintiff's execution of the agreement could itself be no more than an offer, which defendants never accepted.

There is no doubt that the execution and delivery of the purchase and sale agreement by plaintiff, without more, would have operated as an acceptance. The terms of the accompanying letter, however, apparently conditioned the acceptance upon the inclusion of various items of personalty. In assessing the effect of the terms of that letter we must keep in mind certain generally accepted rules. To be effective, an acceptance must be definite and unequivocal. "An offeror is entitled to know in clear terms whether the offeree accepts his proposal. It is not enough that the words of a reply justify a probable inference of assent." 1 Restatement, Contracts § 58, comment a (1932). The acceptance may not impose additional conditions on the offer, nor may it add limitations. "An acceptance which is equivocal or upon condition or with a limitation is a counteroffer and requires acceptance by the original offeror before a contractual relationship can exist." John Hancock Mut. Life Ins. Co. v. Dietlin, 97 R.I. 515, 518, 199 A.2d 311, 313 (1964). Accord, Cavanaugh v. Conway, 36 R.I. 571, 587, 90 A. 1080, 1086 (1914).

However, an acceptance may be valid despite conditional language if the acceptance is clearly independent of the condition. Many cases have so held. Williston states the rule as follows:

> "Frequently an offeree, while making a positive acceptance of the offer, also makes a request or suggestion that some addition or modification be made. So long as it is clear that the meaning of the acceptance is positively and unequivocally to accept the offer whether such request is granted or not, a contract is formed." 1 Williston, Contracts § 79 at 261–62 (3d ed.1957).

Corbin is in agreement with the above view. 1 Corbin, supra, § 84 at 363–65. Thus our task is to decide whether plaintiff's letter is more reasonably interpreted as a qualified acceptance or as an absolute acceptance together with a mere inquiry concerning a collateral matter.

In making our decision we recognize that, as one text states, "The question whether a communication by an offeree is a conditional acceptance or counter-offer is not always easy to answer. It must be determined by the same common-sense process of interpretation that must be applied in so many other cases." 1 Corbin, supra § 82 at 353. In our opinion the language used in plaintiff's letter of September 8 is not consistent with an absolute acceptance accompanied by a request for a gratuitous benefit. We interpret the letter to impose a condition on plaintiff's acceptance of defendants' offer. The letter does not unequivocally state that even without the enumerated items plaintiff is willing to complete the contract. In fact, the letter seeks "confirmation" that the listed items "are a part of the transaction". Thus, far from being an independent, collateral request, the sale of the items in question is explicitly referred to as a part of the real estate transaction. Moreover, the letter goes on to stress the difficulty of finding replacements for these items. This is a further indication that plaintiff did not view the inclusion of the listed items as merely collateral or incidental to the real estate transaction.

A review of the relevant case law discloses that those cases in which an acceptance was found valid despite an accompanying conditional term generally involved a more definite expression of acceptance than the one in the case at bar. E.g., Moss v. Cogle, 267 Ala. 208, 101 So.2d 314 (1958); Jaybe Constr. Co. v. Beco, Inc., 3 Conn.Cir. 406, 216 A.2d 208, 212 (1965); Katz v. Pratt Street Realty Co., 257 Md. 103, 262 A.2d 540 (1970); Nelson v. Hamlin, 258

Mass. 331, 155 N.E. 18 (1927); Duprey v. Donahoe, 52 Wash.2d 129, 323 P.2d 903 (1958).

Accordingly, we hold that since the plaintiff's letter of acceptance dated September 8 was conditional, it operated as a rejection of the defendants' offer and no contractual obligation was created.

The plaintiff's appeal is denied and dismissed, the judgment appealed from is affirmed and the case is remanded to the Superior Court.

Paolino, J., did not participate.

————

RHODE ISLAND DEP'T OF TRANSPORTATION v. PROVIDENCE & WORCESTER R.R., 674 A.2d 1239 (R.I.1996). P & W owned a parcel of waterfront property in East Providence, Rhode Island. There were railroad tracks on the property. A statute, Rhode Island G.L. § 39–6.1–9, provided that "All rail properties within the state offered for sale by any railway corporation ... shall be offered for sale to the state in the first instance at the lowest price at which the railway corporation is willing to sell.... The state shall have a period of not more than thirty (30) days from receipt of the notification to accept the offer." P & W entered into a Real Estate Sales Agreement to sell the property to Promet for $100,000, subject to the State's option. Under the agreement with Promet, P & W was required to remove the tracks from the property. Pursuant to the statute, P & W then offered the property to the State for $100,000. The relevant State official accepted the offer in writing, but added, "Of course, you understand that certain wording in the Real Estate Sales Agreement [with Promet] relating to 'buyer' and obligations concerning the removal of track would be inappropriate to the purpose of the State's purchase." P & W claimed that no contract had been formed because the State's response was a conditional acceptance. Held, for the State:

> This Court has held that a valid acceptance "must be definite and unequivocal," Ardente v. Horan, 117 R.I. 254, 259, 366 A.2d 162, 165 (1976), and that an "acceptance which is equivocal or upon condition or with a limitation is a counteroffer and requires acceptance by the original offeror before a contractual relationship can exist." John Hancock Mutual Life Insurance Co. v. Dietlin, 97 R.I. 515, 518, 199 A.2d 311, 313 (1964). It is not equivocation, however, "if the offeree merely puts into words that which was already reasonably implied in the terms of the offer." 1 Corbin on Contracts, S 3.32 at 478–79 (rev. ed.1993). It is further the case that "an acceptance must receive a reasonable construction" and that "the mere addition of a collateral or immaterial [matter] will not prevent the formation of a contract." Raydon Exploration, Inc. v. Ladd, 902 F.2d 1496, 1500 (10th Cir.1990). See also Hoyt R. Matise Co. v. Zurn, 754 F.2d 560, 566 (5th Cir.1985) ("[t]o transmogrify a purported acceptance into a counteroffer, it must be shown that the acceptance differs in some material respect from the offer").

> The state's letter of acceptance points out that the name of the buyer in the original agreement would have to be changed. In our opinion, this statement simply reflected the obvious necessity to replace "the state" for "Promet" as the named buyer in the deed. Moreover, the letter's refer-

ence to P & W's obligation to Promet to remove tracks from the property as "inappropriate to the purpose of the State's purchase" did not add any terms or conditions to the contract but, instead, constituted a clear benefit to P & W. In pointing out that the "wording" that obligated P & W to remove tracks would be "inappropriate" in an agreement between P & W and the state, the state, in fact, relieved P & W from the obligation and expense it otherwise would have incurred in selling the property to Promet. When an offeree, in its acceptance of an offer, absolves the offeror of a material obligation, the "rules of contract construction and the 'rules of common sense' " preclude construing that absolution as an additional term that invalidates the acceptance. Textron, Inc. v. Aetna Casualty and Surety Co., 638 A.2d 537, 541 (R.I.1994)....

Therefore, we concur with the trial justice who found that the state validly accepted the option extended to it by P & W.

———

RESTATEMENT, SECOND, CONTRACTS § 39

[See Selected Source Materials Supplement]

———

RESTATEMENT, SECOND, CONTRACTS § 39, ILLUSTRATIONS 1–3

1. A offers B to sell him a parcel of land for $5,000, stating that the offer will remain open for thirty days. B replies, "I will pay $4800 for the parcel," and on A's declining that, B writes, within the thirty day period, "I accept your offer to sell for $5,000." There is no contract unless A's offer was [an option supported by consideration], or unless A's reply to the counter-offer manifested an intention to renew his original offer.

2. A makes the same offer to B as that stated in Illustration 1, and B replies, "Won't you take less?" A answers, "No." An acceptance thereafter by B within the thirty-day period is effective. B's inquiry was not a counter-offer, and A's original offer stands.

3. A makes the same offer to B as that stated in Illustration 1. B replies "I am keeping your offer under advisement, but if you wish to close the matter at once I will give you $4800." A does not reply, and within the thirty-day period B accepts the original offer. B's acceptance is effective.

———

PRICE v. OKLAHOMA COLLEGE OF OSTEOPATHIC MEDICINE AND SURGERY, 733 P.2d 1357 (Okla. Ct. App. 1986). Oklahoma College wrote a letter to Price, a member of its faculty, offering a one-year renewal of Price's appointment at an annual salary of $47,117. In the letter, the College asked Price to indicate his acceptance of the offer by signing and returning a copy. The words, "I accept the responsibilities of the appointment under the terms outlined above" were typed at the end of the letter, above a space for

Price's signature. Price signed and returned a copy of the letter, but underneath his signature he wrote, "Signed under protest that salary does not reflect guarantees under present and past Personnel Policies and that proper evaluation procedures were not followed." The College responded that Price's reply was not an acceptance, and that his appointment was terminated. Price sued for breach of contract. Held, for Price.

"The protest language did not in tenor or letter alter or purport to alter any term of the offer; it merely articulated the offeree's opinion that one term of the offer—the salary—had not been determined in accord with 'present and past personnel policies.' Execution of the acceptance was precisely in the manner directed by the offeror. The note added below the acceptance was a precative protest not substantially unlike he had written on the acceptance letter in prior years. The notation amounted to no more than saying I don't like your offer, I don't think it's right or fair, but I accept it. That and nothing more."

RESTATEMENT, SECOND, CONTRACTS § 59

[See Selected Source Materials Supplement]

CISG ART. 19

[See Selected Source Materials Supplement]

UNIDROIT PRINCIPLES OF INTERNATIONAL COMMERCIAL CONTRACTS ART. 2.1.11

[See Selected Source Materials Supplement]

PRINCIPLES OF EUROPEAN CONTRACT LAW ART. 2.208

[See Selected Source Materials Supplement]

NOTE ON THE MIRROR–IMAGE RULE

Under classical contract law, the rule that a conditional acceptance terminates the power of acceptance was accompanied by a closely connected rule known as the mirror-image or ribbon-matching rule. Under that rule, if a purported acceptance varied from the offer in any respect, no matter how minor, no contract was formed. Under modern contract law, the bite of this rule has been softened in two respects. First, UCC § 2–207 applies a special rule in the case of contracts for the sale of goods. Although section 2–207 is not limited in terms to form offers and form acceptances, it is obviously designed primarily to deal with the problems presented by forms, and normally is applied only to forms. UCC § 2–207 will be considered in Chapter 16, infra. Second, Comment a to Restatement Second § 59, which builds on UCC § 2–207, and is supported by some case law, provides that "a definite and seasonal expression of acceptance is operative despite the statement of additional or different terms if the acceptance is not made to depend on assent to the additional or different terms." This leaves open how a court is to determine whether in any given case the acceptance is or is not made to depend on assent to the additional or different terms.

LIVINGSTONE v. EVANS, Alberta Supreme Court, [1925] 4 D.L.R. 769. The correspondence between the parties was as follows: (1) A letter from Seller to Buyer offering to sell certain land for $1800 on terms specified. (2) A telegram from Buyer to Seller: "Send lowest cash price. Will give $1600 cash. Wire." (3) A telegraphic answer from Seller reading simply, "Cannot reduce price." (4) An acceptance from Buyer of the offer contained in Seller's letter, posted after the receipt of Seller's telegram. Held, there was a contract. Buyer's telegram (no. 2 above) being a counter—offer terminated Buyer's power of acceptance until Seller's telegraphic answer (no. 3 above) by implication renewed the offer.

CULTON v. GILCHRIST, 92 Iowa 718, 61 N.W. 384 (1894). A landlord offered his tenant a renewal of a lease on premises then occupied by the tenant. The tenant replied accepting the offer and adding, "Mr. Culton . . . I would like to put a small cookroom at the south side, so we could have some place to cook, wash, as it is very hard for my wife to only have one room. We have stood it quite a while through hot weather. I would like to do this myself, if in the lease you will give me the privilege of taking the same away providing I do not buy." The court stated, "All that is said about this cookroom, and the taking it away is a mere request, which [the landlord] might comply with or not at his election. The acceptance is complete and absolute, and depended in no way upon the matter relating to this cookroom."

RESTATEMENT, SECOND, CONTRACTS § 37

[See Selected Source Materials Supplement]

NOTE ON THE EFFECT OF THE OFFEROR'S DEATH
OR INCAPACITY BEFORE ACCEPTANCE

Under a traditional rule of contract law, the death or incapacity of an offeror terminates the offeree's power of acceptance if the offer is revocable when the death or incapacity occurs. This rule is unexceptionable where the offeree knows or has reason to know of the offeror's death or incapacity before he accepts the offer. The rule is also unexceptionable where, even in the absence of the rule, if a contract is formed the offeror's estate will be excused under the doctrine of changed circumstances. (An example is a contract that involves personal services by the offeror.) The bite of the rule, therefore, is that it applies even when (1) the offeree accepts at a time when he neither knows nor has reason to know of the offeror's death or incapacity and (2) in the absence of the rule, the offeror's death or incapacity would not excuse her estate from performance.

The bite of the rule should not be exaggerated. The rule would normally be inapplicable to offers made by entities that have perpetual existence, such as corporations and governmental bodies. Indeed, the rule would probably be deemed inapplicable to an offer made by most types of business organizations other than sole entrepreneurships—even those types that do not have perpetual existence. Probably too, the rule would be deemed inapplicable to persons who contract in a representative rather than an individual role, such as trustees and executors. Therefore, the principal application of the rule is to cases in which the offer is made by an individual and if a contract was formed, the individual's estate would not be excused by her death or incapacity.

The traditional rule has been criticized on the ground that it defeats the reasonable expectations of offerees who accept when they neither know nor have reason to know of the offeror's death or incapacity. Section 48 of Restatement Second adopts the traditional rule in the black letter, but criticizes the rule in the Comment. "This rule," the Comment states, "seems to be a relic of the obsolete view that a contract requires a 'meeting of minds,' and it is out of harmony with the modern doctrine that a manifestation of assent is effective without regard to actual mental assent."

Occasional cases have rejected the rule. In Swift & Co. v. Smigel, 115 N.J.Super. 391, 279 A.2d 895, 896, 899–900 (App.Div. 1971), aff'd, 60 N.J. 348, 289 A.2d 793 (1972), the offeror had been declared incompetent before the offeree, who did not know of the incompetence, accepted. The contract was held valid. The offer in *Swift* was a guaranty of payment for merchandise supplied to a corporation in which the offeror had a substantial interest. The court stated:

> In the present instance decedent promised plaintiff to make good any bills for provisions incurred by a corporate business enterprise in which he had a one-half stock interest. Had he not done so plaintiff presumably would not have taken on the business risk of selling to the corporation. It would seem to us that if plaintiff neither knew nor had any reason to know of decedent's later adjudication as an incompetent during any portion of the time it was making the deliveries which gave rise to the debts here sued on, plaintiff's reasonable expectations based on dece-

dent's original continuing promise would be unjustifiably defeated by denial of recovery.

If the situation is judged in terms of relative convenience, it would seem easier and more expectable for the guardian of the incompetent to notify at least those people with whom the incompetent had been doing business of the fact of adjudication than for the holder of a guaranty such as here to have to make a specific inquiry as to competency of the guarantor on each occasion of an advance of credit to the principal debtor.

The great majority of the cases, however, have upheld the rule that an offeror's death or incapacity terminates the offeree's power of acceptance. It is easy to understand why this should be so, if the application of the rule was limited to cutting off expectation damages against an individual's estate for nonperformance of a wholly executory contract. As a practical matter, a contract entered into by an individual will normally be worthless to her estate if she dies before performance is to occur, because there will be no practical way for the estate to perform. Think here of a sole entrepreneur who makes an offer in the ordinary course of business and then dies or becomes incapacitated. Consider also that there may be no one who can timely perform the contract on the estate's behalf, because it almost invariably takes time before a representative of an estate is appointed. Accordingly, the courts might understandably be reluctant to saddle an offeror's estate with liability for expectation damages where the offeror died or became incompetent before the offeree accepted.

On the other hand, as Richard Craswell points out, it is often in an offeror's interest that the offeree's power of acceptance not be terminated by the death or incapacity of the offeror unbeknown to the offeree. See Craswell, Offer, Acceptance, and Efficient Reliance, 48 Stan. L. Rev. 481, 515–16 (1996). In particular, in certain cases it is in the offeror's interest to empower the offeree to reliably take an action that the offer is intended to induce. An obvious case of this sort is one like *Swift*, in which the offer consists of a guarantee for an extension of credit by the offeree to a third party, which will benefit the offeror.

The competing considerations that bear on the effect of the death or incapacity of an offeror could be reconciled by a rule that if an offeree accepts an offer that was made by an individual who, unbeknown to the offeree, died or became incompetent after making the offer, the offeree should not be entitled to recover expectation damages against the individual's estate, but should be entitled to recover damages for any justifiable reliance that occurred between the time the offeree accepted and the time he learned of the offeror's death or incompetence.

———

SECTION 3. TERMINATION OF THE OFFEREE'S POWER OF ACCEPTANCE: REVOCATION

DICKINSON v. DODDS

In the Court of Appeal, Chancery Division, 1876.
2 Ch.Div. 463.

On Wednesday, the 10th of June, 1874, the defendant John Dodds signed and delivered to the plaintiff, George Dickinson, a memorandum, of which the material part was as follows:

"I hereby agree to sell to Mr. George Dickinson the whole of the dwellinghouses, garden ground, stabling, and outbuildings thereto belonging, situate at Croft, belonging to me, for the sum of £800. As witness my hand this tenth day of June, 1874.

"£800. [Signed] John Dodds."

"P.S.—This offer to be left over until Friday, 9 o'clock a.m. J.D. (the twelfth), 12th June, 1874.

[Signed] J. Dodds."

The bill alleged that Dodds understood and intended that the plaintiff should have until Friday, 9 a.m., within which to determine whether he would or would not purchase, and that he should absolutely have until that time the refusal of the property at the price of £800, and that the plaintiff in fact determined to accept the offer on the morning of Thursday, the 11th of June, but did not at once signify his acceptance to Dodds, believing that he had the power to accept it until 9 a.m. on the Friday.

In the afternoon of the Thursday the plaintiff was informed by a Mr. Berry that Dodds had been offering or agreeing to sell the property to Thomas Allan, the other defendant. Thereupon the plaintiff, at about half past seven in the evening, went to the house of Mrs. Burgess, the mother-in-law of Dodds, where he was then staying, and left with her a formal acceptance in writing of the offer to sell the property. According to the evidence of Mrs. Burgess this document never in fact reached Dodds, she having forgotten to give it to him.

On the following (Friday) morning, at about seven o'clock, Berry, who was acting as agent for Dickinson, found Dodds at the Darlington railway station, and handed to him a duplicate of the acceptance by Dickinson, and explained to Dodds its purport. He replied that it was too late, as he had sold the property. A few minutes later Dickinson himself found Dodds entering a railway carriage, and handed him another duplicate of the notice of acceptance, but Dodds declined to receive it, saying: "You are too late. I have sold the property."

It appeared that on the day before, Thursday, the 11th of June, Dodds had signed a formal contract for the sale of the property to the defendant Allan for £800, and had received from him a deposit of £40.

The bill in this suit prayed that the defendant Dodds might be decreed specifically to perform the contract of the 10th of June, 1874; that he might be restrained from conveying the property to Allan; that Allan might be restrained from taking any such conveyance; that, if any such conveyance had been or should be made, Allan might be declared a trustee of the property for, and might be directed to convey the property to, the plaintiff; and for damages.

The cause came on for hearing before Vice Chancellor Bacon on the 25th of January, 1876. [It was his opinion that Dodds could withdraw only by giving notice to Dickinson, in spite of Cooke v. Oxley, 3 T.R. 653, and that the contract took effect by the doctrine of relation back as of the time of the offer and hence was prior to the sale to Allan. He therefore decreed specific performance in favor of the plaintiff. From the decision both of the defendants appealed.]

JAMES, L.J., after referring to the document of the 10th of June, 1874, continued:

The document, though beginning "I hereby agree to sell," was nothing but an offer, and was only intended to be an offer, for the plaintiff himself tells us that he required time to consider whether he would enter into an agreement or not. Unless both parties had then agreed, there was no concluded agreement then made; it was in effect and substance only an offer to sell. The plaintiff, being minded not to complete the bargain at that time, added this memorandum: "This offer to be left over until Friday, 9 o'clock a.m. 12th June, 1874." That shows it was only an offer. There was no consideration given for the undertaking or promise, to whatever extent it may be considered binding, to keep the property unsold until 9 o'clock on Friday morning; but apparently Dickinson was of opinion, and probably Dodds was of the same opinion, that he (Dodds) was bound by that promise, and could not in any way withdraw from it, or retract it, until 9 o'clock on Friday morning, and this probably explains a good deal of what afterwards took place. But it is clear settled law, on one of the clearest principles of law, that this promise, being a mere nudum pactum, was not binding, and that at any moment before a complete acceptance by Dickinson of the offer, Dodds was as free as Dickinson himself.

Well, that being the state of things, it is said that the only mode in which Dodds could assert that freedom was by actually and distinctly saying to Dickinson, "Now I withdraw my offer." It appears to me that there is neither principle nor authority for the proposition that there must be an express and actual withdrawal of the offer, or what is called a retraction. It must, to constitute a contract, appear that the two minds were at one, at the same moment of time, that is, that there was an offer continuing up to the time of the acceptance. If there was not such a continuing offer, then the acceptance comes to nothing. Of course it may well be that the one man is bound in some way or other to let the other man know that his mind with regard to the offer has been changed; but in this case, beyond all question, the plaintiff knew that Dodds was no longer minded to sell the property to him as plainly and clearly as if Dodds had told him in so many words, "I withdraw the offer." This is evident from the plaintiff's own statements in the bill.

The plaintiff says in effect that, having heard and knowing that Dodds was no longer minded to sell to him and that he was selling or had sold to some one else, thinking that he could not in point of law withdraw his offer, meaning to fix him to it, and endeavoring to bind him: "I went to the house where he was lodging, and saw his mother-in-law, and left with her an acceptance of the offer, knowing all the while that he had entirely changed his mind. I got an agent to watch for him at 7 o'clock the next morning, and I went to the train just before 9 o'clock, in order that I might catch him and give him my notice of acceptance just before 9 o'clock, and when that occurred he told my agent, and he told me, 'You are too late,' and he then threw back the paper." It is to my mind quite clear that before there was any attempt at acceptance by the plaintiff, he was perfectly well aware that Dodds had changed his mind, and that he had in fact agreed to sell the property to Allan. It is impossible, therefore, to say there was ever that existence of the same mind between the two parties which is essential in point of law to the making of an agreement. I am of opinion, therefore, that the plaintiff has failed to prove that there was any binding contract between Dodds and himself. . . .

[The bill] will be dismissed with costs.

[The concurring opinion of MELLISH, L.J., is omitted.]

———

RESTATEMENT, SECOND, CONTRACTS §§ 42, 43

[See Selected Source Materials Supplement]

———

CISG ART. 16

[See Selected Source Materials Supplement]

———

UNIDROIT PRINCIPLES OF INTERNATIONAL COMMERCIAL CONTRACTS ART. 2.1.4

[See Selected Source Materials Supplement]

———

PRINCIPLES OF EUROPEAN CONTRACT LAW ART. 2.202

[See Selected Source Materials Supplement]

———

NOTE ON CONTRACT PRACTICE

In 1988, Professor Russell Weintraub sent a questionaire to the general counsels of 182 corporations of various sizes, asking for their company's views on certain contracts issues. Weintraub, A Survey of Contract Practice and Policy, 1992 Wisc.L.Rev. 1. Several questions in the survey concerned firm offers. The results were as follows: 76% of the respondents reported that their companies received firm offers. Of these, 95% reported that they relied on the firm offers they received. Correspondingly, 73% percent of the respondents reported that their companies made firm offers to other companies. Of these, 97% reported that they expected offerees to rely on their firm offers.

———

RESTATEMENT, SECOND, CONTRACTS § 45

[See Selected Source Materials Supplement]

RAGOSTA v. WILDER

Supreme Court of Vermont, 1991.
156 Vt. 390, 592 A.2d 367.

Before ALLEN, C.J., and PECK, GIBSON, DOOLEY and MORSE, JJ.

PECK, JUSTICE.

Defendant appeals from a judgment ordering him to convey to plaintiffs a piece of real property known as "The Fork Shop." Defendant argues that the court improperly found that a binding contract existed and that it misapplied the doctrine of equitable estoppel. He also contends that the ruling cannot be upheld under promissory estoppel principles since the court failed to examine the extent to which enforcement of defendant's promise to sell was required to prevent injustice. Because the trial court's ruling cannot stand on contract or equitable estoppel grounds and because the court's analysis of promissory estoppel is inextricably bound in its contractual analysis, we reverse and remand the cause for further proceedings consistent with the principles expressed herein.

In 1985, plaintiffs became interested in purchasing "The Fork Shop" from defendant, but preliminary negotiations between the parties were fruitless. In 1987, plaintiffs learned that defendant was again considering selling "The Fork Shop," [and] mailed him a letter offering to purchase the property along with a check for $2,000 and began arrangements to obtain the necessary financing. By letter dated September 28, 1987, defendant returned the $2,000 check explaining that he had two properties "up for sale" and that he would not sign an acceptance to plaintiffs' offer because "that would tie up both these properties until [there was] a closing." In the letter, he also made the following counter-offer:

> I will sell you The Fork Shop and its property as listed in book 35, at page 135 of the Brookfield Land Records on 17 April 1972, for $88,-000.00—(Eighty-eight thousand dollars), at anytime up until the 1st of November 1987 that you appear with me at the Randolph National Bank with said sum. At which time they will give you a certified deed to this property or to your agent as directed, providing said property has not been sold.

On October 1st, the date plaintiffs received the letter, they called defendant. The court found that during the conversation plaintiffs told defendant that "the terms and conditions of his offer were acceptable and that they would in fact prepare to accept the offer." Defendant assured plaintiffs that there was no one else currently interested in purchasing "The Fork Shop."

On October 6th, plaintiffs informed defendant that they would not close the sale on October 8th as discussed previously but that they would come to Vermont on October 10th. On October 8th, defendant called plaintiffs and informed them that he was no longer willing to sell "The Fork Shop." The trial court found that, at that time, defendant was aware plaintiffs "had processed their loan application and were prepared to close." Plaintiffs informed defendant that they would be at the Randolph National Bank at 10:00 a.m. on October 15th with the $88,000 purchase price and in fact appeared. Defendant did not. Plaintiffs claim they incurred $7,499.23 in loan closing costs.

Plaintiffs sued for specific performance arguing that defendant had contracted to sell the property to them. They alleged moreover that defendant knew they would have to incur costs to obtain financing for the purchase but assured them that the sale would go through and that they relied on his assurances.

The trial court concluded that defendant "made an offer in writing which could only be accepted by performance prior to the deadline." It concluded further that defendant could not revoke his offer on October 8th because plaintiffs, relying on the offer, had already begun performance and that defendant should be estopped from revoking the offer on a theory of equitable estoppel. It ordered defendant to convey to plaintiffs "The Fork Shop" for $88,000. This appeal followed.

I.

Plaintiffs claim that defendant's letter of September 28, 1987 created a contract to sell "The Fork Shop" to them unless the property was sold to another buyer. Rather, defendant's letter contains an offer to sell the property for $88,000, which the trial court found could only be accepted "by performance prior to the deadline," and a promise to keep the offer open unless the property were sold to another buyer. Defendant received no consideration for either promise. In fact, defendant returned plaintiffs' check for $2,000 which would have constituted consideration for the promise to keep the offer open, presumably because he did not wish to make a firm offer. Thus, the promise to keep the offer to sell open was not enforceable and, absent the operation of equitable estoppel, defendant could revoke the offer to sell the property at any time before plaintiffs accepted it. See *Buchannon v. Billings,* 127 Vt. 69, 75, 238 A.2d 638, 642 (1968) ("An option is a continuing offer, and *if supported by a consideration,* it cannot be withdrawn before the time limit.") (emphasis added).

Plaintiffs argue that the actions they undertook to obtain financing, which were detrimental to them, could constitute consideration for the promise to keep the offer to sell open. Their argument is unconvincing. Although plaintiffs are correct in stating that a detriment may constitute consideration, they ignore the rule that "[t]o constitute consideration, a performance or a return promise must be bargained for." Restatement (Second) of Contracts § 71(1) (1981). "A performance or return promise is bargained for if it is sought by the promisor in exchange for his promise and is given by the promisee in exchange for that promise." *Id.* at § 71(2). Plaintiffs began to seek financing even before defendant made a definite offer to sell the property. Whatever detriment they suffered was not in exchange for defendant's promise to keep the offer to sell open.

The trial court ruled that the offer to sell "The Fork Shop" could only be accepted by performance but concluded that in obtaining financing plaintiffs began performance and that therefore defendant could not revoke the offer to sell once plaintiffs incurred the cost of obtaining financing. Section 45 of the Restatement (Second) of Contracts provides that "[w]here an offer invites an offeree to accept by rendering a performance and does not invite a promissory acceptance, an option contract is created when the offeree tenders or begins the invited performance or tenders a beginning of it." However, "[w]hat is begun or tendered must be part of the actual performance invited in order to preclude revocation under this Section." *Id.* at comment f.

Here, plaintiffs were merely engaged in preparation for performance. The court itself found only that "plaintiffs had changed their position in order to tender performance." At most, they obtained financing and assured defendant that they would pay; plaintiffs never tendered to defendant or even began to tender the $88,000 purchase price. Thus, they never accepted defendant's offer and no contract was ever created. See *Multicare Medical Center v. State Social & Health Services,* 114 Wash.2d 572, 584, 790 P.2d 124, 131 (1990) ("under a unilateral contract, an offer cannot be accepted by promising to perform; rather, the offeree must accept, if at all, by performance, and the contract then becomes executed").*

II.

Defendant claims next that the court was not justified in applying equitable estoppel in this case. We agree.

> One who invokes the doctrine of equitable estoppel has the burden of establishing each of its constituent elements. Four essential elements must be established: first, the party to be estopped must know the facts; second, the party being estopped must intend that his conduct shall be acted upon or the acts must be such that the party asserting the estoppel has a right to believe it is so intended; third, the latter must be ignorant of the true facts; and finally, the party asserting the estoppel must rely on the conduct of the party to be estopped to his detriment.

Fisher v. Poole, 142 Vt. 162, 168, 453 A.2d 408, 411–12 (1982) (citations omitted).

Equitable estoppel is inapplicable here because there were no facts known to defendant but unknown to plaintiffs. Plaintiffs cannot have acted on an understanding that defendant would definitely convey the property to them. On its face, defendant's offer stated only that he would convey the property to plaintiffs if he did not convey it to another party first. The trial court acknowledged that if defendant had sold "The Fork Shop" to another party plaintiffs would not have been entitled to relief. Thus, plaintiffs had no assurance that defendant would definitely convey the property to them even if on October 1st defendant told them that there was no one else interested in buying the property at that time. Moreover, plaintiffs engaged in obtaining financing for the purchase even before defendant made any offer to them whatsoever. They understood, at the time they obtained financing for the transaction, that they were assuming a risk that they would be unable to purchase the property in question. Since the plaintiffs had not tendered

---

* Because defendant specified that the manner of acceptance would be performance, plaintiffs' argument that they accepted defendant's offer over the telephone must fail. In fact, plaintiffs admitted in their depositions that they were very worried that the property would be sold to someone else prior to closing. Thus, they should have understood that they had no enforceable contract until closing.

performance and did not establish the elements for the application of equitable estoppel, defendant was entitled to withdraw his offer when he did.

III.

In the course of analyzing the case under part performance and equitable estoppel theories, the trial court cited promissory estoppel principles. It noted, "Plaintiffs relied on the conduct of the Defendant to their detriment when they prepared for and tendered performance" and concluded that defendant's conduct induced plaintiffs to begin performance by obtaining financing.

> A promise which the promisor should reasonably expect to induce action or forbearance on the part of the promisee or a third person and which does induce such action or forbearance is binding if injustice can be avoided only by enforcement of the promise. The remedy granted for breach may be limited as justice requires.

Restatement (Second) of Contracts § 90(1). This principle is distinct from part performance since the action or forbearance involved need not constitute part performance. While the court's order cannot be upheld under a part performance theory, its ruling may be appropriate on promissory estoppel grounds. We cannot affirm the order on those grounds, however, because the trial court, in ruling that the promise must be enforced, erroneously relied on a part performance theory. Cf. *Price v. Price*, 149 Vt. 118, 122, 541 A.2d 79, 82 (1987) (order must be reversed and remanded where court may have relied on inappropriate considerations for its ruling). Under promissory estoppel, plaintiffs are entitled to enforcement of defendant's promise only if the promise induced them to take action "of a definite and substantial character," and if "injustice [*can*] *be avoided only* by enforcement of the promise." *Stacy v. Merchants Bank*, 144 Vt. 515, 521, 482 A.2d 61, 64 (1984) (emphasis added) (citing Restatement (Second) of Contracts § 90).

On remand the court shall consider the case under promissory estoppel only and determine what remedy, if any, is necessary to prevent injustice. In making this determination the court should consider the fact that plaintiffs incurred the expense of obtaining financing although they could not be certain that the property would be sold to them. . . .

Reversed and the cause remanded for further proceedings consistent with the principles expressed herein.

NOTE ON OFFERS FOR UNILATERAL CONTRACTS

The court in *Ragosta* drew a sharp distinction between *preparing* to perform an act pursuant to an offer for a unilateral contract and *beginning* to perform the act. To understand why the court drew this distinction, it is necessary to briefly trace the doctrinal history concerning offers for a unilateral contract—that is, an offer for a contract to be formed by the exchange of a promise (in the form of an offer) and an act, rather than an offer for a contract to be formed by an exchange of promises.

It was a rule of classical contract law that an offer for a unilateral contract could be revoked at any time before the designated act had been completed, even if performance of the act had begun. This rule was exemplified in a pair of famous hypotheticals. In one, A says to B, "I will give you $100 if you walk across the Brooklyn Bridge." After B has walked halfway across the bridge, A overtakes B and revokes. In the other, A offers B $50 to climb a flagpole. After B has climbed halfway up the flagpole, A calls out to B and revokes. The result under classical contract law was the same in both hypotheticals: the revocation was effective, on the ground that an offer for a unilateral contract is revocable until performance of the act has been completed, even if performance had begun. Too bad for B.

The rule that an offer for a unilateral contract is revocable until the act has been completed was justified almost exclusively on the basis of deductive reasoning. The major premises of this reasoning were that only a bargained-for promise was enforceable, and that an offer could be revoked at any time prior to acceptance unless the offeror had made a bargained-for promise to hold the offer open. The minor premises were that an offer for a unilateral contract is not bargained for, and is not accepted until the act of performance that the offer calls for has occurred, that is, has been completed. The deductive conclusion was that an offer for a unilateral contract is revocable until performance has been completed.

The unilateral-contract rule defeated the reasonable expectations of offerees. Tiersma has put this point very well:

> [N]o reasonable person would intentionally create the sort of agreement that the traditional theory of unilateral contracts assumes. Suppose that a person, asserting his freedom to contract and his mastery over his offer, specifically intends to make a promise that will bind him not at the time he makes it, but only after the other party has completed a particular act in exchange. In other words, this promisor wishes to create the traditional unilateral contract. For example, he might tell the offeree that if she paints his house, he will—once she is finished—commit himself to paying her $1000. He makes it clear that he does not wish to be bound until she is completely finished, explaining to her that before she is finished he may revoke with impunity. What rational person would even buy the paint if she believed the speaker had not committed himself? The fact of the matter ... is that very reasonable people spend substantial time and money doing the sorts of things that unilateral contracts attempt to induce them to do. The only rational explanation for such behavior is that people believe the speaker is in fact committed then and there to paying the price if the conditions of the offer are met.

Peter Meijes Tiersma, Reassessing Unilateral Contracts: The Role of Offer, Acceptance and Promise, 26 U.C. Davis L. Rev. 1, 29 (1992).

Furthermore, the unilateral-contract rule was against the interests of offerors as a class. An actor makes an offer for a unilateral contract because she thinks her interests are best served by such an offer. It is in the interests of an actor who makes an offer for a unilateral contract that the offeree act under the offer—otherwise, the offer would not be made—and correspondingly that the offeree begin acting as quickly as reasonably possible. If, however, offers for unilateral contracts were revocable before performance was completed, offerees would not act under such offers, or at least would act at a much lower rate, because of the substantial risks of forfeiture that such action would entail if the offeror revokes before the act has been completed.

The framers of Restatement First—in particular, Williston, as the Reporter—understood that the unilateral-contract rule was unsatisfactory. However, because classical contract law was conceived as an axiomatic system, and the unilateral-contract rule seemed to flow inexorably from some of the axioms, Williston had trouble in figuring out how to break away from the rule without breaking away from the axioms on which he conceived contract law to rest. Williston was willing to bend, but not to break. The result was Section 45 of the First Restatement, which provided:

> If an offer for a unilateral contract is made, and part of the consideration requested in the offer is given or tendered by the offeree in response thereto, the offeror is bound by a contract, the duty of immediate performance of which is conditional on the full consideration being given or tendered within the time stated in the offer, or, if no time is stated therein, within a reasonable time.

Despite the fact that Section 45 liability was triggered only if the offeree took a certain kind of action, Section 45 was not conceptualized as reliance-based. If it had been conceptualized that way, then the section would have been unnecessary, because the problem it addressed could have been solved by its even more famous cousin, Section 90. Instead, the beginning of performance was—and under Restatement Second still is—conceptualized as completing an option contract, enforceable by expectation damages. The theory is as follows: an offer for a unilateral contract carries with it an implied promise that if part of the requested performance is given or tendered, the offeror will not revoke the offer. Rendering (or tendering) part performance completes a bargain for that promise. This makes the promise enforceable as an option under the bargain theory of consideration.

In order to maintain this conceptualization, the text and comment of Section 45, as formulated in both the First and Second Restatements, drew a sharp distinction between beginning to perform and preparing to perform. Under Section 45 of Restatement First, beginning to perform completed a bargain and therefore made the offeror's promise to hold the offer open enforceable. In contrast, action by the offeree other than beginning to perform had no effect under Section 45, because it would not complete a Section 45 bargain—although the Comment to Restatement First added that such action could have an effect under Section 90, which is not bargain-based:

> The main offer [for a unilateral contract] includes as a subsidiary promise, necessarily implied, that if part of the requested performance is given, the offeror will not revoke his offer.... Part performance ... may thus furnish consideration for the subsidiary [promise]. Moreover, merely acting in justifiable reliance on an offer may in some cases serve as sufficient reason for making a promise binding (see § 90).

Section 45 of Restatement Second carries forward the approach of the First Restatement.

The distinction drawn in Section 45, and Ragosta v. Wilder, between beginning to perform and preparing to perform, is not easy to justify. For example, suppose A offers B $10,000 to B if B produces a solution to a famous mathematical problem. B begins by developing some new techniques that will be needed to solve the problem, but will also have independent significance. Has B prepared to perform or has he begun to perform? And why should it matter? As James Gordley observes, under the preparation-versus-performance distinction if the offeree takes one step on the Brooklyn Bridge, the offeror is bound, but if the offeree engages in massive preparations to get ready to cross the Bridge, the offeror is not bound. James Gordley, Enforcing Promises, 82 Cal. L. Rev. 547, 605 (1995).

———

DRENNAN v. STAR PAVING CO.

Supreme Court of California, 1958.
51 Cal.2d 409, 333 P.2d 757.

TRAYNOR, JUSTICE. Defendant appeals from a judgment for plaintiff in an action to recover damages caused by defendant's refusal to perform certain paving work according to a bid it submitted to plaintiff.

On July 28, 1955, plaintiff, a licensed general contractor, was preparing a bid on the "Monte Vista School Job" in the Lancaster school district. Bids had to be submitted before 8:00 p.m. Plaintiff testified that it was customary in that area for general contractors to receive the bids of subcontractors by telephone on the day set for bidding and to rely on them in computing their own bids. Thus on that day plaintiff's secretary, Mrs. Johnson, received by telephone between fifty and seventy-five subcontractors' bids for various parts of the school job. As each bid came in, she wrote it on a special form, which she brought into plaintiff's office. He then posted it on a master cost sheet setting forth the names and bids of all subcontractors. His own bid had to include the names of subcontractors who were to perform one-half of one per cent or more of the construction work, and he had also to provide a bidder's bond of ten per cent of his total bid of $317,385 as a guarantee that he would enter the contract if awarded the work.*

Late in the afternoon, Mrs. Johnson had a telephone conversation with Kenneth R. Hoon, an estimater for defendant. He gave his name and telephone number and stated that he was bidding for defendant for the paving work at the Monte Vista School according to plans and specifications and that his bid was $7,131.60. At Mrs. Johnson's request he repeated his bid. Plaintiff listened to the bid over an extension telephone in his office and posted it on the master sheet after receiving the bid form from Mrs. Johnson. Defendant's was the lowest bid for the paving. Plaintiff computed his own bid accordingly and submitted it with the name of defendant as the subcontractor for the paving. When the bids were opened on July 28th, plaintiff's proved to be the lowest, and he was awarded the contract.

On his way to Los Angeles the next morning plaintiff stopped at defendant's office. The first person he met was defendant's construction engineer, Mr. Oppenheimer. Plaintiff testified: "I introduced myself and he immediately told me that they had made a mistake in their bid to me the night before, they couldn't do it for the price they had bid, and I told him I would expect him to carry through with their original bid because I had used it in compiling my bid and the job was being awarded them. And I would have to go and do the job according to my bid and I would expect them to do the same."

* Under a "bidder's" or "bid" bond, a Surety promises the person who is receiving bids (the "Obligee"), that if the bidder is awarded the contract but refuses to enter into it, the Surety will pay damages up to a stipulated amount (called "the penalty") that is set in the bond. (Footnote by ed.)

Defendant refused to do the paving work for less than $15,000. Plaintiff testified that he "got figures from other people" and after trying for several months to get as low a bid as possible engaged L & H Paving Company, a firm in Lancaster, to do the work for $10,948.60.

The trial court found on substantial evidence that defendant made a definite offer to do the paving on the Monte Vista job according to the plans and specifications for $7,131.60, and that plaintiff relied on defendant's bid in computing his own bid for the school job and naming defendant therein as the subcontractor for the paving work. Accordingly, it entered judgment for plaintiff in the amount of $3,817.00 (the difference between defendant's bid and the cost of the paving to plaintiff) plus costs.

Defendant contends that there was no enforceable contract between the parties on the ground that it made a revocable offer and revoked it before plaintiff communicated his acceptance to defendant.

There is no evidence that defendant offered to make its bid irrevocable in exchange for plaintiff's use of its figures in computing his bid. Nor is there evidence that would warrant interpreting plaintiff's use of defendant's bid as the acceptance thereof, binding plaintiff, on condition he received the main contract, to award the subcontract to defendant. In sum, there was neither an option supported by consideration nor a bilateral contract binding on both parties.

Plaintiff contends, however, that he relied to his detriment on defendant's offer and that defendant must therefore answer in damages for its refusal to perform. Thus the question is squarely presented: Did plaintiff's reliance make defendant's offer irrevocable?

Section 90 of the Restatement of Contracts states: "A promise which the promisor should reasonably expect to induce action or forbearance of a definite and substantial character on the part of the promisee and which does induce such action or forbearance is binding if injustice can be avoided only by enforcement of the promise." This rule applies in this state. . . .

Defendant's offer constituted a promise to perform on such conditions as were stated expressly or by implication therein or annexed thereto by operation of law. (See 1 Williston, Contracts [3rd ed.], § 24A, p. 56, § 61, p. 196.) Defendant had reason to expect that if its bid proved the lowest it would be used by plaintiff. It induced "action . . . of a definite and substantial character on the part of the promisee."

Had defendant's bid expressly stated or clearly implied that it was revocable at any time before acceptance we would treat it accordingly. It was silent on revocation, however, and we must therefore determine whether there are conditions to the right of revocation imposed by law or reasonably inferable in fact. In the analogous problem of an offer for a unilateral contract, the theory is now obsolete that the offer is revocable at any time before complete performance. Thus section 45 of the Restatement of Contracts provides: "If an offer for a unilateral contract is made, and part of the consideration requested in the offer is given or tendered by the offeree in response thereto, the offeror is bound by a contract, the duty of immediate performance of which is conditional on the full consideration being given or tendered within the time stated in the offer, or, if no time is stated therein, within a reasonable time." In explanation, comment *b* states that the "main offer includes as a subsidiary promise, necessarily implied, that if part of the requested performance is given, the offeror will not revoke his offer, and that if tender is made it will be accepted. Part performance or tender may thus furnish consideration for the subsidiary promise. Moreover, merely acting in justifiable reliance on an offer may in some cases serve as sufficient reason for making a promise binding (see § 90)."

Whether implied in fact or law, the subsidiary promise serves to preclude the injustice that would result if the offer could be revoked after the offeree had acted in detrimental reliance thereon. Reasonable reliance resulting in a foreseeable prejudicial change in position affords a compelling basis also for implying a subsidiary promise not to revoke an offer for a bilateral contract.

The absence of consideration is not fatal to the enforcement of such a promise. It is true that in the case of unilateral contracts the Restatement finds consideration for the implied subsidiary promise in the part performance of the bargained-for exchange, but its reference to section 90 makes clear that consideration for such a promise is not always necessary. The very purpose of section 90 is to make a promise binding even though there was no consideration "in the sense of something that is bargained for and given in exchange." (See 1 Corbin, Contracts 634 et seq.) Reasonable reliance serves to hold the offeror in lieu of the consideration ordinarily required to make the offer binding. In a case involving similar facts the Supreme Court of South Dakota stated that "we believe that reason and justice demand that the doctrine [of section 90] be applied to the present facts. We cannot believe that by accepting this doctrine as controlling in the state of facts before us we will abolish the requirement of a consideration in contract cases, in any different sense than an ordinary estoppel abolishes some legal requirement in its application. We are of the opinion, therefore, that the defendants in executing the agreement [which was not supported by consideration] made a promise which they should have reasonably expected would induce the plaintiff to submit a bid based thereon to the Government, that such promise did induce this action, and that injustice can be avoided only by enforcement of the promise." Northwestern Engineering Co. v. Ellerman, 69 S.D. 397, 408, 10 N.W.2d 879, 884; see also, Robert Gordon, Inc. v. Ingersoll–Rand Co., 7 Cir., 117 F.2d 654, 661; cf. James Baird Co. v. Gimbel Bros., 2 Cir., 64 F.2d 344.

When plaintiff used defendant's offer in computing his own bid, he bound himself to perform in reliance on defendant's terms. Though defendant did not bargain for this use of its bid neither did defendant make it idly, indifferent to whether it would be used or not. On the contrary it is reasonable to suppose that defendant submitted its bid to obtain the subcontract. It was bound to realize the substantial possibility that its bid would be the lowest, and that it would be included by plaintiff in his bid. It was to its own interest that the contractor be awarded the general contract; the lower the subcontract bid, the lower the general contractor's bid was likely to be and the greater its chance of acceptance and hence the greater defendant's chance of getting the paving subcontract. Defendant had reason not only to expect plaintiff to rely on its bid but to want him to. Clearly defendant had a stake in plaintiff's reliance on its bid. Given this interest and the fact that plaintiff is bound by his own bid, it is only fair that plaintiff should have at least an opportunity to accept defendant's bid after the general contract has been awarded to him.

It bears noting that a general contractor is not free to delay acceptance after he has been awarded the general contract in the hope of getting a better price. Nor can he reopen bargaining with the subcontractor and at the same time claim a continuing right to accept the original offer. See, R.J. Daum Const. Co. v. Child, Utah, 247 P.2d 817, 823. In the present case plaintiff promptly informed defendant that plaintiff was being awarded the job and that the subcontract was being awarded to defendant.

Defendant contends, however, that its bid was the result of mistake and that it was therefore entitled to revoke it. It relies on the rescission cases of M.F. Kemper Const. Co. v. City of Los Angeles, 37 Cal.2d 696, 235 P.2d 7, and Brunzell Const. Co. v. G.J. Weisbrod, Inc., 134 Cal.App.2d 278, 285 P.2d 989. See also, Lemoge Electric v. San Mateo County, 46 Cal.2d 659, 662, 297 P.2d 638. In those cases, however, the bidder's mistake was known or should have been known to the offeree, and the offeree could be placed in status quo. Of course, if plaintiff had reason to believe that defendant's bid was in error, he could not justifiably rely on it, and section 90 would afford no basis for enforcing it. Robert Gordon, Inc. v. Ingersoll–Rand, Inc., 7 Cir., 117 F.2d 654, 660. Plaintiff, however, had no reason to know that defendant had made a mistake in submitting its bid, since there was usually a variance of 160 per cent between the highest and lowest bids for paving in the desert around Lancaster. He committed himself to performing the main contract in reliance on defendant's figures. Under these circumstances defendant's mistake, far from relieving it of its obligation, constitutes an additional reason for enforcing it, for it misled plaintiff as to the cost of doing the paving. Even had it been clearly understood that defendant's offer was revocable until accepted, it would not necessarily follow that defendant had no duty to exercise reasonable care in preparing its bid. It presented its bid with knowledge of the substantial possibility that it would be used by plaintiff; it could foresee the harm that would ensue from an erroneous underestimate of the cost. Moreover, it was motivated by its own business interest. Whether or not these considerations alone would justify recovery for negligence had the case been tried on that theory (see Biakanja v. Irving, 49 Cal.2d 647, 650, 320 P.2d 16), they are persuasive that defendant's mistake should not defeat recovery under the rule of section 90 of the Restatement, Contracts. As between the subcontractor who made the bid and the general contractor who reasonably relied on it, the loss resulting from the mistake should fall on the party who caused it . . . .

There is no merit in defendant's contention that plaintiff failed to state a cause of action, on the ground that the complaint failed to allege that plaintiff attempted to mitigate the damages or that they could not have been mitigated. Plaintiff alleged that after defendant's default, "plaintiff had to procure the services of the L & H Co. to perform said asphaltic paving for the sum of $10,948.60." Plaintiff's uncontradicted evidence showed that he spent several months trying to get bids from other subcontractors and that he took the lowest bid. Clearly he acted reasonably to mitigate damages. In any event any uncertainty in plaintiff's allegation as to damages could have been raised by special demurrer. Code Civ.Proc. § 430, subd. 9. It was not so raised and was therefore waived. Code Civ.Proc. § 434.

The judgment is affirmed.

GIBSON, C.J., and SHENK, SCHAUER, SPENCE and McCOMB, JJ., concur.

———

UCC § 2–205

[See Selected Source Materials Supplement]

———

DODGE, TEACHING THE CISG IN CONTRACTS, 50 J. Leg. Ed. 72 (2000). "Under the common law, an offer is freely revocable, even if the offeror has promised to hold it open, unless that promise is supported by consideration or reliance. The UCC, of course, changes this rule, allowing a merchant to make an irrevocable offer—a "firm offer"—without the need for consideration. But the UCC's firm-offer rule contains a number of restrictions: the offeror must be a merchant; the offer must be in a signed writing; the offer must contain an "assurance that it will be held open"; and the period of irrevocability may not exceed three months.

"CISG Article 16 allows an offeror to make a firm offer without these limitations:

> (1) Until a contract is concluded an offer may be revoked if the revocation reaches the offeree before he has dispatched an acceptance.

> (2) However, an offer cannot be revoked:

>> (a) if it indicates, whether by stating a fixed time for acceptance or otherwise, that it is irrevocable; or

>> (b) if it was reasonable for the offeree to rely on the offer as being irrevocable and the offeree has acted in reliance on the offer.

"As one can see, Article 16 does not require that the offeror be a merchant or that the offer be in a signed writing, and there is no limit on the period of irrevocability. Article 16 does not even require an express assurance that the offer will be held open. It requires only that the offer 'indicate that it is irrevocable' and it makes clear that an offer may do this 'by stating a fixed time for acceptance.' If an offer simply stated that it would expire after thirty days, the UCC would not treat the offer as 'firm' and would allow the offeror to revoke before the thirty days were up. The CISG, on the other hand, would treat the offer as being irrevocable during the thirty-day period. Article 16(2)(b), like Restatement (Second) § 87(2), provides for an offer to become irrevocable because of the offeree's reliance.

"Article 16 reflects a compromise between the civil law tradition, which presumes that offers are irrevocable, and the common law tradition, which presumes the opposite. Article 16(1) provides that offers are revocable, as under the common law, but Article 16(2) creates broad exceptions that will lead many offers to be irrevocable in practice."

———

PRELOAD TECHNOLOGY, INC. v. A.B. & J. CONSTRUCTION CO., INC., 696 F.2d 1080, 1089 (5th Cir.1983). "Another limitation on the doctrine of promissory estoppel in [suits by a general contractor alleging reliance on a subcontractor's bid] is the prohibition against 'bid shopping,' 'bid chiseling' and related practices sometimes engaged in by general contractors after they have been awarded the general contract and before they subcontract the particular part of the work in dispute. . . . 'Bid shopping' commonly refers to a general contractor's seeking of bids from subcontractors other than the one whose bid amount the general used in calculating its own bid, and often involves the general's informing the other subcontractors of the amount of the low bid and inviting them to undercut it. 'Bid chiseling' usually refers to the general contractor's attempt to negotiate a lower price than that bid from the subcontractor whose bid figure the general employed in calculating its own bid, frequently by threatening to subcontract the work to a third party. . . . When these practices are engaged in, recovery by the general contractor under § 90 may be denied on a variety of theories, viz: that the general contractor did not in fact rely on the subcontractor's bid, or failed to accept it within a reasonable time, or rejected it by a counter-offer, or, perhaps more persuasively, because in such circumstances there is a failure to meet § 90's requirement that 'injustice can be avoided only by enforcement of the promise.' "

ALLEN M. CAMPBELL CO. v. VIRGINIA METAL INDUSTRIES, INC., 708 F.2d 930 (4th Cir.1983). Campbell, a general contractor, proposed to bid on a contract to construct housing. In that connection, Virginia Metal telephoned Campbell and quoted a price to supply hollow metal doors and frames that were required by the contract plans and specification. Campbell was awarded the contract, but Virginia Metal backed out of its bid. Campbell sued. The case was governed by North Carolina law. Held, Virginia Metal was bound to its bid under the theory of promissory estoppel. Although the bid was oral, the UCC Statute of Frauds was not a defense, because under North Carolina law promissory estoppel overcomes the Statute of Frauds.

RESTATEMENT, SECOND, CONTRACTS § 87(2)

[See Selected Source Materials Supplement]

NOTE ON RESTATEMENT SECOND § 87(2)

At first glance, it is not easy to see how the operation of Restatement Second § 87(2) differs from that of § 45, since both sections concern offers that have been relied upon. At least in the view of those who prepared Restatement Second, the difference is rooted in the distinction discussed in the Note on Offers for Unilateral Contracts, supra, between beginning to perform and preparing to perform. According to the Comment to Section 45, that section (which in any event only applies to offers for unilateral contracts) is applicable to beginning to perform, but not to preparing to perform. The

Comment goes on to say, however, that "Preparations to perform may ... constitute justifiable reliance sufficient to make the offeror's promise binding under Section 87(2)."

Thus the framers of the Restatement apparently believed that where an offeree has actually *begun* to perform pursuant to an offer for a unilateral contract, he should automatically be entitled to expectation damages, while in other cases of reliance on an offer, the offeree may appropriately be limited to reliance damages. According to the Comment to Section 87(2), "[i]f the beginning of performance is a reasonable mode of acceptance, it makes the offer *fully enforceable* under § 45 ...; if not, the offeror commonly has no reason to expect part performance before acceptance. But circumstances may be such that the offeree must undergo substantial expense, or undertake substantial commitments, or forego alternatives, in order to put himself in a position to accept by either promise or performance.... Full-scale enforcement of the offered contract is not necessarily appropriate in such cases." (Emphasis added.)

Chapter 11

THE MECHANICS OF A BARGAIN (II)—TRANSACTING AT A DISTANCE

INTRODUCTORY NOTE

The issue often arises in contract law whether a given type of communication is effective when it is dispatched or when it is received. The rules that govern this issue were formulated when the basic modes of communication were usually face-to-face or by mail, and somewhat later, by telephone or telegram. In general, the traditional rule in the contexts of these modes is that a communication is effective when received. However, acceptances have been treated in a special way. Under the traditional rule, if an acceptance is transmitted in a face-to-face context, then like other communications it is effective when received. That is also true if the acceptance is transmitted "by telephone or other medium of substantially instantaneous two-way communication." See Restatement Second § 64. However, if the acceptance is transmitted through a medium that is not substantially instantaneous, such as regular mail, then the acceptance is effective when dispatched, unless the offeror specifies otherwise. (Presumably, the same rule would apply to private express-mail services, such as FedEx.) This rule is known as the *mailbox rule* or the *dispatch rule*. The rule is often associated with a famous English case, Adams v. Lindsell, 1 Barn. & Ald. 681 (K.B. 1818).

Application of the mailbox rule arises in a variety of contexts.

1. *Crossed revocation and acceptance.* The paradigm case for application of the mailbox rule is a crossed revocation and acceptance. For example, assume that A makes an offer by mail to B on June 1. The course of post is two days, so that B receives the offer on June 3. B promptly accepts by mail that day, and his acceptance reaches A on June 5. Meanwhile, on June 2, A has sent B a revocation, which reaches B on June 4. Here A's revocation was dispatched before B's acceptance was dispatched, and was received before B's acceptance was received. Nevertheless, under the mailbox rule a contract is formed, because a revocation is effective only when received (on June 4) while an acceptance is effective when dispatched (on June 3).

An argument in favor of the mailbox rule in this context is that it pushes up the beginning of performance to the earliest possible date. Suppose, for example, that, as in the hypothetical, the course of post is two days, and the offeree is to perform before the offeror. Under the mailbox rule, an offeree can safely begin to perform as soon as he dispatches his acceptance. If we assume that, as seems likely, most offerors do not revoke, then offerors as a class may prefer the mailbox rule, because it is in the interests of offerors that performance begin as soon as possible.

2. *Delay or failure of transmission.* A different question is presented when a mailed acceptance is either delayed or fails to reach the offeror. For example, suppose that Seller offers by mail to sell Blackacre to Buyer, and gives Buyer five days in which to accept. Buyer promptly dispatches a letter of acceptance, but the letter miscarries and never reaches Seller. Seller waits ten days, and having had no word from Buyer, assumes that Buyer is no longer interested and sells Blackacre to someone else. Buyer, who has no reason to anticipate that his acceptance will fail to reach Seller, disposes of premises now in his possession, in the expectation of occupying Blackacre. Is there a contract?

Delay or failure cases are commonly dealt with under the mailbox rule, on the theory that the cases turn on the same issue as crossed-revocation-and-acceptance cases—namely, the issue when does an acceptance take effect. It is apparent, however, that delay or failure cases involve different considerations than those involved in the crossed-revocation-and-acceptance context. In crossed-revocation-and-acceptance cases, the offeror knows that the offeree decided to accept. In delay or failure cases, the offeror is likely to believe that the offeree decided not to accept. Accordingly, if an acceptance takes effect on dispatch in the delay or failure cases, it must either be for reasons other than those that apply to the crossed-revocation-and-acceptance case, or because it is thought wise to avoid nuances and complexities by establishing a categorical rule to cover all types of cases in which the issue is, when does an acceptance take effect.

3. *The date on which contractual liability arises.* Another question involves determining the date on which contractual liability arises. An offer to provide fire insurance is made by mail, and the offeree mails back an acceptance. The property involved is destroyed by fire while the letter of acceptance is en route. Is the loss covered by the insurance contract? A leading case holding that the insurance company is liable under these circumstances is Tayloe v. Merchants' Fire Insurance Co., 50 U.S. (9 How.) 390, 13 L.Ed. 187 (1850).

4. *Interpretation of the offer.* Assume the following facts: On April 1, A makes an offer to B by mail. By its terms, the offer is open until April 5. The course of post is two days. B receives the offer on April 3, and mails an acceptance on April 4. B's acceptance arrives on April 6—that is, B's acceptance is dispatched before April 5, but received after April 5. Should A's offer be interpreted to mean that the acceptance has to be dispatched by April 5, or received by April 5? In such cases, too, the mailbox rule has been applied, so that the offer in the hypothetical is interpreted to mean that the acceptance must be dispatched by April 5, not received by April 5. Falconer v. Mazess, 403 Pa. 165, 168 A.2d 558 (1961). On a companion issue of interpretation, it has been held that where the offeror gives the offeree a fixed period in which to accept the offer, the period begins to run from the date the offer is received,

not from the date it is posted. Caldwell v. Cline, 109 W.Va. 553, 156 S.E. 55 (1930).

––––––

RESTATEMENT, SECOND, CONTRACTS §§ 30, 49, 60, 63–68

[See Selected Source Materials Supplement]

––––––

UCC § 2–206(1)

[See Selected Source Materials Supplement]

––––––

CISG ARTS. 15, 16, 18(2), 20, 22, 23, 24

[See Selected Source Material Supplement]

––––––

UNIDROIT PRINCIPLES OF INTERNATIONAL COMMERCIAL CONTRACTS ARTS. 2.1.3, 2.1.6(2), 2.1.7, 2.1.8, 2.1.10

[See Selected Source Materials Supplement]

––––––

PRINCIPLES OF EUROPEAN CONTRACT LAW ARTS. 2.205(1), 2.206

[See Selected Source Materials Supplement]

––––––

DODGE, TEACHING THE CISG IN CONTRACTS, 50 J. Leg. Ed. 72 (2000). "Under the common law, acceptances are effective upon dispatch, even if they never reach the offeror. This rule performs two functions: it protects the offeree against the possibility of revocation once the acceptance is dispatched, and it places the risk of a lost communication on the offeror. In contrast to the common law mailbox rule, Article 18(2) of the CISG adopts a receipt rule: 'An acceptance of an offer becomes effective at the moment the indication of assent reaches the offeror.' But this provision must be read in conjunction with Article 16(1), which says that 'an offer may be revoked if the revocation reaches the offeree before he has dispatched an acceptance' (emphasis added). In other words, once the offeree has dispatched an acceptance, the offeror may no longer revoke, but if the acceptance is lost in the mail there is no contract. So the CISG and the common law both protect the offeree against the possibility of revocation once the acceptance is dispatched, but the CISG places the risk of a lost communication on the offeree rather than the offeror.

NOTE ON ELECTRONIC COMMERCE

Many contracts are now formed by electronic means. For example, consumers often purchase products from electronic retailers, like Amazon. Similarly, many commercial contracts are undoubtedly formed by an exchange of emails, or by other electronic transactions. One issue raised by electronic contracting concerns the time at which an acceptance is effective. Originally, the paradigmatic means of making an offer were face-to-face and by mail. Where the issue when an acceptance is effective has arisen in the context of a new technology, contract law has often mechanically pigeonholed the technology into one of these two classic paradigms, largely according to whether the technology resembles face-to-face communication, because it involves substantially instantaneous transmission and direct and immediate interaction, or resembles communication through the mail, because it does not inherently involve substantially instantaneous communication and immediate interaction. Thus Restatement Second § 64 provides that "Acceptance given by telephone or other medium of substantially instantaneous two-way communication is governed by the principles applicable to acceptances where the parties are in the presence of each other."

There are relatively few cases concerning new technologies other than telegrams, which are no longer offered in the United States by the basic carrier, Western Union. Of the few cases involving new technologies other than telegrams, most involved telex—which itself has probably been superseded by electronic communications—and concerned the question, where is a contract deemed to be formed for choice-of-law purposes if an acceptance is telexed. American cases held that at least for this purpose a telexed acceptance was effective, and a contract formed, on dispatch.[1]

If a relatively mechanical approach was applied to electronic transmissions, they would seem to fall under the mailbox rule. Although it is true that electronic messages can be transmitted on a virtually instantaneous basis, and that parties using electronic means can engage in direct and immediate interaction, as a practical matter interaction through electronic means usually will not be direct and immediate. Messages sent by electronic messages are not always instantaneously received, are often not read until some time after they have been received, and are often not responded to immediately upon

----

1. For example, in General Time Corp. v. Eye Encounter, Inc., 50 N.C.App. 467, 274 S.E.2d 391 (1981), the court held that where a telexed acceptance was sent from North Carolina, the contract was made in North Carolina, so that suit could be brought in that state. In Norse Petroleum A/S v. LVO International, Inc., 389 A.2d 771 (Del.Super.1978), the court held that if a telexed acceptance was sent from Norway, Norwegian law governed. Two English cases look the other way. In Entores Ld. v. Miles Far East Corp., [1985] 2 Q.B. 327, the court held that where a contract is made by instantaneous communication, such as by telex, the contract is complete only when the acceptance is received by the offeror, so that where a telexed acceptance was sent from Amsterdam to London, the contract was made in England, and an action therefore could be brought on the contract in England. A comparable result was reached in Brinkibon Ltd. v. Stahag Stahl und Stahlwarenhandels GmbH, [1982] All E.R. 293 (H.L.).

being read. On the other hand, transmission is usually close to instantaneous, and the parties usually have an opportunity for almost-instantaneous interaction.

It is an open question whether the dispatch rule will be applied to electronic acceptances. Section 15 of the Uniform Electronic Transactions Act specifies in detail when an electronic record is considered to be sent. However, the Comment to Section 15 provides that although Section 15(a) furnishes rules for determining when an electronic record is sent, "The *effect* of its sending and its import are determined by other law once it is determined that a sending has occurred." (Emphasis added.) Presumably, "other law" includes contract law. In contrast, Section 215 of the Uniform Computer Information Transactions Act (UCITA) is intended to substitute a time-of-receipt rule for the mailbox rule in this case of electronic communication. However, UCITA has only been adopted in two states.

NOTE ON THE CONCEPT OF "RECORD"

With the advent of electronic contracting, the term "record" has been introduced into contract discourse. Under the Electronic Signatures in Global and National Commerce Act and the Uniform Electronic Transactions Act, "record" means "information that is inscribed on a tangible medium or that is stored in an electronic or other medium and is retrievable in perceivable form." "Electronic record," a special type of record, means "a record created, generated, sent, communicated, received, or stored by electronic means." The Comments to Section 2 (Definitions) of the Uniform Electronic Transactions Act state:

10. **"Record."** This is a standard definition designed to embrace all means of communicating or storing information except human memory. It includes any method for storing or communicating information, including "writings." A record need not be indestructible or permanent, but the term does not include oral or other communications which are not stored or preserved by some means. Information that has not been retained other than through human memory does not qualify as a record . . .

6. **"Electronic record."** An electronic record is a subset of the broader defined term "record." It is any record created, used or stored in a medium other than paper. . . .

Information processing systems, computer equipment and programs, electronic data interchange, electronic mail, voice mail, facsimile, telex, telecopying, scanning, and similar technologies all qualify as electronic under this Act. Accordingly information stored on a computer hard drive or disc, faxes, voice mail messages, messages on a telephone answering machine, audio and video tape recordings, among other records, all would be electronic records under this Act.

Chapter 12

THE MECHANICS OF A BARGAIN (III)—MODES OF ACCEPTANCE

NOTE ON THE CONSEQUENCES OF UTILIZING THE WRONG MODE OF ACCEPTANCE

Often it is ambiguous how an offer is to be accepted. If, in such a case, the offeree uses the wrong mode of acceptance (for example, makes an acceptance by promise when the offer requires an acceptance by act), there may be significant consequences. These consequences may occur in the context of a variety of scenarios.

In one scenario, after Offeree accepts an offer, Offeror revokes, claiming that the offer is still revocable, despite the purported acceptance, because Offeree used the wrong mode of acceptance.

In another scenario, after Offeree accepts an offer, some event occurs that would terminate Offeree's power of acceptance by operation of law if a contract has not already been concluded—for example the Offeror dies or becomes incapacitated. Offeror's estate or guardian claims that the acceptance was ineffective because it was in the wrong mode, and that it is now too late to accept because the power of acceptance was terminated by the relevant event.

Typically, although not invariably, issues concerning the consequences of using the wrong mode of acceptance arise where the question is whether the offer was to be accepted by an act, so that it was an offer for a unilateral contract, or by a promise, so that it was an offer for a bilateral contract. Restatement First § 31 provided that "In case of doubt it is presumed that an offer invites the formation of a bilateral contract." That rule was criticized, and in its place Restatement Second § 32 provides that "In case of doubt an offer is interpreted as inviting the offeree to accept either by promising to perform what the offer requests or by rendering the performance, as the offeree chooses." Similarly, UCC § 2–206(1) provides that "Unless otherwise unambiguously indicated by the language or circumstances . . . an offer to make a contract shall be construed as inviting acceptance by any manner . . . reasonable under the circumstances."

The balance of this Chapter will concern issues that arise in connection with acceptance by act (Section 1), acceptance by conduct (Section 2), and silence as acceptance (Section 3).

RESTATEMENT, SECOND, CONTRACTS § 32

[See Selected Source Materials Supplement]

UCC § 2–206(1)

[See Selected Source Materials Supplement]

SECTION 1. ACCEPTANCE BY ACT

KLOCKNER v. GREEN

Supreme Court of New Jersey, 1969.
54 N.J. 230, 254 A.2d 782.

SCHETTINO, J. Plaintiffs, Richard Klockner and Frances Klockner, the stepson and stepgranddaughter respectively of the late Edyth Klockner, brought suit to enforce an alleged oral contract between the deceased and the plaintiffs obligating the deceased to bequeath her estate to the plaintiffs in return for their services to her during her lifetime. Named as defendants were Harry Green, the executor of the estate, William Rhodes, Elizabeth Sylvania and Margaret Rhodes, the surviving next of kin of decedent, and Carolyn Wolf Field, a legatee under decedent's last executed will. (Carolyn Wolf Field did not answer nor appear in this case.)

At the conclusion of plaintiffs' case, the trial court granted defendants' motion to dismiss, holding that the proofs did not reveal the making of a contract because no offer and acceptance nor consideration had been established. The Appellate Division affirmed, holding that since there was no reliance by plaintiffs upon decedent's promise, the statute of frauds barred enforcement of that promise under N.J.S.A. 25:1–5. We granted certification. 53 N.J. 272, 250 A.2d 136 (1969).

Plaintiffs' uncontradicted proofs (as stated above, the motion to dismiss was granted before defendants introduced their case) established that Edyth Klockner, the deceased, and her husband, Richard Klockner's father, executed wills in favor of each other. Although her husband predeceased her, Edyth never revised her will. Accordingly, at her death, approximately three years later, her testamentary disposition had lapsed, and, but for this suit, the bulk of her estate would apparently pass by intestacy to her sole surviving relatives, defendants herein.

Richard Klockner's relationship with decedent, his stepmother, was like that of a natural child to his parent. He performed numerous services for her both before and after his father's death, doing as much and more than could be expected from even one's natural child. On an average, Richard attended to her needs once or twice a week from 1963 to her death in 1966.

Plaintiff, Frances Klockner (daughter of plaintiff, Richard Klockner), similarly spent much time with decedent, having a relationship more like that of mother and daughter than stepgrandmother and stepgranddaughter. Frances spent numerous nights with decedent when the latter felt fearful or alone, and also accompanied her on trips whenever she was needed.

In the early part of 1965 decedent approached Mr. Green, who had represented both her and her husband for many years, to discuss drawing a will. She indicated she wanted to leave her real property to Richard and her personal property to Frances. At Mr. Green's suggestion she prepared a draft of a will, modeled after her earlier will, leaving the bulk of her estate to Richard and Frances. This draft was revised pursuant to suggestions from Mr. Green. Neither was ever executed, however.

Subsequently, in June 1965, decedent discussed with Richard the disposition of her estate. She informed him that she wanted to compensate him for being so helpful, and that if he would agree to continue to look after her and continue to let Frances visit her, she would leave the real property to him and the balance of the estate to Frances. Frances testified that the decedent discussed with her the understanding she had with Richard.

Decedent again contacted Mr. Green and informed him of the understanding she had with plaintiff regarding the disposition of her estate. Using decedent's second draft as a guide, Mr. Green redrafted her will and mailed it to decedent on November 24, 1965. Apparently because of decedent's belief that a will was a premonition of death, this draft remained unexecuted. Decedent became ill suddenly and died in February 1966, never having executed a will subsequent to the mutual will drawn with her husband in 1940.

Both the trial court and the Appellate Division held for defendants because, when questioned on cross-examination, both Richard and Frances testified that they would have continued to perform the services for decedent even if she had not made the promises to compensate them.

It is not disputed that a valid, enforceable contract can be made obligating a person to bequeath property in a specified manner. Accord Davison v. Davison, 13 N.J.Eq. 246 (Ch.1861) (upholding a parol agreement to bequeath real estate in exchange for services); Johnson v. Hubbell, 10 N.J.Eq. 332 (Ch.1855) (holding valid an oral agreement by a father to bequeath property in exchange for a son's conveyance of property to his sister). The question is: was such a contract entered into here?

Although we recognize that alleged agreements to make a particular disposition of one's estate must be subjected to close scrutiny, we have no doubt that decedent here intended to obligate herself to bequeath her property to plaintiffs so long as they continued to serve her as they had prior to her promise. Such a promise, when acted upon, becomes a binding obligation. Decedent bargained for plaintiffs' services and obligated herself to bequeath the property to them when they performed. See 1 Corbin, Contracts, § 63 (1963).

The performance by plaintiffs need not have been induced solely by the offer of compensation. In the Restatement, Contracts § 55 (1932), it is indicated that if an act is requested by the offeror as consideration for a unilateral contract, the act need only be given with the intent of accepting the offer. The examples which illustrate that rule clearly encompass the instant case.

> "A offers a reward for information leading to the conviction of a criminal. . . . B, . . . induced by motives of fear or public duty, would have given the information without hope of reward, but as there is an offer of reward he intends when he gives the information to accept the offer. There is a contract."

In the only New Jersey case discussing this rule, the Court of Errors and Appeals noted that once the contract has been legally concluded, in giving effect to that contract "the motive which induced the party to make the contract or perform it must always be immaterial." Mayor, etc. of Hoboken v. Bailey, 36 N.J.L. 490, 497 (E. & A. 1873). See also 1 Corbin, Contracts § 58 (1963) (recognizing the complexity of motivating causes in human action); Restatement, Second, Contracts § 55 (Tent. Draft No. 1, April 13, 1964) and § 84 (Tent. Draft No. 2, April 30, 1965).

In reviewing the facts of the instant case for purposes of the motion for judgment of dismissal, we must accept as true all the evidence which supports the view of the party against whom the motion is made, and should give him the benefit of all legitimate inferences which may be drawn in his favor. De Rienzo v. Morristown Airport Corp., 28 N.J. 231, 146 A.2d 127 (1958); Cauco v. Galante, 6 N.J. 128, 77 A.2d 793 (1951).

We have no doubt that in the instant case a valid contract was entered into between plaintiffs and Edyth Klockner. Nothing in Richard's testimony indicated that he did not intend to accept the offer notwithstanding his statement that he would have served his stepmother anyway. The testimony of Frances similarly reveals no rejection of the offer despite a similar statement. These statements were merely the normal expressions of affection which naturally flow from the type of relationship which existed between plaintiffs and decedent.

The evidence also fully supports the existence of a bargain by decedent and her belief that she had contracted with plaintiff. Her attempt to execute a will (stymied only by her superstitions), and the testimony of her attorney, while not conclusive, present strong evidence of her intent to carry out her end of the bargain. See Laune v. Chandless, 99 N.J.Eq. 186, 131 A. 634 (Ch.1926) (where the court interpreted the evidence of decedent's attempt to execute a will as indicative of decedent's belief that he had a moral and legal obligation to satisfy the contract); Vreeland v. Vreeland, 53 N.J.Eq. 387, 32 A. 3 (Ch.1895) (where testimony and an undelivered deed were deemed sufficient corroboration of the alleged contract).

Regardless of the apparent existence of a contract, the Appellate Division nevertheless affirmed on the basis that the statute of frauds barred enforcement of the contract. We do not agree that the contract is unenforceable. The rule that a statute of frauds should not be used to work a fraud is well settled. Oral contracts which have been performed by one party are frequently enforced where to do otherwise would work an inequity on the party who has performed. Thus, the cases hold that such performance takes the contract out of the statute of frauds. E.g., Poloha v. Ruman, 137 N.J.Eq. 167, 44 A.2d 411 (Ch.1945) (specifically enforcing parol agreement to leave plaintiff her home if plaintiff would continue to care for decedent and her husband), affirmed per curiam 140 N.J.Eq. 396, 54 A.2d 775 (E. & A.1947); Davison v. Davison, supra

13 N.J.Eq. 246 (holding that plaintiff's part performance took the oral contract out of the statute of frauds)....

We also find no reason on the present record for penalizing plaintiffs because of their professed willingness to serve the widow. Plaintiffs have fully performed, and decedent has received the full benefit of her bargain. Because the decedent has received the full benefit of her bargain, the policy reasons justifying the development of the part performance exception to the statute of frauds have been satisfied. Since at this stage of the proceedings there is no real doubt as to the existence of the contract, the courts should not allow defendants to use the statute of frauds as a device to work a fraud on both plaintiffs and the decedent who at no time gave any indication that her estate should go to someone other than the plaintiffs.

Our discussion of course assumes the truth of the testimony of the plaintiffs and the inferences most favorable to them. We do so, because, as stated at the outset, judgment was granted on motion at the close of plaintiffs' case. We of course do not intend by this opinion to suggest how the testimony should be viewed at the close of the entire case.

We reverse and remand for further proceedings not inconsistent with this opinion.

For reversal and remandment: CHIEF JUSTICE WEINTRAUB and JUSTICES JACOBS, FRANCIS, PROCTOR, HALL, SCHETTINO and HANEMAN–7.

For affirmance: None.

———

DE CICCO v. SCHWEIZER, 221 N.Y. 431, 117 N.E. 807 (1917) (Cardozo, J.) "It will not do to divert the minds of others from a given line of conduct, and then to urge that because of the diversion the opportunity has gone by to say how their minds would otherwise have acted. If the tendency of the promise is to induce them to persevere, reliance and detriment may be inferred from the mere fact of performance. The springs of conduct are subtle and varied. One who meddles with them must not insist upon too nice a measure of proof that the spring which he released was effective to the exclusion of all others."

———

SIMMONS v. UNITED STATES, 308 F.2d 160 (4th Cir.1962). American Brewery sponsored a well–publicized annual American Beer Fishing Derby. Under the Derby rules, the Brewery tagged one of the millions of rockfish in Chesapeake Bay, and named the fish Diamond Jim III. Anyone who caught Diamond Jim III and presented the fish to the brewery, together with the identification tag and an affidavit that the fish was caught on hook and line, would be entitled to a cash prize of $25,000. Simmons caught Diamond Jim III about six weeks after the fish was tagged, and soon thereafter received the cash prize. Simmons knew about the contest, but as an experienced fisherman he also knew that his chances of landing Diamond Jim III were minuscule, and he did not have the fish in mind when he set out to go fishing. Subsequently, the Internal Revenue Service taxed the prize as income. Simmons then filed a claim for refund, on the ground that the payment to him was a gift and therefore was not taxable under § 102 of the Internal Revenue Code, which provides that "Gross income does not include the value of property acquired by gift, bequests, devise, or inheritance." Held, the prize was not a gift.

> ... [U]nder accepted principles of contract law ... the company was legally obligated to award the prize once Simmons had caught the fish and complied with the remaining conditions precedent. The offer of a prize or reward for doing a specified act, like catching a criminal, is an offer for a unilateral contract. For the offer to be accepted and the contract to become binding, the desired act must be performed with knowledge of the offer. The evidence is clear that Simmons knew about the Fishing Derby the morning he caught Diamond Jim III. It is not fatal to his claim for refund that he did not go fishing for the express purpose of catching one of the prize fish. So long as the outstanding offer was known to him, a person may accept an offer for a unilateral contract by rendering performance, even if he does so primarily for reasons unrelated to the offer.

STEPHENS v. MEMPHIS, 565 S.W.2d 213 (Tenn.App.1977) (Nearn, J., dissenting): " ... [T]o base the payment of a reward on 'prior knowledge' ought to be against the public policy of this state.... What policy could be more fraught with impediments to justice and with fraud than one that says to the public, 'Citizens, if you come forward and do your civic duty promptly as you should without knowledge or thought of reward, you shall forfeit all claims to any funds which have been offered by other public-minded citizens to induce the citizenry to come forward and do their duty as they should. However, citizen, if you do not do your duty as you should, but on the contrary, wait until the "pot is right" and you are assured that top dollar will be paid for the information which you ought to have promptly given in the first instance, then you may come forward with your concealed information and you will be amply rewarded for your delay of justice and personal avarice.' To hold 'prior knowledge' necessary for recovery is to make that statement to the people of this state."

BISHOP v. EATON

Supreme Judicial Court of Massachusetts, 1894.
161 Mass. 496, 37 N.E. 665.

Contract, on a guaranty. Writ dated February 2d, 1892. Trial in the Superior Court without a jury, before Braley, J., who found the following facts:

The plaintiff in 1886 was a resident of Sycamore in the State of Illinois, and was to some extent connected in business with Harry H. Eaton, a brother of the defendant. In December, 1886, the defendant in a letter to the plaintiff said, "If Harry needs more money, let him have it, or assist him to get it, and I will see that it is paid."

On January 7th, 1887, Harry Eaton gave his promissory note for two hundred dollars to one Stark, payable in one year. The plaintiff signed the note as surety relying on the letter of the defendant and looked to the defendant solely for reimbursement, if called upon to pay the note. Shortly afterward the plaintiff wrote to the defendant a letter stating that the note had been given and its amount, and deposited the letter in the mail at Sycamore, postage prepaid, and properly addressed to the defendant at his home in Nova Scotia. The letter, according to the testimony of the defendant, was never received by him. At the maturity of the note the time for its payment was extended for a year, but whether with the knowledge or consent of the defendant was in dispute. In August, 1889, in an interview between them, the plaintiff asked the defendant to take up the note still outstanding, and pay it, to which the defendant replied: "Try to get Harry to pay it. If he don't, I will. It shall not cost you anything."

On October 1st, 1891, the plaintiff paid the note, and thereafter made no effort to collect it from Harry Eaton, the maker. The defendant testified that he had no notice of the payment of the note by the plaintiff until December 22d, 1891. . . .

The judge . . . ruled, as matter of law upon the findings of fact, that the plaintiff was entitled to recover, and ordered judgment for him; and the defendant alleged exceptions.

KNOWLTON, J. . . . The defendant requested many rulings in regard to the law applicable to contracts of guaranty, most of which it becomes necessary to consider. The language relied on was an offer to guarantee, which the plaintiff might or might not accept. Without acceptance of it there was no contract, because the offer was conditional and there was no consideration for the promise. But this was not a proposition which was to become a contract only upon the giving of a promise for the promise, and it was not necessary that the plaintiff should accept it in words, or promise to do anything before acting upon it. It was an offer which was to become effective as a contract upon the doing of the act referred to. It was an offer to be bound in consideration of an act to be done, and in such a case the doing of the act constitutes the acceptance of the offer and furnishes the consideration. Ordinarily there is no occasion to notify the offerer of the acceptance of such an offer, for the doing of the act is a sufficient acceptance, and the promisor knows that he is bound when he sees that action has been taken on the faith of his offer. But if the act is of such a kind that knowledge of it will not quickly come to the promisor, the promisee is bound to give him notice of his acceptance within a reasonable time after doing that which constitutes the acceptance. In such a case it is implied in the offer that, to complete the contract, notice shall be given with due diligence, so that the promisor may know that a contract has been made. But where the promise is in consideration of an act to be done, it becomes binding upon the doing of the act so far that the promisee cannot be affected by a subsequent withdrawal of it, if within a reasonable time afterward he notifies the promisor. In accordance with these principles, it has been held in cases like the present, where the guarantor would not know of himself, from the nature of the transaction, whether the offer has been accepted or not, that he is not bound without notice of the acceptance, seasonably given after the performance which constitutes the consideration. Babcock v. Bryant, 12 Pick. 133; Whiting v. Stacy, 15 Gray, 270; Schlessinger v. Dickinson, 5 Allen, 47.

In the present case the plaintiff seasonably mailed a letter to the defendant, informing him of what he had done in compliance with the defendant's request, but the defendant testified that he never received it, and there is no finding that it ever reached him. The judge ruled, as matter of law, that upon the facts found, the plaintiff was entitled to recover, and the question is thus presented whether the defendant was bound by the acceptance when the letter was properly mailed, although he never received it.

When an offer of guaranty of this kind is made, the implication is that notice of the act which constitutes an acceptance of it shall be given in a reasonable way. What kind of a notice is required depends upon the nature of the transaction, the situation of the parties, and the inferences fairly to be drawn from their previous dealings, if any, in regard to the matter. If they are so situated that communication by letter is naturally to be expected, then the deposit of a letter in the mail is all that is necessary. If that is done which is fairly to be contemplated from their relations to the subject-matter and from their course of dealing, the rights of the parties are fixed, and a failure actually to receive the notice will not affect the obligation of the guarantor.

The plaintiff in the case now before us resided in Illinois, and the defendant in Nova Scotia. The offer was made by letter, and the defendant must have contemplated that information in regard to the plaintiff's acceptance or rejection of it would be by letter. It would be a harsh rule which would subject the plaintiff to the risk of the defendant's failure to receive the letter giving notice of his action on the faith of the offer. We are of opinion that the plaintiff, after assisting Harry to get the money, did all that he was required to do when he seasonably sent the defendant the letter by mail informing him of what had been done.

How far such considerations are applicable to the case of an ordinary contract made by letter, about which some of the early decisions are conflicting, we need not now consider....

[A new trial was granted on the ground that when the note became due, it was extended without the consent of the defendant. Because a surety is discharged by an extension of time to the principal debtor, unless the surety consents to the extension, the trial judge should have determined whether the evidence warranted the conclusion that the defendant had consented to the extension.]

RESTATEMENT, SECOND, CONTRACTS § 54

[See Selected Source Materials Supplement]

UCC § 2–206(2)

[See Selected Source Materials Supplement]

SECTION 2.   ACCEPTANCE BY CONDUCT

POLAROID CORP. v. ROLLINS ENVIRONMENTAL SERVICES (NJ), INC.

Supreme Judicial Court of Massachusetts, 1993.
416 Mass. 684, 624 N.E.2d 959.

Before Liacos, C.J., and Wilkins, Abrams, Lynch and Greaney, JJ.

Lynch, Justice.

The defendant appeals from a Superior Court judgment granting the plaintiffs' motion for declaratory relief and ruling that the defendant is obligated to indemnify the plaintiffs for costs associated with a hazardous waste cleanup performed pursuant to the Comprehensive Environmental Response Compensation and Liability Act (CERCLA), 42 U.S.C. §§ 9601 et seq. (1988 & Supp. III 1991). The defendant, Rollins Environmental Services (NJ), Inc. (Rollins), operates a waste disposal facility in Bridgeport, New Jersey, where it disposes of hazardous waste materials through incineration and other chemical and biological processes for customers throughout the country. Polaroid Corporation (Polaroid) and Hooker Chemical Corporation (Hooker), the predecessor company of the plaintiff Occidental Chemical Corporation (Occidental), were customers of Rollins during the 1970's, whereby Rollins disposed of their hazardous wastes.

The plaintiffs' action sought a determination that Rollins was contractually obliged to indemnify them against liability for hazardous waste spills at a temporary storage facility, Bridgeport Rental and Oil Service, Inc. (Bridgeport). Although the complaint sets forth several counts, only the declaratory judgment count is presently before this court. The parties filed cross motions for summary judgment and agreed that there was no dispute as to the material facts.

In her well-reasoned opinion, the trial judge concluded that Polaroid and Occidental have valid, binding, and enforceable indemnification contracts with Rollins under which Rollins is to indemnify and to save the plaintiffs harmless from all liability and loss for releases or a substantial threat of release of hazardous substances at the Bridgeport site.... We transferred this case from the Appeals Court on our own motion and we now affirm.

The judge set forth the following undisputed facts from the pleadings, depositions, affidavits, and exhibits. In early 1976, Polaroid and Rollins entered into an agreement whereby Rollins agreed to perform waste disposal services for Polaroid. Polaroid gave Rollins a copy of Polaroid's "Supplemental General Conditions for Chemical Waste Disposal Services" (supplemental general conditions) and informed Rollins that agreement to the supplemental conditions was an essential condition to any contract between the parties. Rollins made a number of handwritten and initialed changes and then both Rollins and Polaroid signed the supplemental general conditions which provide in pertinent part:

"8. *Precautions*

"You shall perform all services hereunder in a careful and workman-like manner in full compliance with all applicable federal, state and local laws and shall utilize your best efforts to avoid injuries to persons, damage to property or damage to the environment. You further agree to comply with all safety and environmental standards adopted by Polaroid with respect to the handling and transportation, while on Polaroid premises. You further agree to issue certificates of disposal to Polaroid signifying environmentally proper disposal has been accomplished. . . .

"10. *Indemnification*

"You hereby agree to indemnify and save Polaroid harmless from all liability and loss arising from services performed by you or your employ-ees hereunder except where such liability or loss is the result of the negligence of Polaroid or its employees."

From May, 1976, until at least 1980, Rollins provided chemical waste disposal services to Polaroid and transported materials from Polaroid's Massa-chusetts plants to Rollins' New Jersey plant for treatment. Routinely, Polaroid sent Rollins a completed waste data sheet, a written description, and a sample of the waste to enable Rollins to determine whether its facility could properly treat the waste. Rollins would analyze the waste and return a written proposal with the treatment price and shipping cost to Polaroid. Polaroid would then execute a purchase order and Rollins would pick up the waste. All of Polaroid's purchase orders referenced the supplemental general conditions in a list of "documents which constitute this contract." Copies exist only of the fronts of Polaroid's purchase orders, which include the supplemental general conditions. However, the backs of purchase order forms of that general time period, which contain other terms and conditions, are available.

The Occidental Purchase Orders.

Hooker, the predecessor to Occidental, entered into a similar business arrangement with Rollins in late 1970 or early 1971. Hooker operated a chemical manufacturing plant in Hicksville, New York, and contracted with Rollins for waste removal and treatment. Routinely, Hooker submitted pur-chase orders which contained the following indemnity clause typed on their fronts:

"Rollins–Purle (Seller) shall assume all responsibility for injury or damage to the seller, or others, based on or arising out of possession, handling, or use by seller, or by others of any such material for any purpose whatsoever. The seller shall hold and save the buyer harmless of and from any and all claims, demands, damages, actions, and causes of action whatsoever arising from or growing out of possession, handling, or use by seller or by others of materials purchased."

The purchase orders also stated:

"IMPORTANT: ALL TERMS AND CONDITIONS ON THE FACE AND REVERSE SIDE HEREOF ARE A PART OF THIS CONTRACT.

"INSTRUCTIONS:

"1. INVOICE IN DUPLICATE

"2. INCLUDE PACKING LIST WITH ALL SHIPMENTS

"3. FILL IN ACKNOWLEDGMENT COPY AND RETURN IMMEDI-
ATELY

"4. ADVISE AT ONCE IF YOU CANNOT DELIVER ON DATE SPECI-
FIED

"5. PREPAY AND ADD ALL FREIGHT

"6. NO SHIPMENTS ACCEPTED AFTER 3 P.M."

Although Occidental has produced copies of the fronts of the purchase
orders with the preceding language, they have not produced the reverse side
of the documents. From 1971 through 1976, thirteen of the fourteen purchase
orders issued by Hooker contained the preceding indemnity clause and instructions. Rollins never returned the acknowledgement copies of an order
containing the indemnity language. This indemnity language was used on
Hooker's purchase orders without objection from Rollins until January 6,
1977, when Rollins refused a Hooker purchase order because it objected to the
typed indemnity clause. At Rollins' behest, the parties thereafter adopted an
indemnification clause which provided indemnification only for Rollins' negligent acts.

During the course of doing business with both Polaroid and Hooker,
Rollins sometimes stored the plaintiffs' waste materials in the Bridgeport
"tank farm" until Rollins' facility was able to process the waste. Several
hazardous waste spills occurred at Bridgeport during the 1970's. In August of
1988, the United States Environmental Protection Agency (EPA) notified
Polaroid and Occidental that, as waste generators, they were potentially
responsible parties under CERCLA and would be held jointly and severally
liable for investigation and remediation costs incurred by the government.
The EPA asserted that Polaroid was potentially responsible as the generator
of waste shipped to Bridgeport on October 17, 1973, and seven additional
shipments made between August 11, 1976, and April 2, 1977. Occidental is
listed as the generator of waste shipped on June 27, 1974, and August 2, 1974.

The New Jersey Department of Environmental Protection has requested
potentially responsible parties voluntarily to contribute $9,224,189 to the
remediation efforts at the Bridgeport site. Polaroid has paid a small portion
but Occidental has paid nothing. Both Polaroid and Occidental requested
Rollins to defend and to indemnify them with regard to the Bridgeport site
spills but Rollins has refused. . . .

Rollins argues . . . that it rejected the indemnification language by not
returning the acknowledgment copy of the purchase agreement as requested.
Although the purchase orders requested acknowledgement of the terms of the
contract, Rollins routinely completed performance pursuant to the terms of
the purchase order without returning an acknowledgement and without
objecting to the indemnity clause. If an offeror prescribes an exclusive method
of acceptance, only an acceptance in the manner prescribed will bind the
offeror; but if an offeror merely suggests a permitted method of acceptance,
other methods of acceptance are not precluded. Restatement (Second) of
Contracts § 30 comment b (1981).

There is no suggestion from the purchase order that acknowledgement
and return of the purchase order was the sole means of acceptance. Although
silence does not ordinarily manifest assent, the relationship between the
parties or other circumstances may justify the assumption that silence indi-

cates assent to the proposal. *Weichert Co. Realtors v. Ryan,* 128 N.J. 427, 436, 608 A.2d 280 (1992). Moreover, when an offeree accepts the offeror's services without expressing any objection to the offer's essential terms, the offeree has manifested assent to those terms. *Id.* Prior to 1977, Rollins did not give any indication that it rejected the indemnification clause, and it performed pursuant to all of the other terms of the purchase orders issued by Hooker. Although Rollins did object to the indemnification clause in 1977 and negotiated a change with Hooker, there is no indication that the parties understood that the change would be retroactive or otherwise affect past course of dealings. Accordingly, Rollins' performance in compliance with the terms of the agreement without objecting to the indemnity clause constitutes acceptance of the offer's terms. Accord *Allied Steel & Conveyors, Inc. v. Ford Motor Co.,* 277 F.2d 907, 911–913 (6th Cir.1960); *U.S. Ore Corp. v. Commercial Transp. Corp.,* 369 F.Supp. 792, 796 (E.D.La.1974); *Joseph v. Atlantic Basin Iron Works Inc.,* 132 N.Y.S.2d 671, 672–673 (1954), aff'd, 285 A.D. 1147, 143 N.Y.S.2d 601 (1955)....

Judgment affirmed.

SECTION 3.   SILENCE AS ACCEPTANCE

VOGT v. MADDEN

Court of Appeals of Idaho, 1985
110 Idaho 6, 713 P.2d 442

WALTERS, Chief Judge.

Harold and Betty Vogt sued Bob and Neva Madden for damages allegedly resulting from the Maddens' breach, as landlords, of a sharecrop agreement. A jury returned a verdict in favor of the Vogts. The Maddens appeal from the judgment entered on the verdict, presenting three issues. They contend ... that the evidence was insufficient to support the jury's implicit finding that a sharecrop agreement existed between the parties for the year 1981. We agree with the Maddens that it was not proven that a contract existed between the parties for the year 1981 ...

It was undisputed that Harold Vogt had an oral sharecrop agreement with Bob Madden to farm seventy acres of land owned by the Maddens, for the year 1979. It also was undisputed that the parties renewed the agreement for the year 1980. Under their agreement, certain expenses would be borne solely by Vogt, other expenses would be shared equally between Vogt and Madden, and the net profits derived from crops grown on the land would be divided equally between them. When the Vogts eventually filed suit contending a sharecrop agreement existed for the year 1981, Vogt also sought recovery from Madden of $2,000 for the Maddens' share of expenses incurred by Vogt in the years 1979 and 1980.

The dispositive issue in this appeal is whether Vogt and Madden had a sharecrop agreement that Vogt could continue to farm the seventy acres, during 1981. Vogt testified that because no profits had been realized from wheat crops grown on the property in 1979 and 1980, he planned to raise beans on the land in 1981. He testified that he met with Madden several times in August and September, after the wheat crop had been harvested in 1980, concerning the expenses remaining for the years 1979 and 1980. He testified:

> [W]e also discussed the 1981 crop, of what to do then. We had several discussions on this. I met with him two or three, four times—I'm not sure how many—and we both agreed it wasn't the best ground. It isn't number one soil out there, because of the steepness, but I had raised grain for two years, and I had left the straw and stubble on the ground. And I had raised a—let the volunteer grain grow, watered it and plowed it under the first year. And I anticipated plowing under the second year and at that point I told him I thought it would raise a fairly decent crop of pinto beans.
>
> And at that time I told Bob [Madden] that I'd raised two years of grain, plowed under this straw and stubble, and I thought it would raise a crop of pinto beans. And at that time I had decided to do that. I was going to raise the pinto beans on there, along with possibly a few acres of garden beans.
>
> Q: And as a result of that conversation, it was your understanding that you were to farm that; is that correct?
>
> A: Yes.
>
> Q: And when you were discussing the fact of growing the bean crop with Mr. Madden, did he have any objection to that type of crop being grown on his ground?
>
> A: No, not at all.

On cross-examination, Vogt testified as follows:

> Q: You talked about beans, then?
>
> A: Yes, sir.
>
> Q: But Mr. Madden never told you that he wanted to grow beans, did he?
>
> A: No.
>
> Q: He never expressly told you that he would enter into another agreement in the spring of '81?
>
> A: Yes. What we done, we just—I told him I had raised this crop, the wheat and grain for two years, and the third year we could raise a crop of pintos, a crop of beans. And the price of beans at that time was good, and as far as I know that was the way the discussion ended.
>
> Q: But Mr. Madden never agreed one way or another, right?
>
> A: I would say I was under the impression that we had an agreement.
>
> Q: But he never said anything to give you that indication?
>
> A: Honestly, I don't think he said, "Yes, go ahead." No, he didn't say that.

Madden disputed that he and Vogt had agreed to a sharecrop arrangement for the year 1981. He testified that, following one of their discussions over the expense bills for 1979 and 1980,

And I said at that time, I told him, I said, "I just had it. I don't want you to farm it any more. I'll send you what I think is right."

"Harold," I said, "Life's too short to argue over these things, let's just—we're through."

In respect to that same discussion, Vogt denied on rebuttal that Madden had made any statement about Vogt not farming the Maddens' land the next year. In the late fall of 1980, Madden leased the property to another party for the 1981 crop year, thus preventing Vogt from pursuing his plan to raise beans on the land. This lawsuit for damages followed.

By its verdict in favor of Vogt for $18,540, the jury concluded that a sharecrop agreement existed between Vogt and Madden for the year 1981.[1] In order to reach such a conclusion the jury must have disbelieved Madden when he testified he informed Vogt that their relationship was "through," and that he, Madden, did not want Vogt to farm the property any longer. Otherwise, had the jury believed Madden, then clearly the parties would not have had a contract for 1981. If Madden were disbelieved, then the only evidence regarding the creation of a contract between Vogt and Madden for the year 1981 would be Vogt's testimony that he informed Madden of his intent to raise beans on the property in 1981, that Madden did not say "yes" to this proposal, but that Vogt nonetheless was left with the "impression" that a contract had been created.

The question whether silence or inaction may constitute acceptance of an offer was an issue in this case. Over Madden's objection, the jury was given an instruction, No. 18, concerning silence as an acceptance of an offer, creating a contract between the offeror, Vogt, and the offeree, Madden. The instruction was requested by Vogt, demonstrating that Vogt was pursuing a theory that the evidence showed the creation of a sharecrop agreement for 1981 arising because of silence on Madden's part.

The instruction stated:

Silence and inaction may constitute acceptance of an offer to contract, where a party is under a duty to speak or to reject the offer. Such a duty may arise under any one of the following circumstances.

1. Where because of previous dealings it is reasonable that the offeree should notify the offeror if the offeree does not intend to accept.

2. Where an offeree takes the benefit of offered services with reasonable opportunity to reject them and reason to believe the offeror thought the offer was accepted.

3. Where the offeror has stated or given the offeree reason to understand that assent may be manifested by silence or inaction, and the offeree in remaining silent and inactive intends to accept the offer.

This instruction was a slightly modified version of the Restatement (Second) Of Contracts § 69 (1981).[2] The Restatement explains that silence by

---

1. Vogt testified that, had he been allowed to farm the Maddens' property in 1981 under the same sharecrop arrangement as in 1979 and 1980, he would have realized a net profit of $16,540. That figure, when added to the $2,000 owed by Madden to Vogt for the 1979–

80 expenses, totals $18,540, the amount of the verdict.

2. In relevant part, Restatement (Second) of Contracts § 69, at 165 provides:

(1) Where an offeree fails to reply to an offer, his silence and inaction operate as an acceptance in the following cases only:

an offeree ordinarily does not operate as an acceptance of an offer. "The exceptional cases where silence is acceptance fall into two main classes: those where the offeree silently takes offered benefits, and those where one party relies on the other party's manifestation of intention that silence may operate as acceptance." Id. comment a, at 165.

Here, two of the exceptions stated in § 69, and in the court's instruction No. 18, are patently inapplicable because they are wholly unsupported by the evidence. There was no evidence that Madden received "the benefit of offered services" for which Vogt expected to be compensated. See, id. comment b, at 165 ("when the recipient knows or has reason to know that services are being rendered with an expectation of compensation, and by a word could prevent the mistake, his privilege of inaction gives way; under Subsection (1)(a) he is held to an acceptance if he fails to speak."). Vogt did not, in fact, farm the property in 1981. Nor does the evidence show that Vogt stated or gave Madden reason to understand that assent to Vogt's expectation to farm the property might be manifested by silence or inaction, and the evidence does not show that Madden, by remaining silent and inactive intended to accept Vogt's offer. Id. § 69(1)(b).

Finally, the exception arising from "previous dealings" between the parties is inapposite. In their prior dealings, 1979 and 1980, the parties expressly reached oral agreements for sharecropping the farm. After completion of the contract for 1979, a new contract for 1980 did not automatically follow. It was preceded by discussions between Vogt and Madden resulting in an express understanding that Vogt could farm the property in 1980 on a sharecrop basis. We do not believe those previous transactions could give rise to a legitimate conclusion that Vogt's offer to farm the property in 1981 would be accepted in the absence of affirmative notification from Madden that the offer would not be accepted. To the contrary, the previous dealings always resulted in a contract only when both parties expressly agreed.

Absent the applicability of the exceptions stated in Restatement § 69, it is a general rule of law that silence and inaction, or mere silence or failure to reject an offer when it is made, does not constitute an acceptance of the offer. See generally 17 Am.Jur.2d, Contracts § 47, at 385–86 (1964); J. Calamari and J. Perillo, The Law of Contracts § 2–21, at 63–68 (1977). Because none of the exceptions is applicable in this case, we conclude as a matter of law that no contract to sharecrop the Maddens' property in 1981 was created by Madden's silence in response to Vogt's offer to farm the property. We therefore set aside that portion of the judgment awarding damages to the Vogts based on the alleged 1981 contract....

The judgment is reversed in respect to award of any damages for breach of the alleged 1981 contract....

Swanstrom, J., concurs. Burnett, J., voted to grant the petition for rehearing.

(a) Where an offeree takes the benefit of offered services with reasonable opportunity to reject them and reason to know that they were offered with the expectation of compensation.

(b) Where the offeror has stated or given the offeree reason to understand that assent may be manifested by silence or inaction, and the offeree in remaining silent and inactive intends to accept the offer.

(c) Where because of previous dealings or otherwise, it is reasonable that the offeree should notify the offeror if he does not intend to accept.

RESTATEMENT, SECOND, CONTRACTS § 69

[See Selected Source Materials Supplement]

———

CISG ART. 18(1), (3)

[See Selected Source Materials Supplement]

———

UNIDROIT PRINCIPLES OF INTERNATIONAL COMMERCIAL CONTRACTS ART. 2.1.6(3)

[See Selected Source Materials Supplement]

———

PRINCIPLES OF EUROPEAN CONTRACT LAW ART. 2.204(2)

[See Selected Source Materials Supplement]

———

COLE–McINTYRE–NORFLEET CO. v. HOLLOWAY

Supreme Court of Tennessee, 1919.
141 Tenn. 679, 214 S.W. 817, 7 A.L.R. 1683.

LANDSDEN, C.J. This case presents a question of law, which, so far as we are advised, has not been decided by this court in its exact phases. March 26, 1917, a traveling salesman of plaintiff in error [the defendant originally] solicited and received from defendant in error [the plaintiff originally], at his country store in Shelby county, Tenn., an order for certain goods, which he was authorized to sell. Among these goods were 50 barrels of meal. The meal was to be ordered out by defendant in error by the 31st day of July, and afterwards 5 cents per barrel per month was to be charged him for storage.

After the order was given, the defendant in error heard nothing from it until the 26th of May, 1917, when he was in the place of business of plaintiff in error, and told it to begin shipment of the meal on his contract. He was informed by plaintiff in error that it did not accept the order of March 26th, and for that reason the defendant had no contract for meal.

The defendant in error never received confirmation or rejection from plaintiff in error, or other refusal to fill the order. The same traveling salesman of plaintiff in error called on defendant as often as once each week, and this order was not mentioned to defendant, either by him or by his principals, in any way. Between the day of the order and the 26th of May, the day of its alleged rejection, prices on all of the articles in the contract greatly advanced. All of the goods advanced about 50 per cent in value.

Some jobbers at Memphis received orders from their drummers, and filled the orders or notified the purchaser that the orders were rejected; but this method was not followed by plaintiff in error.

The contract provided that it was not binding until accepted by the seller at its office in Memphis, and that the salesman had no authority to sign the contract for either the seller or buyer. It was further stipulated that the order should not be subject to countermand.

It will be observed that plaintiff in error was silent upon both the acceptance and rejection of the contract. It sent forth its salesman to solicit this and other orders. The defendant in error did not have the right to countermand orders and the contract was closed, if and when it was accepted by plaintiff in error. The proof that some jobbers in Memphis uniformly filled such orders unless the purchaser was notified to the contrary is of no value because it does not amount to a custom.

The case, therefore, must be decided upon its facts. The circuit court and the court of civil appeals were both of opinion that the contract was completed because of the lapse of time before plaintiff in error rejected it. The time intervening between the giving of the order by defendant and its alleged repudiation by plaintiff in error was about 60 days. Weekly opportunities were afforded the salesman of plaintiff in error to notify the defendant in error of the rejection of the contract, and, of course, daily occasions were afforded plaintiff in error to notify him by mail or wire. The defendant believed the contract was in force on the 26th of May, because he directed plaintiff in error to begin shipment of the meal on that day. Such shipments were to have been completed by July 31st, or defendant to pay storage charges. From this evidence the circuit court found as an inference of fact that plaintiff in error had not acted within a reasonable time, and therefore its silence would be construed as an acceptance of the contract. The question of whether the delay of plaintiff in error was reasonable or unreasonable was one of fact, and the circuit court was justified from the evidence in finding that the delay was unreasonable. Hence the case, as it comes to us, is whether delay upon the part of plaintiff in error for an unreasonable time in notifying the defendant in error of its action upon the contract is an acceptance of its terms.

We think such delay was unreasonable, and effected an acceptance of the contract. It should not be forgotten that this is not the case of an agent exceeding his authority, or acting without authority. Even in such cases the principal must accept or reject the benefits of the contract promptly and within a reasonable time. Williams v. Storm, 6 Cold. 207.

Plaintiff's agent in this case was authorized to do precisely that which he did do, both as to time and substance. The only thing which was left open by the contract was the acceptance or rejection of its terms by plaintiff in error. It will not do to say that a seller of goods like these could wait indefinitely to decide whether or not he will accept the offer of the proposed buyer. This was all done in the usual course of business, and the articles embraced within the contract were consumable in the use, and some of them would become unfitted for the market within a short time.

It is undoubtedly true that an offer to buy or sell is not binding until its acceptance is communicated to the other party. The acceptance, however, of such an offer, may be communicated by the other party either by a formal acceptance, or acts amounting to an acceptance. Delay in communicating action as to the acceptance may amount to an acceptance itself. When the subject of a contract, either in its nature or by virtue of conditions of the market, will become unmarketable by delay, delay in notifying the other party of his decision will amount to an acceptance by the offerer [offeree?] Otherwise, the offerer [offeree?] could place his goods upon the market, and solicit orders, and yet hold the other party to the contract, while he reserves time to himself to see if the contract will be profitable.

Writ denied.

Response to Petition to Rehear.

An earnest petition to rehear has been filed, and we have re-examined the question with great care. The petition quotes the text of 13 Corpus Juris, p. 276, as follows:

> "An offer made to another, either orally or in writing, cannot be turned into an agreement because the person to whom it is made or sent makes no reply, even though the offer states that silence will be taken as consent, for the offerer cannot prescribe conditions of rejection, so as to turn silence on the part of the offeree into acceptance."

And further:

> "In like manner mere delay in accepting or rejecting an offer cannot make an agreement." . . .

It is a general principle of the law of contracts that, while an assent to an offer is requisite to the formation of an agreement, yet such assent is a condition of the mind, and may be either express or evidenced by circumstances from which the assent may be inferred. Hartford et al. v. Jackson, 24 Conn. 514, 63 Am.Dec. 177; 6 Ruling Case Law, 605; 13 Corpus Juris, 276, 9 Cyc. 258. And see the cases cited in the notes of these authorities. They all agree that acceptance of an offer may be inferred from silence. This is only where the circumstances surrounding the parties afford a basis from which an inference may be drawn from silence. There must be the right and the duty to speak, before the failure to do so can prevent a person from afterwards setting up the truth. We think it is the duty of a wholesale merchant, who sends out his drummers to solicit orders for perishable articles, and articles consumable in the use, to notify his customers within a reasonable time that the orders are not accepted; and if he fails to do so, and the proof shows that he had ample opportunity, silence for an unreasonable length of time will amount to an acceptance, if the offerer is relying upon him for the goods.

The petition to rehear is denied.

HOBBS v. MASSASOIT WHIP CO., 158 Mass. 194, 33 N.E. 495 (1893). Without receiving any specific order for them, the plaintiff had on four or five occasions shipped eelskins to the defendant, for which the defendant had paid. The plaintiff then shipped further eelskins. The defendant retained these eelskins for some months without communicating with the plaintiff, but after a destruction of the skins, the defendant refused to pay for them. The plaintiff sued for the price of the skins. Held, for the plaintiff. The past dealings of the parties were such that the plaintiff had a kind of "standing offer" for eelskins. ". . . Even if the offer was not such that the contract was made as soon as skins corresponding to its terms were sent, sending them did impose on the defendant a duty to act about them; and silence on its part, coupled with a retention of the skins for an unreasonable time, might be found by the jury to warrant the plaintiff in assuming that they were accepted, and thus to amount to an acceptance.''

LOUISVILLE TIN & STOVE CO. v. LAY, 251 Ky. 584, 65 S.W.2d 1002 (1933). Mrs. Lay operated Lay's Variety Store. Her husband, who was insolvent and without credit, operated an independent business known as Lay's Electric Shop. Mr. Lay ordered goods from the plaintiff to be consigned to Lay's Variety Store. When Mrs. Lay was informed that the goods consigned to her store had arrived at the railway depot, she "became angry and said it was her husband's doings." Mrs. Lay directed a drayman to take the goods from the depot to Lay's Electric Shop. Held, when Mrs. Lay assumed control over the disposition of the goods, her acts constituted an acceptance of the shipment, and she became liable to the plaintiff for the price of the goods.

Chapter 13

IMPLIED–IN–LAW AND IMPLIED–IN–FACT CONTRACTS; UNILATERAL CONTRACTS REVISITED

NURSING CARE SERVICES, INC. v. DOBOS

District Court of Appeal of Florida, Fourth District, 1980.
380 So.2d 516.

HURLEY, JUDGE.

Plaintiff, Nursing Care Services, Inc., appeals from that part of a final judgment which disallowed compensation for certain nursing care services. Our review of the record reveals substantial uncontradicted testimony supporting plaintiff's theory of recovery and thus we remand for entry of an amended final judgment.

Mary Dobos, the defendant, was admitted to Boca Raton Community Hospital with an abdominal aneurysm. Her condition was sufficiently serious to cause her doctor to order around-the-clock nursing care. The hospital implemented this order by calling upon the plaintiff which provides individualized nursing services.

Mrs. Dobos received nursing care which in retrospect can be divided into three periods: (1) two weeks of in-hospital care; (2) forty-eight hour post-release care; and (3) two weeks of at-home care. The second period of care (the forty-eight hour post-release care) was removed as an issue at trial when Mrs. Dobos conceded that she or her daughter authorized that period of care. The total bill for all three periods came to $3,723.90; neither the reasonableness of the fee, the competency of the nurses, nor the necessity for the services was contested at trial.

The gist of the defense was that Mrs. Dobos never signed a written contract nor orally agreed to be liable for the nursing services. Testifying about the in-hospital care, she said, "Dr. Rosen did all the work. I don't know what he done (sic), and he says, I needed a nurse." It is undisputed that Mrs. Dobos was mentally alert during her at-home recuperation period. Asked if she ever tried to fire the nurses or dispense with their care, she replied, "I didn't. I didn't know who—I thought maybe if they insist, the doctors insist so much, I thought the Medicare would take care of it, or whatever. I don't know."

331

After a non-jury trial, the court granted judgment for the plaintiff in the sum of $248.00, the cost of the forty-eight hour post-release care. It declined to allow compensation for the first and third periods of care, saying,

"... [T]here certainly was a service rendered, but based on the total surrounding circumstances, I don't think there is sufficient communications and dealings with Mrs. Dobos to make sure that she knew that she would be responsible for those services rendered...."

We concur in the trial court's determination that the plaintiff failed to prove an express contract or a contract implied in fact. It is our view, however, that the uncontradicted testimony provided by plaintiff and defendant alike, clearly established a contract implied in law which entitles the plaintiff to recover.

Contracts implied in law, or as they are more commonly called "quasi contracts", are obligations imposed by law on grounds of justice and equity. Their purpose is to prevent unjust enrichment. Unlike express contracts or contracts implied in fact, quasi contracts do not rest upon the assent of the contracting parties. See generally, 28 Fla.Jur., Restitution and Implied Contracts.

One of the most common areas in which recovery on a contract implied in law is allowed is that of work performed or services rendered. The rationale is that the defendant would be unjustly enriched at the expense of the plaintiff if she were allowed to escape payment for services rendered or work performed. There is, however, an important limitation. Ordinarily liability is imposed to pay for services rendered by another only when the person for whose benefit they were rendered requested the services or knowingly and voluntarily accepted their benefits. *Yeats v. Moody,* 128 Fla. 658, 175 So. 719 (1937); *Strano v. Carr & Carr, Inc.,* 97 Fla. 150, 119 So. 864 (1929); *Taylor v. Thompson,* 359 So.2d 14 (Fla. 1st DCA 1978); and *Tobin & Tobin Insurance Agency, Inc. v. Zeskind,* 315 So.2d 518 (Fla. 3d DCA 1975).

The law's concern that needless services not be foisted upon the unsuspecting has led to the formulation of the "officious intermeddler doctrine." It holds that where a person performs labor for another without the latter's request or implied consent, however beneficial such labor may be, he cannot recover therefor. *Tipper v. Great Lakes Chemical Company,* 281 So.2d 10 (Fla.1973). A notable exception to this rule, however, is that of emergency aid:

A person who has supplied things or services to another, although acting without the other's knowledge or consent, is entitled to restitution therefore from the other if he acted unofficiously and with intent to charge therefore, and the things or services were necessary to prevent the other from suffering serious bodily harm or pain, and the person supplying them had no reason to know that the other would not consent to receiving them, if mentally competent, and it was impossible for the other to give consent or, because of extreme youth or mental impairment, the other's consent would have been immaterial. 66 Am.Jur.2d, Restitution and Implied Contract, § 23.

In the case at bar it is unclear whether Mrs. Dobos, during the period of in-hospital care, understood or intended that compensation be paid. Her condition was grave. She had been placed in the hospital's intensive care unit and thereafter had tubes and other medical equipment attached to her body which necessitated special attention. She was alone, unable to cope and without family assistance. It is worthy of note that at no point during the litigation was there any question as to the propriety of the professional judgment that the patient required special nursing care. To the contrary, the record demonstrates that the in-hospital nursing care was essential to Mrs. Dobos' health and safety. Given these circumstances it would be unconscionable to deny the plaintiff recovery for services which fall squarely within the emergency aid exception. *Tipper v. Great Lakes Chemical Company*, supra.

The third period of care is less difficult. It is unquestioned that during the at-home recuperation, Mrs. Dobos was fully aware of her circumstances and readily accepted the benefits conferred. Given such facts, we believe the rule set down in *Symon v. J. Rolfe Davis, Inc.*, 245 So.2d 278, 279 (Fla. 4th DCA 1971) must govern:

> It is well settled that where services are rendered by one person for another which are knowingly and voluntarily accepted, the law presumes that such services are given and received in expectation of being paid for, and will imply a promise to pay what they are reasonably worth.

A patient's unannounced misconception that the cost of accepted services will be paid by an insurer or Medicare does not absolve her of responsibility to bear the cost of the services.

As a postscript we note that Mrs. Dobos' home recuperation was interrupted by her readmission to the hospital with an apparent heart attack. In this age of burgeoning malpractice actions it is not idle conjecture to ponder what her legal position might have been had the plaintiff unilaterally terminated its services at a time of vital need. To its credit, it did not and therefore it is entitled to just compensation. Accordingly, we remand the cause to the trial court with instructions to enter an amended final judgment for the plaintiff in the sum of $3,723.90 plus interest and court costs.

It is so ordered.

ANSTEAD and LETTS, JJ., concur.

————

SCEVA v. TRUE, 53 N.H. 627 (1873), "We regard it as well settled by the cases referred to in the briefs of counsel, many of which have been commented on at length by Mr. Shirley for the defendant, that an insane person, an idiot, or a person utterly bereft of all sense and reason by the sudden stroke of accident or disease, may be held liable, in assumpsit, for necessaries furnished to him in good faith while in that unfortunate and helpless condition. And the reasons upon which this rests are too broad, as well as too sensible and humane, to be overborne by any deductions which a refined logic may make from the circumstance that in such cases there can be no contract or promise in fact,—no meeting of the minds of the parties. The cases put it on the ground of an implied contract; and by this is not meant, as the defendant's counsel seems to suppose, an actual contract,—that is, an actual meeting of the minds of the parties, an actual, mutual understanding, to be inferred from language, acts, and circumstances, by the jury,—but a contract and promise, said to be implied by the law, where, in point of fact, there was no contract, no mutual understanding, and so no promise. The defendant's counsel says it is usurpation for the court to hold, as matter of law, that there is a contract and a promise, when all the evidence in the case shows that there was not a contract, nor the semblance of one. It is doubtless a legal fiction, invented and used for the sake of the remedy. If it was originally usurpation, certainly it has now become very inveterate, and firmly fixed in the body of the law."

NOTE ON TERMINOLOGY

Three overlapping terms are used in the law to denote cases that involve a recovery based on benefit conferred: restitution, unjust enrichment, and quasi-contract. Because the terms are often used in an imprecise manner, any attempt at precision is somewhat artificial. Within that constraint, however, the following definitions are generally consistent with modern usage:

Unjust enrichment is the general principle that one person should not be unjustly enriched at another's expense.

Restitution has two meanings.

First, restitution is a catchall *substantive* term to describe the body of specific rules that give effect to the principle that one person should not be enriched at another's expense. A typical example would be a case where plaintiff had paid money to defendant by mistake (for example, an overpayment in a settlement of accounts, resulting from a mistake in addition), both parties assuming that the amount paid was the amount actually due. Here defendant has neither committed a tort (the payment was voluntary and there was no fraud), nor expressly or impliedly promised to repay the mistaken overpayment. Certainly, however, she should be required to do so.

Second, restitution is a catchall *remedial* term to describe *remedies* based on a right to recover on the ground of unjust enrichment.

Quasi-contract ("as if it were a contract") is the name given to describe actions at law, as opposed to actions in equity, that are based on unjust enrichment. Those actions are called by a name that includes the word "contract," even though there is often nothing contractual about them, because for historical reasons, discussed in the following Note, the actions were originally brought under a writ, known as assumpsit, that was basically contractual. In general it is said that a quasi-contractual obligation will be imposed when—but only when—two factors are present in the case: (1) the defendant has received a benefit, and (2) retention of the benefit is inequitable. See Woodward, The Law of Quasi Contracts § 7 (1913). Thus, if Uncle freely gives Nephew $1000, he cannot, on later repenting of his generosity, recover the sum given. Nephew has been benefited, but his retention of the benefit is not unjust, because he received the benefit as a gift. Or suppose Meddle decides that the house of his neighbor, Peel, is in need of a coat of paint. During Peel's absence, and without consulting him, Meddle paints the house, and later brings a suit for the value of his services. Peel has perhaps been benefited, but his retention of the benefit would probably not be regarded as unjust, because the benefit was thrust upon Peel without his consent and under circumstances offering no justification for Meddle's interference in Peel's affairs.

NOTE ON IMPLIED–IN–FACT AND IMPLIED–IN–LAW CONTRACTS

In principle, there is a sharp distinction between implied-in-fact and implied-in-law contracts. An *implied-in-fact* contract is a true contract, which differs from a run-of-the-mill contract only in the fact that the parties' assent, while real, is implicit rather than explicit. For example, a winning bidder at an auction, who made her bid by raising her hand, may be said to have made an implied-in-fact contract: the bidder did not expressly say "I bid," or "I offer," or the like, but that is what is implied when she raised her hand in the context of an auction. Or suppose that every day Janet Jones passes a produce store and buys an apple for lunch. One day Jones is in a hurry to catch her bus, so she takes an apple from a bin outside the store, catches the owner's eye, waves the apple at him, and runs off. Here Jones has not explicitly said "I am buying an apple from you, which I will pay for later," but that is implied. In contrast, an *implied-in-law* contract is not a contract at all. Instead, it is a label given to certain kinds of conduct that gives rise to liability for unjust enrichment.

DAY v. CATON

Supreme Judicial Court of Massachusetts, 1876.
119 Mass. 513.

Contract to recover the value of one-half of a brick party wall built by the plaintiff upon and between the adjoining estates, 27 and 29 Greenwich Park, Boston.

At the trial in the Superior Court, before Allen, J., it appeared that, in 1871, the plaintiff, having an equitable interest in lot 29, built the wall in question, placing one half of it on the vacant lot 27, in which the defendant then had an equitable interest. The plaintiff testified that there was an express agreement on the defendant's part to pay him one half the value of the wall when the defendant should use it in building upon lot 27. The defendant denied this, and testified that he never had any conversation with the plaintiff about the wall; and there was no other direct testimony on this point.

The defendant requested the judge to rule that: "(1) The plaintiff can recover in this case only upon an express agreement. (2) If the jury find there was no express agreement about the wall, but the defendant knew that the plaintiff was building upon land in which the defendant had an equitable interest, the defendant's rights would not be affected by such knowledge, and his silence and subsequent use of the wall would raise no implied promise to pay anything for the wall."

The judge refused so to rule, but instructed the jury as follows: "A promise would not be implied from the fact that the plaintiff, with the defendant's knowledge, built the wall and the defendant used it, but it might be implied from the conduct of the parties. If the jury find that the plaintiff undertook and completed the building of the wall with the expectation that the defendant would pay him for it, and the defendant had reason to know that the plaintiff was so acting with that expectation, and allowed him so to act without objection, then the jury might infer a promise on the part of the defendant to pay the plaintiff."

The jury found for the plaintiff, and the defendant alleged exceptions.

DEVENS, J. The ruling that a promise to pay for the wall would not be implied from the fact that the plaintiff, with the defendant's knowledge, built the wall, and that the defendant used it, was substantially in accordance with the request of the defendant, and is conceded to have been correct. Chit.Cont. (11th Ed.) 86; Wells v. Banister, 4 Mass. 514; Knowlton v. Plantation No. 4, 14 Me. 20; Davis v. School Dist., 24 Me. 349.

The [defendant], however, contends that the presiding judge incorrectly ruled that such promise might be inferred from the fact that the plaintiff undertook and completed the building of the wall with the expectation that the defendant would pay him for it, the defendant having reason to know that the plaintiff was acting with that expectation, and allowed him thus to act without objection.

The fact that the plaintiff expected to be paid for the work would certainly not be sufficient of itself to establish the existence of a contract, when the question between the parties was whether one was made. Taft v. Dickinson, 6 Allen, 553. It must be shown that in some manner the party sought to be charged assented to it. If a party, however, voluntarily accepts and avails himself of valuable services rendered for his benefit, when he has the option whether to accept or reject them, even if there is no distinct proof that they were rendered by his authority or request, a promise to pay for them may be inferred. His knowledge that they were valuable, and his exercise of the option to avail himself of them, justify this inference. Abbot v. Hermon, 7 Greenl. (Me.) 118; Hayden v. Madison, 7 Greenl. (Me.) 76. And when one stands by in silence, and sees valuable services rendered upon his real estate by the erection of a structure (of which he must necessarily avail himself afterwards in his proper use thereof), such silence, accompanied with the knowledge on his part that the party rendering the services expects payment therefor, may fairly be treated as evidence of an acceptance of it, and as tending to show an agreement to pay for it.

The maxim, "Qui tacet consentire videtur," is to be construed indeed as applying only to those cases where the circumstances are such that a party is fairly called upon either to deny or admit his liability.* But, if silence may be interpreted as assent where a proposition is made to one which he is bound to deny or admit, so also it may be if he is silent in the face of facts which fairly call upon him to speak. Lamb v. Bunce, 4 Maule & S. 275; Connor v. Hackley, 2 Metc. (Mass.) 613; Preston v. Linen Co., 119 Mass. 400.

If a person saw day after day a laborer at work in his field doing services, which must of necessity inure to his benefit, knowing that the laborer expected pay for his work, when it was perfectly easy to notify him if his services were not wanted, even if a request were not expressly proved, such a request, either previous to or contemporaneous with the performance of the services, might fairly be inferred. But if the fact was merely brought to his attention upon a single occasion and casually, if he had little opportunity to

---

* According to Black's Law Dictionary, the Latin maxim "Qui tacet consentire videtur, ubi tractatur de ejus commodo" means "He who is silent is considered as assenting, when his interest is at stake." (Footnote by ed.)

notify the other that he did not desire the work and should not pay for it, or could only do so at the expense of much time and trouble, the same inference might not be made. The circumstances of each case would necessarily determine whether silence with a knowledge that another was doing valuable work for his benefit and with the expectation of payment indicated that consent which would give rise to the inference of a contract. The question would be one for the jury, and to them it was properly submitted in the case before us by the presiding judge.

Exceptions overruled.

———

BASTIAN v. GAFFORD

Supreme Court of Idaho, 1977.
98 Idaho 324, 563 P.2d 48.

DONALDSON, JUSTICE. On appeal, plaintiff-appellant contends that because the trial court in its decision failed to distinguish between contracts implied in fact and quasi-contracts, the court did not decide this case on the theory alleged in appellant's complaint. We agree and therefore reverse the judgment and remand this case for a new trial.

During March, 1972, the defendant-respondent V.H. Gafford asked plaintiff-appellant Leo Bastian if he would be interested in constructing an office building upon a parcel of respondent's real property located in Twin Falls, Idaho. After several discussions between the parties, appellant orally agreed to construct the building and began drafting the plans therefor. After the plans were substantially completed, respondent contacted First Federal Savings and Loan Association of Twin Falls to seek financing for the building. He was informed that First Federal required a firm bid by a contractor and would not finance the project on a cost-plus basis. Respondent told appellant of the need for a firm bid, but appellant refused to submit one stating that he would only construct the building on a cost-plus basis. Respondent thereafter hired an architect to prepare a second set of plans, and employed another contractor to construct the building using those plans. On June 29, 1972, appellant filed a materialmen's lien upon respondent's real property in the amount of $3,250 for goods and services rendered in preparing the plans. He then commenced this action to foreclose that lien, alleging an implied-in-fact contract to compensate him for his services. After a trial on the merits, however, the court entered judgment for respondent on the ground that respondent had not been unjustly enriched. Since he did not use appellant's plans in constructing the office building, respondent received no benefit from them and was therefore not required to compensate appellant for drafting them.

In basing its decision on unjust enrichment, the trial court failed to distinguish between a quasi-contract and a contract implied in fact. Although unjust enrichment is necessary for recovery based upon quasi-contract, it is irrelevant to a contract implied in fact. *Continental Forest Products, Inc. v. Chandler Supply Co.,* 95 Idaho 739, 518 P.2d 1201 (1974). For appellant to recover under the latter theory, it is not necessary that respondent either use the plans or derive any benefit from them. *Clements v. Jungert,* 90 Idaho 143, 408 P.2d 810 (1965). It is enough that he requested and received them under circumstances which imply an agreement that he pay for appellant's services.

It is apparent from the record that the requested performance may not have been limited to the drafting of the building plans. We express no opinion on what performance was requested, on whether the requested performance was tendered, and on whether the circumstances imply an agreement to compensate appellant.

The judgment is reversed and the cause is remanded for a new trial. Costs to appellants.

McFADDEN, C.J., and SHEPARD, BAKES and BISTLINE, JJ., concur.

WAGENSELLER v. SCOTTSDALE MEMORIAL HOSPITAL

Supreme Court of Arizona, In Banc, 1985.
147 Ariz. 370, 710 P.2d 1025.

FELDMAN, Justice.

Catherine Sue Wagenseller petitioned this court to review a decision of the court of appeals affirming in part the trial court's judgment in favor of Scottsdale Memorial Hospital and certain Hospital employees (defendants). The trial court had dismissed all causes of action on defendants' motion for summary judgment. The court of appeals affirmed in part and remanded, ruling that the only cause of action available to plaintiff was the claim against her supervisor, Kay Smith. *Wagenseller v. Scottsdale Memorial Hospital,* 148 Ariz. 242, 714 P.2d 412 (1984).... We granted review to consider the law of this state with regard to the employment-at-will doctrine. The issues we address are:

1. Is an employer's right to terminate an at-will employee limited by any rules which, if breached, give rise to a cause of action for wrongful termination?

2. If "public policy" or some other doctrine does form the basis for such an action, how is it determined?

3. Did the trial court err, in view of *Leikvold v. Valley View Community Hospital,* 141 Ariz. 544, 688 P.2d 170 (1984), when it determined as a matter of law that the terms of Scottsdale Memorial Hospital's personnel policy manual were not part of the employment contract?

4. Do employment contracts contain an implied covenant of "good faith and fair dealing," and, if so, what is the nature of the covenant? ...

FACTUAL BACKGROUND

Catherine Wagenseller began her employment at Scottsdale Memorial Hospital as a staff nurse in March 1975, having been personally recruited by the manager of the emergency department, Kay Smith. Wagenseller was an "at-will" employee—one hired without specific contractual term. Smith was her supervisor. In August 1978, Wagenseller was assigned to the position of ambulance charge nurse, and approximately one year later was promoted to the position of paramedic coordinator, a newly approved management position in the emergency department. Three months later, on November 1, 1979, Wagenseller was terminated.

Most of the events surrounding Wagenseller's work at the Hospital and her subsequent termination are not disputed, although the parties differ in their interpretation of the inferences to be drawn from and the significance of these events. For more than four years, Smith and Wagenseller maintained a friendly, professional, working relationship. In May 1979, they joined a group consisting largely of personnel from other hospitals for an eight-day camping and rafting trip down the Colorado River. According to Wagenseller, "an uncomfortable feeling" developed between her and Smith as the trip progressed—a feeling that Wagenseller ascribed to "the behavior that Kay Smith was displaying." Wagenseller states that this included public urination, defecation and bathing, heavy drinking, and "grouping up" with other rafters. Wagenseller did not participate in any of these activities. She also refused to join in the group's staging of a parody of the song "Moon River," which allegedly concluded with members of the group "mooning" the audience. Smith and others allegedly performed the "Moon River" skit twice at the Hospital following the group's return from the river, but Wagenseller declined to participate there as well.

Wagenseller contends that her refusal to engage in these activities caused her relationship with Smith to deteriorate and was the proximate cause of her termination. She claims that following the river trip Smith began harassing her, using abusive language and embarrassing her in the company of other staff. Other emergency department staff reported a similar marked change in Smith's behavior toward Wagenseller after the trip, although Smith denied it.

Up to the time of the river trip, Wagenseller had received consistently favorable job performance evaluations. Two months before the trip, Smith completed an annual evaluation report in which she rated Wagenseller's performance as "exceed[ing] results expected," the second highest of five possible ratings. In August and October 1979, Wagenseller met first with Smith and then with Smith's successor,[2] Jeannie Steindorff, to discuss some problems regarding her duties as paramedic coordinator and her attitude toward the job. On November 1, 1979, following an exit interview at which Wagenseller was asked to resign and refused, she was terminated.

She appealed her dismissal in letters to her supervisor and to the Hospital administrative and personnel department, answering the Hospital's stated reasons for her termination, claiming violations of the disciplinary procedure contained in the Hospital's personnel policy manual, and requesting reinstatement and other remedies. When this appeal was denied, Wagenseller brought suit against the Hospital, its personnel administrators, and her supervisor, Kay Smith.

Wagenseller, an "at-will" employee, contends that she was fired for reasons which contravene public policy and without legitimate cause related to job performance. She claims that her termination was wrongful, and that damages are recoverable under both tort and contract theories. The Hospital argues that an "at-will" employee may be fired for cause, without cause, or for "bad" cause. We hold that in the absence of contractual provision such an employee may be fired for good cause or for no cause, but not for "bad" cause.

---

2. Smith left the emergency department on October 1, 1979.

THE EMPLOYMENT–AT–WILL DOCTRINE

History . . .

The at-will rule has been traced to an 1877 treatise by H.G. Wood, in which he wrote:

> With us the rule is inflexible, that a general or indefinite hiring is *prima facie* a hiring at will, and if the servant seeks to make it out a yearly hiring, the burden is upon him to establish it by proof.... [I]t is an indefinite hiring and is determinable at the will of either party....

H.G. Wood, Law of Master and Servant § 134 at 273 (1877). As commentators and courts later would point out, none of the four cases cited by Wood actually supported the rule....

However unsound its foundation, Wood's at-will doctrine was adopted by the New York courts in *Martin v. New York Life Insurance Co.,* 148 N.Y. 117, 42 N.E. 416 (1895), and soon became the generally accepted American rule. In 1932, this court first adopted the rule for Arizona: "The general rule in regard to contracts for personal services, . . . where no time limit is provided, is that they are terminable at pleasure by either party, or at most upon reasonable notice." *Dover Copper Mining Co. v. Doenges,* 40 Ariz. 349, 357, 12 P.2d 288, 291–92 (1932). Thus, an employer was free to fire an employee hired for an indefinite term "for good cause, for no cause, or even for cause morally wrong, without being thereby guilty of legal wrong." . . .

Present-Day Status of the At–Will Rule

In recent years there has been apparent dissatisfaction with the absolutist formulation of the common law at-will rule. . . .

The trend has been to modify the at-will rule by creating exceptions to its operation. Three general exceptions have developed. The most widely accepted approach is the "public policy" exception, which permits recovery upon a finding that the employer's conduct undermined some important public policy. The second exception, based on contract, requires proof of an implied-in-fact promise of employment for a specific duration, as found in the circumstances surrounding the employment relationship, including assurances of job security in company personnel manuals or memoranda. Under the third approach, courts have found in the employment contract an implied-in-law covenant of "good faith and fair dealing" and have held employers liable in both contract and tort for breach of that covenant. Wagenseller raises all three doctrines.

THE PUBLIC POLICY EXCEPTION

The public policy exception to the at-will doctrine began with a narrow rule permitting employees to sue their employers when a statute expressly prohibited their discharge. *See Kouff v. Bethlehem–Alameda Shipyard,* 90 Cal.App.2d 322, 202 P.2d 1059 (1949) (statute prohibiting discharge for serving as an election officer). This formulation was then expanded to include any discharge in violation of a statutory expression of public policy. *See Petermann v. Teamsters Local 396,* 174 Cal.App.2d 184, 344 P.2d 25 (1959) (discharge for refusal to commit perjury). Courts later allowed a cause of action for violation of public policy, even in the absence of a specific statutory prohibition. *See Nees v. Hocks,* 272 Or. 210, 536 P.2d 512 (1975) (discharge for being absent from work to serve on jury duty). The New Hampshire Supreme Court announced perhaps the most expansive rule when it held an employer liable for discharging an employee who refused to go out with her foreman. The court concluded that termination "motivated by bad faith or malice or based on retaliation is not [in] the best interest of the economic system or the public good and constitutes a breach of the employment contract." *Monge v. Beebe Rubber Co.*, 114 N.H. 130, 133, 316 A.2d 549, 551 (1974).[3] Although no other court has gone this far, a majority of the states have now either recognized a cause of action based on the public policy exception or have indicated their willingness to consider it, given appropriate facts.[4] The key to an employee's claim in all of these cases is the proper definition of a public policy that has been violated by the employer's actions.

. . .

[C]ourts have allowed a cause of action where an employee was fired for refusing to violate a specific statute. *E.g., Petermann v. Teamsters Local 396, supra* (declined to commit perjury before a legislative committee); *Tameny v. Atlantic Richfield Co.,* 164 Cal.Rptr. 839, 164 Cal.Rptr. 839, 610 P.2d 1330 (1980) (would not engage in price-fixing); *Sheets v. Teddy's Frosted Foods,* 179 Conn. 471, 427 A.2d 385 (1980) (insisted that employer comply with state Food, Drug, and Cosmetic Act); *Trombetta v. Detroit, Toledo & Ironton Railroad Co.,* 81 Mich.App. 489, 265 N.W.2d 385 (1978) (refused to alter state-mandated pollution control reports); *O'Sullivan v. Mallon,* 160 N.J.Super. 416, 390 A.2d 149 (1978) (would not perform medical procedure for which she was not licensed); *Harless v. First National Bank,* 162 W.Va. 116, 246 S.E.2d 270 (1978) (would not violate consumer protection law). Failure to perform an act which would violate provisions of the Oregon state constitution formed the basis for a cause of action in *Delaney v. Taco Time International,* 297 Or. 10, 681 P.2d 114 (1984) (declined to sign a false and arguably tortious statement regarding a co-employee). Similarly, courts have found terminations improper where to do otherwise would have impinged on the employee's exercise of statutory rights or duties. *E.g., Glenn v. Clearman's Golden Cock Inn,* 192 Cal.App.2d 793, 13 Cal.Rptr. 769 (1961) (right to join a union); *Midgett v. Sackett–Chicago,* 105 Ill.2d 143, 85 Ill.Dec. 475, 473 N.E.2d 1280 (1984) (filing of a workers' compensation claim by a union member protected by a collective bargaining agreement); *Frampton v. Central Indiana Gas Co.,* 260 Ind. 249, 297 N.E.2d 425 (1973) (filing of a workers' compensation claim); *Nees v. Hocks, supra* (requesting not to be excused from jury duty). A division of our court of appeals recently adopted the public policy exception, ruling that the discharge of an at-will employee who refused to conceal a violation of Arizona's theft statute was contrary to public policy. *Vermillion v. AAA Pro Moving & Storage* 146 Ariz. 215 at 216, 704 P.2d 1360 at 1361. (App.1985).

3. Although *Monge* held that the aggrieved employee had a cause of action for breach of her employment contract based on the employer's "bad faith," the New Hampshire Supreme Court later restricted the reach of *Monge,* construing it to apply "only to a situation where an employee is discharged because he performed an act that public policy would encourage, or refused to do that which public policy condemned." *Howard v. Dorr Woolen Co.,* 120 N.H. 295, 297, 414 A.2d 1273, 1274 (1980).

4. Twelve states have recognized a wrongful discharge cause of action for violation of public policy; fifteen additional states have acknowledged a willingness to consider it, if presented with appropriate facts. *See* Shepard & Moran, *"Wrongful" Discharge Litigation,* ILR Report (Fall 1982) and cases decided since the issuance of that report, including *Meredith v. C.E. Walther,* 422 So.2d 761 (Ala.1982); *Parnar v. Americana Hotels,* 65 Hawaii 370, 652 P.2d 625 (1982); *Brockmeyer v. Dun & Bradstreet,* 113 Wis.2d 561, 335 N.W.2d 834 (1983).

The court's ruling, it stated, was the "logical conclusion" to draw from previous decisions of the court of appeals. *Id. See Daniel v. Magma Copper Co.,* 127 Ariz. 320, 620 P.2d 699 (App.1980); *Larsen v. Motor Supply Co.,* 117 Ariz. 507, 573 P.2d 907 (App.1977).

It is difficult to justify this court's further adherence to a rule which permits an employer to fire someone for "cause morally wrong." So far as we can tell, no court faced with a termination that violated a "clear mandate of public policy" has refused to adopt the public policy exception. . . .

We therefore adopt the public policy exception to the at-will termination rule. We hold that an employer may fire for good cause or for no cause. He may not fire for bad cause—that which violates public policy.

We turn then to the questions of where "public policy" may be found and how it may be recognized and articulated. As the expressions of our founders and those we have elected to our legislature, our state's constitution and statutes embody the public conscience of the people of this state. It is thus in furtherance of their interests to hold that an employer may not with impunity violate the dictates of public policy found in the provisions of our statutory and constitutional law.

We do not believe, however, that expressions of public policy are contained only in the statutory and constitutional law, nor do we believe that all statements made in either a statute or the constitution are expressions of public policy. . . .

However, some legal principles, whether statutory or decisional, have a discernible, comprehensive public purpose. A state's criminal code provides clear examples of such statutes. Thus, courts in other jurisdictions have consistently recognized a cause of action for a discharge in violation of a criminal statute. In a seminal case involving the public policy exception, *Petermann v. International Brotherhood of Teamsters Local 396,* 174 Cal. App.2d 184, 344 P.2d 25 (1959), the California Court of Appeals upheld an employee's right to refuse to commit perjury, stating:

> The public policy of this state as reflected in the Penal Code . . . would be seriously impaired if it were to be held that one could be discharged by reason of his refusal to commit perjury. To hold that one's continued employment could be made contingent upon his commission of a felonious act at the instance of his employer would be to encourage criminal conduct upon the part of both the employee and employer and would serve to contaminate the honest administration of public affairs. This is patently contrary to the public welfare.

Id. at 189, 344 P.2d at 27.

Although we do not limit our recognition of the public policy exception to cases involving a violation of a criminal statute, we do believe that our duty will seldom be clearer than when such a violation is involved. We agree with the Illinois Supreme Court that "[t]here is no public policy more basic, nothing more implicit in the concept of ordered liberty, than the enforcement of a State's criminal code." *Palmateer v. International Harvester Co.,* 85 Ill.2d at 132, 52 Ill.Dec. at 16, 421 N.E.2d at 879 (citations omitted).

In the case before us, Wagenseller refused to participate in activities which arguably would have violated our indecent exposure statute, A.R.S.

§ 13–1402. She claims that she was fired because of this refusal. The statute provides:

§ 13–1402. Indecent exposure; classifications

A. A person commits indecent exposure if he or she exposes his or her genitals or anus or she exposes the areola or nipple of her breast or breasts and another person is present, and the defendant is reckless about whether such other person, as a reasonable person, would be offended or alarmed by the act.

B. Indecent exposure is a class 1 misdemeanor. Indecent exposure to a person under the age of fifteen years is a class 6 felony.

.... We are compelled to conclude that termination of employment for refusal to participate in public [mooning] ... is a termination contrary to the policy of this state, even if, for instance, the employer might have grounds to believe that all of the onlookers were voyeurs and would not be offended. In this situation, there might be no crime, but there would be a violation of public policy to compel the employee to do an act ordinarily proscribed by the law. ...

THE "PERSONNEL POLICY MANUAL" EXCEPTION

Although an employment contract for an indefinite term is presumed to be terminable at will, that presumption, like any other presumption, is rebuttable by contrary evidence. *See* Restatement (Second) of Agency § 442; *Leikvold v. Valley View Community Hospital,* 141 Ariz. 544, 547, 688 P.2d 170, 173 (1984). Thus, in addition to relying on the public policy analysis to restrict the operation of the terminable-at-will rule, courts have turned to the employment contract itself, finding in it implied terms that limit the employer's right of discharge. Two types of implied contract terms have been recognized by the courts: implied-in-law terms and implied-in-fact terms. An implied-in-law term arises from a duty imposed by law where the contract itself is silent; it is imposed even though the parties may not have intended it, and it binds the parties to a legally enforceable duty, just as if they had so contracted explicitly. 1 A. *Corbin, Contracts* § 17, at 38 (1960). The covenant of good faith and fair dealing, discussed [below], is an implied-in-law contract term that has been recognized by a small number of courts in the employment-at-will context.

An implied-in-fact contract term, on the other hand, is one that is inferred from the statements or conduct of the parties. *Id.* It is not a promise defined by the law, but one made by the parties, though not expressly. Courts have found such terms in an employer's policy statements regarding such things as job security and employee disciplinary procedures, holding that by the conduct of the parties these statements may become part of the contract, supplementing the verbalized at-will agreement, and thus limiting the employer's absolute right to discharge an at-will employee. *Toussaint v. Blue Cross & Blue Shield of Michigan, supra; Pine River State Bank v. Mettille,* 333 N.W.2d 622 (Minn.1983). Arizona is among the jurisdictions that have recognized the implied-in-fact contract term as an exception to the at-will rule. In *Leikvold v. Valley View Community Hospital, supra,* this court held that a personnel manual can become part of an employment contract and remanded the cause for a jury determination as to whether the particular manual given to Leikvold had become part of her employment contract with Valley View. 141 Ariz. at 548, 688 P.2d at 174.

The relevant facts in the case before us are not dissimilar to those in *Leikvold*. In October 1978, Scottsdale Memorial Hospital established a four-step disciplinary procedure to achieve the Hospital's stated policy of "provid[ing] fair and consistent discipline as required to assist with the improvement of employees' behavior or performance." Subject to 32 listed exceptions, prior to being terminated a Hospital employee must be given a verbal warning, a written performance warning, a letter of formal reprimand, and a notice of dismissal. The manual further qualifies the mandatory procedure by providing that the 32 exceptions "are not inclusive and are only guidelines." In appealing her dismissal, Wagenseller cited violations of this procedure, but the trial court ruled as a matter of law that the manual had not become part of the employment contract between Wagenseller and the Hospital. The court of appeals held that the Hospital's failure to follow the four-step disciplinary procedure did not violate Wagenseller's contract rights because she failed to prove her reliance on the procedure as a part of her employment contract. (Slip op. at 14.) We disagree with both of these rulings.

First, we need look only to *Leikvold* for the rule governing the determination of whether a particular statement by an employer becomes a part of an employment contract:

> Whether any particular personnel manual modifies any particular employment-at-will relationship and becomes part of the particular employment contract is a *question of fact*. Evidence relevant to this factual decision includes the language used in the personnel manual as well as the employer's course of conduct and oral representations regarding it.

141 Ariz. at 548, 688 P.2d at 174 (emphasis added). Thus, we held in *Leikvold* that entry of summary judgment was inappropriate "[b]ecause a material question—whether the policies manual was incorporated into and became part of the terms of the employment contract—remain[ed] in dispute." *Id.* The court may determine as a matter of law the proper construction of contract terms which are "clear and unambiguous." *Id.* Here, the court of appeals ruled, in effect, that the Hospital had adequately disclaimed any liability for failing to follow the procedure it had established. It found this disclaimer in the final item in the Hospital's list of exceptions to its disciplinary procedure: "20. These major and minor infractions are not inclusive and are only guidelines." The court concluded that the effect of this "clear" and "conspicuous" provision was "to create, by its terms, no rights at all." (Slip op. at 14.)

We do not believe this document, read in its entirety, has the clarity that the court of appeals attributed to its individual portions. One reading the document might well infer that the Hospital had established a procedure that would generally apply in disciplinary actions taken against employees. Although such a person would also note the long list of exceptions, he might not conclude from reading the list that an exception would apply in every case so as to swallow the general rule completely. We do not believe that the provision for unarticulated exceptions destroys the entire articulated general policy as a matter of law. Not only does such a result defy common sense, it runs afoul of our reasoning in *Leikvold*, where we addressed this problem directly:

> Employers are certainly free to issue no personnel manual at all or to issue a personnel manual that clearly and conspicuously tells their

employees that the manual is not part of the employment contract and that their jobs are terminable at the will of the employer with or without reason. Such actions, either not issuing a personnel manual or issuing one with clear language of limitation, instill no reasonable expectations of job security and do not give employees any reason to rely on representations in the manual. However, if an employer does choose to issue a policy statement, in a manual or otherwise, and, by its language or by the employer's actions, encourages reliance thereon, the employer cannot be free to only selectively abide by it. Having announced a policy, the employer may not treat it as illusory.

141 Ariz. at 548, 688 P.2d at 174.

We emphasize here that the rule set forth in *Leikvold* is merely a reiteration of employment law as it has existed for centuries, exemplified by the English common law one-year presumption . . . and the at-will employment doctrine itself. The right of discharge without cause is an implied contractual term which is said to exist in an at-will relationship when there are no factual indications to the contrary. The intent to create a different relationship, as well as the parameters of that relationship, are to be discerned from the totality of the parties' statements and actions regarding the employment relationship. *Leikvold*, 141 Ariz. at 548, 688 P.2d at 174.

The general rule is that the determination whether in a particular case a promise should be implied in fact is a question of fact. 1 A. *Corbin, supra,* § 17 at 38; *see also Leikvold*, 141 Ariz. at 548, 688 P.2d at 174. Where reasonable minds may draw different conclusions or inferences from undisputed evidentiary facts, a question of fact is presented. *Dietz v. Waller*, 141 Ariz. 107, 110–111, 685 P.2d 744, 747–48 (1984). "[T]he very essence of [the jury's] function is to select from among conflicting inferences and conclusions that which it considers most reasonable." *Apache Railway Co. v. Shumway*, 62 Ariz. 359, 378, 158 P.2d 142, 150 (1945). We believe that reasonable persons could differ in the inferences and conclusions they would draw from the Hospital's published manual regarding disciplinary policy and procedure. Thus, there are questions of fact as to whether this policy and procedure became a part of Wagenseller's employment contract. *See Leikvold*, 141 Ariz. at 548, 688 P.2d at 174. The trial court therefore erred in granting summary judgment on this issue.

The court of appeals' resolution of the reliance issue also was incorrect. A party may enforce a contractual provision without showing reliance. *Leikvold* does not require a plaintiff employee to show reliance in fact. The employee's reliance on an announced policy is only one of several factors that are relevant in determining whether a particular policy was intended by the parties to modify an at-will agreement. The employer's course of conduct and oral representations regarding the policy, as well as the words of the policy itself, also may provide evidence of such a modification. *Leikvold*, 141 Ariz. at 548, 688 P.2d at 174.

THE "GOOD FAITH AND FAIR DEALING" EXCEPTION

We turn next to a consideration of implied-in-law contract terms which may limit an employer's right to discharge an at-will employee. Wagenseller claims that discharge without good cause breaches the implied-in-law covenant of good faith and fair dealing contained in every contract. . . .

... Were we to adopt such a rule, we fear that we would tread perilously close to abolishing completely the at-will doctrine and establishing by judicial fiat the benefits which employees can and should get *only* through collective bargaining agreements or tenure provisions. *Cf. Fleming v. Pima County,* 141 Ariz. 149, 685 P.2d 1301 (1984) (county employee protected by a merit system was permitted to bring a tort action for wrongful discharge). While we do not reject the propriety of such a rule, we are not persuaded that it should be the result of judicial decision.

In reaching this conclusion, however, we do not feel that we should treat employment contracts as a special type of agreement in which the law refuses to imply the covenant of good faith and fair dealing that it implies in all other contracts. As we noted above, the implied-in-law covenant of good faith and fair dealing protects the right of the parties to an agreement to receive the benefits of the agreement that they have entered into. The denial of a party's right to those benefits, whatever they are, will breach the duty of good faith implicit in the contract. Thus, the relevant inquiry always will focus on the contract itself, to determine what the parties did agree to. In the case of an employment-at-will contract, it may be said that the parties have agreed, for example, that the employee will do the work required by the employer and that the employer will provide the necessary working conditions and pay the employee for work done. What cannot be said is that one of the agreed benefits to the at-will employee is a guarantee of continued employment or tenure. The very nature of the at-will agreement precludes any claim for a prospective benefit. Either employer or employee may terminate the contract at any time.

We do, however, recognize an implied covenant of good faith and fair dealing in the employment-at-will contract, although that covenant does not create a duty for the employer to terminate the employee only for good cause. The covenant does not protect the employee from a "no cause" termination because tenure was never a benefit inherent in the at-will agreement. The covenant does protect an employee from a discharge based on an employer's desire to avoid the payment of benefits already earned by the employee, such as the sales commissions in *Fortune, supra,* but not the tenure required to earn ... pension and retirement benefits .... Thus, plaintiff here has a right to receive the benefits that were a part of her employment agreement with defendant Hospital. To the extent, however, that the benefits represent a claim for prospective employment, her claim must fail. The terminable-at-will contract between her and the Hospital made no promise of continued employment. To the contrary, it was, by its nature, subject to termination by either party at any time, subject only to the legal prohibition that she could not be fired for reasons which contravene public policy.

Thus, because we are concerned not to place undue restrictions on the employer's discretion in managing his workforce and because tenure is contrary to the bargain in an at-will contract, we reject the argument that a no cause termination breaches the implied covenant of good faith and fair dealing in an employment-at-will relationship....

SUMMARY AND CONCLUSIONS

The trial court granted summary judgment against Wagenseller on the count alleging the tort of wrongful discharge in violation of public policy. We adopt the "public policy" exception to the at-will termination rule and hold that the trial court erred in granting judgment against plaintiff on this theory. On remand plaintiff will be entitled to a jury trial if she can make a prima facie showing that her termination was caused by her refusal to perform some act contrary to public policy, or her performance of some act which, as a matter of public policy, she had a right to do. The obverse, however, is that mere dispute over an issue involving a question of public policy is not equivalent to establishing causation as a matter of law and will not automatically entitle plaintiff to judgment. In the face of conflicting evidence or inferences as to the actual reason for termination, the question of causation will be a question of fact.

The trial court granted summary judgment against Wagenseller on the count alleging breach of implied-in-fact provisions of the contract. We hold that this was error. On this record, there is a jury question as to whether the provisions of the employment manual were part of the contract of employment.

We affirm the grant of summary judgment on the count seeking recovery for breach of the implied covenant of good faith and fair dealing. We recognize that covenant as part of this and other contracts, but do not construe it to give either party to the contract rights—such as tenure—different from those for which they contracted. . . .

For the foregoing reasons, we affirm in part and reverse in part. The decision of the court of appeals is vacated and the case remanded to the trial court for proceedings not inconsistent with this opinion.

GORDON, V.C.J., and HAYS and CAMERON, JJ., concur.

HOLOHAN, C.J., concurred in the result except as to the personnel-manual issue. As to that issue, Holohan, C.J. concluded that the personnel manual "was not, as a matter of law, part of the employment contract."]

———

NOTE ON EMPLOYMENT AT WILL

As the court in *Wagenseller* points out, one exception to the at-will rule is that employers cannot discharge an at-will employee for a reason that is prohibited by statute. For example, federal statutes provide that an employee cannot be discharged on the basis of race, religion, gender, age, or disability. See, e.g., Age Discrimination in Employment Act of 1967 § 4(a), 29 U.S.C: § 623(a)(*l*); Civil Rights Act of 1964 § 703(a), 42 U.S.C. § 2000e–2(a)(1); Americans with Disabilities Act, 42 U.S.C. § 12112. A recently adopted federal statute, the Sarbanes–Oxley Act, protects whistleblowers by prohibiting the discharge of an employee of a public company because the employee provided information about, assisted in an investigation of, or testified in a proceeding concerning conduct that the employee reasonably believes violates Securities and Exchange Commission regulations or other relevant laws. 18 U.S.C. § 1514A.

———

PINE RIVER STATE BANK v. METTILLE, 333 N.W.2d 622 (Minn. 1983). "[The employer-defendant argues that the job-security provisions in its personnel handbook] lack enforceability because mutuality of obligation is lacking. Since under a contract of indefinite duration the employee remains free to go elsewhere, why should the employer be bound to its promise not to terminate unless for cause or unless certain procedures are followed? The demand for mutuality of obligation, although appealing in its symmetry, is simply a species of the forbidden inquiry into the adequacy of consideration, an inquiry in which this court has, by and large, refused to engage. *See Estrada v. Hanson,* 215 Minn. 353, 10 N.W.2d 223 (1943). 'If the requirement of consideration is met, there is no additional requirement of . . . equivalence in the values exchanged; or . . . "mutuality of obligation".' Restatement (Second) of Contracts § 79 (1981). We see no merit in the lack of mutuality argument; as we pointed out in *Cardinal Consulting Co. v. Circo Resorts,* 297 N.W.2d 260, 266 (Minn.1980), the concept of mutuality in contract law has been widely discredited and the right of one party to terminate a contract at will does not invalidate the contract. . . . "

NOTE ON MODIFICATION OF EMPLOYEE HANDBOOKS

The cases have differed on an employer's right to modify provisions of an employee handbook that have contractual force. In Asmus v. Pacific Bell, 23 Cal.4th 1, 999 P.2d 71, 96 Cal.Rptr.2d 179 (2000), Pacific Bell had issued the following Management Employment Security Policy (MESP) in 1986: "It will be Pacific Bell's policy to offer all management employees who continue to meet our changing business expectations employment security through reassignment to and retraining for other management positions, even if their present jobs are eliminated. This policy will be maintained so long as there is no change that will materially affect Pacific Bell's business plan achievement."

In January 1990, Pacific Bell notified its managers that industry conditions could force it to discontinue its MESP. In October 1991, Pacific Bell announced it would terminate its MESP on April 1, 1992, so that it could achieve more flexibility in conducting its business and compete more successfully in the marketplace. That same day, Pacific Bell announced it was adopting a new layoff policy (the Management Force Adjustment Program (MFAP)) that replaced the MESP. Employees who chose to continue working for Pacific Bell would receive enhanced pension benefits. Employees who opted to retire in December 1991 would receive additional enhanced pension benefits. Employees who chose to resign in November 1991 would receive these and other benefits, and severance pay equaling the employee's salary and bonus multiplied by a percentage of the employee's years of service.

Former Pacific Bell management employees who were affected by the MESP cancellation brought a suit challenging the cancellation. The plaintiffs had remained with the Pacific Bell for several years after the policy termination, and had received increased pension benefits for their continued employment while working under the new MFAP. Held, for Pacific Bell:

> In a unilateral contract, there is only one promisor, who is under an enforceable legal duty. (1 Corbin on Contracts (1993) § 1.23, p. 87.) The promise is given in consideration of the promisee's act or forbearance. As to the promisee, in general, any act or forbearance, including continuing

to work in response to the unilateral promise, may constitute consideration for the promise. (1 Witkin, Summary of Cal. Law, supra, Contracts, § 213, p. 221; 2 Corbin on Contracts (1995) § 5.9, pp. 40–46; Rest.2d Contracts, §§ 71, 72; Civ.Code, § 1584.) . . .

. . . The parties here disagree on how employers may terminate or modify a unilateral contract that has been accepted by the employees' performance. Plaintiffs assert that Pacific Bell was not entitled to terminate its MESP until it could demonstrate a change materially affecting its business plan, i.e., until the time referred to in a clause in the contract. Pacific Bell asserts that because it formed the contract unilaterally, it could terminate or modify that contract as long as it did so after a reasonable time, gave affected employees reasonable notice, and did not interfere with the employees' vested benefits (e.g., pension and other retirement benefits). . . .

. . . [T]he majority of other jurisdictions that have addressed the question conclude that an employer may terminate or modify a contract with no fixed duration period after a reasonable time period, if it provides employees with reasonable notice, and the modification does not interfere with vested employee benefits. . . .

. . . Just as employers must accept the employees' continued employment as consideration for the original contract terms, employees must be bound by amendments to those terms, with the availability of continuing employment serving as adequate consideration from the employer. When Pacific Bell terminated its original MESP and then offered continuing employment to employees who received notice and signed an acknowledgement to that effect, the employees accepted the new terms, and the subsequent modified contract, by continuing to work. Continuing to work after the policy termination and subsequent modification constituted acceptance of the new employment terms. . . .

In Demasse v. ITT Corp., 194 Ariz. 500, 984 P.2d 1138 (1999), the Arizona Supreme Court reached a different conclusion concerning the modification of employee handbooks:

ITT [the employer] argues that it had the legal power to unilaterally modify the contract by simply publishing a new [1989] handbook. But as with other contracts, an implied-in-fact contract term cannot be modified unilaterally. . . . Once an employment contract is formed—whether the method of formation was unilateral, bilateral, express, or implied—a party may no longer unilaterally modify the terms of that relationship. . . .

The cases ITT cites hold that continued work alone both manifested the Demasse employees' assent to the modification and constituted consideration for it. We disagree with both contentions and the cases that support them. Separate consideration, beyond continued employment, is necessary to effect a modification. . . .

Continued employment after issuance of a new handbook does not constitute acceptance, otherwise the "illusion (and the irony) is apparent: to preserve their right under the [existing contract] . . . plaintiffs would be forced to quit." Doyle, 237 Ill.Dec. 100, 708 N.E.2d at 1145. . . . It is "too much to require an employee to preserve his or her rights under the original employment contract by quitting working." Brodie, 934 P.2d at 1268; see Robinson, 19 F.3d at 364; Torosyan v. Boehringer Ingelheim Pharmaceuticals, Inc., 234 Conn. 1, 662 A.2d 89, 99 (1995). Thus, the employee does not manifest consent to an offer modifying an existing contract without taking affirmative steps, beyond continued performance, to accept....

When ITT distributed the 1989 handbook containing the provisions permitting unilateral modification or cancellation, it did not bargain with those pre–1989 employees who had seniority rights under the old handbooks, did not ask for or obtain their assent, and did not provide consideration other than continued employment. The employees signed a receipt for the "1989 handbook stating that they had received the handbook[,] understood that it was their responsibility to read it, comply with its contents, and contact Personnel if they had any questions concerning the contents." ... The Demasse employees were not informed that continued employment—showing up for work the next day—would manifest assent, constitute consideration, and permit cancellation of any employment rights to which they were contractually entitled. Thus, even if we were to agree that continued employment could provide consideration for rescission of the job security term, that consideration would not have been bargained for and would not support modification.... Our courts have not adopted any conflicting principle.

————

PETTIT, MODERN UNILATERAL CONTRACTS, 63 Boston U.L.Rev. 551 (1983). "[An] important reason for the continued use of unilateral contract analysis in contemporary litigation is that it has proved adaptable to the needs of judges and lawyers in areas unforeseen by [Karl] Llewellyn and apparently by the drafters of the *Second Restatement*. Relatively few of the modern unilateral contracts cases involve traditional commercial exchanges (sales of goods), and it was primarily the traditional commercial context that Llewellyn had in mind when he unleashed his attack on the unilateral contract idea. Llewellyn did not foresee the usefulness in a highly organized society of a concept that allows a plaintiff to assert the defendant's promissory obligation and at the same time preempt the argument that he himself did not undertake any obligation. Many of the modern unilateral contracts cases involve claims by an individual offeree against an organizational offeror—the little guy against the big organization. In this context courts often are quite willing to conclude that the organization made a promise even though the individual did not....

"... [L]awyers and judges recently have been choosing unilateral contract analysis with remarkable and increasing frequency. In assessing this trend toward the unilateral contract, however, it is important to recognize an important change in the way that unilateral contract is being used. In Llewellyn's time, unilateral contract was predominantly a defendant's theory; the plaintiff pressed a bilateral contract argument and the defendant claimed to have made an offer for a unilateral contract which he revoked before the plaintiff's acceptance by performance. In modern times, unilateral contract is predominantly a plaintiff's theory. With some exceptions, courts employ unilateral contract analysis when they find liability and reject it when they deny liability.

"The crucial, difficult question facing the courts in the modern cases is not whether to choose unilateral or bilateral contract analysis, but whether to employ any contractual analysis at all. Judges and lawyers have been expanding contract analysis into new areas and situations. It is no coincidence that they have resorted to unilateral contract in this process. The need to find an enforceable return promise provides some limitation on the use of bilateral contract theory to impose liability. Plaintiffs pursuing a bilateral theory have to prove, and sometimes subject themselves to, their own promissory obligation. Plaintiffs using the unilateral contract device, like tort plaintiffs, have to prove only the defendant's obligation.

"More often than not, the source of the defendant's obligation in modern unilateral contracts cases is an implied, rather than an express, promise. Moreover, the implied promise often takes the following form: 'As long as you keep doing what you've been doing, or are about to do, I'll keep doing what I've been doing, or am about to do.' In other words, the defendant's alleged promise is a promise to maintain the status quo, and the plaintiff's performance is simply continuing the status quo. The only limit on the use of unilateral contract theory is the court's willingness to find the alleged implied promise. Any assessment, therefore, of the appropriateness of modern judicial use of unilateral contract theory must focus on the promissory basis of the asserted obligation: Did the defendant really make a promise and, if so, should that promise serve as the basis for determining the existence and extent of liability?"

Chapter 14

PRELIMINARY NEGOTIATIONS, IN-DEFINITENESS, AND THE DUTY TO BARGAIN IN GOOD FAITH

One of the axioms of classical contract law was that a contract is formed by offer and acceptance. This axiom was at the center of several clusters of rules. One of these clusters concerned preliminary negotiations, indefiniteness, further-document-to-follow provisions, agreements to agree, and the duty to negotiate in good faith. The rules in this cluster are the subject of this Chapter.

One set of these rules concerned the characterization and effect of expressions used in a bargaining context. Under classical contract law, such expressions were characterized as either an offer or acceptance, on the one hand, or as preliminary negotiations, on the other. This was a binary characterization, in which an expression either had immediate legal effect or no legal effect. An offer had the immediate legal effect of creating a power of acceptance in the offeree, and an acceptance had the immediate legal effect of concluding a contract. In contrast, preliminary negotiations had no legal effect. This binary characterization was reflected in binary outcomes: no liability up to the time at which an acceptance of an offer occurred; full liability for expectation damages thereafter.

Another set of rules in this cluster concerned the indefiniteness of agreements. The relationship between the basic rules of offer and acceptance and the rules concerning indefiniteness was not always clear. A basic rule of offer and acceptance is that an expression will not constitute an offer unless it is sufficiently definite. But why then should contract law have another rule about the indefiniteness of *agreements*? If an expression is not sufficiently definite to constitute an offer, no contract can be formed. If an expression is sufficiently definite to constitute an offer, and the offeree assents, what room is left to argue that a resulting agreement is too indefinite?

One possible answer to this question is that the concept of indefiniteness of agreements reflects the brute fact that in reality many contracts are not formed by an offer-and-acceptance sequence. Instead, many contracts are probably formed by simultaneous actions, like signing, shaking hands, concurring that "It's a deal," or the like. In such cases, whether one of the parties used an expression that was sufficiently definite to constitute an offer is usually irrelevant. Instead, indefiniteness bears on whether parties to a joint expression that *looks like* an agreement believed that (1) they had concluded the bargaining process or (2) instead they were still in preliminary negotiations—preliminary, that is, to the conclusion of a bargain. In addition, indefiniteness may be relevant because even if the parties believed they had concluded the bargaining process, the resulting bargain they made may be too indefinite to allow the courts to fashion a remedy for its breach.

Still another set of rules involved fact patterns in which the parties have made an agreement that would look as if it were a completed bargain except for the fact that the parties included in the agreement a provision that contemplated a further, more elaborate agreement. Often, the original agreement would be sufficiently definite to be enforceable but for the presence of such a provision. The question then is, what is the legal significance of the provision? The rule of classical contract law again was binary and static: If the parties intended the further agreement to be only an evidentiary memorial of the terms of their original agreement (for example, to tie together various pieces of correspondence), and the original agreement was otherwise sufficiently definite, then the original agreement was enforceable. If, however, the parties intended not to be bound unless and until the further agreement was executed, so that the further agreement was to be the consummation of their negotiations, then the original agreement was unenforceable. Accordingly, the parties' contemplation of a further agreement either (1) prevented the formation of a contract, in which case there was no liability, or (2) did not, in which case there was a contract on the terms of the original agreement.

Finally, classical contract law did not recognize a duty to negotiate in good faith. On the contrary, it adopted the rule that an agreement to agree was unenforceable, which by implication precluded an obligation to negotiate in good faith.

As will be seen in this Chapter, in regard to these issues modern contract law has made important dynamic departures from the static offer-and-acceptance model of classical contract law.

ACADEMY CHICAGO PUBLISHERS v. CHEEVER

Supreme Court of Illinois, 1991.
144 Ill.2d 24, 161 Ill.Dec. 335, 578 N.E.2d 981.

JUSTICE HEIPLE delivered the opinion of the court:

This is a suit for declaratory judgment. It arose out of an agreement between the widow of the widely published author, John Cheever, and Academy Chicago Publishers. Contact between the parties began in 1987 when the publisher approached Mrs. Cheever about the possibility of publishing a collection of Mr. Cheever's short stories which, though previously published, had never been collected into a single anthology. In August of that year, a publishing agreement was signed which provided, in pertinent part:

> "Agreement made this 15th day of August 1987, between Academy Chicago Publishers or any affiliated entity or imprint (hereinafter referred to as the Publisher) and Mary W. Cheever and Franklin H. Dennis of the USA (hereinafter referred to as Author).

Whereas the parties are desirous of publishing and having published a certain work or works, tentatively titled *The Uncollected Stories of John Cheever* (hereinafter referred to as the Work):

* * * * * *

2. The Author will deliver to the Publisher on a mutually agreeable date one copy of the manuscript of the Work as finally arranged by the editor and satisfactory to the Publisher in form and content.

* * * * * *

5. Within a reasonable time and a mutually agreeable date after delivery of the final revised manuscript, the Publisher will publish the Work at its own expense, in such style and manner and at such price as it deems best, and will keep the Work in print as long as it deems it expedient; but it will not be responsible for delays caused by circumstances beyond its control.''

Academy and its editor, Franklin Dennis, assumed the task of locating and procuring the uncollected stories and delivering them to Mrs. Cheever. Mrs. Cheever and Mr. Dennis received partial advances for manuscript preparation. By the end of 1987, Academy had located and delivered more than 60 uncollected stories to Mrs. Cheever. Shortly thereafter, Mrs. Cheever informed Academy in writing that she objected to the publication of the book and attempted to return her advance.

Academy filed suit in the circuit court of Cook County in February 1988, seeking a declaratory judgment: (1) granting Academy the exclusive right to publish the tentatively titled, ''The Uncollected Stories of John Cheever''; (2) designating Franklin Dennis as the book's editor; and (3) obligating Mrs. Cheever to deliver the manuscript from which the work was to be published. The trial court entered an order declaring, *inter alia:* (1) that the publishing agreement executed by the parties was valid and enforceable; (2) that Mrs. Cheever was entitled to select the short stories to be included in the manuscript for publication; (3) that Mrs. Cheever would comply with her obligations of good faith and fair dealing if she delivered a manuscript including at least 10 to 15 stories totaling at least 140 pages; (4) Academy controlled the design and format of the work to be published, but control must be exercised in cooperation with Mrs. Cheever.

Academy appealed the trial court's order, challenging particularly the declaration regarding the minimum story and page numbers for Mrs. Cheever's compliance with the publishing agreement, and the declaration that Academy must consult with defendant on all matters of publication of the manuscript.

The appellate court affirmed the decision of the trial court with respect to the validity and enforceability of the publishing agreement and the minimum story and page number requirements for Mrs. Cheever's compliance with same. The appellate court reversed the trial court's declaration regarding control of publication, stating that the trial court erred in considering extrinsic evidence to interpret the agreement regarding control of the publication, given the explicit language of the agreement granting exclusive control to Academy. (200 Ill.App.3d 677, 146 Ill.Dec. 386, 558 N.E.2d 349.) Appeal is taken in this court pursuant to Supreme Court Rule 315(a) (134 Ill.2d R. 315(a)).

The parties raise several issues on appeal; this matter, however, is one of contract and we confine our discussion to the issue of the validity and enforceability of the publishing agreement.

While the trial court and the appellate court agreed that the publishing agreement constitutes a valid and enforceable contract, we cannot concur. The principles of contract state that in order for a valid contract to be formed, an "offer must be so definite as to its material terms or require such definite terms in the acceptance that the promises and performances to be rendered by each party are reasonably certain." (1 Williston, Contracts §§ 38 through 48 (3d ed. 1957); 1 Corbin, Contracts §§ 95 through 100 (1963).) Although the parties may have had and manifested the intent to make a contract, if the content of their agreement is unduly uncertain and indefinite no contract is formed. 1 Williston § 37; 1 Corbin § 95.

The pertinent language of this agreement lacks the definite and certain essential terms required for the formation of an enforceable contract. (*Midland Hotel Corp. v. Reuben H. Donnelley Corp.* (1987), 118 Ill.2d 306, 113 Ill.Dec. 252, 515 N.E.2d 61.) A contract "is sufficiently definite and certain to be enforceable if the court is enabled from the terms and provisions thereof, under proper rules of construction and applicable principles of equity, to ascertain what the parties have agreed to do." (*Morey v. Hoffman* (1957), 12 Ill.2d 125, 145 N.E.2d 644.) The provisions of the subject publishing agreement do not provide the court with a means of determining the intent of the parties.

Trial testimony reveals that a major source of controversy between the parties is the length and content of the proposed book. The agreement sheds no light on the minimum or maximum number of stories or pages necessary for publication of the collection, nor is there any implicit language from which we can glean the intentions of the parties with respect to this essential contract term. The publishing agreement is similarly silent with respect to who will decide which stories will be included in the collection. Other omissions, ambiguities, unresolved essential terms and illusory terms are: No date certain for delivery of the manuscript. No definition of the criteria which would render the manuscript satisfactory to the publisher either as to form or content. No date certain as to when publication will occur. No certainty as to style or manner in which the book will be published nor is there any indication as to the price at which such book will be sold, or the length of time publication shall continue, all of which terms are left to the sole discretion of the publisher.

A contract may be enforced even though some contract terms may be missing or left to be agreed upon, but if the essential terms are so uncertain that there is no basis for deciding whether the agreement has been kept or broken, there is no contract. (*Champaign National Bank v. Landers Seed Co.* (1988), 165 Ill.App.3d 1090, 116 Ill.Dec. 742, 519 N.E.2d 957, Restatement (Second) of Contracts § 33 (1981).) Without setting forth adequate terms for compliance, the publishing agreement provides no basis for determining when breach has occurred, and, therefore, is not a valid and enforceable contract.

An enforceable contract must include a meeting of the minds or mutual assent as to the terms of the contract. (*Midland Hotel,* 118 Ill.2d at 313, 113 Ill.Dec. 252, 515 N.E.2d 61.) It is not compelling that [whether?] the parties share a subjective understanding as to the terms of the contract; the parties' conduct may indicate an agreement to the terms of same. (*Steinberg v. Chicago Medical School* (1977), 69 Ill.2d 320, 13 Ill.Dec. 699, 371 N.E.2d 634.) In the instant case, however, no mutual assent has been illustrated. The parties did not and do not share a common understanding of the essential terms of the publishing agreement.

In rendering its judgment, the trial court supplied minimum terms for Mrs. Cheever's compliance, including story and page numbers. It is not uncommon for a court to supply a missing material term, as the reasonable conclusion often is that the parties intended that the term be supplied by implication. However, where the subject matter of the contract has not been decided upon and there is no standard available for reasonable implication, courts ordinarily refuse to supply the missing term. (1 Williston § 42; 1 Corbin § 100.) No suitable standard was available for the trial court to apply. It is our opinion that the trial court incorrectly supplied minimum compliance terms to the publishing agreement, as the agreement did not constitute a valid and enforceable contract to begin with. As noted above, the publishing agreement contains major unresolved uncertainties. It is not the role of the court to rewrite the contract and spell out essential elements not included therein.

In light of our decision that there was no valid and enforceable contract between the parties, we need not address other issues raised on appeal. For the foregoing reasons, the decisions of the trial and appellate courts in this declaratory judgment action are reversed.

Reversed.

JUSTICES CLARK and FREEMAN took no part in the consideration or decision of this opinion.

––––––––

REGO v. DECKER, 482 P.2d 834 (Alaska 1971). "Regarding the rule requiring reasonable certainty and its application to particular factual situations, [our cases] demonstrate that:

> The dream of a mechanical justice is recognized for what it is—only a dream and not even a rosy or desirable one.

"In general it has been said that the primary underlying purpose of the law of contracts is the attempted 'realization of reasonable expectations that have been induced by the making of a promise.' In light of this underlying purpose, two general considerations become relevant to solution of reasonable certainty-specific performance problems. On the one hand, courts should fill gaps in contracts to ensure fairness where the reasonable expectations of the parties are fairly clear. The parties to a contract often cannot negotiate and draft solutions to all the problems which may arise. Except in transactions involving very large amounts of money or adhesion contracts to be imposed on many parties, contracts tend to be skeletal, because the amount of time and money needed to produce a more complete contract would be disproportionate to the value of the transaction to the parties. Courts would impose too great a burden on the business community if the standards of certainty were set too high. On the other hand, the courts should not impose on a party any performance to which he did not and probably would not have agreed. Where the character of a gap in an agreement manifests failure to reach an agreement rather than a sketchy agreement, or where gaps cannot be filled with confidence that the reasonable expectations of the parties are being fulfilled, then specific enforcement should be denied for lack of reasonable certainty.

"Several other considerations affect the standard of certainty. A greater degree of certainty is required for specific performance than for damages, because of the difficulty of framing a decree specifying the performance required, as compared with the relative facility with which a breach may be perceived for purposes of awarding damages. Less certainty is required where the party seeking specific performance has substantially shifted his position in reliance on the supposed contract, than where the contract is wholly unperformed on both sides."

AROK CONSTRUCTION CO. v. INDIAN CONSTRUCTION SERVICES, 174 Ariz. 291, 848 P.2d 870 (1993). "The enforcement of incomplete agreements is a necessary fact of economic life. Business people are not soothsayers, and can neither provide in advance for every unforeseen contingency nor answer every unasked question regarding a commercial agreement. This is especially so with a complex contract for a major construction project. Nor are entrepreneurs perfect at drafting legal documents. Finally, parties may want to bind themselves and at the same time desire to leave some matters open for future resolution in order to maintain flexibility. Thus, courts are often presented with incomplete bargains when the parties intend and desire to be bound.... Refusing the enforcement of obligations the parties intended to create and that marketplace transactions require hardly seems the solution."

RESTATEMENT, SECOND, CONTRACTS §§ 33, 34

[See Selected Source Materials Supplement]

UCC §§ 2–204, 2–305, 2–308, 2–309, 2–310

[See Selected Source Materials Supplement]

CISG ARTS. 14(1), 31, 33, 55, 57, 58

[See Selected Source Materials Supplement]

UNIDROIT PRINCIPLES OF INTERNATIONAL COMMERCIAL CONTRACTS ARTS. 2.1.2, 2.1.13, 2.1.14, 2.1.15, 5.1.7, 5.1.8, 6.1.1, 6.6.6

[See Selected Source Materials Supplement]

————

PRINCIPLES OF EUROPEAN CONTRACT LAW
§§ 2.201(1), 2.301, 6.104, 6.109, 7.01, 7.102

[See Selected Source Materials Supplement]

————

TEACHERS INSURANCE AND ANNUITY ASSOCIATION OF AMERICA v. TRIBUNE CO.

United States District Court, Southern District of New York, 1987.
670 F.Supp. 491.

LEVAL, DISTRICT JUDGE. . . .

[To raise cash that it needed for a number of purposes, including the operation of its newspaper, The New York Daily News, Tribune Company decided to sell the News Building. To this end, Tribune entered negotiations to sell the News Building to LaSalle Partners as part of a complex three-party transaction. The concept of the transaction was as follows: LaSalle would pay for the News Building by giving Tribune a mortgage note secured by a mortgage on the building. This note was to be "nonrecourse," meaning that LaSalle would have no liability under the mortgage note, although the noteholder could foreclose on the Building under the mortgage if the note was not paid.

[Because LaSalle would give Tribune only a nonrecourse note, the LaSalle transaction, taken in itself, would produce no immediate cash for Tribune. However, Tribune would proceed to borrow from a lending institution an amount of money equal to the mortgage note, and in exchange would give the lending institution Tribune's own note for that amount. The loan agreement with the lending institution would provide that Tribune could pay off its own note to the institution by "putting" (delivering to the institution), in place of its own note, the nonrecourse mortgage note that Tribune would receive from LaSalle. To compensate the lending institution for the additional risk inherent in the possible put, Tribune would pay the lender a premium above market interest rates.

[The complex nature of the proposed transaction was largely driven by tax considerations, but there was also an accounting element to the transaction. Tribune believed that because it would have the right to put the mortgage note to the lending institution in full satisfaction of its debt to the institution, it would not be required to include its debt to the institution as a liability on its balance sheet. Instead, Tribune believed, it could employ offset accounting, under which it would set off its debt to the lending institution against the mortgage note, eliminate both its debt and the mortgage note from its balance sheet, and instead describe the debt and mortgage note in the footnotes to its financial statements. This would make Tribune's balance sheet look better, because Tribune would show the cash infusion, but not the debt.

[For tax reasons, it was important that the transaction be completed during 1982. Tribune prepared a list of six leading institutions, including Teachers Insurance and Annuity Association of America ("Teachers" or "TIAA"), that it believed would have the means and flexibility to make a loan with the required specifications. All but Teachers promptly rejected Tribune's proposal. On August 20, Scott Smith, Tribune's Vice President and Treasurer, sent Martha Driver, of Teachers, an Offering Circular, including a term sheet, which described the proposed transaction. Smith's letter stated, "While we are flexible on funds delivery, our objective is to have a firm commitment from a lender by September 15, 1982. Consequently, we need to move the due diligence and negotiation process along very quickly." On September 16, Teachers' Finance Committee met and approved the Tribune loan. Driver then told Smith that TIAA would promptly issue a commitment letter, committing TIAA to make the loan.

[The commitment letter was mailed by TIAA on September 22. It included a two-page term sheet, which was drawn from Tribune's own term sheet and ensuing conversations. TIAA's term sheet covered all the basic economic terms of a loan. Neither TIAA's term sheet nor its commitment letter made reference to the availability of offset accounting. TIAA's letter stated that the loan agreement was "contingent upon the preparation, execution and delivery of documents ... in form and substance satisfactory to TIAA and to TIAA's special counsel," and that the transaction documents would contain the usual and customary representations and warranties, closing conditions, other covenants, and events of default "as we and our special counsel may deem reasonably necessary to accomplish this transaction." The letter concluded by inviting Tribune to "evidence acceptance of the conditions of this letter by having it executed below by a duly authorized officer," and added that "Upon receipt by TIAA of an accepted counterpart of this letter, our agreement to purchase from you and your agreement to issue sell and deliver to us ... the captioned securities, shall become a binding agreement between us."

[The "binding agreement" language in the TIAA commitment letter caused serious concern to Tribune's lawyers. Tribune's outside counsel advised Smith, Tribune's Vice President and Treasurer, not to sign a letter containing "binding agreement" language. But having been turned down by five other lending institutions, Smith did not want to risk losing TIAA's commitment. Therefore, he did not raise a question with TIAA concerning the "binding agreement" language. Instead, he executed the commitment letter on Tribune's behalf, and added a notation that the commitment letter was subject to certain modifications outlined in his covering letter. In the covering letter, Smith wrote that "[O]ur acceptance and agreement is subject to approval by the Company's Board of Directors and the preparation and execution of legal documentation satisfactory to the Company." Smith's covering letter, like TIAA's commitment letter, made no mention of offset accounting.

[On October 28, Tribune's board resolved "that the proper officers of the Company be and they hereby are authorized" to effect the borrowing "with all of the actual terms and conditions to be subject to the prior approval by resolution of the Finance Committee." In the meantime, however, interest rates had dropped rapidly, and were now substantially below the rates that prevailed when TIAA and Tribune had entered into the commitment letter. In addition, Tribune began to be concerned that its accountants would not approve Tribune's use of offset accounting for the transaction.

[On December 6, Tribune closed the sale of the building to LaSalle. TIAA then became concerned that Tribune, which could now borrow at substantially lower rates, was seeking to back out of the transaction, and pressed Tribune to put the loan documents into final form. To this end, TIAA dropped a demand it had made imposing conditions on Tribune's exercise of the put, and it asked for a meeting to iron out all open issues. But the drop in interest rates, together with doubts as to the availability of offset accounting, now made the deal much less attractive to Tribune. Smith therefore replied that there was no point in meeting unless TIAA was willing to agree that Tribune's obligation to close the TIAA loan would be conditional on Tribune's ability to use offset accounting. TIAA responded that Tribune's accounting was not part of the deal. When Tribune exhibited no further interest in pursuing the transaction, TIAA brought suit.]

DISCUSSION

The primary contested issue is as to the nature of the obligations that arose out of the commitment letter agreement:

Tribune contends that although the commitment letter was an undertaking to negotiate, it did not obligate either side to enter into a loan contract that was adverse to its interest. Pointing out that the commitment letter agreement left many terms open, that both sides had reserved the right of approval of satisfactory documentation, and that Tribune had furthermore made its obligation conditioned on the approval of its Board of Directors, it argues that it had no binding commitment to the loan agreement, especially if it found the terms adverse to its interests.

Teachers [TIAA] argues that although the commitment letter did not constitute a concluded *loan agreement,* it was nonetheless a binding commitment which obligated both sides to negotiate in good faith toward a final contract conforming to the agreed terms; it thus committed both sides not to abandon the deal, nor to break it by a demand that was outside the scope of

the agreement. Although Teachers recognizes that the letter agreement left many points unspecified, it argues that the open terms were of minor economic significance and were covered by the provision that "[t]he documents shall contain such representations and warranties, closing conditions, other covenants, events of default and remedies, requirements for delivery of financial statements, and other information and provisions *as are usual and customary in this type of transaction....*" (Emphasis supplied.) ... It argues that these minor open terms did not render the contract illusory or unenforceable. Nor did they indicate an intention of the parties not to be bound when taken together with the express language of "binding agreement." Although it was of course possible for the deal to break without liability on either side by reason of inability of the parties to reach agreement on the open terms, Teachers argues that neither side was free to break the deal over conditions which were either inconsistent with the agreed terms or outside the scope of provisions that would be "usual and customary in this type of transaction."
...

There has been much litigation over preliminary agreements. It is difficult to generalize about their legal effect. They cover a broad scope ranging in innumerable forms and variations from letters of intent which presuppose that no binding obligations will be placed upon any party until final contract documents have been signed, to firm binding commitments which, notwithstanding a need for a more detailed documentation of agreement, can bind the parties to adhere in good faith to the deal that has been agreed. As is commonly the case with contract disputes, prime significance attaches to the intentions of the parties and to their manifestations of intent. Labels such as "letter of intent" or "commitment letter" are not necessarily controlling although they may be helpful indicators of the parties' intentions. Notwithstanding the intention of the parties at the time, if the agreement is too fragmentary, in that it leaves open terms of too fundamental importance, it may be incapable of sustaining binding legal obligation. Furthermore, the conclusion that a preliminary agreement created binding obligations does not necessarily resolve disputes because it leaves open the further question of the nature, scope and extent of the binding obligations.

A primary concern for courts in such disputes is to avoid trapping parties in surprise contractual obligations that they never intended. Ordinarily in contract negotiations, enforceable legal rights do not arise until either the expression of mutual consent to be bound, or some equivalent event that marks acceptance of offer. Contractual liability, unlike tort liability, arises from consent to be bound (or in any event from the manifestation of consent). It is fundamental to contract law that mere participation in negotiations and discussions does not create binding obligation, even if agreement is reached on all disputed terms. More is needed than agreement on each detail, which is overall agreement (or offer and acceptance) to enter into the binding contract.[6] Nor is this principle altered by the fact that negotiating parties may have entered into letters of intent or preliminary agreements if those were made with the understanding that neither side would be bound until final agreement was reached. The Court of Appeals in several recent cases has stressed the importance of recognizing the freedom of negotiating parties from

---

6. *See Winston v. Mediafare Entertainment Corp.,* 777 F.2d 78 (2d Cir.1985); *R.G. Group v. Horn & Hardart Co.,* 751 F.2d 69 (2d Cir. 1984); *Reprosystem, B.V. v. SCM Corp.,* 727 F.2d 257 (2d Cir.), *cert. denied,* 469 U.S. 828, 105 S.Ct. 110, 83 L.Ed.2d 54 (1984).

binding obligations, notwithstanding their having entered into various forms of non-binding preliminary assent. Those decisions have underlined various indicia that can be helpful in making the determination whether a manifestation of preliminary assent amounted to a legally binding agreement.*

Notwithstanding the importance of protecting negotiating parties from involuntary judicially imposed contract, it is equally important that courts enforce and preserve agreements that were intended as binding, despite a need for further documentation or further negotiation. It is, of course, the aim of contract law to gratify, not to defeat, expectations that arise out of intended contractual agreement, despite informality or the need for further proceedings between the parties.

Preliminary contracts with binding force can be of at least two distinct types. One occurs when the parties have reached complete agreement (including the agreement to be bound) on all the issues perceived to require negotiation. Such an agreement is preliminary only in form—only in the sense that the parties desire a more elaborate formalization of the agreement. The second stage is not necessary; it is merely considered desirable. As the Court of Appeals stated with respect to such preliminary agreements in *V'Soske v. Barwick,* 404 F.2d 495, 499 (2d Cir.), *cert. denied,* 394 U.S. 921, 89 S.Ct. 1197, 22 L.Ed.2d 454 (1969), "the mere fact that the parties contemplate memorializing their agreement in a formal document does not prevent their informal agreement from taking effect prior to that event.... Restatement (Second) of Contracts, § 26 (then Tent.Draft No. 1, 1964); 1 Corbin on Contracts § 30 (1950); 1 Williston on Contracts § 28 (3d ed. 1957)."

The second and different sort of preliminary binding agreement is one that expresses mutual commitment to a contract on agreed major terms, while recognizing the existence of open terms that remain to be negotiated. Although the existence of open terms generally suggests that binding agreement has not been reached, that is not necessarily so. For the parties can bind themselves to a concededly incomplete agreement in the sense that they accept a mutual commitment to negotiate together in good faith in an effort to reach final agreement within the scope that has been settled in the preliminary agreement. To differentiate this sort of preliminary agreement from the first, it might be referred to as a binding preliminary commitment. Its binding obligations are of a different order than those which arise out of the first type discussed above. The first type binds both sides to their ultimate contractual objective in recognition that that contract has been reached, despite the anticipation of further formalities. The second type—the binding preliminary commitment—does not commit the parties to their ultimate contractual objective but rather to the obligation to negotiate the open issues in good faith in an attempt to reach the alternate objective within the agreed framework. In the first type, a party may lawfully demand performance of the transaction even if no further steps have been taken following the making of the "preliminary" agreement. In the second type, he may not. What he may

---

* [These factors were summarized as follows in *Winston,* supra note 7.

    ... We have articulated several factors that help determine whether the parties intended to be bound in the absence of a document executed by both sides. The court is to consider (1) whether there has been an express reservation of the right not to be bound in the absence of a writing; (2) whether there has been partial performance of the contract; (3) whether all of the terms of the alleged contract have been agreed upon; and (4) whether the agreement at issue is the type of contract that is usually committed to writing.

(Footnote by ed.)]

demand, however, is that his counter-party negotiate the open terms in good faith toward a final contract incorporating the agreed terms. This obligation does not guarantee that the final contract will be concluded if both parties comport with their obligation, as good faith differences in the negotiation of the open issues may prevent a reaching of final contract. It is also possible that the parties will lose interest as circumstances change and will mutually abandon the negotiation. The obligation does, however, bar a party from renouncing the deal, abandoning the negotiations, or insisting on conditions that do not conform to the preliminary agreement.

It may often be difficult for a court to determine whether a preliminary manifestation of assent should be found to be a binding commitment. The factors mentioned by the Court of Appeals in *Winston*, 777 F.2d 78, and *R.G. Group*, 751 F.2d 69, as relevant to a determination whether final contracts had been reached in preliminary form are also relevant to determination whether preliminary commitments are to be considered binding. But, for this different inquiry, the factors must be applied in a different way. For example, in *R.G. Group*, 751 F.2d at 76, the court identified the ... factor ... "whether there was literally nothing left to negotiate or settle, so that all that remained to be done was to sign what had already been fully agreed to." The existence of open terms is always a factor tending against the conclusion that the parties have reached a binding agreement. But open terms obviously have a somewhat different significance where, unlike *R.G. Group*, the nature of the contract alleged is that it commits the parties in good faith to negotiate the open terms. To consider the existence of open terms as fatal would be to rule, in effect, that preliminary binding commitments cannot be enforced. That is not the law.

In seeking to determine whether such a preliminary commitment should be considered binding, a court's task is, once again, to determine the intentions of the parties at the time of their entry into the understanding, as well as their manifestations to one another by which the understanding was reached. Courts must be particularly careful to avoid imposing liability where binding obligation was not intended. There is a strong presumption against finding binding obligation in agreements which include open terms, call for future approvals and expressly anticipate future preparation and execution of contract documents. Nonetheless, if that is what the parties intended, courts should not frustrate their achieving that objective or disappoint legitimately bargained contract expectations.

Giving legal recognition to preliminary binding commitments serves a valuable function in the marketplace, particularly for relatively standardized transactions like loans. It permits borrowers and lenders to make plans in reliance upon their preliminary agreements and present market conditions. Without such legal recognition, parties would be obliged to expend enormous sums negotiating every detail of final contract documentation before knowing whether they have an agreement, and if so, on what terms. At the same time, a party that does not wish to be bound at the time of the preliminary exchange of letters can very easily protect itself by not accepting language that indicates a "firm commitment" or "binding agreement."

*   *   *   *   *   *

Upon careful consideration of the circumstances and the express terms of this commitment letter, I conclude that it represented a binding preliminary commitment and obligated both sides to seek to conclude a final loan agreement upon the agreed terms by negotiating in good faith to resolve such additional terms as are customary in such agreements. I reject Tribune's contention that its reservation of the right of approval to its Board of Directors left it free to abandon the transaction.

Expression of Intent

The Court of Appeals' first and most important factor looks to the language of the preliminary agreement for indication whether the parties considered it binding or whether they intended not to be bound until the conclusion of final formalities. This factor strongly supports Teachers. The exchange of letters constituting the commitment was replete with the terminology of binding contract, for example:

> If the foregoing properly sets forth your understanding of this transaction, please evidence acceptance of the conditions of this letter by having it executed below by a duly authorized officer ... and by returning one executed counterpart....

> Upon receipt by [Teachers] of an accepted counterpart of this letter, our agreement to purchase from you and your agreement to issue, sell and deliver to us ... the captioned securities, shall become a binding agreement between us.

In signing, Tribune used the words "Accepted and agreed to." Tribune's additional letter of acceptance began "Attached is an executed copy of the Commitment Letter ... for a $76 million loan." The intention to create mutually binding contractual obligations is stated with unmistakable clarity, in a manner not comfortably compatible with Tribune's contention that either side was free to walk away from the deal if it decided its interests were not served thereby.

Tribune argues that this language of binding agreement was effectively contradicted by its statement that "our acceptance and agreement is subject to approval by the Company's Board of Directors and the preparation and execution of legal documentation satisfactory to the Company," as well as by similar reservations in Teachers' letter.

Contracts of preliminary commitment characteristically contain language reserving rights of approval and establishing conditions such as the preparation and execution of documents satisfactory to the contracting party. Although such reservations, considered alone, undoubtedly tend to indicate an intention not to be finally bound, they do not necessarily require that conclusion. Such terms are not to be considered in isolation, but in the context of the overall agreement. Such terms are by no means incompatible with intention to be bound. Since the parties recognize that their deal will involve further documentation and further negotiation of open terms, such reservations make clear the right of a party, or of its Board, to insist on appropriate documentation and to negotiate for or demand protections which are customary for such transactions. In *Reprosystem,* 727 F.2d at 262, and *R.G. Group,* 751 F.2d at 75, the court reasoned that a term stating the agreement would be effective "when executed" could conclusively establish that no binding force was intended prior to execution. That reasoning is of diminished force, however, where the inquiry is not whether the parties had concluded their deal, but only whether they had entered into a binding preliminary commitment which required further steps. Here, the reservation of Board approval and the expressed "contingen[cy] upon the preparation, execution and delivery of documents" did not override and nullify the acknowledgement that a "binding agreement" had been made on the stated terms; those reservations merely recognized that various issues and documentation remained open which also would require negotiation and approval. If full consideration of the circumstances and the contract language indicates that there was a mutual intent to be bound to a preliminary commitment, the presence of such reservations does not free a party to walk away from its deal merely because it later decides that the deal is not in its interest.

The Context of the Negotiations

These conclusions are further reinforced by the particular facts of the negotiation. As Smith's proposal letter of August 20 advised Teachers, Tribune wanted "to have a firm commitment from a lender by September 15, 1982." If such a "firm commitment" meant nothing more than Tribune now contends it does, such a commitment would have been of little value, as the lender would have remained free to abandon the loan if it decided at anytime that the transaction did not suit its purposes, whether because of changed interest rates or for any reason: Tribune wanted a firm commitment because it felt it needed to be sure the transaction would be concluded by the end of the year.

This same thinking governed Tribune's conduct a month later when it received the Teachers' commitment letter. Tribune's lawyers, recognizing that the form of agreement committed Tribune to a "binding" obligation, warned about the consequences of signing it. Tribune, however, wanted Teachers' binding commitment to make the loan. Tribune had been turned down by the five other lenders it considered eligible, and it did not want to risk losing Teachers' commitment. Accordingly, Smith refrained from raising any question about the "binding agreement" language. If he intended by adding the reservation of approval of Tribune's Board of Directors to change the deal fundamentally by freeing Tribune from binding obligations without Teachers noticing the change, he did not accomplish this. Tribune remained committed, as Teachers did. That is to say each was obligated to seek in good faith to conclude a final agreement within the terms specified in the commitment letter, supplemented by such representations, warranties and other conditions as are customary in such transactions. Teachers would not have been free to walk away from the loan by reason of a subsequent decision that the transaction was not in Teachers' interest. Nor could Tribune.

Tribune further contends that, given the uncertainties implicit in the three-cornered deal, neither party could have considered the loan commitment as binding. The agreed terms required Tribune to pay a premium over the prevailing interest rates for the privilege of its option to put the mortgage to Teachers. If Tribune had failed to conclude its deal with LaSalle for the sale of the Building, there would have been no purchase money mortgage and no reason for paying an interest premium.

The argument is not frivolous, but nor is it compelling. If Tribune had failed to sell the News Building and Teachers had nonetheless sought to compel it to take down the loan, Tribune might have succeeded in arguing that the sale of the Building was a mutually agreed implicit condition of the enforceability of the loan agreement. Tribune's argument in those circumstances would have been supported by the references in the commitment letter to the purchase money mortgage resulting from the Building sale.

But, however that dispute would have been resolved had it arisen, it does not compel the conclusion that there was no binding obligation. The Building sale did not fall through. It was concluded on the anticipated terms. If the sale of the Building was an implicit condition of the borrowing, that condition was fulfilled.

Open Terms

Tribune contends that the commitment letter agreement included so many open terms that it could not be deemed a binding contract. It argues also that the numerous open terms indicate a lack of intention on either side to be bound. Neither contention is convincing. Tribune does cite reputable authority to the effect that, notwithstanding language of binding agreement, if a contract fails to include agreement on basic terms of prime importance, it can be considered a nullity. This principle, however, has no application to the present facts. The two page term sheet attached to the commitment letter covered the important economic terms of a loan. The fact that countless pages of relatively conventional minor clauses remained to be negotiated does not render the agreement unenforceable.

The contention is superficially appealing with respect to the mortgage. The commitment letter, although referring to Tribune's optional right to put a mortgage to Teachers in satisfaction of its obligations, did not specify any of the terms of such a mortgage. Absence of agreement on so important a specification as the basic terms of the mortgage would render this agreement illusory. There was, however, no absence of agreement on the basic terms of the mortgage. The references in the commitment letter to the mortgage were understood by both parties as references to the mortgage term sheet that Tribune had furnished to Teachers in its Offering Circular. [The commitment letter stated that the mortgage to be tendered by Tribune "shall preserve the economics proposed for the present Mortgagee (Tribune Company)."] That two-page term sheet described the important economic terms of the proposed LaSalle purchase money mortgage. Notwithstanding its silence as to countless pages of secondary conventional mortgage clauses which remained to be negotiated, it sufficiently specified the important terms to make the commitment letter agreement meaningful and enforceable.

Nor did the existence of open secondary terms compel the conclusion that the parties did not intend to be bound. In support of this argument, Tribune cites the implication of the Court of Appeals in *R.G. Group,* 751 F.2d at 76–77 and *Winston,* 777 F.2d at 80, 82, that the existence of any single open term requires the conclusion that a binding contract had not yet been reached. This takes the Court's observation out of context and distorts its meaning. If the issue is whether the parties have reached final agreement requiring only formal memorialization, the recognized existence of open terms may be a strong indication that they have not. If, on the other hand, as here, the question is whether a preliminary expression of commitment was intended to bind the parties to negotiate the open terms in good faith, the mere fact of the existence of open terms is, of course, far less persuasive. Although the existence of open terms may always be a factor that suggests intention not to be bound, it is by no means conclusive. Where the parties have manifested intention to make a binding agreement, the mere fact of open terms will not permit them to disavow it.

Partial Performance

The factor of partial performance slightly favors Teachers. The evidence shows that for Teachers, its "commitment" to lend involved a budgeting of the funds, albeit somewhat informal. Teachers was in the business of lending its funds. The amount it had available for placement in long-term loans was finite, if large. In its loan budgeting process, Teachers would informally allocate funds which had been so committed. Such allocation reduced the net amount considered available for commitments to new loans. In fact, Teachers advised Tribune that it had only $25 million remaining available to be advanced in 1982 and that the rest would be advanced in 1983.

Tribune argues that because there was no formal segregation, it was of no significance. This misses the point. However informally it was done, the allocation of the loan commitment effectively reserved the funds for the Tribune loan. It reduced the amount of Teachers' funds that it would consider available to competing borrowers. It meant that Teachers would forgo opportunities to procure commitments from other borrowers when its own commitments exhausted its available funds.

In urgently seeking Teachers' "firm commitment" by September 15, Tribune well understood that the commitment would involve a partial performance on Teachers' part. By virtue of the commitment given in September, Tribune was assured that when the time came in December for concluding final documents and drawdown, it would not be told that Teachers had nothing left to lend. Tribune was negotiating to reserve those funds. Teachers acceded and issued the commitment. That constituted a partial performance.

A party's partial performance does not necessarily indicate a belief that the other side is bound. A party may make some partial performance merely to further the likelihood of consummation of a transaction it considers advantageous. This factor was not the subject of highly focused evidence. I have not attached great importance to it and mention it primarily because it is listed among the factors suggested by the Court of Appeals in *R.G. Group* and *Winston.* I conclude, however, that this factor favors the conclusion that both sides considered the commitment binding.

The Customary Form for Such Transactions

The fourth factor mentioned in *R.G. Group,* and *Winston,* is "whether the agreement at issue is the type of contract that is usually committed to writing." 777 F.2d at 80. *See also* 751 F.2d at 77. Of course, the agreement here, unlike those cases, was in writing, but that does not dispose of the issue. To give this factor a broader application, it would better be put in terms of whether in the relevant business community, it is customary to accord binding force to the type of informal or preliminary agreement at issue. The evidence on that question tends to favor Teachers.

Of course it is true, as Tribune argues, that $80 million loans involving mortgages are generally not concluded by means of a four-page letter. But that is not the issue. The question is rather whether the customary practices of the relevant financial community include according such binding force as

Teachers here advocates to such preliminary commitment agreements. Teachers' expert evidence showed that it is within the recognized practices of the financial community to accept that preliminary commitments can be binding. Not all preliminary commitments are binding. Some are not. Some are binding on only one side: Where, for example, the borrower pays a commitment fee for the purpose of binding the lender, the agreement may be in the nature of an option to the borrower to decide by a specified date whether to go ahead with the transaction. In such cases the seller has been paid for its one-sided commitment. Some such preliminary agreements are properly seen as merely letters of intent which leave both sides free to abandon the transaction. The point is that the practices of the marketplace are not rigid or uniform. They encompass a considerable variety of transactions negotiated to suit the needs of the parties, including mutually binding preliminary commitments. Each transaction must be examined carefully to determine its characteristics.

Tribune has failed to show to the court's satisfaction that such binding commitments are outside the usages of the marketplace.

Action by Tribune's Board of Directors

The parties disagree as to whether the Teachers' loan was or was not approved by Tribune's Board of Directors. Tribune contends that the resolutions adopted by its Board on October 28th did not involve any approval whatsoever, but merely a delegation of responsibility to the Finance Committee to approve or disapprove the transaction. Teachers contends that the action of the Board did approve the loan in concept, while delegating to the Finance Committee the right and authority to pass on the particular loan documents. Teachers contends that its interpretation is reinforced by Smith's statement to Driver, when she inquired in late November, that the Board had given "general approval" to the transaction at the October 28 meeting (a statement Smith denies having made).

I need not rule on whether the resolutions adopted by the Board of Directors did or did not constitute approval of the transaction, because nothing turns on this. As noted above, although Tribune had reserved the right of approval of the final transaction to its Board of Directors, this did not mean Tribune could defeat its obligations under the binding agreement of commitment merely by having its Board do nothing. The commitment agreement called for conclusion of the transaction and a $25 million first drawdown before the end of the year. Even if I were to accept Tribune's contention that its Board took no action other than to delegate responsibility to the Finance Committee, that would not justify Tribune's backing out of its binding agreement to negotiate in good faith to reach a complete final contract.

Tribune's argument would construe the commitment letter agreement either as a free option to Tribune to decide over the next three months whether to hold Teachers to its commitment to make the loan, or alternatively as a nonbinding statement of mutual intention. Neither is consistent with either the written agreement or the conduct of the parties. Tribune had requested the "firm commitment" of Teachers to make the loan. Teachers' firm commitment was not given for free but in exchange for Tribune's similarly binding commitment. The reservations as to preparation and execution of documents and as to the satisfaction of Teachers' counsel and Tribune's Board permitted each side to negotiate the implementation of the agreement and to require the inclusion of customary terms in a form which it deemed necessary or appropriate to its protection. But those reservations did not authorize either side to escape its obligation simply by declining to negotiate or to give approval.

In any event, I conclude that Tribune's Board did give approval within the meaning of the agreement. The Minutes reflect that the proper officers were expressly authorized to arrange for the borrowing at a maximum interest rate of 15.25%, "with all of the actual terms and conditions to be subject to the prior approval by resolution of the Finance Committee...." The Resolution went on to say that the "authority granted by this resolution shall expire if not utilized prior to April 30, 1983." (DX 19.) This express authorization to "the proper officers ... to arrange for" the borrowing (which would expire if not acted on by April 30, 1983), surely went beyond a mere delegation to the Finance Committee of the Board's responsibility to approve or disapprove. The fact that the authorization was "subject to" Finance Committee approval recognized rather that there were terms and documents that remained to be negotiated, calling for Board level approval. It did not mean that the Board had done nothing but delegate. On consideration of the minutes and resolutions, as well as the testimony of Tribune officers and directors who were present at the meeting, I find, as Smith later told Driver, that the Board gave "general approval" to the transaction.

Tribune's October 6 letter reserving approval to Tribune's Board did not specify any particular form of Board approval, nor did it require that approval be of the final loan documents. Indeed, it distinguished between the requirements of *"approval* by the Company's Board of Directors" and "the preparation and execution of legal documentation *satisfactory to the Company."* The general approval given was sufficient under the contract.

Tribune's Right to Condition the Loan on Offset Accounting

Tribune contends that its right to carry the loan off-balance-sheet by offset accounting was always deemed an essential condition of the deal. It points out that the Offering Circular which it delivered to Teachers, and the Price Waterhouse background memoranda, which also were delivered to Teachers during the early due diligence and discussion phase, all underlined offset accounting as an important Tribune concern. Nor does Teachers deny that in the early discussions, Smith spoke of Tribune's accounting and tax objectives. The witnesses disagree along predictable lines as to whether Driver told Smith that Teachers would not take the risk of Tribune's accounting treatment. The conflict need not be resolved. For regardless whether Driver orally refused to have Teachers assume the risk of Tribune's right to satisfactory accounting, the signed agreement did not provide for any such condition. The written agreement between the parties contains no basis whatever for the proposition that Tribune's obligation was conditioned on satisfactory assurance that it could report the loan off balance sheet. The fact that Tribune considered this significant is not disputed, but it is not determinative.

Both parties were aware of Tribune's objectives as to both the tax and accounting for the proposed deal. Tribune could, of course, have demanded as a condition of its commitment that it receive satisfactory assurances (in the form of opinion letters of counsel and auditors, or otherwise) as to both deferred taxation and offset accounting. It could have offered to pay a fee for

Teachers' commitment on terms that would have left Tribune free to proceed with the loan or not, at its option. Alternatively, it could have negotiated for the option to prepay if the Internal Revenue Service or the SEC disallowed the desired tax or accounting consequences. The problem was that in September of 1982, Tribune believed that it needed an immediate "firm commitment" from Teachers to be sure of its ability to conclude the transaction as planned within 1982. Had Tribune made such demands, Teachers might well have turned down Tribune's proposal (as the five other institutions had done). Indeed, Tribune was so sensitive to its need for Teachers' firm commitment that when its counsel warned of the consequences of signing the commitment letter with its "binding agreement" language, Tribune disregarded this advice so as not to lose the lender's commitment. Neither the language of the agreement, nor the negotiations of the parties give any support to the contention that offset accounting was a condition of the agreement.

There was perhaps an additional reason why Tribune did not negotiate for offset accounting as a condition of the deal, being that in September and early October it did not have the doubts that it later developed as to the availability of offset accounting. It had received a prior opinion of Price Waterhouse to the effect that the unconditional put would make offset accounting appropriate. Only after the FASB's mid-October exposure draft did Price Waterhouse begin to emphasize doubts about offset accounting and about the position the SEC might take in the event Tribune offered public securities under an SEC registration statement.

Whether the reason was that Tribune was afraid to lose Teachers prompt firm commitment, or that Tribune had not yet worried, as it later did, about the availability of its accounting objective, or simply that Tribune was willing to take the risk to secure this important deal, the fact is that Tribune did not negotiate for and did not obtain its right to offset accounting as a condition of its bargain.

By December of 1982 Tribune faced a completely different set of factors. Interest rates had declined very substantially. The loan agreement that it negotiated with Teachers was no longer to its benefit since it could now borrow money at substantially cheaper cost. Price Waterhouse's newly expressed doubts about the availability of offset accounting gave it further reason to question whether the deal it had made was a good one. With the benefit of two months' hindsight, Tribune most likely would not have entered into the commitment agreement it made in early October. That was, however, the agreement it made.

Conditions Precedent to Enforcement

Tribune contends that even if the commitment letter constituted a valid, enforceable contract, there were conditions precedent to its enforcement that were never satisfied. Teachers' commitment letter stated that the authorization of the loan was "contingent upon the preparation, execution and delivery of" final contract documents; Tribune's response, likewise, stated that "our acceptance and agreement is subject to ... the preparation and execution of legal documentation satisfactory to the Company." Tribune contends that since final contract documents were never prepared, the conditions precedent to the enforceability of the agreement were never satisfied and, accordingly, Tribune cannot be charged with breach. This argument misconceives the meaning of these clauses. The preliminary agreement envisions and requires further and final contract documents without which the loan will not be made; if, through no fault on either party, no final contract were reached, either because the parties in good faith failed to agree on the open secondary terms, or because, as often happens in business, the parties simply lost interest in the transaction and by mutual tacit consent abandoned it without having reached final contract documents, no enforceable rights would survive based on the preliminary commitment. This does not mean that the language of reservation authorized one party to kill the deal simply by refusing to negotiate or to sign the contract documents. Such an interpretation would render language like "binding agreement" and "firm commitment" meaningless.

Tribune's point would be well taken if the negotiations had aborted over inability to reach agreement on the terms of the purchase money mortgage or the put. Indeed, if they had aborted because Teachers had insisted on imposing conditions on the exercise of the put that were incompatible with the initial agreement, Tribune might properly have charged Teachers with breach of the commitment letter agreement.

What in fact happened was the other way around. Tribune broke off contract negotiations by insisting on a condition (satisfactory accounting) that was not within the scope of the agreement. Although Tribune's refusal to go ahead with the contract may well have been motivated in part by doubts as to the availability of offset accounting, I find that that decline in interest rates also substantially influenced Tribune's decision.

Of course it is true that numerous issues remained open at this time. The basic loan agreement was in draft form, recently circulated by Teachers, without any negotiations having taken place over its form and minor terms. Although I find (as a matter of disputed fact) that Teachers had expressed its agreement to a put on terms that were acceptable to Tribune, it is less clear that Teachers had ever stated its acceptance of the form of mortgage that Tribune had concluded with LaSalle. (Teacher's counsel Tencza of the Debevoise firm had recently sent Tribune a letter specifying 35 problematic points in the LaSalle purchase money mortgage.) But the existence of those open points is of no consequence because they did not break the deal. Teachers offered in mid-December to sit down with Tribune and resolve all open issues so that the first drawdown could be made before the end of the year as contemplated in the commitment letter; Tribune declined stating that such a meeting would be of no value unless Teachers was prepared to agree that Tribune's satisfaction as to its accounting would be a condition of its obligation to draw down the loans.

Whatever Teachers' past posture had been as to the mortgage put and terms, there is every reason to believe that it would have acceded to Tribune's demands so long as they were within the terms of the commitment agreement. Given the fact that interest rates had dropped precipitously from the time of the commitment letter, it would have been bad business judgment for Teachers to lose the deal by refusing to agree on points of minor importance. Driver's testimony that Teachers was prepared to agree to Tribune's terms on the purchase money mortgage and the put is entirely credible. But the issue does not depend on a finding as to the likelihood of Teachers acceding to Tribune's demands on those open issues. The point is simply that Teachers, in conformity with its contract obligations, was asking Tribune to sit down and negotiate in good faith towards agreement on the open points, while Tribune refused to negotiate unless Teachers agreed to add a condition that was outside the scope of the bargain. The existence of open points and the failure of the parties to satisfy the condition of execution of final documentation is, therefore, chargeable to Tribune. It cannot rely on those circumstances to escape its contract obligation. . . .

Judgment is granted to the plaintiff.

SO ORDERED.

———

VENTURE ASSOCIATES CORP. v. ZENITH DATA SYSTEMS CORP., 96 F.3d 275 (7th Cir.1996) (Posner, J.). "Damages for breach of an agreement to negotiate may be, although they are unlikely to be, the same as the damages for breach of the final contract that the parties would have signed had it not been for the defendant's bad faith. If, quite apart from any bad faith, the negotiations would have broken down, the party led on by the other party's bad faith to persist in futile negotiations can recover only his reliance damages—the expenses he incurred by being misled, in violation of the parties' agreement to negotiate in good faith, into continuing to negotiate futilely. But if the plaintiff can prove that had it not been for the defendant's bad faith the parties would have made a final contract, then the loss of the benefit of the contract is a consequence of the defendant's bad faith, and, provided that it is a foreseeable consequence, the defendant is liable for that loss—liable, that is, for the plaintiffs consequential damages. . . . The difficulty, which may well be insuperable, is that since by hypothesis the parties had not agreed on *any* of the terms of their contract, it may be impossible to determine what those terms would have been and hence what profit the victim of bad faith would have had. . . . But this goes to the practicality of the remedy, not the principle of it. Bad faith is deliberate misconduct, whereas many breaches of 'final' contracts are involuntary—liability for breach of contract being, in general, strict liability. It would be a paradox to place a lower ceiling on damages for bad faith than on damages for a perfectly innocent breach, though a paradox that the practicalities of proof may require the courts in many or even all cases to accept."

———

Chapter 15

THE PAROL EVIDENCE RULE AND THE INTERPRETATION OF WRITTEN CONTRACTS

This Chapter takes up three related issues.

Section 1 concerns cases in which A and B have admittedly entered into a written contract, but A claims that prior to, or contemporaneously with, making the written contract, the parties entered into a separate agreement that concerned the same subject matter as the written contract, but was not intended to be superseded by the written contract. The treatment of such alleged separate agreements—and more specifically, the issue whether evidence concerning such agreements is admissible—is governed by the *parol evidence rule*. This rule is the subject of Section 1 of this chapter.

Section 2 considers the issue whether, in the admissibility of evidence concerning the *interpretation* of a contract, it should make a difference that the contract is in writing; and if so, what difference it should make. This issue is analytically separate from the issue governed by the parol evidence rule, which concerns the admissibility of evidence concerning whether the parties had a *separate agreement*. The two issues are considered together in this Chapter, partly because courts often run the two issues together, and partly because in practice both issues typically (although not invariably) involve oral evidence that seems to qualify a written contract.

Section 3 further considers the extent to which trade usage, course of performance, and course of dealing may be part of a written contract.

SECTION 1. THE PAROL EVIDENCE RULE

MITCHILL v. LATH
Court of Appeals of New York, 1928.
247 N.Y. 377, 160 N.E. 646, 68 A.L.R. 239.

Action by Catherine C. Mitchill against Charles Lath and another. Judgment of Special Term in plaintiff's favor, directing specific performance of an agreement to remove an icehouse, was affirmed by the Appellate Division (220 App.Div. 776, 221 N.Y.S. 864), and defendants appeal. Judgments of Appellate Division and Trial Term reversed, and complaint dismissed.

ANDREWS, J. In the fall of 1923 the Laths owned a farm. This they wished to sell. Across the road, on land belonging to Lieutenant Governor Lunn, they had an icehouse which they might remove. Mrs. Mitchell looked over the land with a view to its purchase. She found the icehouse objectionable. Thereupon "the defendants orally promised and agreed, for and in consideration of the purchase of their farm by the plaintiff, to remove the said icehouse in the spring of 1924." Relying upon this promise, she made a written contract to buy the property for $8,400, for cash and a mortgage and containing various provisions usual in such papers. Later receiving a deed, she entered into possession, and has spent considerable sums in improving the property for use as a summer residence. The defendants have not fulfilled their promise as to the icehouse, and do not intend to do so. We are not dealing, however, with their moral delinquencies. The question before us is whether their oral agreement may be enforced in a court of equity.

This requires a discussion of the parol evidence rule—a rule of law which defines the limits of the contract to be construed. Glackin v. Bennett, 226 Mass. 316, 115 N.E. 490. It is more than a rule of evidence, and oral testimony, even if admitted, will not control the written contract (O'Malley v. Grady, 222 Mass. 202, 109 N.E. 829), unless admitted without objection (Brady v. Nally, 151 N.Y. 258, 45 N.E. 547). It applies, however, to attempts to modify such a contract by parol. It does not affect a parol collateral contract distinct from and independent of the written agreement. It is, at times, troublesome to draw the line. Williston, in his work on Contracts (section 637) points out the difficulty. "Two entirely distinct contracts," he says, "each for a separate consideration, may be made at the same time, and will be distinct legally. Where, however, one agreement is entered into wholly or partly in consideration of the simultaneous agreement to enter into another, the transactions are necessarily bound together.... Then if one of the agreements is oral and the other in writing, the problem arises whether the bond is sufficiently close to prevent proof of the oral agreement." That is the situation here. It is claimed that the defendants are called upon to do more than is required by their written contract in connection with the sale as to which it deals.

The principle may be clear, but it can be given effect by no mechanical rule. As so often happens, it is a matter of degree, for, as Prof. Williston also says, where a contract contains several promises on each side it is not difficult to put any one of them in the form of a collateral agreement. If this were enough, written contracts might always be modified by parol. Not form, but substance, is the test.

In applying this test, the policy of our courts is to be considered. We have believed that the purpose behind the rule was a wise one, not easily to be abandoned. Notwithstanding injustice here and there, on the whole it works for good. Old precedents and principles are not to be lightly cast aside, unless it is certain that they are an obstruction under present conditions. New York has been less open to arguments that would modify this particular rule, than some jurisdictions elsewhere. Thus in Eighmie v. Taylor, 98 N.Y. 288, it was held that a parol warranty might not be shown, although no warranties were contained in the writing.

Under our decisions before such an oral agreement as the present is received to vary the written contract, at least three conditions must exist: (1) The agreement must in form be a collateral one; (2) it must not contradict express or implied provisions of the written contract; (3) it must be one that parties would not ordinarily be expected to embody in the writing, or, put in another way, an inspection of the written contract, read in the light of surrounding circumstances, must not indicate that the writing appears "to contain the engagements of the parties, and to define the object and measure the extent of such engagement." Or, again, it must not be so clearly connected with the principal transaction as to be part and parcel of it.

The respondent does not satisfy the third of these requirements. It may be, not the second. We have a written contract for the purchase and sale of land. The buyer is to pay $8,400 in the way described. She is also to pay her portion of any rents, interest on mortgages, insurance premiums, and water meter charges. She may have a survey made of the premises. On their part, the sellers are to give a full covenant deed of the premises as described, or as they may be described by the surveyor, if the survey is had, executed, and acknowledged at their own expense; they sell the personal property on the farm and represent they own it; they agree that all amounts paid them on the contract and the expense of examining the title shall be a lien on the property; they assume the risk of loss or damage by fire until the deed is delivered; and they agree to pay the broker his commissions. Are they to do more? Or is such a claim inconsistent with these precise provisions? It could not be shown that the plaintiff was to pay $500 additional. Is it also implied that the defendants are not to do anything unexpressed in the writing?

That we need not decide. At least, however, an inspection of this contract shows a full and complete agreement, setting forth in detail the obligations of each party. On reading it, one would conclude that the reciprocal obligations of the parties were fully detailed. Nor would his opinion alter if he knew the surrounding circumstances. The presence of the icehouse, even the knowledge that Mrs. Mitchill thought it objectionable, would not lead to the belief that a separate agreement existed with regard to it. Were such an agreement made it would seem most natural that the inquirer should find it in the contract. Collateral in form it is found to be, but it is closely related to the subject dealt with in the written agreement—so closely that we hold it may not be proved. . . .

We do not ignore the fact that authorities may be found that would seem to support the contention of the appellant. Such are Erskine v. Adeane (1873) L.R. 8 Ch.App. 756, and Morgan v. Griffith (1871) L.R. 6 Exch. 70, where although there was a written lease a collateral agreement of the landlord to reduce the game was admitted. In this state, Wilson v. Deen might lead to the contrary result. Neither are they approved in New Jersey. Naumberg v. Young, 44 N.J.Law, 331, 43 Am.Rep. 380. Nor in view of later cases in this court can Batterman v. Pierce, 3 Hill, 171, be considered an authority. A line of cases in Massachusetts, of which Durkin v. Cobleigh, 156 Mass. 108, 30 N.E. 474, 17 L.R.A. 270, 32 Am.St.Rep. 436, is an example, have to do with collateral contracts made before a deed is given. But the fixed form of a deed makes it inappropriate to insert collateral agreements, however closely connected with the sale. This may be cause for an exception. Here we deal with the contract on the basis of which the deed to Mrs. Mitchill was given subsequently, and we confine ourselves to the question whether its terms may be modified. . . .

It is argued that what we have said is not applicable to the case as presented. The collateral agreement was made with the plaintiff. The contract of sale was with her husband, and no assignment of it from him appears. Yet the deed was given to her. It is evident that here was a transaction in which she was the principal from beginning to end. We must treat the contract as if in form, as it was in fact, made by her.

Our conclusion is that the judgment of the Appellate Division and that of the Special Term should be reversed and the complaint dismissed, with costs in all courts.

LEHMAN, J. (dissenting). I accept the general rule as formulated by Judge Andrews. I differ with him only as to its application to the facts shown in the record. The plaintiff contracted to purchase land from the defendants for an agreed price. A formal written agreement was made between the sellers and the plaintiff's husband. It is on its face a complete contract for the conveyance of the land. It describes the property to be conveyed. It sets forth the purchase price to be paid. All the conditions and terms of the conveyance to be made are clearly stated. I concede at the outset that parol evidence to show additional conditions and terms of the conveyance would be inadmissible. There is a conclusive presumption that the parties intended to integrate in that written contract every agreement relating to the nature or extent of the property to be conveyed, the contents of the deed to be delivered, the consideration to be paid as a condition precedent to the delivery of the deeds, and indeed all the rights of the parties in connection with the land. The conveyance of that land was the subject-matter of the written contract, and the contract completely covers that subject.

The parol agreement which the court below found the parties had made was collateral to, yet connected with, the agreement of purchase and sale. It has been found that the defendants induced the plaintiff to agree to purchase the land by a promise to remove an icehouse from land not covered by the agreement of purchase and sale. No independent consideration passed to the defendants for the parol promise. To that extent the written contract and the alleged oral contract are bound together. The same bond usually exists wherever attempt is made to prove a parol agreement which is collateral to a written agreement. Hence "the problem arises whether the bond is sufficiently close to prevent proof of the oral agreement." See Judge Andrews' citation from Williston on Contracts, § 637.

Judge Andrews has formulated a standard to measure the closeness of the bond. Three conditions, at least, must exist before an oral agreement may be proven to increase the obligation imposed by the written agreement. I think we agree that the first condition that the agreement "must in form be a collateral one" is met by the evidence. I concede that this condition is met in most cases where the courts have nevertheless excluded evidence of the collateral oral agreement. The difficulty here, as in most cases, arises in connection with the two other conditions.

The second condition is that the "parol agreement must not contradict express or implied provisions of the written contract." Judge Andrews voices doubt whether this condition is satisfied. The written contract has been carried out. The purchase price has been paid; conveyance has been made; title has passed in accordance with the terms of the written contract. The mutual obligations expressed in the written contract are left unchanged by the alleged oral contract. When performance was required of the written contract, the obligations of the parties were measured solely by its terms. By the oral agreement the plaintiff seeks to hold the defendants to other obligations to be performed by them thereafter upon land which was not conveyed to the plaintiff. The assertion of such further obligation is not inconsistent with the written contract, unless the written contract contains a provision, express or implied, that the defendants are not to do anything not expressed in the writing. Concededly there is no such express provision in the contract, and such a provision may be implied, if at all, only if the asserted additional obligation is "so clearly connected with the principal transaction as to be part and parcel of it," and is not "one that the parties would not ordinarily be expected to embody in the writing." The hypothesis so formulated for a conclusion that the asserted additional obligation is inconsistent with an implied term of the contract is that the alleged oral agreement does not comply with the third condition as formulated by Judge Andrews. In this case, therefore, the problem reduces itself to the one question whether or not the oral agreement meets the third condition.

I have conceded that upon inspection the contract is complete. "It appears to contain the engagements of the parties, and to define the object and measure the extent of such engagement;" it constitutes the contract between them, and is presumed to contain the whole of that contract. Eighmie v. Taylor, 98 N.Y. 288. That engagement was on the one side to convey land; on the other to pay the price. The plaintiff asserts further agreement based on the same consideration to be performed by the defendants after the conveyance was complete, and directly affecting only other land. It is true, as Judge Andrews points out, that "the presence of the icehouse, even the knowledge that Mrs. Mitchill thought it objectionable, would not lead to the belief that a separate agreement existed with regard to it"; but the question we must decide is whether or not, *assuming* an agreement was made for the removal of an unsightly icehouse from one parcel of land as an inducement for the purchase of another parcel, the parties would ordinarily or naturally be expected to embody the agreement for the removal of the icehouse from one parcel in the written agreement to convey the other parcel. Exclusion of proof of the oral agreement on the ground that it varies the contract embodied in the writing may be based only upon a finding or presumption that the written contract was intended to cover the oral negotiations for the removal of the icehouse which lead up to the contract of purchase and sale. To determine what the writing was intended to cover, "the document alone will not suffice. What it was intended to cover cannot be known till we know what there was to cover. The question being whether certain subjects of negotiation were intended to be covered, we must compare the writing and the negotiations before we can determine whether they were in fact covered." Wigmore on Evidence (2d Ed.) § 2430.

The subject-matter of the written contract was the conveyance of land. The contract was so complete on its face that the conclusion is inevitable that the parties intended to embody in the writing all the negotiations covering at least the conveyance. The promise by the defendants to remove the icehouse from other land was not connected with their obligation to convey except that one agreement would not have been made unless the other was also made. The plaintiff's assertion of a parol agreement by the defendants to remove the icehouse was completely established by the great weight of evidence. It must prevail unless that agreement was part of the agreement to convey and the entire agreement was embodied in the writing.

The fact that in this case the parol agreement is established by the overwhelming weight of evidence is, of course, not a factor which may be considered in determining the competency or legal effect of the evidence. Hardship in the particular case would not justify the court in disregarding or emasculating the general rule. It merely accentuates the outlines of our problem. The assumption that the parol agreement was made is no longer obscured by any doubts. The problem, then, is clearly whether the parties are presumed to have intended to render that parol agreement legally ineffective and nonexistent by failure to embody it in the writing. Though we are driven to say that nothing in the written contract which fixed the terms and conditions of the stipulated conveyance suggests the existence of any further parol agreement, an inspection of the contract, though it is complete on its face in regard to the subject of the conveyance, does not, I think, show that it was intended to embody negotiations or agreements, if any, in regard to a matter so loosely bound to the conveyance as the removal of an icehouse from land not conveyed.

The rule of integration undoubtedly frequently prevents the assertion of fraudulent claims. Parties who take the precaution of embodying their oral agreements in a writing should be protected against the assertion that other terms of the same agreement were not integrated in the writing. The limits of the integration are determined by the writing, read in the light of the surrounding circumstances. A written contract, however complete, yet covers only a limited field. I do not think that in the written contract for the conveyance of land here under consideration we can find an intention to cover a field so broad as to include prior agreements, if any such were made, to do other acts on other property after the stipulated conveyance was made.

In each case where such a problem is presented, varying factors enter into its solution. Citation of authority in this or other jurisdictions is useless, at least without minute analysis of the facts. The analysis I have made of the decisions in this state leads me to the view that the decision of the courts below is in accordance with our own authorities and should be affirmed.

CARDOZO, C.J., and POUND, KELLOGG and O'BRIEN, JJ., concur with ANDREWS, J.

LEHMAN, J., dissents in opinion in which CRANE, J., concurs.

Judgment accordingly.

———

VON MEHREN, CIVIL LAW ANALOGUES TO CONSIDERATION: AN EXERCISE IN COMPARATIVE ANALYSIS, 72 Harv.L.Rev. 1009, 1011–1012 (1959). "One or more of the interested parties often think that a contractual obligation will be more readily enforced if it is formally divorced from the environment and the motives that produced it. Civil-law theorists, especially the German writers, have discussed such a divorcement in terms of whether the legal system permits an 'abstract' obligation.... [I]n all jurisdictions, a transaction can also be rendered partially abstract by embodying it in an integrating agreement.''

JAMES BRADLEY THAYER, A PRELIMINARY TREATISE ON EVIDENCE 428–429 (1898). Commenting on an opinion of Chief Justice Holt, Thayer remarked: ''The Chief Justice here retires into that lawyer's Paradise where all words have a fixed, precisely ascertained meaning; where men may express their purposes, not only with accuracy, but with fulness; and where, if the writer has been careful, a lawyer, having a document referred to him, may sit in his chair, inspect the text, and answer all questions without raising his eyes. Men have dreamed of attaining for their solemn muniments of title such an absolute security; and some degree of security they have encompassed by giving strict definitions and technical meanings to words and phrases, and by rigid rules of construction. But the fatal necessity of looking outside the text in order to identify persons and things, tends steadily to destroy such illusions and to reveal the essential imperfection of language, whether spoken or written.''

CALAMARI & PERILLO, A PLEA FOR A UNIFORM PAROL EVIDENCE RULE AND PRINCIPLES OF INTERPRETATION

42 Indiana L.J. 333 (1967).

Any reader of advance sheets is well aware that most of the contract decisions reported do not involve offer and acceptance or other subjects usually explored in depth in a course in contracts but rather involve the parol evidence rule and questions of interpretation, topics given scant attention in most courses in contracts.... Much of the fog and mystery surrounding these subjects stems from the fact that there is basic disagreement as to the meaning and effect of the parol evidence rule and as to the appropriate goals to be achieved by the process of contractual interpretation. The cases and treatises of the contract giants tend to conceal this conflict. While frequently masking disagreement by using the same terminology, Professors Williston and Corbin are often poles apart in the meaning they attach to the same term. Often starting from what superficially appear to be the same premises, they frequently advocate different results in similar fact situations. The polarity of their views reflects conflicting value judgments as to policy issues that are as old as our legal system and that are likely to continue as long as courts of law exist. Although many writers and courts have expressed their views on the subject and have made major contributions to it, concentration on the analyses of Professors Williston and Corbin will point up the fundamental bases upon which the conflicting cases and views rest.

The Area of Substantial Agreement

There is a rule of substantive law which states that whenever contractual intent is sought to be ascertained from among several expressions of the parties, an earlier tentative expression will be rejected in favor of a later expression that is final. More simply stated, the contract made by the parties supersedes tentative promises made in earlier negotiations. Consequently, in determining the content of the contract, the earlier tentative promises are irrelevant.

The parol evidence rule comes into play only when the last expression is in writing. Professor Corbin states the rule as follows: "When two parties have made a contract and have expressed it in a writing to which they have both assented as the complete and accurate integration of that contract, evidence, whether parol or otherwise, of antecedent understandings and negotiations will not be admitted for the purpose of varying or contradicting the writing." Professor Williston's formulation is not to the contrary: "Briefly stated," he writes, "this rule requires, in the absence of fraud, duress, mutual mistake, or something of the kind, the exclusion of extrinsic evidence, oral or written, where the parties have reduced their agreement to an integrated writing." Both agree that this, too, is a rule of substantive law that also operates as an exclusionary rule of evidence merely because prior understandings are irrelevant to the process of determining the content of the final contract. The similarity between the parol evidence rule and the rule stated in the preceding paragraph is obvious. The main and important difference is that where the last expression is not in writing the jury determines whether the parties intended the second expression to supersede the first. This is to say that this question of intention is determined as is any other question of intention stemming from oral transactions. Where the later expression is in writing, however, this question is usually determined by the trial judge. At an early date it was felt (and the feeling strongly remains) that writings require the special protection that is afforded by removing this issue from the province of unsophisticated jurors.

The Parol Evidence Rule: The Major Area of Conflict

Apparent agreement by Professors Williston and Corbin, except as noted, on the rules stated above conceals real conflict. The battleground upon which they express disagreement is a major one: the concept of total integration. This, of course, is the area in which most of the cases arise. Both assert that the existence of a total integration depends on the intention of the parties.... It appears, however, that in this context they use the term "intent" in ways that are remarkably dissimilar. A typical fact situation will illustrate this. A agrees to sell and B agrees to purchase Blackacre for $10,000. The contract is in writing and in all respects appears complete on its face. Prior to the signing of the contract A, in order to induce B's assent, orally promises him in the presence of a number of reputable witnesses that if B will sign the contract, A will remove an unsightly shack on A's land across the road from Blackacre. May this promise be proved and enforced? This depends upon whether the writing is a total integration.

Williston argues that if the intention to have a total integration were to be determined by the ordinary process of determining intention, the parol evidence rule would be emasculated. He points out that the mere existence of the collateral oral agreement would conclusively indicate that the parties intended only a partial integration and that the only question that would be presented is whether the alleged prior or contemporaneous agreement was actually made. This would be a question of fact for the jury, thus eliminating the special protection which the trial judge should afford the writing....

... [Williston therefore suggests that] where the writing appears to be a complete instrument expressing the rights and obligations of both parties, it is deemed a total integration unless the alleged additional terms were such as might naturally be made as a separate agreement by parties situated as were the parties to the written contract.

Professor Corbin has an easy task in demolishing the Willistonian approach. In treating the matter of integration as a question of intent, as Professor Williston purports to do, he shows the absurdity of excluding all relevant evidence of intent except the writing itself. But ... Williston, and [courts that follow his view] are unconcerned about the true intention of the parties. Rather, shorn of rote language of fiction indicating a search for intention, they are advocating and applying a rule of form. Since (and even before) the common law had its genesis, there has been a deeply-felt belief that transactions will be more secure, litigation will be reduced, and the temptation to perjury will be removed, if everyone will only use proper forms for his transactions. The Statute of Wills and the Statute of Frauds are but examples of this belief. Professor Corbin, by attacking the apparent arguments of Williston's position has not expressly come to grips with the substance of his position. This is not to suggest that either he or Professor Williston have been unaware of the true nature of their disagreement. Rather, they seem for the most part to have been content not to make explicit the basis of their differing views....

The debate involves the question: is the public better served by giving effect to the parties' entire agreement written and oral, even at the risk of injustice caused by the possibility of perjury and the possibility that superseded documents will be treated as operative, or does the security of transactions require that, despite occasional injustices, persons adopting a formal writing be required, on the penalty of voidness of their oral and written side agreements, to put their entire agreement in the formal writing....

———

RESTATEMENT, FIRST, CONTRACTS §§ 228, 237, 239, 240

§ 228. What is Integration

An agreement is integrated where the parties thereto adopt a writing or writings as the final and complete expression of the agreement. An integration is the writing or writings so adopted.

§ 237. Parol Evidence Rule; Effect of Integration on Prior or Contemporaneous Agreements

Except as stated in [§ 240] the integration of an agreement makes inoperative to add to or to vary the agreement all contemporaneous oral agreements relating to the same subject-matter; and ... all prior oral or written agreements relating thereto....

§ 239. Effect of Partial Integration

Where there is integration of part of the terms of a contract prior written agreements and contemporaneous oral agreements are operative to vary these terms only to the same extent as if the whole contract had been integrated.

§ 240. In What Cases Integration Does Not Affect Prior or Contemporaneous Agreements

(1) An oral agreement is not superseded or invalidated by a subsequent or contemporaneous integration, nor a written agreement by a subsequent integration relating to the same subject-matter, if the agreement is not inconsistent with the integrated contract, and

(a) is made for separate consideration, or

(b) is such an agreement as might naturally be made as a separate agreement by parties situated as were the parties to the written contract. . . .

————

RESTATEMENT, SECOND, CONTRACTS
§§ 209, 210, 213, 214, 215, 216

[See Selected Source Materials Supplement]

————

BRAUCHER, INTERPRETATION AND LEGAL EFFECT IN THE SECOND RESTATEMENT OF CONTRACTS, 81 Colum.L.Rev. 13, 17 (1981). "The core of the 'parol evidence rule' is stated in section 213: a binding integrated agreement discharges inconsistent prior agreements, and a binding completely integrated agreement discharges prior agreements within its scope. These statements, however, merely point to the obvious conclusion; the difficulties arise in determining whether there is an integrated agreement, whether, if so, it is completely or only partially integrated, and whether the prior agreement is consistent with the integrated agreement or within its scope. Those determinations are made in accordance with all relevant evidence, and require interpretation both of the integrated agreement and of the prior agreement. They are made by the court, not by the trier of fact."

————

INTERFORM CO. v. MITCHELL CONSTR. CO., 575 F.2d 1270, 1275–77 (9th Cir.1978). "In practice . . . the difference between the [Corbin and Williston] views is less significant than one might imagine. A writing, which ordinarily and naturally would be an integrated one, generally is one the parties thereto intended to be integrated. Also, the meaning to which the reasonably intelligent person would subscribe generally is that to which the parties did subscribe. . . .

"There are, however, significant differences between the two views. To suggest none exist would reduce the debate between their respective leading protagonists, Williston with regard to the first and Corbin the second, to a triviality. The debate is not that. It relates, as indicated, to the attitude with which judges should approach written contracts. Williston requires the judge to ascertain the legal relations between the parties by reference to those associated with the 'forms' (that is, the natural and normal integration practices and the meaning of words that reasonably intelligent people would employ) to which they should adhere and from which they depart at their peril. Calamari & Perillo 104–05; Williston §§ 633, 638–39. Corbin, on the other hand, directs the judge to fix the legal relations between the parties in accordance with their intention even when the 'forms' they employed suggest otherwise. Corbin §§ 538–42A. A judge, guided by Williston . . . would impose upon the parties the terms of the [contractual documents] as understood by the reasonably intelligent person if [those documents] appear complete and any additional terms ordinarily and naturally would have been included therein. Williston §§ 638–39; Calamari & Perillo 105. A judge, guided by Corbin, would impose upon the parties the agreement that the evidence indicates they in fact reached. . . .

"It is unlikely that any jurisdiction will inflexibly adopt one approach to the exclusion of the other; each is likely to influence the conduct of judges and the disposition of cases. However, it must be acknowledged that the influence of Corbin's way is stronger now . . . , than when he and Williston grappled during the drafting of the American Law Institute's first Restatement, Contracts. . . ."

CISG ART. 8(3)

[See Selected Source Materials Supplement]

DODGE, TEACHING THE CISG IN CONTRACTS, 50 J. Leg. Ed. 72 (2000). "Under the parol evidence rule found in both the common law and the UCC, the parties may not contradict the terms of a final written agreement with evidence of prior or contemporaneous negotiations or agreements. CISG Article 8(3), by contrast, directs a court interpreting a contract to give 'due consideration . . . to all relevant circumstances of the case including the negotiations, any practices which the parties have established between themselves, usages and any subsequent conduct of the parties.' In other words, the CISG lacks a parol evidence rule and allows a court interpreting a written contract to consider not just trade usage, course of dealing, and course of performance, but even the parties' prior negotiations."

UNIDROIT PRINCIPLES OF INTERNATIONAL LAW ART. 4.3

[See Selected Source Materials Supplement]

MASTERSON v. SINE

Supreme Court of California, 1968.
68 Cal.2d 222, 65 Cal.Rptr. 545, 436 P.2d 561.

TRAYNOR, CHIEF JUSTICE.

Dallas Masterson and his wife Rebecca owned a ranch as tenants in common. On February 25, 1958, they conveyed it to Medora and Lu Sine by a grant deed "Reserving unto the Grantors herein an option to purchase the above described property on or before February 25, 1968" for the "same consideration as being paid heretofore plus their depreciation value of any improvements Grantees may add to the property from and after two and a half years from this date." Medora is Dallas' sister and Lu's wife. Since the conveyance Dallas has been adjudged bankrupt. His trustee in bankruptcy and Rebecca brought this declaratory relief action to establish their right to enforce the option.

The case was tried without a jury. Over defendants' objection the trial court admitted extrinsic evidence that by "the same consideration as being paid heretofore" both the grantors and the grantees meant the sum of $50,000 and by "depreciation value of any improvements" they meant the depreciation value of improvements to be computed by deducting from the total amount of any capital expenditures made by defendants grantees the amount of depreciation allowable to them under United States income tax regulations as of the time of the exercise of the option.

The court also determined that the parol evidence rule precluded admission of extrinsic evidence offered by defendants to show that the parties wanted the property kept in the Masterson family and that the option was therefore personal to the grantors and could not be exercised by the trustee in bankruptcy.

The court entered judgment for plaintiffs, declaring their right to exercise the option, specifying in some detail how it could be exercised, and reserving jurisdiction to supervise the manner of its exercise and to determine the amount that plaintiffs will be required to pay defendants for their capital expenditures if plaintiffs decide to exercise the option.

Defendants appeal. They contend that the option provision is too uncertain to be enforced and that extrinsic evidence as to its meaning should not have been admitted. The trial court properly refused to frustrate the obviously declared intention of the grantors to reserve an option to repurchase by an overly meticulous insistence on completeness and clarity of written expression. (See California Lettuce Growers v. Union Sugar Co. (1955) 45 Cal.2d 474, 481, 289 P.2d 785, 49 A.L.R.2d 496; Rivers v. Beadle (1960) 183 Cal.App.2d 691, 695–697, 7 Cal.Rptr. 170.) It properly admitted extrinsic evidence to explain the language of the deed. . . . to the end that the consideration for the option would appear with sufficient certainty to permit specific enforcement. . . . The trial court erred, however, in excluding the extrinsic evidence that the option was personal to the grantors and therefore nonassignable.

When the parties to a written contract have agreed to it as an "integration"—a complete and final embodiment of the terms of an agreement— parol evidence cannot be used to add to or vary its terms. . . . When only part of the agreement is integrated, the same rule applies to that part, but parol evidence may be used to prove elements of the agreement not reduced to writing....

California cases have stated that whether there was an integration is to be determined solely from the face of the instrument ... and that the question for the court is whether it "appears to be a complete ... agreement...." ... Neither of these strict formulations of the rule, however, has been consistently applied. The requirement that the writing must appear incomplete on its face has been repudiated in many cases where parol evidence was admitted "to prove the existence of a separate oral agreement as to any matter on which the document is silent and which is not inconsistent with its terms"—even though the instrument appeared to state a complete agreement.... Even under the rule that the writing alone is to be consulted, it was found necessary to examine the alleged collateral agreement before concluding that proof of it was precluded by the writing alone. (See 3 Corbin, Contracts (1960) § 582, pp. 444–446.) It is therefore evident that "The conception of a writing as wholly and intrinsically self-determinative of the parties' intent to make it a sole memorial of one or seven or twenty-seven subjects of negotiation is an impossible one." (9 Wigmore, Evidence (3d ed. 1940) § 2431, p. 103.) For example, a promissory note given by a debtor to his creditor may integrate all their present contractual rights and obligations, or it may be only a minor part of an underlying executory contract that would never be discovered by examining the face of the note.

In formulating the rule governing parol evidence, several policies must be accommodated. One policy is based on the assumption that written evidence is more accurate than human memory.... This policy, however, can be adequately served by excluding parol evidence of agreements that directly contradict the writing. Another policy is based on the fear that fraud or unintentional invention by witnesses interested in the outcome of the litigation will mislead the finder of facts....

Evidence of oral collateral agreements should be excluded only when the fact finder is likely to be misled. The rule must therefore be based on the credibility of the evidence. One such standard, adopted by section 240(1)(b) of the Restatement [First] of Contracts, permits proof of a collateral agreement if it "is such an agreement as might *naturally* be made as a separate agreement by parties situated as were the parties to the written contract." (Italics added; see McCormick, Evidence (1954) § 216, p. 441; see also 3 Corbin, Contracts (1960) § 583, p. 475, § 594, pp. 568–569; 4 Williston, Contracts (3d ed. 1961) § 638, pp. 1039–1045.) The draftsmen of the Uniform Commercial Code would exclude the evidence in still fewer instances: "If the additional terms are such that if agreed upon, they would *certainly* have been included in the document in the view of the court, then evidence of their alleged making must be kept from the trier of fact." (Com. 3, § 2–202, italics added.)[1]

---

1. Corbin suggests that, even in situations where the court concludes that it would not have been natural for the parties to make the alleged collateral oral agreement, parol evidence of such an agreement should nevertheless be permitted if the court is convinced that the unnatural actually happened in the case being adjudicated. (3 Corbin, Contracts, § 485, pp. 478, 480; cf. Murray, The Parol Evidence Rule: A Clarification (1966) 4 Duquesne L.Rev. 337, 341–342.) This suggestion may be based on a belief that judges are not likely to be misled by their sympathies. If the court believes that the parties intended a collateral

The option clause in the deed in the present case does not explicitly provide that it contains the complete agreement, and the deed is silent on the question of assignability. Moreover, the difficulty of accommodating the formalized structure of a deed to the insertion of collateral agreements makes it less likely that all the terms of such an agreement were included. (See 3 Corbin, Contracts (1960) § 587; 4 Williston, Contracts (3d ed. 1961) § 645; 70 A.L.R. 752, 759 (1931); 68 A.L.R. 245 (1930).) The statement of the reservation of the option might well have been placed in the recorded deed solely to preserve the grantors' rights against any possible future purchasers and this function could well be served without any mention of the parties' agreement that the option was personal. There is nothing in the record to indicate that the parties to this family transaction, through experience in land transactions or otherwise, had any warning of the disadvantages of failing to put the whole agreement in the deed. This case is one, therefore, in which it can be said that a collateral agreement such as that alleged "might naturally be made as a separate agreement." *A fortiori,* the case is not one in which the parties "would certainly" have included the collateral agreement in the deed.

It is contended, however, that an option agreement is ordinarily presumed to be assignable if it contains no provisions forbidding its transfer or indicating that its performance involves elements personal to the parties. (Mott v. Cline (1927) 200 Cal. 434, 450, 253 P. 718; Altman v. Blewett (1928) 93 Cal.App. 516, 525, 269 P. 751.) The fact that there is a written memorandum, however, does not necessarily preclude parol evidence rebutting a term that the law would otherwise presume. In American Industrial Sales Corp. v. Airscope, Inc., supra, 44 Cal.2d 393, 397–398, 282 P.2d 504, we held it proper to admit parol evidence of a contemporaneous collateral agreement as to the place of payment of a note, even though it contradicted the presumption that a note, silent as to the place of payment, is payable where the creditor resides. (For other examples of this approach, see Richter v. Union Land etc. Co. (1900) 129 Cal. 367, 375, 62 P. 39 [presumption of time of delivery rebutted by parol evidence]; Wolters v. King (1897) 119 Cal. 172, 175–176, 51 P. 35 [presumption of time of payment rebutted by parol evidence]; Mangini v. Wolfschmidt, Ltd., supra, 165 Cal.App.2d 192, 198–201, 331 P.2d 728 [presumption of duration of an agency contract rebutted by parol evidence]; Zinn v. Ex–Cell–O Corp. (1957) 148 Cal.App.2d 56, 73–74, 306 P.2d 1017; see also Rest., Contracts, § 240, com. c.)[2] Of course a statute may preclude parol

---

agreement to be effective, there is no reason to keep the evidence from the jury.

2. Counsel for plaintiffs direct our attention to numerous cases that they contend establish that parol evidence may never be used to show a collateral agreement contrary to a term that the law presumes in the absence of an agreement. In each of these cases, however, the decision turned upon the court's belief that the writing was a complete integration and was no more than an application of the rule that parol evidence cannot be used to vary the terms of a completely integrated agreement....

In Standard Box Co. v. Mutual Biscuit Co. (1909) 10 Cal.App. 746, 750, 103 P. 938, 940, the [court excluded] evidence of an agreement for a time of performance other than the "rea-

sonable time" implied by law in a situation where the writing, although stating no time of performance, was "clear and complete when aided by that which is imported into it by legal implication." This decision was simply an application of the then-current theory regarding integration. The court regarded the instrument as a complete integration, and it therefore precluded proof of collateral agreements. Since it is now clear that integration cannot be determined from the writing alone, the decision is not authoritative insofar as it finds a complete integration. There is no reason to believe that the court gave any independent significance to implied terms. Had the court found from the writing alone that there was no integration, there is nothing to indicate that it would have excluded proof contrary to terms it would have otherwise presumed....

evidence to rebut a statutory presumption.... Here, however, there is no such statute. In the absence of a controlling statute the parties may provide that a contract right or duty is nontransferable.... Moreover, even when there is no explicit agreement—written *or* oral—that contractual duties shall be personal, courts will effectuate a presumed intent to that effect if the circumstances indicate that performance by substituted person would be different from that contracted for....

In the present case defendants offered evidence that the parties agreed that the option was not assignable in order to keep the property in the Masterson family. The trial court erred in excluding that evidence.

The judgment is reversed.

PETERS, TOBRINER, MOSK, and SULLIVAN, JJ., concur.

Dissenting Opinion

BURKE, JUSTICE.

I dissent....

The court properly admitted parol evidence to explain the intended meaning of the "same consideration" and "depreciation value" phrases of the written option to purchase defendants' land, as the intended meaning of those phrases was not clear. However, there was nothing ambiguous about the *granting* language of the option and not the slightest suggestion in the document that the option was to be nonassignable. Thus, to permit such words of limitation to be added by parol is to *contradict* the absolute nature of the grant, and to directly violate the parol evidence rule.

Just as it is unnecessary to state in a deed to "lot X" that the house located thereon goes with the land, it is likewise unnecessary to add to "I grant an option to Jones" the words *"and his assigns"* for the option to be assignable.... California statutes expressly declare that it *is* assignable, and only if I add language in writing showing my intent to withhold or restrict the right of assignment may the grant be so limited. Thus, to seek to restrict the grant by parol is to *contradict* the written document in violation of the parol evidence rule....

McCOMB, J., concurs.

Rehearing denied; McCOMB and BURKE, JJ., dissenting.

UCC § 2–202

[See Selected Source Materials Supplement]

INTERFORM v. MITCHELL CONSTR. CO., 575 F.2d 1270, 1277 (9th Cir. 1978). "... [UCC § 2–202] reflects Corbin's influence. It precludes contradiction of 'confirmatory memoranda' by prior or contemporaneous oral agreements when the writing was *'intended* by the parties as a final expression of their agreement' and permits the introduction of consistent additional terms 'unless the court finds the writing to have been *intended* also as a complete and exclusive statement of the terms of the agreement.' (Italics added). The focus plainly is on the intention of the parties, not the integration practices of reasonable persons acting normally and naturally. This is Corbin's focus. Furthermore, [Official Comment 1 rejects] certain rules more applicable to Williston's approach than to Corbin's...."

HUNT FOODS AND INDUSTRIES, INC. v. DOLINER

Supreme Court of New York, Appellate Division, First Department 1966.
26 A.D.2d 41, 270 N.Y.S.2d 937.

Before BREITEL, J.P., and RABIN, STEVENS, STEUER and CAPOZZOLI, JJ.

STEUER, JUSTICE. In February 1965 plaintiff corporation undertook negotiations to acquire the assets of Eastern Can Company. The stock of the latter is owned by defendant George M. Doliner and his family to the extent of 73%. The balance is owned by independent interests. At a fairly early stage of the negotiations agreement was reached as to the price to be paid by plaintiff ($5,922,500 if in cash, or $5,730,000 in Hunt stock), but several important items, including the form of the acquisition, were not agreed upon. At this point it was found necessary to recess the negotiations for several weeks. The Hunt negotiators expressed concern over any adjournment and stated that they feared that Doliner would use their offer as a basis for soliciting a higher bid from a third party. To protect themselves they demanded an option to purchase the Doliner stock. Such an option was prepared and signed by George Doliner and the members of his family and at least one other person associated with him who were stockholders. It provides that Hunt has the option to buy all of the Doliner stock at $5.50 per share. The option is to be exercised by giving notice on or before June 1, 1965, and if notice is not given the option is void. If given, Hunt is to pay the price and the Doliners to deliver their stock within seven days thereafter. The agreement calls for Hunt to pay $1,000 for the option, which was paid. To this point there is substantial accord as to what took place.

Defendant claims that when his counsel called attention to the fact that the option was unconditional in its terms, he obtained an understanding that it was only to be used in the event that he solicited an outside offer; and that plaintiff insisted that unless the option was signed in unconditional form negotiations would terminate. Plaintiff contends there was no condition. Concededly, on resumption of negotiations the parties failed to reach agreement and the option was exercised. Defendants declined the tender and refused to deliver the stock.

Plaintiff moved for summary judgment for specific performance. We do not believe that summary judgment lies. Plaintiff's position is that the condition claimed could not be proved under the parol evidence rule, and, eliminating that, there is no defense to the action.

The parol evidence rule, at least as that term refers to contracts of sale,[3] is now contained in Section 2–202 of the Uniform Commercial Code, which reads:

---

3. While article 2 of the Uniform Commercial Code which contains this section does not deal with the sale of securities, this section applies to article 8, dealing with securities. Cf.

"Terms with respect to which the confirmatory memoranda of the parties agree or which are otherwise set forth in a writing intended by the parties as a final expression of their agreement with respect to such terms as are included therein may not be contradicted by evidence of any prior agreement or of a contemporaneous oral agreement but may be explained or supplemented

" * * *

"(b) by evidence of consistent additional terms unless the court finds the writing to have been intended also as a complete and exclusive statement of the terms of the agreement."

The term (that the option was not to be exercised unless Doliner sought outside bids), admittedly discussed but whose operative effect is disputed, not being set out in the writing, is clearly "additional" to what is in the writing. So the first question presented is whether that term is "consistent" with the instrument. In a sense any oral provision which would prevent the ripening of the obligations of a writing is inconsistent with the writing. But that obviously is not the sense in which the word is used (Hicks v. Bush, 10 N.Y.2d 488, 491, 225 N.Y.S.2d 34, 180 N.E.2d 425). To be inconsistent the term must contradict or negate a term of the writing. A term or condition which has a lesser effect is provable.

The Official Comment prepared by the drafters of the Code contains this statement:

"If the additional terms are such that, if agreed upon, they would certainly have been included in the document in the view of the court, then evidence of their alleged making must be kept from the trier of fact." (McKinney's Uniform Commercial Code, Part 1, p. 158)

Special Term interpreted this language as not only calling for an adjudication by the court in all instances where proof of an "additional oral term" is offered, but making that determination exclusively the function of the court. We believe the proffered evidence to be inadmissible only where the writing contradicts the existence of the claimed additional term (Meadow Brook Nat. Bank v. Bzura, 20 A.D.2d 287, 290, 246 N.Y.S.2d 787, 790). The conversations in this case, some of which are not disputed, and the expectation of all the parties for further negotiations, suggest that the alleged oral condition precedent cannot be precluded as a matter of law or as factually impossible. It is not sufficient that the existence of the condition is implausible. It must be impossible (cf. Millerton Agway Coop. v. Briarcliff Farms, 17 N.Y.2d 57, 63–64, 268 N.Y.S.2d 18, 215 N.E.2d 341).

The order should be reversed on the law and the motion for summary judgment denied with costs and disbursements to abide the event.

Order and judgment . . . unanimously reversed, on the law, with $50 costs and disbursements to abide the event, and plaintiff's motion for summary judgment denied. All concur.

Agar v. Orda, 264 N.Y. 248, 190 N.E. 479, 90 A.L.R. 269; Official Comment, McKinney's Uniform Commercial Code, Part 1, pp. 96–97;

Note, 65 Col.L.Rev. 880, 890–1. All parties and Special Term so regarded it.

ALASKA NORTHERN DEVELOPMENT, INC. v. ALYESKA PIPE-LINE SERVICE CO., 666 P.2d 33 (Alaska 1983), cert. denied, 464 U.S. 1041, 104 S.Ct. 706, 79 L.Ed.2d 170 (1984). "The narrow view of consistency expressed in *Hunt Foods* has been criticized. In Snyder v. Herbert Greenbaum & Associates, Inc., 38 Md.App. 144, 380 A.2d 618 (Md.App.1977), the court held that the parol evidence of a contractual right to unilateral rescission was inconsistent with a written agreement for the sale and installation of carpeting. The court defined 'inconsistency' as used in section 2–202(b) as 'the absence of reasonable harmony in terms of the language and respective obligations of the parties.' Id. 380 A.2d at 623 (emphasis in original) (citing U.C.C. § 1–205(4)). Accord: Luria Brothers & Co. v. Pielet Brothers Scrap Iron & Metal, Inc., 600 F.2d 103, 111 (7th Cir.1979); Southern Concrete Services, Inc. v. Mableton Contractors, Inc., 407 F.Supp. 581 (N.D.Ga.1975), aff'd mem., 569 F.2d 1154 (5th Cir.1978).

"We agree with this view of inconsistency and reject the view expressed in *Hunt Foods*.[4] Under this definition of inconsistency, it is clear that the proffered parol evidence limiting the owner committee's right of final approval to price is inconsistent with the integrated term that unconditionally gives the committee the right to approval. Therefore, the superior court was correct in refusing to admit parol evidence on this issue."

UCC § 2–209(2), (4), (5)

[See Selected Source Materials Supplement]

UNIDROIT PRINCIPLES OF INTERNATIONAL COMMERCIAL CONTRACTS ART. 2.1.18

[See Selected Source Materials Supplement]

PRINCIPLES OF EUROPEAN CONTRACT LAW ART. 2.106

[See Selected Source Materials Supplement]

------

4. *Hunt Foods* was implicitly rejected in Johnson v. Curran, 633 P.2d 994, 996–97 (Alaska 1981) (parol evidence concerning an early termination right based on nightclub owner's dissatisfaction with the band's per-formance was inconsistent with parties' written contract specifying definite time without mention of any right of early termination and thus inadmissible).

SECTION 2. THE INTERPRETATION OF WRITTEN CONTRACTS

STEUART v. McCHESNEY

Supreme Court of Pennsylvania, 1982.
498 Pa. 45, 444 A.2d 659.

Before O'BRIEN, C.J., and ROBERTS, NIX, LARSEN, FLAHERTY, McDERMOTT and HUTCHINSON, JJ.

OPINION OF THE COURT

FLAHERTY, JUSTICE.

This is an appeal from an Order of the Superior Court which reversed a Decree of the Court of Common Pleas of the Thirty–Seventh Judicial District construing a Right of First Refusal affecting the sale of certain real property.

On June 8, 1968, the appellant, Lepha I. Steuart, and her husband, James A. Steuart (now deceased), executed an agreement granting to the appellees, William C. McChesney and Joyce C. McChesney, husband and wife, a Right of First Refusal on a parcel of improved farmland. The agreement provided:

> (a) During the lifetime of said Steuarts, should said Steuarts obtain a Bona Fide Purchaser for Value, the said McChesneys may exercise their right to purchase said premises at a value equivalent to the market value of the premises according to the assessment rolls as maintained by the County of Warren and Commonwealth of Pennsylvania for the levying and assessing of real estate taxes; provided, however, that the date of valuation shall be that upon which the said Steuarts notify said McChesneys, in writing, of the existence of a Bona Fide Purchaser.

On July 6, 1977, the subject property was appraised by a real estate broker at a market value of $50,000. Subsequently, on October 10, 1977 and October 13, 1977 respectively, appellant received bona fide offers of $35,000 and $30,000 for the land. Upon receiving notice of these offers, the appellees sought to exercise their right to purchase the property by tendering $7,820. This amount was exactly twice the assessed value of the property as listed on the tax rolls maintained in Warren County, it being the practice in that County to value real estate for tax assessment purposes at 50% of market value. The tender was refused, however, by appellant, who then commenced an action in equity seeking to cancel the Right of First Refusal, or, in the alternative, to have the agreement construed as requiring that the exercise price be that of a bona fide third party offer or fair market value as determined independently of assessed value. Appellees, requesting a conveyance of the subject premises for $7,820, sought specific performance.

The primary issue on appeal concerns the price at which the Right of First Refusal may be exercised. The Court of Common Pleas, after hearing testimony, held that the formula of twice the assessed value was intended to serve as "a mutual protective minimum price for the premises rather than to be the controlling price without regard to a market third party offer." The agreement was, therefore, construed as granting appellees a preemptive right to purchase the land for $35,000, the amount of the first bona fide offer received. The Superior Court reversed, holding that the plain language of the agreement required that assessed market value, alone, determine the exercise price. We agree.

It is well established that the intent of the parties to a written contract is to be regarded as being embodied in the writing itself, and when the words are clear and unambiguous the intent is to be discovered only from the express language of the agreement. *Estate of Breyer,* 475 Pa. 108, 379 A.2d 1305 (1977); *Felte v. White,* 451 Pa. 137, 302 A.2d 347 (1973).... As this Court stated in *East Crossroads Center, Inc. v. Mellon–Stuart Co.,* 416 Pa. at 230–231, 205 A.2d at 866, "[w]hen a written contract is clear and unequivocal, its meaning must be determined by its contents alone. It speaks for itself and a meaning cannot be given to it other than that expressed. Where the intention of the parties is clear, there is no need to resort to extrinsic aids or evidence." Hence, where language is clear and unambiguous, the focus of interpretation is upon the terms of the agreement as *manifestly expressed,* rather than as, perhaps, silently intended.

Application of the plain meaning rule of interpretation has, however, been subjected to criticism as being unsound in theory. "The fallacy consists in assuming that there is or ever can be *some one real* or absolute meaning." 9 Wigmore, *Evidence* § 2462 (Chadbourn rev. 1981). "[S]ome of the surrounding circumstances always must be known before the meaning of the words can be plain and clear; and proof of the circumstances may make a meaning plain and clear when in the absence of such proof some other meaning may also have seemed plain and clear." 3 Corbin, *Contracts* § 542 (1960). "It is indeed desirable that it be made as difficult as is reasonably feasible for an unscrupulous person to establish a meaning that was foreign to what was in fact understood by the parties to the contract. However, this result can be achieved without the aid of an inflexible rule." Murray, *Contracts,* § 110 (1974).

While adhering to the plain meaning rule of construction, this Court, too, has cautioned:

> We are not unmindful of the dangers of focusing only upon the words of the writing in interpreting an agreement. A court must be careful not to "retire into that lawyer's Paradise where all words have a fixed, precisely ascertained meaning; where men may express their purposes, not only with accuracy, but with fullness; and where, if the writer has been careful, a lawyer, having a document referred to him, may sit in his chair inspect the text, and answer all questions without raising his eyes." Thayer, Preliminary Treatise on Evidence 428, quoted in 3 Corbin on Contracts § 535 n. 16 (1960).

Estate of Breyer, 475 Pa. at 115, 379 A.2d at 1309 n. 5 (1977). Indeed, whether the language of an agreement is clear and unambiguous may not be apparent without cognizance of the context in which the agreement arose:

> The flexibility of or multiplicity in the meaning of words is the principal source of difficulty in the interpretation of language. Words are the conduits by which thoughts are communicated, yet scarcely any of them have such a fixed and single meaning that they are incapable of denoting more than one thought. In addition to the multiplicity in meaning of words set forth in the dictionaries there are the meanings imparted to them by trade customs, local uses, dialects, telegraphic codes, etc. One meaning crowds a word full of significance, while another almost empties the utterance of any import.

Hurst v. Lake & Co., Inc., 141 Or. 306, 310, 16 P.2d 627, 629 (1932), quoted in 4 Williston, *Contracts* § 609 (3d ed. 1961).

Nevertheless, the rationale for interpreting contractual terms in accord with the plain meaning of the language expressed is multifarious, resting in part upon what is viewed as the appropriate role of the courts in the interpretive process: "[T]his Court long ago emphasized that '[t]he parties [have] the right to make their own contract, and it is not the function of this Court to re-write it, or to give it a construction in conflict with . . . the accepted and plain meaning of the language used.' *Hagarty v. William Akers, Jr. Co.,* 342 Pa. 236, 20 A.2d 317 (1941)." *Felte v. White,* 451 Pa. at 144, 302 A.2d at 351. " 'It is not the province of the court to alter a contract by construction or to make a new contract for the parties; its duty is confined to the interpretation of the one which they have made for themselves, without regard to its wisdom or folly.' [13 C.J. § 485, p. 524]" *Moore v. Stevens Coal Co.,* 315 Pa. 564, 568, 173 A. 661, 662 (1934).

In addition to justifications focusing upon the appropriate role of the courts in the interpretive process, the plain meaning approach to construction has been supported as generally best serving the ascertainment of the contracting parties' mutual intent. "When the parties have reduced their agreement to writing, the writing is to be taken to be the final expression of their intention." 17A C.J.S. *Contracts* § 296(2). "Where the contract evidences care in its preparation, it will be presumed that its words were employed deliberately and with intention." 17A C.J.S. *Contracts* § 296(2). "In determining what the parties intended by their contract, the law must look to what they clearly expressed. Courts in interpreting a contract do not assume that its language was chosen carelessly." *Moore v. Stevens Coal Co.,* 315 Pa. at 568, 173 A. at 662. Neither can it be assumed that the parties were ignorant of the meaning of the language employed. *See Fogel Refrigerator Co. v. Oteri,* 391 Pa. 188, 137 A.2d 225, 231 (1958).

Accordingly, the plain meaning approach enhances the extent to which contracts may be relied upon by contributing to the security of belief that the final expression of *consensus ad idem* will not later be construed to import a meaning other than that clearly expressed. *Cf.* McCormick, *The Parol Evidence Rule as a Procedural Device for Control of the Jury,* 41 Yale L.J. 365, 365–366 (1932). Likewise, resort to the plain meaning of language hinders parties dissatisfied with their agreement from creating a myth as to the true meaning of the agreement through subsequently exposed extrinsic evidence. Absent the plain meaning rule, nary an agreement could be conceived, which, in the event of a party's later disappointment with his stated bargain, would not be at risk to having its true meaning obfuscated under the guise of examining extrinsic evidence of intent. Even if the dissatisfied party in good faith believed that the agreement, as manifest, did not express the *consensus ad idem,* his post hoc judgment would be inclined to be colored by belief as to what should have been, rather than what strictly was, intended. Hence, the plain meaning approach to interpretation rests upon policies soundly based, and the judiciousness of that approach warrants reaffirmation.

In the instant case, the language of the Right of First Refusal, viewed in context, is express and clear and is, therefore, not in need of interpretation by reference to extrinsic evidence. The plain meaning of the agreement in question is that if, during the lifetime of the appellant, a bona fide purchaser for value should be obtained, the appellees may purchase the property "at a value equivalent to the market value of the premises according to the assessment rolls as maintained by the County of Warren and Commonwealth of Pennsylvania for the levying and assessing of real estate taxes." Indeed, a more clear and unambiguous expression of the Right of First Refusal's exercise price would be onerous to conceive. By conditioning exercise of the Right of First Refusal upon occurrence of the triggering event of there being obtained a bona fide offer, protection was afforded against a sham offer, made not in good faith, precipitating exercise of the preemptive right. The clear language of the agreement, however, in no manner links determination of the exercise price to the magnitude of the bona fide offer received through that triggering mechanism.

Were the present agreement to be regarded as ambiguous, so as to enable a court to consider extrinsic evidence of the meaning intended, as was done in the Court of Common Pleas, the policy of resorting to extrinsic evidence only when confronted with unclear or ambiguous language would be enervated. Certainly, the words of the Right of First Refusal are not indefinite, doubtful, or uncertain in their signification, so as to be regarded as unclear. Nor is the language reasonably or fairly susceptible to being understood in more than one sense so as to be regarded as ambiguous. "A patent ambiguity is that which appears on the face of the instrument, and arises from the defective, obscure, or insensible language used." *Black's Law Dictionary* 105 (rev. 4th ed. 1968). In contrast, a latent ambiguity arises from extraneous or collateral facts which make the meaning of a written agreement uncertain although the language thereof, on its face, appears clear and unambiguous. *Easton v. Washington County Insurance Co.,* 391 Pa. 28, 137 A.2d 332 (1957). "The usual instance of a latent ambiguity is one in which a writing refers to a particular person or thing and is thus apparently clear on its face, but upon application to external objects is found to fit two or more of them equally." *Id.* at 35, 137 A.2d at 336. In holding that an ambiguity is present in an agreement, a court must not rely upon a strained contrivancy to establish one; scarcely an agreement could be conceived that might not be unreasonably contrived into the appearance of ambiguity. Thus, the meaning of language cannot be distorted to establish the ambiguity. *Anstead v. Cook,* 291 Pa. 335, 337, 140 A. 139, 140, (1927). The instant agreement, not being reasonably susceptible to being understood in more than one sense, whether by patent or latent ambiguity, does not present language in need of extrinsic clarification.

By construing the clause in question to merely signify that the exercise price be, *in effect, "not less than"* the market value of the premises according to the assessment rolls, the Court of Common Pleas ignored the clearly expressed intent that the exercise price be *"equivalent* to the market value of the premises according to the assessment rolls." To no extent is the term "equivalent", meaning "equal",[5] interchangeable with "not less than", and, since the parties specified the former, they shall be deemed to have intended the same. Hence, any divergence between the exercise price and the bona fide offer cannot be eliminated by construction where no ambiguity exists. Nor is

---

5. "Equivalent carries with it the idea of value in some way (Latin *aequus,* equal, plus *valere,* to be strong or valuable). When something adds up to something else in value or worth or significance or importance, the two are said to be equivalent the one to the other; when two or more things are exactly the same they are properly said to be equal. *Equal* is the simpler term, and applies to simpler considerations." J.B. Opdycke, *Mark My Words,* at 568–569 (1940).

there freedom, under the guise of construction, to redraft the Right of First Refusal simply because of the realization, at the time when rights under the agreement are to be exercised, that the market price according to the assessment rolls falls substantially short of the bona fide offers received.

Appellant contends that, based upon equitable considerations, specific performance at the assessed market value of $7,820 should be denied; in particular, the divergence between assessed market value and the amount of the bona fide offers assertedly renders an award of specific performance inequitable. As this Court has established, however, " '[i]nadequacy of consideration is not ground for refusing to decree specific performance of a contract to convey real estate, unless there is evidence of fraud or unfairness in the transaction sufficient to make it inequitable to compel performance ...' *Welsh v. Ford,* 282 Pa. 96, 99, 127 A. 431, 432 (1925)...."... Appellant alleges that an attorney employed solely by the appellees drafted the Right of First Refusal agreement, and that she was unfairly induced to enter the agreement without representation of her interests. This position ignores, however, an express finding of fact by the Court of Common Pleas, amply supported by testimony of record, that at the time of the preliminary negotiation and drafting of the agreement the parties were all represented by the same attorney. Hence, appellant's assertion is without merit.

Order affirmed.

ROBERTS, J., files a dissenting opinion in which LARSEN, J., joins.

ROBERTS, JUSTICE, dissenting.

I dissent. Although the contract at issue mandates that appellees may purchase appellant's property at "the market value of the premises according to the assessment rolls as maintained by the County of Warren ...," it is by no means clear that $7,820 is the price which appellees should pay.

The omission from the contract of a specific future purchase price was intentional because, according to the draftsman, the parties "wanted to reflect either increase or decrease of the assessed value as of [the] time" of appellees' exercise of the option to buy. To assure the accuracy and currency of this "reflection" of the change in assessed value, the parties provided that "the date of valuation shall be that upon which the said Steuarts notify said McChesneys, in writing, of the existence of a Bona Fide purchaser."

Written notice of appellant's receipt of an offer for the property was delivered to appellees on or about October 25, 1977. At that time, the assessed value of the property, as recorded on the tax rolls of Warren County, was $3,910, or 50% of the "market value" of $7,820. However, from the testimony of the draftsman, it would appear that the property had not been reassessed since 1972, when the assessed value was increased by only $405.

Section 602 of the Fourth to Eighth Class County Assessment Law provides:

> "It shall be the duty of the chief assessor to assess, rate and value all subjects and objects of local taxation ... according to the actual value thereof.... [R]eal property shall be assessed at a value based upon an established predetermined ratio ... not exceeding seventy-five per centum (75%) of its actual value or the price for which the same would separately bona fide sell...."

72 P.S. § 5453.602(a) (1964). As this Court stated in *Brooks Building Tax Assessment Case,* 391 Pa. 94, 97, 137 A.2d 273, 274 (1958),

> "[t]he term 'actual value' means 'market value' [citing cases]. And market value has been defined as the price which a purchaser, willing but not obliged to buy, would pay an owner, willing but not obliged to sell, taking into consideration all uses to which the property is adapted and might in reason be applied."

Accord, *Buhl Foundation v. Board of Property Assessment,* 407 Pa. 567, 570, 180 A.2d 900, 902 (1962).

Here, where appellant received bona fide offers of $30,000, $35,000, and $50,000 for her property, there can be no doubt that the actual value of appellant's property in 1977 was at least four times greater than the value according to the outdated assessment on the Warren County tax rolls. It is the height of unfairness to grant appellees' requested decree for specific performance at a price based on a valuation which took place in 1972. In effect, appellees are receiving a substantial windfall simply because Warren County has apparently failed to maintain accurate assessments "according to the actual value" of appellant's property, as required by law.

In these circumstances, I would remand this case to the Court of Common Pleas of Warren County for a determination of what the proper assessed value of appellant's property would have been on October 25, 1977, the "date of valuation," with directions to enter a decree of specific performance in favor of appellees at a "market value" based upon that determination.

LARSEN, J., joins in this dissenting opinion.

———

MELLON BANK, N.A. v. AETNA BUSINESS CREDIT, INC., 619 F.2d 1001, 1011 (3d Cir.1980). "A court must have a reference point to determine if words may reasonably admit of different meanings. Under a 'four corners' approach a judge sits in chambers and determines from his point of view whether the written words before him are ambiguous. An alternative approach is for the judge to hear the proffer of the parties and determine if there is objective indicia that, from the linguistic reference point of the parties, the terms of the contract are susceptible of differing meanings. We believe the latter to be the correct approach.

"It is the role of the judge to consider the words of the contract, the alternative meaning suggested by counsel, and the nature of the objective evidence to be offered in support of that meaning. The trial judge must then determine if a full evidentiary hearing is warranted. If a *reasonable* alternative interpretation is suggested, even though it may be alien to the judge's linguistic experience, objective evidence in support of that interpretation should be considered by the fact finder."

———

AMOCO PRODUCTION CO. v. WESTERN SLOPE GAS CO., 754 F.2d 303, 308 (10th Cir. 1985). "Under the UCC, the lack of facial ambiguity in the contract language is basically irrelevant to whether extrinsic evidence ought to be considered by the court as an initial matter. A judge first must consider the circumstances and purposes surrounding the making of the writing before he or she can determine whether it is in fact ambiguous. '[I]t is proper to consider the contract's commercial setting even though the contract is not facially ambiguous.' . . .

"[U]nder section 2–202, there is no longer an assumption that the parties intended a writing to be the complete expression of their agreement. In fact, the assumption is to the contrary unless the court expressly finds that the parties intended the contract to be completely integrated. . . . See generally, Interform Co. v. Mitchell, 575 F.2d 1270, 1274–78 (9th Cir.1978). Only if in light of the circumstances and purposes of the contract the judge finds it unambiguous should he or she prohibit parol evidence to explain its meaning."

PACIFIC GAS & ELECTRIC CO. v. G.W. THOMAS DRAYAGE & RIGGING CO.

Supreme Court of California, 1968.
69 Cal.2d 33, 69 Cal.Rptr. 561, 442 P.2d 641.

TRAYNOR, CHIEF JUSTICE. Defendant appeals from a judgment for plaintiff in an action for damages for injury to property under an indemnity clause of a contract.

In 1960 defendant entered into a contract with plaintiff to furnish the labor and equipment necessary to remove and replace the upper metal cover of plaintiff's steam turbine. Defendant agreed to perform the work "at [its] own risk and expense" and to "indemnify" plaintiff "against all loss, damage, expense and liability resulting from . . . injury to property, arising out of or in any way connected with the performance of this contract." Defendant also agreed to procure not less than $50,000 insurance to cover liability for injury to property. Plaintiff was to be an additional named insured, but the policy was to contain a cross-liability clause extending the coverage to plaintiff's property.

During the work the cover fell and injured the exposed rotor of the turbine. Plaintiff brought this action to recover $25,144.51, the amount it subsequently spent on repairs. During the trial it dismissed a count based on negligence and thereafter secured judgment on the theory that the indemnity provision covered injury to all property regardless of ownership.

Defendant offered to prove by admissions of plaintiff's agents, by defendant's conduct under similar contracts entered into with plaintiff, and by other proof that in the indemnity clause the parties meant to cover injury to property of third parties only and not to plaintiff's property.[6] Although the trial court observed that the language used was "the classic language for a third party indemnity provision" and that "one could very easily conclude that . . . its whole intendment is to indemnify third parties," it nevertheless

---

6. Although this offer of proof might ordinarily be regarded as too general to provide a ground for appeal . . . since the court repeatedly ruled that it would not admit extrinsic evidence to interpret the contract and sustained objections to all questions seeking to elicit such evidence, no formal offer of proof was required. . . .

held that the "plain language" of the agreement also required defendant to indemnify plaintiff for injuries to plaintiff's property. Having determined that the contract had a plain meaning, the court refused to admit any extrinsic evidence that would contradict its interpretation.

When a court interprets a contract on this basis, it determines the meaning of the instrument in accordance with the " ... extrinsic evidence of the judge's own linguistic education and experience." (3 Corbin on Contracts (1960 ed.) [1964 Supp. § 579, p. 225, fn. 56].) The exclusion of testimony that might contradict the linguistic background of the judge reflects a judicial belief in the possibility of perfect verbal expression. (9 Wigmore on Evidence (3d ed. 1940) § 2461, p. 187.) This belief is a remnant of a primitive faith in the inherent potency and inherent meaning of words.

The test of admissibility of extrinsic evidence to explain the meaning of a written instrument is not whether it appears to the court to be plain and unambiguous on its face, but whether the offered evidence is relevant to prove a meaning to which the language of the instrument is reasonably susceptible. . . .

A rule that would limit the determination of the meaning of a written instrument to its four-corners merely because it seems to the court to be clear and unambiguous, would either deny the relevance of the intention of the parties or presuppose a degree of verbal precision and stability our language has not attained.

Some courts have expressed the opinion that contractual obligations are created by the mere use of certain words, whether or not there was any intention to incur such obligations.[7] Under this view, contractual obligations flow, not from the intention of the parties but from the fact that they used certain magic words. Evidence of the parties' intention therefore becomes irrelevant.

In this state, however, the intention of the parties as expressed in the contract is the source of contractual rights and duties.[8] A court must ascertain and give effect to this intention by determining what the parties meant by the words they used. Accordingly, the exclusion of relevant, extrinsic evidence to explain the meaning of a written instrument could be justified only if it were feasible to determine the meaning the parties gave to the words from the instrument alone.

If words had absolute and constant referents, it might be possible to discover contractual intention in the words themselves and in the manner in which they were arranged. Words, however, do not have absolute and constant referents. "A word is a symbol of thought but has no arbitrary and fixed meaning like a symbol of algebra or chemistry, ..." (Pearson v. State Social Welfare Board (1960) 54 Cal.2d 184, 195, 5 Cal.Rptr. 553, 559, 353 P.2d 33, 39.) The meaning of particular words or groups of words varies with the " ... verbal context and surrounding circumstances and purposes in view of the

7. "A contract has, strictly speaking, nothing to do with the personal, or individual, intent of the parties. A contract is an obligation attached by the mere force of law to certain acts of the parties, usually words, which ordinarily accompany and represent a known intent." (Hotchkiss v. National City Bank of New York (S.D.N.Y.1911) 200 F. 287, 293. . . .)

8. "A contract must be so interpreted as to give effect to the mutual intention of the parties as it existed at the time of contracting, so far as the same is ascertainable and lawful." (Civ.Code, § 1636 . . .)

linguistic education and experience of their users and their hearers or readers (not excluding judges).... A word has no meaning apart from these factors; much less does it have an objective meaning, one true meaning." (Corbin, The Interpretation of Words and the Parol Evidence Rule (1965) 50 Cornell L.Q. 161, 187.) Accordingly, the meaning of a writing " ... can only be found by interpretation in the light of all the circumstances that reveal the sense in which the writer used the words. The exclusion of parol evidence regarding such circumstances merely because the words do not appear ambiguous to the reader can easily lead to the attribution to a written instrument of a meaning that was never intended. [Citations omitted.]" (Universal Sales Corp. v. Cal. Press Mfg. Co., supra, 20 Cal.2d 751, 776, 128 P.2d 665, 679 (concurring opinion); see also, e.g., Garden State Plaza Corp. v. S.S. Kresge Co. (1963) 78 N.J.Super. 485, 189 A.2d 448, 454....

Although extrinsic evidence is not admissible to add to, detract from, or vary the terms of a written contract, these terms must first be determined before it can be decided whether or not extrinsic evidence is being offered for a prohibited purpose. The fact that the terms of an instrument appear clear to a judge does not preclude the possibility that the parties chose the language of the instrument to express different terms. That possibility is not limited to contracts whose terms have acquired a particular meaning by trade usage, but exists whenever the parties' understanding of the words used may have differed from the judge's understanding.

Accordingly, rational interpretation requires at least a preliminary consideration of all credible evidence offered to prove the intention of the parties.[9] (Civ.Code, § 1647; Code Civ.Proc. § 1860; see also 9 Wigmore on Evidence, op. cit. supra, § 2470, fn. 11, p. 227.) Such evidence includes testimony as to the "circumstances surrounding the making of the agreement ... including the object, nature and subject matter of the writing ..." so that the court can "place itself in the same situation in which the parties found themselves at the time of contracting." (Universal Sales Corp. v. Cal. Press Mfg. Co., supra, 20 Cal.2d 751, 761, 128 P.2d 665, 671; Lemm v. Stillwater Land & Cattle Co., supra, 217 Cal. 474, 480–481, 19 P.2d 785.) If the court decides, after considering this evidence, that the language of a contract, in the light of all the circumstances, is "fairly susceptible of either one of the two interpretations contended for...." ... extrinsic evidence relevant to prove either of such meanings is admissible.[10]

In the present case the court erroneously refused to consider extrinsic evidence offered to show that the indemnity clause in the contract was not intended to cover injuries to plaintiff's property. Although that evidence was not necessary to show that the indemnity clause was reasonably susceptible of

9. When objection is made to any particular item of evidence offered to prove the intention of the parties, the trial court may not yet be in a position to determine whether in the light of all of the offered evidence, the item objected to will turn out to be admissible as tending to prove a meaning of which the language of the instrument is reasonably susceptible or inadmissible as tending to prove a meaning of which the language is not reasonably susceptible. In such case the court may admit the evidence conditionally by either reserving its ruling on the objection or by admitting the evidence subject to a motion to strike. (See Evid.Code, § 403.)

10. Extrinsic evidence has often been admitted in such cases on the stated ground that the contract was ambiguous (e.g., Universal Sales Corp. v. Cal. Press Mfg. Co., supra, 20 Cal.2d 751, 761, 128 P.2d 665). This statement of the rule is harmless if it is kept in mind that the ambiguity may be exposed by extrinsic evidence that reveals more than one possible meaning.

the meaning contended for by defendant, it was nevertheless relevant and admissible on that issue. Moreover, since that clause was reasonably susceptible of that meaning, the offered evidence was also admissible to prove that the clause had that meaning and did not cover injuries to plaintiff's property.[11] Accordingly, the judgment must be reversed. . . .

PETERS, MOSK, BURKE, SULLIVAN, and PEEK, JJ., concur.

McCOMB, J., dissents.

———

GARDEN STATE PLAZA CORP. v. S.S. KRESGE CO., 78 N.J.Super. 485, 189 A.2d 448 (1963). "[T]he parol evidence rule does not even come into play until it is first determined what the true agreement of the parties is—i.e., what they meant by what they wrote down. Only when that is determined is one in an appropriate position to raise the bar of the parol evidence rule to prevent alteration or impugnment of the agreement by the asserted contradictory prior or contemporaneous agreement. In other words, interpretation and construction must necessarily precede protection against forbidden contradiction or modification. And in the process of interpretation and construction of the integrated agreement all relevant evidence pointing to meaning is admissible because experience teaches that language is so poor an instrument for communication or expression of intent that ordinarily all surrounding circumstances and conditions must be examined before there is any trustworthy assurance of derivation of contractual intent, even by reasonable judges of ordinary intelligence, from any given set of words which the parties have

---

11. The court's exclusion of extrinsic evidence in this case would be error even under a rule that excluded such evidence when the instrument appeared to the court to be clear and unambiguous on its face. The controversy centers on the meaning of the word "indemnify" and the phrase "all loss, damage, expense and liability." The trial court's recognition of the language as typical of a third party indemnity clause and the double sense in which the word "indemnify" is used in statutes and defined in dictionaries demonstrate the existence of an ambiguity. (Compare Civ.Code, § 2772, "Indemnity is a contract by which one engages to save another from a legal consequence of the conduct of one of the parties, or of some other person," with Civ.Code, § 2527, "Insurance is a contract whereby one undertakes to indemnify another against loss, damage, or liability, arising from an unknown or contingent event." Black's Law Dictionary (4th ed. 1951) defines "indemnity" as "A collateral contract or assurance, by which one person engages to secure another against an anticipated loss or to prevent him from being damnified by the legal consequences of an act or forbearance on the part of one of the parties or of some third person." Stroud's Judicial Dictionary (2d ed. 1903) defines it as a "Contract . . . to indemnify against a liability. . . ." One of the definitions given to "indemnify" by Webster's Third New Internat. Dict. (1961 ed.) is "to exempt from incurred penalties or liabilities.")

Plaintiff's assertion that the use of the word "all" to modify "loss, damage, expense and liability" dictates an all inclusive interpretation is not persuasive. If the word "indemnify" encompasses only third-party claims, the word "all" simply refers to all such claims. The use of the words "loss," "damage," and "expense" in addition to the word "liability" is likewise inconclusive. These words do not imply an agreement to reimburse for injury to an indemnitee's property since they are commonly inserted in third-party indemnity clauses, to enable an indemnitee who settles a claim to recover from his indemnitor without proving his liability. (Carpenter Paper Co. v. Kellogg (1952) 114 Cal.App.2d 640, 651, 251 P.2d 40. . . .

The provision that defendant perform the work "at his own risk and expense" and the provisions relating to insurance are equally inconclusive. By agreeing to work at its own risk defendant may have released plaintiff from liability for any injuries to defendant's property arising out of the contract's performance, but this provision did not necessarily make defendant an insurer against injuries to plaintiff's property. Defendant's agreement to procure liability insurance to cover damages to plaintiff's property does not indicate whether the insurance was to cover all injuries or only injuries caused by defendant's negligence.

committed to paper as their contract. Construing a contract of debatable meaning by resort to surrounding and antecedent circumstances and negotiations for light as to the meaning of the words used is never a violation of the parol evidence rule. And debatability of meaning is not always discernible at the first reading of a contract by a new mind. More often it becomes manifest upon exposure of the specific disputed interpretations in the light of the attendant circumstances.... Of course, in order to justify the use of evidence of extrinsic circumstances to establish a contended—for interpretation of disputed contractual language, that interpretation must be one 'which the written words will bear.' ... As stated in the Restatement, Contracts (1932), § 242, comment, p. 342, 'Previous negotiations cannot give to an integrated agreement a meaning completely alien to anything its words can possibly express.' "

SECTION 3. TRADE USAGE, COURSE OF PERFORMANCE AND COURSE OF DEALING AS PART OF A WRITTEN CONTRACT

NANAKULI PAVING AND ROCK CO. v. SHELL OIL CO.

United States Court of Appeals, Ninth Circuit, 1981.
664 F.2d 772.

Before BROWNING, CHIEF JUDGE, and KENNEDY, CIRCUIT JUDGE, and HOFFMAN,* DISTRICT JUDGE.

HOFFMAN, DISTRICT JUDGE:

[Prior to 1963, there were two major paving contractors on Oahu: Nanakuli and Hawaiian Bitumals ("H.B."). Of these, H.B. was by far the largest, in part because it had a special relationship with Chevron, which supplied asphalt, a major element in paving construction. Shell Oil, like Chevron, was a major worldwide oil company, but partly because of the relationship between H.B. and Chevron, Shell had only a small percentage of the asphalt market in Hawaii and had no asphalt terminals in Hawaii.

[In 1963, Nanakuli and Shell entered into a five-year contract under which Nanakuli agreed to buy its asphalt requirements from Shell, and Shell agreed to supply these requirements. The contract gave Nanakuli an assured source of supply, so that it could compete on equal terms with H.B., and gave Shell the potential for drastically expanding its asphalt sales in Hawaii. In 1969, a new contract was executed. The term of this contract was until December 31, 1975, at which point each party had an option to cancel on 6 months' notice.

[In February 1976, Nanakuli sued Shell for breach of the 1969 contract. That contract provided that the price of asphalt to Nanakuli would be "Shell's

* Honorable Walter E. Hoffman, Senior United States District Judge for the Eastern District of Virginia, sitting by designation.

posted price at the time of delivery"—that is, the price Shell posted, at the time of delivery, for sale to all buyers. Nanakuli argued that notwithstanding this price term, Nanakuli was entitled to "price protection" under both trade usage and course of performance, and that Shell had breached the contract by refusing to give such protection. "Price protection" means that a supplier will not increase the price charged to a contractor, despite an increase in the supplier's posted price, without advance notice, and instead will apply the posted price that is in place at the time the contractor made a bid, and that is incorporated by the contractor into its bid, long enough to allow the contractor to order the asphalt needed on the job. Nanakuli claimed that Shell breached the 1969 contract in January 1974 by failing to price protect Nanakuli on 7,200 tons of asphalt when Shell raised the price for asphalt from $44 to $76. The jury returned a verdict of $220,800 for Nanakuli. The district court set aside this verdict, and granted Shell's motion for judgment n.o.v.]

. . . We reinstate the jury verdict because we find that, viewing the evidence as a whole, there was substantial evidence to support a finding by reasonable jurors that Shell breached its contract by failing to provide protection for Nanakuli in 1974. . . .

[W]e hold that, under the facts of this case, a jury could reasonably have found that Shell's acts on two occasions to price protect Nanakuli were not ambiguous and therefore indicated Shell's understanding of the terms of the agreement with Nanakuli rather than being a waiver by Shell of those terms.[12]

[We also] hold that, although the express price terms of Shell's posted price of delivery may seem, at first glance, inconsistent with a trade usage of price protection at time of increases in price, a closer reading shows that the jury could have reasonably construed price protection as consistent with the express term. We reach this holding for several reasons. First, we are persuaded by a careful reading of the U.C.C., one of whose underlying purposes is to promote flexibility in the expansion of commercial practices and which rather drastically overhauls this particular area of the law. The Code would have us look beyond the printed pages of the contract to usages and the entire commercial context of the agreement in order to reach the "true understanding" of the parties. Second, decisions of other courts in similar situations have managed to reconcile such trade usages with seemingly contradictory express terms where the prior course of dealings between the parties, trade usages, and the actual performance of the contract by the parties showed a clear intent by the parties to incorporate those usages into the agreement or to give to the express term the particular meaning provided by those usages, even at times varying the apparent meaning of the express terms. Third, the delineation by thoughtful commentators of the degree of consistency demanded between express terms and usage is that a usage should be allowed to modify the apparent agreement, as seen in the written terms, as long as it does not totally negate it. We believe the usage here falls within the limits set forth by commentators and generally followed in the better reasoned decisions. The manner in which price protection was actually

12. In addition, Shell's Bohner volunteered on direct for Shell that Shell price protected Nanakuli again after 1974 on the only two occasions of later price increases in 1977 and 1978. Although not constituting a course of performance, since the occasions took place under different contracts, these two additional instances of price protection could have reinforced the jury's impression that Shell's earlier actions were a carrying out of the price term.

practiced in Hawaii was that it only came into play at times of price increases and only for work committed prior to those increases on non-escalating contracts. Thus, it formed an exception to, rather than a total negation of, the express price term of "Shell's Posted Price at time of delivery." Our decision is reinforced by the overwhelming nature of the evidence that price protection was routinely practiced by all suppliers in the small Oahu market of the asphaltic paving trade and therefore was known to Shell; that it was a realistic necessity to operate in that market and thus vital to Nanakuli's ability to get large government contracts and to Shell's continued business growth on Oahu; and that it therefore constituted an intended part of the agreement, as that term is broadly defined by the Code, between Shell and Nanakuli. . . .

II

Trade Usage Before and After 1969

The key to price protection being so prevalent in 1969 that both parties would intend to incorporate it into their contract is found in one reality of the Oahu asphaltic paving market: the largest paving contracts were let by government agencies and none of the three levels of government—local, state, or federal—allowed escalation clauses for paving materials. If a paver bid at one price and another went into effect before the award was made, the paving company would lose a great deal of money, since it could not pass on increases to any government agency or to most general contractors. Extensive evidence was presented that, as a consequence, aggregate suppliers routinely price protected paving contractors in the 1960's and 1970's, as did the largest asphaltic supplier in Oahu, Chevron. Nanakuli presented documentary evidence of routine price protection by aggregate suppliers as well as two witnesses: Grosjean, Vice–President for Marketing of Ameron H.C. & D., and Nihei, Division Manager of Lone Star Industries for Pacific Cement and Aggregate (P.C. & A.). Both testified that price protection to their knowledge had always been practiced: at H.C. & D. for many years prior to Grosjean's arrival in 1962 and at P.C. & A. routinely since Nihei's arrival in 1960. Such protection consisted of advance notices of increases, coupled with charging the old price for work committed at that price or for enough time to order the tonnage committed. The smallness of the Oahu market led to complete trust among suppliers and pavers. H.C. & D. did not demand that Nanakuli or other pavers issue purchase orders or sign contracts for aggregate before incorporating its aggregate prices into bids. Nanakuli would merely give H.C. & D. a list of projects it had bid at the time H.C. & D. raised its prices, without documentation. "Their word and letter is good enough for us," Grosjean testified. Nihei said P.C. & A. at the time of price increases would get a list of either particular projects bid by a paver or simply total tonnage bid at the old price. "We take either one. We take their word for it." None of the aggregate companies had a contract with Nanakuli expressly stating price protection would be given; Nanakuli's contract with P.C. & A. merely set out that P.C. & A. would not charge Nanakuli more than it charged its other customers.

The evidence about Chevron's practice of price protection came in the form of an affidavit by Bery Jameyson, Chevron's Division Manager–Asphalt in California. He stated that Chevron had routinely price protected H.B. on work bid for many years, the last occasion prior to the signing of the 1969 contracts between Nanakuli and Shell being a price increase put into effect on March 7, 1969, with the understanding that H.B. would be protected on work bid, which amounted to 12,000 tons. In answer to Shell's protest that such evidence was not relevant without the contract itself, Nanakuli introduced the contract into evidence. Much like the contract at issue here, it provided that the price to H.B. would be a given percentage of the price Chevron set for a specified crude oil in California. No mention was made of price protection in the written contract between H.B. and Chevron.

In addition to evidence of trade usages existing in 1969 when the contract at issue was signed, the District Judge let in evidence of the continuation of that trade usage after 1969, over Shell's protest. He stated that, giving a liberal reading to Section 1–205, he felt that later evidence was relevant to show that the expectation of the parties that a given usage would be observed was justified. The basis for incorporating a trade usage into a contract under the U.C.C. is the justifiable expectation of the parties that it will be observed. That later evidence consisted here of more price protection by the aggregate companies on Oahu, as well as continued asphalt price protection. Chevron after 1969 continued price protecting H.B. on Oahu and, on raising prices in 1979, price protected Nanakuli on the island of Molokai, where Nanakuli purchased its asphalt from Chevron. Additionally, Shell price protected Nanakuli in 1977 and 1978 on Oahu.[13]

III

Shell's Course of Performance of the 1969 Contract

The Code considers actual performance of a contract as the most relevant evidence of how the parties interpreted the terms of that contract. In 1970 and 1971, the only points at which Shell raised prices between 1969 and 1974, it price protected Nanakuli by holding its old price for four and three months, respectively, after announcing a price increase. In the late summer of 1970, Shell had announced a price increase from $35 to $40 a ton effective September 1, 1970. When Nanakuli protested to Bohner [Shell's Hawaiian representative] that it should be price protected on work already committed, Blee [a Shell asphalt official in San Francisco, to whom Bohner reported] wrote Bohner an in-house memo that, if Bohner could not "convince" Nanakuli to go along with the price increase on September 1, he should try to "bargain" to get Nanakuli to accept the price raise by at least the first of the year, which was what was finally agreed upon. During that four-month period, Nanakuli bought 3,300 tons. Shell announced a second increase in October, 1970, from $40 to $42 effective December 31st. Before that increase went into effect, on November 25 Shell increased the [amount of the] raise to $4, making the price $44 as of the first of the year.[14] Shell again agreed to price protect Nanakuli by holding the price at $40, which had been the official price since September 1, for three months from January to March, 1971. Shell

13. We do not need to decide whether usage evidence after a contract was signed is admissible to show that a party's reliance on a given usage was justifiable, given its continuation, because part of that evidence dealing with asphalt prices was admissible to show the reasonably commercial standards of fair dealing prevalent in the trade in 1974 and the part dealing with the continuation of price protec-tion by aggregate suppliers, after 1969 was not so extensive as to be prejudicial to Shell....

14. That November letter also announced a "new pricing policy" of Shell, setting out a requirement that firm contractual commitments be made with Shell within 15 days of accepting a bid.

did not actually raise prices again until January, 1974, but at several points it believed that increases would be necessary and gave several months' advance notice of those possible increases. Those actions were in accord with Shell's own policy, as professed by Bohner, and that of other asphalt and aggregate suppliers: to give at least several months' advance notice of price increases. On January 14, 1971, Shell wrote its asphalt customers that the maximum 1971 increase would be to $46. On July 9, 1971, another letter promised the price would not go over $50 in 1972. In addition, Bohner volunteered on direct the information that Shell price protected Nanakuli on the only two occasions of price increases after 1974 by giving 6 months' advance notice in 1977 and 3 or 4 months' advance notice in 1978, a practice he described as "in effect carryover pricing," his term for price protection. By its actions, Bohner testified, Shell allowed Nanakuli time to make arrangements to buy up tonnage committed at the old price, that is, to "chew up" tonnage bid or contracted. Shell apparently offered this testimony to impress the jury with its subsequent good faith toward Nanakuli. In fact, it also may have reinforced the impression of the universality of price protection in the asphaltic paving trade on Oahu and, by showing Shell's adherence to that practice on every relevant occasion except 1974, have highlighted for the jury what was the commercially reasonable standard of fair dealing in effect on Oahu in 1974....

VI

Waiver or Course of Performance

Course of performance under the Code is the action of the parties in carrying out the contract at issue, whereas course of dealing consists of relations between the parties *prior* to signing that contract. Evidence of the latter was excluded by the District Judge; evidence of the former consisted of Shell's price protection of Nanakuli in 1970 and 1971. Shell protested that the jury could not have found that those two instances of price protection amounted to a course of performance of its 1969 contract, relying on two Code comments. First, one instance does not constitute a course of performance. "A single occasion of conduct does not fall within the language of this section...." Haw.Rev.Stat. § 490:2–208, Comment 4. Although the Comment rules out one instance, it does not further delineate how many acts are needed to form a course of performance. The prior occasions here were only two, but they constituted the only occasions before 1974 that would call for such conduct. In addition, the language used by a top asphalt official of Shell in connection with the first price protection of Nanakuli indicated that Shell felt that Nanakuli was entitled to some form of price protection. On that occasion in 1970 Blee, who had negotiated the contract with Nanakuli and was familiar with exactly what terms Shell was bound to by that agreement, wrote of the need to "bargain" with Nanakuli over the extent of price protection to be given, indicating that some price protection was a legal right of Nanakuli's under the 1969 agreement.

Shell's second defense is that the Comment expresses a preference for an interpretation of waiver.

3. Where it is difficult to determine whether a particular act merely sheds light on the meaning of the agreement or represents a waiver of a term of the agreement, the preference is in favor of "waiver" whenever such construction, plus the application of the provisions on the reinstate-

ment of rights waived . . ., is needed to preserve the flexible character of commercial contracts and to prevent surprise or other hardship.

Id., Comment 3. The preference for waiver only applies, however, where acts are ambiguous. It was within the province of the jury to determine whether those acts were ambiguous, and if not, whether they constituted waivers or a course of performance of the contract. The jury's interpretation of those acts as a course of performance was bolstered by evidence offered by Shell that it again price protected Nanakuli on the only two occasions of post–1974 price increases, in 1977 and 1978.[15]

VII

*Express Terms as Reasonably Consistent With
Usage In Course of Performance*

Perhaps one of the most fundamental departures of the Code from prior contract law is found in the parol evidence rule and the definition of an agreement between two parties. Under the U.C.C., an agreement goes beyond the written words on a piece of paper. " 'Agreement' means the bargain of the parties in fact as found in their language or by implication from other circumstances including course of dealing or usage of trade or course of performance as provided in this chapter (sections 490:1–205 and 490:2–208)." *Id.* § 490:1–201(3). Express terms, then, do not constitute the entire agreement, which must be sought also in evidence of usages, dealings, and performance of the contract itself. The purpose of evidence of usages, which are defined in the previous section, is to help to understand the entire agreement.

> [Usages are] a factor in reaching the commercial meaning of the agreement which the parties have made. The language used is to be interpreted as meaning what it may fairly be expected to mean to parties involved in the particular commercial transaction in a given locality or in a given vocation or trade. . . . Part of the agreement of the parties . . . is to be sought for in the usages of trade which furnish the background and give particular meaning to the language used, and are the framework of common understanding controlling any general rules of law which hold only when there is no such understanding.

Id. § 490:1–205, Comment 4. Course of dealings is more important than usages of the trade, being specific usages between the two parties to the contract. "[C]ourse of dealing controls usage of trade." *Id.* § 490:1–205(4). It "is a sequence of previous conduct between the parties to a particular transaction which is fairly to be regarded as establishing a common basis of understanding for interpreting their expressions and other conduct." *Id.* § 490:1–205(1). Much of the evidence of prior dealings between Shell and Nanakuli in negotiating the 1963 contract and in carrying out similar earlier contracts was excluded by the court.[16]

---

15. Bohner testified on direct for Shell at the 1978 trial that the two later instances of price protection occurred "this" year and "last" year, by which he could have meant 1976 and 1977. Bohner's testimony was that on those later occasions Shell gave Nanakuli six and three or four months' notice of an increase to allow Nanakuli to buy tonnage it had committed at the old price. He defined Shell's actions as "in effect carryover pricing." The jury's finding was reasonable in light of the circumstances of universal price protection by asphalt and aggregate suppliers, as well as by Shell on all price increases except 1974.

16. *See* footnote 31, *supra.*

A commercial agreement, then, is broader than the written paper and its meaning is to be determined not just by the language used by them in the written contract but "by their action, read and interpreted in the light of commercial practices and other surrounding circumstances. The measure and background for interpretation are set by the commercial context, which may explain and supplement even the language of a formal or final writing." *Id.,* Comment 1. Performance, usages, and prior dealings are important enough to be admitted always, even for a final and complete agreement; only if they cannot be reasonably reconciled with the express terms of the contract are they not binding on the parties. "The express terms of an agreement and an applicable course of dealing or usage of trade shall be construed wherever reasonable as consistent with each other; but when such construction is unreasonable express terms control both course of dealing and usage of trade and course of dealing controls usage of trade." *Id.* § 490:1–205(4).

Of these three, then, the most important evidence of the agreement of the parties is their actual performance of the contract. *Id.* The operative definition of course of performance is as follows: "Where the contract for sale involves repeated occasions for performance by either party with knowledge of the nature of the performance and opportunity for objection to it by the other, any course of performance accepted or acquiesced in without objection shall be relevant to determine the meaning of the agreement." *Id.* § 490:2–208(1). "Course of dealing ... is restricted, literally, to a sequence of conduct between the parties previous to the agreement. However, the provisions of the Act on course of performance make it clear that a sequence of conduct after or under the agreement may have equivalent meaning (Section 2–208)." *Id.* 490:1–205, Comment 2. The importance of evidence of course of performance is explained: "The parties themselves know best what they have meant by their words of agreement and their action under that agreement is the best indication of what that meaning was. This section thus rounds out the set of factors which determines the meaning of the 'agreement' ..." *Id.* § 490:2–208, Comment 1. "Under this section a course of performance is always relevant to determine the meaning of the agreement." *Id.,* Comment 2.

Our study of the Code provisions and Comments, then, form the first basis of our holding that a trade usage to price protect pavers at times of price increases for work committed on nonescalating contracts could reasonably be construed as consistent with an express term of seller's posted price at delivery. Since the agreement of the parties is broader than the express terms and includes usages, which may even add terms to the agreement,[17] and since the commercial background provided by those usages is vital to an understanding of the agreement, we follow the Code's mandate to proceed on the assumption that the parties have included those usages unless they cannot reasonably be construed as consistent with the express terms.

Federal courts usually have been lenient in not ruling out consistent additional terms or trade usage for apparent inconsistency with express terms. The leading case on the subject is *Columbia Nitrogen Corp. v. Royster Co.,* 451 F.2d 3 (4th Cir.1971). Columbia, the buyer, had in the past primarily produced and sold nitrogen to Royster. When Royster opened a new plant that

---

17. "The agreement of the parties includes that part of their bargain found in course of dealing, usage of trade, or course of performance. These sources are relevant not only to the interpretation of express contract terms, but may themselves constitute contract terms." White & Summers, *supra,* § 3–3 at 84.

produced more phosphate than it needed, the parties reversed roles and signed a sales contract for Royster to sell excess phosphate to Columbia. The contract terms set out the price that would be charged by Royster and the amount to be sold. It provided for the price to go up if certain events occurred but did not provide for price declines. When the price of nitrogen fell precipitously, Columbia refused to accept the full amount of nitrogen specified in the contract after Royster refused to renegotiate the contract price. The District Judge's exclusion of usage of the trade and course of dealing to explain the express quantity term in the contract was reversed. Columbia had offered to prove that the quantity set out in the contract was a mere projection to be adjusted according to market forces. Ambiguity was not necessary for the admission of evidence of usage and prior dealings.[18] Even though the lengthy contract was the result of long and careful negotiations and apparently covered every contingency, the appellate court ruled that "the test of admissibility is not whether the contract appears on its face to be complete in every detail, but whether the proffered evidence of course of dealing and trade usage reasonably can be construed as consistent with the express terms of the agreement." *Id.* at 9. The express quantity term could be reasonably construed as consistent with a usage that such terms would be mere projections for several reasons: (1) the contract did not expressly state that usage and dealings evidence would be excluded; (2) the contract was silent on the adjustment of price or quantities in a declining market; (3) the minimum tonnage was expressed in the contract as Products Supplied, not Products Purchased; (4) the default clause of the contract did not state a penalty for failure to take delivery; and (5) apparently most important in the court's view, the parties had deviated from similar express terms in earlier contracts in times of declining market. *Id.* at 9–10. As here, the contract's merger clause said that there were no oral agreements. The court explained that its ruling "reflects the reality of the marketplace and avoids the overly legalistic interpretations which the Code seeks to abolish." *Id.* at 10. The Code assigns dealing and usage evidence "unique and important roles" and therefore "overly simplistic and overly legalistic interpretation of a contract should be shunned." *Id.* at 11.

Usage and an oral understanding led to much the same interpretation of a quantity term specifying delivery of 500 tons of stainless-steel solids in *Michael Schiavone & Sons, Inc. v. Securalloy Co.*, 312 F.Supp. 801 (D.Conn. 1970). In denying summary judgment for plaintiff-buyer, the court ruled that defendant-seller could attempt to prove that the quantity term was modified by an oral understanding, in line with a trade usage, that seller would only supply as many tons as he could, with 500 tons the upper limit. The court reasoned that an additional term with a lesser effect than total contradiction or negation of a contract term can be a consistent term and "[e]vidence that the quantity to be supplied by defendant was orally understood to be up to

---

18. As discussed earlier, the District Judge here mistakenly equated ambiguity with admissibility. He said, "I think this is a close case. On the face of the contract it would seem to be unambiguous," although acknowledging that liberal commentators on the Code would let in evidence of usage and performance even without ambiguity. He only let in usage evidence because Shell's answer to interrogatory 11 provided some ambiguity, ... saying "I think if these can be consistently used to explain the apparently unambiguous terms, they should be allowed in." In fact, this court has ruled that ambiguity is not necessary to admit usage evidence. *Board of Trade of San Francisco v. Swiss Credit Bank*, 597 F.2d 146, 148 (9th Cir.1979).

500 tons cannot be said to be inconsistent with the terms of the written contract which specified the quantity as '500 Gross Ton.'" *Id.* at 804....

Probably the two leading cases that have rejected usage evidence as inconsistent with express terms are *Southern Concrete Services, Inc. v. Mableton Contractors, Inc.*, 407 F.Supp. 581 (N.D.Ga.1975), *aff'd*, 569 F.2d 1154 (5th Cir.1978) (unpublished opinion), and *Division of Triple T Service, Inc. v. Mobil Oil Corp.*, 60 Misc.2d 720, 304 N.Y.S.2d 191 (Sup.Ct.1969). In *Southern Concrete* the District Court, distinguishing its facts from those in *Columbia Nitrogen, supra,* held that evidence of a trade usage and an agreement to additional terms was not admissible. The usage allegedly was that contract quantity specifications were not mandatory on either buyer or seller. The court acknowledged that U.C.C. § 2–202 "was meant to liberalize the common law parol evidence rule to allow evidence of agreements outside the contract, without a prerequisite finding that the contract was ambiguous" and "requires that contracts be interpreted in light of the commercial context in which they were written and not by the rules on legal construction." *Southern Concrete, supra,* at 582–83. Nevertheless, the court held, the express quantity term in the contract and the usage could not be construed as reasonably consistent. "A construction which negates the express terms of the contract by allowing unilateral abandonment of its specifications is patently unreasonable." *Id.* at 585. The court's attempt to differentiate its facts from those in *Columbia Nitrogen* was unsuccessful; the distinctions discussed were very minor. The difference between the two results should depend less on such subtle variations in contract language and more on the strength of the usage evidence and whether the parties are or should be aware of the usage and thus should be bound by it. The court in *Southern Concrete* acknowledged that *Columbia Nitrogen* is not the only case at odds with its holding that a usage that quantities are projections cannot modify a seemingly unambiguous quantity term. *Southern Concrete, supra,* at 585–86.

The other leading case cited by Shell is a New York case, *Triple T, supra.* Because the express term of the franchise agreement gave either party the right to terminate 90–days' notice, the court refused to find as reasonably consistent with that term a usage of the trade that a gasoline franchisor could only terminate a dealer for "cause". "[T]he express terms of the contract cover the entire area of termination and negate plaintiff's argument that the custom or usage in the trade implicitly adds the words 'with cause' in the termination clause. The contract is unambiguous and no sufficient basis appears for a construction which would insert words to limit the effect of the termination clause." *Id.* at 203. The court then held that only consistent usages are admissible, which is an incorrect reading of the Code. Usage is always admissible, even though the express term controls in the event of inconsistency, which is a jury question.

Higher New York courts have not been as quick to reject evidence of additional terms for inconsistency as was the Supreme Court in *Triple T* in rejecting usage evidence.... *Hunt Foods & Industries, Inc. v. Doliner*, 26 App.Div.2d 41, 270 N.Y.S.2d 937 (1966) [p. 541, supra]....

... Here the evidence was overwhelming that all suppliers to the asphaltic paving trade price protected customers under the same types of circumstances. Chevron's contract with H.B. was a similar long-term supply contract between a buyer and seller with very close relations, on a form supplied by the seller, covering sales of asphalt, and setting the price at seller's posted price, with no mention of price protection. . . .

Because the stock printed forms cannot always reflect the changing methods of business, members of the trade may do business with a standard clause in the forms that they ignore in practice. If the trade consistently ignores obsolete clauses at variance with actual trade practices, a litigant can maintain that it is reasonable that the courts also ignore the clauses. . . .

Kirst, [Usage of Trade and Course of Dealing: Subversion of the UCC Theory, [1977] U.Ill.L. Forum 811] at 824. *Levie,* [Trade Usage and Custom . . ., 40 N.Y.U.L.Rev. 1101 (1965)], at 1112, writes, "Astonishing as it will seem to most practicing attorneys, under the Code it will be possible in some cases to use custom to contradict the written agreement. . . . Therefore usage may be used to 'qualify' the agreement, which presumably means to 'cut down' express terms although not to negate them entirely." Here, the express price term was "Shell's Posted Price at time of delivery." A total negation of that term would be that the buyer was to set the price. It is a less than complete negation of the term that an unstated exception exists at times of price increases, at which times the old price is to be charged, for a certain period or for a specified tonnage, on work already committed at the lower price on nonescalating contracts. Such a usage forms a broad and important exception to the express term, but does not swallow it entirely. Therefore, we hold that, under these particular facts, a reasonable jury could have found that price protection was incorporated into the 1969 agreement between Nanakuli and Shell and that price protection was reasonably consistent with the express term of seller's posted price at delivery. . . .

[The court also held that in light of the universal practice in the asphaltic paving trade of giving advance notice of a price increase, Shell could not have exercised good faith in raising its price by $32, effective January 1, in a letter written on December 31 and only received on January 4.]

Because the jury could have found for Nanakuli on its price protection claim under either theory, we reverse the judgment of the District Court and reinstate the jury verdict for Nanakuli in the amount of $220,800, plus interest according to law.

REVERSED AND REMANDED WITH DIRECTIONS TO ENTER FINAL JUDGMENT.

KENNEDY, CIRCUIT JUDGE, concurring specially:

The case involves specific pricing practices, not an allegation of unfair dealing generally. Our opinion should not be interpreted to permit juries to import price protection or a similarly specific contract term from a concept of good faith that is not based on well-established custom and usage or other objective standards of which the parties had clear notice. Here, evidence of custom and usage regarding price protection in the asphaltic paving trade was not contradicted in major respects, and the jury could find that the parties knew or should have known of the practice at the time of making the contract. In my view, these are necessary predicates for either theory of the case, namely, interpretation of the contract based on the course of its performance or a finding that good faith required the seller to hold the price. With these observations, I concur.

——————

C–THRU CONTAINER CORP. v. MIDLAND MFG. CO., 533 N.W.2d 542 (Iowa 1995). C–Thru and Midland entered into a contract under which Midland purchased bottle-making equipment from C–Thru. Under the contract, Midland could pay for the equipment by supplying commercially acceptable bottles to C–Thru. If Midland failed to supply the bottles, C–Thru could demand the purchase price of the equipment in cash. C–Thru claimed that Midland had breached the contract by being incapable of producing commercially acceptable bottles, and demanded that Midland pay the purchase price of the equipment. Midland contended that it had not breached the contract because C–Thru had not ordered any bottles. C–Thru responded that the practice in the bottling industry was that before the purchaser places an order, the bottle manufacturer provides sample bottles to verify that it is capable of producing commercially acceptable bottles, and that C–Thru had not provided such samples. C–Thru argued that evidence of this practice was inadmissible under the parol evidence rule, because the contract was complete and unambiguous. Held, evidence that there was such a practice was admissible.

We first reject Midland's argument that evidence of trade usage is admissible only when the contract is ambiguous. There is no such requirement in [UCC § 2–202]. Moreover, the official comment to [§ 2–202] . . . states that this section "definitely rejects" a requirement that the language of the contract be ambiguous as a condition precedent to the admission of trade-usage evidence. . . .

We also hold that even a "complete" contract may be explained or supplemented by parol evidence of trade usages.[19] . . . As the official comment to section 2–202 states, commercial sales contracts "are to be read on the assumption that the course of prior dealings between the parties and the usages of trade were taken for granted when the document was phrased." U.C.C. § 2–202 cmt. 2 (1977). Therefore, even a completely integrated contract may be supplemented by practices in the industry that do not contradict express terms of the contract.

That brings us to the remaining argument made by Midland—that C–Thru may not use parol evidence to add a new term to the agreement. Section [2–202] says that when parol evidence shows a usage of trade that does not contradict a contract term, the evidence is admissible to "supplement" the contract. We look to the common meaning of the word "supplement." . . . "Supplement" means "to add . . . to." Webster's Third New Int'l Dictionary 2297 (1993). Consequently, the trade-usage evidence upon which C–Thru relies is admissible even though it adds a new term to the contract. White & Summers, § 3–3 (usage of trade may itself constitute a contract term).

——————

19. The contract here stated that "[t]his agreement constitutes the entire agreement between C–Thru and Midland and supersedes any and all prior agreements between them."

NOTE ON THE PLAIN–MEANING RULE
AND THE PAROL EVIDENCE RULE

Strictly speaking, the plain meaning (or "four corners") rule, that extrinsic evidence cannot be introduced to help interpret a written contract unless the contract is ambiguous on its face, is not the same as the parol evidence rule. At least in theory, the plain meaning rule is a principle of interpretation; the parol evidence rule is not. Furthermore, the term *extrinsic evidence* is broader than the term *parol evidence*, because extrinsic evidence includes not only evidence of other agreements, but evidence of the circumstances surrounding the making of a contract. Thus many plain-meaning-rule opinions, like Steuart v. McChesney, don't even mention the parol evidence rule.

However, the two rules are similar in certain fundamental respects. Both aim, properly or misguidedly, to preserve what proponents of the rules perceive to be the integrity of writings. Both operate to preclude the introduction of evidence concerning, but not contained in, a written contract. Both focus largely on the exclusion of oral evidence, which is often referred to as parol evidence even in plain-meaning-rule cases. The two rules differ in that the parol evidence rule normally does not preclude evidence of the *circumstances* under which a written contract was made, as opposed to evidence of *agreements* not embodied in the written contract, while the plain–meaning rule may preclude even evidence concerning circumstances.

Although in principle the parol evidence rule applies only to alleged parol agreements, in practice courts often apply the rule to exclude interpretive evidence that in the courts' view would lead to an interpretation that the writing "cannot bear."

Part IV

FORM CONTRACTS IN COMMERCIAL AND CONSUMER CONTEXTS

———

The problems raised by form contracts have been a major preoccupation of contract–law scholars since the middle of the twentieth century. The primary areas of concern have been the enforceability of preprinted terms and the import of preprinted terms in determining whether a form sent in response to an offer constitutes an acceptance.

The phenomenon of rational ignorance plays a powerful role in both concerns. The provisions of a contract can be divided into performance and nonperformance terms. Performance terms specify the performance each party must render. All other provisions are normally nonperformance terms. The most important types of performance terms concern the description of the subject-matter of the contract, quantity, price, delivery terms, and payment terms. Nonperformance terms cover a wide range of issues, such as how and when notice of default must be given, limitations on warranties, excuse, and so forth. Most preprinted terms are nonperformance terms that concern low-probability future risks. Call a party who prepares a form contract a form-giver, and a party who receives a form contract a form-taker. A form-giver typically offers a package consisting of a commodity (using that term in a broadly defined manner, to include goods, realty, and services) and a form contract that states the terms on which the commodity will be purchased or sold. Each part of the package, in turn, consists of a number of attributes: The commodity has physical attributes, such as size, shape, and color. The form contract has business and legal attributes, most of which are nonperformance terms. Typically, the most important performance terms—description, quantity, price, delivery, payment—will be custom-tailored to each transaction, and individually filled into the form. In contrast, the nonperformance terms and the less important performance terms (such as provisions concerning crating or notice of shipment) will typically be preprinted.

To make an optimum substantive decision, a form-taker who is choosing between a variety of commodities of a given type would carefully deliberate not only on the characteristics of the commodities, but also on the business and legal attributes of each form contract that is coupled with each commodity that he is considering. Analyzing all the terms of a form contract in this manner, however, will often be unduly costly. First, a form contract often contains a very large number of terms. Form insurance contracts, for example, often contain forty, fifty, or more terms. Moreover, the meaning and effect of the preprinted terms will very often be inaccessible to laypersons. In part, this is because the terms are often written in highly technical prose. Even if the terms are written clearly, however, the form-taker usually will be unable fully to understand their effects, because preprinted terms characteristically vary the form-taker's baseline legal rights, and most form-takers do not know their baseline legal rights. The verbal and legal obscurity of preprinted terms renders the cost of searching out and deliberating on the preprinted terms of various form contracts exceptionally high. In contrast, the low probability that these nonperformance terms will ever come into play heavily discounts the benefits of search and deliberation.

Furthermore, the length and complexity of a form contract is often not correlated to the dollar value of the transaction. Often, therefore, the cost of thorough search and deliberation on preprinted terms, let alone the cost of legal advice about the meaning and effect of the terms, would be prohibitive in relation to the benefits. A rational form-taker faced with preprinted terms whose effect he knows he will find difficult or impossible to fully understand, which involve risks that probably will never mature, which are unlikely to be worth the cost of search and deliberation, and which probably aren't subject to negotiation in any event, will typically decide to remain ignorant of many or most preprinted terms.

There is, however, a fundamental imbalance in this respect between the form-taker and the form-giver. For the form-taker, any given form contract is normally a one-shot transaction. This is one reason why the costs of searching and deliberating on the preprinted terms, or of retaining a lawyer to evaluate them, will normally far exceed the benefits of search and deliberation. For the form-giver, however, a form contract is a high-volume, repeat transaction. Thus, a rational form-giver will spend a significant amount of time and money, including money for legal services, to prepare a form contract that is optimal from his perspective. These asymmetrical incentives almost always work to heavily slant form contracts in favor of form-givers.

The law has responded to these problems through Section 2–207(1) of the Uniform Commercial Code, and through the common law doctrines of unfair surprise and reasonable expectations, which sharply limit the effect of preprinted terms in the contexts of contract formation and contract enforceability, respectively. The former issue is the subject of Chapter 16; the latter issue is the subject of Chapter 17.

Chapter 16

CONTRACT FORMATION IN A FORM–CONTRACT SETTING

SECTION 1. BATTLE OF THE FORMS: THE BASIC ISSUES

NOTE ON THE BATTLE OF THE FORMS

When goods are supplied by a commercial seller to a commercial buyer, in most cases there is no document covering the transaction that is called on its face a "contract." Often the buyer will send to the seller a form the buyer calls a "purchase order." At the bottom of this form, or on the reverse side, there will appear certain preprinted terms, often loosely designated in the form as "conditions." These terms may be fairly extensive, and include shipping instructions, provisions making the order cancellable for delays in delivery, provisions covering crating charges, provisions for the arbitration of disputes, etc. Usually the purchase-order form will state that the order is given "subject to" the conditions stated. Generally the purchase order will request an "acknowledgment," although occasionally the word "acceptance" is used. The buyer sometimes hopefully provides a tear sheet or a separate form, requesting the seller to sign and return this form as an "acknowledgment" of the order.

Often the seller, instead of accepting the buyer's purchase order, or returning the buyer's "acknowledgment" form, sends the buyer the seller's own form, frequently called a "sales order." Or the first document may be a "sales order" sent by the seller to the buyer. This will be like the buyer's "purchase order," and will itself be "subject to" certain preprinted terms or "conditions" printed at the bottom or on the back.

The chances that the preprinted terms in the sales order will coincide with those in the purchase order are negligible. Sometimes, to strengthen its position, the seller will repeat its terms (or perhaps a different set of terms) on the invoice that is sent when the goods are shipped, stating in this form that the goods are shipped "subject to the following conditions." The buyer, anticipating that the seller will decorate the back of its invoice with fine print, may stipulate in its purchase order that if the terms stated in the invoice do not agree with the buyer's purchase order, the terms of the purchase order will control.

The result is that instead of an orderly negotiation of the terms of the sale, we have the parties engaged in a battle of forms, each jockeying for position and each attempting to get the other to indicate assent to its form. Sometimes a seller's sales order is signed by the buyer, and a buyer's purchase order is signed by the seller. Thus, the same transaction is covered by two different forms, stipulating inconsistent terms. More commonly, neither party is willing to sign the other's form, so that each party states in writing its terms of the sale, but neither expressly indicates assent to the terms proposed by the other.

The battle of the forms had a special bite under the *mirror-image* (or *ribbon-matching*) rule of classical contract law. Under this rule, any difference between an offer and a purported acceptance, no matter how minor, prevented the formation of a contract. Since the seller's form and the buyer's form seldom if ever matched, the exchange of a purchase order and a sales order (or counterpart forms) would seldom if ever constitute a contract under the mirror-image rule.

But the matter did not end there. Under another rule, an offer can be accepted by conduct. Putting the two rules together, if no contract was formed by the exchange of forms, but the seller shipped the goods and the buyer accepted them, a contract was deemed to have been made, consisting of the terms in whichever form was sent last. The theory was that the first form was an offer, the responding form was a counter-offer, and the goods were shipped and accepted pursuant to that counter-offer. For example, suppose the buyer began a transaction by sending a purchase order, and the seller responded by sending back a nonconforming sales order. Under the mirror-image rule, there would be no contract at that point. However, the sales order would not be without legal effect; instead, under traditional principles it would be a counter-offer. Now suppose the seller shipped the goods and the buyer accepted the shipment. The buyer was deemed to have accepted pursuant to the sales order/counter-offer, so that the terms of the resulting contract were those set by the seller. Similarly, suppose the seller began a transaction be sending a sales order, the buyer responded with a nonconforming purchase order, the seller shipped the goods, and the buyer accepted the shipment. In that case, the terms of the contract would be those set in the purchase order, because the buyer's nonconforming purchase order would be a counter-offer, and the seller's shipment would be deemed an acceptance of that counter-offer. This analysis was often called the "last-shot" approach, because if the goods were shipped and accepted, the terms of the contract were those set by whichever party fired the last shot in the battle of the forms.

UCC §§ 2–204(1), 2–204, 2–207

[See Selected Source Materials Supplement]

ABA TASK FORCE REPORT ON ARTICLE 2, 16 Del.J.Corp.Law. 981, 1063–64 (1991). "The premise that underlies [UCC] section 2–207 is that pre–printed boilerplate terms in each party's form are not read. Indeed, they cannot reasonably be expected to be read by the other party."

NOTE ON WHAT CONSTITUTES AN ACCEPTANCE UNDER UCC § 2–207

UCC § 2–207 applies only if there has been a "definite and [seasonable] expression of acceptance," but leaves open what constitutes a definite and seasonable expression of acceptance. In most cases under § 2–207 the offeror has sent a form to the offeree; the offeree has returned to the offeror another form whose individualized (non-preprinted) terms match the individualized terms of the offer; virtually no other terms match; and the courts have explicitly or implicitly held that the return form nevertheless constitutes an "expression of acceptance" under § 2–207. Indeed, that is the paradigm case at which § 2–207 was directed.

Where, however, the parties don't employ forms, even a small difference between the offer and the response may prevent a response from being an acceptance under § 2–207, at least if the parties have been bargaining about that difference.

For example, in Koehring Co. v. Glowacki, 77 Wis.2d 497, 253 N.W.2d 64 (1977), Koehring circulated a letter listing nine items of surplus machinery that were available for sale at its plant on an "as is, where is" basis. The term "as is, where is" meant that the buyer would bear the cost and risk of loading the machinery onto its truck. Glowacki telephoned Koehring, inquiring as to price. Koehring responded that Glowacki must bid $16,500, and that the bid must be in the form of a telegram. Glowacki telegraphed a bid of only $16,000. Koehring called Glowacki, reiterating that the bid must be $16,500. Glowacki then sent a second telegram, which bid $16,500, but including the statement "FOB [free on board], our truck, your plant, loaded." The term "FOB ... loaded" meant that the seller would bear the cost and risk of loading the machinery onto the buyer's truck. Koehring responded with a telegram "accepting" the bid, but restating that the machinery was sold "as is, where is." In a suit by Koehring, the court held that no contract had been formed:

> As the trial court properly held in the present case, before we reach the question of additional or different terms added to a contract, we must first inquire whether or not any contract ever existed. Here the defendant's telegram was an offer to purchase at a price of $16,500 "FOB, our truck, your plant, loaded." Plaintiff's response was a counteroffer to sell at the price of $16,500 on an "as is, where is" basis. There was no "meeting of the minds" or agreement of the parties prior to the exchange of telegrams. No such "meeting of the minds" or agreement resulted from the exchange of telegrams. This being so, we do not reach the issue as to whether additional or differing terms do or do not destroy an agreement of the parties since there is no valid contract in the first place.

> In the case before us, we deal with an initial and continuing absence of agreement between the parties as to whether the sales price included loading risks and costs. The second telegram of defendant, offering $16,500 "FOB, our truck, your plant, loaded," was an offer. The respond-

ing telegram of plaintiff, all tools sold on an "as is, where is" basis, while labeled an acceptance, was actually a rejection of the defendant's offer and a counteroffer. This being the situation, it follows, as the trial court concluded, that there was here no contract or agreement between these two parties either preceding or derived from their exchange of telegrams.

CISG ART. 19

[See Selected Source Materials Supplement]

UNIDROIT PRINCIPLES OF INTERNATIONAL COMMERCIAL CONTRACTS ARTS. 2.1.12, 2.1.22

[See Selected Source Materials Supplement]

PRINCIPLES OF EUROPEAN CONTRACT LAW ART. 2.209

[See Selected Source Materials Supplement]

GARDNER ZEMKE CO. v. DUNHAM BUSH, INC.

Supreme Court of New Mexico, 1993.
115 N.M. 260, 850 P.2d 319.

FRANCHINI, JUSTICE.

This case involves a contract for the sale of goods and accordingly the governing law is the Uniform Commercial Code—Sales, as adopted in New Mexico. NMSA 1978, §§ 55–2–101 to–2–725 (Orig.Pamp. & Cum.Supp.1992) (Article 2). In the course of our discussion, we will also refer to pertinent general definitions and principles of construction found in NMSA 1978, Sections 55–1–101 to–1–209 (Orig.Pamp. & Cum.Supp.1992). Section 55–2–103(4). The case presents us with our first opportunity to consider a classic "battle of the forms" scenario arising under Section 55–2–207. Appellant Gardner Zemke challenges the trial court's judgment that a Customer's Acknowledgment (Acknowledgment) sent by appellee manufacturer Dunham Bush, in response to a Gardner Zemke Purchase Order (Order), operated as a counteroffer, thereby providing controlling warranty terms under the contract formed by the parties. We find merit in appellants' argument and remand for the trial court's reconsideration.

I.

Acting as the general contractor on a Department of Energy (DOE) project, Gardner Zemke issued its Order to Dunham Bush for air-conditioning equipment, known as chillers, to be used in connection with the project. The

Order contained a one-year manufacturer's warranty provision and the requirement that the chillers comply with specifications attached to the Order. Dunham Bush responded with its preprinted Acknowledgment containing extensive warranty disclaimers, a statement that the terms of the Acknowledgment controlled the parties' agreement, and a provision deeming silence to be acquiescence to the terms of the Acknowledgment.

The parties did not address the discrepancies in the forms exchanged and proceeded with the transaction. Dunham Bush delivered the chillers, and Gardner Zemke paid for them. Gardner Zemke alleges that the chillers provided did not comply with their specifications and that they incurred additional costs to install the nonconforming goods. Approximately five or six months after start up of the chillers, a DOE representative notified Gardner Zemke of problems with two of the chillers. In a series of letters, Gardner Zemke requested on-site warranty repairs. Through its manufacturer's representative, Dunham Bush offered to send its mechanic to the job site to inspect the chillers and absorb the cost of the service call only if problems discovered were within any component parts it provided. Further, Dunham Bush required that prior to the service call a purchase order be issued from the DOE, to be executed by Dunham Bush for payment for their services in the event their mechanic discovered problems not caused by manufacturing defects. Gardner Zemke rejected the proposal on the basis that the DOE had a warranty still in effect for the goods and would not issue a separate purchase order for warranty repairs.

Ultimately, the DOE hired an independent contractor to repair the two chillers. The DOE paid $24,245.00 for the repairs and withheld $20,000.00 from its contract with Gardner Zemke.[1] This breach of contract action then ensued, with Gardner Zemke alleging failure by Dunham Bush to provide equipment in accordance with the project plans and specifications and failure to provide warranty service.

II.

On cross-motions for summary judgment, the trial court granted partial summary judgment in favor of Dunham Bush, ruling that its Acknowledgment was a counteroffer to the Gardner Zemke Order and that the Acknowledgment's warranty limitations and disclaimers were controlling. Gardner Zemke filed an application for interlocutory appeal from the partial summary judgment in this Court, which was denied. A bench trial was held in December 1991, and the trial court again ruled the Acknowledgment was a counteroffer which Gardner Zemke accepted by silence and that under the warranty provisions of the Acknowledgment, Gardner Zemke was not entitled to damages.

On appeal, Gardner Zemke raises two issues: (1) the trial court erred as a matter of law in ruling that the Acknowledgment was a counteroffer; and (2) Gardner Zemke proved breach of contract and contract warranty, breach of code warranties, and damages.

---

1. The government has the right to set off the remaining $4,245.00 from any other Gardner Zemke government contract. *See Project*

Map, Inc. v. United States, 203 Ct.Cl. 52, 486 F.2d 1375 (1973) (per curiam).

III.

Karl N. Llewellyn, the principal draftsman of Article 2, described it as "[t]he heart of the Code." Karl N. Llewellyn, *Why We Need the Uniform Commercial Code,* 10 U.Fla.L.Rev. 367, 378 (1957). Section 2–207 is characterized by commentators as a "crucial section of Article 2" and an "iconoclastic Code section." *Bender's Uniform Commercial Code Service* (Vol. 3, Richard W. Duesenberg & Lawrence P. King, Sales & Bulk Transfers Under The Uniform Commercial Code) § 3.01 at 3–2 (1992). Recognizing its innovative purpose and complex structure Duesenberg and King further observe Section 2–207 "is one of the most important, subtle, and difficult in the entire Code, and well it may be said that the product as it finally reads is not altogether satisfactory." *Id.* § 3.02 at 3–13.

Section 55–2–207 provides:

(1) A definite and seasonable expression of acceptance or a written confirmation which is sent within a reasonable time operates as an acceptance even though it states terms additional to or different from those offered or agreed upon, unless acceptance is expressly made conditional on assent to the additional or different terms.

(2) The additional terms are to be construed as proposals for addition to the contract. Between merchants such terms become part of the contract unless:

(a) the offer expressly limits acceptance to the terms of the offer;

(b) they materially alter it; or,

(c) notification of objection to them has already been given or is given within a reasonable time after notice of them is received.

(3) Conduct by both parties which recognizes the existence of a contract is sufficient to establish a contract for sale although the writings of the parties do not otherwise establish a contract. In such case the terms of the particular contract consist of those terms on which the writings of the parties agree, together with any supplementary terms incorporated under any other provisions of this act [this chapter].

Relying on Section 2–207(1), Gardner Zemke argues that the trial court erred in concluding that the Dunham Bush Acknowledgment was a counteroffer rather than an acceptance. Gardner Zemke asserts that even though the Acknowledgment contained terms different from or in addition to the terms of their Order, it did not make acceptance expressly conditional on assent to the different or additional terms and therefore should operate as an acceptance rather than a counteroffer.

At common law, the "mirror image" rule applied to the formation of contracts, and the terms of the acceptance had to exactly imitate or "mirror" the terms of the offer. *Idaho Power Co. v. Westinghouse Elec. Corp.,* 596 F.2d 924, 926 (9th Cir.1979). If the accepting terms were different from or additional to those in the offer, the result was a counteroffer, not an acceptance. *Id.; see also Silva v. Noble,* 85 N.M. 677, 678–79, 515 P.2d 1281, 1282–83 (1973). Thus, from a common law perspective, the trial court's conclusion that the Dunham Bush Acknowledgment was a counteroffer was correct.

However, the drafters of the Code "intended to change the common law in an attempt to conform contract law to modern day business transactions." *Leonard Pevar Co. v. Evans Prods. Co.*, 524 F.Supp. 546, 551 (D.Del.1981). As Professors White and Summers explain:

> The rigidity of the common law rule ignored the modern realities of commerce. Where preprinted forms are used to structure deals, they rarely mirror each other, yet the parties usually assume they have a binding contract and act accordingly. Section 2–207 rejects the common law mirror image rule and converts many common law counteroffers into acceptances under 2–207(1).

James J. White & Robert S. Summers, *Handbook of the Law Under the Uniform Commercial Code* § 1–3 at 29–30 (3d ed. 1988) (footnotes omitted).

On its face, Section 2–207(1) provides that a document responding to an offer and purporting to be an acceptance will be an acceptance, despite the presence of additional and different terms. Where merchants exchange preprinted forms and the essential contract terms agree, a contract is formed under Section 2–207(1). Duesenberg & King, § 3.04 at 3–47 to–49. A responding document will fall outside of the provisions of Section 2–207(1) and convey a counteroffer, only when its terms differ radically from the offer, or when "acceptance is expressly made conditional on assent to the additional or different terms"—whether a contract is formed under Section 2–207(1) here turns on the meaning given this phrase.

Dunham Bush argues that the language in its Acknowledgment makes acceptance expressly conditional on assent to the additional or different terms set forth in the Acknowledgment. The face of the Acknowledgment states:

> IT IS UNDERSTOOD THAT OUR ACCEPTANCE OF THIS ORDER IS SUBJECT TO THE TERMS AND CONDITIONS ENUMERATED ON THE REVERSE SIDE HEREOF, IT BEING STRICTLY UNDERSTOOD THAT THESE TERMS AND CONDITIONS BECOME A PART OF THIS ORDER AND THE ACKNOWLEDGMENT THEREOF.

The following was among the terms and conditions on the reverse side of the Acknowledgment.

> Failure of the Buyer to object in writing within five (5) days of receipt thereof to Terms of Sale contained in the Seller's acceptance and/or acknowledgment, or other communications, shall be deemed an acceptance of such Terms of Sale by Buyer.

In support of its contention that the above language falls within the "expressly conditional" provision of Section 2–207, Dunham Bush urges that we adopt the view taken by the First Circuit in *Roto–Lith, Ltd. v. F.P. Bartlett & Co.*, 297 F.2d 497 (1st Cir.1962). There, Roto–Lith sent an order for goods to Bartlett, which responded with an acknowledgment containing warranty disclaimers, a statement that the acknowledgment reflected the terms of the sale, and a provision that if the terms were unacceptable Roto–Lith should notify Bartlett at once. *Id.* at 498–99. Roto–Lith did not protest the terms of the acknowledgment and accepted and paid for the goods. The court held the Bartlett acknowledgment was a counteroffer that became binding on Roto–Lith with its acceptance of the goods, reasoning that "a response which states a condition materially altering the obligation solely to the disadvantage of the offeror" falls within the "expressly conditional" language of 2–207(1). *Id.* at 500.

Dunham Bush suggests that this Court has demonstrated alliance with the principles of *Roto–Lith* in *Fratello v. Socorro Electric Cooperative, Inc.,* 107 N.M. 378, 758 P.2d 792 (1988). *Fratello* involved the terms of a settlement agreement in which one party sent the other party a proposed stipulated order containing an additional term. In the context of the common law, we cited *Roto–Lith* in support of the proposition that the additional term made the proposed stipulation a counteroffer. *Fratello,* 107 N.M. at 381, 758 P.2d at 795.

We have never adopted *Roto–Lith* in the context of the Code and decline to do so now. While ostensibly interpreting Section 2–207(1), the First Circuit's analysis imposes the common law doctrine of offer and acceptance on language designed to avoid the common law result. *Roto–Lith* has been almost uniformly criticized by the courts and commentators as an aberration on Article 2 jurisprudence. *Leonard Pevar Co.,* 524 F.Supp. at 551 (and cases cited therein); Duesenberg & King, § 3.05[1] at 3–61 to–62; White & Summers, § 1–3 at 36–37.

Mindful of the purpose of Section 2–207 and the spirit of Article 2, we find the better approach suggested in *Dorton v. Collins & Aikman Corp.,* 453 F.2d 1161 (6th Cir.1972). In *Dorton,* the Sixth Circuit considered terms in acknowledgment forms sent by Collins & Aikman similar to the terms in the Dunham Bush Acknowledgment. The Collins & Aikman acknowledgments provided that acceptance of orders was subject to the terms and conditions of their form, together with at least seven methods in which a buyer might acquiesce to their terms, including receipt and retention of their form for ten days without objection. *Id.* at 1167–68.

Concentrating its analysis on the concept of the offeror's "assent," the Court reasoned that it was not enough to make acceptance expressly conditional on additional or different terms; instead, the expressly conditional nature of the acceptance must be predicated on the offeror's "assent" to those terms. *Id.* at 1168. The Court concluded that the "expressly conditional" provision of Section 2–207(1) "was intended to apply only to an acceptance which clearly reveals that the offeree is unwilling to proceed with the transaction unless he is assured of the offeror's assent to the additional or different terms therein." *Id.* This approach has been widely accepted. *Diatom, Inc. v. Pennwalt Corp.,* 741 F.2d 1569, 1576–77 (10th Cir.1984); *Reaction Molding Technologies, Inc. v. General Elec. Co.,* 588 F.Supp. 1280, 1288 (E.D.Pa.1984); *Idaho Power Co.,* 596 F.2d at 926–27.

We agree with the court in *Dorton* that the inquiry focuses on whether the offeree clearly and unequivocally communicated to the offeror that its willingness to enter into a bargain was conditioned on the offeror's "assent" to additional or different terms. An exchange of forms containing identical dickered terms, such as the identity, price, and quantity of goods, and conflicting undickered boilerplate provisions, such as warranty terms and a provision making the bargain subject to the terms and conditions of the offeree's document, however worded, will not propel the transaction into the "expressly conditional" language of Section 2–207(1) and confer the status of counteroffer on the responsive document.

While *Dorton* articulates a laudable rule, it fails to provide a means for the determination of when a responsive document becomes a counteroffer. We adopt the rule in *Dorton* and add that whether an acceptance is made expressly conditional on assent to different or additional terms is dependent on the commercial context of the transaction. Official Comment 2 to Section 55–2–207 suggests that "[u]nder this article a proposed deal which in commercial understanding has in fact been closed is recognized as a contract." While the comment applies broadly and envisions recognition of contracts formed under a variety of circumstances, it guides us to application of the concept of "commercial understanding" to the question of formation. *See* 2 William D. Hawkland, *Uniform Commercial Code Series* § 2–207:02 at 160 (1992) ("The basic question is whether, in commercial understanding, the proposed deal has been closed.").

Discerning whether "commercial understanding" dictates the existence of a contract requires consideration of the objective manifestations of the parties' understanding of the bargain. It requires consideration of the parties' activities and interaction during the making of the bargain; and when available, relevant evidence of course of performance, Section 55–2–208; and course of dealing and usage of the trade, Section 55–1–205. The question guiding the inquiry should be whether the offeror could reasonably believe that in the context of the commercial setting in which the parties were acting, a contract had been formed. This determination requires a very fact specific inquiry. *See* John E. Murray, Jr., *Section 2–207 Of The Uniform Commercial Code: Another Word About Incipient Unconscionability,* 39 U.Pitt.L.Rev., 597, 632–34 (1978) (discussing *Dorton* and identifying the commercial understanding of the reasonable buyer as the "critical inquiry").

Our analysis does not yield an iron clad rule conducive to perfunctory application. However, it does remain true to the spirit of Article 2, as it calls the trial court to consider the commercial setting of each transaction and the reasonable expectations and beliefs of the parties acting in that setting. *Id.* at 600; § 55–1–102(2)(b) (stating one purpose of the act is "to permit the continued expansion of commercial practices through custom, usage and agreement of the parties").

The trial court's treatment of this issue did not encompass the scope of the inquiry we envision. We will not attempt to make the factual determination necessary to characterize this transaction on the record before us. Not satisfied that the trial court adequately considered all of the relevant factors in determining that the Dunham Bush Acknowledgment functioned as a counteroffer, we remand for reconsideration of the question.

In the event the trial court concludes that the Dunham Bush Acknowledgment constituted an acceptance, it will face the question of which terms will control in the exchange of forms. In the interest of judicial economy, and because this determination is a question of law, we proceed with our analysis.

IV.

The Gardner Zemke Order provides that the "[m]anufacturer shall replace or repair all parts found to be defective during initial year of use at no additional cost." Because the Order does not include any warranty terms, Article 2 express and implied warranties arise by operation of law. Section 55–2–313 (express warranties), § 55–2–314 (implied warranty of merchantability), § 55–2–315 (implied warranty of fitness for a particular purpose). The Dunham Bush Acknowledgment contains the following warranty terms.

> WARRANTY: We agree that the apparatus manufactured by the Seller will be free from defects in material and workmanship for a period of one year under normal use and service and when properly installed: and our obligation under this agreement is limited solely to repair or replacement at our option, at our factories, of any part or parts thereof which shall within one year from date of original installation or 18 months from date of shipment from factory to the original purchaser, whichever date may first occur be returned to us with transportation charges prepaid which our examination shall disclose to our satisfaction to have been defective. THIS AGREEMENT TO REPAIR OR REPLACE DEFECTIVE PARTS IS EXPRESSLY IN LIEU OF AND IS HEREBY DISCLAIMER OF ALL OTHER EXPRESS WARRANTIES, AND IS IN LIEU OF AND IN DISCLAIMER AND EXCLUSION OF ANY IMPLIED WARRANTIES OF MERCHANTABILITY AND FITNESS FOR A PARTICULAR PURPOSE, AS WELL AS ALL OTHER IMPLIED WARRANTIES, IN LAW OR EQUITY, AND OF ALL OTHER OBLIGATIONS OR LIABILITIES ON OUR PART. THERE ARE NO WARRANTIES WHICH EXTEND BEYOND THE DESCRIPTION HEREOF.... Our obligation to repair or replace shall not apply to any apparatus which shall have been repaired or altered outside our factory in any way.

The one proposition on which most courts and commentators agree at this point in the construction of the statute is that Section 2–207(3) applies only if a contract is not found under Section 2–207(1). *Dorton*, 453 F.2d at 1166; Duesenberg & King, § 3.03[1] at 3–40; 2 Hawkland, § 2–207:04 at 178–79; White & Summers, § 1–3 at 35. However, there are courts that disagree even with this proposition. *See Westinghouse Elec. Corp. v. Nielsons, Inc.*, 647 F.Supp. 896 (D.Colo.1986) (dealing with different terms, finding a contract under 2–207(1) and proceeding to apply 2–207(2) and 2–207(3)).

The language of the statute makes it clear that "additional" terms are subject to the provisions of Section 2–207(2). However, a continuing controversy rages among courts and commentators concerning the treatment of "different" terms in a Section 2–207 analysis. While Section 2–207(1) refers to both "additional or different" terms, Section 2–207(2) refers only to "additional" terms. The omission of the word "different" from Section 55–2–207(2) gives rise to the questions of whether "different" terms are to be dealt with under the provisions of Section 2–207(2), and if not, how they are to be treated. That the terms in the Acknowledgment are "different" rather than "additional" guides the remainder of our inquiry and requires that we join the fray. Initially, we briefly survey the critical and judicial approaches to the problem posed by "different" terms.

One view is that, in spite of the omission, "different" terms are to be analyzed under Section 2–207(2). 2 Hawkland, § 2–207:03 at 168. The foundation for this position is found in Comment 3, which provides "[w]hether or not additional or different terms will become part of the agreement depends upon the provisions of Subsection (2)." Armed with this statement in Comment 3, proponents point to the ambiguity in the distinction between "different" and "additional" terms and argue that the distinction serves no clear purpose. *Steiner v. Mobil Oil Corp.*, 20 Cal.3d 90, 141 Cal.Rptr. 157, 165–66 n.

5, 569 P.2d 751, 759–60 n. 5 (1977); *Boese–Hilburn Co. v. Dean Machinery Co.*, 616 S.W.2d 520, 527 (Mo.Ct.App.1981). Following this rationale in this case, and relying on the observation in Comment 4 that a clause negating implied warranties would "materially alter" the contract, the Dunham Bush warranty terms would not become a part of the contract, and the Gardner Zemke warranty provision, together with the Article 2 warranties would control. § 55–2–207(2)(b).

Another approach is suggested by Duesenberg and King who comment that the ambiguity found in the treatment of "different" and "additional" terms is more judicially created than statutorily supported. While conceding that Comment 3 "contributes to the confusion," they also admonish that "the Official Comments do not happen to be the statute." Duesenberg & King, § 3.05 at 3–52. Observing that "the drafters knew what they were doing, and that they did not sloppily fail to include the term 'different' when drafting subsection (2)," Duesenberg and King postulate that a "different" term in a responsive document operating as an acceptance can never become a part of the parties' contract under the plain language of the statute. *Id.* § 3.03[1] at 3–38.

The reasoning supporting this position is that once an offeror addresses a subject it implicitly objects to variance of that subject by the offeree, thereby preventing the "different" term from becoming a part of the contract by prior objection and obviating the need to refer to "different" terms in Section 55–2–207(2). *Id.* § 3.05[1] at 3–77; *Air Prods. & Chems. Inc. v. Fairbanks Morse, Inc.*, 58 Wis.2d 193, 206 N.W.2d 414, 423–25 (1973). Professor Summers lends support to this position. White & Summers, § 1–3 at 34. Although indulging a different analysis, following this view in the case before us creates a result identical to that flowing from application of the provisions of Section 2–207(2) as discussed above—the Dunham Bush warranty provisions fall out, and the stated Gardner Zemke and Article 2 warranty provisions apply.

Yet a third analysis arises from Comment 6, which in pertinent part states:

> Where clauses on confirming forms sent by both parties conflict each party must be assumed to object to a clause of the other conflicting with one on the confirmation sent by himself. As a result the requirement that there be notice of objection which is found in Subsection (2) is satisfied and the conflicting terms do not become a part of the contract. The contract then consists of the terms originally expressly agreed to, terms on which the confirmations agree, and terms supplied by this act, including Subsection (2).

The import of Comment 6 is that "different" terms cancel each other out and that existing applicable code provisions stand in their place. The obvious flaws in Comment 6 are the use of the words "confirming forms," suggesting the Comment applies only to variant confirmation forms and not variant offer and acceptance forms, and the reference to Subsection 55–2–207(2)—arguably dealing only with "additional" terms—in the context of "different" terms. Of course, Duesenberg and King remind us that Comment 6 "is only a comment, and a poorly drawn one at that." Duesenberg & King, § 3.05[1] at 3–79.

The analysis arising from Comment 6, however, has found acceptance in numerous jurisdictions including the Tenth Circuit. *Daitom, Inc. v. Pennwalt Corp.*, 741 F.2d 1569, 1578–79 (10th Cir.1984). Following a discussion similar to the one we have just indulged, the court found this the preferable approach. *Id.* at 1579; *accord Southern Idaho Pipe & Steel Co. v. Cal–Cut Pipe & Supply, Inc.,* 98 Idaho 495, 567 P.2d 1246, 1254–55 (1977), *appeal dismissed and cert. denied,* 434 U.S. 1056, 98 S.Ct. 1225, 55 L.Ed.2d 757 (1978). Professor White also finds merit in this analysis. White & Summers, § 1–3 at 33–35. Application of this approach here cancels out the parties' conflicting warranty terms and allows the warranty provisions of Article 2 to control.

We are unable to find comfort or refuge in concluding that any one of the three paths drawn through the contours of Section 2–207 is more consistent with or true to the language of the statute. We do find that the analysis relying on Comment 6 is the most consistent with the purpose and spirit of the Code in general and Article 2 in particular. We are mindful that the overriding goal of Article 2 is to discern the bargain struck by the contracting parties. However, there are times where the conduct of the parties makes realizing that goal impossible. In such cases, we find guidance in the Code's commitment to fairness, Section 55–1–102(3); good faith, Sections 55–1–203 & –2–103(1)(b); and conscionable conduct, Section 55–2–302.

While Section 2–207 was designed to avoid the common law result that gave the advantage to the party sending the last form, we cannot conclude that the statute was intended to shift that advantage to the party sending the first form. Such a result will generally follow from the first two analyses discussed. We adopt the third analysis as the most even-handed resolution of a difficult problem. We are also aware that under this analysis even though the conflicting terms cancel out, the Code may provide a term similar to one rejected. We agree with Professor White that "[a]t least a term so supplied has the merit of being a term that the draftsmen considered fair." White & Summers, § 1–3 at 35.

Due to our disposition of this case, we do not address the second issue raised by Gardner Zemke. On remand, should the trial court conclude a contract was formed under Section 2–207(1), the conflicting warranty provisions in the parties' forms will cancel out, and the warranty provisions of Article 2 will control.

IT IS SO ORDERED.

BACA, J., and PATRICIO M. SERNA, DISTRICT JUDGE (sitting by designation).

––––––––

NOTE ON GARDNER ZEMKE

The rule approved in *Gardner Zemke,* that when a contract is formed under UCC § 2–207 conflicting terms in the offer and acceptance cancel each other out, is commonly referred to as the "knockout" rule, because under the rule conflicting terms knock each other out of the parties' agreement. In Dorton v. Collins & Aikman Corp., 453 F.2d 1161 (6th Cir.1972), the court applied the knockout rule where one of the conflicting terms was implied, rather than express.

––––––––

DIAMOND FRUIT GROWERS, INC. v. KRACK CORP.

United States Court of Appeals, Ninth Circuit, 1986.
794 F.2d 1440.

Before FLETCHER, ALARCON, and WIGGINS, CIRCUIT JUDGES.

WIGGINS, CIRCUIT JUDGE:

Metal–Matic, Inc. (Metal–Matic) appeals from judgment entered after a jury verdict in favor of Krack Corporation (Krack) on Krack's third-party complaint against Metal–Matic. Metal–Matic also appeals from the district court's denial of its motion for judgment n.o.v. We have jurisdiction under 28 U.S.C. § 1291 (1982) and affirm.

FACTS AND PROCEEDINGS BELOW

Krack is a manufacturer of cooling units that contain steel tubing it purchases from outside suppliers. Metal–Matic is one of Krack's tubing suppliers. At the time this dispute arose, Metal–Matic had been supplying tubing to Krack for about ten years. The parties followed the same course of dealing during the entire ten years. At the beginning of each year, Krack sent a blanket purchase order to Metal–Matic stating how much tubing Krack would need for the year. Then, throughout the year as Krack needed tubing, it sent release purchase orders to Metal–Matic requesting that tubing be shipped. Metal–Matic responded to Krack's release purchase orders by sending Krack an acknowledgment form and then shipping the tubing.[2]

Metal–Matic's acknowledgment form disclaimed all liability for consequential damages and limited Metal–Matic's liability for defects in the tubing to refund of the purchase price or replacement or repair of the tubing. As one would expect, these terms were not contained in Krack's purchase order. The following statement was printed on Metal–Matic's form: "Metal–Matic, Inc.'s acceptance of purchaser's offer or its offer to purchaser is hereby expressly made conditional to purchaser's acceptance of the terms and provisions of the acknowledgment form." This statement and the disclaimer of liability were on the back of the acknowledgment form. However, printed at the bottom of the front of the form in bold-face capitals was the following statement: "SEE REVERSE SIDE FOR TERMS AND CONDITIONS OF SALE."

On at least one occasion during the ten-year relationship between Metal–Matic and Krack, Allen Zver, Krack's purchasing manager, discussed the limitation of warranty and disclaimer of liability terms contained in Metal–Matic's acknowledgment form with Robert Van Krevelen, Executive Vice President of Metal–Matic. Zver told Van Krevelen that Krack objected to the terms and tried to convince him to change them, but Van Krevelen refused to do so. After the discussions, Krack continued to accept and pay for tubing from Metal–Matic.[3]

---

2. The blanket purchase order apparently did no more than establish Krack's willingness to purchase an amount of tubing during the year. The parties' conduct indicates that they intended to establish their contract based on Krack's release purchase orders and Metal–Matic's acknowledgments sent in response to those purchase orders.

3. Krack contends that there is no evidence of when these discussions took place. That is not the case. Van Krevelen testified that at least some discussions were held before this incident arose. That testimony is not contradicted.

In February 1981, Krack sold one of its cooling units to Diamond Fruit Growers, Inc. (Diamond) in Oregon, and in September 1981, Diamond installed the unit in a controlled-atmosphere warehouse. In January 1982, the unit began leaking ammonia from a cooling coil made of steel tubing.

After Diamond discovered that ammonia was leaking into the warehouse, Joseph Smith, the engineer who had been responsible for building Diamond's controlled-atmosphere warehouses, was called in to find the source of the leak. Smith testified that he found a pinhole leak in the cooling coil of the Krack cooling unit. Smith inspected the coil while it was still inside the unit. He last inspected the coil on April 23, 1982. The coil then sat in a hall at Diamond's warehouse until May, 1984, when John Myers inspected the coil for Metal–Matic.

Myers cut the defective tubing out of the unit and took it to his office. At his office, he did more cutting on the tubing. After Myers inspected the tubing, it was also inspected by Bruce Wong for Diamond and Paul Irish for Krack.

Diamond sued Krack to recover the loss in value of fruit that it was forced to remove from the storage room as a result of the leak. Krack in turn brought a third-party complaint against Metal–Matic and Van Huffel Tube Corporation (Van Huffel), another of its tubing suppliers, seeking contribution or indemnity in the event it was held liable to Diamond. At the close of the evidence, both Metal–Matic and Van Huffel moved for a directed verdict on the third party complaint. The court granted Van Huffel's motion based on evidence that the failed tubing was not manufactured by Van Huffel. The court denied Metal–Matic's motion.

The jury returned a verdict in favor of Diamond against Krack. It then found that Krack was entitled to contribution from Metal–Matic for thirty percent of Diamond's damages. Metal–Matic moved for judgment n.o.v. The court denied that motion and entered judgment on the jury verdict.

Metal–Matic raises two grounds for reversal. First, Metal–Matic contends that as part of its contract with Krack, it disclaimed all liability for consequential damages and specifically limited its liability for defects in the tubing to refund of the purchase price or replacement or repair of the tubing. Second, Metal–Matic asserts that the evidence does not support a finding that it manufactured the tubing in which the leak developed or that it caused the leak. We address each of these contentions in turn....

DISCUSSION

. . .

If the contract between Metal–Matic and Krack contains Metal–Matic's disclaimer of liability, Metal–Matic is not liable to indemnify Krack for part of Diamond's damages. Therefore, the principal issue before us on this appeal is whether Metal–Matic's disclaimer of liability became part of the contract between these parties.

Relying on Uniform Commercial Code (U.C.C.) § 2–207, Or.Rev.Stat. § 72.2070 (1985), Krack argues that Metal–Matic's disclaimer did not become part of the contract. Metal–Matic, on the other hand, argues that section 2–207 is inapplicable to this case because the parties discussed the disclaimer, and Krack assented to it.

Krack is correct in its assertion that section 2–207 applies to this case. One intended application of section 2–207 is to commercial transactions in which the parties exchange printed purchase order and acknowledgment forms. *See* U.C.C. § 2–207 comment 1. The drafters of the U.C.C. recognized that "[b]ecause the [purchase order and acknowledgment] forms are oriented to the thinking of the respective drafting parties, the terms contained in them often do not correspond." *Id.* Section 2–207 is an attempt to provide rules of contract formation in such cases. In this case, Krack and Metal–Matic exchanged purchase order and acknowledgment forms that contained different or additional terms. This, then, is a typical section 2–207 situation. The fact that the parties discussed the terms of their contract after they exchanged their forms does not put this case outside section 2–207. *See* 3 R. Duesenburg & L. King, *Sales and Bulk Transfers under the Uniform Commercial Code* (Bender's U.C.C. Service) § 3.05[2] (1986). Section 2–207 provides rules of contract formation in cases such as this one in which the parties exchange forms but do not agree on all the terms of their contract.

Generally, section 2–207(1) "converts a common law counteroffer into an acceptance even though it states additional or different terms." *Idaho Power,* 596 F.2d at 926; *see* U.C.C. § 2–207(1). The only requirement under section 2–207(1) is that the responding form contain a definite and seasonable expression of acceptance. The terms of the responding form that correspond to the offer constitute the contract. Under section 2–207(2), the additional terms of the responding form become proposals for additions to the contract. Between merchants the additional terms become part of the contract unless the offer is specifically limited to its terms, the offeror objects to the additional terms, or the additional terms materially alter the terms of the offer. U.C.C. § 2–207(2); *see* J. White & R. Summers, § 1–2 at 32.

However, section 2–207(1) is subject to a proviso. If a definite and seasonable expression of acceptance expressly conditions acceptance on the offeror's assent to additional or different terms contained therein, the parties' differing forms do not result in a contract unless the offeror assents to the additional terms. *See* J. White & R. Summers, § 1–2 at 32–33. If the offeror assents, the parties have a contract and the additional terms are a part of that contract. If, however, the offeror does not assent, but the parties proceed with the transaction as if they have a contract, their performance results in formation of a contract. U.C.C. § 2–207(3). In that case, the terms of the contract are those on which the parties' forms agree plus any terms supplied by the U.C.C. *Id.; see Boise Cascade Corp. v. Etsco, Ltd.,* 39 U.C.C.Rep.Serv. (Callaghan) 410, 414 (D.Or.1984); J. White & R. Summers, § 1–2 at 34.

In this case, Metal–Matic expressly conditioned its acceptance on Krack's assent to the additional terms contained in Metal–Matic's acknowledgment form. That form tracks the language of the section 2–207(1) proviso, stating that "Metal–Matic, Inc.'s acceptance . . . is hereby *expressly made conditional* to purchaser's acceptance of the terms and provisions of the acknowledgment form." (emphasis added). *See C. Itoh & Co.,* 552 F.2d at 1235. Therefore, we must determine whether Krack assented to Metal–Matic's limitation of liability term.

Metal–Matic argues that Krack did assent to the limitation of liability term. This argument is based on the discussions between Zver for Krack and Van Krevelen for Metal–Matic. Some time during the ten-year relationship between the companies, these two men discussed Krack's objections to the warranty and liability limitation terms in Metal–Matic's acknowledgment form. Krack attempted to persuade Metal–Matic to change its form, but Metal–Matic refused to do so. After the discussions, the companies continued to do business as in the past. Metal–Matic contends that Krack assented to the limitation of liability term when it continued to accept and pay for tubing after Metal–Matic insisted that the contract contain its terms.

To address Metal–Matic's argument, we must determine what constitutes assent to additional or different terms for purposes of section 2–207(1). The parties have not directed us to any cases that analyze this question and our research has revealed none. We therefore look to the language and structure of section 2–207 and to the purposes behind that section to determine the correct standard.

One of the principles underlying section 2–207 is neutrality. If possible, the section should be interpreted so as to give neither party to a contract an advantage simply because it happened to send the first or in some cases the last form. *See* J. White & R. Summers, § 1–2 at 26–27. Section 2–207 accomplishes this result in part by doing away with the common law's "last shot" rule. *See* 3 R. Duesenberg & L. King, § 3.05[1][a][iii] at 3–73. At common law, the offeree/counterofferor gets all of its terms simply because it fired the last shot in the exchange of forms. Section 2–207(3) does away with this result by giving neither party the terms it attempted to impose unilaterally on the other. *See id.* at 3–71. Instead, all of the terms on which the parties' forms do not agree drop out, and the U.C.C. supplies the missing terms.

Generally, this result is fair because both parties are responsible for the ambiguity in their contract. The parties could have negotiated a contract and agreed on its terms, but for whatever reason, they failed to do so. Therefore, neither party should get its terms. *See* 3 R. Duesenberg & L. King, § 3.05[2] at 3–88. However, as White and Summers point out, resort to section 2–207(3) will often work to the disadvantage of the seller because he will "wish to undertake less responsibility for the quality of his goods than the Code imposes or else wish to limit his damages liability more narrowly than would the Code." J. White & R. Summers, § 1–2 at 34. Nevertheless, White and Summers recommend that section 2–207(3) be applied in such cases. *Id.* We agree. Application of section 2–207(3) is more equitable than giving one party its terms simply because it sent the last form. Further, the terms imposed by the code are presumably equitable and consistent with public policy because they are statutorily imposed. *See* 3 R. Duesenberg & L. King, § 3.05[2] at 3–88.

With these general principles in mind, we turn now to Metal–Matic's argument that Krack assented to the disclaimer when it continued to accept and pay for tubing once Metal–Matic indicated that it was willing to sell tubing only if its warranty and liability terms were part of the contract. Metal–Matic's argument is appealing. Sound policy supports permitting a seller to control the terms on which it will sell its products, especially in a case in which the seller has indicated both in writing and orally that those are the only terms on which it is willing to sell the product. Nevertheless, we reject Metal–Matic's argument because we find that these considerations are outweighed by the public policy reflected by Oregon's enactment of the U.C.C.

If we were to accept Metal–Matic's argument, we would reinstate to some extent the common law's last shot rule. To illustrate, assume that the parties in this case had sent the same forms but in the reverse order and that Krack's form contained terms stating that Metal–Matic is liable for all consequential damages and conditioning acceptance on Metal–Matic's assent to Krack's terms. Assume also that Metal–Matic objected to Krack's terms but Krack refused to change them and that the parties continued with their transaction anyway. If we applied Metal–Matic's argument in that case, we would find that Krack's term was part of the contract because Metal–Matic continued to ship tubing to Krack after Krack reaffirmed that it would purchase tubing only if Metal–Matic were fully liable for consequential damages. Thus, the result would turn on which party sent the last form, and would therefore be inconsistent with section 2–207's purpose of doing away with the last shot rule.

That result is avoided by requiring a specific and unequivocal expression of assent on the part of the offeror when the offeree conditions its acceptance on assent to additional or different terms. If the offeror does not give specific and unequivocal assent but the parties act as if they have a contract, the provisions of section 2–207(3) apply to fill in the terms of the contract. Application of section 2–207(3) is appropriate in that situation because by going ahead with the transaction without resolving their dispute, both parties are responsible for introducing ambiguity into the contract. Further, in a case such as this one, requiring the seller to assume more liability than it intends is not altogether inappropriate. The seller is most responsible for the ambiguity because it inserts a term in its form that requires assent to additional terms and then does not enforce that requirement. If the seller truly does not want to be bound unless the buyer assents to its terms, it can protect itself by not shipping until it obtains that assent. *See C. Itoh & Co.,* 552 F.2d at 1238.

We hold that because Krack's conduct did not indicate unequivocally that Krack intended to assent to Metal–Matic's terms, that conduct did not amount to the assent contemplated by section 2–207(1). *See* 3 R. Duesenberg & L. King, § 3.05[1][a][iii] at 3–74....

[The court also concluded that the evidence supported the findings that Metal–Matic manufactured the tubing that failed, and caused the defect.]

The jury verdict is supported by the evidence and consistent with the U.C.C. Therefore, the district court did not err in denying Metal–Matic's motion for a directed verdict.

AFFIRMED.

SECTION 2. "ROLLING CONTRACTS"

ProCD, INC. v. ZEIDENBERG

United States Court of Appeals, Seventh Circuit, 1996.
86 F.3d 1447.

EASTERBROOK, Circuit Judge.

Must buyers of computer software obey the terms of shrinkwrap licenses? The district court held not ... [on the ground that] they are not contracts because the licenses are inside the box rather than printed on the outside.... [W]e disagree with the district judge's conclusion.... Shrinkwrap licenses are enforceable unless their terms are objectionable on grounds applicable to contracts in general (for example, if they violate a rule of positive law, or if they are unconscionable). Because no one argues that the terms of the license at issue here are troublesome, we remand with instructions to enter judgment for the plaintiff.

I

ProCD, the plaintiff, has compiled information from more than 3,000 telephone directories into a computer database. We may assume that this database cannot be copyrighted, although it is more complex, contains more information (nine-digit zip codes and census industrial codes), is organized differently, and therefore is more original than the single alphabetical directory at issue in Feist Publications, Inc. v. Rural Telephone Service Co., 499 U.S. 340, 111 S.Ct. 1282, 113 L.Ed.2d 358 (1991). See Paul J. Heald, The Vices of Originality, 1991 Sup.Ct. Rev. 143, 160–68. ProCD sells a version of the database, called SelectPhone (trademark), on CD–ROM discs. (CD–ROM means "compact disc—read only memory." The "shrinkwrap license" gets its name from the fact that retail software packages are covered in plastic or cellophane "shrinkwrap," and some vendors, though not ProCD, have written licenses that become effective as soon as the customer tears the wrapping from the package. Vendors prefer "end user license," but we use the more common term.) A proprietary method of compressing the data serves as effective encryption too. Customers decrypt and use the data with the aid of an application program that ProCD has written. This program, which is copyrighted, searches the database in response to users' criteria (such as "find all people named Tatum in Tennessee, plus all firms with 'Door Systems' in the corporate name"). The resulting lists (or, as ProCD prefers, "listings") can be read and manipulated by other software, such as word processing programs.

The database in SelectPhone (trademark) cost more than $10 million to compile and is expensive to keep current. It is much more valuable to some users than to others. The combination of names, addresses, and SIC codes enables manufacturers to compile lists of potential customers. Manufacturers and retailers pay high prices to specialized information intermediaries for such mailing lists; ProCD offers a potentially cheaper alternative. People with nothing to sell could use the database as a substitute for calling long distance information, or as a way to look up old friends who have moved to unknown towns, or just as an electronic substitute for the local phone book. ProCD decided to engage in price discrimination, selling its database to the general public for personal use at a low price (approximately $150 for the set of five discs) while selling information to the trade for a higher price. It has adopted some intermediate strategies too: access to the SelectPhone (trademark) database is available via the America Online service for the price America Online charges to its clients (approximately $3 per hour), but this service has been tailored to be useful only to the general public.

If ProCD had to recover all of its costs and make a profit by charging a single price—that is, if it could not charge more to commercial users than to the general public—it would have to raise the price substantially over $150. The ensuing reduction in sales would harm consumers who value the information at, say, $200. They get consumer surplus of $50 under the current arrangement but would cease to buy if the price rose substantially. If because of high elasticity of demand in the consumer segment of the market the only way to make a profit turned out to be a price attractive to commercial users alone, then all consumers would lose out—and so would the commercial clients, who would have to pay more for the listings because ProCD could not obtain any contribution toward costs from the consumer market.

To make price discrimination work, however, the seller must be able to control arbitrage. An air carrier sells tickets for less to vacationers than to business travelers, using advance purchase and Saturday-night-stay requirements to distinguish the categories. A producer of movies segments the market by time, releasing first to theaters, then to pay-per-view services, next to the videotape and laserdisc market, and finally to cable and commercial tv. Vendors of computer software have a harder task. Anyone can walk into a retail store and buy a box. Customers do not wear tags saying "commercial user" or "consumer user." Anyway, even a commercial-user-detector at the door would not work, because a consumer could buy the software and resell to a commercial user. That arbitrage would break down the price discrimination and drive up the minimum price at which ProCD would sell to anyone.

Instead of tinkering with the product and letting users sort themselves— for example, furnishing current data at a high price that would be attractive only to commercial customers, and two-year-old data at a low price—ProCD turned to the institution of contract. Every box containing its consumer product declares that the software comes with restrictions stated in an enclosed license. This license, which is encoded on the CD–ROM disks as well as printed in the manual, and which appears on a user's screen every time the software runs, limits use of the application program and listings to non-commercial purposes.

Matthew Zeidenberg bought a consumer package of SelectPhone (trademark) in 1994 from a retail outlet in Madison, Wisconsin, but decided to ignore the license. He formed Silken Mountain Web Services, Inc., to resell the information in the SelectPhone (trademark) database. The corporation makes the database available on the Internet to anyone willing to pay its price—which, needless to say, is less than ProCD charges its commercial customers. Zeidenberg has purchased two additional SelectPhone (trademark) packages, each with an updated version of the database, and made the latest information available over the World Wide Web, for a price, through his corporation. ProCD filed this suit seeking an injunction against further dissemination that exceeds the rights specified in the licenses (identical in each of the three packages Zeidenberg purchased). The district court held the licenses ineffectual because their terms do not appear on the outside of the packages. The court added that the second and third licenses stand no different from the first, even though they are identical, because they might have been different, and a purchaser does not agree to—and cannot be bound by—terms that were secret at the time of purchase. 908 F.Supp. at 654.

II

Following the district court, we treat the licenses as ordinary contracts accompanying the sale of products, and therefore as governed by the common law of contracts and the Uniform Commercial Code. Whether there are legal differences between "contracts" and "licenses" (which may matter under the copyright doctrine of first sale) is a subject for another day. See Microsoft Corp. v. Harmony Computers & Electronics, Inc., 846 F.Supp. 208 (E.D.N.Y. 1994). Zeidenberg does not argue that Silken Mountain Web Services is free of any restrictions that apply to Zeidenberg himself, because any effort to treat the two parties as distinct would put Silken Mountain behind the eight ball on ProCD's argument that copying the application program onto its hard disk violates the copyright laws. Zeidenberg does argue, and the district court held, that placing the package of software on the shelf is an "offer," which the customer "accepts" by paying the asking price and leaving the store with the goods. Peeters v. State, 154 Wis. 111, 142 N.W. 181 (1913). In Wisconsin, as elsewhere, a contract includes only the terms on which the parties have agreed. One cannot agree to hidden terms, the judge concluded. So far, so good—but one of the terms to which Zeidenberg agreed by purchasing the software is that the transaction was subject to a license. Zeidenberg's position therefore must be that the printed terms on the outside of a box are the parties' contract—except for printed terms that refer to or incorporate other terms. But why would Wisconsin fetter the parties' choice in this way? Vendors can put the entire terms of a contract on the outside of a box only by using microscopic type, removing other information that buyers might find more useful (such as what the software does, and on which computers it works), or both. The "Read Me" file included with most software, describing system requirements and potential incompatibilities, may be equivalent to ten pages of type; warranties and license restrictions take still more space. Notice on the outside, terms on the inside, and a right to return the software for a refund if the terms are unacceptable (a right that the license expressly extends), may be a means of doing business valuable to buyers and sellers alike. See E. Allan Farnsworth, 1 Farnsworth on Contracts § 4.26 (1990); Restatement (2d) of Contracts § 211 comment a (1981) ("Standardization of agreements serves many of the same functions as standardization of goods and services; both are essential to a system of mass production and distribution. Scarce and costly time and skill can be devoted to a class of transactions rather than the details of individual transactions."). Doubtless a state could forbid the use of standard contracts in the software business, but we do not think that Wisconsin has done so.

Transactions in which the exchange of money precedes the communication of detailed terms are common. Consider the purchase of insurance. The buyer goes to an agent, who explains the essentials (amount of coverage, number of years) and remits the premium to the home office, which sends back a policy. On the district judge's understanding, the terms of the policy are irrelevant because the insured paid before receiving them. Yet the device of payment, often with a "binder" (so that the insurance takes effect immediately even though the home office reserves the right to withdraw coverage later), in advance of the policy, serves buyers' interests by accelerating effectiveness and reducing transactions costs. Or consider the purchase of an airline ticket. The traveler calls the carrier or an agent, is quoted a price, reserves a seat, pays, and gets a ticket, in that order. The ticket contains elaborate terms, which the traveler can reject by canceling the reservation. To use the ticket is to accept the terms, even terms that in retrospect are disadvantageous. See Carnival Cruise Lines, Inc. v. Shute, 499 U.S. 585, 111

S.Ct. 1522, 113 L.Ed.2d 622 (1991); see also Vimar Seguros y Reaseguros, S.A. v. M/V Sky Reefer, 515 U.S. 528, 115 S.Ct. 2322, 132 L.Ed.2d 462 (1995) (bills of lading). Just so with a ticket to a concert. The back of the ticket states that the patron promises not to record the concert; to attend is to agree. A theater that detects a violation will confiscate the tape and escort the violator to the exit. One could arrange things so that every concertgoer signs this promise before forking over the money, but that cumbersome way of doing things not only would lengthen queues and raise prices but also would scotch the sale of tickets by phone or electronic data service.

Consumer goods work the same way. Someone who wants to buy a radio set visits a store, pays, and walks out with a box. Inside the box is a leaflet containing some terms, the most important of which usually is the warranty, read for the first time in the comfort of home. By Zeidenberg's lights, the warranty in the box is irrelevant; every consumer gets the standard warranty implied by the UCC in the event the contract is silent; yet so far as we are aware no state disregards warranties furnished with consumer products. Drugs come with a list of ingredients on the outside and an elaborate package insert on the inside. The package insert describes drug interactions, contraindications, and other vital information—but, if Zeidenberg is right, the purchaser need not read the package insert, because it is not part of the contract.

Next consider the software industry itself. Only a minority of sales take place over the counter, where there are boxes to peruse. A customer may place an order by phone in response to a line item in a catalog or a review in a magazine. Much software is ordered over the Internet by purchasers who have never seen a box. Increasingly software arrives by wire. There is no box; there is only a stream of electrons, a collection of information that includes data, an application program, instructions, many limitations ("MegaPixel 3.14159 cannot be used with BytePusher 2.718"), and the terms of sale. The user purchases a serial number, which activates the software's features. On Zeidenberg's arguments, these unboxed sales are unfettered by terms—so the seller has made a broad warranty and must pay consequential damages for any shortfalls in performance, two "promises" that if taken seriously would drive prices through the ceiling or return transactions to the horse-and-buggy age.

According to the district court, the UCC does not countenance the sequence of money now, terms later. (Wisconsin's version of the UCC does not differ from the Official Version in any material respect, so we use the regular numbering system. Wis. Stat. § 402.201 corresponds to UCC § 2–201, and other citations are easy to derive.) One of the court's reasons—that by proposing as part of the draft Article 2B a new UCC § 2–2203 that would explicitly validate standard-form user licenses, the American Law Institute and the National Conference of Commissioners on Uniform Laws have conceded the invalidity of shrinkwrap licenses under current law, see 908 F.Supp. at 655–56—depends on a faulty inference.

To propose a change in a law's *text* is not necessarily to propose a change in the law's *effect*. New words may be designed to fortify the current rule with a more precise text that curtails uncertainty. To judge by the flux of law review articles discussing shrinkwrap licenses, uncertainty is much in need of reduction—although businesses seem to feel less uncertainty than do scholars, for only three cases (other than ours) touch on the subject, and none directly addresses it. See Step–Saver Data Systems, Inc. v. Wyse Technology, 939 F.2d 91 (3d Cir.1991); Vault Corp. v. Quaid Software Ltd., 847 F.2d 255, 268–70 (5th Cir.1988); Arizona Retail Systems, Inc. v. Software Link, Inc., 831 F.Supp. 759 (D.Ariz.1993). As their titles suggest, these are not consumer transactions. *Step–Saver* is a battle-of-the-forms case, in which the parties exchange incompatible forms and a court must decide which prevails. See Northrop Corp. v. Litronic Industries, 29 F.3d 1173 (7th Cir.1994) (Illinois law); Douglas G. Baird & Robert Weisberg, Rules, Standards, and the Battle of the Forms: A Reassessment of § 2–207, 68 Va. L.Rev. 1217, 1227–31 (1982). Our case has only one form; UCC § 2–207 is irrelevant. *Vault* holds that Louisiana's special shrinkwrap-license statute is preempted by federal law, a question to which we return. And *Arizona Retail Systems* did not reach the question, because the court found that the buyer knew the terms of the license before purchasing the software. What then does the current version of the UCC have to say? We think that the place to start is § 2–204(1): "A contract for sale of goods may be made in any manner sufficient to show agreement, including conduct by both parties which recognizes the existence of such a contract." A vendor, as master of the offer, may invite acceptance by conduct, and may propose limitations on the kind of conduct that constitutes acceptance. A buyer may accept by performing the acts the vendor proposes to treat as acceptance. And that is what happened. ProCD proposed a contract that a buyer would accept by *using* the software after having an opportunity to read the license at leisure. This Zeidenberg did. He had no choice, because the software splashed the license on the screen and would not let him proceed without indicating acceptance. So although the district judge was right to say that a contract can be, and often is, formed simply by paying the price and walking out of the store, the UCC permits contracts to be formed in other ways. ProCD proposed such a different way, and without protest Zeidenberg agreed. Ours is not a case in which a consumer opens a package to find an insert saying "you owe us an extra $10,000" and the seller files suit to collect. Any buyer finding such a demand can prevent formation of the contract by returning the package, as can any consumer who concludes that the terms of the license make the software worth less than the purchase price. Nothing in the UCC requires a seller to maximize the buyer's net gains.

Section 2–606, which defines "acceptance of goods", reinforces this understanding. A buyer accepts goods under § 2–606(1)(b) when, after an opportunity to inspect, he fails to make an effective rejection under § 2–602(1). ProCD extended an opportunity to reject if a buyer should find the license terms unsatisfactory; Zeidenberg inspected the package, tried out the software, learned of the license, and did not reject the goods. We refer to § 2–606 only to show that the opportunity to return goods can be important; acceptance of an offer differs from acceptance of goods after delivery, see Gillen v. Atalanta Systems, Inc., 997 F.2d 280, 284 n. 1 (7th Cir.1993); but the UCC consistently permits the parties to structure their relations so that the buyer has a chance to make a final decision after a detailed review.

Some portions of the UCC impose additional requirements on the way parties agree on terms. A disclaimer of the implied warranty of merchantability must be "conspicuous." UCC § 2–316(2), incorporating UCC § 1–201(10). Promises to make firm offers, or to negate oral modifications, must be "separately signed." UCC §§ 2–205, 2–209(2). These special provisos reinforce the impression that, so far as the UCC is concerned, other terms may be as inconspicuous as the forum-selection clause on the back of the cruise ship ticket in *Carnival Lines*. Zeidenberg has not located any Wisconsin case—for that matter, any case in any state—holding that under the UCC the ordinary terms found in shrinkwrap licenses require any special prominence, or otherwise are to be undercut rather than enforced. In the end, the terms of the license are conceptually identical to the contents of the package. Just as no court would dream of saying that SelectPhone (trademark) must contain 3,100 phone books rather than 3,000, or must have data no more than 30 days old, or must sell for $100 rather than $150—although any of these changes would be welcomed by the customer, if all other things were held constant—so, we believe, Wisconsin would not let the buyer pick and choose among terms. Terms of use are no less a part of "the product" than are the size of the database and the speed with which the software compiles listings. Competition among vendors, not judicial revision of a package's contents, is how consumers are protected in a market economy. Digital Equipment Corp. v. Uniq Digital Technologies, Inc., 73 F.3d 756 (7th Cir.1996). ProCD has rivals, which may elect to compete by offering superior software, monthly updates, improved terms of use, lower price, or a better compromise among these elements. As we stressed above, adjusting terms in buyers' favor might help Matthew Zeidenberg today (he already has the software) but would lead to a response, such as a higher price, that might make consumers as a whole worse off. . . .

REVERSED AND REMANDED.

NOTE

Stewart MacCauley, a noted Contracts scholar at the University of Wisconsin, posted the following message concerning *ProCD* on a Contracts listserve: "We have a box of the ProCD disks that were involved in that case. The notice that you were to look inside was in yellow type in a sentence mixed in with others. The typeface is very very small, and the notice is on the bottom flap of the box next to the bar code. I cannot believe that many people would see it. The few who did wouldn't understand that they were buying far less than it might seem.

"However, the defendant in the case was a graduate student in computer sciences at the UW–Madison. He had consulted my colleague John Kidwell about the assertion of a copyright to telephone book listings. He might have known apart from what he read on the box. Of course, there is no evidence of that in the record."

HILL v. GATEWAY 2000, 105 F.3d 1147 (7th Cir. 1997) (Easterbrook, J.). "A customer picks up the phone, orders a computer, and gives a credit card number. Presently a box arrives, containing the computer and a list of terms, said to govern unless the customer returns the computer within 30 days. Are these terms effective as the parties' contract, or is the contract term-free because the order-taker did not read any terms over the phone and elicit the customer's assent?

"One of the terms in the box containing a Gateway 2000 system was an arbitration clause. Rich and Enza Hill, the customers, kept the computer more than 30 days before complaining about its components and performance. They filed suit in federal court.... Gateway asked the district court to enforce the arbitration clause; the judge refused....

"ProCD, Inc. v. Zeidenberg, 86 F.3d 1447 (7th Cir. 1996), holds that terms inside a box of software bind consumers who use the software after an opportunity to read the terms and to reject them by returning the product.... Gateway shipped computers with the same sort of accept-or-return offer ProCD made to users of its software....

"Plaintiffs ask us to limit *ProCD* to software, but where's the sense in that? *ProCD* is about the law of contract, not the law of software. Payment preceding the revelation of full terms is common for air transportation, insurance, and many other endeavors. Practical considerations support allowing vendors to enclose the full legal terms with their products. Cashiers cannot be expected to read legal documents to customers before ringing up sales. If the staff at the other end of the phone for direct-sales operations such as Gateway's had to read the four-page statement of terms before taking the buyer's credit card number, the droning voice would anesthetize rather than enlighten many potential buyers. Others would hang up in a rage over the waste of their time. And oral recitation would not avoid customers' assertions (whether true or feigned) that the clerk did not read term X to them, or that they did not remember or understand it. Writing provides benefits for both sides of commercial transactions. Customers as a group are better off when vendors skip costly and ineffectual steps such as telephonic recitation, and use instead a simple approve-or-return device. Competent adults are bound by such documents, read or unread....

"For their second sally, the Hills contend that *ProCD* should be limited to executory contracts (to licenses in particular), and therefore does not apply because both parties' performance of this contract was complete when the box arrived at their home. This is legally and factually wrong: legally because the question at hand concerns the *formation* of the contract rather than its *performance*, and factually because both contracts were incompletely performed. *ProCD* did not depend on the fact that the seller characterized the transaction as a license rather than as a contract; we treated it as a contract for the sale of goods and reserved the question whether for other purposes a "license" characterization might be preferable. 86 F.3d at 1450. All debates about characterization to one side, the transaction in *ProCD* was no more executory than the one here: Zeidenberg paid for the software and walked out of the store with a box under his arm, so if arrival of the box with the product ends the time for revelation of contractual terms, then the time ended in *ProCD* before Zeidenberg opened the box. But of course *ProCD* had not completed performance with delivery of the box, and neither had Gateway. One element of the transaction was the warranty, which obliges sellers to fix defects in their products. The Hills have invoked Gateway's warranty and are not satisfied with its response, so they are not well positioned to say that Gateway's obligations were fulfilled when the motor carrier unloaded the box. What is more, both ProCD and Gateway promised to help customers to use their products. Long-term service and information obligations are common in the computer business, on both hardware and software sides. Gateway offers 'lifetime service' and has a round-the-clock telephone hotline to fulfil this promise. Some vendors spend more money helping customers use their products than on developing and manufacturing them. The document in Gateway's box includes promises of future performance that some consumers value highly; these promises bind Gateway just as the arbitration clause binds the Hills....

"At oral argument the Hills propounded still another distinction: the box containing ProCD's software displayed a notice that additional terms were within, while the box containing Gateway's computer did not. The difference is functional, not legal. Consumers browsing the aisles of a store can look at the box, and if they are unwilling to deal with the prospect of additional terms can leave the box alone, avoiding the transactions costs of returning the package after reviewing its contents. Gateway's box, by contrast, is just a shipping carton; it is not on display anywhere. Its function is to protect the product during transit, and the information on its sides is for the use of handlers (Fragile! "This Side Up!") rather than would-be purchasers.

"Perhaps the Hills would have had a better argument if they were first alerted to the bundling of hardware and legal-ware after opening the box and wanted to return the computer in order to avoid disagreeable terms, but were dissuaded by the expense of shipping. What the remedy would be in such a case—could it exceed the shipping charges?—is an interesting question, but one that need not detain us because the Hills knew before they ordered the computer that the carton would include *some* important terms, and they did not seek to discover these in advance. Gateway's ads state that their products come with limited warranties and lifetime support. How limited was the warranty—30 days, with service contingent on shipping the computer back, or five years, with free onsite service? What sort of support was offered? Shoppers have three principal ways to discover these things. First, they can ask the vendor to send a copy before deciding whether to buy. The Magnuson–Moss Warranty Act requires firms to distribute their warranty terms on request, 15 U.S.C. § 2302(b)(1)(A); the Hills do not contend that Gateway would have refused to enclose the remaining terms too. Concealment would be bad for business, scaring some customers away and leading to excess returns from others. Second, shoppers can consult public sources (computer magazines, the Web sites of vendors) that may contain this information. Third, they may inspect the documents after the product's delivery. Like Zeidenberg, the Hills took the third option. By keeping the computer beyond 30 days, the Hills accepted Gateway's offer, including the arbitration clause."

M.A. MORTENSON, CO. v. TIMBERLINE SOFTWARE CORP., 140 Wash.2d 568, 998 P.2d 305 (2000). "We find the approach of the *ProCD* [and] *Hill* ... courts persuasive and adopt it to guide our analysis under [UCC § 2–204]. We conclude because [UCC § 2–204] allows a contract to be formed 'in any manner sufficient to show agreement ... even though the moment of its making is undetermined,' it allows the formation of 'layered contracts' similar to those envisioned by *ProCD* [and] *Hill*...."

KLOCEK v. GATEWAY, INC., 104 F.Supp.2d 1332 (D. Kan. 2000). "The Court is not persuaded that Kansas or Missouri courts would follow the Seventh Circuit reasoning in *Hill* and *ProCD*. In each case the Seventh Circuit concluded without support that UCC § 2–207 was irrelevant because the cases involved only one written form. *See ProCD*, 86 F.3d at 1452 (citing no authority); *Hill*, 105 F.3d at 1150 (citing *ProCD*). This conclusion is not supported by the statute or by Kansas or Missouri law. Disputes under § 2–207 often arise in the context of a "battle of forms," . . . but nothing in its language precludes application in a case which involves only one form. The statute provides:

Additional terms in acceptance or confirmation.

(1) A definite and seasonable expression of acceptance or a written confirmation which is sent within a reasonable time operates as an acceptance even though it states terms additional to or different from those offered or agreed upon, unless acceptance is expressly made conditional on assent to the additional or different terms.

(2) The additional terms are to be construed as proposals for addition to the contract [if the contract is not between merchants]. . . .

". . . By its terms, § 2–207 applies to an acceptance or written confirmation. It states nothing which requires another form before the provision becomes effective."

———

SPECHT v. NETSCAPE COMMUNICATIONS CORP.

United States Court of Appeals, Second Circuit, 2002.
306 F.3d 17.

Before McLAUGHLIN, LEVAL, and SOTOMAYOR, Circuit Judges.

SOTOMAYOR, Circuit Judge.

This is an appeal from a judgment of the Southern District of New York denying a motion by defendants-appellants Netscape Communications Corporation and its corporate parent, America Online, Inc. (collectively, "defendants" or "Netscape"), to compel arbitration and to stay court proceedings. In order to resolve the central question of arbitrability presented here, we must address issues of contract formation in cyberspace. Principally, we are asked to determine whether plaintiffs-appellees ("plaintiffs"), by acting upon defendants' invitation to download free software made available on defendants' webpage, agreed to be bound by the software's license terms (which included the arbitration clause at issue), even though plaintiffs could not have learned of the existence of those terms unless, prior to executing the download, they had scrolled down the webpage to a screen located below the download button. We agree with the district court that a reasonably prudent Internet user in circumstances such as these would not have known or learned of the existence of the license terms before responding to defendants' invitation to download the free software, and that defendants therefore did not provide reasonable notice of the license terms. In consequence, plaintiffs' bare act of downloading the software did not unambiguously manifest assent to the arbitration provision contained in the license terms.

We also agree with the district court that plaintiffs' claims relating to the software at issue—a "plug-in" program entitled SmartDownload ("Smart-Download" or "the plug-in program"), offered by Netscape to enhance the functioning of the separate browser program called Netscape Communicator ("Communicator" or "the browser program")—are not subject to an arbitration agreement contained in the license terms governing the use of Communicator. . . .

We therefore affirm the district court's denial of defendants' motion to compel arbitration and to stay court proceedings.

BACKGROUND

. . . FACTS

In three related putative class actions, plaintiffs alleged that, unknown to them, their use of SmartDownload transmitted to defendants private information about plaintiffs' downloading of files from the Internet, thereby effecting an electronic surveillance of their online activities in violation of two federal statutes, the Electronic Communications Privacy Act, 18 U.S.C. § § 2510 *et seq.,* and the Computer Fraud and Abuse Act, 18 U.S.C. § 1030.

Specifically, plaintiffs alleged that when they first used Netscape's Communicator—a software program that permits Internet browsing—the program created and stored on each of their computer hard drives a small text file known as a "cookie" that functioned "as a kind of electronic identification tag for future communications" between their computers and Netscape. Plaintiffs further alleged that when they installed SmartDownload—a separate software "plug-in"[2] that served to enhance Communicator's browsing capabilities—SmartDownload created and stored on their computer hard drives another string of characters, known as a "Key," which similarly functioned as an identification tag in future communications with Netscape. According to the complaints in this case, each time a computer user employed Communicator to download a file from the Internet, SmartDownload "assume[d] from Communicator the task of downloading" the file and transmitted to Netscape the address of the file being downloaded together with the cookie created by Communicator and the Key created by SmartDownload. These processes, plaintiffs claim, constituted unlawful "eavesdropping" on users of Netscape's software products as well as on Internet websites from which users employing SmartDownload downloaded files.

In the time period relevant to this litigation, Netscape offered on its website various software programs, including Communicator and SmartDownload, which visitors to the site were invited to obtain free of charge. It is undisputed that five of the six named plaintiffs—Michael Fagan, John Gibson, Mark Gruber, Sean Kelly, and Sherry Weindorf—downloaded Communicator from the Netscape website. These plaintiffs acknowledge that when they proceeded to initiate installation[3] of Communicator, they were automatically

---

2. Netscape's website defines "plug-ins" as "software programs that extend the capabilities of the Netscape Browser in a specific way—giving you, for example, the ability to play audio samples or view video movies from within your browser." (http://wp.net-scape.com/plugins/) SmartDownload purportedly made it easier for users of browser programs like Communicator to download files from the Internet without losing their progress when they paused to engage in some other task, or if their Internet connection was severed. *See Specht,* 150 F.Supp.2d at 587.

3. There is a difference between downloading and installing a software program. When a user downloads a program from the Internet to

shown a scrollable text of that program's license agreement and were not permitted to complete the installation until they had clicked on a "Yes" button to indicate that they accepted all the license terms.[4] If a user attempted to install Communicator without clicking "Yes," the installation would be aborted. All five named user plaintiffs[5] expressly agreed to Communicator's license terms by clicking "Yes." The Communicator license agreement that these plaintiffs saw made no mention of SmartDownload or other plug-in programs, and stated that "[t]hese terms apply to Netscape Communicator and Netscape Navigator"[6] and that "all disputes relating to this Agreement (excepting any dispute relating to intellectual property rights)" are subject to "binding arbitration in Santa Clara County, California."

Although Communicator could be obtained independently of SmartDownload, all the named user plaintiffs, except Fagan, downloaded and installed Communicator in connection with downloading SmartDownload.[7] Each of these plaintiffs allegedly arrived at a Netscape webpage[8] captioned "Smart-Download Communicator" that urged them to "Download With Confidence Using SmartDownload!" At or near the bottom of the screen facing plaintiffs was the prompt "Start Download" and a tinted button labeled "Download." By clicking on the button, plaintiffs initiated the download of SmartDownload. Once that process was complete, SmartDownload, as its first plug-in task, permitted plaintiffs to proceed with downloading and installing Communicator, an operation that was accompanied by the clickwrap display of Communicator's license terms described above.

The signal difference between downloading Communicator and download-ing SmartDownload was that no clickwrap presentation accompanied the

his or her computer, the program file is stored on the user's hard drive but typically is not operable until the user installs or executes it, usually by double-clicking on the file and causing the program to run.

4. This kind of online software license agreement has come to be known as "click-wrap" (by analogy to "shrinkwrap," used in the licensing of tangible forms of software sold in packages) because it "presents the user with a message on his or her computer screen, requiring that the user manifest his or her assent to the terms of the license agreement by clicking on an icon. The product cannot be obtained or used unless and until the icon is clicked." *Specht,* 150 F.Supp.2d at 593–94 (footnote omitted). Just as breaking the shrink-wrap seal and using the enclosed computer program after encountering notice of the existence of governing license terms has been deemed by some courts to constitute assent to those terms in the context of tangible software, *see, e.g., ProCD, Inc. v. Zeidenberg,* 86 F.3d 1447, 1451 (7th Cir.1996), so clicking on a webpage's clickwrap button after receiving notice of the existence of license terms has been held by some courts to manifest an Internet user's assent to terms governing the use of downloadable intangible software, *see, e.g., Hotmail Corp. v. Van$ Money Pie Inc.,* 47 U.S.P.Q.2d 1020, 1025 (N.D.Cal.1998).

5. The term "user plaintiffs" here and else-where in this opinion denotes those plaintiffs

who are suing for harm they allegedly incurred as computer users, in contrast to plaintiff Specht, who alleges that he was harmed in his capacity as a website owner. [Ed.—The portion of the opinion concerning Specht is omitted.]

6. While Navigator was Netscape's "stand-alone" Internet browser program during the period in question, Communicator was a "software suite" that comprised Navigator and other software products. All five named user plaintiffs stated in affidavits that they had obtained upgraded versions of Communica-tor. . . .

7. Unlike the four other user plaintiffs, Fa-gan chose the option of obtaining Netscape's browser program without first downloading SmartDownload. As discussed below, Fagan al-legedly obtained SmartDownload from a sepa-rate "shareware" website unrelated to Net-scape. [Ed.—In a subsequent portion of the opinion, the court held that Fagan's legal posi-tion was the same as that of the other user plaintiffs. This portion of the opinion is omit-ted.]

8. For purposes of this opinion, the term "webpage" or "page" is used to designate a document that resides, usually with other web-pages, on a single Internet website and that contains information that is viewed on a com-puter monitor by scrolling through the docu-ment. To view a webpage in its entirety, a user typically must scroll through multiple screens.

latter operation. Instead, once plaintiffs Gibson, Gruber, Kelly, and Weindorf had clicked on the "Download" button located at or near the bottom of their screen, and the downloading of SmartDownload was complete, these plaintiffs encountered no further information about the plug-in program or the existence of license terms governing its use.[9] The sole reference to SmartDownload's license terms on the "SmartDownload Communicator" webpage was located in text that would have become visible to plaintiffs only if they had scrolled down to the next screen.

Had plaintiffs scrolled down instead of acting on defendants' invitation to click on the "Download" button, they would have encountered the following invitation: "Please review and agree to the terms of the *Netscape SmartDownload software license agreement* before downloading and using the software." Plaintiffs Gibson, Gruber, Kelly, and Weindorf averred in their affidavits that they never saw this reference to the SmartDownload license agreement when they clicked on the "Download" button. They also testified during depositions that they saw no reference to license terms when they clicked to download SmartDownload, although under questioning by defendants' counsel, some plaintiffs added that they could not "remember" or be "sure" whether the screen shots of the SmartDownload page attached to their affidavits reflected precisely what they had seen on their computer screens when they downloaded SmartDownload.[10]

In sum, plaintiffs Gibson, Gruber, Kelly, and Weindorf allege that the process of obtaining SmartDownload contrasted sharply with that of obtaining Communicator. Having selected SmartDownload, they were required neither to express unambiguous assent to that program's license agreement nor even to view the license terms or become aware of their existence before proceeding with the invited download of the free plug-in program. Moreover, once these plaintiffs had initiated the download, the existence of SmartDownload's license terms was not mentioned while the software was running or at any later point in plaintiffs' experience of the product.

Even for a user who, unlike plaintiffs, did happen to scroll down past the download button, SmartDownload's license terms would not have been immediately displayed in the manner of Communicator's clickwrapped terms. Instead, if such a user had seen the notice of SmartDownload's terms and then clicked on the underlined invitation to review and agree to the terms, a hypertext link would have taken the user to a separate webpage entitled "License & Support Agreements." The first paragraph on this page read, in pertinent part:

> The use of each Netscape software product is governed by a license agreement. You must read and agree to the license agreement terms BEFORE acquiring a product. Please click on the appropriate link below to review the current license agreement for the product of interest to you

---

9. Plaintiff Kelly, a relatively sophisticated Internet user, testified that when he clicked to download SmartDownload, he did not think that he was downloading a software program at all, but rather that SmartDownload "was merely a piece of download technology." He later became aware that SmartDownload was residing as software on his hard drive when he attempted to download electronic files from the Internet.

10. In the screen shot of the SmartDownload webpage attached to Weindorf's affidavit, the reference to license terms is partially visible, though almost illegible, at the bottom of the screen. In the screen shots attached to the affidavits of Gibson, Gruber, and Kelly, the reference to license terms is not visible.

before acquisition. For products available for download, you must read and agree to the license agreement terms BEFORE you install the software. If you do not agree to the license terms, do not download, install or use the software.

Below this paragraph appeared a list of license agreements, the first of which was *License Agreement for Netscape Navigator and Netscape Communicator Product Family* (Netscape Navigator, Netscape Communicator and Netscape SmartDownload)." If the user clicked on that link, he or she would be taken to yet another webpage that contained the full text of a license agreement that was identical in every respect to the Communicator license agreement except that it stated that its "terms apply to Netscape Communicator, Netscape Navigator, and Netscape SmartDownload." The license agreement granted the user a nonexclusive license to use and reproduce the software, subject to certain terms:

> BY CLICKING THE ACCEPTANCE BUTTON OR INSTALLING OR USING NETSCAPE COMMUNICATOR, NETSCAPE NAVIGATOR, OR NETSCAPE SMARTDOWNLOAD SOFTWARE (THE "PRODUCT"), THE INDIVIDUAL OR ENTITY LICENSING THE PRODUCT ("LICENSEE") IS CONSENTING TO BE BOUND BY AND IS BECOMING A PARTY TO THIS AGREEMENT. IF LICENSEE DOES NOT AGREE TO ALL OF THE TERMS OF THIS AGREEMENT, THE BUTTON INDICATING NON–ACCEPTANCE MUST BE SELECTED, AND LICENSEE MUST NOT INSTALL OR USE THE SOFTWARE.

Among the license terms was a provision requiring virtually all disputes relating to the agreement to be submitted to arbitration:

> Unless otherwise agreed in writing, all disputes relating to this Agreement (excepting any dispute relating to intellectual property rights) shall be subject to final and binding arbitration in Santa Clara County, California, under the auspices of JAMS/EndDispute, with the losing party paying all costs of arbitration....

II. PROCEEDINGS BELOW

In the district court, defendants moved to compel arbitration and to stay court proceedings pursuant to the Federal Arbitration Act ("FAA"), 9 U.S.C. § 4, arguing that the disputes reflected in the complaints, like any other dispute relating to the SmartDownload license agreement, are subject to the arbitration clause contained in that agreement. Finding that Netscape's webpage, unlike typical examples of clickwrap, neither adequately alerted users to the existence of SmartDownload's license terms nor required users unambiguously to manifest assent to those terms as a condition of downloading the product, the court held that the user plaintiffs had not entered into the SmartDownload license agreement. *Specht,* 150 F.Supp.2d at 595–96.

The district court also ruled that the separate license agreement governing use of Communicator, even though the user plaintiffs had assented to its terms, involved an independent transaction that made no mention of SmartDownload and so did not bind plaintiffs to arbitrate their claims relating to SmartDownload. *Id.* at 596. ...

DISCUSSION

I. Standard of Review and Applicable Law

A district court's denial of a motion to compel arbitration is reviewed *de novo*. . . .

The FAA provides that a "written provision in any . . . contract evidencing a transaction involving commerce to settle by arbitration a controversy thereafter arising out of such contract or transaction . . . shall be valid, irrevocable, and enforceable, save upon such grounds as exist at law or in equity for the revocation of any contract." 9 U.S.C. § 2. It is well settled that a court may not compel arbitration until it has resolved "the question of the very existence" of the contract embodying the arbitration clause. *Interocean Shipping Co. v. Nat'l Shipping & Trading Corp.*, 462 F.2d 673, 676 (2d Cir.1972). "[A]rbitration is a matter of contract and a party cannot be required to submit to arbitration any dispute which he has not agreed so to submit."

The district court properly concluded that in deciding whether parties agreed to arbitrate a certain matter, a court should generally apply state-law principles to the issue of contract formation. . . . The district court further held that California law governs the question of contract formation here; the parties do not appeal that determination. . . .

In sum, we conclude that the district court properly decided the question of reasonable notice and objective manifestation of assent as a matter of law on the record before it, and we decline defendants' request to remand for a full trial on that question. . . .

III. Whether the User Plaintiffs Had Reasonable Notice of and Manifested Assent to the SmartDownload License Agreement

Whether governed by the common law or by Article 2 of the Uniform Commercial Code ("UCC"), a transaction, in order to be a contract, requires a manifestation of agreement between the parties. *See Windsor Mills, Inc. v. Collins & Aikman Corp.*, 25 Cal.App.3d 987, 991, 101 Cal.Rptr. 347, 350 (1972) ("[C]onsent to, or acceptance of, the arbitration provision [is] necessary to create an agreement to arbitrate."); *see also* Cal. Com.Code § 2204(1) ("A contract for sale of goods may be made in any manner sufficient to show agreement, including conduct by both parties which recognizes the existence of such a contract.").[13] Mutual manifestation of assent, whether by written or spoken word or by conduct, is the touchstone of contract. *Binder v. Aetna Life Ins. Co.*, 75 Cal.App.4th 832, 848, 89 Cal.Rptr.2d 540, 551 (1999); *cf.* Restatement (Second) of Contracts § 19(2) (1981) ("The conduct of a party is not effective as a manifestation of his assent unless he intends to engage in the conduct and knows or has reason to know that the other party may infer from

---

13. The district court concluded that the SmartDownload transactions here should be governed by "California law as it relates to the sale of goods, including the Uniform Commercial Code in effect in California." *Specht,* 150 F.Supp.2d at 591. It is not obvious, however, that UCC Article 2 ("sales of goods") applies to the licensing of software that is downloadable from the Internet. *Cf. Advent Sys. Ltd. v. Unisys Corp.,* 925 F.2d 670, 675 (3d Cir.1991). . .

We need not decide today whether UCC Article 2 applies to Internet transactions in downloadable products. The district court's analysis and the parties' arguments on appeal show that, for present purposes, there is no essential difference between UCC Article 2 and the common law of contracts. We therefore apply the common law, with exceptions as noted.

his conduct that he assents."). Although an onlooker observing the disputed transactions in this case would have seen each of the user plaintiffs click on the SmartDownload "Download" button, *see Cedars Sinai Med. Ctr. v. Mid-West Nat'l Life Ins. Co.*, 118 F.Supp.2d 1002, 1008 (C.D.Cal.2000) ("In California, a party's intent to contract is judged objectively, by the party's outward manifestation of consent."), a consumer's clicking on a download button does not communicate assent to contractual terms if the offer did not make clear to the consumer that clicking on the download button would signify assent to those terms, *see Windsor Mills*, 25 Cal.App.3d at 992, 101 Cal.Rptr. at 351 ("[W]hen the offeree does not know that a proposal has been made to him this objective standard does not apply."). California's common law is clear that "an offeree, regardless of apparent manifestation of his consent, is not bound by inconspicuous contractual provisions of which he is unaware, contained in a document whose contractual nature is not obvious." *Id.; see also Marin Storage & Trucking, Inc. v. Benco Contracting & Eng'g, Inc.*, 89 Cal.App.4th 1042, 1049, 107 Cal.Rptr.2d 645, 651 (2001) (same).

Arbitration agreements are no exception to the requirement of manifestation of assent. "This principle of knowing consent applies with particular force to provisions for arbitration." *Windsor Mills*, 101 Cal.Rptr. at 351. Clarity and conspicuousness of arbitration terms are important in securing informed assent. "If a party wishes to bind in writing another to an agreement to arbitrate future disputes, such purpose should be accomplished in a way that each party to the arrangement will fully and clearly comprehend that the agreement to arbitrate exists and binds the parties thereto." *Commercial Factors Corp. v. Kurtzman Bros.*, 131 Cal.App.2d 133, 134–35, 280 P.2d 146, 147–48 (1955) (internal quotation marks omitted). Thus, California contract law measures assent by an objective standard that takes into account both what the offeree said, wrote, or did and the transactional context in which the offeree verbalized or acted.

A. The Reasonably Prudent Offeree of Downloadable Software

Defendants argue that plaintiffs must be held to a standard of reasonable prudence and that, because notice of the existence of SmartDownload license terms was on the next scrollable screen, plaintiffs were on "inquiry notice" of those terms.[14] We disagree with the proposition that a reasonably prudent offeree in plaintiffs' position would necessarily have known or learned of the existence of the SmartDownload license agreement prior to acting, so that plaintiffs may be held to have assented to that agreement with constructive notice of its terms. *See* Cal. Civ.Code § 1589 ("A voluntary acceptance of the benefit of a transaction is equivalent to a consent to all the obligations arising from it, so far as the facts are known, or ought to be known, to the person accepting."). It is true that "[a] party cannot avoid the terms of a contract on the ground that he or she failed to read it before signing." *Marin Storage & Trucking*, 89 Cal.App.4th at 1049, 107 Cal.Rptr.2d at 651. But courts are quick to add: "An exception to this general rule exists when the writing does not appear to be a contract and the terms are not called to the attention of the recipient. In such a case, no contract is formed with respect to the undisclosed term." *Id.; cf. Cory v. Golden State Bank*, 95 Cal.App.3d 360, 364,

---

14. "Inquiry notice" is "actual notice of circumstances sufficient to put a prudent man upon inquiry." *Cal. State Auto. Ass'n Inter-* *Ins. Bureau v. Barrett Garages, Inc.*, 257 Cal. App.2d 71, 64 Cal.Rptr. 699, 703 (Cal.Ct.App. 1967) (internal quotation marks omitted).

157 Cal.Rptr. 538, 541 (1979) ("[T]he provision in question is effectively hidden from the view of money order purchasers until after the transactions are completed. . . . Under these circumstances, it must be concluded that the Bank's money order purchasers are not chargeable with either actual or constructive notice of the service charge provision, and therefore cannot be deemed to have consented to the provision as part of their transaction with the Bank.").

Most of the cases cited by defendants in support of their inquiry-notice argument are drawn from the world of paper contracting. *See, e.g., Taussig v. Bode & Haslett,* 134 Cal. 260, 66 P. 259 (1901) (where party had opportunity to read leakage disclaimer printed on warehouse receipt, he had duty to do so); *In re First Capital Life Ins. Co.,* 34 Cal.App.4th 1283, 1288, 40 Cal. Rptr.2d 816, 820 (1995) (purchase of insurance policy after opportunity to read and understand policy terms creates binding agreement); *King v. Larsen Realty, Inc.,* 121 Cal.App.3d 349, 356, 175 Cal.Rptr. 226, 231 (1981) (where realtors' board manual specifying that party was required to arbitrate was "readily available," party was "on notice" that he was agreeing to mandatory arbitration); *Cal. State Auto. Ass'n Inter–Ins. Bureau v. Barrett Garages, Inc.,* 257 Cal.App.2d 71, 76, 64 Cal.Rptr. 699, 703 (1967) (recipient of airport parking claim check was bound by terms printed on claim check, because [an] "ordinarily prudent" person would have been alerted to the terms); *Larrus v. First Nat'l Bank,* 122 Cal.App.2d 884, 888, 266 P.2d 143, 147 (1954) ("clearly printed" statement on bank card stating that depositor agreed to bank's regulations provided sufficient notice to create agreement, where party had opportunity to view statement and to ask for full text of regulations, but did not do so); *see also Hux v. Butler,* 339 F.2d 696, 700 (6th Cir.1964) (constructive notice found where "slightest inquiry" would have disclosed relevant facts to offeree); *Walker v. Carnival Cruise Lines,* 63 F.Supp.2d 1083, 1089 (N.D.Cal.1999) (under California and federal law, "conspicuous notice" directing the attention of parties to existence of contract terms renders terms binding) (quotation marks omitted); *Shacket v. Roger Smith Aircraft Sales, Inc.,* 651 F.Supp. 675, 691 (N.D.Ill.1986) (constructive notice found where "minimal investigation" would have revealed facts to offeree).

As the foregoing cases suggest, receipt of a physical document containing contract terms or notice thereof is frequently deemed, in the world of paper transactions, a sufficient circumstance to place the offeree on inquiry notice of those terms. "Every person who has actual notice of circumstances sufficient to put a prudent man upon inquiry as to a particular fact, has constructive notice of the fact itself in all cases in which, by prosecuting such inquiry, he might have learned such fact." Cal. Civ.Code § 19. These principles apply equally to the emergent world of online product delivery, pop-up screens, hyperlinked pages, clickwrap licensing, scrollable documents, and urgent admonitions to "Download Now!". What plaintiffs saw when they were being invited by defendants to download this fast, free plug-in called SmartDownload was a screen containing praise for the product and, at the very bottom of the screen, a "Download" button. Defendants argue that under the principles set forth in the cases cited above, a "fair and prudent person using ordinary care" would have been on inquiry notice of SmartDownload's license terms. *Shacket,* 651 F.Supp. at 690.

We are not persuaded that a reasonably prudent offeree in these circumstances would have known of the existence of license terms. Plaintiffs were responding to an offer that did not carry an immediately visible notice of the existence of license terms or require unambiguous manifestation of assent to those terms. Thus, plaintiffs' "apparent manifestation of ... consent" was to terms "contained in a document whose contractual nature [was] not obvious." *Windsor Mills,* 25 Cal.App.3d at 992, 101 Cal.Rptr. at 351. Moreover, the fact that, given the position of the scroll bar on their computer screens, plaintiffs may have been aware that an unexplored portion of the Netscape webpage remained below the download button does not mean that they reasonably should have concluded that this portion contained a notice of license terms. In their deposition testimony, plaintiffs variously stated that they used the scroll bar "[o]nly if there is something that I feel I need to see that is on—that is off the page," or that the elevated position of the scroll bar suggested the presence of "mere[ ] formalities, standard lower banner links" or "that the page is bigger than what I can see." Plaintiffs testified, and defendants did not refute, that plaintiffs were in fact unaware that defendants intended to attach license terms to the use of SmartDownload.

We conclude that in circumstances such as these, where consumers are urged to download free software at the immediate click of a button, a reference to the existence of license terms on a submerged screen is not sufficient to place consumers on inquiry or constructive notice of those terms.[15] The SmartDownload webpage screen was "printed in such a manner that it tended to conceal the fact that it was an express acceptance of [Netscape's] rules and regulations." *Larrus,* 266 P.2d at 147. Internet users may have, as defendants put it, "as much time as they need[ ]" to scroll through multiple screens on a webpage, but there is no reason to assume that viewers will scroll down to subsequent screens simply because screens are there. When products are "free" and users are invited to download them in the absence of reasonably conspicuous notice that they are about to bind themselves to contract terms, the transactional circumstances cannot be fully analogized to those in the paper world of arm's-length bargaining. In the next two sections, we discuss case law and other legal authorities that have addressed the circumstances of computer sales, software licensing, and online transacting. Those authorities tend strongly to support our conclusion that plaintiffs did not manifest assent to SmartDownload's license terms.

B. Shrinkwrap Licensing and Related Practices

Defendants cite certain well-known cases involving shrinkwrap licensing and related commercial practices in support of their contention that plaintiffs became bound by the SmartDownload license terms by virtue of inquiry notice. For example, in *Hill v. Gateway 2000, Inc.,* 105 F.3d 1147 (7th Cir.1997), the Seventh Circuit held that where a purchaser had ordered a computer over the telephone, received the order in a shipped box containing the computer along with printed contract terms, and did not return the computer within the thirty days required by the terms, the purchaser was bound by the contract. *Id.* at 1148–49. In *ProCD, Inc. v. Zeidenberg,* the same court held that where an individual purchased software in a box containing license terms which were displayed on the computer screen every time the

---

15. We do not address the district court's alternative holding that notice was further vitiated by the fact that the reference to Smart-Download's license terms, even if scrolled to, was couched in precatory terms ("a mild request") rather than mandatory ones. *Specht,* 150 F.Supp.2d at 596.

user executed the software program, the user had sufficient opportunity to review the terms and to return the software, and so was contractually bound after retaining the product. *ProCD*, 86 F.3d at 1452; *cf. Moore v. Microsoft Corp.*, 293 A.D.2d 587, 587, 741 N.Y.S.2d 91, 92 (2d Dep't 2002) (software user was bound by license agreement where terms were prominently displayed on computer screen before software could be installed and where user was required to indicate assent by clicking "I agree"); *Brower v. Gateway 2000, Inc.*, 246 A.D.2d 246, 251, 676 N.Y.S.2d 569, 572 (1st Dep't 1998) (buyer assented to arbitration clause shipped inside box with computer and software by retaining items beyond date specified by license terms); *M.A. Mortenson Co. v. Timberline Software Corp.*, 93 Wash.App. 819, 970 P.2d 803, 809 (1999) (buyer manifested assent to software license terms by installing and using software), *aff'd*, 140 Wash.2d 568, 998 P.2d 305 (2000); *see also I.Lan Sys.*, 183 F.Supp.2d at 338 (business entity "explicitly accepted the clickwrap license agreement [contained in purchased software] when it clicked on the box stating 'I agree' ").

These cases do not help defendants. To the extent that they hold that the purchaser of a computer or tangible software is contractually bound after failing to object to printed license terms provided with the product, *Hill* and *Brower* do not differ markedly from the cases involving traditional paper contracting discussed in the previous section. Insofar as the purchaser in *ProCD* was confronted with conspicuous, mandatory license terms every time he ran the software on his computer, that case actually undermines defendants' contention that downloading in the absence of conspicuous terms is an act that binds plaintiffs to those terms. In *Mortenson,* the full text of license terms was printed on each sealed diskette envelope inside the software box, printed again on the inside cover of the user manual, and notice of the terms appeared on the computer screen every time the purchaser executed the program. *Mortenson,* 970 P.2d at 806. In sum, the foregoing cases are clearly distinguishable from the facts of the present action.

C. Online Transactions

Cases in which courts have found contracts arising from Internet use do not assist defendants, because in those circumstances there was much clearer notice than in the present case that a user's act would manifest assent to contract terms. *See, e.g., Hotmail Corp. v. Van$ Money Pie Inc.*, 47 U.S.P.Q.2d 1020, 1025 (N.D.Cal.1998) (granting preliminary injunction based in part on breach of "Terms of Service" agreement, to which defendants had assented); *America Online, Inc. v. Booker,* 781 So.2d 423, 425 (Fla.Dist.Ct.App.2001) (upholding forum selection clause in "freely negotiated agreement" contained in online terms of service); *Caspi v. Microsoft Network, L.L.C.,* 323 N.J.Super. 118, 732 A.2d 528, 530, 532–33 (N.J.Super.Ct.App.Div.1999) (upholding forum selection clause where subscribers to online software were required to review license terms in scrollable window and to click "I Agree" or "I Don't Agree"); *Barnett v. Network Solutions, Inc.,* 38 S.W.3d 200, 203–04 (Tex.App.2001) (upholding forum selection clause in online contract for registering Internet domain names that required users to scroll through terms before accepting or rejecting them); *cf. Pollstar v. Gigmania, Ltd.,* 170 F.Supp.2d 974, 981–82 (E.D.Cal.2000) (expressing concern that notice of license terms had appeared in small, gray text on a gray background on a linked webpage, but concluding that it was too early in the case to order dismissal).

After reviewing the California common law and other relevant legal authority, we conclude that under the circumstances here, plaintiffs' downloading of SmartDownload did not constitute acceptance of defendants' license terms. Reasonably conspicuous notice of the existence of contract terms and unambiguous manifestation of assent to those terms by consumers are essential if electronic bargaining is to have integrity and credibility. We hold that a reasonably prudent offeree in plaintiffs' position would not have known or learned, prior to acting on the invitation to download, of the reference to SmartDownload's license terms hidden below the "Download" button on the next screen. We affirm the district court's conclusion that the user plaintiffs, including Fagan, are not bound by the arbitration clause contained in those terms.

IV. Whether Plaintiffs' Assent to Communicator's License Agreement Requires Them To Arbitrate Their Claims Regarding SmartDownload

Plaintiffs do not dispute that they assented to the license terms governing Netscape's Communicator. The parties disagree, however, over the scope of that license's arbitration clause. Defendants contend that the scope is broad enough to encompass plaintiffs' claims regarding SmartDownload, even if plaintiffs did not separately assent to SmartDownload's license terms and even though Communicator's license terms did not expressly mention SmartDownload. Thus, defendants argue, plaintiffs must arbitrate. . . .

After careful review of these allegations, we conclude that plaintiffs' claims "present no question involving construction of the [Communicator license agreement], and no questions in respect of the parties' rights and obligations under it." *Collins & Aikman,* 58 F.3d at 23. It follows that the claims of the five user plaintiffs are beyond the scope of the arbitration clause contained in the Communicator license agreement. Because those claims are not arbitrable under that agreement or under the SmartDownload license agreement, to which plaintiffs never assented, we affirm the district court's holding that the five user plaintiffs may not be compelled to arbitrate their claims. . . .

CONCLUSION

For the foregoing reasons, we affirm the district court's denial of defendants' motion to compel arbitration and to stay court proceedings.

Chapter 17

INTERPRETATION AND UNCON-
SCIONABILITY IN A FORM–
CONTRACT SETTING

LLEWELLYN, THE COMMON LAW TRADITION:
DECIDING APPEALS

362–371 (1960).

The impetus to the form-pad is clear, for any business unit: by standardizing terms, and by standardizing even the spot on the form where any individually dickered term appears, one saves all the time and skill otherwise needed to dig out and record the meaning of variant language; one makes check-up, totaling, follow-through, etc., into routine operations; one has duplicates (in many colors) available for the administration of a multidepartment business; and so on more. The content of the standardized terms accumulates experience, it avoids or reduces legal risks and also confers all kinds of operating leeways and advantages, all without need of either consulting counsel from instance to instance or of bargaining with the other parties. Not to be overlooked, either, is the tailoring of the crude misfitting hand-me-down pattern of the "general law" "in the absence of agreement" to the particular detailed working needs of your own line of business—whether apartment rentals, stock brokerage, international grain trade, installment selling of appliances, flour milling, sugar beet raising, or insurance. It would be a heartwarming scene, a triumph of private attention to what is essentially private self-government in the lesser transactions of life or in those areas too specialized for the blunt, slow tools of the legislature—if only all businessmen and all their lawyers would be reasonable.

But power, like greed, if it does not always corrupt, goes easily to the head. So that the form-agreements tend either at once or over the years, and often by whole lines of trade, into a massive and almost terrifying jug-handled character; the one party lays his head into the mouth of a lion—either, and mostly, without reading the fine print, or occasionally in hope and expectation (not infrequently solid) that it will be a sweet and gentle lion. The more familiar instances, perhaps, are the United Realtors' Standard Lease, almost

451

any bank's collateral note or agreement, almost any installment sale form, an accident insurance policy, a steamship ticket, a beet sugar refinery contract with a farmer or a flour miller's with its customer; or, on a lesser scale, the standard nonwarranty given by seed companies or auto manufacturers. In regard to such, one notes four things: (1) sometimes language which seems at first sight horrifying may have good human and economic stimulus; thus, suits for loss of crop before a farmer jury are pretty terrible things to face for the price of a few bags of seed; and (2) there are crooked claims and there are irrationally unreasonable ones—each with its jury risk—as well as solid ones; and only a clause which in law bars the claim absolutely can free an outfit like an insurance company to deal fairly though "in its discretion" with the latter class. On the other hand, (3) boiler-plate clauses can and often do run far beyond any such need or excuse, sometimes ... involving flagrant trickery; and (4) not all "dominant" parties are nice lions, and even nice lions can make mistakes.

There is a fifth and no less vital thing to note: Where the form is drawn with a touch of Mr. Dooley's "gentlemanly restraint," or where, as with the overseas grain contracts or the Pacific Coast dried fruit contracts or the Worth Street Rules on textiles, two-fisted bargainers on either side have worked out in the form a balanced code to govern the particular line or trade or industry, there is every reason for a court to assume both fairness and wisdom in the terms, and to seek in first instance to learn, understand, and fit both its own thinking and its action into the whole design. Contracts of this kind (so long as reasonable in the net) are a road to better than official-legal regulation of our economic life....

... [T]he true answer to the whole problem seems, amusingly, to be one which could occur to any court or any lawyer, at any time, as readily as to a scholar who had spent a lifetime on the subject—though I doubt if it could occur to anyone without the inquiry and analysis in depth which we owe to the scholarly work.

The answer, I suggest, is this: Instead of thinking about "assent" to boilerplate clauses, we can recognize that so far as concerns the specific, there is no assent at all. What has in fact been assented to, specifically, are the few dickered terms, and the broad type of the transaction, and but one thing more. That one thing more is a blanket assent (not a specific assent) to any not unreasonable or indecent terms the seller may have on his form, which do not alter or eviscerate the reasonable meaning of the dickered terms. The fine print which has not been read has no business to cut under the reasonable meaning of those dickered terms which constitute the dominant and only real expression of agreement....

The queer thing is that where the transaction occurs without the fine print present, courts do not find this general line of approach too hard to understand: thus ... [I cannot] see a court having trouble, where a short memo agrees in due course to sign "our standard contract," in rejecting an outrageous form as not being fairly within the reasonable meaning of the term. The clearest case to see is the handing over of a blank check: no court, judging as between the parties, would fail to reach for the circumstances, in determining whether the amount filled in had gone beyond the reasonable.

Why, then, can we not face the fact where boiler-plate is present? There has been an arm's length deal, with dickered terms. There has been accompanying that basic deal another which, if not on any fiduciary basis, at least involves a plain expression of confidence, asked and accepted, with a corresponding limit on the powers granted: the boiler-plate is assented to en bloc, "unsight, unseen," on the implicit assumption and to the full extent that (1) it does not alter or impair the fair meaning of the dickered terms when read alone, and (2) that its terms are neither in the particular nor in the net manifestly unreasonable and unfair. Such is the reality, and I see nothing in the way of a court's operating on that basis, to truly effectuate the only intention which can in reason be worked out as common to the two parties, granted good faith. And if the boiler-plate party is not playing in good faith, there is law enough to bar that fact from benefiting it. We had a hundred years of sales law in which any sales transaction with explicit words resulted in two several contracts for the one consideration: that of sale, and the collateral one of warranty. The idea is applicable here, for better reason: any contract with boiler-plate results in *two* several contracts: the *dickered* deal, and the collateral one of *supplementary* boiler-plate.

Rooted in sense, history, and simplicity, it is an answer which could occur to anyone.

WEAVER v. AMERICAN OIL CO.

Supreme Court of Indiana, 1971.
257 Ind. 458, 276 N.E.2d 144.

Action for a declaratory judgment to determine whether exculpatory and indemnity clauses of gas station lease were enforceable. The Circuit Court, Marshall County, Roy Sheneman, J., upheld enforceability, and lessee appealed. The Appellate Court, 261 N.E. 99, reversed and remanded. On rehearing, 262 N.E.2d 663, the prior opinion was modified, and petition to transfer appeal was granted. . . .

ARTERBURN, CHIEF JUSTICE. In this case the appellee oil company presented to the appellant-defendant leasee, a filling station operator, a printed form contract as a lease to be signed, by the defendant, which contained, in addition to the normal leasing provisions, a "hold harmless" clause which provided in substance that the leasee operator would hold harmless and also indemnify the oil company for any negligence of the oil company occurring on the leased premises. The litigation arises as a result of the oil company's own employee spraying gasoline over Weaver and his assistant and causing them to be burned and injured on the leased premises. This action was initiated by American Oil and Hoffer (Appellees) for a declaratory judgment to determine the liability of appellant Weaver, under the clause in the lease. The trial court entered judgment holding Weaver liable under the lease.

Clause three [3] of the lease reads as follows:

"Lessor, its agents and employees shall not be liable for any loss, damage, injuries, or other casualty of whatsoever kind or by whomsoever caused to the person or property of anyone (including Lessee) on or off the premises, arising out of or resulting from Lessee's use, possession or operation thereof, or from defects in the premises whether apparent or hidden, or from the installation[,] existence, use, maintenance, condition, repair, alteration, removal or replacement of any equipment thereon, whether due in whole or in part to negligent acts or omissions of Lessor, its agents or employees; and Lessee for himself, his heirs, executors, administrators, successors and assigns, hereby agrees to indemnify and hold Lessor, its agents and employees, harmless from and against all claims, demands, liabilities, suits or actions (including all reasonable expenses and attorneys' fees incurred by or imposed on the Lessor in connection therewith) for such loss, damage, injury or other casualty. Lessee also agrees to pay all reasonable expenses and attorneys' fees incurred by Lessor in the event that Lessee shall default under the provisions of this paragraph."

It will be noted that this lease clause not only exculpated the lessor oil company from its liability for its negligence, but also compelled Weaver to indemnify them for any damages or loss incurred as a result of its negligence. The appellate court held the exculpatory clause invalid, 261 N.E.2d 99, but the indemnifying clause valid, 262 N.E.2d 663. In our opinion, both these provisions must be read together since one may be used to effectuate the result obtained through the other. We find no ground for any distinction and we therefore grant the petition to transfer the appeal to this court.

This is a contract, which was submitted (already in printed form) to a party with lesser bargaining power. As in this case, it may contain unconscionable or unknown provisions which are in fine print. Such is the case now before this court.

The facts reveal that Weaver had left high school after one and a half years and spent his time, prior to leasing the service station, working at various skilled and unskilled labor oriented jobs. He was not one who should be expected to know the law or understand the meaning of technical terms. The ceremonious activity of signing the lease consisted of nothing more than the agent of American Oil placing the lease in front of Mr. Weaver and saying "sign", which Mr. Weaver did. There is nothing in the record to indicate that Weaver read the lease; that the agent asked Weaver to read it; or that the agent, in any manner, attempted to call Weaver's attention to the "hold harmless" clause in the lease. Each year following, the procedure was the same. A salesman, from American Oil, would bring the lease to Weaver, at the station, and Weaver would sign it. The evidence showed that Weaver had never read the lease prior to signing and that the clauses in the lease were never explained to him in a manner from which he could grasp their legal significance. The leases were prepared by the attorneys of American Oil Company, for the American Oil Company, and the agents of the American Oil Company never attempted to explain the conditions of the lease nor did they advise Weaver that he should consult legal counsel, before signing the lease. The superior bargaining power of American Oil is patently obvious and the significance of Weaver's signature upon the legal document amounted to nothing more than a mere formality to Weaver for the substantial protection of American Oil.

Had this case involved the sale of goods it would have been termed an "unconscionable contract" under sec. 2–302 of the Uniform Commercial Code. . . .

"It is not the policy of the law to restrict business dealings or to relieve a party of his own mistakes of judgment, but where one party has taken advantage of another's necessities and distress to obtain an unfair advantage over him, and the latter, owing to his condition, has encumbered himself with a heavy liability or an onerous obligation for the sake of a small or inadequate present gain, there will be relief granted." Stiefler v. McCullough (1933), 97 Ind.App. 123, 174 N.E. 823.

The facts of this case reveal that in exchange for a contract which, if the clause in question is enforceable, may cost Mr. Weaver potentially thousands of dollars in damages for negligence of which he was not the cause, Weaver must operate the service station seven days a week for long hours, at a total yearly income of $5,000–$6,000. The evidence also reveals that *the clause was in fine print and contained no title heading* which would have identified it as an indemnity clause. It seems a deplorable abuse of justice to hold a man of poor education, to a contract prepared by the attorneys of American Oil, for the benefit of American Oil which was presented to Weaver on a "take it or leave it basis".

Justice Frankfurter of the United States Supreme Court spoke on the question of inequality of bargaining power in his dissenting opinion in United States v. Bethlehem Steel Corp. (1942), 315 U.S. 289, 326, 62 S.Ct. 581, 599, 86 L.Ed. 855, 876.

> "(I)t is said that familiar principles would be outraged if Bethlehem were denied recovery on these contracts. But is there any principle which is more familiar or more firmly embedded in the history of Anglo–American law than the basic doctrine that the courts will not permit themselves to be used as instruments of inequity and injustice? Does any principle in our law have more universal application than the doctrine that courts will not enforce transactions in which the relative positions of the parties are such that one has unconscionably taken advantage of the necessities of the other?" . . .

The traditional contract is the result of free bargaining of parties who are brought together by the play of the market, and who meet each other on a footing of approximate economic equality. In such a society there is no danger that freedom of contract will be a threat to the social order as a whole. But in present-day commercial life the standardized mass contract has appeared. It is used primarily by enterprises with strong bargaining power and position. The weaker party, in need of the good or services, is frequently not in a position to shop around for better terms, either because the author of the standard contract has a monopoly (natural or artificial) or because all competitors use the same clauses.

Judge Frankfurter's dissent was written nearly twenty years ago. It represents a direction and philosophy which the law . . . at that time was taking and is now compelled to accept in our modern society over the old principle known as the *parol evidence rule*. The parol evidence rule states that an agreement or contract, signed by the parties, is *conclusively presumed* to represent an integration or meeting of the minds of the parties. This is an archaic rule from the old common law. The objectivity of the rule has as its only merit its simplicity of application which is far outweighed by its failure in many cases to represent the actual agreement, particularly where a printed form prepared by one party [which] contains hidden clauses unknown to the other party is submitted and signed. The law should seek the truth or the subjective understanding of the parties in this more enlightened age. The burden should be on the party submitting such "a package" in printed form to show that the other party had knowledge of any unusual or unconscionable terms contained therein. The principle should be the same as that applicable to implied warranties, namely that a package of goods sold to a purchaser is fit for the purposes intended and contains no harmful materials other than that represented. Caveat lessee is no more the current law than caveat emptor. Only in this way can justice be served and the true meaning of freedom of contract preserved. The analogy is rational. We have previously pointed out a similar situation in the Uniform Commercial Code, which prohibits unconscionable contract clauses in sales agreements.

When a party can show that the contract, which is sought to be enforced, was in fact an unconscionable one, due to a prodigious amount of bargaining power on behalf of the stronger party, which is used to the stronger party's advantage and is unknown to the lesser party, causing a great hardship and risk on the lesser party, the contract provision, or the contract as a whole, if the provision is not separable, should not be enforceable on the grounds that the provision is contrary to public policy. The party seeking to enforce such a contract has the burden of showing that the provisions were explained to the other party and *came to his knowledge* and there was in fact *a real and voluntary meeting of the minds and not merely an objective meeting.* ...

We do not mean to say or infer that parties may not make contracts exculpating one of his negligence and providing for indemnification, but it must be done *knowingly* and *willingly* as in insurance contracts made for that very purpose.

It is the duty of the courts to administer justice and that role is not performed, in this case, by enforcing a written instrument, not really an agreement of the parties as shown by the evidence here, although signed by the parties. The parol evidence rule must yield to the equities of the case. The appeal is transferred to this court and the judgment of the trial court is reversed with direction to enter judgment for the appellant.

GIVAN, DEBRULER and HUNTER, JJ., concur.

[The dissenting opinion of Justice Prentice is omitted.]

————

RESTATEMENT, SECOND, CONTRACTS § 211

[See Selected Source Materials Supplement]

————

UNIDROIT PRINCIPLES OF INTERNATIONAL COMMERCIAL CONTRACTS ARTS. 2.1.19, 2.1.22

[See Selected Source Materials Supplement]

————

PRINCIPLES OF EUROPEAN CONTRACT LAW ART. 4.110

[See Selected Source Materials Supplement]

DARNER MOTOR SALES v. UNIVERSAL UNDERWRITERS

Supreme Court of Arizona, En Banc, 1984.
140 Ariz. 383, 682 P.2d 388.

FELDMAN, JUSTICE.

Darner Motor Sales, Inc., dba Darner Leasing Co. (Darner Motors), petitions for review of a memorandum decision of the court of appeals (Darner Motor Sales, Inc. v. Universal Underwriters Insurance Company, No. 1 CA–CIV 5796, filed February 22, 1983). That decision affirmed a summary judgment in favor of Universal Underwriters Insurance Company (Universal) and their agent, John Brent Doxsee (Doxsee), who were the third party defendants impleaded by Darner Motors. We granted review because we believe that the issues presented call into question the clarity and consistency of a large body of Arizona law dealing with insurance coverage. We have jurisdiction pursuant to Ariz. Const. Art. 6, § 5(3) and Rule 23, Rules of Civ.App.P., 17A A.R.S.

FACTS

Darner Motors is in the automobile sales, service and leasing business. Prior to transacting business with Universal, Darner Motors' various operations were insured under several policies issued by The Travelers Company (Travelers). In October of 1973, Doxsee, an insurance agent who was a full-time employee of Universal, contacted Joel Darner to solicit insurance business. The following month, Darner purchased a Universal "U–Drive policy" through Doxsee. This policy insured Darner Motors and the lessees of its cars for automobile liability risk. Darner Motors was covered in limits of $100,000 for any one injury and $300,000 (100/300) for all injuries arising out of any one accident. The lessees were covered in limits of 15/30. The rest of Darner Motors' business risks continued to be insured under a "dealership package policy" issued by Travelers.

It is unclear from the record, but this situation presumably continued until April of 1975, a renewal date of the Travelers policy. In April of 1975, Universal "picked up" the entire insurance "package" for Darner Motors' various business activities. This "package" consisted of a Universal "Unicover" policy which included coverage for garagekeeper's liability, premises liability, property coverage, crime coverage, customer car coverage, and plate glass insurance. The parties describe this as an "umbrella policy," so it is possible that, in addition to covering multiple risks, it also contained excess coverage over other policies which provided primary coverage.[1] In addition to

---

1. It is difficult to tell just what was or was not insured under this "umbrella policy" since a copy of the policy is not part of the record, even though the coverage contained in that policy is the precise issue in the case.

the umbrella policy, Universal also renewed the U–Drive policy, which provided coverage to the lessees of Darner Motors.[2]

Substantial controversy exists with regard to many of the factual allegations. However, according to Darner, he informed Doxsee that renewal of lessee coverage was to be in the same limits as applied to Darner Motors in the original U–Drive policy. When the new U–Drive policy arrived after renewal in April of 1975, Darner examined it and noticed that the limits of coverage for lessees were 15/30. After reading this, Darner claims that he called Doxsee. He was concerned because his rental contract contained a representation of greater coverage (100/300) and because he felt that it would be better for his business operation if his lessees had the higher coverage. Darner told Doxsee that the liability limits of the U–Drive policy did not conform to their prior agreement, and asked Doxsee to come to Darner Motors and discuss the matter. Doxsee did call upon Mr. Darner at the latter's office. Although Doxsee could not recall the subsequent conversation, both Darner and his former sales manager, Jack Hadley, testified about the discussion. Their deposition testimony would support a finding that Doxsee told Darner not to worry about the limits because, although the U–Drive policy provided only 15/30 coverage, the all-risk clause of the umbrella policy would provide additional coverage to limits of 100/300.[3]

At some time after he received the U–Drive policy and, presumably, also after his discussions with Doxsee, Darner did receive a copy of the umbrella policy. That policy was evidently quite lengthy and forbidding. Darner admits never reading it; he explained this omission by pointing out that "it's like reading a book" and stating that, following his conversations with Doxsee, "I didn't think I needed to." Darner's office manager testified that she never really read the policy either and saw little need to do so in view of the fact that Doxsee would occasionally appear, remove pages from the loose-leaf binder and insert new pages. So far as the record shows, the printed, boiler-plate provisions contained in the loose-leaf type, "book length," all-risk policy were neither negotiated before nor discussed after the policy was delivered. The parties seem to have confined themselves to a discussion of the objectives that would be realized from the purchase of the policy rather than an attempt to negotiate the wording of the policy.

Approximately twenty months after the conversation between Darner and Doxsee concerning coverage under the Universal policies, Darner Motors rented a car to Dwayne Crawford. The transaction was in the ordinary course of business, except that the form used for the rental agreement was the "old type," which contained a representation of coverage in the amount of 100/300. While driving the vehicle under this rental contract, Crawford negligently injured a pedestrian and caused severe injuries. The pedestrian sued Crawford, who looked to Universal for coverage. Universal claimed that lessee's

2. Lessors are required to provide such insurance to their lessees, A.R.S. § 28–324. The statute also provides that if the lessor fails to do so, it is jointly and severally liable for all damages caused by the lessee while driving the leased vehicle.

3. As might be expected, although Doxsee does not remember the substance of the conversation, he is quite sure he could have told Darner no such thing. Darner's testimony was impeached by evidence that he subsequently reduced the limits on his rental forms from 100/300 to 15/30. Darner explains this by stating that Doxsee told him that it was better to represent the coverage limits at the minimum required by the state so as to discourage plaintiffs' lawyers from pursuing claims for their badly injured clients. As in most such cases, who told what to whom is hotly contested, and there is much to be said for both versions of the facts.

coverage on the "U–Drive" policy was limited to 15/30. Crawford then sued Darner Motors under the rental agreement warranty that coverage was provided in limits of 100/300. Darner Motors called upon Universal to provide additional coverage under the umbrella policy. The umbrella policy did contain the higher limits, but Universal claimed that lessees were not parties "insured" as that term was defined in the all-risk policy. Universal was therefore unwilling to provide coverage in excess of the $15,000 limit of the U–Drive policy. Darner Motors then filed a third-party complaint, naming Universal and Doxsee as third party defendants.

Eventually, the pedestrian recovered $60,000 from Crawford. Universal paid $15,000 of this amount, and Darner Motors has either paid or is liable to Crawford for the remainder. Darner Motors claims that Universal and Doxsee are obligated to indemnify it against that loss. To support that contention, Darner Motors advances the following theories:

(1) Universal is estopped to deny coverage for lessees under the umbrella policy in amounts less than 100/300;

(2) The umbrella policy should be reformed so that it does contain such coverage;

(3) If no coverage is found through estoppel or reformation, then the loss incurred by Darner Motors was caused by the negligence of Universal and its agent, Doxsee, and should be borne by them;

(4) If no coverage exists by way of estoppel or reformation, then the loss incurred by Darner Motors is the result of fraud committed by Universal and its agent, Doxsee.

After considerable discovery, Universal and Doxsee moved for summary judgment, contending that there was no genuine issue of fact and that they were entitled to judgment as a matter of law. The motion was granted and judgment entered against Darner Motors. The court of appeals affirmed; pointing out that Darner Motors had not claimed that the umbrella policy was ambiguous, the court held that the insured's failure to read the policy prevented recovery on any theory, even though the contents of the policy did not comport with the representations of the insurance agent and those same representations were a part of the reason that the insured failed to read the policy.

The court of appeals stated that under Arizona law an insured who had received a copy of an unambiguous policy could not "expand the insurer's liability beyond the terms of the ... policy issued...." We believe this statement is too broad, though we acknowledge that the law is, at best, confused on this subject. In an attempt to bring some clarity and logic to the question, we have reviewed our cases and will discuss each of the theories advanced by Darner Motors. Before doing so, however, we must consider the inherent nature of an insurance contract and of the issues presented by the fact situation before us.

CONTRACT LAW AND INSURANCE POLICIES

Since this is an appeal from summary judgment, we must view the facts in the light most favorable to the party against whom judgment was taken. *Gulf Insurance Co. v. Grisham*, 125 Ariz. 123, 124, 613 P.2d 283, 284 (1980). Taking the facts in that light, the question we must decide is whether the courts will enforce an unambiguous provision contrary to the negotiated agreement made by the parties because, after the insurer's representations of coverage, the insured failed to read the insurance contract which was in his possession.[4]

Implicit in the reasoning of the court of appeals is the concept that the insurance policies purchased by Darner constitute *the* contract between Darner and Universal. Darner is considered to be bound by the terms contained within the documents. The court of appeals held:

> Because Mr. Darner received a copy of the umbrella policy and made no contention that it was ambiguous or confusing, he cannot expand the insurer's liability beyond the terms of the umbrella policy issued by Universal.

(slip op. at 7). Basic to this holding is the principle that the oral agreement between Doxsee and Darner cannot be shown to vary the terms of the insurance policy. This, indeed, was at one time the majority view. See cases cited in 12 Appleman, *Insurance Law and Practice* § 7155 (1981); similar language is contained in *Parks v. American Casualty Co. of Reading, Pa.,* 117 Ariz. 339, 572 P.2d 801 (1977); *Sellers v. Allstate Insurance Company,* 113 Ariz. 419, 422, 555 P.2d 1113, 1116 (1976); *see also Western Farm Bureau Mut. Ins. Co. v. Barela,* 79 N.M. 149, 441 P.2d 47 (1968). Some cases, including those from our own state, hold that since insurance policies are like other contracts, where the meaning and intent of the parties is "clear" from the words used in the instrument, the courts cannot "rewrite" the policy by considering the actual "words" used in striking the bargain. Thus, the rule of interpretation is stated to be that the intention of the parties as derived from the language used within the four corners of the instrument must prevail. *See, e.g., Rodemich v. State Farm Mutual Auto. Insurance Co.,* 130 Ariz. 538, 539, 637 P.2d 748, 749 (App.1981) (a vehicle which turned over and was damaged when the driver swerved to avoid an animal was not covered under the "upset" clause of a comprehensive risk policy because "upsets" resulting from attempts to avoid collision with animals were not covered unless there was actual contact). . . .

. . . Artificial results derived from application of ordinary rules of contract construction to insurance policies have made courts struggle to find some method of reaching a sensible resolution within the conceptual bounds of treating standardized, formal contracts as if they were traditional "agreements," reached by bargaining between the parties. This difficult task is often accomplished by the use of various constructs which enable courts to reach a desired result by giving lip service to traditional contract rules. One of the most prominent of these methods is the well recognized principle of resolving ambiguities against the insurer. *See Almadova v. State Farm Mutual Automo-*

---

4. In characterizing the issue in this manner, we acknowledge that the insured did read the terms of the policy covering lessees and did discover the error in that policy. He was told by the agent that the umbrella policy provided the additional coverage. He did not read the provisions of the umbrella policy. Although that policy is not part of the record, we assume that it contains a clause or clauses defining the word "insured" in such a manner that lessees are excluded from the class of persons insured by the policy. We assume further that this definitional exclusion is clear and unambiguous. Therefore, it could have been found, read and understood by Darner. Of course we have no way of knowing that these assumptions are correct; however, it was the appellant's burden to make an adequate record on appeal. Since the appellant failed to offer the policy in evidence at the trial, we settle all factual uncertainty in favor of supporting the judgment of the trial court.

bile Ins. Co., 133 Ariz. 81, 649 P.2d 284 (1982). The limitations of this principle have been discussed by Professor Robert Keeton, who comments that

> [t]he principle of resolving ambiguities against the draftsman is simply an inadequate explanation of the results of some cases. The conclusion is inescapable that courts have sometimes invented ambiguity where none existed, then resolved the invented ambiguity contrary to the plainly expressed terms of the contract document.

Keeton, *Insurance Law Rights at Variance with Policy Provisions,* 83 Harv. L.Rev. 961, 972 (1970) (footnotes omitted). Our court of appeals has attempted to avoid the problem of invented ambiguity by stating the principle that courts should not create ambiguities in order to rewrite the policy. Cf. *Barber v. Old Republic Life Ins. Co.,* 132 Ariz. 602, 604, 647 P.2d 1200, 1202 (App.1982) with *State Farm v. Gibbs, supra.* However, we also follow the rule of construction that where different jurisdictions reach different conclusions regarding the language of an insurance contract "ambiguity is established," *Federal Insurance Co. v. P.A.T. Homes, Inc.,* 113 Ariz. 136, 138, 547 P.2d 1050, 1052 (1976); thus, we may find ourselves justly criticized for accepting the inventions of other courts. It is also illogical to hold that an unexpected, unknown ambiguity in a clause which the parties did not negotiate, write or read should permit them to show the true terms of the agreement, but that the lack of such an ambiguity prevents them from so doing.

Such systems of logic—or illogic—have been criticized by Keeton, *supra,* and others for failing to recognize the realities of the insurance business and the methods used in modern insurance practice. *See, e.g., Zuckerman v. Transamerica Ins. Co.,* 133 Ariz. 139, 144–46, 650 P.2d 441, 446–48 (1982); *Harr v. Allstate Insurance Co.,* 54 N.J. 287, 301–04, 255 A.2d 208, 216–18 (1969); Restatement of Contracts (Second) § 211, comment b, and authorities cited in the reporter's note thereto; Abraham, *Judge–Made Law and Judge–Made Insurance: Honoring the Reasonable Expectations of the Insured,* 67 Va.L.Rev. (1981); Murray, *The Parol Evidence Process and Standardized Agreements under the Restatement (Second) of Contracts,* 123 U.Pa.L.Rev. 1342 (1975).

Abraham, *supra,* argues that "insurance law should be brought into the mainstream of our jurisprudence," and notes that "in many states, a principle authorizing the courts to honor the 'reasonable expectations' of the insured is emerging." *Id.* at 1151. "Emergence" is probably an inaccurate description of the use of the reasonable expectations test since, if correctly understood, that doctrine has long been a basic principle in the law of contracts.

> That portion of the field of law that is classified and described as the law of contracts attempts the realization of *reasonable expectations that have been induced* by the making of a promise.

1 Corbin, *Contracts* § 1, at 2 (1963) (emphasis supplied). We have previously recognized the doctrine of "reasonable expectations." *Zuckerman v. Transamerica Ins. Co.,* 133 Ariz. at 146, 650 P.2d at 448; *Sparks v. Republic Nat. Life Ins. Co.,* 132 Ariz. 529, 536–37, 647 P.2d 1127, 1134–35, *cert. denied,* 459 U.S. 1070, 74 L.Ed.2d 632, 103 S.Ct. 490 (1982). Of course, if not put in proper perspective, the reasonable expectations concept is quite troublesome, since most insureds develop a "reasonable expectation" that every loss will be covered by their policy. Therefore, the reasonable expectation concept must be

limited by something more than the fervent hope usually engendered by loss. Such a limitation is easily found in the postulate contained in Corbin's work—that the expectations to be realized are those that "have been induced by the making of a promise." 1 Corbin, *supra* § 1 at 2.

We think it better, then, to start the analysis by attempting to determine what expectations have been induced. We note the concept that contracts are not merely printed words. The words, of course, are usually of paramount importance. However, other matters are also significant. 3 Corbin, *supra* §§ 538, 549. It is important to recognize that although the writing "may be coextensive with the agreement, it is not the agreement but only evidence thereof." Murray, *supra*, 123 U.Pa.L.Rev. at 1389. Murray adds that "if the writing is normally executed absent understanding of its fine print provisions, it is less worthy as evidence of the true agreement." *Id.* at 1373. Llewellyn puts the proposition another way:

> The fine print which has not been read has no business to cut under the reasonable meaning of those dickered terms which constitute the dominant and only real expression of agreement, but much of [the writing] commonly belongs in [the contract].

Llewellyn, *The Common Law Tradition* 370 (1960). Thus, Llewellyn concludes, "any contract with boiler-plate results in *two* several contracts: the *dickered* deal and the collateral one of *supplementary* boiler-plate." *Id.* at 371 (emphasis in original).

If we continue to look at an insurance policy as a contract between the insured and insurer, the foregoing analysis compels the conclusion that the problem is simply the application of the parol evidence rule. The traditional view of the law of contracts is that a written agreement adopted by the parties will be viewed as an integrated contract which binds those parties to the terms expressed within the four corners of the agreement. Thus, the parties may not vary or expand the agreement by introducing parol evidence to show understandings or antecedent agreements which are in some way contrary to the terms of the contract. *Restatement (Second) of Contracts* § 215. This rule is applied with varying degrees of exactitude to insurance policies. Cases from this state reflect that attitude. *See Sparks v. Republic Nat. Life Ins. Co., supra; Isaak v. Massachusetts Indemnity Life Ins. Co.,* 127 Ariz. 581, 623 P.2d 11 (1981); *Dairyland Mutual Ins. Co. v. Andersen,* 102 Ariz. 515, 433 P.2d 963 (1967); *but see Southern Casualty v. Hughes,* 33 Ariz. 206, 263 P. 584 (1928); *Ranger Insurance Co. v. Phillips,* 25 Ariz.App. 426, 544 P.2d 250 (1976).

When faced with harsh or illogical results, such as those produced by application of the parol evidence rule to most insurance contracts, the law usually reacts by recognizing exceptions which permit courts to avoid injustice. The ambiguity rule is, of course, one of those exceptions. Others, advanced with varying success, are the doctrines of waiver and estoppel. In our view, a better rationale is to be found by application of *established principles of contract law*. In so doing, however, we must remember that the usual insurance policy is a special kind of contract. It is largely adhesive; some terms are bargained for, but most terms consist of boilerplate, not bargained for, neither read nor understood by the buyer, and often not even fully understood by the selling agent. In contracts, as in other fields, the common law has evolved to accommodate the practices of the marketplace. Thus, in insurance law, as in other areas of contract law, the parol evidence rule has not been strictly applied to enforce an illusory "bargain" set forth in a *standardized contract* when that "bargain" was never really made and would, if applied, defeat the true agreement which was supposedly contained in the policy. *Sparks v. Republic National Life Insurance Co.,* 132 Ariz. at 537, 647 P.2d at 1135. *See also Zuckerman v. Transamerica Insurance Co.,* 133 Ariz. at 144, 650 P.2d at 446.

Sparks and *Zuckerman* reflect this court's attempt to bring some degree of logic and predictability into the field of insurance. What is needed, however, is recognition of a general rule of contract law. We believe that the current formulation of the *Restatement (Second) of Contracts* contains a workable resolution of the problem. The Restatement approach is basically a modification of the parol evidence rule when dealing with contracts containing boilerplate provisions which are not negotiated, and often not even read by the parties.

Standardized Agreements

(1) Except as stated in Subsection (3), where a party to an agreement signs or otherwise manifests assent to a writing and has reason to believe that like writings are regularly used to embody terms of agreements of the same type, he adopts the writing as an integrated agreement with respect to the terms included in the writing.

(2) Such a writing is interpreted wherever reasonable as treating alike all those similarly situated, without regard to their knowledge or understanding of the standard terms of the writing.

(3) Where the other party has reason to believe that the party manifesting such assent would not do so if he knew that the writing contained a particular term, the term is not part of the agreement.

Restatement (Second) of Contracts § 211. We believe that the comments to this section of the Restatement support the wisdom of the rule formulated. Comment (a) points out that standardization of agreements is essential

> to a system of mass production and distribution. Scarce and costly time and skill can be devoted to a class of transactions rather than to details of individual transactions.... Sales personnel and customers are freed from attention to numberless variations and can focus on meaningful choice among a limited number of significant features: transaction-type, style, quantity, price, or the like. Operations are simplified and costs reduced, to the advantage of all concerned.

Subsections (1) and (2) of § 211 reflect the reality of the marketplace. Thus, those who make use of a standardized form of agreement neither expect nor desire their customers "to understand or even to read the standard terms." *Id.* comment (b). On the other hand, customers "trust to the good faith of the party using the form [and] ... understand that they are assenting to the terms not read or not understood, subject to such limitations as the law may impose." *Id.* The limitations that the law may impose are that standard terms

> may be superseded by separately negotiated or added terms (§ 203), they are construed against the draftsman (§ 206), and they are subject to the

overriding obligation of good faith (§ 205) and to the power of the court to refuse to enforce an unconscionable contract or term (§ 208).

Id. comment (c).[5]

Subsection (3) of § 211 is the Restatement's codification of and limitation on the "reasonable expectation" rule as applied to standardized agreements. The comment reads as follows:

> Although customers typically adhere to standardized agreements and are bound by them without even appearing to know the standard terms in detail, they are not bound to unknown terms which are beyond the range of reasonable expectation.... [An insured] who adheres to the [insurer's] standard terms does not assent to a term if the [insurer] has reason to believe that the [insured] would not have accepted the agreement if he had known that the agreement contained the particular term. Such a belief or assumption may be shown by the prior negotiations or inferred from the circumstances. Reason to believe may be inferred from the fact that the term is bizarre or oppressive, from the fact that it eviscerates the non-standard terms explicitly agreed to, or from the fact that it eliminates the dominant purpose of the transaction. The inference is reinforced if the adhering party never had an opportunity to read the term, or if it is illegible or otherwise hidden from view. This rule is closely related to the policy against unconscionable terms and the rule of interpretation against the draftsman.

Id. comment (f). We believe the analysis contained in the comments to the cited sections in the Restatement is a sensible rationale for interpretation of the usual type of insuring agreement.[6]

This treatment of insurance law is neither radical nor new. All that is new in the "changed" Restatement is the articulation of the rule. Some cases long ago recognized the underlying principles....

... Missing has been the articulation or formulation of some general rule to explain results of many past cases and to provide a pragmatic, honest approach to the resolution of future disputes. Hopefully, the adoption of § 211 of the Restatement as the rule for standardized contracts will provide greater predictability and uniformity of results—a benefit to both the insurance industry and the consumer.

In adopting this rule, we do not create a special field of contract law, we merely adopt a rule of integration which recognizes the method by which people do business. Indeed, the law pertaining to nonstandardized, negotiated contracts long ago began to move in the same direction. "Ordinary" contract law now recognizes that an agreement may be "partially integrated," or "completely integrated," depending upon "the degree to which the parties intended the writing to express their agreement." E. Farnsworth, *Contracts,* § 7.3 at 452 (1982). The relationship between the degree of integration and the application of the parol evidence rule has been the subject of much

5. The Section numbers in this quote refer to sections in the Restatement (Second) of Contracts.

6. It would, of course, also be applicable to other transactions handled in a similar manner. We note, for example, that contracts for transport by rail, airline or bus; for rental of cars, trucks and other equipment; credit card and charge account "rules" and terms; bills of lading, invoices and many other commercial documents are "sold" or "made" in the same manner as most insurance policies. On the other hand, there are some insurance transactions which are still the product of negotiation which includes the terms of the policy. Such contracts are not affected by § 211 because it applies only to standardized agreements such as the average automobile, general liability, or fire policy.

scholarly controversy. The authors of the leading contract treatises, Williston and Corbin, present differing views. "The point in dispute is whether the fact that the writing appears on its face to be a complete and exclusive statement of the terms of the agreement establishes conclusively that the agreement is completely integrated." Farnsworth, *supra* at 455. If it does, Williston would restrict interpretation to the four corners of the document. *Id.; See 4 Williston on Contracts* §§ 600A, 629, 633 (3d ed. 1961). Corbin argues that account should always be taken of all the surrounding circumstances to determine the extent of the integration *and* the interpretation of the agreement. Farnsworth, *supra* at 456; 3 Corbin, *supra,* § 582.

Recent decisions, the Uniform Commercial Code and the Restatement (Second) of Contracts have all favored Corbin's view. Farnsworth, *supra* at 453. *See also* Braucher, *Interpretation and Legal Effect in the Second Restatement of Contracts,* 81 Colum.L.Rev. 12 (1981). Arizona has followed the modern trend and adopted the Corbin view. . . .

It would be anomalous, indeed, to follow this view for contracts with bargained terms but to cling to the rejected rule in cases involving standardized form contracts. It would be even more anomalous if reasonable expectations induced by promises or conduct of a party are to be considered in determining integration or interpreting the words of a negotiated ... agreement but disregarded when dealing with boilerplate, so that regardless of intent or even actual agreement, the parties are bound by provisions that were never discussed, examined, read or understood.

The general rule of contract interpretations adopted by the Restatement and based on Corbin's viewpoint is a modern view which takes into account the realities of present day commercial practice. See, Trakman, *Interpreting Contracts: A Common Law Dilemma,* 59 Canadian Bar Review 241 (1981). The rule which we adopt today for interpretation of standardized contracts recognizes modern commercial practice by business entities which use automated equipment to effect a large volume of transactions through use of standardized forms. It parallels the general rule which applies to all contracts by attempting to discover the intent of the parties, in so far as intent existed, and attempts to ascertain the real agreement so far as it was expressed or conveyed by implication. However, it recognizes that most provisions of standardized agreements are not the result of negotiation; often, neither customer nor salesperson are aware of the contract provisions. The rule adopted today recognizes reality and the needs of commerce; it allows businesses that use such forms to write their own contract. It charges the customer with knowledge that the contract being "purchased" is or contains a form applied to a vast number of transactions and includes terms which are unknown (or even unknowable); it binds the customer to such terms. However, the rule stops short of granting the drafter of the contract license to accomplish any result. It holds the drafter to good faith and terms which are conscionable; it requires drafting of provisions which can be understood if the customer does attempt to check on his rights; it does not give effect to boilerplate terms which are contrary to either the expressed agreement or the purpose of the transaction as known to the contracting parties. From the standpoint of the judicial system, the rule recognizes the true origin of standardized contract provisions, frees the courts from having to write a contract for the parties, and removes the temptation to create ambiguity or invent intent in order to reach a result.

The rule does not set a premium on failure to read. Those who negotiate their transactions will be held to the same rules as have previously obtained with regard to the duty to read. The rule which we adopt applies to contracts (or parts of contracts) made up of standardized forms which, because of the nature of the enterprise, customers will not be expected to read and over which they have no real power of negotiation.[7]

To apply the old rule and interpret such contracts according to the imagined intent of the parties is to perpetuate a fiction which can do no more than bring the law into ridicule. To those troubled by the change in the law, we point out that the fundamental change occurred first in business practice. The change in legal analysis does no more than reflect the change in methods of doing business. To acknowledge standardized contracts for what they are— rules written by commercial enterprises—and to enforce them as written, subject to those reasonable limitations provided by law, is to recognize the reality of the marketplace as it now exists, while imposing just limits on business practice. These, we think, have always been the proper functions of contract law.

We turn, then, to the facts of this case. We have adopted a rule of law which, in proper circumstances, will relieve the insured from certain clauses of an agreement which he did not negotiate, probably did not read, and probably would not have understood had he read them. Does this case present a proper circumstance? If so, by what process is this to be accomplished? How is the restatement rule to be given effect?

Equitable Estoppel

The elements of estoppel are "conduct by which one ... induces another to believe ... in certain material facts, which inducement results in acts in reliance thereon, justifiably taken, which cause injury...." *Sahlin v. American Casualty Company of Reading,* 103 Ariz. 57, 59, 436 P.2d 606, 608 (1968) (quoting *Builders Supply Corp. v. Marshall,* 88 Ariz. 89, 94, 352 P.2d 982, 985 (1960)).

The majority rule is considered to be "that the doctrines of waiver and estoppel are not available to bring within the coverage of an insurance policy risks not covered by its terms, or expressly excluded therefrom." Annot. 1 A.L.R.3d 1149, 1147 (1965). Indeed, the annotation lists only two jurisdictions (Idaho and South Dakota) that clearly take the contrary view. *Id.* at 1150–51. However, since the annotation was published several other states have adopted the view that estoppel may be available under certain circumstances.

---

7. It cannot be seriously contended, for instance, that airline companies, car rental agencies, and the like expect their customers to line up, demand copies of the various instruments which set forth the "contract" and require explanations of the various terms. The usual "contract" for air transportation provides an example; it begins as follows:

Conditions of Contract

As used in this contract "ticket" means this passenger ticket and baggage check, of which these conditions and the notices form part, "carriage" is equivalent to "transportation", "carrier" means all air carriers that carry or undertake to carry the passenger or his baggage hereunder or perform any other service incidental to such air carriage, "Warsaw Convention" means the convention for the unification of certain rules relating to international carriage by air signed at Warsaw, 12th of October, 1929, or that convention as amended at the Hague, 28th September, 1955, whichever may be applicable.

Uniform Passenger Ticket and Baggage Check, ATC version, printed on the back of the standard form of ticket in general use by airlines in the United States. Fortunately, we have not yet been required to interpret this contract by conjuring up some supposed intent of the passenger.

Harr v. Allstate Insurance Co., 54 N.J. 287, 255 A.2d 208 (1969); *King v. Travelers Ins. Co.,* 84 N.M. 550, 505 P.2d 1226 (1973); *Hunter v. Farmers Insurance Group,* 554 P.2d 1239, 1243 (Wyo.1976).

. . . The "majority rule" is eroding. *See* 16C Appleman, *supra,* § 9166 at 153–58, § 9167 at 162–65 (1981). Given our view of contract theory and the policy considerations in *Sparks* and *Zuckerman,* there are strong reasons to recognize a rule which allows an insured to raise the issue of estoppel to establish coverage contrary to the limitations in the boiler-plate policy when the insurer's agent had represented the coverage as greater than the language found in the printed policy. The fact that the insured has not read the insurance policy "word for word" is not, as a matter of law, an absolute bar to his theory of estoppel. *See Northwestern National Ins. Co. v. Chambers,* 24 Ariz. 86, 94, 206 P. 1081, 1084 (1922) (disapproving of the rule of *caveat emptor* in insurance transactions). It is for the trier of fact to determine whether, under circumstances such as this, the appellant had a duty to read. *Heiner,* 74 Ariz. at 156, 245 P.2d at 418. *See generally,* Macaulay, *Private Legislation and the Duty to Read—Business Run by IBM Machine, the Law of Contracts and Credit Cards,* 19 Vand.L.Rev. 1051, 1051–69 (1966).

The facts of the case at bench are within the exception to interpretation contained in subsection (3) to *Restatement (Second) of Contracts,* § 211. The coverage limits for lessees were separately negotiated. The standard boiler-plate definition of the word "insured", excluding lessees, was not bargained for, not written by and not read by the parties. It need not be allowed to "undercut the dickered deal." We therefore adopt the rationale of the New Jersey Supreme Court in *Harr*[8] and recognize equitable estoppel as a device to prevent enforcement of those boiler-plate terms of the insurance contract which are more limited than the coverage expressly agreed upon by the parties. As applied to this case, the rule adopted means simply that if the fact finder determines that Darner and Doxsee did agree upon lessee's coverage in limits of 100/300, and if, by justifiably relying on Doxsee's assurances or for some other justifiable reason, Darner was unaware of the limitation in the umbrella policy, Universal would be estopped to assert the definitional exclusion which eliminates Darner's lessee from the class of persons insured. Thus, we do not limit the assertion of estoppel by the insured to cases in which an insurance policy has not been delivered prior to the loss. Since the parol evidence rule does not necessarily prevent establishing the true agreement, estoppel may apply where, from the nature of the transaction, the fact finder is able to determine that the insured acted reasonably in not reading the particular provision of the policy.[9]

---

8. . . . where an insurer or its agent misrepresents, even though innocently, the coverage of an insurance contract or the exclusions therefrom, to an insured before or at the inception of the contract, and the insured reasonably relies thereupon to his ultimate detriment, the insurer is estopped to deny coverage after a loss on a risk or from a peril actually not covered by the terms of the policy. The proposition is one of elementary and simple justice. By justifiably relying on the insurer's superior knowledge, the insured has been prevented from procuring the desired coverage elsewhere. To reject this approach because a new contract is thereby made for the parties would be an unfortunate triumph of form over substance. . . .

9. The jury could find, for instance, that the insured acted reasonably in failing to read standard boilerplate which defined insured—particularly in view of Doxsee's assurances regarding the limits. On the other hand, if the limit problem is clearly disclosed in the declaration page, and Darner also failed to read that, the fact finder might find that estoppel was not applicable under the principles of § 211. The key question is whether the clause or provision was one bargained for and agreed upon, in which case it is enforced as written

Reformation

"Where reformation is sought because of the mistake of one party only, it is essential that fraud or inequitable conduct be found in the other." *Korrick v. Tuller,* 42 Ariz. 493, 498, 27 P.2d 529, 531 (1933). "Inequitable conduct which would justify reformation when there is unilateral mistake takes the form of knowledge on the part of one party of the other's mistake." *Isaak v. Massachusetts Indemnity Life Ins. Co.,* 127 Ariz. at 584, 623 P.2d at 14. "Ordinarily, the terms of the policy should control, although the statement of an agent well may ground an action for reformation." 16C Appleman, *supra,* § 9167 at 165. Moreover, one whose inequitable conduct has caused the instrument to be "accepted with provisions at variance with the true agreement may not set up the other party's negligence in failing to read the instrument. * * *" *Lane v. Mathews,* 75 Ariz. 1, 5, 251 P.2d 303 (1952) (quoting 76 C.J.S., Reformation of Instruments, § 46 at 400).

According to Universal, Darner was simply mistaken about the extent of coverage under his umbrella policy. Darner avers that, if so, this resulted from Doxsee's failure to properly explain the terms of the policy. There is no dispute that Darner told Doxsee he was concerned about having only 15/30 coverage for lessees. There is clearly a factual dispute regarding Doxsee's appreciation of Darner's concern. Arguably, Doxsee had knowledge of Darner's "mistaken" understanding of the agreement. Thus it may be that "the true contract of insurance in this case ... arose out of the oral agreement between the parties and not that as evidenced by the written policy." *Ranger Insurance Co. v. Phillips,* 25 Ariz.App. 426, 430, 544 P.2d 250, 254 (1976); *See also A.I.D. Ins. Services v. Riley,* 25 Ariz.App. 132, 135, 541 P.2d 595, 598 (1975).

The same disputed material facts which demand trial on the merits regarding the estoppel remedy can also be marshalled under the reformation theory. Under the provisions of *Restatement (Second) of Contracts,* § 211 the form provisions at variance with the bargained deal or contrary to the dominant purpose of the transaction are "not part of the agreement." They should be eliminated, so that the bargains made will be realized. The written agreement may be reformed to state the true agreement. Accordingly, summary judgment on reformation was error.

[As to Darner's negligence theory, the court held that an insurance agent owes a duty to the insured to exercise reasonable care, skill, and prudence in procuring insurance; that whether the insured's not reading the policies constitutes contributory negligence turns on the reasonableness of not reading the policies and relying on the agent's statements; and that the issue was one for the trier of fact. As to Darner's fraud theory, the court held that it could not say that the allegations on which the fraud count was based were wholly without merit.]

For the foregoing reasons we vacate the decision of the court of appeals and reverse the trial court's summary judgment as to the counts of equitable estoppel, reformation of the contract, negligent misrepresentation and fraud. Because of this disposition of the substantive matters, the court of appeals' award of attorney's fees is vacated.

and interpreted, or whether it was part of the standardized form which the customer would not ordinarily be expected to read, in which case it would be enforced as written, subject to the constraints and limitations of § 211.

GORDON, V.C.J., and HAYS, J., concur.

[The concurring opinion of Cameron, J., and the dissenting opinion of Holohan, C.J., are omitted.]

———

GORDINIER v. AETNA CASUALTY & SURETY CO., 154 Ariz. 266, 742 P.2d 277 (1987). The Arizona Court here elaborated on *Darner* as follows: " . . . As a synthesis of the cases and authorities demonstrates, Arizona courts will not enforce even unambiguous boilerplate terms in standardized insurance contracts in a *limited* variety of situations:

"1. Where the contract terms, although not ambiguous to the court, cannot be understood by the reasonably intelligent consumer who might check on his or her rights, the court will interpret them in light of the objective, reasonable expectations of the average insured (*see* . . . *Wainscott v. Ossenkop,* 633 P.2d 237 (Alaska 1981) (application of "resident of same household" definition, while not technically ambiguous, defeats reasonable expectations of spouse));

"2. Where the insured did not receive full and adequate notice of the term in question, and the provision is either unusual or unexpected, or one that emasculates apparent coverage . . . ;

"3. Where some activity which can be reasonably attributed to the insurer would create an objective impression of coverage in the mind of a reasonable insured . . . ;

"4. Where some activity reasonably attributable to the insurer has induced a particular insured reasonably to believe that he has coverage, although such coverage is expressly and unambiguously denied by the policy. . . .

———

FARM BUREAU MUTUAL INSURANCE CO. v. SANDBULTE, 302 N.W.2d 104 (Iowa 1981). "The rationale of the reasonable expectation doctrine is that, in a contract of adhesion, such as an insurance policy, form must not be exalted over substance, and that the reasonable expectations of the insured may not be frustrated 'even though painstaking study of the policy provisions would have negated those expectations.' Rodman v. State Farm Mutual Insurance Co., 208 N.W.2d at 906 (quoting Keeton, Insurance Law— Basic Text § 6.3(a), at 351 (1971)); *see also* C & J Fertilizer, Inc., 227 N.W.2d at 176–77. Reasonable expectations giving rise to application of the doctrine may be established by proof of the underlying negotiations or inferred from the circumstances. Restatement (Second) of Contracts § 237, at 541 (comment f). The doctrine will apply here if the exclusion (1) is bizarre or oppressive, (2) eviscerates terms explicitly agreed to, or (3) eliminates the dominant purpose of the transaction. *Id.* The doctrine is well illustrated by C & J Fertilizer: Under the terms of a burglary policy the insurer agreed '[t]o pay for loss by burglary or by robbery of a watchman, while the premises are not open for business. . . .' In the definition section of the policy, however, burglary was defined in such a way as to exclude any occurrence which was not evidenced by marks left on the exterior of the premises. This definition was not consistent with a layman's concept of the crime, nor with its legal interpretation. In effect, the definition overrode the dominant purpose for purchasing the policy and in effect eviscerated the coverage specifically bargained for, protecting against burglary. 227 N.W.2d at 176–77.''

Part V

MISTAKE AND UNEXPECTED CIRCUMSTANCES

Chapter 18

MISTAKE

Suppose that A and B enter into a contract that is either based on or reflects some kind of mistake made by A, or by A and B jointly. After the mistake is discovered, A claims that because of the mistake the contract should either be unenforceable, if it has not been performed, or reversible, if it has been.

The problems raised by claims of this kind have been a source of persistent difficulty in contract law. In part this difficulty results from the complex nature of the underlying issues. Intuitively, there seems to be a serious tension between the concept that a mistake may be a ground for relief in contractual transactions, on the one hand, and such basic ideas of contract law as risk-shifting, the security of transactions, and rewards for knowledge, skill, and diligence, on the other. Much of the difficulty, however, results from the use of legal categories and doctrinal rules that are not based on a functional analysis.

Traditionally, the subject of mistake in contract law has been divided into four categories: misunderstanding, mutual mistake, unilateral mistake, and mistake in transcription. These names are somewhat misleading, because often they are not descriptive of the kind of mistake cases that normally fall within each category. Despite the somewhat misleading nature of the names of these categories, they will be used as Section headings in this Chapter. In part, this is because the names of the categories are traditional. Another reason is that the traditional *categories* are functional, even if their names are not. The cases in each traditional category concern a different kind of mistake, even though the kind of mistake each category concerns may not be the kind described in the category's title.

This Chapter will consider four types of mistake: mechanical errors, mistranscriptions, shared mistaken factual assumptions, and unshared mistaken factual assumptions. ("Misunderstanding" cases have been considered in Chapter 9, Section 1, supra.)

SECTION 1. UNILATERAL MISTAKES (MECHANICAL ERRORS)

A common kind of mistake in everyday life consists of physical blunders, like spilling coffee. This kind of mistake, although manifested externally, normally results from an error in the mechanics of an actor's internal machinery, such as a lapse of concentration, a loss of balance, or an error in hand-eye coordination. Such errors are almost invariably transient. If an actor spilled every cup of coffee he handled, we would not characterize his spills as mistakes, but instead would conclude that he had a disability.

A counterpart to transient physical blunders consists of intellectual blunders that result from transient errors in the mechanics of an actor's internal machinery. For example, as a result of a transient error in the mechanics of an actor's mental machinery, the actor may write "65" when he intends to write "56" or may incorrectly add a column of figures.

Mistakes of this kind—that is, physical or intellectual blunders that result from transient errors in the mechanics of an actor's internal machinery—may be thought of as *mechanical errors*. Mechanical errors resemble the kind of mistake sometimes made in the transcription of DNA. Almost invariably, that transcription is correct. Every once in a while, it goes transiently awry.

Although contract law does not use the term "mechanical errors," in fact virtually all cases that are categorized as involving "unilateral mistakes" are essentially mechanical-error cases.

DONOVAN v. RRL CORP.

Supreme Court of California, 2001.
26 Cal.4th 261, 109 Cal.Rptr.2d 807, 27 P.3d 702.

GEORGE, C.J.

Defendant RRL Corporation is an automobile dealer doing business under the name Lexus of Westminster. Because of typographical and proofreading errors made by a local newspaper, defendant's advertisement listed a price for a used automobile that was significantly less than the intended sales price. Plaintiff Brian J. Donovan read the advertisement and, after examining the vehicle, attempted to purchase it by tendering the advertised price. Defendant refused to sell the automobile to plaintiff at that price, and plaintiff brought this action against defendant for breach of contract. The municipal court entered judgment for defendant on the ground that the mistake in the advertisement precluded the existence of a contract. The appellate department of the superior court and the Court of Appeal reversed, relying in part upon Vehicle Code section 11713.1, subdivision (e), which makes it unlawful for an automobile dealer not to sell a motor vehicle at the advertised price while the vehicle remains unsold and before the advertisement expires.

We conclude that a contract satisfying the statute of frauds arose from defendant's advertisement and plaintiff's tender of the advertised price, but that defendant's unilateral mistake of fact provides a basis for rescinding the contract. Although Vehicle Code section 11713.1, subdivision (e), justifies a reasonable expectation on the part of consumers that an automobile dealer intends that such an advertisement constitute an offer, and that the offer can be accepted by paying the advertised price, this statute does not supplant governing common law principles authorizing rescission of a contract on the ground of mistake. As we shall explain, rescission is warranted here because the evidence establishes that defendant's unilateral mistake of fact was made in good faith, defendant did not bear the risk of the mistake, and enforcement of the contract with the erroneous price would be unconscionable. Accordingly, we shall reverse the judgment of the Court of Appeal.

I

While reading the April 26, 1997, edition of the Costa Mesa Daily Pilot, a local newspaper, plaintiff noticed a full-page advertisement placed by defendant. The advertisement promoted a "PRE–OWNED COUP–A–RAMA SALE!/ 2–DAY PRE–OWNED SALES EVENT" and listed, along with 15 other used automobiles, a 1995 Jaguar XJ6 Vanden Plas. The advertisement described the color of this automobile as sapphire blue, included a vehicle identification number, and stated a price of $25,995. The name Lexus of Westminster was displayed prominently in three separate locations in the advertisement, which included defendant's address along with a small map showing the location of the dealership. The following statements appeared in small print at the bottom of the advertisement: "All cars plus tax, lic., doc., smog & bank fees. On approved credit. Ad expires 4/27/97[.]"

Also on April 26, 1997, plaintiff visited a Jaguar dealership that offered other 1995 Jaguars for sale at $8,000 to $10,000 more than the price specified in defendant's advertisement. The following day, plaintiff and his spouse drove to Lexus of Westminster and observed a blue Jaguar displayed on an elevated ramp. After verifying that the identification number on the sticker was the same as that listed in defendant's April 26 Daily Pilot advertisement, they asked a salesperson whether they could test drive the Jaguar. Plaintiff mentioned that he had seen the advertisement and that the price "looked really good." The salesperson responded that, as a Lexus dealer, defendant might offer better prices for a Jaguar automobile than would a Jaguar dealer. At that point, however, neither plaintiff nor the salesperson mentioned the specific advertised price.

After the test drive, plaintiff and his spouse discussed several negative characteristics of the automobile, including high mileage, an apparent rust problem, and worn tires. In addition, it was not as clean as the other Jaguars they had inspected. Despite these problems, they believed that the advertised price was a very good price and decided to purchase the vehicle. Plaintiff told the salesperson, "Okay. We will take it at your price, $26,000." When the salesperson did not respond, plaintiff showed him the advertisement. The salesperson immediately stated, "That's a mistake."

After plaintiff asked to speak with an individual in charge, defendant's sales manager also told plaintiff that the price listed in the advertisement was a mistake. The sales manager apologized and offered to pay for plaintiff's fuel, time, and effort expended in traveling to the dealership to examine the automobile. Plaintiff declined this offer and expressed his belief that there had been no mistake. Plaintiff stated that he could write a check for the full purchase price as advertised. The sales manager responded that he would not sell the vehicle at the advertised price. Plaintiff then requested the sales price. After performing some calculations, and based upon defendant's $35,000 investment in the automobile, the sales manager stated that he would sell it to plaintiff for $37,016. Plaintiff responded, "No, I want to buy it at your advertised price, and I will write you a check right now." The sales manager again stated that he would not sell the vehicle at the advertised price, and plaintiff and his spouse left the dealership.

Plaintiff subsequently filed this action against defendant for breach of contract, fraud, and negligence. In addition to testimony consistent with the facts set forth above, the following evidence was presented to the municipal court, which acted as the trier of fact.

Defendant's advertising manager compiles information for placement in advertisements in several local newspapers, including the Costa Mesa Daily Pilot. Defendant's advertisement published in the Saturday, April 19, 1997, edition of the Daily Pilot listed a 1995 Jaguar XJ6 Vanden Plas but did not specify a price for that automobile; instead, the word "Save" appeared in the space where a price ordinarily would have appeared. The following Thursday afternoon, defendant's sales manager instructed the advertising manager to delete the 1995 Jaguar from all advertisements and to substitute a 1994 Jaguar XJ6 with a price of $25,995. The advertising manager conveyed the new information to a representative of the Daily Pilot that same afternoon.

Because of typographical and proofreading errors made by employees of the Daily Pilot, however, the newspaper did not replace the description of the 1995 Jaguar with the description of the 1994 Jaguar, but did replace the word "Save" with the price of $25,995. Thus, the Saturday, April 26, edition of the Daily Pilot erroneously advertised the 1995 Jaguar XJ6 Vanden Plas at a price of $25,995. The Daily Pilot acknowledged its error in a letter of retraction sent to defendant on April 28. No employee of defendant reviewed a proof sheet of the revised Daily Pilot advertisement before it was published, and defendant was unaware of the mistake until plaintiff attempted to purchase the automobile.

Except for the 1995 Jaguar XJ6 Vanden Plas, defendant intended to sell each vehicle appearing in the April 26, 1997, Daily Pilot advertisement at the advertised price. Defendant's advertisements in the April 26 editions of several other newspapers correctly listed the *1994* Jaguar XJ6 with a price of $25,995. In May 1997, defendant's advertisements in several newspapers listed the 1995 Jaguar XJ6 Vanden Plas for sale at $37,995. Defendant subsequently sold the automobile for $38,399.

The municipal court entered judgment for defendant. During the trial, the court ruled that plaintiff had not stated a cause of action for negligence, and it precluded plaintiff from presenting evidence in support of such a claim. After the close of evidence and presentation of argument, the municipal court concluded as a matter of law that a newspaper advertisement for an automobile generally constitutes a valid contractual offer that a customer may accept by tendering payment of the advertised price. The court also determined that such an advertisement satisfies the requirements of the statute of frauds when the dealer's name appears in the advertisement. Nevertheless, the municipal court held that in the present case there was no valid offer because defendant's unilateral mistake of fact vitiated or negated contractual intent.

The court made factual findings that defendant's mistake regarding the advertisement was made in good faith and was not intended to deceive the public. The municipal court also found that plaintiff was unaware of the mistake before it was disclosed to him by defendant's representatives....

[T]he Court of Appeal reversed the judgment of the municipal court and held that defendant's advertisement constituted a contractual offer that invited acceptance by the act of tendering the advertised price, which plaintiff performed. Acknowledging that the question was close, ... the Court of Appeal reasoned that Vehicle Code section 11713.1, subdivision (e), "tips the scale in favor of ... construing the advertisement as an offer...." The court disagreed with the municipal court's conclusion that defendant's unilateral mistake of fact, unknown to plaintiff at the time he tendered the purchase price, precluded the existence of a valid offer. With regard to the contention that defendant should not bear the risk of an error resulting solely from the negligence of the newspaper, the Court of Appeal made a factual finding based upon the appellate record (Code Civ. Proc., § 909) that defendant's failure to review a proof sheet for the Daily Pilot advertisement constituted negligence that contributed to the placement of the erroneous advertisement.

We granted defendant's petition for review...

IV

[The court first concluded that defendant's advertisement for the sale of the Jaguar automobile constituted an offer that was accepted by plaintiff's tender of the advertised price (this portion of the case is set out in Chapter 10, Section 1, supra), and that the resulting contract satisfied the statute of frauds.]

[W]e next consider whether defendant can avoid enforcement of the contract on the ground of mistake....

A party may rescind a contract if his or her consent was given by mistake. (Civ.Code, § 1689, subd. (b)(1).) A factual mistake by one party to a contract, or unilateral mistake, affords a ground for rescission in some circumstances. Civil Code section 1577 states in relevant part: "Mistake of fact is a mistake, not caused by the neglect of a legal duty on the part of the person making the mistake, and consisting in: [¶] 1. An unconscious ignorance or forgetfulness of a fact past or present, material to the contract...."....

Under the first Restatement of Contracts, unilateral mistake did not render a contract voidable unless the other party knew of or caused the mistake. (1 Witkin, ... Contracts, § 370, p. 337; see Rest., Contracts, § 503.) In *Germain etc. Co. v. Western Union etc. Co.* (1902) 137 Cal. 598, 602, 70 P. 658, this court endorsed a rule similar to that of the first Restatement. Our opinion indicated that a seller's price quotation erroneously transcribed and delivered by a telegraph company contractually could bind the seller to the incorrect price, unless the buyer knew or had reason to suspect that a mistake had been made. Some decisions of the Court of Appeal have adhered to the approach of the original Restatement. (See, e.g., *Conservatorship of O'Connor* (1996) 48 Cal.App.4th 1076, 1097–1098, 56 Cal.Rptr.2d 386, and cases cited therein.) Plaintiff also advocates this approach and contends that rescission is unavailable to defendant, because plaintiff was unaware of the mistaken price in defendant's advertisement when he accepted the offer.

The Court of Appeal decisions reciting the traditional rule do not recognize that in *M.F. Kemper Const. Co. v. City of L.A.* (1951) 37 Cal.2d 696, 701, 235 P.2d 7 (*Kemper*), we acknowledged but rejected a strict application of the foregoing Restatement rule regarding unilateral mistake of fact. The plaintiff in *Kemper* inadvertently omitted a $301,769 item from its bid for the defendant city's public works project—approximately one-third of the total contract price. After discovering the mistake several hours later, the plaintiff immediately notified the city and subsequently withdrew its bid. Nevertheless, the city accepted the erroneous bid, contending that rescission of the offer was unavailable for the plaintiff's unilateral mistake.

Our decision in *Kemper* recognized that the bid, when opened and announced, resulted in an irrevocable option contract conferring upon the city a right to accept the bid, and that the plaintiff could not withdraw its bid unless the requirements for rescission of this option contract were satisfied. (*Kemper, supra,* 37 Cal.2d at pp. 700, 704, 235 P.2d 7.) We stated: "Rescission may be had for mistake of fact if the mistake is material to the contract and was not the result of neglect of a legal duty, if enforcement of the contract as made would be unconscionable, and if the other party can be placed in statu quo. [Citations.]" (*Id.* at p. 701, 235 P.2d 7.) Although the city knew of the plaintiff's mistake before it accepted the bid, and this circumstance was relevant to our determination that requiring the plaintiff to perform at the mistaken bid price would be unconscionable (*id.* at pp. 702–703, 235 P.2d 7), we authorized rescission of the city's option contract even though the city had not known of or contributed to the mistake before it opened the bid.

Similarly, in *Elsinore Union etc. Sch. Dist. v. Kastorff* (1960) 54 Cal.2d 380, 6 Cal.Rptr. 1, 353 P.2d 713 (*Elsinore*), we authorized the rescission of an erroneous bid even where the contractor had assured the public agency, after the agency inquired, that his figures were accurate, and where the agency already had accepted the bid before it was aware of the mistake. In this situation, the other party clearly had no reason to know of the contractor's mistake before it accepted the bid.

The decisions in *Kemper* and *Elsinore* establish that California law does not adhere to the original Restatement's requirements for rescission based upon unilateral mistake of fact—i.e., only in circumstances where the other party knew of the mistake or caused the mistake. Consistent with the decisions in *Kemper* and *Elsinore,* the Restatement Second of Contracts authorizes rescission for a unilateral mistake of fact where "the effect of the mistake is such that enforcement of the contract would be unconscionable." (Rest.2d Contracts, § 153, subd. (a).)[6] The comment following this section recognizes "a growing willingness to allow avoidance where the consequences of the mistake are so grave that enforcement of the contract would be unconscionable." (*Id.,* com. a, p. 394.) Indeed, two of the illustrations recognizing this additional ground for rescission in the Restatement Second of Contracts are based in part upon this court's decisions in *Kemper* and *Elsinore.* (Rest.2d Contracts, § 153, com. c, illus. 1, 3, pp. 395, 396, and

---

6. Section 153 of the Restatement Second of Contracts states: "Where a mistake of one party at the time a contract was made as to a basic assumption on which he made the contract has a material effect on the agreed exchange of performances that is adverse to him, the contract is voidable by him if he does not bear the risk of the mistake under the rule stated in § 154, and [¶] (a) the effect of the mistake is such that enforcement of the contract would be unconscionable, or [¶] (b) the other party had reason to know of the mistake or his fault caused the mistake."

Reporter's Note, pp. 400–401.... Although the most common types of mistakes falling within this category occur in bids on construction contracts, section 153 of the Restatement Second of Contracts is not limited to such cases. (Rest.2d Contracts, § 153, com. b, p. 395.)

Because the rule in section 153, subdivision (a), of the Restatement Second of Contracts, authorizing rescission for unilateral mistake of fact where enforcement would be unconscionable, is consistent with our previous decisions, we adopt the rule as California law. As the author of one treatise recognized more than 40 years ago, the decisions that are inconsistent with the traditional rule "are too numerous and too appealing to the sense of justice to be disregarded." (3 Corbin, Contracts (1960) § 608, p. 675, fn. omitted.) We reject plaintiff's contention and the Court of Appeal's conclusion that, because plaintiff was unaware of defendant's unilateral mistake, the mistake does not provide a ground to avoid enforcement of the contract.

Having concluded that a contract properly may be rescinded on the ground of unilateral mistake of fact as set forth in section 153, subdivision (a), of the Restatement Second of Contracts, we next consider whether the requirements of that provision, construed in light of our previous decisions, are satisfied in the present case. Where the plaintiff has no reason to know of and does not cause the defendant's unilateral mistake of fact, the defendant must establish the following facts to obtain rescission of the contract: (1) the defendant made a mistake regarding a basic assumption upon which the defendant made the contract; (2) the mistake has a material effect upon the agreed exchange of performances that is adverse to the defendant; (3) the defendant does not bear the risk of the mistake; and (4) the effect of the mistake is such that enforcement of the contract would be unconscionable. We shall consider each of these requirements below.

A significant error in the price term of a contract constitutes a mistake regarding a basic assumption upon which the contract is made, and such a mistake ordinarily has a material effect adverse to the mistaken party. (See, e.g., *Elsinore, supra,* 54 Cal.2d at p. 389, 6 Cal.Rptr. 1, 353 P.2d 713 [7 percent error in contract price]; *Lemoge Electric v. County of San Mateo* (1956) 46 Cal.2d 659, 661–662, 297 P.2d 638 [6 percent error]; *Kemper, supra,* 37 Cal.2d at p. 702, 235 P.2d 7 [28 percent error]; *Brunzell Const. Co. v. G.J. Weisbrod, Inc.* (1955) 134 Cal.App.2d 278, 286, 285 P.2d 989 [20 percent error]; Rest.2d Contracts, § 152, com. b, illus. 3, p. 387 [27 percent error].) In establishing a material mistake regarding a basic assumption of the contract, the defendant must show that the resulting imbalance in the agreed exchange is so severe that it would be unfair to require the defendant to perform. (Rest.2d Contracts, § 152, com. c, p. 388.) Ordinarily, a defendant can satisfy this requirement by showing that the exchange not only is less desirable for the defendant, but also is more advantageous to the other party. (*Ibid.*)

Measured against this standard, defendant's mistake in the contract for the sale of the Jaguar automobile constitutes a material mistake regarding a basic assumption upon which it made the contract. Enforcing the contract with the mistaken price of $25,995 would require defendant to sell the vehicle to plaintiff for $12,000 less than the intended advertised price of $37,995—an error amounting to 32 percent of the price defendant intended. The exchange of performances would be substantially less desirable for defendant and more desirable for plaintiff. Plaintiff implicitly concedes that defendant's mistake was material.

The parties and amici curiae vigorously dispute, however, whether defendant should bear the risk of its mistake. Section 154 of the Restatement Second of Contracts states: "A party bears the risk of a mistake when [¶] (a) the risk is allocated to him by agreement of the parties, or [¶] (b) he is aware, at the time the contract is made, that he has only limited knowledge with respect to the facts to which the mistake relates but treats his limited knowledge as sufficient, or [¶] (c) the risk is allocated to him by the court on the ground that it is reasonable in the circumstances to do so." Neither of the first two factors applies here. Thus, we must determine whether it is reasonable under the circumstances to allocate to defendant the risk of the mistake in the advertisement.

Civil Code section 1577, as well as our prior decisions, instructs that the risk of a mistake must be allocated to a party where the mistake results from that party's neglect of a legal duty. (*Kemper, supra,* 37 Cal.2d at p. 701, 235 P.2d 7.) It is well established, however, that ordinary negligence does not constitute neglect of a legal duty within the meaning of Civil Code section 1577. (*Kemper, supra,* 37 Cal.2d at p. 702, 235 P.2d 7.) For example, we have described a careless but significant mistake in the computation of the contract price as the type of error that sometimes will occur in the conduct of reasonable and cautious businesspersons, and such an error does not necessarily amount to neglect of legal duty that would bar equitable relief. (*Ibid.;* see also *Sun 'n Sand, Inc. v. United California Bank* (1978) 21 Cal.3d 671, 700–701, 148 Cal.Rptr. 329, 582 P.2d 920 (plur. opn. of Mosk, J.); *Elsinore, supra,* 54 Cal.2d at pp. 388–389, 6 Cal.Rptr. 1, 353 P.2d 713.)

A concept similar to neglect of a legal duty is described in section 157 of the Restatement Second of Contracts, which addresses situations in which a party's fault precludes relief for mistake. Only where the mistake results from "a failure to act in good faith and in accordance with reasonable standards of fair dealing" is rescission unavailable. (Rest.2d Contracts, § 157.) This section, consistent with the California decisions cited in the preceding paragraph, provides that a mistaken party's failure to exercise due care does not necessarily bar rescission under the rule set forth in section 153.

"The mere fact that a mistaken party could have avoided the mistake by the exercise of reasonable care does not preclude ... avoidance ... [on the ground of mistake]. Indeed, since a party can often avoid a mistake by the exercise of such care, the availability of relief would be severely circumscribed if he were to be barred by his negligence. Nevertheless, in *extreme cases* the mistaken party's fault is a proper ground for denying him relief for a mistake that he otherwise could have avoided.... [T]he rule is stated in terms of good faith and fair dealing.... [A] failure to act in good faith and in accordance with reasonable standards of fair dealing during pre-contractual negotiations does not amount to a breach. Nevertheless, under the rule stated in this Section, the failure bars a mistaken party from relief based on a mistake that otherwise would not have been made. During the negotiation stage each party is held to a degree of responsibility appropriate to the justifiable expectations of the other. The terms 'good faith' and 'fair dealing' are used, in this context, in much the same sense as in ... Uniform Commercial Code § 1–203." (Rest.2d Contracts, § 157, com. a, pp. 416–417, italics added.) Section 1201, subdivision (19), of the California Uniform Commercial Code defines "good faith," as used in section 1203 of that code, as "honesty in fact in the conduct or transaction concerned." . . .

[The municipal court made an express finding of fact that "the mistake on the part of [defendant] was made in good faith[;] it was an honest mistake, not intended to deceive the public. . . ." The Court of Appeal correctly recognized that "[w]e must, of course, accept the trial court's finding that there was a 'good faith' mistake that caused the error in the advertisement." The evidence presented at trial compellingly supports this finding.]

Defendant regularly advertises in five local newspapers. Defendant's advertising manager, Crystal Wadsworth, testified that ordinarily she meets with Kristen Berman, a representative of the Daily Pilot, on Tuesdays, Wednesdays, and Thursdays to review proof sheets of the advertisement that will appear in the newspaper the following weekend. When Wadsworth met with Berman on Wednesday, April 23, 1997, defendant's proposed advertisement listed a 1995 Jaguar XJ6 Vanden Plas without specifying a price, as it had the preceding week. On Thursday, April 24, a sales manager instructed Wadsworth to substitute a 1994 Jaguar XJ6 with a price of $25,995. The same day, Wadsworth met with Berman and conveyed to her this new information. Wadsworth did not expect to see another proof sheet reflecting this change, however, because she does not work on Friday, and the Daily Pilot goes to press on Friday and the edition in question came out on Saturday, April 26.

Berman testified that the revised advertisement was prepared by the composing department of the Daily Pilot. Berman proofread the advertisement, as she does all advertisements for which she is responsible, but Berman did not notice that it listed the 1995 Jaguar XJ6 Vanden Plas for sale at $25,995, instead of listing the 1994 Jaguar at that price. Both Berman and Wadsworth first learned of the mistake on Monday, April 28, 1997. Defendant's sales manager first became aware of the mistake after plaintiff attempted to purchase the automobile on Sunday, April 27. Berman confirmed in a letter of retraction that Berman's proofreading error had led to the mistake in the advertisement.

Defendant's erroneous advertisement in the Daily Pilot listed 16 used automobiles for sale. Each of the advertisements prepared for several newspapers in late April 1997, except for the one in the Daily Pilot, correctly identified the 1994 Jaguar XJ6 for sale at a price of $25,995. In May 1997, defendant's advertisements in several newspapers listed the 1995 Jaguar XJ6 Vanden Plas for sale at $37,995, and defendant subsequently sold the automobile for $38,399. Defendant had paid $35,000 for the vehicle.

Evidence at trial established that defendant adheres to the following procedures when an incorrect advertisement is discovered. Defendant immediately contacts the newspaper and requests a letter of retraction. Copies of any erroneous advertisements are provided to the sales staff, the error is explained to them, and the mistake is circled in red and posted on a bulletin board at the dealership. The sales staff informs customers of any advertising errors of which they are aware.

No evidence presented at trial suggested that defendant knew of the mistake before plaintiff attempted to purchase the automobile, that defendant intended to mislead customers, or that it had adopted a practice of deliberate indifference regarding errors in advertisements. Wadsworth regularly reviews proof sheets for the numerous advertisements placed by defendant, and representatives of the newspapers, including the Daily Pilot, also proofread defendant's advertisements to ensure they are accurate. Defendant follows procedures for notifying its sales staff and customers of errors of which it becomes aware. The uncontradicted evidence established that the Daily Pilot made the proofreading error resulting in defendant's mistake.

Defendant's fault consisted of failing to review a proof sheet reflecting the change made on Thursday, April 24, 1997, and/or the actual advertisement appearing in the April 26 edition of the Daily Pilot—choosing instead to rely upon the Daily Pilot's advertising staff to proofread the revised version. Although, as the Court of Appeal found, such an omission might constitute negligence, it does not involve a breach of defendant's duty of good faith and fair dealing that should preclude equitable relief for mistake. In these circumstances, it would not be reasonable for this court to allocate the risk of the mistake to defendant.

As indicated above, the Restatement Second of Contracts provides that during the negotiation stage of a contract "each party is held to a degree of responsibility appropriate to the justifiable expectations of the other." (Rest.2d Contracts, § 157, com. a, p. 417.) No consumer reasonably can expect 100 percent accuracy in each and every price appearing in countless automobile advertisements listing numerous vehicles for sale. The degree of responsibility plaintiff asks this court to impose upon automobile dealers would amount to strict contract liability for any typographical error in the price of an advertised automobile, no matter how serious the error or how blameless the dealer. We are unaware of any other situation in which an individual or business is held to such a standard under the law of contracts. Defendant's good faith, isolated mistake does not constitute the type of extreme case in which its fault constitutes the neglect of a legal duty that bars equitable relief. Therefore, . . . defendant's conduct in the present case does not preclude rescission.

The final factor defendant must establish before obtaining rescission based upon mistake is that enforcement of the contract for the sale of the 1995 Jaguar XJ6 Vanden Plas at $25,995 would be unconscionable. Although the standards of unconscionability warranting rescission for mistake are similar to those for unconscionability justifying a court's refusal to enforce a contract or term, the general rule governing the latter situation (Civ.Code, § 1670.5) is inapplicable here, because unconscionability resulting from mistake does not appear at the time the contract is made. (Rest.2d Contracts, § 153, com. c, p. 395; 1 Witkin, *supra,* Contracts, § 370, pp. 337–338.)

An unconscionable contract ordinarily involves both a procedural and a substantive element: (1) oppression or surprise due to unequal bargaining power, and (2) overly harsh or one-sided results. (*Armendariz v. Foundation Health Psychcare Services, Inc.* (2000) 24 Cal.4th 83, 114, 99 Cal.Rptr.2d 745, 6 P.3d 669.) Nevertheless, " 'a sliding scale is invoked which disregards the regularity of the procedural process of the contract formation, that creates the terms, in proportion to the greater harshness or unreasonableness of the substantive terms themselves.' [Citations.]" (*Ibid.*) For example, the Restatement Second of Contracts states that "[i]nadequacy of consideration does not of itself invalidate a bargain, but gross disparity in the values exchanged may be an important factor in a determination that a contract is unconscionable and may be sufficient ground, without more, for denying specific performance." (Rest.2d Contracts, § 208, com. c, p. 108.) In ascertaining whether rescission is warranted for a unilateral mistake of fact, substantive unconscionability often will constitute the determinative factor, because the oppression and surprise ordinarily results from the mistake—not from inequality in bargaining power. Accordingly, even though defendant is not the weaker party to the contract and its mistake did not result from unequal bargaining power, defendant was surprised by the mistake, and in these circumstances overly harsh or one-sided results are sufficient to establish unconscionability entitling defendant to rescission.

Our previous cases support this approach. In *Kemper, supra,* 37 Cal.2d 696, 235 P.2d 7, we held that enforcement of the city's option to accept a construction company's bid, which was 28 percent less than the intended bid, would be unconscionable. Our decision reasoned that (1) the plaintiff gave prompt notice upon discovering the facts entitling it to rescind, (2) the city therefore was aware of the clerical error before it exercised the option, (3) the city already had awarded the contract to the next lowest bidder, (4) the company had received nothing of value it was required to restore to the city, and (5) "the city will not be heard to complain that it cannot be placed in statu quo because it will not have the benefit of an inequitable bargain." (*Id.* at p. 703, 235 P.2d 7.) Therefore, "under all the circumstances, it appears that it would be unjust and unfair to permit the city to take advantage of the company's mistake." (*Id.* at pp. 702–703, 235 P.2d 7.) Nothing in our decision in *Kemper* suggested that the mistake resulted from surprise related to inequality in the bargaining process. (Accord, *Farmers Sav. Bank, Joice v. Gerhart* (Iowa 1985) 372 N.W.2d 238, 243–245 [holding unconscionable the enforcement of sheriff's sale against bank that overbid because of a mistake caused by negligence of its own attorney].) Similarly, in *Elsinore, supra,* 54 Cal.2d 380, 6 Cal.Rptr. 1, 353 P.2d 713, we authorized rescission of a bid based upon a clerical error, without suggesting any procedural unconscionability, even where the other party afforded the contractor an opportunity to verify the accuracy of the bid before it was accepted.

In the present case, enforcing the contract with the mistaken price of $25,995 would require defendant to sell the vehicle to plaintiff for $12,000 less than the intended advertised price of $37,995—an error amounting to 32 percent of the price defendant intended. Defendant subsequently sold the automobile for slightly more than the intended advertised price, suggesting that that price reflected its actual market value. Defendant had paid $35,000 for the 1995 Jaguar and incurred costs in advertising, preparing, displaying, and attempting to sell the vehicle. Therefore, defendant would lose more than $9,000 of its original investment in the automobile. Plaintiff, on the other hand, would obtain a $12,000 windfall if the contract were enforced, simply because he traveled to the dealership and stated that he was prepared to pay the advertised price.

These circumstances are comparable to those in our prior decisions authorizing rescission on the ground that enforcing a contract with a mistaken price term would be unconscionable. Defendant's 32 percent error in the price exceeds the amount of the errors in cases such as *Kemper* and *Elsinore.* For example, in *Elsinore, supra,* 54 Cal.2d at page 389, 6 Cal.Rptr. 1, 353 P.2d 713, we authorized rescission for a $6,500 error in a bid that was intended to be $96,494—a mistake of approximately 7 percent in the intended contract price. As in the foregoing cases, plaintiff was informed of the mistake as soon as defendant discovered it. Defendant's sales manager, when he first learned of the mistake in the advertisement, explained the error to plaintiff, apologized, and offered to pay for plaintiff's fuel, time, and effort expended in traveling to the dealership to examine the automobile. Plaintiff refused this offer to be restored to the status quo. Like the public agencies in *Kemper* and *Elsinore,* plaintiff should not be permitted to take advantage of defendant's honest mistake that resulted in an unfair, one-sided contract. (Cf. *Drennan v. Star Paving Co.* (1958) 51 Cal.2d 409, 415–416, 333 P.2d 757 [no rescission of mistaken bid where other party detrimentally altered his position in reasonable reliance upon the bid and could not be restored to the status quo].) . . .

. . . [U]nder the circumstances, enforcement of the contract for the sale of the 1995 Jaguar XJ6 Vanden Plas at the $25,995 mistaken price would be unconscionable. The other requirements for rescission on the ground of unilateral mistake have been established. Defendant entered into the contract because of its mistake regarding a basic assumption, the price. The $12,000 loss that would result from enforcement of the contract has a material effect upon the agreed exchange of performances that is adverse to defendant. Furthermore, defendant did not neglect any legal duty within the meaning of Civil Code section 1577 or breach any duty of good faith and fair dealing in the steps leading to the formation of the contract. Plaintiff refused defendant's offer to compensate him for his actual losses in responding to the advertisement. "The law does not penalize for negligence beyond requiring compensation for the loss it has caused." (3 Corbin, Contracts, *supra,* § 609, p. 684.) In this situation, it would not be reasonable for this court to allocate the risk of the mistake to defendant.

Having determined that defendant satisfied the requirements for rescission of the contract on the ground of unilateral mistake of fact, we conclude that the municipal court correctly entered judgment in defendant's favor.

V

The judgment of the Court of Appeal is reversed.

KENNARD, J., CHIN, J., and BROWN, J., concur.

[The dissenting Opinion by WERDEGAR, J. in which Baxter, J., concurred, is omitted. Judge Werdegar agreed that an enforceable contract was formed between the parties but dissented from the grant of rescission on the ground that the defendant had not sought rescission either in the trial court or on appeal.]

————

RESTATEMENT, SECOND, CONTRACTS §§ 153, 154

[See Selected Source Materials Supplement]

————

NOTE ON UNILATERAL MISTAKE

It is sometimes said that relief for unilateral mistake will not be granted unless the parties "can be placed in status quo in the equity sense, i.e. rescission must not result in prejudice to the other party except for the loss of his bargain." James T. Taylor & Son, Inc. v. Arlington Independent School District, 160 Tex. 617, 335 S.W.2d 371 (1960). Taken literally, this would preclude relief when there has been *any* reliance by the nonmistaken party. Such a rule would be unnecessary to serve the purposes intended, and expressions like that in *James T. Taylor* should be read to mean that relief will not be granted unless the other party has either not relied *or* cannot be restored to his precontractual position by the award of reliance damages.

SECTION 2.   MISTAKES IN TRANSCRIPTION; REFORMATION

TRAVELERS INS. CO. v. BAILEY

Supreme Court of Vermont, 1964.
124 Vt. 114, 197 A.2d 813.

BARNEY, JUSTICE. The plaintiff insurance company has come into equity asking for reformation of the annuity provisions of a life insurance policy on the basis of mistake. Thirty years after issuance of the original policy it tendered the defendant insured an amended policy which he refused. On trial, the chancellor found that the amended policy represented the true insuring agreement originally entered into by the parties and allowed reformation. The defendant appealed.

At the instance of his mother, the defendant, when nineteen, submitted an application to an agent of the plaintiff for a life insurance policy. The plan requested in the application was one insuring the defendant's life for five thousand dollars, with an annuity at age sixty-five for five hundred dollars a year for the balance of his life, ten years certain. When the application was accepted and the policy prepared in the home office of the plaintiff, the correct descriptive information was inserted on the wrong policy form. The printed portion of the form used yielded the correct life insurance contract, but produced an annuity obligation to pay five hundred dollars a month for life, one hundred months certain. The application was made a part of the policy, by its terms. In accordance with its usual practice, the plaintiff did not retain a copy of the policy itself but kept a record of the information permitting reproduction of the policy if the occasion demanded.

The premiums were regularly paid on the policy issued in 1931, and about the middle of 1961 the actual policy came into the possession of the defendant for the first time. The semi-annual premiums charged and paid were identical with the prescribed premium for five thousand dollars of life insurance with annuity at age sixty-five of five hundred dollars annually, with payment for ten years certain. This $40.90 semi-annual premium was applicable only to that policy plan, issued at the defendant's then age of nineteen, and no other. The plaintiff had no rate for and did not sell a policy for five thousand dollars life insurance with an annuity at age sixty-five of five hundred dollars monthly, payment for one hundred months certain.

After being told by a third party that his policy could not have the provisions he claimed for it, the defendant took the policy to the office of the defendant's agent that sold the policy and made inquiry. Shortly thereafter, in late 1961, the amended policy was tendered. There is no evidence that the defendant then knew that his original policy provided for an annuity payment larger than he was entitled to in view of the premium paid and the life insurance coverage purchased.

Vermont law, like that of many jurisdictions, imposes upon the party seeking reformation the duty of establishing, beyond a reasonable doubt, the true agreement to which the contract in question is to be reformed. deNeergaard v. Dillingham, 123 Vt. 327, 331, 187 A.2d 494. That this was accomplished, in the judgment of the chancellor, is demonstrated by this finding in particular:

> "The only agreement that the plaintiff and defendant made was for $5000 insurance with annuity of $500 per year at attained age 65, ten years certain."

Adequate evidentiary support for all findings of fact, including this one, made in this case by the chancellor, appears from the transcript of the evidence.

Indeed, in his appeal, the defendant does not question any of the findings relating to the facts already recited. His principal attack on the decision relates to the chancellor's finding that the mistake in issuing the policy furnished the defendant came about through no fault of the defendant, but solely through the negligence and inattention of the plaintiff. This, says the defendant, is a finding of unilateral mistake, and therefore, under the authority of New York Life Insurance Co. v. Kimball, 93 Vt. 147, 153, 106 A. 676, is not grounds for reformation....

In [that case] Justice Miles commented ... "The law of a case cannot be determined from a brief quotation of portions of the opinion separate from the facts of a case, especially where the law upon the subject has many exceptions, as in the subject now under consideration." This thought is particularly applicable to cases dealing with mistake and reformation....

One variety of classification [of cases involving mistake] is suggested by the difference between a subsequent erroneous recording or transcription of a contract already in fact agreed to by the parties, and a mistake or misunderstanding [which] occurs while the parties are seeking to arrive at or believe they are arriving at an agreement. In the first case an agreement already exists, while in the second considerations of mutuality, together with knowledge of and responsibility for the mistake, weigh heavily in determining whether or not an enforceable agreement, or a right to relief, exists. Unfortunately, language appropriate to the second situation has sometimes been transposed to the first, where it may be both inappropriate and misleading. See 3 Corbin on Contracts § 608 (1960).

Where, as here, an antecedent contract has been established by the requisite measure of proof, equity will act to bring the erroneous writing into conformity with the true agreement. Burlington Building & Loan Ass'n v. Cummings, 111 Vt. 447, 453, 17 A.2d 319. On the basis of the maxim, "Equity regards that as done which ought to be done," equity will deal generously with the correction of mistakes. Stone v. Blake, 118 Vt. 424, 427, 110 A.2d 702, 704. This power has been regularly and frequently invoked in connection with real estate transactions, but there is nothing that requires that equity limit its application to that kind of case.

Other courts have exercised the equitable power of reformation in similar cases. In New England Mutual Life Insurance Co. v. Jones, D.C., 1 F.Supp. 984, a clerical mistake in the policy was discovered after the death of the insured when a double indemnity benefit claim for accidental death was made. The policy provided for double indemnity on the basis of the face amount of the policy, but in the blank space stating the obligation the figure $5000.00 had been entered. This considerably increased the double indemnity figure above that computed on the face amount of the policy. Premiums had been assessed and paid on the basis of the correct figure. Reformation was allowed.

In Stamen v. Metropolitan Life Insurance Co., 41 N.J.Super. 135, 124 A.2d 328, the insured received a policy, after a series of policy conversions, which inadvertently included a provision for disability benefits. The original application accepted by the company requested a policy without such provision, and the premiums had been assessed on the basis that no such benefits were payable. Reformation was allowed. . . .

Each of these cases speak of the reformation as justified either because there was "mutuality" of mistake or because the policy holder knew or ought to have known that there was a variation between the policy described in the accepted application and the one handed the insured. To insist on enforcement of the contract once knowledge of the error is acquired by the insured is held to be unconscionable, and classified as then a unilateral mistake known to the other party, which supports reformation. If the mistake exists in the writing unknown to both parties, it is classified as "mutual" and reformation is allowed.

Since these cases support reformation irrespective of the insured's knowledge of the existence of the mistake conferring a benefit on him beyond the bargain, talk of "mutual" or "unilateral" mistake seems to be of little help in this kind of situation. . . .

If, in this kind of case, talk of "mutuality" of mistake is unnecessary, much confusion can be avoided. Invariably, two mistakes are involved. There is a natural tendency to concentrate on the making of the clerical error in the writing as the critical mistake involved, when the true crucial error is mistaken belief of the parties about the correctness of the written instrument. When a test of "mutuality" is applied to the clerical error, the confusion is compounded, since the concern of the court should be with the belief or knowledge of the parties. The concept of "mutuality" adds nothing to the right to a remedy in this type of case. It is important as a concept in other, different, reformation situations. Applying to all the common linguistic label of "mutuality" gives to unlike situations an illusion of similarity. This invites the misapplication of principles, sound for one type of situation, to a different type, for which they are unsound.

Accordingly, we hold that where there has been established beyond a reasonable doubt a specific contractual agreement between parties, and a subsequent erroneous rendition of the terms of the agreement in a material particular, the party penalized by the error is entitled to reformation, if there has been no prejudicial change of position by the other party while ignorant of the mistake. If such change of position can equitably be taken into account and adjusted for in the decree, reformation may be possible even then. Mutual Life Ins. Co. of Baltimore v. Metzger, 167 Md. 27, 172 A. 610; see also Brown v. Lamphear, 35 Vt. 252. Mistakes generally occur through some carelessness, and failure to discover a mistake may be in some degree negligent, but unless some prejudice to the other party's rights under the true contract results, so as to make its enforcement inequitable, reformation will not be refused because of the presence of some negligence. Ward v. Lyman, 108 Vt. 464, 471, 188 A. 892; Mutual Life Insurance Co. of Baltimore v. Metzger, supra, 167 Md. 27, 30, 172 A. 610.

Change of position is raised as an issue by the defendant. It cannot be said that the defendant acted in reliance on the terms of the policy which, he testified, were not exactly known by him until he received the policy in 1961. But he argues that the mere passage of time, in this case thirty years, should overcome the chancellor's finding to the contrary and establish a change of position. But clearly this aging process was inevitable, and not a prejudicial act induced by the mistaken term in the policy. The defendant has not demonstrated that he was prejudiced by the existence of the error. Ward v. Lyman, supra, 108 Vt. 464, 471, 188 A. 892.

Reformation was properly granted.

Decree affirmed.

———

RESTATEMENT, SECOND, OF CONTRACTS § 155

[See Selected Source Materials Supplement]

———

CHIMART ASSOCIATES v. PAUL, 66 N.Y.2d 570, 498 N.Y.S.2d 344, 489 N.E.2d 231 (1986). "Because the thrust of a reformation claim is that a writing does not set forth the actual agreement of the parties, generally neither the parol evidence rule nor the Statute of Frauds applies to bar proof, in the form of parol or extrinsic evidence, of the claimed agreement.... However, this obviously recreates the very danger against which the parol evidence rule and Statute of Frauds were supposed to protect—the danger that a party, having agreed to a written contract that turns out to be disadvantageous, will falsely claim the existence of a different, oral contract.... To this end ... reformation has been limited both substantively and procedurally. Substantively, for example, reformation based upon mistake is not available where the parties purposely contract based upon uncertain or contingent events....

"Procedurally, there is a 'heavy presumption that a deliberately prepared and executed written instrument [manifests] the true intention of the parties' ... and a correspondingly high order of evidence is required to overcome that presumption.... The proponent of reformation must 'show in no uncertain terms, not only that mistake or fraud exists, but exactly what was really agreed upon between the parties'...."

SECTION 3.   MUTUAL MISTAKES (SHARED MISTAKEN ASSUMPTIONS)

Another important type of mistake in contract law consists of a mistaken factual assumption about the present state of the world outside the mind of the actor who holds the assumption. Mistaken factual assumptions differ from mechanical errors, because they do not involve blunders that result from transient errors in a party's mental or physical machinery. They differ from mistranscriptions, because they do not turn on whether a writing is erroneous.

A mistaken factual assumption may either be shared by both parties to a contract or held by only one of the parties. Traditionally, shared mistaken factual assumptions have been treated under the heading of *mutual mistake*, meaning a mistake that is shared by both parties. This terminology fails to differentiate among shared mistakes according to their functional characteristics. Some kinds of shared mistakes should provide a basis for relief, while others should not. For example, if Team A trades Player P to Team B, and both teams share a mistake about just how fast or how strong P is, that mistake should not and would not give either team the right to rescind the trade. Even shared mistakes that should provide a basis for relief fall into different functional categories that require differing treatment. For example, in mistranscription cases the parties both mistakenly believe that the writing properly transcribes the bargain. The appropriate remedy here normally is reformation, not recission.

In short, that a mistake is shared is relevant but it is not critical. What is critical is the character of the shared mistake. That character is captured in the term *shared mistaken factual assumptions* or, for short, *shared mistaken assumptions*.

In analyzing shared assumptions from the perspective of mistake, it is useful to begin with shared assumptions that are made explicit in a contract. If a contract is explicitly based on a shared assumption that turns out to have been mistaken, normally the mistake should furnish a basis for relief under a relatively straightforward interpretation of the language of the contract. For example, suppose A agrees to sell a plot of land, Tenacre, to B, and the contract provides, "This agreement is made on the assumption that Tenacre is zoned for commercial use." If it turns out that Tenacre is not zoned for commercial use, it is pretty clear that under the contract, B should be entitled to rescission.

Now suppose a shared mistaken assumption is tacit rather than explicit. The concept of a tacit assumption has been explicated as follows by Lon Fuller: Words like "intention," "assumption," "expectation" and "understanding" all seem to imply a conscious state involving an awareness of alternatives and a deliberate choice among them. It is, however, plain that there is a psychological state that can be described as a "tacit assumption", which does not involve a consciousness of alternatives. The absent-minded professor stepping from his office into the hall as he reads a book "assumes" that the floor of the hall will be there to receive him. His conduct is conditioned and directed by this assumption, even though the possibility that the floor has been removed does not "occur" to him, that is, is not present in his conscious mental processes.

A more colloquial expression that captures the concept of a tacit assumption is "taken for granted." A tacit assumption is so deeply embedded in an actor's mind that it simply doesn't occur to the actor to make the assumption explicit—any more than it occurs to Fuller's professor to think to himself, every time he is about to walk through a door, "Remember to check that the floor is still in place." Of course, if actors had infinite time and no costs, they would ransack their minds to think through every one of their tacit assumptions, and make each of those assumptions explicit. But actors do not have infinite time and they do have costs. Normally, it would be irrational for a potential contracting party to take the time to determine, and make explicit, every tacit assumption that he holds, because the costs of doing so would often approach or exceed the expected profit from the contract. It would also normally be virtually impossible to make such a determination. As Randy Barnett has stated:

> [When we add] to the infinity of knowledge about the present world the inherent uncertainty of future events ... we immediately can see that the seductive idea that a contract can ... articulate every contingency that might arise before ... performance is sheer fantasy. For this reason, contracts must be silent on an untold number of items. And many of these silent assumptions that underlie every agreement are as basic as the assumption that the sun will rise tomorrow. They are simply too basic to merit mention.

Randy E. Barnett, Contracts: Cases and Doctrine 1163 (2d ed. 1999).

WITTGENSTEIN, PHILOSOPHICAL INVESTIGATIONS 33 (1953 tr.) "Someone says to me: 'Show the children a game.' I teach them gaming with dice, and the other says, 'I didn't mean that sort of game.' Must the exclusion of the game with dice have come before his mind when he gave the order?"

SHERWOOD v. WALKER

Supreme Court of Michigan, 1887.
66 Mich. 568, 33 N.W. 919, 11 Am.St.Rep. 531.

Morse, J. Replevin for a cow. Suit commenced in justice's court; judgment for plaintiff; appealed to circuit court of Wayne county, and verdict and judgment for plaintiff in that court. The defendants bring error, and set out 25 assignments of the same.

The main controversy depends upon the construction of a contract for the sale of the cow. The plaintiff claims that the title passed, and bases his action upon such claim. The defendants contend that the contract was executory, and by its terms no title to the animal was acquired by plaintiff. The defendants reside at Detroit, but are in business at Walkerville, Ontario, and have a farm at Greenfield, in Wayne county, upon which were some blooded cattle supposed to be barren as breeders. The Walkers are importers and breeders of polled Angus cattle. The plaintiff is a banker living at Plymouth, in Wayne county. He called upon the defendants at Walkerville for the purchase of some of their stock, but found none there that suited him. Meeting one of the defendants afterwards, he was informed that they had a few head upon their Greenfield farm. He was asked to go out and look at them, with the statement at the time that they were probably barren, and would not breed. May 5, 1886, plaintiff went out to Greenfield and saw the cattle. A few days thereafter, he called upon one of the defendants with the view of purchasing a cow, known as "Rose 2d of Aberlone." After considerable talk it was agreed that defendants would telephone Sherwood at his home in Plymouth in reference to the price. The second morning after this talk he was called up by telephone, and the terms of the sale were finally agreed upon. He was to pay five and one-half cents per pound, live weight, fifty pounds shrinkage. He was asked how he intended to take the cow home, and replied that he might ship her from King's cattle-yard. He requested defendants to confirm the sale in writing, which they did by sending him the following letter:

"Walkerville, May 15, 1886.

"T.C. Sherwood, President, etc.—Dear Sir: We confirm sale to you of the cow Rose 2d of Aberlone, lot 56 of our catalogue, at five and a half cents per pound, less fifty pounds shrink. We inclose herewith order on Mr. Graham for the cow. You might leave check with him, or mail to us here, as you prefer.

"Yours truly,
Hiram Walker & Sons."

The order upon Graham enclosed in the letter read as follows:

"Walkerville, May 15, 1886.

"George Graham: You will please deliver at King's cattle-yard to Mr. T.C. Sherwood, Plymouth, the cow Rose 2d of Aberlone, lot 56 of our catalogue. Send halter with the cow, and have her weighed.

"Yours truly,
Hiram Walker & Sons."

On the twenty-first of the same month the plaintiff went to defendants' farm at Greenfield, and presented the order and letter to Graham, who informed him that the defendants had instructed him not to deliver the cow. Soon after, the plaintiff tendered to Hiram Walker, one of the defendants, $80, and demanded the cow. Walker refused to take the money or deliver the cow. The plaintiff then instituted this suit. After he had secured possession of the cow under the writ of replevin, the plaintiff caused her to be weighed by the constable who served the writ, at a place other than King's cattle-yard. She weighed 1,420 pounds.

When the plaintiff, upon the trial in the circuit court, had submitted his proofs showing the above transaction, defendants moved to strike out and exclude the testimony from the case, for the reason that it was irrelevant and did not tend to show that the title to the cow passed, and that it showed that the contract of sale was merely executory. The court refused the motion, and an exception was taken.

The defendants then introduced evidence tending to show that at the time of the alleged sale it was believed by both the plaintiff and themselves that the cow was barren and would not breed; that she cost $850, and if not barren would be worth from $750 to $1,000; that after the date of the letter, and the order to Graham, the defendants were informed by said Graham that in his judgment the cow was with calf, and therefore they instructed him not to deliver her to plaintiff, and on the twentieth of May, 1886, telegraphed plaintiff what Graham thought about the cow being with calf, and that consequently they could not sell her. The cow had a calf in the month of October following.

On the nineteenth of May, the plaintiff wrote Graham as follows:

"Plymouth, May 19, 1886

"Mr. George Graham, Greenfield—Dear Sir: I have bought Rose or Lucy from Mr. Walker, and will be there for her Friday morning, nine or ten o'clock. Do not water her in the morning.

"Yours, etc., T.C. Sherwood"

Plaintiff explained the mention of the two cows in this letter by testifying that, when he wrote this letter, the order and letter of defendants was at his home, and, writing in a hurry, and being uncertain as to the name of the cow, and not wishing his cow watered, he thought it would do no harm to name them both, as his bill of sale would show which one he had purchased. Plaintiff also testified that he asked defendants to give him a price on the balance of their herd at Greenfield, as a friend thought of buying some, and received a letter dated May 17, 1886, in which they named the price of five cattle, including Lucy, at $90, and Rose 2d at $80. When he received the letter he called defendants up by telephone, and asked them why they put Rose 2d in the list, as he had already purchased her. They replied that they knew he had, but thought it would make no difference if plaintiff and his friend concluded to take the whole herd.

The foregoing is the substance of all the testimony in the case.

The circuit judge instructed the jury that if they believed the defendants, when they sent the order and letter to plaintiff, meant to pass the title to the cow, and that the cow was intended to be delivered to plaintiff, it did not matter whether the cow was weighed at any particular place, or by any particular person; and if the cow was weighed afterwards, as Sherwood testified, such weighing would be a sufficient compliance with the order. If they believed that defendants intended to pass the title by writing, it did not matter whether the cow was weighed before or after suit brought, and the plaintiff would be entitled to recover.

The defendants submitted a number of requests which were refused. The substance of them was that the cow was never delivered to plaintiff, and the title to her did not pass by the letter and order; and that under the contract, as evidenced by these writings, the title did not pass until the cow was weighed and her price thereby determined; and that, if the defendants only agreed to sell a cow that would not breed, then the barrenness of the cow was a condition precedent to passing title, and plaintiff cannot recover. The court also charged the jury that it was immaterial whether the cow was with calf or not. It will therefore be seen that the defendants claim that, as a matter of law, the title of this cow did not pass, and that the circuit judge erred in submitting the case to the jury, to be determined by them, upon the intent of the parties as to whether or not the title passed with the sending of the letter and order by the defendants to the plaintiff. . . .

It appears from the record that both parties supposed this cow was barren and would not breed, and she was sold by the pound for an insignificant sum as compared with her real value if a breeder. She was evidently sold and purchased on the relation of her value for beef, unless the plaintiff had learned of her true condition, and concealed such knowledge from the defendants. Before the plaintiff secured the possession of the animal, the defendants learned that she was with calf, and therefore of great value, and undertook to rescind the sale by refusing to deliver her. The question arises whether they had a right to do so. The circuit judge ruled that this fact did not avoid the sale and it made no difference whether she was barren or not. I am of the opinion that the court erred in this holding. I know that this is a close question, and the dividing line between the adjudicated cases is not easily discerned. But it must be considered as well settled that a party who has given an apparent consent to a contract of sale may refuse to execute it, or he may avoid it after it has been completed, if the assent was founded, or the contract made, upon the mistake of a material fact,—such as the subject-matter of the sale, the price, or some collateral fact materially inducing the agreement; and this can be done when the mistake is mutual. . . .

If there is a difference or misapprehension as to the substance of the thing bargained for; if the thing actually delivered or received is different in substance from the thing bargained for, and intended to be sold,—then there is no contract; but if it be only a difference in some quality or accident, even though the mistake may have been the actuating motive to the purchaser or seller, or both of them, yet the contract remains binding. "The difficulty in every case is to determine whether the mistake or misapprehension is as to the substance of the whole contract, going, as it were, to the root of the matter, or only to some point, even though a material point, an error as to which does not affect the substance of the whole consideration." Kennedy v. Panama, etc., Mail Co., L.R. 2 Q.B. 580, 588. It has been held, in accordance with the principles above stated, that where a horse is bought under the belief that he is sound, and both vendor and vendee honestly believe him to be sound, the purchaser must stand by his bargain, and pay the full price, unless there was a warranty.

It seems to me, however, in the case made by this record, that the mistake or misapprehension of the parties went to the whole substance of the agreement. If the cow was a breeder, she was worth at least $750; if barren, she was worth not over $80. The parties would not have made the contract of sale except upon the understanding and belief that she was incapable of breeding, and of no use as a cow. It is true she is now the identical animal that they thought her to be when the contract was made; there is no mistake as to the identity of the creature. Yet the mistake was not of the mere quality of the animal, but went to the very nature of the thing. A barren cow is substantially a different creature than a breeding one. There is as much difference between them for all purposes of use as there is between an ox and a cow that is capable of breeding and giving milk. If the mutual mistake had simply related to the fact whether she was with calf or not for one season, then it might have been a good sale, but the mistake affected the character of the animal for all time, and for its present and ultimate use. She was not in fact the animal, or the kind of animal, the defendants intended to sell or the plaintiff to buy. She was not a barren cow, and, if this fact had been known, there would have been no contract. The mistake affected the substance of the whole consideration, and it must be considered that there was no contract to sell or sale of the cow as she actually was. The thing sold and bought had in fact no existence. She was sold as a beef creature would be sold; she is in fact a breeding cow, and a valuable one. The court should have instructed the jury that if they found that the cow was sold, or contracted to be sold, upon the understanding of both parties that she was barren, and useless for the purpose of breeding, and that in fact she was not barren, but capable of breeding, then the defendants had a right to rescind, and refuse to deliver, and the verdict should be in their favor.

The judgment of the court below must be reversed, and a new trial granted, with costs of this court to defendants.

CAMPBELL, C.J., and CHAMPLIN, J., concurred.

SHERWOOD, J. (dissenting). I do not concur in the opinion given by my brethren in this case. . . .

As has already been stated by my brethren, the record shows that the plaintiff is a banker and a farmer as well, carrying on a farm, and raising the best breeds of stock, and lived in Plymouth, in the county of Wayne, 23 miles from Detroit; that the defendants lived in Detroit, and were also dealers in stock of the higher grades; that they had a farm at Walkerville, in Canada, and also one in Greenfield in said county of Wayne, and upon these farms the defendants kept their stock. The Greenfield farm was about 15 miles from the plaintiff's. In the spring of 1886 the plaintiff, learning that the defendants had some "polled Angus cattle" for sale, was desirous of purchasing some of that breed, and meeting the defendants, or some of them, at Walkerville, inquired about them, and was informed that they had none at Walkerville, "but had a few head left on their farm in Greenfield, and asked the plaintiff to go and see them, stating that in all probability they were sterile and would not breed." . . . The record further shows that the defendants, when they sold the cow, believed the cow was not with calf, and barren; that from what the plaintiff had been told by defendants (for it does not appear he had any other knowledge or facts from which he could form an opinion) he believed the cow was farrow, but still thought she could be made to breed. The foregoing shows the entire interview and treaty between the parties as to the sterility and qualities of the cow sold to the plaintiff. The cow had a calf in the month of October.

There is no question but that the defendants sold the cow representing her of the breed and quality they believed the cow to be, and that the purchaser so understood it. And the buyer purchased her believing her to be of the breed represented by the sellers, and possessing all the qualities stated, and even more. He believed she would breed. There is no pretense that the plaintiff bought the cow for beef, and there is nothing in the record indicating that he would have bought her at all only that he thought she might be made to breed. Under the foregoing facts,—and these are all that are contained in the record material to the contract,—it is held that because it turned out that the plaintiff was more correct in his judgment as to one quality of the cow than the defendants, and a quality, too, which could not by any possibility be positively known at the time by either party to exist, the contract may be annulled by the defendants at their pleasure. I know of no law, and have not been referred to any, which will justify any such holding, and I think the circuit judge was right in his construction of the contract between the parties.

It is claimed that a mutual mistake of a material fact was made by the parties when the contract of sale was made. There was no warranty in the case of the quality of the animal. When a mistaken fact is relied upon as ground for rescinding, such fact must not only exist at the time the contract is made, but must have been known to one or both of the parties. Where there is no warranty, there can be no mistake of fact when no such fact exists, or, if in existence, neither party knew of it, or could know of it; and that is precisely this case. If the owner of a Hambletonian horse had speeded him, and was only able to make him go a mile in three minutes, and should sell him to another, believing that was his greatest speed, for $300, when the purchaser believed he could go much faster, and made the purchase for that sum, and a few days thereafter, under more favorable circumstances, the horse was driven a mile in 2 min. 16 sec., and was found to be worth $20,000, I hardly think it would be held, either at law or in equity, by any one, that the seller in such case could rescind the contract. The same legal principles apply in each case.

In this case neither party knew the actual quality and condition of this cow at the time of the sale. The defendants say, or rather said, to the plaintiff, "they had a few head left on their farm in Greenfield, and asked plaintiff to go and see them, stating to plaintiff that in all probability they were sterile and would not breed." Plaintiff did go as requested, and found there these cows, including the one purchased, with a bull. The cow had been exposed, but neither knew she was with calf or whether she would breed. The defendants thought she would not, but the plaintiff says that he thought she could be made to breed, but believed she was not with calf. The defendants sold the cow for what they believed her to be, and the plaintiff bought her as he believed she was, after the statements made by the defendants. No conditions whatever were attached to the terms of sale by either party. It was in fact as absolute as it could well be made, and I know of no precedent as authority by which this court can alter the contract thus made by these parties in writing, and interpolate in it a condition by which, if the *defendants should be mistaken in their belief that the cow was barren,* she could be returned to them and their contract should be annulled. It is not the duty of courts to destroy contracts when called upon to enforce them, after they have been legally made. There was no mistake of any material fact by either of the parties in the case as would license the vendors to rescind. There was no difference between the parties, nor misapprehension, as to the substance of the thing bargained for, which was a cow supposed to be barren by one party, and believed not to be by the other. As to the quality of the animal, subsequently developed, both parties were equally ignorant, and as to this each party took his chances. If this were not the law, there would be no safety in purchasing this kind of stock.

I entirely agree with my brethren that the right to rescind occurs whenever "the thing actually delivered or received is different in substance from the thing bargained for, and intended to be sold; but if it be only a difference in some quality or accident, even though the misapprehension may have been the actuating motive" of the parties in making the contract, yet it will remain binding. In this case the cow sold was the one delivered. What might or might not happen to her after the sale formed no element in the contract. . . .

NESTER v. MICHIGAN LAND & IRON CO., 69 Mich. 290, 37 N.W. 278 (1888). In September 1885, Michigan Land entered into a written contract with Nester, under which Michigan Land sold to Nester all the merchantable pine on certain land. Michigan Land made no representation to Nester that it intended Nester to rely upon, or that he did rely upon, in making his purchase. Prior to the sale, Michigan Land's agent told Nester that if he purchased the timber he had to do so on the basis of his own estimate. Nester had such an estimate made, and knew that an estimate could not be made with any degree of certainty—to use the language of his estimate, that "it is all guesswork any way." After the purchase, Nester sued to reduce the purchase price by 50% on the ground that both parties were mistaken in their estimate of the quality of the timber on the land; that a large portion of the timber was unsound; and that in consequence of the amount of decayed timber, the yield of merchantable pine furnished only about half the quantity of such pine that was anticipated or estimated. The case was decided by the Michigan Supreme Court, one year after Sherwood v. Walker. The opinion was written by Judge Sherwood, who had dissented in Sherwood v. Walker, and then had become Chief Judge of the Court. Held, for Michigan Land.

"We know of no case which will sustain the complainant's case upon the facts before us. That of *Sherwood v. Walker* . . . will come the nearest to it of any referred to. That is, however, somewhat different upon its facts, and the rule applied in that case can never be resorted to except in a case where all the facts and circumstances are precisely the same as in that." There were no dissents.

GRIFFITH v. BRYMER

King's Bench Div., 1903.
19 T.L.R. 434.

This was an action brought by Mr. Murray Griffith, of 8, Seamoreplace, Park-lane against Colonel W.E. Brymer, M.P., of 8, St. James's-street to recover the sum of £100 paid on an agreement to hire a certain room at 8, St. James's-street for the purpose of viewing the Coronation Procession on June 26, 1902.

The facts, so far as material, were as follows:—At 11 a.m. on June 24, 1902, the plaintiff entered into a verbal agreement with Messrs. Pope, Roach, and Co., the defendant's agents, to take the room for the purpose of viewing the procession on June 26, and handed over his cheque for £100. It was admitted that the decision to operate on the King, which rendered the procession impossible, had been reached at about 10 a.m. that morning. But neither party was aware of this fact when the agreement was entered into and the cheque given; and it was contended for the plaintiff that, as both parties were under a misconception with regard to the existing state of facts about which they were contracting, the plaintiff was entitled to the return of his money. In the course of the argument Clark v. Lindsay, 19 T.L.R. 202, 88 L.T. 198, and Blakeley v. Muller, 19 T.L.R. 186, were cited.

Mr. Justice Wright held that the principle of such cases as Coutourier v. Hastie, 8 Ex., 40, applied to this case, and expressed his agreement with the law as laid down by Mr. Justice Channell in Clark v. Lindsay. The agreement was made on the supposition by both parties that nothing had happened which made performance impossible. This was a missupposition of the state of facts which went to the whole root of the matter. The contract was therefore void, and the plaintiff was entitled to recover his £100.

————

EVERETT v. ESTATE OF SUMSTAD, 95 Wash.2d 853, 631 P.2d 366 (1981). The Mitchells owned a small secondhand store. In August 1978, they attended Alexander's Auction, where they frequently shopped to obtain merchandise for their own use and for use as inventory in their business. At the auction, the Mitchells purchased for $50 a used safe that had a locked inside compartment. Several days after the auction, the Mitchells took the safe to a locksmith to have the locked compartment opened. The locksmith found $32,207 inside, and a controversy arose whether the Mitchells were entitled to the money. An affidavit of the Mitchells stated:

> [W]e saw that the top outer-most door with a combination lock was open, and that the inner door was locked shut. That inner door required a key to open, and we learned that the safe would have to be taken to a locksmith to get the inner door opened because no key was available. We also learned that the combination for the outer lock was unknown. The auctioneer told the bidders that both this and the other safe had come from an estate, that both were still locked, that neither had been opened, and that the required combinations and key were unavailable for either.

The auctioneer's affidavit stated:

> I told the crowd at the auction that [the safes] were from an estate, that they were still locked and had never been opened by me and that I didn't have the combinations.

Held, for the Mitchells.

"A sale is a consensual transaction. The subject matter which passes is to be determined by the intent of the parties as revealed by the terms of their agreement in light of the surrounding circumstances. . . .

" . . . Under these circumstances, we hold reasonable persons would conclude that the auctioneer manifested an objective intent to sell the safe and its contents and that the parties mutually assented to enter into that sale of the safe and the contents of the locked compartment."

RESTATEMENT, SECOND, CONTRACTS §§ 151, 152, 154

[See Selected Source Materials Supplement]

UNIDROIT PRINCIPLES OF INTERNATIONAL COMMERCIAL CONTRACTS ARTS. 3.4, 3.5, 3.18

[See Selected Source Materials Supplement]

PRINCIPLES OF EUROPEAN CONTRACT LAW ART. 4.103

[See Selected Source Materials Supplement]

LENAWEE COUNTY BOARD OF HEALTH v. MESSERLY

Supreme Court of Michigan, 1982.
417 Mich. 17, 331 N.W.2d 203.

RYAN, JUSTICE.

In March of 1977, Carl and Nancy Pickles, appellees, purchased from appellants, William and Martha Messerly, a 600–square-foot tract of land upon which is located a three-unit apartment building. Shortly after the transaction was closed, the Lenawee County Board of Health condemned the property and obtained a permanent injunction which prohibits human habitation on the premises until the defective sewage system is brought into conformance with the Lenawee County sanitation code.

We are required to determine whether appellees should prevail in their attempt to avoid this land contract on the basis of mutual mistake and failure of consideration. We conclude that the parties did entertain a mutual misapprehension of fact, but that the circumstances of this case do not warrant rescision.

I

The facts of the case are not seriously in dispute. In 1971, the Messerlys acquired approximately one acre plus 600 square feet of land. A three-unit apartment building was situated upon the 600–square–foot portion. The trial court found that, prior to this transfer, the Messerlys' predecessor in title, Mr. Bloom, had installed a septic tank on the property without a permit and in violation of the applicable health code. The Messerlys used the building as an income investment property until 1973 when they sold it, upon [a] land contract, to James Barnes who likewise used it primarily as an income-producing investment.

Mr. and Mrs. Barnes, with the permission of the Messerlys, sold approximately one acre of the property in 1976, and the remaining 600 square feet and building were offered for sale soon thereafter when Mr. and Mrs. Barnes defaulted on their land contract. Mr. and Mrs. Pickles evidenced an interest in the property, but were dissatisfied with the terms of the Barnes–Messerly land contract. Consequently, to accommodate the Pickleses' preference to enter into a land contract directly with the Messerlys, Mr. and Mrs. Barnes executed a quit-claim deed which conveyed their interest in the property back to the Messerlys. After inspecting the property, Mr. and Mrs. Pickles executed a new land contract with the Messerlys on March 21, 1977. It provided for a purchase price of $25,500. A clause was added to the end of the land contract form which provides:

> "17. Purchaser has examined this property and agrees to accept same in its present condition. There are no other or additional written or oral understandings."

Five or six days later, when the Pickleses went to introduce themselves to the tenants, they discovered raw sewage seeping out of the ground. Tests conducted by a sanitation expert indicated the inadequacy of the sewage system. The Lenawee County Board of Health subsequently condemned the property and initiated this lawsuit in the Lenawee Circuit Court against the Messerlys as land contract vendors, and the Pickleses, as vendees, to obtain a permanent injunction proscribing human habitation of the premises until the property was brought into conformance with the Lenawee County sanitation code. The injunction was granted, and the Lenawee County Board of Health was permitted to withdraw from the lawsuit by stipulation of the parties.

When no payments were made on the land contract, the Messerlys filed a cross-complaint against the Pickleses seeking foreclosure, sale of the property, and a deficiency judgment. Mr. and Mrs. Pickles then counterclaimed for rescission against the Messerlys, and filed a third-party complaint against the Barneses, which incorporated, by reference, the allegations of the counterclaim against the Messerlys. In count one, Mr. and Mrs. Pickles alleged failure of consideration. Count two charged Mr. and Mrs. Barnes with willful concealment and misrepresentation as a result of their failure to disclose the condition of the sanitation system. Additionally, Mr. and Mrs. Pickles sought to hold the Messerlys liable in equity for the Barneses' alleged misrepresentation. The Pickleses prayed that the land contract be rescinded.

After a bench trial, the court concluded that the Pickleses had no cause of action against either the Messerlys or the Barneses as there was no fraud or misrepresentation. This ruling was predicated on the trial judge's conclusion that none of the parties knew of Mr. Bloom's earlier transgression or of the resultant problem with the septic system until it was discovered by the Pickleses, and that the sanitation problem was not caused by any of the parties. The trial court held that the property was purchased "as is", after inspection and, accordingly, its "negative * * * value cannot be blamed upon an innocent seller". Foreclosure was ordered against the Pickleses, together with a judgment against them in the amount of $25,943.09.[1]

---

1. The parties stipulated that this amount was due on the land contract, assuming that the contract was valid and enforceable.

Mr. and Mrs. Pickles appealed from the adverse judgment. The Court of Appeals unanimously affirmed the trial court's ruling with respect to Mr. and Mrs. Barnes but, in a two-to-one decision, reversed the finding of no cause of action on the Pickleses' claims against the Messerlys. *Lenawee County Board of Health v. Messerly,* 98 Mich.App. 478, 295 N.W.2d 903 (1980). It concluded that the mutual mistake between the Messerlys and the Pickleses went to a basic, as opposed to a collateral, element of the contract,[2] and that the parties intended to transfer income-producing rental property but, in actuality, the vendees paid $25,500 for an asset without value.[3]

We granted the Messerlys' application for leave to appeal. 411 Mich. 900 (1981).[4]

II

We must decide initially whether there was a mistaken belief entertained by one or both parties to the contract in dispute and, if so, the resultant legal significance.[5]

A contractual mistake "is a belief that is not in accord with the facts". 1 Restatement Contracts, 2d, § 151, p. 383. The erroneous belief of one or both of the parties must relate to a fact in existence at the time the contract is executed. *Richardson Lumber Co. v. Hoey,* 219 Mich. 643, 189 N.W. 923 (1922); *Sherwood v. Walker,* 66 Mich. 568, 580, 33 N.W. 919 (1887) (Sherwood, J., dissenting). That is to say, the belief which is found to be in error may not be, in substance, a prediction as to a future occurrence or non-occurrence. *Henry v. Thomas,* 241 Ga. 360, 245 S.E.2d 646 (1978); *Hailpern v. Dryden,* 154 Colo. 231, 389 P.2d 590 (1964). But see *Denton v. Utley,* 350 Mich. 332, 86 N.W.2d 537 (1957).

The Court of Appeals concluded, after a *de novo* review of the record, that the parties were mistaken as to the income-producing capacity of the property in question. 98 Mich.App. 487–488, 295 N.W.2d 903. We agree. The vendors and the vendees each believed that the property transferred could be utilized as income-generating rental property. All of the parties subsequently learned that, in fact, the property was unsuitable for any residential use.

Appellants assert that there was no mistake in the contractual sense because the defect in the sewage system did not arise until after the contract was executed. The appellees respond that the Messerlys are confusing the date of the inception of the defect with the date upon which the defect was discovered.

2. Mr. and Mrs. Pickles did not appeal the trial court's finding that there was no fraud or misrepresentation by the Messerlys or Mr. and Mrs. Barnes. Likewise, the propriety of that ruling is not before this Court today.

3. The trial court found that the only way that the property could be put to residential use would be to pump and haul the sewage, a method which is economically unfeasible, as the cost of such a disposal system amounts to double the income generated by the property. There was speculation by the trial court that the adjoining land might be utilized to make the property suitable for residential use, but,

in the absence of testimony directed at that point, the court refused to draw any conclusions. The trial court and the Court of Appeals both found that the property was valueless, or had a negative value.

4. The Court of Appeals decision to affirm the trial court's finding of no cause of action against Mr. and Mrs. Barnes has not been appealed to this Court and, accordingly, the propriety of that ruling is not before us today.

5. We emphasize that this is a bifurcated inquiry. Legal or equitable remedial measures are not mandated in every case in which a mutual mistake has been established.

This is essentially a factual dispute which the trial court failed to resolve directly. Nevertheless, we are empowered to draw factual inferences from the facts found by the trial court. GCR 1963, 865.1(6).

An examination of the record reveals that the septic system was defective prior to the date on which the land contract was executed. The Messerlys' grantor installed a nonconforming septic system without a permit prior to the transfer of the property to the Messerlys in 1971. Moreover, virtually undisputed testimony indicates that, assuming ideal soil conditions, 2,500 square feet of property is necessary to support a sewage system adequate to serve a three-family dwelling. Likewise, 750 square feet is mandated for a one-family home. Thus, the division of the parcel and sale of one acre of the property by Mr. and Mrs. Barnes in 1976 made it impossible to remedy the already illegal septic system within the confines of the 600–square–foot parcel.

Appellants do not dispute these underlying facts which give rise to an inference contrary to their contentions.

Having determined that when these parties entered into the land contract they were laboring under a mutual mistake of fact, we now direct our attention to a determination of the legal significance of that finding.

A contract may be rescinded because of a mutual misapprehension of the parties, but this remedy is granted only in the sound discretion of the court. *Harris v. Axline,* 323 Mich. 585, 36 N.W.2d 154 (1949). Appellants argue that the parties' mistake relates only to the quality or value of the real estate transferred, and that such mistakes are collateral to the agreement and do not justify rescission, citing *A & M Land Development Co. v. Miller,* 354 Mich. 681, 94 N.W.2d 197 (1959).

In that case, the plaintiff was the purchaser of 91 lots of real property. It sought partial rescission of the land contract when it was frustrated in its attempts to develop 42 of the lots because it could not obtain permits from the county health department to install septic tanks on these lots. This Court refused to allow rescission because the mistake, whether mutual or unilateral, related only to the value of the property. . . .

Appellees contend, on the other hand, that in this case the parties were mistaken as to the very nature of the character of the consideration and claim that the pervasive and essential quality of this mistake renders rescission appropriate. They cite in support of that view *Sherwood v. Walker,* 66 Mich. 568, 33 N.W. 919 (1887), the famous "barren cow" case. . . .

As the parties suggest, the foregoing precedent arguably distinguishes mistakes affecting the essence of the consideration from those which go to its quality or value, affording relief on a per se basis for the former but not the latter. See, *e.g., Lenawee County Board of Health v. Messerly,* 98 Mich.App. 478, 492, 295 N.W.2d 903 (1980) (Mackenzie, J., concurring in part).

However, the distinctions which may be drawn from *Sherwood* and *A & M Land Development Co.* do not provide a satisfactory analysis of the nature of a mistake sufficient to invalidate a contract. Often, a mistake relates to an underlying factual assumption which, when discovered, directly affects value, but simultaneously and materially affects the essence of the contractual consideration. It is disingenuous to label such a mistake collateral. *McKay v. Coleman,* 85 Mich. 60, 48 N.W. 203 (1891). Corbin, Contracts (One Vol. ed.), § 605, p. 551.

Appellant and appellee both mistakenly believed that the property which was the subject of their land contract would generate income as rental property. The fact that it could not be used for human habitation deprived the property of its income-earning potential and rendered it less valuable. However, this mistake, while directly and dramatically affecting the property's value, cannot accurately be characterized as collateral because it also affects the very essence of the consideration. "The thing sold and bought [income generating rental property] had in fact no existence". *Sherwood v. Walker,* 66 Mich. 578, 33 N.W. 919.

We find that the inexact and confusing distinction between contractual mistakes running to value and those touching the substance of the consideration serves only as an impediment to a clear and helpful analysis for the equitable resolution of cases in which mistake is alleged and proven. Accordingly, the holdings of *A & M Land Development Co.* and *Sherwood* with respect to the material or collateral nature of a mistake are limited to the facts of those cases.

Instead, we think the better-reasoned approach is a case-by-case analysis whereby rescission is indicated when the mistaken belief relates to a basic assumption of the parties upon which the contract is made, and which materially affects the agreed performances of the parties. *Denton v. Utley,* 350 Mich. 332, 86 N.W.2d 537 (1957); *Farhat v. Rassey,* 295 Mich. 349, 294 N.W. 707 (1940); *Richardson Lumber Co. v. Hoey,* 219 Mich. 643, 189 N.W. 923 (1922). 1 Restatement Contracts, 2d, § 152, pp. 385–386. Rescission is not available, however, to relieve a party who has assumed the risk of loss in connection with the mistake. *Denton v. Utley,* 350 Mich. 344–345, 86 N.W.2d 537; *Farhat v. Rassey,* 295 Mich. 352, 294 N.W. 707; Corbin, Contracts (One Vol. ed.), § 605, p. 552; 1 Restatement Contracts, 2d, §§ 152, 154, pp. 385–386, 402–406.

All of the parties to this contract erroneously assumed that the property transferred by the vendors to the vendees was suitable for human habitation and could be utilized to generate rental income. The fundamental nature of these assumptions is indicated by the fact that their invalidity changed the character of the property transferred, thereby frustrating, indeed precluding, Mr. and Mrs. Pickles' intended use of the real estate. Although the Pickleses are disadvantaged by enforcement of the contract, performance is advantageous to the Messerlys, as the property at issue is less valuable absent its income-earning potential. Nothing short of rescission can remedy the mistake. Thus, the parties' mistake as to a basic assumption materially affects the agreed performances of the parties.

Despite the significance of the mistake made by the parties, we reverse the Court of Appeals because we conclude that equity does not justify the remedy sought by Mr. and Mrs. Pickles.

Rescission is an equitable remedy which is granted only in the sound discretion of the court. *Harris v. Axline,* 323 Mich. 585, 36 N.W.2d 154 (1949); *Hathaway v. Hudson,* 256 Mich. 694, 239 N.W. 859 (1932). A court need not grant rescission in every case in which the mutual mistake relates to a basic assumption and materially affects the agreed performance of the parties.

In cases of mistake by two equally innocent parties, we are required, in the exercise of our equitable powers, to determine which blameless party should assume the loss resulting from the misapprehension they shared.[6] Normally that can only be done by drawing upon our "own notions of what is reasonable and just under all the surrounding circumstances".[7]

Equity suggests that, in this case, the risk should be allocated to the purchasers. We are guided to that conclusion, in part, by the standards announced in § 154 of the Restatement of Contracts 2d, for determining when a party bears the risk of mistake. . . . Section 154(a) suggests that the court should look first to whether the parties have agreed to the allocation of the risk between themselves. While there is no express assumption in the contract by either party of the risk of the property becoming uninhabitable, there was indeed some agreed allocation of the risk to the vendees by the incorporation of an "as is" clause into the contract which, we repeat, provided:

> "Purchaser has examined this property and agrees to accept same in its present condition. There are no other or additional written or oral understandings."

That is a persuasive indication that the parties considered that, as between them, such risk as related to the "present condition" of the property should lie with the purchaser. If the "as is" clause is to have any meaning at all, it must be interpreted to refer to those defects which were unknown at the time that the contract was executed.[8] Thus, the parties themselves assigned the risk of loss to Mr. and Mrs. Pickles.

We conclude that Mr. and Mrs. Pickles are not entitled to the equitable remedy of rescission and, accordingly, reverse the decision the Court of Appeals.

WILLIAMS, C.J., and COLEMAN, FITZGERALD, KAVANAGH and LEVIN, JJ., concur.

RILEY, J., not participating.

UCC §§ 2–312, 2–313, 2–314, 2–315

[See Selected Source Materials Supplement]

---

6. This risk-of-loss analysis is absent in both *A & M Land Development Co.* and *Sherwood,* and this omission helps to explain, in part, the disparate treatment in the two cases. Had such an inquiry been undertaken in *Sherwood,* we believe that the result might have been different. Moreover, a determination as to which party assumed the risk in *A & M Land Development Co.* would have alleviated the need to characterize the mistake as collateral so as to justify the result denying rescission. Despite the absence of any inquiry as to the assumption of risk in those two leading cases, we find that there exists sufficient precedent to warrant such an analysis in future cases of mistake.

7. *Hathaway v. Hudson,* 256 Mich. 702, 239 N.W. 859, quoting 9 C.J., p. 1161.

8. An "as is" clause waives those implied warranties which accompany the sale of a new home, *Tibbitts v. Openshaw,* 18 Utah 2d 442, 425 P.2d 160 (1967), or the sale of goods. M.C.L. § 440.2316(3)(a); M.S.A. § 19.2316(3)(a). Since implied warranties protect against latent defects, an "as is" clause will impose upon the purchaser the assumption of the risk of latent defects, such as an inadequate sanitation system, even when there are no implied warranties.

SECTION 4. NONDISCLOSURE

NOTE ON NONDISCLOSURE

Suppose that A and B propose to enter into a contract for the purchase and sale of a commodity (by which I mean anything that can be bought or sold). A knows a material fact, F, concerning the commodity. B does not know F. The problem raised by such a case is whether A must disclose the relevant fact, F, to B. Traditionally, the issue raised by this problem has been cast in terms of whether the knowing party, A, has a duty to disclose. This terminology is functional and convenient. However, if we focus on the unknowing party, B, the issue is mistake, because in the paradigmatic nondisclosure case in contract law, A knows F is the case while B tacitly and mistakenly assumes that Not–F is the case.

HILL v. JONES

Arizona Court of Appeals, 1986.
151 Ariz. 81, 725 P.2d 1115.

MEYERSON, Judge.

Must the seller of a residence disclose to the buyer facts pertaining to past termite infestation? This is the primary question presented in this appeal. Plaintiffs Warren G. Hill and Gloria R. Hill (buyers) filed suit to rescind an agreement to purchase a residence. Buyers alleged that Ora G. Jones and Barbara R. Jones (sellers) had made misrepresentations concerning termite damage in the residence and had failed to disclose to them the existence of the damage and history of termite infestation in the residence. . . .

. . . The trial court granted summary judgment, finding that there was "no genuinely disputed issue of material fact and that the law favors the . . . defendants." . . . Buyers have appealed from the judgment and sellers have cross-appealed from the trial court's ruling on attorney's fees.

I. FACTS

In 1982, buyers entered into an agreement to purchase sellers' residence for $72,000. The agreement was entered after buyers made several visits to the home. The purchase agreement provided that sellers were to pay for and place in escrow a termite inspection report stating that the property was free from evidence of termite infestation. Escrow was scheduled to close two months later.

One of the central features of the house is a parquet teak floor covering the sunken living room, the dining room, the entryway and portions of the halls. On a subsequent visit to the house, and when sellers were present, buyers noticed a small "ripple" in the wood floor on the step leading up to the dining room from the sunken living room. Mr. Hill asked if the ripple could be termite damage. Mrs. Jones answered that it was water damage. A few years previously, a broken water heater in the house had in fact caused water damage in the area of the dining room and steps which necessitated that some repairs be made to the floor. No further discussion on the subject, however, took place between the parties at that time or afterwards.

Mr. Hill, through his job as maintenance supervisor at a school district, had seen similar "ripples" in wood which had turned out to be termite damage. Mr. Hill was not totally satisfied with Mrs. Jones's explanation, but he felt that the termite inspection report would reveal whether the ripple was due to termites or some other cause.

The termite inspection report stated that there was no visible evidence of infestation. The report failed to note the existence of physical damage or evidence of previous treatment. The realtor notified the parties that the property had passed the termite inspection. Apparently, neither party actually saw the report prior to close of escrow.

After moving into the house, buyers found a pamphlet left in one of the drawers entitled "Termites, the Silent Saboteurs." They learned from a neighbor that the house had some termite infestation in the past. Shortly after the close of escrow, Mrs. Hill noticed that the wood on the steps leading down to the sunken living room was crumbling. She called an exterminator who confirmed the existence of termite damage to the floor and steps and to wood columns in the house. The estimated cost of repairing the wood floor alone was approximately $5,000.

Through discovery after their lawsuit was filed, buyers learned the following. When sellers purchased the residence in 1974, they received two termite guarantees that had been given to the previous owner by Truly Nolen, as well as a diagram showing termite treatment at the residence that had taken place in 1963. The guarantees provided for semi-annual inspections and annual termite booster treatments. The accompanying diagram stated that the existing damage had not been repaired. The second guarantee, dated 1965, reinstated the earlier contract for inspection and treatment. Mr. Jones admitted that he read the guarantees when he received them. Sellers renewed the guarantees when they purchased the residence in 1974. They also paid the annual fee each year until they sold the home.

On two occasions during sellers' ownership of the house but while they were at their other residence in Minnesota, a neighbor noticed "streamers" evidencing live termites in the wood tile floor near the entryway. On both occasions, Truly Nolen gave a booster treatment for termites. On the second incident, Truly Nolen drilled through one of the wood tiles to treat for termites. The neighbor showed Mr. Jones the area where the damage and treatment had occurred. Sellers had also seen termites on the back fence and had replaced and treated portions of the fence.

Sellers did not mention any of this information to buyers prior to close of escrow. They did not mention the past termite infestation and treatment to the realtor or to the termite inspector. There was evidence of holes on the patio that had been drilled years previously to treat for termites. The inspector returned to the residence to determine why he had not found evidence of prior treatment and termite damage. He indicated that he had not seen the holes in the patio because of boxes stacked there. It is unclear whether the boxes had been placed there by buyers or sellers. He had not found the damage inside the house because a large plant, which buyers had purchased from sellers, covered the area. After investigating the second time, the inspector found the damage and evidence of past treatment. He acknowledged that this information should have appeared in the report. He complained, however, that he should have been told of any history of termite infestation and treatment before he performed his inspection and that it was customary for the inspector to be given such information.

Other evidence presented to the trial court was that during their numerous visits to the residence before close of escrow, buyers had unrestricted access to view and inspect the entire house. Both Mr. and Mrs. Hill had seen termite damage and were therefore familiar with what it might look like. Mr. Hill had seen termite damage on the fence at this property. Mrs. Hill had noticed the holes on the patio but claimed not to realize at the time what they were for. Buyers asked no questions about termites except when they asked if the "ripple" on the stairs was termite damage. Mrs. Hill admitted she was not "trying" to find problems with the house because she really wanted it. . . .

III. DUTY TO DISCLOSE

The principal legal question presented in this appeal is whether a seller has a duty to disclose to the buyer the existence of termite damage in a residential dwelling known to the seller, but not to the buyer, which materially affects the value of the property. For the reasons stated herein, we hold that such a duty exists.

This is not the place to trace the history of the doctrine of caveat emptor. Suffice it to say that its vitality has waned during the latter half of the 20th century. E.g., Richards v. Powercraft Homes, Inc., 139 Ariz. 242, 678 P.2d 427 (1984) (implied warranty of workmanship and habitability extends to subsequent buyers of homes); see generally Quashnock v. Frost, 299 Pa.Super. 9, 445 A.2d 121 (1982); Ollerman v. O'Rourke Co., 94 Wis.2d 17, 288 N.W.2d 95 (1980). The modern view is that a vendor has an affirmative duty to disclose material facts where:

    1. Disclosure is necessary to prevent a previous assertion from being a misrepresentation or from being fraudulent or material;

    2. Disclosure would correct a mistake of the other party as to a basic assumption on which that party is making the contract and if nondisclosure amounts to a failure to act in good faith and in accordance with reasonable standards of fair dealing;

    3. Disclosure would correct a mistake of the other party as to the contents or effect of a writing, evidencing or embodying an agreement in whole or in part;

    4. The other person is entitled to know the fact because of a relationship of trust and confidence between them.

Restatement (Second) of Contracts § 161 (1981) (Restatement); See Restatement (Second) of Torts § 551 (1977).

Arizona courts have long recognized that under certain circumstances there may be a "duty to speak." Van Buren v. Pima Community College Dist. Bd., 113 Ariz. 85, 87, 546 P.2d 821, 823 (1976); Batty v. Arizona State Dental Bd., 57 Ariz. 239, 254, 112 P.2d 870, 877 (1941). As the supreme court noted in the context of a confidential relationship, "[s]uppression of a material fact which a party is bound in good faith to disclose is equivalent to a false representation." Leigh v. Loyd, 74 Ariz. 84, 87, 244 P.2d 356, 358 (1952); National Housing Indus. Inc. v. E.L. Jones Dev. Co., 118 Ariz. 374, 379, 576 P.2d 1374, 1379 (1978).

Thus, the important question we must answer is whether under the facts of this case, buyers should have been permitted to present to the jury their claim that sellers were under a duty to disclose their (sellers') knowledge of termite infestation in the residence. This broader question involves two inquiries. First, must a seller of residential property advise the buyer of material facts within his knowledge pertaining to the value of the property? Second, may termite damage and the existence of past infestation constitute such material facts?

The doctrine imposing a duty to disclose is akin to the well-established contractual rules pertaining to relief from contracts based upon mistake. Although the law of contracts supports the finality of transactions, over the years courts have recognized that under certain limited circumstances it is unjust to strictly enforce the policy favoring finality. Thus, for example, even a unilateral mistake of one party to a transaction may justify rescission. Restatement § 153.

There is also a judicial policy promoting honesty and fair dealing in business relationships. This policy is expressed in the law of fraudulent and negligent misrepresentations. Where a misrepresentation is fraudulent or where a negligent misrepresentation is one of material fact, the policy of finality rightly gives way to the policy of promoting honest dealings between the parties. See Restatement § 164(1).

Under certain circumstances nondisclosure of a fact known to one party may be equivalent to the assertion that the fact does not exist. For example "[w]hen one conveys a false impression by the disclosure of some facts and the concealment of others, such concealment is in effect a false representation that what is disclosed is the whole truth." State v. Coddington, 135 Ariz. 480, 481, 662 P.2d 155, 156 (App.1983). Thus, nondisclosure may be equated with and given the same legal effect as fraud and misrepresentation. One category of cases where this has been done involves the area of nondisclosure of material facts affecting the value of property, known to the seller but not reasonably capable of being known to the buyer.

Courts have formulated this "duty to disclose" in slightly different ways. For example, the Florida Supreme Court recently declared that "where the seller of a home knows of facts materially affecting the value of the property which are not readily observable and are not known to the buyer, the seller is under a duty to disclose them to the buyer." Johnson v. Davis, 480 So.2d 625, 629 (Fla.1985) (defective roof in three-year old home). In California, the rule has been stated this way:

> [W]here the seller knows of facts materially affecting the value or desirability of the property which are known or accessible only to him and also knows that such facts are not known to, or within the reach of the diligent attention and observation of the buyer, the seller is under a duty to disclose them to the buyer.

Lingsch v. Savage, 213 Cal.App.2d 729, 735, 29 Cal.Rptr. 201, 204 (1963); contra Ray v. Montgomery, 399 So.2d 230 (Ala.1980); see generally W. Prosser

& W. Keeton, The Law of Torts § 106 (5th ed.1984). We find that the Florida formulation of the disclosure rule properly balances the legitimate interests of the parties in a transaction for the sale of a private residence and accordingly adopt it for such cases.

As can be seen, the rule requiring disclosure is invoked in the case of material facts.[22] Thus, we are led to the second inquiry—whether the existence of termite damage in a residential dwelling is the type of material fact which gives rise to the duty to disclose. The existence of termite damage and past termite infestation has been considered by other courts to be sufficiently material to warrant disclosure. See generally Annot., 22 A.L.R.3d 972 (1968)....

Although sellers have attempted to draw a distinction between live termites[23] and past infestation, the concept of materiality is an elastic one which is not limited by the termites' health. "A matter is material if it is one to which a reasonable person would attach importance in determining his choice of action in the transaction in question." Lynn v. Taylor, 7 Kan.App.2d at 371, 642 P.2d at 134–35. For example, termite damage substantially affecting the structural soundness of the residence may be material even if there is no evidence of present infestation. Unless reasonable minds could not differ, materiality is a factual matter which must be determined by the trier of fact. The termite damage in this case may or may not be material. Accordingly, we conclude that buyers should be allowed to present their case to a jury.

Sellers argue that even assuming the existence of a duty to disclose, summary judgment was proper because the record shows that their "silence ... did not induce or influence" the buyers. This is so, sellers contend, because Mr. Hill stated in his deposition that he intended to rely on the termite inspection report. But this argument begs the question. If sellers were fully aware of the extent of termite damage and if such information had been disclosed to buyers, a jury could accept Mr. Hill's testimony that had he known of the termite damage he would not have purchased the house.

Sellers further contend that buyers were put on notice of the possible existence of termite infestation and were therefore "chargeable with the knowledge which [an] inquiry, if made, would have revealed." Godfrey v. Navratil, 3 Ariz.App. 47, 51, 411 P.2d 470 (1966) (quoting Luke v. Smith, 13 Ariz. 155, 162, 108 P. 494, 496 (1910)). It is also true that "a party may ... reasonably expect the other to take normal steps to inform himself and to draw his own conclusions." Restatement § 161 comment d. Under the facts of this case, the question of buyers' knowledge of the termite problem (or their diligence in attempting to inform themselves about the termite problem) should be left to the jury.[24]

... Reversed and remanded.

CONTRERAS, P.J., and YALE McFATE, J. (Retired), concur.

---

22. Arizona has recognized that a duty to disclose may arise where the buyer makes an inquiry of the seller, regardless of whether or not the fact is material. Universal Inv. Co. v. Sahara Motor Inn, Inc., 127 Ariz. 213, 215, 619 P.2d 485, 487 (1980). The inquiry by buyers whether the ripple was termite damage imposed a duty upon sellers to disclose what information they knew concerning the existence of termite infestation in the residence.

23. Sellers acknowledge that a duty of disclosure would exist if live termites were present. Obde v. Schlemeyer, 56 Wash.2d 449, 353 P.2d 672 (1960).

24. Sellers also contend that they had no knowledge of any existing termite damage in the house. An extended discussion of the facts on this point is unnecessary. Simply stated, the facts are in conflict on this issue.

RESTATEMENT, SECOND, CONTRACTS §§ 159, 161

[See Selected Source Materials Supplement]

RESTATEMENT, SECOND, CONTRACTS
§ 161, ILLUSTRATIONS 7, 10, 11

7. A, seeking to induce B to make a contract to sell land, knows that B does not know that the land has appreciably increased in value because of a proposed shopping center but does not disclose this to B. B makes the contract. Since B's mistake is not one as to a basic assumption ... A's non-disclosure is not equivalent to an assertion that the value of the land has not appreciably increased.... The contract is not voidable by B....

10. A, seeking to induce B to make a contract to sell A land, learns from government surveys that the land contains valuable mineral deposits and knows that B does not know this, but does not disclose this to B. B makes the contract. A's non-disclosure does not amount to a failure to act in good faith and in accordance with reasonable standards of fair dealing and is therefore not equivalent to an assertion that the land does not contain valuable mineral deposits. The contract is not voidable by B.

11. The facts being otherwise as stated in Illustration 10, A learns of the valuable mineral deposits from trespassing on B's land and not from government surveys. A's non-disclosure is equivalent to an assertion that the land does not contain valuable mineral deposits, and this assertion is a misrepresentation....

UNITED STATES v. DIAL, 757 F.2d 163 (7th Cir.1985), cert. denied, 474 U.S. 838, 106 S.Ct. 116, 88 L.Ed.2d 95 (1985) (Posner, J.). "Fraud in the common law sense of deceit is committed by deliberately misleading another by words, by acts, or, in some instances—notably where there is a fiduciary relationship, which creates a duty to disclose all material facts—by silence. Liability is narrower for nondisclosure than for active misrepresentation, since the former sometimes serves a social purpose; for example, someone who bought land from another thinking that it had oil under it would not be required to disclose the fact to the owner, because society wants to encourage people to find out the true value of things, and it does this by allowing them to profit from their knowledge.... But if someone asks you to break a $10 bill, and you give him two $1 bills instead of two $5's because you know he cannot read and won't know the difference, that is fraud. Even more clearly is it fraud to fail to 'level' with one to whom one owes fiduciary duties. The essence of a fiduciary relationship is that the fiduciary agrees to act as his principal's alter ego rather than to assume the standard arm's length stance of traders in a market. Hence the principal is not armed with the usual wariness that one has in dealing with strangers; he trusts the fiduciary to deal with him as frankly as he would deal with himself—he has bought candor."

Chapter 19

THE EFFECT OF UNEXPECTED CIRCUMSTANCES

INTRODUCTORY NOTE

The issue considered in this Chapter is when, and to what extent, unexpected circumstances bear on the parties' rights under a contract. In many crucial respects, the modern legal rules that govern this issue are comparable to the rules that govern mutual mistake, in that both sets of rules focus on assumptions and risk. A major difference between the two kinds of cases is practical: In general, mutual-mistake cases usually involve attempts to either rescind the contract, or justify nonperformance, before either party has done much under the contract. In contrast, in unexpected-circumstances cases the relevant circumstances usually become salient only after performance has begun. The legal treatment of unexpected-circumstances cases is often rendered more complex and difficult as a result of this practical difference.

The cases considered in this chapter are generally dealt with under the legal rubrics *impossibility*, *impracticability*, and *frustration*. Roughly speaking, the three doctrines arose in that order: First, the courts recognized that impossibility might be a defense; next, that impracticability might be a defense; and finally, that frustration of the purpose of a contract might be a defense. In this Chapter, these three doctrines will be taken up more or less in that order ("more or less," because the doctrines overlap), under the general heading of unexpected circumstances.

TAYLOR v. CALDWELL
In the Queen's Bench, 1863.
3 Best & S. 826.

Blackburn, J. In this case the plaintiffs and defendants had, on May 27th, 1861, entered into a contract by which the defendants agreed to let the plaintiffs have the use of The Surrey Gardens and Music Hall on four days then to come, viz., June 17th, July 15th, August 5th, and August 19th, for the purpose of giving a series of four grand concerts, and day and night fêtes, at the Gardens and Hall on those days respectively; and the plaintiffs agreed to take the Gardens and Hall on those days, and pay £100 for each day.

510

The parties inaccurately call this a "letting," and the money to be paid, a "rent"; but the whole agreement is such as to show that the defendants were to retain the possession of the Hall and Gardens so that there was to be no demise of them, and that the contract was merely to give the plaintiffs the use of them on those days. Nothing, however, in our opinion, depends on this. The agreement then proceeds to set out various stipulations between the parties as to what each was to supply for these concerts and entertainments, and as to the manner in which they should be carried on. The effect of the whole is to show that the existence of the Music Hall in the Surrey Gardens in a state fit for a concert was essential for the fulfilment of the contract,—such entertainments as the parties contemplated in their agreement could not be given without it.

After the making of the agreement, and before the first day on which a concert was to be given, the Hall was destroyed by fire. This destruction, we must take it on the evidence, was without the fault of either party, and was so complete that in consequence the concerts could not be given as intended. And the question we have to decide is whether, under these circumstances, the loss which the plaintiffs have sustained is to fall upon the defendants. [The damages claimed in the declaration were for moneys paid by the plaintiffs in advertising the concerts and for sums expended and expenses incurred by them in preparing for the concerts.] The parties when framing their agreement evidently had not present to their minds the possibility of such a disaster, and have made no express stipulation with reference to it, so that the answer to the question must depend upon the general rules of law applicable to such a contract.

There seems no doubt that where there is a positive contract to do a thing, not in itself unlawful, the contractor must perform it or pay damages for not doing it, although in consequence of unforeseen accidents the performance of his contract has become unexpectedly burdensome or even impossible. The law is so laid down in 1 Roll.Abr. 450, Condition (G), and in the note (2) to Walton v. Waterhouse (2 Wms.Saund. 421a, 6th Ed.) and is recognized as the general rule by all the judges in the much discussed case of Hall v. Wright (E.B. & E. 746). But this rule is only applicable when the contract is positive and absolute, and not subject to any condition either express or implied; and there are authorities which, as we think, establish the principle that where, from the nature of the contract, it appears that the parties must from the beginning have known that it could not be fulfilled unless when the time for the fulfilment of the contract arrived some particular specified thing continued to exist, so that, when entering into the contract, they must have contemplated such continuing existence as the foundation of what was to be done; there, in the absence of any express or implied warranty that the thing shall exist, the contract is not to be construed as a positive contract, but as subject to an implied condition that the parties shall be excused in case, before breach, performance becomes impossible from the perishing of the thing without default of the contractor.

There seems little doubt that this implication tends to further the great object of making the legal construction such as to fulfill the intention of those who entered into the contract. For in the course of affairs men in making such contracts in general would, if it were brought to their minds, say that there should be such a condition . . . .

There is a class of contracts in which a person binds himself to do something which requires to be performed by him in person; and such promises, e.g. promises to marry, or promises to serve for a certain time, are never in practice qualified by an express exception of the death of the party; and therefore in such cases the contract is in terms broken if the promisor dies before fulfilment. Yet it was very early determined that, if the performance is personal, the executors are not liable; Hyde v. The Dean of Windsor (Cro.Eliz. 552, 553). See 2 Wms.Exors. 1560 (5th Ed.), where a very apt illustration is given. "Thus," says the learned author, "if an author undertakes to compose a work, and dies before completing it, his executors are discharged from this contract; for the undertaking is merely personal in its nature, and by the intervention of the contractor's death, has become impossible to be performed." For this he cites a dictum of Lord Lyndhurst in Marshall v. Broadhurst (1 Tyr. 348, 349) and a case mentioned by Patteson, J., in Wentworth v. Cock (10 A. & E. 42, 45–46). In Hall v. Wright (E.B. & E. 746, 749), Crompton, J., in his judgment, puts another case. "Where a contract depends upon personal skill, and the act of God renders it impossible, as, for instance, in the case of a painter employed to paint a picture who is struck blind, it may be that the performance might be excused."

It seems that in those cases the only ground on which the parties or their executors can be excused from the consequences of the breach of the contract, is, that from the nature of the contract there is an implied condition of the continued existence of the life of the contractor, and perhaps in the case of the painter, of his eyesight. In the instances just given the person, the continued existence of whose life is necessary to the fulfilment of the contract, is himself the contractor, but that does not seem in itself to be necessary to the application of the principle, as is illustrated by the following example. In the ordinary form of an apprentice deed, the apprentice binds himself in unqualified terms to "serve until the full end and term of seven years to be fully complete and ended," during which term it is covenanted that the apprentice his master "faithfully shall serve," and the father of the apprentice in equally unqualified terms binds himself for the performance by the apprentice of all and every covenant on his part. (See the form, 2 Chitty on Pleading, 370 [7th Ed.] by Greening.) It is undeniable that if the apprentice dies within the seven years, the covenant of the father that he shall perform his covenant to serve for seven years is not fulfilled, yet surely it cannot be that an action would lie against the father. Yet the only reason why it would not is that he is excused because of the apprentice's death.

These are instances where the implied condition is of the life of a human being, but there are others in which the same implication is made as to the continued existence of a thing. For example, where a contract of sale is made amounting to a bargain and sale, transferring presently the property in specific chattels, which are to be delivered by the vendor at a future day; there, if the chattels, without the fault of the vendor, perish in the interval, the purchaser must pay the price, and the vendor is excused from performing his contract to deliver, which has thus become impossible.

That this is the rule of the English law is established by the case of Rugg v. Minett (11 East, 210), where the article that perished before delivery was turpentine, and it was decided that the vendor was bound to refund the price of all those lots in which the property had not passed; but was entitled to retain without deduction the price of those lots in which the property had passed, though they were not delivered, and though in the conditions of sale, which are set out in the report, there was no express qualification of the promise to deliver on payment. It seems in that case rather to have been taken for granted than decided that the destruction of the thing sold before delivery excused the vendor from fulfilling his contract to deliver on payment. . . .

It may, we think, be safely asserted to be now English law, that in all contracts of loan of chattels or bailments if the performance of the promise of the borrower or bailee to return the things lent or bailed, becomes impossible because it has perished, this impossibility (if not arising from the fault of the borrower or bailee from some risk which he has taken upon himself) excuses the borrower or bailee from the performance of his promise to redeliver the chattel.

The great case of Coggs v. Bernard (1 Smith's L.C. 171 [5th Ed.] 2 L.Raym. 909) is now the leading case on the law of bailments, and Lord Holt, in that case, referred so much to the civil law that it might perhaps be thought that this principle was there derived direct from the civilians, and was not generally applicable in English law except in the case of bailments; but the case of Williams v. Lloyd (W. Jones, 179), above cited, shows that the same law had been already adopted by the English law as early as the Book of Assizes. The principle seems to us to be that, in contracts in which the performance depends on the continued existence of a given person or thing, a condition is implied that the impossibility of performance arising from the perishing of the person or thing shall excuse the performance.

In none of these cases is the promise in words other than positive, nor is there any express stipulation that the destruction of the person or thing shall excuse the performance; but that excuse is by law implied, because from the nature of the contract it is apparent that the parties contracted on the basis of the continued existence of the particular person or chattel. In the present case, looking at the whole contract, we find that the parties contracted on the basis of the continued existence of the Music Hall at the time when the concerts were to be given, that being essential to their performance.

We think, therefore, that the Music Hall having ceased to exist, without fault of either party, both parties are excused, the plaintiffs from taking the gardens and paying the money, the defendants from performing their promise to give the use of the Hall and Gardens and other things. Consequently the rule must be absolute to enter the verdict for the defendants.

Rule absolute.

TACIT ASSUMPTIONS—CONTINUED

In *Taylor v. Caldwell* the court says that when framing their agreement the parties "had not present to their minds the possibility" of a disaster affecting the Music Hall, and concludes that the parties "must have contemplated" the "continuing existence" of the Hall "as the foundation" of their agreement.

Is there a contradiction here? The court seems to say that the parties did not think of the possibility of the Hall's burning and therefore assumed that it would not burn. But how can the parties assume that no fire will occur when the possibility of a fire was never present to their minds? If this possibility was not present to their minds, would it not be more accurate to say that they assumed nothing about a fire, either that it would or would not occur?

The difficulty here can be resolved through the concept of tacit assumptions discussed in the previous Chapter. As pointed out in that Chapter, words like "intention," "assumption," "expectation" and "understanding" all seem to imply a *conscious* state involving an awareness of alternatives and a deliberate choice among them. It is, however, plain that there is a psychological state that can be described as a "tacit assumption," which does not involve a consciousness of alternatives. In experiments with animals the relative strength of such "assumptions" can be roughly measured. If a rat is trained for months to run through a particular maze, the sudden interposition of a barrier in one of the paths will have a very disruptive effect on its behavior. For some time after encountering the barrier, the rat will be likely to engage in random and apparently pointless behavior, running in circles, scratching itself, etc. The degree to which the barrier operates disruptively reflects the strength of the "assumption" made by the rat that the barrier would not be there. If the maze has been frequently changed, and the rat has only recently become accustomed to the maze's present form, the introduction of a barrier will act less disruptively. In such a case, after a relatively short period of random behavior the rat will begin to act purposively, will retrace its steps, seek other outlets, etc. In this situation the "assumption" that the path would not be obstructed has not been deeply etched into the rat's nervous system; the rat behaves as if it "half-expected" some such impediment.

In a similar way, where parties have entered into a contract, an unexpected obstacle to performance may operate disruptively in varying degrees depending on the context. To one who has contracted to carry goods by truck over a road traversing a mountain pass, a landslide filling the pass may be a very disruptive and unexpected event. But one who contracts to build a road through the mountains might view the same event, occurring during the course of construction, as a temporary set-back and a challenge to her resourcefulness. One who contracts to deliver goods a year from now at a fixed price certainly "takes into account" the possibility of some fluctuation in price levels, but may feel that a ten-fold inflation is contrary to an "assumption" or "expectation" that price variations would occur within the "normal" range, and that this expectation was "the foundation of the agreement."

In spite of hopeful beginnings that promise a more comprehensive psychological treatment of human behavior, for the time being the only methods available for dealing with problems like that raised by Taylor v. Caldwell are essentially those resting on intuition and introspection. We "just know" that the burning of a music hall violates a tacit assumption of the parties who executed a contract for hiring it for a few days; we "just know" that a two per cent increase in the price of beans does not violate a tacit assumption underlying a contract to deliver a ton of beans for a fixed price.

————

OCEAN TRAMP TANKERS CORP. v. V/O SOVFRACHT, [1964] 2 Q.B. 226 (1963) (Denning, M.R.). "It was originally said that the doctrine of frustration was based on an implied term. In short, that the parties, if they had foreseen the new situation, would have said to one another: 'If that happens, of course, it is all over between us.' But the theory of an implied term has now been discarded by everyone, or nearly everyone, for the simple reason that it does not represent the truth. The parties would not have said: 'It is all over between us.' They would have differed about what was to happen. Each would have sought to insert reservations or qualifications of one kind or another.''

MINERAL PARK LAND CO. v. HOWARD, 172 Cal. 289, 156 P. 458 (1916). Plaintiff owned certain land in a ravine. Defendants had made a contract with public authorities to construct a concrete bridge across the ravine. In August 1911, the parties made a contract under which plaintiff granted defendants the right to haul gravel and earth from its land, and defendants agreed to take from that land all the gravel and earth necessary for the fill and cement work on the bridge. Defendants used 101,000 cubic yards in this work but procured 50,869 of those cubic yards from persons other than plaintiff, and plaintiff sued for breach of contract. The trial court found as follows: Plaintiff's land contained earth and gravel far in excess of 101,000 cubic yards of earth and gravel, but only 50,131 of these cubic yards, the amount taken by defendants, was above the water level. No greater quantity could have been taken by ordinary means, but only by employing a steam dredger, and earth and gravel taken in this way could not have been used without first having been dried. Defendants removed all the earth and gravel from plaintiff's land "that was practical to take and remove from a financial standpoint." Any greater amount could have been taken only at an expense of 10 or 12 times the usual cost per yard. It was not "advantageous or practical" to have taken more material from plaintiff's land, although it was not impossible. Held, defendant was excused:

> . . . When [the parties] stipulated that all of the earth and gravel needed for this purpose should be taken from plaintiff's land, they contemplated and assumed that the land contained the requisite quantity, available for use. The defendants were not binding themselves to take what was not there. And, in determining whether the earth and gravel were "available," we must view the conditions in a practical and reasonable way. Although there was gravel on the land, it was so situated that the defendants could not take it by ordinary means, nor except at a prohibitive cost. To all fair intents then, it was impossible for defendants to take it.

> "... A thing is impossible in legal contemplation when it is not practicable; and a thing is impracticable when it can only be done at an excessive and unreasonable cost." 1 Beach on Contr. § 216. We do not mean to intimate that the defendants could excuse themselves by showing the existence of conditions which would make the performance of their obligation more expensive than they had anticipated, or which would entail a loss upon them. But, where the difference in cost is so great as here, and has the effect, as found, of making performance impracticable,

the situation is not different from that of a total absence of earth and gravel.

UNITED STATES v. WEGEMATIC CORP.

United States Court of Appeals, Second Circuit, 1966.
360 F.2d 674.

Before LUMBARD, CHIEF JUDGE, and FRIENDLY and ANDERSON, CIRCUIT JUDGES.

FRIENDLY, CIRCUIT JUDGE. The facts developed at trial in the District Court for the Southern District of New York, fully set forth in a memorandum by Judge Graven, can be briefly summarized: In June 1956 the Federal Reserve Board invited five electronics manufacturers to submit proposals for an intermediate-type, general-purpose electronic digital computing system or systems; the invitation stressed the importance of early delivery as a consideration in determining the Board's choice. Defendant, a relative newcomer in the field, which had enjoyed considerable success with a smaller computer known as the ALWAC III–E, submitted a detailed proposal for the sale or lease of a new computer designated as the ALWAC 800. It characterized the machine as "a truly revolutionary system utilizing all of the latest technical advances," and featured that "maintenance problems are minimized by the use of highly reliable magnetic cores for not only the high speed memory but also logical elements and registers." Delivery was offered nine months from the date the contract or purchase order was received. In September the Board acted favorably on the defendant's proposal, ordering components of the ALWAC 800 with an aggregate cost of $231,800. Delivery was to be made on June 30, 1957, with liquidated damages of $100 per day for delay. The order also provided that in the event the defendant failed to comply "with any provision" of the agreement, "the Board may procure the services described in the contract from other sources and hold the Contractor responsible for any excess cost occasioned thereby." Defendant accepted the order with enthusiasm.

The first storm warning was a suggestion by the defendant in March 1957 that the delivery date be postponed. In April it informed the Board by letter that delivery would be made on or before October 30 rather than as agreed, the delay being due to the necessity of "a redesign which we feel has greatly improved this equipment"; waiver of the stipulated damages for delay was requested. The Board took the request under advisement. On August 30 defendant wrote that delivery would be delayed "possibly into 1959"; it suggested use of ALWAC III–E equipment in the interim and waiver of the $100 per day "penalty." The Board also took this request under advisement but made clear it was waiving no rights. In mid-October defendant announced that "due to engineering difficulties it has become impracticable to deliver the ALWAC 800 Computing System at this time"; it requested cancellation of the contract without damages. The Board set about procuring comparable equipment from another manufacturer; on October 6, 1958, International Business Machines Corporation delivered an IBM 650 computer, serving substantially the same purpose as the ALWAC 800, at a rental of $102,000 a year with an option to purchase for $410,450.

In July 1958 the Board advised defendant of its intention to press its claim for damages; this suit followed. The court awarded the United States $46,300 for delay under the liquidated damages clause, $179,450 for the excess cost of the IBM equipment, and $10,056 for preparatory expenses useless in operating the IBM system—a total of $235,806, with 6% interest from October 6, 1958.

The principal point of the defense, which is the sole ground of this appeal, is that delivery was made impossible by "basic engineering difficulties" whose correction would have taken between one and two years and would have cost a million to a million and a half dollars, with success likely but not certain. Although the record does not give an entirely clear notion what the difficulties were, two experts suggested that they may have stemmed from the magnetic cores, used instead of transistors to achieve a solid state machine, which did not have sufficient uniformity at this stage of their development. Defendant contends that under federal law, which both parties concede to govern, see Cargill, Inc. v. Commodity Credit Corp., 275 F.2d 745, 751–753 (2 Cir.1960), the "practical impossibility" of completing the contract excused its defaults in performance. . . .

We find persuasive the defendant's suggestion of looking to the Uniform Commercial Code as a source for the "federal" law of sales. . . .

Section 2–615 of the UCC, entitled "Excuse by failure of presupposed conditions," provides that:

> "Except so far as a seller may have assumed a greater obligation . . . delay in delivery or non-delivery . . . is not a breach of his duty under a contract for sale if performance as agreed has been made impracticable by the occurrence of a contingency the nonoccurrence of which was a basic assumption on which the contract was made". . . .

The latter part of the test seems a somewhat complicated way of putting Professor Corbin's question of how much risk the promisor assumed. Recent Developments in the Law of Contracts, 50 Harv.L.Rev. 449, 465–66 (1937); 2 Corbin, Contracts § 1333, at 371. We see no basis for thinking that when an electronics system is promoted by its manufacturer as a revolutionary breakthrough, the risk of the revolution's occurrence falls on the purchaser; the reasonable supposition is that it has already occurred or, at least, that the manufacturer is assuring the purchaser that it will be found to have when the machine is assembled. As Judge Graven said: "The Board in its invitation for bids did not request invitations to conduct a development program for it. The Board requested invitations from manufacturers for the furnishing of a computer machine." Acceptance of defendant's argument would mean that though a purchaser makes his choice because of the attractiveness of a manufacturer's representation and will be bound by it, the manufacturer is free to express what are only aspirations and gamble on mere probabilities of fulfillment without any risk of liability. In fields of developing technology, the manufacturer would thus enjoy a wide degree of latitude with respect to performance while holding an option to compel the buyer to pay if the gamble should pan out. See Austin Co. v. United States, 314 F.2d 518, 521, 161 Ct.Cl. 76, cert. denied, 375 U.S. 830, 84 S.Ct. 75, 11 L.Ed.2d 62 (1963). We do not think this the common understanding—above all as to a contract where the manufacturer expressly agreed to liquidated damages for delay and authorized the purchaser to resort to other sources in the event of non-delivery. Contrast

National Presto Industries, Inc. v. United States, 338 F.2d 99, 106–112, 167 Ct.Cl. 749 (1964), cert. denied, 380 U.S. 962 (1965). If a manufacturer wishes to be relieved of the risk that what looks good on paper may not prove so good in hardware, the appropriate exculpatory language is well known and often used.

Beyond this the evidence of true impracticability was far from compelling. The large sums predicted by defendant's witnesses must be appraised in relation not to the single computer ordered by the Federal Reserve Board, evidently for a bargain price, but to the entire ALWAC 800 program as originally contemplated. Although the record gives no idea what this was, even twenty-five machines would gross $10,000,000 if priced at the level of the comparable IBM equipment. While the unanticipated need for expending $1,000,000 or $1,500,000 on redesign might have made such a venture unattractive, as defendant's management evidently decided, the sums are thus not so clearly prohibitive as it would have them appear. What seemingly did become impossible was on-time performance; the issue whether if defendant had offered prompt rectification of the design, the Government could have refused to give it a chance and still recover not merely damages for delay but also the higher cost of replacement equipment, is not before us.

Affirmed.

TRANSATLANTIC FINANCING CORP. v. UNITED STATES

United States Court of Appeals, District of Columbia Circuit, 1966.
363 F.2d 312.

Before DANAHER, WRIGHT and McGOWAN, CIRCUIT JUDGES.

J. SKELLY WRIGHT, CIRCUIT JUDGE. This appeal involves a voyage charter between Transatlantic Financing Corporation, operator of the SS CHRISTOS, and the United States covering carriage of a full cargo of wheat from a United States Gulf port to a safe port in Iran. The District Court dismissed a libel filed by Transatlantic against the United States for costs attributable to the ship's diversion from the normal sea route caused by the closing of the Suez Canal. We affirm.

On July 26, 1956, the Government of Egypt nationalized the Suez Canal Company and took over operation of the Canal. On October 2, 1956, during the international crisis which resulted from the seizure, the voyage charter in suit was executed between representatives of Transatlantic and the United States. The charter indicated the termini of the voyage but not the route. On October 27, 1956, the SS CHRISTOS sailed from Galveston for Bandar Shapur, Iran, on a course which would have taken her through Gibraltar and the Suez Canal. On October 29, 1956, Israel invaded Egypt. On October 31, 1956, Great Britain and France invaded the Suez Canal Zone. On November 2, 1956, the Egyptian Government obstructed the Suez Canal with sunken vessels and closed it to traffic.

On or about November 7, 1956, Beckmann, representing Transatlantic, contacted Potosky, an employee of the United States Department of Agriculture, who appellant concedes was unauthorized to bind the Government, requesting instructions concerning disposition of the cargo and seeking an agreement for payment of additional compensation for a voyage around the Cape of Good Hope. Potosky advised Beckmann that Transatlantic was expected to perform the charter according to its terms, that he did not believe Transatlantic was entitled to additional compensation for a voyage around the Cape, but that Transatlantic was free to file such a claim. Following this discussion, the CHRISTOS changed course for the Cape of Good Hope and eventually arrived in Bandar Shapur on December 30, 1956.

Transatlantic's claim is based on the following train of argument. The charter was a contract for a voyage from a Gulf port to Iran. Admiralty principles and practices, especially stemming from the doctrine of deviation, require us to imply into the contract the term that the voyage was to be performed by the "usual and customary" route. The usual and customary route from Texas to Iran was, at the time of contract, via Suez, so the contract was for a voyage from Texas to Iran via Suez. When Suez was closed this contract became impossible to perform. Consequently, appellant's argument continues, when Transatlantic delivered the cargo by going around the Cape of Good Hope, in compliance with the Government's demand under claim of right, it conferred a benefit upon the United States for which it should be paid in *quantum meruit*.

The doctrine of impossibility of performance has gradually been freed from the earlier fictional and unrealistic strictures of such tests as the "implied term" and the parties' "contemplation." Page, The Development of the Doctrine of Impossibility of Performance, 18 Mich.L.Rev. 589, 596 (1920). See generally 6 Corbin, Contracts §§ 1320–1372 (rev. ed. 1962); 6 Williston, Contracts §§ 1931–1979 (rev. ed. 1938). It is now recognized that " 'A thing is impossible in legal contemplation when it is not practicable; and a thing is impracticable when it can only be done at an excessive and unreasonable cost.' " Mineral Park Land Co. v. Howard, 172 Cal. 289, 293, 156 P. 458, 460, L.R.A. 1916F, 1 (1916). Accord, Whelan v. Griffith Consumers Company, D.C.Mun.App., 170 A.2d 229 (1961); Restatement, Contracts § 454 (1932); Uniform Commercial Code (U.L.A.) § 2–615, comment 3. The doctrine ultimately represents the ever-shifting line, drawn by courts hopefully responsive to commercial practices and mores, at which the community's interest in having contracts enforced according to their terms is outweighed by the commercial senselessness of requiring performance.[1] When the issue is raised, the court is asked to construct a condition of performance based on the changed circumstances, a process which involves at least three reasonably definable steps. First, a contingency—something unexpected—must have occurred. Second, the risk of the unexpected occurrence must not have been allocated either by agreement or by custom. Finally, occurrence of the contingency must have rendered performance commercially impracticable.[2] Unless the court finds these three requirements satisfied, the plea of impossibility must fail.

1. While the impossibility issue rarely arises, as it has here, in a suit to recover the cost of an alternative method of performance, compare Annot., 84 A.L.R.2d 12, 19 (1962), there is nothing necessarily inconsistent in claiming commercial impracticability for the method of performance actually adopted; the concept of impracticability assumes performance was physically possible. Moreover, a rule making nonperformance a condition precedent to recovery would unjustifiably encourage disappointment of expectations.

2. Compare Uniform Commercial Code § 2–615(a). . . .

The first requirement was met here. It seems reasonable, where no route is mentioned in a contract, to assume the parties expected performance by the usual and customary route at the time of contract. Since the usual and customary route from Texas to Iran at the time of contract[3] was through Suez, closure of the Canal made impossible the expected method of performance. But this unexpected development raises rather than resolves the impossibility issue, which turns additionally on whether the risk of the contingency's occurrence had been allocated and, if not, whether performance by alternative routes was rendered impracticable.

Proof that the risk of a contingency's occurrence has been allocated may be expressed in or implied from the agreement. Such proof may also be found in the surrounding circumstances, including custom and usages of the trade. See 6 Corbin, supra, § 1339, at 394–397; 6 Williston, supra, § 1948, at 5457–5458. The contract in this case does not expressly condition performance upon availability of the Suez route. Nor does it specify "via Suez" or, on the other hand, "via Suez or Cape of Good Hope." Nor are there provisions in the contract from which we may properly imply that the continued availability of Suez was a condition of performance.[4] Nor is there anything in custom or trade usage, or in the surrounding circumstances generally, which would support our constructing a condition of performance. The numerous cases requiring performance around the Cape when Suez was closed, see e.g., Ocean Tramp Tankers Corp. v. V/O Sovfracht (The Eugenia), [1964] 2 Q.B. 226, and cases cited therein, indicate that the Cape route is generally regarded as an alternative means of performance. So the implied expectation that the route would be via Suez is hardly adequate proof of an allocation to the promisee of the risk of closure. In some cases, even an express expectation may not amount to a condition of performance.[5] The doctrine of deviation supports our assumption that parties normally expect performance by the usual and customary route, but it adds nothing beyond this that is probative of an allocation of the risk.[6]

3. ... It may be that very often the availability of a customary route at the time of performance other than the route expected to be used at the time of contract should result in denial of relief under the impossibility theory; certainly if *no* customary route is available at the time of performance the contract is rendered impossible. But the same customarily used alternative route may be practicable in one set of circumstances and impracticable in another, as where the goods are unable to survive the extra journey. Moreover, ... the alternative route, in our case around the Cape, may be practicable at some time during performance, for example while the vessel is still in the Atlantic Ocean, and impracticable at another time during performance, for example after the vessel has traversed most of the Mediterranean Sea....

4. The charter provides that the vessel is "in every way fitted for *the voyage*" (emphasis added), and the "P. & I. Bunker Deviation Clause" refers to "the contract voyage" and the "direct and/or customary route." Appellant argues that these provisions require implication of a voyage by the direct and customary route. Actually they prove only what we are willing to accept—that the parties expected the usual and customary route would be used. The provisions in no way condition performance upon nonoccurrence of this contingency....

5. [The court here quoted UCC § 2–614(1).]

6. The deviation doctrine, drawn principally from admiralty insurance practice, implies into all relevant commercial instruments naming the termini of voyages the usual and customary route between those points. 1 Arnould, Marine Insurance and Average § 376, at 522 (10th ed. 1921). Insurance is cancelled when a ship unreasonably "deviates" from this course, for example by extending a voyage or by putting in at an irregular port, and the shipowner forfeits the protection of clauses of exception which might otherwise have protected him from his common law insurer's liability to cargo. See Gilmore & Black [on Admiralty] § 2–6, at 59–60. This practice, properly qualified see id. § 3–41, makes good sense, since insurance rates are computed on the basis of the implied course, and deviations in the course increasing the anticipated risk make the insurer's calculations meaningless. Arnould, supra, § 14, at 26.

If anything, the circumstances surrounding this contract indicate that the risk of the Canal's closure may be deemed to have been allocated to Transatlantic. We know or may safely assume that the parties were aware, as were most commercial men with interests affected by the Suez situation, see The Eugenia, supra, that the Canal might become a dangerous area. No doubt the tension affected freight rates, and it is arguable that the risk of closure became part of the dickered terms. Uniform Commercial Code § 2–615, comment 8. We do not deem the risk of closure so allocated, however. Foreseeability or even recognition of a risk does not necessarily prove its allocation.[7] Compare Uniform Commercial Code § 2–615, Comment 1; Restatement, Contracts § 457 (1932). Parties to a contract are not always able to provide for all the possibilities of which they are aware, sometimes because they cannot agree, often simply because they are too busy. Moreover, that some abnormal risk was contemplated is probative but does not necessarily establish an allocation of the risk of the contingency which actually occurs. In this case, for example, nationalization by Egypt of the Canal Corporation and formation of the Suez Users Group did not necessarily indicate that the Canal would be blocked even if a confrontation resulted.[8] The surrounding circumstances do indicate, however, a willingness by Transatlantic to assume abnormal risks, and this fact should legitimately cause us to judge the impracticability of performance by an alternative route in stricter terms than we would were the contingency unforeseen.

We turn then to the question whether occurrence of the contingency rendered performance commercially impracticable under the circumstances of this case. The goods shipped were not subject to harm from the longer, less temperate Southern route. The vessel and crew were fit to proceed around the Cape. Transatlantic was no less able than the United States to purchase insurance to cover the contingency's occurrence. If anything, it is more reasonable to expect owner-operators of vessels to insure against the hazards of war. They are in the best position to calculate the cost of performance by alternative routes (and therefore to estimate the amount of insurance required), and are undoubtedly sensitive to international troubles which uniquely affect the demand for and cost of their services. The only factor operating here in appellant's favor is the added expense, allegedly $43,972.00 above and beyond the contract price of $305,842.92, of extending a 10,000 mile voyage by approximately 3,000 miles. While it may be an overstatement to say that increased cost and difficulty of performance never constitute impracticability, to justify relief there must be more of a variation between expected cost and

Thus the route, so far as insurance contracts are concerned, is crucial, whether express or implied. But even here, the implied term is not inflexible. Reasonable deviations do not result in loss of insurance, at least so long as established practice is followed ... The doctrine's only relevance, therefore, is that it provides additional support for the assumption we willingly make that merchants agreeing to a voyage between two points expect that the usual and customary route between those points will be used. The doctrine provides no evidence of an allocation of the risk of the route's unavailability.

7. See Note, The Fetish of Impossibility in the Law of Contracts, 53 Colum.L.Rev. 94, 98 n. 23 (1953), suggesting that foreseeability is properly used "as a *factor* probative of assumption of the risk of impossibility." (Emphasis added.)

8. Sources cited in the briefs indicate formation of the Suez Canal Users Association on October 1, 1956, was viewed in some quarters as an implied threat of force. See N.Y. Times, Oct. 2, 1956, p. 1, col. 1, noting, on the day the charter in this case was executed, that "Britain has declared her freedom to use force as a last resort if peaceful methods fail to achieve a satisfactory settlement." Secretary of State Dulles was able, however, to view the statement as evidence of the canal users' "dedication to a just and peaceful solution." The Suez Problem 369–370 (Department of State Pub. 1956).

the cost of performing by an available alternative than is present in this case, where the promisor can legitimately be presumed to have accepted some degree of abnormal risk, and where impracticability is urged on the basis of added expense alone.

We conclude, therefore, as have most other courts considering related issues arising out of the Suez closure, that performance of this contract was not rendered legally impossible. Even if we agreed with appellant, its theory of relief seems untenable. When performance of a contract is deemed impossible it is a nullity. In the case of a charter party involving carriage of goods, the carrier may return to an appropriate port and unload its cargo, The Malcolm Baxter, Jr., 277 U.S. 323, 48 S.Ct. 516, 72 L.Ed. 901 (1928), subject of course to required steps to minimize damages. If the performance rendered has value, recovery in *quantum meruit* for the entire performance is proper. But here Transatlantic has collected its contract price, and now seeks *quantum meruit* relief for the additional expense of the trip around the Cape. If the contract is a nullity, Transatlantic's theory of relief should have been *quantum meruit* for the entire trip, rather than only for the extra expense. Transatlantic attempts to take its profit on the contract, and then force the Government to absorb the cost of the additional voyage. When impracticability without fault occurs, the law seeks an equitable solution, see 6 Corbin, supra, § 1321, and *quantum meruit* is one of its potent devices to achieve this end. There is no interest in casting the entire burden of commercial disaster on one party in order to preserve the other's profit. Apparently the contract price in this case was advantageous enough to deter appellant from taking a stance on damages consistent with its theory of liability. In any event, there is no basis for relief.

Affirmed.

AMERICAN TRADING & PRODUCTION CORP. v. SHELL INT'L MARINE LTD., 453 F.2d 939 (2d Cir.1972). American chartered the vessel Washington Trader to Shell for a voyage with a full cargo of lube oil from Beaumont, Texas to Bombay, India. The charter provided for a freight rate in accordance with the then–prevailing American Tanker Rate Schedule of $14.25 per long ton of cargo, plus seventy–five percent. In addition, there was a charge of $.85 per long ton for passage through the Suez Canal. On May 14, 1967, the Washington Trader departed from Beaumont with a cargo of 16,183.32 long tons of lube oil. Freight of $417,327.36 was paid to American in advance. American advised the Washington Trader by radio to bunker (take on additional fuel) at Ceuta in Spanish Morocco at the Strait of Gibraltar due to possible diversion because of the Suez Canal crisis. The vessel arrived at Ceuta on May 30, bunkered, and sailed for the Canal on May 31. On June 5, American cabled the ship's master, advised him of reports of trouble in the Canal, and suggested delay in entering it pending clarification. That day the Canal was closed due to the state of war which had developed. The vessel then proceeded westward, back through the Strait of Gibraltar and around the Cape, and eventually arrived in Bombay on July 15th, some 30 days later than initially expected, traveling a total of 18,055 miles, instead of the 9,709 miles that it would have sailed if the Canal had been open. American billed Shell

$131,978.44 as extra compensation. Shell refused to pay, and American brought suit. Held, for Shell:

> Appellant ... seeks to distinguish *Transatlantic* because in that case the change in course was in the mid-Atlantic and added some 300 miles to the voyage while in this case the WASHINGTON TRADER had traversed most of the Mediterranean and thus had added some 9000 miles to the contemplated voyage. It should be noted that although both the time and the length of the altered passage here exceeded those in the *Transatlantic,* the additional compensation sought here is just under one third of the contract price. Aside from this however, it is a fact that the master of the WASHINGTON TRADER was alerted by radio on May 29th, 1967 of a "possible diversion because of Suez Canal crisis," but nevertheless two days later he had left Ceuta (opposite Gibraltar) and proceeded across the Mediterranean. While we may not speculate about the foreseeability of a Suez crisis at the time the contract was entered, there does not seem to be any question but that the master here had been actually put on notice before traversing the Mediterranean that diversion was possible. Had the WASHINGTON TRADER then changed course, the time and cost of the Mediterranean trip could reasonably have been avoided, thereby reducing the amount now claimed.

————

RESTATEMENT, SECOND, CONTRACTS § 261, Illustration 10: "[Several months after the nationalization of the Suez Canal, during the international crisis resulting from its seizure, A contracts to carry a cargo of B's wheat on A's ship from Galveston, Texas to Bandar Shapur, Iran, for a flat rate. The contract does not specify the route, but the voyage would normally be through the Strait of Gibraltar and the Suez Canal. The] Suez Canal is closed while A's ship is in the Canal, preventing the completion of the voyage. A's duty to carry B's cargo is discharged, and A is not liable to B for breach of contract."

————

UCC §§ 1–103, 2–509, 2–510, 2–613, 2–614, 2–615, 2–616

[See Selected Source Materials Supplement]

————

RESTATEMENT, SECOND, CONTRACTS §§ 261–272

[See Selected Source Materials Supplement]

————

CISG ARTS. 66–69

[See Selected Source Materials Supplement]

————

UNIDROIT PRINCIPLES OF INTERNATIONAL COMMERCIAL CONTRACTS ARTS. 6.2.1, 6.2.2, 6.2.3, 7.1.7

[See Selected Source Materials Supplement]

PRINCIPLES OF EUROPEAN CONTRACT LAW ARTS. 4.102, 6.111, 8.108

[See Selected Source Materials Supplement]

ABA TASK FORCE REPORT ON ARTICLE 2, 16 Del.J.Corp.Law 981, 1201 (1991). "The comments [to UCC § 2–615] should make clear that the section adopts the limited obligation theory of contract. That is, the parties ordinarily do not intend to allocate the risk of unforeseen events, thus leaving a gap in the contract. Should the unforeseen event occur, a court is to fill the gap. More specifically, the court should allocate the risk of the event based on what is fair under the circumstances, not on some supposed implicit agreement–based risk allocation which never occurred."

AMERICAN INSTITUTE OF ARCHITECTS, GENERAL CONDITIONS OF THE CONTRACT FOR CONSTRUCTION, AIA DOC A201, ARTICLES 4, 11 (1987)

[See Selected Source Materials Supplement]

ALBRE MARBLE & TILE CO. v. JOHN BOWEN CO.

Supreme Judicial Court of Massachusetts, 1959.
338 Mass. 394, 155 N.E.2d 437.

Before SPALDING, WILLIAMS, COUNIHAN and WHITTEMORE, JJ.

SPALDING, JUSTICE. The declaration in this action of contract contains four counts. The plaintiff in counts 1 and 2 seeks damages for the defendant's alleged breach of two subcontracts under which the plaintiff agreed to supply labor and materials to the defendant as general contractor of the Chronic Disease Hospital and Nurses' Home in Boston.[12] In counts 3 and 4 the plaintiff seeks to recover the value of work and labor furnished by it to the defendant at the defendant's request. The defendant's substitute answer in defence to the first two counts states that the performance of the subcontracts became impossible when the defendant's general contract with the Commonwealth was declared invalid by this court in Gifford v. Commissioner of Public Health, 328 Mass. 608, 105 N.E.2d 476. The defendant's answer to counts 3

---

12. Count 1 relates to tile work and count 2 relates to marble work.

and 4 (based on quantum meruit) states that no payment could be demanded because the plaintiff did not possess an architect's certificate for the work done. . . .

The defendant filed a motion, accompanied by an affidavit, for the immediate entry of judgment in its favor. . . . The plaintiff filed a counter affidavit. After hearing, the motion was allowed, and the plaintiff duly claimed an exception.

[The court concluded that the granting of defendant's motion for judgment on counts 1 and 2 was proper.]

We turn now to counts 3 and 4 by which the plaintiff seeks a recovery for the fair value of work and labor furnished to the defendant prior to the termination of the general contract. The plaintiff seeks recovery in count 3 for "preparation of samples, shop drawings, tests and affidavits" in connection with the tile work; in count 4 recovery for similar work in connection with the marble contract is sought.

The defendant in its affidavit maintains that the tile and marble work to be furnished by the plaintiff could not have been done until late in the construction process; that no tile or marble was actually installed in the building; and that the expenses incurred by the plaintiff prior to the time the general contract was declared invalid consisted solely of expenditures in preparation for performance. Relying on the decision in Young v. Chicopee, 186 Mass. 518, 72 N.E. 63, the defendant maintains that where a building contract has been rendered impossible of performance a plaintiff may not recover for expenses incurred in preparation for performance, but may recover only for the labor and materials "wrought into" the structure. Therefore, the defendant says, the plaintiff should take nothing here.

The plaintiff places its reliance upon a clause appearing in both contracts which provides in part: "It is agreed you [the plaintiff] will furnish and submit all necessary or required samples, shop drawings, tests, affidavits, etc., for approval, all as ordered or specified. . . ." The plaintiff in effect concedes that no labor or materials were actually wrought into the structure, but argues that the contract provision quoted above placed its preparatory efforts under the supervision of the defendant, and that this circumstance removes this case from the ambit of those decisions which apply the "wrought-in" principle. . . .

The problem of allocating losses where a building contract has been rendered impossible of performance by a supervening act not chargeable to either party is a vexed one. In situations where the part performance of one party measurably exceeds that of the other the tendency has been to allow recovery for the fair value of work done in the actual performance of the contract and to deny recovery for expenditures made in reliance upon the contract or in preparing to perform. This principle has sometimes been expressed in terms of "benefit" or "lack of benefit." In other words, recovery may be had only for those expenditures which, but for the supervening act, would have enured to the benefit of the defendant as contemplated by the contract. See, e.g. Young v. Chicopee, 186 Mass. 518, 520, 72 N.E. 63. The "wrought-in" principle applied in building contract cases is merely a variant of this principle. It has long been recognized that this theory is unworkable if the concept of benefit is applied literally. In M. Ahern Co. v. John Bowen Co. Inc., 334 Mass. 36, 41, 133 N.E.2d 484, 487, we quoted with approval the statement of Professor Williston that "It is enough that the defendant has actually received in part performance of the contract something for which when completed he had agreed to pay a price." Williston on Contracts (Rev. ed.) § 1976.

Although the matter of denial of reliance expenditures in impossibility situations seems to have been discussed but little in judicial opinions, it has, however, been the subject of critical comment by scholars. See Fuller and Perdue, The Reliance Interest in Contract Damages, 46 Yale L.J. 52, 373, 379–383. Note, 46 Mich.L.Rev. 401. In England the recent frustrated contracts legislation provides that the court may grant recovery for expenditures in reliance on the contract or in preparation to perform it where it appears *"just to do so having regard to all the circumstances of the case"* (emphasis supplied). 6 & 7 George VI, c. 40.

We are of opinion that the plaintiff here may recover for those expenditures made pursuant to the specific request of the defendant as set forth in the contract clause quoted above. A combination of factors peculiar to this case justifies such a holding without laying down the broader principle that in every case recovery may be had for payments made or obligations reasonably incurred in preparation for performance of a contract where further performance is rendered impossible without fault by either party. See Boston Plate & Window Glass Co. v. John Bowen Co. Inc., 335 Mass. 697, 702, 141 N.E.2d 715.

The factors which determine the holding here are these: First, this is not a case of mere impossibility by reason of a supervening act. The opinion of this court in M. Ahern Co. v. John Bowen Co. Inc., 334 Mass. 36, 133 N.E.2d 484, points out that the defendant's involvement in creating the impossibility was greater than that of its subcontractors. The facts regarding the defendant's conduct are set forth in that opinion and need not be restated.* Although the defendant's conduct was not so culpable as to render it liable for breach of contract (Boston Plate & Window Glass Co. v. John Bowen Co. Inc., 335 Mass. 697, 141 N.E.2d 715), nevertheless, it was a contributing factor to a loss sustained by the plaintiff which as between the plaintiff and the defendant the latter ought to bear to the extent herein permitted.

We attach significance to the clause in the contract, which was prepared by the defendant, specifically requesting the plaintiff to submit samples, shop drawings, tests, affidavits, etc., to the defendant. This is not a case in which all efforts in preparation for performance were solely within the discretion and control of the subcontractor. We are mindful that in Young v. Chicopee, 186 Mass. 518, 72 N.E. 63, recovery of the value of materials brought to the construction site at the specific request of the defendant therein was denied. But in that case the supervening act rendering further performance impossible was a fire not shown to have been caused by the fault of either party. We are not disposed to extend that holding to a situation in which the defendant's fault is greater than the plaintiff's.

Moreover, the acts requested here by their very nature could not be "wrought into" the structure. In Angus v. Scully, 176 Mass. 357, 57 N.E. 674, 49 A.L.R. 562, recovery for the value of services rendered by house movers was allowed although the house was destroyed midway in the moving. The

---

* The defendant had presented its bid for the hospital construction project in such a manner as to cause the bid to appear to be the lowest although in fact it was not. (Footnote by ed.)

present case comes nearer to the rationale of the *Angus* case than to that of the *Young* case. . . .

We hold that the damages to be assessed are limited solely to the fair value of those acts done in conformity with the specific request of the defendant as contained in the contract. Expenses incurred prior to the execution of the contract, such as those arising out of preparing the plaintiff's bid, are not to be considered.

The plaintiff's exceptions as to counts 1 and 2 are overruled and are sustained as to counts 3 and 4; as to those counts the case is remanded to the Superior Court for further proceedings in conformity with this opinion. The appeal is dismissed.

So ordered.

MISSOURI PUBLIC SERVICE CO. v. PEABODY COAL CO.

Missouri Court of Appeals, Western District, 1979.
583 S.W.2d 721, cert. denied, 444 U.S. 865, 100 S.Ct. 135, 62 L.Ed.2d 88.

Before SHANGLER, P.J., SWOFFORD, C.J., and TURNAGE, J.

SWOFFORD, CHIEF JUDGE.

This is an appeal from a decree of specific performance involving a contract between the parties wherein the appellant (Peabody) agreed to supply the respondent (Public Service) with coal for the production of electricity at the power plants of Public Service in Jackson County, Missouri over a long term. Faced with escalating costs, Peabody unsuccessfully attempted to negotiate a higher price per ton for coal furnished under the contract, and failing in such attempts, declared its intention to discontinue coal shipments. Public Service thereupon elected to consider this position of Peabody to be an anticipatory breach of the contract and thereafter instituted this action to require specific performance of the contract as it was written.

The resolution of this appeal depends upon the underlying basic facts concerning the contractual relationship of the parties. Public Service is a state-regulated public utility supplying electricity and serving the consumers in 28 Missouri counties. In anticipation of need for expanded capacity, it constructed a large coal burning power plant at Sibley, Missouri in Jackson County, and simultaneously undertook negotiations with several coal suppliers, including Peabody, for a 10–year coal supply agreement to meet the requirements of the plant. Letters of intent were signed in 1966 with Peabody and one other coal supplier. At that time, the supply of coal was described as a "buyers market" in which coal suppliers and natural gas companies competed vigorously for the business of energy producers.

Negotiations progressed between the parties to the point where Peabody made an offer to Public Service to supply its coal needs at the Sibley plant for a period of ten years at a base price of $5.40 per net ton, subject to certain price adjustments from time to time relating to costs of labor, taxes, compliance with government regulations, and increase in transportation costs, as reflected in railroad tariffs. Peabody's offer also contained an inflation escalator clause based upon the Consumer Price Index published by the United States Department of Labor. Public Service rejected this offer because of the price adjustment features, but negotiations continued and ultimately resulted in the drafting by Peabody of an agreement essentially the same as the original offer in the area of price adjustments except that the inflation escalator clause was changed so that it would be based upon the Industrial Commodities Index, also published by the United States Department of Labor, but unlike the Consumer Price Index, based, in large part, upon material production costs. This final agreement was formally executed by the parties on December 22, 1967.

Performance under the agreement was profitable for Peabody during the first two years of operation thereunder. Thereafter, production costs began to outpace the price adjustment features of the contract to the extent that in 1974, Peabody requested modification of the price adjustment features. Public Service rejected all proposed modifications in this area but did offer a modification to provide for an increase of $1.00 in the original cost per net ton. This proposal was rejected by Peabody.

On September 16, 1974, a meeting was held between officials of Public Service and Peabody at the Jackson County, Missouri home office of Public Service. At this meeting Public Service again flatly rejected Peabody's proposed modifications of the contract. Peabody thereupon declared that unless these proposed modifications were met, coal shipments to Public Service would cease and the contract would be considered by Peabody to be inoperative. Contact and negotiations continued during which Public Service adamantly refused to agree to the proposed modifications and declared its intentions to hold Peabody to the terms of the original contract. Peabody, by letter dated May 6, 1975, mailed from its principal office in St. Louis, Missouri, advised Public Service that upon the expiration of 60 days all coal shipments under the contract would cease, if the contract modifications were not agreed to by Public Service.

It is undisputed that Peabody possessed adequate coal supplies and ability to perform the contract. Rather, excuse from performance is claimed upon the basis of excessive economic loss under the agreement, absent modification; that excuse from performance was lawful upon the doctrine of "commercial impracticability" under Section 400.2–615 RSMo 1969.

Peabody claimed and the evidence tended to establish that the loss was occasioned largely because the escalation clause in the contract was based upon the Industrial Commodities Index which in years prior to the execution of the contract had been an accurate measure of inflation but had ceased to be an effective measure due to the 1973 oil embargo, runaway inflation and the enactment of new and costly mine safety regulations. Public Service conceded a weakening of this significant function of the Industrial Commodities Index but introduced evidence, including admissions by Peabody, that the events bringing this about were foreseeable at the time of the execution of the contract.

Peabody introduced evidence that its losses under the contract were in excess of 3.4 million dollars at the time of the trial. Peabody's evidence showed that 60% of these claimed losses were not due to inadequacy of the price adjustment features of the contract to track inflation, but rather to reduction in price caused by lower calorific and higher waste content of the coal received than that originally contemplated under the terms of the contract. It is apparently not disputed that had the escalation clause been based upon the Consumer Price Index, Peabody's purported losses would have been substantially reduced.

That Peabody sustained loss under the contract seems clear, although the extent and cause thereof was in sharp dispute. Public Service, over objection, was permitted to show that since performance of the contract began, Peabody had experienced an approximate three-fold increase in the value of its coal reserves, presumably brought about by the same inflationary trend and other causes to which it ascribes its loss under the contract.

This cause was tried without a jury and the court entered its decree of specific performance, from which judgment Peabody appealed. Under such circumstances, the judgment must be affirmed unless there is no substantial evidence to support it, or it is against the weight of the evidence, or erroneously declares or applies the law. Rule 73.01; *Murphy v. Carron,* 536 S.W.2d 30, 32[1] (Mo. banc 1976). The issues upon this appeal are essentially legal in nature, and are, in part at least, issues of first impression in Missouri. These legal issues are governed by the terms and provisions of Chapter 400, Uniform Commercial Code, RSMo 1969 (effective July 1, 1965) (U.C.C.) and in force at the time of the execution of the sales contract here involved....

... Peabody strongly urges, as a ground for reversal of the decree, that the court erred in entering the decree because Public Service acted in bad faith in its refusal to accede to a price modification of the contract and thus Public Service breached the contract. In so doing, Peabody relies upon the U.C.C. provisions imposing the obligation of good faith upon both buyer and seller as an inherent part of all contracts for the sale of goods. Section 400.1–203 under General Provisions of U.C.C. provides:

"Obligation of good faith

"Every contract or duty within this chapter imposes an obligation of good faith in its performance or enforcement."

Section 400.2–103(1)(b) under the provisions of U.C.C. relating to Sales, [provides] in part:

"Definitions and index of definitions ...

" 'Good faith' in the case of a merchant means honesty in fact and the observance of reasonable commercial standards of fair dealing in the trade...."

Such good faith, honesty and adherence to commercial or business standards are also inherent in the right to maintain an equitable action for specific performance of a contract as in the case at bar. There is no evidence or present claim that Public Service acted in any particular outside the boundaries thus imposed in the original negotiations, offer and counteroffers and final execution of the sales contract here in question nor in the performance of the obligations thereunder preceding the breach by repudiation. Peabody's charge is based entirely upon the refusal of Public Service to accede to Peabody's demands for price modification, which refusal, it asserts, constituted bad faith and thus placed the onus of breach upon Public Service. Neither the law of contracts generally nor the terms of U.C.C. relied upon by Peabody lend support to this theory. The contract here involved was settled as a result of arm's length dealing with no cloud of dishonesty, lack of good faith or failure to adhere to standard business or commercial practice upon the part of either party. The fact that foreseeable economic trends or developments resulted in loss of anticipated profits or, as here claimed, actual financial loss, does not prevent Public Service from refusal of a modification of price and to take advantage of a good bargain. Such is particularly true here, for the reason that Public Service is a utility impressed with public interest and any increase in its cost in producing electricity would reflect in its rates to its public and private consumers. For this reason, its good faith, if it had agreed to a gratuitous modification upward of its costs, might properly be called into question. Indeed, in the case of *U.S. for the Use and Benefit of Crane Co. v. Progressive Enterprises, Inc.,* 418 F.Supp. 662 (E.D.Va.1976), strongly relied upon by Peabody, the court held in similar circumstances that the purchaser "possessed the contractual right to refuse to modify and to demand performance on the original terms" (at l.c. 664). Where an enforceable, untainted contract exists, refusing modification of price and seeking specific performance of valid covenants does not constitute bad faith or breach of contract, and the trial court properly so held.

The appellant's final allegation of error is that the trial court erred in refusing to relieve or excuse it from its obligations under the contract upon the basis of "commercial impracticability" under Section 400.2–615 RSMo 1969 (U.C.C.), which section reads, in part:

"Excuse by failure of presupposed conditions

"Except so far as a seller may have assumed a greater obligation and subject to the preceding section on substituted performance:

"(a) Delay in delivery or nondelivery in whole or in part by a seller who complies with paragraphs (b) and (c)[13] is not a breach of his duty under a contract for sale *if performance as agreed has been made impracticable by the occurrence of a contingency the nonoccurrence of which was a basic assumption on which the contract was made* or by compliance in good faith with any applicable foreign or domestic governmental regulation or order whether or not it later proves to be invalid. . . ." (Emphasis supplied)

The comments accompanying this section treat it as dealing with the doctrine of "commercial impracticability" and central to this concept is that the doctrine may be applicable upon the occurrence of a supervening, unforeseen event not within the reasonable contemplation of the parties at the time the contract was made. Such occurrence must go to the heart of the contract.

Further light is shed upon the provisions of Section 400.2–615, in Comment No. 4, accompanying that section, which states:

"4. *Increased cost alone does not excuse performance* unless the rise in cost is due to some unforeseen contingency which alters *the essential nature of the performance.* Neither is a rise or a collapse in the market in itself a justification, *for that is exactly the type of business risk which business contracts made at fixed prices are intended to cover.* But a severe shortage of raw materials or of supplies due to a contingency such as war, embargo, local crop failure, unforeseen shutdown of major sources of

---

13. Subparagraphs (b) and (c) cover situations where a seller's capacity to perform the contract is only partially impaired and for allo-cation of his curtailed production among all of his customers and notice to the buyers. These provisions are not applicable here.

supply or the like, which either causes a marked increase in cost or altogether prevents the seller from securing supplies necessary to his performance, is within the contemplation of this section." (Emphasis added)

In the case of *Transatlantic Financing Corp. v. United States,* 124 U.S.App.D.C. 183, 186, 363 F.2d 312, 315[3] (1966) the court articulates the ingredients necessary to establish the claim of "commercial impracticability" as (1) the occurrence of a contingency; (2) the nonoccurrence of which was a *basic assumption* upon which the contract was made; and (3) by which occurrence further performance has become commercially impracticable. The ... statute is drawn in such general terms ... to provide flexibility in its application and full scope for the application of equitable principles and considerations with which the doctrine of commercial impracticability is imbued, as recognized in the *Transatlantic Financing Corp.* decision, *supra.* When so viewed and applied, a wide variety of commercial situations often unique to the particular case under consideration are subject to scrutiny. This is particularly true in a case such as the one at bar, where the claim of commercial impracticability is based primarily upon the fact that the performance of the contract results in great financial loss to Peabody due to increase in cost of production (due to the causes enumerated) which were not foreseeable at the time the contract was made. In this connection, Peabody argues that in the resolution of this issue, only the contract in litigation should be considered by the court and that the factors of Peabody's financial condition, experience in the production of coal, resources, availability of the raw material (coal reserves) and other factors should be disregarded. This argument is without merit and Peabody cites no authority in support thereof. Those factors have a direct bearing and evidentiary value in determining the question of foreseeability of the occurrence triggering the loss. See e.g. *Eastern Airlines, Inc. v. Gulf Oil Corp.,* 415 F.Supp. 429 (S.D.Fla.1975). A commercial, governmental or business trend affecting a contract's value which would be foreseeable to a party with wide experience and knowledge in the field and, perhaps, not [foreseeable] to a party with less; a loss to a party with vast resources and ample supply of raw materials to perform a bad bargain would be less harmful than to a party without them; and, the application of the doctrine and the equitable principles inherent therein might call for relief in one instance and not another based upon these factors, and others, outside the strict confines of the contract itself.

Further, the trial court is put upon inquiry and finding (under the statute) that the nonoccurrence of the event was a "basic assumption on which the contract was made" and that the occurrence of such event "alters the essential nature of the performance thereunder." See: *Eastern Airlines v. Gulf Oil Corp., supra; United States v. Wegematic Corp.,* 360 F.2d 674 (2d Cir.1966); *Neal–Cooper Grain Co. v. Texas Gulf Sulphur Co.,* 508 F.2d 283 (7th Cir.1974); 6 Corbin on Contracts, Section 1333 (Rev.Ed.1962); 6 Williston on Contracts, Section 1952 (Rev.Ed.1938).

A recent case which is strikingly similar to the case at bar is *Iowa Electric Light & Power Co. v. Atlas Corporation,* 23 U.C.C.Rep.Service (U.S., N.D.Iowa 5/4/78). In that case, the Iowa Electric entered into a contract in 1973 whereby it was to purchase approximately 700,000 pounds of uranium concentrate from Atlas, at a beginning price per pound of $7.10, over an extended period for use in the production of electric energy. The contract contained an escalation clause providing for an automatic inflationary price per pound increase of $0.12329 cents per day or [3.75¢] per month on July 15th of each year so that the contract price by 1978 would be approximately $8.45 per pound. Because of late deliveries, Iowa Electric by way of a proceeding in injunction, in the nature of specific performance, sought to insure deliveries under the terms and at the price established in the contract, and Atlas counterclaimed seeking to reform the contract by judicial decree so as to provide a higher price per pound for the product upon the basis of commercial impracticability. The case was tried upon the counterclaim by stipulation of the parties and the court denied Atlas the relief sought and dismissed its counterclaim.

The basis upon which Atlas sought relief was that unforeseen factors had so drastically increased its costs and resulted in burdensome losses amounting to approximately $1,800,000.00 in 1976 and projected to losses of approximately $4,000,000.00 in fiscal years 1977–1979. Atlas attributed the increase in its costs to the Arab oil embargo and OPEC cartel, unexpected federal environmental and occupational safety regulations, inflation in wages and costs of chemicals and equipment, and certain uranium market conditions. Atlas produced evidence that its costs had increased to $17.40 per pound and that the open market price per pound in 1977 was $43.00 per pound. The court held, among other things:

(1) That the term " 'impracticable' as used in U.C.C. § 2–615 does not mean impossible and each situation should be viewed in the context of reasonable commercial relationships"; that "Atlas must show that the increase is more than onerous or expensive and that it had no part in stimulating that increase"; and that the "burden of proving each element of impracticability is on the party claiming excuse".

(2) That, although some of the factors which resulted in the increased cost of production may have been unforeseen and the total impact was not contemplated by the parties during contract negotiations, prior to contract there was good reason to anticipate rising costs and drastically increased expense arising from inflation and governmental environmental and safety regulations.

(3) It was not clear that Atlas was not in a position to protect itself contractually from some of the risks; that some of the increased costs resulted from internal corporate decisions; and, that increased costs were partially due to rise in the market price of uranium, the fact that Atlas' reserve in Alkaline ores used in processing uranium were rapidly becoming exhausted, facts known to Atlas at the time the contract was negotiated.

The court in *Iowa Electric* refused to reform the contract principally upon the basis of the failure of Atlas to sustain its burden of proof to establish "commercial impracticability", but the facts there are so similar the case stands for an acceptable precedent in the case at bar.

It should again be emphasized that in the negotiations leading to the contract now before this Court an escalator clause was agreed upon to cover the contingencies of increase in Peabody's costs due to wages reflected by labor contracts; payments for unemployment, social security taxes and Workmen's Compensation insurance premiums; costs of compliance with federal, state and local laws, regulations or orders; railroad tariffs; and, increase in the costs of material and supplies, explosives, electric power and administrative and supervisory expense based upon the Industrial Commodities Index of the Department of Labor. There is no evidence nor, indeed, serious claim, that Public Service did not abide by the letter of these provisions, and in addition, prior to suit, agreed to a further price increase of $1.00 per net ton, which Peabody rejected.

The facts as shown by the record lead to the conclusion that at least some of the loss resulted from the fact that for some unexplained reason the Industrial Commodities Index lagged behind the Consumer Price Index, the measuring factor first proposed by Peabody, in reflecting inflationary cost increases. That such indexes were based upon different commercial and economic factors was presumably known by both parties since each was skilled and experienced in those areas and the divergence between the indexes could not be said to be unforeseeable. Be that as it may, Peabody agreed to the use of the Industrial Commodities Index factor.

The other claim made by Peabody alleged to bring it within the doctrine of "commercial impracticability", is the Arab oil embargo. Such a possibility was common knowledge and had been thoroughly discussed and recognized for many years by our government, media economists and business, and the fact that the embargo was imposed during the term of the contract here involved was foreseeable. Peabody failed to demonstrate that this embargo affected its ability to secure oil or petroleum products necessary to its mining production albeit at inflated cost. In fact, as previously stated, this embargo can reasonably be said to have, at least indirectly, contributed to the marked appreciation to the value of Peabody's coal reserves by forcing the market value of that alternative source of energy upward in this country.

It is apparent that Peabody did make a bad bargain and an unprofitable one under its contract with Public Service resulting in a loss, the cause and size of which is disputed. But this fact alone does not deal with either the "basic assumption" on which the contract was negotiated or alter the "essential nature of the performance" thereunder so as to constitute "commercial impracticability". The court below properly decreed specific performance.

The judgment is affirmed.

All concur.

GEORGIA POWER CO. v. CIMARRON COAL CORP., 526 F.2d 101 (6th Cir.1975), cert. denied, 425 U.S. 952, 96 S.Ct. 1727, 48 L.Ed.2d 195 (1976). Georgia Power and Cimarron Coal entered into a coal supply agreement which provided that for a period of ten years beginning January 1, 1970, Cimarron would sell and Georgia Power would purchase designated quantities of coal. The Agreement provided for a base price of $4.03 per ton, subject to adjustment from time to time. Specific provisions of the Agreement provided formulas or methods for adjusting the base price for changes in certain labor costs, supplies, and governmental requirements. The Agreement also contained the following provisions:

20.01 *Arbitration.* Any unresolved controversy between the parties, arising under this Agreement shall, at the request of either party, be submitted to arbitration under the rules of the American Arbitration Association....

26.01 *Adjustments for Gross Inequities.* Any gross proven inequity that may result in unusual economic conditions not contemplated by the parties at the time of the execution of this Agreement may be corrected by mutual consent. Each party shall in the case of a claim of gross inequity furnish the other with whatever documentary evidence may be necessary to assist in affecting a settlement.

Nothing contained in this section shall be construed as relieving either the Purchaser or Seller from any of its respective obligations hereunder solely because of the existence of a claim of inequity or the failure of the parties to reach an agreement with respect thereto.

During 1973 and 1974, there was a rapid escalation in the market price of coal. In 1974, Cimarron requested adjustments in the base price under the gross-inequities provision of the Agreement, claiming that a gross inequity had resulted from the disparity between the market price of coal and the price being paid under the Agreement. Cimarron pointed out that the current adjusted base price under the Agreement was $10.00 per ton, while coal of the same quality was selling for $19.00 to $32.00 per ton on the open market. Georgia Power refused to make the requested adjustment, and Cimarron petitioned for arbitration on the ground that the parties had an "unresolved controversy" within the meaning of § 20.01. Held, Cimarron had a right to require a dispute under the gross-inequities provision to be resolved by arbitration.

"... The gross inequities provision deals with a possible adjustment in price which might be required because of unforeseeable changes in the economic climate of the coal industry. This provision lacks the specific details of the other portions of the Agreement dealing with price adjustment, but that arises from the fact that it is something of a 'catch-all' provision designed to take care of the kinds of changes which cannot be predicted in detail, but which experience teaches do occur. In the absence of language withdrawing this provision from the arbitration requirement it is the duty of the court to resolve any doubts in favor of arbitration."

KRELL v. HENRY

In the Court of Appeal, 1903.
[1903] 2 K.B. 740.

Appeal from a decision of DARLING, J.

The plaintiff, Paul Krell, sued the defendant, C.S. Henry, for £50, being the balance of a sum of £75, for which the defendant had agreed to hire a flat at 56A, Pall Mall on the days of June 26 and 27, for the purpose of viewing the processions to be held in connection with the coronation of His Majesty. The defendant denied his liability, and counterclaimed for the return of the sum of £25, which had been paid as a deposit, on the ground that, the processions not having taken place owing to the serious illness of the King, there had been a total failure of consideration for the contract entered into by him.

The facts, which were not disputed, were as follows. The plaintiff on leaving the country in March, 1902, left instructions with his solicitor to let his suite of chambers at 56A, Pall Mall on such terms and for such period (not exceeding six months) as he thought proper. On June 17, 1902, the defendant noticed an announcement in the windows of the plaintiff's flat to the effect that windows to view the coronation processions were to be let. The defendant interviewed the housekeeper on the subject, when it was pointed out to him what a good view of the procession could be obtained from the premises, and he eventually agreed with the housekeeper to take the suite for the two days in question for a sum of £75.

On June 20 the defendant wrote the following letter to the plaintiff's solicitor:—

"I am in receipt of yours of the 18th instant, inclosing form of agreement for the suite of chambers on the third floor at 56A, Pall Mall, which I have agreed to take for the two days, the 26th and 27th instant, for the sum of £75. For reasons given you I cannot enter into the agreement, but as arranged over the telephone I inclose herewith cheque for £25 as deposit, and will thank you to confirm to me that I shall have the entire use of these rooms during the days (not the nights) of the 26th and 27th instant. You may rely that every care will be taken of the premises and their contents. On the 24th inst. I will pay the balance, viz., £50, to complete the £75 agreed upon."

On the same day the defendant received the following reply from the plaintiff's solicitor:—

"I am in receipt of your letter of today's date inclosing cheque for £25 deposit on your agreeing to take Mr. Krell's chambers on the third floor at 56A, Pall Mall for the two days, the 26th and 27th June, and I confirm the agreement that you are to have the entire use of these rooms during the days (but not the nights), the balance, £50, to be paid to me on Tuesday next the 24th instant."

The processions not having taken place on the days originally appointed, namely, June 26 and 27, the defendant declined to pay the balance of £50 alleged to be due from him under the contract in writing of June 20 constituted by the above two letters. Hence the present action.

Darling J., on August 11, 1902, held upon the authority of Taylor v. Caldwell and The Moorcock (1889, 14 P.D. 64), that there was an implied condition in the contract that the procession should take place, and gave judgment for the defendant on the claim and counterclaim.

The plaintiff appealed.

Spencer Bower, K.C., and Holman Gregory, for the plaintiff. In the contract nothing is said about the coronation procession, but it is admitted that both parties expected that there would be a procession, and that the price to be paid for the rooms was fixed with reference to the expected procession. Darling J. held that both the claim and the counterclaim were governed by Taylor v. Caldwell, and that there was an implied term in the contract that the procession should take place. It is submitted that the learned judge was wrong. If he was right, the result would be that in every case of this kind an unremunerated promisor will be in effect an insurer of the hopes and expectations of the promisee.... In order that the person who has contracted to pay the price should be excused from doing so, there must be (1) no default on his part; (2) either the physical extinction or the not coming into existence of the subject-matter of the contract; (3) the performance of the contract must have been thereby rendered impossible.

In the present case there has been no default on the part of the defendant. But there has been no physical extinction of the subject-matter, and the performance of the contract was quite possible. . . .

VAUGHAN WILLIAMS, L.J. read the following written judgment:—The real question in this case is the extent of the application in English law of the principle of the Roman law which has been adopted and acted on in many English decisions, and notably in the case of Taylor v. Caldwell. . . . It is said, on the one side, that the specified thing, state of things, or condition the continued existence of which is necessary for the fulfilment of the contract, so that the parties entering into the contract must have contemplated the continued existence of that thing, condition, or state of things as the foundation of what was to be done under the contract, is limited to things which are either the subject-matter of the contract or a condition or state of things, present or anticipated, which is expressly mentioned in the contract. But, on the other side, it is said that the condition or state of things need not be expressly specified, but that it is sufficient if that condition or state of things clearly appears by extrinsic evidence to have been assumed by the parties to be the foundation or basis of the contract, and the event which causes the impossibility is of such a character that it cannot reasonably be supposed to have been in the contemplation of the contracting parties when the contract was made. In such a case the contracting parties will not be held bound by the general words which, though large enough to include, were not used with reference to a possibility of a particular event rendering performance of the contract impossible. I do not think that the principle of the civil law as introduced into the English law is limited to cases in which the event causing the impossibility of performance is the destruction or nonexistence of some thing which is the subject-matter of the contract or of some condition or state of things expressly specified as a condition of it. I think that you first have to ascertain, not necessarily from the terms of the contract, but, if required, from necessary inferences, drawn from surrounding circumstances recognized by both contracting parties, what is the substance of the contract, and then to ask the question whether that substantial contract needs for its foundation the assumption of the existence of a particular state of things. If it does, this will limit the operation of the general words, and in such case, if the contract becomes impossible of performance by reason of the nonexistence of the state of things assumed by both contracting parties as the foundation of the contract, there will be no breach of the contract thus limited. . . .

In my judgment [in this case] the use of the rooms was let and taken for the purpose of seeing the Royal procession. It was not a demise of the rooms, or even an agreement to let and take the rooms. It is a licence to use rooms for a particular purpose and none other. And in my judgment the taking place of those processions on the days proclaimed along the proclaimed route, which passed 56A, Pall Mall, was regarded by both contracting parties as the foundation of the contract; and I think that it cannot reasonably be supposed to have been in the contemplation of the contracting parties, when the contract was made, that the coronation would not be held on the proclaimed days, or the processions not take place on those days along the proclaimed route; and I think that the words imposing on the defendant the obligation to accept and pay for the use of the rooms for the named days, although general and unconditional, were not used with reference to the possibility of the particular contingency which afterwards occurred.

It was suggested in the course of the argument that if the occurrence, on the proclaimed days, of the coronation and the procession in this case were the foundation of the contract, and if the general words are thereby limited or qualified, so that in the event of the non-occurrence of the coronation and procession along the proclaimed route they would discharge both parties from further performance of the contract, it would follow that if a cabman was engaged to take some one to Epsom on Derby Day at a suitable enhanced price for such a journey, say £10, both parties to the contract would be discharged in the contingency of the race at Epsom for some reason becoming impossible; but I do not think this follows, for I do not think that in the cab case the happening of the race would be the foundation of the contract. No doubt the purpose of the engager would be to go to see the Derby, and the price would be proportionately high; but the cab had no special qualifications for the purpose which led to the selection of the cab for this particular occasion. Any other cab would have done as well. Moreover, I think, that under the cab contract, the hirer, even if the race went off, could have said, "Drive me to Epsom; I will pay you the agreed sum; you have nothing to do with the purpose for which I hired the cab," and that if the cabman refused he would have been guilty of a breach of contract, there being nothing to qualify his promise to drive the hirer to Epsom on a particular day. Whereas in the case of the coronation, there is not merely the purpose of the hirer to see the coronation procession, but it is the coronation procession and the relative position of the rooms which is the basis of the contract as much for the lessor as the hirer; and I think that if the King, before the coronation day and after the contract, had died, the hirer could not have insisted on having the rooms on the days named. It could not in the cab case be reasonably said that seeing the Derby race was the foundation of the contract, as it was of the licence in this case. Whereas in the present case, where the rooms were offered and taken, by reason of their peculiar suitability from the position of the rooms for a view of the coronation procession, surely the view of the coronation procession was the foundation of the contract, which is a very different thing from the purpose of the man who engaged the cab—namely, to see the race—being held to be the foundation of the contract.

Each case must be judged by its own circumstances. In each case one must ask oneself, first, what, having regard to all the circumstances, was the foundation of the contract? Secondly, was the performance of the contract prevented? Thirdly, was the event which prevented the performance of the contract of such a character that it cannot reasonably be said to have been in the contemplation of the parties at the date of the contract? If all these questions are answered in the affirmative (as I think they should be in this case), I think both parties are discharged from further performance of the contract. . . .

This disposes of the plaintiff's claim for £50 unpaid balance of the price agreed to be paid for the use of the rooms. The defendant at one time set up a cross-claim for the return of the £25 he paid at the date of the contract. As that claim is now withdrawn it is unnecessary to say anything about it. . . . I think this appeal ought to be dismissed.

[The concurring opinions of Romer, L.J., and Stirling, L.J., are omitted.] Appeal dismissed.

WLADIS, COMMON LAW AND UNCOMMON EVENTS: THE DEVELOPMENT OF THE DOCTRINE OF IMPOSSIBILITY OF PERFORMANCE IN ENGLISH CONTRACT LAW, 75 Geo.L.J. 1575, 1609, 1618 (1987). "The facts giving rise to the coronation cases may be stated briefly: Edward VII was to be crowned on Thursday, June 26, 1902, in Westminster Abbey. There was to be a coronation procession that day between the royal residence at Buckingham Palace and the Abbey, and a lengthier one [on June 27] throughout the city of London. In addition, on Saturday, June 28, a naval review of the fleet was to take place. Flats were let, grandstands erected, and seats sold along the routes of the processions. Boats were also chartered to take the public to the naval review. However, during the morning of June 24 it was determined that Edward, who had been suffering from appendicitis, needed to undergo surgery. Later that day it was announced that the coronation would be postponed and the naval review not held. . . .

" . . . The coronation events were not canceled, but only postponed. The procession [scheduled for] June 26 eventually took place on August 9 and proceeded along the same route as had originally been planned. The procession scheduled for June 27 occurred on October 25 and followed as nearly as possible the original route. Even the naval review that had been canceled was rescheduled and held on August 16."

ALFRED MARKS REALTY CO. v. HOTEL HERMITAGE CO., 170 App.Div. 484, 156 N.Y.S. 179 (1915). In January 1914, plaintiff undertook the publication of a "Souvenir and Program of International Yacht Races," the races being scheduled to take place in September. Defendant contracted for an advertisement in this program. Under its contract, defendant was to pay for the advertisement "upon publication and delivery of one copy." Early in August, plaintiff put out an anticipatory issue of about 3000 copies. In mid-August, the races were cancelled because of the outbreak of the European war. On August 25, a copy of the program was sent to defendant, with a demand for payment. Defendant did not pay, and plaintiff sued for the agreed price of the advertisement. Held, for defendant. Cancellation of the races frustrated the entire design of the project; a souvenir cannot recall what has not taken place. The partial and anticipatory issue of the program before the cancellation of the races did not constitute "publication" in the sense of the contract.

LA CUMBRE GOLF & COUNTRY CLUB v. SANTA BARBARA HOTEL CO., 205 Cal. 422, 271 P. 476 (1928). Santa Barbara Hotel Co. owned and operated the Ambassador Hotel. Under a contract between Santa Barbara and the La Cumbre Golf and Country Club, La Cumbre extended privileges at its club to guests at the Ambassador. In 1920, Santa Barbara wanted to purchase and operate a bus between the Ambassador and the club, provided the golf privileges were extended over an additional period of time. Accordingly, the parties made a contract for a period ending December 31, 1923, under which La Cumbre agreed that it would grant all the privileges of membership to guests at the Ambassador, and Santa Barbara agreed to be responsible for the guests' greens fees and to pay La Cumbre $300 a month. In April 1921, the Ambassador burned down. Santa Barbara stopped making payments under the contract, and La Cumbre sued for the balance due, $7200. Held, for Santa Barbara. It was an implied condition of the contract that there would be guests in the Ambassador.

*

Part VI

PROBLEMS INVOLVING PERSONS OTHER THAN THE PARTIES TO THE ORIGINAL CONTRACT

Chapter 20

THIRD–PARTY BENEFICIARIES

PRELIMINARY ANALYSIS OF THE PROBLEM OF THIS CHAPTER

The basic situation dealt with in this Chapter can be stated as follows: A promises B for a valid consideration that A will render a designated performance. The performance will benefit C. To what extent shall the law protect C's interest in the contract between A and B?

This problem can be attacked in two different ways: In a formal way, as a problem of legal doctrine, or in a substantive way, as a problem of policy, morals, and experience. Under a formal methodology, the problem is one of deducing C's rights, or lack of rights, from some general premise. Under a substantive methodology, the problem is one of developing the best set of rules by applying the relevant policy, moral, and empirical propositions. The crucial inquiries from a substantive point of view are: Is there a need to grant legal protection to C's interest in the contract? If so, what undesirable consequences, if any, would be entailed in granting that protection?

When the question is raised in this form, it is at once apparent that it is necessary to know something about the objectives of the parties. For example, in exacting the promise from A, B's motive may have been that of conferring a gift on C, who is perhaps a favorite nephew or other relative. If B dies before A has conferred the promised benefit on C, then if C is denied a right to enforce the contract, it may not be carried out at all, because B's executor, who may represent legatees who are in competition with C, will have no incentive to bring a suit on C's behalf. In this particular situation, therefore, there is a sound reason for permitting a suit by C, because otherwise B's intent may be defeated. On the other hand, to grant a broad and unlimited protection to C's interest in the agreement may be going too far. For example, if B has not died but is still alive and now wishes to rescind or modify the agreement between himself and A, how shall we resolve a possible conflict of interest between B and C? A has promised only one performance, and in that sense is subject to one claim only. But B is interested in that claim as promisee and as the one who furnished the consideration for it, while C is interested in it as the designated recipient of the benefit. How shall we partition the control over this claim between B and C when they come in conflict?

A closer study of these concrete problems must be postponed until actual cases are presented. It is apparent, however, that substantive methodology for resolving this problem inevitably drives the courts in the direction of a close inquiry into the objectives and motives of the parties. That is not true of formal methodology. The formal methodology of classical contract law assumed that before any inquiry is made concerning the advisability of permitting or denying a suit by C, weight, perhaps decisive weight, must be given to an obstacle supposedly thought to be presented by an axiomatic premise, namely, that only a person who is a party to a contract can sue on it or have rights under it.

The objection that C is not "a party to the contract" was more specifically defined in three different ways: (1) The promise by A was not made *to* C, but to B. (The objection that C was not the promisee is one that was chiefly raised in American jurisdictions.) (2) The *consideration* did not move from C, but from B. (This seems to have been the controlling objection in England.) (3) C did not *assent* to the contract, because the expression of agreement ran between A and B. (This is the objection that has been most bothersome for legal theorists in the civil law.) The first objection assumes that only one to whom a promise is made can enforce the promise; the second, that only one who furnishes the consideration has rights under a contract; the third, that only one who has joined in the expression of mutual assent has rights under a contract.

None of these axiomatic objections involves any conscious weighing of the advantages or disadvantages of allowing suit by C, nor is there any such weighing even of the premise that only one who is a party to a contract can have rights on it. Rather, this premise is, in Holmes's expression, taken on inspiration and authority.

––––––––

Nomenclature is important in analyzing third-party beneficiary problems. In the Notes in this Chapter, the term *third-party beneficiary* will be used to mean a person who is not a party to a contract, but who would benefit from its performance. The term *promisor* will be used to mean a person who has made a legally enforceable promise, the performance of which would benefit a third-party beneficiary. The term *promisee* will be used to mean the person to whom this promise is made. The term *contract* will be used to mean an enforceable agreement between a promisor and a promisee, the performance of which would benefit a third party. The term *contracting parties* will be used to refer to the promisor and the promisee, taken together. This nomenclature is somewhat artificial, because in bilateral contracts each party is both a promisor and a promisee. Typically, however, a third-party beneficiary would be benefited only by the performance of one of the parties—the party who will be called the promisor.

––––––––

RESTATEMENT, SECOND, OF CONTRACTS
§ 302, ILLUSTRATIONS 16–19

16. B contracts with A to erect an expensive building on A's land. C's adjoining land would be enhanced in value by the performance of the contract. C is [only] an incidental beneficiary [and cannot bring suit under the contract].

17. B contracts with A to buy a new car manufactured by C. C is [only] an incidental beneficiary [and cannot bring suit under the contract], even though the promise can only be performed if money is paid to C.

18. A, a labor union, promises B, a trade association, not to strike against any member of B during a certain period. One of the members of B charters a ship from C on terms under which such a strike would cause financial loss to C. C is [only] an incidental beneficiary of A's promise [and cannot bring suit under the contract].

19. A contracts to erect a building for C. B then contracts with A to supply lumber needed for the building. C is [only] an incidental beneficiary of B's promise, and B is [only] an incidental beneficiary of C's promise to pay A for the building [and neither can bring suit under the other's contract].

———

LAWRENCE v. FOX

Court of Appeals of New York, 1859.
20 N.Y. 268.

Appeal from the Superior Court of the City of Buffalo. On the trial before Mr. Justice Masten, it appeared by the evidence of a bystander that one Holly, in November, 1857, at the request of the defendant, loaned and advanced to him $300, stating at the time that he owed that sum to the plaintiff for money borrowed of him, and had agreed to pay it to him the then next day; that the defendant in consideration thereof, at the time of receiving the money, promised to pay it to the plaintiff the then next day. Upon this state of facts the defendant moved for a nonsuit, upon three several grounds, viz.: That there was no proof tending to show that Holly was indebted to the plaintiff, that the agreement by the defendant with Holly to pay the plaintiff was void for want of consideration, and that there was no privity between the plaintiff and defendant. The court overruled the motion, and the counsel for the defendant excepted. The cause was then submitted to the jury, and they found a verdict for the plaintiff for the amount of the loan and interest, $344.66, upon which judgment was entered, from which the defendant appealed to the Superior Court, at General Term, where the judgment was affirmed, and the defendant appealed to this court. The cause was submitted on printed arguments.

H. Gray, J. The first objection raised on the trial amounts to this: That the evidence of the person present, who heard the declarations of Holly giving directions as to the payment of the money he was then advancing to the defendant, was mere hearsay and, therefore, not competent. Had the plaintiff sued Holly for this sum of money no objection to the competency of this evidence would have been thought of; and if the defendant had performed his promise by paying the sum loaned to him to the plaintiff, and Holly had afterward sued him for its recovery, and this evidence had been offered by the defendant, it would doubtless have been received without an objection from any source. All the defendant had the right to demand in this case was evidence which, as between Holly and the plaintiff, was competent to establish the relation between them of debtor and creditor. For that purpose the evidence was clearly competent; it covered the whole ground and warranted the verdict of the jury.

But it is claimed that notwithstanding this promise was established by competent evidence, it was void for the want of consideration. It is now more than a quarter of a century since it was settled by the Supreme Court of this state—in an able and painstaking opinion by the late Chief Justice Savage, in which the authorities were fully examined and carefully analyzed—that a promise in all material respects like the one under consideration was valid; and the judgment of that court was unanimously affirmed by the Court for the Correction of Errors. Farley v. Cleveland, 4 Cow. 432, 15 Am.Dec. 387; s.c. in error, 9 Cow. 639.

In that case one Moon owed Farley and sold to Cleveland a quantity of hay, in consideration of which Cleveland promised to pay Moon's debt to Farley; and the decision in favor of Farley's right to recover was placed upon the ground that the hay received by Cleveland from Moon was a valid consideration for Cleveland's promise to pay Farley, and that the subsisting liability of Moon to pay Farley was no objection to the recovery.

The fact that the money advanced by Holly to the defendant was a loan to him for a day, and that it thereby became the property of the defendant, seemed to impress the defendant's counsel with the idea that because the defendant's promise was not a trust fund placed by the plaintiff [Holly?] in the defendant's hands, out of which he was to realize money as from the sale of a chattel or the collection of a debt, the promise although made for the benefit of the plaintiff could not inure to his benefit. The hay which [Moon] delivered to [Cleveland] was not to be paid to Farley, but the debt incurred by Cleveland for the purchase of the hay, like the debt incurred by the defendant for money borrowed, was what was to be paid.

That case has been often referred to by the courts of this state, and has never been doubted as sound authority for the principle upheld by it. Barker v. Bucklin, 2 Denio, 45, 43 Am.Dec. 726; Canal Co. v. Westchester County Bank, 4 Denio, 97. It puts to rest the objection that the defendant's promise was void for want of consideration. The report of that case shows that the promise was not only made to Moon but to the plaintiff Farley. In this case the promise was made to Holly and not expressly to the plaintiff; and this difference between the two cases presents the question, raised by the defendant's objection, as to the want of privity between the plaintiff and defendant. As early as 1806 it was announced by the Supreme Court of this state, upon what was then regarded as the settled law of England, "That where one person makes a promise to another for the benefit of a third person, that third person may maintain an action upon it." Schemerhorn v. Vanderheyden, 1 Johns. 140, 3 Am.Dec. 304, has often been reasserted by our courts and never departed from . . . .

The same principle is adjudged in several cases in Massachusetts. I will refer to but a few of them. . . . In Hall v. Marston [1822, 17 Mass. 575], the court say: "It seems to have been well settled that if A promises B for a valuable consideration to pay C, the latter may maintain assumpsit for the money;" and in Brewer v. Dyer [1851, 7 Cush. 337, 340], the recovery was upheld, as the court said, "upon the principle of law *long recognized and clearly* established, that when one person, for a valuable consideration, engages with another, by a simple contract, to do some act for the benefit of a third, the latter, who would enjoy the benefit of the act, may maintain an action for the breach of such engagement; that it does not rest upon the ground of any actual or supposed relationship between the parties as some of the earlier cases would seem to indicate, but upon the broader and more satisfactory basis, that the law operating on the act of the parties creates the duty, establishes a privity, and implies the promise and obligation on which the action is founded." . . .

But it is urged that because the defendant was not in any sense a trustee of the property of Holly for the benefit of the plaintiff, the law will not imply a promise. I agree that many of the cases where a promise was implied were cases of trusts, created for the benefit of the promisor [beneficiary?]. The case of Felton v. Dickinson, 10 Mass. 287, and others that might be cited are of that class; but concede them all to have been cases of trusts, and it proves nothing against the application of the rule to this case. The duty of the trustee to pay the cestui que trust, according to the terms of the trust, implies his promise to the latter to do so. In this case the defendant, upon ample consideration received from Holly, promised Holly to pay his debt to the plaintiff; the consideration received and the promise to Holly made it as plainly his duty to pay the plaintiff as if the money had been remitted to him for that purpose, and as well implied a promise to do so as if he had been made a trustee of property to be converted into cash with which to pay. The fact that a breach of the duty imposed in the one case may be visited, and justly, with more serious consequences than in the other, by no means disproves the payment to be a duty in both. The principle illustrated by the example so frequently quoted (which concisely states the case in hand) "that a promise made to one for the benefit of another, he for whose benefit it is made may bring an action for its breach," has been applied to trust cases, not because it was exclusively applicable to those cases, but because it was a principle of law, and as such applicable to those cases.

It was also insisted that Holly could have discharged the defendant from his promise, though it was intended by both parties for the benefit of the plaintiff, and, therefore, the plaintiff was not entitled to maintain this suit for the recovery of a demand over which he had no control. It is enough that the plaintiff [Holly?] did not release the defendant from his promise, and whether he could or not is a question not now necessarily involved; but if it was, I think it would be found difficult to maintain the right of Holly to discharge a judgment recovered by the plaintiff upon confession or otherwise, for the breach of the defendant's promise; and if he could not, how could he discharge the suit before judgment, or the promise before suit, made as it was for the plaintiff's benefit and in accordance with legal presumption accepted by him (Berly v. Taylor, 5 Hill, 577–584 et seq.), until his dissent was shown.

The cases cited, and especially that of Farley v. Cleveland, established the validity of a parol promise; it stands then upon the footing of a written one. Suppose the defendant had given his note in which for value received of Holly, he had promised to pay the plaintiff and the plaintiff had accepted the promise, retaining Holly's liability. Very clearly Holly could not have discharged that promise, be the right to release the defendant as it may. No one can doubt that he owes the sum of money demanded of him, or that in accordance with his promise it was his duty to have paid it to the plaintiff; nor can it be doubted that whatever may be the diversity of opinion elsewhere, the adjudications in this state, from a very early period, approved by experience, have established the defendant's liability; if, therefore, it could be shown that a more strict and technically accurate application of the rules applied, would lead to a different result (which I by no means concede), the effort should not be made in the face of manifest justice.

The judgment should be affirmed.

JOHNSON, CH. J., DENIO, SELDEN, ALLEN and STRONG, JS. concurred. JOHNSON, CH. J., and DENIO, J., were of opinion that the promise was to be regarded as made to the plaintiff through the medium of his agent, whose action he could ratify when it came to his knowledge, though taken without his being privy thereto.

COMSTOCK, J. (Dissenting). The plaintiff had nothing to do with the promise on which he brought this action. It was not made to him, nor did the consideration proceed from him. If he can maintain the suit, it is because an anomaly has found its way into the law on this subject. In general, there must be privity of contract. The party who sues upon a promise must be the promisee, or he must have some legal interest in the undertaking. In this case, it is plain that Holly, who loaned the money to the defendant, and to whom the promise in question was made, could at any time have claimed that it should be performed to himself personally. He had lent the money to the defendant, and at the same time directed the latter to pay the sum to the plaintiff. This direction he could countermand, and if he had done so, manifestly the defendant's promise to pay according to the direction would have ceased to exist. The plaintiff would receive a benefit by a complete execution of the arrangement, but the arrangement itself was between other parties, and was under their exclusive control. If the defendant had paid the money to Holly, his debt would have been discharged thereby. So Holly might have released the demand or assigned it to another person, or the parties might have annulled the promise now in question, and designated some other creditor of Holly as the party to whom the money should be paid. It has never been claimed that in a case thus situated the right of a third person to sue upon the promise rested on any sound principle of law. We are to inquire whether the rule has been so established by positive authority....

The cases in which some trust was involved are also frequently referred to as authority for the doctrine now in question, but they do not sustain it. If A. delivers money or property to B., which the latter accepts upon a trust for the benefit of C., the latter can enforce the trust by an appropriate action for that purpose. Berly v. Taylor, 5 Hill, 577. If the trust be of money, I think the beneficiary may assent to it and bring the action for money had and received to his use. If it be of something else than money, the trustee must account for it according to the terms of the trust, and upon principles of equity. There is some authority even for saying that an express promise founded on the possession of a trust fund may be enforced by an action at law in the name of the beneficiary, although it was made to the creator of the trust. Thus, in Comyn's Digest (Action on the Case upon Assumpsit, B, 15), it is laid down that if a man promise a pig of lead to A., and his executor give lead to make a pig to B., who assumes to deliver it to A., an assumpsit lies by A. against him. The case of Delaware & H. Canal Co. v. Westchester County Bank, 4 Denio, 97, involved a trust because the defendants had received from a third party a bill of exchange under an agreement that they would endeavor to collect it, and would pay over the proceeds when collected to the plaintiffs. A fund received under such an agreement does not belong to the person who receives it. He must account for it specifically; and perhaps there is no gross violation of principle in permitting the equitable owner of it to sue upon an express promise to pay it over. Having a specific interest in the thing, the undertaking to account for it may be regarded as in some sense made with him through the author of the trust. But further than this we cannot go without violating plain rules of law. In the case before us there was nothing in the nature of a trust or agency. The defendant borrowed the money of Holly and received it as his own. The plaintiff had no right in the fund, legal or equitable. The promise to repay the money created an obligation in favor of the lender to whom it was made and not in favor of any one else. . . .

The question was also involved in some confusion by the earlier cases in Massachusetts. Indeed, the Supreme Court of that State seems at one time to have made a nearer approach to the doctrine on which this action must rest, than the courts of this State have ever done. (10 Mass., 287; 17 id., 400.) But in the recent case of Mellen, Administratrix v. Whipple (1854, 1 Gray, 317) the subject was carefully reviewed and the doctrine utterly overthrown. . . .

The judgment of the court below should, therefore, be reversed, and a new trial granted.

Grover, J., also dissented.

Judgment affirmed.

NOTE ON LAWRENCE v. FOX

An obvious question in *Lawrence v. Fox* is why Holly engaged in the relatively unusual transaction described in the case—a one-day loan of what was then a relatively large amount of money—and why Lawrence followed the winding path of suing Fox rather than the straight path of suing Holly. On the basis of historical spadework and some leaps of deduction, Professor Jon Waters has suggested that Lawrence may have sued Fox rather than Holly because Holly's debt to Lawrence was a gambling debt, unenforceable at law. A gambling milieu might also, perhaps, explain the unusual nature of the Holly–Fox transaction. Waters, The Property in the Promise, 98 Harv.L.Rev. 1109 (1985). More conventional explanations of why Lawrence sued Fox would be that Holly was insolvent or outside the jurisdiction.

SEAVER v. RANSOM

Court of Appeals of New York, 1918.
224 N.Y. 233, 120 N.E. 639, 2 A.L.R. 1187.

Action by Marion E. Seaver against Matt C. Ransom and another, as executors, etc., of Samuel A. Beman, deceased. From a judgment of the Appellate Division (180 App.Div. 734, 168 N.Y.S. 454), affirming judgment for plaintiff, defendants appeal. Affirmed.

POUND, J. Judge Beman and his wife were advanced in years. Mrs. Beman was about to die. She had a small estate, consisting of a house and lot in Malone and little else. Judge Beman drew his wife's will according to her instructions. It gave $1,000 to plaintiff, $500 to one sister, plaintiff's mother, and $100 each to another sister and her son, the use of the house to her husband for life, and remainder to the American Society for the Prevention of Cruelty to Animals. She named her husband as residuary legatee and executor. Plaintiff was her niece, 34 years old, in ill health, sometimes a member of the Beman household. When the will was read to Mrs. Beman she said that it was not as she wanted it; she wanted to leave the house to plaintiff. She had no other objection to the will, but her strength was waning, and, although the judge offered to write another will for her, she said she was afraid she would not hold out long enough to enable her to sign it. So the judge said, if she would sign the will he would leave plaintiff enough in his will to make up the difference. He avouched the promise by his uplifted hand with all solemnity and his wife then executed the will. When he came to die, it was found that his will made no provision for the plaintiff.

This action was brought and plaintiff recovered judgment in the trial court on the theory that Beman had obtained property from his wife and induced her to execute the will in the form prepared by him by his promise to give plaintiff $6,000, the value of the house, and that thereby equity impressed his property with a trust in favor of plaintiff. Where a legatee promises the testator that he will use property given him by the will for a particular purpose, a trust arises. O'Hara v. Dudley, 95 N.Y. 403, 47 Am.Rep. 53; Trustees of Amherst College v. Ritch, 151 N.Y. 282, 45 N.E. 876, 37 L.R.A. 305; Ahrens v. Jones, 169 N.Y. 555, 62 N.E. 666, 88 Am.St.Rep. 620. Beman received nothing under his wife's will but the use of the house in Malone for life. Equity compels the application of property thus obtained to the purpose of the testator, but equity cannot so impress a trust, except on property obtained by the promise. Beman was bound by his promise, but no property was bound by it; no trust in plaintiff's favor can be spelled out.

An action on the contract for damages, or to make the executors trustees for performance, stands on different ground. Farmers' Loan & Trust Co. v. Mortimer, 219 N.Y. 290, 294, 295, 114 N.E. 389, Ann.Cas.1918E, 1159. The Appellate Division properly passed to the consideration of the question whether the judgment could stand upon the promise made to the wife, upon a valid consideration, for the sole benefit of plaintiff. The judgment of the trial court was affirmed by a return to the general doctrine laid down in the great case of Lawrence v. Fox, 20 N.Y. 268, which has since been limited as herein indicated.

Contracts for the benefit of third persons have been the prolific source of judicial and academic discussion. Williston, Contracts for the Benefit of a

Third Person, 15 Harvard Law Review, 767; Corbin, Contracts for the Benefit of Third Persons, 27 Yale Law Journal, 1008. The general rule, both in law and equity (Phalen v. United States Trust Co., 186 N.Y. 178, 186, 78 N.E. 943, 7 L.R.A., N.S., 734, 9 Ann.Cas. 595), was that privity between a plaintiff and a defendant is necessary to the maintenance of an action on the contract. The consideration must be furnished by the party to whom the promise was made. The contract cannot be enforced against the third party, and therefore it cannot be enforced by him. On the other hand, the right of the beneficiary to sue on a contract made expressly for his benefit has been fully recognized in many American jurisdictions, either by judicial decision or by legislation, and is said to be "the prevailing rule in this country." Hendrick v. Lindsay, 93 U.S. 143, 23 L.Ed. 855; Lehow v. Simonton, 3 Colo. 346. It has been said that "the establishment of this doctrine has been gradual and is a victory of practical utility over theory, of equity over technical subtlety." Brantly on Contracts (2d Ed.) p. 253. The reasons for this view are that it is just and practical to permit the person for whose benefit the contract is made to enforce it against one whose duty it is to pay. Other jurisdictions still adhere to the present English rule (7 Halsbury's Laws of England, 342, 343; Jenks' Digest of English Civil Law, § 229) that a contract cannot be enforced by or against a person who is not a party (Exchange Bank v. Rice, 107 Mass. 37, 9 Am.Rep. 1). But see, also Forbes v. Thorpe, 209 Mass. 570, 95 N.E. 955; Gardner v. Denison, 217 Mass. 492, 105 N.E. 359, 51 L.R.A., N.S., 1108.

In New York the right of the beneficiary to sue on contracts made for his benefit is not clearly or simply defined. It is at present confined, first, to cases where there is a pecuniary obligation running from the promisee to the beneficiary, "a legal right founded upon some obligation of the promisee in the third party to adopt and claim the promise as made for his benefit." Farley v. Cleveland, 4 Cow. 432, 15 Am.Dec. 387; Lawrence v. Fox, supra; Garnsey v. Rogers, 47 N.Y. 233, 7 Am.Rep. 440; Vrooman v. Turner, 69 N.Y. 280, 25 Am.Rep. 195; Lorillard v. Clyde, 122 N.Y. 498, 25 N.E. 917, 10 L.R.A. 113; Durnherr v. Rau, 135 N.Y. 219, 32 N.E. 49; Townsend v. Rackham, 143 N.Y. 516, 38 N.E. 731; Sullivan v. Sullivan, 161 N.Y. 554, 56 N.E. 116. Secondly, to cases where the contract is made for the benefit of the wife (Buchanan v. Tilden, 158 N.Y. 109, 52 N.E. 724, 44 L.R.A. 170, 70 Am.St.Rep. 454; Bouton v. Welch, 170 N.Y. 554, 63 N.E. 539), affianced wife (De Cicco v. Schweizer, 221 N.Y. 431, 117 N.E. 807, L.R.A.1918E, 1004, Ann.Cas.1918C, 816), or child (Todd v. Weber, 95 N.Y. 181, 193, 47 Am.Rep. 20; Matter of Kidd, 188 N.Y. 274, 80 N.E. 924) of a party to the contract. The close relationship cases go back to the early King's Bench Case (1677), long since repudiated in England, of Dutton v. Poole, 2 Lev. 211. See Schemerhorn v. Vanderheyden, 1 Johns. 139, 3 Am.Dec. 304. The natural and moral duty of the husband or parent to provide for the future of wife or child sustains the action on the contract made for their benefit. "This is the farthest the cases in this state have gone," says Cullen, J., in the marriage settlement case of Borland v. Welch, 162 N.Y. 104, 110, 56 N.E. 556.

The right of the third party is also upheld, in, thirdly, the public contract cases (Little v. Banks, 85 N.Y. 258; Pond v. New Rochelle Water Co., 183 N.Y. 330, 76 N.E. 211, 1 L.R.A., N.S., 958, 5 Ann.Cas. 504; Smyth v. City of New York, 203 N.Y. 106, 96 N.E. 409; Farnsworth v. Boro Oil & Gas Co., 216 N.Y. 40, 48, 109 N.E. 860; Rigney v. N.Y.C. & H.R.R. Co., 217 N.Y. 31, 111 N.E. 226; Matter of International Ry. Co. v. Rann, 224 N.Y. 83, 120 N.E. 153. Cf.

German Alliance Ins. Co. v. Home Water Supply Co., 226 U.S. 220, 33 S.Ct. 32, 57 L.Ed. 195, 42 L.R.A., N.S., 1000), where the municipality seeks to protect its inhabitants by covenants for their benefit; and, fourthly the cases where, at the request of a party to the contract, the promise runs directly to the beneficiary although he does not furnish the consideration (Rector, etc. v. Teed, 120 N.Y. 583, 24 N.E. 1014; F.N. Bank of Sing Sing v. Chalmers, 144 N.Y. 432, 439, 39 N.E. 331; Hamilton v. Hamilton, 127 App.Div. 871, 875, 112 N.Y.S. 10). It may be safely said that a general rule sustaining recovery at the suit of the third party would include but few classes of cases not included in these groups, either categorically or in principle.

The desire of the childless aunt to make provision for a beloved and favorite niece differs imperceptibly in law or in equity from the moral duty of the parent to make testamentary provision for a child. The contract was made for the plaintiff's benefit. She alone is substantially damaged by its breach. The representatives of the wife's estate have no interest in enforcing it specifically. It is said in Buchanan v. Tilden that the common law imposes moral and legal obligations upon the husband and the parent not measured by the necessaries of life. It was, however, the love and affection or the moral sense of the husband and the parent that imposed such obligations in the cases cited, rather than any common-law duty of husband and parent to wife and child. If plaintiff had been a child of Mrs. Beman, legal obligation would have required no testamentary provision for her, yet the child could have enforced a covenant in her favor identical with the covenant of Judge Beman in this case. De Cicco v. Schweizer, supra. The constraining power of conscience is not regulated by the degree of relationship alone. The dependent or faithful niece may have a stronger claim than the affluent or unworthy son. No sensible theory of moral obligation denies arbitrarily to the former what would be conceded to the latter. We might consistently either refuse or allow the claim of both, but I cannot reconcile a decision in favor of the wife in Buchanan v. Tilden based on the moral obligations arising out of near relationship with a decision against the niece here on the ground that the relationship is too remote for equity's ken. No controlling authority depends upon so absolute a rule. In Sullivan v. Sullivan, supra, the grandniece lost in a litigation with the aunt's estate, founded on a certificate of deposit payable to the aunt "or in case of her death to her niece"; but what was said in that case of the relations of plaintiff's intestate and defendant does not control here, any more than what was said in Durnherr v. Rau, supra, on the relation of husband and wife, and the inadequacy of mere moral duty, as distinguished from legal or equitable obligation, controlled the decision in Buchanan v. Tilden. Borland v. Welch, supra, deals only with the rights of volunteers under a marriage settlement not made for the benefit of collaterals. Kellogg, P.J., writing for the court below well said: "The doctrine of Lawrence v. Fox is progressive, not retrograde. The course of the late decisions is to enlarge, not to limit, the effect of that case."

The court in that leading case attempted to adopt the general doctrine that any third person, for whose direct benefit a contract was intended, could sue on it. The headnote thus states the rule. Finch, J., in Gifford v. Corrigan, 117 N.Y. 257, 262, 22 N.E. 756, 6 L.R.A. 610, 15 Am.St.Rep. 508, says that the case rests upon that broad proposition; Edward T. Bartlett, J., in Pond v. New Rochelle Water Co., 183 N.Y. 330, 337, 76 N.E. 211, 213, 1 L.R.A., N.S., 958, 5 Ann.Cas. 504, calls it "the general principle"; but Vrooman v. Turner, supra, confined its application to the facts on which it was decided. "In every case in which an action has been sustained," says Allen, J., "there has been a debt or duty owing by the promisee to the party claiming to sue upon the promise." 69 N.Y. 285, 25 Am.Rep. 195. As late as Townsend v. Rackham, 143 N.Y. 516, 523, 38 N.E. 731, 733, we find Peckham, J., saying that, "to maintain the action by the third person, there must be this liability to him on the part of the promisee." Buchanan v. Tilden went further than any case since Lawrence v. Fox in a desire to do justice rather than to apply with technical accuracy strict rules calling for a legal or equitable obligation. In Embler v. Hartford Steam Boiler Inspection & Ins. Co., 158 N.Y. 431, 53 N.E. 212, 44 L.R.A. 512, it may at least be said that a majority of the court did not avail themselves of the opportunity to concur with the views expressed by Gray, J., who wrote the dissenting opinion in Buchanan v. Tilden, to the effect that an employee could not maintain an action on an insurance policy issued to the employer which covered injuries to employees. In Wright v. Glen Telephone Co., 48 Misc. 192, 195, 95 N.Y.S. 101, the learned presiding justice who wrote the opinion in this case said at Trial Term: "The right of a third person to recover upon a contract made by other parties for his benefit must rest upon the peculiar circumstances of each case rather than upon the law of some other case." "The case at bar is decided upon its peculiar facts." Edward T. Bartlett, J., in Buchanan v. Tilden.

But, on principle, a sound conclusion may be reached. If Mrs. Beman had left her husband the house on condition that he pay the plaintiff $6,000, and he had accepted the devise, he would have become personally liable to pay the legacy, and plaintiff could have recovered in an action at law against him, whatever the value of the house. Gridley v. Gridley, 24 N.Y. 130; Brown v. Knapp, 79 N.Y. 136, 143; Dinan v. Coneys, 143 N.Y. 544, 547, 38 N.E. 715; Blackmore v. White [1899] 1 Q.B. 293, 304. That would be because the testatrix had in substance bequeathed the promise to plaintiff, and not because close relationship or moral obligation sustained the contract. The distinction between an implied promise to a testator for the benefit of a third party to pay a legacy and an unqualified promise on a valuable consideration to make provision for the third party by will is discernible, but not obvious. The tendency of American authority is to sustain the gift in all such cases and to permit the donee beneficiary to recover on the contract. Matter of Edmundson's Estate (1918) 259 Pa. 429, 103 A. 277, 2 A.L.R. 1150. The equities are with the plaintiff, and they may be enforced in this action, whether it be regarded as an action for damages or an action for specific performance to convert the defendants into trustees for plaintiff's benefit under the agreement.

The judgment should be affirmed with costs.

HOGAN, CARDOZO, and CRANE, JJ., concur. HISCOCK, C.J., and COLLIN and ANDREWS, JJ., dissent.

Judgment affirmed.

———

RESTATEMENT, FIRST, CONTRACTS § 133

§ 133. Definition of Donee Beneficiary, Creditor Beneficiary, Incidental Beneficiary

(1) Where performance of a promise in a contract will benefit a person other than the promisee, that person is, except as stated in Subsection (3):

(a) a donee beneficiary if it appears from the terms of the promise in view of the accompanying circumstances that the purpose of the promisee in obtaining the promise of all or part of the performance thereof is to make a gift to the beneficiary or to confer upon him a right against the promisor to some performance neither due nor supposed or asserted to be due from the promisee to the beneficiary;

(b) a creditor beneficiary if no purpose to make a gift appears from the terms of the promise in view of the accompanying circumstances and performance of the promise will satisfy an actual or supposed or asserted duty of the promisee to the beneficiary, or a right of the beneficiary against the promisee which has been barred by the Statute of Limitations or by a discharge in bankruptcy, or which is unenforceable because of the Statute of Frauds;

(c) an incidental beneficiary if neither the facts stated in Clause (a) nor those stated in Clause (b) exist. . . .

[Ed. note: Under §§ 135 and 136, a donee or creditor beneficiary has legally enforceable rights under the contract; an incidental beneficiary does not.]

RESTATEMENT, SECOND, CONTRACTS §§ 302, 304, 315

[See Selected Source Materials Supplement]

SCARPITTI v. WEBORG

Supreme Court of Pennsylvania, 1992.
530 Pa. 366, 609 A.2d 147.

Before NIX, C.J., and LARSEN, FLAHERTY, McDERMOTT, ZAPPALA, PAPADAKOS and CAPPY, JJ.

LARSEN, Justice.

This case presents the question of whether purchasers of lots in a residential subdivision, who are required by subdivision restrictions recorded of public record to have their house construction plans reviewed and approved by an architect retained by the subdivision developer, are intended beneficiaries of the implied contract between the developer and the architect, and, as a result, have a cause of action against the architect for any breach of said contract for his alleged failure to properly review and approve the plans of other lot purchasers in the subdivision.

Appellees, lot owners in the Winchester subdivision, instituted an action against appellant, architect William Weborg, seeking damages for his arbitrary enforcement of the subdivision restrictions. Appellant's preliminary objections in the nature of a demurrer were sustained by the trial court and appellees' complaint dismissed with prejudice. On appeal, the Superior Court reversed, 400 Pa.Super. 632, 576 A.2d 1144, and held that appellees had a cause of action as third party beneficiaries of the implied contract between appellant and the subdivision developer. We agree.

We begin by noting that for purposes of review of a dismissal on the pleadings in the nature of a demurrer, the averments of the petition, except to the extent they constitute conclusions of law, must be taken as true. *Cianfrani v. Com., State Employees' Retirement Bd.*, 505 Pa. 294, 479 A.2d 468 (1984). The question presented by a demurrer is whether, on the facts averred, the law says with certainty that no recovery is possible, and where a doubt exists as to whether a demurrer should be sustained, this doubt should be resolved in favor of overruling it. *Muhammad v. Strassburger, et al.*, 526 Pa. 541, 587 A.2d 1346 (1991), *cert. denied*, 502 U.S. 867, 112 S.Ct. 196, 116 L.Ed.2d 156 (1991).

Viewed in light of the aforementioned standards, the complaint avers that appellees William and Susan Scarpitti and Joseph and Judith Hines purchased residential lots located in the Winchester South Subdivision in Erie, Pennsylvania, from Winchester Development Company, Inc. (Winchester), the successor in interest to the original developer Red Dog Realty Partnership (Partnership). Each of the lots purchased by the Scarpittis and the Hineses are, and were at the time of purchase, subject to certain recorded deed restrictions. Restriction No. 2 provides that:

> No more than one single family dwelling with no less than a two car nor more than a two and one-half car attached garage, shall be erected on any lot in the subdivision.

Restriction No. 7 provides that:

> No dwelling, tennis court, swimming pool, fence, or other structure shall be erected or maintained on any lot in the subdivision unless the plans therefore, showing the nature, kind, shape, height, material, color scheme, and location of said structure, and the elevation and grading plans of the lot to be built upon, shall have been submitted to and approved in writing by the architectural firm of William Weborg Associates or such other authority as the Partnership, by a duly recorded amendment to these Restrictions, may designate for that purpose.

In accordance with Restriction No. 7, appellees submitted their construction plans to William Weborg, appellant, for approval. Appellees' plans were disapproved by appellant because their plans contained three car garages in violation of Restriction No. 2. Subsequently, based upon appellant's denial, appellees constructed homes with two or two and one-half car garages in accordance with Restriction No. 2. Some time later, however, appellant approved plans of other lot owners in the Winchester South Subdivision for homes with three car garages.[1]

Appellant asserts that no privity of contract existed between the parties thereby precluding a contract claim, and no legal duty existed between the

---

1. These plans that were approved by appellant which included three car garages were designed by appellant in his private capacity as a professional architect, and then approved by appellant in his capacity as the subdivision architect charged with reviewing construction plans and enforcing deed restrictions.

parties thereby precluding a tort claim. Appellees contend that a cause of action exists against appellant under a contractual third party beneficiary theory. Under this analysis, appellees assert that they were intended beneficiaries of the implied contract which retained appellant for the purpose of approving construction plans and enforcing the recorded restrictions of the Winchester South Subdivision, pursuant to Restriction No. 7.

The current rule in Pennsylvania for designation of a party as a third party beneficiary was first articulated in the seminal case of *Spires v. Hanover Fire Insurance Co.,* 364 Pa. 52, 70 A.2d 828 (1950) (plurality opinion). In *Spires,* we held that in order for a third party beneficiary to have standing to recover on a contract, both contracting parties must have expressed an intention that the third party be a beneficiary, and that intention must have affirmatively appeared in the contract itself. *Spires v. Hanover Fire Insurance Co.,* 364 Pa. at 57, 70 A.2d at 830–31. But, in *Guy v. Liederbach,* 501 Pa. 47, 459 A.2d 744 (1983), we carved out an exception to the *Spires* rule, and allowed the beneficiary of a will to recover for legal malpractice against an attorney, despite the fact that the beneficiary was not in privity of contract with the attorney and was not named specifically as an intended beneficiary of the contract. In so doing, we adopted the Restatement (Second) of Contracts, § 302 (1979), as a guide for analysis of third party beneficiary claims in Pennsylvania. Restatement (Second) of Contracts, § 302 (1979) states:

Intended and Incidental Beneficiaries

(1) Unless otherwise agreed between promisor and promisee, a beneficiary of a promise is an intended beneficiary if recognition of a right to performance in the beneficiary is appropriate to effectuate the intentions of the parties and either

(a) the performance of the promise will satisfy an obligation of the promisee to pay money to the beneficiary; or

(b) the circumstances indicate that the promisee intends to give the beneficiary the benefit of the promised performance.

(2) An incidental beneficiary is a beneficiary who is not an intended beneficiary.

Restatement (Second) of Contracts § 302 (1979).

Consequently, this Court in *Guy* concluded:

There is thus a two part test for determining whether one is an intended third party beneficiary: (1) the recognition of the beneficiary's right must be "appropriate to effectuate the intention of the parties," and (2) the performance must "satisfy an obligation of the promisee to pay money to the beneficiary" or "the circumstances indicate that the promisee intends to give the beneficiary the benefit of the promised performance."

Guy v. Liederbach, 501 Pa. at 60, 459 A.2d at 751. The first part of the test sets forth a standing requirement which leaves discretion with the court to determine whether recognition of third party beneficiary status would be appropriate. The second part defines the two types of claimants who may be intended as third party beneficiaries. If a party satisfies both parts of the test, a claim may be asserted under the contract. *Id.*

Appellant argues that the holding in *Guy* was intended to have very limited application, and that the Restatement (Second) of Contracts, § 302 (1979) applies only where the court is faced with a legatee of a will as a possible third party beneficiary. Appellant cites numerous Superior Court opinions refusing to extend *Guy* to a new class of beneficiaries, contending that these cases stand for the proposition that *Guy* was intended to apply only to cases sufficiently similar on the facts. . . . In all of these cases, the Superior Court, although refusing to extend *Guy,* found that the third party was not an intended beneficiary either because there was no underlying contract, recognition of a right to performance was not appropriate to effectuate the intentions of the parties, or there was no clear intention to benefit the third party at the time the contract was entered into. Additionally, this Court never limited its holding in *Guy* to the facts of the case; rather, what this Court said in *Guy* was that "We believe that Restatement (Second) of Contracts § 302 (1979) provides an analysis of third party beneficiaries which permits a properly restricted cause of action for beneficiaries such as appellee. In adopting this standard, . . ." *Guy v. Liederbach,* 501 Pa. at 59, 459 A.2d at 751. It is clear from the language of the opinion in *Guy* that this Court was adopting the Restatement (Second) of Contracts § 302 (1979) as the law of Pennsylvania. Nothing in the holding of *Guy* precludes appellees from being included in the narrow class of third party beneficiaries envisioned by this Court, if they show that they meet the requirements of § 302.

Accordingly, we hold that a party becomes a third party beneficiary only where both parties to the contract express an intention to benefit the third party in the contract itself, *Spires, supra, unless,* the circumstances are so compelling that recognition of the beneficiary's right is appropriate to effectuate the intention of the parties, and the performance satisfies an obligation of the promisee to pay money to the beneficiary or the circumstances indicate that the promisee intends to give the beneficiary the benefit of the promised performance. *Guy, supra.*

Applying these principles to the case at bar, we find that appellees are intended third party beneficiaries of the implied contract between appellant and Winchester. The underlying contract is between appellant [promisor] and Winchester [promisee], whereby appellant promises to review all building plans and enforce the recorded subdivision restrictions. Obviously, the purpose of this agreement was to make the lots more attractive to prospective purchasers by assuring that other homeowners in the subdivision would be required to abide by the recorded subdivision restrictions. The third party beneficiary relationship, therefore, was within the contemplation of the promisor and the promisee at the time of contracting. It is the homeowners who have the greatest interest in uniform enforcement of restrictions and it is the homeowners who were benefitted by the establishment of a vehicle to enforce the restrictions. Hence, they were reasonable in relying upon the promise as manifesting an intention to confer a right on them. Although the agreement between appellant and Winchester does not expressly manifest an intent to benefit the subdivision homeowners, we find that recognition of a right to uniform enforcement of the deed restrictions in appellees is appropriate to effectuate the intention of the parties.

In this case, the architect is the promisor, promising to enforce deed restrictions which carry out the developer's intention to benefit the homeowners. The developer, the promisee, intends that the homeowners have the benefit of the architect's performance. Thus, it is patently clear that the parties, by establishing a vehicle for the enforcement of deed restrictions, intended to benefit the homeowners who purchased lots in the Winchester South Subdivision, at the time the contract was entered into. Although not individually named, appellee homeowners were part of a limited class of persons intended to benefit from the agreement between appellant and Winchester, thus satisfying the second prong of *Guy* and subsection (b) of § 302 Restatement (Second) of Contracts (1979). In fact, we have not been informed of any other purpose for the employment of appellant to review construction plans, but for the benefit of the homeowners in the subdivision. Accordingly, we find that appellees, as third party beneficiaries, have a cause of action in accord with the principles of the Restatement (Second) of Contracts § 302 (1979), and *Guy*.

Appellant also contends that the availability to appellees of alternative sources of redress takes the case out of the holding of *Guy*. Appellant suggests that appellees institute suit against either Winchester or the offending homeowners in the subdivision. Although part of what made a cause of action appropriate in *Guy* was the fact that Mrs. Guy would have been left without recourse or remedy if we denied her third party beneficiary status, the critical point in *Guy* was that the beneficiary was an *intended* beneficiary, intended by the promisee to receive the benefit of the promised performance. Nevertheless, the Superior Court found, and we agree, that subdivision Restriction No. 23 precludes homeowners from bringing suit against the developer. Said subdivision restriction reads as follows:

> No delay or omission on the part of the Partnership or the owner of any other lot in the subdivision in exercising any right, power, or remedy herein provided for in the event of breach of any part of the provisions, conditions, restrictions, and covenants herein contained shall be construed as a waiver thereof or acquiescence therein; and no right of action shall accrue nor shall any action be brought or maintained by anyone whomsoever against the Partnership for or on account of the failure or neglect of the Partnership to exercise any right, power, or remedy herein provided for in the event of such breach.

Pursuant to this provision, the developer has no duty to enforce the subdivision restrictions and is essentially insulated from liability by virtue of this disclaimer. However, there is no such disclaimer that applies to appellant. Appellant, pursuant to his agreement with Winchester, assumed the duty of enforcing the subdivision restrictions and cannot now try to insulate himself from liability by bringing himself within the ambit of Restriction No. 23.[2]

We find, therefore, that the circumstances of this case are sufficiently compelling to warrant the application of the exception created in *Guy v. Liederbach*. Accordingly, the judgment of the Superior Court is affirmed. The case is remanded to the trial court with instructions to reinstate the complaint and proceed consistent with this opinion.

NIX, C.J., and FLAHERTY and ZAPPALA, JJ., concur in the result.

––––––––––

2. We do not decide the propriety of a suit against the offending homeowners, since the existence of an alternative remedy does not preclude one from being a third party beneficiary, entitled to assert a claim under the contract.

UCC § 2–318

[See Selected Source Materials Supplement]

RESTATEMENT, SECOND, CONTRACTS § 313

[See Selected Source Materials Supplement]

MARTINEZ v. SOCOMA COMPANIES, INC.

Supreme Court of California, 1974.
11 Cal.3d 394, 113 Cal.Rptr. 585, 521 P.2d 841.

WRIGHT, CHIEF JUSTICE. Plaintiffs brought this class action on behalf of themselves and other disadvantaged unemployed persons, alleging that defendants failed to perform contracts with the United States government under which defendants agreed to provide job training and at least one year of employment to certain numbers of such persons. Plaintiffs claim that they and the other such persons are third party beneficiaries of the contracts and as such are entitled to damages for defendants' nonperformance. General demurrers to the complaint were sustained without leave to amend, apparently on the ground that plaintiffs lacked standing to sue as third party beneficiaries. Dismissals were entered as to the demurring defendants, and plaintiffs appeal.

We affirm the judgments of dismissal. As will appear, the contracts nowhere state that either the government or defendants are to be liable to persons such as plaintiffs for damages resulting from the defendants' nonperformance. The benefits to be derived from defendants' performance were clearly intended not as gifts from the government to such persons but as a means of executing the public purposes stated in the contracts and in the underlying legislation. Accordingly, plaintiffs were only incidental beneficiaries and as such have no right of recovery.

The complaint names as defendants Socoma Companies, Inc. ("Socoma"), Lady Fair Kitchens, Incorporated ("Lady Fair"), Monarch Electronics International, Inc. ("Monarch"), and eleven individuals of whom three are alleged officers or directors of Socoma, four of Lady Fair, and four of Monarch. Lady Fair and the individual defendants associated with it, a Utah corporation and Utah residents respectively, did not appear in the trial court and are not parties to this appeal.

The complaint alleges that under 1967 amendments to the Economic Opportunity Act of 1964 (81 Stat. 688–690, 42 U.S.C.A. §§ 2763–2768, repealed by 86 Stat. 703 (1972)) "the United States Congress instituted Special Impact Programs with the intent to benefit the residents of certain neighborhoods having especially large concentrations of low income persons and suffering from dependency, chronic unemployment and rising tensions." Funds to administer these programs were appropriated to the United States

Department of Labor. The department subsequently designated the East Los Angeles neighborhood as a "Special Impact area" and made federal funds available for contracts with local private industry for the benefit of the "hard-core unemployed residents" of East Los Angeles.

On January 17, 1969, the corporate defendants allegedly entered into contracts with the Secretary of Labor, acting on behalf of the Manpower Administration, United States Department of Labor (hereinafter referred to as the "Government"). Each such defendant entered into a separate contract and all three contracts are made a part of the complaint as exhibits. Under each contract the contracting defendant agreed to lease space in the then vacant Lincoln Heights jail building owned by the City of Los Angeles, to invest at least $5,000,000 in renovating the leasehold and establishing a facility for the manufacture of certain articles, to train and employ in such facility for at least 12 months, at minimum wage rates, a specified number of East Los Angeles residents certified as disadvantaged by the Government, and to provide such employees with opportunities for promotion into available supervisorial-managerial positions and with options to purchase stock in their employer corporation. Each contract provided for the lease of different space in the building and for the manufacture of a different kind of product. As consideration, the Government agreed to pay each defendant a stated amount in installments. Socoma was to hire 650 persons and receive $950,000; Lady Fair was to hire 550 persons and receive $999,000; and Monarch was to hire 400 persons and receive $800,000. The hiring of these persons was to be completed by January 17, 1970.

Plaintiffs were allegedly members of a class of no more than 2,017 East Los Angeles residents who were certified as disadvantaged and were qualified for employment under the contracts. Although the Government paid $712,500 of the contractual consideration to Socoma, $299,700 to Lady Fair, and $240,000 to Monarch, all of these defendants failed to perform under their respective contracts, except that Socoma provided 186 jobs of which 139 were wrongfully terminated, and Lady Fair provided 90 jobs, of which all were wrongfully terminated.

The complaint contains 11 causes of action. The second, fourth, and sixth causes of action seek damages of $3,607,500 against Socoma, $3,052,500 against Lady Fair, and $2,220,000 against Monarch, calculated on the basis of 12 months' wages at minimum rates and $1,000 for loss of training for each of the jobs the defendant contracted to provide. The third and fifth causes of action seek similar damages for the 139 persons whose jobs were terminated by Socoma and the 90 persons whose jobs were terminated by Lady Fair. . . .

Each cause of action alleges that the "express purpose of the [Government] in entering into [each] contract was to benefit [the] certified disadvantaged hardcore unemployed residents of East Los Angeles [for whom defendants promised to provide training and jobs] and none other, and those residents are thus the express third party beneficiaries of [each] contract."

The general demurrers admitted the truth of all the material factual allegations of the complaint, regardless of any possible difficulty in proving them (Alcorn v. Anbro Engineering, Inc. (1970) 2 Cal.3d 493, 496, 86 Cal. Rptr. 88, 468 P.2d 216), but did not admit allegations which constitute conclusions of law (Faulkner v. Cal. Toll Bridge Authority (1953) 40 Cal.2d 317, 329, 253 P.2d 659) or which are contrary to matters of which we must take judicial notice (Chavez v. Times–Mirror Co. (1921) 185 Cal. 20, 23, 195 P. 666). (See Witkin, Cal. Procedure (2d ed. 1970) Pleading, §§ 328, 800.) When a complaint is based on a written contract which it sets out in full, a general demurrer to the complaint admits not only the contents of the instrument but also any pleaded meaning to which the instrument is reasonably susceptible. (Coast Bank v. Minderhout (1964) 61 Cal.2d 311, 315, 38 Cal.Rptr. 505, 392 P.2d 265.) Moreover, where, as here, the general demurrer is to an *original* complaint and is sustained without leave to amend, "the issues presented are whether the complaint states a cause of action, and if not, whether there is a reasonable possibility that it could be amended to do so." (MacLeod v. Tribune Publishing Co. (1959) 52 Cal.2d 536, 542, 343 P.2d 36, 38; see 3 Witkin, Cal.Procedure (2d ed. 1971) Pleading, § 845.) Thus, we must determine whether the pleaded written contracts support plaintiffs' claim either on their face or under any interpretation to which the contracts are reasonably susceptible and which is pleaded in the complaint or could be pleaded by proper amendment. This determination must be made in light of applicable federal statutes and other matters we must judicially notice. (Evid.Code, §§ 451, 459, subd. (a).)

Plaintiffs contend they are third party beneficiaries under Civil Code section 1559, which provides: "A contract, made expressly for the benefit of a third person, may be enforced by him at any time before the parties thereto rescind it." This section excludes enforcement of a contract by persons who are only incidentally or remotely benefited by it. (Lucas v. Hamm (1961) 56 Cal.2d 583, 590, 15 Cal.Rptr. 821, 824, 364 P.2d 685, 688.) American law generally classifies persons having enforceable rights under contracts to which they are not parties as either creditor beneficiaries or donee beneficiaries. (Restatement, Contracts, §§ 133, subds. (1), (2), 135, 136, 147; 2 Williston on Contracts (3d ed. 1959) § 356; 4 Corbin on Contracts (1951) § 774; see Restatement, Second, Contracts (Tentative Drafts 1973) § 133, coms. b, c.) California decisions follow this classification. . . .

A person cannot be a creditor beneficiary unless the promisor's performance of the contract will discharge some form of legal duty owed to the beneficiary by the promisee. (Hartman Ranch Co. v. Associated Oil Co. (1937) 10 Cal.2d 232, 244, 73 P.2d 1163; Restatement, Contracts § 133, subd. (1)(b).) Clearly the Government (the promisee) at no time bore any legal duty toward plaintiffs to provide the benefits set forth in the contracts and plaintiffs do not claim to be creditor beneficiaries.

A person is a donee beneficiary only if the promisee's contractual intent is either to make a gift to him or to confer on him a right against the promisor. (Restatement, Contracts § 133, subd. (1)(a).) If the promisee intends to make a gift, the donee beneficiary can recover if such donative intent must have been understood by the promisor from the nature of the contract and the circumstances accompanying its execution. (Lucas v. Hamm, supra, 56 Cal.2d at pp. 590–591, 15 Cal.Rptr. 821, 364 P.2d 685.) This rule does not aid plaintiffs, however, because, as will be seen, no intention to make a gift can be imputed to the Government as promisee.

Unquestionably plaintiffs were among those whom the Government intended to benefit through defendants' performance of the contracts which recite that they are executed pursuant to a statute and a presidential directive calling for programs to furnish disadvantaged persons with training and employment opportunities. However, the fact that a Government program for social betterment confers benefits upon individuals who are not required to render contractual consideration in return does not necessarily imply that the benefits are intended as gifts. Congress' power to spend money in aid of the general welfare (U.S. Const., art. I, § 8) authorizes federal programs to alleviate national unemployment. (Helvering v. Davis (1937) 301 U.S. 619, 640–645, 57 S.Ct. 904, 81 L.Ed. 1307.) The benefits of such programs are provided not simply as gifts to the recipients but as a means of accomplishing a larger public purpose. The furtherance of the public purpose is in the nature of consideration to the Government, displacing any governmental intent to furnish the benefits as gifts. (See County of Alameda v. Janssen (1940) 16 Cal.2d 276, 281, 106 P.2d 11; Allied Architects v. Payne (1923) 192 Cal. 431, 438–439, 221 P. 209.)

Even though a person is not the intended recipient of a gift, he may nevertheless be "a donee beneficiary if it appears from the terms of the promise in view of the accompanying circumstances that the purpose of the promisee in obtaining the promise ... is ... to *confer upon him a right against the promisor* to some performance neither due nor supposed or asserted to be due from the promisee to the beneficiary." (Restatement, Contracts § 133, subd. (1)(a) (italics supplied); Gourmet Lane, Inc. v. Keller (1963) 222 Cal.App.2d 701, 705, 35 Cal.Rptr. 398.) The Government may, of course, deliberately implement a public purpose by including provisions in its contracts which expressly confer on a specified class of third persons a direct right to benefits, or damages in lieu of benefits, against the private contractor. But a governmental intent to confer such a direct right cannot be inferred simply from the fact that the third persons were intended to enjoy the benefits. The Restatement, Contracts makes this clear in dealing specifically with contractual promises to the Government to render services to members of the public: "A promisor bound to the United States or to a State or municipality by contract to do an act or render a service to some or all of the members of the public, *is subject to no duty* under the contract to such members to give compensation for the injurious consequences of performing or attempting to perform it, or of failing to do so, unless, ... *an intention is manifested in the contract,* as interpreted in the light of the circumstances surrounding its formation, *that the promisor shall compensate members of the public for such injurious consequences....*" (Restatement, Contracts § 145 (italics supplied);[1] see City & County of San Francisco v. Western Air Lines, Inc. (1962) 204 Cal.App.2d 105, 121, 22 Cal.Rptr. 216.)

The present contracts manifest no intent that the defendants pay damages to compensate plaintiffs or other members of the public for their nonperformance. To the contrary, the contracts' provisions for retaining the Government's control over determination of contractual disputes and for

---

1. The corresponding language in the Tentative Drafts of the Restatement, Second, Contracts (1973), section 145, is: "[A] promisor who contracts with a government or governmental agency to do an act for or render a service to the public *is not subject to contractual liability* to a member of the public for consequential damages resulting from performance or failure to perform unless ... the terms of the promise provide for such liability...."

The language omitted in this quotation and the quotation in the accompanying text relates to the creditor beneficiary situation in which the government itself would be liable for nonperformance of the contract. As noted earlier, plaintiffs do not claim to be creditor beneficiaries.

limiting defendants' financial risks indicate a governmental purpose to exclude the direct rights against defendants claimed here.

Each contract provides that any dispute of fact arising thereunder is to be determined by written decision of the Government's contracting officer, subject to an appeal to the Secretary of Labor, whose decision shall be final unless determined by a competent court to have been fraudulent, capricious, arbitrary, in bad faith, or not supported by substantial evidence. These administrative decisions may include determinations of related questions of law although such determinations are not made final. The efficiency and uniformity of interpretation fostered by these administrative procedures would tend to be undermined if litigation such as the present action, to which the Government is a stranger, were permitted to proceed on the merits.

In addition to the provisions on resolving disputes each contract contains a "liquidated damages" provision obligating the contractor to refund all amounts received from the Government, with interest, in the event of failure to acquire and equip the specified manufacturing facility, and, for each employment opportunity it fails to provide, to refund a stated dollar amount equivalent to the total contract compensation divided by the number of jobs agreed to be provided. This liquidated damages provision limits liability for the breaches alleged by plaintiffs to the refunding of amounts received and indicates an absence of any contractual intent to impose liability directly in favor of plaintiffs, or, as claimed in the complaint, to impose liability for the value of the promised performance. To allow plaintiffs' claim would nullify the limited liability for which defendants bargained and which the Government may well have held out as an inducement in negotiating the contracts.

It is this absence of any manifestation of intent that defendants should pay compensation for breach to persons in the position of plaintiffs that distinguishes this case from Shell v. Schmidt (1954) 126 Cal.App.2d 279, 272 P.2d 82, relied on by plaintiffs. The defendant in *Shell* was a building contractor who had entered into an agreement with the federal government under which he received priorities for building materials and agreed in return to use the materials to build homes with required specifications for sale to war veterans at or below ceiling prices. Plaintiffs were 12 veterans, each of whom had purchased a home that failed to comply with the agreed specifications. They were held entitled to recover directly from the defendant contractor as third party beneficiaries of his agreement with the government. The legislation under which the agreement was made included a provision empowering the government to obtain payment of monetary compensation by the contractor to the veteran purchasers for deficiencies resulting from failure to comply with specifications. Thus, there was "an intention ... manifested in the contract ... that the promisor shall compensate members of the public for such injurious consequences [of nonperformance]."[2]

2. In contrast to *Shell*, supra, is City & County of San Francisco v. Western Air Lines, Inc., supra, 204 Cal.App.2d 105, 22 Cal.Rptr. 216. There, Western Air Lines claimed to be a third party beneficiary of agreements between the federal government and the City and County of San Francisco under which the city received federal funds for the development of its airport subject to a written condition that the airport "be available for public use on fair and reasonable terms and without unjust discrimination." Western Air Lines asserted that it had been charged for its use of the airport at a higher rate than some other air carriers in violation of the contractual condition, and therefore was entitled to recover the excess charges from the city. One of the reasons given by the court on appeal for rejecting this contention was the absence of any provision or indication of intent in the agreements between

Plaintiffs contend that section 145 of the Restatement, Contracts, previously quoted, does not preclude their recovery because it applies only to promises made to a governmental entity "to do an act or render a service to ... the public," and, plaintiffs assert they and the class they represent are identified persons set apart from "the public." Even if this contention were correct it would not follow that plaintiffs have standing as third party beneficiaries under the Restatement. The quoted provision of section 145 "is a special application of the principles stated in §§ 133(1a), 135 [on donee beneficiaries]" (Restatement, Contracts § 145, com. a), delineating certain circumstances which preclude government contractors' liability to third parties. Section 145 itself does not purport to confer standing to sue on persons who do not otherwise qualify under basic third party beneficiary principles.[3] As pointed out above, plaintiffs are not donee beneficiaries under those basic principles because it does not appear from the terms and circumstances of the contract that the Government intended to make a gift to plaintiffs or to confer on them a legal right against the defendants.

Moreover, contrary to plaintiffs' contention, section 145 of the Restatement, Contracts does preclude their recovery because the services which the contracts required the defendants to perform *were* to be rendered to "members of the public" within the meaning of that section. Each contract recites it is made under the "Special Impact Programs" part of the Economic Opportunity Act of 1964 and pursuant to a presidential directive for a test program of cooperation between the federal government and private industry in an effort to provide training and jobs for thousands of the hard-core unemployed or under-employed. The congressional declaration of purpose of the Economic Opportunity Act as a whole points up the public nature of its benefits on a national scale. Congress declared that the purpose of the act was to "strengthen, supplement, and coordinate efforts in furtherance of [the] policy" of "opening to everyone the opportunity for education and training, the opportunity to work, and the opportunity to live in decency and dignity" so that the "United States can achieve its full economic and social potential as a nation." (42 U.S.C.A. § 2701.)

In providing for special impact programs, Congress declared that such programs were directed to the solution of critical problems existing in particular neighborhoods having especially large concentration of low-income persons, and that the programs were intended to be of sufficient size and scope to have an appreciable impact in such neighborhoods in arresting tendencies toward dependency, chronic unemployment, and rising community tensions. (42 U.S.C.A. former § 2763.) Thus the contracts here were designed not to benefit individuals as such but to utilize the training and employment of disadvantaged persons as a means of improving the East Los Angeles neighborhood. Moreover, the means by which the contracts were intended to accomplish this community improvement were not confined to provision of the particular benefits on which plaintiffs base their claim to damages—one year's employment at minimum wages plus $1,000 worth of training to be provided to each of 650 persons by one defendant, 400 by another, and 550 by another. Rather the objective was to be achieved by establishing permanent industries in which local residents would be permanently employed and would

the government and the city to compensate third parties for noncompliance....

3. The same is true of the Tentative Draft of section 145 of the Restatement, Second, Contracts....

have opportunities to become supervisors, managers and part owners. The required minimum capital investment of $5,000,000 by each defendant and the defendants' 22–year lease of the former Lincoln Heights jail building for conversion into an industrial facility also indicates the broad, long-range objective of the program. Presumably, as the planned enterprises prospered, the quantity and quality of employment and economic opportunity that they provided would increase and would benefit not only employees but also their families, other local enterprises and the government itself through reduction of law enforcement and welfare costs.

The fact that plaintiffs were in a position to benefit more directly than certain other members of the public from performance of the contract does not alter their status as incidental beneficiaries. (See Restatement, Contracts § 145, illus. 1: C, a member of the public cannot recover for injury from B's failure to perform a contract with the United States to carry mail over a certain route.)[4] For example, in City & County of San Francisco v. Western Air Lines, Inc., supra, 204 Cal.App.2d 105, 22 Cal.Rptr. 216, the agreement between the federal government and the city for improvement of the airport could be considered to be of greater benefit to air carriers using the airport than to many other members of the public. Nevertheless, Western, as an air carrier, was but an incidental, not an express, beneficiary of the agreement and therefore had no standing to enforce the contractual prohibition against discrimination in the airport's availability for public use. The court explains the distinction as follows: "None of the documents under consideration confers on Western the rights of a third-party beneficiary. The various contracts and assurances created benefits and detriments as between only two parties—the United States and the city. Nothing in them shows any intent of the contracting parties to confer any benefit directly and expressly upon air carriers such as the defendant. It is true that air carriers, including Western, may be *incidentally* benefited by City's assurances in respect to nondiscriminatory treatment at the airport. They may also be incidentally benefited by the fact that, through federal aid, a public airport is improved with longer runways, brighter beacons, or larger loading ramps, or by the fact a new public airport is provided for a community without one. The various documents and agreements were part of a federal aid program directed to the promoting of a national transportation system. Provisions in such agreements, including the nondiscrimination clauses, were intended to advance such federal aims and not for the benefit of those who might be affected by the sponsor's failure to perform." (204 Cal.App.2d at p. 120, 22 Cal.Rptr. at p. 225.)

For the reasons above stated we hold that plaintiffs and the class they represent have no standing as third party beneficiaries to recover the damages sought in the complaint under either California law or the general contract principles which federal law applies to government contracts.

The judgments of dismissal are affirmed.

McComb, Sullivan, and Clark, JJ., concur.

Burke, Justice (dissenting).

---

4. This illustration is repeated in Tentative Draft, Restatement, Second, Contracts, section 145, illustration 1.

I dissent. The certified hard-core unemployed of East Los Angeles were the express, not incidental, beneficiaries of the contracts in question and, therefore, have standing to enforce those contracts. . . .

The majority err . . . because the congressional purpose was to benefit *both* the communities in which the impact programs are established *and* the individual impoverished persons in such communities.[5] The benefits from the instant contracts were to accrue directly to the members of plaintiffs' class, as a reading of the contracts clearly demonstrates.[6] These direct benefits to members of plaintiffs' class were not merely the *"means of executing the public purposes,"* as the majority contend . . . , but were the *ends* in themselves and one of the public purposes to which the legislation and subsequent contracts were addressed. Accordingly, I cannot agree with the majority that "the contracts here were designed *not* to benefit individuals as such but to utilize the training and employment of disadvantaged persons as a *means* of improving the East Los Angeles neighborhood." (. . . italics added.)

The intent of the contracts themselves is expressed in their preambles. . . . By these provisions, the contracting parties clearly state as one of their purposes their intent to find jobs for the hard-core unemployed.

In accord with this expressed intent, the substantive provisions of the contracts confer a direct benefit upon the class seeking to enforce them. The contracts call for the hiring of stated numbers of hard-core unemployed from the East Los Angeles Special Impact Area for a period of at least one year at a starting minimum wage of $2.00 per hour for the first 90 days and a minimum wage of $2.25 per hour thereafter, or for the prevailing wage for the area, whichever is higher. In addition to requiring appropriate job training for such employees, the contracts also require "That the Contractor will arrange for the orderly promotion of persons so employed into available supervisory-managerial and other positions, and will arrange for all contract employees to obtain a total ownership interest not exceeding thirty (30) percent in the Contractor through an appropriate stock purchase plan. . . ." The scope of the stock purchase plans is detailed in each of the contracts. . . .

The language of section 133 [of the Restatement,[7]], standing alone, could reasonably suggest that members of the general public are "donee beneficia-

5. Evidence of Congress' purpose to aid the *individual* impoverished persons in such communities can be gleaned from 42 U.S.C.A. § 2701, wherein Congress declared that if our country is to achieve its full potential, "every individual" must be given "the opportunity for education and training, the opportunity to work, and the opportunity to live in decency and dignity." Congress implemented this general policy of assisting our impoverished citizens in various ways, including the Special Impact Program involved in this case. Yet, contrary to the majority, nothing indicates that Congress' *exclusive* purpose in doing so was to assist the neighborhoods and communities in which these persons live. It seems clear that Congress intended *both* the communities and the individuals to be direct beneficiaries of the program. It is incorrect to label one as an intended *direct* beneficiary and the other as merely *incidental*.

6. In the contracts, the defendants agreed to provide training and jobs to a specified class of persons, whom plaintiffs represent. The government's express intent, therefore, was to confer a benefit, namely training and jobs, upon an ascertainable identifiable class and not simply the general public itself.

7. Comment (c) to section 133 of the Restatement, Contracts states in part that "By gift is meant primarily some performance or right which is not paid for by the recipient and which is apparently designed to benefit him." Thus, section 133 states essentially the same rule as that enunciated in Shell v. Schmidt, supra, 126 Cal.App.2d 279, 290–291, 272 P.2d 82. Section 133 has been followed by the California courts. (Hartman Ranch Co. v. Associated Oil Co., supra, 10 Cal.2d 232, 244, 73 P.2d 1163; Southern Cal. Gas Co. v. ABC Construction Co., 204 Cal.App.2d 747, 752, 22 Cal.Rptr. 540.)

ries" under any contract whose purpose is to confer a "gift" upon them. Section 145 qualifies this broad language and treats the general public merely as incidental, not direct, beneficiaries under contracts made for the general public benefit, unless the contract manifests a clear intent to compensate such members of the public in the event of a breach. Section 145 does not, however, entirely preclude application of the "donee beneficiary" concept to every government contract. Whenever, as in the instant case, such a contract expresses an intent to benefit directly a particular person or ascertainable class of persons, section 145 is, by its terms, inapplicable and the contract may be enforced by the beneficiaries pursuant to the general provisions of section 133. Thus, I would conclude that section 145 is consistent with the holding of Shell v. Schmidt, supra, 126 Cal.App.2d 279, 272 P.2d 82, and the City and County of San Francisco v. Western Air Lines, Inc., supra, 204 Cal.App.2d 105, 22 Cal.Rptr. 216....

The majority contend that the inclusion of liquidated damage clauses in each of the contracts limits defendants' financial risks and was intended to preclude the assertion of third party claims.... Yet, these clauses simply provide for various refunds of monies advanced by the government in the event of a default. These so-called "liquidated damages" clauses nowhere purport to limit damages to the specified refunds. Nothing in the contracts limits the right of the government or, more importantly, plaintiffs' class, to seek additional relief....

The majority also rely on the fact that, "The present contracts manifest no intent that the defendants pay damages to compensate plaintiffs or other members of the public for their nonperformance." ... Therefore, it assertedly follows that giving plaintiffs the right to monetary benefits in lieu of performance would give to plaintiffs and the class they represent benefits never contemplated nor intended under the contracts. This argument disregards both the fact that the class was to receive a direct monetary benefit under the contracts in the form of wages, and that under well settled contract law, an aggrieved party is entitled to be compensated for all the detriment proximately caused by a breach of contract (Civ.Code, § 3300)....

It is my conclusion, therefore, that the trial court erred in sustaining the demurrer without leave to amend. I would order the trial court to determine the propriety of plaintiffs' class action prior to proceeding upon the merits of the complaint.

TOBRINER and MOSK, JJ., concur.

———

ZIGAS v. SUPERIOR COURT, 120 Cal.App.3d 827, 174 Cal.Rptr. 806 (1981). The petitioners were tenants of an apartment building that was financed with a federally insured mortgage, pursuant to the National Housing Act. A provision of the financing agreement required the landlords to charge no more than the schedule of rents approved by the Department of Housing and Urban Development (HUD). Petitioners sought damages for the landlords' violation of that provision, by overcharges. Held, the tenants could sue the landlords as third–party beneficiaries.

"California law clearly allows third-party suits for breaches of contract where no government agency is a party to the contract.... Whether such suits are allowed when the government contracts with a private party depends upon analysis of the decisions in Shell v. Schmidt (1954) 126 Cal.App.2d 279 [272 P.2d 82] and Martinez v. Socoma Companies Inc., supra, 11 Cal.3d 394."

"[U]nder *Martinez,* standing to sue as a third-party beneficiary to a government contract depends on the intent of the parties as manifested by the contract and the circumstances surrounding its formation.... We therefore must determine, from the terms of the contract between HUD and real parties [landlords] and the attendant circumstances, whether there was manifested an intention that petitioners be compensated in the event of real parties' nonperformance.... [W]e are of the view that the case falls within *Shell;* that is to say, appellants [tenants] were direct beneficiaries of the contract and have standing, and not, as in *Martinez,* incidental beneficiaries without standing.

"We explicate:

"1. In *Martinez,* the contract between the government and Socoma provided that if Socoma breached the agreement, Socoma would refund to the government that which the government had paid Socoma pursuant to the contract between them. Thus, it is clear in *Martinez* that it was the government that was out of pocket as a consequence of the breach and should be reimbursed therefor, not the people to be trained and given jobs. In the case at bench, as in *Shell,* the government suffered no loss as a consequence of the breach, it was the renter here and the veteran purchaser in *Shell* that suffered the direct pecuniary loss.

"2. Unlike *Martinez,* too, in the case at bench, no governmental administrative procedure was provided for the resolution of disputes arising under the agreement. Thus, to permit this litigation would in no way affect the 'efficiency and uniformity of interpretation fostered by these administrative procedures.' (Martinez v. Socoma Companies, Inc., supra, 11 Cal.3d at p. 402.) On the contrary, as we earlier noted, lawsuits such as this promote the federal interest by inducing compliance with HUD agreements.

"3. In *Martinez,* the court held that 'To allow plaintiffs' claim would nullify the limited liability for which defendants bargained and which the Government may well have held out as an inducement in negotiating the contracts.' ... Here, there is no 'limited liability.' As we shall point out, real parties are liable under the agreement, *without limitation,* for breach of the agreement.

"4. Further, in *Martinez,* the contracts 'were designed not to benefit individuals as such but to utilize the training and employment of disadvantaged persons as a means of improving the East Los Angeles neighborhood.' ... Moreover, the training and employment programs were but one aspect of a 'broad, long-range objective' ... contemplated by the agreement and designed to benefit not only those to be trained and employed but also 'other local enterprises and the government itself through reduction of law enforcement and welfare costs.' ...

"Here, on the other hand, as in *Shell,* the purpose of the Legislature and of the contract between real parties and HUD is narrow and specific: to provide moderate rental housing for families with children; in *Shell,* to provide moderate priced homes for veterans.

"5. Finally, we believe the agreement itself manifests an intent to make tenants direct beneficiaries, not incidental beneficiaries, of [the landlords'] promise to charge no more than the HUD approved rent schedule.

"Section 4(a) and 4(c) of the agreement, providing that there can be no increase in rental fees, over the approved rent schedule, without the prior approval in writing of HUD, were obviously designed to protect the tenant against arbitrary increases in rents, precisely that which is alleged to have occurred here. Certainly, it was not intended to benefit the government as a guarantor of the mortgage....

"We are supported in our view by section 17 of the Agreement which specifically provides that [the landlords] are personally liable, '(a) for funds ... of the project coming into their hands which, by the provisions [of the Agreement] *they are not entitled to retain;* and (b) for their own acts and deeds or acts and deeds of other [sic] which they have authorized in violation of the provisions [of the Agreement].' ...

"By the allegations of the complaint, [the landlords] have 'retained' in excess of $2 million in violation of the Agreement. Therefore, they are liable for that sum. To whom should they be liable? To ask the question is to answer it. It is not the government from whom the money was exacted; it was taken from the tenants. Therefore, it should be returned to the tenants."

————————

H.B. DEAL & CO. v. HEAD, 221 Ark. 47, 251 S.W.2d 1017 (1952). The Government made a contract with Deal calling for the construction by Deal of an ordnance plant. A provision in the contract required Deal to pay his laborers time–and–a–half for overtime. The Fair Labor Standards Act laid down a similar requirement for employees engaged in certain classes of work. Employees of Deal brought an action against him under the Act and, in the alternative, under the contract. Held, the Act was inapplicable to Deal's construction job, but the employees could sue under the contract, because the Government placed the time–and–a–half provision in the contract for their benefit.

————————

H.R. MOCH CO. v. RENSSELAER WATER CO., 247 N.Y. 160, 159 N.E. 896 (1928). A waterworks company entered into a contract with a city whereby the company: (1) agreed to furnish the city with water for sewer flushing, for street sprinkling, and for public buildings, and to provide service at fire hydrants at the rate of $42.50 a year for each hydrant; and (2) agreed to provide private and industrial takers with water at reasonable rates. The plaintiff was a property owner who alleged that his property was destroyed by fire in consequence of the failure of the waterworks company to comply with its contract with the city by providing a sufficient head of water at the fire hydrants. A demurrer to the complaint was sustained. The court said (through Cardozo, Ch. J.) that since the city did not owe its inhabitants a legal duty to provide them with water for the purpose of extinguishing fires, the contract between the city and the waterworks company could not be construed as an agreement to discharge a duty of the city to its inhabitants.

That being so, the plaintiff had no rights as a third–party beneficiary unless "an intention appears that the promisor [the waterworks company] is to be answerable to individual members of the public as well as to the city for any loss ensuing from the failure to fulfil the promise. No such intention is discernible here."

The court conceded that "every city contract, not improvident or wasteful, is for the benefit of the public." But before the injured member of the public can have a right against the party contracting with the city, the benefit must not be merely "incidental and secondary," but rather "must be primary and immediate in such a sense and to such a degree as to bespeak the assumption of a duty to make reparation directly to the individual members of the public if the benefit is lost." Illustrating the principle the court said, "A promisor undertakes to supply fuel for heating a public building. He is not liable for breach of contract to a visitor who finds the building without fuel, and thus [catches] a cold. . . . The carrier of the mails under contract with the government is not answerable to the merchant who has lost the benefit of the bargain through negligent delay. The householder is without a remedy against manufacturers of hose and engines, though prompt performance of their contracts would have stayed the ravages of fire. 'The law does not spread its protection so far.' " If the defendant were liable to this plaintiff, the court said, the defendant would also be liable to all the property owners in the city if the whole city were laid low through a spreading of the fire. "A promisor will not be deemed to have had in mind the assumption of a risk so overwhelming for any trivial reward." (The court also held that the plaintiff had no cause of action for a common–law tort or for breach of a statutory duty.)

LA MOUREA v. RHUDE, 209 Minn. 53, 295 N.W. 304 (1940). Defendants contracted to do certain sewer-construction work, involving blasting, for the city of Duluth. The contract provided that defendants should be "liable for any damages done to the work or other structure or public or private property and injuries sustained by persons" in the course of defendants' operations. Plaintiff sued for damage to his real estate caused by defendants' blasting. The court affirmed an order overruling a demurrer to the complaint, rejecting defendants' argument "that this promise was one to indemnify the city and nothing more."

NOTE ON THE POWER OF THE CONTRACTING PARTIES TO VARY THE PROMISOR'S DUTY TO THE BENEFICIARY

Restatement First drew a sharp line between the power of the contracting practice to vary the promisor's duty to a creditor beneficiary, on the one hand, and to a donee beneficiary, on the other. Section 143 provided that:

A discharge of the promisor by the promisee in a contract or a variation thereof by them is effective against a *creditor* beneficiary if, (a) the creditor beneficiary does not bring suit upon the promise or otherwise materially change his position in reliance thereon before he knows of the discharge or variation, and (b) the promisee's action is not a fraud on creditors.

However, Section 142 provided that:

> Unless the power to do so is reserved, the duty of the promisor to the *donee* beneficiary cannot be released by the promisee or affected by any agreement between the promisee and the promisor....

(Emphasis added in both cases.)

The rule of Restatement First § 142 was dramatically exemplified by Illustration 2:

> A promises B to pay A's son, C, $1000 a year for five years, in consideration of which B promises A to pay B's daughter D, who is C's wife, the same amount. Before C or D learn of this contract A and B mutually agree to rescind it. C and D can treat the agreement of rescission as inoperative to destroy their respective rights to enforce the original contract.

Restatement Second § 311 drops the rule of Restatement First § 142, and gives unified treatment to all intended beneficiaries. However, Section 311 introduces new qualifications on the power of the contracting parties to vary the promisor's duty to the beneficiary.

RESTATEMENT, SECOND, CONTRACTS §§ 309, 311

[See Selected Source Materials Supplement]

ROUSE v. UNITED STATES

United States Court of Appeals, District of Columbia Circuit, 1954.
94 U.S.App.D.C. 386, 215 F.2d 872.

EDGERTON, CIRCUIT JUDGE. Bessie Winston gave Associated Contractors, Inc., her promissory note for $1,008.37, payable in monthly installments of $28.01, for a heating plant in her house. The Federal Housing Administration guaranteed the note and the payee endorsed it for value to the lending bank, the Union Trust Company.

Winston sold the house to Rouse. In the contract of sale Rouse agreed to assume debts secured by deeds of trust and also "to assume payment of $850 for heating plant payable $28 per Mo." Nothing was said about the note.

Winston defaulted on her note. The United States paid the bank, took an assignment of the note, demanded payment from Rouse, and sued him for $850 and interest.

Rouse alleged as defenses (1) that Winston fraudulently misrepresented the condition of the heating plant and (2) that Associated Contractors did not install it satisfactorily. The District Court struck these defenses and granted summary judgment for the plaintiff. The defendant Rouse appeals.

Since Rouse did not sign the note he is not liable on it. D.C.Code 1951, § 28–119; N.I.L. Sec. 18. He is not liable to the United States at all unless his contract with Winston makes him so. The contract says the parties to it are not "bound by any terms, conditions, statements, warranties or representations, oral or written" not contained in it. But this means only that the written contract contains the entire agreement. It does not mean that fraud cannot be set up as a defense to a suit on the contract. Rouse's promise to "assume payment of $850 for heating plant" made him liable to Associated Contractors, Inc., only if and so far as it made him liable to Winston; one who promises to make a payment to the promisee's creditor can assert against the creditor any defense that the promisor could assert against the promisee. Accordingly Rouse, if he had been sued by the corporation, would have been entitled to show fraud on the part of Winston. He is equally entitled to do so in this suit by an assignee of the corporation's claim. It follows that the court erred in striking the first defense. We do not consider whether Winston's alleged fraud, if shown, would be a complete or only a partial defense to this suit, since that question has not arisen and may not arise.

We think the court was right in striking the second defense. "If the promisor's agreement is to be interpreted as a promise to discharge whatever liability the promisee is under, the promisor must certainly be allowed to show that the promisee was under no enforceable liability.... On the other hand, if the promise means that the promisor agrees to pay a sum of money to A, to whom the promisee says he is indebted, it is immaterial whether the promisee is actually indebted to that amount or at all.... Where the promise is to pay a specific debt ... this interpretation will generally be the true one."[9]

The judgment is reversed and the cause remanded with instructions to reinstate the first defense.

Reversed and remanded.

9. 2 [Williston, Contracts, rev. ed. 1936] § 399.

Chapter 21

ASSIGNMENT AND NEGOTIATION

The last Chapter concerned cases in which A and B made a contract that benefited a third party, who wants to enforce the contract. This Chapter concerns cases in which A and B have made a contract that did not benefit a third party at the outset, but in which A subsequently either (1) assigned (that is, transferred) or attempted to assign, to a third party, his rights under a contract, or (2) delegated or attempted to delegate, to a third party, his duties under a contract. A number of different issues can arise in this context, including what rights are assignable, what duties are delegable, and what formalities are required to make an effective assignment.

SECTION 1.   INTRODUCTION

NOTE ON THE ECONOMIC SIGNIFICANCE OF THE ASSIGNMENT OF CLAIMS

A transfer of an intangible asset, such as a claim, by sale, gift, or as security, is called an *assignment*. A claim that is transferable is said to be *assignable*. Not all kinds of claims are transferable. Which kinds of claims are transferable, and which are not, depends on deeply held social norms. Under early English common law, the assignment of a claim (or "chose in action") was legally impossible. If Debtor B owed Creditor A $10, and A purported to transfer his claim against B to Third Party T, the courts early held that literally nothing happened to the claim by virtue of the attempted transfer. B still owed A, not T, and T gained no rights against B.

Most claims are held by creditors, and the rules concerning the assignability of claims eventually changed as the credit system matured. The economic institution of credit can exist in at least a limited way even if claims are not assignable. Money can be lent, and goods can be sold in return for promises of future payment, in a society that knows nothing of the transfer of claims. However, the assignability of claims greatly increases the power of the credit system.

To discover what the assignability of creditors' claims adds to the credit system, it is necessary to analyze first what can be accomplished by that system even in the absence of a power in creditors to assign their claims. Without doubt, one of the principal advantages of the credit system lies in the flexibility it introduces into economic relations. Any existing distribution of economic power (that is, of control over the processes of production and distribution) runs the risk of becoming stagnated. Indeed, from the standpoint of world history the stagnant economy may be regarded as normal. Where economic power rests on private ownership, the institution of private property can easily degenerate into something equivalent to a caste system.

One of the elements that may prevent this from occurring is the device of credit. In a society in which it is possible to obtain present assets in return for a promise of future payment, those who are enterprising may find it possible to improve their economic condition. If A anticipates an increased demand for soy beans, and others have confidence in A's judgment, A can, by borrowing money and investing it in the lease of a farm, bring about an increased production of that commodity. If A has accurately predicted the demand, she will not only have increased her wealth by making a profit on her investment, but will also have given economic activity a desirable direction that it would not have taken had she been living in a society in which borrowing was unknown.

The flexibility of economic processes that results from the availability of credit is increased where it is possible to assign claims. Suppose A hold claims for $5,000 each against D, E, and F. If A is unable to assign these claims, although they represent wealth, they do not represent present control over the economy. For example, suppose A is reasonably sure that there will soon be a greatly increased demand for some commodity. If A has no liquid assets, and A's claims cannot be transferred to raise funds, A's ownership of the claims does not enable him to bring about an increase in the production of that commodity. On the other hand, if the claims are assignable, then by transferring the claims he owns to someone else, A can obtain funds whose investment may result in an expansion of some branch of the economy.

The assignability of claims therefore converts what would otherwise be merely an expectancy of future control over economic factors of production and distribution into present control. By dispersing control over a larger group, assignability widens the pool of human knowledge and increases the opportunity for a productive application of human energies.*

CLAPP v. ORIX CREDIT ALLIANCE, INC.

Court of Appeals of Oregon, 2004.
192 Or.App. 320, 84 P.3d 833.

Before LANDAU, Presiding Judge, and ARMSTRONG and BREWER, Judges.

BREWER, J.

This is an action for money had and received arising from the insured loss of a vehicle in a secured transaction. On appeal, plaintiff assigns error to the

---

* For a brief history of the law concerning the assignability of claims, see Appendix D.

trial court's denial of her motion for summary judgment and its grant of the cross-motion for summary judgment of defendant Orix Credit Alliance, Inc. (Orix). We review the summary judgment record to determine whether there are any genuine issues of material fact and whether either moving party is entitled to judgment as a matter of law.... We reverse and remand.

The material facts are undisputed. Plaintiff is an independent truck driver. Defendant Laser Express, Inc., (Laser) is an interstate common carrier with whom plaintiff contracted to provide truck driving services. Orix is a commercial finance company. In 1996, plaintiff decided to purchase a highway tractor. Laser agreed to act as an undisclosed agent for plaintiff. [That is, Laser held itself out to the seller as if it were buying the truck on its own behalf, rather than as an agent acting on behalf of Clapp, the plaintiff.] Laser entered into a conditional sale contract note (the contract) that documented its installment purchase of the tractor. Orix is the vendor's assignee under the contract.

By the terms of the contract, Laser granted Orix a security interest in the tractor. The contract provided that "[b]uyer [Laser] shall not assign this contract note without the prior written consent of Holder [Orix]." Plaintiff made the down payment toward the purchase of the tractor, and she also made all payments received by Orix on the contract. In May 1998, Laser, as assignor, and plaintiff, as assignee, entered into an assignment of contract (the assignment) by the terms of which Laser transferred its interest in the contract to plaintiff. Orix did not give prior consent to the assignment.

The assignment provides, in part:

"1. [Laser], (as assignor, and vendee under contract) does hereby convey, assign, sell, transfer and set over unto [plaintiff], assignee, all of its right, title and interest in and to the written and attached contract of sale dated on or about December 26, 1996, together with any and all other documents relating to the sale by [Orix's assignor] and as assigned, conveyed to or otherwise delivered to [Orix]....

"2. [Laser] does hereby direct [Orix], its successors or assigns, to deliver, upon completion of all payments provided in the aforementioned contract, the title to said vehicle to [plaintiff], to be hers absolutely, free and clear of any claims by [Laser].

"3. [Laser] also hereby conveys to [plaintiff] all of its right, title and interest in the property described in the contract and the legal title thereto, which is pledged to secure the performance of the vendee's obligations created thereby....

"5. The parties hereto recognize that this assignment shall not relieve [Laser] from its obligations due on the contract between [Orix] and [Laser]. Therefore, [plaintiff] does hereby agree to indemnify, defend and hold harmless [Laser] from any and all obligations due under the contract and the payments due thereon for the purchase of the aforementioned vehicle."

In March 1999, the tractor was totally destroyed in a roll-over accident. Plaintiff notified Orix of the loss, and she advised Orix that she claimed the net insurance proceeds in excess of the balance due on the contract. Orix received $27,500 from the insurer for the loss of the tractor. Orix applied the insurance proceeds in full satisfaction of the contract balance, leaving a credit balance of $9,950.39. On May 10, 1999, plaintiff delivered a copy of the assignment to Orix, and she reasserted her demand for payment of the net insurance proceeds. On May 12, 1999, Orix nevertheless issued a check for the proceeds to Laser. Plaintiff then commenced this action against Laser and Orix for conversion and money had and received.

Plaintiff filed a motion for partial summary judgment against Orix on her claim for money had and received, in which she asserted that she was entitled, by virtue of the assignment, to the net insurance proceeds from the loss of the truck. Orix filed a cross-motion for summary judgment on both of plaintiff's claims, arguing that the prohibition of assignment contained in the contract invalidated the assignment and that, even if it did not, the assignment did not transfer the right to receive the insurance proceeds. The trial court denied plaintiff's motion for summary judgment, and it granted Orix's cross-motion. The court assumed that the prohibition was ineffective to prevent the assignment, but it agreed with Orix that "the assignment is a limited assignment and plaintiff is not entitled to net insurance proceeds under this agreement." On appeal, the parties renew their arguments made before the trial court.

[The court began by holding that the assignment included the right to receive the net insurance proceeds payable as a result of the loss of the truck.]

The issue remains whether the prohibition of assignment without [Orix's] prior consent restricted the assignment of *rights* in the contract or whether it applied only to the delegation of the contractual *obligations* thereby created. Because the contract encompassed both a sale of goods and a secured transaction, that issue is governed by the provisions of Articles 2 and 9 of the Uniform Commercial Code (UCC).

UCC § 2–210,* relating to assignments of contracts for the sale of goods, provides, in part:

> "(2) Except as otherwise provided in UCC § 9–406, unless otherwise agreed, all rights of either seller or buyer can be assigned except where the assignment would materially change the duty of the other party, or increase materially the burden or risk imposed on the other party by the contract, or impair materially the chance of the other party obtaining return performance. A right to damages for breach of the whole contract or a right arising out of the assignor's due performance of the entire obligation of the assignor can be assigned despite agreement otherwise....

> "(4) Unless the circumstances indicate the contrary a prohibition of assignment of 'the contract' is to be construed as barring only the delegation to the assignee of the assignor's performance."

The contract prohibited Laser from assigning the "contract note without the prior written consent of Holder." By its terms, the prohibition focused on the vendee's *obligations* under the contract; it referred to the vendor as "[h]older," that is, the person toward whom contractual obligations are owed.

---

* For simplicity, the court's citations to sections of the Oregon UCC have been converted   to citations to the UCC itself. (Footnote by ed.)

See UCC § 1–201(20) (defining the "holder" of a negotiable instrument as "the person in possession of the negotiable instrument"). Nothing in the contract or the summary judgment record suggests that the prohibition was concerned with the assignment of the vendee's rights under the contract. Further, there was no evidence that such an assignment would materially change Orix's duty, or increase materially the burden or risk imposed on Orix by the contract, or materially impair its chance of obtaining return performance. *See* UCC § 2–210(2). Thus, the prohibition did not prevent the transfer to plaintiff of Laser's rights under the contract. *See* UCC § 2–210(4).

That conclusion is consistent with UCC § 9–401(2), which governs the alienability of a debtor's rights in collateral under Article 9. UCC § 9–401(2) provides that "[a]n agreement between the debtor and secured party which prohibits a transfer of the debtor's rights in collateral or makes the transfer a default does not prevent the transfer from taking effect." This case concerns the assignment of the right to receive the proceeds of collateral for the debt owed to Orix under the contract.[3] Those proceeds, in turn, constituted collateral. *See* UCC § 9–102(a)(12)(A)(stating that the term "collateral" includes "[p]roceeds to which a security interest attaches"). The prohibition therefore was ineffective to prevent the transfer of Laser's rights in the insurance proceeds to plaintiff from taking effect. *See* UCC § 9–401(2).

Because Orix had notice of the assignment when it paid the net insurance proceeds to Laser, it remained liable to plaintiff, the assignee of the right to receive the insurance proceeds. *See State Farm Ins. v. Pohl*, 255 Or. 46, 50, 464 P.2d 321 (1970) (stating that, "[w]hen a person obtains a right against a third person by subrogation or assignment, the law is that if the third person has notice of the subrogation or assignment and nevertheless pays the assignor or subrogor, rather than the assignee or subrogee, the third person continues to be liable to the assignee or subrogee"); *see also McCallums, Inc. v. Mountain Title Co.*, 60 Or.App. 693, 697, 654 P.2d 1157 (1982) (holding that "an obligor on a chose in action who has notice of the assignment of the beneficial interest in the chose in action is liable to the assignee if the obligation is paid other than by the terms of the assignment"). It follows that the trial court erred in denying plaintiff's motion for summary judgment and in granting Orix's cross-motion for summary judgment.

Reversed and remanded for entry of order granting plaintiff's motion for partial summary judgment.

UCC ARTICLE 9, § 9–406(a)

PRE–2000 UCC ARTICLE 9, § 9–318(3)*

[See Selected Source Materials Supplement]

---

3. UCC § 9–201 provides, in part:

"(a) As used in this chapter . . .

"(64) 'Proceeds,' . . . means the following property . . .

"(E) To the extent of the value of collateral and to the extent payable to the debtor or the secured party, insurance payable by reason of the loss or nonconformity of, defects or infringement of rights in, or damage to, the collateral."

* Article 9 of the UCC was completely revised in the late 1990's. The revision became effective in 2000. Because the great bulk of

ERTEL v. RADIO CORPORATION OF AMERICA, 261 Ind. 573, 307 N.E.2d 471 (1974). "[UCC] § 9–318(3) clearly delineates the legal relationship between the account debtor ... and the assignee ... once the account debtor receives adequate notification of an assignment. The account debtor, upon receipt of said notification, is duty–bound to pay the assignee and not the assignor. Payment to an assignor, after notification of assignment, does not relieve the account debtor of his obligation to pay the assignee unless the assignee consents to such a collection process. (See Official Comment No. 3, 9–318.) The account debtor's failure to pay the assignee after receiving due notification gives rise to an assignee's claim for wrongful payment."

NOTE ON WHAT FORMALITIES ARE NECESSARY TO MAKE AN EFFECTIVE ASSIGNMENT

What formalities, if any, are required to make an assignment effective?

1. *Gratuitous assignments.* An assignment is a form of transfer. Just as the owner of a physical object may make a gift of the commodity by transferring it to a donee, so the owner of a claim against an obligor may make a gift of the claim by assigning it to a donee. Such assignments are usually referred to as gratuitous assignments. This leaves open the question of what formalities are required to make a gratuitous assignment.

In the case of a physical commodity, a gift is completed—and therefore irrevocable—if the donor either delivers the commodity to the donee or executes a writing in which he transfers ownership of the commodity to the donee. In contrast, claims cannot be physically delivered, because they are intangible. Accordingly, a gratuitous transfer of a claim can be made even by a donor-assignor's oral statement to the donee-assignee by which the donor makes a present assignment of the claim to the donee. Such an assignment is effective against the obligor—the person who owes money or some other performance that gives rise to the assigned claim—but without more, the claim is *revocable* by the donor-assignor. For example, suppose A, having lent $1,000 to B, orally assigns his $1,000 claim against B to T. T then sues B on the claim, asserting that he has become the assignee of the claim through A's oral gift. At the time of the suit, A is alive and has done nothing inconsistent with the assignment. B defends against T's suit on the ground that A's claim against her could not be validly transferred by an oral gift. According to Restatement Second, judgment should go for T on these facts. The oral gift of a claim is effective so long as the assignor remains alive, is not bankrupt, and has not repudiated the assignment.

Now suppose that a gratuitous assignor repudiates his gratuitous assignment by a revocation communicated to the assignee, or makes a later assignment of the same claim to another person, or dies or becomes incapacitated. Without more, the assignment will be revoked by the occurrence of any of these events. However, there are ways to make even a gratuitous assign-

cases decided prior to the time this Casebook was written were based on the pre–2000 version of Article 9—and also because many or most of the relevant rules in the prior and current version of Article 9 are highly comparable—both versions will be cross-referenced in this Chapter unless indicated otherwise.

ment irrevocable. Restatement Second § 332 sets out the following rules to govern when a gratuitous assignment is revocable or irrevocable:

(1) Unless a contrary intention is manifested, a gratuitous assignment is *irrevocable* if

(a) the assignment is in a writing either signed or under seal that is delivered by the assignor; or

(b) the assignment is accompanied by delivery of a writing of a type customarily accepted as a symbol or as evidence of the right assigned.

(2) Except as stated in this Section, a gratuitous assignment is *revocable* and the right of the assignee is terminated by the assignor's death or incapacity, by a subsequent assignment by the assignor, or by notification from the assignor received by the assignee or by the obligor.

(3) A gratuitous assignment ceases to be revocable to the extent that before the assignee's right is terminated he obtains

(a) payment or satisfaction of the obligation, or

(b) judgment against the obligor, or

(c) a new contract of the obligor by novation.

(4) A gratuitous assignment is irrevocable to the extent necessary to avoid injustice where the assignor should reasonably expect the assignment to induce action or forbearance by the assignee or a sub-assignee and the assignment does induce such action or forbearance. . . .

(Emphasis added.)

2. *Assignments for value.* Absent statute, an assignment made for value is fully effective and irrevocable, even though oral. Today, however, most although not all assignments are governed by the UCC—in particular, by Article 9 (see Section 3, infra)—and an assignment may need to be in writing to satisfy a relevant UCC Statute of Frauds provision. See Appendix A, Section 10, infra.

———

SPEELMAN v. PASCAL, 10 N.Y.2d 313, 222 N.Y.S.2d 324, 178 N.E.2d 723 (1961). The Estate of George Bernard Shaw licensed a corporation, which was almost wholly owned by Gabriel Pascal, to do a musical play and a musical motion picture based one of Shaw's plays, *Pygmalion*. The license was to terminate if within a certain period the corporation did not arrange with Lerner and Lowe, or similar well–known composers, to write the musical and arrange to produce it. While the license still had two years to run, Pascal signed and delivered to Kingman the following letter: "Dear Miss Kingman: This is to confirm to you our understanding that I give you from my shares of profits of the Pygmalion Musical stage version five per cent (5%) in England, and two per cent (2%) of my shares of profits in the United States. From the film version, five per cent (5%) from my profit shares all over the world. As soon as the contracts are signed, I will send a copy of this letter to my lawyer, Edwin Davies, in London, and he will confirm to you this arrangement in a legal form. This participation in my shares of profits is a present to you, in recognition for your loyal work for me as my Executive Secretary." Four and one–half months later, Pascal died. Held, delivery of the letter constituted a completed gift by way of assignment. Therefore, the gift was not revoked by Pascal's death.

SECTION 2.   ASSIGNABILITY OF RIGHTS AND DELEGABILITY OF DUTIES

EVENING NEWS ASS'N v. PETERSON

United States District Court, District of Columbia, 1979.
477 F.Supp. 77.

BARRINGTON D. PARKER, DISTRICT JUDGE. The question presented in this litigation is whether a contract of employment between an employee and the owner and licensee of a television station, providing for the employee's services as a newscaster-anchorman, was assigned when the station was sold and acquired by a new owner and licensee.

Plaintiff Evening News Association (Evening News) a Michigan Corporation, acquired station WDVM–TV (Channel 9) a District of Columbia television station from Post–Newsweek Stations, Inc. (Post–Newsweek) in June of 1978. At that time, the defendant Gordon Peterson was and had been employed for several years as a newscaster-anchorman by Post–Newsweek. This defendant is a citizen of the State of Maryland. The plaintiff claims that Peterson's employment contract was assignable without the latter's consent, was indeed assigned, and thus otherwise enforceable. The defendant contends, however, that his Post–Newsweek contract required him to perform unique and unusual services and because of the personal relationship he had with Post–Newsweek the contract was not assignable.

Mr. Peterson was employed by the plaintiff for more than one year after the acquisition and received the compensation and all benefits provided by the Post–Newsweek contract. In early August, 1979, he tendered his resignation to the plaintiff. At that time the defendant had negotiated an employment contract with a third television station located in the District of Columbia, a competitor of the plaintiff. The Evening News then sued Peterson, seeking a declaration of the rights and legal relations of the parties under the contract and permanent injunctive relief against the defendant.

Following an accelerated briefing schedule and an expedited bench trial on the merits, the Court concludes that the contract was assignable and that Evening News is entitled to appropriate permanent injunctive relief against the defendant Gordon Peterson.

In accordance with Rule 52(a) Fed.R.Civ.P., the Court's findings of fact and conclusions of law in support of that determination are set forth.

FINDINGS OF FACT

The defendant was employed by Post–Newsweek Stations, Inc. from 1969 to 1978. During that period he negotiated several employment contracts. Post–Newsweek had a license to operate television station WTOP–TV (Channel 9) in the District of Columbia. In June of 1978, following approval by the Federal Communications Commission, Post–Newsweek sold its operating license to Evening News and Channel 9 was then designated WDVM–TV. A June 26, 1978, Bill of Sale and Assignment and Instrument of Assumption and Indemnity between the two provided in pertinent part:

> PNS has granted, bargained, sold, conveyed and assigned to ENA, ... all the property of PNS ... including, ... all right, title and interest, legal or equitable, of PNS in, to and under all agreements, contracts and commitments listed in Schedule A hereto....

When Evening News acquired the station, Peterson's Post–Newsweek employment contract, dated July 1, 1977, was included in the Bill of Sale and Assignment. The contract was for a three-year term ending June 30, 1980, and could be extended for two additional one-year terms, at the option of Post–Newsweek. The significant and relevant duties and obligations under that contract required Peterson:

> to render services as a news anchorman, and to perform such related services as news gathering, writing and reporting, and the organization and preparation of program material, to the extent required by the Stations, as are consistent with [his] primary responsibility as a news anchorman.... [To participate] personally as a newsman, announcer, on-the-air personality or other performer in any news, public affairs, documentary, news analysis, interview, special events or other program or segment of any program, designated by ... and to the extent required by the Stations ... as may reasonably be required by the Stations....

As compensation the defendant was to receive a designated salary which increased each year from 1977 through the fifth (option) year. Post–Newsweek was also obligated to provide additional benefits including term life insurance valued at his 1977 base salary, disability insurance, an annual clothing allowance and benefits to which he was entitled as provided in an underlying collective bargaining agreement with the American Federation of Television and Radio Artists.

There was no express provision in the 1977 contract concerning its assignability or nonassignability. However, it contained the following integration clause:

This agreement contains the entire understanding of the parties ... and this agreement cannot be altered or modified except in a writing signed by both parties.

A.

Aside from the various undisputed documents and exhibits admitted into evidence, there were sharp conflicts in testimony concerning various events and what was said and done by the parties and their representatives, both before and after the Evening News' acquisition. As trier of fact, having heard and seen the several witnesses testify and after assessing and determining their credibility, the Court makes the following additional findings.

The defendant's duties, obligations and performance under the 1977 contract did not change in any significant way after the Evening News' acquisition. In addition, the Evening News met all of its required contract obligations to the defendant and its performance after acquisition in June, 1978, was not materially different from that of Post–Newsweek.

Mr. Peterson testified that he had "almost a family relationship" with James Snyder, News Director, and John Baker, Executive Producer, for Post–Newsweek, which permitted and promoted a free exchange of ideas, frank expressions of dissent and criticism and open lines of communication. These men left Channel 9 when Post–Newsweek relinquished its license, and they have since been replaced by Evening News personnel. According to Mr. Peterson, the close relationship and rapport which existed between him and them was an important factor as he viewed the contract; these relationships made the contract in his view nonassignable and indeed their absence at the Evening News prevented defendant from contributing his full efforts. Even if Mr. Peterson's contentions are accepted, it should be noted that he contracted with the Post–Newsweek corporation and not with the News Director and Executive Producer of that corporation. Indeed, the 1977 contract makes no reference to either officer, except to provide that vacations should be scheduled and coordinated through the News Director. Had the defendant intended to condition his performance on his continued ability to work with Snyder and Baker, one would have expected the contract to reflect that condition.

The close, intimate and personal relationship which Mr. Peterson points to as characterizing his association with Post–Newsweek and its personnel, was highly subjective and was supported only by his testimony. The Court cannot find that Peterson contracted with Post–Newsweek in 1977 to work with particular individuals or because of a special policy-making role he had been selected to perform in the newsroom. For the fourteen-month period of Peterson's employment at the Evening News, there is no showing that he was in any way circumscribed, limited in his work or otherwise disadvantaged in his performance. Nor is there any credible evidence that the News Director or other top personnel of Evening News were rigid, inflexible, warded off any of Mr. Peterson's criticisms or even that at any time he gave suggestions and criticisms which were ignored or rejected. Finally, the Court does not find that Post–Newsweek contracted with Peterson because of any peculiarly unique qualities or because of a relationship of personal confidence with him.

B.

In his direct testimony, Mr. Peterson expressed a degree of disappointment because of Evening News' failure to keep apace with advances in technology and to seize opportunities for live in-depth coverage of current events. He characterized the plaintiff's news coverage as "less aggressive" than what he had experienced with Post–Newsweek.

On cross-examination, however, he was shown an exhibit comparing the broadcast of special assignments reported and produced by him for two one-year periods, one before and one after the June, 1978 acquisition. While he admitted to its accuracy with some reservation, the exhibit clearly showed that a comparable number of such assignments of similar quality, were broadcast within the two years. He also conceded that for the same period Evening News received two Peabody awards, an award for best editorials, and a number of Emmy awards for public affairs exceeding those received in prior years by Post–Newsweek. Finally, he acknowledged that Channel 9 still maintained the highest ratings for audience viewing among the television stations in the Washington, D.C. market area.

A great amount of testimony was generated as to when Peterson learned of the Evening News' acquisition and what then occurred relative to the assignment of the contract. The testimony on this issue was conflicting, largely cumulative and as now viewed, over-emphasized by the parties. The Court finds that the defendant gained first knowledge of a possible sale and transfer of the station in December, 1977. At that time, the president of Post–Newsweek publicly announced to the station's employees, including Peterson, that an agreement in principle had been reached, subject to approval by the Federal Communications Commission. At no time from December, 1977, until December, 1978, did the defendant or his attorney ever indicate or venture an opinion that the contract was not assignable. Indeed, through at least April, 1979, the defendant's attorney made representations that assignment of the contract presented no problem to his client.

In summary, the Court finds that the performance required of Mr. Peterson under the 1977 contract was (1) not based upon a personal relationship or one of special confidence between him and Post–Newsweek or its employees, and (2) was not changed in any material way by the assignment to the Evening News.

Conclusions of Law

There is diversity of citizenship; the amount in controversy exceeds $10,000; and the Court has jurisdiction over this proceeding by virtue of 28 U.S.C.A. § 1332.

A.

The distinction between the assignment of a right to receive services and the obligation to provide them is critical in this proceeding. This is so because duties under a personal services contract involving special skill or ability are generally not delegable by the one obligated to perform, absent the consent of the other party. The issue, however, is not whether the personal services Peterson is to perform are delegable but whether Post–Newsweek's right to receive them is assignable.

Contract rights as a general rule are assignable. Munchak Corp. v. Cunningham, 457 F.2d 721 (4th Cir.1972); Meyer v. Washington Times Co., 64 App.D.C. 218, 76 F.2d 988 (D.C.Cir.) cert. denied 295 U.S. 734, 55 S.Ct. 646, 79 L.Ed. 1682 (1935); 4 A. Corbin, Contracts § 865 (1951); Restatement, Contracts § 151 (1932). This rule, however, is subject to exception where the assignment would vary materially the duty of the obligor, increase materially the burden of risk imposed by the contract, or impair materially the obligor's chance of obtaining return performance. Corbin § 868; Restatement § 152. There has been no showing, however, that the services required of Peterson by the Post–Newsweek contract have changed in any material way since the Evening News entered the picture. Both before and after, he anchored the same news programs. Similarly he has had essentially the same number of special assignments since the transfer as before. Any additional policymaking role that he formerly enjoyed and is now denied was neither a condition of his contract nor factually supported by other than his own subjective testimony.

The general rule of assignability is also subject to exception where the contract calls for the rendition of personal services based on a relationship of confidence between the parties. *Munchak,* 457 F.2d at 725; *Meyer,* 64 App.

D.C. at 219, 76 F.2d at 989. As Corbin has explained this limitation on assignment:

> In almost all cases where a "contract" is said to be non-assignable because it is "personal," what is meant is not that the contractor's right is not assignable, but that the performance required by his duty is a personal performance and that an attempt to perform by a substituted person would not discharge the contractor's duty.

Corbin § 865. In *Munchak,* the Court concluded that a basketball player's personal services contract could be assigned by the owner of the club to a new owner, despite a contractual prohibition on assignment to another club, on the basis that the services were to the club. The Court found it "inconceivable" that the player's services "could be affected by the personalities of successive corporate owners." 457 F.2d at 725. The policy against the assignment of personal service contracts, as the Court noted, "is to prohibit an assignment of a contract in which the obligor undertakes to serve only the original obligee." 457 F.2d at 726.

Given the silence of the contract on assignability, its merger clause, and the usual rule that contract rights are assignable, the Court cannot but conclude on the facts of this case that defendant's contract was assignable. Mr. Peterson's contract with Post–Newsweek gives no hint that he was to perform as other than a newscaster-anchorman for their stations. Nor is there any hint that he was to work with particular Post–Newsweek employees or was assured a policy-making role in concert with any given employees. Defendant's employer was a corporation, and it was for Post–Newsweek Stations, Inc. that he contracted to perform. The corporation's duties under the contract did not involve the rendition of personal services to defendant; essentially they were to compensate him. Nor does the contract give any suggestion of a relation of special confidence between the two or that defendant was expected to serve the Post–Newsweek stations only so long as the latter had the license for them. . . .

C.

Plaintiff's argument that defendant has waived any objection to the assignment by accepting the contract benefits and continuing to perform for the Evening News for over a year has perhaps some merit. If defendant has doubts about assignability, he should have voiced them when he learned of the planned transfer or at least at the time of transfer. His continued performance without reservation followed by the unanticipated tender of his resignation did disadvantage Evening News in terms of finding a possible replacement for him and possibly in lost revenues. The Court, however, concludes that the contract was assignable in the first instance and thus it is not necessary to determine whether defendant's continued performance constitutes a waiver of objection to the assignment.

During the course of this trial Edwin W. Pfeiffer, an executive officer of WDVM–TV, testified that Mr. Peterson allegedly stated "if the Judge decides I should stay, I will stay." Assuming that he did not overstate Mr. Peterson's position and that Mr. Peterson was quoted in appropriate context, the television audience of the Washington, D.C. metropolitan area should anticipate his timely reappearance as news anchorman for station WDVM–TV. Of course, the avenue of appeal is always available.

An order consistent with this Memorandum Opinion will be entered. Counsel for the plaintiff shall submit immediately an appropriate order.

———

RESTATEMENT, SECOND, CONTRACTS §§ 317, 322

[See Selected Source Materials Supplement]

———

UCC § 2–210(2), (4)

[See Selected Source Materials Supplement]

———

RESTATEMENT, SECOND, CONTRACTS § 322, ILLUSTRATIONS 1, 2

1. A holds a policy of industrial insurance issued to him by the B Insurance Company. After lapse for failure to pay premiums, B refuses to pay the "cash surrender value" provided for in the policy. A and others similarly situated assign their claims to C for collection. The assignment is effective without regard to any contractual prohibition of assignment.

2. A and B contract for the sale of land by B to A. A fully performs the contract, becomes entitled to specific performance on B's refusal to convey the land, and then assigns his rights to C. C is entitled to specific performance against B without regard to any contractual prohibition of assignment. . . .

———

UCC ARTICLE 9, § 9–306(d)

PRE–2000 UCC ARTICLE 9, § 9–318(4)

[See Selected Source Materials Supplement]

———

MACKE CO. v. PIZZA OF GAITHERSBURG, INC.

Court of Appeals of Maryland, 1970.
259 Md. 479, 270 A.2d 645.

Argued before HAMMOND, C.J., and BARNES, FINAN, SINGLEY, SMITH and DIGGES, JJ.

SINGLEY, JUDGE. The appellees and defendants below, Pizza of Gaithersburg, Inc.; Pizzeria, Inc.; The Pizza Pie Corp., Inc. and Pizza Oven, Inc., four corporations under the common ownership of Sidney Ansell, Thomas S. Sherwood and Eugene Early and the same individuals as partners or proprietors (the Pizza Shops) operated at six locations in Montgomery and Prince George's Counties. The appellees had arranged to have installed in each of their locations cold drink vending machines owned by Virginia Coffee Service, Inc., and on 30 December 1966, this arrangement was formalized at five of the locations, by contracts for terms of one year, automatically renewable for a like term in the absence of 30 days' written notice. A similar contract for the sixth location, operated by Pizza of Gaithersburg, Inc., was entered into on 25 July 1967.

On 30 December 1967, Virginia's assets were purchased by The Macke Company (Macke) and the six contracts were assigned to Macke by Virginia. In January, 1968, the Pizza Shops attempted to terminate the five contracts having the December anniversary date, and in February, the contract which had the July anniversary date.

Macke brought suit in the Circuit Court for Montgomery County against each of the Pizza Shops for damages for breach of contract. From judgments for the defendants, Macke has appealed.

The lower court based the result which it reached on two grounds: first, that the Pizza Shops, when they contracted with Virginia, relied on its skill, judgment and reputation, which made impossible a delegation of Virginia's duties to Macke; and second, that the damages claimed could not be shown with reasonable certainty. These conclusions are challenged by Macke.

In the absence of a contrary provision—and there was none here—rights and duties under an executory bilateral contract may be assigned and delegated, subject to the exception that duties under a contract to provide personal services may never be delegated, nor rights be assigned under a contract where *delectus personae* was an ingredient of the bargain.[1] 4 Corbin on Contracts § 865 (1951) at 434; 6 Am.Jur.2d, Assignments § 11 (1963) at 196. Crane Ice Cream Co. v. Terminal Freezing & Heating Co., 147 Md. 588, 128 A. 280 (1925) held that the right of an individual to purchase ice under a contract which by its terms reflected a knowledge of the individual's needs and reliance on his credit and responsibility could not be assigned to the corporation which purchased his business. In Eastern Advertising Co. v. McGaw & Co., 89 Md. 72, 42 A. 923 (1899), our predecessors held that an advertising agency could not delegate its duties under a contract which had been entered into by an advertiser who had relied on the agency's skill, judgment and taste.

---

1. Like all generalizations, this one is subject to an important exception. Uniform Commercial Code § 9–318 makes ineffective a term in any contract prohibiting the assignment of a contract right: i.e., a right to payment. Compare Restatement, Contracts § 151(c) (1932).

The six machines were placed on the appellees' premises under a printed "Agreement–Contract" which identified the "customer," gave its place of business, described the vending machine, and then provided:

"Terms

"1. The Company will install on the Customer's premises the above listed equipment and will maintain the equipment in good operating order and stocked with merchandise.

"2. The location of this equipment will be such as to permit accessibility to persons desiring use of same. This equipment shall remain the property of the Company and shall not be moved from the location at which installed, except by the Company.

"3. For equipment requiring electricity and water, the Customer is responsible for electrical receptacle and water outlet within ten (10) feet of the equipment location. The Customer is also responsible to supply the Electrical Power and Water needed.

"4. The Customer will exercise every effort to protect this equipment from abuse or damage.

"5. The Company will be responsible for all licenses and taxes on the equipment and sale of products.

"6. This Agreement–Contract is for a term of one (1) year from the date indicated herein and will be automatically renewed for a like period, unless thirty (30) day written notice is given by either party to terminate service.

"7. Commission on monthly sales will be paid by the Company to the Customer at the following rate:...."

The rate provided in each of the agreements was "30% of Gross Receipts to $300.00 monthly[,] 35% over [$]300.00," except for the agreement with Pizza of Gaithersburg, Inc., which called for "40% of Gross Receipts."

We cannot regard the agreements as contracts for personal services. They were either a license or concession granted Virginia by the appellees, or a lease of a portion of the appellees' premises, with Virginia agreeing to pay a percentage of gross sales as a license or concession fee or as rent, see Charlotte Coca–Cola Bottling Co. v. Shaw, 232 N.C. 307, 59 S.E.2d 819 (1950) and Herbert's Laurel–Ventura, Inc. v. Laurel Ventura Holding Corp., 58 Cal.App.2d 684, 138 P.2d 43, 46–47 (1943), and were assignable by Virginia unless they imposed on Virginia duties of a personal or unique character which could not be delegated, S & L Vending Corp. v. 52 Thompkins Ave. Restaurant, Inc., 26 A.D.2d 935, 274 N.Y.S.2d 697 (1966).

The appellees earnestly argue that they had dealt with Macke before and had chosen Virginia because they preferred the way it conducted its business. Specifically, they say that service was more personalized, since the president of Virginia kept the machines in working order, that commissions were paid in cash, and that Virginia permitted them to keep keys to the machines so that minor adjustments could be made when needed. Even if we assume all this to be true, the agreements with Virginia were silent as to the details of the working arrangements and contained only a provision requiring Virginia to "install ... the above listed equipment and ... maintain the equipment in good operating order and stocked with merchandise." We think the Supreme

Court of California put the problem of personal service in proper focus a century ago when it upheld the assignment of a contract to grade a San Francisco street:

> "All painters do not paint portraits like Sir Joshua Reynolds, nor landscapes like Claude Lorraine, nor do all writers write dramas like Shakespeare or fiction like Dickens. Rare genius and extraordinary skill are not transferable, and contracts for their employment are therefore personal, and cannot be assigned. But rare genius and extraordinary skill are not indispensable to the workmanlike digging down of a sand hill or the filling up of a depression to a given level, or the construction of brick sewers with manholes and covers, and contracts for such work are not personal, and may be assigned." Taylor v. Palmer, 31 Cal. 240 at 247–248 (1866).

See also Devlin v. Mayor, Aldermen and Commonalty of the City of New York, 63 N.Y. 8, at 17 (1875). Moreover, the difference between the service the Pizza Shops happened to be getting from Virginia and what they expected to get from Macke did not mount up to such a material change in the performance of obligations under the agreements as would justify the appellees' refusal to recognize the assignment, Crane Ice Cream Co. v. Terminal Freezing & Heating Co., supra, 147 Md. 588, 128 A. 280....

As we see it, the delegation of duty by Virginia to Macke was entirely permissible under the terms of the agreements. In so holding, we do not put ourselves at odds with Eastern Advertising Co. v. McGaw, supra, 89 Md. 72, 42 A. 923, for in that case, the agreement with the agency contained a provision that "the advertising cards were to be 'subject to the approval of Eastern Advertising Company as to style and contents' ", at 82, 42 A. at 923, which the court found to import that reliance was being placed on the agency's skill, judgment and taste, at 88, 42 A. 923.

Having concluded that the Pizza Shops had no right to rescind the agreements, we turn to the question of damages.

[The court concluded that damages could be shown with reasonable certainty.]

Judgment reversed as to liability; judgment entered for appellant for costs, on appeal and below; case remanded for a new trial on the question of damages.

BRITISH WAGGON CO. v. LEA & CO., [1880] 5 Q.B.D. 149 "[W]e cannot suppose that in stipulating for the repair of these waggons by the company—a rough description of work which ordinary workmen conversant with the business would be perfectly able to execute—the defendants attached any importance to whether the repairs were done by the company, or by any one with whom the company might enter into a subsidiary contract to do the work. All that the hirers, the defendants, cared for in this stipulation was that the waggons should be kept in repair; it was indifferent to them by whom the repairs should be done. Thus if ... the company had entered into a contract with any competent party to do the repairs, and so had procured them to be done, we cannot think that this would have been a departure from the terms of the contract to keep the waggons in repair.... [I]t is difficult to see how in repairing a carriage when necessary, or painting it once a year, preference would be given to one coachmaker over another. Much work is contracted for, which it is known can only be executed by means of subcontracts; much is contracted for as to which it is indifferent to the party for whom it is to be done, whether it is done by the immediate party to the contract, or by someone on his behalf. In all these cases the maxim qui facit per alium facit per se [he who acts through another acts himself] applies."

————

BASHIR v. MOAYEDI, 627 A.2d 997 (D.C.App.1993). This was a suit by an obligee under a contract against the obligor, Bashir. Bashir defended on the ground that it had delegated its obligations to Daou, who assumed the obligations. The court rejected this defense: "... [T]he general rule with respect to delegation is that a delegant cannot free herself from liability by delegating her duties of performance to another.... Were this not the case, 'every solvent person could obtain freedom from his debts by delegating them to an insolvent.' ... Thus, while [the assumption by Daou of the obligations of Bashir,] may have rendered [Daou] liable to appellant Bashir, that assumption did not discharge appellant Bashir's duty to [the obligee]. In arguing otherwise ... Bashir confuses delegation of performance of an obligation with delegation of responsibility for the performance of an obligation."

————

RESTATEMENT, SECOND, CONTRACTS §§ 318, 328

[See Selected Source Materials Supplement]

————

UCC § 2–210(1)

[See Selected Source Materials Supplement]

————

NOTE ON THE RIGHT OF THE OBLIGEE UNDER A CONTRACT TO DEMAND PERFORMANCE FROM AN ASSIGNEE OF THE CONTRACT

Assume that A and B have a contract, and that after the contract is made, one of two transaction types occurs between A and a third party, T.

In a *Type I Transaction*, A makes an agreement with T under which A assigns the contract to T, and T expressly promises A to perform the obligations that A owes to B under the contract. Because T has promised to discharge A's preexisting legal obligations to B, B is a creditor beneficiary of T's promise. Therefore, it is well-established that in a Type I Transaction B can enforce T's promise. (Note that A will remain liable to B, even though T is also liable, because a party to a contract cannot get out of its obligations by delegating them. As between A and T, however, T will be ultimately liable.)

A *Type II Transaction* is identical to a Type I Transaction except that although A assigns the contract to T, T does not expressly agree to perform the obligations that A owes under the contract. In such a case, the agreement between A and T should normally be interpreted to mean that T has *impliedly* agreed to perform A's obligations. This interpretation of a Type II Transaction reflects both the usual way in which A and T probably would understand their transaction and the business economics of such transactions. Although there are transactions in which A would be willing to transfer all his benefits under a contract to T while remaining primarily liable for all the contract's burdens, such transactions are not typical. T should therefore be liable to B by virtue of his implied promise, just as he would be liable to B in a Type I Transaction by virtue of his express promise.

This interpretation of a Type II Transaction is adopted in both Restatement Second § 328 and UCC § 2–310(2). However, the majority rule in the case law is that T is not liable to B in a Type II Transaction, unless the transaction falls within UCC Article 2. Moreover, even the rule stated in Restatement Second § 328 is made subject to the caveat that "The American Law Institute expresses no opinion as to whether the rule ... applies to an assignment by a purchaser of his rights under a contract for the sale of land." This caveat was adopted in deference to Langel v. Betz, 250 N.Y. 159, 164 N.E. 890 (1928), a leading case that applied the majority rule to a contract for the sale of real estate.

———

*

Part VII

PROBLEMS OF PERFORMANCE

———

Part VII of this book concerns problems of performance. These problems fall into a variety of categories.

Chapter 22 concerns the obligation to perform a contract in good faith. This obligation is important not only in itself, but because it directly or indirectly provides a foundation for many other doctrines concerning performance.

Chapter 23 concerns the doctrine of substantial performance. In cases to which this doctrine is applicable, a contracting party is entitled to bring suit on the contract if his performance is substantially what she promised to do, even though not exactly what she promised to do, subject to an offset to reflect the shortfall in her performance.

Chapter 24 concerns express conditions. An express condition differs from a promise in that it imposes no obligation, but instead provides that a contracting party either does not come under a duty to perform unless a certain state of affairs exists, or is released from a duty to perform if a certain state of affairs exists.

Chapter 25 concerns (1) the order in which performance under a contract must occur when the contract is not explicit on that issue, and (2) when a breach by one party makes it permissible for the other party to treat the contract as at an end.

Finally, Chapter 26 concerns the effect of a repudiation of a contract by one of the parties before that party's performance is due; the consequences that arise when it appears that one party will be unable to perform under the contract, although she has not yet either breached or repudiated the contract; and cases in which one party may justifiably insist that the other provide adequate assurance that performance will be forthcoming.

Chapter 22

THE OBLIGATION TO PERFORM IN GOOD FAITH

RESTATEMENT, SECOND, CONTRACTS § 237, ILLUSTRATIONS 6, 7: "6. A contracts to sell and B to buy on 30 days credit 3,000 tons of iron rails at a stated price. B purchases iron rails heavily from various sources for use in his business, and in consequence A has difficulty in securing 3,000 tons and the market price is substantially increased. A fails to deliver the rails. B has a claim against A for breach of contract. B's purchase of iron rails from other sources for use in his business is not a failure of performance because B is under no duty to refrain from purchasing for that purpose. A's failure to deliver the rails is therefore a breach.

"7. The facts being otherwise as stated in Illustration 6, B maliciously buys iron rails heavily from various sources in order to prevent A from performing his contract with B. B has no claim against A. B's malicious purchase of iron rails from other sources is a material breach of his duty of good faith and fair dealing . . ., which operates as the non-occurrence of a condition of A's duty to deliver the rails, discharging it."

KIRKE LA SHELLE CO. v. PAUL ARMSTRONG CO., 263 N.Y. 79, 188 N.E. 163 (1933). "[I]n every contract there is an implied covenant that neither party shall do anything which will have the effect of destroying or injuring the rights of the other party to receive the fruits of the contract, which means that in every contract there exists an implied covenant of good faith and fair dealing."

RESTATEMENT, SECOND, CONTRACTS § 205

[See Selected Source Materials Supplement]

PRE–2001 UCC ARTICLE 1 (IN FORCE IN MOST STATES), §§ 1–201(19), 1–203,

UCC § 2–103(1)(b)

2001 VERSION OF ARTICLE 1, § 1–201(20)

[See Selected Source Materials Supplement]

————

NOTE ON THE UCC DEFINITIONS OF GOOD FAITH

The UCC is promulgated by the National Conference of Commissioners on Uniform State Law (NCCUSL) and the American Law Institute (ALI). However, the UCC is only effective to the extent it is adopted by state legislatures. Prior to 2001, Section 1–201(19) of Article 1 (General Provisions) defined good faith narrowly, to mean "honesty in fact in the conduct or transaction concerned." In contrast, Section 2–201 of Article 2 (Sale of Goods) defined good faith broadly, to mean, in the case of a merchant, "honesty in fact and the observance of reasonable commercial standards of fair dealing in the trade."

In 2001, NCCUSL and the ALI promulgated a revised official version of UCC Article 1. Section 1–201(20) of the revised official version of Article 1 defined good faith broadly, for all Articles of the UCC except Article 5, to mean "honesty in fact and the observance of reasonable commercial standards of fair dealing." The adoption of this broad definition in the revised official version of Article 1 rendered superfluous the broad definition of good faith in the official version of Article 2. Accordingly, that definition was deleted from the official version of Article 2. However, as of early 2006 only sixteen states had adopted the revised official version of Article 1. Furthermore, about half those states did not adopt the definition of good faith in revised Article 1 and retained the prior definition of good faith in Article 2. Accordingly, in most states the enacted definitions of good faith in Articles 1 and 2 continue as they were prior to 2001—that is, continue to be as set forth in the first paragraph of this Note.

————

CISG ART. 7(1)

[See Selected Source Materials Supplement]

————

UNIDROIT PRINCIPLES OF INTERNATIONAL COMMERCIAL CONTRACTS ART. 1.7

[See Selected Source Materials Supplement]

————

PRINCIPLES OF EUROPEAN CONTRACT LAW ART. 1.201

[See Selected Source Materials Supplement]

———

E. ALLAN FARNSWORTH, GOOD FAITH IN CONTRACT PERFORMANCE, IN GOOD FAITH AND FAULT IN CONTRACT LAW*

... What [is meant] by "good faith" in the context of performance of contracts?

The most restrictive answer is that the duty of good faith is "simply a rechristening of fundamental principles of contract law," as Justice Antonin Scalia put it in the days when he was a federal Court of Appeals judge. Three decades ago, in [an] article on good faith, I took much the same position, to which Scalia alluded in observing "correct ... is the perception of Professor Farnsworth that the significance of the doctrine is 'in implying terms in the agreement.'" This restrictive answer has not satisfied ... academics, however, and their search for the meaning of good faith has sparked a spirited debate.

In 1968, Professor Robert Summers published an influential article on good faith in which he sketched the contours of this mandate in terms of an "excluder" analysis. He suggested "that in cases of doubt, a lawyer will determine more accurately what the judge means by using the phrase "good faith" if he does not ask what good faith itself means, but rather asks: "What ... does the judge intend to rule out by his use of this phrase?" Summers argued that "good faith ... is best understood as an 'excluder'—it is a phrase which has no general meaning or meanings of its own, but which serves to exclude many heterogeneous forms of bad faith." This excluder analysis ... found its way into the commentary to the good faith provision in the Restatement 2d....

In 1980, Professor Steven Burton, of the University of Iowa, in a major article on good faith, introduced "forgone opportunity analysis." Taking a swipe at Summers by lamenting that "neither courts or commentators have articulated an operational standard that distinguishes good faith performance from bad faith performance," he attempted to fashion a standard based on the expectations of the parties. "Good faith," he argued, "limits the exercise of discretion in performance conferred on one party by the contract," so it is bad faith to use discretion "to recapture opportunities forgone upon contracting" as determined by the other party's expectations—in other words, to refuse "to pay the expected cost of performance"....

Courts have looked to all three of these views—Burton's, Summers', and mine—for support, often without recognizing a conflict among them, which is scarcely surprising, because in the context of performance the meaning of good faith may turn on which of its several functions is in issue. Sometimes

---

* J. Beatson & W. Friedman, eds., 1995. Reprinted by permission of Oxford University Press.

good faith is the basis of a limitation on the exercise of discretion conferred on a party, as under Burton's view. Sometimes good faith is the basis for proscribing behaviors which violate basic standards of decency, as under Summers' view. Sometimes it is merely the basis of an implied term to fill a gap or deal with an omitted case, as under [my] view. . . .

——————

SOUTHWEST SAVINGS AND LOAN ASS'N v. SUNAMP SYSTEMS, 172 Ariz. 553, 838 P.2d 1314 (Ariz. Ct. App. 1992). "If contracting parties cannot profitably use their contractual powers without fear that a jury will second-guess them under a vague standard of good faith, the law will impair the predictability that an orderly commerce requires. Yet contracting parties, hard as they may try, cannot reduce every understanding to a stated term. Instances inevitably arise where one party exercises discretion retained or unforeclosed under a contract in such a way as to deny the other a reasonably expected benefit of the bargain. . . . The law of good faith, though inexact, attempts a remedy for such abuse. *See* Steven J. Burton, *Breach of Contract and the Common Law Duty to Perform in Good Faith,* 94 Harv. L.Rev. 369, 385–86 (1980):

> The good faith performance doctrine may be said to permit the exercise of discretion for any purpose—including ordinary business purposes—reasonably within the contemplation of the parties. A contract thus would be breached by a failure to perform in good faith if a party uses its discretion for a reason outside the contemplated range—a reason beyond the risks assumed by the party claiming a breach.

(Footnotes omitted.) *See also* Restatement (Second) of Contracts § 205 cmt. a (1981) ("Good faith performance or enforcement of a contract emphasizes faithfulness to an agreed common purpose and consistency with the justified expectations of the other party. . . .").

"Consistently with [these formulations], our supreme court has decided in a variety of contexts that a contracting party may exercise a retained contractual power in bad faith. In insurance bad faith cases, for example, the supreme court has determined that an insurance company may act in bad faith by manipulating its power to evaluate and adjust claims in such a way as to defeat the reasonable expectations of its insured. *See, e.g., Rawlings,* 151 Ariz. at 153–57, 726 P.2d at 569–73; *cf. Farmers Ins. Exch. v. Henderson,* 82 Ariz. 335, 338–40, 313 P.2d 404, 407–09 (1957) (insurance company may act in bad faith by refusing to settle litigation against insured). In wrongful termination cases the supreme court has held that an employer-at-will may fire an employee for no cause, but may not exercise this power abusively for bad cause. *See, e.g., Wagenseller v. Scottsdale Memorial Hosp.,* 147 Ariz. 370, 385–86, 710 P.2d 1025, 1040–41 (1985).

"In this case, therefore, inquiry does not end with recognition that Southwest had contractual authority to freeze, and ultimately terminate, SunAmp's credit line. The question is whether the jury might reasonably have found that Southwest wrongfully exercised this power "for a reason beyond the risks" that SunAmp assumed in its loan agreement, Burton, *supra,* 147

Ariz. at 386, 710 P.2d at 1041, or for a reason inconsistent with SunAmp's 'justified expectations,' Restatement, *supra,* § 205 cmt. a.''

BLOOR v. FALSTAFF BREWING CORP.

United States Court of Appeals, Second Circuit, 1979.
601 F.2d 609.

Before MOORE, FRIENDLY and MESKILL, CIRCUIT JUDGES.

FRIENDLY, CIRCUIT JUDGE. This action, wherein federal jurisdiction is predicated on diversity of citizenship, 28 U.S.C.A. § 1332, was brought in the District Court for the Southern District of New York, by James Bloor, Reorganization Trustee of Balco Properties Corporation, formerly named P. Ballantine & Sons (Ballantine), a venerable and once successful brewery based in Newark, N.J. He sought to recover from Falstaff Brewing Corporation (Falstaff) for breach of a contract dated March 31, 1972, wherein Falstaff bought the Ballantine brewing labels, trademarks, accounts receivable, distribution systems and other property except the brewery. The price was $4,000,000 plus a royalty of fifty cents on each barrel of the Ballantine brands sold between April 1, 1972 and March 31, 1978. Although other issues were tried, the appeals concern only two provisions of the contract. These are:

8. *Certain other covenants of buyer.* (a) After the Closing Date the [Buyer] will use its best efforts to promote and maintain a high volume of sales under the Proprietary Rights.

2(a)(v) [The Buyer will pay a royalty of $.50 per barrel for a period of 6 years], provided, however, that if during the Royalty Period the Buyer substantially discontinues the distribution of beer under the brand name ''Ballantine'' (except as the result of a restraining order in effect for 30 days issued by a court of competent jurisdiction at the request of a governmental authority), it will pay to the Seller a cash sum equal to the years and fraction thereof remaining in the Royalty Period times $1,100,000, payable in equal monthly installments on the first day of each month commencing with the first month following the month in which such discontinuation occurs....

Bloor claimed that Falstaff had breached the best efforts clause, 8(a), and indeed that its default amounted to the substantial discontinuance that would trigger the liquidated damage clause, 2(a)(v). In an opinion that interestingly traces the history of beer back to Domesday Book and beyond, Judge Brieant upheld the first claim and awarded damages but dismissed the second. Falstaff appeals from the former ruling, Bloor from the latter. Both sides also dispute the court's measurement of damages for breach of the best efforts clause.

We shall assume familiarity with Judge Brieant's excellent opinion, 454 F.Supp. 258 (S.D.N.Y.1978), from which we have drawn heavily, and will state only the essentials. Ballantine had been a family owned business, producing low-priced beers primarily for the northeast market, particularly New York, New Jersey, Connecticut and Pennsylvania. Its sales began to decline in 1961, and it lost money from 1965 on. On June 1, 1969, Investors Funding Corporation (IFC), a real estate conglomerate with no experience in brewing, acquired substantially all the stock of Ballantine for $16,290,000. IFC increased advertising expenditures, levelling off in 1971 at $1 million a year. This and other promotional practices, some of dubious legality, led to steady growth in Ballantine's sales despite the increased activities in the northeast of the "nationals"[3] which have greatly augmented their market shares at the expense of smaller brewers. However, this was a profitless prosperity; there was no month in which Ballantine had earnings and the total loss was $15,500,000 for the 33 months of IFC ownership.

After its acquisition of Ballantine, Falstaff continued the $1 million a year advertising program, IFC's pricing policies, and also its policy of serving smaller accounts not solely through sales to independent distributors, the usual practice in the industry, but by use of its own warehouses and trucks— the only change being a shift of the retail distribution system from Newark to North Bergen, N.J., when brewing was concentrated at Falstaff's Rhode Island brewery. However, sales declined and Falstaff claims to have lost $22 million in its Ballantine brand operations from March 31, 1972 to June 1975. Its other activities were also performing indifferently, although with no such losses as were being incurred in the sale of Ballantine products, and it was facing inability to meet payrolls and other debts. In March and April 1975 control of Falstaff passed to Paul Kalmanovitz, a businessman with 40 years experience in the brewing industry. After having first advanced $3 million to enable Falstaff to meet its payrolls and other pressing debts, he later supplied an additional $10 million and made loan guarantees, in return for which he received convertible preferred shares in an amount that endowed him with 35% of the voting power and became the beneficiary of a voting trust that gave him control of the board of directors.

Mr. Kalmanovitz determined to concentrate on making beer and cutting sales costs. He decreased advertising, with the result that the Ballantine advertising budget shrank from $1 million to $115,000 a year. In late 1975 he closed four of Falstaff's six retail distribution centers, including the North Bergen, N.J. depot, which was ultimately replaced by two distributors servicing substantially fewer accounts. He also discontinued various illegal practices that had been used in selling Ballantine products. What happened in terms of sales volume is shown in plaintiff's exhibit 114 J, a chart which we reproduce in the margin. With 1974 as a base, Ballantine declined 29.72% in 1975 and 45.81% in 1976 as compared with a 1975 gain of 2.24% and a 1976 loss of 13.08% for all brewers excluding the top 15. Other comparisons are similarly devastating, at least for 1976. Despite the decline in the sale of its own labels as well as Ballantine's, Falstaff, however, made a substantial financial recovery. In 1976 it had net income of $8.7 million and its year-end working capital had increased from $8.6 million to $20.2 million and its cash and certificates of deposit from $2.2 million to $12.1 million.

3. Miller's, Schlitz, Anheuser–Busch, Coors and Pabst.

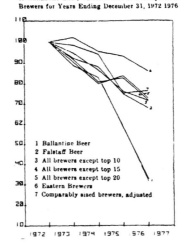

4. Percentage Increase or Decline in Sales Volume of Ballantine Beer, Falstaff Beer and Comparable Brewers for Years Ending December 31, 1972 1976

1 Ballantine Beer
2 Falstaff Beer
3 All brewers except top 10
4 All brewers except top 15
5 All brewers except top 20
6 Eastern Brewers
7 Comparably sized brewers, adjusted

Seizing upon remarks made by the judge during the trial that Falstaff's financial standing in 1975 and thereafter "is probably not relevant" and a footnote in the opinion, 454 F.Supp. at 267 n. 7,[4] appellate counsel for Falstaff contend that the judge read the best efforts clause as requiring Falstaff to maintain Ballantine's volume by any sales methods having a good prospect of increasing or maintaining sales or, at least, to continue lawful methods in use at the time of purchase, no matter what losses they would cause. Starting from this premise, counsel reason that the judge's conclusion was at odds with New York law, stipulated by the contract to be controlling, as last expressed by the Court of Appeals in Feld v. Henry S. Levy & Sons, Inc., 37 N.Y.2d 466, 373 N.Y.S.2d 102, 335 N.E.2d 320 (1975). . . . [in which] the court said that, absent a cancellation on six months' notice for which the contract provided:

> defendant was expected to continue to perform in good faith and could cease production of the bread crumbs, a single facet of its operation, only in good faith. Obviously, a bankruptcy or genuine imperiling of the very existence of its entire business caused by the production of the crumbs would warrant cessation of production of that item; the yield of less profit from its sale than expected would not. Since bread crumbs were but a part of defendant's enterprise and since there was a contractual right of cancellation, good faith required continued production until cancellation, even if there be no profit. In circumstances such as these and without more, defendant would be justified, in good faith, in ceasing production of the single item prior to cancellation only if its losses from continuance would be more than trivial, which, overall, is a question of fact.

4. "Even if Falstaff's financial position had been worse in mid–1975 than it actually was, and even if Falstaff had continued in that state of impecuniosity during the term of the contract, performance of the contract is not excused where the difficulty of performance arises from financial difficulty or economic hardship. As the New York Court of Appeals stated in 407 E. 61st Garage, Inc. v. Savoy Corp., 23 N.Y.2d 275, 281, 296 N.Y.S.2d 338, 344, 244 N.E.2d 37, 41 (1968):

"[W]here impossibility or difficulty of performance is occasioned only by financial difficulty or economic hardship, even to the extent of insolvency or bankruptcy, performance of a contract is not excused.' (Citations omitted.)"

37 N.Y.2d 471–72, 373 N.Y.S.2d 106, 335 N.E.2d 323.[5] Falstaff argues from this that it was not bound to do anything to market Ballantine products that would cause "more than trivial" losses.

We do not think the judge imposed on Falstaff a standard as demanding as its appellate counsel argues that he did. Despite his footnote 7, see note 6 supra, he did not in fact proceed on the basis that the best efforts clause required Falstaff to bankrupt itself in promoting Ballantine products or even to sell those products at a substantial loss. He relied rather on the fact that Falstaff's obligation to "use its best efforts to promote and maintain a high volume of sales" of Ballantine products was not fulfilled by a policy summarized by Mr. Kalmanovitz as being:

We sell beer and you pay for it....

We sell beer, F.O.B. the brewery. You come and get it.

—however sensible such a policy may have been with respect to Falstaff's other products. Once the peril of insolvency had been averted, the drastic percentage reductions in Ballantine sales as related to any possible basis of comparison ... required Falstaff at least to explore whether steps not involving substantial losses could have been taken to stop or at least lessen the rate of decline. The judge found that, instead of doing this, Falstaff had engaged in a number of misfeasances and nonfeasances which could have accounted in substantial measure for the catastrophic drop in Ballantine sales shown in the chart, see 454 F.Supp. at 267–72. These included the closing of the North Bergen depot which had serviced "Mom and Pop" stores and bars in the New York metropolitan area; Falstaff's choices of distributors for Ballantine products in the New Jersey and particularly the New York areas, where the chosen distributor was the owner of a competing brand; its failure to take advantage of a proffer from Guinness–Harp Corporation to distribute Ballantine products in New York City through its Metrobeer Division; Falstaff's incentive to put more effort into sales of its own brands which sold at higher prices despite identity of the ingredients and were free from the $.50 a barrel royalty burden; its failure to treat Ballantine products evenhandedly with Falstaff's; its discontinuing the practice of setting goals for salesmen; and the general Kalmanovitz policy of stressing profit at the expense of volume. In the court's judgment, these misfeasances and nonfeasances war-

5. The text of the *Feld* opinion did not refer to the case cited by Judge Brieant in the preceding footnote, 407 East 61st Garage, Inc. v. Savoy Fifth Avenue Corporation, 23 N.Y.2d 275, 296 N.Y.S.2d 338, 244 N.E.2d 37 (1968), which might suggest a more onerous obligation here. The Court of Appeals there reversed a summary judgment in favor of the defendant, which had discontinued operating the Savoy Hilton Hotel because of substantial financial losses, in alleged breach of a five-year contract with plaintiff wherein the defendant had agreed to use all reasonable efforts to provide the garage with exclusive opportunity for storage of the motor vehicles of hotel guests. Although the court did use the language quoted by Judge Brieant, the actual holding was simply that "an issue of fact is presented whether the agreement did import an implied promise by Savoy to fulfill its obligations for an entire five-year period." 23 N.Y.2d at 281, 296 N.Y.S.2d at 343, 244 N.E.2d at 41.

Other cases suggest that under New York law a "best efforts" clause imposes an obligation to act with good faith in light of one's own capabilities. In Van Valkenburgh v. Hayden Publishing Co., 30 N.Y.2d 34, 330 N.Y.S.2d 329, 281 N.E.2d 142 (1972), the court held a publisher liable to an author when, in clear bad faith after a contract dispute, he hired another to produce a book very similar to plaintiff's and then promoted it to those who had been buying the latter. On the other hand, a defendant having the exclusive right to sell the plaintiff's product may sell a similar product if necessary to meet outside competition, so long as he accounts for any resulting loses the plaintiff can show in the sales of the licensed product. Parev Products Co. v. I. Rokeach & Sons, 124 F.2d 147 (2 Cir.1941)....

ranted a conclusion that, even taking account of Falstaff's right to give reasonable consideration to its own interests, Falstaff had breached its duty to use best efforts as stated in the *Van Valkenburgh* decision, supra, 30 N.Y.2d at 46, 330 N.Y.S.2d at 334, 281 N.E.2d at 145.

Falstaff levels a barrage on these findings. The only attack which merits discussion is its criticism of the judge's conclusion that Falstaff did not treat its Ballantine brands evenhandedly with those under the Falstaff name. We agree that the subsidiary findings "that Falstaff but not Ballantine had been advertised extensively in Texas and Missouri" and that "[i]n these same areas Falstaff, although a 'premium' beer, was sold for extended periods below the price of Ballantine," while literally true, did not warrant the inference drawn from them. Texas was Falstaff territory and, with advertising on a cooperative basis, it was natural that advertising expenditures on Falstaff would exceed those on Ballantine. The lower price for Falstaff was a particular promotion of a bicentennial can in Texas, intended to meet a particular competitor.

However, we do not regard this error as undermining the judge's ultimate conclusion of breach of the best efforts clause. While that clause clearly required Falstaff to treat the Ballantine brands as well as its own, it does not follow that it required no more. With respect to its own brands, management was entirely free to exercise its business judgment as to how to maximize profit even if this meant serious loss in volume. Because of the obligation it had assumed under the sales contract, its situation with respect to the Ballantine brands was quite different. The royalty of $.50 a barrel on sales was an essential part of the purchase price. Even without the best efforts clause Falstaff would have been bound to make a good faith effort to see that substantial sales of Ballantine products were made, unless it discontinued under clause 2(a)(v) with consequent liability for liquidated damages. Cf. Wood v. Duff–Gordon, 222 N.Y. 88, 118 N.E. 214 (1917) (Cardozo, J.). Clause 8 imposed an added obligation to use "best efforts to promote and maintain a *high* volume of sales...." (emphasis supplied). Although we agree that even this did not require Falstaff to spend itself into bankruptcy to promote the sales of Ballantine products, it did prevent the application to them of Kalmanovitz' philosophy of emphasizing profit *über alles* without fair consideration of the effect on Ballantine volume. Plaintiff was not obliged to show just what steps Falstaff could reasonably have taken to maintain a high volume for Ballantine products. It was sufficient to show that Falstaff simply didn't care about Ballantine's volume and was content to allow this to plummet so long as that course was best for Falstaff's overall profit picture, an inference which the judge permissibly drew. The burden then shifted to Falstaff to prove there was nothing significant it could have done to promote Ballantine sales that would not have been financially disastrous.

Having correctly concluded that Falstaff had breached its best efforts covenant, the judge was faced with a difficult problem in computing what the royalties on the lost sales would have been. There is no need to rehearse the many decisions that, in a situation like this, certainty is not required; "[t]he plaintiff need only show a 'stable foundation for a reasonable estimate of royalties he would have earned had defendant not breached' ".... After carefully considering other possible bases, the court arrived at the seemingly sensible conclusion that the most nearly accurate comparison was with the combined sales of Rheingold and Schaefer beers, both, like Ballantine, being "price" beers sold primarily in the northeast, and computed what Ballantine sales would have been if its brands had suffered only the same decline as a composite of Rheingold and Schaefer....

... It is true ... that the award may overcompensate the plaintiff since Falstaff was not necessarily required to do whatever Rheingold and Shaefer did. But that is the kind of uncertainty which is permissible in favor of a plaintiff who has established liability in a case like this....

We can dispose quite briefly of the portion of the plaintiff's cross-appeal which claims error in the rejection of his contention that Falstaff's actions triggered the liquidated damage clause. One branch of this puts heavy weight on the word "distribution"; the claim is that the closing of the North Bergen center and Mr. Kalmanovitz' general come-and-get-it philosophy was, without more, a substantial discontinuance of "distribution". On this basis plaintiff would be entitled to invoke the liquidated damage clause even if Falstaff's new methods had succeeded in checking the decline in Ballantine sales. Another fallacy is that, countrywide, Falstaff substantially increased the number of distributors carrying Ballantine labels. Moreover the term "distribution", as used in the brewing industry, does not require distribution by the brewer's own trucks and employees. The norm rather is distribution through independent wholesalers. Falstaff's default under the best efforts clause was not in returning to that method *simpliciter* but in its failure to see to it that wholesale distribution approached in effectiveness what retail distribution had done.

Plaintiff contends more generally that permitting a decline of 63.12% in Ballantine sales from 1974 to 1977 was the equivalent of quitting the game. However, as Judge Brieant correctly pointed out, a large part of this drop was attributable "to the general decline of the market share of the smaller brewers" as against the "nationals", 454 F.Supp. at 266, and even the 518,899 barrels sold in 1977 were not a negligible amount of beer.

The judgment is affirmed. Plaintiff may recover two-thirds of his costs.

WOOD v. LUCY, LADY DUFF–GORDON

[Chapter 2, supra]

UCC § 2–306

[See Selected Source Materials Supplement]

MARKET STREET ASSOCIATES v. FREY

United States Court of Appeals, Seventh Circuit, 1991.
941 F.2d 588.

POSNER, Circuit Judge.

Market Street Associates Limited Partnership and its general partner appeal from a judgment for the defendants, General Electric Pension Trust and its trustees, entered upon cross-motions for summary judgment in a diversity suit that pivots on the doctrine of "good faith" performance of a contract. Cf. Robert Summers, " 'Good Faith' in General Contract Law and the Sales Provisions of the Uniform Commercial Code," 54 Va.L.Rev. 195, 232–43 (1968). Wisconsin law applies—common law rather than Uniform Commercial Code, because the contract is for land rather than for goods, UCC § 2–102; Wis.Stat. § 402.102, and because it is a lease rather than a sale and Wisconsin has not adopted UCC art. 2A, which governs leases....

... In 1968, J.C. Penney Company, the retail chain, entered into a sale and leaseback arrangement with General Electric Pension Trust in order to finance Penney's growth. Under the arrangement Penney sold properties to the pension trust which the trust then leased back to Penney for a term of 25 years. Paragraph 34 of the lease entitles the lessee to "request Lessor [the pension trust] to finance the costs and expenses of construction of additional Improvements upon the Premises," provided the amount of the costs and expenses is at least $250,000. Upon receiving the request, the pension trust "agrees to give reasonable consideration to providing the financing of such additional Improvements and Lessor and Lessee shall negotiate in good faith concerning the construction of such Improvements and the financing by Lessor of such costs and expenses." Paragraph 34 goes on to provide that, should the negotiations fail, the lessee shall be entitled to repurchase the property at a price roughly equal to the price at which Penney sold it to the pension trust in the first place, plus 6 percent a year for each year since the original purchase. So if the average annual appreciation in the property exceeded 6 percent, a breakdown in negotiations over the financing of improvements would entitle Penney to buy back the property for less than its market value (assuming it had sold the property to the pension trust in the first place at its then market value).

One of these leases was for a shopping center in Milwaukee. In 1987 Penney assigned this lease to Market Street Associates, which the following year received an inquiry from a drugstore chain that wanted to open a store in the shopping center, provided (as is customary) that Market Street Associates built the store for it. Whether Market Street Associates was pessimistic about obtaining financing from the pension trust, still the lessor of the shopping center, or for other reasons, it initially sought financing for the project from other sources. But they were unwilling to lend the necessary funds without a mortgage on the shopping center, which Market Street Associates could not give because it was not the owner but only the lessee. It decided therefore to try to buy the property back from the pension trust. Market Street Associates' general partner, Orenstein, tried to call David Erb of the pension trust, who was responsible for the property in question. Erb did not return his calls, so Orenstein wrote him, expressing an interest in buying the property and asking him to "review your file on this matter and call me so that we can discuss it further." At first, Erb did not reply. Eventually Orenstein did reach Erb, who promised to review the file and get back to him. A few days later an associate of Erb called Orenstein and indicated an interest in selling the property for $3 million, which Orenstein considered much too high.

That was in June of 1988. On July 28, Market Street Associates wrote a letter to the pension trust formally requesting funding for $2 million in improvements to the shopping center. The letter made no reference to paragraph 34 of the lease; indeed, it did not mention the lease. The letter asked Erb to call Orenstein to discuss the matter. Erb, in what was becoming a habit of unresponsiveness, did not call. On August 16, Orenstein sent a second letter—certified mail, return receipt requested—again requesting financing and this time referring to the lease, though not expressly to paragraph 34.

The heart of the letter is the following two sentences: "The purpose of this letter is to ask again that you advise us immediately if you are willing to provide the financing pursuant to the lease. If you are willing, we propose to enter into negotiation to amend the ground lease appropriately." The very next day, Market Street Associates received from Erb a letter, dated August 10, turning down the original request for financing on the ground that it did not "meet our current investment criteria": the pension trust was not interested in making loans for less than $7 million. On August 22, Orenstein replied to Erb by letter, noting that his letter of August 10 and Erb's letter of August 16 had evidently crossed in the mails, expressing disappointment at the turn-down, and stating that Market Street Associates would seek financing elsewhere. That was the last contact between the parties until September 27, when Orenstein sent Erb a letter stating that Market Street Associates was exercising the option granted it by paragraph 34 to purchase the property upon the terms specified in that paragraph in the event that negotiations over financing broke down.

The pension trust refused to sell, and this suit to compel specific performance followed. Apparently the price computed by the formula in paragraph 34 is only $1 million. The market value must be higher, or Market Street Associates wouldn't be trying to coerce conveyance at the paragraph 34 price; whether it is as high as $3 million, however, the record does not reveal.

The district judge granted summary judgment for the pension trust on two grounds that he believed to be separate although closely related. The first was that, by failing in its correspondence with the pension trust to mention paragraph 34 of the lease, Market Street Associates had prevented the negotiations over financing that are a condition precedent to the lessee's exercise of the purchase option from taking place. Second, this same failure violated the duty of good faith, which the common law of Wisconsin, as of other states, reads into every contract. In re Estate of Chayka, 47 Wis.2d 102, 107, 176 N.W.2d 561, 564 (1970); Super Valu Stores, Inc. v. D–Mart Food Stores, Inc., 146 Wis.2d 568, 577, 431 N.W.2d 721, 726 (App.1988); Ford Motor Co. v. Lyons, 137 Wis.2d 397, 442, 405 N.W.2d 354, 372 (App.1987); Sunds Defibrator AB v. Beloit Corp., 930 F.2d 564, 566 (7th Cir.1991); Restatement (Second) of Contracts § 205 (1981); 2 E. Allan Farnsworth, Farnsworth on Contracts § 7.17a (1990). In support of both grounds the judge emphasized a statement by Orenstein in his deposition that it had occurred to him that Erb mightn't know about paragraph 34, though this was unlikely (Orenstein testified) because Erb or someone else at the pension trust would probably check the file and discover the paragraph and realize that if the trust refused to negotiate over the request for financing, Market Street Associates, as Penney's assignee, would be entitled to walk off with the property for (perhaps) a song. The judge inferred that Market Street Associates didn't want financing from the pension trust—that it just wanted an opportunity to buy the property at a bargain price and hoped that the pension trust wouldn't realize the implications of turning down the request for financing. Market

Street Associates should, the judge opined, have advised the pension trust that it was requesting financing pursuant to paragraph 34, so that the trust would understand the penalty for refusing to negotiate.

We begin our analysis by setting to one side two extreme contentions by the parties. The pension trust argues that the option to purchase created by paragraph 34 cannot be exercised until negotiations over financing break down; there were no negotiations; therefore they did not break down; therefore Market Street Associates had no right to exercise the option. This argument misreads the contract. Although the option to purchase is indeed contingent, paragraph 34 requires the pension trust, upon demand by the lessee for the financing of improvements worth at least $250,000, "to give reasonable consideration to providing the financing." The lessor who fails to give reasonable consideration and thereby prevents the negotiations from taking place is breaking the contract; and a contracting party cannot be allowed to use his own breach to gain an advantage by impairing the rights that the contract confers on the other party. Variance, Inc. v. Losinske, 71 Wis.2d 31, 40, 237 N.W.2d 22, 26 (1976); Ethyl Corp. v. United Steelworkers of America, 768 F.2d 180, 185 (7th Cir.1985); Spanos v. Skouras Theatres Corp., 364 F.2d 161, 169 (2d Cir.1966) (en banc) (Friendly, J.); 3A Corbin on Contracts § 767, at p. 540 (1960). Often, it is true, if one party breaks the contract, the other can walk away from it without liability, can in other words exercise self-help. First National Bank v. Continental Illinois National Bank, 933 F.2d 466, 469 (7th Cir.1991). But he is not required to follow that course. He can stand on his contract rights.

But what exactly are those rights in this case? The contract entitles the lessee to reasonable consideration of its request for financing, and only if negotiations over the request fail is the lessee entitled to purchase the property at the price computed in accordance with paragraph 34. It might seem therefore that the proper legal remedy for a lessor's breach that consists of failure to give the lessee's request for financing reasonable consideration would not be an order that the lessor sell the property to the lessee at the paragraph 34 price, but an order that the lessor bargain with the lessee in good faith. But we do not understand the pension trust to be arguing that Market Street Associates is seeking the wrong remedy. We understand it to be arguing that Market Street Associates has no possible remedy. That is an untenable position.

Market Street Associates argues, with equal unreason as it seems to us, that it could not have broken the contract because paragraph 34 contains no express requirement that in requesting financing the lessee mention the lease or paragraph 34 or otherwise alert the lessor to the consequences of his failing to give reasonable consideration to granting the request. There is indeed no such requirement (all that the contract requires is a demand). But no one says there is. The pension trust's argument, which the district judge bought, is that either as a matter of simple contract interpretation or under the compulsion of the doctrine of good faith, a provision requiring Market Street Associates to remind the pension trust of paragraph 34 should be read into the lease.

It seems to us that these are one ground rather than two. A court has to have a reason to interpolate a clause into a contract. The only reason that has been suggested here is that it is necessary to prevent Market Street Associates from reaping a reward for what the pension trust believes to have been Market Street's bad faith. So we must consider the meaning of the contract duty of "good faith." The Wisconsin cases are cryptic as to its meaning though emphatic about its existence, so we must cast our net wider. We do so mindful of Learned Hand's warning, that "such words as 'fraud,' 'good faith,' 'whim,' 'caprice,' 'arbitrary action,' and 'legal fraud' ... obscure the issue." Thompson–Starrett Co. v. La Belle Iron Works, 17 F.2d 536, 541 (2d Cir. 1927). Indeed they do. Summers, supra, at 207–20; 2 Farnsworth on Contracts, supra, § 7.17a, at pp. 328–32. The particular confusion to which the vaguely moralistic overtones of "good faith" give rise is the belief that every contract establishes a fiduciary relationship. A fiduciary is required to treat his principal as if the principal were he, and therefore he may not take advantage of the principal's incapacity, ignorance, inexperience, or even naivete. Olympia Hotels Corp. v. Johnson Wax Development Corp., 908 F.2d 1363, 1373–74 (7th Cir.1990); United States v. Dial, 757 F.2d 163, 168 (7th Cir.1985); Faultersack v. Clintonville Sales Corp., 253 Wis. 432, 435–37, 34 N.W.2d 682, 683–84 (1948); Schweiger v. Loewi & Co., 65 Wis.2d 56, 64–65, 221 N.W.2d 882, 888 (1974); Meinhard v. Salmon, 249 N.Y. 458, 463–64, 164 N.E. 545, 546 (1928) (Cardozo, C.J.). If Market Street Associates were the fiduciary of General Electric Pension Trust, then (we may assume) it could not take advantage of Mr. Erb's apparent ignorance of paragraph 34, however exasperating Erb's failure to return Orenstein's phone calls was and however negligent Erb or his associates were in failing to read the lease before turning down Orenstein's request for financing.

But it is unlikely that Wisconsin wishes, in the name of good faith, to make every contract signatory his brother's keeper, especially when the brother is the immense and sophisticated General Electric Pension Trust, whose lofty indifference to small (= < $7 million) transactions is the signifier of its grandeur. In fact the law contemplates that people frequently will take advantage of the ignorance of those with whom they contract, without thereby incurring liability. Restatement, supra, § 161, comment d. The duty of honesty, of good faith even expansively conceived, is not a duty of candor. You can make a binding contract to purchase something you know your seller undervalues. Laidlaw v. Organ, 15 U.S. (2 Wheat.) 178, 181 n. 2, 4 L.Ed. 214 (1817); Teamsters Local 282 Pension Trust Fund v. Angelos, 762 F.2d 522, 528 (7th Cir.1985); United States v. Dial, supra, 757 F.2d at 168; 1 Farnsworth on Contracts, supra, § 4.11, at pp. 406–10; Anthony T. Kronman, "Mistake, Disclosure, Information, and the Law of Contracts," 7 J. Legal Stud. 1 (1978).

That of course is a question about formation, not performance, and the particular duty of good faith under examination here relates to the latter rather than to the former. But even after you have signed a contract, you are not obliged to become an altruist toward the other party and relax the terms if he gets into trouble in performing his side of the bargain. Kham & Nate's Shoes No. 2, Inc. v. First Bank, 908 F.2d 1351, 1357 (7th Cir.1990). Otherwise mere difficulty of performance would excuse a contracting party—which it does not. Northern Indiana Public Service Co. v. Carbon County Coal Co., 799 F.2d 265, 276–78 (7th Cir.1986); Jennie–O Foods, Inc. v. United States, 217 Ct.Cl. 314, 580 F.2d 400, 409 (1978) (per curiam); 2 Farnsworth on Contracts, supra, § 7.17a, at p. 330.

But it is one thing to say that you can exploit your superior knowledge of the market—for if you cannot, you will not be able to recoup the investment you made in obtaining that knowledge—or that you are not required to spend money bailing out a contract partner who has gotten into trouble. It is another thing to say that you can take deliberate advantage of an oversight by your contract partner concerning his rights under the contract. Such taking advantage is not the exploitation of superior knowledge or the avoidance of unbargained-for expense; it is sharp dealing. Like theft, it has no social product, and also like theft it induces costly defensive expenditures, in the form of overelaborate disclaimers or investigations into the trustworthiness of a prospective contract partner, just as the prospect of theft induces expenditures on locks. See generally Steven J. Burton, "Breach of Contract and the Common Law Duty to Perform in Good Faith," 94 Harv.L.Rev. 369, 393 (1980).

The form of sharp dealing that we are discussing might or might not be actionable as fraud or deceit. That is a question of tort law and there the rule is that if the information is readily available to both parties the failure of one to disclose it to the other, even if done in the knowledge that the other party is acting on mistaken premises, is not actionable. Kamuchey v. Trzesniewski, 8 Wis.2d 94, 98 N.W.2d 403 (1959); Southard v. Occidental Life Ins. Co., 36 Wis.2d 708, 154 N.W.2d 326 (1967); Lenzi v. Morkin, 103 Ill.2d 290, 82 Ill.Dec. 644, 469 N.E.2d 178 (1984); Guyer v. Cities Service Oil Co., 440 F.Supp. 630 (E.D.Wis.1977); W. Page Keeton et al., Prosser and Keeton on the Law of Torts § 106, at p. 737 (5th ed. 1984). All of these cases, however, with the debatable exception of *Guyer*, involve failure to disclose something in the negotiations leading up to the signing of the contract, rather than failure to disclose after the contract has been signed. (*Guyer* involved failure to disclose during the negotiations leading up to a renewal of the contract). The distinction is important, as we explained in Maksym v. Loesch, 937 F.2d 1237, 1242 (7th Cir.1991). Before the contract is signed, the parties confront each other with a natural wariness. Neither expects the other to be particularly forthcoming, and therefore there is no deception when one is not. Afterwards the situation is different. The parties are now in a cooperative relationship the costs of which will be considerably reduced by a measure of trust. So each lowers his guard a bit, and now silence is more apt to be deceptive. Cf. AMPAT/Midwest, Inc. v. Illinois Tool Works Inc., 896 F.2d 1035, 1040–41 (7th Cir.1990).

Moreover, this is a contract case rather than a tort case, and conduct that might not rise to the level of fraud may nonetheless violate the duty of good faith in dealing with one's contractual partners and thereby give rise to a remedy under contract law. Burton, supra, at 372 n. 17. This duty is, as it were, halfway between a fiduciary duty (the duty of *utmost* good faith) and the duty merely to refrain from active fraud. Despite its moralistic overtones it is no more the injection of moral principles into contract law than the fiduciary concept itself is. Tymshare, Inc. v. Covell, 727 F.2d 1145, 1152 (D.C.Cir.1984); Summers, supra, at 204–07, 265–66. It would be quixotic as well as presumptuous for judges to undertake through contract law to raise the ethical standards of the nation's business people. The concept of the duty of good faith like the concept of fiduciary duty is a stab at approximating the terms the parties would have negotiated had they foreseen the circumstances that have given rise to their dispute. The parties want to minimize the costs of performance. To the extent that a doctrine of good faith designed to do this by reducing defensive expenditures is a reasonable measure to this end, interpolating it into the contract advances the parties' joint goal.

It is true that an essential function of contracts is to allocate risk, and would be defeated if courts treated the materializing of a bargained-over, allocated risk as a misfortune the burden of which is required to be shared between the parties (as it might be within a family, for example) rather than borne entirely by the party to whom the risk had been allocated by mutual agreement. But contracts do not just allocate risk. They also (or some of them) set in motion a cooperative enterprise, which may to some extent place one party at the other's mercy. "The parties to a contract are embarked on a cooperative venture, and a minimum of cooperativeness in the event unforeseen problems arise at the performance stage is required even if not an explicit duty of the contract." AMPAT/Midwest, Inc. v. Illinois Tool Works, Inc., supra, 896 F.2d at 1041. The office of the doctrine of good faith is to forbid the kinds of opportunistic behavior that a mutually dependent, cooperative relationship might enable in the absence of rule. " 'Good faith' is a compact reference to an implied undertaking not to take opportunistic advantage in a way that could not have been contemplated at the time of drafting, and which therefore was not resolved explicitly by the parties." Kham & Nate's Shoes No. 2, Inc. v. First Bank, supra, 908 F.2d at 1357. The contractual duty of good faith is thus not some newfangled bit of welfare-state paternalism or (pace Duncan Kennedy, "Form and Substance in Private Law Adjudication," 89 Harv.L.Rev. 1685, 1721 (1976)) the sediment of an altruistic strain in contract law, and we are therefore not surprised to find the essentials of the modern doctrine well established in nineteenth-century cases, a few examples being Bush v. Marshall, 47 U.S. (6 How.) 284, 291, 12 L.Ed. 440 (1848); Chicago, Rock Island & Pac. R.R. v. Howard, 74 U.S. (7 Wall.) 392, 413, 19 L.Ed. 117 (1868); Marsh v. Masterson, 101 N.Y. 401, 410–11, 5 N.E. 59, 63 (1886), and Uhrig v. Williamsburg City Fire Ins. Co., 101 N.Y. 362, 4 N.E. 745 (1886).

The emphasis we are placing on postcontractual versus precontractual conduct helps explain the pattern that is observed when the duty of contractual good faith is considered in all its variety, encompassing not only good faith in the *performance* of a contract but also good faith in its *formation*, Summers, supra, at 220–32, and in its enforcement. Harbor Ins. Co. v. Continental Bank Corp., 922 F.2d 357, 363 (7th Cir.1990). The formation or negotiation stage is precontractual, and here the duty is minimized. It is greater not only at the performance but also at the enforcement stage, which is also postcontractual. "A party who hokes up a phony defense to the performance of his contractual duties and then when that defense fails (at some expense to the other party) tries on another defense for size can properly be said to be acting in bad faith." Id.; see also Larson v. Johnson, 1 Ill.App.2d 36, 46, 116 N.E.2d 187, 191–92 (1953). At the formation of the contract the parties are dealing in present realities; performance still lies in the future. As performance unfolds, circumstances change, often unforeseeably; the explicit terms of the contract become progressively less apt to the governance of the parties' relationship; and the role of implied conditions—and with it the scope and bite of the good-faith doctrine—grows.

We could of course do without the term "good faith," and maybe even without the doctrine. We could, as just suggested, speak instead of implied conditions necessitated by the unpredictability of the future at the time the contract was made. Farnsworth, "Good Faith Performance and Commercial Reasonableness under the Uniform Commercial Code," 30 U.Chi.L.Rev. 666, 670 (1963). Suppose a party has promised work to the promisee's "satisfaction." As Learned Hand explained, "he may refuse to look at the work, or to exercise any real judgment on it, in which case he has prevented performance and excused the condition." Thompson–Starrett Co. v. La Belle Iron Works, supra, 17 F.2d at 541. See also Morin Building Products Co. v. Baystone Construction, Inc., 717 F.2d 413, 415 (7th Cir.1983). That is, it was an implicit condition that the promisee examine the work to the extent necessary to determine whether it was satisfactory; otherwise the performing party would have been placing himself at the complete mercy of the promisee. The parties didn't write this condition into the contract either because they thought such behavior unlikely or failed to foresee it altogether. In just the same way—to switch to another familiar example of the operation of the duty of good faith—parties to a requirements contract surely do not intend that if the price of the product covered by the contract rises, the buyer shall be free to increase his "requirements" so that he can take advantage of the rise in the market price over the contract price to resell the product on the open market at a guaranteed profit. Empire Gas Corp. v. American Bakeries Co., 840 F.2d 1333 (7th Cir.1988). If they fail to insert an express condition to this effect, the court will read it in, confident that the parties would have inserted the condition if they had known what the future held. Of similar character is the implied condition that an exclusive dealer will use his best efforts to promote the supplier's goods, since otherwise the exclusive feature of the dealership contract would place the supplier at the dealer's mercy. Wood v. Duff–Gordon, 222 N.Y. 88, 118 N.E. 214 (1917) (Cardozo, J.).

But whether we say that a contract shall be deemed to contain such implied conditions as are necessary to make sense of the contract, or that a contract obligates the parties to cooperate in its performance in "good faith" to the extent necessary to carry out the purposes of the contract, comes to much the same thing. They are different ways of formulating the overriding purpose of contract law, which is to give the parties what they would have stipulated for expressly if at the time of making the contract they had had complete knowledge of the future and the costs of negotiating and adding provisions to the contract had been zero.

The two formulations would have different meanings only if "good faith" were thought limited to "honesty in fact," an interpretation perhaps permitted but certainly not compelled by the Uniform Commercial Code, see Summers, supra, at 207–20—and anyway this is not a case governed by the UCC. We need not pursue this issue. The dispositive question in the present case is simply whether Market Street Associates tried to trick the pension trust and succeeded in doing so. If it did, this would be the type of opportunistic behavior in an ongoing contractual relationship that would violate the duty of good faith performance however the duty is formulated. There is much common sense in Judge Reynolds' conclusion that Market Street Associates did just that. The situation as he saw it was as follows. Market Street Associates didn't want financing from the pension trust (initially it had looked elsewhere, remember), and when it learned it couldn't get the financing without owning the property, it decided to try to buy the property. But the pension trust set a stiff price, so Orenstein decided to trick the pension trust into selling at the bargain price fixed in paragraph 34 by requesting financing and hoping that the pension trust would turn the request down without noticing the paragraph. His preliminary dealings with the pension trust made this hope a realistic one by revealing a sluggish and hidebound bureaucracy unlikely to have retained in its brontosaurus's memory, or to be able at short notice to retrieve, the details of a small lease made twenty years earlier. So by requesting financing without mentioning the lease Market Street Associates might well precipitate a refusal before the pension trust woke up to paragraph 34. It is true that Orenstein's second letter requested financing "pursuant to the lease." But when the next day he received a reply to his first letter indicating that the pension trust was indeed oblivious to paragraph 34, his response was to send a lulling letter designed to convince the pension trust that the matter was closed and could be forgotten. The stage was set for his thunderbolt: the notification the next month that Market Street Associates was taking up the option in paragraph 34. Only then did the pension trust look up the lease and discover that it had been had.

The only problem with this recital is that it construes the facts as favorably to the pension trust as the record will permit, and that of course is not the right standard for summary judgment. The facts must be construed as favorably to the nonmoving party, to Market Street Associates, as the record permits (that Market Street Associates filed its own motion for summary judgment is irrelevant, as we have seen). When that is done, a different picture emerges. On Market Street Associates' construal of the record, $3 million was a grossly excessive price for the property, and while $1 million might be a bargain it would not confer so great a windfall as to warrant an inference that if the pension trust had known about paragraph 34 it never would have turned down Market Street Associates' request for financing cold. And in fact the pension trust may have known about paragraph 34, and either it didn't care or it believed that unless the request mentioned that paragraph the pension trust would incur no liability by turning it down. Market Street Associates may have assumed and have been entitled to assume that in reviewing a request for financing from one of its lessees the pension trust would take the time to read the lease to see whether it bore on the request. Market Street Associates did not desire financing from the pension trust initially—that is undeniable—yet when it discovered that it could not get financing elsewhere unless it had the title to the property it may have realized that it would have to negotiate with the pension trust over financing before it could hope to buy the property at the price specified in the lease.

On this interpretation of the facts there was no bad faith on the part of Market Street Associates. It acted honestly, reasonably, without ulterior motive, in the face of circumstances as they actually and reasonably appeared to it. The fault was the pension trust's incredible inattention, which misled Market Street Associates into believing that the pension trust had no interest in financing the improvements regardless of the purchase option. We do not usually excuse contracting parties from failing to read and understand the contents of their contract; and in the end what this case comes down to—or so at least it can be strongly argued—is that an immensely sophisticated enterprise simply failed to read the contract. On the other hand, such enterprises make mistakes just like the rest of us, and deliberately to take advantage of your contracting partner's mistake during the performance stage (for we are not talking about taking advantage of superior knowledge at the formation stage) is a breach of good faith. To be able to correct your contract partner's mistake at zero cost to yourself, and decide not to do so, is a species of opportunistic behavior that the parties would have expressly forbidden in the contract had they foreseen it. The immensely long term of the lease amplified the possibility of errors but did not license either party to take advantage of them.

The district judge jumped the gun in choosing between these alternative characterizations. The essential issue bearing on Market Street Associates' good faith was Orenstein's state of mind, a type of inquiry that ordinarily cannot be concluded on summary judgment, and could not be here. If Orenstein believed that Erb knew or would surely find out about paragraph 34, it was not dishonest or opportunistic to fail to flag that paragraph, or even to fail to mention the lease, in his correspondence and (rare) conversations with Erb, especially given the uninterest in dealing with Market Street Associates that Erb fairly radiated. To decide what Orenstein believed, a trial is necessary. As for the pension trust's intimation that a bench trial (for remember that this is an equity case, since the only relief sought by the plaintiff is specific performance) will add no illumination beyond what the summary judgment proceeding has done, this overlooks the fact that at trial the judge will for the first time have a chance to see the witnesses whose depositions he has read, to hear their testimony elaborated, and to assess their believability.

The judgment is reversed and the case is remanded for further proceedings consistent with this opinion.

REVERSED AND REMANDED.

———

WAGENSELLER v. SCOTTSDALE MEMORIAL HOSPITAL

[Chapter 13, supra]

———

Chapter 23

THE DOCTRINE OF SUBSTANTIAL PERFORMANCE

This Chapter concerns the following question: Suppose A and B have entered into a contract under which A is to render some designated performance and B is to pay a designated amount for the performance. A renders performance, but the performance is not perfect; that is, there is some difference between the performance that A promised and the performance that she rendered. Under what circumstances, if any, can A sue B on the contract for expectation damages (with an offset for the defects in A's performance), rather than being limited to suing B in restitution for the value of the benefit that A conferred on B?

It turns out that the answer to this question depends to at least some extent on the subject-matter of the contract. The general principle, considered in Section 1, is that A can sue B on the contract if she has rendered "substantial performance." However, special rules, considered in Section 2, are applicable to contracts for the sale of goods.

SECTION 1. THE GENERAL PRINCIPLE

JACOB & YOUNGS v. KENT

Court of Appeals of New York, 1921.
230 N.Y. 239, 129 N.E. 889, 23 A.L.R. 1429.

CARDOZO, J. The plaintiff built a country residence for the defendant at a cost of upwards of $77,000, and now sues to recover a balance of $3,483.46, remaining unpaid. The work of construction ceased in June, 1914, and the defendant then began to occupy the dwelling. There was no complaint of defective performance until March, 1915. One of the specifications for the plumbing work provides that "all wrought-iron pipe must be well galvanized, lap welded pipe of the grade known as 'standard pipe' of Reading manufacture."

The defendant learned in March, 1915, that some of the pipe, instead of being made in Reading, was the product of other factories. The plaintiff was accordingly directed by the architect to do the work anew. The plumbing was then encased within the walls except in a few places where it had to be exposed. Obedience to the order meant more than the substitution of other pipe. It meant the demolition at great expense of substantial parts of the completed structure. The plaintiff left the work untouched, and asked for a certificate that the final payment was due. Refusal of the certificate was followed by this suit.

The evidence sustains a finding that the omission of the prescribed brand of pipe was neither fraudulent nor wilful. It was the result of the oversight and inattention of the plaintiff's subcontractor. Reading pipe is distinguished from Cohoes pipe and other brands only by the name of the manufacturer stamped upon it at intervals of between six and seven feet. Even the defendant's architect, though he inspected the pipe upon arrival, failed to notice the discrepancy. The plaintiff tried to show that the brands installed, though made by other manufacturers, were the same in quality, in appearance, in market value, and in cost as the brand stated in the contract—that they were indeed, the same thing, though manufactured in another place. The evidence was excluded, and a verdict directed for the defendant. The Appellate Division reversed, and granted a new trial.

We think the evidence, if admitted would have supplied some basis for the inference that the defect was insignificant in its relation to the project. The courts never say that one who makes a contract fills the measure of his duty by less than full performance. They do say, however, that an omission, both trivial and innocent, will sometimes be atoned for by allowance of the resulting damage, and will not always be the breach of a condition to be followed by a forfeiture.... The distinction is akin to that between dependent and independent promises, or between promises and conditions. Anson on Contracts (Corbin's Ed.) § 367; 2 Williston on Contracts, § 842. Some promises are so plainly independent that they can never by fair construction be conditions of one another. Rosenthal Paper Co. v. Nat. Folding Box & Paper Co., 226 N.Y. 313, 123 N.E. 766; Bogardus v. N.Y. Life Ins. Co., 101 N.Y. 328, 4 N.E. 522. Others are so plainly dependent that they must always be conditions. Others, though dependent and thus conditions when there is departure in point of substance, will be viewed as independent and collateral when the departure is insignificant. 2 Williston on Contracts, §§ 841, 842; Eastern Forge Co. v. Corbin, 182 Mass. 590, 592, 66 N.E. 419; Robinson v. Mollett, L.R., 7 Eng. & Ir.App. 802, 814; Miller v. Benjamin, 142 N.Y. 613, 37 N.E. 631. Considerations partly of justice and partly of presumable intention are to tell us whether this or that promise shall be placed in one class or in another. The simple and the uniform will call for different remedies from the multifarious and the intricate. The margin of departure within the range of normal expectation upon a sale of common chattels will vary from the margin to be expected upon a contract for the construction of a mansion or a "skyscraper." There will be harshness sometimes and oppression in the implication of a condition when the thing upon which labor has been expended is incapable of surrender because united to the land, and equity and reason in the implication of a like condition when the subject-matter, if defective, is in shape to be returned. From the conclusion that promises may not be treated as dependent to the extent of their uttermost minutiae without sacrifice of justice, the progress is a short one to the conclusion that they may not be so treated without a perversion of intention. Intention not otherwise revealed may be presumed to hold in contemplation the reasonable and probable. If something else is in view, it must not be left to implication. There will be no assumption of a purpose to visit venial faults with oppressive retribution.

Those who think more of symmetry and logic in the development of legal rules than of practical adaptation to the attainment of a just result will be troubled by a classification where the lines of division are so wavering and blurred. Something doubtless, may be said on the score of consistency and certainty in favor of a stricter standard. The courts have balanced such considerations against those of equity and fairness, and found the latter to be the weightier. The decisions in this state commit us to the liberal view, which is making its way, nowadays, in jurisdictions slow to welcome it. Dakin & Co. v. Lee, 1916, 1 K.B. 566, 579. Where the line is to be drawn between the important and the trivial cannot be settled by a formula. "In the nature of the case precise boundaries are impossible." 2 Williston on Contracts, § 841. The same omission may take on one aspect or another according to its setting. Substitution of equivalents may not have the same significance in fields of art on the one side and in those of mere utility on the other. Nowhere will change be tolerated, however, if it is so dominant or pervasive as in any real or substantial measure to frustrate the purpose of the contract. Crouch v. Gutmann, 134 N.Y. 45, 51, 31 N.E. 271, 30 Am.St.Rep. 608. There is no general license to install whatever, in the builder's judgment, may be regarded as "just as good." Easthampton L. & C. Co., Ltd. v. Worthington, 186 N.Y. 407, 412, 79 N.E. 323. The question is one of degree, to be answered, if there is doubt, by the triers of the facts (Crouch v. Gutmann; Woodward v. Fuller, supra), and, if the inferences are certain, by the judges of the law (Easthampton L. & C. Co., Ltd. v. Worthington, supra). We must weigh the purpose to be served, the desire to be gratified, the excuse for deviation from the letter, the cruelty of enforced adherence. Then only can we tell whether literal fulfillment is to be implied by law as a condition. This is not to say that the parties are not free by apt and certain words to effectuate a purpose that performance of every term shall be a condition of recovery. That question is not here. This is merely to say that the law will be slow to impute the purpose, in the silence of the parties, where the significance of the default is grievously out of proportion to the oppression of the forfeiture. The wilful transgressor must accept the penalty of his transgression. Schultze v. Goodstein, 180 N.Y. 248, 251, 73 N.E. 21; Desmond–Dunne Co. v. Friedman–Doscher Co., 162 N.Y. 486, 490, 56 N.E. 995. For him there is no occasion to mitigate the rigor of implied conditions. The transgressor whose default is unintentional and trivial may hope for mercy if he will offer atonement for his wrong. Spence v. Ham [163 N.Y. 220, 57 N.E. 412].

In the circumstances of this case, we think the measure of the allowance is not the cost of replacement, which would be great, but the difference in value, which would be either nominal or nothing.... It is true that in most cases the cost of replacement is the measure. Spence v. Ham, supra. The owner is entitled to the money which will permit him to complete, unless the cost of completion is grossly and unfairly out of proportion to the good to be attained. When that is true, the measure is the difference in value....

The order should be affirmed, and judgment absolute directed in favor of the plaintiff upon the stipulation, with costs in all courts. . . .

[The dissenting opinion of McLaughlin, J. is omitted.]

***

R. DANZIG, THE CAPABILITY PROBLEM IN CONTRACT LAW 120–23 (1978). "The contract [in Jacob & Youngs v. Kent] specified a standard of pipe [wrought iron] which cost 30% more than steel pipe—then the most widely used (and now the almost universally used) pipe. The makers of wrought iron pipe, however, claimed that the savings due to durability and low maintenance more than made up for the added expense. . . .

"The Reading Company was by its account the largest manufacturer of wrought iron pipe in the country. . . .

". . . According to a pipe wholesaler interviewed in New York City in 1975, genuine wrought iron pipe was manufactured in the pre-war period by four largely noncompeting companies: Reading, Cohoes, Byers and Southchester. According to this informant, all of these brands 'were of the same quality and price. The manufacturer's name would make absolutely no difference in pipe or in price.' . . .

"Why then was Reading Pipe specified? Apparently because it was the normal trade practice to assure wrought iron pipe quality by naming a manufacturer. In contemporary trade bulletins put out by Byers and Reading, prospective buyers were cautioned that some steel pipe manufacturers used iron pipe and often sold under misleading names like 'wrought pipe.' To avoid such inferior products, Byers warned: 'When wrought iron pipe is desired, the specifications often read "genuine wrought iron pipe" but as this does not always exclude wrought iron containing steel scrap, it is safer to mention the name of a manufacturer known not to use scrap.' "

***

BRUNER v. HINES, 295 Ala. 111, 324 So.2d 265 (1975). "The doctrine of substantial performance is a necessary inroad on the pure concept of freedom of contracts. The doctrine recognizes countervailing interests of private individuals and society; and, to some extent, it sacrifices the preciseness of the individual's contractual expectations to society's need for facilitating economic exchange. This is not to say that the rule of substantial performance constitutes a moral or ethical compromise; rather, the wisdom of its application adds legal efficacy to promises by enforcing the essential purposes of contracts and by eliminating trivial excuses for nonperformance."

***

GOETZ & SCOTT, THE MITIGATION PRINCIPLE: TOWARD A GENERAL THEORY OF CONTRACTUAL OBLIGATION, 69 Va.L.Rev. 967, 1010 (1983). "The substantial performance doctrine reduces opportunistic claims by softening the breacher–nonbreacher distinction, thereby removing opportunities to exploit inadvertent breaches.''

JARDINE ESTATES, INC. v. DONNA BROOK CORP., 42 N.J.Super. 332, 126 A.2d 372 (1956). "Substantial performance is compliance in good faith with all important particulars of the contract.... [For the doctrine to apply,] a builder's default should not be willful, nor the defects so serious as to deprive the property of its value for the intended use, nor so pervade the whole work that a deduction in damages will not be fair compensation. 3 Williston on Contracts (Rev. ed.), § 805, p. 2256 et seq....

"Appellant stresses that since there was a verdict in its favor for incomplete and defective work in a sum equal to 31% of the contract price, it is conclusive that there was not substantial performance. We do not agree. The matter is not to be determined on a percentage basis, for the cost of remedying defects may sometimes even exceed the outlay for original construction."

VINCENZI v. CERRO, 186 Conn. 612, 442 A.2d 1352 (1982). "The principal claim of the defendants is that the doctrine of substantial performance was inapplicable in this case because the plaintiffs were guilty of a wilful or intentional breach of contract by failing to complete all of the work required.... We have in several cases approved the common statement that a contractor who is guilty of a 'wilful' breach cannot maintain an action upon the contract.... The contemporary view, however, is that even a conscious and intentional departure from the contract specifications will not necessarily defeat recovery, but may be considered as one of the several factors involved in deciding whether there has been full performance. 3A Corbin, Contract § 707; 2 Restatement (Second), Contracts § 237, comment D. The pertinent inquiry is not simply whether the breach was 'wilful' but whether the behavior of the party in default 'comports with standard of good faith and fair dealing.' 2 Restatement (Second), Contracts § 241(e); see comment f. Even an adverse conclusion on this point is not decisive but is to be weighted with other factors, such as the extent to which the owner will be deprived of a reasonably expected benefit and the extent to which the builder may suffer forfeiture, in deciding whether there has been substantial performance. Id.; see § 237, comment d."

KREYER v. DRISCOLL

Supreme Court of Wisconsin, 1968.
39 Wis.2d 540, 159 N.W.2d 680.

This is a suit to recover the contract price of an oral contract to construct a home for the defendants Winfred M. Driscoll and Ann Driscoll. The defense alleged a breach of contract and a failure to substantially perform. The case was tried to the court which found the plaintiff Robert J. Kreyer, doing business as R.J. Kreyer Construction Company and the defendants Driscolls entered into a contract about December 1, 1961, for the construction of a dwelling house according to drawings and specifications at a cost of $47,046.62, which was to be completed in the fall of 1962. Extras were found to amount to $2,787.83. There were difficulties in completing the house and a refusal by the Driscolls to pay the plaintiff because of alleged breaches on his part. However, the court found the plaintiff substantially performed the contract and deducted from the contract price $740 for imperfect workmanship; $1,233.32 damages for unreasonable delay in completion; $23,460 for payments made to the plaintiff; and $13,433.32 for payments made directly by the Driscolls to subcontractors either for lien satisfactions or on their accounts, $4,650 of which was work performed after difficulties arose between the plaintiff and the Driscolls. Judgment was entered in favor of the plaintiff for the balance, namely, $10,967.81, and the Driscolls appealed and the plaintiff cross appealed for interest.

HALLOWS, CHIEF JUSTICE. The plaintiff complains the findings of fact as to terms of the building contract are in error because they omit: (1) The plaintiff was to receive payment in four draws as the job progressed; (2) he was to use the draw money only for Driscolls' house; and (3) the plaintiff was to submit lien waivers to show for what he had used the draw money. The record is voluminous and contains much evidence relating to these three issues. The evidence is conflicting but it does appear the plaintiff was to receive payment in four draws on condition that he submit waivers of liens as a condition precedent to drawing on the mortgage money of the Driscolls after the first instalment payment. Some of the liens presented stated amounts in excess of that actually paid the subcontractors and some were for amounts in excess of material furnished. Apparently some of the money was used to pay bills other than for material used in Driscolls' house.

It is not material in the view we take of this case whether findings on this issue were made. We point out, however, that the Driscolls did not request the findings they now claim should have been made. The trial court found the plaintiff duly performed all the conditions of the contract with the exception of the defective work and the delay. The evidence does not sustain this finding in respect to the completion of the home.

The trial court thought the plaintiff substantially performed the contract because only $4,650 of uncompleted work remained at the time the plaintiff and the Driscolls reached an impasse. The trial court also concluded the Driscolls looked to the plaintiff to continue the contract and did not rescind it. We do not think that recission is a necessary condition precedent to a defense to substantial performance. The Driscolls were dissatisfied with the plaintiff's performance and notified him. They could accept so much of the work as the plaintiff performed without waiving full performance. Manthey v. Stock (1907), 133 Wis. 107, 113 N.W. 443. If the Driscolls had valid grounds to rescind the contract, that would have precluded substantial performance of the contract and required the plaintiff to sue in *quantum meruit*. However, failure to rescind does not make performance substantial which is unsubstantial.

The doctrine of substantial performance is an equitable doctrine and constitutes an exception in building contracts to the general rule requiring complete performance of the contract. To recover on an uncompleted construction contract on a claim of having substantially, but not fully, performed it, the contractor must make a good faith effort to perform and substantially perform his agreement. Nees v. Weaver (1936), 222 Wis. 492, 269 N.W. 266, 107 A.L.R. 1405. This doctrine of substantial performance was explained and the cases discussed in Manthey v. Stock, supra, and further explained and cases discussed in Plante v. Jacobs (1960) . . . .

Most of the cases considering the doctrine of substantial performance involved defective work or work contrary to the terms of the contract which required substantial amounts of money to conform the work to the terms of the contract. In some cases, while the work was completed the performance of the subject of the contract did not meet the object and purpose of the contract. In the present case, we have on the findings of the court only an incompleteness in respect to the construction work and a cost of completing the dwelling to the owner which was readily ascertainable. Such a case by its nature presents a less difficult case of substantial performance than those involving defective work or inability of the subject matter to meet performance standards. But we should not consider as controlling the fact that the owner can obtain all he contracted for by self-help and by the expenditure of money.

Here, the defendant considered he had to take an active part in finishing the house because he could not trust the plaintiff to complete the house free of liens because of his prior conduct. We think the owner has a right to contract for the completed structure or work and in the building of a house the contract price pays for the relief from trouble and personal effort on the part of the owner in respect to building. Consequently, a dispensation in favor of the contractor on the theory of substantial performance should be granted in cases of incompleteness only when such details are inconsiderable and not the fault of the contractor. See Manthey v. Stock, supra.

The court made no finding on the good faith of the plaintiff and if we presume an affirmative finding on that question was impliedly made, we still do not consider it a saving grace because the plaintiff did not construct the house to the point of completeness which could be called substantial performance. In Plante v. Jacobs, supra, at 572, 103 N.W.2d at 298, we stated, "No mathematical rule relating to the percentage of the price, of cost of completion, or of completeness can be laid down to determine substantial performance of a building contract." At that time there remained to be done: Approximately one half of the plumbing at a cost of $800; one half of the electrical work at a cost of about $800; one half of the heating at a cost of about $800; one half of the tile work at a cost of about $1,500; and all the linoleum at a cost of $560; and about one fourth of the decorating.

We do not think a contractor who leaves this much work unfinished has substantially complied with his contract to completely build a home according to plans and specifications. It may be true that he should not be denied compensation, but neither should he be entitled to recover on the contract for substantially complete performance. We think the trial court was in error in granting recovery on the theory of substantial performance, but the plaintiff has a cause of action to be reimbursed for his services and material on the theory of *quantum meruit*. See Plante v. Jacobs, supra.

In Valentine v. Patrick Warren Construction Co. (1953), 263 Wis. 143, 56 N.W.2d 860, the rule was laid down in respect to restitution in favor of a plaintiff who is in default. In this case we adopted the rule found in Restatement, Second, Contracts, pp. 623–624, sec. 357(1), which provides that where a defendant justifiably refuses to perform his contract because of the plaintiff's breach but the plaintiff has rendered part performance which is of a net benefit to the defendant, the plaintiff can get judgment with some exceptions for the amount of such benefit in excess of the harm he has caused the defendant by his breach but in no case exceeding a ratable proportion of the agreed compensation. Under this rule, the defendant with knowledge of the plaintiff's breach must assent to the rendition of the part performance or accept the benefit of it. This is what the trial court found the Driscolls did by not rescinding the contract.

Illustration 3 to this rule is on all fours with the facts of this case and the computation made by the trial court is the computation which would be made under this section. The same rule as stated in 5 Williston, Contracts (rev.), pp. 41–44, secs. 1482–1483, is that the true measure of quasi-contractual recovery where the performance is incomplete but readily remedial is the unpaid contract price less the cost of completion and other additional harm to the defendant except that it must never exceed the benefit actually received by the defendant. This is the net benefit by which the defendant is enriched.

In this case the Driscolls have a house which now meets the conditions of the contract with adjustments made for delay in performance and for minor faulty work. It would be unjust to allow them to retain the $10,967.81. They should not receive a windfall because of the plaintiff's breach. It is immaterial to the Driscolls whether subcontractors are paid or not. There are no valid liens against their home and their agreement was not a third-party-beneficiary contract for subcontractors. The trial court found the dwelling was reasonably worth the purchase price and thus the amount found due the plaintiff by the court does not exceed the benefit actually received by [the] Driscolls. It would be useless to send this case back for a retrial which would reach the same result on the facts found. We therefore hold the amount of the judgment found by the lower court was not justified on the theory of substantial performance but is justified on the theory of *quantum meruit* or restitution.

On the cross appeal the plaintiff asks for interest on the amount of the judgment, but recovery is not now on the contract and this question is moot. In equity the plaintiff is not entitled to interest and, likewise, neither party should have costs on this appeal.

Judgment affirmed; costs denied to both parties.

———

O.W. GRUN ROOFING & CONSTR. CO. v. COPE, 529 S.W.2d 258 (Tex.Civ.App.1975). Grun agreed to install a new russet–colored shingle roof on Cope's home for $648. As actually installed, the roof had yellow streaks but was structurally sound. Cope refused to pay, and Grun filed a mechanic's lien. Cope then sued to set aside the lien and for damages equal to the difference between (i) the $648 price under the contract with Grun and (ii) the cost of installing a new roof, which was 20% higher. The trial court set aside the lien and awarded Cope $123, based on the cost to install a new roof ($648 plus 20% for price increases). Affirmed:

. . . It should not come as a shock to anyone to adopt a rule to the effect that a person has, particularly with respect to his home, to choose for himself and to contract for something which exactly satisfies that choice, and not to be compelled to accept something else. In the matter of homes and their decoration, as much as, if not more than, in many other fields, mere taste or preference, almost approaching whimsy, may be controlling with the homeowner, so that variations which might, under other circumstances, be considered trifling, may be inconsistent with that "substantial performance" on which liability to pay must be predicated. [M]ere incompleteness or deviations which may be easily supplied or remedied after the contractor has finished his work, and the cost of which to the owner is not excessive and readily ascertainable, present less cause for hesitation in concluding that the performance tendered constitutes substantial performance, since in such cases the owner can obtain complete satisfaction by merely spending some money and deducting the amount of such expenditure from the contract price.

In the case before us there is evidence to support the conclusion that plaintiff can secure a roof of uniform coloring only by installing a completely new roof. We cannot say, as a matter of law, that the evidence establishes that in this case that a roof which so lacks uniformity in color as to give the appearance of a patch job serves essentially the same purpose as a roof of uniform color which has the appearance of being a new roof. We are not prepared to hold that a contractor who tenders a performance so deficient that it can be remedied only by completely redoing the work for which the contract called has established, as a matter of law, that he has substantially performed his contractual obligation.

A recovery by Grun in quantum meruit for benefit conferred was denied:

. . . [T]he evidence does not conclusively establish that plaintiff has received any benefit from defendant's defective performance. As already pointed out, there is evidence that plaintiff will have to install a completely new roof.

———

SECTION 2. CONTRACTS FOR THE SALE OF GOODS

———

UCC §§ 2–508, 2–601, 2–608, 2–612

[See Selected Source Materials Supplement]

———

CISG ARTS. 35(1), 37, 45, 46, 48, 49

[See Selected Source Materials Supplement]

———

J. WHITE & R. SUMMERS, UNIFORM COMMERCIAL CODE § 8–2 (5th ed. 2000). "At the outset one should understand the significance of a self–help remedy which permits the buyer to return the goods to the seller (that is, rejection or revocation of acceptance). In these cases the buyer is freed from its obligation to pay the price, and the buyer has a right to recover that part of the price already paid. Moreover, except in unusual circumstances, the buyer need not resell the goods. One should understand the economic difference between the status of the buyer who has rejected and the status of the buyer who has accepted and sued for breach of warranty. The typical buyer who accepts and sues for breach of warranty under 2–714 will recover only for injury proximately resulting from defects in the goods at the time of sale. If, for example, the purchased automobile had a cracked piston that will cost $500 to repair (and the value of the car is so diminished by $500), buyer will recover that $500. On the other hand, if buyer rejects the goods, buyer is first recompensed for the losses resulting from the seller's failure to perform its end of the contract (for example, by a suit under 2–713 or 2–712); more important, buyer escapes the bargain, and throws any loss resulting from depreciation of the goods back upon the seller.

"The importance of goods oriented remedies can be illustrated by an example from a commodity market. Assume that the seller delivers 10,000 bushels of potatoes and that 100 of those bushels are rotten. If the buyer accepts the potatoes, it will have a cause of action under 2–714, and it will recover money approximately equivalent to the value of those 100 bushels. If, on the other hand, the buyer rejects the entire delivery, if the seller cannot cure, and if the price of the potatoes has fallen substantially, the buyer's rejection may save it thousands of dollars by allowing the purchase of conforming goods on the market at a much lower price than specified in the contract. Rejection avoids the economic injury of a bad bargain as well."

NOTE ON THE PERFECT–TENDER RULE AND THE UCC

Prior to the adoption of the Uniform Commercial Code, the doctrine of substantial performance was not applicable to contracts for the sale of goods. Instead, at least in theory and often in practice, a buyer could refuse to accept a delivery of goods that in any way failed to conform to the contract. This rule was known as the perfect-tender rule, because a buyer of goods could reject any tender of delivery that was not perfect. A leading case was Norrington v. Wright, 115 U.S. 188, 6 S.Ct. 12, 29 L.Ed. 366 (1885). UCC § 2–601 nominally preserves the perfect-tender rule for the sale of goods. However, other provisions of the UCC strip away much or most of the significance of this Section.

1. *Revocation of acceptance.* First, UCC § 2–601 applies only where a buyer rejects goods. It does not apply where the buyer accepts goods and then discovers a defect. Under UCC § 2–608, a buyer may revoke acceptance in such a case, but only if the nonconformity substantially impairs the value of the goods to her.

There are other limitations on the buyer's right to revoke acceptance under § 2–608, even if the nonconformity does substantially impair the value of the goods to him. If the buyer accepted the goods knowing that they were nonconforming, she can revoke her acceptance only if she accepted on the reasonable assumption that the nonconformity would be cured (for example, because the seller promised cure), and the nonconformity was not seasonably cured. If the buyer accepted the goods without knowing that they were nonconforming, she can revoke her acceptance only if her acceptance was reasonably induced either by the difficulty of discovering the defect before acceptance or by the seller's assurances.

2. *Installment contracts.* Section 2–601 is also inapplicable to installment contracts, that is, contracts that require or authorize the delivery of goods in separate lots, to be separately accepted. Such contracts are covered by Section 2–612. Under Section 2–612(2), a buyer normally can reject a nonconforming installment only if the nonconformity substantially impairs the value of the installment and cannot be cured. Furthermore, under Section 2–612(3) a buyer cannot treat the whole installment contract as breached on the ground of a nonconformity or default with respect to one or more installments, unless those nonconformities or defaults substantially impair the value of the whole contract.

3. *Cure.* The perfect-tender rule is also significantly ameliorated by Section 2–508, the "cure" provision. Under Section 2–508(1), in the case of a single-delivery (non-installment) contract, if a tender of goods is rejected because it is nonconforming, and the time for performance has not yet expired, the seller may cure the defect by making a conforming delivery within the contract time. Even more significantly, under Section 2–508(2) if a tender of goods is rejected because it is nonconforming, and the seller had reasonable grounds to believe that the tender would be acceptable with a money allowance or otherwise, the seller has a further reasonable time to substitute a conforming tender even if the time for performance has expired.

4. *Good Faith.* Under UCC § 1–203, "Every contract ... within [the UCC] imposes an obligation of good faith in its performance or enforcement." Under UCC § 1–201(19), at a minimum good faith requires "honesty in fact in the conduct or transaction concerned." Under UCC § 2–103(1)(b), in the case of a merchant, in contracts for the sale of goods, good faith means not only honesty in fact but also "the observance of reasonable commercial standards of fair dealing in the trade."* A buyer who seized on a minor defect to justify a rejection that was really based on the fact that the contract is no longer favorable to her might not satisfy this minimum obligation. As stated in Printing Center of Texas, Inc. v. Supermind Publishing Co., 669 S.W.2d 779 (Tex.App.1984):

> Once the contract of the parties has been determined, the evidence must be reviewed to see if the right goods were tendered at the right time and place. If the evidence does establish nonconformity in some respect, the buyer is entitled to reject if he rejects in good faith. [UCC] § 1–203 provides that, "Every contract or duty within this Act imposes an obligation of good faith in its performance or enforcement." Since the rejection of goods is a matter of performance, the buyer is obligated to act in good faith when he rejects the goods. When the buyer is a merchant, his standard of good faith rejection requires honesty in fact and observ-

---

* The UCC sections quoted in this passage are those in force in most states. See Note on The Duty to Perform in Good Faith under the   UCC and Restatement Second, Chapter 22, supra.

ance of reasonable commercial standards of fair dealing in the trade. [UCC § 2–103(2)].... Evidence of circumstances which indicate that the buyer's motivation in rejecting the goods was to escape the bargain, rather than to avoid acceptance of a tender which in some respect impairs the value of the bargain to him, would support a finding of rejection in bad faith. Neumiller Farms Inc. v. Cornett, 368 So.2d 272 (Ala.1979). Thus, evidence of rejection of the goods on account of a minor defect in a falling market would in some instances be sufficient to support a finding that the buyer acted in bad faith when he rejected the goods.

RAMIREZ v. AUTOSPORT, 88 N.J. 277, 440 A.2d 1345 (1982). "In the nineteenth century, sellers were required to deliver goods that complied exactly with the sales agreement. See Filley v. Pope, 115 U.S. 213, 220, 6 S.Ct. 19, 21, 29 L.Ed. 372, 373 (1885) (buyer not obliged to accept otherwise conforming scrap iron shipped to New Orleans from Leith, rather than Glasgow, Scotland, as required by contract); Columbian Iron Works & Dry-Dock Co. v. Douglas, 84 Md. 44, 47, 34 A. 1118, 1120–1121 (1896) (buyer who agreed to purchase steel scrap from United States cruisers not obliged to take any other kind of scrap). That rule, known as the 'perfect tender' rule, remained part of the law of sales well into the twentieth century. By the 1920's the doctrine was so entrenched in the law that Judge Learned Hand declared '[t]here is no room in commercial contracts for the doctrine of substantial performance.' Mitsubishi Goshi Kaisha v. J. Aaron & Co., Inc., 16 F.2d 185, 186 (2 Cir.1926).

"The harshness of the rule led courts to seek to ameliorate its effect and to bring the law of sales in closer harmony with the law of contracts, which allows rescission only for material breaches. LeRoy Dyal Co. v. Allen, 161 F.2d 152, 155 (4 Cir.1947). See 5 Corbin, Contracts § 1104 at 464 (1951); 12 Williston, Contracts § 1455 at 14 (3 ed. 1970). Nevertheless, a variation of the perfect tender rule appeared in the Uniform Sales Act. N.J.S.A. 46:30–75 (purchasers permitted to reject goods or rescind contracts for any breach of warranty).... The chief objection to the continuation of the perfect tender rule was that buyers in a declining market would reject goods for minor non-conformities and force the loss on surprised sellers....

"To the extent that a buyer can reject goods for any nonconformity, the UCC retains the perfect tender rule.... Section 2–601 authorizes a buyer to reject goods if they 'or the tender of delivery fail in any respect to conform to the contract.' ... The Code, however, mitigates the harshness of the perfect tender rule and balances the interests of buyer and seller."

COMMENTS OF GRANT GILMORE, IN ALI–ABA, ADVANCED ALI–ABA COURSE OF STUDY ON BANKING AND SECURED TRANSACTIONS UNDER THE UNIFORM COMMERCIAL CODE 145 (1968). "There was a considerable controversy in the early days of the Code as to why the Code had, apparently, although stating the strong substantial performance role in § 2–612 with respect to installment contracts, restated what many people considered [the] exploded theory of perfect tender in § 2–

601. I think at that point few people realized how much substantial performance there was buried in other, apparently unrelated, sections of the code to cut back § 2–601. There was considerable tendency in the academic discussions of the problem in law review articles to say that § 2–601 was all wrong and what the draftsman ought to have done was to have adopted a straight substantial performance rule all the way through.

"I remember hearing Professor Llewellyn discuss this problem once. He put it this way: He said that one of his advisers in the early years of drafting the sales article had been a Mr. Hiram Thomas of Boston, a Boston lawyer, for whom Llewellyn had great admiration, indeed reverence. Llewellyn said there was one meeting at which Hiram Thomas explained why it was that the perfect tender rule of § 2–601 was right with respect to ordinary contracts and the substantial performance rule of § 2–612 was right with respect to installment contracts. Anyone who heard Mr. Thomas that day, said Llewellyn, would be in no doubt that both sections were right. Unfortunately, said Llewellyn, he had since forgotten exactly what it was that Mr. Thomas said, and Mr. Thomas had since died, so that there was no way of reconstructing just why it was that § 2–601 was a good section of its type and § 2–612 was a good section of its type. But Professor Llewellyn was adamant that they were both right and that Mr. Thomas had once known the reason. (Laughter)"

T.W. OIL, INC. v. CONSOLIDATED EDISON CO.

Court of Appeals of New York, 1982.
57 N.Y.2d 574, 457 N.Y.S.2d 458, 443 N.E.2d 932.

FUCHSBERG, JUDGE.

In the first case to wend its way through our appellate courts on this question, we are asked, in the main, to decide whether a seller who, acting in good faith and without knowledge of any defect, tenders nonconforming goods to a buyer who properly rejects them, may avail itself of the cure provision of subdivision (2) of section 2–508 of the Uniform Commercial Code. We hold that, if seasonable notice be given, such a seller may offer to cure the defect within a reasonable period beyond the time when the contract was to be performed so long as it has acted in good faith and with a reasonable expectation that the original goods would be acceptable to the buyer.

The factual background against which we decide this appeal is based on either undisputed proof or express findings at Trial Term. In January, 1974, midst the fuel shortage produced by the oil embargo, the plaintiff (then known as Joc Oil USA, Inc.) purchased a cargo of fuel oil whose sulfur content was represented to it as no greater than 1%. While the oil was still at sea en route to the United States in the tanker *MT Khamsin*, plaintiff received a certificate from the foreign refinery at which it had been processed informing it that the sulfur content in fact was .52%. Thereafter, on January 24, the plaintiff entered into a written contract with the defendant (Con Ed) for the sale of this oil. The agreement was for delivery to take place between January 24 and January 30, payment being subject to a named independent testing agency's confirmation of quality and quantity. The contract, following a trade custom to round off specifications of sulfur content at, for instance, 1%, .5% or .3%, described that of the *Khamsin* oil as .5%. In the course of the negotiations, the plaintiff learned that Con Ed was then authorized to buy and burn oil with a sulfur content of up to 1% and would even mix oils containing more and less to maintain that figure.

When the vessel arrived, on January 25, its cargo was discharged into Con Ed storage tanks in Bayonne, New Jersey.[1] In due course, the independent testing people reported a sulfur content of .92%. On this basis, acting within a time frame whose reasonableness is not in question, on February 14 Con Ed rejected the shipment. Prompt negotiations to adjust the price failed; by February 20, plaintiff had offered a price reduction roughly responsive to the difference in sulfur reading, but Con Ed, though it could use the oil, rejected this proposition out of hand. It was insistent on paying no more than the latest prevailing price, which, in the volatile market that then existed, was some 25% below the level which prevailed when it agreed to buy the oil.

The very next day, February 21, plaintiff offered to cure the defect with a substitute shipment of conforming oil scheduled to arrive on the *S.S. Appollonian Victory* on February 28. Nevertheless, on February 22, the very day after the cure was proffered, Con Ed, adamant in its intention to avail itself of the intervening drop in prices, summarily rejected this proposal too. The two cargos were subsequently sold to third parties at the best price obtainable, first that of the *Appollonian* and, sometime later, after extraction from the tanks had been accomplished, that of the *Khamsin*.[2]

There ensued this action for breach of contract,[3] which, after a somewhat unconventional trial course, resulted in a nonjury decision for the plaintiff in the sum of $1,385,512.83, essentially the difference between the original contract price of $3,360,667.14 and the amount received by the plaintiff by way of resale of the *Khamsin* oil at what the court found as a matter of fact was a negotiated price which, under all the circumstances,[4] was reasonably procured in the open market. To arrive at this result, the Trial Judge, while ruling against other liability theories advanced by the plaintiff, which, in particular, included one charging the defendant with having failed to act in good faith in the negotiations for a price adjustment on the *Khamsin* oil (Uniform Commercial Code, § 1–203), decided as a matter of law that subdivision (2) of section 2–508 of the Uniform Commercial Code was available to the plaintiff even if it had no prior knowledge of the nonconformity. Finding that in fact plaintiff had no such belief at the time of the delivery, that what turned out to be a .92% sulfur content was "within the range of contemplation of reasonable acceptability" to Con. Ed., and that seasonable notice of an intention to cure was given, the court went on to hold that plaintiff's "reasonable and timely offer to cure" was improperly rejected (*sub nom. Joc Oil USA v. Consolidated Edison Co. of N.Y.*, 107 Misc.2d 376, 390, 434

---

1. The tanks already contained some other oil, but Con Ed appears to have had no concern over the admixture of the differing sulfur contents. In any event, the efficacy of the independent testing required by the contract was not impaired by the commingling.

2. Most of the *Khamsin* oil was drained from the tanks and sold at $10.75 per barrel. The balance was retained by Con Ed in its mixed form at $10.45 per barrel. The original price in January had been $17.875 per barrel.

3. The plaintiff originally also sought an affirmative injunction to compel Con Ed to accept the *Khamsin* shipment or, alternatively, the *Appollonian* substitute. However, when a preliminary injunction was denied on the ground that the plaintiff had an adequate remedy at law, it amended its complaint to pursue the latter remedy alone.

4. These circumstances included the fact that the preliminary injunction was not denied until April so that, by the time the *Khamsin* oil was sold in May, almost three months had gone by since its rejection.

N.Y.S.2d 623 [Shanley N. Egeth, J.]). The Appellate Division, 84 A.D.2d 970, 447 N.Y.S.2d 572, having unanimously affirmed the judgment entered on this decision, the case is now here by our leave (CPLR 5602, subd. [a], par. 1, cl. [i]).

In support of its quest for reversal, the defendant now asserts that the trial court erred . . . in failing to interpret subdivision (2) of section 2–508 of the Uniform Commercial Code to limit the availability of the right to cure after date of performance to cases in which the seller knowingly made a nonconforming tender and . . . in calculating damages on the basis of the resale of the nonconforming cargo rather than of the substitute offered to replace it. For the reasons which follow, we find [these assertions] unacceptable. . . .

. . . Fairly interpreted, did subdivision (2) of section 2–508 of the Uniform Commercial Code require Con Ed to accept the substitute shipment plaintiff tendered? In approaching this question, we, of course, must remember that a seller's right to cure a defective tender, as allowed by both subdivisions of section 2–508, was intended to act as a meaningful limitation on the absolutism of the old perfect tender rule, under which, no leeway being allowed for any imperfections, there was, as one court put it, just "no room * * * for the doctrine of substantial performance" of commercial obligations (*Mitsubishi Goshi Kaisha v. Aron & Co.*, 16 F.2d 185, 186 [Learned Hand, J.]; see Note, Uniform Commercial Code, § 2–508; Seller's Right to Cure Non–Conforming Goods, 6 Rutgers—Camden L.J. 387–388).

In contrast, to meet the realities of the more impersonal business world of our day, the code, to avoid sharp dealing, expressly provides for the liberal construction of its remedial provisions (§ 1–102) so that "good faith" and the "observance of reasonable commercial standards of fair dealing" be the rule rather than the exception in trade (see § 2–103, subd. [1], par. [b]), "good faith" being defined as "honesty in fact in the conduct or transaction concerned" (Uniform Commercial Code, § 1–201, subd. [19]). As to section 2–508 in particular, the code's Official Comment advises that its mission is to safeguard the seller "against surprise as a result of sudden technicality on the buyer's part" (Uniform Commercial Code, § 2–106, Comment 2; see, also, Peters, Remedies for Breach of Contracts Relating to the Sale of Goods under the Uniform Commercial Code: A Roadmap for Article Two, 73 Yale L.J. 199, 210; 51 N.Y.Jur., Sales, § 101, p. 41).

Section 2–508 may be conveniently divided between provisions for cure offered when "the time for performance has not yet expired" (subd. [1]), a precode concept in this State (*Lowinson v. Newman*, 201 App.Div. 266, 194 N.Y.S. 253), and ones which, by newly introducing the possibility of a seller obtaining "a further reasonable time to substitute a conforming tender" (subd. [2]), also permit cure beyond the date set for performance. In its entirety the section reads as follows:

"(1) Where any tender or delivery by the seller is rejected because nonconforming and the time for performance has not yet expired, the seller may seasonably notify the buyer of his intention to cure and may then within the contract time make a conforming delivery.

"(2) Where the buyer rejects a non-conforming tender which the seller had reasonable grounds to believe would be acceptable with or without money allowance the seller may if he seasonably notifies the buyer have a further reasonable time to substitute a conforming tender."

Since we here confront circumstances in which the conforming tender came after the time of performance, we focus on subdivision (2). On its face, taking its conditions in the order in which they appear, for the statute to apply (1) a buyer must have rejected a nonconforming tender, (2) the seller must have had reasonable grounds to believe this tender would be acceptable (with or without money allowance), and (3) the seller must have "seasonably" notified the buyer of the intention to substitute a conforming tender within a reasonable time.[5]

In the present case, none of these presented a problem. The first one was easily met for it is unquestioned that, at .92%, the sulfur content of the *Khamsin* oil did not conform to the .5% specified in the contract and that it was rejected by Con Ed. The second, the reasonableness of the seller's belief that the original tender would be acceptable, was supported not only by unimpeached proof that the contract's .5% and the refinery certificate's .52% were trade equivalents, but by testimony that, by the time the contract was made, the plaintiff knew Con Ed burned fuel with a content of up to 1%, so that, with appropriate price adjustment, the *Khamsin* oil would have suited its needs even if, at delivery, it was, to the plaintiff's surprise, to test out at .92%. Further, the matter seems to have been put beyond dispute by the defendant's readiness to take the oil at the reduced market price on February 20. Surely, on such a record, the trial court cannot be faulted for having found as a fact that the second condition too had been established.

As to the third, the conforming state of the *Appollonian* oil is undisputed, the offer to tender it took place on February 21, only a day after Con Ed finally had rejected the *Khamsin* delivery and the *Appollonian* substitute then already was en route to the United States, where it was expected in a week and did arrive on March 4, only four days later than expected. Especially since Con Ed pleaded no prejudice (unless the drop in prices could be so regarded), it is almost impossible, given the flexibility of the Uniform Commercial Code definitions of "seasonable" and "reasonable" (n. 7, *supra*), to quarrel with the finding that the remaining requirements of the statute also had been met.

Thus lacking the support of the statute's literal language, the defendant nonetheless would have us limit its application to cases in which a seller *knowingly* makes a nonconforming tender which it has reason to believe the buyer will accept. For this proposition, it relies almost entirely on a critique in Nordstrom, Law of Sales (§ 105), which rationalizes that, since a seller who believes its tender is conforming would have no reason to think in terms of a reduction in the price of the goods, to allow such a seller to cure after the time for performance had passed would make the statutory reference to a money allowance redundant.[6] Nordstrom, interestingly enough, finds it useful to

5. Essentially a factual matter, "seasonable" is defined in subdivision (3) of section 1–204 of the Uniform Commercial Code as "at or within the time agreed or if no time is agreed at or within a reasonable time". At least equally factual in character, a "reasonable time" is left to depend on the "nature, purpose and circumstances" of any action which is to be taken (Uniform Commercial Code, § 1–204, subd. [2]).

6. The premise for such an argument, which ignores the policy of the code to prevent buyers from using insubstantial remediable or price adjustable defects to free themselves from unprofitable bargains (Hawkland, Sales and Bulk Sales Under the Uniform Commercial Code, pp. 120–122), is that the words "with or without money allowance" apply only to sellers who believe their goods will be acceptable with

buttress this position by the somewhat dire prediction, though backed by no empirical or other confirmation, that, unless the right to cure is confined to those whose nonconforming tenders are knowing ones, the incentive of sellers to timely deliver will be undermined. To this it also adds the somewhat moralistic note that a seller who is mistaken as to the quality of its goods does not merit additional time (Nordstrom, *loc. cit.*). Curiously, recognizing that the few decisions extant on this subject have adopted a position opposed to the one for which it contends, Con Ed seeks to treat these as exceptions rather than exemplars of the rule (e.g., *Wilson v. Scampoli,* 228 A.2d 848 (D.C.App.) [goods obtained by seller from their manufacturer in original carton resold unopened to purchaser; seller held within statute though it had no reason to believe the goods defective]; *Appleton State Bank v. Lee,* 33 Wis.2d 690, 148 N.W.2d 1 [seller mistakenly delivered sewing machine of wrong brand but otherwise identical to one sold; held that seller, though it did not know of its mistake, had a right to cure by substitution]).[7]

That the principle for which these cases stand goes far beyond their particular facts cannot be gainsaid. These holdings demonstrate that, in dealing with the application of subdivision (2) of section 2–508, courts have been concerned with the reasonableness of the seller's belief that the goods would be acceptable rather than with the seller's pretender knowledge or lack of knowledge of the defect (*Wilson v. Scampoli, supra;* compare *Zabriskie Chevrolet v. Smith,* 99 N.J.Super. 441, 240 A.2d 195).

It also is no surprise then that the aforementioned decisional history is a reflection of the mainstream of scholarly commentary on the subject....

White and Summers, for instance, put it well, and bluntly. Stressing that the code intended cure to be "a remedy which should be carefully cultivated and developed by the courts" because it "offers the possibility of conforming the law to reasonable expectations and of thwarting the chiseler who seeks to escape from a bad bargain" ..., the authors conclude, as do we, that a seller should have recourse to the relief afforded by subdivision (2) of section 2–508 of the Uniform Commercial Code as long as it can establish that it had reasonable grounds, tested objectively, for its belief that the goods would be accepted (*ibid.,* at p 321). It goes without saying that the test of reasonableness, in this context, must encompass the concepts of "good faith" and "commercial standards of fair dealing" which permeate the code (Uniform Commercial Code, § 1–201, subd. [19]; §§ 1–203, 2–103, subd. [1], par. [b]).

As to the damages issue raised by the defendant, we affirm without reaching the merits. At no stage of the proceedings before the trial court did the defendant object to the plaintiff's proposed method for their calculation....

COOKE, C.J., and JASEN, GABRIELLI, JONES, WACHTLER and MEYER, JJ., concur.

Order affirmed.

---

such an allowance and not to sellers who believe their goods will be acceptable without such an allowance. But, since the words are part of a phrase which speaks of an otherwise unqualified belief that the goods will be acceptable, unless one strains for an opposite interpretation, we find insufficient reason to doubt that it intends to include both those who find a need to offer an allowance and those who do not.

7. The only New York case to deal with this section involved a seller who knowingly tendered a "newer and improved version of the model that was actually ordered" on the contract delivery date. The court held he had reasonable grounds to believe the buyer would accept the newer model (*Bartus v. Riccardi,* 55 Misc.2d 3, 284 N.Y.S.2d 222 [Utica City Ct., Hymes, J.]).

ZABRISKIE CHEVROLET v. SMITH, 99 N.J.Super. 441, 240 A.2d 195 (1968). Zabriskie Chevrolet, a new-car dealership, sold a new 1966 Chevrolet to Smith. As soon as Smith's wife drove off from the dealership, it became evident that the car had very serious problems. As a result, Smith stopped payment on his check and notified Zabriskie that the sale was canceled. Zabriskie then towed the car back, determined that the transmission was defective, replaced the transmission with a transmission it removed from a car on its showroom floor, and asked Smith to take delivery of the repaired car under the contract. When Smith refused to take delivery, Zabriskie brought suit. Held, Zabriskie did not have a right to cure the defective delivery:

"A 'cure' which endeavors by substitution to tender a chattel not within the agreement or contemplation of the parties is invalid.

"For a majority of people the purchase of a new car is a major investment, rationalized by the peace of mind that flows from its dependability and safety. Once their faith is shaken, the vehicle loses not only its real value in their eyes, but becomes an instrument whose integrity is substantially impaired and whose operation is fraught with apprehension. The attempted cure in the present case was ineffective."

MIDWEST MOBILE DIAGNOSTIC IMAGING, L.L.C. v. DYNAMICS CORPORATION OF AMERICA, 965 F.Supp. 1003 (W.D.Mich.1997). "[W]hich standard of conformity applies to cure under an installment contract, perfect tender or substantial impairment? Looking to the rationale behind § 2–612, the court notes that the very purpose of allowing the seller time to cure under this section is to permit it additional time to meet the obligations of the contract. The assumption is that, because the parties have an ongoing relationship, the seller should be given an opportunity to make up the deficiency. This section was not designed to allow the seller to have a never-ending series of chances to bring the item into conformity with the contract. Nor was it enacted to force the buyer to accept a nonconforming product as satisfaction of the contract. Consequently, it is logical that a tender of cure should be required to meet the higher "perfect tender" standard. On its face, however, § 2–612, which generally defines a buyer's right to reject goods under an installment contract, requires only substantial impairment in this context as well. Thus, there is some question as to which is the appropriate standard. The answer is not crucial [here] however, since the trailer in this case fails under *both* standards."

Chapter 24

EXPRESS CONDITIONS

SECTION 1. INTRODUCTION

NOTE ON THE DIFFERENCE BETWEEN
PROMISES AND CONDITIONS

Up to now, the materials in this casebook have chiefly concerned promises. This Chapter concerns another basic set of contractual building blocks—express conditions. As previously discussed, the term "express condition" normally refers to an explicit contractual provision that either: (1) A party to the contract does not come under a duty to perform unless and until some designated state of affairs occurs or fails to occur; or (2) If some designated state of affairs occurs or fails to occur, a party's duty to perform is suspended or terminated. For example, Corporation A may agree to merge with Corporation B, but only on condition that the Commissioner of Internal Revenue rules that the transaction will be tax-free. Or, C may agree to purchase D's house, but only on condition that a termite-inspection report shows no infestation.

Why would parties use an express condition rather than a promise? In some cases, it is because neither party is willing to promise that the state of affairs in question will occur. In the merger hypothetical, for example, neither A nor B would normally be willing to promise that the Commissioner will issue a favorable ruling. In the sale-of-the-house hypothetical, D may not know whether the house is infested with termites, and therefore may not be willing to promise that there is no infestation.

Another possible reason for using express conditions, rather than promises, is to avoid—or at least attempt to avoid—the doctrine of substantial performance. Under that doctrine, if A promises to perform construction for B according to agreed-upon specifications, a slight deviation from the specifications will render A liable to a claim for damages by B, but may not prevent A from holding B to his promise to pay for the job, with an offset for the damages. On the other hand, if the contract expressly states that it is a condition to B's liability to A that A's performance meets the designated specifications, then B's chance of escaping liability for the contract price because of a departure from the specifications is improved.

As the next several cases illustrate, it is not always easy to determine whether a given contractual provision is a promise or a condition. The issue whether a given contractual provision is a promise or a condition is further confused by the fact that under modern contract terminology, where A and B have a contract, A's substantial performance of *his* promises may be an *implied condition* to B's obligation to perform *her* promises. This issue will be taken up in Chapter 25, infra.

The organization of this Chapter is as follows: Section 2 will explore the differences between the operation of promises and conditions. Section 3 concerns issues of interpretation in determining whether a contractual provision is a promise or a condition. Sections 4 and 5 concern two recurring kinds of conditions—conditions of cooperation, in which one party's cooperation is deemed to be a condition to the other party's duty to perform, and conditions of satisfaction, in which a duty to pay for a performance is made conditional on satisfaction with the performance. Section 6 concerns excuses for the nonfulfillment of conditions.

SECTION 2. THE DISTINCTIONS BETWEEN THE OPERATION OF A PROMISE AND THE OPERATION OF A CONDITION

OPPENHEIMER & CO. v. OPPENHEIM, APPEL, DIXON & CO.

Court of Appeals of New York, 1995.
86 N.Y.2d 685, 660 N.E.2d 415, 636 N.Y.S.2d 734.

CIPARICK, Justice.

The parties entered into a letter agreement setting forth certain conditions precedent to the formation and existence of a sublease between them. The agreement provided that there would be no sublease between the parties "unless and until" plaintiff delivered to defendant the prime landlord's written consent to certain "tenant work" on or before a specified deadline. If this condition did not occur, the sublease was to be deemed "null and void." Plaintiff provided only oral notice on the specified date. The issue presented is whether the doctrine of substantial performance applies to the facts of this case. We conclude it does not for the reasons that follow.

I.

In 1986, plaintiff Oppenheimer & Co. moved to the World Financial Center in Manhattan, a building constructed by Olympia & York Company (O & Y). At the time of its move, plaintiff had three years remaining on its existing lease for the 33rd floor of the building known as One New York Plaza. As an incentive to induce plaintiff's move, O & Y agreed to make the rental payments due under plaintiff's rental agreement in the event plaintiff was unable to sublease its prior space in One New York Plaza.

In December 1986, the parties to this action entered into a conditional letter agreement to sublease the 33rd floor. Defendant already leased space on the 29th floor of One New York Plaza and was seeking to expand its operations. The proposed sublease between the parties was attached to the letter agreement. The letter agreement provided that the proposed sublease would be executed only upon the satisfaction of certain conditions. Pursuant to paragraph 1(a) of the agreement, plaintiff was required to obtain "the Prime Landlord's written notice of confirmation, substantially to the effect that [defendant] is a subtenant of the Premises reasonably acceptable to Prime Landlord." If such written notice of confirmation were not obtained "on or before December 30, 1986, then this letter agreement and the Sublease shall be deemed null and void and of no further force and effect and neither party shall have any rights against nor obligations to the other."

Assuming satisfaction of the condition set forth in paragraph 1(a), defendant was required to submit to plaintiff, on or before January 2, 1987, its plans for "tenant work" involving construction of a telephone communication linkage system between the 29th and 33rd floors. Paragraph 4(c) of the letter agreement then obligated plaintiff to obtain the prime landlord's "written consent" to the proposed "tenant work" and deliver such consent to defendant on or before January 30, 1987. Furthermore, if defendant had not received the prime landlord's written consent by the agreed date, both the agreement and the sublease were to be deemed "null and void and of no further force and effect," and neither party was to have "any rights against nor obligations to the other." Paragraph 4(d) additionally provided that, notwithstanding satisfaction of the condition set forth in paragraph 1(a), the parties "agree not to execute and exchange the Sublease unless and until the conditions set forth in paragraph (c) above are timely satisfied."

The parties extended the letter agreement's deadlines in writing and plaintiff timely satisfied the first condition set forth in paragraph 1(a) pursuant to the modified deadline. However, plaintiff never delivered the prime landlord's written consent to the proposed tenant work on or before the modified final deadline of February 25, 1987. Rather, plaintiff's attorney telephoned defendant's attorney on February 25 and informed defendant that the prime landlord's consent had been secured. On February 26, defendant, through its attorney, informed plaintiff's attorney that the letter agreement and sublease were invalid for failure to timely deliver the prime landlord's written consent and that it would not agree to an extension of the deadline. The document embodying the prime landlord's written consent was eventually received by plaintiff on March 20, 1987, 23 days after expiration of paragraph 4(c)'s modified final deadline.

Plaintiff commenced this action for breach of contract, asserting that defendant waived and/or was estopped by virtue of its conduct[1] from insisting on physical delivery of the prime landlord's written consent by the February 25 deadline. Plaintiff further alleged in its complaint that it had substantially performed the conditions set forth in the letter agreement.

At the outset of trial, the court issued an order in *limine* barring any reference to substantial performance of the terms of the letter agreement.

---

1. Plaintiff argued that it could have met the deadline, but failed to do so only because defendant, acting in bad faith, induced plaintiff into delaying delivery of the landlord's consent. Plaintiff asserted that the parties had previously extended the agreement's deadlines as a matter of course.

Nonetheless, during the course of trial, the court permitted the jury to consider the theory of substantial performance, and additionally charged the jury concerning substantial performance. Special interrogatories were submitted. The jury found that defendant had properly complied with the terms of the letter agreement, and answered in the negative the questions whether defendant failed to perform its obligations under the letter agreement concerning submission of plans for tenant work, whether defendant by its conduct waived the February 25 deadline for delivery by plaintiff of the landlord's written consent to tenant work, and whether defendant by its conduct was equitably estopped from requiring plaintiff's strict adherence to the February 25 deadline. Nonetheless, the jury answered in the affirmative the question, "Did plaintiff substantially perform the conditions set forth in the Letter Agreement?," and awarded plaintiff damages of $1.2 million.

Defendant moved for judgment notwithstanding the verdict. Supreme Court granted the motion, ruling as a matter of law that "the doctrine of substantial performance has no application to this dispute, where the Letter Agreement is free of all ambiguity in setting the deadline that plaintiff concededly did not honor." The Appellate Division reversed the judgment on the law and facts, and reinstated the jury verdict. The Court concluded that the question of substantial compliance was properly submitted to the jury and that the verdict should be reinstated because plaintiff's failure to deliver the prime landlord's written consent was inconsequential.

This Court granted defendant's motion for leave to appeal and we now reverse.

II.

Defendant argues that no sublease or contractual relationship ever arose here because plaintiff failed to satisfy the condition set forth in paragraph 4(c) of the letter agreement. Defendant contends that the doctrine of substantial performance is not applicable to excuse plaintiff's failure to deliver the prime landlord's written consent to defendant on or before the date specified in the letter agreement and that the Appellate Division erred in holding to the contrary. Before addressing defendant's arguments and the decision of the court below, an understanding of certain relevant principles is helpful.

A condition precedent is "an act or event, other than a lapse of time, which, unless the condition is excused, must occur before a duty to perform a promise in the agreement arises" (Calamari and Perillo, Contracts S 11–2, at 438 [3d ed.]; see, Restatement [Second] of Contracts S 224; see also, Merritt Hill Vineyards v. Windy Hgts. Vineyard, 61 N.Y.2d 106, 112–113, 472 N.Y.S.2d 592, 460 N.E.2d 1077). Most conditions precedent describe acts or events which must occur before a party is obliged to perform a promise made pursuant to an existing contract, a situation to be distinguished conceptually from a condition precedent to the formation or existence of the contract itself (see, M.K. Metals v. Container Recovery Corp., 645 F.2d 583). In the latter situation, no contract arises "unless and until the condition occurs" (Calamari and Perillo, Contracts § 11–5, at 440 [3d ed]).

Conditions can be express or implied. Express conditions are those agreed to and imposed by the parties themselves. Implied or constructive conditions are those "imposed by law to do justice" (Calamari and Perillo, Contracts § 11–8, at 444 [3d ed]). Express conditions must be literally performed, whereas constructive conditions, which ordinarily arise from language of promise, are subject to the precept that substantial compliance is sufficient. The importance of the distinction has been explained by Professor Williston:

> "Since an express condition depends for its validity on the manifested intention of the parties, it has the same sanctity as the promise itself. Though the court may regret the harshness of such a condition, as it may regret the harshness of a promise, it must, nevertheless, generally enforce the will of the parties unless to do so will violate public policy. Where, however, the law itself has imposed the condition, in absence of or irrespective of the manifested intention of the parties, it can deal with its creation as it pleases, shaping the boundaries of the constructive condition in such a way as to do justice and avoid hardship". (5 Williston, Contracts § 669, at 154 [3d ed].)

In determining whether a particular agreement makes an event a condition courts will interpret doubtful language as embodying a promise or constructive condition rather than an express condition. This interpretive preference is especially strong when a finding of express condition would increase the risk of forfeiture by the obligee (see, Restatement [Second] of Contracts § 227 [1]).

Interpretation as a means of reducing the risk of forfeiture cannot be employed if "the occurrence of the event as a condition is expressed in unmistakable language" (Restatement [Second] of Contracts § 229, comment a, at 185; see, § 227, comment b [where language is clear, "(t)he policy favoring freedom of contract requires that, within broad limits, the agreement of the parties should be honored even though forfeiture results"]). Nonetheless, the nonoccurrence of the condition may yet be excused by waiver, breach or forfeiture. The Restatement posits that "[t]o the extent that the non-occurrence of a condition would cause disproportionate forfeiture, a court may excuse the non-occurrence of that condition unless its occurrence was a material part of the agreed exchange" (Restatement [Second] of Contracts § 229).

Turning to the case at bar, it is undisputed that the critical language of paragraph 4(c) of the letter agreement unambiguously establishes an express condition precedent rather than a promise, as the parties employed the unmistakable language of condition ("if," "unless and until"). There is no doubt of the parties' intent and no occasion for interpreting the terms of the letter agreement other than as written.

Furthermore, plaintiff has never argued, and does not now contend, that the nonoccurrence of the condition set forth in paragraph 4(c) should be excused on the ground of forfeiture.[2] Rather, plaintiff's primary argument from the inception of this litigation has been that defendant waived or was equitably estopped from invoking paragraph 4(c). Plaintiff argued secondarily that it substantially complied with the express condition of delivery of written notice on or before February 25th in that it gave defendant oral notice of consent on the 25th.

---

2. The Restatement defines the term "forfeiture" as "the denial of compensation that results when the obligee loses [its] right to the agreed exchange after [it] has relied substan-tially, as by preparation or performance on the expectation of that exchange" (§ 229, comment b).

Contrary to the decision of the Court below, we perceive no justifiable basis for applying the doctrine of substantial performance to the facts of this case. The flexible concept of substantial compliance "stands in sharp contrast to the requirement of strict compliance that protects a party that has taken the precaution of making its duty expressly conditional" (2 Farnsworth, Contracts § 8.12, at 415 [2d ed 1990]). If the parties "have made an event a condition of their agreement, there is no mitigating standard of materiality or substantiality applicable to the non-occurrence of that event" (Restatement [Second] of Contracts § 237, comment d, at 220). Substantial performance in this context is not sufficient, "and if relief is to be had under the contract, it must be through excuse of the non-occurrence of the condition to avoid forfeiture" (id.; see, Brown–Marx Assocs. v. Emigrant Sav. Bank, 703 F.2d 1361, 1367–1368 [11th Cir.]; see also, Childres, Conditions in the Law of Contracts, 45 NYU L.Rev. 33, 35).

Here, it is undisputed that plaintiff has not suffered a forfeiture or conferred a benefit upon defendant. Plaintiff alludes to a $1 million licensing fee it allegedly paid to the prime landlord for the purpose of securing the latter's consent to the subleasing of the premises. At no point, however, does plaintiff claim that this sum was forfeited or that it was expended for the purpose of accomplishing the sublease with defendant. It is further undisputed that O & Y, as an inducement to effect plaintiff's move to the World Financial Center, promised to indemnify plaintiff for damages resulting from failure to sublease the 33rd floor of One New York Plaza. Consequently, because the critical concern of forfeiture or unjust enrichment is simply not present in this case, we are not presented with an occasion to consider whether the doctrine of substantial performance is applicable, that is, whether the courts should intervene to excuse the nonoccurrence of a condition precedent to the formation of a contract.

The essence of the Appellate Division's holding is that the substantial performance doctrine is universally applicable to all categories of breach of contract, including the nonoccurrence of an express condition precedent. However, as discussed, substantial performance is ordinarily not applicable to excuse the nonoccurrence of an express condition precedent . . .

III.

In sum, the letter agreement provides in the clearest language that the parties did not intend to form a contract "unless and until" defendant received written notice of the prime landlord's consent on or before February 25, 1987. Defendant would lease the 33rd floor from plaintiff only on the condition that the landlord consent in writing to a telephone communication linkage system between the 29th and 33rd floors and to defendant's plans for construction effectuating that linkage. This matter was sufficiently important to defendant that it would not enter into the sublease "unless and until" the condition was satisfied. Inasmuch as we are not dealing here with a situation where plaintiff stands to suffer some forfeiture or undue hardship, we perceive no justification for engaging in a "materiality-of-the-nonoccurrence" analysis. To do so would simply frustrate the clearly expressed intention of the parties. Freedom of contract prevails in an arm's length transaction between sophisticated parties such as these, and in the absence of countervailing public policy concerns there is no reason to relieve them of the consequences of their bargain. If they are dissatisfied with the consequences of their agreement, "the time to say so [was] at the bargaining table" [Maxton Bldrs. v. Lo Galbo, 68 N.Y.2d 373, 509 N.Y.S.2d 507, 502 N.E.2d 184].

Finally, the issue of substantial performance was not for the jury to resolve in this case. A determination whether there has been substantial performance is to be answered, "if the inferences are certain, by the judges of the law" (Jacob & Youngs v. Kent, 230 N.Y. 239, 243, 129 N.E. 889 supra).

Accordingly, the order of the Appellate Division should be reversed, with costs, and the complaint dismissed.

Chief Judge KAYE, C.J., and Judges SIMONS, TITONE, BELLACOSA, SMITH and LEVINE, JJ., concur.

Order reversed, etc.

———

MERRITT HILL VINEYARDS, INC. v. WINDY HEIGHTS VINEYARD, INC.

Court of Appeals of New York, 1984.
61 N.Y.2d 106, 472 N.Y.S.2d 592, 460 N.E.2d 1077.

KAYE, JUDGE.

. . .

In September, 1981, plaintiff, Merritt Hill Vineyards, entered into a written agreement with defendants, Windy Heights Vineyard and its sole shareholder Leon Taylor, to purchase a majority stock interest in respondents' Yates County vineyard, and tendered a $15,000 deposit. The agreement provides that "[i]f the sale contemplated hereby does not close, Taylor shall retain the deposit as liquidated damages unless Taylor or Windy Heights failed to satisfy the conditions specified in Section 3 thereof." Section 3, in turn, lists several "conditions precedent" to which the obligation of purchaser to pay the purchase price and to complete the purchase is subject. Among the conditions are that, by the time of the closing, Windy Heights shall have obtained a title insurance policy in a form satisfactory to Merritt Hill, and Windy Heights and Merritt Hill shall have received confirmation from the Farmers Home Administration that certain mortgages on the vineyard are in effect and that the proposed sale does not constitute a default.

In April, 1982, at the closing, plaintiff discovered that neither the policy nor the confirmation had been issued. Plaintiff thereupon refused to close and demanded return of its deposit. When defendants did not return the deposit, plaintiff instituted this action, asserting two causes of action, one for return of the deposit, and one for approximately $26,000 in consequential damages allegedly suffered as a result of defendants' failure to perform.

Special Term denied plaintiff's motion for summary judgment on both causes of action. The Appellate Division unanimously reversed Special Term's order, granted plaintiff's motion for summary judgment as to the cause of action for return of the deposit, and . . . granted summary judgment in favor of defendants, dismissing plaintiff's second cause of action for consequential damages. Both plaintiff and defendants appealed from that decision. . . .

... [P]laintiff's right to return of its deposit or to consequential damages depends upon whether the undertaking to produce the policy and mortgage confirmation is a promise or a condition.

A promise is "a manifestation of intention to act or refrain from acting in a specified way, so made as to justify a promisee in understanding that a commitment has been made." (Restatement, Contracts 2d, § 2, subd. [1].) A *condition,* by comparison, is "an event, not certain to occur, which must occur, unless its non-occurrence is excused, before performance under a contract becomes due." (Restatement, Contracts 2d, § 224.) Here, the contract requirements of a title insurance policy and mortgage confirmation are expressed as conditions of plaintiff's performance rather than as promises by defendants. The requirements are contained in a section of the agreement entitled "Conditions Precedent to Purchaser's Obligation to Close," which provides that plaintiff's obligation to pay the purchase price and complete the purchase of the vineyard is "subject to" fulfillment of those requirements. No words of promise are employed.* Defendants' agreement to sell the stock of the vineyard, not those conditions, was the promise by defendants for which plaintiff's promise to pay the purchase price was exchanged.

Defendants' failure to fulfill the conditions of section 3 entitles plaintiff to a return of its deposit but not to consequential damages. While a contracting party's failure to fulfill a condition excuses performance by the other party whose performance is so conditioned, it is not, without an independent promise to perform the condition, a breach of contract subjecting the nonfulfilling party to liability for damages (Restatement, Contracts 2d, § 225, subds. [1], [3]; 3A Corbin, Contracts, § 663; 5 Williston, Contracts [Jaeger–3d ed.], § 665). This is in accord with the parties' expressed intent, for section 1 of their agreement provides that if defendants fail to satisfy the conditions of section 3 plaintiff's deposit will not be returned. It does not provide for payment of damages.

On the merits of this case the Appellate Division thus correctly determined that plaintiff was entitled to the return of its deposit but not to consequential damages.

Accordingly, the order of the Appellate Division should be affirmed.

Cooke, C.J., and Jasen, Jones, Wachtler and Meyer, JJ., concur.

Simons, J., taking no part.

Order affirmed, without costs.

––––––

* Plaintiff contends that the failure to produce the policy and confirmation is also a breach of section 5, entitled "Representations, Warranties and Agreements." A provision may be both a condition and a promise, if the parties additionally promise to perform a condition as part of their bargain. Such a promise is not present here. The only provision of section 5 conceivably relevant is that "Windy Heights has good and marketable title to the Property and all other properties and assets * * * as of December 31, 1980". But this is quite different from the conditions of section 3 that a title insurance policy and mortgage confirmation be produced at the closing, which took place in April, 1982. Both the complaint and plaintiff's affidavits are premised on nonperformance of section 3 of the agreement, not section 5. [Footnote by the court.]

SECTION 3.   PROBLEMS OF INTERPRETATION IN DISTINGUISHING BETWEEN CONDITIONS AND PROMISES

HOWARD v. FEDERAL CROP INSURANCE CORP.

United States Court of Appeals, Fourth Circuit, 1976.
540 F.2d 695.

Before Russell, Field and Widener, Circuit Judges.

Widener, Circuit Judge:

Plaintiff-appellants sued to recover for losses to their 1973 tobacco crop due to alleged rain damage. The crops were insured by defendant-appellee, Federal Crop Insurance Corporation (FCIC). Suits were brought in a state court in North Carolina and removed to the United States District Court. The three suits are not distinguishable factually so far as we are concerned here and involve identical questions of law. They were combined for disposition in the district court and for appeal. The district court granted summary judgment for the defendant and dismissed all three actions. We remand for further proceedings. Since we find for the plaintiffs as to the construction of the policy, we express no opinion on the procedural questions.

Federal Crop Insurance Corporation, an agency of the United States, in 1973, issued three policies to the Howards, insuring their tobacco crops, to be grown on six farms, against weather damage and other hazards.

The Howards (plaintiffs) established production of tobacco on their acreage, and have alleged that their 1973 crop was extensively damaged by heavy rains, resulting in a gross loss to the three plaintiffs in excess of $35,000. The plaintiffs harvested and sold the depleted crop and timely filed notice and proof of loss with FCIC, but, prior to inspection by the adjuster for FCIC, the Howards had either plowed or disked under the tobacco fields in question to prepare the same for sowing a cover crop of rye to preserve the soil. When the FCIC adjuster later inspected the fields, he found the stalks had been largely obscured or obliterated by plowing or disking and denied the claims, apparently on the ground that the plaintiffs had violated a portion of the policy which provides that the stalks on any acreage with respect to which a loss is claimed shall not be destroyed until the corporation makes an inspection.

The holding of the district court is best capsuled in its own words:

> "The inquiry here is whether compliance by the insureds with this provision of the policy was a condition precedent to the recovery. The court concludes that it was and that the failure of the insureds to comply worked a forfeiture of benefits for the alleged loss."

... Paragraph 5 of the tobacco endorsement is entitled *Claims*. Pertinent to this case are subparagraphs 5(b) and 5(f), which are as follows:

> "5(b) *It shall be a condition precedent* to the payment of any loss that the insured establish the production of the insured crop on a unit and

that such loss has been directly caused by one or more of the hazards insured against during the insurance period for the crop year for which the loss is claimed, and furnish any other information regarding the manner and extent of loss as may be required by the Corporation. (Emphasis added)"

"5(f) The tobacco stalks on any acreage of tobacco of types 11a, 11b, 12, 13, or 14 with respect to which a loss is claimed *shall not be destroyed until the Corporation makes an inspection.* (Emphasis added)"

The arguments of both parties are predicated upon the same two assumptions. First, if subparagraph 5(f) creates a condition precedent, its violation caused a forfeiture of plaintiffs' coverage. Second, if subparagraph 5(f) creates an obligation (variously called a promise or covenant) upon plaintiffs not to plow under the tobacco stalks, defendant may recover from plaintiffs (either in an original action, or, in this case, by a counterclaim, or as a matter of defense) for whatever damage it sustained because of the elimination of the stalks. However, a violation of subparagraph 5(f) would not, under the second premise, standing alone, cause a forfeiture of the policy.

Generally accepted law provides us with guidelines here. There is a general legal policy opposed to forfeitures. *United States v. One Ford Coach,* 307 U.S. 219, 226, 59 S.Ct. 861, 83 L.Ed. 1249 (1939); *Baca v. Commissioner of Internal Revenue,* 326 F.2d 189, 191 (5th Cir.1964). Insurance policies are generally construed most strongly against the insurer. *Henderson v. Hartford Accident & Indemnity Co.,* 268 N.C. 129, 150 S.E.2d 17, 19 (1966). When it is doubtful whether words create a promise or a condition precedent, they will be construed as creating a promise. *Harris and Harris Const. Co. v. Crain and Denbo, Inc.,* 256 N.C. 110, 123 S.E.2d 590, 595 (1962). The provisions of a contract will not be construed as conditions precedent in the absence of language plainly requiring such construction. *Harris,* 123 S.E.2d at 596. And *Harris,* at 123 S.E.2d 590, 595, cites *Jones v. Palace Realty Co.,* 226 N.C. 303, 37 S.E.2d 906 (1946), and *Restatement of the Law, Contracts,* § 261.

Plaintiffs rely most strongly upon the fact that the term "condition precedent" is included in subparagraph 5(b) but not in subparagraph 5(f). It is true that whether a contract provision is construed as a condition or an obligation does not depend entirely upon whether the word "condition" is expressly used. Appleman, *Insurance Law and Practice* (1972), vol. 6A, § 4144. However, the persuasive force of plaintiffs' argument in this case is found in the use of the term "condition precedent" in subparagraph 5(b) but not in subparagraph 5(f). Thus, it is argued that the ancient maxim to be applied is that the expression of one thing is the exclusion of another. . . .

The *Restatement [First] of the Law of Contracts* states:

"§ 261. INTERPRETATION OF DOUBTFUL WORDS AS PROMISE OR CONDITION.

Where it is doubtful whether words create a promise or an express condition, they are interpreted as creating a promise; but the same words may sometimes mean that one party promises a performance and that the other party's promise is conditional on that performance."

Two illustrations (one involving a promise, the other a condition) are used in the *Restatement:*

"2. A, an insurance company, issues to B a policy of insurance containing promises by A that are in terms conditional on the happening of certain events. The policy contains this clause: 'provided, in case differences shall arise touching any loss, *the matter shall be submitted to impartial arbitrators,* whose award shall be binding on the parties.' This is a promise to arbitrate and does not make an award a condition precedent of the insurer's duty to pay.

3. A, an insurance company, issues to B an insurance policy in usual form containing this clause: 'In the event of disagreement as to the amount of loss it shall be ascertained by two appraisers and an umpire. The loss shall *not be payable until 60 days after the award of the appraisers when such an appraisal is required.*' This provision is not merely a promise to arbitrate differences but makes an award a condition of the insurer's duty to pay in case of disagreement." (Emphasis added)

We believe that subparagraph 5(f) in the policy here under consideration fits illustration 2 rather than illustration 3. Illustration 2 specifies something to be done, whereas subparagraph 5(f) specifies something not to be done. Unlike illustration 3, subparagraph 5(f) does not state any conditions under which the insurance shall "not be payable," or use any words of like import. We hold that the district court erroneously held, on the motion for summary judgment, that subparagraph 5(f) established a condition precedent to plaintiffs' recovery which forfeited the coverage.

From our holding that defendant's motion for summary judgment was improperly allowed, it does not follow the plaintiffs' motion for summary judgment should have been granted, for if subparagraph 5(f) be not construed as a condition precedent, there are other questions of fact to be determined. At this point, we merely hold that the district court erred in holding, on the motion for summary judgment, that subparagraph 5(f) constituted a condition precedent with resulting forfeiture.

The explanation defendant makes for including subparagraph 5(f) in the tobacco endorsement is that it is necessary that the stalks remain standing in order for the Corporation to evaluate the extent of loss and to determine whether loss resulted from some cause not covered by the policy. However, was subparagraph 5(f) inserted because without it the Corporation's opportunities for proof would be more difficult, or because they would be impossible? Plaintiffs point out that the Tobacco Endorsement, with subparagraph 5(f), was adopted in 1970, and crop insurance goes back long before that date. Nothing is shown as to the Corporation's prior 1970 practice of evaluating losses. Such a showing might have a bearing upon establishing defendant's intention in including 5(f). Plaintiffs state, and defendant does not deny, that another division of the Department of Agriculture, or the North Carolina Department, urged that tobacco stalks be cut as soon as possible after harvesting as a means of pest control. Such an explanation might refute the idea that plaintiffs plowed under the stalks for any fraudulent purpose. Could these conflicting directives affect the reasonableness of plaintiffs' interpretation of defendant's prohibition upon plowing under the stalks prior to adjustment?

We express no opinion on these questions because they were not before the district court and are mentioned to us largely by way of argument rather than from the record. No question of ambiguity was raised in the court below or here and no question of the applicability of paragraph 5(c) to this case was alluded to other than in the defendant's pleadings, so we also do not reach those questions. Nothing we say here should preclude FCIC from asserting as a defense that the plowing or disking under of the stalks caused damage to FCIC if, for example, the amount of the loss was thereby made more difficult or impossible to ascertain whether the plowing or disking under was done with bad purpose or innocently. To repeat, our narrow holding is that merely plowing or disking under the stalks does not of itself operate to forfeit coverage under the policy.

The case is remanded for further proceedings not inconsistent with this opinion.

VACATED AND REMANDED.

RESTATEMENT, SECOND, CONTRACTS § 227

[See Selected Source Materials Supplement]

SECTION 4. CONDITIONS OF COOPERATION; PREVENTION; THE IMPLICATION OF A PROMISE FROM AN EXPRESS CONDITION

VANADIUM CORP. v. FIDELITY & DEPOSIT CO.
Circuit Court of Appeals, Second Circuit, 1947.
159 F.2d 105.

CLARK, CIRCUIT JUDGE. This action against a surety on a bond securing performance of a contract of sale of mining leases was originally brought in the Supreme Court of the State of New York and came to the district court below through removal by defendant because of the diverse citizenship of the parties. The principal on the bond, Horace Ray Redington, then intervened as a party defendant. Since the contract of sale was not completed, plaintiff vendee by its terms became entitled to repayment of the consideration paid in advance of $13,000, unless its own acts justified defendants' refusal to make the refund. Accordingly the issues below concerned the defenses raised by defendants that plaintiff had refused that co-operation required by law in obtaining completion of the contract. These defenses, three in number, were upheld as legally sufficient by the District Court against attack by motions before and after verdict and by requests to charge. The jury having found for defendants, this appeal from the resulting judgment brings the issues of the validity of the defenses before us.

The two original mining leases were made in 1939 and 1940 to three lessees, John F. Wade, Thomas F. V. Curran, and Redington, and covered various lands belonging to the Navajo tribe of Indians in the Navajo Reservation in Arizona. The lands produced vanadium-bearing ore, vanadium being a critical war material. Since Indian lands were involved, all transfers required the approval of the Secretary of the Interior. 25 U.S.C.A. § 396a et seq.; 25 CFR § 186.26. The contract here in question was made by Redington with plaintiff on June 3, 1942. By it, in return for the payment of $13,000 which he acknowledged, Redington assigned to plaintiff his interest in the two leases, "subject only to approval by the Secretary of Interior." It also contained a provision that in the event the assignments were not approved, Redington would repay the purchase price and the agreement would be deemed cancelled. Redington further agreed to furnish a bond with appropriate surety for the return of the money in the event that his assignments "aforesaid shall not be approved by the Secretary of Interior of the United States within a period of six (6) months from the date hereof." At the same time Redington executed formal assignments of his interests in the leases, and he and the corporate defendant executed the bond in suit. By the latter the principal and surety bound themselves to return all amounts paid Redington "under protection of this bond." It also provided that plaintiff should be held harmless against all loss or damage arising "by reason of any invalidation of this purchase agreement."

From the beginning, however, it appears that the stumbling block was the unwillingness of the other two owners to go along with plaintiff's plans. But plaintiff was not in the dark as to this situation; while it held only an option from, and before closing with, Redington, it had approached the other owners for a purchase of their interest, and had been refused. After taking the assignments from Redington, plaintiff tried to reopen negotiations with the others, either for purchase or for joint operations of the mines; but its proposals were again repulsed. Under date of June 7, 1942, Curran notified it that Wade, acting for all the owners, had made a contract with the Metals Reserve Corporation (a government corporation) for the entire output of ore from the properties for the duration of the war. Curran added that they would do all possible to get the largest possible tonnage from the leases, on their contract with the Metals Reserve Corporation, and "will welcome any aid you may give that will promote this end." It is defendants' contention that this information as to the prior right of the Metals Reserve Corporation to the output caused plaintiff's desire for the Redington interests to cool; and this disposal of the output obviously ran counter to plaintiff's program of securing a large flow of ore to a government-financed processing plant at Monticello, Utah, being built for operation by plaintiff on a fee basis. Plaintiff denies any lack of co-operation, calling attention to its general offers otherwise appearing as late as August 28, 1942, in a letter of that date to the Assistant Commissioner of Indian Affairs. But so far as an issue of fact was presented, that was resolved by the jury against the plaintiff.

Actually the proof adequately supported the allegations of fact of all the defenses. These were, first, that plaintiff refused reasonable assurances to the Department of an intent to co-operate with Curran and Wade in an amicable operation of the mines; second, that prior to November 18, 1942, it withdrew its request for approval of the assignments and caused the Department to withhold approval; and third, that after November 18, it prevented reconsideration of the disapproval already made. Thus when the Assistant Commissioner notified plaintiff by letter of September 4 of the official intent to disapprove the assignments because of plaintiff's failure to work out an operating agreement with Curran and Wade, plaintiff's immediate reaction was to perfect its rights against the surety by formal demand upon the latter and by request to the Department for final certification of the Secretary's disapproval. True, it acknowledged the communication from the Assistant Commissioner by letter of September 8; but this, like other acts of the plaintiff during the period, was subject to various interpretations, depending upon the background. For in this acknowledgment it expressed regret at the withholding of approval, since it had hoped to increase production of vanadium ore by "our co-operation" with the owners of the leases and that the maximum amount of ore would be removed from the claims, tendered "any assistance that we may properly offer to accomplish that end," and closed by stating that it was "immediately notifying" Redington and taking steps to secure the return of funds it had advanced. Further, there was evidence that in October it refused to give the assurances desired by the Department of its intent to co-operate with the other owners, but indeed went so far as to tell the General Superintendent of the Navajo Service in Arizona of its lack of further interest in the assignments. Accordingly the Assistant Secretary of the Interior, acting on a recommendation from the office of the Department Solicitor reciting that the officers of plaintiff had stated that they were no longer interested in obtaining the assignments, formally disapproved the assignments November 18, 1942.

The evidence is yet more direct on the issue that plaintiff prevented reconsideration of the disapproval after November 18, 1942. Here plaintiff's position is that its rights became fixed on that date and that later reconsideration could not affect them. It is not contested that the Assistant Secretary, on the appeal of Redington and his counsel, was prepared to reconsider the matter if the plaintiff would go along, and so wired plaintiff's president on November 28, saying that the disapproval was "being reconsidered with view to approving assignments. Wire your position," to which plaintiff's answer, November 30, was, "Our position therefore must be to respectfully request no reconsideration of your position." And so the Assistant Secretary on December 3 notified the parties that without "a joint request for reconsideration by both parties to the assignment," no further consideration could be given the matter. Plaintiff now argues that it understood the original assignments and contract to be dead, and hence was refusing merely to enter into an entirely new contract, not interfering with approval of those assignments or preventing fulfillment of the original conditions. But this seems only a different verbalization of its same argument that the time period granted for performance in the contract must be further restricted by an earlier disapproval by the Secretary. Of course it overlooks completely the Assistant Secretary's explicit statement that the action *disapproving* the Redington *assignments* was being reconsidered with a view to approval.

On the record, therefore, there seems to be no doubt of the plaintiff's complete disinterest in the Redington assignments at this time. But clearly it is in error in asserting that the rights of the parties became finally fixed on November 18, 1942. For the explicit provision of the contract, calling for the bond here in question, required only refund of the consideration if the Secretary did not approve within six months, i.e., by December 3, 1942. Nothing is said to suggest that the period is shortened by an earlier notice of disapproval. Particularly under the circumstances here where the Secretary was prepared to reconsider, it would be harsh to add to the contract such a provision which the parties themselves did not choose to incorporate in it. The District Court was correct in considering the third defense as on the same plane as the others.

The question therefore is reduced to that of the extent of plaintiff's legal duty in the premises. Professor Williston says that "wherever the cooperation of the promisee is necessary for the performance of the promise, there is a condition implied in fact that the cooperation will be given." 3 Williston on Contracts, Rev.Ed.1936, § 887A, p. 2495. See to the same effect, § 677, p. 1956; 2 Restatement, Contracts, 1932, § 395, comment c. Here an obligation to attempt in good faith to secure the prerequisite of the Secretary's approval would appear to rest upon both parties. . . . Indeed plaintiff may well have the heavier burden, for, as its counsel contended at the trial, it seems that the assignee must file the assignment for approval and apparently no one else can legally do so. It was surely not the intent of the parties when they made an apparently binding assignment that the plaintiff should have the power to invalidate the assignment by not filing it for approval. On the contrary, it must have been assumed that plaintiff would seasonably file it and in good faith seek its approval. Silverman v. Isaac Goldmann Realty Corp., 232 App.Div. 292, 249 N.Y.S. 505. And plainly plaintiff was obligated to refrain from positive actions to prevent approval by the Secretary. Patterson v. Meyerhofer, 204 N.Y. 96, 97 N.E. 472; Carns v. Bassick, 187 App.Div. 280, 175 N.Y.S. 670; Irving Trust Co. v. Park & Tilford Import Corp., 250 App.Div. 570, 294 N.Y.S. 822. Hence on the facts, as the jury could and did find them, the defendants' contractual duty herein was discharged by plaintiff's breach of a condition precedent. 2 Restatement, Contracts, 1932, § 395.

The court's denial of the plaintiff's various motions and requests to charge and its submission of the case to the jury with a brief, but adequate, charge were therefore without error. . . .

Affirmed.

WINSLOW v. MELL, 48 Wash.2d 581, 295 P.2d 319 (1956). Plaintiff alleged that defendant had broken a contract to finance plaintiff's logging operation on (1) 200 acres of timberland owned by defendant, and (2) an adjoining tract owned by Crown Zellerbach, provided that defendant obtained the timber rights on that tract. At the trial, plaintiff failed to show that defendant had obtained timber rights on the Crown Zellerbach tract. Held, the jury should not have been permitted to consider the claim based on that tract. "The appellant's promise that the respondent could also log the Crown Zellerbach tract was conditioned upon appellant's acquisition of the timber rights. There was no duty on the part of the appellant to acquire the Crown Zellerbach timber so that respondent might log it. Its acquisition was at appellant's option or pleasure."

LACH v. CAHILL, 138 Conn. 418, 85 A.2d 481 (1951). Lach signed an agreement with Cahill to purchase Cahill's house for $18,000, and paid a deposit of $1,000. The contract contained the following provision: "This agreement is contingent upon buyer being able to obtain mortgage in the sum of $12,000 on the premises...." Lach then applied to six banks for a $12,000 mortgage, but was denied. thereafter, Lach wrote to Cahill that he was unable to secure a mortgage in the amount of $12,000, and requested the return of the deposit. Cahill offered to take back a purchase–money mortgage payable on demand, or to obtain a mortgage from another person, but he specified no terms. Lach had already made a deposit on another house, and declined Cahill's offer. Lach then sued for the return of his deposit. The trial court held for Lach. Affirmed.

" ... The decisive issues in the case are whether the ability of the plaintiff to secure a $12,000 mortgage was a condition precedent to his duty to perform his promise to purchase and whether he made a reasonable effort to secure the mortgage.

"The ... language used, read in the light of the situation of the parties, expressed an intention that the plaintiff should not be held to an agreement to purchase unless he could secure a mortgage for $12,000 on reasonable terms as to the amount and time of instalment payments.

"The condition in the contract implied a promise by the plaintiff that he would make reasonable efforts to secure a suitable mortgage.... The performance or nonperformance of this implied promise was a matter for the determination of the trial court. The conclusion reached upon the facts was proper."

SECTION 5.   CONDITIONS OF SATISFACTION

INTRODUCTORY NOTE

Often a contract provides that one party, A, need not pay for the performance of the other party, B, unless A is satisfied with the performance. The question then arises whether A may escape liability even though his dissatisfaction, while honest, is unreasonable. In the determination of this question, the following factors would probably be influential:

(1) The language used. Did the contract say, for example, that A must be "personally satisfied," or merely that the performance must be "satisfactory"?

(2) The degree to which it is possible to apply an objective standard to the performance in question. For example, there is a decided difference in this respect between a contract to install a furnace and a contract to paint a portrait. The inclination to interpret "satisfaction" as the actual personal satisfaction of A would obviously be stronger in the later case.

(3) The degree to which A will be enriched at B's expense if the contract is interpreted to require A's personal satisfaction. If A retains and uses in his house a furnace installed by B, and seeks to escape liability to pay anything for the furnace by declaring that he is not satisfied with its performance, the

case would be a very strong one for B. Recovery in B's favor might be supported either on the basis of interpretation—the word "satisfaction" being interpreted to mean satisfaction of a reasonable person—or on the theory that one who has failed to comply with a condition may nevertheless recover the value of the benefit conferred on the other party. The case is less strong for B if he has, for example, painted a portrait under a contract whereby A is not to pay unless he is satisfied, and A refuses to accept the portrait. Here B has lost the value of his own performance, but A has not been enriched.

(4) The degree of forfeiture that will be imposed on B if A escapes liability to pay for B's performance.

The chief lesson that the draftsman should derive from the cases in this field is that even though the words used in the contract may seem clearly to imply that the actual, personal satisfaction of the defendant is a condition to his liability, in certain cases the courts may nevertheless construe the contract to require only such performance as would satisfy a reasonable person.

McCARTNEY v. BADOVINAC, 62 Colo. 76, 160 P. 190 (1916). A diamond had been stolen from Mrs. Ragsdale. Her husband, Dr. Ragsdale, accused Mrs. McCartney of the theft. Mr. McCartney then hired Badovinac, a private detective, to investigate the affair. Badovinac was to receive $500 for his services when he had "to the satisfaction of the said McCartney" determined whether the diamond was stolen, and if so, who had taken it. Badovinac's investigations led him to the uncomforting conclusion that Mrs. McCartney had in fact stolen the diamond, and he put his proofs before McCartney. On McCartney's refusal to pay, Badovinac brought suit. The case was tried without a jury. The trial judge found that Badovinac had clearly established that Mrs. McCartney had taken the jewel. McCartney, however, testified on the stand that he was not satisfied that his wife was the thief. Held, McCartney's statement that he is not satisfied is not conclusive of the issue. On these facts the trial judge properly found that McCartney's answers on the stand were "a mere subterfuge and pretext." A judgment for Badovinac was affirmed.

MORIN BUILDING PRODUCTS CO. v. BAYSTONE CONSTRUCTION, INC.

United States Court of Appeals, Seventh Circuit, 1983.
717 F.2d 413.

Before POSNER and COFFEY, CIRCUIT JUDGES and FAIRCHILD, SENIOR CIRCUIT JUDGE.

POSNER, CIRCUIT JUDGE.

This appeal from a judgment for the plaintiff in a diversity suit requires us to interpret Indiana's common law of contracts. General Motors, which is not a party to this case, hired Baystone Construction, Inc., the defendant, to build an addition to a Chevrolet plant in Muncie, Indiana. Baystone hired Morin Building Products Company, the plaintiff, to supply and erect the aluminum walls for the addition. The contract required that the exterior siding of the walls be of "aluminum type 3003, not less than 18 B & S gauge, with a mill finish and stucco embossed surface texture to match finish and texture of existing metal siding." The contract also provided "that all work shall be done subject to the final approval of the Architect or Owner's [General Motors'] authorized agent, and his decision in matters relating to artistic effect shall be final, if within the terms of the Contract Documents"; and that "should any dispute arise as to the quality or fitness of materials or workmanship, the decision as to acceptability shall rest strictly with the Owner, based on the requirement that all work done or materials furnished shall be first class in every respect. What is usual or customary in erecting other buildings shall in no wise enter into any consideration or decision."

Morin put up the walls. But viewed in bright sunlight from an acute angle the exterior siding did not give the impression of having a uniform finish, and General Motors' representative rejected it. Baystone removed Morin's siding and hired another subcontractor to replace it. General Motors approved the replacement siding. Baystone refused to pay Morin the balance of the contract price ($23,000) and Morin brought this suit for the balance, and won.

The only issue on appeal is the correctness of a jury instruction which, after quoting the contractual provisions requiring that the owner (General Motors) be satisfied with the contractor's (Morin's) work, states: "Notwithstanding the apparent finality of the foregoing language, however, the general rule applying to satisfaction in the case of contracts for the construction of commercial buildings is that the satisfaction clause must be determined by objective criteria. Under this standard, the question is not whether the owner was satisfied in fact, but whether the owner, as a reasonable person, should have been satisfied with the materials and workmanship in question." There was much evidence that General Motors' rejection of Morin's exterior siding had been totally unreasonable. Not only was the lack of absolute uniformity in the finish of the walls a seemingly trivial defect given the strictly utilitarian purpose of the building that they enclosed, but it may have been inevitable; "mill finish sheet" is defined in the trade as "sheet having a nonuniform finish which may vary from sheet to sheet and within a sheet, and may not be entirely free from stains or oil." If the instruction was correct, so was the judgment. But if the instruction was incorrect—if the proper standard is not whether a reasonable man would have been satisfied with Morin's exterior siding but whether General Motors' authorized representative in fact was— then there must be a new trial to determine whether he really was dissatisfied, or whether he was not and the rejection therefore was in bad faith.

Some cases hold that if the contract provides that the seller's performance must be to the buyer's satisfaction, his rejection—however unreasonable—of the seller's performance is not a breach of the contract unless the rejection is in bad faith. See, e.g., *Stone Mountain Properties, Ltd. v. Helmer*, 139 Ga.App. 865, 869, 229 S.E.2d 779, 783 (1976). But most cases conform to the position stated in section 228 of the Restatement (Second) of Contracts (1979): if "it is practicable to determine whether a reasonable person in the position of the obligor would be satisfied, an interpretation is preferred under which the condition [that the obligor be satisfied with the obligee's performance] occurs if such a reasonable person in the position of the obligor would be satisfied." See Farnsworth, Contracts 556–59 (1982); Annot., 44 A.L.R.2d

1114, 1117, 1119–20 (1955). *Indiana Tri—City Plaza Bowl, Inc. v. Estate of Glueck*, 422 N.E.2d 670, 675 (Ind.App.1981), consistently with hints in earlier Indiana cases, see *Andis v. Personett*, 108 Ind. 202, 206, 9 N.E. 101, 103 (1886); *Semon, Bache & Co. v. Coppes, Zook & Mutschler Co.*, 35 Ind.App. 351, 355, 74 N.E. 41, 43 (1905), adopts the majority position as the law of Indiana.

We do not understand the majority position to be paternalistic; and paternalism would be out of place in a case such as this, where the subcontractor is a substantial multistate enterprise. The requirement of reasonableness is read into a contract not to protect the weaker party but to approximate what the parties would have expressly provided with respect to a contingency that they did not foresee, if they had foreseen it. Therefore the requirement is not read into every contract, because it is not always a reliable guide to the parties' intentions. In particular, the presumption that the performing party would not have wanted to put himself at the mercy of the paying party's whim is overcome when the nature of the performance contracted for is such that there are no objective standards to guide the court. It cannot be assumed in such a case that the parties would have wanted a court to second-guess the buyer's rejection. So "the reasonable person standard is employed when the contract involves commercial quality, operative fitness, or mechanical utility which other knowledgeable persons can judge.... The standard of good faith is employed when the contract involves personal aesthetics or fancy." *Indiana Tri–City Plaza Bowl, Inc. v. Estate of Glueck, supra*, 422 N.E.2d at 675; see also *Action Engineering v. Martin Marietta Aluminum*, 670 F.2d 456, 460–61 (3d Cir.1982).

We have to decide which category the contract between Baystone and Morin belongs in. The particular in which Morin's aluminum siding was found wanting was its appearance, which may seem quintessentially a matter of "personal aesthetics," or as the contract put it, "artistic effect." But it is easy to imagine situations where this would not be so. Suppose the manager of a steel plant rejected a shipment of pig iron because he did not think the pigs had a pretty shape. The reasonable-man standard would be applied even if the contract had an "acceptability shall rest strictly with the Owner" clause, for it would be fantastic to think that the iron supplier would have subjected his contract rights to the whimsy of the buyer's agent. At the other extreme would be a contract to paint a portrait, the buyer having reserved the right to reject the portrait if it did not satisfy him. Such a buyer wants a portrait that will please him rather than a jury, even a jury of connoisseurs, so the only question would be his good faith in rejecting the portrait. *Gibson v. Cranage*, 39 Mich. 49 (1878).

This case is closer to the first example than to the second. The building for which the aluminum siding was intended was a factory—not usually intended to be a thing of beauty. That aesthetic considerations were decidedly secondary to considerations of function and cost is suggested by the fact that the contract specified mill-finish aluminum, which is unpainted. There is much debate in the record over whether it is even possible to ensure a uniform finish within and among sheets, but it is at least clear that mill finish usually is not uniform. If General Motors and Baystone had wanted a uniform finish they would in all likelihood have ordered a painted siding. Whether Morin's siding achieved a reasonable uniformity amounting to satisfactory commercial quality was susceptible of objective judgment; in the language of the Restatement, a reasonableness standard was "practicable."

But this means only that a requirement of reasonableness would be read into this contract if it contained a standard owner's satisfaction clause, which it did not; and since the ultimate touchstone of decision must be the intent of the parties to the contract we must consider the actual language they used. The contract refers explicitly to "artistic effect," a choice of words that may seem deliberately designed to put the contract in the "personal aesthetics" category whatever an outside observer might think. But the reference appears as number 17 in a list of conditions in a general purpose form contract. And the words "artistic effect" are immediately followed by the qualifying phrase, "if within the terms of the Contract Documents," which suggests that the "artistic effect" clause is limited to contracts in which artistic effect is one of the things the buyer is aiming for; it is not clear that he was here. The other clause on which Baystone relies, relating to the quality or fitness of workmanship and materials, may seem all-encompassing, but it is qualified by the phrase, "based on the requirement that all work done or materials furnished shall be first class in every respect"—and it is not clear that Morin's were not. This clause also was not drafted for this contract; it was incorporated by reference to another form contract (the Chevrolet Division's "Contract General Conditions"), of which it is paragraph 35. We do not disparage form contracts, without which the commercial life of the nation would grind to a halt. But we are left with more than a suspicion that the artistic-effect and quality-fitness clauses in the form contract used here were not intended to cover the aesthetics of a mill-finish aluminum factory wall.

If we are right, Morin might prevail even under the minority position, which makes good faith the only standard but presupposes that the contract conditioned acceptance of performance on the buyer's satisfaction in the particular respect in which he was dissatisfied. Maybe this contract was not intended to allow General Motors to reject the aluminum siding on the basis of artistic effect. It would not follow that the contract put Morin under no obligations whatsoever with regard to uniformity of finish. The contract expressly required it to use aluminum having "a mill finish . . . to match finish . . . of existing metal siding." The jury was asked to decide whether a reasonable man would have found that Morin had used aluminum sufficiently uniform to satisfy the matching requirement. This was the right standard if, as we believe, the parties would have adopted it had they foreseen this dispute. It is unlikely that Morin intended to bind itself to a higher and perhaps unattainable standard of achieving whatever perfection of matching that General Motors' agent insisted on, or that General Motors would have required Baystone to submit to such a standard. Because it is difficult—maybe impossible—to achieve a uniform finish with mill-finish aluminum, Morin would have been running a considerable risk of rejection if it had agreed to such a condition, and it therefore could have been expected to demand a compensating increase in the contract price. This would have required General Motors to pay a premium to obtain a freedom of action that it could not have thought terribly important, since its objective was not aesthetic. If a uniform finish was important to it, it could have gotten such a finish by specifying painted siding.

All this is conjecture; we do not know how important the aesthetics were to General Motors when the contract was signed or how difficult it really would have been to obtain the uniformity of finish it desired. The fact that General Motors accepted the replacement siding proves little, for there is evidence that the replacement siding produced the same striped effect, when viewed from an acute angle in bright sunlight, that Morin's had. When in doubt on a difficult issue of state law it is only prudent to defer to the view of the district judge, *Murphy v. White Hen Pantry Co.,* 691 F.2d 350, 354 (7th Cir.1982), here an experienced Indiana lawyer who thought this the type of contract where the buyer cannot unreasonably withhold approval of the seller's performance.

Lest this conclusion be thought to strike at the foundations of freedom of contract, we repeat that if it appeared from the language or circumstances of the contract that the parties really intended General Motors to have the right to reject Morin's work for failure to satisfy the private aesthetic taste of General Motors' representative, the rejection would have been proper even if unreasonable. But the contract is ambiguous because of the qualifications with which the terms "artistic effect" and "decision as to acceptability" are hedged about, and the circumstances suggest that the parties probably did not intend to subject Morin's rights to aesthetic whim.

AFFIRMED.

MATTEI v. HOPPER

[Chapter 2, supra]

RESTATEMENT, SECOND, CONTRACTS § 227, ILLUSTRATIONS 5–8: "5. A contracts with B to repair B's building for $20,000, payment to be made 'on the satisfaction of C, B's architect, and the issuance of his certificate.' A makes the repairs, but C refuses to issue his certificate, and explains why he is not satisfied. Other experts in the field consider A's performance to be satisfactory and disagree with C's explanation. A has no claim against B. . . . If C is honestly not satisfied, B is under no duty to pay A, and it makes no difference if his dissatisfaction was not reasonable.

"6. The facts being otherwise as stated in Illustration 5, C refuses to issue his certificate although he admits that he is satisfied. A has a claim against B for $20,000. The quoted language will be interpreted so that the requirement of the certificate is merely evidentiary and the condition occurs when there is, as here, adequate evidence that C is honestly satisfied.

"7. The facts being otherwise as stated in Illustration 5, C does not make a proper inspection of the work and gives no reasons for his dissatisfaction. A has a claim against B for $20,000. In using the quoted language, A and B assumed that C would exercise an honest judgment and by failing to make a proper inspection, C did not exercise such a judgment. . . .

"8. The facts being otherwise as stated in Illustration 5, C makes a gross mistake with reference to the facts on which his refusal to give a certificate is based. A has a claim against B for $20,000. In using the quoted language, A and B assumed that C would exercise his judgment without a gross mistake as to the facts. . . . ''

SECTION 6.   EXCUSE

AETNA CASUALTY AND SURETY CO. v. MURPHY

Supreme Court of Connecticut, 1988.
206 Conn. 409, 538 A.2d 219.

PETERS, CHIEF JUSTICE.

The sole issue in this appeal is whether an insured who belatedly gives notice of an insurable claim can nonetheless recover on the insurance contract by rebutting the presumption that his delay has been prejudicial to the insurance carrier. The plaintiff, Aetna Casualty and Surety Company, brought an action against the defendant, George A. Murphy III, to recover for damage he allegedly caused to a building it had insured. The defendant then filed a third party complaint impleading his comprehensive liability insurer, Federal Insurance Company, Chubb Group of Insurance Companies (hereinafter Chubb), as third party defendant. Chubb successfully moved for summary judgment on the ground that Murphy, the defendant and third party plaintiff, had inexcusably and unreasonably delayed in complying with the notice provisions of the insurance contract. The defendant appeals from this judgment. We find no error.

The underlying facts are undisputed. The defendant, George A. Murphy III, a dentist, terminated a lease with Hopmeadow Professional Center Associates on or about November 30, 1982. The manner in which he had dismantled his office gave rise to a claim for damages to which the plaintiff, Aetna Casualty and Surety Company, became subrogated. Although served with the plaintiff's complaint on November 21, 1983, the defendant gave no notice of the existence of this claim to Chubb until January 10, 1986. The motion to implead Chubb as third party defendant was filed on May 14, 1986, and granted on June 2, 1986.

Chubb moved for summary judgment on its three special defenses,* alleging Murphy's noncompliance with the terms of his insurance policy. Its first claim was that it was entitled to judgment because Murphy had ignored two provisions in the Chubb policy imposing notice requirements on its policyholders. The first of these provisions states: "In the event of an occurrence, written notice . . . shall be given by or for the insured to the company . . . as soon as practicable." The other states: "If claim is made or suit is brought against the insured, the insured shall immediately forward to

---

* Chubb, the third party defendant, had filed three special defenses, although the trial court ruled on only one. The first special defense relied on Murphy's admitted failure to give written notice of loss as soon as practicable and to forward notice of the claim against him immediately upon its filing by the plaintiff.

The second and third special defenses related to questions of coverage: whether the loss suffered by Murphy was excluded as having been "expected or intended from the standpoint of the insured" or as falling outside the policy definitions of "occurrence."

the company every demand, notice, summons, or other process received by him or his representative." In his answer to Chubb's special defenses, Murphy admitted his failure to comply with these provisions. Accordingly, his affidavit opposing summary judgment raised no question of fact but relied on his argument that, as a matter of law, an insurer may not deny coverage because of late notice without a showing, on its part, that it has been prejudiced by its insured's delay.

The trial court granted Chubb's motion for summary judgment on its first special defense. It found that Murphy's two year delay in giving notice to Chubb was inexcusable and unreasonable, and concluded that such a delay "voids coverage and insurer's duties under the contract [of insurance]...."

On appeal, Murphy challenges only the trial court's conclusion of law. Despite his inexcusable and unreasonable delay in giving notice, he maintains that he is entitled to insurance coverage because Chubb has failed to allege or to show prejudice because of his late notice.

As Murphy concedes, the trial court's decision accurately reflects numerous holdings of this court that, absent waiver, an unexcused, unreasonable delay in notification constitutes a failure of condition that entirely discharges an insurance carrier from any further liability on its insurance contract....

In our appraisal of the continued vitality of this line of cases, it is noteworthy that they do not reflect a searching analysis of what role prejudice, or its absence, should play in the enforcement of such standard clauses in insurance policies. That issue was put on the table, but not resolved, by a vigorous dissent in *Plasticrete Corporation v. American Policyholders Ins. Co.,* 184 Conn. 231, 240–44, 439 A.2d 968 (1981) (*Bogdanski, J.,* dissenting). The time has come for us to address it squarely.

We are confronted, in this case, by a conflict between two competing principles in the law of contracts. On the one hand, the law of contracts supports the principle that contracts should be enforced as written, and that contracting parties are bound by the contractual provisions to which they have given their assent. Among the provisions for which the parties may bargain are clauses that impose conditions upon contractual liability. "If the occurrence of a condition is required by the agreement of the parties, rather than as a matter of law, a rule of strict compliance traditionally applies." E. Farnsworth, Contracts (1982) § 8.3, p. 544; see *Grenier v. Compratt Construction Co.,* 189 Conn. 144, 148, 454 A.2d 1289 (1983); *Brauer v. Freccia,* 159 Conn. 289, 293–94, 268 A.2d 645 (1970); *Strimiska v. Yates,* 158 Conn. 179, 185–86, 257 A.2d 814 (1969). On the other hand, the rigor of this traditional principle of strict compliance has increasingly been tempered by the recognition that the occurrence of a condition may, in appropriate circumstances, be excused in order to avoid a 'disproportionate forfeiture.' See, e.g., 2 Restatement (Second), Contracts (1981) § 229;** *Johnson Controls, Inc. v. Bowes,*

** The Restatement (Second) of Contracts (1981) § 229, entitled "Excuse of a Condition to Avoid Forfeiture," provides: "To the extent that the non-occurrence of a condition would cause disproportionate forfeiture, a court may excuse the non-occurrence of that condition unless its occurrence was a material part of the agreed exchange."

Comment b elaborates on the concept of "disproportionate forfeiture" as follows: "The rule stated in the present Section is, of necessity, a flexible one, and its application is within the sound discretion of the court. Here, as in § 227(1), 'forfeiture' is used to refer to the denial of compensation that results when the obligee loses his right to the agreed exchange after he has relied substantially, as by prepara-

381 Mass. 278, 280, 409 N.E.2d 185 (1980); 3A A. Corbin, Contracts (1960 & Sup.1984) § 754; E. Farnsworth, supra, § 8.7, pp. 570–71; 5 S. Williston, Contracts (3d Ed. Jaeger 1961) §§ 769 through 811.

In numerous cases, this court has held that, especially in the absence of conduct that is "wilful," a contracting party may, despite his own departure from the specifications of his contract, enforce the obligations of the other party with whom he has dealt in good faith. In construction contracts, a builder's deviation from contract specifications, even if such a departure is conscious and intentional, will not totally defeat the right to recover in an action against the owner on the contract. *Grenier v. Compratt Construction Co.,* supra, 148–49, 454 A.2d 1289; *Vincenzi v. Cerro,* 186 Conn. 612, 615, 442 A.2d 1352 (1982). In contracts for the sale of real property, the fact that a contract states a date for performance does not necessarily make time of the essence. *Kakalik v. Bernardo,* 184 Conn. 386, 392, 439 A.2d 1016 (1981); see *Ravitch v. Stollman Poultry Farms, Inc.,* 165 Conn. 135, 148, 328 A.2d 711 (1973). A purchaser of real property does not, despite his knowing default, forfeit the right to seek restitution of sums of money earlier paid under the contract of sale, even when such payments are therein characterized as liquidated damages. *Vines v. Orchard Hills, Inc.,* 181 Conn. 501, 509, 435 A.2d 1022 (1980); *Pierce v. Staub,* 78 Conn. 459, 466, 62 A. 760 (1906). Finally, despite a failure to deliver contract goods, a seller need not pay an amount contractually designated as liquidated damages to a buyer who has suffered no damages attributable to the seller's breach. *Norwalk Door Closer Co. v. Eagle Lock & Screw Co.,* 153 Conn. 681, 689, 220 A.2d 263 (1966).

This case law demonstrates that, in appropriate circumstances, a contracting party, despite his own default, may be entitled to relief from the rigorous enforcement of contract provisions that would otherwise amount to a forfeiture. On the question of what circumstances warrant such relief, no better guidelines have ever been proffered than those articulated by Judge Benjamin Cardozo in the celebrated case of *Jacob & Youngs, Inc. v. Kent,* 230 N.Y. 239, 129 N.E. 889 (1921). Discussing the interpretation of contracts to ascertain how the parties intended to govern their contractual relationship, Cardozo first notes that "[t]here will be no assumption of a [contractual] purpose to visit venial faults with oppressive retribution." Id., 242, 129 N.E. 889. The opinion then continues: "Those who think more of symmetry and logic in the development of legal rules than of practical adaptation to the attainment of a just result will be troubled by a classification where the lines of division are so wavering and blurred. Something, doubtless, may be said on the score of consistency and certainty in favor of a stricter standard. The courts have balanced such considerations against those of equity and fairness, and found the latter to be the weightier.... Where the line is to be drawn between the important and the trivial cannot be settled by a formula. 'In the nature of the case precise boundaries are impossible' (2 Williston on Contracts, sec. 841). The same omission may take on one aspect or another

tion or performance on the expectation of that exchange. See Comment b to § 227. The extent of the forfeiture in any particular case will depend on the extent of that denial of compensation. In determining whether the forfeiture is 'disproportionate,' a court must weigh the extent of the forfeiture by the obligee against the importance to the obligor of the risk from which he sought to be protected and the degree to which that protection will be lost if the nonoccurrence of the condition is excused to the extent required to prevent forfeiture. *The character of the agreement may, as in the case of insurance agreements, affect the rigor with which the requirement is applied.*" (Emphasis added.)

according to its setting.... The question is one of degree, to be answered, if there is doubt, by the triers of the facts ... and, if the inferences are certain, by the judges of the law.... We must weigh the purpose to be served, the desire to be gratified, the excuse for deviation from the letter, the cruelty of enforced adherence. Then only can we tell whether literal fulfilment is to be implied by law as a condition."*** Id., 242–43, 129 N.E. 889.

In the setting of this case, three considerations are central. First, the contractual provisions presently at issue are contained in an insurance policy that is a "contract of adhesion," the parties to this form contract having had no occasion to bargain about the consequences of delayed notice. Second, enforcement of these notice provisions will operate as a forfeiture because the insured will lose his insurance coverage without regard to his dutiful payment of insurance premiums. Third, the insurer's legitimate purpose of guaranteeing itself a fair opportunity to investigate accidents and claims can be protected without the forfeiture that results from presuming, irrebuttably, that late notice invariably prejudices the insurer.

There can be no question that the insurance policy in this case is a "contract of adhesion." That term was first introduced into American legal vocabulary by Professor Edwin Patterson, who noted that life insurance contracts are contracts of adhesion because "[t]he contract is drawn up by the insurer and the insured, who merely 'adheres' to it, has little choice as to its terms." E. Patterson, "The Delivery of a Life–Insurance Policy," 33 Harv. L.Rev. 198, 222 (1919). Standardized contracts of insurance continue to be prime examples of contracts of adhesion, whose most salient feature is that they are not subject to the normal bargaining processes of ordinary contracts. *Nationwide Ins. Co. v. Gode,* 187 Conn. 386, 404, 446 A.2d 1059 (1982) (*Shea, J.,* dissenting); *Weaver Bros., Inc. v. Chappel,* 684 P.2d 123, 125 (Alaska 1984); *Cooper v. Government Employees Ins. Co.,* 51 N.J. 86, 93, 237 A.2d 870 (1968); *Great American Ins. Co. v. C.G. Tate Construction Co.,* 303 N.C. 387, 392–93, 279 S.E.2d 769 (1981); *Brakeman v. Potomac Ins. Co.,* 472 Pa. 66, 72–73, 371 A.2d 193 (1977); F. Kessler, "Contracts of Adhesion—Some Thoughts about Freedom of Contract," 43 Colum.L.Rev. 629, 631–32 (1943). The fact that the notice provisions in the Chubb insurance policy were an inconspicuous part of a printed form; cf. General Statutes §§ 42a–1–201(10) and 42a–2–316(2); supports the characterization of these clauses as a "contract of adhesion." Nothing in the record suggests that they were brought to Murphy's attention or that, if they had been, their terms would have been subject to negotiation.

It is equally clear that literal enforcement of the notice provisions in this case will discharge Chubb from any further liability to Murphy with regard to the present claims for insurance coverage. That indeed is the necessary purport of Chubb's special defense and the consequence of the trial court's ruling on its motion for summary judgment. The operative effect of noncompliance with the notice provisions is a forfeiture of the interests of the insured that is, in all likelihood, disproportionate. *Johnson Controls, Inc. v. Bowes,* supra, 381 Mass. at 280–81, 409 N.E.2d 185.

*** The court's opinion in *Jacob & Youngs, Inc. v. Kent,* 230 N.Y. 239, 243, 129 N.E. 889 (1921), suggests that the parties may, by express contractual language, "effectuate a purpose that performance of every term shall be a condition of recovery." That observation is not easy to reconcile with the fact that the record in the case discloses the existence of a clause specifically permitting rejection, whenever discovered, of any work of the contractor that failed "fully" to conform with contract specifications "in every respect." See J. Dawson, W. Harvey & S. Henderson, Contracts and Contract Remedies (4th Ed.1982) pp. 816–17.

In determining whether an insured is entitled to relief from such a disproportionate forfeiture, loss of coverage must be weighed against an insurer's legitimate interest in protection from stale claims. "The purpose of a policy provision requiring the insured to give the company prompt notice of an accident or claim is to give the insurer an opportunity to make a timely and adequate investigation of all the circumstances.... And further, if the insurer is thus given the opportunity for a timely investigation, reasonable compromises and settlements may be made, thereby avoiding prolonged and unnecessary litigation." 8 J. Appleman, Insurance Law and Practice (Rev.Ed. 1981) § 4731, pp. 2–5. If this legitimate purpose can be protected by something short of automatic enforcement of the notice provisions, then their strict enforcement is unwarranted.

In our judgment, a proper balance between the interests of the insurer and the insured requires a factual inquiry into whether, in the circumstances of a particular case, an insurer has been prejudiced by its insured's delay in giving notice of an event triggering insurance coverage. If it can be shown that the insurer suffered no material prejudice from the delay, the nonoccurrence of the condition of timely notice may be excused because it is not, in Restatement terms, "a material part of the agreed exchange." Literal enforcement of notice provisions when there is no prejudice is no more appropriate than literal enforcement of liquidated damages clauses when there are no damages. *Norwalk Door Closer Co. v. Eagle Lock & Screw Co.,* supra, 153 Conn. at 689, 220 A.2d 263.

A significant number of cases in other jurisdictions lend support to our conclusion that, absent a showing of material prejudice, an insured's failure to give timely notice does not discharge the insurer's continuing duty to provide insurance coverage. Most of these decisions place the burden of proof on the issue of prejudice on the insurer.... In a few jurisdictions, although prejudice from delay is presumed, that presumption is rebuttable if the insured can demonstrate an actual lack of material prejudice.... By contrast to these cases which afford some latitude for factual inquiry into prejudice, some jurisdictions continue to enforce delayed notice provisions literally....

In light of existing related precedents in this jurisdiction, although we are persuaded that the existence or nonexistence of prejudice from delayed notice should be determined on a factual basis, the burden of establishing lack of prejudice must be borne by the insured. It is the insured who is seeking to be excused from the consequences of a contract provision with which he has concededly failed to comply. His position is akin to that of the defaulting purchaser of real property in *Vines v. Orchard Hills, Inc.,* supra, 181 Conn. at 510, 435 A.2d 1022, where we held that, "[t]o prove unjust enrichment, in the ordinary case, the purchaser, because he is the party in breach, must prove that the damages suffered by his seller are less than the moneys received from the purchaser.... It may not be easy for the purchaser to prove the extent of the seller's damages, it may even be strategically advantageous for the seller to come forward with relevant evidence of the losses he has incurred and may expect to incur on account of the buyer's breach. Nonetheless, only if the breaching party satisfies his burden of proof that the innocent party has sustained a net gain may a claim for unjust enrichment be sustained." Principles of unjust enrichment and restitution bear a family resemblance to those involved in considerations of forfeiture. Under both sets of principles, the law has come to permit a complainant to seek a fair allocation of profit and loss despite the complainant's own failure to comply fully with his contract obligations. The determination of what is fair, as a factual matter, must however depend upon a proper showing by the complainant who seeks this extraordinary relief.

Applying these principles to the present case, we conclude that the trial court was correct in granting summary judgment, although not for the reason upon which it relied. *A & H Corporation v. Bridgeport,* 180 Conn. 435, 443, 430 A.2d 25 (1980); *Favorite v. Miller,* 176 Conn. 310, 317, 407 A.2d 974 (1978). Chubb, the third party defendant, was not automatically discharged because of the delay of Murphy, the third party plaintiff, in giving notice of an insured occurrence. Chubb was, however, entitled to summary judgment because Murphy's affidavit opposing summary judgment contained no factual basis for a claim that Chubb had not been materially prejudiced by Murphy's delay.

There is no error.

In this opinion ARTHUR H. HEALEY, CALLAHAN and GLASS, JJ., concurred.

COVELLO, J., concurred in the result.

RESTATEMENT, SECOND, CONTRACTS § 229

[See Selected Source Materials Supplement]

RESTATEMENT, SECOND, CONTRACTS § 229, ILLUSTRATIONS 1, 2

1. A contracts to build a house for B, using pipe of Reading manufacture. In return, B agrees to pay $75,000 in progress payments, each payment to be made "on condition that no pipe other than that of Reading manufacture has been used." Without A's knowledge, a subcontractor mistakenly uses pipe of Cohoes manufacture which is identical in quality and is distinguishable only by the name of the manufacturer which is stamped on it. The mistake is not discovered until the house is completed, when replacement of the pipe will require destruction of substantial parts of the house. B refuses to pay the unpaid balance of $10,000. A court may conclude that the use of Reading rather than Cohoes pipe is so relatively unimportant to B that the forfeiture that would result from denying A the entire balance would be disproportionate, and may allow recovery by A subject to any claim for damages for A's breach of his duty to use Reading pipe.

2. A, an ocean carrier, carries B's goods under a contract providing that it is a condition of A's liability for damage to cargo that "written notice of claim for loss or damage must be given within 10 days after removal of goods." B's cargo is damaged during carriage and A knows of this. On removal of the goods, B notes in writing on the delivery record that the cargo is damaged, and five days later informs A over the telephone of a claim for that damage and invites A to participate in an inspection within the ten day period. A inspects the goods within the period, but B does not give written

notice of its claim until 25 days after removal of the goods. Since the purpose of requiring the condition of written notice is to alert the carrier and enable it to make a prompt investigation, and since this purpose had been served by the written notice of damage and the oral notice of claim, the court may excuse the non-occurrence of the condition to the extent required to allow recovery by B.

RESTATEMENT, SECOND, CONTRACTS § 230

[See Selected Source Materials Supplement]

RESTATEMENT, SECOND, CONTRACTS § 230, ILLUSTRATIONS 1, 2

1. A, an insurance company, insures the property of B under a policy providing that no recovery can be had if suit is not brought on the policy within two years after a loss. A loss occurs and B lets two years pass before bringing suit. A's duty to pay B for the loss is discharged and B cannot maintain the action on the policy.

2. The facts being otherwise as stated in Illustration 1, B lives in a foreign country and is prevented by the outbreak of war from bringing suit against A for two years. A's duty to pay B for the loss is not discharged and B can maintain an action on the policy when the war is ended.

RESTATEMENT, SECOND, CONTRACTS § 271

[See Selected Source Materials Supplement]

RESTATEMENT, SECOND, CONTRACTS § 271, ILLUSTRATIONS 1, 2

1. A contracts with B to repair B's building for $20,000, payment to be made "on the satisfaction of C, B's architect, and the issuance of his certificate." A properly makes the repairs, but C dies before he is able to give a certificate. Since presentation of the architect's certificate is not a material part of the agreed exchange and forfeiture would otherwise result, the occurrence of the condition is excused, and A has a claim against B for $20,000. . . .

2. A, an insurance company, issues to B a policy of accidental injury insurance which provides that notice within 14 days of an accident is a condition of A's duty. B is injured as a result of an accident covered by the policy but is so mentally deranged that he is unable to give notice for 20 days.

B gives notice as soon as he is able. Since the giving of notice within 14 days is not a material part of the agreed exchange, and forfeiture would otherwise result, the non-occurrence of the condition is excused and B has a claim against A under the policy.

————

RESTATEMENT, SECOND, CONTRACTS § 84

[See Selected Source Materials Supplement]

————

VANADIUM CORP. v. FIDELITY & DEPOSIT CO.

[Section 4, supra]

————

Chapter 25

BREACH AND RESPONSE

Section 1 of this Chapter considers the question, in the absence of an express condition, when can it be fairly implied that one party to a contract does not come under a duty to perform unless the other party has either performed or tendered performance? Section 2 of this Chapter considers a related problem: Suppose that A is to perform first, and performs less than perfectly. That is, suppose that A both performs and breaches. Because A has breached, B can sue A for damages for the breach. Depending on the facts, B may also have a right to *terminate* the contract as a result of A's breach. Section 3 considers the question, when does A's breach give B a right to terminate the contract, and what are the consequences if B terminates when A's breach does not give B the right to terminate?

SECTION 1. THE ORDER OF PERFORMANCE

Once it is accepted that contracted-for performances are mutually dependant, the question arises, in what order must the performances be rendered when the contract does not itself dictate the order of performance? This question arises in two closely related contexts:

(1) In the first context, A claims that B has not performed and is therefor in breach. B responds that she is not in breach because she was not obliged to perform until A had performed—or at least had tendered performance—and A had neither performed nor tendered. It must then be decided which party's performance was to come first, or alternatively whether the parties' performances were to be exchanged simultaneously.

(2) The second context is the flip side of the first: When must one party perform, or at least tender performance, to put the other party in breach?

The courts have developed somewhat elaborate rules to determine the order of performance for these purposes, which are reflected in Restatement Second §§ 233, 234.

RESTATEMENT, SECOND, CONTRACTS §§ 233, 234

[See Selected Source Materials Supplement]

RESTATEMENT, SECOND, CONTRACTS
§ 234, ILLUSTRATIONS 1–5, 9

1. A promises to sell land to B, delivery of the deed to be on July 1. B promises to pay A $50,000, payment to be made on July 1. Delivery of the deed and payment of the price are due simultaneously.

2. A promises to sell land to B, the deed to be delivered on July 1. B promises to pay A $50,000, no provision being made for the time of payment. Delivery of the deed and payment of the price are due simultaneously.

3. A promises to sell land to B and B promises to pay A $50,000, no provision being made for the time either of delivery of the deed or of payment. Delivery of the deed and payment of the price are due simultaneously.

4. A promises to sell land to B, delivery of the deed to be on or before July 1. B promises to pay A $50,000, payment to be on or before July 1. Delivery of the deed and payment of the price are due simultaneously.

5. A promises to sell land to B, delivery of the deed to be on or before July 1. B promises to pay A $50,000, payment to be on or before August 1. Delivery of the deed and payment of the [price] are not due simultaneously . . . . .

9. A contracts to do the concrete work on a building being constructed by B for $10 a cubic yard. In the absence of language or circumstances indicating the contrary, payment by B is not due until A has finished the concrete work. . . .

UCC §§ 2–507, 2–511

[See Selected Source Materials Supplement]

CISG ART. 58

[See Selected Source Materials Supplement]

UNIDROIT PRINCIPLES OF INTERNATIONAL COMMERCIAL CONTRACTS ARTS. 6.1.4, 7.1.3

[See Selected Source Materials Supplement]

PRINCIPLES OF EUROPEAN CONTRACT
LAW ARTS. 7.104, 9.201

[See Selected Source Materials Supplement]

NOTE ON CONCURRENT CONDITIONS

Seller and Buyer enter into a contract for the sale of Blackacre for $60,000 cash. May 2 is set for the delivery of the deed and the payment of the purchase price. Nothing is said about which performance is to come first. The natural implication is that the two performances will be simultaneous: the deed and the money will be passed across the table at the same time.

Suppose that in such a case one party brings suit for damages against the other, claiming that the other is in default? As part of his case, the party bringing suit must allege and show that it was the other party who was in default, not himself. If both parties stayed at home, and neither approached the other with a proposal for completing the sale, neither should be allowed to recover damages from the other. Accordingly, the rule is that where performances are to be simultaneous, neither party can recover damages unless he has done something to put the other party in default. This would usually mean making a definite offer to perform and having at the time the capacity to carry out the offer.

It is commonly said that such a case involves *concurrent conditions,* meaning that concurrent performance by each party is a condition to the other party's obligation to perform. The term "concurrent conditions" is something of a misnomer. What the term really means is that where the performances of the *promises* in a contract are to be concurrent, then it is normally a condition to a suit by either party for damages for breach of the contract that he must tender his own performance to put the other party in default.

Intermixed with problems concerning the order of performance are issues that are raised when one party lacks the ability to perform.

SECTION 2. ABILITY TO PERFORM

KANAVOS v. HANCOCK BANK & TRUST CO., 395 Mass. 199, 479 N.E.2d 168 (1985). "The weight of authority in this country is that the financial ability of a prospective buyer of property is a material issue in his action for damages against a repudiating defendant for breach of an agreement to sell that property for an established price. See 5 S. Williston, Contracts § 699, at 352–353 (Jaeger ed. 1961), and 6 S. Williston, Contracts § 882, at 394 (Jaeger ed. 1962); 4 A. Corbin, Contracts § 978, at 924–925 (1951); Restatement (Second) of Contracts § 254, comment a (1981) (the duty of a repudiating party 'to pay damages is discharged if it subsequently appears that there would have been a total failure of performance by the injured party').... We have taken the view that, even where promises were not concurrent, a plaintiff could only recover nominal or small damages against a defendant who repudiated a contract, where it would have been impossible for the plaintiff to perform a contractual obligation arising shortly after the defendant's breach. See *Randall v. Peerless Motor Car Co.*, 212 Mass. 352, 382, 99 N.E. 221 (1912)....

"If, as we have concluded, [the ability of the plaintiff, Kanavos,] to match the offer which the bank accepted is material to his right to recover, the question then is whether the burden of proof should be placed on Kanavos to show his ability or on the bank to show his lack of ability. The general rule is that the plaintiff must prove his ability to perform his obligations under a contract of the type involved here.... There is not, however, a unanimity of view in this country on the placing of the burden of proof in such a case....

"The burden was on Kanavos to prove his ability to finance the purchase of the stock. The fact of his ability to do so was an essential part of establishing the defendant's liability. Circumstances concerning his ability to raise $760,000 for the stock were far better known to him than to the bank. It is, of course, true that the bank created the problem by selling the stock to another in violation of its contractual obligation, and one could argue that, therefore, it should take the risk of failing to establish Kanavos's inability to purchase the stock. Such an argument, however, has not been generally accepted, for to do so would in effect place on the defendant the burden of disproving a fact essential to the plaintiff's case."

SECTION 3. MATERIAL BREACH: FAILURE OF PERFORMANCE BY ONE PARTY AS AN EXCUSE FOR NONPERFORMANCE BY THE OTHER

RESTATEMENT, SECOND, CONTRACTS § 237

[See Selected Source Materials Supplement]

K & G CONSTR. CO. v. HARRIS

Court of Appeals of Maryland, 1960.
223 Md. 305, 164 A.2d 451.

Before BRUNE, C.J., and HENDERSON, HAMMOND, PRESCOTT and HORNEY, JJ.

PRESCOTT, JUDGE. Feeling aggrieved by the action of the trial judge of the Circuit Court for Prince George's County, sitting without a jury, in finding a judgment against it in favor of a subcontractor, the appellant, the general contractor on a construction project, appealed.[1]

The principal question presented is: Does a contractor, damaged by a subcontractor's failure to perform a portion of his work in a workmanlike manner, have a right, under the circumstances of this case, to withhold, in partial satisfaction of said damages, an installment payment, which, under the terms of the contract, was due the subcontractor, unless the negligent performance of his work excused its payment?

The appeal is presented on a case stated in accordance with Maryland Rule 826g.

The statement, in relevant part, is as follows:

"... K & G Construction Company, Inc. (hereinafter called Contractor), plaintiff and counter-defendant in the Circuit Court and appellant herein, was owner and general contractor of a housing subdivision project being constructed (herein called Project). Harris and Brooks (hereinafter called Subcontractor), defendants and counter-plaintiffs in the Circuit Court and appellees herein, entered into a contract with Contractor to do excavating and earth-moving work on the Project. Pertinent parts of the contract are set forth below:

" 'Section 3. The Subcontractor agrees to complete the several portions and the whole of the work herein sublet by the time or times following:

" '(a) Without delay, as called for by the Contractor.

" '(b) It is expressly agreed that time is of the essence of this contract, and that the Contractor will have the right to terminate this contract and employ a substitute to perform the work in the event of delay on the part of Subcontractor, and Subcontractor agrees to indemnify the Contractor for any loss sustained thereby, provided, however, that nothing in this paragraph shall be construed to deprive Contractor of any rights or remedies it would otherwise have as to damage for delay.

" 'Section 4. (b) Progress payments will be made each month during the performance of the work. Subcontractor will submit to Contractor, by the 25th of each month, a requisition for work performed during the preceding month. Contractor will pay these requisitions, less a retainer equal to ten per cent (10%), by the 10th of the months in which such requisitions are received.[2]

" '(c) No payments will be made under this contract until the insurance requirements of Sec. 9 hereof have been complied with. . . .

" 'Section 8. . . . All work shall be performed in a workmanlike manner, and in accordance with the best practices.

" 'Section 9. Subcontractor agrees to carry, during the progress of the work, . . . liability insurance against . . . property damage, in such amounts and with such companies as may be satisfactory to

---

1. There are two appellees; the statement of the case refers to them as "subcontractor." We shall do likewise.

2. This section is not a model for clarity.

Contractor and shall provide Contractor with certificates showing the same to be in force.'

"While in the course of his employment by the Subcontractor on the Project, a bulldozer operator drove his machine too close to Contractor's house while grading the yard, causing the immediate collapse of a wall and other damage to the house. The resulting damage to contractor's house was $3,400.00. Subcontractor had complied with the insurance provision (Sec. 9) of the aforesaid contract. Subcontractor reported said damages to their liability insurance carrier. The Subcontractor and its insurance carrier refused to repair damage or compensate Contractor for damage to the house, claiming that there was no liability on the part of the Subcontractor.

"Contractor gave no written notice to Subcontractor for any services rendered or materials furnished by the Contractor to the Subcontractor

. . .

"Contractor was generally satisfied with Subcontractor's work and progress as required under Sections 3 and 8 of the contract until September 12, 1958, with the exception of the bulldozer accident of August 9, 1958.

"Subcontractor performed work under the contract during July, 1958, for which it submitted a requisition by the 25th of July, as required by the contract, for work done prior to the 25th of July, payable under the terms of the contract by Contractor on or before August 10, 1958. Contractor was current as to payments due under all preceding monthly requisitions from Subcontractor. The aforesaid bulldozer accident damaging Contractor's house occurred on August 9, 1958. Contractor refused to pay Subcontractor's requisition due on August 10, 1958, because the bulldozer damage to Contractor's house had not been repaired or paid for. Subcontractor continued to work on the project until the 12th of September, 1958, at which time they discontinued working on the project because of Contractor's refusal to pay the said work requisition and notified Contractor by registered letters of their position and willingness to return to the job, but only upon payment. At that time, September 12, 1958, the value of the work completed by Subcontractor on the project for which they had not been paid was $1,484.50.

"Contractor later requested Subcontractor to return and complete work on the Project which Subcontractor refused to do because of nonpayment of work requisitions of July 25 and thereafter. Contractor's house was not repaired by Subcontractor nor compensation paid for the damage.

"It was stipulated that Subcontractor had completed work on the Project under the contract for which they had not been paid in the amount of $1,484.50 and that if they had completed the remaining work to be done under the contract, they would have made a profit of $1,340.00 on the remaining uncompleted portion of the contract. It was further stipulated that it cost the Contractor $450.00 above the contract price to have another excavating contractor complete remaining work required under the contract. It was the opinion of the Court that if judgment were in favor of the Subcontractor, it should be for the total amount of $2,824.50.

"... Contractor filed suit against the Subcontractor in two counts: (1), for the aforesaid bulldozer damage to Contractor's house, alleging negligence of the Subcontractor's bulldozer operator, and (2) for the $450.00 costs above the contract price in having another excavating subcontractor complete the uncompleted work in the contract. Subcontractor filed a counter-claim for recovery of work of the value of $1,484.50 for which they had not received payment and for loss of anticipated profits on uncompleted portion of work in the amount of $1,340.00. By agreement of the parties, the first count of Contractor's claim, i.e., for aforesaid bulldozer damage to Contractor's house, was submitted to jury who found in favor of Contractor in the amount of $3,400.00. Following the finding by the jury, the second count of the Contractor's claim and the counter-claims of the Subcontractor, by agreement of the parties, were submitted to the Court for determination, without jury. All of the facts recited herein above were stipulated to by the parties to the Court. Circuit Court Judge Fletcher found for counter-plaintiff Subcontractor in the amount of $2,824.50 from which Contractor has entered this appeal."

The $3,400 judgment has been paid.

It is immediately apparent that our decision turns upon the respective rights and liabilities of the parties under that portion of their contract whereby the subcontractor agreed to do the excavating and earth-moving work in "a workmanlike manner, and in accordance with the best practices," with time being of the essence of the contract, and the contractor agreed to make progress payments therefor on the 10th day of the months following the performance of the work by the subcontractor.[3] The subcontractor contends, of course, that when the contractor failed to make the payment due on August 10, 1958, he breached his contract and thereby released him (the subcontractor) from any further obligation to perform. The contractor, on the other hand, argues that the failure of the subcontractor to perform his work in a workmanlike manner constituted a material breach of the contract, which justified his refusal to make the August 10 payment; and, as there was no breach on his part, the subcontractor had no right to cease performance on September 12, and his refusal to continue work on the project constituted another breach, which rendered him liable to the contractor for damages. The vital question, more tersely stated, remains: Did the contractor have a right, under the circumstances, to refuse to make the progress payment due on August 10, 1958?

... Promises are mutually dependent if the parties intend *performance* by one to be conditioned upon *performance* by the other, and, if they be mutually dependent, they may be (a) precedent, i.e., a promise that is to be performed before a corresponding promise on the part of the adversary party is to be performed, (b) subsequent, i.e., a corresponding promise that is not to be performed until the other party to the contract has performed a precedent covenant, or (c) concurrent, i.e., promises that are to be performed at the same time by each of the parties, who are respectively bound to perform each....

---

3. The statement of the case does not show the exact terms concerning the remuneration to be paid the subcontractor. It does not disclose whether he was to be paid a total lump sum, by the cubic yard, by the day, or in some other manner. It does state that the excavation finally cost the contractor $450 more than the "contract price."

... The modern rule, which seems to be of almost universal application, is that there is a presumption that mutual promises in a contract are dependent and are to be so regarded, whenever possible....

Considering the presumption that promises and counter-promises are dependent and the statement of the case, we have no hesitation in holding that the promise and counter-promise under consideration here were mutually dependent, that is to say, the parties intended performance by one to be conditioned on performance by the other; and the subcontractor's promise was, by the explicit wording of the contract, precedent to the promise of payment, monthly, by the contractor. In Shapiro Engineering Corp. v. Francis O. Day Co., 215 Md. 373, 380, 137 A.2d 695, we stated that it is the general rule that where a total price for work is fixed by a contract, the work is not rendered divisible by progress payments. It would indeed present an unusual situation if we were to hold that a building contractor, who has obtained someone to do work for him and has agreed to pay each month for the work performed in the previous month, has to continue the monthly payments, irrespective of the degree of skill and care displayed in the performance of work, and his only recourse is by way of suit for ill-performance. If this were the law, it is conceivable, in fact, probable, that many contractors would become insolvent before they were able to complete their contracts....

We hold that when the subcontractor's employee negligently damaged the contractor's wall, this constituted a breach of the subcontractor's promise to perform his work in a "workmanlike manner, and in accordance with the best practices." Gaybis v. Palm, 201 Md. 78, 85, 93 A.2d 269; Johnson v. Metcalfe, 209 Md. 537, 544, 121 A.2d 825; 17 C.J.S. Contracts § 515; Weiss v. Sheet Metal Fabricators, 206 Md. 195, 203, 110 A.2d 671. And there can be little doubt that the breach was material: the damage to the wall amounted to more than double the payment due on August 10. Speed v. Bailey, 153 Md. 655, 661, 662, 139 A. 534. 3A Corbin, Contracts, § 708, says: "The failure of a contractor's [in our case, the subcontractor's] performance to constitute 'substantial' performance may justify the owner [in our case, the contractor] in refusing to make a progress payment.... If the refusal to pay an installment is justified on the owner's [contractor's] part, the contractor [subcontractor] is not justified in abandoning work by reason of that refusal. His abandonment of the work will itself be a wrongful repudiation that goes to the essence, even if the defects in performance did not." See also Restatement, Contracts § 274; F.H. McGraw & Co. v. Sherman Plastering Co., D.C.Conn., 60 F.Supp. 504, 512, affirmed 2 Cir., 149 F.2d 301 ... and compare Williston, op. cit., §§ 805, 841 and 842. Professor Corbin, in § 954, states further: "The unexcused failure of a contractor to render a promised performance when it is due is always a breach of contract ... Such failure may be of such great importance as to constitute what has been called herein a 'total' breach.... For a failure of performance constituting such a 'total' breach, an action for remedies that are appropriate thereto is at once maintainable. Yet the injured party is not required to bring such action. He has the option of treating the non-performance as a 'partial' breach only...." In permitting the subcontractor to proceed with work on the project after August 9, the contractor, obviously, treated the breach by the subcontractor as a partial one. As the promises were mutually dependent and the subcontractor had made a material breach in his performance, this justified the contractor in refusing to make the August 10 payment; hence, as the contractor was not in default, the subcontractor again breached the contract when he, on September 12, discontinued work on the project, which rendered him liable (by the express terms of the contract) to the contractor for his increased cost in having the excavating done—a stipulated amount of $450. Cf. Keystone Engineering Corp. v. Sutter, 196 Md. 620, 628, 78 A.2d 191. . . .

Judgment against the appellant reversed; and judgment entered in favor of the appellant against the appellees for $450, the appellees to pay the costs.

———

E. ALLAN FARNSWORTH, CONTRACTS § 8.13 (4th ed. 2004). "A contract is said to be divisible if the performances to be exchanged can be divided into corresponding pairs of part performances in such a way that a court will treat the parts of each pair as if the parties had agreed that they were equivalents. . . .

"Suppose, for example, that a builder has made a contract to build three houses at $100,000 each for a total price of $300,000. The builder breaks the contract by building only one of the houses and claims its price of $100,000. Will a court allow the builder to recover on the contract to build three houses, even though the builder has not substantially performed it? It will, if it regards the contract as divisible into three pairs of part performances, each pair consisting of the building of a house and the payment of $100,000. The builder is then entitled to recover $100,000 on the contract for the house that was built, less such damages as the owner can prove were suffered by the builder's breach in not building the other two. Indeed, if the contract is divisible, the builder is entitled to recover on the contract for building the first house even if performance of that part of the contract is only substantial. The builder's recovery will then be reduced by damages resulting from the defects in the first house as well as from the failure to build the other two houses.

"How does a court decide whether a contract is divisible? As the Supreme Court of Colorado warned that 'there is no set formula which furnishes a foolproof method for determining in a given case just which contracts are severable and which are entire.' The Restatement Second lays down two requirements: it must be possible to apportion the parties' performances into corresponding pairs of part performances; and it must be proper to regard the parts of each pair as agreed equivalents."

———

WALKER & CO. v. HARRISON

Supreme Court of Michigan, 1957.
347 Mich. 630, 81 N.W.2d 352.

Before the Entire Bench, except BOYLES, J.

SMITH, JUSTICE. This is a suit on a written contract. The defendants are in the dry-cleaning business. Walker & Company, plaintiff, sells, rents, and services advertising signs and billboards. These parties entered into an agreement pertaining to a sign. The agreement is in writing and is termed a "rental agreement." It specifies in part that:

"The lessor agrees to construct and install, at its own cost, one 18′ 9″ high × 8′ 8″ wide pylon type d.f. neon sign with electric clock and flashing lamps.... The lessor agrees to and does hereby lease or rent unto the said lessee the said SIGN for the term, use and rental and under the conditions, hereinafter set out, and the lessee agrees to pay said rental....

"(a) The term of this lease shall be 36 months....

"(b) The rental to be paid by lessee shall be $148.50 per month for each and every calendar month during the term of this lease;....

"(d) *Maintenance.* Lessor at its expense agrees to maintain and service the sign together with such equipment as supplied and installed by the lessor to operate in conjunction with said sign under the terms of this lease; this service is to include cleaning and repainting of sign in original color scheme as often as deemed necessary by lessor to keep sign in first class advertising condition and make all necessary repairs to sign and equipment installed by lessor...."

At the "expiration of this agreement," it was also provided, "title to this sign reverts to lessee." This clause is in addition to the printed form of agreement and was apparently added as a result of defendants' concern over title, they having expressed a desire "to buy for cash" and the salesman, at one time, having "quoted a cash price."

The sign was completed and installed in the latter part of July, 1953. The first billing of the monthly payment of $148.50 was made August 1, 1953, with payment thereof by defendants on September 3, 1953. This first payment was also the last. Shortly after the sign was installed, someone hit it with a tomato. Rust, also, was visible on the chrome, complained defendants, and in its corners were "little spider cobwebs." In addition, there were "some children's sayings written down in here." Defendant Herbert Harrison called Walker for the maintenance he believed himself entitled to under subparagraph (d) above. It was not forthcoming. He called again and again. "I was getting, you might say, sorer and sorer.... Occasionally, when I started calling up, I would walk around where the tomato was and get mad again. Then I would call up on the phone again." Finally, on October 8, 1953, plaintiff not having responded to his repeated calls, he telegraphed Walker that:

"You Have Continually Voided Our Rental Contract By Not Maintaining Signs As Agreed As We No Longer Have A Contract With You Do Not Expect Any Further Remuneration."

Walker's reply was in the form of a letter. After first pointing out that "your telegram does not make any specific allegations as to what the failure of maintenance comprises," and stating that "We certainly would appreciate your furnishing us with such information," the letter makes reference to a prior collateral controversy between the parties, "wondering if this refusal on our part prompted your attempt to void our rental contract," and concludes as follows:

"We would like to call your attention to paragraph G in our rental contract, which covers procedures in the event of a Breach of Agreement. In the event that you carry out your threat to make no future monthly payments in accordance with the agreement, it is our intention to enforce the conditions outlined under paragraph G[1] through the proper legal channels. We call to your attention that your monthly rental payments are due in advance at our office not later than the 10th day of each current month. You are now approximately 30 days in arrears on your September payment. Unless we receive both the September and October payments by October 25th, this entire matter will be placed in the hands of our attorney for collection in accordance with paragraph G which stipulates that the entire amount is forthwith due and payable.''

No additional payments were made and Walker sued in assumpsit for the entire balance due under the contract, $5,197.50, invoking paragraph (g) of the agreement. Defendants filed answer and claim of recoupment, asserting that plaintiff's failure to perform certain maintenance services constituted a prior material breach of the agreement, thus justifying their repudiation of the contract and grounding their claim for damages. The case was tried to the court without a jury and resulted in a judgment for the plaintiff. The case is before us on a general appeal.

Defendants urge upon us again and again, in various forms, the proposition that Walker's failure to service the sign, in response to repeated requests, constituted a material breach of the contract and justified repudiation by them. Their legal proposition is undoubtedly correct. Repudiation is one of the weapons available to an injured party in event the other contractor has committed a material breach. But the injured party's determination that there has been a material breach, justifying his own repudiation, is fraught with peril, for should such determination, as viewed by a later court in the calm of its contemplation, be unwarranted, the repudiator himself will have been guilty of material breach and himself have become the aggressor, not an innocent victim.

What is our criterion for determining whether or not a breach of contract is so fatal to the undertaking of the parties that it is to be classed as "material"? There is no single touchstone. Many factors are involved. They are well stated in section 275 of [the] Restatement, Law of Contracts in the following terms:

"In determining the materiality of a failure fully to perform a promise the following circumstances are influential:

"(a) The extent to which the injured party will obtain the substantial benefit which he could have reasonably anticipated;

---

1. (g) *Breach of Agreement.* Lessee shall be deemed to have breached this agreement by default in payment of any installment of the rental herein provided for; abandonment of the sign or vacating premises where the sign is located; termination or transfer of lessee's interest in the premises by insolvency, appointment of a receiver for lessee's business; filing of a voluntary or involuntary petition in bankruptcy with respect to lessee or the violation of any of the other terms or conditions hereof. In the event of such default, the lessor may, upon notice to the lessee, which notice shall conclusively be deemed sufficient if mailed or delivered to the premises where the sign was or is located, take possession of the sign and declare the balance of the rental herein provided for to be forthwith due and payable, and lessee hereby agrees to pay such balance upon any such contingencies. Lessor may terminate this lease and without notice, remove and repossess said sign and recover from the lessee such amounts as may be unpaid for the remaining unexpired term of this agreement. Time is of the essence of this lease with respect to the payment of rentals herein provided for. Should lessee after lessor has declared the balance of rentals due and payable, pay the full amount of rental herein provided, he shall then be entitled to the use of the sign, under all the terms and provisions hereof, for the balance of the term of this lease. . . .

"(b) The extent to which the injured party may be adequately compensated in damages for lack of complete performance;

"(c) The extent to which the party failing to perform has already partly performed or made preparations for performance;

"(d) The greater or less hardship on the party failing to perform in terminating the contract;

"(e) The wilful, negligent or innocent behavior of the party failing to perform;

"(f) The greater or less uncertainty that the party failing to perform will perform the remainder of the contract."*

We will not set forth in detail the testimony offered concerning the need for servicing. Granting that Walker's delay (about a week after defendant Herbert Harrison sent his telegram of repudiation Walker sent out a crew and took care of things) in rendering the service requested was irritating, we are constrained to agree with the trial court that it was not of such materiality as to justify repudiation of the contract, and we are particularly mindful of the lack of preponderant evidence contrary to his determination. Jones v. Eastern Michigan Motorbuses, 287 Mich. 619, 283 N.W. 710. The trial court, on this phase of the case, held as follows:

"Now Mr. Harrison phoned in, so he testified, a number of times. He isn't sure of the dates but he sets the first call at about the 7th of August and he complained then of the tomato and of some rust and some cobwebs. The tomato, according to the testimony, was up on the clock; that would be outside of his reach, without a stepladder or something. The cobwebs are within easy reach of Mr. Harrison and so would the rust be. I think that Mr. Bueche's argument that these were not materially a breach would clearly be true as to the cobwebs and I really can't believe in the face of all the testimony that there was a great deal of rust seven days after the installation of this sign. And that really brings it down to the tomato. And, of course, when a tomato has been splashed all over your clock, you don't like it. But he says he kept calling their attention to it, although the rain probably washed some of the tomato off. But the stain remained, and they didn't come. I really can't find that that was such a material breach of the contract as to justify rescission. I really don't think so."

Nor, we conclude, do we. There was no valid ground for defendants' repudiation and their failure thereafter to comply with the terms of the contract was itself a material breach, entitling Walker, upon this record, to judgment.

The question of damages remains. The parties, particularly appellants, have discussed at some length whether this contract is one of sale or of lease. Through much of its content it appears merely to be an ordinary lease, but when we come to its end we find that title, without more, is to pass to the "lessee" at the expiration of the agreement. Is the so-called rent merely the payment of a sale price in installments? We need not, in the light of the terms of the particular contract, and upon the record, vex this question, despite illustrious aid offered us by 2 Williston on Sales, § 336, extensive annotations in 17 A.L.R. 1435, 43 A.L.R. 1257, 92 A.L.R. 323, and 175 A.L.R. 1366, and

* The citation is to Restatement First. (Footnote by ed.)

the comprehensive analysis of Dalzell in 1 Oregon Law Review 9, "Lease–Contracts as a Means of Conveying Title to Chattels." For the parties before us have agreed, with particularity, as to remedies in event of breach, the remedy here sought, as provided, being acceleration of "rentals" due. The trial court cut down such sum by the amount that service would have cost Walker during the unexpired portion of the agreement (Restatement, Contracts, § 335) and as to such diminution Walker does not complain or cross-appeal. Judgment was, therefore, rendered for the cash price of the sign, for such services and maintenance as were extended and accepted, and interest upon the amount in default. There was no error.

Affirmed. Costs to appellee.

———

ZULLA STEEL, INC. v. A & M GREGOS, INC., 174 N.J.Super. 124, 415 A.2d 1183 (1980). Defendant was the prime contractor for the expansion of a post office. Plaintiff was a subcontractor. Plaintiff started performing under its contract in summer 1975. It continued working into 1976, when it left the job because it was not paid progress payments in accordance with its contract. On March 23, 1976, defendant telegraphed plaintiff to return to the job or its contract would be terminated. Plaintiff did not return. The trial court held that defendant had committed a material breach, and plaintiff was entitled to stop performing and sue for damages. Affirmed.

"The trial judge held that defendant, by reason of its delinquencies in payments, had breached the contract with plaintiff, and we agree.... Plaintiff presented substantial credible evidence that defendant's failure to pay plaintiff meant that plaintiff could not pay its [own] subcontractor and thus could not complete its contract with defendant. The trial judge accepted this testimony and so do we....

"Since defendant breached its contract we must determine whether the breach justified plaintiff in abandoning the project. It is true that it has been held that where a contract is entire so that the payment of the consideration in installments is not for a particular performance, nonpayment does not justify the contractor in failing to complete the work.... But there is contrary authority.... Certainly the current approach in contract construction is to honor the expressed or presumed intention of the parties.... We find it impossible to believe that in a major construction project the parties would expect that a subcontractor would be obliged to continue working even though there were material delays in payment to it. Ordinarily the parties would expect that the subcontractor would be using the installment payments to satisfy its own expenses. While we do not suggest that every delay in payment will justify a contractor in terminating performance under an installment contract, here there was a substantial underpayment for a prolonged period of time. In these circumstances we hold that plaintiff was justified in discontinuing performance."

———

RESTATEMENT, SECOND, CONTRACTS §§ 241, 242

[See Selected Source Materials Supplement]

————

CISG ARTS. 25, 49

[See Selected Source Materials Supplement]

————

UNIDROIT PRINCIPLES OF INTERNATIONAL COMMERCIAL CONTRACTS ARTS. 7.3.1, 7.3.5, 7.3.6

[See Selected Source Materials Supplement]

————

PRINCIPLES OF EUROPEAN CONTRACT LAW ARTS. 9.301, 9.302, 9.305, 9.307–309

[See Selected Source Materials Supplement]

————

NOTE ON THE CONCEPT OF CURE UNDER RESTATEMENT SECOND

Recall that one way in which the UCC limited the perfect-tender rule, in contracts for the sale of goods, was by introducing the concept of cure. Restatement Second § 237 introduces a version of cure into all contracts, not merely contracts for the sale of goods.

§ 237. Effect on Other Party's Duties of a Failure to Render Performance

     ... [I]t is a condition of each party's remaining duties to render performances to be exchanged under an exchange of promises that there be no *uncured* material failure by the other party to render any such performance due at an earlier time.*

The Comment adds:

     ... Under the rule stated in this Section, a material failure of performance, including defective performance as well as an absence of performance, operates as the non-occurrence of a condition. [T]he non-occurrence of a condition has two possible effects on the duty subject to that condition.... The first is that of preventing performance of the duty from becoming due, at least temporarily.... The second is that of discharging the duty when the condition can no longer occur.... A material failure of performance has, under this Section, these effects on

———

* Emphasis throughout this Note is added.

the other party's remaining duties of performance with respect to the exchange. It prevents performance of those duties from becoming due, at least temporarily, and it discharges those duties *if it has not been cured* during the time in which performance can occur....

Illustrations:

1. A contracts to build a house for B for $50,000, progress payments to be made monthly in an amount equal to 85% of the price of the work performed during the preceding month, the balance to be paid on the architect's certificate of satisfactory completion of the house. Without justification B fails to make a $5,000 progress payment. A thereupon stops work on the house and a week goes by. A's failure to continue the work is not a breach and B has no claim against A. B's failure to make the progress payment is an uncured material failure of performance which operates as the non-occurrence of a condition of A's remaining duties of performance under the exchange. If B offers to make the delayed payment and in all the circumstances *it is not too late to cure* the material breach, A's duties to continue the work are not discharged. A has a claim against B for damages for partial breach because of the delay.

2. The factors being otherwise as stated in Illustration 1, B fails to make the progress payment or to give any explanation or assurances for one month. If, in all the circumstances, it is now *too late for B to cure* his material failure of performance by making the delayed payment, A's duties to continue the work are discharged. Because B's failure to make the progress payment was a breach, A also has a claim against B for total breach of contract....

Similarly, Restatement Second § 241 provides:

§ 241. Circumstances Significant in Determining Whether a Failure Is Material

In determining whether a failure to render or to offer performance is material, the following circumstances are significant ...

(d) the likelihood that the party failing to perform or to offer to perform *will cure his failure,* taking account of all the circumstances including any reasonable assurances....

———

UNIDROIT PRINCIPLES OF INTERNATIONAL COMMERCIAL CONTRACTS ART. 7.1.4

[See Selected Source Materials Supplement]

———

PRINCIPLES OF EUROPEAN CONTRACT LAW ART. 8.104

[See Selected Source Materials Supplement]

———

Chapter 26

ANTICIPATORY BREACH, PROSPECTIVE INABILITY TO PERFORM, AND ADEQUATE ASSURANCE OF PERFORMANCE

This Chapter concerns the following related topics: (1) The effect of a repudiation of a contract by a party before the party's performance is due. (2) The consequences that arise when it appears that one party to a contract will be unable to perform although she has not repudiated the contract. (3) Whether and when a party to a contract may justifiably insist that the other party provide adequate assurance that performance will be forthcoming.

SECTION 1.   ANTICIPATORY BREACH

HOCHSTER v. DE LA TOUR

In the Queen's Bench, 1853.
2 Ellis & Bl. 678.

This was an action for breach of contract. On the trial, before Erle, J., at the London sittings in last Easter Term, it appeared that plaintiff was a courier, who, in April, 1852, was engaged by defendant to accompany him on a tour to commence on June 1st, 1852, on the terms mentioned in the declaration. On May 11th, 1852, defendant wrote to plaintiff that he had changed his mind, and declined his services. He refused to make him any compensation. The action was commenced on May 22d. The plaintiff, between the commencement of the action and June 1st, obtained an engagement with Lord Ashburton, on equally good terms, but not commencing till July 4th. The defendant's counsel objected that there could be no breach of the contract before the 1st of June. The learned judge was of a contrary opinion, but reserved leave to enter a nonsuit on this objection. The other questions were left to the jury, who found for plaintiff.

Hugh Hill, in the same term, obtained a rule nisi to enter a nonsuit or arrest the judgment. In last Trinity Term.

Hannon showed cause.... If one party to an executory contract gave the other notice that he refused to go on with the bargain, in order that the other side might act upon that refusal in such a manner as to incapacitate himself from fulfilling it, and he did so act, the refusal could never be retracted; and, accordingly, in Cort v. Ambergate & c. R. Co. (17 Q.B. 127) this court after considering the cases, decided that in such a case the plaintiff might recover, though he was no longer in a position to fulfil his contract. That was a contract under seal to manufacture and supply iron chairs. The purchasers discharged the vendors from manufacturing the goods; and it was held that an action might be maintained by the vendors. It is true, however, that in that case the writ was issued after the time when the chairs ought to have been received. In the present case, if the writ had been issued on the 2nd of June, Cort v. Ambergate & c. R. Co. would have been expressly in point. The question, therefore, comes to be: Does it make any difference that the writ was issued before the 1st of June? If the dicta of Parke, B., in Phillpotts v. Evans, 5 M. & W. 475, are to be taken as universally applicable it does make a difference; but they cannot be so taken. In a contract to marry at a future day, a marriage of the man before that day is a breach. Short v. Stone, 8 Q.B. 358. The reason of this is, that the marriage is a final refusal to go on with the contract. It is not on the ground that the defendant has rendered it impossible to fulfil the contract; for, as was argued in vain in Short v. Stone, the first wife might be dead before the day came. So also, on a contract to assign a term of years on a day future, a previous assignment to a stranger is a breach. Lovelock v. Franklyn, 8 Q.B. 371. [Lord Campbell, C.J. It probably will not be disputed that an act on the part of the defendant incapacitating himself from going on with the contract would be a breach. But how does the defendant's refusal in May incapacitate him from travelling in June? It was possible that he might do so.] It was; but the plaintiff, who, so long as the engagement subsisted, was bound to keep himself disengaged and make preparations so as to be ready and willing to travel with the defendant on the 1st of June, was informed by the defendant that he would not go on with the contract, in order that the plaintiff might act upon that information; and the plaintiff then was entitled to engage himself to another, as he did. In Planche v. Colburn (8 Bing. 14) the plaintiff had contracted with defendants to write a work for "The Juvenile Library"; and he was held to be entitled to recover on their discontinuing the publication; yet the time for the completion of the contract, that is for the work being published in "The Juvenile Library," had not arrived, for that would not be till a reasonable time after the author had completed the work. Now in that case the author never did complete the work. [Lord Campbell, C.J. It certainly would have been cruelly hard if the author had been obliged, as a condition precedent to redress, to compose a work which he knew could never be published. Crompton, J. When a party announces his intention not to fulfil the contract, the other side may take him at his word and rescind the contract. That word "rescind" implies that both parties have agreed that the contract shall be at an end as if it had never been. But I am inclined to think that the party may also say: "Since you have announced that you will not go on with the contract, I will consent that it shall be at an end from this time; but I will hold you liable for the damage I have sustained; and I will proceed to make that damage as little as possible by making the best use I can of my liberty." This is the principle of those cases in which there has been a discussion as to the measure of damages to which a servant is entitled on a wrongful dismissal. They were all considered in Elderton v. Emmens (6 C.B. 160). Lord Campbell, C.J. The counsel in support of the rule have to answer a very able argument.]

Hugh Hill and Deighton, contra. In Cort v. Ambergate & c. R. Co., the writ was taken out after the time for completing the contract. That case is consistent with the defendant's position, which is, that an act incapacitating the defendant, in law, from completing the contract is a breach, because it is implied that the parties to a contract shall keep themselves legally capable of performing it; but that an announcement of an intention to break the contract when the time comes is no more than an offer to rescind. It is evidence, till retracted, of a dispensation with the necessity of readiness and willingness on the other side; and, if not retracted, it is, when the time for performance comes, evidence of a continued refusal; but till then it may be retracted. Such is the doctrine in Phillpotts v. Evans (5 M. & W. 475) and Ripley v. McClure (4 Exch. 345). [Crompton, J. May not the plaintiff, on notice that the defendant will not employ him, look out for other employment, so as to diminish the loss?] If he adopts the defendant's notice, which is in legal effect an offer to rescind, he must adopt it altogether. [Lord Campbell, C.J. So that you say the plaintiff, to preserve any remedy at all, was bound to remain idle. Erle, J. Do you go one step further? Suppose the defendant, after the plaintiff's engagement with Lord Ashburton, had retracted his refusal and required the plaintiff to travel with him on the 1st of June, and the plaintiff had refused to do so, and gone with Lord Ashburton instead? Do you say that the now defendant could in that case have sued the now plaintiff for a breach of contract?] It would be, in such a case, a question of fact for a jury, whether there had not been an exoneration. In Phillpotts v. Evans, it was held that the measure of damages was the market price at the time when the contract ought to be completed. If a refusal before that time is a breach, how could these damages be ascertained? [Coleridge, J. No doubt it was possible, in this case, that, before the 1st of June, the plaintiff might die, in which case the plaintiff would have gained nothing had the contract gone on. Lord Campbell, C.J. All contingencies should be taken into account by the jury in assessing the damages. Crompton, J. That objection would equally apply to the action by a servant for dismissing him before the end of his term, and so disabling him from earning his wages; yet that action may be brought immediately on the dismissal; note to Cutter v. Powell (6 T.R. 320)]. It is quite possible that the plaintiff himself might have intended not to go on; no one can tell what intention is. [Lord Campbell, C.J. The intention of the defendant might be proved by showing that he entered in his diary a memorandum to that effect; and, certainly, no action would lie for entering such a memorandum. But the question is as to the effect of a communication to the other side, made that he might know that intention and act upon it.] . . .

Lord Campbell, C.J., now delivered the judgment of the Court.

On this motion in arrest of judgment, the question arises, whether if there be an agreement between A and B, whereby B engages to employ A on and from a future day for a given period of time, to travel with him into a foreign country as a courier, and to start with him in that capacity on that day, A being to receive a monthly salary during the continuance of such service, B may, before the day, refuse to perform the agreement and break and renounce it, so as to entitle A before the day to commence an action against B to recover damages for breach of the agreement; A having been ready and willing to perform it, till it was broken and renounced by B. The defendant's counsel very powerfully contended that, if the plaintiff was not contented to dissolve the contract and to abandon all remedy upon it, he was bound to remain ready and willing to perform it till the day when the actual employment as courier in the service of the defendant was to begin; and that there could be no breach of the agreement before that day to give a right of action.

But it cannot be laid down as a universal rule that, where by agreement an act is to be done on a future day, no action can be brought for a breach of the agreement till the day for doing the act has arrived. If a man promises to marry a woman on a future day, and before that day marries another woman, he is instantly liable to an action for breach of promise of marriage. Short v. Stone (8 Q.B. 358). If a man contracts to execute a lease on and from a future day for a certain term, and before that day executes a lease to another for the same term, he may be immediately sued for breaking the contract. Ford v. Tiley (6 B. & C. 325). So, if a man contracts to sell and deliver specific goods on a future day, and before the day he sells and delivers them to another, he is immediately liable to an action at the suit of the person with whom he first contracted to sell and deliver them. Bowdell v. Parsons (10 East. 359). One reason alleged in support of such an action is, that the defendant has, before the day, rendered it impossible for him to perform the contract at the day, but this does not necessarily follow; for prior to the day fixed for doing the act, the first wife may have died, a surrender of the lease executed might be obtained, and the defendant might have repurchased the goods so as to be in a situation to sell and deliver them to the plaintiff. Another reason may be that, where there is a contract to do an act on a future day, there is a relation constituted between the parties in the meantime by the contract, and that they impliedly promise that in the meantime neither will do anything to the prejudice of the other inconsistent with that relation. As an example, a man and woman engaged to marry are affianced to one another during the period between the time of the engagement and the celebration of the marriage.

In this very case of traveler and courier, from the day of the hiring till the day when the employment was to begin, they were engaged to each other; and it seems to be a breach of an implied contract if either of them renounces the engagement. This reasoning seems in accordance with the unanimous decision of the Exchequer Chamber in Elderton v. Emmens (6 C.B. 160), which we have followed in subsequent cases in this court. The declaration in the present case, in alleging a breach, states a great deal more than a passing intention on the part of the defendant which he may repent of, and could only be proved by evidence that he had utterly renounced the contract, or done some act which rendered it impossible for him to perform it.

If the plaintiff has no remedy for breach of the contract unless he treats the contract as in force, and acts upon it down to the 1st of June, 1852, it follows that, till then, he must enter into no employment which will interfere with his promise "to start with the defendant on such travels on the day and year," and that he must then be properly equipped in all respects as a courier for a three months' tour on the continent of Europe. But it is surely much more rational, and more for the benefit of both parties, that, after the renunciation of the agreement by the defendant, the plaintiff should be at liberty to consider himself absolved from any future performance of it, retaining his right to sue for any damage he has suffered from the breach of it. Thus, instead of remaining idle and laying out money in preparations which must be useless, he is at liberty to seek service under another employer, which would go in mitigation to the damages to which he would otherwise be entitled for a breach of the contract. It seems strange that the defendant, after renouncing the contract, and absolutely declaring that he will never act under it, should be permitted to object that faith is given to his assertion, and that an opportunity is not left to him of changing his mind. If the plaintiff is barred of any remedy by entering into an engagement inconsistent with starting as a courier with the defendant on the 1st of June, he is prejudiced by putting faith in the defendant's assertion: and it would be more consonant with principle, if the defendant were precluded from saying that he had not broken the contract when he declared that he entirely renounced it.

Suppose that the defendant, at the time of his renunciation, had embarked on a voyage for Australia, so as to render it physically impossible for him to employ the plaintiff as a courier on the continent of Europe in the months of June, July and August, 1852: according to decided cases, the action might have been brought before the 1st of June; but the renunciation may have been founded on other facts, to be given in evidence, which would equally have rendered the defendant's performance of the contract impossible. The man who wrongfully renounces a contract into which he has deliberately entered cannot justly complain if he is immediately sued for a compensation in damages by the man whom he has injured; and it seems reasonable to allow an option to the injured party, either to sue immediately, or to wait till the time when the act was to be done, still holding it as prospectively binding for the exercise of this option, which may be advantageous to the innocent party, and cannot be prejudicial to the wrongdoer.

An argument against the action before the 1st of June is urged from the difficulty of calculating the damages, but this argument is equally strong against an action before the 1st of September, when the three months would expire. In either case, the jury in assessing the damages would be justified in looking to all that had happened, or was likely to happen, to increase or mitigate the loss of the plaintiff down to the day of trial. We do not find any decision contrary to the view we are taking of this case. . . .

Upon the whole, we think that the declaration in this case is sufficient. It gives us great satisfaction to reflect that, the question being on the record, our opinion may be reviewed in a court of error. In the meantime we must give judgment for the plaintiff.

Judgment for plaintiff.

———

UNIQUE SYSTEMS, INC. v. ZOTOS INTERNATIONAL, INC., 622 F.2d 373 (8th Cir.1980). On January 30, 1974, Lilja contracted to manufacture and sell to Zotos, for resale by Zotos, 15,000 hair–spray systems that Lilja would develop. In an amendment to the contract, the parties agreed that Zotos's stocking and distribution of the systems would commence in "month one," defined as a "mutually agreed date in the year 1974." Later, Zotos began to fear a softening of the market, and indicated that it would not proceed unless Lilja would agree to a market test of completed systems. In light of Zotos's refusal to proceed without the market–test period, Lilja considered the contract repudiated, and brought suit. Held, for Lilja.

"If a party to a contract demands of the other party a performance to which he has no right under the contract and states definitely that, unless his demand is complied with, he will not render his promised performance, an anticipatory repudiation has been committed. 4 Corbin, Contracts § 973 (1951). When Zotos told Lilja in August of 1975 that it would not proceed until market tests were performed with results subject to Zotos's approval, Zotos repudiated the contract and was in total breach. No market tests were required by the contract, a fact that Zotos admits that it knew."

———

THERMO ELECTRON CORP. v. SCHIAVONE CONSTRUCTION CO., 958 F.2d 1158 (1st Cir.1992). " ... Thermo repudiated only if it 'insist[ed] ... upon terms' ... to *the point where that insistence 'amounts to a statement of intention not to perform except on conditions which go beyond the contract.'* Restatement (Second) of Contracts § 250 cmt. b, at 273 (quoting U.C.C. § 2–610 cmt. 2) (emphasis added). Commentators have pointed out that there 'must be a definite and unequivocal manifestation of intention [not to render performance].... A mere request for a change in the terms or a request for cancellation of the contract is not in itself enough to constitute a repudiation.' 4 Arthur L. Corbin, Corbin on Contracts § 973, at 905–06 (1951) (footnotes omitted). A party's statements or actions 'must be sufficiently positive to be reasonably understood as meaning that the breach will actually occur. A party's expressions of doubt as to its willingness or ability to perform do not constitute a repudiation.' E. Allan Farnsworth, Contracts § 8.21, at 663 (2d ed. 1990); accord Restatement (Second) of Contracts § 250 cmt. b, at 273."

———

TAYLOR v. JOHNSTON, 15 Cal.3d 130, 123 Cal.Rptr. 641, 539 P.2d 425 (1975). "When a promisor repudiates a contract, the injured party faces an election of remedies: He can treat the repudiation as an anticipatory breach and immediately seek damages for breach of contract, thereby terminating the contractual relation between the parties, or he can treat the repudiation as an empty threat, wait until the time for performance arrives and exercise his remedies for actual breach if a breach does in fact occur at such time.... However, if the injured party disregards the repudiation and treats the contract as still in force, and the repudiation is retracted prior to the time of performance, then the repudiation is nullified and the injured party is left with his remedies, if any, invocable at the time of performance."

———

UNITED STATES v. SEACOAST GAS CO., 204 F.2d 709 (5th Cir. 1953), cert. denied 346 U.S. 866, 74 S.Ct. 106, 98 L.Ed. 377 (1953). Seacoast had entered into a contract to supply gas to a federal housing project. While performance of the contract was in progress, Seacoast wrote to the Public

Housing Authority that because of the Authority's alleged breach of the contract, Seacoast intended to cancel the contract as of November 15, 1947. It was admitted that this letter constituted an anticipatory breach. The Authority notified Seacoast that it did not recognize any right in Seacoast to stop performance, and proposed to advertise for bids to ensure a continued supply of gas if Seacoast's breach persisted. Thereafter, the Authority advertised for bids, and, having received the low bid from Trion Company on November 6, notified Seacoast that unless Seacoast retracted its repudiation of the contract within three days, Trion's bid would be accepted and Seacoast would be held liable for breach of contract.

Seacoast did not retract within the time fixed. On November 10, the Authority accepted Trion's bid and began preparations to execute a contract with Trion for a price above that provided in the Seacoast contract. On November 13 (two days before the November 15 termination date that Seacoast had fixed in its notice), Seacoast admitted that it had no right to cancel the contract and retracted its notice. On November 17, the Authority signed a contract with Trion. In a suit by the Authority, Seacoast defended on the ground that it had retracted its notice of repudiation, and given assurance of its intention to continue to perform, before the Authority had actually signed the new contract, and that since the Authority had not then substantially changed its position or suffered any damages the retraction was timely and healed the breach. Held, Seacoast's retraction was ineffective.

"All that is required to close the door to repentance is definite action indicating that the anticipatory breach has been accepted as final, and this requisite can be supplied either by the filing of a suit or a firm declaration, as here, that unless within a fixed time the breach is repudiated, it will be accepted."

NOTE ON REMEDIES FOR THE BREACH OF A CONTRACT IN WHICH ALL THE DUTIES ON ONE SIDE HAVE BEEN PERFORMED

There is a rule of contract law that (1) if A and B have a contract, all of A's duties have been performed, and the only duty remaining for B is to perform a series of separate acts in the future, then (2) in the case of breach by B, A can bring suit on the basis of the acts that are due and unperformed, but cannot bring suit based on the remaining future acts unless and until there is a breach of the duty to perform those acts. Contracts that fall within this rule are often characterized as having become "unilateral," because by the hypothesis only one party remains obliged to perform under the contract. Although this rule is conventionally dealt with under the category of anticipatory breach, it is applicable to a present breach as well. And although the issue addressed by this rule can arise regardless of the nature of the unperformed duty, as a practical matter the rule is usually invoked only when B's sole remaining unperformed duty is to make a series of payments in installments.

In Minor v. Minor, 184 Cal.App.2d 118, 7 Cal.Rptr. 455 (1960), the court stated the following rationale for the rule:

... [A] party who has fully performed need only await counter-performance; he is entitled to no more than such performance upon the future dates to which he has agreed. On the other hand, [a] party who has not yet performed must be ready to, or actually, undertake, further performance. To call upon him to do so in the face of a repudiation of the other contracting party may cause him unmerited hardship. Hence his claim for immediate total performance is greater than that of his dormant counterpart who has fully performed.

This rationale strikes most commentators as thin. As the court in *Minor* went on to note: "[T]he dissenting critics point out that to gain a rather tenuous 'logical consistency,' we incongruously award judgment for future installments to the party who has not yet performed, and deny such judgment to the party who has fully performed." Perhaps the rule is simply an historical anachronism, or perhaps it represents a crude compromise between those who support the doctrine of anticipatory repudiation and those who oppose it. In some cases, the courts have circumvented the rule on the ground that the injured party party had some conceivable remaining obligation, no matter how minor. See, e.g., Long Island R.R. Co. v. Northville Industries Corp., 41 N.Y.2d 455, 393 N.Y.S.2d 925, 362 N.E.2d 558 (1977).

An obvious problem with the rule is that in theory it could force the injured party to bring one suit after another for each unpaid installment. In practice, however, in most cases the defendant will probably conform her conduct to the court's initial decision, and pay the remaining installments voluntarily. Furthermore, rule or no rule, if the defendant continues to withhold installments even after an initial judgement in the injured party's favor, the courts are unlikely to require the injured party to keep bringing one suit after another. Thus in Greguhn v. Mutual of Omaha Ins. Co., 23 Utah 2d 214, 461 P.2d 285 (1969), a disability-payment case, the court limited the plaintiff's judgment to installments already due, but added:

The verdict and the decision of the trial court amounts to a determination that the plaintiff is entitled to the monthly payments as specified in the insurance policies so long as he is totally and permanently disabled. Defendants are not relieved of the obligation of making the payments unless the plaintiff should recover or die. Should the defendants fail in the future to make payment in accordance with the terms of the policies without just cause or excuse and the plaintiff is compelled to file another action for delinquent installments, the court at that time should be able to fashion such relief as will compel performance.

———

RESTATEMENT, SECOND, CONTRACTS §§ 250, 253, 256

[See Selected Source Materials Supplement]

———

UCC §§ 2–610, 2–611, 2–708(1), 2–713, 2–723

[See Selected Source Materials Supplement]

CISG ART. 72

[See Selected Source Materials Supplement]

UNIDROIT PRINCIPLES OF INTERNATIONAL COMMERCIAL CONTRACTS ART. 7.3.3

[See Selected Source Materials Supplement]

OLOFFSON v. COOMER

Appellate Court of Illinois, Third District, 1973.
11 Ill.App.3d 918, 296 N.E.2d 871.

ALLOY, PRESIDING JUSTICE. Richard Oloffson, d/b/a Rich's Ag Service appeals from a judgment of the circuit court of Bureau County in favor of appellant against Clarence Coomer in the amount of $1,500 plus costs. The case was tried by the court without a jury.

Oloffson was a grain dealer. Coomer was a farmer. Oloffson was in the business of merchandising grain. Consequently, he was a "merchant" within the meaning of section 2–104 of the Uniform Commercial Code. (Ill.Rev.Stat. 1969, ch. 26 § 2–104). Coomer, however, was simply in the business of growing rather than merchandising grain. He, therefore, was not a "merchant" with respect to the merchandising of grain.

On April 16, 1970, Coomer agreed to sell to Oloffson, for delivery in October and December of 1970, 40,000 bushels of corn. Oloffson testified at the trial that the entire agreement was embodied in two separate contracts, each covering 20,000 bushels and that the first 20,000 bushels were to be delivered on or before October 30 at a price of $1.12¾ per bushel and the second 20,000 bushels were to be delivered on or before December 15, at a price of $1.12¼ per bushel. Coomer, in his testimony, agreed that the 40,000 bushels were to be delivered but stated that he was to deliver all he could by October 30 and the balance by December 15.

On June 3, 1970, Coomer informed Oloffson that he was not going to plant corn because the season had been too wet. He told Oloffson to arrange elsewhere to obtain the corn if Oloffson had obligated himself to deliver to any third party. The price for a bushel of corn on June 3, 1970, for future delivery, was $1.16. In September of 1970, Oloffson asked Coomer about delivery of the corn and Coomer repeated that he would not be able to deliver. Oloffson, however, persisted. He mailed Coomer confirmations of the April 16 agreement. Coomer ignored these. Oloffson's attorney then requested that Coomer perform. Coomer ignored this request likewise. The scheduled delivery dates referred to passed with no corn delivered. Oloffson then covered his obligation to his own vendee by purchasing 20,000 bushels at $1.35 per bushel and 20,000 bushels at $1.49 per bushel. The judgment from which Oloffson appeals awarded Oloffson as damages, the difference between the contract and the market prices on June 3, 1970, the day upon which Coomer first advised Oloffson he would not deliver.

Oloffson argues on this appeal that the proper measure of his damages was the difference between the contract price and the market price on the dates the corn should have been delivered in accordance with the April 16 agreement. Plaintiff does not seek any other damages. The trial court prior to entry of judgment, in an opinion finding the facts and reviewing the law, found that plaintiff was entitled to recover judgment only for the sum of $1,500 plus costs as we have indicated which is equal to the amount of the difference between the minimum contract price and the price on June 3, 1970, of $1.16 per bushel (taking the greatest differential from $1.12¼ per bushel multiplied by 40,000 bushels). We believe the findings and the judgment of the trial court were proper and should be affirmed.

It is clear that on June 3, 1970, Coomer repudiated the contract "with respect to performance not yet due." Under the terms of the Uniform Commercial Code the loss would impair the value of the contract to the remaining party in the amount as indicated. (Ill.Rev.Stat.1969, ch. 26, § 2–610.) As a consequence, on June 3, 1970, Oloffson, as the "aggrieved party", could then:

> "(a) for a commercially reasonable time await performance by the repudiating party; or

> (b) resort to any remedy for breach (Section 2–703 or Section 2–711), even though he has notified the repudiating party that he would await the latter's performance and has urged retraction; . . . "

If Oloffson chose to proceed under subparagraph (a) referred to, he could have awaited Coomer's performance for a "commercially reasonable time." As we indicate in the course of this opinion, that "commercially reasonable time" expired on June 3, 1970. The Uniform Commercial Code made a change in existing Illinois law in this respect, in that, prior to the adoption of the Code, a buyer in a position as Oloffson was privileged to await a seller's performance until the date that, according to the agreement, such performance was scheduled. To the extent that a "commercially reasonable time" is less than such date of performance, the Code now conditions the buyer's right to await performance. (See Ill.Rev.Stat.Ann.1969, ch. 26, § 2–610, Illinois Code Comment, Paragraph (a)).

If, alternatively, Oloffson had proceeded under subparagraph (b) by treating the repudiation as a breach, the remedies to which he would have been entitled were set forth in section 2–711 (Ill.Rev.Stat.1969, ch. 26, § 2–711), which is the only applicable section to which section 2–610(b) refers, according to the relevant portion of 2–711:

> "(1) Where the seller fails to make delivery or repudiates or the buyer rightfully rejects or justifiably revokes acceptance then with respect to any goods involved, and with respect to the whole if the breach goes to

the whole contract (Section 2–612), the buyer may cancel and whether or not he has done so may in addition to recovering so much of the price as has been paid

"(a) 'cover' and have damages under the next section as to all the goods affected whether or not they have been identified to the contract; or

"(b) recover damages for non-delivery as provided in this Article (Section 2–713). . . ."

Plaintiff, therefore, was privileged under Section 2–610 of the Uniform Commercial Code to proceed either under subparagraph (a) or under subparagraph (b). At the expiration of the "commercially reasonable time" specified in subparagraph (a), he in effect would have a duty to proceed under subparagraph (b) since subparagraph (b) directs reference to remedies generally available to a buyer upon a seller's breach.

Oloffson's right to await Coomer's performance under section 2–610(a) was conditioned upon his:

(i) waiting no longer than a "commercially reasonable time"; and

(ii) dealing with Coomer in good faith.

Since Coomer's statement to Oloffson on June 3, 1970, was unequivocal and since "cover" easily and immediately was available to Oloffson in the well-organized and easily accessible market for purchases of grain to be delivered in the future, it would be unreasonable for Oloffson on June 3, 1970, to have awaited Coomer's performance rather than to have proceeded under Section 2–610(b) and, thereunder, to elect then to treat the repudiation as a breach. Therefore, if Oloffson were relying on his right to effect cover under section 2–711(1)(a), June 3, 1970, might for the foregoing reason alone have been the day on which he acquired cover.

Additionally, however, the record and the finding of the trial court indicates that Oloffson adhered to a usage of trade that permitted his customers to cancel the contract for a future delivery of grain by making known to him a desire to cancel and paying to him the difference between the contract and market price on the day of cancellation. There is no indication whatever that Coomer was aware of this usage of trade. The trial court specifically found, as a fact, that, in the context in which Oloffson's failure to disclose this information occurred, Oloffson failed to act in good faith. According to Oloffson, he didn't ask for this information:

"I'm no information sender. If he had asked I would have told him exactly what to do. . . . I didn't feel my responsibility. I thought it his to ask, in which case I would tell him exactly what to do."

We feel that the words "for a commercially reasonable time" as set forth in Section 2–610(a) must be read relatively to the obligation of good faith that is defined in Section 2–103(1)(b) and imposed expressly in Section 1–203. (Ill.Rev.Stat.1969, ch. 26, § 2–103(1)(b) and § 1–203.)

The Uniform Commercial Code imposes upon the parties the obligation to deal with each other in good faith regardless of whether they are merchants. The Sales Article of the Code specifically defines good faith, "in the case of a merchant . . . [as] honesty in fact and the observance of reasonable commercial standards of fair dealing in the trade." For the foregoing reasons and likewise because Oloffson's failure to disclose in good faith might itself have been responsible for Coomer's failure to comply with the usage of trade which we must assume was known only to Oloffson, we conclude that a commercially reasonable time under the facts before us expired on June 3, 1970.

Imputing to Oloffson the consequences of Coomer's having acted upon the information that Oloffson in good faith should have transmitted to him, Oloffson knew or should have known on June 3, 1970, the limit of damages he probably could recover. If he were obligated to deliver grain to a third party, he knew or should have known that unless he covered on June 3, 1970, his own capital would be at risk with respect to his obligation to his own vendee. Therefore, on June 3, 1970, Oloffson, in effect, had a duty to proceed under subparagraph (b) of Section 2–610 and under subparagraphs (a) and (b) of subparagraph 1 of Section 2–711. If Oloffson had so proceeded under subparagraph (a) of Section 2–711, he should have effected cover and would have been entitled to recover damages all as provided in section 2–712, which requires that he would have had to cover in good faith without unreasonable delay. Since he would have had to effect cover on June 3, 1970, according to section 2–712(2), he would have been entitled to exactly the damages which the trial court awarded him in this cause.

Assuming that Oloffson had proceeded under subparagraph (b) of Section 2–711, he would have been entitled to recover from Coomer under Section 2–713 and Section 2–723 of the Commercial Code, the difference between the contract price and the market price on June 3, 1970, which is the date upon which he learned of the breach. This would produce precisely the same amount of damages which the trial court awarded him. [See: Ill.Rev.Stat.1969, ch. 26 § 2–723(1)].

Since the trial court properly awarded the damages to which plaintiff was entitled in this cause, the judgment of the circuit court of Bureau County is, therefore, affirmed.

Affirmed.

STOUDER and SCOTT, JJ., concur.

———

SECTION 2. PROSPECTIVE INABILITY TO PERFORM AND ADEQUATE ASSURANCE OF PERFORMANCE

———

UCC §§ 2–609, 2–702(1), 2–705(1)

[See Selected Source Materials Supplement]

———

RESTATEMENT, SECOND, CONTRACTS § 251

[See Selected Source Materials Supplement]

CISG ART. 71

[See Selected Source Materials Supplement]

UNIDROIT PRINCIPLES OF INTERNATIONAL COMMERCIAL CONTRACTS ART. 7.3.4

[See Selected Source Materials Supplement]

PRINCIPLES OF EUROPEAN CONTRACT LAW ART. 8.105

[See Selected Source Materials Supplement]

PITTSBURGH–DES MOINES STEEL CO. v. BROOKHAVEN MANOR WATER CO.

United States Court of Appeals, Seventh Circuit, 1976.
532 F.2d 572.

Seller of one-million gallon water tank brought action against buyer for repudiation of the sales contract and buyer counterclaimed for breach of contract. The United States District Court for the Northern District of Illinois, Thomas R. McMillen, J., entered judgment notwithstanding the verdict in favor of the buyer and seller appealed. . . .

Before CLARK, ASSOCIATE JUSTICE (Retired),* and CUMMINGS and PELL, CIRCUIT JUDGES.

PELL, CIRCUIT JUDGE. This is an appeal by the Pittsburgh–Des Moines Steel Company (hereinafter PDM) from the district court's entry of a judgment notwithstanding the verdict against PDM on its complaint for repudiation of contract and for Brookhaven Manor Water Company (hereinafter Brookhaven) on its counterclaim for breach of contract and from the district court's subsequent adjudgment of damages. The questions raised on appeal are whether the district court erred in entering judgment notwithstanding the verdict in favor of Brookhaven on the liability issue and whether error was committed in the district court's subsequent assessment of damages against PDM.

---

* Associate Justice Tom C. Clark, United States Supreme Court, Retired, is sitting by designation.

The record discloses the following series of events. On July 24, 1968, PDM, a designer, fabricator, and engineer of steel products, submitted a proposal to Brookhaven for the construction of a one-million-gallon water tank for $175,000. The original proposal incorporated, as terms of payment, 60 percent upon receipt of materials in PDM's plant, 30 percent upon completion of erection, and 10 percent upon completion of testing, or within 30 days after the tank had been made ready for testing. The original terms were not satisfactory to Brookhaven's president, Irving Betke, and were subsequently changed. The altered payment term provided that 100% of the contract price was due and payable within 30 days after the tank had been tested and accepted. The altered proposal was signed and accepted by Brookhaven on November 26, 1968.

Sometime during the following month Norman Knuttel, PDM's district manager who had prepared and signed the original and revised proposals, talked to a representative of the Arbanas Construction Company which company had contracted with Brookhaven for the construction of the tank foundation. Knuttel was informed that Brookhaven had received a loan from Diversified Finance Corporation. Although this information as to the receipt of the loan was incorrect, Brookhaven had negotiated with Diversified for a loan for the purpose of the construction which negotiations continued into the following year. Under date of January 3, 1969, PDM's credit manager wrote Diversified with a copy to Betke which letter in part was as follows:

> "[W]e hereby request a letter assuring that $175,000.00 for payment of the referenced project will be held in escrow and fully committed to payment to us upon completion of referenced elevated tank.

> "As a matter of good business we are holding this order in abeyance until receipt of such notification."

The contract contained no provision for escrow financing. Brookhaven, through Betke, took no action upon the receipt of the copy of the letter. Subsequently, after further correspondence and meetings, resulting primarily from Brookhaven's not having secured a planned loan of $275,000.00 from Diversified Finance, PDM's credit manager sent an air mail, special delivery letter to Betke, dated March 19, 1969, which suggested that Betke "mail us your personal guarantee of payment of $175,000.00 as per the contract, to protect us in the interim between now and the time your loan is completed."

While the contract specified the payment of the amount mentioned no later than 30 days after completion of the tank, it was silent as to any reference to a personal guarantee by Betke. The letter concluded as follows:

> "Upon receipt of such guarantee, we could immediately set in motion our shop fabrication which would result in earlier completion of your new tank.

> "When your loan is completed we will still require a letter of instructions to be forwarded from you to your bank, or other financial institution which extends this loan, that $175,000.00 is to be held in escrow for disbursement only to Pittsburgh–Des Moines Steel Company in accordance with our contract."

The construction of the water tower was scheduled to begin on April 15, 1969. A crew had been scheduled for the site three months previously, and a crew was ready to appear there on April 15, 1969. As matters transpired, however, the tank was never installed at Brookhaven's site. On March 31, 1969, Betke sent PDM Comptroller Harry Kelly his personal financial statement, but he did not send PDM his personal guarantee for the loan. After Betke failed to provide his personal guarantee of the $175,000.00 contract price, PDM took no further steps toward performance.[1] On April 22, 1969, Kelly, PDM Secretary–Treasurer Tom Morris, PDM Sales Manager Dwight Long, and Betke attended a meeting on the Brookhaven premises. Although the record reveals somewhat inconsistent versions of the details of that meeting, it appears that Morris told Betke that PDM would complete the fabrication of the tank and deliver it to the job site within a matter of weeks but that Betke replied that he had no need for the tank until the following year.

Further efforts to implement the contract broke down completely after April 22, 1969. Brookhaven's installation of the reinforced concrete foundation for the tank had been accomplished at a cost to it of $18,895. Subsequent to the March meeting, Brookhaven purchased additional land and developed two wells which provided an adequate water supply. Brookhaven later sold all its assets, including both equipment and land, to the City of Darien. At the trial of the damages issue, an expert in demolition testified that the cost of removing the reinforced concrete foundation would be about $7,000. On the basis of this testimony, which was proffered upon the legal theory that Brookhaven had a right to recover the cost of the removal, the district court found that the total amount of damages sustained by Brookhaven was the sum of $25,895.00 and entered judgment in its favor for that amount....

II.   Claimed Bases of Liability

Under the contract as executed, into which prior negotiations had been merged, Brookhaven's performance of its principal obligation to pay the purchase price was not due until after the completion of construction. Nevertheless within a period of time shortly more than one month after the contract became effective, PDM was requesting that a prospective lender of the funds to Brookhaven should hold the entire $175,000.00 in escrow. This was not a request that a lending institution give a letter of intent or otherwise confirm that it would make a particular loan when the payment became due after completion of construction. Instead the letter explicitly would, if honored, have required Brookhaven to complete all necessary loan papers and to arrange for the consummation of the loan, the proceeds of which would then be held by Diversified for some months until the work was completed. It is no answer to say that perhaps Brookhaven could have arranged for the escrowed fund to have been invested in some safe, readily liquidable form which might offset in part at least the loss to Brookhaven resulting from having to pay interest on money already borrowed. PDM having purported to agree not to ask for progress payments during the course of construction, more than half of which would have been due before the first act took place by PDM on the construction site, it now was substituting another requirement clearly beyond

---

1. The record indicates that as of April 22, 1969, the foundation, the construction of which was the obligation of Brookhaven, had been completed and two-thirds of the required tankage parts, which were the obligation of PDM, had been fabricated. However, it is also noted that as late as March 19, 1969, PDM had written Betke that upon the receipt of the guarantee, the shop could immediately set in motion fabrication. It is not clear whether PDM did anything to dispel the clear inference to Betke that there would be no fabrication, or at least further fabrication, until the guarantee had been received.

any requirement contemplated in the contract which would not have put the purchase price in hand but would nevertheless have it where it could be available for the picking at the appropriate time. The contract is silent as to any right of PDM to insist Brookhaven provide any such guarantee during the period before completion of construction. Further, PDM made it quite clear that it was "holding this order in abeyance until receipt of" notification that the money was being so held. We find no basis for an inference that at this time Brookhaven was not ready, willing and able to perform its obligations under the contract nor that it would not be able to pay when it owed. The fact that there had been negotiations for a loan of money that would not be needed for some months, which negotiations had not come to fruition, does not support such an inference. Two months after the letter to Diversified, PDM reaffirmed its lack of retreat from the position of requiring assurance that the money would be forthcoming.

PDM argues that its position was in accordance with Section 2–609 of the Uniform Commercial Code (UCC) enacted into law in Illinois as Ill.Rev.Stat. ch. 26, sec. 2–609. . . .

. . . The question . . . is whether PDM's actions subsequent to the execution of the contract were within the protection provided by § 2–609. We hold that they were not.

The performance to which PDM was entitled was the full payment of the purchase price within a specified time after the completion of the tank. While we have a substantial question as to whether PDM made a written demand as required by the statute, in keeping with our concept that the UCC should be liberally construed, we do not desire to rest our decision on a formalistic approach. Letters were written which conveyed what PDM wanted done before they would pursue their obligations under the contract. The fundamental problem is that these letters, if they be deemed to be in the nature of a demand, demanded more than that to which PDM was entitled and the demand was not founded upon what in our opinion was an actuating basis for the statute's applicability.

We do not construe § 2–609 as being a vehicle without more for an implied term being inserted in a contract when a substantially equivalent term was expressly waived in the contract. The something more to trigger applicability of the statute is that the expectation of due performance on the part of the other party entertained at contracting time no longer exists because of "reasonable grounds for insecurity" arising. We find that PDM's actions in demanding either the escrowing of the purchase price or a personal guarantee lacked the necessary predicate of reasonable grounds for insecurity having arisen. The contract negates the existence of any basis for insecurity at the time of the contract when PDM was willing to wait 30 days beyond completion for payment. The fact that Brookhaven had not completed its loan negotiations does not constitute reasonable grounds for insecurity when the money in question was not to be needed for some months. Reasonable business men prefer in the absence of some compulsive reason not to commence paying interest on borrowed money until the time for the use for that money is at hand. The credit manager's January letter that the order was being held in abeyance until receipt of notification of escrowing was based upon a "matter of good business," but not upon any change of condition bearing upon Brookhaven's ability to discharge its payment obligation under the contract. With regard to the later request for a personal guarantee, it is not uncommon for an individual to decline assuming obligations of a corporation in which he is a shareholder. Indeed, the use of the corporate device frequently has as a principal purpose the limitation on individual exposure to liability. If an unfavorable risk in dealing with a corporation exists at contracting time, good business judgment may well indicate that an assurance be secured before contracting that there will be individual shareholder back-up. None of this occurred and the record is silent as to any reasonable grounds for insecurity arising thereafter.

It is true that one officer of PDM testified that the company did not send a crew because we questioned whether we might be paid for the project "at that time." Some more objective factual basis than a subjective questioning, in our opinion, is needed to demonstrate reasonable grounds for insecurity. Likewise, another PDM officer testified that it was the company's normal and regular procedure not to erect a structure "until we have reason to believe that the funds to pay for the structure *are* available." The time of which he was speaking was a time at which there was no contractual requirement that the funds be available. The funds were only required to be available after completion of installation. He testified further that the normal procedure was not to erect until satisfactory arrangements were made. None of this subjectively normal procedure was imposed as a provision in the contract which in view of the withdrawn provision for progress payments showed reasonably to Brookhaven that not only payment, but arrangements for payment, would not be necessary until after completion.

We, of course, would not deprive PDM of resort to § 2–609 if there had been a demonstration that reasonable grounds for insecurity had arisen. The proof in that respect was lacking. The comptroller and supervisor of PDM's credit department testified that he had access to all of the credit information that the company had regarding Brookhaven, that he had reviewed that information, and that he was unaware of any change in the financial condition of Brookhaven between November of 1968 and the end of 1969. Finally, we note that despite the professed subjective questioning in April as to whether PDM might be paid, the credit manager as early as January had said that the job would be held in abeyance until arrangements had been made for escrowing and a month after the questioning, the questioning officer had offered to proceed with construction in exchange for an interest in Brookhaven, an unlikely course if Brookhaven were financially in a questionable condition. There was also testimony with the same inference that PDM was not fearful of Brookhaven's financial stability or ability to pay in connection with PDM lending to Brookhaven the amount involved at an interest rate of 9½% which rate was then unacceptable to Brookhaven. If the buyer was unable to pay for the performance of the contract, it is difficult to see that it was better able to pay a promissory note. We do not fault Brookhaven for its rejection of various proposals advanced by PDM each of which amounted to a rewriting of the contract in the absence of a proper § 2–609 basis. The fact, if it were a fact, that Brookhaven may not have had a large amount of cash lying in the bank in a checking account, not an unusual situation for a real estate developer, does not support the belief that it, as a company with substantial assets, would fail to meet its obligations as they fell due. Section 2–609 is a protective device when reasonable grounds for insecurity arise; it is not a pen for rewriting a contract in the absence of those reasonable grounds having arisen, particularly when the proposed rewriting involves the very factors which had been waived by the one now attempting to wield the pen. The situation is made no more persuasive for PDM when it is recalled that that company was the original scrivener.

Brookhaven's request to put off the contract for a year clearly came after PDM's repudiation of the contract and was indicative of nothing more than that Brookhaven was willing to undertake a new arrangement with PDM a year hence. Pursuant to § 2–610 of the UCC, Brookhaven was entitled to suspend its own performance by virtue of the anticipatory repudiation by PDM and to resort to available remedies, including damages pursuant to § 2–711 of the Code.[2] . . .

For the reasons hereinbefore set out the judgment of the district court is affirmed.

CUMMINGS, CIRCUIT JUDGE (concurring).

Although I agree with the result reached in the majority opinion, I differ with the reasoning. Reasonable men could certainly conclude that PDM had legitimate grounds to question Brookhaven's ability to pay for the water tank. When the contract was signed, the parties understood that Brookhaven would obtain a loan to help pay for the project. When the loan failed to materialize, a prudent businessman would have "reasonable grounds for insecurity." I disagree that there must be a fundamental change in the financial position of the buyer before the seller can invoke the protection of UCC § 2–609. Rather, I believe that the Section was designed to cover instances where an underlying condition of the contract, even if not expressly incorporated into the written document, fails to occur. See Comment 3 to UCC § 2–609. Whether, in a specific case, the breach of the condition gives a party "reasonable grounds for insecurity" is a question of fact for the jury.

UCC § 2–609, however, does not give the alarmed party a right to redraft the contract. Whether the party invoking that provision is merely requesting an assurance that performance will be forthcoming or whether he is attempting to alter the contract is a mixed question of law and fact, depending in part upon the court's interpretation of the obligations imposed on the parties. In this case, PDM would have been assured only if significant changes in the contract were made, either by receiving Betke's personal guarantee, by attaining escrow financing or by purchasing an interest in Brookhaven. The district court could properly conclude as a matter of law that these requests by PDM demanded more than a commercially "adequate assurance of due performance."

J. WHITE & R. SUMMERS, UNIFORM COMMERCIAL CODE § 6–2 (5th ed. 2000). "All demands for adequate assurance call for more than was originally promised under the contract, and that is precisely what 2–609 authorizes. If, for example, it was appropriate to sell on open credit at the

----

2. . . . [W]e find no merit in PDM's argument that even if its January action could be construed as an anticipatory repudiation under § 2–610, its subsequent actions demonstrated a retraction of the anticipatory repudiation pursuant to § 2–611. That section requires a clear indication to the aggrieved party "that the repudiating party intends to perform." PDM only made it clear throughout that it intended to perform if Brookhaven gave assurances not required of it legally or contractually.

outset of a contract but subsequent events cause insecurity, 2–609 calls for modification of the contract to provide greater security to the seller than the seller could have demanded, absent such insecurity. Thus it is the very purpose of 2–609 to authorize one party to insist upon more than the contract gives. Of course there are limits. One can demand only 'adequate' assurances. If a party demands and receives specific assurances, then absent a further change of circumstances, the assurances demanded and received are adequate, and the party who has demanded the assurances is bound to proceed. Of course, the party receiving assurances is entitled to conforming performance. Read properly section 2–609 will mitigate the lawyer's dilemma about what to advise a client upon an apparent repudiation."

NORCON POWER PARTNERS v. NIAGARA MOHAWK POWER CORP.

Court of Appeals of New York, 1998.
92 N.Y.2d 458, 705 N.E.2d 656, 682 N.Y.S.2d 664.

BELLACOSA, J.

The doctrine, known as demand for adequate assurance of future performance, is at the heart of a Federal lawsuit that stems from a 1989 contract between Norcon Power Partners, L.P., an independent power producer, and Niagara Mohawk Power Corporation, a public utility provider. Niagara Mohawk undertook to purchase electricity generated at Norcon's Pennsylvania facility. The contract was for 25 years, but the differences emerged during the early years of the arrangement.

The case arrives on this Court's docket by certification of the substantive law question from the United States Court of Appeals for the Second Circuit. Our Court is presented with an open issue that should be settled within the framework of New York's common-law development. We accepted the responsibility to address this question involving New York contract law:

> "Does a party have the right to demand adequate assurance of future performance when reasonable grounds arise to believe that the other party will commit a breach by non-performance of a contract governed by New York law, where the other party is solvent and the contract is not governed by the U.C.C.?" (Norcon Power Partners v. Niagara Mohawk Power Corp., 110 F.3d 6, 9 (2d Cir.1997).)

As framed by the particular dispute, we answer the law question in the affirmative with an appreciation of this Court's traditional common-law developmental method, and as proportioned to the precedential sweep of our rulings.

I.

The Second Circuit Court of Appeals describes the three pricing periods, structure and details [of the contract between the parties] as follows:

> "In the first period, Niagara Mohawk pays Norcon six cents per kilowatt-hour for electricity. In the second and third periods, the price paid by Niagara Mohawk is based on its 'avoided cost.' The avoided cost reflects the cost that Niagara Mohawk would incur to generate electricity

itself or purchase it from other sources. In the second period, if the avoided cost falls below a certain floor price (calculated according to a formula), Niagara Mohawk is obligated to pay the floor price. By the same token, if the avoided cost rises above a certain amount (calculated according to a formula), Niagara Mohawk's payments are capped by a ceiling price. An 'adjustment account' tracks the difference between payments actually made by Niagara Mohawk in the second period and what those payments would have been if based solely on Niagara Mohawk's avoided cost.

"In the third period, the price paid by Niagara Mohawk is based on its avoided cost without any ceiling or floor price. Payments made by Niagara Mohawk in the third period are adjusted to account for any balance existing in the adjustment account that operated in the second period. If the adjustment account contains a balance in favor of Niagara Mohawk—that is, the payments actually made by Niagara Mohawk in the second period exceeded what those payments would have been if based solely on Niagara Mohawk's avoided cost—then the rate paid by Niagara Mohawk will be reduced to reflect the credit. If the adjustment account contains a balance in favor of Norcon, Niagara Mohawk must make increased payments to Norcon. If a balance exists in the adjustment account at the end of the third period, the party owing the balance must pay the balance in full within thirty days of the termination of the third period" (Norcon Power Partners v. Niagara Mohawk Power Corp., 110 F.3d 6, 7, supra).

In February 1994, Niagara Mohawk presented Norcon with a letter stating its belief, based on revised avoided cost estimates, that substantial credits in Niagara Mohawk's favor would accrue in the adjustment account during the second pricing period. "[A]nalysis shows that the Cumulative Avoided Cost Account will reach over $610 million by the end of the second period." Anticipating that Norcon would not be able to satisfy the daily escalating credits in the third period, Niagara Mohawk demanded that "Norcon provide adequate assurance to Niagara Mohawk that Norcon will duly perform all of its future repayment obligations."

Norcon promptly sued Niagara Mohawk in the United States District Court, Southern District of New York. It sought a declaration that Niagara Mohawk had no contractual right under New York State law to demand adequate assurance, beyond security provisions negotiated and expressed in the agreement. Norcon also sought a permanent injunction to stop Niagara Mohawk from anticipatorily terminating the contract based on the reasons described in the demand letter. Niagara Mohawk counterclaimed. It sought a counter declaration that it properly invoked a right to demand adequate assurance of Norcon's future payment performance of the contract.

The District Court granted Norcon's motion for summary judgment. It reasoned that New York common law recognizes the exceptional doctrine of demand for adequate assurance only when a promisor becomes insolvent, and also when the statutory sale of goods provision under UCC 2–609, is involved. Thus, the District Court ruled in Norcon's favor because neither exception applied, in fact or by analogy to the particular dispute (decided sub nom. Encogen Four Partners v. Niagara Mohawk Power Corp., 914 F.Supp. 57 (S.D.N.Y.1996)).

The Second Circuit Court of Appeals preliminarily agrees (110 F.3d 6, supra) with the District Court that, except in the case of insolvency, no common-law or statutory right to demand adequate assurance exists under New York law which would affect non-UCC contracts, like the instant one. Because of the uncertainty concerning this substantive law question the Second Circuit certified the question to our Court as an aid to its correct application of New York law, and with an eye toward settlement of the important precedential impact on existing and future non-UCC commercial law matters and disputes.

II.

Our analysis should reference a brief review of the evolution of the doctrine of demands for adequate assurance. Its roots spring from the doctrine of anticipatory repudiation (see, Garvin, Adequate Assurance of Performance: Of Risk, Duress, and Cognition, 69 U. Colo. L. Rev. 71, 77 [1998]). Under that familiar precept, when a party repudiates contractual duties "prior to the time designated for performance and before" all of the consideration has been fulfilled, the "repudiation entitles the nonrepudiating party to claim damages for total breach" (Long Is. R.R. Co. v. Northville Indus. Corp., 41 N.Y.2d 455, 463, 393 N.Y.S.2d 925, 362 N.E.2d 558; see, II Farnsworth, Contracts § 8.20; Restatement [Second] of Contracts § 253; UCC 2–610). A repudiation can be either "a statement by the obligor to the obligee indicating that the obligor will commit a breach that would of itself give the obligee a claim for damages for total breach" or "a voluntary affirmative act which renders the obligor unable or apparently unable to perform without such a breach" (Restatement [Second] of Contracts § 250; see, II Farnsworth, Contracts § 8.21; UCC 2–610, Comment 1).

That switch in performance expectation and burden is readily available, applied and justified when a breaching party's words or deeds are unequivocal. Such a discernible line in the sand clears the way for the nonbreaching party to broach some responsive action. When, however, the apparently breaching party's actions are equivocal or less certain, then the nonbreaching party who senses an approaching storm cloud, affecting the contractual performance, is presented with a dilemma, and must weigh hard choices and serious consequences. One commentator has described the forecast options in this way:

> "If the promisee regards the apparent repudiation as an anticipatory repudiation, terminates his or her own performance and sues for breach, the promisee is placed in jeopardy of being found to have breached if the court determines that the apparent repudiation was not sufficiently clear and unequivocal to constitute an anticipatory repudiation justifying nonperformance. If, on the other hand, the promisee continues to perform after perceiving an apparent repudiation, and it is subsequently determined that an anticipatory repudiation took place, the promisee may be denied recovery for post-repudiation expenditures because of his or her failure to avoid those expenses as part of a reasonable effort to mitigate damages after the repudiation" (Crespi, The Adequate Assurances Doctrine after U.C.C. § 2–609: A Test of the Efficiency of the Common Law, 38 Vill. L. Rev. 179, 183 [1993]). . . .

III.

The Uniform Commercial Code settled on a mechanism for relieving some of this uncertainty. It allows a party to a contract for the sale of goods to demand assurance of future performance from the other party when reasonable grounds for insecurity exist (see, UCC 2–609; II Farnsworth, Contracts § 8.23). When adequate assurance is not forthcoming, repudiation is deemed confirmed, and the nonbreaching party is allowed to take reasonable actions as though a repudiation had occurred (see, 4 Anderson, Uniform Commercial Code § 2–609:3 [3d ed. 1997 rev.]).

UCC 2–609 provides, in relevant part:

"(1) A contract for sale imposes an obligation on each party that the other's expectation of receiving due performance will not be impaired. When reasonable grounds for insecurity arise with respect to the performance of either party the other may in writing demand adequate assurance of due performance and until he receives such assurance may if commercially reasonable suspend any performance for which he has not already received the agreed return.

"(4) After receipt of a justified demand failure to provide within a reasonable time not exceeding thirty days such assurance of due performance as is adequate under the circumstances of the particular case is a repudiation of the contract."

In theory, this UCC relief valve recognizes that "the essential purpose of a contract between commercial [parties] is actual performance and that a continuing sense of reliance and security that the promised performance will be forthcoming when due, is an important feature of the bargain" (UCC 2–609, Comment 1). In application, section 2–609 successfully implements the laudatory objectives of quieting the doubt a party fearing repudiation may have, mitigating the dilemma flowing from that doubt, and offering the nonbreaching party the opportunity to interpose timely action to deal with the unusual development (see, II Farnsworth, Contracts § 8.23a . . .).

Indeed, UCC 2–609 has been considered so effective in bridging the doctrinal, exceptional and operational gap related to the doctrine of anticipatory breach that some States have imported the complementary regimen of demand for adequate assurance to common-law categories of contract law, using UCC 2–609 as the synapse (see, e.g., Lo Re v. Tel–Air Communications, 200 N.J.Super. 59, 490 A.2d 344 [finding support in UCC 2–609 and Restatement (Second) of Contracts § 251 for applying doctrine of adequate assurance to contract to purchase radio station]; Conference Ctr. v. TRC—The Research Corp. of New England, 189 Conn. 212, 455 A.2d 857 [analogizing to UCC 2–609, as supported by Restatement (Second) of Contracts § 251, in context of constructive eviction]).

Commentators have helped nudge this development along. They have noted that the problems redressed by UCC 2–609 are not unique to contracts for sale of goods, regulated under a purely statutory regime. Thus, they have cogently identified the need for the doctrine to be available in exceptional and qualifying common-law contractual settings and disputes because of similar practical, theoretical and salutary objectives (e.g., predictability, definiteness, and stability in commercial dealings and expectations) (see, e.g., Campbell, op.

cit., at 1299–1304; see generally, White, Eight Cases and Section 251, 67 Cornell L. Rev. 841 [1982]; Dowling, op. cit.).

The American Law Institute through its Restatement (Second) of Contracts has also recognized and collected the authorities supporting this modern development. Its process and work settled upon this black letter language:

> "(1) Where reasonable grounds arise to believe that the obligor will commit a breach by non-performance that would of itself give the obligee a claim for damages for total breach under § 243, the obligee may demand adequate assurance of due performance and may, if reasonable, suspend any performance for which he has not already received the agreed exchange until he receives such assurance.

> "(2) The obligee may treat as a repudiation the obligor's failure to provide within a reasonable time such assurance of due performance as is adequate in the circumstances of the particular case" (Restatement [Second] of Contracts § 251).

Modeled on UCC 2–609, § 251 tracks "the principle that the parties to a contract look to actual performance 'and that a continuing sense of reliance and security that the promised performance will be forthcoming when due, is an important feature of the bargain'" (Restatement [Second] of Contracts § 251, comment a, quoting UCC 2–609, Comment 1). The duty of good faith and fair dealing in the performance of the contract is also reflected in section 251 (see, Restatement [Second] of Contracts § 251, comment a).

Some States have adopted Restatement § 251 as their common law of contracts, in varying degrees and classifications (see, e.g., Carfield & Sons v. Cowling, 616 P.2d 1008 [Colo] [construction contract]; L.E. Spitzer Co. v. Barron, 581 P.2d 213 [Alaska] [construction contract]; Drinkwater v. Patten Realty Corp., 563 A.2d 772 [Me] [sale of real estate]; Jonnet Dev. Corp. v. Dietrich Indus., 316 Pa.Super. 533, 463 A.2d 1026 [real estate lease]; but see, Mollohan v. Black Rock Contr., 160 W.Va. 446, 235 S.E.2d 813 [declining to adopt section 251, except to the extent that failure to give adequate assurance on demand may be some evidence of repudiation]).

IV.

New York, up to now, has refrained from expanding the right to demand adequate assurance of performance beyond the Uniform Commercial Code (see, Sterling Power Partners v. Niagara Mohawk Power Corp., 239 A.D.2d 191, 657 N.Y.S.2d 407, appeal dismissed 92 N.Y.2d 877, 677 N.Y.S.2d 783, 700 N.E.2d 322; Schenectady Steel Co. v. Trimpoli Gen. Constr. Co., 43 A.D.2d 234, 350 N.Y.S.2d 920, affd. on other grounds 34 N.Y.2d 939, 359 N.Y.S.2d 560, 316 N.E.2d 875). The only other recognized exception is the insolvency setting (see, Hanna v. Florence Iron Co...., 222 N.Y. 290, 118 N.E. 629; Pardee v. Kanady, 100 N.Y. 121, 2 N.E. 885; Updike v. Oakland Motor Car Co., 229 App.Div. 632, 242 N.Y.S. 329). Hence, the need for this certified question emerged so this Court could provide guidance towards a correct resolution of the Federal lawsuit by settling New York law with a modern pronouncement governing this kind of contract and dispute.

Niagara Mohawk, before our Court through the certified question from the Federal court, urges a comprehensive adaptation of the exceptional demand tool. This wholesale approach has also been advocated by the commentators (see generally, Dowling, op. cit.; Campbell, op. cit.). Indeed, it is even reflected in the breadth of the wording of the certified question.

This Court's jurisprudence, however, usually evolves by deciding cases and settling the law more modestly (Rooney v. Tyson, 91 N.Y.2d 685, 694, 674 N.Y.S.2d 616, 697 N.E.2d 571, citing Cardozo, Nature of the Judicial Process, in Selected Writings of Benjamin Nathan Cardozo, at 115, 134 [Margaret E. Hall ed. 1947] [observing that Judges proceed interstitially]). The twin purposes and functions of this Court's work require significant professional discipline and judicious circumspection.

We conclude, therefore, that it is unnecessary, while fulfilling the important and useful certification role, to promulgate so sweeping a change and proposition in contract law, as has been sought, in one dramatic promulgation. That approach might clash with our customary incremental common-law developmental process, rooted in particular fact patterns and keener wisdom acquired through observations of empirical application of a proportioned, less than absolute, rule in future cases.

It is well to note the axiom that deciding a specific case, even with the precedential comet's tail its rationale illuminates, is very different from enacting a statute of general and universal application (see, Breitel, The Lawmakers, 2 Benjamin N. Cardozo Memorial Lectures 761, 788 [1965] ["(P)rocedurally, courts are limited to viewing the problem as presented in a litigated case within the four corners of its record. A multiplication of cases will broaden the view because of the multiplication of records, but the limitation still persists because the records are confined by the rules of procedure, legal relevance, and evidence."]).

Experience and patience thus offer a more secure and realistic path to a better and fairer rule, in theory and in practical application. Therefore, this Court chooses to take the traditionally subtler approach, consistent with the proven benefits of the maturation process of the common law, including in the very area of anticipatory repudiation which spawns this relatively newer demand for assurance corollary (see, Garvin, op. cit., at 77–80; Robertson, op. cit., at 307–310; Dowling, op. cit., at 1359–1362; see also, Breitel, op. cit., at 781–782 [1965] ["The commonplace, for which the Holmeses and the Cardozos had to blaze a trail in the judicial realm, assumes the rightness of courts in making interstitial law, filling gaps in the statutory and decisional rules, and at a snail-like pace giving some forward movement to the developing law. Any law creation more drastic than this is often said and thought to be an invalid encroachment on the legislative branch."]).

This Court is now persuaded that the policies underlying the UCC 2–609 counterpart should apply with similar cogency for the resolution of this kind of controversy. A useful analogy can be drawn between the contract at issue and a contract for the sale of goods. If the contract here was in all respects the same, except that it was for the sale of oil or some other tangible commodity instead of the sale of electricity, the parties would unquestionably be governed by the demand for adequate assurance of performance factors in UCC 2–609. We are convinced to take this prudent step because it puts commercial parties in these kinds of disputes at relatively arm's length equilibrium in terms of reliability and uniformity of governing legal rubrics. The availability of the doctrine may even provide an incentive and tool for parties to resolve their own differences, perhaps without the necessity of judicial intervention. Open, serious renegotiation of dramatic developments and changes in unusual contractual expectations and qualifying circumstances would occur because of and with an eye to the doctrine's application.

The various authorities, factors and concerns, in sum, prompt the prudence and awareness of the usefulness of recognizing the extension of the doctrine of demand for adequate assurance, as a common-law analogue. It should apply to the type of long-term commercial contract between corporate entities entered into by Norcon and Niagara Mohawk here, which is complex and not reasonably susceptible of all security features being anticipated, bargained for and incorporated in the original contract. Norcon's performance, in terms of reimbursing Niagara Mohawk for credits, is still years away. In the meantime, potential quantifiable damages are accumulating and Niagara Mohawk must weigh the hard choices and serious consequences that the doctrine of demand for adequate assurance is designed to mitigate. This Court needs to go no further in its promulgation of the legal standard as this suffices to declare a dispositive and proportioned answer to the certified question.

Accordingly, the certified question should be answered in the affirmative.

Chief Judge KAYE and Judges SMITH, LEVINE, CIPARICK and WESLEY concur.

Following certification of a question by the United States Court of Appeals for the Second Circuit and acceptance of the question by this Court pursuant to section 500.17 of the Rules of the Court of Appeals (22 NYCRR 500.17), and after hearing argument by counsel for the parties and consideration of the briefs and the record submitted, certified question answered in the affirmative.

NOTE ON AFFIRMATIVE RECOVERY UNDER
UCC § 2–609

Although UCC § 2–609 is normally used as a defense by a buyer or seller who has stopped performing on the ground of insecurity, Subsection (4) provides that "[a]fter receipt of a justified demand [for assurance,] failure to provide within a reasonable time not exceeding thirty days such assurance of due performance as is adequate under the circumstances of the particular case is a repudiation of the contract." A repudiation is itself a breach, and therefore gives rise to a right of action by a party who rightfully but unsuccessfully demanded assurance. See Creusot–Loire International, Inc. v. Coppus Engineering Corp., 585 F.Supp. 45 (S.D.N.Y.1983); Universal Builders Corp. v. United Methodist Convalescent Homes, Inc., 7 Conn.App. 318, 508 A.2d 819 (1986).

*

Appendix A

THE STATUTE OF FRAUDS

Analysis

SECTION 1.   INTRODUCTION

Under the Statute of Frauds, certain types of contracts are unenforceable against a party unless the contract is in writing, or evidenced by a writing (or, to use the terminology of the Statute, by a "memorandum") signed by the party to be charged, that is, the party sought to be held liable under the contract. (For ease of exposition, in the balance of this Appendix this requirement, where applicable, will be referred to simply as a requirement that a contract be in writing.) The purpose of this Appendix is to provide an introduction to the most significant types of problems that can arise under the Statute.

This Appendix includes a number of Examples, in the form of hypothetical cases and their resolutions. The resolutions offered in the Examples are those that would normally be rendered in a typical American jurisdiction, although not necessarily in every jurisdiction.

A note on terminology: When a contract is of a type that is covered by the Statute, and is not in writing, the contract is said to be "within the Statute." However, when an exception to the Statute applies, the contract is said to be "taken out of the Statute" by virtue of the exception. Thus a contract that is within the Statute and is not in writing is unenforceable unless it is taken out of the Statute by an exception. If it is taken out of the Statute, the contract is enforceable although not in writing.

SECTION 2. THE TEXT OF THE ORIGINAL STATUTE

The original English Statute of Frauds was passed in 1677. Its title was "An Act for Prevention of Frauds and Perjuries." It contained twenty-five sections, and attempted to prevent fraud in the proof of many different kinds of legal transactions—not only in the area of contracts, but also in the areas of assignments, deeds to land, trusts, and wills. To insure a trustworthy memorial of what occurred, and thereby to prevent perjury, many sections of the Statute required a signed writing to make particular kinds of acts or transactions enforceable. In some cases an additional formality, such as attestation by witnesses, was required. In others, an alternative formality was permitted, such as providing that a will may be effectively revoked if it is canceled, torn, or obliterated by the testator or under his immediate direction. Certain sections of the Statute related to matters of procedure and land law that had only an indirect relation to the general object of the Statute.

The provisions of the original Statute that are chiefly relevant to contract law are Sections 4 and 17, reproduced below. In the balance of this Appendix, references to "the Statute of Frauds" or "the Statute" refer to those two sections and their modern counterparts. Spelling and punctuation have been modernized, and some liberties have been taken with the original in the paragraphing and numbering of subsections.

Section 4

And be it further enacted . . . that . . . no action shall be brought

(1) whereby to charge any executor or administrator upon any special promise to answer damages out of his own estate; or

(2) whereby to charge the defendant upon any special promise to answer for the debt, default or miscarriages of another person; or

(3) to charge any person upon any agreement made upon consideration of marriage; or

(4) upon any contract or sale of lands, tenements or hereditaments, or any interest in or concerning them; or

(5) upon any agreement that is not to be performed within the space of one year from the making thereof;

unless the agreement upon which such action shall be brought, or some memorandum or note thereof, shall be in writing, and signed by the party to be charged therewith, or some other person thereunto by him lawfully authorized.

Section 17

[The "sale-of-goods" section]

And be it further enacted ... that ... no contract for the sale of any goods, wares or merchandises for the price of ten pounds sterling or upwards shall be allowed to be good, except

     (a) the buyer shall accept part of the goods so sold and actually receive the same; or

     (b) give something in earnest to bind the bargain or in part payment; or

     (c) that some note or memorandum in writing of the said bargain be made and signed by the parties to be charged by such contract or their agents thereunto lawfully authorized.

(Note that the Statute uses the terms "agreement" and "contract" interchangeably. The same usage will be followed in this Appendix.)

SECTION 3. THE PURPOSE OF THE STATUTE

Legislation that makes the enforceability of an act or transaction depend upon the observance of certain formalities may be adopted for a variety of reasons. In contract law, Austin discerned two principal reasons for requiring formalities: (1) "to provide evidence of the existence and purport of the contract, in case of controversy," and (2) "to prevent inconsiderate [not well-thought-through] engagements." J. Austin, Fragments—On Contracts, 2 Lectures on Jurisprudence 940 (4th ed., 1879).

Certainly the Statute of Frauds was intended to serve the first purpose. It was an act to prevent "frauds and perjuries," and stated in its preamble that it was aimed at "many fraudulent practices which are commonly endeavored to be upheld by perjury, and subornation of perjury." To handicap the plaintiff who might seek to establish a contract by perjured testimony, the Statute required him to base his case on a writing signed by the defendant. In this respect the purpose of the Statute was evidentiary. It sought a trustworthy memorial of the transaction and its terms.

On the other hand, it is clear that the Statute could also have had another purpose, that which Austin described as preventing "inconsiderate engagements." When a person is not bound unless and until she has signed a writing, a procedure has been established that will tend to prevent persons from slipping into legal undertakings without a full appreciation of what they are doing, because the writing may serve as a warning or deterrent against hasty action.

If the drafters of the Statute of Frauds had this second object in mind, they left no trace of it in the historical records of the time or in the language of the act they drew up. On the other hand, the judges who have interpreted the Statute have occasionally assumed that ensuring deliberation in the making of contracts was a collateral and secondary purpose of the Statute. Thus in Warden v. Jones, 1857, 2 De.Gex & J. 76, 83–84, the court said, "The law has ... wisely forbidden [oral proof of contracts in consideration of marriage]. Persons are so likely to be led into such promises inconsiderately, that the law has wisely required them to be manifested by writing." Expressions tending toward the same thought will be found in cases involving some other sections of the Statute, particularly the "suretyship" provision, section 4(2).

However, there are holdings that can only be justified on the view that the sole purpose of the Statute is to ensure reliable evidence of the contract. If the purpose of the Statute was to protect persons against hasty engagements, it would seem that the Statute could not be satisfied simply by a writing that repudiates the contract. Indeed, Restatement Second provides that in the case of a contract in consideration of marriage, "a subsequent writing does not satisfy the Statute unless made as a memorandum of the agreement," because "[t]he marriage provision ... performs a cautionary function" as well as an evidentiary one. Restatement Second § 133, comment a. See also Restatement Second § 124, comment d. However, the general rule is that a writing that sets forth an earlier oral contract but repudiates the contract serves as a memorandum that satisfies the Statute. Restatement Second § 133.

Example No. 1:

As part of a land-development scheme, Susan Slide wanted to buy Blackacre, owned by Oliver Oakapple. Slide enters an agreement for the purchase of Blackacre for $40,000. This agreement is incorporated in an elaborate written contract, which Oakapple signs but Slide does not. When the development scheme collapses, Slide wishes to escape her obligation. Oakapple writes a letter to Slide reminding her of the contract, which he encloses, demanding performance. Slide returns the contract, with a letter that reads: "It is true that I entered an oral contract with you on the terms of the enclosed written document. However, the law requires that the contract or a memorandum of it be signed by the party to be charged therewith. You will note that I did not sign this contract, and therefore I am not bound by it. Hoping this incident will teach you some law, Yours truly, Susan Slide."

The decision will go for Oakapple. Slide has provided Oakapple with a signed memorandum of the contract, which will take the contract out of the Statute and permit a successful suit against her.

The conclusions in this Section may be summarized as follows: Everyone agrees that the primary purpose of the Statute of Frauds is to ensure reliable evidence of certain types of contracts on which suit is brought. Cases like *Example No. 1* indicate that the courts usually view the "memorandum" that is required by the Statute, in the absence of a written contract, not as a writing designed to warn a party against "inconsiderate engagements," but as a means of ensuring the existence of a contract and its terms. On the other hand, some cases discern, as a secondary purpose of the Statute, ensuring against hasty action, and this conception of the Statute may influence the interpretation of some of its provisions.

SECTION 4. AMERICAN VARIATIONS ON THE ENGLISH THEME

Ambit. All the American states except Louisiana, Maryland, and New Mexico copied Section 4 of the English Statute of Frauds, and in Maryland and New Mexico the Statute of Frauds is in force by judicial decision. See Restatement Second, ch. 5, Statutory Note. Some states originally omitted Section 17 from their Statutes of Frauds, but the substance of Section 17 was later incorporated in the Uniform Commercial Code. Other states have in a very few instances left out particular provisions of Section 4 of the original Statute, or more commonly have extended the requirement of a writing to transactions not included in the English Statute. One common extension requires a suit to recover a real estate broker's commission to be founded on a written agreement. A contract to make a will is sometimes required to be in writing. Many statutes require a promise to pay certain types of barred or discharged debts to be in writing.

Phraseology. Sometimes American enactments of the original statute introduce minor changes in phraseology. For example, instead of saying "no action shall be brought" on a specified type of oral contract (section 4 of the English Statute), or that the oral contract shall not "be allowed to be good" (section 17 of the English Statute), a Statute of Frauds may simply say that oral contracts of certain types shall be "void." Though the word "void" is probably not to be taken in a literal sense, its use may have some influence in the application of a Statute of Frauds.

Another change sometimes introduced in American Statutes of Frauds is to say that "the contract" must be in writing, instead of following the language of the English Statute, which requires only that "the agreement" or "some memorandum or note thereof" be in writing. This change may be significant as destroying the efficacy of a memorandum executed for some purpose other than that of serving as a statement of the agreement. (See *Example No. 1.* Slide's letter is perhaps a memorandum of the agreement; it is certainly not "the contract.")

SECTION 5. CONTRACTS FOR THE SALE OF AN INTEREST IN LAND (SECTION 4(4))

Section 4(4) covers broadly and somewhat verbosely contracts for the sale of any kind of interest in land. The price, value, or extent of the interest is immaterial.

Example No. 2:

Jim Joad orally agrees with Jane Jukes that he will sell her his eroded tract, Redacre, for ten cents. The contract is within section 4(4) of the Statute of Frauds.

Test. In determining what constitutes an interest in land for purposes of the Statute of Frauds, the test applied is generally that furnished by the law of property. Restatement Second § 127.

Example No. 3:

To obtain a shortcut from his farm to the highway, Paul Pass wants the right to drive through Bilbo Block's land. The parties orally agree that in consideration of the payment of $1000, Pass shall have that right during his life. This contract falls within Section 4(4), because it is a contract for the sale of an interest in land. If the parties had called in a lawyer to draw up the papers for their transaction, the lawyer would have treated this right as an "easement," a familiar heading in books dealing with interests in land.

Example No. 4:

Richard Rocksie, a theatre proprietor, who owns his theatre and the land on which it rests, orally agrees with Julia Roberts that if she will attend the theater's opening night, he will give her a pass, good for life, to sit in seat F11, sixth-row center, for all future performances.

This contract is not within section 4(4). The right to sit in a certain seat during a theatrical performance would not be viewed generally as an interest in the land. No lawyer with a sense of linguistic proprieties would call this right an "easement."

Conveyances. The language of section 4(4) speaks of "any contract *or* sale" of lands. One might assume that this covers either a contract *to* convey, or a *present* conveyance by way of sale. Actually, however, present conveyances are covered by the first three sections of the Statute of Frauds, which have not been reproduced in this Appendix. Accordingly, it is safe to assume that despite its language, section 4(4) really means any contract for the sale of an interest in land, with the qualification that the term "contract or sale of lands ... or any interest concerning them" is used here in a broad sense that includes contracts to devise land by will or to exchange land for something other than money, as well as the more common contract to convey land by deed in return for an agreed money price. (Restatement Second § 125, comments a, c, and Illustrations.)

Leases. In very general terms, the first three Sections of the original Statute state that a writing is necessary to create or transfer an interest in land, except that a tenancy at will and, under certain conditions, a lease not to exceed three years, may be created orally. The substance of these provisions is very generally carried over into American Statutes of Frauds, but the exception for oral short-term leases is usually reduced to either one year or two years.

SECTION 6. CONTRACTS FOR THE SALE OF GOODS

The basic provision. In this country, Section 17 of the Statute of Frauds (the sale-of-goods section) was eventually succeeded by UCC § 2–201:

§ 2–201. Formal Requirements; Statute of Frauds

(1) Except as otherwise provided in this section a contract for the sale of goods for the price of $500 or more is not enforceable by way of action or defense unless there is some writing sufficient to indicate that a contract for sale has been made between the parties and signed by the party against whom enforcement is sought or by his authorized agent or

broker. A writing is not insufficient because it omits or incorrectly states a term agreed upon but the contract is not enforceable under this paragraph beyond the quantity of goods shown in such writing.

(2) Between merchants if within a reasonable time a writing in confirmation of the contract and sufficient against the sender is received and the party receiving it has reason to know its contents, it satisfies the requirements of subsection (1) against such party unless written notice of objection to its contents is given within 10 days after it is received.

(3) A contract which does not satisfy the requirements of subsection (1) but which is valid in other respects is enforceable

(a) if the goods are to be specially manufactured for the buyer and are not suitable for sale to others in the ordinary course of the seller's business and the seller, before notice of repudiation is received and under circumstances which reasonably indicate that the goods are for the buyer, has made either a substantial beginning of their manufacture or commitments for their procurement; or

(b) if the party against whom enforcement is sought admits in his pleading, testimony or otherwise in court that a contract for sale was made, but the contract is not enforceable under this provision beyond the quantity of goods admitted; or

(c) with respect to goods for which payment has been made and accepted or which have been received and accepted....

Three points are worth noting at the outset.

First, UCC § 2–201(1) relates only to the sale of "goods"—that is, physical property other than realty, or what the comment to the UCC calls "movables." It does not include sales of "choses in action" or other intangibles.

Second, the writing required by UCC § 2–201(1) need only be "sufficient to indicate that a contract for sale has been made between the parties." There is no requirement that the writing either specify the kind of goods involved or state the price. Curiously, there is not even a requirement that the quantity of goods sold be stated, but this apparent looseness is illusory, because subsection (1) provides that "the contract is not enforceable ... beyond the quantity of goods shown in such writing." Accordingly, if no quantity is shown the extent of enforcement is zero; if the oral agreement was for 1000 units, while the writing says 500 units, the contract is enforceable only to the extent of 500 units. (The UCC does not itself deal with the possibility of reforming the writing to correct a mistake. Presumably, if both parties intended the writing to state 1000 units, a court might in a proper case reform the memorandum, which then would become enforceable to the extent of 1000 units. See Section 25 of this Appendix.)

Third, UCC § 2–201 applies only if the price is $500 or more. However, if the price is $500 or more, and § 2–201 is not satisfied, the entire contract (not merely that portion of the contract in excess of $500) is unenforceable.

Exceptions. As indicated by introductory clause to UCC § 2–201, the basic requirement of section 2–201(1) is subject to several exceptions.

Part performance. Subsection (3)(c) provides that "A contract which does not satisfy the requirements of [section 2–201(1)] but which is valid in other respects is enforceable . . . with respect to goods for which payment has been made and accepted or which have been received and accepted. . . .'' Even in the absence of subsection (3)(c), if a buyer has accepted goods she would be liable for the value of the goods under the law of unjust enrichment. See Section 19 of this Appendix. The significance of subsection (3)(c) is that if seller sues under the law of unjust enrichment, he would be entitled to recover only the value of the goods at the time they were accepted by the buyer. In contrast, under subsection (3)(c) the seller can recover the contract price of the accepted goods.

Goods made specially to order. Suppose a patient orders a dental bridge from his dentist and orally agrees to pay a price of $2000. The dentist faithfully prepares the bridge to fit the patient's teeth, but when the time comes for installation of the bridge, the patient refuses to pay for it or to receive and accept it. If this contract was held to be a contract for the sale of goods, and unenforceable unless in writing, a serious injustice would be done to the dentist, who will obviously have some difficulty finding a market for the bridge that the patient rejected. Subsection (3)(a) deals with this problem by providing that "A contract which does not satisfy the requirements of [§ 2–201(1)] but which is valid in other respects is enforceable . . . if [i] the goods are to be specially manufactured for the buyer and [ii] are not suitable for sale to others in the ordinary course of the seller's business and [iii] the seller, before notice of repudiation is received and under circumstances which reasonably indicate that the goods are for the buyer, has made either a substantial beginning of their manufacture or commitments for their procurement. . . ." (Subdivisions inserted by ed.)

Receipt of confirmation. Subsection (2) adds another exception to the requirement of a writing for a contract for the sale of goods, based upon modern methods of contracting. That subsection provides, "Between merchants if within a reasonable time a writing in confirmation of the contract and sufficient against the sender is received and the party receiving it has reason to know its contents, it satisfies the requirements of [§ 2–201(1)] against such party unless written notice of objection to its contents is given within 10 days after it is received." Note that subsection (2) is confined to transactions between merchants. (For the UCC definition of "merchant," see UCC § 2–104(1).)

Admissions. Subsection (3)(b) provides that "A contract which does not satisfy the requirements of [§ 2–201(1)] but which is valid in other respects is enforceable . . . if the party against whom enforcement is sought admits in his pleading, testimony or otherwise in court that a contract for sale was made, but the contract is not enforceable under this provision beyond the quantity of goods admitted. . . ." The weight of authority is that the admission may be involuntary as well as voluntary. Accordingly, under subsection 3(b) a plaintiff can bring suit on an oral contract and then try to make the defendant admit, in discovery proceedings or on cross-examination, that the oral contract was in fact made. Indeed, there is much authority that where a complaint is based on an oral contract for the sale of goods it should ordinarily not be dismissed on motion before the plaintiff has had the chance to depose the defendant, because the plaintiff should have an opportunity to elicit such an admission. See, e.g., ALA, Inc. v. CCAIR, Inc., 29 F.3d 855 (3d Cir. 1994) (decided under an analogous statute); Theta Products, Inc. v. Zippo Mfg. Co., 81 F. Supp. 2d 346 (D.R.I. 1999). This is as it should be. The Statute of Frauds is designed to protect against the danger that a plaintiff may, by perjury, establish a contract to the jury's satisfaction where there was no contract in fact. If the defendant *admits* the contract existed, the purpose of the Statute is satisfied.

The CISG. So far, we have been dealing only with the provisions of the UCC that concern when a contract for the sale of goods must be in writing. Many international contracts for the sale of goods are governed by the CISG (Convention for the International Sale of Goods) rather than the UCC. Article 11 of the CISG provides that "A contract of sale need not be concluded in or evidenced by writing and is not subject to any other requirement as to form." See Dodge, Teaching the CISG in Contracts, 50 J. Leg. Ed. 72 (2000).

SECTION 7. SOME OTHER FORMAL REQUIREMENTS IN THE UNIFORM COMMERCIAL CODE

The UCC has several other provisions that bear on the requirement of a writing. In particular:

1. UCC § 9–203 provides that security interests in most types of collateral that are already not in the creditor's possession are enforceable only if described in a security agreement that is authenticated by the debtor.

2. UCC § 8–113 provides that "A contract or modification of a contract for the sale or purchase of a security is enforceable whether or not there is a writing signed or record authenticated by a party against whom enforcement is sought, even if the contract or modification is not capable of performance within one year of its making."

3. UCC § 1–206 ("Statute of Frauds for Kinds of Personal Property Not Otherwise Covered") provides:

> (1) Except in the cases described in subsection (2) of this section a contract for the sale of personal property is not enforceable by way of action or defense beyond five thousand dollars in amount or value of remedy unless there is some writing which indicates that a contract for sale has been made between the parties at a defined or stated price, reasonably identifies the subject matter, and is signed by the party against whom enforcement is sought or by his authorized agent.

> (2) Subsection (1) of this section does not apply to contracts for the sale of goods (Section 2–201) nor of securities (Section 8–113) nor of security agreements (Section 9–203).

Note that no matter how great is the price, UCC § 1–206 is only applicable if the value of the *remedy* is $5,000 or more.

SECTION 8. AGREEMENTS NOT TO BE PERFORMED WITHIN ONE YEAR FROM THE MAKING THEREOF (SECTION 4(5))

Section 4(5) of the Statute of Frauds concerns actions "upon any agreement that is not to be performed within the space of one year from the making thereof."

To the casual reader, the language of section 4(5) contains no warning of the interpretation the courts have put on this section. It will be easier to understand this interpretation if one considers first the problem that faced courts that had to apply the section.

There was no mystery about the reason for requiring a signed writing in the case of a contract not to be performed within one year; in Holt's words, "the design of the statute was, not to trust to the memory of witnesses for a longer time than one year." Smith v. Westall, 1697, 1 Lord Raymond 317. The trouble lay, not in any obscurity of purpose, but in a failure to provide an apt means for effectuating that purpose.

In the first place, there is no direct relation between the time when a witness may be called to testify and the time that is required to perform the contract; a contract might be scheduled for completion within one month and yet first come into proof in court two years later. Furthermore, the drafters failed to ask themselves what should be done in the case of a contract as to which it is impossible to say in advance how much time its performance will require. For example, the performance of a contract to support A for life might be completed within a month if A died so soon, or might on the other hand stretch over decades if A were sufficiently long-lived. In a case coming up for decision shortly after the Statute was enacted, it was suggested that the validity of the contract should depend on the actual course of events. (Smith v. Westall, supra.) But this solution was never accepted, and could not be. Parties need to know from the outset, or at least as soon as trouble develops, whether they have a contract. To make the existence of a binding contract depend upon later events would invite all kinds of jockeying for position and produce an intolerable confusion.

The courts were, then, confronted with a statute that simply could not be applied in a way to carry out the likely conceived intention of its drafters. One stab at a solution that easily comes to mind is to measure expected duration for performance according to the expectation of the parties when they entered the contract. There are, in fact, a few cases that speak as if this were the governing principle, but this way out is scarcely acceptable. Where the time that will be required for performance is uncertain, there is usually no reason to suppose that the parties have made some calculation of probabilities and have in their minds some expected duration, such as six months or five years. Where a contract requires that A be supported for the rest of his life, the parties do not know how long A will live, and know that they do not know.

Accordingly, most courts have said that the applicability of Section 4(5) depends not on what actually happens, or on what the parties thought would happen, but on what *could have* happened. When the contract was entered, was there any *possibility* that it could have been performed within a year? If so, it is not within the Statute and is therefore enforceable although oral.

Restatement Second § 130. As stated by Chief Justice Peters in C.R. Klewin, Inc. v. Flagship Properties, Inc., 220 Conn. 569, 600 A.2d 772 (1991):

> ... [The] issue can be framed as follows: in the exclusion from the statute of frauds of all contracts except those "whose performance cannot possibly be completed within a year" ... what meaning should be attributed to the word "possibly"? One construction of "possibly" would encompass only contracts whose completion within a year would be inconsistent with the express terms of the contract. An alternate construction would include as well contracts ... in which, while no time period is expressly specified, it is ... realistically impossible for performance to be completed within a year. We now hold that the former and not the latter is the correct interpretation. "The critical test ... is whether 'by its terms' the agreement is not to be performed within a year, so that the statute will not apply where "the alleged agreement contain[s] [no] provision which directly or indirectly regulated the time for performance." Freedman v. Chemical Construction Corporation, 43 N.Y.2d 260, 265, 372 N.E.2d 12, 401 N.Y.S.2d 176 (1977). "It is the law of this state, as it is elsewhere, that a contract is not within this clause of the statute unless its terms are so drawn that it cannot by any possibility be performed fully within one year." (Emphasis added.) Burkle v. Superflow Mfg. Co., ... 137 Conn. at 492, 78 A.2d 698....
>
> We therefore hold that an oral contract that does not say, in express terms, that performance is to have a specific duration beyond one year is, as a matter of law.... enforceable because it is outside the prescriptive force of the statute regardless of how long completion of performance will actually take.

Under this rule, an oral agreement to hire A for life is not within the Statute of Frauds, because there is a possibility that the agreement can be performed within a year through the death of A within that time. It is immaterial that in fact A lives and works on the job for twenty years. If A is then discharged, he can base a suit against the employer on proof of the oral agreement made years before, when he accepted employment. (*Warning.* In some states it is specifically provided that a contract that is not to be completed before the end of a lifetime *is* within the Statute. A few cases reach the same result. See, e.g., McInerney v. Charter Golf, Inc., 176 Ill.2d 482, 680 N.E.2d 1347 (1997), where the court so held over a vigorous dissent.)

SECTION 9.   WHAT KIND OF WRITING WILL SATISFY THE STATUTE

The issue, what type of writing is required to satisfy the Statute of Frauds, has become recast in recent years, because the broader concept of a *record* has for many purposes, including the Statute, replaced the narrower concept of a *writing*. That complication will be put aside for the moment, and discussed in the next Section of this Appendix. Much of the discussion in this Section will use the term "writing," because that is the traditional term used in the Statute and in most of the cases decided until fairly recently. The discussion of the term "record" in the next Section will build on the discussion of the term "writing" in this Section, because most of the points made in this Section apply to a record as well.

The principal points to note are the following:

First. Unless the relevant Statute requires "the contract" to be in writing, the Statute is satisfied by almost any kind of signed document (using the term *document* extremely broadly, for present purposes only, to include both writings and records) that evidences the terms of the parties' agreement. This result follows from the language of section 4, which states, in effect, that there must either be a written contract *or* some memorandum or note *of* the contract.

Second. The requirement of a "signed" document does not mean that a document must be signed by the party in her own hand and with her full name. Any symbol used with an intent to authenticate a document will suffice. For instance, an "O.K." with initials is sufficient. Even a photocopied or computer-printed name will count as a signature if it reflects an intent to authenticate a document.

The UCC defines the term "signed" to include "any symbol executed or adopted by a party with present intention to authenticate a writing." UCC § 1–201(39) (as in force in most states). The Comment states: "The inclusion of authentication in the definition of 'signed' is to make clear that as the term is used in [the Code] a complete signature is not necessary. Authentication may be printed, stamped, or written; it may be by initials or by thumbprint. It may be on any part of the document and in appropriate cases may be found in a billhead or letterhead. No catalog of possible authentications can be complete and the court must use common sense and commercial experience in passing upon these matters. The question always is whether the symbol was executed or adopted by the party with present intention to authenticate the writing."

Restatement Second is somewhat broader, in that it allows either actual or apparent intent to suffice. Restatement Second § 134. Farnsworth wrote similarly that the "modern test is whether the other party reasonably believes that the asserted signer's intention is to authenticate the writing as the asserted signer's own." E. Allan Farnsworth, Contracts, § 6.8 (4th ed. 2004). In Donovan v. RRL Corp., 26 Cal.4th 261, 27 P.3d 702 (Cal. 2001), the court held that "[w]hen an advertisement constitutes an offer, the printed name of the merchant is intended to authenticate the advertisement as that of the merchant.... In other words, where the advertisement reasonably justifies the recipient's understanding that the communication was intended as an offer, the offeror's intent to authenticate his or her name as a signature can be established from the face of the advertisement."

Third. If an agreement or memorandum is to satisfy the Statute, it must state the terms of the contract with reasonable adequacy. A document that failed to identify the parties, the subject-matter, and the essential terms would normally not be sufficient. On the other hand, the courts do not demand perfection, and some degree of ambiguity or ellipsis is not fatal.

Fourth. An adequate statement of the terms of the contract would normally reveal the consideration that made the promise or promises binding. However, it is not uncommon for a surety to guarantee a debt in writing without stating the consideration for her own undertaking as surety—which may be, for example, an advance made by the creditor to the debtor or an extension of time granted by the creditor to the debtor. An early English case construing section 4(2) of the Statute of Frauds declared such a memorandum to be fatally defective. Some American courts have followed this English decision; more have refused to. In 1856 the English law was changed by a statute that dispensed with the need for stating the consideration in a written guaranty.

In the United States there are a variety of statutes concerning whether the consideration must be stated to make a document effective. Some statutes say the consideration *must* be stated; some say the consideration need not be stated in a guaranty; some say the consideration need not be stated in any case. It is the last form of statute that gives the most difficulty. Does it mean, for example, that a written contract to sell land is effective although it makes no mention of the price, or states the price incorrectly? The cases are divided, but some have gone so far as to accept this conclusion. And note that the UCC Statute of Frauds, § 2–201, does not require the price to be stated in the writing. See *Ninth*, infra.

Fifth. Generally the document need not be signed by both parties, but only by the "party to be charged." This may result in a contract that can be enforced in one direction only.

Sixth. Even where no single document exists that is sufficient to satisfy the Statute, a memorandum that satisfies the statute may sometimes be obtained by piecing together several documents. If the documents are physically attached, or contain internal references to one another, there is no difficulty. More doubtful is the question whether piecing together is permissible where doing so rests entirely on oral evidence or general appearances. Some cases hold that sufficient connection between writings is established by reference in the documents to the same subject matter or transaction; other cases require that the connection be established by examination of the writings alone.

Seventh. A memorandum may fail to satisfy the Statute of Frauds because it does not *correctly* state the agreement. Restatement Second § 131, comment g. (But note that UCC § 2–201(1) specifically provides otherwise in the case of a sale of goods.)

SECTION 10. ELECTRONIC CONTRACTING AND THE STATUTE OF FRAUDS

Within the last few years, the concept and term record has come into use in place of the concept and term *writing*. A *record* is defined slightly differently in different statutes, but at its core the term has the meaning given by section 2(13) of the Uniform Electronic Transactions Act, discussed below: "information that is inscribed on a tangible medium or that is stored in an electronic or other medium and is retrievable in perceivable form." In connection with the shift from *writing* to *record*, two important legislative developments have affected the issue of what kinds of records and signatures satisfy the Statute of Frauds.

UETA. First, the Uniform Electronics Transactions Act (UETA) was promulgated in 1999 by the National Conference of Commissioners on Uniform State Laws, and has been adopted by almost all the states. UETA § 7 provides as follows:

(a) A record or signature may not be denied legal effect or enforceability solely because it is in electronic form.

(b) A contract may not be denied legal effect or enforceability solely because an electronic record was used in its formation.

(c) If a law requires a record to be in writing, an electronic record satisfies the law.

(d) If a law requires a signature, an electronic signature satisfies the law.

The terms used in section 7 are defined in section 2. Section 2(13) provides that the term "record" means "information that is inscribed on a tangible medium or that is stored in an electronic or other medium and is retrievable in perceivable form." The Comment to section 2(13) states:

This is a standard definition designed to embrace all means of communicating or storing information except human memory. It includes any method for storing or communicating information, including "writings." A record need not be indestructible or permanent, but the term does not include oral or other communications which are not stored or preserved by some means. Information that has not been retained other than through human memory does not qualify as a record. As in the case of the terms "writing" or "written," the term "record" does not establish the purposes, permitted uses or legal effect which a record may have under any particular provision of substantive law.

Section 2(8) provides that the term "electronic signature" means "an electronic sound, symbol, or process attached to or logically associated with a record and executed or adopted by a person with the intent to sign the record." The Comment to section 2(8) states:

The idea of a signature is broad and not specifically defined. Whether any particular record is "signed" is a question of fact. Proof of that fact must be made under other applicable law. This Act simply assures that the signature may be accomplished through electronic means. No specific technology need be used in order to create a valid signature. One's voice on an answering machine may suffice if the requisite intention is present. Similarly, including one's name as part of an electronic mail communication also may suffice, as may the firm name on a facsimile.... In any case the critical element is the intention to execute or adopt the sound or symbol or process for the purpose of signing the related record.... It is that intention that is understood in the law as a part of the word "sign", without the need for a definition.

This Act establishes, to the greatest extent possible, the equivalency of electronic signatures and manual signatures. Therefore the term "signature" has been used to connote and convey that equivalency....

This definition includes as an electronic signature the standard webpage click through process. For example, when a person orders goods or services through a vendor's website, the person will be required to provide information as part of a process which will result in receipt of the goods or services. When the customer ultimately gets to the last step and clicks "I agree," the person has adopted the process and has done so with the intent to associate the person with the record of that process. The actual effect of the electronic signature will be determined from all the surrounding circumstances[;] however, the person adopted a process which the circumstances indicate s/he intended to have the effect of getting the goods/services and being bound to pay for them. The adoption of the process carried the intent to do a legally significant act, the hallmark of a signature.

Another important aspect of this definition lies in the necessity that the electronic signature be linked or logically associated with the record. In the paper world, it is assumed that the symbol adopted by a party is attached to or located somewhere in the same paper that is intended to be authenticated, e.g., an allonge firmly attached to a promissory note, or the classic signature at the end of a long contract. These tangible manifestations do not exist in the electronic environment, and accordingly, this definition expressly provides that the symbol must in some way be linked to, or connected with, the electronic record being signed. . . .

The Illustrations to UETA § 7 exemplify how this section operates:

Illustration 1: A sends the following e-mail to B: "I hereby offer to buy widgets from you, delivery next Tuesday. /s/ A." B responds with the following e-mail: "I accept your offer to buy widgets for delivery next Tuesday. /s/ B." The e-mails may not be denied effect solely because they are electronic. In addition, the e-mails . . . qualify as records under the Statute of Frauds. However, because there is no quantity stated in either record, the parties' agreement would be unenforceable under existing UCC Section 2–201(1).

Illustration 2: A sends the following e-mail to B: "I hereby offer to buy 100 widgets for $1000, delivery next Tuesday. /s/ A." B responds with the following e-mail: "I accept your offer to purchase 100 widgets for $1000, delivery next Tuesday. /s/ B." In this case the analysis is the same as in Illustration 1 except that here the records otherwise satisfy the requirements of UCC Section 2–201(1). The transaction may not be denied legal effect solely because there is not a pen and ink "writing" or "signature".

E-Sign. The second major legislative development affecting records and signatures is the Electronic Signatures in Global and National Commerce Act ("E–Sign"). E–Sign is a federal statute which is generally comparable to UETA as regards the effect of electronic records and electronic signatures. Because E–Sign is a federal statute, it would normally preempt UETA. However, E–Sign specifically recognizes and avoids preempting UETA, and on the contrary, provides that with limited exceptions, states may preempt E–sign by adopting UETA. Because all but four states have adopted UETA, UETA generally takes precedence over E–Sign.

SECTION 11. THE EFFECT OF PART PERFORMANCE OF, OR RELIANCE UPON, AN ORAL CONTRACT WITHIN THE STATUTE—INTRODUCTION

This Section will consider the following question: A has entered an oral contract with B, and A has broken the contract after B acted upon it. Should B be given any recovery? This question is best approached if it is first put in general terms, without reference to specific provisions the Statute of Frauds.

The basic opposing considerations that must be weighed in answering this question are: (1) the dangers involved in founding a legal liability on mere spoken words; and (2) the possible hardship to A resulting from a denial of relief on the oral agreement.

To balance these opposing considerations, it is necessary to know the particular hardship of which A complains and the specific measure of relief that he demands. Three situations may be distinguished: (1) B seeks restitutionary damages for a benefit that he conferred on A under the oral contract. (2) B seeks reliance damages for losses he incurred in reliance on the oral contract, but A received no benefit as the result of B's reliance. (3) B seeks expectation damages for the value of the performance promised by A.

The next three Sections of this Appendix take up these three classes of claims.

———

SECTION 12. THE RESTITUTION OF BENEFITS CONFERRED UNDER THE ORAL AGREEMENT

It is well settled that normally B may recover the value of any benefits he conferred on A under an oral contract that falls within the Statute of Frauds.

Example No. 5:

Under an oral contract with Marian Means, Steven Smock, an artist, agrees to paint a mural in Means's home in exchange for a conveyance of Passacre. After full performance by Smock, Means refuses to give him a deed to Passacre.

Although this transaction is a contract for the sale of land within Section 4(4) of the Statute of Frauds, Smock can recover the value of the mural.

There are two explanations for reconciling this result with the Statute of Frauds. One explanation is normative; the other is doctrinal.

The normative explanation is that to allow a party to retain benefits that she has received under a contract that is unenforceable only because not in writing would be a result too unjust for the law to countenance.

The doctrinal explanation is that the Statute of Frauds only bars actions to enforce a contract, and doctrinally a suit for restitution is not an action to enforce the contract. Such an action is based not on contract law, but on an entirely separate body of law, the law of unjust enrichment and restitution. Correspondingly, the measure of recovery in a suit in restitution is basically different from the measure of recovery in a suit on the contract. In a suit on the contract, the plaintiff's recovery is measured by the value of the performance promised by the defendant. In *Example No. 14*, this would be the value of Passacre. In contrast, in a suit in restitution the plaintiff's recovery is measured by the value of his own performance as received by the defendant. In *Example No. 14*, this would be the value of the mural. A suit in contract is based on redressing a breach of contract; a suit in restitution is based on preventing unjust enrichment.

SECTION 13.   REIMBURSEMENT FOR RELIANCE ON THE ORAL CONTRACT

Suppose a plaintiff seeks, not restitution for a benefit conferred under a contract that is unenforceable under the Statute of Frauds, but damages based on losses that he incurred in acting under the contract, which losses did not result in a benefit to the defendant. The issue here is not as clear-cut as it is in the case of a benefit conferred under a contract that is unenforceable under the Statute of Frauds.

Normatively, a rule that allowed a defendant to retain a benefit that has been conferred upon her under a contract that is unenforceable only because it is not in writing would be more shocking to the sense of justice than a rule that a defendant need not reimburse the plaintiff for his losses under such contract, where those losses did not result in a benefit to the defendant. (This is not to say that a rule of the second kind would be just; only that the injustice is less intense in the reliance case than in the restitution case.)

Doctrinally, unlike an action to recover the value of a benefit conferred, which is brought under the law of unjust enrichment and restitution, an action to recover reliance damages is a suit under contract law. Such an action therefore runs more squarely into the Statute of Frauds than an action to recover the value of a benefit conferred.

At least until recently, the prevailing view has been that it would be contrary to the Statute of Frauds to allow a recovery for losses from reliance on a contract that is unenforceable under the Statute when those losses did not benefit the defendant. Today, that view is gradually changing. Two of the leading cases are Monarco v. Lo Greco, 35 Cal.2d 621, 220 P.2d 737 (1950) and Alaska Airlines v. Stephenson, 217 F.2d 295 (9th Cir.1954).

In Monarco v. Lo Greco, Christie Lo Greco's mother and stepfather orally promised Christie that if he would stay on the family farm and help in its management, they would leave him the bulk of their property. Christie did as they asked, and the family farm prospered. However, Christie's stepfather left the property to his grandson. The court held for Christie, despite Section 4(4) of the Statute of Frauds (the land section) on the basis of Christie's reliance. The opinion qualified the reliance exception to the Statute of Frauds by stating that reliance was a ground for overcoming the Statute only "where either an unconscionable injury or unjust enrichment would result from refusal to enforce the contract."

In Alaska Airlines v. Stephenson, Alaska Airlines orally promised to give an airline pilot a two-year written contract as soon as the airline obtained a required certificate to fly between Seattle and Alaska. In reliance on this promise, the pilot let his right to return to his previous employer expire. The airline broke its promise. Here too the court held that the pilot's reliance overcame the Statute. See also, e.g., Alaska Democratic Party v. Rice, 934 P.2d 1313 (Alaska 1997).

Going one step further, Restatement Second § 139 gives full recognition to the reliance principle in the Statute of Frauds area. Furthermore, under the principle embodied in this section, a relying promisee may be entitled to expectation damages:

§ 139. Enforcement by Virtue of Action in Reliance

(1) A promise which the promisor should reasonably expect to induce action or forbearance on the part of the promisee or a third person and which does induce the action or forbearance is enforceable notwithstanding the Statute of Frauds if injustice can be avoided only by enforcement of the promise. The remedy granted for breach is to be limited as justice requires.

(2) In determining whether injustice can be avoided only by enforcement of the promise, the following circumstances are significant:

(a) the availability and adequacy of other remedies, particularly cancellation and restitution;

(b) the definite and substantial character of the action or forbearance in relation to the remedy sought;

(c) the extent to which the action or forbearance corroborates evidence of the making and terms of the promise, or the making and terms are otherwise established by clear and convincing evidence;

(d) the reasonableness of the action or forbearance;

(e) the extent to which the action or forbearance was foreseeable by the promisor. . . .

Comment . . .

d. Partial enforcement; particular remedies. The same factors which bear on whether any relief should be granted also bear on the character and extent of the remedy. In particular, the remedy of restitution is not ordinarily affected by the Statute of Frauds . . . ; where restitution is an adequate remedy, other remedies are not made available by the rule stated in this Section. Again, when specific enforcement is available . . . an ordinary action for damages is commonly less satisfactory, and justice then does not require enforcement in such an action. . . . In some cases it may be appropriate to measure relief by the extent of the promisee's reliance rather than by the terms of the promise. See § 90. . . .

Restatement Second § 139 has undoubtedly reinforced the tendency of the courts to adopt a reliance exception to the Statute of Frauds. However, not all courts adopt the reliance exception. See, e.g., Stearns v. Emery–Waterhouse Co., 596 A.2d 72 (Maine 1991) ("We affirm that equitable estoppel, based upon a promisor's fraudulent conduct, can avoid application of the statute of frauds and that this principle applies to a fraudulent promise of employment. But we decline [the plaintiff's] invitation to accept *promissory* estoppel as permitting avoidance of the statute in employment contracts that require longer than one year to perform"). Furthermore, some courts that adopt the reliance exception continue to qualify the exception in the same manner as *Monarco.*

The cases are divided on whether the reliance exception applies to UCC § 2–201. Some cases take the position that the exceptions in § 2–201 should be deemed to be exclusive of any others, partly to promote uniformity in the application of the Code. See, e.g., Renfroe v. Ladd, 701 S.W.2d 148 (Ky.App. 1985); Lige Dickson Co. v. Union Oil Co., 96 Wash.2d 291, 635 P.2d 103 (1981). Other cases take the position that the reliance exception applies to cases that fall within § 2–201 because UCC § 1–103 provides that "Unless displaced by the particular provisions of this Act, the principles of law and equity, including . . . the law relative to . . . estoppel . . . or other validating or invalidating cause shall supplement its provisions." See, e.g., Allen M. Campbell Co. v. Virginia Metal Industries, 708 F.2d 930 (4th Cir.1983); Ralston Purina Co. v. McCollum, 271 Ark. 840, 611 S.W.2d 201 (1981).

SECTION 14.   THE RIGHT TO THE "VALUE OF THE BARGAIN" WHERE THERE HAS BEEN PART PERFORMANCE OF, OR RELIANCE UPON, THE ORAL CONTRACT

From the standpoint of a plaintiff who has acted under an oral contract falling within the Statute of Frauds, the state of the law summarized in the last two Sections of this Appendix is unsatisfactory in two respects: (1) Despite some straining in that direction, the law does not in all cases reimburse the plaintiff's losses in acting under the contract. (2) Where the plaintiff has performed his side of the contract, it would often be to his advantage if his measure of recovery was the value of the performance promised by the defendant, rather than the value of his own performance. If the plaintiff seeks the former measure simply to realize the advantage of a profitable bargain, we may say that this objective is contrary to the Statute of Frauds. But a plaintiff's right to restitution is clearly recognized by the cases, and the plaintiff has legitimate grounds for complaint if this right is impaired in practice by the imposition of an uncertain measure of recovery. He may point out that the uncertainty in the amount of his claim not only jeopardizes his recovery in case of actual litigation, but (and this is more important in practice) impairs his bargaining power in any negotiations looking toward a settlement without litigation.

This objection has particular application where the benefit conferred on the defendant by the plaintiff's performance does not have a definite market value, and the defendant has promised to pay a flat sum of money for the performance. As an original question, it would seem sensible to avoid the hazards and doubts involved in measuring the value of the plaintiff's performance in such cases by taking, as the value of that performance, the amount the defendant promised to pay for it. By way of reinforcing this argument, the plaintiff may point out that his having acted under the contract is a voucher of his good faith and corroborative evidence that a contract did in fact exist; it thus serves in some measure as a substitute for a writing.

Against this reasoning stands, of course, the plain language of the Statute of Frauds itself. One section of the original Statute of Frauds—section 17, the sale-of-goods section (now supplanted by the UCC)—expressly recognized and gave legal effect to the kind of considerations advanced above, by providing that the plaintiff could sue for the contract price if certain kinds of part performance had occurred. The omission of part-performance exceptions in section 4 of the Statute might seem to indicate that there could be no recovery of the contract price in cases falling within that section, even if the contract had been partly performed or had otherwise given rise to a serious change of position.

In spite of the force of the last argument, the courts, by a process extending over the centuries, have read into certain provisions of the Statute of Frauds exceptions under which the Statute becomes inapplicable, and the plaintiff can bring suit under the contract for expectation damages, where the contract has been fully or even partly performed on one side. The exact nature of the part-performance exceptions vary from provision to provision of the Statute. A summary of the law on this question follows.

The Suretyship Section

Generally no exception to the Statute of Frauds is read into the suretyship section of the Statute in favor of a party who performs on the basis of an oral guaranty. For example, if Seller delivers goods to Buyer in reliance on Surety's oral promise to answer for Buyer's obligation to pay the price, Surety does not thereby become bound.

The Marriage Section

It is generally assumed that an oral contract upon consideration of marriage is not taken out of the Statute of Frauds simply because the marriage has taken place in reliance on the promise. (There are, however, cases enforcing the oral agreement where a serious change of position, involving acts in addition to marriage, has occurred.)

The Land Section

In the case of contracts for the sale of an interest in land ("land contracts"), a part-performance exception—perhaps more accurately, a part-performance-and-reliance exception—has become institutionalized and has been built into an imposing body of case law.

The traditional rules. Traditionally, the cases in this area make explicit two different considerations: (1) The equity in favor of a party who has acted under the oral contract and who will suffer hardship if the contract is not enforced. (2) The evidentiary value of acts of reliance or part performance in pointing to the existence of a contract. Because these considerations may appear in varying degrees, there are strict and liberal applications of the part-performance exception in this context. Furthermore, some decisions place greater weight on the evidentiary significance of acts of performance or reliance, while others place greater weight on the element of hardship.

In discussing the case law on the part-performance exception for land contracts, it is necessary to distinguish between acts under the contract by the *vendor* and acts under the contract by the *purchaser*.

A *vendor* is entitled to recover the price under an oral contract for the sale of land as soon as the vendor has actually conveyed the land to the purchaser. Restatement Second § 125(3). Thus the vendor can obtain the price promised by the purchaser, and with it the benefit of the vendor's oral bargain, instead of being thrown back upon either an action in restitution for the reasonable value of the land or a suit in equity to compel a reconveyance of the land (specific restitution).

Where it is the *purchaser* who acts under the oral contract, the law is more complicated. A good summary of the traditional rule in this area was set out in Restatement First § 197. That Section provided that an oral agreement for the sale of an interest in land becomes *specifically enforceable* if "the purchaser with the assent of the vendor (a) makes valuable improvements on the land, or (b) takes possession thereof or retains a possession thereof existing at the time of the bargain, and also pays a portion or all of the purchase price."

As indicated by Restatement First § 197, under the traditional rule payment of all or part of the purchase price does not alone make the contract enforceable, although there are some cases to the contrary. The theory is that such a payment does not identify the land sold. (However, the payment can be recovered in a suit for restitution.) Similarly, under the traditional rule the purchaser's act of taking possession does not alone make the contract enforceable by the plaintiff. The theory is that although taking possession may have evidentiary value as indicating some kind of agreement and identifying its object, taking possession is as consistent with a lease as with a sale, and may not always involve a serious change of position by the purchaser.

These limitations are by no means universally respected by the courts. In addition to some cases indicating that taking possession is sufficient, even without payment of the purchase price, there are many cases holding that the rendition of services over a long period will suffice to take the contract out of the Statute. This type of holding is found typically in "care-for-me-for-the-rest-of-my-life-and-you-can-have-the-farm-when-I-am-gone" contracts.

Concerning the traditional rule that certain acts by the purchaser under a land contract may make the contract specifically enforceable, the following points should be noted.

(1) This rule was developed by courts of equity, and therefore it is generally assumed to affect only the purchaser's right to specific performance, and not to give the purchaser a right to recover damages measured by the value of the land. Restatement Second § 129, Comment c. In contrast, the *vendor's* right to the price after conveying land under an oral contract is a right to sue at law.

(2) Generally it is the purchaser who, having made improvements or otherwise acted under the contract, brings suit for specific performance against the vendor. There are cases, however, holding that the same acts under the contract by the purchaser that will create in him a right to specific performance will also create a right to specific performance in the vendor. Here it is not the hardship to the plaintiff-vendor that makes the oral contract enforceable, but either (1) the evidentiary value of the purchaser's acts, or (2) a notion that if it is fair for the purchaser to enforce the contract, equality of treatment should allow the vendor to sue on the same set of facts.

(3) In a few jurisdictions, the courts have stated that they do not recognize the principle that part performance of an oral contract for the sale of an interest in land will make the contract specifically enforceable.

(4) There is a general tendency to very liberally enforce an oral contract that settles a disputed boundary. Where parties are in dispute or doubt about

the boundary between their lands, and orally agree to settle the issue by running a fence or other marker along a designated line, generally the agreement becomes enforceable as soon as any action is taken under it. Restatement Second § 128(1).

The rule in Restatement Second. Restatement Second § 129 completely reconceptualizes and reformulates the part-performance exception for land contracts, by making the exception center on reliance. That section provides:

> A contract for the transfer of an interest in land may be specifically enforced notwithstanding failure to comply with the Statute of Frauds if it is established that the party seeking enforcement, in reasonable reliance on the contract and on the continuing assent of the party against whom enforcement is sought, has so changed his position that injustice can be avoided only by specific enforcement.

Whether the law in this area will shift to the rule stated in Restatement Second § 129 remains to be seen.

The One–Year Provision

Taking as a guide Restatement Second § 130 and many cases, the part-performance rule concerning the one-year provision—section 4(5)—is as follows: As soon as one side of the contract has been fully performed the promise of the other party becomes binding, whether or not that promise can be performed within one year. (The rationale of this rule is seldom discussed. Perhaps the explanation lies in the fact that difficulties intrinsic to section 4(5) had already compelled so much departure from the literal meaning of the section (see Section 10 of this Appendix) that the courts have felt free to take further liberties with its language in order to make its operation more equitable.) Piecing this principle together with the basic interpretation of section 4(5), it may be said that an oral contract is either not within or is taken out of the one-year provision if (1) the whole contract *could* have been performed within one year, although neither party has as yet fully performed or (2) one party has fully performed, no matter how long it took for performance to take place.

Caution: The case law is more ambiguous than the rule laid down by Restatement Second, and the general tendency of the law is less favorable to removing the oral contract from the Statute's one-year provision as a result of part performance. According to some cases, if the defendant's performance will require more than a year, the fact that the plaintiff has fully performed is immaterial. Under this view, the plaintiff's only relief is in restitution. Still other cases say that full performance on one side will take the contract out of the Statute only if that performance itself takes place within one year after the contract is made.

————

SECTION 15.   ORAL RESCISSION

The problem of the validity of an oral rescission arises chiefly in connection with the following situation: The original contract was in writing, and its terms were such as to bring it within the Statute of Frauds. In short, the contract had to be in writing—as it was—to be enforceable. The contract is then orally rescinded by the parties' mutual agreement. As a general proposition, in such cases the rescission is effective, on the theory that the rescission does not call for the performance of any duties, and therefore does not fall within any of the classes covered by the Statute. See *Example No. 4* in Section 6 of this Appendix; Restatement Second § 148 and comment a.

This general proposition requires two qualifications:

1. *Sale of land.* Where the rescinded contract is for the sale of land, and the original transaction was fully executed, the rescission itself effectively calls for a conveyance—albeit a reconveyance—and therefore falls within the Statute. Suppose the original contract was executory at the time the contract of rescission was entered into? Even here, there are cases saying that the rescission is ineffective unless in writing. The theory of these cases is that an executory contract to sell land creates a present property interest in the purchaser, so that a rescission of such a contract also involves the reconveyance of an interest in land. However, according to Restatement Second § 148, comment c, "[t]he prevailing rule"—which is adopted by Restatement Second—"is that an executory land contract may be rescinded orally like other contracts within the Statute. . . ."

2. *Sale of goods.* If the original contract was for the sale of goods, and title had already passed to the buyer, "rescission" is really a resale of the goods, and comes within UCC § 2–201 if the amount involved is sufficient. Restatement Second § 148, comment b and Illustration 2.

SECTION 16.   ORAL MODIFICATIONS

Generally speaking, a modification of a contract falls within the Statute of Frauds if, but only if, the new agreement that results from putting together the original agreement and the modification is within the Statute. However, a special rule applies to modifications of contracts for the sale of goods, which are governed by UCC § 2–209(3). That section provides:

> The requirements of the statute of frauds section of this Article (Section 2–201) must be satisfied if [a contract for the sale of goods] as modified is within its provisions.

Comment 3 adds:

> The Statute of Frauds provisions of this Article are expressly applied to modifications by subsection (3). Under those provisions the "delivery and acceptance" test is limited to the goods which have been accepted, that is, to the past. "Modification" for the future cannot therefore be conjured up by oral testimony if the price involved is $500.00 or more since such modification must be shown at least by an authenticated memo. And since a memo is limited in its effect to the quantity of goods set forth in it there is safeguard against oral evidence.

The Comment suggests that *any* modification of a contract for the sale of goods must be in writing. This position was taken in Zemco Mfg., Inc. v. Navistar Int'l Transp. Corp., 186 F.3d 815 (7th Cir. 1999), decided by the Seventh Circuit under Indiana law. In 1983, the parties entered into a written contract for the sale of parts. Originally, the contract was to last one year, but it was extended to 1987 by successive written agreements. After 1987, the parties orally agreed to extend the contract. Navistar argued that the oral contract extensions were unenforceable under the Statute of Frauds. The Seventh Circuit agreed.

In contrast, White & Summers comment, "Assuming that a party can establish a modifying agreement, must one show that it was reduced to writing? Section 2–209(3) states that '[t]he requirements of the statute of frauds section of this Article (2–201) must be satisfied if the contract as modified is within its provisions.' The impact of this provision is not clear. We see at least the following possible interpretations: (1) that if the original contract was within 2–201, any modification thereof must also be in writing; (2) that a modification must be in writing if the term it adds brings the entire deal within 2–201 for the first time, as where the price is modified from $400 to $500; (3) that a modification must be in writing if it falls in 2–201 on its own; (4) that the modification must be in writing if it changes the quantity term of an original agreement that fell within 2–201; and (5) some combination of the foregoing. Given the purposes of the basic statute of frauds section 2–201, we believe interpretations (2), (3), and (4) are each justified, subject, of course, to the exceptions in 2–201 itself and to any general supplemental principles of estoppel." J. White & R. Summers, Uniform Commercial Code § 1–6 (5th ed. 2000).

Finally there is emergent in this area another doctrine of part performance or reliance, according to which an oral modification becomes effective if action has been taken under it. Restatement Second § 150. In this connection, UCC § 2–209(4) provides that an attempt at modification that does not satisfy § 2–209(3) can operate as a waiver, and § 2–209(5) provides that such a waiver cannot be retracted if retraction would be unjust in view of a material change of position in reliance on the waiver.

Index

References are to Pages

†